Where to Stay
Contents

Key to Symbols
Inside Back Cover

Front cover: Potash Farm, Felsted, Essex.
Spine: Holly Cottage, Wroxham, Norfolk.
Back cover: (clockwise from left)
Giffords Hall, Hartest, Suffolk;
Holmfield, Kendal, Cumbria;
Causa Grange, Rosley, near Caldbeck, Cumbria.

This *Where to Stay* guide is designed to give you all the information you need to help you find accommodation in England in the right place, at the right price and with the facilities and services that are right for you.

Welcome to the

Sure Signs of where to stay

All accommodation in *Where to Stay* has been inspected – or is awaiting inspection – under the English Tourist Board's official National Grading and Classification Scheme. You'll find many listings in *Where to Stay* provide the reassurance of both a classification and quality grading: the Crown classification (Listed and One to Five Crown) shows you the range of services and facilities provided to guests; Quality Grading (De Luxe, Highly Commended, Commended or Approved) indicates the overall standard of welcome, service and accommodation.

So where you see a rating in an accommodation entry, you'll know that our inspectors have checked it out before you check in.

Easy to use

A comprehensive town index and full-colour location maps pinpoint all those cities, towns and villages with listings to help you quickly find accommodation in the area you wish to visit. Accommodation entries are listed alphabetically by place within eleven tourist board regions; thumbnail town descriptions give you a quick picture of each place.

Guide

You'll find all the essential information you need presented in a straightforward and easy-to-read style: a description of the establishment, prices, accommodation details and at-a-glance symbols showing additional services and facilities.

Useful information

Starting on page 385 you'll find Information Pages full of useful advice on such things as bookings, deposits, cancellations, complaints, etc.

A Sign of Quality

Knowing what to expect is vital when choosing a place to stay whether you're taking a short break, are away on business, or visiting family and friends. Whatever type of accommodation you are looking for, you'll find that establishments in *Where to Stay* offer the reassurance provided by the English Tourist Board's National Quality Grading and Classification Scheme.

Classification of facilities

An establishment's assessment under the Scheme will usually consist of two parts: the first, using the Crown symbol, classifies the range of services and facilities provided for guests; the second, from De Luxe to Approved, indicates the overall quality standard of these services and facilities.

The range of services and facilities provided is classified under one of six bands: from **Listed** (clean and comfortable accommodation, but limited range of services and facilities) to **Five Crown** (providing full range of services and facilities). Quite simply, the more Crowns, the wider the range.

Please note that a higher number of Crowns does not necessarily imply that the quality on offer is superior to that available at an establishment with fewer Crowns.

Quality grading

A separate quality grading indicates the overall standard of services and facilities. Graded establishments are awarded one of the following quality gradings:

DE LUXE (excellent overall standard)
HIGHLY COMMENDED (very good overall standard)
COMMENDED (good overall standard)
APPROVED (acceptable overall standard).

Before awarding a quality grading, Tourist Board inspectors check in as a guest, only identifying themselves after paying the bill. They assess the warmth of welcome and level of care and service they receive, as well as the standard and state of the decor, furnishings and fittings. Their overall assessment takes the nature and size of the establishments into account; you will therefore find that all types of accommodation have been able to achieve a Highly Commended or De Luxe quality grading.

If no quality grade appears alongside the Crown classification, it means the proprietor has yet to invite an inspector to do a quality assessment. However, from next year all the establishments participating in the Tourist Board's National Grading and Classification Scheme will be graded for quality as well as classified for their facilities.

Range of facilities

Listed and then **One** to **Five Crown** tell you the range of facilities provided. The more Crowns, the wider the range. Below is an indication of some of the facilities you can expect under each classification.

Listed Clean and comfortable accommodation, but limited range of facilities and services.

🏵 There will be additional facilities, including washbasin and chair in your bedroom, and you will have the use of a telephone.

🏵🏵 There will be a colour TV in your bedroom or in a lounge and you can enjoy morning tea/coffee in your room. At least some of the bedrooms will have a private bath (or shower) and WC.

🏵🏵🏵 At least half of the bedrooms will have private bath (or shower) en-suite. You will also be able to order a hot evening meal.

🏵🏵🏵🏵 Your bedroom will have a colour TV, radio and telephone; 90% of bedrooms will have private bath and/or shower and WC en-suite. There will be lounge service until midnight and evening meals can be ordered up to 2030 hours.

🏵🏵🏵🏵🏵 Every bedroom will have private bath, fixed shower and WC en-suite. The restaurant will be open for breakfast, lunch and dinner (or you can take meals in your room from breakfast until midnight) and you will benefit from an all-night lounge service. A night porter will also be on duty.

Lodge accommodation

The Lodge classification covers purpose-built bedroom accommodation that you will find along major roads and motorways. The range of facilities is indicated by **One** to **Three Moon** symbols. A separate quality grading indicates the overall standard of these facilities.

🌑 Your bedroom will have at least a washbasin and radio or colour TV. Tea/coffee may be from a vending machine in a public area.

🌑🌑 Your room will have colour TV, tea/coffee-making facilities and en-suite bath or shower with WC.

🌑🌑🌑 You will find colour TV and radio, tea/coffee-making facilities and comfortable seating in your bedroom and there will be a bath, shower and WC en-suite. The reception will be manned throughout the night.

Accessible Scheme

If you have difficulty walking or are a wheelchair user, it is important to be able to identify those establishments that will be able to cater for your requirements. If you book accommodation displaying an Accessible symbol, there's no longer any guesswork involved. Establishments can be awarded one of three categories of accessibility:

♿ Category 1 accessible to all wheelchair users including those travelling independently

♿ Category 2 accessible to a wheelchair user with assistance

♿ Category 3 accessible to a wheelchair user able to walk short distances and up at least three steps.

See page 10 for a full list of establishments in this guide who have an accessible symbol.

Finding a Place to Stay

Where to Stay makes it quick and easy to find accommodation that offers the quality and range of facilities you're looking for in the area you plan to visit.

Regional sections

The guide is divided into eleven regional sections corresponding to England's tourist regions. For an explanation of which counties each section covers, refer to the colour-coded map on page 12.

Each regional section contains an alphabetical listing of the region's cities, towns and villages with their accommodation establishments. A brief introduction, giving a flavour of the region, is followed by a selection of ideas on interesting places to visit – a sketch map shows where you can find these.

The town index on page 407 and colour location maps at the back of the guide show all cities, towns and villages with accommodation listings in this guide. Use these as a quick and easy way to find suitable accommodation.

Town index

If the place you plan to visit is included in the town index, turn to the page number given to find accommodation available there. Also check that location on the colour maps to find other places nearby which also have accommodation listings in this guide.

Location maps

If the place you want is not in the town index – or you only have a general idea of where you wish to stay – use the colour location maps to find places in the area which have accommodation listings in this guide. The town index will then guide you to the appropriate page.

The place for you

Each accommodation listing contains detailed information to enable you to make a judgement as to its suitability. This information has been provided by the proprietors themselves, and our aim has been to ensure that it is as objective and factual as possible.

Below the establishment name you will find the Crown classification, **Listed** or **One** to **Five Crown**, which indicates the range of services and facilities provided; the quality grading, **De Luxe, Highly Commended, Commended** or **Approved**, tells you the overall standard of services and facilities offered.

At-a-glance symbols at the end of the entry give you additional information on the services and facilities offered - a full key is given on the flap on the back cover. There's no need to flick back and forth between pages, just fold out the flap and you can check them as you go.

Accessibility

If you are a wheelchair user or have difficulty walking, look for the Accessible symbol. You will find a full list of entries with accommodation categorised under the Accessible Scheme on page 10.

Check for changes

Please remember that changes may have occurred since the guide went to press or may occur during 1996. When you have found a suitable place to stay, we do advise you to contact the establishment to check not only its availability, but also to confirm prices and any specific facilities, which may be important to you. The coupons at the back of the guide will help with your enquiries.

When you are happy with everything make your booking and, if you have time, confirm it in writing.

Further Information

You may also find it useful to read the information pages at the back of the guide (see page 385), particularly the section on cancellations.

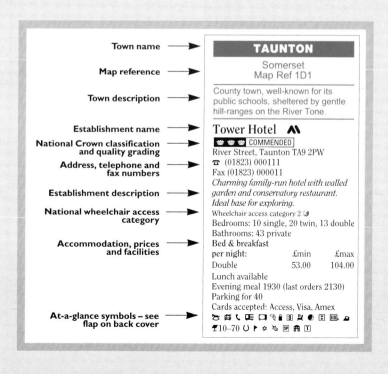

Town name →	**TAUNTON**
Map reference →	Somerset Map Ref 1D1
Town description →	County town, well-known for its public schools, sheltered by gentle hill-ranges on the River Tone.
Establishment name →	Tower Hotel
National Crown classification and quality grading →	COMMENDED
Address, telephone and fax numbers →	River Street, Taunton TA9 2PW ☎ (01823) 000111 Fax (01823) 000011
Establishment description →	*Charming family-run hotel with walled garden and conservatory restaurant. Ideal base for exploring.*
National wheelchair access category →	Wheelchair access category 2
Accommodation, prices and facilities →	Bedrooms: 10 single, 20 twin, 13 double Bathrooms: 43 private Bed & breakfast

per night:	£min	£max
Double	53.00	104.00

Lunch available
Evening meal 1930 (last orders 2130)
Parking for 40
Cards accepted: Access, Visa, Amex

At-a-glance symbols – see flap on back cover →

A Look at Some of the Best

The award of a DE LUXE quality grade recognises an establishment's excellent overall standard of such things as warmth of welcome, general atmosphere and ambience, efficiency of service, as well as the quality of facilities and standard of fittings.

Hope House, Tynemouth, Tyne & Wear

Causa Grange, Rosley, Cumbria

Broadview, Crewkerne, Somerset
Causa Grange, Rosley, Cumbria
Holmfield, Kendal, Cumbria
Hope House, Tynemouth, Tyne & Wear
Isbourne Manor House, Winchcombe, Gloucestershire
Meadowland, Bath, Avon
Middle Ord Manor House, Berwick-upon-Tweed, Northumberland
The Old Parsonage, Royal Tunbridge Wells, Kent
Pickett Howe, Buttermere, Cumbria
Shawswell Country House, Rendcomb, Gloucestershire
Tavern House, Tetbury, Gloucestershire

The inspector's overall assessment takes the nature and size of an establishment into account; you will therefore find all types of accommodation can achieve a DE LUXE quality grading.

These pages feature those establishments in *Where to Stay* that have achieved the highest quality grade of DE LUXE. Use the Town Index at the back of the guide to find page numbers for their fully detailed entries.

The Old Parsonage

Use Your *i*'s

Tourist Information *i*

When it comes to your next England break, the first stage of your journey could be closer than you think. You've probably got a Tourist Information Centre nearby. But you might not have realised that it's there to serve the local community – as well as visitors.

So make us your first stop. We'll be happy to help you, wherever you're heading.

Many Information Centres can provide you with maps and guides, helping you plan well in advance. And sometimes it's even possible for us to book your accommodation, too.

A visit to your nearest Information Centre can pay off in other ways as well. We can point you in the right direction when it comes to finding out about all the special events which are happening in the local region.

In fact, we can give you details of places to visit within easy reach... and perhaps tempt you to plan a day trip or weekend away.

Across the country, there are more than 550 Tourist Information Centres so you're never far away. You'll find the address of your nearest Tourist Information Centre in your local Phone Book.

National Accessible Scheme

Throughout Britain, the Tourist Boards are inspecting all types of places to stay, on holiday or business, that provide accessible accommodation for wheelchair users and others who may have difficulty walking.

The Tourist Boards recognise three categories of accessibility:

Category 1
Accessible to all wheelchair users including those travelling independently.

Category 2
Accessible to a wheelchair user with assistance.

Category 3
Accessible to a wheelchair user able to walk short distances and up at least three steps.

If you have additional needs or special requirements of any kind, we strongly recommend that you make sure these can be met by your chosen establishment before you confirm your booking.

The criteria the Tourist Boards have adopted do not, necessarily, conform to British Standards or to Building Regulations. They reflect what the Boards understand to be acceptable to meet the practical needs of wheelchair users.

The following establishments listed in this *Where to Stay* guide had been inspected and given an access category at the time of going to press. Use the Town Index at the back of the guide to find page numbers for their full entries.

⚙ Category 1

- WIMBORNE MINSTER, DORSET
  - Northill House

⚙ Category 2

- GARBOLDISHAM, NORFOLK
  - Ingleneuk Lodge
- LITTLEHAMPTON, WEST SUSSEX
  - Bracken Lodge Guest House

⚙ Category 3

- AMBLESIDE, CUMBRIA
  - Borrans Park Hotel
  - Rowanfield Country Guesthouse
- ARUNDEL, WEST SUSSEX
  - Mill Lane House
- BOSCASTLE, CORNWALL
  - The Old Coach House
- BRIDGNORTH, SHROPSHIRE
  - Haven Pasture
- CONGLETON, CHESHIRE
  - Sandhole Farm
- ELLERBY, N. YORKSHIRE
  - Ellerby Hotel
- HENLEY-ON-THAMES
  - Holmwood
- LENHAM, KENT
  - Dog and Bear Hotel
- LINCOLN, LINCOLNSHIRE
  - Garden House
- NAILSWORTH, GLOUCESTERSHIRE
  - Apple Orchard House
- PARKEND, GLOUCESTERSHIRE
  - The Fountain Inn
- RICHMOND, N. YORKSHIRE
  - Mount Pleasant Farm
- SANDBACH, CHESHIRE
  - Canal Centre and Village Store
- SARRE, KENT
  - Crown Inn (The Famous Cherry Brandy House)
- SHEFFIELD, S. YORKSHIRE
  - University of Sheffield
- STRATFORD-UPON-AVON, WARWICKSHIRE
  - Church Farm
- SWAFFHAM, NORFOLK
  - Glebe Bungalow
- THIRSK, N. YORKSHIRE
  - Doxford House
- ULLSWATER, CUMBRIA
  - Waterside House

- WARWICK, WARWICKSHIRE
  - Fulbrook Edge
  - Woodside
- WINCHESTER, HAMPSHIRE
  - Shawlands
- WISBECH, CAMBRIDGESHIRE
  - Crown Lodge Hotel
  - Stratton Farm
- YOXALL, STAFFORDSHIRE
  - The Moat

❏ The National Accessible Scheme forms part of the Tourism for All Campaign that is being promoted by all three National Tourist Boards. Additional help and guidance on finding suitable holiday accommodation for those with special needs can be obtained from:

Holiday Care Service
2 Old Bank Chambers, Station Road, Horley, Surrey RH6 9HW.
Tel: (01293) 774535.
Fax: (01293) 784647.
Minicom: (01293) 776943.

England's Tourist Regions

England is divided into 11 tourist regions, each of which has its own section in this guide. The regions are shown on the map and also listed opposite together with an index which identifies the region in which each county is located.

Location maps showing all the places with accommodation listed in this guide and an index to the place names can be found at the back of the guide.

Northumbria

Cumbria

Yorkshire & Humberside

North West

Middle England

East Anglia

Heart of England

London

South East England

South of England

West Country

The England for Excellence Awards
Winners 1994

The England for Excellence Awards were created by the English Tourist Board to recognise and reward the highest standards of excellence and quality in all major sectors of tourism in England. The coveted Leo statuette, presented each year to winners, has become firmly established as the ultimate accolade in the English tourism industry.

Over the past seven years the Leo has been won by all types and sizes of business with one common attribute – excellence in the facilities and services they offer.

Hotel of the Year
Sponsored by Yellow Pages
Linthwaite House Hotel (Four Crown, De Luxe)
Bowness-on-Windermere, Cumbria

Bed and Breakfast of the Year
Sponsored by Ordnance Survey
Pickett Howe Country Guesthouse (Three Crown, De Luxe)
Buttermere Valley, Cumbria

Caravan Holiday Park of the Year
Sponsored by the National Caravan Council
Hoburne Park (Five Tick), Christchurch, Dorset

Self-Catering Holiday of the Year
Sponsored by Country Holidays Group
Beech Farm Holiday Cottages (Four Key, De Luxe)
Pickering, North Yorkshire

Visitor Attraction of the Year
Sponsored by American Express Europe Limited
Warwick Castle, Warwickshire

Holiday Destination of the Year
Sponsored by Marks & Spencer
The Furness & Cartmel Peninsulas: Southern Lakeland

Tourism for All Award
Sponsored by Jarvis Hotels
Snibston Discovery Park, Coalville, Leicestershire

Tourism Information Centre of the Year
Sponsored by National Express
Malton Tourist Information Centre, North Yorkshire

Tourism and the Environment Award
Sponsored by Center Parcs
South Devon Green Tourism Initiative, Totnes, Devon

Travel Journalist of the Year
Sponsored by Hilton National
Alison Rice, Editor, BBC Holidays Magazine

Outstanding Contribution to English Tourism Award
Sponsored by Hilton International
The National Trust

Where to Stay in England '96

Hotels & Guesthouses £8.99
Bed & Breakfast, Farmhouses, Inns & Hostels £7.99
Self-Catering Holiday Homes £5.99

Somewhere Special £6.99
Families Welcome £4.99

AT-A-GLANCE SYMBOLS

At-a-glance symbols at the end of each accommodation entry give information about services and facilities. A handy guide to these symbols can be found inside the back cover flap, which can be kept open for easy reference.

BOOKING ENQUIRIES

When enquiring about accommodation you may find it helpful to use the accommodation coupons towards the end of the guide. These should be mailed direct to the establishments in which you are interested. Do please remember to include your name and address.

Where to Stay in England

Published by: English Tourist Board, Thames Tower, Black's Road, Hammersmith, London W6 9EL.
ISBN: 0 86143 196 0
Managing Editor: Jane Collinson
Compilation & Production: Guide Associates, Croydon
Design: Celsius, Winchester
Colour Photography: Nigel Corrie (front cover), Celsius, Glyn Williams and Britain on View
Illustrations: Susie Louis
Cartography: Colin Earl Cartography, Alton, and Line & Line, Thames Ditton
Typesetting: Computaprint, London, and Celsius
Printing & Binding: Pindar plc, Scarborough
Advertisement Sales: Madison Bell Ltd, 3 St. Peter's Street, Islington Green, London N1 8JD.
Telephone: (0171) 359 7737.
© English Tourist Board (except where stated)

Important:
The information contained in this guide has been published in good faith on the basis of information submitted to the English Tourist Board by the proprietors of the premises listed, who have paid for their entries to appear. The English Tourist Board cannot guarantee the accuracy of the information in this guide and accepts no responsibility for any error or misrepresentation. All liability for loss, disappointment, negligence or other damage caused by reliance on the information contained in this guide, or in the event of bankruptcy, or liquidation, or cessation of trade of any company, individual or firm mentioned, is hereby excluded. Please check carefully all prices and other details before confirming a reservation.

The English Tourist Board
The Board is a statutory body created by the Development of Tourism Act 1969 to develop and market England's tourism. Its main objectives are to provide a welcome for people visiting England; to encourage people living in England to take their holidays there; and to encourage the provision and improvement of tourist amenities and facilities in England. The Board has a statutory duty to advise the Government on tourism matters relating to England and, with Government approval and support, administers the national classification and grading schemes for tourist accommodation in England.

London

London is studded with good things as richly and thickly as a Victorian plum pudding. There's something for everyone: more than 100 museums and galleries; dozens of historic houses and gardens; some of the world's most famous shops and markets; and all the well-known sightseeing spots – Madame Tussaud's, Buckingham Palace, London Zoo....

London's parks are the green lungs of the capital – tree-dotted open spaces in the heart of the city. They're a haven for strolling in, for picnicking, or simply cooling street-dusty heels.

Don't miss the chance to see a West End show while you're in town, or one of London's many sparky, surprising fringe productions. And make sure you eat out in one of the thousands of interesting restaurants.

Greater London, comprising the 32 London boroughs

For more information on London, contact:

London Tourist Board and Convention Bureau, 26 Grosvenor Gardens, London SW1W 0DU

Tel: (0171) 730 3450

Fax: (0171) 730 9367

Where to Go in London – see pages 18–20

Where to Stay in London – see pages 24–34

London

You will find hundreds of interesting places to visit during your stay in London, just some of which are listed in these pages. Contact any Tourist Information Centre in the region for more ideas on days out in the London.

Bankside Gallery
48 Hopton Street, London SE1 9JH
Tel: (0171) 928 7521
Changing exhibitions of watercolours and prints. Home of The Royal Watercolour Society and The Royal Society of Painter-Etchers and Engravers.

British Museum
Great Russell Street, London
WC1B 3DG
Tel: (0171) 636 1555
One of the great museums of the world showing the works of man from all over the world from prehistoric times to the present day. British Library Exhibition Galleries are in the museum.

Cabinet War Rooms
Clive Steps, King Charles Street, London SW1A 2AQ
Tel: (0171) 930 6961
The underground headquarters used by Winston Churchill and the British Government during the Second World War; includes Cabinet Room, transatlantic telephone room and map room.

Chessington World of Adventures
Leatherhead Road, Chessington, Surrey KT9 2NE
Tel: (01372) 729560
A world of adventure, fun, exciting theme areas, rides, circus and the famous zoo. Rides include "Revenge of Ramases", "Vampire", "Terror Tomb", "Professor Burp's Bubble Works" and "Toytown Truckers".

Commonwealth Institute
Kensington High Street, London
W8 6NQ
Tel: (0171) 603 4535
Three floors of exhibition galleries depicting the history, landscape, wildlife and culture of 50 Commonwealth countries.

Design Museum
Shad Thames, London SE1 2YD
Tel: (0171) 403 6933
A study collection showing the development of design in mass production. Review of new products, graphics gallery and changing programme of exhibitions.

Fenton House
Windmill Hill, London
NW3 6RT
Tel: (0171) 435 3471
William and Mary house containing Benton Fletcher collection of early keyboard instruments and Binning collection of porcelain and furniture.

Guards Museum
Wellington Barracks, Birdcage Walk, London SW1E 6HQ
Tel: (0171) 414 3271
Collection of uniforms, colours and artefacts spanning over 300 years' history of the Foot Guards.

Guinness World of Records
The Trocadero, Coventry Street, Piccadilly Circus, London
W1V 7FD
Tel: (0171) 439 7331
Exhibition using models, videos,

computers and electronic displays to bring to life the Guinness Book of Records.

Hampton Court Palace
Hampton Court, Surrey
KT8 9AU
Tel: (0181) 781 9500
Oldest Tudor palace in England. Tudor kitchens, tennis courts, maze, state apartments and King's apartments.

HMS Belfast
Morgan's Lane, Tooley Street, London SE1 2JH
Tel: (0171) 407 6434
Naval museum in 11,500-tonne World War II cruiser moored on the Thames. Seven decks to explore.

Imperial War Museum
Lambeth Road, London SE1 6HZ
Tel: (0171) 416 5000
The story of 20th C war from Flanders to the Gulf. Features include Blitz Experience, Trench Experience and Operation Jericho.

Kew Bridge Steam Museum
Green Dragon Lane, Brentford, Middlesex TW8 0EN
Tel: (0181) 568 4757
Victorian waterworks housing massive steam-powered pumping engines. Steam railway, waterwheel, history of water. Tea room and shop.

London Zoo
Regent's Park, London NW1 4RY
Tel: (0171) 722 3333
Over 8,000 animals including giant panda, venomous snakes, penguins and piranhas. Daily events, Lifewatch Conservation Centre and Moonlight World.

Madame Tussaud's
Marylebone Road, London NW1 5LR
Tel: (0171) 935 6861
Wax figures in themed settings, including The Garden Party, Superstars, The Chamber of Horrors and The Spirit of London.

Museum of London
150 London Wall, London EC2Y 5HN
Tel: (0171) 600 3699
Galleries illustrate over 2,000 years of the capital's social history. Regular temporary exhibitions, lunchtime lecture programme.

Museum of the Moving Image
South Bank, Waterloo, London SE1 8XT
Tel: (0171) 928 3535
A celebration of cinema and television. 44 exhibition areas, offering plenty of hands-on participation, and a cast of actors to tell visitors more.

National Army Museum
Royal Hospital Road, London SW3 4HT
Tel: (0171) 730 0717
Histories of the British Army from 1485, the Indian Army up to independence in 1947 and colonial land forces. Battle of Waterloo exhibition.

National Gallery
Trafalgar Square, London WC2N 5DN
Tel: (0171) 839 3321
Western painting from 1260 to 1920, including work by Van Gogh, Rembrandt, Cezanne, Turner, Gainsborough, Leonardo da Vinci, Renoir and Botticelli.

National Maritime Museum
Romney Road, Greenwich, London SE10 9NF
Tel: (0181) 858 4422
Britain's maritime heritage illustrated through actual and model ships, paintings, uniforms, navigation and astronomy instruments, archives and photographs. Queen's House.

National Portrait Gallery
St Martin's Place, London WC2H 0HE
Tel: (0171) 306 0055
Collection of portraits of famous men and women from Middle Ages to the present day.

National Postal Museum
King Edward Building, King Edward Street, London EC1A 1LP

Tel: (0171) 239 5420
One of the most important and extensive collections of postage stamps in the world, including Phillips and Berne collections. Temporary exhibitions.

Natural History Museum
Cromwell Road, London
SW7 5BD
Tel: (0171) 938 9123
Home of the wonders of the natural world, one of the most popular museums in the world and one of London's finest landmarks.

Old Royal Observatory
Flamsteed House, Greenwich Park, Greenwich, London
SE10 9NF
Tel: (0181) 858 4422
Museum of space and time. Greenwich Meridian, working telescopes and planetarium, timeball, intricate clocks, computer simulations, Wren's Octagon Room.

Pollock's Toy Museum
1 Scala Street, London W1P 1LT
Tel: (0171) 636 3452
Toys of all kinds, including dolls, dolls' houses, teddy bears, tin toys, folk toys, toy theatres.

Royal Air Force Museum
Grahame Park Way, Hendon, London NW9 5LL
Tel: (0181) 205 2266
Three halls displaying over 70 full-size aircraft. "Battle of Britain Experience", flight simulator, jet trainer, free film shows.

Science Museum
Exhibition Road, South

Kensington, London SW7 2DD
Tel: (0171) 938 8000
National Museum of Science and Industry. Full-size replica of Apollo II Lunar Lander, launch pad, Wellcome Museum of History of Medicine, flight lab, food for thought, optics.

The Story of Telecommunications
145 Queen Victoria Street, London EC4V 4AT
Tel: (0171) 248 7444
Museum telling the story of telecommunications with set pieces and hands-on exhibits.

The Theatre Museum
1E Tavistock Street, Covent Garden, London WC2E 7PA
Tel: (0171) 836 7891
Five galleries include permanent display of history of performance in the UK. Collection includes theatre, ballet, dance, rock and pop music, musical stage.

Tower Hill Pageant
Tower Hill Terrace, London
EC3N 4EE
Tel: (0171) 709 0081
Automatic vehicles transport visitors past tableaux depicting the history of the City and its port. Display of archaeological finds, shops, restaurant.

Find Out More
A free information pack about holidays and attractions in London is available on written request from: **London Tourist Board and Convention Bureau**, 26 Grosvenor Gardens, London SW1W 0DU.

Tourist Information

Tourist and leisure information can be obtained from Tourist Information Centres throughout England. Details of centres and other information services in Greater London are given below. The symbol 🛏 means that an accommodation booking service is provided.

Tourist Information Centres

Points of arrival

Victoria Station, Forecourt, SW1 🛏
Easter–October, daily 0800–1900. November–Easter, reduced opening hours.

Liverpool Street Underground Station, EC2 🛏
Monday 0815–1900.
Tuesday–Saturday 0815–1800.
Sunday 0830–1645.

Heathrow Terminals 1, 2, 3 Underground Station Concourse (Heathrow Airport) 🛏
Daily 0830–1800.

Heathrow Terminal 3 Arrivals Concourse 🛏
Waterloo International Arrivals Hall 🛏
The above information centres provide a London and Britain tourist information service, offer a hotel accommodation booking service, stock free and saleable publications on Britain and London and sell theatre tickets, tourist tickets for bus and underground and tickets for sightseeing tours.

Inner London

British Travel Centre 🛏
12 Regent Street, Piccadilly Circus, SW1Y 4PQ
Monday–Friday 0900–1830.
Saturday–Sunday 1000–1600
(0900–1700 Saturdays May–September).

East End Visitor Centre
107a Commercial Street, E1 6BG

Tel: (0181) 375 2549
Monday–Friday 0930–1630.

Greenwich Tourist Information Centre 🛏
46 Greenwich Church Street, SE10 9BL
Tel: (0181) 858 6376
April–September, daily 1015–1645. October–March, reduced opening hours.

Hackney Museum and Tourist Information Centre
Central Hall, Mare Street, E8
Tel: (0181) 986 6914
Tuesday–Friday 1000–1700.
Saturday 1330–1700.

Islington Tourist Information Centre 🛏
44 Duncan Street, E1 8BL
Tel: (0171) 278 8787
Monday–Saturday 1000–1700.

Lewisham Tourist Information Centre
Lewisham Library, Lewisham High Street, SE13
Tel: (0181) 297 8317
Monday 1000–1700.
Tuesday-Thursday 1000–2000.
Friday and Saturday 0900–1700.

Selfridges 🛏
Oxford Street, W1. Basement Services Arcade
Tel: (0171) 629 1234
Open during normal store hours.

Southwark Tourist Information Centre
Hay's Galleria, Tooley Street, SE1
Tel: (0171) 403 8299
Monday–Friday 1100–1730.
Saturday, Sunday 1200–1730.
Closed weekends and 1100-1600 weekdays in winter.

Outer London

Bexley Tourist Information Centre 🛏
Central Library, Townley Road, Bexleyheath DA6 7HJ
Tel: (0181) 303 9052
Monday, Tuesday, Thursday 0930–2000.
Friday 0930–1730.
Saturday 0930–1700.

Also at Hall Place Visitor Centre 🛏
Bourne Road, Bexley
Tel: (01322) 558676
June–September, daily 1130–1630.

Croydon Tourist Information Centre 🛏
Katharine Street, Croydon CR9 1ET
Tel: (0181) 253 1009
Monday–Wednesday and Friday 0900–1800. Thursday 0930–1800.
Saturday 0900–1700.
Sunday 1200–1700.

Harrow Tourist Information Centre
Civic Centre, Station Road, Harrow HA1 2XF
Tel: (0181) 424 1103
Monday–Friday 0900–1700.

Hillingdon Tourist Information Centre
Central Library, 14 High Street, Uxbridge UB8 1HD
Tel: Uxbridge (01895) 250706
Monday, Tuesday and Thursday 0930–2000. Friday and Wednesday 0930–1730.
Saturday 0930–1600.

Hounslow Tourist Information Centre
24 The Treaty Centre, Hounslow

High Street, Hounslow TW3 1ES
Tel: (0181) 572 8279
Monday, Wednesday, Saturday
0930–1730. Tuesday, Thursday
0930–2000.

**Redbridge Tourist
Information Centre**
Town Hall, High Road, Ilford,
Essex IG1 1DD
Tel: (0181) 478 3020
Monday–Friday 0830–1700.

**Richmond Tourist
Information Centre**
Old Town Hall, Whittaker
Avenue, Richmond upon Thames
TW9 1TP
Tel: (0181) 940 9125
Monday–Friday 1000–1800.
Saturday 1000–1700.
May–October, also Sunday
1015–1615.

**Twickenham Tourist
Information Centre**
44, York Street, Twickenham
TW1 3BZ
Tel: (0181) 891 7272
Monday–Friday 0900–1700.

Visitorcall
The London Tourist Board and
Convention Bureau's 'phone guide
to London operates 24 hours a
day. To access a full range of
information call 0839 123456. To
access specific lines dial 0839 123
followed by:

What's on this week – 400
What's on next 3 months – 401
Sunday in London – 407
Rock and pop concerts – 422
Popular attractions – 480
Where to take children – 424
Museums – 429
Palaces (including Buckingham
Palace) – 481
Current exhibitions – 403
Changing the Guard – 411
Popular West End shows – 416
Pubs and restaurants – 485
Calls cost 39p per minute cheap rate,
49p per minute at all other times.

To order a Visitorcall card please
call (0171) 971 0026. Information
for callers using push-button
telephones: (0171) 971 0027.

Artsline
London's information and advice
service for disabled people on
arts and entertainment. Call
(0171) 388 2227.

Hotel Accommodation Service
The London Tourist Board and
Convention Bureau helps visitors
to find and book accommodation
at a wide range of prices in hotels
and guesthouses, including budget
accommodation, throughout the
Greater London area.

Reservations are made with
hotels which are members of LTB,
denoted in this guide with the
symbol ▲▲ by their name.
Reservations can be made by
credit card holders via the
telephone accommodation
reservations service on (0171)
824 8844 by simply giving the
reservations clerk your card
details (Access or Visa) and room
requirements. LTB takes an
administrative booking fee. The
service operates Monday–Friday
0930–1730.

Reservations on arrival are
handled at the Tourist Information
Centres operated by LTB at
Victoria Station, Liverpool Street
Station, Waterloo International,
Selfridges and Heathrow. Go to
any of them on the day when you
need accommodation. A
communication charge and a
refundable deposit are payable
when making a reservation.

Which part of London?
The majority of tourist
accommodation is situated in the
central parts of London and is
therefore very convenient for
most of the city's attractions and
night life.

However, there are many hotels
in outer London which provide
other advantages, such as easier
parking. In the "Where to Stay"
pages which follow, you will find
accommodation listed under
INNER LONDON (covering the
E1 to W14 London Postal Area)
and OUTER LONDON (covering
the remainder of Greater
London). Colour maps 6 and 7 at
the back of the guide show place
names and London Postal Area
codes and will help you to locate
accommodation in your chosen
area of London.

LONDON INDEX

If you are looking for accommodation in a particular establishment in London and you know its name, this index will give you the page number of the full entry in the guide.

BOOKING ENQUIRIES

When enquiring about accommodation you may find it helpful to use the accommodation coupons towards the end of the guide. These should be mailed direct to the establishments in which you are interested. Do please remember to include your name and address.

WHERE TO STAY

Accommodation entries in this section are listed under **Inner London** (covering the E1 to W14 London Postal Area) and **Outer London** (covering the remainder of Greater London) – see the colour location maps 6 and 7 at the back of this guide. If you want to look up a particular establishment, you can use the index to establishments (preceding page) to find the page number.

At-a-glance symbols at the end of each accommodation entry give information about services and facilities. A handy guide to these symbols can be found inside the back cover flap, which can be kept open for easy reference.

INNER LONDON

Colour maps 6 & 7 at the back of the guide show place names and London Postal Area codes and will help you to locate accommodation in your chosen area of London.

LONDON E4

25 Eglington Road
Listed
North Chingford, London E4 7AN
☎ (0181) 529 1140
Fax (0181) 508 3837
Comfortable Edwardian period family home with exclusive facilities in quiet suburb, easy access to City. Solar-heated swimming pool in landscaped garden. Gourmet meals on request.
Bedrooms: 1 double, 1 twin
Bathrooms: 1 public

Bed & breakfast per night:	£min	£max
Single	29.00	
Double	58.00	

Half board per person:	£min	£max
Daily	40.00	

Lunch available
Evening meal 1700 (last orders 2300)

LONDON E10

Sleeping Beauty Motel
APPROVED
543 Lea Bridge Road, Leyton, London E10 7EB
☎ (0181) 556 8080
Fax (0181) 556 8080

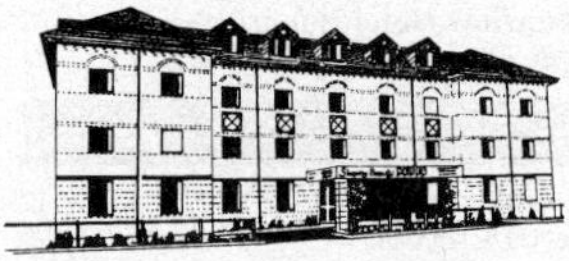

All rooms en-suite with bath and showers, satellite TV. Lift, bar, car park. Warm and friendly atmosphere. Prices are per room.
Bedrooms: 16 double, 21 twin, 4 triple
Bathrooms: 41 private

Bed & breakfast per night:	£min	£max
Single	35.00	40.00
Double	35.00	40.00

Parking for 34
Cards accepted: Access, Visa, Diners, Amex, Switch/Delta

LONDON N1

Kandara Guest House
Listed
68 Ockendon Road, London N1 3NW
☎ (0171) 226 5721 & 226 3379
Small family-run guesthouse near the Angel, Islington. Free street parking and good public transport to West End and City.
Bedrooms: 4 single, 3 double, 2 twin, 1 triple
Bathrooms: 3 public

Bed & breakfast per night:	£min	£max
Single	24.00	25.00
Double	34.00	36.00

Cards accepted: Access, Visa

LONDON N7

Five Kings Guest House
59 Anson Road, Tufnell Park, London N7 0AR
☎ (0171) 607 3996 & 607 6466
Privately-run guesthouse in a quiet residential area. 15 minutes to central London. Unrestricted parking in road.
Bedrooms: 6 single, 3 double, 3 twin, 2 triple, 2 family rooms; suites available
Bathrooms: 9 private, 3 public, 2 private showers

Bed & breakfast per night:	£min	£max
Single	17.00	24.00
Double	28.00	36.00

Cards accepted: Access, Visa

LONDON N13

71 Berkshire Gardens
Listed
Palmers Green, London N13 6AA
☎ (0181) 888 5573
2-storey house with garden, 5 minutes' bus ride from Wood Green Piccadilly line underground station. Car parking available.
Bedrooms: 1 single, 1 double, 1 twin
Bathrooms: 1 private, 1 public

Bed & breakfast per night:	£min	£max
Single	11.00	13.00
Double	22.00	26.00

Half board per person:	£min	£max
Daily	15.00	18.00

Lunch available
Evening meal 1800 (last orders 2000)
Parking for 1
🦽 10 ⊠ 🍳 ▢ 🖕 🔌 🅤🅛 🛈 Ⓢ ✂ 🅜 📺 🞖, 🖴 ✿ ✕ 🐾 ⚲

LONDON N19

Parkland Walk Guest House
Listed **COMMENDED**

12 Hornsey Rise Gardens, London
N19 3PR
☎ (0171) 263 3228 & (01973) 382982
Fax (0171) 831 9489
*Friendly Victorian family house in
residential area, Highgate/Crouch End.
Near many restaurants and convenient
for central London. Non-smokers only.
Recent British Tourist Authority award
winner - Best Small Hotel in London
competition.*
Bedrooms: 3 single, 1 double, 1 twin,
1 family room
Bathrooms: 4 private, 1 public

Bed & breakfast

per night:	£min	£max
Single	23.00	35.00
Double	42.00	55.00

Cards accepted: Amex
🦽 ⊠ 🍳 ▢ 🖕 🔌 🅤🅛 🛈 Ⓢ ✂ 🅜 📺 🞖, 🖴
📲8 ✿ ✕ 🐾

LONDON N22

Pane Residence
Listed

154 Boundary Road, Wood Green,
London N22 6AE
☎ (0181) 889 3735
*In a pleasant location 6 minutes' walk
from Turnpike Lane underground
station and near Alexandra Palace.
Kitchen facilities available.*
Bedrooms: 1 single, 1 double, 1 twin
Bathrooms: 1 public

Bed & breakfast

per night:	£min	£max
Single	15.50	17.50
Double	23.00	26.00

Parking for 2
🦽 1 🍳 🖕 🅤🅛 🛈 🞖, 🖴 ✿ ✕ 🐾

LONDON NW4

Rilux House
♛♛

1 Lodge Road, London NW4 4DD
☎ (0181) 203 0933
Fax (0181) 203 6446
*High standard, all private facilities,
kitchenette and garden. Quiet. Close to
underground, buses, M1, 20 minutes
West End. Convenient for Wembley,
easy route to Heathrow, direct trains to
Gatwick and Luton airports. Languages
spoken.*
Bedrooms: 1 single, 1 double
Bathrooms: 2 private

Bed & breakfast

per night:	£min	£max
Single	25.00	27.50
Double	40.00	45.00

Parking for 1
🦽 🛶 📞 🍳 ▢ 🖕 🔌 🅤🅛 🛈 ✂ 🅜 📺 🞖, 🖴
✿ ✕ 🐾 🅞🅐🅟 ⚲ 🆂🅿 🆃

LONDON NW10

30 All Souls Avenue
Listed

Willesden, London NW10 6AR
☎ (0181) 965 6051
Fax (0181) 965 6051
*Family-run house, 20 minutes from
Baker Street.*
Bedrooms: 1 single, 2 twin
Bathrooms: 2 public

Bed & breakfast

per night:	£min	£max
Single	15.00	18.00
Double	28.00	34.00

Half board

per person:	£min	£max
Daily	18.00	20.00
Weekly	100.00	140.00

🦽 8 🍳 ▢ 🖕 🔌 🅤🅛 Ⓢ ✂ 🅜 🞖, 🖴 ✿
✕ 🐾

J and T Guest House
Listed

98 Park Avenue North, Willesden
Green, London NW10 1JY
☎ (0181) 452 4085
Fax (0181) 450 2503
*Small guesthouse in north west London
close to underground. Easy access to
Wembley Stadium complex. 5 minutes
from M1.*
Bedrooms: 1 single, 1 double, 3 twin,
1 triple
Bathrooms: 6 private

Bed & breakfast

per night:	£min	£max
Single	29.00	32.00
Double	40.00	49.00

Parking for 2
Cards accepted: Access, Visa
🦽 🛶 📞 🍳 ▢ 🖕 🔌 🅤🅛 🞖, 🖴 ✕ 🐾 🆃

LONDON SE6

41 Minard Road
Listed **COMMENDED**

Catford, London SE6 1NP
☎ (0181) 697 2596
*English home in quiet residential area
off A205 South Circular Road. 10
minutes' walk to Hither Green station
for 20-minute journey to central
London.*
Bedrooms: 1 single, 2 twin
Bathrooms: 1 public

Bed & breakfast

per night:	£min	£max
Single	17.00	17.00
Double	34.00	34.00

Evening meal 1700 (last orders 2000)
🦽 ⊠ ▢ 🖕 🔌 🅤🅛 🛈 🅜 📺 🞖, 🖴 ✿ ✕ 🐾 🆂🅿

LONDON SE12

Kingsland House
Listed

45 Southbrook Road, Lee, London
SE12 8LJ
☎ (0181) 318 4788
*Detached house in conservation area,
close to Blackheath and Greenwich and
with easy access to City and West End.
Off A205 South Circular Road and 8
minutes' walk from Lee station. Homely
atmosphere.*
Bedrooms: 1 single, 3 twin
Bathrooms: 2 public

Bed & breakfast

per night:	£min	£max
Single	20.00	22.00
Double	36.00	40.00

🦽 🍳 ▢ 🖕 🅤🅛 🞖, 🖴 ✿ 🐾

LONDON SE21

Diana Hotel
♛♛

88 Thurlow Park Road, London
SE21 8HY
☎ (0181) 670 3250
Fax (0181) 761 9152
*Comfortable and friendly family-run
hotel near Dulwich Village, a pleasant
suburb 10 minutes from central
London.*
Bedrooms: 1 single, 4 double, 3 twin,
2 triple, 1 family room
Bathrooms: 4 private, 2 public,
1 private shower

Bed & breakfast

per night:	£min	£max
Single	28.00	38.00
Double	38.00	48.00

Evening meal 1800 (last orders 1930)
Parking for 3
Cards accepted: Access, Visa
🦽 🛶 ▢ 🖕 🅜 📺 🞖, 🖴 🐾 🆂🅿 🆃

LONDON SE22

Bedknobs ♨
Listed **COMMENDED**

58 Glengarry Road, East Dulwich,
London SE22 8QD
☎ (0181) 299 2004
*Carefully restored Victorian family-run
house offering many home comforts,
good service and a warm welcome. BTA
London B&B Award 1992.*
Bedrooms: 1 double, 1 twin, 1 triple
Bathrooms: 2 public

Bed & breakfast

per night:	£min	£max
Single	21.00	29.50
Double	40.00	48.00

🦽 🍳 ▢ 🖕 🔌 🅤🅛 🛈 Ⓢ ✂ 🞖, 🖴 ✕ 🐾

We advise you to confirm
your booking in writing.

LONDON SW1

Brindle House Hotel ♈
Listed

1 Warwick Place North, London
SW1V 1QW
☎ (0171) 828 0057
Fax (0171) 931 8805
*Small and quiet (off main road) bed
and breakfast ideally located for
Victoria bus, train and underground
stations. Good atmosphere.*
Bedrooms: 4 single, 4 double, 2 twin,
2 triple
Bathrooms: 2 public, 5 private
showers

Bed & breakfast

per night:	£min	£max
Single	25.00	29.00
Double	38.00	44.00

Cards accepted: Access, Visa, Diners,
Amex

Caswell Hotel
Listed

25 Gloucester Street, London
SW1V 2DB
☎ (0171) 834 6345
*Pleasant, family-run hotel, near Victoria
coach and rail stations, yet in a quiet
location.*
Bedrooms: 1 single, 6 double, 6 twin,
3 triple, 2 family rooms
Bathrooms: 7 private, 5 public

Bed & breakfast

per night:	£min	£max
Single	26.00	48.00
Double	34.00	62.00

Chester House ♈
Listed

134 Ebury Street, London SW1W 9QQ
☎ (0171) 730 3632 & 824 8445
Fax (0171) 824 8446
*Small, friendly bed and breakfast close
to Sloane Square and 10 minutes' walk
from Harrods. Convenient for public
transport.*
Bedrooms: 3 single, 2 double, 5 twin,
2 triple
Bathrooms: 7 private, 2 public

Bed & breakfast

per night:	£min	£max
Single	27.00	38.00
Double	40.00	60.00

Cards accepted: Access, Visa, Diners,
Amex

Colliers Hotel ♈

97 Warwick Way, London SW1V 1QL
☎ (0171) 834 6931 & 828 0210
Fax (0171) 834 8439
*Modern-style family hotel with spacious
rooms. Very clean, budget priced,
centrally located. Ideal for easy
connections to London's major tourist
spots.*
Bedrooms: 4 single, 6 double, 6 twin,
1 triple, 1 family room
Bathrooms: 2 private, 3 public,
4 private showers

Bed & breakfast

per night:	£min	£max
Single	22.00	26.00
Double	30.00	36.00

Cards accepted: Access, Visa, Diners,
Amex

Elizabeth Hotel ♈

37 Eccleston Square, Victoria, London
SW1V 1PB
☎ (0171) 828 6812

*Friendly, quiet hotel overlooking
magnificent gardens of stately
residential square (circa 1835), close to
Belgravia and within 5 minutes' walk of
Victoria.*
Bedrooms: 6 single, 7 double, 6 twin,
10 triple, 11 family rooms
Bathrooms: 39 private, 2 public,
1 private shower

Bed & breakfast

per night:	£min	£max
Single	36.00	55.00
Double	55.00	80.00

Ad Display advertisement appears on
this page

Georgian House Hotel ♈

35 St. George's Drive, London
SW1V 4DG
☎ (0171) 834 1438
Fax (0171) 976 6085
*Traditional B&B in a quiet residential
area of City of Westminster within
walking distance of Victoria station,
shopping areas and important sights.
Student rooms.*
Bedrooms: 8 single, 12 double, 2 twin,
7 triple, 5 family rooms
Bathrooms: 20 private, 3 public,
5 private showers

Bed & breakfast

per night:	£min	£max
Single	18.00	32.00
Double	31.00	47.00

Cards accepted: Access, Visa, Switch/
Delta

Stanley House Hotel ♈

19-21 Belgrave Road, London
SW1V 1RB
☎ (0171) 834 5042 & 834 7292
Fax (0171) 834 8439
*Modern-style family hotel with spacious
rooms, all with intercom and radio.
Telex available.*
Bedrooms: 3 single, 5 double, 12 twin,
8 triple, 13 family rooms
Bathrooms: 30 private, 5 public

Bed & breakfast

per night:	£min	£max
Single	20.00	25.00
Double	30.00	42.00

Cards accepted: Access, Visa, Diners,
Amex

Windermere Hotel ♠

👑👑👑 COMMENDED

142-144 Warwick Way, Victoria,
London SW1V 4JE
☎ (0171) 834 5163 & 834 5480
Fax (0171) 630 8831
*Winner of the 1992 BTA Trophy, Small
Hotel Award. Winner of the Certificate
of Distinction in 1991. A friendly,
charming hotel with well-appointed
rooms and a licensed restaurant.*
Bedrooms: 3 single, 11 double, 5 twin,
1 triple, 3 family rooms
Bathrooms: 19 private, 2 public

Bed & breakfast

per night:	£min	£max
Single	34.00	55.00
Double	48.00	82.00

Lunch available
Evening meal 1800 (last orders 2130)
Cards accepted: Access, Visa, Amex,
Switch/Delta

🛏🍴📞🖨🔒🛎Ⓢ✂🅿📺◑🛗, 📠
✈ OAP 🐾 SP Ⓣ

LONDON SW5

London Tourist Hotel ♠

👑👑 COMMENDED

15 Penywern Road, Earl's Court,
London SW5 9TT
☎ (0171) 370 4356
Fax (0171) 370 7923
Telex 299471

*Situated within 2 minutes' walk of
Earl's Court underground, with direct
connections to Heathrow, Victoria and
Piccadilly Circus. Newly refurbished, all
rooms with en-suite facilities, colour TV,
telephone and hairdryer. Children
under 3 free of charge.*
Bedrooms: 9 single, 4 double, 13 twin,
6 triple
Bathrooms: 32 private

Bed & breakfast

per night:	£min	£max
Single	38.00	48.00
Double	54.00	68.00

Cards accepted: Access, Visa, Diners,
Amex

🛏🍴📞🖨🔒🅿📺◑🔲🛗,📠✆30
❄ OAP 🐾 SP Ⓣ

Merlyn Court Hotel ♠

👑👑

2 Barkston Gardens, London
SW5 0EN
☎ (0171) 370 1640
Fax (0171) 370 4986

*Well-established, family-run, good value
hotel in quiet Edwardian square, close
to Earl's Court and Olympia. Direct
underground link to Heathrow, the West
End and rail stations. Car park nearby.*
Bedrooms: 4 single, 4 double, 4 twin,
2 triple, 3 family rooms
Bathrooms: 11 private, 6 public,
1 private shower

Bed & breakfast

per night:	£min	£max
Single	25.00	45.00
Double	35.00	55.00

Cards accepted: Access, Visa

🛏🍴📞🖨🔒🅄🛎✂🅿📺🛗,📠 OAP
🐾 SP Ⓣ

Swiss House Hotel ♠

Listed COMMENDED

171 Old Brompton Road, London
SW5 0AN
☎ (0171) 373 2769 & 373 9383
Fax (0171) 373 4983

Continued ▶

LONDON SW5

Continued

Very clean, comfortable and conveniently situated hotel near London museums, shopping/exhibition centres. Gloucester Road underground station is within easy walking distance. Recent winner of BTA award for best value B&B in London.
Bedrooms: 5 single, 5 double, 2 twin, 4 triple
Bathrooms: 14 private, 1 public
Bed & breakfast

per night:	£min	£max
Single	34.00	50.00
Double	60.00	64.00

Cards accepted: Access, Visa, Diners, Amex, Switch/Delta

Windsor House ⋀

Listed

12 Penywern Road, London SW5 9ST
☎ (0171) 373 9087
Fax (0171) 385 2417

Budget-priced bed and breakfast establishment in Earl's Court. Easily reached from airports and motorway. The West End is minutes away by underground. NCP parking.
Bedrooms: 2 single, 4 double, 4 twin, 1 triple, 7 family rooms
Bathrooms: 10 private, 6 public, 6 private showers
Bed & breakfast

per night:	£min	£max
Single	24.00	36.00
Double	30.00	46.00

Ad Display advertisement appears on this page

York House Hotel ⋀

28 Philbeach Gardens, London SW5 9EA
☎ (0171) 373 7519 & 373 7579
Fax (0171) 370 4641
Conveniently located close to the Earl's Court and Olympia Exhibition Centres and the West End. Underground direct to Heathrow Airport.
Bedrooms: 20 single, 6 double, 3 twin, 5 triple, 4 family rooms
Bathrooms: 1 private, 9 public
Bed & breakfast

per night:	£min	£max
Single	25.00	26.00
Double	40.00	42.00

Cards accepted: Access, Visa, Diners, Amex

LONDON SW7

Abcone Hotel ⋀

APPROVED

10 Ashburn Gardens, London SW7 4DG
☎ (0171) 370 3383
Fax (0171) 373 3082
Close to Gloucester Road underground and convenient for High Street Kensington, Knightsbridge, Olympia, Earl's Court, museums and Hyde Park.
Bedrooms: 17 single, 15 double, 3 twin
Bathrooms: 28 private, 5 public

BOOKING ENQUIRIES

When enquiring about accommodation you may find it helpful to use the accommodation coupons towards the end of the guide. These should be mailed direct to the establishments in which you are interested. Do please remember to include your name and address.

LONDON SW7

Continued

Bed & breakfast

per night:	£min	£max
Single	39.00	74.00
Double	50.00	89.00

Evening meal 1900 (last orders 2130)
Cards accepted: Access, Visa, Diners, Amex

Five Sumner Place Hotel ⋀

`Listed` `HIGHLY COMMENDED`

5 Sumner Place, South Kensington, London SW7 3EE
☎ (0171) 584 7586
Fax (0171) 823 9962
Recent winner of the Best Small Hotel in London Award. Situated in South Kensington, the most fashionable area. This family owned and run hotel offers first-class service and personal attention.
Bedrooms: 3 single, 10 double
Bathrooms: 13 private, 1 public

Bed & breakfast

per night:	£min	£max
Single	62.00	89.00
Double	89.00	111.00

Cards accepted: Access, Visa, Diners, Amex

LONDON SW14

The Plough Inn

`APPROVED`

42 Christchurch Road, East Sheen, London SW14 7AF
☎ (0181) 876 7833 & 876 4533
Fax (0181) 876 7833

Delightful old pub, part 16th C, next to Richmond Park. En-suite accommodation, traditional ales, home-cooked food.
Bedrooms: 4 double, 3 twin
Bathrooms: 7 private

Bed & breakfast

per night:	£min	£max
Single	50.00	52.00
Double	65.00	70.00

Half board

per person:	£min	£max
Daily	56.00	66.00

Lunch available
Evening meal 1930 (last orders 2130)
Parking for 4
Cards accepted: Access, Visa, Amex

LONDON SW19

Compton Guest House

`Listed`

65 Compton Road, Wimbledon, London SW19 7QA
☎ (0181) 947 4488 & 879 3245
Family-run guesthouse in pleasant, peaceful area, 5 minutes from Wimbledon station (British Rail and District Line). Easy access to the West End, central London, M1, M2, M3, M4 and M25. Quality rooms, with excellent service. About 12 minutes' walk to Wimbledon tennis courts.
Bedrooms: 2 single, 1 double, 2 twin, 1 triple, 2 family rooms
Bathrooms: 2 public

Bed & breakfast

per night:	£min	£max
Single	26.00	36.00
Double	38.00	58.00

Parking for 2

LONDON W1

Bentinck House Hotel ⋀

20 Bentinck Street, London W1M 5RL
☎ (0171) 935 9141
Fax (0171) 224 5903
Telex 8954111
Family-run bed and breakfast hotel in the heart of London's fashionable West End, close to Bond Street underground and Oxford Street.
Bedrooms: 8 single, 1 double, 3 twin, 5 triple
Bathrooms: 12 private, 4 public

Bed & breakfast

per night:	£min	£max
Single	43.00	55.00
Double	65.00	75.00

Half board

per person:	£min	£max
Daily	35.00	65.00
Weekly	240.00	450.00

Evening meal 1800 (last orders 2200)
Cards accepted: Access, Visa, Diners, Amex

The Bickenhall Hotel ⋀

119 Gloucester Place, London W1H 3PJ
☎ (0171) 935 3401
Fax (0171) 224 0614
Well-appointed Georgian house in the heart of London's West End. Convenient for shops, theatres and sightseeing.
Bedrooms: 5 single, 3 double, 3 twin, 6 triple, 2 family rooms
Bathrooms: 15 private, 1 public

Bed & breakfast

per night:	£min	£max
Single	35.00	55.00
Double	55.00	75.00

Cards accepted: Access, Visa, Diners, Amex

The Edward Lear Hotel ⋀

30 Seymour Street, London W1H 5WD
☎ (0171) 402 5401
Fax (0171) 706 3766
Family-run Georgian town residence, once the home of Edward Lear, famous poet and painter, with informal but efficient atmosphere and in a central location. 1 minute from Oxford Street and Marble Arch.
Bedrooms: 13 single, 4 double, 10 twin, 2 triple, 2 family rooms
Bathrooms: 4 private, 6 public, 9 private showers

Bed & breakfast

per night:	£min	£max
Single	39.50	52.50
Double	49.50	62.50

Cards accepted: Access, Visa, Switch/Delta

Lincoln House Hotel ⋀

`COMMENDED`

33 Gloucester Place, London W1H 3PD
☎ (0171) 486 7630
Fax (0171) 486 0166
Attractively refurbished Georgian hotel with en-suite rooms. Superb location, admirable standard of facilities and services, competitively priced in the heart of London's West End.
Bedrooms: 6 single, 8 double, 4 twin, 3 triple, 1 family room
Bathrooms: 22 private, 1 public

Bed & breakfast

per night:	£min	£max
Single	52.00	55.00
Double	65.00	79.00

Cards accepted: Access, Visa, Diners, Amex, Switch/Delta

Wigmore Court Hotel ⋀

`COMMENDED`

23 Gloucester Place, Portman Square, London W1H 3PB
☎ (0171) 935 0928
Fax (0171) 487 4254
Small, clean, fully refurbished family hotel. Large en-suite rooms - ideal for families. 3 minutes' walk to Oxford Street. Competitively priced.
Bedrooms: 5 single, 6 double, 4 twin, 3 triple, 2 family rooms
Bathrooms: 18 private, 1 public

> **Please mention this guide when making a booking.**

Bed & breakfast

per night:	£min	£max
Single	25.00	50.00
Double	35.00	70.00

Cards accepted: Access, Visa, Diners

☎ ⚹ ✆ ▤ ▢ ⓊⓁ ㋫ 📺 ◐ ▥ ◨ ✶ ⒹⒶⓅ ✽ ⓈⓅ ㊟ ⓣ

Wyndham Hotel

Listed

30 Wyndham Street, London
W1H 1DD
☎ (0171) 723 7204 & 723 9400
Fax (0171) 723 7204
*Small family-run B&B in a Georgian
terrace, around the corner from Baker
Street and a short walk from Oxford
Street.*
Bedrooms: 5 single, 4 double, 2 twin
Bathrooms: 1 public, 10 private
showers

Bed & breakfast

per night:	£min	£max
Single	30.00	32.00
Double	40.00	42.00

☎ ⚹ ▢ ✿ ⓊⓁ ✁ ◐ ▥ ◨ ✶ ⚵

LONDON W2

Abbey Court Hotel ⋀

Listed

174 Sussex Gardens, London W2 1TP
☎ (0171) 402 0704
Fax (0171) 262 2055
*Central London hotel, reasonable
prices. Within walking distance of
Lancaster Gate, Paddington station and
Hyde Park. Car parking available at
modest charge.*
Bedrooms: 14 single, 17 double,
7 twin, 10 triple, 2 family rooms
Bathrooms: 50 private, 1 public

Bed & breakfast

per night:	£min	£max
Single	22.00	36.00
Double	28.00	55.00

Parking for 20
Cards accepted: Access, Visa, Amex

☎ ⚹ ▤ ▢ ⓊⓁ ▥ 📺 ◐ ▥ ◨ ✝ ✶ ⒹⒶⓅ
✽ ⓈⓅ

Ad Display advertisement appears on
page 29

Barry House ⋀

APPROVED

12 Sussex Place, London W2 2TP
☎ (0171) 723 7340 & 723 0994
Fax (0171) 723 9775

*We believe in family-like care.
Comfortable en-suite rooms with TV,
telephone and hospitality tray. Located
close to Hyde Park, the West End,*

*Paddington Station and many tourist
attractions.*
Bedrooms: 3 single, 3 double, 9 twin,
3 family rooms
Bathrooms: 14 private, 2 public

Bed & breakfast

per night:	£min	£max
Single	28.00	36.00
Double	48.00	56.00

Cards accepted: Access, Visa, Diners,
Amex, Switch/Delta

☎ ⚹ ✆ ▢ ⓊⓁ ✁ Ⓢ ▥ 📺 ◐ ▥
◨ Ⓤ ✶ ⒹⒶⓅ ✽ ⓈⓅ ⓣ

Beverley House Hotel ⋀

☸☸☸

142 Sussex Gardens, London W2 1UB
☎ (0171) 723 3380
Fax (0171) 262 0324
*Refurbished bed and breakfast hotel,
serving traditional English breakfast
and offering high standards at low
prices. Close to Paddington station,
Hyde Park and museums.*
Bedrooms: 6 single, 5 double, 6 twin,
6 triple
Bathrooms: 23 private

Bed & breakfast

per night:	£min	£max
Single	35.00	45.00
Double	40.00	60.00

Evening meal 1800 (last orders 2200)
Parking for 2
Cards accepted: Access, Visa, Diners,
Amex

☎ ⚹ ✆ ▤ ▢ ㋫ ▥ 📺 ◐ ▥ ◨ ✽ ⓈⓅ ⓣ

Europa House Hotel ⋀

Listed **APPROVED**

151 Sussex Gardens, London W2 2RY
☎ (0171) 723 7343 & 402 1923
Fax (0171) 224 9331
*Close to Hyde Park and convenient for
the Heathrow Airbus link. All rooms
with en-suite facilities, tea and coffee
making facilities, colour TV. English
breakfast included.*
Bedrooms: 2 single, 2 double, 7 twin,
5 triple, 2 family rooms
Bathrooms: 18 private, 1 public

Bed & breakfast

per night:	£min	£max
Single	28.00	34.00
Double	42.00	48.00

Parking for 1
Cards accepted: Access, Visa, Diners

☎ ⚹ ✆ ▢ ✿ ⓊⓁ Ⓢ ▥ 📺 ◐ ▥ ◨ ✶ ⒹⒶⓅ ✽
ⓈⓅ ⓣ

Hyde Park Rooms Hotel ⋀

Listed

137 Sussex Gardens, Hyde Park,
London W2 2RX
☎ (0171) 723 0225 & 723 0965
*Small centrally located private hotel
with personal service. Clean,
comfortable and friendly. Within
walking distance of Hyde Park and
Kensington Gardens. Car parking
available.*
Bedrooms: 5 single, 6 double, 2 twin,
1 family room
Bathrooms: 8 private, 2 public

Bed & breakfast

per night:	£min	£max
Single	20.00	24.00
Double	30.00	36.00

Parking for 3
Cards accepted: Access, Visa, Diners,
Amex, Switch/Delta

☎ ⚹ ▢ ㋫ ⓊⓁ ◐ ▥ ◨ Ⓤ ✶ ⒹⒶⓅ ✽ ⓈⓅ
㊟ ⓣ

Nayland Hotel ⋀

☸☸☸ **COMMENDED**

132-134 Sussex Gardens, London
W2 1UB
☎ (0171) 723 4615
Fax (0171) 723 3292
*Centrally located, close to many
amenities and within walking distance
of Hyde Park and Oxford Street. Quality
you can afford.*
Bedrooms: 11 single, 8 double,
17 twin, 5 triple
Bathrooms: 41 private

Bed & breakfast

per night:	£min	£max
Single	38.00	52.00
Double	46.00	64.00

Evening meal 1800 (last orders 2100)
Parking for 5
Cards accepted: Access, Visa, Diners,
Amex

☎ ⚹ ✆ ▤ ▢ ㋫ ▥ 📺 ◐ ▤ ▥ ◨ ✶
⚵ ㊟ ⓣ

Rhodes House Hotel ⋀

☸☸ **COMMENDED**

195 Sussex Gardens, London W2 2RJ
☎ (0171) 262 5617 & 262 0537
Fax (0171) 723 4054

*Rooms with private facilities and
satellite TV, telephone, refrigerator,
hairdryer and tea/coffee-making
facilities. Friendly atmosphere. Families
especially welcome. Excellent transport
for sightseeing and shopping.*
Bedrooms: 3 single, 3 double, 4 twin,
4 triple, 4 family rooms
Bathrooms: 16 private, 1 public

Bed & breakfast

per night:	£min	£max
Single	40.00	58.75
Double	50.00	70.50

Cards accepted: Access, Visa

☎ ⚹ ✆ ▢ ✿ ㋫ ⓊⓁ ▥ 📺 ◐ ▥ ◨ ✶ ⚵
✽ ⓈⓅ ⓣ

Sass House Hotel ⋀

Listed

10 & 11 Craven Terrace, London
W2 3QD
☎ (0171) 262 2325
Fax (0171) 262 0889

Continued ▶

LONDON W2

Continued

Budget accommodation, convenient for central London, Hyde Park and West End. Paddington and Lancaster Gate underground stations nearby. Easy access to tourist attractions.
Bedrooms: 4 single, 4 double, 4 twin, 6 triple
Bathrooms: 3 public

Bed & breakfast

per night:	£min	£max
Single	18.00	
Double	24.00	

Cards accepted: Access, Visa, Amex

[Ad] Display advertisement appears on page 29

Westpoint Hotel ⚑
Listed
170-172 Sussex Gardens, London W2 1TP
☎ (0171) 402 0281
Fax (0171) 224 9114
Inexpensive accommodation in central London. Close to Paddington and Lancaster Gate underground stations. Easy access to tourist attractions and Hyde Park.
Bedrooms: 12 single, 15 double, 16 twin, 14 triple, 6 family rooms
Bathrooms: 31 private, 10 public, 9 private showers

Bed & breakfast

per night:	£min	£max
Single	22.00	36.00
Double	26.00	48.00

Parking for 15
Cards accepted: Access, Visa, Diners, Amex

[Ad] Display advertisement appears on page 29

LONDON W5

Corfton Guest House
42 Corfton Road, Ealing, London W5 2HT
☎ (0181) 998 1120
Close to Ealing Broadway station, in a quiet residential area of considerable character.
Bedrooms: 3 single, 4 double, 1 twin, 2 triple
Bathrooms: 6 private, 2 public

Bed & breakfast

per night:	£min	£max
Single	15.00	26.00
Double	23.00	30.00

Parking for 6

Creffield Lodge ⚑
Listed
2-4 Creffield Road, Ealing, London W5 3HN
☎ (0181) 993 2284
Fax (0181) 992 7082
Telex 935114

Victorian-style property on ground and two upper floors, located in quiet residential road, adjacent to 150-bedroom Carnarvon Hotel.
Bedrooms: 10 single, 4 double, 4 twin, 1 triple
Bathrooms: 5 private, 5 public

Bed & breakfast

per night:	£min	£max
Single	32.00	50.00
Double	52.00	70.00

Half board

per person:	£min	£max
Daily	48.00	66.00

Lunch available
Evening meal 1830 (last orders 2130)
Parking for 20
Cards accepted: Access, Visa, Diners, Amex

Grange Lodge Hotel
48-50 Grange Road, Ealing, London W5 5BX
☎ (0181) 567 1049
Fax (0181) 579 5350
Quiet, comfortable hotel within a few hundred yards of the underground station. Midway between central London and Heathrow.
Bedrooms: 7 single, 1 double, 2 twin, 4 triple
Bathrooms: 9 private, 2 public

Bed & breakfast

per night:	£min	£max
Single	30.00	35.00
Double	40.00	46.00

Parking for 10
Cards accepted: Access, Visa, Switch/Delta

43 Inglis Road
London W5 3RL
☎ (0181) 992 9990
Victorian house with a garden. 200 yards from transport links to central London and airports
Bedrooms: 1 single, 1 double, 1 twin
Bathrooms: 2 public

Bed & breakfast

per night:	£min	£max
Single	20.00	22.00
Double	38.00	42.00

LONDON W8

Demetriou Guest House ⚑
Listed **APPROVED**
9 Strathmore Gardens, London W8 4RZ
☎ (0171) 229 6709
Small, privately-owned B & B at reasonable prices. Very close to Kensington Gardens and Hyde Park and convenient for all amenities.
Bedrooms: 1 single, 2 double, 3 twin, 3 triple
Bathrooms: 8 private, 3 public

Bed & breakfast

per night:	£min	£max
Single	30.00	
Double	46.00	50.00

LONDON W11

Mrs L Stephan
Listed
152 Kensington Park Road, London W11 2EP
☎ (0171) 727 7174
Pleasantly situated Victorian terrace house, close to all amenities. Clients receive individual attention in homely and friendly surroundings.
Bedrooms: 2 double, 1 triple
Bathrooms: 1 public

Bed & breakfast

per night:	£min	£max
Double	20.00	24.00

LONDON WC1

Euro Hotel
53 Cartwright Gardens, London WC1H 9EL
☎ (0171) 387 6789 & 387 8777
Fax (0171) 383 5044
Centrally located hotel close to the West End and British Museum. Bright, spacious rooms with TV, radio, direct-dial telephone, tea/coffee facilities, video films, satellite channel.
Bedrooms: 8 single, 2 double, 11 twin, 11 triple, 3 family rooms
Bathrooms: 16 private, 19 public, 8 private showers

Bed & breakfast

per night:	£min	£max
Single	32.50	39.50
Double	49.50	59.50

Cards accepted: Access, Visa, Amex, Switch/Delta

St. Athan's Hotel M
Listed

20 Tavistock Place, Russell Square,
London WC1H 9RE
☎ (0171) 837 9140 & 837 9627
Fax (0171) 833 8352
Small family-run hotel offering bed and breakfast.
Bedrooms: 16 single, 15 double,
15 twin, 4 triple, 5 family rooms
Bathrooms: 15 private, 12 public
Bed & breakfast

per night:	£min	£max
Single	20.00	34.00
Double	30.00	44.00

Lunch available
Cards accepted: Access, Visa, Diners, Amex

Thanet Hotel
Listed COMMENDED

8 Bedford Place, London WC1B 5JA
☎ (0171) 580 3377 & 636 2869
Fax (0171) 323 6676
Comfortable, family-run hotel, with colour TV, tea and coffee and direct-dial telephones. All en-suite rooms. Next to British Museum, close to London's famous Theatreland. Full English breakfast.
Bedrooms: 4 single, 4 double, 4 twin,
1 triple, 1 family room
Bathrooms: 14 private
Bed & breakfast

per night:	£min	£max
Single	49.00	49.00
Double	65.00	65.00

Cards accepted: Access, Visa, Diners, Amex, Switch/Delta

LONDON WC2

Hotel Strand Continental M
Listed

143 The Strand, London WC2R 1JA
☎ (0171) 836 4880
Small hotel with friendly atmosphere, near theatres and famous London landmarks.
Bedrooms: 10 single, 8 double, 2 twin,
2 triple
Bathrooms: 6 public
Bed & breakfast

per night:	£min	£max
Single	25.00	30.00
Double	33.00	38.00

National gradings and classifications were correct at the time of going to press but are subject to change. Please check at the time of booking.

OUTER LONDON

Colour maps 6 & 7 at the back of the guide show place names and London Postal Area codes and will help you to locate accommodation in your chosen area of London.

CROYDON

Iverna
Listed

1 Annandale Road, Addiscombe,
Croydon CR0 7HP
☎ (0181) 654 8639
Large house in a quiet road, close to East Croydon station. London Victoria 15 minutes away. No smoking in public areas.
Bedrooms: 3 single, 1 twin
Bathrooms: 1 public
Bed & breakfast

per night:	£min	£max
Single	20.00	22.00
Double	38.00	40.00

Parking for 2

HEATHROW AIRPORT

See under Hounslow, West Drayton

HOUNSLOW

Tourist Information Centre
☎ (0181) 572 8279

Hounslow Hotel M
APPROVED

41 Hounslow Road, Feltham,
Middlesex TW14 0AU
☎ (0181) 890 2358
Fax (0181) 751 6103
Small family hotel with good parking facilities, close to motorways, major tourist attractions and Heathrow Airport. Central London 30 minutes. Good restaurant - bar snacks and a la carte. All rooms en-suite with colour TV, welcome tray and telephone. Free parking.
Bedrooms: 15 single, 3 double, 3 twin,
2 triple
Bathrooms: 23 private
Bed & breakfast

per night:	£min	£max
Single	36.00	40.00
Double	44.00	48.00

Lunch available
Evening meal 1830 (last orders 2130)
Parking for 56
Cards accepted: Access, Visa, Diners, Amex

We advise you to confirm your booking in writing.

PURLEY

Stocks
Listed

51 Selcroft Road, Purley, Surrey
CR8 1AJ
☎ (0181) 660 3054
Central London 20 minutes by train. Convenient for M25, M23 and Gatwick Airport.
Bedrooms: 1 single, 1 double, 1 triple
Bathrooms: 1 private, 1 public
Bed & breakfast

per night:	£min	£max
Single	20.00	22.00
Double	40.00	44.00

Parking for 3
Open January-November

SIDCUP

"The Chimneys"
Listed

6 Clarence Road, Sidcup, Kent
DA14 4DL
☎ (0181) 309 1460 & Mobile 0378 022179
Comfortable and friendly Victorian home, within easy walking distance of station and amenities. 30 minutes to central London by train, 10 minutes from M20, M25.
Bedrooms: 1 double, 1 twin
Bathrooms: 1 public
Bed & breakfast

per night:	£min	£max
Single	18.00	
Double	30.00	

Half board

per person:	£min	£max
Daily	22.00	25.00
Weekly	154.00	175.00

WEMBLEY

Elm Hotel M
APPROVED

1-7 Elm Road, Wembley, Middlesex
HA9 7JA
☎ (0181) 902 1764
Fax (0181) 903 8365
Ten minutes' walk (1200 yards) from Wembley Stadium and Conference Centre. 150 yards from Wembley Central underground and mainline station.
Bedrooms: 6 single, 9 double, 9 twin,
1 triple, 2 family rooms; suites available
Bathrooms: 24 private, 1 public
Bed & breakfast

per night:	£min	£max
Single	34.00	42.00
Double	45.00	55.00

Continued ▶

WEMBLEY		
Continued		

Half board
per person:	£min	£max
Daily	39.00	47.00
Weekly	250.00	329.00

Evening meal 1800 (last orders 2000)
Parking for 7
Cards accepted: Access, Visa, Switch/
Delta

WEST DRAYTON		

The Alice House

`Listed` `APPROVED`

9 Hollycroft Close, Sipson, West
Drayton, Middlesex UB7 OJJ
☎ (0181) 897 9032

*Small, clean and comfortable
guesthouse. Convenient for Heathrow
Airport, but with no noise from flight
path. Car service to airport available.
Evening meal by arrangement. Close
M4, M25. London 40 minutes. Parking.*
Bedrooms: 1 single, 1 double, 1 twin
Bathrooms: 1 public

Bed & breakfast
per night:	£min	£max
Single	28.00	32.00
Double	38.00	42.00

Evening meal 1800 (last orders 2000)
Parking for 6

Please mention this guide
when making a booking.

AT-A-GLANCE SYMBOLS

At-a-glance symbols at the end of each
accommodation entry give information about
services and facilities. A handy guide to these
symbols can be found inside the back cover flap,
which can be kept open for easy reference.

BOOKING ENQUIRIES

When enquiring about accommodation you
may find it helpful to use the accommodation
coupons towards the end of the guide. These
should be mailed direct to the establishments
in which you are interested. Do please
remember to include your name and address.

Cumbria

It won't fail to astonish you. With its towering crags and great glimmering lakes, the Lake District is simply breathtakingly beautiful. Wordsworth called it 'the loveliest spot that man hath ever found'.

It's a paradise for walkers, climbers and watersports enthusiasts; and for the less energetic there are pretty villages, the Lake District National Park with its busy events calendar, visitor centres, working farms, museums and steam boat trips to enjoy.

West of Lakeland is Cumbria's coast – from the red cliffs of St Bees with its nesting seabirds, to the gentle charms of Grange-over-Sands. To the north, you can explore the wild North Pennines and Borderlands; to the southeast, the tranquil Eden valley.

The County of Cumbria

For more information on Cumbria, contact:

Cumbria Tourist Board, Ashleigh, Holly Road, Windermere, Cumbria LA23 2AQ

Tel: (015394) 44444

Fax: (015394) 44041

Where to Go in Cumbria – see pages 36–39

Where to Stay in Cumbria – see pages 40–57

Cumbria

Where to go and what to see
You will find hundreds of interesting places to visit during your stay in Cumbria, just some of which are listed in these pages. The number against each name will help you locate it on the map (page 39). Contact any Tourist Information Centre in the region for more ideas on days out in Cumbria.

1 Birdoswald Roman Fort
Gilsland, Cumbria CA6 7DD
Tel: (016977) 47602
Remains of Roman fort on Hadrian's Wall, with excellent views of Irthing Gorge. Visitor centre.

2 Tullie House Museum and Art Gallery
Castle Street, Carlisle, Cumbria CA3 8TP
Tel: (01228) 34781
Major tourist complex housing museum, art gallery, education facility, lecture theatre, shops, garden restaurant, terrace bars.

3 South Tynedale Railway
Railway Station, Alston, Cumbria CA9 3JB
Tel: (01434) 381696
2ft gauge railway following part of the route of the former Alston to Haltwhistle branch line through South Tynedale.

4 Four Seasons Farm Experience
Sceugh Mire, Southwaite, Cumbria CA4 0LS
Tel: (016974) 73753
An open farm where you can meet the animals and try your hand at some farming skills and other activities.

5 Senhouse Roman Museum
The Battery, Sea Brows, Maryport, Cumbria CA15 6JD
Tel: (01900) 816168
Largest collection of Roman altars and inscriptions from a single site. Museum shows what Roman life was like in the North West.

6 Hutton-in-the-Forest
Skelton, Cumbria CA11 9TH
Tel: (017684) 84449
14th C Pele Tower with later additions. Tapestries, furniture, paintings, china, armour. Formal gardens, dovecote, lake and woods with specimen trees.

7 Mirehouse
Underskiddaw, Cumbria CA12 4QE
Tel: (017687) 72287
Manuscripts and portraits with many literary connections, Victorian schoolroom/nursery, antiques quiz, woodland and lakeside walk, 4 adventure playgrounds.

8 Acorn Bank Garden
Temple Sowerby, Cumbria CA10 1SP
Tel: (017683) 61893
Spring bulbs, walled garden, outstanding herb garden, wild garden. 16th C house in garden is not normally open to the public.

9 Dalemain Historic House and Gardens
Dacre, Penrith, Cumbria CA11 OHB
Tel: (017684) 86450
Historic house with Georgian furniture. Westmorland and Cumberland Yeomanry Museum.

Agricultural bygones, adventure playground, licensed restaurant, gardens.

⑩ Lakeland Bird of Prey Centre
Old Walled Garden, Lowther, Cumbria CA10 2HH
Tel: (01931) 712746
Most types of hawk, falcon, buzzard, owl and eagle are displayed either in aviaries or "blocked out".

⑪ Whinlatter Forest Park Visitor Centre
Braithwaite, Cumbria CA12 5TW
Tel: (017687) 78469
Interpretative forestry exhibition with audio-visual presentations. Working model of forest operations, lecture theatre, shop, walks, trails, orienteering.

⑫ Dove Cottage and Wordsworth Museum
Town End, Grasmere, Cumbria LA22 9SH
Tel: (015394) 35544
Wordsworth's home 1799–1808. Poet's possessions, museum with manuscripts, farmhouse reconstruction, paintings and drawings. Year-round programme of events.

⑬ Rydal Mount
Ambleside, Cumbria LA22 9LU
Tel: (015394) 33002

Wordsworth's home for 37 years, with first editions, portraits, memorabilia. Garden landscaped by the poet.

⑭ Eskdale Corn Mill
Boot, Cumbria CA19 1TG
Tel: (019467) 23335
Historic water-powered corn mill near Dalegarth station, approached by a packhorse bridge. Early wooden machinery, waterfalls, exhibition.

⑮ Brockhole – Lake District National Park Visitor Centre
Windermere, Cumbria LA23 1LJ
Tel: (015394) 46601
Exhibitions include the National Park Story, slide shows and films. Shop, gardens, grounds, adventure playground, dry stone walling area, trails, events. Restaurant, tearoom.

⑯ The World of Beatrix Potter Exhibition
The Old Laundry, Crag Brow, Bowness-on-Windermere, Cumbria LA23 3BX
Tel: (015394) 88444
Exhibition interpreting the life and works of Beatrix Potter, comprising 9-screen video wall recreating scenes in three dimensions and film.

⑰ Steam Yacht Gondola
Pier Cottage, Coniston, Cumbria LA21 8AJ
Tel: (015394) 41288

Steam-powered yacht, launched 1859 and now completely renovated with opulent saloon, carries 86 passengers. Piers at Coniston, Park-a-Moor and Brantwood.

⑱ Muncaster Castle, Gardens and Owl Centre
Ravenglass, Cumbria CA18 1RQ
Tel: (01229) 717614
14th C pele tower with 15th and 19th C additions. Gardens with exceptional collection of rhododendrons and azaleas. Extensive collection of owls.

⑲ Ravenglass and Eskdale Railway and Museum
Ravenglass, Cumbria CA18 1SW
Tel: (01229) 717171
England's oldest narrow gauge railway, running for 7 miles through glorious scenery to the foot of the country's highest hills. Most trains are steam-hauled.

⑳ Kendal Museum
Station Road, Kendal, Cumbria LA9 6BT
Tel: (01539) 721374
Outstanding natural history gallery with reconstructions of Lake District habitats, world wildlife gallery, Westmorland gallery on local history, Alfred Wainwright display.

㉑ Sizergh Castle
Kendal, Cumbria LA8 8AE

Tel: (015395) 60070
Castle with 14th C pele tower, 15th C great hall and 16th C wings. Stuart connections. Rock garden, rose garden, daffodils.

22 Levens Hall
Kendal, Cumbria
LA8 0PD
Tel: (015395) 60321
Elizabethan mansion incorporating a pele tower. Topiary garden laid out in 1694, plant centre, steam collection, picnic and play areas, shop.

23 Graythwaite Hall Gardens
Newby Bridge, Cumbria
LA12 8BA
Tel: (015395) 31248
Rhododendrons, azaleas and flowering shrubs. Laid out by T. Mawson 1888–1890.

24 Windermere Iron Steamboat Company
Lakeside Pier, Newby Bridge, Cumbria
LA12 8AS
Tel: (015395) 31188
Three steamers sailing Windermere, also motor launches and ferry service from Lakeside to Fell Foot. Booking offices at Lakeside, Bowness and Ambleside.

25 Lakeside and Haverthwaite Railway
Haverthwaite Station, Ulverston, Cumbria LA12 8AL
Tel: (015395) 31594
Standard gauge steam railway operating a daily service at Easter and from May to October. Display of steam and diesel locomotives.

26 Heron Glass
The Gill, Ulverston, Cumbria
LA12 7BL
Tel: (01229) 581121
New visitor centre with glass-makers transforming molten glass into artistic shapes.

27 Holker Hall and Gardens
Cark in Cartmel, Cumbria
LA11 7PL
Tel: (015395) 58328
Victorian wing, formal and woodland garden, deer park, motor museum, adventure playground, gift shop. Exhibitions, including Timeless Toys and Teddies.

28 Heron Corn Mill and Museum of Papermaking
Waterhouse Mills, Beetham, Cumbria LA7 7AR

Tel: (015395) 63363
Restored working corn mill with 14ft high breastshot waterwheel. Museum of Papermaking.

29 The Dock Museum
North Road, Barrow-in-Furness, Cumbria LA14 2PW
Tel: (01229) 870871
Based in the unique setting of a 19th C dry dock, the museum presents the story of steel shipbuilding for which Barrow-in-Furness is famous.

Find Out More

Further information about holidays and attractions in Cumbria is available from:
Cumbria Tourist Board,
Ashleigh, Holly Road,

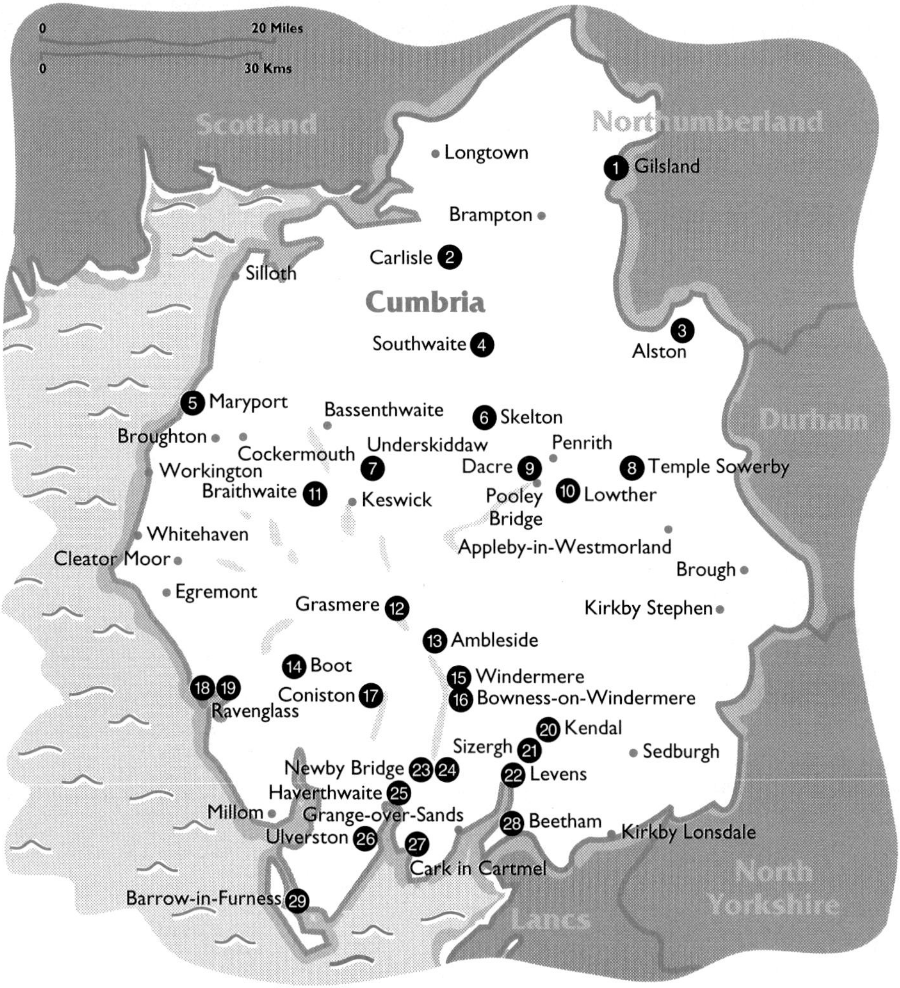
0
20 Miles
0
30 Kms
Scotland
Northumberland
Longtown
1 Gilsland
Brampton
Carlisle 2
Silloth
Cumbria
Southwaite 4
3 Alston
Durham
5 Maryport
Bassenthwaite
6 Skelton
Broughton
Cockermouth
Underskiddaw
Penrith
Workington
7
Dacre 9
8 Temple Sowerby
Braithwaite 11
Keswick
Pooley Bridge
10 Lowther
Whitehaven
Appleby-in-Westmorland
Cleator Moor
Brough
Egremont
Grasmere 12
Kirkby Stephen
13 Ambleside
14 Boot
15 Windermere
18 19
Coniston 17
16 Bowness-on-Windermere
Ravenglass
20 Kendal
Sizergh 21
Sedburgh
Newby Bridge 23 24
22 Levens
Haverthwaite 25
Millom
Grange-over-Sands
28 Beetham
Kirkby Lonsdale
Ulverston 26
27
Cark in Cartmel
North Yorkshire
Barrow-in-Furness 29
Lancs

Windermere, Cumbria LA23 2AQ
Tel: (015394) 44444
These publications are available from the Cumbrian Tourist Board:

- **Cumbria The Lake District Touring Map** – including tourist information and touring caravan and camping parks. £3.45. Laminated poster £2.95.
- **Days Out in Cumbria** – over 200 ideas for a great day out. £1.25.
- **Short Walks – Good for Families** – route descriptions, maps and information for 14 walks in lesser-known areas of Cumbria. 95p.
- **Wordsworth's Lake District** – folded map showing major Wordsworthian sites plus biographical details. 60p. Japanese language version £1. Laminated poster £1.
- **Explore Cumbria by Car** – route descriptions, maps and information for 10 circular motor tours. 95p.

WHERE TO STAY

Accommodation entries in this regional section are listed in alphabetical order of place name, and then in alphabetical order of establishment.

Map references refer to the colour location maps at the back of this guide. The first figure is the map number; the letter and figure which follow indicate the grid reference on the map.

At-a-glance symbols at the end of each accommodation entry give information about services and facilities. A handy guide to these symbols can be found inside the back cover flap, which can be kept open for easy reference.

AMBLESIDE

Cumbria
Map ref 5A3

Market town situated at the head of Lake Windermere and surrounded by fells. The historic town centre is now a conservation area and the country around Ambleside is rich in historic and literary associations. Good centre for touring, walking and climbing.

Borrans Park Hotel ⋀
� HIGHLY COMMENDED
Borrans Road, Ambleside LA22 0EN
☎ (015394) 33454
Peacefully situated between the village and lake. Enjoy candlelit dinners, 120 fine wines, and four-poster bedrooms with private spa baths.
Wheelchair access category 3 ♿
Bedrooms: 9 double, 1 twin, 2 triple
Bathrooms: 12 private

Bed & breakfast

per night:	£min	£max
Single	29.00	49.00
Double	58.00	78.00

Half board

per person:	£min	£max
Daily	40.00	55.00
Weekly	229.00	325.00

Evening meal 1900 (last orders 1800)
Parking for 20
Cards accepted: Access, Visa
⌖♣☎♨☐♦🅿🛏S✗⅍Ⅲ, ⌂
✿✗🐾↘SP

Glenside ⋀
⌖ COMMENDED
Old Lake Road, Ambleside LA22 0DP
☎ (015394) 32635
17th C farm cottage, comfortable bedrooms with original oak beams, TV

---

lounge. Between town and lake, ideal centre for walking. Private parking.
Bedrooms: 2 double, 1 twin
Bathrooms: 1 public

Bed & breakfast

per night:	£min	£max
Single	14.00	16.00
Double	28.00	32.00

Parking for 3
Open February-November
⌖5♨ⅦⅢ♦🅿✗⅍Ⅳ Ⅲ, 🐾🐾OAPT

Hideaway Cottage
⌖⌖⌖
McIver Lane, Ambleside LA22 0DU
☎ (015394) 34858
A cottage/bungalow offering ground floor only facilities. In a quiet woodland location only 2 minutes' stroll from Lake Windermere. Prices below are per room.
Bedrooms: 3 double
Bathrooms: 3 private

Bed & breakfast

per night:	£min	£max
Double	30.00	40.00

Parking for 3
Open February-December
⌖10♨☐♦ⅦⅢ♦🅿✗⅍Ⅳ Ⅲ, ⌂✿
✗🐾

High Wray Farm
⌖ Listed COMMENDED
High Wray, Ambleside LA22 0JE
☎ (015394) 32280

173-acre livestock farm. Charming 17th C farmhouse once owned by Beatrix

---

Potter. In quiet location, ideal centre for touring or walking. Panoramic views and lake shore walks close by.
Bedrooms: 2 double, 1 twin
Bathrooms: 1 private, 1 public

Bed & breakfast

per night:	£min	£max
Single	14.00	16.00
Double	28.00	32.00

Parking for 7
⌖♣☐ⅦⅢ🅿S✗⅍Ⅳ Ⅲ, ⌂✿🐾
SP🐾

The Howes
Listed COMMENDED
Stockghyll Brow, Ambleside LA22 0QZ
☎ (015394) 32444
Private detached house near Stockghyll Waterfalls with 2 ground floor en-suite bedrooms.
Bedrooms: 1 double, 1 twin
Bathrooms: 2 private

Bed & breakfast

per night:	£min	£max
Double	37.00	44.00

Parking for 2
⌖5♨⌧☐♦♨ⅦⅢ🅿⌂✿🐾SP

Laurel Villa ⋀
⌖⌖⌖ HIGHLY COMMENDED
Lake Road, Ambleside LA22 0DB
☎ (015394) 33240
Detached Victorian house, visited by Beatrix Potter. En-suite bedrooms overlooking the fells. Within easy reach of Lake Windermere and the village. Private car park.
Bedrooms: 7 double, 1 twin
Bathrooms: 8 private

Bed & breakfast

per night:	£min	£max
Single	50.00	50.00
Double	60.00	80.00

Half board

per person:	£min	£max
Daily	50.00	60.00

Evening meal 1900 (last orders 1700)
Parking for 10
Cards accepted: Access, Visa

[symbols]

Lyndale ♨

[symbols]

Low Fold, Lake Road, Ambleside
LA22 ODN
☎ (015394) 34244
*Spacious Victorian guesthouse, midway
between lake and village. Some en-suite
rooms. Good fell views. A warm
welcome awaits you.*
Bedrooms: 2 single, 2 double, 1 twin,
1 triple
Bathrooms: 2 private, 2 public
Bed & breakfast

per night:	£min	£max
Single	14.50	16.50
Double	29.00	39.00

[symbols]

Meadowbank

Listed APPROVED

Rydal Road, Ambleside LA22 9BA
☎ (015394) 32710
*Country house in private garden with
ample parking in grounds. Overlooking
meadowland and fells, yet a level, easy
walk to Ambleside. Good walking base.*
Bedrooms: 1 single, 2 double, 2 twin,
2 triple
Bathrooms: 3 private, 2 public
Bed & breakfast

per night:	£min	£max
Single	19.00	22.00
Double	38.00	44.00

Parking for 10
[symbols]

Mill Cottage ♨

Listed APPROVED

Rydal Road, Ambleside LA22 9AN
☎ (015394) 34830
*Grade II listed restaurant and
guesthouse in riverside location
adjacent to the famous Bridge House.*
Bedrooms: 4 double, 1 twin, 1 family
room
Bathrooms: 3 private, 1 public
Bed & breakfast

per night:	£min	£max
Single	16.00	18.00
Double	32.00	36.00

Evening meal 1830 (last orders 2100)
[symbols]

The Old Vicarage ♨

COMMENDED

Vicarage Road, Ambleside LA22 9DH
☎ (015394) 33364
Fax (015394) 34734

*Quietly situated in own grounds in
heart of village. Car park, quality en-
suite accommodation, friendly service.
Family-run. Pets welcome.*
Bedrooms: 7 double, 1 twin, 1 triple,
1 family room
Bathrooms: 10 private
Bed & breakfast

per night:	£min	£max
Single	28.00	
Double	46.00	

Parking for 12
Cards accepted: Access, Visa, Switch/
Delta
[symbols]

Riverside Lodge Country House ♨

COMMENDED

Nr. Rothay Bridge, Ambleside
LA22 OEH
☎ (015394) 34208

*Georgian country house of character
with 2 acres of grounds through which
the River Rothay flows. 500 yards from
the centre of Ambleside.*
Bedrooms: 1 single, 2 double, 1 twin,
1 triple
Bathrooms: 5 private
Bed & breakfast

per night:	£min	£max
Double	38.00	57.00

Parking for 20
Cards accepted: Access, Visa
[symbols]

Rowanfield Country Guesthouse ♨

HIGHLY COMMENDED

Kirkstone Road, Ambleside LA22 9ET
☎ (015394) 33686

*Idyllic setting, panoramic lake and
mountain views. Laura Ashley style*

*decor. Scrumptious food created by
proprietor/chef. Special break prices.*
Wheelchair access category 3 ♿
Bedrooms: 5 double, 1 twin, 1 triple
Bathrooms: 7 private
Bed & breakfast

per night:	£min	£max
Double	50.00	56.00

Half board

per person:	£min	£max
Daily	41.00	44.00
Weekly	248.00	264.00

Evening meal 1900 (last orders 1900)
Parking for 8
Open March-December
Cards accepted: Access, Visa, Switch/
Delta
[symbols]

Smallwood House Hotel ♨

APPROVED

Compston Road, Ambleside LA22 9DJ
☎ (015394) 32330
*Family-run hotel in central position,
offering warm and friendly service,
good home cooking and value-for-money
quality and standards.*
Bedrooms: 7 double, 3 twin, 3 triple,
2 family rooms
Bathrooms: 15 private, 2 public
Bed & breakfast

per night:	£min	£max
Single	17.00	25.50
Double	34.00	41.00

Half board

per person:	£min	£max
Daily	28.00	35.00
Weekly	205.00	230.00

Lunch available
Evening meal 1800 (last orders 2000)
Parking for 11
[symbols]

Tock How Farm ♨

Listed

High Wray, Ambleside LA22 0JF
☎ (015394) 36481
*300-acre mixed farm. Overlooking
beautiful Blelham Tarn. Panoramic
views of Coniston, the Langdales and
Lake Windermere. Home-made
preserves a speciality.*
Bedrooms: 1 double, 1 triple
Bathrooms: 1 public
Bed & breakfast

per night:	£min	£max
Single	18.00	20.00
Double	28.00	32.00

Evening meal from 1800
Parking for 3
[symbols]

Windlehurst Guesthouse ♨

[symbols]

Millans Park, Ambleside LA22 9AG
☎ (015394) 33137
*Victorian house in quiet location close
to village. Commanding views of
Loughrigg Fell. Comfortable rooms,*
Continued ▶

AMBLESIDE

Continued

friendly service. Non-smoking. Dogs welcome.
Bedrooms: 1 single, 2 double, 2 triple, 1 family room
Bathrooms: 2 private, 2 public
Bed & breakfast

per night:	£min	£max
Single	14.50	18.00
Double	28.00	44.00

Parking for 6

APPLEBY-IN-WESTMORLAND

Cumbria
Map ref 5B3

Former county town of Westmorland, at the foot of the Pennines in the Eden Valley. The castle was rebuilt in the 17th C, except for its Norman keep, ditches and ramparts. It now houses a Rare Breeds Survival Trust Centre. Good centre for exploring the Eden Valley.
Tourist Information Centre
☎ *(017683) 51177*

Asby Grange Farm

Great Asby, Appleby-in-Westmorland
CA16 6HF
☎ (017683) 52881
300-acre mixed farm. 18th C farmhouse in beautiful and peaceful countryside, 5 miles south of Appleby. Ideal for touring Lakes and Yorkshire Dales. Convenient for M6.
Bedrooms: 1 double, 1 triple
Bathrooms: 1 public
Bed & breakfast

per night:	£min	£max
Double	26.00	30.00

Parking for 4
Open April-October

Bongate House ⚊

COMMENDED

Appleby-in-Westmorland CA16 6UE
☎ (017683) 51245
Family-run Georgian guesthouse on the outskirts of a small market town. Large garden. Relaxed friendly atmosphere, good home cooking.
Bedrooms: 1 single, 3 double, 2 twin, 1 triple, 1 family room
Bathrooms: 5 private, 1 public
Bed & breakfast

per night:	£min	£max
Single	17.00	19.50
Double	34.00	39.00

Half board

per person:	£min	£max
Daily	25.00	27.50
Weekly	160.00	180.00

Evening meal 1900 (last orders 1800)
Parking for 10

Bridge End Farm

HIGHLY COMMENDED

Kirkby Thore, Penrith CA10 1UZ
☎ Kirkby Thore (017683) 61362
450-acre arable & dairy farm. Relax in 18th C farmhouse in Eden Valley. Spacious rooms overlooking Pennine Hills, alongside River Eden. Delicious home-made breakfast and dinners.
Bedrooms: 2 double, 1 twin
Bathrooms: 3 private, 1 public
Bed & breakfast

per night:	£min	£max
Single	18.00	20.00
Double	36.00	38.00

Half board

per person:	£min	£max
Daily	26.50	180.00
Weekly	180.00	

Evening meal 1800 (last orders 1930)
Parking for 3

Dufton Hall Farm

APPROVED

Dufton, Appleby-in-Westmorland
CA16 6DD
☎ (017683) 51573
60-acre mixed farm. Part of ancient hall, and working hill farm in village centre. 3.5 miles north-east of Appleby-in-Westmorland and close to Pennine Way.
Bedrooms: 2 double, 1 twin
Bathrooms: 3 private
Bed & breakfast

per night:	£min	£max
Single	20.00	
Double	30.00	

Half board

per person:	£min	£max
Daily	25.00	

Evening meal 1800 (last orders 1900)
Parking for 3
Open April-October

Howgill House ⚊

COMMENDED

Appleby-in-Westmorland CA16 6UW
☎ (017683) 51574 & 51240
Private family-run house standing in a large garden. On B6542, half a mile from the town centre.
Bedrooms: 1 single, 1 twin, 2 triple
Bathrooms: 3 private
Bed & breakfast

per night:	£min	£max
Single	15.00	
Double	28.00	

Parking for 6
Open April-September

ARNSIDE

Cumbria
Map ref 5A3

Small coastal village in an Area of Outstanding Natural Beauty, with spectacular views across the Kent Estuary to the Lakeland hills. Excellent base for bird-watching. The incoming tide creates an impressive tidal bore.

Willowfield Hotel ⚊

COMMENDED

The Promenade, Arnside, Carnforth, Lancashire LA5 0AD
☎ (01524) 761354
Non-smoking, relaxed, family-run hotel with panoramic outlook over estuary to Lakeland hills. Good home cooking and quiet situation.
Bedrooms: 2 single, 3 double, 3 twin, 2 triple
Bathrooms: 6 private, 2 public
Bed & breakfast

per night:	£min	£max
Single	18.00	22.00
Double	36.00	44.00

Half board

per person:	£min	£max
Daily	28.00	32.00
Weekly	182.00	210.00

Evening meal from 1830
Parking for 10
Cards accepted: Visa

BORROWDALE

Cumbria
Map ref 5A3

Stretching south of Derwentwater to Seathwaite in the heart of the Lake District, the valley is walled by high fellsides. It can justly claim to be the most scenically impressive valley in the Lake District. Excellent centre for walking and climbing.

Scawdel

Listed

Grange-in-Borrowdale, Keswick
CA12 5UQ
☎ Keswick (017687) 77271
Detached house with private parking in Grange village, 4 miles from Keswick. Excellent mountain views from most windows. Rooms have comfortable seating and orthopaedic beds.
Bedrooms: 2 double, 1 twin
Bathrooms: 1 public
Bed & breakfast

per night:	£min	£max
Single	17.50	25.00
Double	31.00	35.00

Parking for 4

Yew Craggs Guest House

Listed

Rosthwaite, Keswick CA12 5XB
☎ (017687) 77260
*Beside Rosthwaite Bridge in the centre
of the Borrowdale Valley. Good for
walking, superb views in all directions.*
Bedrooms: 3 double, 2 triple
Bathrooms: 1 public
Bed & breakfast

per night:	£min	£max
Double	28.00	38.00

Parking for 6
Open February-November

BRAITHWAITE

Cumbria
Map ref 5A3

Braithwaite nestles at the foot of
the Whinlatter Pass and has a
magnificent backdrop of the
mountains forming the Coledale
Horseshoe.

Coledale Inn ♠

Braithwaite, Keswick CA12 5TN
☎ (017687) 78272
*Victorian country house hotel and
Georgian inn, in a peaceful hillside
position away from traffic, with superb
mountain views. Families and pets
welcome.*
Bedrooms: 1 single, 6 double, 1 twin,
3 triple, 1 family room
Bathrooms: 12 private
Bed & breakfast

per night:	£min	£max
Single	18.00	21.00
Double	46.00	52.00

Lunch available
Evening meal 1830 (last orders 2100)
Parking for 15
Cards accepted: Access, Visa

BRAMPTON

Cumbria
Map ref 5B3

Excellent centre for exploring
Hadrian's Wall. Wednesday is
market day around the Moot Hall
in this delightful sandstone-built
town. Wall plaque marks the site
of Bonnie Prince Charlie and his
Jacobite army headquarters whilst
they laid siege to Carlisle Castle in
1745.

Hare & Hounds Inn

Talkin Village, Brampton CA8 1LE
☎ (016977) 3456
*Typical country inn with a cosy
atmosphere and real ale, only 500 yards
from the golf-course and Talkin Tarn.*

*with boating, fishing, swimming,
windsurfing and birdwatching.*
Bedrooms: 1 single, 2 double, 1 twin
Bathrooms: 2 private, 1 public
Bed & breakfast

per night	£min	£max
Single	16.00	25.00
Double	26.00	35.00

Half board

per person:	£min	£max
Daily	20.00	28.00
Weekly	130.00	196.00

Lunch available
Evening meal 1900 (last orders 2100)
Parking for 18

Howard House Farm ♠

HIGHLY COMMENDED

Gilsland, Carlisle CA6 7AN
☎ Gilsland (016977) 47285
*250-acre livestock farm. Peaceful farm
in comfortable and friendly
surroundings, 7 miles north-east of
Brampton and centre of Roman Wall.
Birdoswald 2 miles, Housesteads 6
miles.*
Bedrooms: 1 double, 1 twin, 1 triple
Bathrooms: 1 private, 2 public
Bed & breakfast

per night:	£min	£max
Double	34.00	40.00

Half board

per person:	£min	£max
Daily	22.00	30.00
Weekly	115.00	

Evening meal 1800 (last orders 1800)
Parking for 4

BROUGHTON-IN-FURNESS

Cumbria
Map ref 5A3

Old market village whose historic
charter to hold fairs is still
proclaimed every year on the first
day of August in the market
square. Good centre for touring
the pretty Duddon Valley.

Black Cock Inn

Princes Street, Broughton-in-Furness
LA20 6HQ
☎ (01229) 716529
Fax (01229) 716774
*16th C listed inn serving home-made
fare and traditional ales. A haven
within easy reach of Windermere,
Coniston and the beautiful Duddon
Valley.*
Bedrooms: 1 double, 2 twin, 1 family
room
Bathrooms: 1 public
Bed & breakfast

per night:	£min	£max
Single	15.50	17.50
Double	31.00	35.00

Lunch available
Evening meal 1800 (last orders 2130)
Cards accepted: Access, Visa, Switch/
Delta

Cobblers Cottage ♠

COMMENDED

Griffin Street, Broughton-in-Furness
LA20 6HH
☎ (01229) 716413

*Quaint 17th C cottage offering delicious
food in a cosy and relaxed atmosphere.
Ideally situated for exploring South
Lakes and beautiful Duddon Valley.*
Bedrooms: 2 double, 1 twin
Bathrooms: 1 private, 1 public
Bed & breakfast

per night:	£min	£max
Single	16.00	18.50
Double	32.00	37.00

Half board

per person:	£min	£max
Daily	25.00	30.50
Weekly	168.00	206.50

Evening meal 1900 (last orders 1700)

BUTTERMERE

Cumbria
Map ref 5A3

Small village surrounded by high
mountains, between Buttermere
Lake and Crummock Water. An
ideal centre for walking and
climbing the nearby peaks and for
touring.

Pickett Howe ♠

DE LUXE

Buttermere Valley, Cockermouth
CA13 9UY
☎ Lorton (01900) 85444
Fax (01900) 85209

*National winner of English Tourist
Board's "England for Excellence"
award. Luxuriously appointed and
peacefully situated 17th C farmhouse,
renowned for creative cooking, relaxing
atmosphere and jacuzzis!*
Bedrooms: 3 double, 1 twin
Bathrooms: 4 private

Continued ▶

BUTTERMERE

Continued

Bed & breakfast

per night:	£min	£max
Double	35.00	35.00

Half board

per person:	£min	£max
Daily	56.00	56.00
Weekly	364.00	364.00

Evening meal from 1915
Parking for 6
Open April-November
Cards accepted: Access, Visa
📺 10 📞🖭🖵✆🍴🕯🛈 Ⓢ ✂ 🛏 🏧 🚗 ♪ ❄ 🐾 🏮 Ⓣ

CALDBECK

Cumbria
Map ref 5A2

Quaint limestone village lying on the northern fringe of the Lake District National Park. John Peel, the famous huntsman who is immortalised in song, is buried in the churchyard. The fells surrounding Caldbeck were once heavily mined, being rich in lead, copper and barytes.

Friar Hall ♠
🏚

Caldbeck, Wigton CA7 8DS
☎ (016974) 78633
140-acre mixed farm. In the lovely village of Caldbeck overlooking the river. Ideal for touring the Lakes and Scottish Borders. On Cumbria Way route.
Bedrooms: 2 double, 1 triple
Bathrooms: 2 public

Bed & breakfast

per night:	£min	£max
Single	18.00	19.00
Double	33.00	35.00

Parking for 3
Open March-October
📺🖵✆ Ⓤ 🛏 📺 🚗 🐾

Parkend Restaurant and Country Hotel
🏚🏚🏚 COMMENDED

Parkend, Caldbeck, Wigton CA7 8HH
☎ (016974) 78494
17th C farmhouse restaurant with en-suite rooms. Situated 1.5 miles west of Caldbeck in the northern fells of the Lake District National Park.
Bedrooms: 3 double
Bathrooms: 3 private

Bed & breakfast

per night:	£min	£max
Single		28.00
Double		48.00

Evening meal 1730 (last orders 2200)
Parking for 16
Cards accepted: Access, Visa, Amex
📺🖭🖵✆🍴🛈 Ⓢ ✂ 🛏 📺 🖩 🚗 ❄ 🐾 🆂🅿 🏮

Swaledale Watch ♠
🏚🏚

Whelpo, Caldbeck, Wigton CA7 8HQ
☎ (016974) 78409
300-acre mixed farm. Enjoy great comfort, fine food, beautiful surroundings and peaceful countryside on this working farm, central for touring or walking the rolling northern fells.
Bedrooms: 2 double, 2 triple
Bathrooms: 4 private

Bed & breakfast

per night:	£min	£max
Single	17.00	18.00
Double	34.00	34.00

Half board

per person:	£min	£max
Daily		26.00
Weekly		182.00

Evening meal 1900 (last orders 1400)
Parking for 10
📺🖭🖵✆ Ⓤ 🛈 Ⓢ ✂ 🛏 📺 🖩 🚗 ❄ ✕ 🐾

CARLISLE

Cumbria
Map ref 5A2

Cumbria's only city is rich in history. Attractions include the small red sandstone cathedral and 900-year-old castle with magnificent view from the keep. Award-winning Tullie House Museum and Art Gallery brings 2,000 years of Border history dramatically to life. Excellent centre for shopping.
Tourist Information Centre
☎ (01228) 512444

Beech Croft
🏚🏚🏚 COMMENDED

Aglionby, Carlisle CA4 8AQ
☎ (01228) 513762
Spacious, modern, detached house in a delightful rural setting. 1 mile on the A69 from M6 junction 43. High quality accommodation in a friendly family atmosphere.
Bedrooms: 1 single, 2 double
Bathrooms: 3 private

Bed & breakfast

per night:	£min	£max
Single	18.00	25.00
Double	36.00	40.00

Parking for 4
📺 3 🖭🖵✆ Ⓤ Ⓢ ✂ 🛏 📺 🖩 🚗 ❄ 🐾

Corner House Hotel and Bar ♠
🏚🏚🏚

4 Grey Street, Off London Road, Carlisle CA1 2JP
☎ (01228) 33239 & 46628
Warm welcome, friendly bar, games room with pool/darts. Sky TV in lounge. Hen and stag parties welcome. All rooms en-suite. 5 minutes from city

centre, bus/train stations and easy access M6, junctions 42/43.
Bedrooms: 4 single, 2 double, 3 twin, 1 triple
Bathrooms: 10 private, 1 public

Bed & breakfast

per night:	£min	£max
Single	18.00	25.00
Double	32.00	35.00

Half board

per person:	£min	£max
Daily	21.50	30.00
Weekly	129.50	143.00

Lunch available
Evening meal 1730 (last orders 2030)
📺🔥🖭🖵✆ Ⓤ 🍴🛈 Ⓢ 📺 🖩 🚗 🔍 ⊕ 🐾 🆂🅿

Craighead
🏚 COMMENDED

6 Hartington Place, Carlisle CA1 1HL
☎ (01228) 596767
Grade II listed Victorian town house with spacious rooms and original features. Short walk to city centre, bus and rail stations. Friendly and comfortable. Fresh farm food.
Bedrooms: 1 single, 1 double, 1 twin, 1 family room
Bathrooms: 2 public

Bed & breakfast

per night:	£min	£max
Single	15.00	17.00
Double	28.00	32.00

📺🖭🖵✆ Ⓤ Ⓢ 📺 🖩 🚗 ⊳ 🐾 🆂🅿 🏮 Ⓣ

Croft End ♠
Listed

Hurst, Ivegill, Carlisle CA4 0NL
☎ (017684) 84362
Rural bungalow situated midway junction 41 and 42 of M6, 3 miles west of Southwaite service area.
Bedrooms: 2 double
Bathrooms: 1 public

Bed & breakfast

per night:	£min	£max
Single	15.00	16.00
Double	30.00	30.00

Parking for 4
📺 1 ✕🔥🖭🖵✆ Ⓤ ✂ 📺 🖩 🚗 ❄ ✕ 🐾

The Gill Farm ♠
🏚

Blackford, Carlisle CA6 4EL
☎ Kirklinton (01228) 75326
124-acre arable & livestock farm. Ideal halfway stopping place or a good base for touring Cumbria's beauty spots. In peaceful countryside, 3 miles from M6 junction 44. From Carlisle go north to Blackford, fork right at sign for Longpark, Cliff and Scaleby, after 100 yards turn right, half a mile turn left, Gill Farm on left up this road.
Bedrooms: 1 double, 1 twin, 1 triple
Bathrooms: 2 public

Bed & breakfast per night:	£min	£max
Single	17.50	20.00
Double	31.00	34.00

Parking for 6
Open January-November
🕿 ♨ UL M TV IIII, ♨ ✓ ✿ 🐾 SP 🏠 T

Howard Lodge Guesthouse
APPROVED
90 Warwick Road, Carlisle CA1 1JU
🕿 (01228) 29842
Large Victorian house on main road, 400 metres from city centre. Recently refurbished with en-suite facilities. Satellite TV and welcome tray in all rooms.
Bedrooms: 1 double, 1 twin, 1 triple, 2 family rooms
Bathrooms: 3 private, 2 public, 1 private shower

Bed & breakfast per night:	£min	£max
Single	15.00	20.00
Double	30.00	40.00

Half board per person:	£min	£max
Daily	20.00	25.00
Weekly	140.00	175.00

Evening meal 1800 (last orders 2200)
Parking for 1
🕿 ☐ ♨ UL ♨ S TV IIII, ♨ ✿ 🐾 SP T

New Pallyards ⋔
COMMENDED
Hethersgill, Carlisle CA6 6HZ
🕿 Nicholforest (01228) 577308
Fax (01228) 577308
65-acre mixed farm. Warmth and hospitality await you in this 18th C modernised farmhouse. Country setting, easily accessible from M6, A7, M74. En-suite rooms. National award winner.
Bedrooms: 1 single, 2 double, 1 twin, 1 triple
Bathrooms: 4 private, 1 public, 1 private shower

Bed & breakfast per night:	£min	£max
Single	20.00	25.00
Double	34.00	40.00

Half board per person:	£min	£max
Daily	28.00	32.00
Weekly	150.00	168.00

Evening meal 1900 (last orders 1930)
Parking for 7
Cards accepted: Access, Visa, Amex
🕿 ♨ ♨ ♨ ⤫ M TV IIII, ♨ ☂ ∪ ✎ ✓ ✿ OAP ♨ SP T

Streethead Farm
COMMENDED
Ivegill, Carlisle CA4 0NG
🕿 Southwaite (016974) 73327
211-acre mixed & dairy farm. Distant hills, log fires, en-suite bedrooms on working farm between Penrith and Carlisle (8 miles). 10 minutes from junctions 41 and 42 of M6. Ideal for Lakes or Scotland. Brochure available.

Bedrooms: 1 double, 1 triple
Bathrooms: 2 private, 1 public

Bed & breakfast per night:	£min	£max
Single	16.00	18.00
Double	32.00	36.00

Half board per person:	£min	£max
Weekly	105.00	119.00

Parking for 2
Open March-October
🕿 7 ♨ ♨ UL S TV IIII, ✿ ✓ 🐾 SP 🏠

Cumbria
Map ref 5A3

Picturesque conserved village based on a 12th C priory with a well-preserved church and gatehouse. Just half a mile outside the Lake District National Park, this is a peaceful base for walking and touring, with historic houses and beautiful scenery.

Eeabank House
♨
123 Station Road, Cark in Cartmel, Grange-over-Sands LA11 7NY
🕿 Flookburgh (015395) 58818
Family-run guesthouse close to Holker Hall and gardens. Easy access to Lakes, good country walks. Ideal for touring.
Bedrooms: 1 double, 1 twin, 1 triple
Bathrooms: 2 private, 1 public

Bed & breakfast per night:	£min	£max
Single	17.50	19.50
Double	35.00	39.00

Half board per person:	£min	£max
Daily	24.50	26.50
Weekly	162.00	176.00

Lunch available
Evening meal 1830 (last orders 2100)
Parking for 3
Cards accepted: Access, Visa
🕿 ♨ ♨ ♨ S M TV IIII, ♨ ✿ 🐾 OAP ♨ SP

Cumbria
Map ref 5A3

Small village set in tranquil countryside in an upland area of great beauty. Noted for its 16th C church with 3-tiered pulpit.

Lightwood Farmhouse
COMMENDED
Cartmel Fell, Bowland Bridge, Grange-over-Sands LA11 6NP
🕿 Newby Bridge (015395) 31454
17th C farmhouse with original oak beams. Extensive views, large garden with streams. Home cooking. Just off the A592 near Bowland Bridge.
Bedrooms: 4 double, 3 twin, 2 triple

Bathrooms: 6 private, 1 public

Bed & breakfast per night:	£min	£max
Double	46.00	50.00

Evening meal from 1900
Parking for 10
Cards accepted: Access, Visa
🕿 ♨ ♨ S ⤫ M TV IIII, ♨ ✿ ✕ 🐾 ♨ 🏠

Cumbria
Map ref 5A2

Ancient market town at confluence of Rivers Cocker and Derwent. Birthplace of William Wordsworth in 1770. The house where he was born is at the end of the town's broad, tree-lined main street and is now owned by the National Trust. Good touring base for the Lakes.
Tourist Information Centre
🕿 (01900) 822634

Crag End Farm
Listed **APPROVED**
Rogerscale, Lorton, Cockermouth CA13 0RG
🕿 Lorton (01900) 85658
250-acre mixed farm. In lovely surroundings and ideal for families, this peaceful working family farm is convenient for the Lakes, the shops and many walks. Home cooking using home-grown produce.
Bedrooms: 1 single, 2 double, 1 twin, 1 family room
Bathrooms: 2 public

Bed & breakfast per night:	£min	£max
Single	17.00	
Double	34.00	

Half board per person:	£min	£max
Daily	25.00	
Weekly	175.00	

Evening meal from 1900
Parking for 10
Open February-November
🕿 UL S ⤫ TV ✿ 🐾 🏠

The symbol 🏵 within an entry indicates participation in the Welcome Host programme – a nationally recognised customer care initiative which aims to promote the highest standards of service and a warm welcome for all visitors.

CONISTON

Cumbria
Map ref 5A3

Born from the mining industry, this village lies at the north end of Coniston Water. The scenery to the rear of the village is dominated by Coniston Old Man. Its most famous resident was John Ruskin, whose home, Brantwood, is open to the public. Good centre for walking.

Arrowfield Country Guest House ⚠

👑👑 HIGHLY COMMENDED

Little Arrow, Coniston LA21 8AU
☎ (015394) 41741
Elegant Lakeland house in rural setting, offering quality accommodation. Immediate access to fells. Superb breakfasts, including home-made bread and jams.
Bedrooms: 1 single, 2 double, 2 twin
Bathrooms: 2 private, 1 public

Bed & breakfast

per night:	£min	£max
Single	17.50	21.00
Double	32.00	46.00

Parking for 6
Open March-November

Brigg House ⚠

👑👑 HIGHLY COMMENDED

Torver, Coniston LA21 8AY
☎ (015394) 41592
Country house in beautiful setting at the foot of Coniston Old Man. All rooms en-suite. Varied breakfast menu. Non-smoking.
Bedrooms: 2 double, 1 twin
Bathrooms: 3 private, 1 public

Bed & breakfast

per night:	£min	£max
Double	38.00	40.00

Parking for 4
Open March-November

Thwaite Cottage ⚠

👑 COMMENDED

Waterhead, Coniston LA21 8AJ
☎ (015394) 41367
Beautiful 17th C cottage in secluded position. 5 minutes' walk from village, 200 yards from lake. 2 acres of garden and woodland. Non-smokers only, please.
Bedrooms: 2 double, 1 triple
Bathrooms: 2 public

Bed & breakfast

per night:	£min	£max
Double	34.00	34.00

Parking for 3

Yewdale Hotel ⚠

👑👑👑 COMMENDED

Yewdale Road, Coniston LA21 8LU
☎ (015394) 41280
Built of local materials in 1896 as a bank, now a modern hotel skilfully refurbished throughout. Reduced rate breaks available.
Bedrooms: 5 double, 2 twin, 3 triple
Bathrooms: 7 private, 2 public

Bed & breakfast

per night:	£min	£max
Single	21.95	31.50
Double	43.90	63.00

Half board

per person:	£min	£max
Daily	32.90	42.45
Weekly	126.00	192.00

Lunch available
Evening meal (last orders 2100)
Parking for 6
Cards accepted: Access, Visa

DALSTON

Cumbria
Map ref 5A2

Village in undulating countryside on the banks of the River Caldew. The churchyard is burial place to two Bishops of Carlisle.

Barn Close

Listed

Gaitsgill, Dalston, Carlisle CA5 7AH
☎ Raughton Head (016974) 76558
Dated 1703, in tranquil countryside with a secluded garden. Easy access M6 (junction 42), Carlisle and Borders. Inns nearby.
Bedrooms: 2 double, 1 twin
Bathrooms: 2 public

Bed & breakfast

per night:	£min	£max
Single	17.00	17.00
Double	34.00	34.00

Parking for 4
Open May-October

DENT

Cumbria
Map ref 5B3

Very picturesque village with narrow cobbled streets, lying within the boundaries of the Yorkshire Dales National Park.

Sun Inn ⚠

Listed APPROVED

Main Street, Dent, Sedbergh LA10 5QL
☎ (01539) 625208
17th C inn with original beams, in an outstanding conservation area. Reputation for good value bar meals
and serves beer from the local Dent Brewery.
Bedrooms: 1 double, 1 twin, 1 triple
Bathrooms: 1 public

Bed & breakfast

per night:	£min	£max
Single	17.00	
Double	34.00	

Lunch available
Evening meal 1830 (last orders 2030)
Parking for 20
Cards accepted: Access, Visa, Switch/Delta

ESKDALE

Cumbria
Map ref 5A3

Several minor roads lead to the west end of this beautiful valley, or it can be approached via the east over the Hardknott Pass, the Lake District's steepest pass. Scafell Pike and Bow Fell lie to the north and a miniature railway links the Eskdale Valley with Ravenglass on the coast.

Woolpack Inn ⚠

👑

Boot, Eskdale CA19 1TH
☎ (01946) 723230
Comfortable hotel serving home-cooked food, set in beautiful scenery at the head of the Eskdale Valley.
Bedrooms: 3 double, 4 twin, 1 family room
Bathrooms: 1 public, 4 private showers

Bed & breakfast

per night:	£min	£max
Single	19.00	23.50
Double	38.00	47.00

Half board

per person:	£min	£max
Daily	25.95	38.50
Weekly	180.00	215.50

Lunch available
Evening meal 1830 (last orders 2100)
Parking for 40
Cards accepted: Access, Visa

The symbol ⊛ within an entry indicates participation in the Welcome Host programme – a nationally recognised customer care initiative which aims to promote the highest standards of service and a warm welcome for all visitors.

GRASMERE

Cumbria
Map ref 5A3

Described by William Wordsworth as "the loveliest spot that man hath ever found", this village, famous for its gingerbread, is in a beautiful setting overlooked by Helm Grag. Wordsworth lived at Dove Cottage. The cottage and museum are open to the public.

Beck Allans ♠
Listed   HIGHLY COMMENDED

College Street, Grasmere, Ambleside LA22 9SZ
☎ (015394) 35563
Fax (015394) 35563
Lakeland guesthouse hidden in the delightful well timbered grounds of Beck Allans Holiday Apartments. Centre of village, adjacent River Rothay, super views. Accommodation includes 2-bedroom family suite. Aga-cooked breakfast. Sky movies.
Bedrooms: 3 double, 1 twin
Bathrooms: 4 private

Bed & breakfast per night:	£min	£max
Single	20.50	29.00
Double	41.00	58.00

Parking for 15
Open January-November
Cards accepted: Access, Visa

Craigside House ♠
♨♨   COMMENDED

Grasmere, Ambleside LA22 9SG
☎ (015394) 35292
Delightfully furnished Victorian house on the edge of the village near Dove Cottage. In a large, peaceful garden overlooking the lake and hills.
Bedrooms: 2 double, 1 twin
Bathrooms: 3 private

Bed & breakfast per night:	£min	£max
Single	26.00	46.00
Double	52.00	60.00

Parking for 6

The Harwood ♠
Listed

Red Lion Square, Grasmere, Ambleside LA22 9SP
☎ (015394) 35248
Fax (015394) 35545
Family-run hotel in the heart of Grasmere. Comfortable rooms all with private facilities and TV. Ideal for exploring the Lake District.
Bedrooms: 1 single, 6 double
Bathrooms: 7 private

Bed & breakfast per night:	£min	£max
Single	16.50	23.50
Double	33.00	51.00

Lunch available

Parking for 8
Cards accepted: Access, Visa, Switch/Delta

Travellers Rest ♠
Listed

Grasmere, Ambleside LA22 9RR
☎ (015394) 35604
Charming 17th C inn nestling in the heart of Lakeland and with superb views. Cumbrian hospitality includes good food, real ales, open fires and comfortable accommodation.
Bedrooms: 1 single, 4 double, 2 twin
Bathrooms: 2 public

Bed & breakfast per night:	£min	£max
Single	15.95	36.95
Double	31.90	53.90

Half board per person:	£min	£max
Daily	25.95	36.95
Weekly	181.65	258.65

Lunch available
Evening meal 1900 (last orders 2130)
Parking for 45

Woodland Crag Guest House ♠
♨♨   HIGHLY COMMENDED

Howe Head Lane, Grasmere, Ambleside LA22 9SG
☎ (015394) 35351
Charming Victorian Lakeland-stone house with lake and fell views. Beautiful walks radiate from here. Peacefully situated in landscaped grounds on edge of village. No smoking, please.
Bedrooms: 2 single, 2 double, 1 twin
Bathrooms: 3 private, 1 public

Bed & breakfast per night:	£min	£max
Single	24.00	26.00
Double	50.00	54.00

Parking for 5

GRAYRIGG

Cumbria
Map ref 5B3

Village on the A685 north of Kendal. Important in the development of the Quaker church.

Punchbowl House
♨♨   COMMENDED

Grayrigg, Kendal LA8 9BU
☎ (01539) 824345
Spacious Victorian farmhouse with log fires, in peaceful surroundings between Lakes and dales. Non-smoking.
Bedrooms: 2 double, 1 twin
Bathrooms: 1 private, 1 public

Bed & breakfast per night:	£min	£max
Single	15.50	26.00
Double	31.00	37.00

Parking for 6

GREENODD

Cumbria
Map ref 5A3

Village 3 miles north-east of Ulverston on the Cumbria Cycle Way route.

Machell Arms ♠
♨   APPROVED

Greenodd Village, Ulverston LA12 7QZ
☎ Ulverston (01229) 861 246
Family-run pub in hillside village. 5 miles Windermere, 5 miles Coniston Water. Log fire, home-made food and real ale. Warm welcome.
Bedrooms: 2 triple, 1 family room
Bathrooms: 1 public

Bed & breakfast per night:	£min	£max
Single	15.50	17.50
Double	28.00	30.00

Half board per person:	£min	£max
Daily	23.00	26.00
Weekly	145.00	165.00

Lunch available
Evening meal 1800 (last orders 2030)
Parking for 7

HAWKSHEAD

Cumbria
Map ref 5A3

Lying near Esthwaite Water, this village has great charm and character. Its small squares are linked by flagged or cobbled alleys and the main square is dominated by the market house, or Shambles, where the butchers had their stalls in days gone by.

Balla Wray Cottage ♠
Listed

High Wray, Ambleside LA22 0JQ
☎ Ambleside (015394) 32401
Lakeland-stone cottage on west side of Windermere, in quiet secluded position with views over the lake. Quality facilities. Brochure available.
Bedrooms: 1 double, 1 twin
Bathrooms: 2 private

Bed & breakfast per night:	£min	£max
Single	20.00	22.50
Double	40.00	45.00

Parking for 2

HAWKSHEAD

Continued

The Drunken Duck Inn ⚑

😃😃😃 **COMMENDED**

Barngates, Ambleside LA22 0NG
☎ Ambleside (015394) 36347
*An old-fashioned inn amidst
magnificent scenery. Oak-beamed bars,
cosy log fires and charming bedrooms.
Good food and beers.*
Bedrooms: 9 double, 1 twin
Bathrooms: 10 private

Bed & breakfast

per night:	£min	£max
Single	43.75	50.00
Double	59.50	79.00

Lunch available
Evening meal 1830 (last orders 2100)
Parking for 60
Cards accepted: Access, Visa, Switch/
Delta

📺🖁📻☎📖♨🅿🍴🛗🅢✒🎿🖩◨🍽🎂10♪
✓❀🚗🐾 SP

The Sun Inn ⚑

😃😃😃 **COMMENDED**

Hawkshead, Ambleside LA22 0NT
☎ Windermere (015394) 36236
Fax (015394) 36674
*19th C inn with original beams. A
family-run business with friendly
atmosphere, good food and wine. Very
good value for money, families
welcome.*
Bedrooms: 6 double
Bathrooms: 6 private

Bed & breakfast

per night:	£min	£max
Double	48.00	58.00

Half board

per person:	£min	£max
Weekly	99.00	135.00

Lunch available
Evening meal 1800 (last orders 2130)
Parking for 6
Cards accepted: Access, Visa

📺1📖♨🍴🅢✒🎿📻🖩◨🍴🚗🐾
SP🏛

KENDAL

Cumbria
Map ref 5B3

The "Auld Grey Town" lies in the
valley of the River Kent with a
backcloth of limestone fells.
Situated just outside the Lake
District National Park, it is a good
centre for touring the Lakes and
surrounding country. Ruined castle,
reputed birthplace of Catherine
Parr.
Tourist Information Centre
☎ *(01539) 725758*

Fairways Guest House

😃😃 **COMMENDED**

102 Windermere Road, Kendal
LA9 5EZ
☎ (01539) 725564

*On the main Kendal-Windermere road.
Victorian guesthouse with en-suite
facilities. TV, tea and coffee in all
rooms. Four-poster bedrooms. Private
parking.*
Bedrooms: 3 double
Bathrooms: 3 private, 1 public

Bed & breakfast

per night:	£min	£max
Single	17.00	20.00
Double	32.00	36.00

Parking for 4

📺🖁📻📖♨🖩🍴🅢✒🎿🖩◨🚗🍴🍴
🚗🐾

Garnett House Farm ⚑

😃😃 **COMMENDED**

Burneside, Kendal LA9 5SF
☎ (01539) 724542
*270-acre mixed farm. 15th C farmhouse
set in lovely countryside 10 minutes
from Windermere. During January,
February and March - 3 nights for
£42.00, en-suite £48.00.*
Bedrooms: 4 double
Bathrooms: 3 private, 2 public

Bed & breakfast

per night:	£min	£max
Double	30.00	

Half board

per person:	£min	£max
Daily	23.00	

Evening meal 1830 (last orders 1730)
Parking for 6

📺📖♨🖩🍴📻🖩🚗❀🍴🚗🏛

Gateside Farm

Listed **COMMENDED**

Windermere Road, Kendal LA9 5SE
☎ (01539) 721036
*300-acre dairy & livestock farm.
Traditional Lakeland farm easily
accessible from the motorway and on
the main tourist route through
Lakeland. One night and short stays are
welcome.*
Bedrooms: 3 double, 1 twin, 1 family
room
Bathrooms: 2 private, 2 public

Bed & breakfast

per night:	£min	£max
Single	16.00	20.00
Double	32.00	40.00

Evening meal (last orders 1700)
Parking for 7

📺📖♨🖩🍴🖩❀🚗 SP

Holmfield ⚑

Listed **DE LUXE**

41 Kendal Green, Kendal LA9 5PP
☎ (01539) 720790
Fax (01539) 720790
*Superb location. Elegant Edwardian
house in large gardens. Panoramic
views, swimming pool, croquet.
Spacious bathrooms, lovely bedrooms,
including four-poster. No smoking.*
Bedrooms: 2 double, 1 twin
Bathrooms: 2 private, 2 public

Bed & breakfast

per night:	£min	£max
Single	18.00	25.00
Double	36.00	42.00

Parking for 7

📺13🥂📻📖♨🖩🍴🅢✒🎿🖩◨🍴
🖩🚗❀☼🍴🚗 SP🏛 Ⓣ

Lyndhurst ⚑

😃

8 South Road, Kendal LA9 5QH
☎ (01539) 727281
*Terraced house providing comfortable
accommodation, in a quiet area with
river view. 10 minutes' walk from the
town.*
Bedrooms: 2 single, 2 double, 1 twin,
1 triple
Bathrooms: 2 public

Bed & breakfast

per night:	£min	£max
Single	14.50	15.50
Double	29.00	31.00

Parking for 4

📺♨🖩✒🖩📻🖩◨🚗🍴🚗

Newalls Farmhouse ⚑

Listed **COMMENDED**

Skelsmergh, Kendal LA9 6NU
☎ (01539) 723202
*500-acre dairy farm. Tastefully
modernised farmhouse, with visitors'
own private entrance into a large
garden. Pubs and restaurants within 2
miles. Warm welcome assured.*
Bedrooms: 1 double, 1 triple
Bathrooms: 1 public

Bed & breakfast

per night:	£min	£max
Single		15.00
Double	26.00	28.00

Parking for 2
Open April-October

📺3📖♨🖩✒🖩📻🖩◨🚗∪❀🍴
🚗🏛

Park Lea

😃😃 **COMMENDED**

15 Sunnyside, Kendal LA9 7DJ
☎ (01539) 740986
Fax (01539) 740986
*Delightful Victorian house close to
castle and river, overlooking parkland.
Abbot Hall, Brewery Arts and town
centre 5 minutes' walk.*
Bedrooms: 2 double, 1 twin
Bathrooms: 3 private

Bed & breakfast

per night:	£min	£max
Single	14.00	18.00
Double	28.00	36.00

Parking for 2

📺📖♨🖩✒🎿🅢🖩📻🖩◨🚗❀🚗

Riverbank House

😃😃 **COMMENDED**

Garnett Bridge, Kendal LA8 9AZ
☎ Selside (01539) 823254
*Family-built country house with 20
acres of pastureland bordered by river.*

Foot of Longsleddale Valley, 5 miles north of Kendal.
Bedrooms: 2 double, 1 twin
Bathrooms: 1 public
Bed & breakfast

per night:	£min	£max
Single	14.00	15.00
Double	28.00	30.00

Parking for 4

🕭 👬 Ⓤ 🅐 ⅍ 📺 🖪 🥢 ☼ 🐾

7 Thorny Hills

🍽 COMMENDED

Kendal LA9 7AL
☎ (01539) 720207
Beautiful, unspoilt Georgian town house. Peaceful, pretty location close to town centre. Good home cooking. Self-catering available. Non-smokers only, please.
Bedrooms: 2 double, 1 twin
Bathrooms: 3 private
Bed & breakfast

per night:	£min	£max
Single	17.00	19.00
Double	34.00	38.00

Half board

per person:	£min	£max
Daily	26.00	26.00

Evening meal from 1800
Parking for 3
Open January-November

🕭 🖵 👬 Ⓤ Ⓢ ⅍ 🅐 🛋 ☼ 🥢 🐾 🏠

KESWICK

Cumbria
Map ref 5A3

Beautifully positioned town beside Derwentwater and below the mountains of Skiddaw and Blencathra. Excellent base for walking, climbing, watersports and touring. Motor-launches operate on Derwentwater and motor boats, rowing boats and canoes can be hired.
Tourist Information Centre
☎ *(017687) 72645*

Acorn House Hotel 🕼

🍽🍽 HIGHLY COMMENDED

Ambleside Road, Keswick CA12 4DL
☎ (017687) 72553
Delightful Georgian house in own grounds. All bedrooms are of a high standard. Close to town centre. Ideal base for touring Lake District.
Bedrooms: 6 double, 1 twin, 3 triple
Bathrooms: 10 private
Bed & breakfast

per night:	£min	£max
Single	25.00	35.00
Double	45.00	56.00

Parking for 10
Open February-November
Cards accepted: Access, Visa

🕭 ▼6 🖳 🛢🖵 👬 Ⓢ ⅍ 🅐 🛋 ☼ 🥢 🐾 🏠 Ⓣ

Avondale Guest House 🕼

🍽🍽 COMMENDED

20 Southey Street, Keswick CA12 4EF
☎ (017687) 72735
Comfortable, homely guesthouse near town centre, lake and parks. Good home cooking. A non-smoking establishment.
Bedrooms: 1 single, 4 double, 1 twin
Bathrooms: 4 private, 1 public
Bed & breakfast

per night:	£min	£max
Single	14.50	18.50
Double	29.00	37.00

Half board

per person:	£min	£max
Daily	24.50	28.50
Weekly	168.00	188.00

Evening meal 1830 (last orders 1900)
Cards accepted: Access, Visa, Switch/Delta

🕭 ▼12 🖳🖵 👬 🛢 Ⓢ ⅍ 🅐 🛒 🛋 🥢 🐾 🕭 🆂🅿 Ⓣ

Bank Tavern

Listed

47 Main Street, Keswick CA12 5DS
☎ (017687) 72663
A country pub in the town centre.
Bedrooms: 2 double, 2 twin, 1 triple
Bathrooms: 1 public
Bed & breakfast

per night:	£min	£max
Single	14.00	16.00
Double	28.00	32.00

Lunch available
Evening meal 1800 (last orders 2100)
Parking for 5

🕭 👬 🛢 🅐 📺 🛋 🛋 🐾 ⚲

The Bay Tree 🕼

🍽🍽 COMMENDED

1 Wordsworth Street, Keswick CA12 4HU
☎ (017687) 73313
Friendly guesthouse with lovely views over river and Fitz Park to mountains. 3 minutes' walk from town centre. Home-cooked food.
Bedrooms: 4 double, 1 twin
Bathrooms: 1 private, 1 public
Bed & breakfast

per night:	£min	£max
Double	29.00	38.00

Half board

per person:	£min	£max
Daily	27.00	31.50
Weekly	182.00	213.50

Lunch available
Evening meal 1900 (last orders 1600)

🕭 ▼10 👬 🛢 Ⓢ ⅍ 🅐 🛋 🛋 🥢 🐾 🆂🅿

Beckstones Farm 🕼

🍽🍽 COMMENDED

Thornthwaite, Keswick CA12 5SQ
☎ Braithwaite (017687) 78510
4-acre smallholding. Converted Georgian farmhouse in a typical Lakeland setting, with extensive views of the mountains and Thornthwaite Forest. 3 miles west of Keswick.

Bedrooms: 3 double, 2 triple
Bathrooms: 5 private, 1 public
Bed & breakfast

per night:	£min	£max
Single	20.00	21.00
Double	40.00	42.00

Evening meal 1830 (last orders 1000)
Parking for 8
Open February-November

🕭 ▼6 👬 🛢 Ⓢ ⅍ 🅐 📺 🛋 🛋 ☼ 🐾

Birkrigg Farm

Listed APPROVED

Newlands, Keswick CA12 5TS
☎ Braithwaite (017687) 78278
250-acre mixed farm. Pleasantly and peacefully located in the Newlands Valley. 5 miles from Keswick on the Braithwaite to Buttermere road.
Bedrooms: 1 single, 2 double, 1 twin, 1 triple, 1 family room
Bathrooms: 2 public
Bed & breakfast

per night:	£min	£max
Single	15.00	16.00
Double	30.00	32.00

Parking for 6
Open March-November

🕭 Ⓤ 🛢 ⅍ 🅐 📺 🛋 🛋 ☼ 🥢 🐾

The Bungalows Guest House

🍽🍽 COMMENDED

Sunnyside, Threlkeld, Keswick CA12 4SD
☎ Threlkeld (017687) 79679
Bed and breakfast accommodation, furnished to a high standard, serving full English breakfasts. Excellent views of the surrounding fells. Self-catering also available.
Bedrooms: 1 double, 2 triple, 1 family room
Bathrooms: 4 private, 1 public
Bed & breakfast

per night:	£min	£max
Single	25.00	
Double	35.00	40.00

Parking for 14

🕭 🖳 🖵 🛢 🖲 Ⓤ 🛢 Ⓢ ⅍ 🅐 🅞 🛋 🛋 Ủ ▶ ☼ 🐾 🅞🅐🅟 🆂🅿 Ⓣ

Dancing Beck

☎

Underskiddaw, Keswick CA12 4PZ
☎ (017687) 73800
Lakeland house, with views of Derwent Valley and Lakeland mountains, 2.5 miles from Keswick, just off A591 Keswick-Carlisle road.
Bedrooms: 1 double, 2 twin
Bathrooms: 3 private, 1 public
Bed & breakfast

per night:	£min	£max
Single	18.00	22.00
Double	36.00	40.00

Parking for 3
Open March-October

🕭 🖳 👬 Ⓤ 🖲 🛢 🅐 📺 🛋 🛋 ☼ 🥢 🐾 🏠

KESWICK

Continued

Hazeldene Hotel ▲

⚜⚜ APPROVED

The Heads, Keswick CA12 5ER
☎ (017687) 72106
Fax (017687) 75435
Beautiful and central with open views of Skiddaw and Borrowdale and Newlands Valleys. Midway between town centre and Lake Derwentwater.
Bedrooms: 5 single, 9 double, 4 twin, 4 triple
Bathrooms: 20 private, 2 public

Bed & breakfast per night:	£min	£max
Single	22.00	28.00
Double	44.00	56.00

Half board per person:	£min	£max
Daily	36.00	42.00
Weekly	236.00	275.00

Evening meal 1830 (last orders 1600)
Parking for 18
Open February-November
🛇📞🖨🕯📶🗑♿📺🖩 ♨🍺🐾

Keskadale Farm

Listed

Newlands Valley, Keswick CA12 5TS
☎ Braithwaite (017687) 78544
300-acre livestock farm. Traditional Lakeland farm 6 miles from Keswick, 2.5 miles from Buttermere. Pleasantly situated in the Newland Valley with magnificent views from all bedrooms. A warm welcome awaits you.
Bedrooms: 2 double, 1 twin
Bathrooms: 1 public

Bed & breakfast per night:	£min	£max
Double	30.00	34.00

Parking for 6
Open March-November
🛇📭🕯🖳🏠🗑💲🎿📺🖩. ♨►❄✳ 🐴🏠

King's Arms Hotel ▲

⚜⚜ COMMENDED

Main Street, Keswick CA12 5BL
☎ (017687) 72083

Charming 18th C coaching inn, oak-beamed bar/lounge, air-conditioned, refurbished restaurant. Traditional English home-cooking. Bedrooms of high quality, all en-suite with colour TV, tea/coffee makers. Free use of leisure club.
Bedrooms: 6 double, 5 twin, 2 triple
Bathrooms: 13 private

Bed & breakfast per night:	£min	£max
Single	34.50	42.00
Double	45.00	54.00

Half board per person:	£min	£max
Daily	32.00	35.00
Weekly	175.00	184.00

Lunch available
Evening meal 1800 (last orders 2200)
Cards accepted: Access, Visa, Switch/Delta
🛇📭🗑🕯🏠🖳🗑. ♨💲🎿❄🇺🇾🏠
🐾 🆂🏠 🅃

Kings Head Hotel ▲

⚜⚜ APPROVED

Thirlspot, Keswick CA12 4TN
☎ (017687) 72393
Fax (017687) 72309
Situated at the foot of Helvellyn on the main A591, approximately 5 miles south of Keswick. This 16th C former coaching inn is family-run and offers a wide range of real ales and wines, with good food and comfortable accommodation.
Bedrooms: 3 single, 8 double, 3 twin, 2 triple, 1 family room
Bathrooms: 17 private, 1 public

Bed & breakfast per night:	£min	£max
Single	16.95	26.95
Double	31.90	53.90

Half board per person:	£min	£max
Daily	26.95	36.95
Weekly	188.65	258.65

Lunch available
Evening meal 1800 (last orders 2130)
Parking for 60
Cards accepted: Access, Visa, Switch/Delta
🛇📞📭🗑🕯🏠🖳🗑🎿🅼📺🖩.♨🍺100
🍺🇺🇾►❄🐾 🆂🏠

Lonnin Garth ▲

⚜⚜ COMMENDED

Lonnin Garth, Portinscale, Keswick CA12 5RS
☎ (017687) 74095
An interesting house with character and lovely views, set in mature grounds overlooking northern fells on the outskirts of Keswick.
Bedrooms: 3 double, 2 twin
Bathrooms: 2 private, 1 public

Bed & breakfast per night:	£min	£max
Single	16.50	18.50
Double	33.00	37.00

Parking for 6
🛇5📭🕯🖳🕯🏠🆂🎿🅼🖩.✳🐾🐾🐾

Richmond House ▲

⚜⚜⚜

37-39 Eskin Street, Keswick CA12 4DG
☎ (017687) 73965
Family-run guesthouse, home-from-home, easy walking distance to town
centre and lake. Vegetarians catered for. Non-smokers only, please.
Bedrooms: 2 single, 5 double, 1 twin, 1 triple
Bathrooms: 7 private, 2 public

Bed & breakfast per night:	£min	£max
Single	14.00	15.50
Double	28.00	36.00

Half board per person:	£min	£max
Daily	22.50	24.00
Weekly	155.00	175.00

Evening meal 1900 (last orders 1700)
Cards accepted: Access, Visa, Amex
🛇5📭🕯🏠🖳🕯🏠🆂🎿📺🖩.♨🍺20
🍺🐾🏠

Rickerby Grange ▲

⚜⚜ COMMENDED

Portinscale, Keswick CA12 5RH
☎ (017687) 72344

Detached country hotel in its own gardens, in a quiet village on the outskirts of Keswick. Provides imaginative cooking, a cosy bar and quiet lounge. Ground floor bedrooms available.
Bedrooms: 1 single, 7 double, 1 twin, 3 triple
Bathrooms: 12 private

Bed & breakfast per night:	£min	£max
Single	25.00	27.00
Double	50.00	54.00

Half board per person:	£min	£max
Daily	36.00	38.00
Weekly	235.00	235.00

Evening meal 1900 (last orders 1800)
Parking for 14
Open February-November
🛇5🖳🕯📭🗑🕯🎿🖩.♨✳🐾🐾🆂

Watendlath Guest House ▲

Listed COMMENDED

15 Acorn Street, Keswick CA12 4EA
☎ (017687) 74165
Within easy walking distance of the lake, hills and town centre. We offer a warm and friendly welcome and traditional English breakfast.
Bedrooms: 4 double, 1 twin
Bathrooms: 2 private, 1 public

Bed & breakfast per night:	£min	£max
Double	30.00	34.00

Open January-October
🛇📭🗑🗑🖳🗑🖩.♨🗡🐾🐾🆂

Whitehouse Guest House

COMMENDED

15 Ambleside Road, Keswick
CA12 4DL
☎ (017687) 73176

Fully refurbished, small, friendly guesthouse 5 minutes' walk from the town centre. Colour TV, electric blankets, tea/coffee. Most rooms with en-suite facilities.

Bedrooms: 4 double
Bathrooms: 3 private, 1 public, 1 private shower

Bed & breakfast per night:	£min	£max
Double	30.00	35.00

Parking for 3
Open March-October

KIRKBY STEPHEN

Cumbria
Map ref 5B3

Old market town close to the River Eden, with many fine Georgian buildings and an attractive market square. St Stephen's Church is known as the "Cathedral of the Dales". Good base for exploring the Eden Valley and the Dales.

The Old Rectory

Listed HIGHLY COMMENDED

Crosby Garrett, Kirkby Stephen
CA17 4PW
☎ (017683) 72074

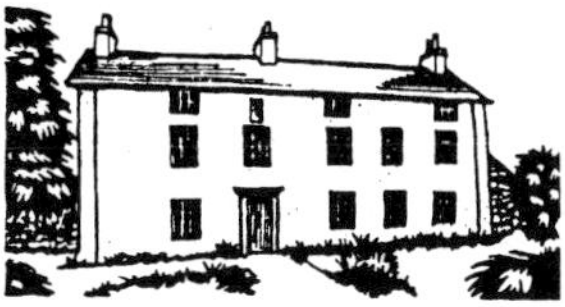

A Grade II listed 17th C rectory, recently restored retaining oak beams and panelled rooms, in unique village setting. Ideal for walking or exploring Eden, Lakes or dales. Aga cooking.*

Bedrooms: 2 double, 1 twin
Bathrooms: 3 private

Bed & breakfast per night:	£min	£max
Single	20.00	26.00
Double	36.00	40.00

Half board per person:	£min	£max
Daily	27.00	30.00

Evening meal 1800 (last orders 2100)
Parking for 3

Please check prices and other details at the time of booking.

LAMBRIGG

Cumbria
Map ref 5B3

Holme Park Hall

Listed

Lambrigg, Kendal LA8 0DJ
☎ Kendal (01539) 824336

Family-run bed and breakfast in early Victorian country house, situated in picturesque location only 1.5 miles from junction 37 of M6 motorway. On Dalesway Walk.

Bedrooms: 1 triple, 1 family room
Bathrooms: 2 private, 1 public

Bed & breakfast per night:	£min	£max
Single	10.00	15.00

Half board per person:	£min	£max
Daily	20.00	

Evening meal from 1800
Parking for 6
Open February-November
20

LAMPLUGH

Cumbria
Map ref 5A3

Near the A5086 between Cockermouth and Cleator Moor, Lamplugh is a scattered village famous for its "Lamplugh Pudding". Ideal touring base for the western Lake District.

Briscoe Close Farm

Listed COMMENDED

Scalesmoor, Lamplugh, Workington
CA14 4TZ
☎ (01946) 861633

Bungalow close to family-run farm. Near Loweswater and Ennerdale, half a mile from A5086. Home cooking using produce grown on farm.

Bedrooms: 2 double
Bathrooms: 1 public

Bed & breakfast per night:	£min	£max
Single	15.00	16.00
Double	30.00	

Half board per person:	£min	£max
Daily	22.00	
Weekly	150.00	

Evening meal from 1900
Parking for 2

The accommodation coupons at the back will help you when contacting proprietors.

LANGDALE

Cumbria
Map ref 5A3

The two Langdale valleys (Great Langdale and Little Langdale) lie in the heart of beautiful mountain scenery. The craggy Langdale Pikes are almost 2500 ft high. An ideal walking and climbing area and base for touring.

Britannia Inn

COMMENDED

Elterwater, Ambleside LA22 9HP
☎ (015394) 37210
Fax (015394) 37311

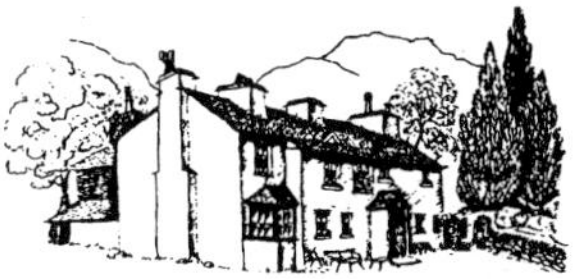

A 400-year-old traditional Lake District inn on a village green in the beautiful Langdale Valley. A warm welcome to all. TV, telephone, welcome tray, hairdryer available in bedrooms.

Bedrooms: 1 single, 9 double, 3 twin
Bathrooms: 10 private, 1 public

Bed & breakfast per night:	£min	£max
Single	17.00	49.00
Double	34.00	53.00

Lunch available
Evening meal 1930 (last orders 1930)
Parking for 10
Cards accepted: Access, Visa, Switch/Delta

LAZONBY

Cumbria
Map ref 5B2

Busy, working village of stone cottages, set beside the River Eden amid sweeping pastoral landscape. Good fishing available.

Bracken Bank Lodge

Lazonby, Penrith CA10 1AX
☎ (01768) 898241
Fax (01768) 898221

Guesthouse and sporting lodge. Field parties catered for. 6 miles from Penrith, signposted to Lazonby on A6.

Bedrooms: 4 single, 3 double, 3 twin
Bathrooms: 4 public

Bed & breakfast per night:	£min	£max
Single	21.15	
Double	42.30	

Continued ▶

LAZONBY

Continued

Half board per person:	£min	£max
Daily	38.70	

Lunch available
Evening meal 2000 (last orders 2000)
Parking for 10

🛌🏠🛇🚭🏧📺🗒🍽25 ♪ ✓ ❀ 🐎 ✍ SP

LEVENS

Cumbria
Map ref 5B3

Village at the southern tip of Scout Scar, overlooking the Lyth Valley. Just outside the village is Levens Hall, an Elizabethan mansion with topiary gardens open to the public.

Olde Peat Cotes

Listed

Olde Peat Cotes, Sampool Lane, Levens, Kendal LA8 8EH
☎ Sedgwick (015395) 60096
Modern bungalow with homely atmosphere, lovely views and beautiful garden. Fishing available on River Kent. Historic farmhouse next door.
Bedrooms: 1 double, 1 twin
Bathrooms: 1 public

Bed & breakfast per night:	£min	£max
Single	10.00	
Double	20.00	

Parking for 2

🛌🎿🏠🖳🏧🚭📺🗒 ♪ ❀ 🐎

LONGTOWN

Cumbria
Map ref 5A2

Perfect base from which to explore the magnificent Borderlands, lying adjacent to the site of the Battle of Solway Moss fought in 1542 between the English and the Scots. Handsome bridge and England's largest sheep market.
Tourist Information Centre
☎ *(01228) 791876*

Craigburn 🏠

😊😊😊 COMMENDED

Penton, Longtown, Carlisle CA6 5QP
☎ Nicholforest (01228) 577214
Fax (01228) 577214

250-acre mixed farm. One of the best farmhouses for delicious food. Beautiful

bedrooms, some four-poster beds. Pets' corner.
Bedrooms: 3 double, 1 twin, 2 triple
Bathrooms: 6 private

Bed & breakfast per night:	£min	£max
Single	19.00	20.00
Double	38.00	40.00

Half board per person:	£min	£max
Daily	29.00	30.00
Weekly	162.00	168.00

Evening meal 1800 (last orders 1400)
Parking for 20
Cards accepted: Access, Visa

🛌🚪♿🎣🏧🛇🚭📺🗒 ♿🍴☀❀🐎 SP T

LOW LORTON

Cumbria
Map ref 5A3

Winder Hall 🏠

😊😊 HIGHLY COMMENDED

Low Lorton, Cockermouth CA13 9UP
☎ Cockermouth (01900) 85107
Old manor house, 1630, on the River Cocker in quiet lakeland village. Spacious and comfortable accommodation. Fell views. Ample parking.
Bedrooms: 1 double, 1 triple
Bathrooms: 2 private

Bed & breakfast per night:	£min	£max
Single	25.00	27.00
Double	40.00	52.00

Parking for 7
Open April-November

🛌4🖳♿🏧🛇🚭📺🗒 ♿✓❀ ✗🐎🏠

LOWESWATER

Cumbria
Map ref 5A3

Scattered village lying between Loweswater, one of the smaller lakes, and Crummock Water. Mountains surround this quiet valley of three lakes, giving some marvellous views.

Brook Farm

😊 COMMENDED

Thackthwaite, Loweswater, Cockermouth CA13 0RP
☎ Lorton (01900) 85606
300-acre hill farm. In quiet surroundings and a good walking area, 5 miles from Cockermouth. Carrying sheep and suckler cows.
Bedrooms: 1 double, 1 twin
Bathrooms: 1 public

Bed & breakfast per night:	£min	£max
Single	16.00	18.00
Double	32.00	36.00

Half board per person:	£min	£max
Daily	23.00	25.00
Weekly	161.00	175.00

Evening meal from 1900
Parking for 3
Open May-October

🐎♿🖳🛇✓🚭📺❀🐎

MAULDS MEABURN

Cumbria
Map ref 5B3

Large village with the River Lyvennet flowing through the middle. The word Meaburn is derived from the old English Maed meaning meadow.

Meaburn Hill Farm

Listed HIGHLY COMMENDED

Meaburn Hill, Maulds Meaburn, Penrith CA10 3HN
☎ Ravensworth (01931) 715205
Fax (01931) 715205

200-acre livestock farm. Lovely 16th C farmhouse overlooking village green and river, in hidden valley near Appleby. Enjoy real country breakfasts, afternoon teas, log fires and antique-furnished rooms. A very special welcome in a little piece of lost England.
Bedrooms: 2 double, 1 twin
Bathrooms: 3 private

Bed & breakfast per night:	£min	£max
Double	38.00	45.00

Evening meal (last orders 0800)
Parking for 3
Open March-December

🛌🚪♿🎣🏧🛇✓🚭📺🗒 ♿🍴10 ✎ ∪▸✓❀✗🐎🏠

ORTON

Cumbria
Map ref 5B3

Small, attractive village with the background of Orton Scar, it has some old buildings and a spacious green. George Whitehead, the itinerant Quaker preacher, was born here in 1636.

Vicarage 🏠

Listed COMMENDED

Orton, Penrith CA10 3RQ
☎ (015396) 24873
Fax (015396) 24873
Warm, comfortable accommodation in a working vicarage overlooking rooftops

and fells. Ideal for walkers visiting the Lakes and Yorkshire Dales.
Bedrooms: 1 double, 2 twin
Bathrooms: 1 public

Bed & breakfast

per night:	£min	£max
Single	16.00	
Double	32.00	

Half board

per person:	£min	£max
Daily	25.00	

Evening meal 1900 (last orders 2100)
Parking for 2

🏠🏊🍴♨⛰🅰📞⛱✂📺⬛.🔌❄🐾 📶 T

PENRITH

Cumbria
Map ref 5B2

Ancient and historic market town, the northern gateway to the Lake District. Penrith Castle was built as a defence against the Scots. Its ruins, open to the public, stand in the public park. High above the town is the Penrith Beacon, made famous by William Wordsworth.
Tourist Information Centre
☎ *(01768) 867466*

Glendale ⋀
Listed COMMENDED
4 Portland Place, Penrith CA11 7QN
☎ (01768) 862579
Victorian town house overlooking pleasant family gardens. Spacious family rooms. Children and pets welcome. Special diets catered for on request.
Bedrooms: 1 single, 1 double, 3 triple
Bathrooms: 1 public

Bed & breakfast

per night:	£min	£max
Single	17.00	17.00
Double	31.00	31.00

Parking for 1

🏠📞♨⛰🅰📞✂📺⬛.🔌📶 SP

Holmewood Guest House ⋀
Listed COMMENDED
5 Portland Place, Penrith CA11 7QN
☎ (01768) 863072
Large Victorian terraced house run by proprietress and providing good facilities. Ideal for Lake District and stopover to or from Scotland.
Bedrooms: 1 double, 3 triple, 1 family room
Bathrooms: 1 private, 2 public

Bed & breakfast

per night:	£min	£max
Single	16.50	19.00
Double	30.00	45.00

Parking for 1

🏠📞♨⛰🅰📞⬛.🔌✂🐾 SP

Hornby Hall Country House ⋀
Listed HIGHLY COMMENDED
Hornby Hall Farm, Brougham, Penrith CA10 2AR
☎ Culgaith (01768) 891114 & Mobile 0831 482108
Fax (01768) 88248

850-acre mixed farm. 16th C farmhouse with original dining hall. Fishing on Eamont available. Easy reach of Lakes and Yorkshire Dales. Home-cooked local produce.
Bedrooms: 2 single, 2 double, 3 twin
Bathrooms: 2 private, 3 public

Bed & breakfast

per night:	£min	£max
Single	19.00	29.50
Double	48.00	59.00

Half board

per person:	£min	£max
Daily	29.00	45.00
Weekly	174.00	270.00

Evening meal 1900 (last orders 2100)
Parking for 10
Cards accepted: Access, Visa

🏠🏊♨⛰🅰📞✂📺⬛.🔌🍴25🌙❄ 🐾 📶 🏧

ROSLEY

Cumbria
Map ref 5A2

Village on the B5805 from Wigton.

Causa Grange ⋀
🏆 DE LUXE
Rosley, Wigton CA7 8DD
☎ Wigton (016973) 45358
Charming Victorian house set in the heart of the countryside yet only 8 miles from historic Carlisle. Overlooking Caldbeck Fells towards Lake District. Fine food and furnishings, log fires and a warm welcome.
Bedrooms: 1 double, 1 twin
Bathrooms: 2 private, 1 public

Bed & breakfast

per night:	£min	£max
Single	21.00	25.00
Double	40.00	48.00

Half board

per person:	£min	£max
Daily	31.00	36.00
Weekly	190.00	245.00

Evening meal 1800 (last orders 2100)
Parking for 9

⛰🅰♨⛰🅰📞✂📺⬛.🔌❄✂🐾 📶 🏧

ST BEES

Cumbria
Map ref 5A3

Small seaside village with fine Norman church and a public school founded in the 16th C. Dramatic red sandstone cliffs make up impressive St Bees Head, parts of which are RSPB reserves and home to puffins and black guillemot. Start or finishing point of Wainwright's Coast to Coast Walk.

Stonehouse
Listed APPROVED
Main Street, Next to Railway Station, St Bees CA27 0DE
☎ Whitehaven (01946) 822 224
Modernised Georgian listed farmhouse, conveniently and attractively situated next to station, shops and hotels. Start of Coast to Coast Walk. Golf-course, long-stay car park.
Bedrooms: 1 single, 2 double, 2 twin, 1 family room
Bathrooms: 1 private, 3 public

Bed & breakfast

per night:	£min	£max
Single	18.00	25.00
Double	30.00	36.00

Parking for 8

🏠🏊🍴📞♨⛰🅰📞⬛.🔌⛱❄ DAP 📶 🏧 T

SATTERTHWAITE

Cumbria
Map ref 5A3

Secluded village with visitors' centre, set in the heart of the Grizedale Forest. Forest trails, forest sculptures, theatre and pretty waterfalls nearby.

Eagles Head Inn
Listed
Satterthwaite, Ulverston LA12 8LN
☎ Ulverston (01229) 860237
Village inn in picturesque Grizedale Forest, 3.5 miles from Hawkshead.
Bedrooms: 3 double, 1 twin
Bathrooms: 4 private, 1 public

Bed & breakfast

per night:	£min	£max
Single	17.00	19.00
Double	34.00	36.00

Half board

per person:	£min	£max
Daily	27.00	28.00

Lunch available
Evening meal 1900 (last orders 2100)
Parking for 10

🏠6📞♨⛰🅰✂📺🍴❄🐾🔌

SAWREY

Cumbria
Map ref 5A3

Far Sawrey and Near Sawrey lie near Esthwaite Water. Both villages are small but Near Sawrey is famous for Hill Top Farm, home of Beatrix Potter, now owned by the National Trust and open to the public.

The Glen ⚍

Listed

Far Sawrey, Ambleside LA22 0LQ
☎ Windermere (015394) 43370
Comfortable old country house in peaceful surroundings with magnificent views. Ideal for walking and touring. Good home-cooking. Log fire.
Bedrooms: 3 double, 1 twin, 1 triple
Bathrooms: 5 private

Bed & breakfast

per night:	£min	£max
Single	26.00	27.00
Double	38.00	40.00

Half board

per person:	£min	£max
Daily	30.00	31.00
Weekly	183.50	190.00

Evening meal 1930 (last orders 0900)
Parking for 6

SEDBERGH

Cumbria
Map ref 5B3

This busy market town set below the Howgill Fells is an excellent centre for walkers and touring the Dales and Howgills. The noted boys' school was founded in 1525.

Dalesman Country Inn

COMMENDED

Main Street, Sedbergh LA10 5BN
☎ (015396) 21183
On entering Sedbergh from the M6 the Dalesman is the first inn on the left. 17th C but recently refurbished by local craftsmen. 10% discount on weekly bookings. Winter breaks available.
Bedrooms: 1 single, 3 double, 1 twin
Bathrooms: 5 private

Bed & breakfast

per night:	£min	£max
Single	28.00	38.00
Double	48.00	50.00

Lunch available
Evening meal 1800 (last orders 2130)
Parking for 12
Cards accepted: Access, Visa

We advise you to confirm your booking in writing.

SHAP

Cumbria
Map ref 5B3

Village lying nearly 1000 ft above sea-level, amongst impressive moorland scenery. Shap Abbey, open to the public, is hidden in a valley nearby. Most of the ruins date from the early 13th C, but the tower is 16th C. The famous Shap granite and limestone quarries are nearby.

Kings Arms Hotel ⚍

Listed

Main Street, Shap, Penrith CA10 3NU
☎ (01931) 716277
Comfortable friendly accommodation on the fringe of the Lake District near M6 junction 39. Directly on the Coast to Coast Walk.
Bedrooms: 2 double, 2 twin, 2 triple
Bathrooms: 2 public

Bed & breakfast

per night:	£min	£max
Single	20.00	
Double	36.00	

Lunch available
Evening meal 1830 (last orders 2000)
Parking for 15
Cards accepted: Access

SILECROFT

Cumbria
Map ref 5A3

Quiet, coastal community offering pebble and sand beaches, 9-hole golf-course, coastal walks and access to Black Combe and the Whicham Valley.

Miners Arms ⚍

COMMENDED

Silecroft, Millom LA18 5LP
☎ Millom (01229) 772325 & 773397
Small, friendly coaching inn 5 minutes' drive from the beach and golf-course. Hospitality enjoyed by visitors and locals alike.
Bedrooms: 2 double, 2 twin
Bathrooms: 4 private, 1 public

Bed & breakfast

per night:	£min	£max
Single	20.00	20.00
Double	32.00	32.00

Half board

per person:	£min	£max
Daily	25.00	30.00

Lunch available
Evening meal 1800 (last orders 2200)
Parking for 50

TEBAY

Cumbria
Map ref 5B3

Village lying amongst high fells at the north end of the Lune Gorge.

Primrose Cottage

Listed

Orton Road, Tebay, Penrith CA10 3TL
☎ Penrith (015396) 24791
Approximately 50 yards from M6, junction 38. Overnight stops/short breaks, excellent facilities. Close to Lakes and Yorkshire Dales.
Bedrooms: 2 double, 1 twin
Bathrooms: 1 private, 2 public

Bed & breakfast

per night:	£min	£max
Single	15.00	20.00
Double	30.00	35.00

Half board

per person:	£min	£max
Daily	22.00	25.00
Weekly	140.00	165.00

Lunch available
Parking for 6

TROUTBECK

Cumbria
Map ref 5A3

On the Penrith to Keswick road, Troutbeck was the site of a series of Roman camps. The village now hosts a busy weekly sheep market.

Lane Head Farm Guest House ⚍

Troutbeck, Penrith CA11 0SY
☎ Threlkeld (017687) 79220
Charming 17th C former farmhouse in quiet location, 4 miles from Ullswater lake. Good home cooking, table licence. Log fire, some en-suite and four-poster rooms.
Bedrooms: 6 double, 2 twin, 1 family room
Bathrooms: 5 private, 1 public

Bed & breakfast

per night:	£min	£max
Single	20.00	25.00
Double	32.00	45.00

Half board

per person:	£min	£max
Daily	24.00	30.00

Lunch available
Evening meal 1900 (last orders 2000)
Parking for 10

Please mention this guide when making a booking.

ULLSWATER

Cumbria
Map ref 5A3

This beautiful lake, which is over 7 miles long, runs from Glenridding to Pooley Bridge. Lofty peaks ranging around the lake make an impressive background. A steamer service operates along the lake between Pooley Bridge, Howtown and Glenridding in the summer.

Bridge End Farm ⋀

COMMENDED

Hutton, Hutton John, Penrith CA11 0LZ
☎ Greystoke (017684) 83273
14-acre mixed farm. Warmest hospitality in 17th C farmhouse, situated in own grounds with gardens to river. Lakeland fell views. 5 miles west of M6, half a mile A66, 3 miles Ullswater.
Bedrooms: 2 double, 1 twin, 1 triple
Bathrooms: 4 private
Bed & breakfast

per night:	£min	£max
Double	30.00	35.00

Half board

per person:	£min	£max
Daily	23.00	25.00
Weekly	150.00	160.00

Evening meal 1830 (last orders 1700)
Parking for 6
Open April-October
➣ 10 ⅢⅢ ◨ ⬚ ＴＶ ▦ ◨ ✿ ✕ ⬚ 🏢

Netherdene Guest House ⋀

COMMENDED

Troutbeck, Penrith CA11 0SJ
☎ Greystoke (017684) 83475
Traditional country house in its own quiet grounds, with extensive mountain views, offering comfortable well-appointed rooms with personal attention. Ideal base for touring Lakeland.
Bedrooms: 1 single, 1 double, 1 twin, 1 triple
Bathrooms: 4 private, 1 public
Bed & breakfast

per night:	£min	£max
Single	20.00	23.00
Double	33.00	38.00

Half board

per person:	£min	£max
Daily	25.50	27.00
Weekly	165.00	175.00

Evening meal 1830 (last orders 1600)
Parking for 6
➣ 7 ▢ ◨ ⅢⅢ ✕ ◨ ▦ ⬚ ✿ ✕ ⬚ 🏢

Tymparon Hall

COMMENDED

Newbiggin, Stainton, Penrith CA11 0HS
☎ Greystoke (017684) 83236

150-acre livestock farm. Delightful 18th C manor house with colourful summer garden in excellent location. Lake Ullswater a 10-minute drive.
Bedrooms: 3 double
Bathrooms: 2 private, 1 public
Bed & breakfast

per night:	£min	£max
Single	20.00	22.00
Double	38.00	42.00

Half board

per person:	£min	£max
Daily	30.00	32.00
Weekly	185.00	190.00

Evening meal 1830 (last orders 1430)
Open April-October
➣ ⬚ ◨ ⅢⅢ ⓵ ◨ ◨ ＴＶ ▦ ⬚ ✿ ⬚ ᴰᴬᴾ ˢᴾ

Waterside House ⋀

COMMENDED

Watermillock, Penrith CA11 0JH
☎ Pooley Bridge (017684) 86038
Beautiful lakeside house (1771) set in 10 acres of gardens and meadows on Ullswater's glorious shores. Peaceful and comfortable, an idyllic retreat from pressures. On A592 to Patterdale, 2 miles south of Pooley Bridge.
Wheelchair access category 3 ♿
Bedrooms: 5 double, 1 twin, 1 triple
Bathrooms: 4 private, 3 public
Bed & breakfast

per night:	£min	£max
Double	40.00	70.00

Lunch available
Evening meal 1800 (last orders 2130)
Cards accepted: Access, Visa
➣ ⬚ ♿ ◨ ◨ ⓵ ◨ ✕ ◨ ＴＶ ▦ ⓣ20 ✈ ✿ ⬚ ˢᴾ 🏢

White Lion Inn ⋀

Listed

Patterdale, Penrith CA11 0NW
☎ Patterdale (017684) 82214
Old world country inn with friendly atmosphere, on Lake Ullswater near Helvellyn. An ideal centre for walking, fishing and sailing. Traditional beer.
Bedrooms: 1 single, 2 double, 4 twin, 1 triple
Bathrooms: 1 private, 1 public
Bed & breakfast

per night:	£min	£max
Single	21.00	
Double	42.00	

Lunch available
Evening meal 1830 (last orders 2145)
Parking for 50
➣ ▢ ⬚ ⓵ ⓢ ▦ ◡ ✈ ⌁ ⬚

UNDERBARROW

Cumbria
Map ref 5A3

At the foot of limestone escarpment Scout Scar, Underbarrow is close to the National Trust's Brigsteer Woods, west of Kendal. A quiet, spread-out village, overlooking the Lyth Valley.

Tranthwaite Hall

Listed COMMENDED

Underbarrow, Kendal LA8 8HG
☎ Crosthwaite (015395) 68285
260-acre dairy/sheep farm. Magnificent 11th C farmhouse, with oak beams and doors, offering immaculate accommodation. Ideal location for touring Lakeland.
Bedrooms: 1 double, 1 triple
Bathrooms: 2 private, 1 public
Bed & breakfast

per night:	£min	£max
Single	18.00	20.00
Double	32.00	38.00

Parking for 3
➣ ⬚ ◨ ✕ ◨ ＴＶ ▦ ✿ ⬚ ˢᴾ 🏢

WINDERMERE

Cumbria
Map ref 5A3

Once a tiny hamlet before the introduction of the railway in 1847, now adjoins Bowness which is on the lakeside. Centre for sailing and boating. A good way to see the lake is a trip on a passenger steamer. Steamboat Museum has a fine collection of old boats.
Tourist Information Centre
☎ *(015394) 46499*

Aaron Slack ⋀

COMMENDED

48 Ellerthwaite Road, Windermere LA23 2BS
☎ (015394) 44649 & Mobile 0374 638714
Small, friendly guesthouse for non-smokers in a quiet part of Windermere, close to all amenities and concentrating on personal service.
Bedrooms: 2 double, 1 twin
Bathrooms: 3 private
Bed & breakfast

per night:	£min	£max
Single	14.00	21.00
Double	28.00	40.00

Cards accepted: Access, Visa, Amex
➣ 12 ▯ ▢ ⬚ ◨ ⓵ ⓢ ✕ ◨ ▦ ⬚ ✕ ⬚ ⬚ ⓣ

Beckside Cottage ⋀

Listed

4 Park Road, Windermere LA23 2AW
☎ (015394) 42069 & 88105

Continued ▶

WINDERMERE

Continued

Comfortable cottage with en-suite bedrooms. Full central heating, colour TV, tea/coffee and radio in all rooms. Full English breakfast served. Ideally situated, close to Windermere village.
Bedrooms: 1 single, 2 double, 1 triple
Bathrooms: 4 private

Bed & breakfast

per night:	£min	£max
Single	15.00	18.00
Double	30.00	36.00

Parking for 3

The Common Farm

Windermere LA23 1JQ
☎ (015394) 43433
200-acre dairy farm. Picturesque and homely 17th C farmhouse in peaceful surroundings, less than 1 mile from Windermere village.
Bedrooms: 1 double, 1 family room
Bathrooms: 1 public

Bed & breakfast

per night:	£min	£max
Double	28.00	32.00

Parking for 4
Open March-November

Fairfield Country House Hotel ⋔

COMMENDED

Brantfell Road, Bowness-on-Windermere, Windermere LA23 3AE
☎ (015394) 46565
Fax (015394) 46565
Small, friendly 200-year-old country house with half an acre of peaceful secluded gardens. 2 minutes' walk from Lake Windermere and village. Private car park, leisure facilities.
Bedrooms: 1 single, 5 double, 1 twin, 1 triple, 1 family room
Bathrooms: 9 private, 1 public

Bed & breakfast

per night:	£min	£max
Single	24.00	28.00
Double	48.00	56.00

Half board

per person:	£min	£max
Daily	39.00	43.00
Weekly	255.00	285.00

Evening meal 1900 (last orders 1900)
Parking for 14
Cards accepted: Access, Visa

Fir Trees ⋔

HIGHLY COMMENDED

Lake Road, Windermere LA23 2EQ
☎ (015394) 42272
Fax (015394) 42272
Well-situated and handsome Victorian gentleman's residence offering elegant accommodation. Lovely bedrooms,

scrumptious breakfasts and warm hospitality, all at exceptional value for money.
Bedrooms: 5 double, 1 twin, 1 triple
Bathrooms: 7 private

Bed & breakfast

per night:	£min	£max
Single	19.50	31.00
Double	39.00	52.00

Parking for 8
Cards accepted: Access, Visa, Amex

Holly Lodge ⋔

COMMENDED

6 College Road, Windermere
LA23 1BX
☎ (015394) 43873
Fax (015394) 43873
Traditional Lakeland stone guesthouse, built in 1854. In a quiet area off the main road, close to the village centre, buses, railway station and all amenities.
Bedrooms: 1 single, 5 double, 2 twin, 3 triple
Bathrooms: 6 private, 2 public

Bed & breakfast

per night:	£min	£max
Single	17.00	20.00
Double	34.00	40.00

Half board

per person:	£min	£max
Daily	27.00	30.00

Evening meal from 1900
Parking for 7

Kirkwood Guest House ⋔

COMMENDED

Prince's Road, Windermere LA23 2DD
☎ (015394) 43907
Large Victorian house conveniently situated in a quiet location between Windermere and Bowness. En-suite rooms, honeymoon suite, four-poster beds. Tours arranged.
Bedrooms: 4 double, 2 triple, 1 family room
Bathrooms: 7 private

Bed & breakfast

per night:	£min	£max
Double	20.00	50.00

Parking for 1
Cards accepted: Access, Visa

Laurel Cottage ⋔

COMMENDED

St. Martin's Square, Bowness-on-Windermere, Windermere LA23 3EF
☎ (015394) 45594
Fax (015394) 45594
Charming early 17th C cottage with front garden, situated in centre of Bowness. Superb selection of restaurants within one minute's stroll.
Bedrooms: 2 single, 10 double, 1 twin, 2 triple
Bathrooms: 10 private, 2 public

Bed & breakfast

per night:	£min	£max
Single	21.00	23.00
Double	34.00	52.00

Parking for 8
Cards accepted: Access

Lindisfarne

Listed

Sunny Bank Road, Windermere
LA23 2EN
☎ (015394) 46295
Traditional detached Lakeland stone house, colour TVs, tea and coffee facilities, en-suite rooms. Ideally situated in quiet area, close to lake, shops and scenic walks.
Bedrooms: 2 double, 1 twin, 1 family room
Bathrooms: 4 private, 2 public

Bed & breakfast

per night:	£min	£max
Single	15.00	20.00
Double	26.00	35.00

Half board

per person:	£min	£max
Daily	23.00	28.00
Weekly	138.00	168.00

Evening meal 1800 (last orders 2000)
Parking for 4

New Hall Bank

Listed

Fallbarrow Road, Bowness-on-Windermere, Windermere LA23 3AJ
☎ (015394) 43558
In a quiet area within 2 minutes' walking distance of town centre and the lake. Ample parking space. Lake views.
Bedrooms: 2 single, 7 double, 3 triple, 2 family rooms
Bathrooms: 2 public, 1 private shower

Bed & breakfast

per night:	£min	£max
Single	16.00	20.00
Double	30.00	40.00

Parking for 16

Oldfield House ⋔

COMMENDED

Oldfield Road, Windermere LA23 2BY
☎ (015394) 88445
Fax (015394) 43250

Friendly, informal atmosphere within a traditionally-built Lakeland residence. Quiet central location, free use of swimming and leisure club.

Bedrooms: 2 single, 3 double, 1 triple, 1 family room
Bathrooms: 7 private, 1 public

Bed & breakfast

per night:	£min	£max
Single	20.00	29.50
Double	36.00	55.00

Parking for 7
Open February-December
Cards accepted: Access, Visa, Amex, Switch/Delta

The Poplars ⋀

COMMENDED

Lake Road, Windermere LA23 2EQ
☎ (015394) 42325 & 46690
Small family-run guesthouse on the main lake road, offering en-suite accommodation coupled with fine cuisine and homely atmosphere. Golf and fishing can be arranged.
Bedrooms: 1 single, 3 double, 2 twin, 1 triple
Bathrooms: 6 private, 1 public

Bed & breakfast

per night:	£min	£max
Single	18.50	21.00
Double	37.00	42.00

Half board

per person:	£min	£max
Daily	29.50	32.00
Weekly	199.50	217.00

Evening meal 1800 (last orders 1800)
Parking for 7

St. John's Lodge ⋀

COMMENDED

Lake Road, Windermere LA23 2EQ
☎ (015394) 43078
Small private hotel midway between Windermere and the lake, managed by the chef/proprietor and convenient for all amenities and services. Facilities of local sports and leisure club available to guests.
Bedrooms: 1 single, 9 double, 2 twin, 2 triple
Bathrooms: 14 private

Bed & breakfast

per night:	£min	£max
Single	20.00	25.00
Double	37.00	50.00

Half board

per person:	£min	£max
Daily	30.00	35.00
Weekly	198.00	225.00

Evening meal 1900 (last orders 1800)
Parking for 11
Open February-November
Cards accepted: Access, Visa

Upper Oakmere ⋀

Listed

3 Upper Oak Street, Windermere LA23 2LB
☎ (015394) 45649

Ideal location, 100 yards from main High Street. Friendly atmosphere, home cooking. Single people/party bookings. Open all year. Pets welcome
Bedrooms: 1 single, 3 double, 1 twin
Bathrooms: 1 public

Bed & breakfast

per night:	£min	£max
Single	12.00	16.50
Double	24.00	33.00

Half board

per person:	£min	£max
Daily	19.50	24.00
Weekly	136.50	168.00

Evening meal 1830 (last orders 1900)
Parking for 2

Villa Lodge

COMMENDED

Cross Street, Windermere LA23 1AE
☎ (015394) 43318
Fax (015394) 43318

Friendliness and cleanliness guaranteed. Peacefully situated in quiet cul-de-sac overlooking Windermere village. Splendid views. Safe private parking.
Bedrooms: 1 single, 4 double, 2 twin, 1 family room
Bathrooms: 7 private

Bed & breakfast

per night:	£min	£max
Single	17.00	20.00
Double	30.00	50.00

Parking for 7
Open February-October, December
Cards accepted: Access, Visa

Westbourne Hotel ⋀

COMMENDED

Biskey Howe Road, Bowness-on-Windermere, Windermere LA23 2JR
☎ (015394) 43625
In a peaceful area of Bowness within a short walk of the lake and shops. Highly recommended by our regular guests for comfort, decor and efficient, friendly service.
Bedrooms: 1 single, 5 double, 2 twin, 1 triple
Bathrooms: 9 private

Bed & breakfast

per night:	£min	£max
Single	28.00	32.00
Double	38.00	55.00

Evening meal 1830 (last orders 1900)
Parking for 10
Cards accepted: Access, Visa, Amex

White Lodge Hotel ⋀

COMMENDED

Lake Road, Windermere LA23 2JS
☎ (015394) 43624
Victorian family-owned hotel with good home cooking, only a short walk from Bowness Bay. All bedrooms have private bathroom, colour TV and tea making facilities, some with lake views and four-posters.
Bedrooms: 2 single, 7 double, 2 twin, 1 triple
Bathrooms: 12 private

Bed & breakfast

per night:	£min	£max
Single	23.00	29.00
Double	46.00	56.00

Half board

per person:	£min	£max
Daily	33.00	40.00
Weekly	230.00	255.00

Lunch available
Evening meal 1900 (last orders 2000)
Parking for 20
Open March-November
Cards accepted: Access, Visa

WORKINGTON

Cumbria
Map ref 5A2

A deep-water port on the west Cumbrian coast. There are the ruins of the 14th C Workington Hall, where Mary Queen of Scots stayed in 1568.
Tourist Information Centre
☎ *(01900) 602923*

Morven Guest House ⋀

Siddick Road, Siddick, Workington CA14 1LE
☎ (01900) 602118 & 602002
Detached house north-west of Workington. Ideal base for touring the Lake District and west Cumbria. Large car park.
Bedrooms: 2 single, 1 double, 2 twin, 1 triple
Bathrooms: 4 private, 1 public

Bed & breakfast

per night:	£min	£max
Single	20.00	32.00
Double	36.00	46.00

Half board

per person:	£min	£max
Daily	30.00	42.00
Weekly	175.00	

Lunch available
Evening meal 1800 (last orders 1600)
Parking for 20

USE YOUR *i*'S

There are more than 550 Tourist Information Centres throughout England offering friendly help with accommodation and holiday ideas as well as suggestions of places to visit and things to do. There may well be a centre in your home town which can help you before you set out. You'll find the address of your nearest Tourist Information Centre in your local Phone Book.

COUNTRY CODE

♣ Enjoy the countryside and respect its life and work ♣ Guard against all risk of fire ♣ Fasten all gates ♣ Keep your dogs under close control ♣ Keep to public paths across farmland ♣ Use gates and stiles to cross fences, hedges and walls ♣ Leave livestock, crops and machinery alone ♣ Take your litter home ♣ Help to keep all water clean ♣ Protect wildlife, plants and trees ♣ Take special care on country roads ♣ Make no unnecessary noise

Northumbria

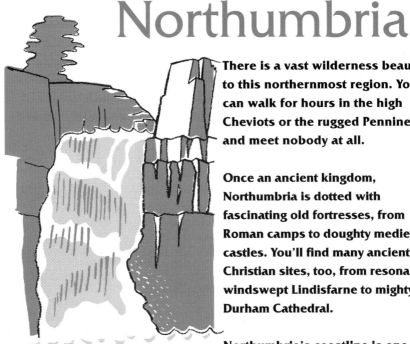

There is a vast wilderness beauty to this northernmost region. You can walk for hours in the high Cheviots or the rugged Pennines and meet nobody at all.

Once an ancient kingdom, Northumbria is dotted with fascinating old fortresses, from Roman camps to doughty medieval castles. You'll find many ancient Christian sites, too, from resonant, windswept Lindisfarne to mighty Durham Cathedral.

Northumbria's coastline is one of its glories, and includes the lovely, great stretch of unspoilt Northumberland Heritage coast. It also offers sandy beaches, quiet fishing villages and lively seaside resorts.

Don't leave the region without visiting Tyneside and Catherine Cookson country, a land of good old-fashioned pubs, industrial heritage and northern down-to-earth friendliness.

The Counties of Cleveland, Durham, Northumberland and Tyne & Wear

For more information on Northumbria, contact:

Northumbria Tourist Board,
Aykley Heads, Durham DH1 5UX

Tel: (0191) 384 6905

Fax: (0191) 386 0899

Where to Go in Northumbria –
see pages 60–63

Where to Stay in Northumbria –
see pages 64–76

Northumbria

Where to go and what to see

You will find hundreds of interesting places to visit during your stay in Northumbria, just some of which are listed in these pages. The number against each name will help you locate it on the map (page 63). Contact any Tourist Information Centre in the region for more ideas on days out in Northumbria.

1 Lindisfarne Castle
Holy Island, Berwick-upon-Tweed, Northumberland
TD15 2SH
Tel: (01289) 89244
Tudor fort converted into a private home in 1903 for Edward Hudson by the architect Edwin Lutyens.

2 Bamburgh Castle
Bamburgh, Northumberland
NE69 7DF
Tel: (01668) 214208
Magnificent coastal castle completely restored in 1900. Collections of china, porcelain, furniture, paintings, arms and armour.

3 Farne Islands
Seahouses, off Northumberland coast
Bird reserve holding around 55,000 pairs of breeding birds of 21 species. Also home to a large colony of grey seals.

4 Alnwick Castle
Alnwick, Northumberland
NE66 1NQ
Tel: (01665) 510777
Home of the Percys, Dukes of Northumberland, since 1309. Largest inhabited castle in England after Windsor.

5 Cragside House, Gardens and Grounds
Cragside, Rothbury, Northumberland NE65 7PX
Tel: (01669) 20333
House built 1864–95 for the first Lord Armstrong, Tyneside industrialist. First house to be lit by electricity generated by water power.

6 Morpeth Chantry Bagpipe Museum
The Chantry, Bridge Street, Morpeth, Northumberland
NE61 1PJ
Tel: (01670) 519466
Set in a 13th C church building,

museum showing the history and development of Northumbrian small pipes and the music.

7 Chesters Roman Fort
Chollerford, Humshaugh, Hadrian's Wall, Northumberland
NE46 4EP
Tel: (01434) 681379
Fort built for 500 cavalrymen. Remains include 5 gateways, barrack blocks, commandant's house and headquarters. Finest military bathhouse in Britain.

8 Sea Life Centre
Grand Parade, Long Sands, Tynemouth, Tyne & Wear
NE30 4JF
Tel: (0191) 257 6100
Over 30 hi-tech displays provide encounters with thousands of amazing sea creatures.

9 Wet 'N Wild
Rotary Way, North Shields, Tyne

& Wear NE29 6DA
Tel: (0191) 296 1333
Tropical indoor waterpark. A brand new fun water playground to provide the UK's wildest and wettest indoor rapid experience.

⑩ Housesteads Roman Fort
Hadrian's Wall, Northumberland
NE47 6NN
Tel: (01434) 344363
Best preserved and most impressive of the Roman forts. Vercovicium was 5-acre fort with extensive civil settlement.

⑪ Souter Point Lighthouse
Coast Road, Whitburn, South Shields, Tyne & Wear SR6 7NH
Tel: (0191) 529 3061
Lighthouse and associated buildings were constructed in 1871 and contained the most advanced lighthouse technology of the day.

⑫ MetroCentre
Gateshead, Tyne & Wear
NE11 9XX
Tel: (0191) 493 2046
Over 350 shops with spacious malls, garden court, Mediterranean village, antique village, Roman forum, over 50 eating outlets, cinema, superbowl. Metroland indoor theme park with roller-coaster, dodgems, pirate ship, live entertainment.

⑬ Gibside Chapel and Grounds
Gibside, Burnopfield, Newcastle upon Tyne, NE16 6BG
Tel: (01207) 542255
Mausoleum of 5 members of the Bowes family, built to a design by James Paine between 1760 and 1812. Restored in 1965. Avenue of Turkey Oak trees.

⑭ Wildfowl and Wetlands Trust
Washington, Tyne & Wear
NE38 8LE
Tel: (0191) 416 5454
Collection of 1,250 wildfowl of 108 varieties. Viewing gallery, picnic areas, hides and winter wild bird feeding station (bird food available). Flamingoes.

⑮ Beamish – The North of England Open Air Museum
Beamish, Co Durham DH9 0RG
Tel: (01207) 231811
Open air museum of northern life around the turn of the century. Buildings re-erected to form a town with shops and houses. Colliery village, station and working farm.

⑯ Durham Castle
Palace Green, Durham DH1 3RW
Tel: (0191) 374 3863
Castle with fine bailey founded in 1072, Norman chapel dating from 1080, kitchens and great hall dating from 1499 and 1284 respectively.

⑰ Durham Cathedral
Durham, DH1 3EQ
Tel: (0191) 386 2367
Widely considered to be the finest example of Norman church architecture in England. Tombs of St Cuthbert and the Venerable Bede.

⑱ Killhope Leadmining Centre
Cowshill, St John's Chapel, Co Durham DL13 1AR
Tel: (01388) 537505
Most complete lead mining site in Great Britain. Includes crushing mill with 34ft water wheel, reconstruction of Victorian machinery and miners' accommodation.

⑲ High Force Waterfall
Forest-in-Teesdale, Middleton-in-Teesdale, Co Durham
Tel: (01833) 40209
Most majestic of the waterfalls on the River Tees. The falls are only a short walk from a bus stop, car park and picnic area.

⑳ Raby Castle
Staindrop, Co Durham DL2 3AH
Tel: (01833) 660202
Medieval castle in 200-acre park. 600-year-old kitchen and carriage collection. Walled gardens and deer park.

㉑ Saltburn Smugglers Heritage Centre
Ship Inn, Saltburn-by-the-Sea,

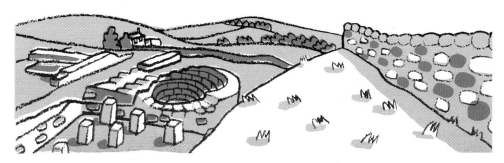

Cleveland TS12 1HF
Tel: (01287) 625252
Offers the sights, sounds and smells of Saltburn's smuggling heritage, with tales of John Andrew, "King of the Smugglers".

22 Butterfly World
Preston Park, Yarm Road, Stockton-on-Tees, Cleveland TS18 3RH
Tel: (01642) 791414
Indoor tropical garden with exotic free-flying butterflies plus fascinating insects and reptiles.

23 Green Dragon Museum
Theatre Yard, Stockton-on-Tees, Cleveland TS18 1AT
Tel: (01642) 674308
Local history museum recording

development of Stockton. "1825, the Birth of Railways" is an exciting audio-visual show.

24 Preston Hall Museum
Yarm Road, Stockton-on-Tees, Cleveland TS18 3RH
Tel: (01642) 781184
Social history museum with period street and rooms, working craftsmen, arms, armour, costume and toys. Set in 116 acres of beautiful parkland, with aviary, pitch and putt.

25 Captain Cook Birthplace Museum
Stewart Park, Marton, Middlesbrough, Cleveland TS7 6AS
Tel: (01642) 311211
Early life and voyages of Captain Cook and the countries he visited. Exhibitions changed monthly.

26 Ormesby Hall
Church Lane, Ormesby, Middlesbrough, Cleveland TS7 9AS
Tel: (01642) 324188
Mid-18th C house with fine decorative plasterwork, Jacobean doorway, stable block. Attributed to Carr of York.

Find Out More

Further information about holidays and attractions in Northumbria is available from:
Northumbria Tourist Board, Aykley Heads, Durham DH1 5UX
Tel: (0191) 384 6905

These publications are available free from the Northumbria Tourist Board:
- **Northumbria Breaks 1996**
- **Bed & Breakfast Touring Map** – Northumbria and Cumbria
- **Great Days Out** – regional attraction guide
- **Freedom Caravan and Camping Guide** – Northumbria, Yorkshire &

Berwick-upon-Tweed

1 Holy Island
3 Farne Islands
2 Bamburgh

Belford •

Scotland

Wooler •

Alnwick **4**

Rothbury **5**

Amble •

• Kielder   • Otterburn

Northumberland

• Bellingham   Morpeth **6**   • Ashington

• Blyth

Whitley Bay

Chollerford **7**   North Shields   **8** Tynemouth

Haltwhistle •   Hexham •   **9**   South Shields

10   Newcastle upon Tyne •   Jarrow

Housesteads •   Prudhoe •   Gateshead **12** Whitburn **11**   **Tyne & Wear**

Haydon Bridge   Burnopfield **13**   **14** Sunderland

Consett •   **15** Beamish Washington

Stanley

Durham **16** **17**

18 Cowshill   Peterlee •

Crook •

Forest-in-Teesdale **19**   **Durham**   Hartlepool

Redcar

Cumbria   Staindrop **20**   • Bishop Auckland   Middlesbrough   Saltburn-
21 by-the-Sea

Barnard Castle •   Stockton-on-Tees **22** **23** **24** **25** **26**   • Guisborough

Darlington •   Marton   **Cleveland**

North Yorkshire

Humberside, Cumbria and
North West
- **Festivals & Events** – annual
  listing of events in region
- **Schools Out** – educational
  brochure

Also available are (prices include
postage and packaging):
- **Northumbria touring map
  and guide** £4.75
- **Leisure Guide to
  Northumbria** £10.99

- **Walk Northumbria** £6.50

WHERE TO STAY

Accommodation entries in this regional section are listed in alphabetical order of place name, and then in alphabetical order of establishment.

Map references refer to the colour location maps at the back of this guide. The first figure is the map number; the letter and figure which follow indicate the grid reference on the map.

At-a-glance symbols at the end of each accommodation entry give information about services and facilities. A handy guide to these symbols can be found inside the back cover flap, which can be kept open for easy reference.

ALNMOUTH

Northumberland
Map ref 5C1

Quiet village with pleasant old buildings, at the mouth of the River Aln where extensive dunes and sands stretch along Alnmouth Bay. 18th C granaries, some converted to dwellings, still stand.

High Buston Hall ♠

🏵🏵🏵 HIGHLY COMMENDED

High Buston, Alnmouth, Alnwick NE66 3QH
☎ Alnwick (01665) 830341
Fax (01665) 830341
Elegant listed Georgian house with commanding coastal views. Comfortable and stylish with traditional furnishings. Relaxed atmosphere, warm hospitality and peaceful village setting.
Bedrooms: 2 double, 1 twin
Bathrooms: 3 private

Bed & breakfast

per night:	£min	£max
Single	30.00	45.00
Double	55.00	60.00

Parking for 9
Open January-November

🏵🖵💧Ⓢ✂🗏🗺🛏💻🗂♪12🗘🌢✗
🗂 SP ♨ ◎

The symbols ❶ 🌓 🌕 indicate categories of accessibility for wheelchair users. They are explained in full in the information pages at the back of this guide.

ALNWICK

Northumberland
Map ref 5C1

Ancient and historic market town, entered through the Hotspur Tower, an original gate in the town walls. The medieval castle, the second biggest in England and still the seat of the Dukes of Northumberland, was restored from ruin in the 18th C.
Tourist Information Centre
☎ *(01665) 510665*

Lindisfarne Guest House

Listed

6 Bondgate Without, Alnwick NE66 1PP
☎ (01665) 603430
Traditional stone-built Northumbrian house built in early 19th C. Converted to provide guesthouse of considerable charm and comfort.
Bedrooms: 1 single, 1 double, 1 triple, 1 family room
Bathrooms: 2 public

Bed & breakfast

per night:	£min	£max
Single	14.00	16.00
Double	28.00	32.00

Evening meal 1800 (last orders 1700)
🏵🖵💧🗏Ⓢ🗺🛏💻🗂♪🗂

Masons Arms ♠

🏵🏵🏵 COMMENDED

Stamford Cott, Rennington, Alnwick NE66 3RX
☎ (01665) 577275
Fax (01665) 577894

Country inn offering real ale and good food. En-suite bedrooms. 3.5 miles from A1 towards coast and beaches, on B1340.
Bedrooms: 2 double, 1 twin, 2 triple; suite available
Bathrooms: 5 private

Bed & breakfast

per night:	£min	£max
Single	35.00	35.00
Double	47.00	47.00

Lunch available
Evening meal 1900 (last orders 2100)
Parking for 20
Cards accepted: Access, Visa, Switch/ Delta
🏵14🖵💧💻🗂♪20🗘✗🗂

Norfolk ♠

🏵🏵 HIGHLY COMMENDED

41 Blakelaw Road, Alnwick NE66 1BA
☎ (01665) 602892
Private detached house in quiet area. Tastefully furnished, comfort assured. Delicious 4-course evening meals using own garden produce. No smoking throughout.
Bedrooms: 1 double, 1 twin
Bathrooms: 2 private

Bed & breakfast

per night:	£min	£max
Double	37.00	

Half board		
per person:	£min	£max
Daily	25.50	
Weekly	175.00	

Evening meal 1830 (last orders 1700)
Parking for 2
Open April-October
🛏 ♨ ♦ ⛳ ⑪ ✕ 🐾 📺 ⭐, 🚗 ❄ ✠ 🚲 [OAP] [SP]

BAMBURGH

Northumberland
Map ref 5C1

Village with a spectacular red sandstone castle standing 150 ft above the sea. On the village green the magnificent Norman church stands opposite a museum containing mementoes of the heroine Grace Darling.

Glenander Guest House ♠♠
🏆🏆 HIGHLY COMMENDED
27 Lucker Road, Bamburgh NE69 7BS
☎ (01668) 214336
Built early this century and recently carefully and tastefully modernised, providing quality accommodation. All rooms en-suite with hospitality trays, hairdryers, colour TV. All day access.
Bedrooms: 1 double, 2 twin
Bathrooms: 3 private
Bed & breakfast

per night:	£min	£max
Single	20.00	30.00
Double	36.00	55.00

🛏 6 ⛳🍴 ♦ ⑪ ✕ 🐾 📺 ⭐, 🚗 🚲 [OAP] [SP]

Mizen Head Hotel ♠♠
🏆🏆🏆 APPROVED
Lucker Road, Bamburgh NE69 7BS
☎ (01668) 214254
Privately-owned, fully licensed hotel in own grounds, with accent on good food and service. Convenient for beaches, castle and golf. 2 minutes' walk from village centre.
Bedrooms: 2 single, 6 double, 4 twin, 4 family rooms
Bathrooms: 11 private, 2 public
Bed & breakfast

per night:	£min	£max
Single	21.00	40.00
Double	42.00	71.00

Half board

per person:	£min	£max
Daily	31.50	48.00
Weekly	217.00	290.00

Lunch available
Evening meal 1830 (last orders 2000)
Parking for 30
Cards accepted: Access, Visa
🛏 🖵 ♦ 🛈 [S] 📺 ⭐, 🚗 🍴30 ❄ ✠ [SP] [T]

Individual proprietors have supplied all details of accommodation. As changes can occur, we advise you to confirm the information at the time of booking.

BARNARD CASTLE

Durham
Map ref 5B3

High over the Tees, a thriving market town with a busy market square. Bernard Baliol's 12th C castle (now ruins) stands nearby. The Bowes Museum, housed in a grand 19th C French chateau, holds fine paintings and furniture. Nearby are some magnificent buildings.
Tourist Information Centre
☎ *(01833) 690909*

East Mellwaters Farm ♠♠
🏆🏆🏆 COMMENDED
Bowes, Barnard Castle, County Durham DL12 9RH
☎ Teesdale (01833) 628269
350-acre livestock farm. On A66, 2 miles west of Bowes. 17th C farmhouse in attractive setting with views. Sleep in modern comfort, dine by traditional open-fire range. Home-made bread.
Bedrooms: 1 single, 2 double, 1 twin, 1 triple
Bathrooms: 5 private
Bed & breakfast

per night	£min	£max
Single	18.00	20.00
Double	34.00	36.00

Half board

per person:	£min	£max
Daily	28.00	35.00
Weekly	168.00	180.00

Lunch available
Evening meal 1730 (last orders 1900)
Parking for 12
Cards accepted: Access, Visa
🛏 🖵 ♦ 🛈 [S] ✕ ⭐, 🚗 🍴15 🐾 ✠ 🚲 [SP] 🎣 ●

George & Dragon Inn
Listed
Boldron, Barnard Castle, County Durham DL12 9RF
☎ Teesdale (01833) 638215
Attractive inn in beautiful Teesdale, offering comfortable accommodation and friendly hospitality.
Bedrooms: 1 double, 1 twin
Bathrooms: 1 public
Bed & breakfast

per night:	£min	£max
Single	15.50	16.00
Double	31.00	32.00

Half board

per person:	£min	£max
Daily	20.00	21.00
Weekly	140.00	140.00

Lunch available
Evening meal 1900 (last orders 1730)
Parking for 20
🛏 🖵 ♦ 🛈 [S] ⭐ 📺 ⭐, 🚲

Old Well Inn ♠♠
🏆🏆 COMMENDED
21 The Bank, Barnard Castle, County Durham DL12 8PH
☎ Teesdale (01833) 690130
Fax (01833) 690140
Historic inn and popular restaurant, tastefully decorated, with spacious en-suite bedrooms. Home-cooked food and real ales. North Pennines Area of Outstanding Natural Beauty.
Bedrooms: 1 double, 2 twin
Bathrooms: 2 private, 1 public
Bed & breakfast

per night	£min	£max
Single	28.00	35.00
Double	40.00	45.00

Lunch available
Evening meal 1900 (last orders 2130)
Cards accepted: Access, Visa, Amex, Switch/Delta
🛏 🛒 ♨ ♦ ⛳ 🛈 [S] ✕ ⭐ ⭐, 🚗 🍴 ✠ 🚲 [OAP] 🎣 ●

BARNINGHAM

Durham
Map ref 5B3

Village 4 miles south-east of Barnard Castle.

Stangfoot Farm
Listed
Barningham, Richmond, North Yorkshire DL11 7EA
☎ Teesdale (01833) 621343
50-acre livestock farm. Stangfoot is a working farm on the Scargill to Reeth road at the foot of the Stang Forest. 3 miles south of A66.
Bedrooms: 1 single, 1 double, 1 twin
Bathrooms: 1 private, 1 public
Bed & breakfast

per night:	£min	£max
Single	14.00	
Double	28.00	

Half board

per person:	£min	£max
Daily	20.00	
Weekly	140.00	

Open April-October
🛏 6 🍳 ♨ ⛳ ⑪ ✕ 📺 ⭐, 🚗 🐾 ❄ ✠ 🚲 🎣

The symbol ● within an entry indicates participation in the Welcome Host programme – a nationally recognised customer care initiative which aims to promote the highest standards of service and a warm welcome for all visitors.

BERWICK-UPON-TWEED

Northumberland
Map ref 5B1

Guarding the mouth of the Tweed, England's northernmost town with the best 16th C city walls in Europe. The handsome Guildhall and barracks date from the 18th C. Three bridges cross to Tweedmouth, the oldest built in 1634.
Tourist Information Centre
☎ (01289) 330733

Ladythorne House

[Listed] [COMMENDED]

Cheswick, Berwick-upon-Tweed
TD15 2RW
☎ (01289) 387382
Grade II listed building, dated 1721, set in farmland. Only 15 minutes' walk from the beaches.
Bedrooms: 1 single, 1 double, 2 twin, 2 triple
Bathrooms: 3 public

Bed & breakfast per night:	£min	£max
Single	11.00	15.00
Double	22.00	30.00

Parking for 8
[UL] [S] [TV] [SP]

Middle Ord Manor House

[DE LUXE]

Middle Ord Farm, Berwick-upon-Tweed TD15 2XQ
☎ (01289) 306323

550-acre mixed farm. Award-winning accommodation within Georgian farmhouse - "England for Excellence" silver award 1994; "Pride of Northumbria" best B&B award 1993 and 1994. Central for touring Borders, coast and Holy Island.
Bedrooms: 2 double, 1 twin
Bathrooms: 2 private, 1 public

Bed & breakfast per night:	£min	£max
Single	26.00	
Double	46.00	

Parking for 6
Open April-October
[UL] [TV]

The Old Vicarage Guest House

[HIGHLY COMMENDED]

24 Church Road, Tweedmouth, Berwick-upon-Tweed TD15 2AN
☎ (01289) 306909

Spacious, detached 19th C vicarage, refurbished to a high standard. 10 minutes' walk from town centre and beautiful beaches.
Bedrooms: 1 single, 4 double, 1 twin, 1 triple
Bathrooms: 4 private, 1 public

Bed & breakfast per night:	£min	£max
Single	14.00	17.00
Double	28.00	46.00

Parking for 4
[UL] [S] [OAP] [SP] [T]

8 Ravensdowne

[HIGHLY COMMENDED]

Berwick-upon-Tweed TD15 1HX
☎ (01289) 307883
Sally Duke offers a year-round welcome in this listed Georgian townhouse, adjacent to the historic town walls. All-day access. Pets by arrangement.
Bedrooms: 2 single, 1 double, 2 twin
Bathrooms: 2 private, 2 public

Bed & breakfast per night:	£min	£max
Single	16.00	25.00
Double	32.00	40.00

Parking for 5
[UL] [TV]

BISHOP AUCKLAND

Durham
Map ref 5C2

Busy market town on the bank of the River Wear. The Palace, a castellated Norman manor house altered in the 18th C, stands in beautiful gardens. Entered from the market square by a handsome 18th C gatehouse, the park is a peaceful retreat of trees and streams.
Tourist Information Centre
☎ (01388) 604922

Five Gables

Binchester, Bishop Auckland, County Durham DL14 8AT
☎ Weardale (01388) 608204
300 yards from A688 between Bishop Auckland and Spennymoor. Victorian house with views over countryside and Weardale. Within easy reach of popular tourist attractions in the North of England.
Bedrooms: 1 double, 1 triple
Bathrooms: 2 private

Bed & breakfast per night:	£min	£max
Single	20.00	
Double	27.50	35.00

Parking for 2
5 [UL] [S] [TV] [SP]

BOWES

Durham
Map ref 5B3

Old stone village high up on a Roman road crossing the Pennines. Settled since Roman times, the town has a sturdy Norman castle keep and an ancient church with a Norman font and Roman inscribed stone.

Ancient Unicorn Inn

Bowes, Barnard Castle, County Durham DL12 9HN
☎ Teesdale (01833) 628321
16th C inn on the A66 with comfortable bedrooms, extensive bar menu. Ideal base for exploring the Lakes, Northumbria, Yorkshire Dales and Yorkshire Wolds.
Bedrooms: 2 twin, 1 triple
Bathrooms: 3 private

Bed & breakfast per night:	£min	£max
Single	20.00	20.00
Double	32.00	32.00

Lunch available
Evening meal 1930 (last orders 2130)
Parking for 20
[OAP]

CARTERWAY HEADS

Northumberland
Map ref 5B2

Small hamlet on the A68, high on the moors at the head of the Derwent Valley overlooking Derwent reservoir.

Greenhead House

[COMMENDED]

A68, Carterway Heads, Consett DH8 9TP
☎ Edmundbyers (01207) 255676
18th C stone, former coaching inn at A68 Carterway Heads crossroads to Edmundbyers and Shotley Bridge. Rooms and garden with uninterrupted views. Evening meals by arrangement. All rooms en-suite. Table licence.
Bedrooms: 2 double, 1 twin
Bathrooms: 3 private

Bed & breakfast per night:	£min	£max
Single	15.00	20.00
Double	30.00	

Half board per person:	£min	£max
Daily	20.00	25.00
Weekly	140.00	175.00

Lunch available
Evening meal 1800 (last orders 2000)
Parking for 10

CASTLESIDE

Durham
Map ref 5B2

Village on the edge of the North Pennines on the A68, one of the main routes from England to Scotland.

Castlenook Guest House M
♛♛

18-20 Front Street, Castleside, Consett, County Durham DH8 9AR
☎ Consett (01207) 506634
On the A68 within easy reach of Durham City, Hadrian's Wall, Beamish Museum and MetroCentre. Excellent village amenities.
Bedrooms: 1 double, 2 twin
Bathrooms: 3 private
Bed & breakfast

per night:	£min	£max
Single	20.00	20.00
Double	30.00	32.00

Evening meal 1700 (last orders 1850)
Parking for 7

Willerby Grange Farm M
♛ COMMENDED

Allensford, Castleside, Consett, County Durham DH8 9BA
☎ Consett (01207) 508752
Situated in beautiful Derwent Valley, self-contained apartments available also for bed and breakfast. Pony trekking nearby, livery on site. Easy travelling distance to Beamish Museum, Gateshead MetroCentre, Hadrian's Wall. Moorland and woodland walks. Approximately 1 kilometre off A68 at Allensford.
Bedrooms: 3 double, 2 twin
Bathrooms: 3 private, 1 public
Bed & breakfast

per night:	£min	£max
Single	25.00	30.00
Double	40.00	50.00

Parking for 100
Cards accepted: Access, Visa, Diners, Amex

National gradings and classifications were correct at the time of going to press but are subject to change. Please check at the time of booking.

CHESTER-LE-STREET

Durham
Map ref 5C2

Originally a Roman military site, town with modern commerce and light industry on the River Wear. The ancient church replaced a wooden sanctuary which sheltered the remains of St Cuthbert for 113 years. The Anker's house beside the church is now a museum.

Waldridge Fell House
♛♛ HIGHLY COMMENDED

Waldridge Lane, Waldridge, Chester-Le-Street, County Durham DH2 3RY
☎ (0191) 389 1908
Former village chapel, stone-built in 1868. Panoramic views and country walks. Children half price. One and a half miles from cricket ground.
Bedrooms: 3 triple, 2 family rooms
Bathrooms: 1 private, 1 public, 1 private shower
Bed & breakfast

per night:	£min	£max
Single	22.00	
Double	36.00	

Parking for 8

CONSETT

Durham
Map ref 5B2

Former steel town on the edge of rolling moors. Modern development includes the shopping centre and a handsome Roman Catholic church, designed by a local architect. To the west, the Derwent Reservoir provides water sports and pleasant walks.

Bee Cottage Farm M
♛♛ HIGHLY COMMENDED

Castleside, Consett, County Durham DH8 9HW
☎ (01207) 508224

46-acre livestock farm. 1.5 miles west of the A68, between Castleside and Tow Law. Unspoilt views. Ideally located for Beamish Museum and Durham. No smoking in main farmhouse.
Bedrooms: 1 single, 3 double, 2 twin, 1 triple, 2 family rooms
Bathrooms: 3 private, 5 public

Bed & breakfast

per night:	£min	£max
Single	25.00	
Double	40.00	

Half board

per person:	£min	£max
Daily	32.00	
Weekly	224.00	

Lunch available
Evening meal 2015 (last orders 2130)
Parking for 20

CORBRIDGE

Northumberland
Map ref 5B2

Small town on the River Tyne. Close by are extensive remains of the Roman military town Corstopitum, with a museum housing important discoveries from excavations. The town itself is attractive with shady trees, a 17th C bridge and interesting old buildings, notably a 14th C vicarage.

Dilston Mill M
Listed COMMENDED

Corbridge NE45 5QZ
☎ Hexham (01434) 633493
Fax (01434) 633513
Historic former watermill, with medieval foundations, on the banks of Devils Water. Overlooked by the ruined tower of Dilston Castle. Comfort, warm welcome, wonderful setting. Close to all amenities.
Bedrooms: 1 double, 1 twin, 1 triple
Bathrooms: 3 private, 1 public
Bed & breakfast

per night:	£min	£max
Single	16.50	23.00
Double	36.00	38.00

Parking for 3

Fellcroft M
♛♛ HIGHLY COMMENDED

Station Road, Corbridge NE45 5AY
☎ Hexham (01434) 632384
Well-appointed stone-built Edwardian house with full private facilities and colour TV in all bedrooms. Quiet road in country setting, half a mile south of market square. Excellent choice of eating places nearby. Non-smokers only, please. 10 per cent reduction for weekly half board stays.
Bedrooms: 2 twin
Bathrooms: 2 private
Bed & breakfast

per night:	£min	£max
Single	18.50	20.50
Double	31.00	33.00

Continued ▶

CORBRIDGE

Continued

Half board

per person:	£min	£max
Daily	23.00	28.00

Evening meal 1900 (last orders 1945)
Parking for 3

⛵🕯️🍴⌨️♨️🐾🆔🔲🅱️Ⓢ✂️🐴📺🍽️🅿️ 🌼🚐

Fox & Hounds Hotel ⚔

🏵🏵🏵 **COMMENDED**

Stagshaw Bank, Corbridge NE45 5QW
☎ Hexham (01434) 633024
Fax (01434) 633024

*400-year-old coaching inn with a 70-seat
conservatory restaurant. Owners operate
and live on premises.*
Bedrooms: 4 double, 4 twin
Bathrooms: 8 private

Bed & breakfast

per night:	£min	£max
Single	25.00	25.00
Double	40.00	40.00

Half board

per person:	£min	£max
Daily	25.00	30.00
Weekly	175.00	200.00

Lunch available
Evening meal 1700 (last orders 2130)
Parking for 40

⛵🕯️🍴⌨️♨️🆔Ⓢ🐴Ⓞ🍽️🅿️🐿️🌼 🏠Ⓣ

Thornbrough High House

Listed **COMMENDED**

Corbridge NE45 5PR
☎ Hexham (01434) 633080
*500-acre mixed farm. Stone-built, Grade
II listed farmhouse and buildings with
outstanding views over Tyne Valley.
Surrounded by lovely gardens, quiet
situation.*
Bedrooms: 1 double, 2 twin
Bathrooms: 3 private

Bed & breakfast

per night:	£min	£max
Single	25.00	28.00
Double	38.00	40.00

Half board

per person:	£min	£max
Daily	35.00	40.00

Evening meal 1830 (last orders 2000)
Parking for 11

⛵🕯️♨️🔲🆔🐴📺🍽️🌼🚐🏠

COTHERSTONE

Durham
Map ref 5B3

Village 3 miles north-west of
Barnard Castle with remains of
Norman castle.

Glendale

🏵🏵 **HIGHLY COMMENDED**

Cotherstone, Barnard Castle, County
Durham DL12 9UH
☎ Teesdale (01833) 650384
*Dormer bungalow with beautiful
gardens and large pond, in quiet, rural
surroundings. Take Briscoe road from
Cotherstone for 200 yards.*
Bedrooms: 3 double
Bathrooms: 3 private, 1 public

Bed & breakfast

per night:	£min	£max
Single	18.00	22.00
Double	30.00	30.00

Parking for 4
Open January-December

⛵10🧺🍴⌨️♨️🐾🔲🆔✂️🐴🍽️🅿️Ⓤ ▶🌼🚐Ⓢ🅿️

COWSHILL

Durham
Map ref 5B2

Alston and Kilhope Riding Centre ⚔

🏵🏵🏵

Low Cornriggs Farm, Cowshill, Bishop
Auckland, County Durham DL13 1AQ
☎ Bishop Auckland (01388) 537600
*60-acre mixed farm. 200-year-old
farmhouse with magnificent views, on
the Weardale Way. Licensed dining
room, log fires, all food fresh and
home-made. Horse riding.*
Bedrooms: 1 double, 2 twin
Bathrooms: 3 private, 1 public

Bed & breakfast

per night:	£min	£max
Single	16.00	18.00
Double	31.00	35.00

Half board

per person:	£min	£max
Daily	25.50	27.50
Weekly	170.50	179.00

Lunch available
Evening meal 1930 (last orders 2100)
Parking for 6

⛵1🎹♨️🐾🆔Ⓢ✂️📺🍽️🅿️10Ⓤ ▶🐎✎🌼Ⓓ🐾Ⓢ🏠Ⓣ

Individual proprietors
have supplied all details of
accommodation. As changes
can occur, we advise you to
confirm the information at
the time of booking.

CRASTER

Northumberland
Map ref 5C1

Small fishing village with a fine
northward view of Dunstanburgh
Castle. Fishing cobles in the tiny
harbour, stone cottages at the
water's edge and a kippering shed
where Craster's famous delicacy is
produced give the village its
unspoilt charm.

Cottage Inn ⚔

🏵🏵🏵 **COMMENDED**

Dunstan Village, Craster, Alnwick
NE66 3ZS
☎ Embleton (01665) 576658
*Family-run inn half a mile from the sea.
All rooms are ground floor and have
garden view. Noted for food. Special
breaks available.*
Bedrooms: 2 double, 8 twin
Bathrooms: 10 private

Bed & breakfast

per night:	£min	£max
Single		35.00
Double		59.00

Half board

per person:	£min	£max
Daily		45.50
Weekly		202.50

Lunch available
Evening meal 1800 (last orders 2130)
Parking for 30
Cards accepted: Access, Visa

⛵🧺🕯️🍴♨️Ⓢ✂️🍽️🅿️🅠Ⓤ▶🌼✗ 🐾Ⓢ

DURHAM

Durham
Map ref 5C2

Ancient city with its Norman castle
and cathedral set on a bluff high
over the Wear. A market and
university town and regional
centre, spreading beyond the
market-place on both banks of the
river.
Tourist Information Centre
☎ *(0191) 384 3720*

Bay Horse Inn ⚔

🏵🏵🏵 **COMMENDED**

Brandon Village, Durham, County
Durham DH7 8ST
☎ (0191) 378 0498
*Ten stone-built chalets 3 miles from
Durham city centre. All have shower,
toilet, TV, tea and coffee facilities and
telephone. Ample car parking.*
Bedrooms: 3 double, 6 twin, 1 family
room
Bathrooms: 10 private

Bed & breakfast

per night:	£min	£max
Single	30.00	
Double	39.00	

Lunch available
Evening meal 1900 (last orders 2200)

Parking for 25
Cards accepted: Access, Visa
♿🛁🖨✆📞♦🧇🍴✂🖨🏨◨🛏▸❄ 🚲Ⓣ

Castledene

Listed **COMMENDED**

37 Nevilledale Terrace, Durham,
County Durham DH1 4QG
☎ (0191) 384 8386
*Edwardian end-of-terrace house half a
mile west of the market place. Within
walking distance of the riverside,
cathedral and castle.*
Bedrooms: 2 twin
Bathrooms: 1 public
Bed & breakfast

per night:	£min	£max
Single		22.00
Double		35.00

Parking for 6
♿7♦Ⓤ🛏Ⓣ🏨◨🚲

Trevelyan College ⋀

😊😊😊

Elvet Hill Road, Durham, County
Durham DH1 3LN
☎ (0191) 374 3765 & 374 3768
Fax (0191) 374 3789
*Set in parkland within easy walking
distance of Durham City. Comfortable
Cloister Bar, TV lounges, ample
parking. Standard and en-suite rooms
available.*
Bedrooms: 253 single, 8 double,
27 twin
Bathrooms: 58 private, 47 public
Bed & breakfast

per night:	£min	£max
Single	18.00	28.00
Double	33.00	51.50

Half board

per person:	£min	£max
Daily	27.00	37.00

Lunch available
Evening meal 1830 (last orders 1930)
Parking for 100
Open March-April, June-September,
December
♿🛁♦🛏Ⓢ🛏Ⓣ🏨◨🚲🏆300▸❄🍴
🏨◉

EGLINGHAM

Northumberland
Map ref 5B1

Small village north of Alnwick with
a medieval church which stands
on the site of a former Saxon
church. South of the village lies an
ancient earthwork called the
Ringses with 3 stone and earth
ramparts.

Ash Tree House ⋀

😊 **HIGHLY COMMENDED**

The Terrace, Eglingham, Alnwick
NE66 2UA
☎ Powburn (01665) 578533
*A warm Northumbrian welcome with
good home cooking awaits you in this
lovely stone-built home set in the*

---

*glorious North Northumbrian
countryside. Winner of the Lion Heart
Award for Hospitality 1994.*
Bedrooms: 1 double, 1 twin
Bathrooms: 1 public
Bed & breakfast

per night:	£min	£max
Single	17.00	17.00
Double	34.00	34.00

Half board

per person:	£min	£max
Daily	27.00	27.00
Weekly	189.00	189.00

Evening meal 1900 (last orders 2000)
Parking for 3
♿10Ⓤ🍴✂🛏Ⓣ🏨❄✈🚲🐎SP◉

EMBLETON

Northumberland
Map ref 5C1

Coastal village beside a golf-
course spread along the edge of
Embleton Bay. The old church was
extensively restored in the 19th C.
The vicarage incorporates a
medieval pele tower.

Doxford Farmhouse ⋀

😊😊 **COMMENDED**

Chathill NE67 5DY
☎ Charlton Mires (01665) 579235
Fax (01665) 579215

*400-acre mixed farm. Listed Georgian
farmhouse set in wooded grounds.
Pollution-free beaches and moorland are
within easy reach. Lake and woodland
nature trail. Home cooking and home-
made bread.*
Bedrooms: 1 double, 1 twin, 1 triple,
1 family room; suite available
Bathrooms: 1 private, 1 public
Bed & breakfast

per night:	£min	£max
Single	16.00	24.00
Double	32.00	36.00

Half board

per person:	£min	£max
Daily	26.00	34.00
Weekly	175.00	200.00

Evening meal 1830 (last orders 1400)
Parking for 8
Cards accepted: Visa
♿🛁🖨♦🛏Ⓢ✂🛏Ⓣ🏨◨🚲🏆24
♦🌲🔍◡♪❄🐎🏨

We advise you to confirm
your booking in writing.

FALSTONE

Northumberland
Map ref 5B2

Remote village on the edge of
Kielder Forest where it spreads
beneath the heathery slopes of the
south-west Cheviots along the
valley of the North Tyne. Just 1
mile west lies Kielder Water, a
vast man-made lake which adds
boating and fishing to forest
recreations.

Blackcock Inn ⋀

😊😊😊 **COMMENDED**

Falstone, Hexham NE48 1AA
☎ Hexham (01434) 240200
Fax (01434) 240036

*Traditional old country village inn close
to Kielder Water, offering cask ale, good
food and comfortable accommodation.
Non-smokers 10% discount.*
Bedrooms: 2 single, 2 double
Bathrooms: 4 private, 1 public
Bed & breakfast

per night:	£min	£max
Single	25.00	27.50
Double	45.00	50.00

Lunch available
Evening meal 1900 (last orders 2100)
Parking for 12
♿🍴♦🧇🍴Ⓢ✂🛏Ⓣ🍴🏨🚲♦◡
♪❄🐎SPⓉ

FOREST-IN-TEESDALE

Durham
Map ref 5B2

An area in Upper Teesdale of
widely-dispersed farmsteads set in
wild but beautiful scenery with
High Force Waterfall and Cauldron
Snout. Once the hunting park of
the Earls of Darlington.

Langdon Beck Hotel

Listed

Forest-in-Teesdale, Barnard Castle,
County Durham DL12 0XP
☎ Teesdale (01833) 622267
*Pleasant inn in the magnificent area of
Upper Teesdale where a friendly
welcome and home cooking are
assured. Ideal for walkers and nature
lovers.*
Bedrooms: 4 single, 1 double, 1 twin,
1 triple
Bathrooms: 2 private, 2 public
Continued ▶

FOREST-IN-TEESDALE

Continued

Bed & breakfast per night:	£min	£max
Single	19.00	22.00
Double	38.00	44.00

Half board per person:	£min	£max
Daily	26.00	29.00
Weekly	176.00	197.00

Lunch available
Evening meal 1830 (last orders 1830)
Parking for 15
Open January-November

HALLINGTON

Northumberland
Map ref 5B2

Hamlet 7 miles north of Corbridge.
Next to two reservoirs. Hallington
Hall (not open to public).

Cuan Dor Cottage ⋔
HIGHLY COMMENDED

Hallington, Newcastle upon Tyne
NE19 2LW
☎ Hexham (01434) 672412
*Converted farm building offering
comfortable en-suite accommodation in
quiet hamlet. 3.5 miles off A68 and 7
miles from Corbridge. Freshly prepared
meals and a warm welcome assured.*
Bedrooms: 1 double, 1 twin
Bathrooms: 2 private

Bed & breakfast per night:	£min	£max
Double	36.00	42.00

Half board per person:	£min	£max
Daily	25.50	28.50
Weekly	160.00	180.00

Lunch available
Evening meal from 1950
Parking for 4

The symbol ⊛ within an
entry indicates participation
in the Welcome Host
programme – a nationally
recognised customer care
initiative which aims to
promote the highest
standards of service and a
warm welcome for all visitors.

HALTWHISTLE

Northumberland
Map ref 5B2

Small market town with interesting
12th C church, old inns and
blacksmith's smithy. North of the
town are several important sites
and interpretation centres of
Hadrian's Wall. Ideal centre for
archaeology, outdoor activity or
touring holidays.
Tourist Information Centre
☎ *(01434) 322002*

Broomshaw Hill Farm ⋔
HIGHLY COMMENDED

Willia Road, Haltwhistle NE49 9NP
☎ Hexham (01434) 320866
Fax (01434) 320866
*5-acre livestock farm. Attractive
modernised 18th C stone-built
farmhouse. On conjunction of bridleway
and footpath, both leading to Hadrian's
Wall 1 mile away.*
Bedrooms: 2 double, 1 twin
Bathrooms: 1 private, 1 public

Bed & breakfast per night:	£min	£max
Double	32.00	40.00

Evening meal 1830 (last orders 0900)
Parking for 8
Open February-October

Hall Meadows ⋔
COMMENDED

Main Street, Haltwhistle NE49 0AZ
☎ (01434) 321021
*Built in 1888, a large family house with
pleasant garden in the centre of town.
Ideally placed for Hadrian's Wall.*
Bedrooms: 1 single, 1 double, 1 twin
Bathrooms: 1 public

Bed & breakfast per night:	£min	£max
Single	16.00	16.00
Double	30.00	30.00

Parking for 3

Oaky Knowe Farm ⋔
Listed COMMENDED

Haltwhistle NE49 0NB
☎ Hexham (01434) 320648
*300-acre livestock farm. Overlooking the
Tyne Valley, within walking distance of
Haltwhistle and the Roman Wall, this
comfortable farmhouse offers friendly
family holidays.*
Bedrooms: 1 twin, 2 triple
Bathrooms: 1 public

Bed & breakfast per night:	£min	£max
Single	16.00	17.00
Double	28.00	30.00

Half board per person:	£min	£max
Daily	22.00	25.00
Weekly	145.00	170.00

Evening meal 1700 (last orders 1530)
Parking for 8

HAMSTERLEY FOREST

Durham
Map ref 5B2

*See also Barnard Castle, Bishop
Auckland, Tow Law*
2 miles west of Witton-Le-Wear
with visitor centre, walks, forest
drive and cycling routes.

Grove House ⋔⋔
HIGHLY COMMENDED

Redford, Hamsterley Forest, Bishop
Auckland, County Durham DL13 3NL
☎ Witton-le-Wear (0138848) 8203
*Country house in the heart of
Hamsterley Forest with fishing, walking
and birdwatching close at hand. Ideal
for families to enjoy tranquil
countryside.*
Bedrooms: 1 double, 2 twin
Bathrooms: 3 private

Bed & breakfast per night:	£min	£max
Single	19.50	25.00
Double	39.00	50.00

Half board per person:	£min	£max
Daily	32.00	37.50
Weekly	202.00	217.00

Evening meal 1800 (last orders 2100)
Parking for 20

HAYDON BRIDGE

Northumberland
Map ref 5B2

Small town on the banks of the
South Tyne with an ancient
church, built of stone from sites
along the Roman Wall just north.
Ideally situated for exploring
Hadrian's Wall and the Border
country.

Sewing Shields Farm ⋔
Listed COMMENDED

Hadrian's Wall, Haydon Bridge,
Hexham NE47 6NW
☎ Hexham (01434) 684418
*2000-acre hill farm. 17th C listed
farmhouse, situated on top of Hadrian's
Wall, 1 mile east of Housesteads, 5
miles north of Haydon Bridge.
Breathtaking views.*
Bedrooms: 1 double, 1 twin, 1 family
room
Bathrooms: 2 public

Bed & breakfast per night:	£min	£max
Single	15.00	15.00
Double	30.00	30.00

Half board

per person:	£min	£max
Daily	22.50	22.50
Weekly	150.00	150.00

Evening meal from 1800
Parking for 6
🛇🏕🌢⚲ⓊⓁ🛆Ⓢ✕🐾ⓉⓋ📷.🛋Ⓤ☼ 🐴ᴰᴬᴾ🛇ⓈⓅ🎻

HEIGHINGTON

Durham
Map ref 5C3

Village 2 miles south-west of Newton Aycliffe. Built around a large green giving fine views of the Tees Valley.

Eldon House ⚠

👑👑 HIGHLY COMMENDED

East Green, Heighington, Darlington, County Durham DL5 6PP
☎ Aycliffe (01325) 312270
17th C manor house with large garden overlooking the village green. Large, comfortable, well-appointed rooms. Ample parking. Tennis court. Coal/wood fire in sitting room.
Bedrooms: 3 twin
Bathrooms: 3 private

Bed & breakfast

per night:	£min	£max
Single	27.00	32.00
Double	40.00	45.00

Parking for 6
🛇🌢ⓊⓁ🛆Ⓜ📷.🛋✎☼🐴🎻

HEXHAM

Northumberland
Map ref 5B2

Old coaching and market town near Hadrian's Wall. Since pre-Norman times a weekly market has been held in the centre with its market-place and abbey park, and the richly-furnished 12th C abbey church has a superb Anglo-Saxon crypt.
Tourist Information Centre
☎ *(01434) 605225*

Anick Grange

👑 COMMENDED

Hexham NE46 4LP
☎ (01434) 603807
363-acre mixed farm. 17th C farmhouse 1 mile from Hexham. Superb open views. Comfortable, informal and a warm welcome.
Bedrooms: 1 single, 1 twin, 1 triple
Bathrooms: 1 private, 1 public

Bed & breakfast

per night:	£min	£max
Single	15.00	15.00
Double	30.00	34.00

Parking for 4
Open April-September
🛇1🌢ⓊⓁⓉⓋ📷.Ⓤ🐴

Dene House ⚠

👑👑 HIGHLY COMMENDED

Juniper, Hexham NE46 1SJ
☎ (01434) 673413

Stone farmhouse with beamed ceilings, log fires and flowers everywhere. Very quietly situated in 9 acres of farmland, 4 miles south of Hexham.
Bedrooms: 1 single, 1 double, 1 twin
Bathrooms: 2 private, 1 public

Bed & breakfast

per night:	£min	£max
Single	18.00	18.00
Double	36.00	36.00

Half board

per person:	£min	£max
Daily	28.00	28.00
Weekly	180.00	180.00

Evening meal 1800 (last orders 1900)
Parking for 3
🛇🎘🌢ⓊⓁ🛆Ⓢ✕🐾ⓉⓋ📷.🛋☼🐴

Laburnum House ⚠

👑 HIGHLY COMMENDED

23 Leazes Crescent, Hexham NE46 3JZ
☎ (01434) 601828
Very comfortable, spacious, Victorian family home 10-12 minutes' walk from town centre. Good home cooking. Ideal for Hadrian's Wall and Northumbria.
Bedrooms: 2 single, 1 double, 1 twin
Bathrooms: 1 public

Bed & breakfast

per night:	£min	£max
Single	16.00	18.00
Double	32.00	36.00

Half board

per person:	£min	£max
Daily	26.00	28.00

Evening meal 1900 (last orders 1900)
🛇12🎘🖵🌢⚲ⓊⓁ🛆Ⓢ✕🐾📷.🛋✕ 🐴◉

Peth Head Cottage ⚠

👑👑 HIGHLY COMMENDED

Juniper Village, Steel, Hexham NE47 0LA
☎ (01434) 673286
Fax (01434) 673038

Rose-covered stone cottage in quiet hamlet. Charming bedrooms and attractive lounge for guests. Picturesque

rural location, ideal for walking and touring holidays.
Bedrooms: 1 single, 1 double, 1 twin
Bathrooms: 3 private

Bed & breakfast

per night:	£min	£max
Single	18.00	18.00
Double	36.00	36.00

Parking for 5
🛇🎘🌢⚲ⓊⓁ🛆✕ⓉⓋ📷.🛋▸☼✕ 🐴Ⓣ

Rose and Crown Inn ⚠

👑👑👑 HIGHLY COMMENDED

Main Street, Slaley, Hexham NE47 0AA
☎ (01434) 673263
Warm, friendly, family-run business with good wholesome home cooking and a la carte restaurant. All bedrooms en-suite. In Slaley, 5 miles south-east of Hexham.
Bedrooms: 1 single, 2 twin
Bathrooms: 3 private

Bed & breakfast

per night:	£min	£max
Single	17.50	25.00
Double	35.00	50.00

Half board

per person:	£min	£max
Daily	27.50	35.00
Weekly	175.00	225.00

Lunch available
Evening meal 1830 (last orders 2200)
Parking for 32
Cards accepted: Access, Visa
🛇🎘🖵⚲🛆Ⓢ✕🐾📷.🛋▸☼✕🐴 🛇ⓈⓅ🎻Ⓣ

Rye Hill Farm ⚠

👑👑 COMMENDED

Slaley, Hexham NE47 0AH
☎ (01434) 673259
Fax (01434) 673259

30-acre livestock farm. Warm and comfortable barn conversion, 5 miles south of Hexham, where you can enjoy the peace of rural life. Noted for the food and the friendly atmosphere.
Bedrooms: 2 double, 2 twin, 2 family rooms
Bathrooms: 6 private, 1 public

Bed & breakfast

per night:	£min	£max
Single	18.00	20.00
Double	36.00	40.00

Continued ▶

HEXHAM

Continued

Half board

per person:	£min	£max
Daily	28.00	30.00
Weekly	183.40	196.00

Evening meal 1930 (last orders 1700)
Parking for 6

Stotsfold Hall ⋀

Steel, Hexham NE47 0HP
☎ (01434) 673270
Beautiful house surrounded by 15 acres of gardens and woodland with streams and flowers. 6 miles south of Hexham.
Bedrooms: 2 single, 1 double, 1 twin
Bathrooms: 3 public

Bed & breakfast

per night:	£min	£max
Single	18.50	18.50
Double	37.00	37.00

Parking for 6

HOLY ISLAND

Northumberland
Map ref 5B1

Still an idyllic retreat, tiny island and fishing village and cradle of northern Christianity. It is approached from the mainland at low water by a causeway. The clifftop castle (National Trust) was restored by Sir Edwin Lutyens.

Britannia

Holy Island, Berwick-upon-Tweed
TD15 2RX
☎ Berwick-upon-Tweed (01289) 389218
Comfortable, friendly bed and breakfast in centre of Holy Island. Hot and cold water, tea-making facilities in all rooms. TV lounge. En-suite available.
Bedrooms: 1 double, 1 twin, 1 triple
Bathrooms: 1 private, 1 public

Bed & breakfast

per night:	£min	£max
Single		17.00
Double	34.00	34.00

Parking for 4
Open March–October

North View ⋀

COMMENDED

Marygate, Holy Island, Berwick-upon-Tweed TD15 2SD
☎ Berwick-upon-Tweed (01289) 389222
400-year-old listed building on historic and beautiful island. Ideally situated for visiting many of Northumberland's tourist attractions.

Bedrooms: 2 double, 1 twin
Bathrooms: 3 private

Bed & breakfast

per night:	£min	£max
Single	22.00	27.00
Double	44.00	

Half board

per person:	£min	£max
Daily	31.00	38.00

Lunch available
Evening meal 1900 (last orders 2100)
Parking for 6
Cards accepted: Access, Visa

KIELDER FOREST

Northumberland

See under Falstone, West Woodburn

KIELDER WATER

Northumberland
Map ref 5B2

A magnificent man-made lake, the largest in Northern Europe, with over 27 miles of shoreline. On the edge of the Northumberland National Park and near the Scottish border, Kielder can be explored by car, on foot or by ferry.

The Pheasant Inn (by Kielder Water) ⋀

COMMENDED

Stannersburn, Falstone, Hexham
NE48 1DD
☎ Hexham (01434) 240382

Historic inn with beamed ceilings and open fires. Home cooking. Fishing, riding and all water sports nearby. Close to Kielder Water, Hadrian's Wall and the Scottish border.
Bedrooms: 4 double, 3 twin, 1 family room
Bathrooms: 8 private

Bed & breakfast

per night:	£min	£max
Single	25.00	30.00
Double	50.00	52.00

Half board

per person:	£min	£max
Daily	35.00	45.00

Lunch available
Evening meal 1900 (last orders 2100)
Parking for 30

LESBURY

Northumberland
Map ref 5C1

Village 1 mile north-west of Alnmouth near the Northumberland coast.

Dukes Ryde ⋀

COMMENDED

Longhoughton Road, Lesbury, Alnwick
NE66 3AT
☎ Alnwick (01665) 830855
Delightful and imposing early 20th C house set in secluded gardens, on the outskirts of Lesbury village, near beaches and golf-courses.
Bedrooms: 1 double, 1 twin
Bathrooms: 1 private, 1 public

Bed & breakfast

per night:	£min	£max
Single	20.00	25.00
Double	37.00	40.00

Parking for 6

MIDDLESBROUGH

Cleveland
Map ref 5C3

Boom-town of the mid 19th C, today's Teesside industrial and conference town has a modern shopping complex and predominantly modern buildings. An engineering miracle of the early 20th C is the Transporter Bridge which replaced an old ferry.
Tourist Information Centre
☎ *(01642) 243425 or 264330*

Maltby Farm ⋀

APPROVED

Maltby, Middlesbrough TS8 0BP
☎ (01642) 590121
187-acre mixed farm. Traditional Yorkshire farmhouse, over 200 years old, looking south on to the Cleveland Hills.
Bedrooms: 1 single, 1 twin, 1 triple
Bathrooms: 1 public

Bed & breakfast

per night:	£min	£max
Single	15.00	16.00
Double	30.00	32.00

Half board

per person:	£min	£max
Daily	21.00	22.00
Weekly	132.00	135.00

Evening meal 1800 (last orders 2000)
Parking for 6
Open April–October

Please mention this guide
when making a booking.

MIDDLETON-IN-TEESDALE

Durham
Map ref 5B3

Small stone town of hillside terraces overlooking the river, developed by the London Lead Company in the 18th C. Five miles up-river is the spectacular 70-ft waterfall, High Force.

Bowbank House
♛♛♛ HIGHLY COMMENDED

Lunedale, Middleton-in-Teesdale, Barnard Castle, County Durham DL12 0NT
☎ (01833) 640637

Bowbank was built at the turn of the 18th C. A typical Georgian property, with original stone roof, internal beams, coal fires and beautiful gardens.
Bedrooms: 2 double, 1 twin
Bathrooms: 3 private
Bed & breakfast

per night:	£min	£max
Single	20.00	25.00
Double	32.00	36.00

Parking for 4
🛇 8 🖳 🖵 🖩 🌂 🏺 ⓤ 🖊 ✂ 🐾 ⅏ 🖵 ⅏ ☐ ✿ 🛫 🐾 🎪

Brunswick House ⚐
♛♛♛ COMMENDED

55 Market Place, Middleton-in-Teesdale, Barnard Castle, County Durham DL12 0QH
☎ Teesdale (01833) 640393

18th C listed stone-built guesthouse retaining much character and many original features. Comfort, friendly service and home cooking are assured.
Bedrooms: 2 double, 1 twin, 1 family room
Bathrooms: 4 private
Bed & breakfast

per night:	£min	£max
Single	20.00	27.50
Double	40.00	40.00

Half board

per person:	£min	£max
Daily	32.95	
Weekly		195.00

Lunch available
Evening meal 1930 (last orders 1900)
Parking for 5
Cards accepted: Access, Visa
🛇 🖳 🖵 🏺 🌂 🏺 🖊 ✂ 🐾 ⅏ 🖵 ⅏ ☐ ✿ 🛫 🐾
SP 🎪

NEWCASTLE UPON TYNE

Tyne and Wear
Map ref 5C2

Commercial and cultural centre of the North East, with a large indoor shopping centre, Quayside market, museums and theatres which offer an annual 6 week season by the Royal Shakespeare Company. Norman castle keep, medieval alleys, old Guildhall.
Tourist Information Centre
☎ *(0191) 261 0610 or 230 0030 or 214 4422 (Newcastle Airport)*

Grosvenor Hotel ⚐
♛♛♛ APPROVED

Grosvenor Road, Jesmond, Newcastle upon Tyne NE2 2RR
☎ (0191) 281 0543
Fax (0191) 281 9217
Friendly hotel in quiet residential suburb, offering a wide range of facilities. Close to city centre.
Bedrooms: 17 single, 8 double, 9 twin, 6 triple
Bathrooms: 32 private, 5 public
Bed & breakfast

per night:	£min	£max
Single	15.00	40.00
Double	35.00	60.00

Half board

per person:	£min	£max
Daily	20.00	45.00
Weekly	120.00	270.00

Lunch available
Evening meal 1830 (last orders 2100)
Parking for 30
Cards accepted: Access, Visa, Diners, Amex, Switch/Delta
🛇 🖧 🖾 ☎ 🖳 🖵 🏺 🌂 🏺 🖊 S 🐾 ⅏ ● 🖩
🖵 🎯 120 DAP 🌂 SP T

NORHAM

Northumberland
Map ref 5B1

Border village on the salmon-rich Tweed, dominated by its dramatic castle ruin. Near Castle Street is the church, like the castle destroyed after the Battle of Flodden, but rebuilt. Norham Station Railway Museum is just outside the town.

Dromore House ⚐
Listed

12 Pedwell Way, Norham, Berwick-upon-Tweed TD15 2LD
☎ Berwick-upon-Tweed (01289) 382313
Guesthouse in a small village on the River Tweed, between the Cheviot and

Lammermuir Hills. Quiet beaches are within easy reach.
Bedrooms: 1 double, 1 twin, 1 triple
Bathrooms: 2 private, 1 public
Bed & breakfast

per night:	£min	£max
Single	16.00	19.00
Double	32.00	38.00

Half board

per person:	£min	£max
Daily	23.00	26.00
Weekly	161.00	182.00

Evening meal 1700 (last orders 1900)
Parking for 3
🛇 🖧 🖵 🏺 ⓤ 🏺 🖊 ⅏ 🖩 🐾 🎪

PETERLEE

Durham
Map ref 5C2

New Town named after the miners' leader. Just outside the town is the Castle Eden country park and nature reserve.
Tourist Information Centre
☎ *(0191) 586 4450*

Golden Calf Hotel
♛

Front Street, Hesleden, Hartlepool, Cleveland TS27 4PH
☎ Wellfield (01429) 836493
Family-run inn with friendly service. Only 1 mile from A19 on Castle Eden road. 15 minutes to Teesside, 35 minutes to Newcastle, 12 miles to A1.
Bedrooms: 2 double, 2 triple
Bathrooms: 1 public
Bed & breakfast

per night:	£min	£max
Single	13.00	
Double	26.00	

Lunch available
Evening meal 1900 (last orders 2200)
Parking for 20
🛇 🖵 🏺 🏺 S 🐾 ⅏ 🖩 ◀ ▶ 🐾 ⟋ 🎪

REDCAR

Cleveland
Map ref 5C3

Lively holiday resort near Teesside with broad sandy beaches, a fine racecourse, a large indoor funfair at Coatham and other seaside amusements. Britain's oldest existing lifeboat can be seen at the Zetland Museum.

Tudor Lodge
7 Turner Street, Redcar TS10 1AY
☎ (01642) 474883
Private hotel, 2 minutes' walk from the seafront and shopping centre, and 5 minutes from the leisure centre.
Bedrooms: 4 single, 2 double, 3 twin, 1 triple
Bathrooms: 4 public

Continued ▶

REDCAR

Continued

Bed & breakfast

per night:	£min	£max
Single	12.50	15.00
Double	21.00	26.00

Half board

per person:	£min	£max
Daily	16.00	19.50
Weekly	112.00	136.50

Lunch available
Evening meal 1800 (last orders 2000)
🛏🗘🛆🛗🛎📺◐🖳, 🚗🏍

Waterside House
♨

35 Newcomen Terrace, Redcar
TS10 1DB
☎ (01642) 481062
Large terraced property overlooking the sea, close to town centre and leisure centre. Warm, friendly atmosphere with true Yorkshire hospitality.
Bedrooms: 2 single, 3 triple, 1 family room
Bathrooms: 2 public

Bed & breakfast

per night:	£min	£max
Single	14.00	16.00
Double	25.00	27.00

Half board

per person:	£min	£max
Daily	19.50	22.50
Weekly	136.50	157.50

Evening meal 1700 (last orders 1900)
🛏🗘🛆🖳🛗📺🖳, 🚗 SP

ROTHBURY

Northumberland
Map ref 5B1

Old market town on the River Coquet near the Simonside Hills. It makes an ideal centre for walking and fishing or for exploring this beautiful area from the coast to the Cheviots. Cragside House and Gardens (National Trust) are open to the public.

Thropton Demesne Farmhouse ♨

♨♨ HIGHLY COMMENDED

Thropton, Morpeth NE65 7LT
☎ (01669) 620196
24-acre mixed farm. Traditional farmhouse peacefully situated in the picturesque Coquet Valley. Spectacular views. Ideally placed for fishing, golf and walking.
Bedrooms: 1 double, 1 twin, 1 triple
Bathrooms: 3 private

Bed & breakfast

per night:	£min	£max
Single	25.00	38.00
Double	36.00	38.00

Parking for 6
🛏🗘🛆🖳🛗🗝🛗🖳, 🚗✳ SP 🏠

RYTON

Tyne and Wear
Map ref 5C2

On a wooded site above the Tyne, Ryton has a 12th C church with a Jacobean screen and good 19th C oak carving. Small pit working, notable for the spectacular 1826 Stargate Explosion, ceased in 1967. Easy access to the A1, Hadrian's Wall and rural Northumbria.

Barmoor Old Manse ♨

Listed APPROVED

The Old Manse, Barmoor, Ryton NE40 3BD
☎ (0191) 413 2438
Large stone Victorian house, built as manse for Congregational church in 1862. Delightful garden. Near MetroCentre, Roman Wall and Beamish Museum.
Bedrooms: 1 double, 2 twin
Bathrooms: 1 public

Bed & breakfast

per night:	£min	£max
Single	16.00	
Double	32.00	

Parking for 2
🛏🖳🗘🛆🖳🗝🛗🖳, 🚗✳🏍 SP

SALTBURN-BY-THE-SEA

Cleveland
Map ref 5C3

Set on fine cliffs just north of the Cleveland Hills, a gracious Victorian resort with later developments and wide, firm sands. A handsome Jacobean mansion at Marske can be reached along the sands.
Tourist Information Centre
☎ *(01287) 622422*

Boulby Barns Farm

Listed

Easington, Loftus, Saltburn-by-the-Sea TS13 4UT
☎ Guisborough (01287) 641306
7-acre mixed farm. Traditional stone farmhouse with accommodation on a working smallholding in the national park. Situated half a mile from A174, close to Boulby Cliffs and the Cleveland Way, with views of moors and sea.
Bedrooms: 1 double, 2 twin
Bathrooms: 2 public

Bed & breakfast

per night:	£min	£max
Single	15.00	17.50
Double	30.00	35.00

Parking for 8
Open April-November
🛏5🛆🖳🗝📺🖳, 🚗🏍

SEAHOUSES

Northumberland
Map ref 5C1

Small modern resort developed around a 19th C herring port. Just offshore, and reached by boat from here, are the rocky Farne Islands (National Trust) where there is an important bird reserve. The bird observatory occupies a medieval pele tower.

'Leeholme' ♨

Listed COMMENDED

93 Main Street, Seahouses NE68 7TS
☎ (01665) 720230
A warm welcome awaits you at this small homely bed and breakfast. 5 minutes' walk to Seahouses harbour and shops. Hearty breakfast assured.
Bedrooms: 1 double, 1 twin
Bathrooms: 1 public

Bed & breakfast

per night:	£min	£max
Single	14.00	
Double	28.00	

Parking for 2
Open March-October
🛏🖳🗘🛆🖳🛗▮🗝🖳, 🚗◖▸🏍

Rowena ♨

Listed

99 Main Street, Seahouses NE68 7TS
☎ (01665) 721309
Comfortable bed and breakfast accommodation, 5 minutes' walk from the harbour where boats leave to visit the Farne Islands.
Bedrooms: 1 single, 1 double, 1 twin, 1 triple
Bathrooms: 1 private, 1 public

Bed & breakfast

per night:	£min	£max
Single	15.00	15.00
Double	30.00	34.00

Parking for 3
🛏🛆🖳🗘🛆🖳 S 🖳, 🚗✳🏍

West Side Guest House
♨

9 King Street, Seahouses NE68 7XN
☎ (01665) 720508
Guesthouse in the village centre, within walking distance of the harbour and other facilities.
Bedrooms: 1 single, 2 double, 1 twin
Bathrooms: 2 public

Bed & breakfast

per night:	£min	£max
Single	15.00	
Double	29.00	

Parking for 6
Open March-October
🛏🛆🖳🗝📺🖳, 🏍

SPENNYMOOR

Durham
Map ref 5C2

Booming coal and iron town from the 18th C until early in the present century when traditional industry gave way to lighter manufacturing and trading estates were built. On the moors south of the town there are fine views of the Wear Valley.

Idsley House ⚠

███ HIGHLY COMMENDED

4 Green Lane, Spennymoor, County Durham DL16 6HD
☎ Bishop Auckland (01388) 814237
Long-established detached guesthouse on A167/A688 run by local family. Ideal for Durham City. Suitable for business or pleasure. Ample safe parking on premises.
Bedrooms: 1 single, 1 double, 2 twin, 1 triple
Bathrooms: 4 private, 1 public
Bed & breakfast

per night:	£min	£max
Single	18.00	25.00
Double	33.00	35.00

Parking for 8
🛇📠🖵🕯🏧♿🛂📺▥🌀☆

STAINDROP

Durham
Map ref 5B3

Village 5 miles north-east of Barnard Castle, not far from Raby Castle, one of the most impressive castles in the north of England.

Gazebo House

███ HIGHLY COMMENDED

4 North Green, Staindrop, Darlington, County Durham DL2 3JN
☎ Teesdale (01833) 660222
Fax (01833) 660222

18th C house with listed gazebo (illustrated) in garden. Adjacent Raby Park and Castle. Ideal base for Lake District and Yorkshire Dales.
Bedrooms: 1 double, 1 twin
Bathrooms: 2 private
Bed & breakfast

per night:	£min	£max
Single	18.00	
Double	38.00	

Half board

per person:	£min	£max
Daily	30.00	

Evening meal 1900 (last orders 2200)
🛇📞📠🖵♿🕯🏧📺▥🌀☆🚗🏠

SUNDERLAND

Tyne and Wear
Map ref 5C2

Ancient coal and shipbuilding port on Wearside, with important glassworks since the 17th C. Today's industrial complex dates from the 19th C. Modern building includes the Civic Centre.
Tourist Information Centre
☎ *(0191) 565 0990 or 565 0960*

Bed & Breakfast Stop ⚠

Listed COMMENDED

183 Newcastle Road, Fulwell, Sunderland, Tyne & Wear SR5 1NR
☎ (0191) 548 2291
Tudor-style semi-detached house on the A1018 Newcastle to Sunderland road. 5 minutes to the railway station and 10 minutes to the seafront and city centre.
Bedrooms: 1 single, 1 twin, 1 triple
Bathrooms: 1 public
Bed & breakfast

per night:	£min	£max
Single	15.00	16.00
Double	28.00	30.00

Half board

per person:	£min	£max
Daily	21.00	22.00
Weekly	133.00	140.00

Evening meal 1800 (last orders 1200)
Parking for 3
🛇3🖵♿▥🌀📺▥🚗🏠SP

Grange Guest House

Listed

12 Saint Georges Terrace, Roker, Sunderland, Tyne & Wear SR6 9LX
☎ (0191) 565 9550
Small, family guesthouse, close to the sea. All rooms en-suite with colour TV and tea/coffee facilities. Secure parking on request.
Bedrooms: 1 double, 2 twin
Bathrooms: 3 private
Bed & breakfast

per night:	£min	£max
Single	20.00	20.00
Double	30.00	30.00

Parking for 6
🛇♿🖵♿▥🏧⌷🌀▥🚗☆⨯🐕⌷DAP
📺SP

The town index at the back of this guide gives page numbers of all places with accommodation.

TOW LAW

Durham
Map ref 5B2

Old industrial town 8 miles north-west of Bishop Auckland.

Greenwell Farm ⚠

███ COMMENDED

Nr. Wolsingham, Tow Law, County Durham DL13 4PH
☎ Weardale (01388) 527248
300-acre mixed farm. Friendly hospitality in this comfortable 17th C farmhouse, set in peaceful countryside. Ideal for touring, cricket and fishing. Farm nature trail and wildlife.
Bedrooms: 1 double, 1 triple
Bathrooms: 2 private, 1 public
Bed & breakfast

per night:	£min	£max
Single	18.50	21.00
Double	37.00	40.00

Half board

per person:	£min	£max
Daily	28.50	31.00
Weekly	199.00	217.00

Evening meal 1800 (last orders 2100)
Parking for 8
🛇🖵♿▥🕯🛂📺🚗⌷10☉♨⨯
☆🚗🏠◉

TYNEMOUTH

Tyne and Wear
Map ref 5C2

At the mouth of the Tyne, old Tyneside resort adjoining North Shields with its fish quay and market. The pier is overlooked by the gaunt ruins of a Benedictine priory and a castle. Splendid sands, amusement centre and park.

Hope House ⚠

███ DE LUXE

47 Percy Gardens, Tynemouth, North Shields NE30 4HH
☎ (0191) 257 1989
Fax (0191) 257 1989
Double-fronted Victorian house with superb coastal views from most rooms. Tastefully furnished, with large bedrooms. Fine cuisine and quality wines.
Bedrooms: 2 double, 1 twin
Bathrooms: 3 private, 1 public
Bed & breakfast

per night:	£min	£max
Single	32.50	42.50
Double	39.50	49.50

Lunch available
Evening meal 1800 (last orders 2100)
Parking for 5
Cards accepted: Access, Visa, Diners, Amex
🛇📠🖵♿🕯🏧🛂◉⌷▥🚗◆♨
♨⨯🚗⌷DAP📺SP🏠⊤◉

WARKWORTH

Northumberland
Map ref 5C1

A pretty village overlooked by its
medieval castle. A 14th C fortified
bridge across the wooded Coquet
gives a superb view of 18th C
terraces climbing to the castle.
Upstream is a curious 14th C
Hermitage and in the market
square is the Norman church of St
Lawrence.

Beck 'N' Call ⚠
HIGHLY COMMENDED

Birling West Cottage, Warkworth,
Morpeth NE65 0XS
☎ Alnwick (01665) 711653
Country cottage set in half an acre of
terraced gardens with stream. First
cottage on the right entering Warkworth
from Alnwick.
Bedrooms: 2 double, 1 triple
Bathrooms: 2 private, 2 public

Bed & breakfast

per night:	£min	£max
Single	17.00	19.00

Parking for 4

Bide A While ⚠
Listed **COMMENDED**

4 Beal Croft, Warkworth, Morpeth
NE65 0XL
☎ Alnwick (01665) 711753
Bungalow on small executive housing
estate of 8 dwellings.
Bedrooms: 1 double, 1 family room
Bathrooms: 1 public, 1 private shower

Bed & breakfast

per night:	£min	£max
Single	17.00	18.00
Double	30.00	34.00

Parking for 3

North Cottage ⚠
HIGHLY COMMENDED

Birling, Warkworth, Morpeth
NE65 0XS
☎ Alnwick (01665) 711263

> At-a-glance symbols are
> explained on the flap inside
> the back cover.

Attractive cottage, with ground floor, en-
suite non-smoking rooms. Extensive
gardens, with patio where visitors are
welcome to relax. Off-street parking.
Bedrooms: 1 single, 2 double, 1 twin
Bathrooms: 3 private, 1 public

Bed & breakfast

per night:	£min	£max
Single	18.00	18.00
Double	36.00	36.00

Parking for 8

WEST WOODBURN

Northumberland
Map ref 5B2

Small hamlet on the River Rede in
rolling moorland country.

Bay Horse Inn
⚜⚜

West Woodburn, Hexham NE48 2RX
☎ Hexham (01434) 270218
18th C coaching inn beside River Rede.
On A68 between Corbridge and
Otterburn and near Bellingham.
Bedrooms: 1 double, 2 twin, 2 triple
Bathrooms: 2 public, 1 private shower

Bed & breakfast

per night:	£min	£max
Single	18.00	20.00
Double	32.00	36.00

Lunch available
Evening meal 1900 (last orders 2100)
Parking for 25
Cards accepted: Access, Visa, Switch/
Delta

Toad Hall ⚠
HIGHLY COMMENDED

1 Woodburn Park, West Woodburn,
Hexham NE48 2RA
☎ Bellingham (01434) 270013
New spacious bungalow just off A68.
Near village with post office/shop and 2
public houses. Historic area and
beautiful scenery.
Bedrooms: 1 double, 1 twin, 1 triple
Bathrooms: 3 private

Bed & breakfast

per night:	£min	£max
Single	16.00	16.00
Double	36.00	40.00

Half board

per person:	£min	£max
Daily	24.00	30.00
Weekly	157.00	195.00

Evening meal from 1900
Parking for 4
Open March-October

WHITLEY BAY

Tyne and Wear
Map ref 5C2

Traditional seaside resort with long
beaches of sand and rock and
many pools to explore. St Mary's
lighthouse is open to the public.
Tourist Information Centre
☎ *(0191) 200 8535*

Windsor Hotel ⚠
COMMENDED

South Parade, Whitley Bay NE26 2RF
☎ (0191) 251 8888 & 297 0272

Private hotel close to the seafront and
town centre. An excellent base in the
north east for business or pleasure.
Bedrooms: 5 single, 16 double,
43 twin
Bathrooms: 64 private

Bed & breakfast

per night:	£min	£max
Single	40.00	60.00
Double	45.00	60.00

Half board

per person:	£min	£max
Daily	45.00	70.00
Weekly	210.00	350.00

Lunch available
Evening meal 1800 (last orders 2130)
Parking for 26
Cards accepted: Access, Visa, Diners,
Amex, Switch/Delta

North West

This region is packed with colour and character, a great intricate mosaic of cities, coast and countryside.

Visit the humming centres of Manchester and Liverpool with their industrial heritage, fabulous art collections and stunning Victorian architecture. Treat yourself a ticket to hear an international orchestra, or shop at the markets, malls and mill shops. But for a different city flavour altogether, visit elegant, ancient-walled Chester.

The countryside is full of variety too, from the pretty villages of the Wirral to the rolling border country and tow paths of Cheshire; while a day at the sea offers everything from the glitter of Blackpool's golden mile, to the tranquillity and birdlife of the Dee estuary.

The Counties of Cheshire, Greater Manchester, Lancashire and Merseyside

For more information on the North West, contact:
North West Tourist Board
Swan House, Swan Meadow Road,
Wigan Pier, Wigan, Lancashire WN3 5BB
Tel: (01942) 821222
Fax: (01942) 820002
Where to Go in the North West –
see pages 78–81
Where to Stay in the North West –
see pages 82–90

North West

Where to go and what to see

You will find hundreds of interesting places to visit during your stay in North West England, just some of which are listed in these pages. The number against each name will help you locate it on the map (page 81). Contact any Tourist Information Centre in the region for more ideas on days out in the North West.

1 Frontierland Western Theme Park
Marine Road, Morecambe, Lancashire LA4 4DG
Tel: (01524) 410024
Over 30 Wild West thrill rides and attractions, including Texas Tornado, Perculator, Stampede Roller Coaster. "Fun house" indoor complex.

2 Lancaster Castle
Shire Hall, Castle Parade, Lancaster LA1 1YJ
Tel: (01524) 64998
Collection of coats of arms, dungeons, Crown Court, Grand Jury Room, Jane Scott's chair, external tour of castle walls.

3 Sandcastle
Promenade, Blackpool, Lancashire FY4 1BB
Tel: (01253) 343602
Leisure pool, wave pool, giant slides, amusements, live entertainment, bars, cafés, showbar, shops, nightclub, children's playground, beer garden.

4 Blackpool Pleasure Beach
Ocean Boulevard, Blackpool, Lancashire FY4 1EZ
Tel: (01253) 341033
Europe's greatest amusement park: Space Invader, Big Dipper, Revolution, etc. Funshineland for children. Summer season ice show, illusion show in Horseshoe Bar.

5 Blackpool Sea Life Centre
The Promenade, Blackpool, Lancashire FY1 5AA
Tel: (01253) 22445
Tropical sharks up to 8ft in length housed in 100,000-gallon display with underwater walk-through tunnel.

6 Blackpool Tower
The Promenade, Blackpool, Lancashire FY1 4BJ
Tel: (01253) 22242
Tower Ballroom, Bug World, Jungle Jim's playground, Out of this World, Undersea World, laser fantasy, lift ride. Tower Circus. Children's entertainment in Hornpipe Galley.

7 Ribchester Museum of Childhood
Church Street, Ribchester, Lancashire PR3 3YE
Tel: (01254) 878520
Childhood toys, dolls, dolls' houses, 20-piece model fairground, Tom Thumb replica. Collectors' toy shop.

8 Pleasureland Amusement Park
Marine Drive, The Fun Coast, Southport, Merseyside PR8 1RX
Tel: (01704) 532717
Traditional amusement park with wide variety of thrilling and family rides.

9 Camelot Theme Park
Park Hall Road, Charnock Richard, Lancashire PR7 5LP
Tel: (01257) 453044
Magical kingdom offering over 100 thrilling rides, fantastic medieval entertainment and lots of family fun.

⑩ Wildfowl and Wetland Centre
Martin Mere, Burscough, Lancashire L40 0TA
Tel: (01704) 895181
45 acres of gardens with over 1,600 ducks, geese and swans of 120 different kinds. Two flocks of flamingoes. 300-acre wild area with 20-acre lake.

⑪ East Lancashire Railway
Bolton Street Station, Bury, Lancashire BL9 0EY
Tel: (0161) 764 7790
Eight-mile-long preserved railway operated principally by steam traction. Transport museum nearby.

⑫ Wigan Pier
Wallgate, Wigan, Lancashire WN3 4EU
Tel: (01942) 323666
"The Way We Were" – life in Wigan in 1900. Cotton machinery hall, world's largest steam-operated mill engine, waterbuses, shops, Victorian classroom, picnic gardens.

⑬ Granada Studios Tour
Water Street, Manchester M60 9EA
Tel: (0161) 832 9090
The only major TV theme park in Europe, giving a unique insight into the fascinating world behind the TV screen. Visit three of the most famous streets on TV.

⑭ Museum of Science and Industry in Manchester
Liverpool Road, Castlefield, Manchester M3 4JP
Tel: (0161) 832 2244
Based in the world's oldest passenger railway station, 15 galleries amaze, amuse and entertain.

⑮ Knowsley Safari Park
Prescot, Merseyside L34 4AN
Tel: (0151) 430 9009
Five-mile drive through game reserves, set in 400 acres of parkland containing lions, tigers, elephants, rhinos, etc. Large picnic areas, children's amusement park.

⑯ Albert Dock
The Colonnades, Albert Dock, Liverpool L3 4AA
Tel: (0151) 708 7334
Britain's largest Grade I listed historic building. Restored 4-sided dock, including shops, bars, restaurants, entertainment, marina and maritime museum.

⑰ Tate Gallery Liverpool
Albert Dock, Liverpool L3 4BB
Tel: (0151) 709 3223
North of England venue for the national collection of modern art.

⑱ Catalyst: The Museum of the Chemical Industry
Gossage Building, Mersey Road, Widnes, Cheshire WA8 0DF
Tel: (0151) 420 1121
Dramatic riverside observation gallery with interactive microcomputers, video and other displays telling the story of the chemical industry in Widnes and Runcorn.

⑲ Dunham Massey Hall and Park
Altrincham, Cheshire WA14 4SJ
Tel: (0161) 941 1025
Historic house, garden and park with restaurant and shop.

⑳ Bramall Hall
Bramall Park, Bramhall, Cheshire SK7 3NX
Tel: (0161) 485 3708
Important Elizabethan manor house in 60 acres of landscaped grounds. Wall paintings, furniture, medieval stained glass, Victorian kitchen.

㉑ Lyme Park
Disley, Cheshire SK12 2NX
Tel: (01663) 762023
National Trust country estate with 1,377 acres of moorland, woodland and park. Magnificent house with 17 acres of historic gardens.

㉒ Quarry Bank Mill
Styal, Cheshire SK9 4LA
Tel: (01625) 527468
Georgian water-powered cotton spinning mill, with four floors of displays and demonstrations.

㉓ Lady Lever Art Gallery
Port Sunlight Village, Bebington,
Merseyside L62 5EQ
Tel: (0151) 645 3623
*The first Lord Leverhulme's
magnificent collection of British
paintings, 1750–1900, plus
Wedgwood and oriental porcelain,
British furniture.*

**㉔ Port Sunlight Heritage
Centre**
95 Greendale Road, Port Sunlight,
Merseyside L62 4XE
Tel: (0151) 644 6466
*Display showing creation of village,
with photographs, drawings, models
in listed building.*

**㉕ Norton Priory Museum and
Gardens**
Tudor Road, Runcorn, Cheshire
WA7 1SX
Tel: (01928) 569895

*Excavated Augustinian priory,
remains of church, cloister and
chapter house. Later site of Tudor
mansion and Georgian house.*

㉖ Boat Museum
Dock Yard Road, Ellesmere Port,
Cheshire L65 4EF
Tel: (0151) 355 5017
*Over 50 historic craft – largest floating
collection in the world. Restored
buildings, traditional cottages,
workshops, steam engines, boat
trips, shop, etc.*

㉗ Arley Hall and Gardens
Arley, Northwich, Cheshire
CW9 6NA
Tel: (01565) 777353
*Early Victorian house and 15th C
tythe barn in 12 acres of magnificent
gardens. Collection of watercolours
of the area. Woodland walk,
craftsmen, shop.*

㉘ Macclesfield Silk Museum
The Heritage Centre, Roe Street,
Macclesfield, Cheshire SK11 6UT
Tel: (01625) 613210
*Information centre, town history
exhibition, silk museum, Sunday
school, history exhibition, guided trails,
tearoom, shop. Auditorium seats 450.*

**㉙ Jodrell Bank Science
Centre and Arboretum**
Lower Withington, Cheshire
SK11 9DL
Tel: (01477) 571339
*Exhibition and interactive exhibits on
astronomy, space, satellites, energy,
the environment. Planetarium, the
Lovell telescope, 35-acre arboretum.*

Find Out More

Further information about holidays and attractions in the North West is available from: **North West Tourist Board**, Swan House, Swan Meadow Road, Wigan Pier, Wigan, Lancashire WN3 5BB Tel: (01942) 821222

These publications are available free from the North West Tourist Board:

- **North West Welcome**
  Guide
- **Discover England's North West**
- **Group Travel Guide**
- **Bed & Breakfast map**
- **Caravan & Camping Parks Guide**

WHERE TO STAY

Accommodation entries in this regional section are listed in alphabetical order of place name, and then in alphabetical order of establishment.

Map references refer to the colour location maps at the back of this guide. The first figure is the map number; the letter and figure which follow indicate the grid reference on the map.

At-a-glance symbols at the end of each accommodation entry give information about services and facilities. A handy guide to these symbols can be found inside the back cover flap, which can be kept open for easy reference.

ALDERLEY EDGE

Cheshire
Map ref 4B2

Picturesque town taking its name from the wooded escarpment towering above the Cheshire plain, with fine views and walks. A romantic local legend tells of the Wizard and sleeping warriors who will save the country in crisis. Excellent shops. Chorley Hall, nearby, boasts a moat.

Dean Green Farm

👑👑👑 HIGHLY COMMENDED

Nusery Lane, Nether Alderley, Macclesfield SK10 4TX
☎ Chelford (01625) 861401

131-acre beef farm. Situated between A34 and A535 at Nether Alderley. Grade II oak-beamed farmhouse surrounded by pastureland looking towards Alderley Edge. Convenient for Knutsford, Wilmslow and Macclesfield.

Bedrooms: 1 double
Bathrooms: 1 private

Bed & breakfast per night:	£min	£max
Single		29.37
Double		58.75

Half board per person:	£min	£max
Daily		44.06

Evening meal 1800 (last orders 2100)
Parking for 10
🛏 ☐ 🫖 💨 [UL] 🔒 🪑 [TV] ♨ 🧺 🎾 🐟 🔫 ✿ 🐕 🚐 🏠

We advise you to confirm your booking in writing.

ALTRINCHAM

Greater Manchester
Map ref 4A2

Altrincham preserves the best of the old at its fascinating Old Market Place, with the best of the new on pedestrianised George Street. International fashion and high style interior design rub shoulders with unique boutiques and local speciality shops.
Tourist Information Centre
☎ (0161) 912 5931

Ashley Mill ▲

👑 HIGHLY COMMENDED

Ashley Mill Lane, Ashley, Altrincham, Cheshire WA14 3PU
☎ (0161) 928 5751

17th C mill house set in 5 acres of delightful Cheshire countryside. A haven of peace and tranquillity, yet only 10 minutes from Manchester Airport. Car parking available for airport.

Bedrooms: 1 single, 2 double, 1 twin
Bathrooms: 1 public

Bed & breakfast per night:	£min	£max
Single	20.00	
Double	40.00	

Evening meal from 1830
Parking for 32
🐴 10 🛏 ☐ 🫖 💨 [UL] 🔒 [S] 🚭 🪑 [TV] ♨ 🧺 ✿ 🐕 🚐 🍃 🏠

Rooftree

Listed HIGHLY COMMENDED

40 Arthog Road, Hale, Altrincham, Cheshire WA15 0LU
☎ (0161) 980 4906
Fax (0161) 980 4906

Welcome to superb accommodation in lovely, detached, non-smoking house in quiet location. Airport and M56 only 10 minutes away. TV in all rooms. Evening meals. Secure parking.

Bedrooms: 2 single, 1 twin
Bathrooms: 1 public

Bed & breakfast per night:	£min	£max
Single	20.00	20.00
Double	40.00	40.00

Half board per person:	£min	£max
Daily	27.00	27.00

Evening meal from 1700
Parking for 5
🐴 🛏 ☐ 🫖 💨 [UL] [S] 🚭 🪑 [TV] ♨ 🧺 ⚑ ✿ 🐕 🚐

BACUP

Lancashire
Map ref 4B1

Best preserved cotton town in Britain, surrounded by stretches of moorland and close to the South Yorkshire border. The Natural History Society Museum has collections of 19th C relics, geology and natural history.

Pasture Bottom Farm

👑 APPROVED

Bacup OL13 9UZ
☎ (01706) 873790

100-acre beef farm. Farmhouse bed and breakfast ideally situated for walking Rossendale and Lancashire Moor. Local attractions include a textile museum, Ski Rossendale and hang-gliding at Whitworth.

Bedrooms: 2 twin
Bathrooms: 1 public

Bed & breakfast per night:	£min	£max
Single	13.50	13.50
Double	27.00	27.00

Half board

per person:	£min	£max
Daily	20.50	20.50
Weekly	143.50	143.50

Evening meal 1900 (last orders 1900)
Parking for 3

🛇🖵♿🛁ℹ️TV🖩🅿️🅗

BLACKPOOL

Lancashire
Map ref 4A1

Britain's largest fun resort, with Blackpool Pleasure Beach, 3 piers and the famous Tower. Host to the spectacular autumn illuminations - "the greatest free show on earth".
Tourist Information Centre
☎ *(01253) 21623*

Ashbeian Hotel

😀😀😀 COMMENDED

49 High Street, Blackpool FY1 2BN
☎ (01253) 26301
En-suite bedrooms, good parking. Privately owned. Splendid menus. Terrific value. Just off seafront, an easy walk to everything.
Bedrooms: 1 single, 2 double, 2 triple
Bathrooms: 5 private

Bed & breakfast

per night:	£min	£max
Single	16.00	25.00
Double	30.00	42.00

Half board

per person:	£min	£max
Daily	22.00	31.00
Weekly	100.00	150.00

Evening meal 1700 (last orders 1930)

🛇5🖵♿🚶ℹ️SℳℳTV🖩🅿️OAP
SP🅗

Sunray ⋀

😀😀😀 COMMENDED

42 Knowle Avenue, Blackpool
FY2 9TQ
☎ (01253) 351937
Fax (01253) 593307
Modern semi in quiet residential part of north Blackpool. Friendly personal service and care. 1.75 miles north of tower along promenade. Turn right at Uncle Tom's Cabin. Sunray is about 300 yards on left.
Bedrooms: 3 single, 2 double, 2 twin, 2 triple
Bathrooms: 9 private, 1 public

Bed & breakfast

per night:	£min	£max
Single	25.00	28.00
Double	50.00	56.00

Half board

per person:	£min	£max
Daily	37.00	40.00
Weekly	222.00	240.00

Evening meal 1750 (last orders 1500)
Parking for 6
Cards accepted: Access, Visa, Amex

🛇📞📠🖵♿🚶🔌ℹ️S ℳ TV🖩🅿️❋🤎
OAP SP🅗

BURNLEY

Lancashire
Map ref 4B1

"A town amidst the Pennines", set in the glorious Lancashire countryside. Towneley Hall has fine period rooms and is home to Burnley's art gallery and museum. The Kay-Shuttleworth collection of lace and embroidery can be seen at Gawthorpe Hall (National Trust).
Tourist Information Centre
☎ *(01282) 455485*

Ormerod Hotel

😀😀 HIGHLY COMMENDED

121-123 Ormerod Road, Burnley
BB11 3QW
☎ (01282) 423255
Small bed and breakfast hotel in quiet, pleasant surroundings facing local parks. Recently refurbished, all en-suite facilities. 5 minutes from town centre.
Bedrooms: 4 single, 2 double, 2 twin, 2 triple
Bathrooms: 10 private

Bed & breakfast

per night:	£min	£max
Single	19.00	25.00
Double	35.00	37.00

Parking for 7

🛇📠🖵♿🛁ℹ️SℳTV🖩🅿️🅗

BURWARDSLEY

Cheshire
Map ref 4A2

The Pheasant Inn

😀😀😀 COMMENDED

Higher Burwardsley, Tattenhall, Chester CH3 9PF
☎ Tattenhall (01829) 770434
Fax (01829) 771097

300-year-old inn, half-timber and sandstone construction, nestling on the top of the Peckforton Hills. Accommodation in delightfully converted barn affording pleasant views towards Chester.
Bedrooms: 5 double, 2 twin, 1 triple
Bathrooms: 8 private

Bed & breakfast

per night:	£min	£max
Single	45.00	
Double	60.00	

Lunch available
Evening meal 1930 (last orders 2130)
Parking for 60

Cards accepted: Access, Visa, Diners, Amex

🛇📠📞🖵♿🔌🛁ℹ️SℳℳTV🖩🅿️
🍴❋🤎❋SP🏠🅗

CHESTER

Cheshire
Map ref 4A2

Roman and medieval walled city rich in architectural and archaeological treasures. Fine timber-framed and plaster buildings. Shopping in the Rows (galleried arcades reached by steps from the street). 14th C cathedral, castle and zoo.
Tourist Information Centre
☎ *(01244) 317962 or 351609 or 322220*

Cheyney Lodge Hotel ⋀

😀😀😀 COMMENDED

77-79 Cheyney Road, Chester
CH1 4BS
☎ (01244) 381925
Small, friendly hotel of unusual design, featuring indoor garden and fish pond. 10 minutes' walk from city centre and on main bus route. Personally supervised with emphasis on good food.
Bedrooms: 1 single, 4 double, 2 twin, 1 triple
Bathrooms: 8 private

Bed & breakfast

per night:	£min	£max
Single	24.00	24.00
Double	38.00	42.00

Half board

per person:	£min	£max
Daily	26.50	29.50

Lunch available
Evening meal 1800 (last orders 2000)
Parking for 12
Cards accepted: Access, Visa

🛇📠🎾🖵🖵♿🛁ℹ️S🖩🅿️❋✗SP🅗

Eaton House

😀😀

36 Eaton Road, Handbridge, Chester
CH4 7EN
☎ (01244) 671346
140-year-old Victorian house with all modern facilities, in pleasant conservation area, near river and town centre.
Bedrooms: 3 double
Bathrooms: 2 private, 1 public

Bed & breakfast

per night:	£min	£max
Double	29.00	34.00

Parking for 3

🖵🖵♿🚶🔌ℹ️🅿️✗🤎

Grove House ⋀

😀😀 HIGHLY COMMENDED

Holme Street, Tarvin, Chester
CH3 8EQ
☎ Tarvin (01829) 740893
Fax (01829) 741769

Continued ▶

CHESTER
Continued

Warm welcome in relaxing environment. Spacious, comfortable rooms, attractive garden. Ample parking. Within easy reach of Chester (4 miles) and major North West and North Wales tourist attractions.
Bedrooms: 1 single, 1 double, 1 twin
Bathrooms: 1 private, 1 public

Bed & breakfast
per night:	£min	£max
Single	18.50	
Double	40.00	

Parking for 8

Mitchells of Chester
HIGHLY COMMENDED
Green Gables House, 28 Hough Green, Chester CH4 8JQ
☎ (01244) 679004

Tastefully restored, elegant Victorian residence, with steeply pitched slated roofs, a sweeping staircase, antique furniture in tall rooms with moulded cornices. Compact landscaped gardens. Close to city centre.
Bedrooms: 1 single, 1 double, 1 twin, 1 family room
Bathrooms: 4 private, 1 public

Bed & breakfast
per night:	£min	£max
Single	25.00	29.00
Double	39.00	39.00

Parking for 5

Moorings
HIGHLY COMMENDED
14 Sandy Lane, Chester CH3 5UL
☎ (01244) 324485
Award-winning B & B in elegant riverside Victorian house with terraced gardens to River Dee. Idyllic rural aspect yet within easy walking distance of city centre.
Bedrooms: 2 double, 1 twin
Bathrooms: 3 private, 1 public

Bed & breakfast
per night:	£min	£max
Single	19.50	23.00
Double	30.00	39.00

Open February-December

Newton Hall
HIGHLY COMMENDED
Tattenhall, Chester CH3 9AY
☎ Tattenhall (01829) 770153
140-acre dairy & livestock farm. Bed and breakfast accommodation in 16th C oak-beamed farmhouse, 6 miles from Chester off A41. Lovely gardens, views of Beeston and Peckforton castles.
Bedrooms: 1 single, 1 double, 1 twin
Bathrooms: 1 private, 1 public

Bed & breakfast
per night:	£min	£max
Single	20.00	25.00
Double	36.00	40.00

Parking for 3

Tickeridge House
Whitchurch Road, Milton Green, Chester CH3 9DS
☎ Tattenhall (01829) 770443
Chester 5 miles, off A41 at Milton Green. Worth looking for and certainly worth staying. Beautifully appointed house with all rooms on ground floor. Very warm welcome. Succulent full English breakfast. Look forward to meeting you, all facilities for your comfort.
Bedrooms: 1 double, 1 twin, 1 triple
Bathrooms: 2 private, 1 public

Bed & breakfast
per night:	£min	£max
Single	17.50	20.00
Double	30.00	37.00

Parking for 6
Cards accepted: Visa

CLITHEROE
Lancashire
Map ref 4A1

Intriguing town with an 800-year-old castle keep and a wide range of award-winning shops. Good base for touring Ribble Valley, Trough of Bowland and Pennine moorland. Country market on Tuesdays and Saturdays.
Tourist Information Centre
☎ *(01200) 25566*

Lower Standen Farm ⋀
Whalley Road, Clitheroe BB7 1PP
☎ (01200) 24176
30-acre mixed farm. 17th C farmhouse. Excellent for walking holidays.
Bedrooms: 2 double, 1 twin
Bathrooms: 1 private, 1 public

Bed & breakfast
per night:	£min	£max
Single	15.00	15.00
Double	30.00	34.00

Parking for 3

COLNE
Lancashire
Map ref 4B1

Old market town with mixed industries bordering the moorland Bronte country. Nearby are the ruins of Wycoller House, featured in Charlotte Bronte's "Jane Eyre" as Ferndean Manor.

Blakey Hall Farm
Listed
Red Lane, Colne BB8 9TD
☎ (01282) 863121
120-acre dairy farm. Built in early 16th C, surrounded by rolling fields. Oliver Cromwell reputed to have stayed at this farm, which has a warm welcome awaiting you.
Bedrooms: 1 double, 2 twin
Bathrooms: 1 private, 1 public

Bed & breakfast
per night:	£min	£max
Single	17.00	22.00
Double	34.00	44.00

Half board
per person:	£min	£max
Daily	24.50	29.50
Weekly	171.50	206.50

Evening meal 1900 (last orders 2100)
Parking for 4

148 Keighley Road
HIGHLY COMMENDED
Colne BB8 0PJ
☎ (01282) 862002
Edwardian town house. Comfortable, attractive bedrooms. Friendly and helpful hosts. Close to open countryside. Non-smokers only, please.
Bedrooms: 1 single, 2 double
Bathrooms: 1 private, 1 public

Bed & breakfast
per night:	£min	£max
Single	16.00	16.00
Double	32.00	36.00

Parking for 1

Middle Beardshaw Head Farm
Listed APPROVED
Burnley Road, Trawden, Colne BB8 8PP
☎ (01282) 865257
15-acre dairy farm. 17th-18th C Lancashire longhouse with oak beams, panelling, log fires. Panoramic views with pools, woods and stream. Half mile from Trawden. Caravan and camping site on farm, with bathroom, hot shower and electricity.

Bedrooms: 2 single, 1 double, 1 family room
Bathrooms: 2 public, 2 private showers

Bed & breakfast

per night:	£min	£max
Single	17.50	20.00
Double	35.00	40.00

Half board

per person:	£min	£max
Daily	26.00	28.50
Weekly	180.00	198.00

Evening meal 1900 (last orders 2030)
Parking for 10

Turnpike House

COMMENDED

6 Keighley Road, Colne BB8 0JL
☎ (01282) 869596
Come and relax in our Victorian house with garden. Ideal for exploring Bronte country, Pendle, Forest of Bowland, Yorkshire Dales. Follow Lancashire Mill Trail. A warm welcome awaits you. Walkers welcome.
Bedrooms: 1 single, 1 double, 1 triple
Bathrooms: 1 public

Bed & breakfast

per night:	£min	£max
Single	14.00	15.00
Double	28.00	30.00

Half board

per person:	£min	£max
Daily	20.00	21.00

Evening meal 1800 (last orders 1930)
Parking for 1

CONGLETON

Cheshire
Map ref 4B2

Important cattle market and silk town on the River Dane, now concerned with general textiles. Nearby are Little Moreton Hall, a Tudor house surrounded by a moat, the Bridestones, a chambered tomb, and Mow Cop, topped by a folly.
Tourist Information Centre
☎ *(01260) 271095*

Sandhole Farm

HIGHLY COMMENDED

Hulme Walfield, Congleton CW12 2JH
☎ Marton Heath (01260) 224419
Fax (01260) 224766
200-acre arable and mixed farm. Charming en-suite accommodation in tastefully converted stables adjacent to attractive traditional farmhouse. Two miles north of Congleton on A34.
Wheelchair access category 3 🦽
Bedrooms: 1 single, 6 double, 9 twin, 1 triple, 1 family room
Bathrooms: 18 private, 2 public

Bed & breakfast

per night:	£min	£max
Single		33.00
Double		43.00

Parking for 40
Cards accepted: Access, Visa, Diners

CREWE

Cheshire
Map ref 4A2

Famous for its railway junction, this small market town is at the heart of the beautiful south Cheshire countryside and well located for visiting local attractions.

The Hand and Trumpet Inn

COMMENDED

Main Road, Wrinehill, Crewe CW3 9BJ
☎ (01270) 820048
Fax (01270) 820087
A comfortable rural inn, convenient for Crewe and the Potteries. Set in landscaped gardens, husband and wife operated.
Bedrooms: 4 double, 2 twin
Bathrooms: 4 private, 2 public

Bed & breakfast

per night:	£min	£max
Single	25.00	28.00
Double	30.00	35.00

Half board

per person:	£min	£max
Daily	30.00	

Lunch available
Evening meal 1900 (last orders 2200)
Parking for 20
Cards accepted: Access, Visa, Diners

GREAT ECCLESTON

Lancashire
Map ref 4A1

Cartford Hotel

Cartford Lane, Little Eccleston, Preston PR3 0YP
☎ (01995) 670166
A country riverside pub and coaching inn, with 1.5 miles of fishing rights. Within easy reach of Blackpool and the Lake District.
Bedrooms: 5 double, 1 twin
Bathrooms: 6 private

Bed & breakfast

per night:	£min	£max
Single	27.50	32.50
Double	39.50	45.50

Lunch available
Evening meal 1900 (last orders 2130)
Parking for 100
Cards accepted: Access, Visa

HOLMES CHAPEL

Cheshire
Map ref 4A2

Large village with some interesting 18th C buildings and St Luke's Church encased in brick hiding the 15th C original.

Tiree

Listed

5 Middlewich Road, Cranage, Holmes Chapel, Crewe CW4 8HG
☎ (01477) 533716
Modern house set in open country 3 miles from the M6 (junction 18) and close to the A50, 2 miles north of Holmes Chapel.
Bedrooms: 1 single, 1 double, 1 twin
Bathrooms: 1 public

Bed & breakfast

per night:	£min	£max
Single	16.00	16.00
Double	30.00	30.00

Parking for 4

INGLEWHITE

Lancashire
Map ref 4A1

Latus Hall Farm

Listed COMMENDED

Inglewhite, Preston PR3 2LN
☎ Brock (01995) 640368

100-acre dairy farm. 300-year-old farmhouse. 7 miles north of Preston, 2.5 miles from A6 at Bilsborrow. Oak beams, log fires and a warm welcome.
Bedrooms: 2 double, 1 twin
Bathrooms: 2 public

Bed & breakfast

per night:	£min	£max
Single	13.50	
Double	27.00	30.00

Parking for 6

The symbols 🦽 🦽 🦽 indicate categories of accessibility for wheelchair users. They are explained in full in the information pages at the back of this guide.

KNUTSFORD

Cheshire
Map ref 4A2

Delightful town with many buildings of architectural and historic interest. The setting of Elizabeth Gaskell's "Cranford". Annual May Day celebration and decorative "sanding" of the pavements are unique to the town. Popular Heritage Centre.
Tourist Information Centre
☎ *(01565) 632611 or 632210*

Laburnum Cottage Guest House ⋀

HIGHLY COMMENDED

Knutsford Road, Mobberley, Knutsford WA16 7PU
☎ Mobberley (01565) 872464
Fax (01565) 872464
Small country house in Cheshire countryside on B5085 close to Tatton Park, 6 miles from Manchester Airport, 4 miles from M6 exit 19 and 4 miles from M56. Taxi service to airport. Non-smokers only please. Winner of NWTB Place to Stay '93 Guesthouse Award and Cheshire Tourist Board B&B of the Year 93/94.
Bedrooms: 2 single, 1 double, 2 twin
Bathrooms: 3 private, 1 public

Bed & breakfast

per night:	£min	£max
Single	28.00	38.00
Double	40.00	48.00

Parking for 12

LANCASTER

Lancashire
Map ref 5A3

Interesting old county town on the River Lune with history dating back to Roman times. Norman castle, St Mary's Church, Customs House, City and Maritime Museums, Ashton Memorial and Butterfly House are among places of note. Good centre for touring the Lake District.
Tourist Information Centre
☎ *(01524) 32878*

Lancaster Town House ⋀

COMMENDED

11 Newton Terrace, Caton Road, Lancaster LA1 3PB
☎ (01524) 65527
Ideal for touring the area, close to M6 motorway. All rooms en-suite with colour TV. Four-poster bedroom. Full breakfast menu.
Bedrooms: 1 single, 3 double, 1 twin
Bathrooms: 5 private

Bed & breakfast

per night:	£min	£max
Single	22.00	25.00
Double	34.50	40.00

Middle Holly Cottage ⋀

COMMENDED

Middle Holly, Forton, Preston PR3 1AH
☎ Forton (01524) 792399
Former coaching inn, set in rural surroundings. Adjacent A6 Lancaster road, 7 miles south of city centre, 5 minutes from university, 3 miles south of M6 junction 33. Convenient for all North Lancashire areas and only 30 minutes' drive to Lakes.
Bedrooms: 1 single, 2 double, 1 twin, 1 triple
Bathrooms: 5 private

Bed & breakfast

per night:	£min	£max
Single	24.50	29.50
Double	37.50	42.50

Parking for 11
Cards accepted: Access, Visa

LIVERPOOL

Merseyside
Map ref 4A2

Exciting city, famous for the Beatles, football, the Grand National, theatres and nightlife. Liverpool has a magnificent waterfront, 2 cathedrals, 3 historic houses, museum, galleries and a host of attractions.
Tourist Information Centre
☎ *(0151) 709 3631 or 708 8854*

Anna's

COMMENDED

65 Dudlow Lane, Calderstones, Liverpool L18 2EY
☎ (0151) 722 3708
Fax (0151) 722 8699
Large family house with friendly atmosphere, in select residential area close to all amenities. Direct transport routes to city centre. 1 mile from end of M62 motorway.
Bedrooms: 1 double, 3 twin
Bathrooms: 1 public

Bed & breakfast

per night:	£min	£max
Single	18.50	18.50
Double	30.00	33.00

Parking for 6

Somersby Guest House

COMMENDED

57 Green Lane, off Menlove Avenue, Liverpool L18 2EP
☎ (0151) 722 7549
Attractive house with secure parking, delightfully situated in exclusive area
with easy access to city centre, airport and M62.
Bedrooms: 2 double, 1 twin
Bathrooms: 2 public

Bed & breakfast

per night:	£min	£max
Single	20.00	20.00
Double	35.00	35.00

Parking for 6

MACCLESFIELD

Cheshire
Map ref 4B2

Cobbled streets and quaint old buildings stand side by side with modern shops and three markets. Centuries of association with the silk industry; museums feature working exhibits and social history. Stunning views of the Peak District National Park.
Tourist Information Centre
☎ *(01625) 504114*

Sandpit Farm

COMMENDED

Messuage Lane, Marton, Macclesfield SK11 9HS
☎ Marton Heath (01260) 224254
110-acre arable farm. Comfortable, oak-beamed house with hot and cold water in single. Twin and double rooms en-suite. Convenient for stately homes and National Trust properties. Easy access to the Peak District, Chester and Manchester Airport. 4 miles north of Congleton and 1 mile west of A34.
Bedrooms: 1 single, 1 double, 1 twin
Bathrooms: 2 private, 1 public

Bed & breakfast

per night:	£min	£max
Single	14.00	18.00
Double	28.00	36.00

Parking for 4

MALPAS

Cheshire
Map ref 4A2

Millhey Farm

Barton, Malpas SY14 7HY
☎ Broxton (01829) 782431
140-acre mixed farm. Typical, lovely Cheshire black and white part-timbered farmhouse in conservation area, 9 miles from Chester, close to Welsh Border country. On A534, just off A41.
Bedrooms: 1 twin, 1 triple
Bathrooms: 2 private, 1 public

Bed & breakfast

per night:	£min	£max
Single	15.00	15.00
Double	30.00	30.00

Parking for 2

MANCHESTER

Greater Manchester
Map ref 4B1

The Gateway to the North, offering one of Britain's largest selections of arts venues and theatre productions, a wide range of chain stores and specialist shops, a legendary, lively nightlife, spectacular architecture and a plethora of eating and drinking places.
Tourist Information Centre
☎ *(0161) 234 3157 or 234 3158 or 436 3344 (Manchester Airport Terminal 1)*

Parkside Guest House
☸☸

58 Cromwell Road, Off Edge Lane, Stretford, Manchester M32 8QJ
☎ (0161) 865 2860
Clean, comfortable, convenient. In a quiet pleasant area near Old Trafford football/cricket grounds. 15 minutes from airport and city centre by Metro. M63 exit 7. A warm and friendly welcome assured.
Bedrooms: 1 single, 2 twin, 1 family room
Bathrooms: 3 private, 1 public

Bed & breakfast per night:	£min	£max
Single	18.50	20.00
Double	33.00	35.00

Parking for 3
☸7🛏🍴📺♿⛰🛎✕🏊🚗🅣

MANCHESTER AIRPORT

See under Alderley Edge, Altrincham, Knutsford, Manchester, Stockport, Styal

NANTWICH

Cheshire
Map ref 4A2

Old market town on the River Weaver made prosperous in Roman times by salt springs. Fire destroyed the town in 1583 and many buildings were rebuilt in Elizabethan style. Churche's Mansion (open to the public) survived the fire.
Tourist Information Centre
☎ *(01270) 610983 or 610880*

Lea Farm
☸☸ COMMENDED

Wrinehill Road, Wybunbury, Nantwich CW5 7NS
☎ Crewe (01270) 841429
160-acre dairy farm. Charming farmhouse in beautiful gardens where peacocks roam. Comfortable lounge, pool/snooker, fishing pool. Ideal surroundings.
Bedrooms: 2 double, 1 triple
Bathrooms: 2 private, 1 public

Bed & breakfast per night:	£min	£max
Single	16.00	19.00
Double	29.00	31.00

Half board per person:	£min	£max
Daily	22.00	26.00
Weekly	142.00	170.00

Evening meal 1800 (last orders 1900)
Parking for 22
☸📺🍴♿⛰🛎🏊✕📺🚗∪♪✓❄🚗

Stoke Grange Farm
☸☸ COMMENDED

Chester Road, Nantwich CW5 6BT
☎ (01270) 625525
120-acre mixed & dairy farm. Attractive farmhouse dating from 1838. Spacious, en-suite bedrooms, comfortable lounge and games room. Splendid views. Cheshire Development Award winner 1991/92.
Bedrooms: 1 double, 2 twin
Bathrooms: 2 private, 1 public

Bed & breakfast per night:	£min	£max
Single	17.50	20.00
Double	35.00	40.00

Parking for 10
☸📺🍴♿⛰🛎🏊📺�🔌🚗⛳✓❄✕🚗

NORTHWICH

Cheshire
Map ref 4A2

An important salt-producing town since Roman times, Northwich has been replanned with a modern shopping centre and a number of black and white buildings. Unique Anderton boat-lift on northern outskirts of town.

Barratwich
Listed

Cuddington Lane, Cuddington, Northwich CW8 2SZ
☎ Sandiway (01606) 882412
Attractive cottage set in lovely countryside, yet only 1 mile from A49 and A556. Close to Delamere Forest, 12 miles from Chester. Comfortable rooms.
Bedrooms: 1 single, 2 twin
Bathrooms: 1 public

Bed & breakfast per night:	£min	£max
Single	16.00	16.00
Double	32.00	32.00

Half board per person:	£min	£max
Daily	25.00	25.00
Weekly	175.00	175.00

Evening meal 1900 (last orders 1400)
Parking for 4
☸3📺🍴♿⛰🛎🏊⛰🚗❄🚗🏧

Springfield Guest House ⋀
☸☸ COMMENDED

Chester Road, Delamere, Oakmere, Northwich CW8 2HB
☎ Sandiway (01606) 882538
Family guesthouse erected in 1863. On A556 close to Delamere Forest, midway between Chester and M6 motorway junction 19. Manchester Airport 25 minutes' drive.
Bedrooms: 4 single, 1 double, 1 twin, 1 family room
Bathrooms: 2 private, 1 public

Bed & breakfast per night:	£min	£max
Single	19.00	19.00
Double	35.00	35.00

Parking for 12
Open March-November and Christmas
☸📺♿⛰🛎🏊📺⛰❄✕🚗🏧

OLDHAM

Greater Manchester
Map ref 4B1

The magnificent mill buildings which made Oldham one of the world's leading cotton-spinning towns still dominate the landscape. Ideally situated on the edge of the Peak District, it is now a centre of culture, sport and shopping.
Tourist Information Centre
☎ *(0161) 627 1024*

Boothstead Farm
Listed COMMENDED

Rochdale Road, Denshaw, Oldham OL3 5UE
☎ Saddleworth (01457) 878622
200-acre livestock farm. 18th C farmhouse on fringe of Saddleworth (A640) between junctions 21 and 22 of M62 motorway.
Bedrooms: 1 double, 1 twin
Bathrooms: 1 public

Bed & breakfast per night:	£min	£max
Single	17.50	20.00
Double	34.00	38.00

Parking for 4
☸4🍴♿⛰📺⛰✕🚗🏧

PRESTON

Lancashire
Map ref 4A1

Scene of decisive Royalist defeat by Cromwell in the Civil War and later of riots in the Industrial Revolution. Local history exhibited in Harris Museum.
Tourist Information Centre
☎ *(01772) 253731*

Olde Duncombe House ⋀
☸☸☸ HIGHLY COMMENDED

Garstang Road, Bilsborrow, Preston PR3 0RE
☎ Brock (01995) 640336

Continued ▶

PRESTON

Continued

Traditional cottage-style bed and breakfast establishment set in rural surroundings alongside the picturesque Lancaster canal. 4 miles north of M6, junction 32.
Bedrooms: 5 double, 2 twin, 2 triple
Bathrooms: 9 private

Bed & breakfast

per night:	£min	£max
Single	29.50	32.50
Double	39.50	45.00

Lunch available
Evening meal 1800 (last orders 2030)
Parking for 12
Cards accepted: Access, Visa

Smithy Farm

`Listed`

Huntingdonhall Lane, Dutton,
Longridge, Preston PR3 2ZT
☎ Ribchester (01254) 878250
Set in the beautiful Ribble Valley, 20 minutes from the M6. Homely atmosphere, children half price.
Bedrooms: 2 double, 1 twin
Bathrooms: 1 public

Bed & breakfast

per night:	£min	£max
Single	15.00	
Double	25.00	

Half board

per person:	£min	£max
Daily	17.00	
Weekly	119.00	

Evening meal 1900 (last orders 2130)
Parking for 4

RIBBLE VALLEY

See under Clitheroe

ROCHDALE

Greater Manchester
Map ref 4B1

Pennine mill town made prosperous by wool and later cotton-spinning, famous for the Co-operative Movement started in 1844 by a group of Rochdale working men. Birthplace of John Bright (Corn Law opponent) and more recently Gracie Fields. Fine neo-Gothic town hall.
Tourist Information Centre
☎ (01706) 356592

Leaches Farm Bed and Breakfast

`Listed`

Leaches Farm, Ashworth Valley,
Rochdale, Lancashire OL11 5UN
☎ (01706) 41116/7 & 228520

140-acre livestock farm. 18th C Pennine hill farmhouse with panoramic views and moorland walks. 10 minutes from M62/M66.
Bedrooms: 1 single, 1 double, 1 twin
Bathrooms: 1 public

Bed & breakfast

per night:	£min	£max
Single	18.00	
Double	36.00	

Parking for 6

SADDLEWORTH

Greater Manchester
Map ref 4B1

The stone-built villages of Saddleworth are peppered with old mill buildings and possess a unique Pennine character. The superb scenery of Saddleworth Moor provides an ideal backdrop for canal trips, walking and outdoor pursuits.
Tourist Information Centre
☎ (01457) 870336 or 874093

Farrars Arms

56 Oldham Road, Grasscroft, Oldham OL4 4HL
☎ (01457) 872124
Old world public house with lots of character, in a lovely area of Saddleworth.
Bedrooms: 1 single, 1 double, 1 twin
Bathrooms: 1 public

Bed & breakfast

per night:	£min	£max
Single	20.00	25.00
Double	38.00	38.00

Lunch available
Evening meal 1700 (last orders 1930)
Parking for 23
Cards accepted: Access, Visa, Amex

Globe Farm Guest House

`COMMENDED`

Huddersfield Road, Standedge, Delph, Oldham OL3 5LU
☎ (01457) 873040
18-acre mixed farm. Quarter of a mile from the Pennine Way and high walking country. Bed and breakfast accommodation, 28-bed bunkhouse (self-catering or with meals) and small campsite.
Bedrooms: 3 single, 2 double, 1 twin, 1 triple
Bathrooms: 7 private

Bed & breakfast

per night:	£min	£max
Single	18.00	20.00
Double	35.00	38.00

Half board

per person:	£min	£max
Daily	24.00	26.00
Weekly	150.00	

Evening meal 1830 (last orders 1900)
Parking for 20
Cards accepted: Access, Visa

ST MICHAEL'S ON WYRE

Lancashire
Map ref 4A1

Village near Blackpool with interesting 13th C church of St Michael containing medieval stained glass window depicting sheep shearing, and clock tower bell made in 1548.

Compton House

`COMMENDED`

Garstang Road, St Michael's on Wyre, Preston PR3 0TE
☎ St. Michaels (01995) 679378
Fax (01995) 679378
Well-furnished country house in own grounds in a picturesque village, near M6 and 40 minutes from Lake District. Fishing in the Wyre. "Best-Kept Guesthouse" award 1995.
Bedrooms: 1 single, 1 double, 2 twin
Bathrooms: 4 private

Bed & breakfast

per night:	£min	£max
Single	17.50	
Double	35.00	

Parking for 6

SANDBACH

Cheshire
Map ref 4A2

Small Cheshire town, originally important for salt production. Contains narrow, winding streets, timbered houses and a cobbled market-place. Town square has 2 Anglo-Saxon crosses to commemorate the conversion to Christianity of the King of Mercia's son.

Canal Centre and Village Store

`Listed` `COMMENDED`

Hassall Green, Sandbach CW11 0YB
☎ Crewe (01270) 762266

The house and shop, built circa 1777 at the side of Lock 57 on the Trent and

Mersey Canal, have served canal users for over 200 years. Off A533 near Sandbach and junction 17 on M6 - signposted. Gift shop, tearooms, store and licensed restaurant (Tues-Sat from 7pm).
Wheelchair access category 3 ♿
Bedrooms: 1 single, 3 double, 2 twin
Bathrooms: 2 private, 1 public
Bed & breakfast

per night:	£min	£max
Single	16.00	18.00
Double	32.00	36.00

Lunch available
Evening meal 1900 (last orders 2130)
Parking for 7
Cards accepted: Access, Visa, Switch/Delta
🛇🔥🍽️📖♿👜🆔Ⓢ⊁🅿📺🖥️🚗❄🐎

Moss Cottage Farm
🛏️ HIGHLY COMMENDED
Hassall Road, Winterley, Sandbach CW11 0RU
☎ Crewe (01270) 583018
Beamed farmhouse in quiet location just off A534, with lovely walks, fishing and golf. All rooms have tea-making facilities and hand basins. Evening meals by arrangement.
Bedrooms: 1 single, 1 double, 1 twin
Bathrooms: 2 public
Bed & breakfast

per night:	£min	£max
Single	15.00	16.50
Double	30.00	33.00

Evening meal 1700 (last orders 2000)
Parking for 10
🛇📬♿🍵🖥️🅿🔌⊁🅿📺🖥️🚗❄🐎

SIDDINGTON
Cheshire
Map ref 4B2

Golden Cross Farm
🛏️🛏️
Siddington, Macclesfield SK11 9JP
☎ Marton Heath (01260) 224358
45-acre dairy farm. Beautiful old farmhouse in the heart of Cheshire countryside. Lots of character. Adjacent Siddington Church. Closed over Christmas and New Year period. Non-smokers preferred.
Bedrooms: 2 single, 2 double
Bathrooms: 1 private, 2 public
Bed & breakfast

per night:	£min	£max
Single	15.00	18.00
Double	30.00	36.00

Parking for 6
🛇👜🖥️⊁🅿📺🖥️🚗❄🏹🐎

> Establishments should be open throughout the year unless otherwise stated in the entry.

SINGLETON
Lancashire
Map ref 4A1

Ancient parish dating from 1175, mentioned in Domesday Book. Chapel and day school dating back to 1865. Mainly rural area to the north of St Anne's.

Old Castle Farm ⋀⋀
Listed APPROVED
Garstang Road, Singleton, Blackpool FY6 8ND
☎ Poulton-le-Fylde (01253) 883839
Take junction 3 off M55, follow Fleetwood sign to first traffic lights. Turn right, travel 200 yards on A586 to bungalow on the right.
Bedrooms: 1 double, 1 twin, 1 triple
Bathrooms: 1 public
Bed & breakfast

per night:	£min	£max
Single	15.00	
Double	30.00	

Parking for 20
Open April-October
🛇👜🖥️Ⓢ🅿📺🖥️🏹🐎

SOUTHPORT
Merseyside
Map ref 4A1

Delightful Victorian resort noted for its gardens, sandy beaches and six golf-courses, particularly Royal Birkdale. Attractions include the Atkinson Art Gallery, Southport Railway Centre, Pleasureland and the annual Southport Flower Show. Excellent shopping.
Tourist Information Centre
☎ *(01704) 533333*

Sandy Brook Farm ⋀⋀
🛏️🛏️ APPROVED
52 Wyke Cop Road, Scarisbrick, Southport PR8 5LR
☎ Scarisbrick (01704) 880337
27-acre arable farm. Small, comfortable farmhouse in rural area of Scarisbrick, offering a friendly welcome. 3.5 miles from seaside town of Southport.
Bedrooms: 1 single, 1 double, 2 twin, 1 triple, 1 family room
Bathrooms: 6 private
Bed & breakfast

per night:	£min	£max
Single	18.50	18.50
Double	31.00	31.00

Parking for 9
🛇👜♿🖥️Ⓢ📺🖥️🚗🐎

> Colour maps at the back of this guide pinpoint all places which have accommodation listings in the guide.

STOCKPORT
Greater Manchester
Map ref 4B2

Once an important cotton-spinning and manufacturing centre, Stockport has an impressive railway viaduct, a shopping precinct built over the River Mersey and Vernon Park Museum nearby. Lyme Hall and Vernon Park Museum nearby.
Tourist Information Centre
☎ *(0161) 474 3320 or 474 3321*

Needhams Farm ⋀⋀
🛏️🛏️🛏️ COMMENDED
Uplands Road, Werneth Low, Gee Cross, Hyde, Cheshire SK14 3AQ
☎ (0161) 368 4610
Fax (0161) 367 9106
30-acre beef farm. 500-year-old farmhouse with exposed beams in all rooms and an open fire in bar/dining room. Excellent views. Well placed for Manchester city and the airport.
Bedrooms: 1 single, 4 double, 1 twin, 1 triple
Bathrooms: 5 private, 1 public
Bed & breakfast

per night:	£min	£max
Single	17.00	19.00
Double	30.00	32.00

Half board

per person:	£min	£max
Daily	24.00	26.00

Lunch available
Evening meal 1900 (last orders 2130)
Parking for 12
Cards accepted: Access, Visa, Amex
🛇🐟📬📖♿🍵🔌🆔Ⓢ⊁🅿📺🖥️🚗
🍴📖❄🐎 OAP ⊠ SP 🏧 T

Northumbria House
🛏️ COMMENDED
35 Corbar Road, Stockport, Cheshire SK2 6EP
☎ (0161) 483 4000
Edwardian house set in a large garden in a quiet, residential area close to bus, rail stations and airport. Lots of tourist information. German and French spoken. Non-smokers only, please.
Bedrooms: 1 double, 1 twin
Bathrooms: 1 public
Bed & breakfast

per night:	£min	£max
Single	16.00	18.00
Double	30.00	34.00

Parking for 3
👜🔌🆔Ⓢ⊁🅿📺🖥️🚗❄🏹🐎

Shire Cottage Farmhouse ⋀⋀
🛏️🛏️ COMMENDED
Benches Lane, Chisworth, Hyde, Cheshire SK14 6RY
☎ Glossop (01457) 866536
180-acre mixed farm. Opposite Woodheys Restaurant off the A626 Stockport to Glossop road, close to the Peak District, Buxton, Derwent Dams ▸
Continued ▸

STOCKPORT

Continued

and Kinder Scout. 20 minutes from the airport, 16 miles from Manchester city centre. Swimming, horse riding, fishing and boating nearby.
Bedrooms: 1 single, 1 double, 1 twin, 1 triple
Bathrooms: 2 private, 2 public

Bed & breakfast

per night:	£min	£max
Single	17.00	24.00
Double	32.00	38.00

Parking for 7

🖚🛌🖵♨🖢🖵ⓘⓢ🅜📺🖩▣⌣✿
🚗 ᴼᴬᴾ ⌦ 🆂🅿

STYAL

Cheshire
Map ref 4B2

Willow Cottage 𝕄

♔ HIGHLY COMMENDED

56 Hollin Lane, Styal, Wilmslow
SK9 4JH
☎ Wilmslow (01625) 523630
Comfortable modern dormer bungalow set in rural surroundings yet convenient for motorways, airport, restaurants and Styal Country Park and Mill. Free transport to and from airport.
Bedrooms: 1 single, 1 twin
Bathrooms: 1 public

Bed & breakfast

per night:	£min	£max
Single	17.00	20.00
Double	34.00	38.00

Parking for 6
Cards accepted: Access, Visa
🖚3🖵🖵♨🖢🖵ⓤⓛ⌦📺🖩▣✿✈
🚗ⓣ

TARPORLEY

Cheshire
Map ref 4A2

Old town with gabled houses and medieval church of St Helen containing monuments to the Done family, a historic name in this area. Spectacular ruins of 13th C Beeston Castle nearby.

Swan Hotel at Tarporley 𝕄

♔♔♔ COMMENDED

50 High Street, Tarporley CW6 0AG
☎ (01829) 733838
Fax (01829) 732932

Historic Georgian coaching inn, attractively and traditionally furnished. High standard of food and warm welcome. Well-appointed bedrooms. Close to Oulton Park, the Oakland and Portal golf-courses. Also, walking on the Sandstone Trail.
Bedrooms: 3 single, 7 double, 10 twin
Bathrooms: 20 private

Bed & breakfast

per night:	£min	£max
Single	42.95	44.95
Double	47.95	52.95

Half board

per person:	£min	£max
Daily	40.00	56.95

Lunch available
Evening meal 1800 (last orders 2200)
Parking for 28
Cards accepted: Access, Visa, Amex
🖚🖧🖣🖵♨ⓘⓢ🖩▣🔱100🕴✿🆑
🆂🅿🏠

WILLINGTON

Cheshire
Map ref 4A2

Roughlow Farm

♔♔ COMMENDED

Willington, Tarporley CW6 0PG
☎ Kelsall (01829) 751199
Fax (01829) 751199
18th C sandstone farmhouse in idyllic situation with magnificent views to Shropshire and Wales. Elegant house with comfortable bedrooms, private bathrooms, large garden and tennis court. Very peaceful situation, 10 minutes from Chester.
Bedrooms: 3 twin
Bathrooms: 3 private

Bed & breakfast

per night:	£min	£max
Single	20.00	25.00
Double	40.00	50.00

Parking for 11

🖚6♨🖢ⓤⓛ⌦📺🖩▣⌫⌣🕴✿✈🚗

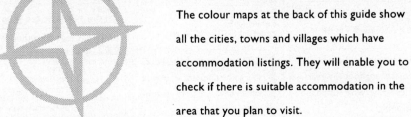

CHECK THE MAPS

The colour maps at the back of this guide show all the cities, towns and villages which have accommodation listings. They will enable you to check if there is suitable accommodation in the area that you plan to visit.

Yorkshire & Humberside

The high heather uplands of the North York Moors; the fells and chattering streams of the Dales; the wild landscapes of Brontë country – these are the region's great and lovely wildernesses. Here you can ramble, canoe, ride a steam railway, or simply find peace and solitude.

Not all of the region is high and wild, of course. There are quiet vales and rolling Wolds to be explored; and the coastline strung with pretty villages.

For buzzing excitement, visit the busy seaside resorts of Scarborough or Bridlington with all the family attractions anyone could dream of. Or pay a visit to some of the best museums in England – from fascinating industrial heritage sites, working mills and mines to the whizz-bang excitement of the Eureka museum.

The Counties of North Yorkshire, South Yorkshire, West Yorkshire and Humberside

For more information on Yorkshire & Humberside, contact:

Yorkshire & Humberside Tourist Board
312 Tadcaster Road, York YO2 2HF
Tel: (01904) 707961 or 707070
(24-hour brochure line)
Fax: (01904) 701414

Where to Go in Yorkshire & Humberside – see pages 92–95
Where to Stay in Yorkshire & Humberside – see pages 96–118

Yorkshire & Humberside

Where to go and what to see

You will find hundreds of interesting places to visit during your stay in Yorkshire & Humberside, just some of which are listed in these pages.

The number against each name will help you locate it on the map (page 95). Contact any Tourist Information Centre in the region for more ideas on days out in the Yorkshire & Humberside.

1 Scarborough Millennium
Harbourside, Scarborough, North Yorkshire YO11 1PG
Tel: (01723) 501000
A time-travel experience unlike any other. An epic adventure through 1,000 years from 966 to 1966.

2 North Yorkshire Moors Railway
Pickering Station, Pickering, North Yorkshire YO18 7AJ
Tel: (01751) 472508
18-mile railway through the magnificent scenery of the North York Moors National Park.

3 Flamingo Land Family Funpark, Zoo and Holiday Village
Kirby Misperton, North Yorkshire YO17 0UX
Tel: (01653) 668287
One-price family funpark with over 100 attractions, shows and Europe's largest privately-owned zoo.

4 Fountains Abbey and Studley Royal Park
Ripon, North Yorkshire HG4 3DZ
Tel: (01765) 608888
Largest monastic ruin in Britain, founded by Cistercian monks in 1132. Landscaped garden laid out 1720–40 with lake, formal watergarden and temples, deer park.

5 Dalby Forest Drive and Visitor Centre
Low Dalby, North Yorkshire YO18 7LS
Tel: (01751) 460295
9-mile scenic drive with picnic places, waymarked walks, wayfaring course. Visitor centre with forestry exhibition.

6 Castle Howard
Malton, North Yorkshire YO6 7DA
Tel: (01653) 648444
Set in 1,000 acres of parkland with nature walks, scenic lake and stunning rose gardens. Important furniture and works of art.

7 Eden Camp Modern History Theme Museum
Malton, North Yorkshire YO17 0SD
Tel: (01653) 697777
Modern history theme museum depicting civilian way of life in Britain during World War II. Based in a genuine ex-Prisoner of War camp with original buildings.

8 Sewerby Hall, Park and Zoo
Sewerby, Bridlington, North

Humberside YO15 1EA
Tel: (01262) 673769
Zoo, aviary, old English walled garden, bowls, putting, golf, children's corner, museum, art gallery, Amy Johnson collection, novel train from park to North Beach.

⑨ Yorkshire Dales Falconry and Conservation Centre
Crows Nest, Giggleswick, North Yorkshire LA2 8AS
Tel: (01729) 825164
Falconry centre with many species of birds of prey from around the world including vultures, eagles, hawks, falcons and owls. Free-flying displays, lecture room and aviaries.

⑩ Beningbrough Hall
Shipton-by-Beningbrough, York, North Yorkshire YO6 1DD
Tel: (01904) 470666
Handsome Baroque house built in 1716 with nearly 100 pictures from the National Portrait Gallery. Victorian laundry, potting shed, garden, adventure playground, National Trust shop.

⑪ Skipton Castle
Skipton, North Yorkshire BD23 1AQ
Tel: (01756) 792442
One of the most complete and well-preserved medieval castles in England. Beautiful Conduit Court with famous yew.

⑫ Bolton Abbey Estate
Bolton Abbey, North Yorkshire BD23 6EX
Tel: (01756) 710533
Ruins of 12th C priory in parkland setting by River Wharfe. Nature trails, fishing, fell walking in picturesque countryside.

⑬ Ripley Castle
Ripley, North Yorkshire HG3 3AY
Tel: (01423) 770152
Ingilby family home since 1345. Fine armour, furniture, chandeliers, panelling, priest's hiding hole.

⑭ Jorvik Viking Centre
Coppergate, York YO1 1NT
Tel: (01904) 643211
Visitors travel in electric cars down a time tunnel to a re-creation of Viking York. Excavated remains of Viking houses and display of objects found.

⑮ National Railway Museum
Leeman Road, York YO2 4XJ
Tel: (01904) 621261
Experience nearly 200 years of technical and social history of the railways and see how they shaped the world.

⑯ York Castle Museum
The Eye of York, York YO1 1RY
Tel: (01904) 653611
Popular museum of everyday life with reconstructed streets and period rooms, Edwardian park,

costume and jewellery, arms and armour, craft workshops.

⑰ York Minster
Deangate, York YO1 2JA
Tel: (01904) 624426
The largest Gothic cathedral in England. Museum of Saxon and Norman remains, chapter house and crypt. Unrivalled views from Norman tower.

⑱ Harewood House
Harewood, Leeds, West Yorkshire LS17 9LQ
Tel: (0113) 288 6225
18th C Carr/Adam house, Capability Brown landscape. Fine Sevres and Chinese porcelain, English and Italian paintings, Chippendale furniture. Exotic bird garden.

⑲ Leeds City Art Gallery and Henry Moore Centre
The Headrow, Leeds, West Yorkshire LS1 3AA
Tel: (0113) 247 8248
19th and 20th C paintings, sculptures, prints and drawings. Permanent collection of 20th C sculpture in Henry Moore Centre.

⑳ Tropical World
Canal Gardens, Roundhay Park, Leeds LS8 1DF
Tel: (0113) 266 1850
Greenhouses, butterfly house, tropical house, jungle experience, aquaria, insects and fish.

㉑ Museum of Army Transport
Beverley, Humberside HU17 ONG
Tel: (01482) 860445
*Army road, rail, sea and air exhibits
excitingly displayed in two exhibition
halls, plus the huge, last remaining
Blackburn Beverley aircraft. D-Day
exhibition.*

**㉒ National Museum of
Photography, Film and
Television**
Pictureville, Bradford, West
Yorkshire BD1 1NQ
Tel: (01274) 307610
*The largest cinema screen (Imax) in
Britain. Kodak Museum. Fly on a
magic carpet, operate TV camera,
become a newsreader for a day.*

㉓ Eureka!
Discovery Road, Halifax,
West Yorkshire HX1 2NE
Tel: (01422) 330069
*Designed especially for
children between 5 and 12
years of age. Visitors can
touch, listen and smell as well
as look at exhibitions about
the body, work and
communications.*

㉔ Piece Hall
Halifax, West Yorkshire
HX1 1RE
Tel: (01422) 358087
*Historic colonnaded cloth hall,
surrounding open-air
courtyard and comprising 40
speciality shops, art gallery,
weekly markets, new
Calderdale Kaleidoscope
display, Tourist Information
Centre.*

**㉕ Yorkshire Mining
Museum**
Caphouse Colliery, New
Road, Overton, Wakefield,
West Yorkshire WF4 4RH
Tel: (01924) 848806
Exciting award-winning
*museum of the Yorkshire coalfield,
including guided underground tour of
authentic old workings.*

㉖ Yorkshire Sculpture Park
Bretton, West Yorkshire WF4 4LG
Tel: (01924) 830302
*Beautiful parkland containing
regular exhibitions of contemporary
sculpture. Permanent collections
include work by Barbara Hepworth
and Henry Moore.*

㉗ Normanby Hall
Normanby, South Humberside
DN15 9HU
Tel: (01724) 720588
*Regency mansion by Sir Robert
Smirke, architect of British Museum.
Furnished and decorated in period,
with displays of costume.*

**㉘ National Fishing Heritage
Centre**
Alexandra Dock, Grimsby,
Humberside DN31 1UF
Tel: (01472) 344867
*Spectacular 1950s steam trawler
experience. See, hear, smell and
touch a series of re-created
environments. Museum displays,
aquarium, shop.*

**㉙ Cusworth Hall Museum of
South Yorkshire Life**
Cusworth Lane, Doncaster, South
Yorkshire DN5 7TU
Tel: (01302) 782342
*Georgian mansion in landscaped
park containing Museum of South
Yorkshire Life. Special educational
facilities.*

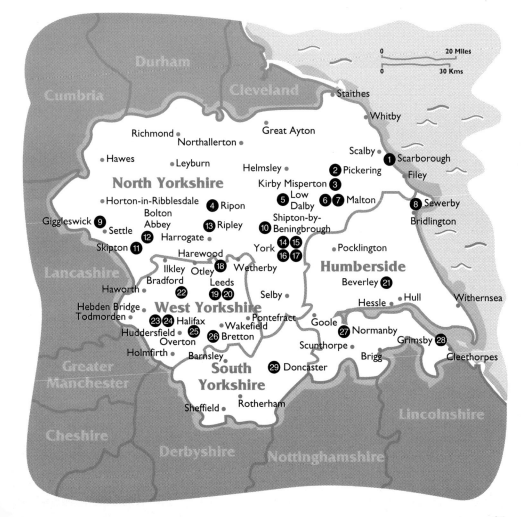

WHERE TO STAY

Accommodation entries in this regional section are listed in alphabetical order of place name, and then in alphabetical order of establishment.

Map references refer to the colour location maps at the back of this guide. The first figure is the map number; the letter and figure which follow indicate the grid reference on the map.

At-a-glance symbols at the end of each accommodation entry give information about services and facilities. A handy guide to these symbols can be found inside the back cover flap, which can be kept open for easy reference.

AMPLEFORTH

North Yorkshire
Map ref 5C3

Stone-built village in Hambleton Hills. Famous for its abbey and college, a Benedictine public school, founded in 1802, of which Cardinal Hume was once abbot.

Carr House Farm **M**

⚜️⚜️ COMMENDED

Shallowdale, Ampleforth, York
YO6 4ED
☎ Coxwold (01347) 868526
375-acre mixed farm. "Good food, welcome, walking" in peaceful "Herriot/Heartbeat" countryside. Romantic en-suite four-poster bedrooms. Just 30 minutes from York. Featured in the "Observer".
Bedrooms: 3 double
Bathrooms: 3 private

Bed & breakfast

per night:	£min	£max
Single	15.00	
Double	30.00	

Half board

per person:	£min	£max
Daily	23.00	

Evening meal 1800 (last orders 1800)
Parking for 3

🐾7🛏🏕🖥�TV🎒🚲U♪⭐ ✓❄✕🚜🏕T

The symbol **M** after an establishment name indicates membership of a Regional Tourist Board.

ASKRIGG

North Yorkshire
Map ref 5B3

The name of this dales village means "ash tree ridge". It is centred on a steep main street of high, narrow 3-storey houses and thrived on cotton and later wool in 18th C. Once famous for its clock making.

Home Farm

Listed HIGHLY COMMENDED

Stalling Busk, Askrigg, Leyburn
DL8 3DH
☎ Wensleydale (01969) 650360
65-acre mixed farm. Licensed 17th C beamed, dales farmhouse with log fires, beautiful Victorian and antique furnishings, brass bedsteads and patchwork quilts. Traditional cooking and home-made bread.
Bedrooms: 3 double
Bathrooms: 2 public

Bed & breakfast

per night:	£min	£max
Double	29.00	32.00

Half board

per person:	£min	£max
Daily	24.00	25.50

Evening meal 1900 (last orders 1800)
Parking for 4

🐾🛏️📺�⭐🖥�TV🎒🚲U✓❄🚜
OAP SP

Milton House **M**

⚜️⚜️

Askrigg, Leyburn DL8 3HJ
☎ Wensleydale (01969) 650217
Large, comfortable, family house in a beautiful dales village, central for touring or walking. Colour TV lounge and wholesome Yorkshire cooking.
Bedrooms: 3 double

Bathrooms: 3 private

Bed & breakfast

per night:	£min	£max
Double	37.00	

Half board

per person:	£min	£max
Daily	28.50	

Evening meal 1900 (last orders 1900)
Parking for 3

🐾🖥�📺🖥�TV🎒🚜❄

Thornsgill Guest House **M**

⚜️⚜️ HIGHLY COMMENDED

Moor Road, Askrigg, Leyburn
DL8 3HH
☎ Wensleydale (01969) 650617
Spacious, early 20th C family house in the Yorkshire Dales National Park. En-suite bedrooms. Wholesome Yorkshire food. Relaxed friendly atmosphere.
Bedrooms: 2 double, 1 twin
Bathrooms: 3 private

Bed & breakfast

per night:	£min	£max
Double	41.00	

Half board

per person:	£min	£max
Daily	33.50	

Evening meal from 1830
Parking for 3

🐾10🖥�📺�⭐🖥�TV🎒🚜❄🚜

The symbols ♿ ♿ ♿ indicate categories of accessibility for wheelchair users. They are explained in full in the information pages at the back of this guide.

AYSGARTH

North Yorkshire
Map ref 5B3

Famous for its beautiful Falls - a series of 3 cascades extending for half a mile on the River Ure in Wensleydale. There is a coach and carriage museum at Yore Mill and a National Park Centre.

Palmer Flatt Hotel ⚘

👑👑👑

Aysgarth, Leyburn DL8 3SR
☎ (01969) 663228
Fax (01969) 663182
Family-owned hotel offering guests a warm welcome, in the heart of Wensleydale, near Aysgarth Falls.
Bedrooms: 6 double, 2 twin, 1 family room
Bathrooms: 9 private
Bed & breakfast

per night:	£min	£max
Single	24.50	30.00
Double	45.00	55.00

Lunch available
Evening meal 1900 (last orders 2130)
Parking for 30
Cards accepted: Access, Visa
🛇🏵💷🖵♨🛀📶♿📺⁆🛏🍴30♦
🦮🌣🐾 SP 🏤

BEDALE

North Yorkshire
Map ref 5C3

Ancient church of St Gregory and Georgian Bedale Hall occupy commanding positions over this market town situated in good hunting country. The hall, which contains interesting architectural features including great ballroom and flying-type staircase, now houses a library and museum.

The Old Vicarage ⚘

Listed HIGHLY COMMENDED
Crakehall, Bedale DL8 1HE
☎ (01677) 422967

Georgian stone vicarage in pretty village, with charming gardens and herbacious plants for sale. Relax with tea and crumpets in front of the fire after walking the dales. Home-made preserves.
Bedrooms: 3 double, 2 twin
Bathrooms: 2 private, 1 public

Bed & breakfast

per night:	£min	£max
Single	25.00	35.00
Double	40.00	50.00

Parking for 10
🛇7💷🖵♨🛀🎱♿📺⁆📶♿🍴🦮
SP 🏤

BEVERLEY

Humberside
Map ref 4C1

Beverley's most famous landmark is its beautiful medieval Minster with Percy family tomb. Many attractive squares and streets, notably Wednesday and Saturday Market, North Bar Gateway and the Museum of Army Transport, Flemingate. Famous racecourse.
Tourist Information Centre
☎ *(01482) 867430 or 883898*

Eastgate Guest House ⚘

👑👑 COMMENDED
7 Eastgate, Beverley, North Humberside HU17 0DR
☎ Hull (01482) 868464
Fax (01482) 871899
Family-run Victorian guesthouse, established and run by the same proprietor for 27 years. Close to the town centre, Beverley Minster, Museum of Army Transport and railway station.
Bedrooms: 6 single, 3 double, 3 twin, 3 triple, 3 family rooms
Bathrooms: 7 private, 3 public
Bed & breakfast

per night:	£min	£max
Single	17.50	30.00
Double	30.00	44.00

🛇🏵🖵 UL S 🛁♿📺⁆📶♿🍴 DAP SP

BINGLEY

West Yorkshire
Map ref 4B1

Bingley Five-Rise is an impressive group of locks on the Leeds and Liverpool Canal. Town claims to have first bred the Airedale terrier originally used for otter hunting. Among fine Georgian houses is Myrtle Grove where John Wesley stayed. East Riddlesden Hall is nearby.

Five Rise Locks Hotel ⚘

👑👑👑 HIGHLY COMMENDED
Beck Lane, Bingley BD16 4DD
☎ Bradford (01274) 565296
Fax (01274) 568828
Newly renovated Victorian mill owner's house set in a quiet position in its own grounds. Relaxed atmosphere, varied menu and wine list. Prices are per room.
Bedrooms: 6 double, 3 twin
Bathrooms: 9 private

Bed & breakfast

per night:	£min	£max
Single	42.00	45.00
Double	42.00	45.00

Half board

per person:	£min	£max
Daily	30.00	34.00

Evening meal 1915 (last orders 2015)
Parking for 15
Cards accepted: Access, Visa, Switch/Delta
🛇🦮♿💷🖵♨🛀 S 🍴🛏📺⁆💷🛇
⁆20♦🅿🌣🍴📶 SP 🏤 T

BISHOP THORNTON

North Yorkshire
Map ref 5C3

Small village in Nidderdale, near Brimham Rocks.

Hatton House Farm

Listed HIGHLY COMMENDED
Colber Lane, Bishop Thornton, Harrogate HG3 3JA
☎ Harrogate (01423) 770315
150-acre dairy & livestock farm. Farmhouse accommodation with special emphasis on well-presented, home-cooked food. Open all year round. No smoking indoors, please.
Bedrooms: 2 double, 1 twin
Bathrooms: 1 public
Bed & breakfast

per night:	£min	£max
Single	18.00	22.00
Double	36.00	40.00

Evening meal 1830 (last orders 1800)
Parking for 10
🛇♨ UL 🛀 S 🍴🛏📺⁆💷🛇🙾🌣
🍴🦮

BISHOP WILTON

Humberside
Map ref 4C1

Village on the edge of the wolds, 5 miles east of Stamford Bridge.

Fleece Inn

👑👑
Bishop Wilton, York YO4 1RU
☎ (01759) 368251
Country inn in unspoilt village at foot of the wolds. Freehouse offering a variety of real ales, traditional meals and fine wines. Most bedrooms have tea and coffee making facilities.
Bedrooms: 2 double, 1 twin, 1 family room
Bathrooms: 4 private, 1 public
Bed & breakfast

per night:	£min	£max
Single	25.00	
Double	40.00	

Evening meal 1900 (last orders 2130)
Parking for 20
🛇🖵♨🛀🛏📺⁆📶🍴

BISHOP WILTON

Continued

High Belthorpe
📷 APPROVED

High Belthorpe, Bishop Wilton, York
YO4 1SB
☎ Stamford Bridge (01759) 368238
450-acre arable farm. Set on an ancient moated site in the Yorkshire Wolds, this large farmhouse has a private lake, extensive stabling and fabulous country walks.
Bedrooms: 1 double, 1 family room
Bathrooms: 1 public
Bed & breakfast

per night:	£min	£max
Single	16.12	

Evening meal 1800 (last orders 2000)
Parking for 3
🐕 🖤 ⓤⓛ 📺 ➡️ 🖉 ✿ 🐎 🏛

BRADFORD

West Yorkshire
Map ref 4B1

City founded on wool, with fine Victorian and modern buildings. Attractions include the cathedral, city hall, Cartwright Hall, Lister Park, Moorside Mills Industrial Museum and National Museum of Photography, Film and Television.
Tourist Information Centre
☎ *(01274) 753678*

Brow Top Farm
📷 HIGHLY COMMENDED

Baldwin Lane, Clayton, Bradford
BD14 6PS
☎ (01274) 882178
300-acre mixed farm. Newly renovated farmhouse.
Bedrooms: 2 double, 1 twin
Bathrooms: 3 private
Bed & breakfast

per night:	£min	£max
Single	20.00	20.00
Double	30.00	30.00

Parking for 4
🐕 🖵 🖤 ⓠ ⓤⓛ 📺 🖩 ➡️ ✿ ✕ 🐎

Carlton House Guest House
Listed

Thornton Road, Thornton, Bradford
BD13 3QE
☎ (01274) 833397
Detached, Victorian house in open countryside between the Bronte villages of Thornton and Haworth.
Bedrooms: 1 double, 1 twin, 1 triple
Bathrooms: 3 private
Bed & breakfast

per night:	£min	£max
Single	20.00	
Double	32.00	

Parking for 6
🐕 🖵 🖤 ⓠ ⓤⓛ 👜 ⓢ 🖩 ➡️ ✿ ✕ 🐎

Ivy Guest House ⋀
Listed

3 Melbourne Place, Bradford BD5 0HZ
☎ (01274) 727060
Large, detached, listed house built of Yorkshire stone. Close to city centre, National Museum of Photography, Film and Television and Alhambra Theatre.
Bedrooms: 3 single, 2 double, 4 twin, 1 triple
Bathrooms: 3 public
Bed & breakfast

per night:	£min	£max
Single	18.00	18.00
Double	30.00	30.00

Lunch available
Evening meal 1800 (last orders 2000)
Parking for 12
Cards accepted: Access, Visa, Diners, Amex, Switch/Delta
🐕 🖵 🖤 ⓤⓛ 👜 ⓢ 🖩 📺 🖩 ➡️ 📆20 ✿ ✕ 🖳 ✎ 🅢🅟 🏛 Ⓣ

BRAYTON

North Yorkshire
Map ref 4C1

Village south-west of Selby on the west bank of Selby Canal.

West Cottage ⋀
📷

Mill Lane, Brayton, Selby YO8 9LD
☎ Selby (01757) 213318
Always a warm welcome at this country cottage in a quiet location. Large garden, ample parking, convenient for York and with easy access to M62 and A1.
Bedrooms: 1 triple
Bathrooms: 1 private
Bed & breakfast

per night:	£min	£max
Single	18.00	24.00
Double	32.00	35.00

Parking for 5
🐕 📆12 🖵 🖤 ⓤⓛ ⓢ ✕ 🖩 📺 🖩 ➡️ ⚲ ↺ ✿ ✕ 🐎 🏛

BRIGG

Humberside
Map ref 4C1

Small town at an ancient crossing of the River Ancholme, granted a weekly Thursday market and annual horsefair by Henry III in 1235.
Tourist Information Centre
☎ *(01652) 657053*

Holcombe House ⋀
📷 COMMENDED

34 Victoria Road, Barnetby, South Humberside DN38 6JR
☎ Barnetby (01652) 680655 & Mobile 0850 764002
Pleasant, homely accommodation in centre of Barnetby village. 5 minutes from M180 and railway station, 3 miles

from Humberside Airport, 10 minutes from Brigg, 15-30 minutes from Grimsby, Scunthorpe and Hull.
Bedrooms: 3 single, 3 twin, 2 triple
Bathrooms: 4 private, 2 public, 1 private shower
Bed & breakfast

per night:	£min	£max
Single	15.00	25.00
Double	30.00	40.00

Half board

per person:	£min	£max
Daily	22.50	42.50
Weekly	157.50	297.50

Evening meal 1900 (last orders 2000)
Parking for 4
Cards accepted: Access, Visa
🐕 🅗 🖵 🖤 ⓤⓛ ⓢ 🅜 📺 🖩 ➡️ ✕ 🐎

COXWOLD

North Yorkshire
Map ref 5C3

This well-known beauty spot in Hambleton and Howardian Hills is famous as home of Laurence Sterne, the 18th C country parson and author of "Tristram Shandy" books who, in 1760, lived at Shandy Hall, now open to the public.

Wakendale House
📷 COMMENDED

Oldstead Grange, Coxwold, York
YO6 4BJ
☎ (01347) 868351
160-acre mixed farm. Comfortable accommodation with a friendly family in an attractive farmhouse set in lovely countryside. Ideal for walking and sightseeing.
Bedrooms: 1 double, 2 twin
Bathrooms: 1 public
Bed & breakfast

per night:	£min	£max
Double	30.00	32.00

Parking for 5
Open March-November
🐕 🖤 ⓤⓛ 📺 🖩 ➡️ ✿ ✕ 🐎

CROPTON

North Yorkshire
Map ref 5C3

Moorland village at the top of a high ridge with stone houses, some of cruck construction, a Victorian church and the remains of a 12th C moated castle. Cropton Forest nearby.

Burr Bank Cottage ⋀
📷 HIGHLY COMMENDED

Cropton, Pickering YO18 8HL
☎ Lastingham (01751) 417777
Fax (01751) 417777
Stone cottage in 50 acres with extensive views. Peaceful, well-appointed accommodation, a warm welcome and home cooking.

Bedrooms: 1 double, 1 twin
Bathrooms: 2 private

Bed & breakfast

per night:	£min	£max
Single	21.00	21.00
Double	42.00	42.00

Half board

per person:	£min	£max
Daily	33.00	33.00
Weekly	210.00	210.00

Evening meal 1900 (last orders 1900)
Parking for 10

🥾🛁📞🖭🖥♿🔍🐾 UL ⊁ Ħ TV 🛏 🅿 ∪ ✿ 🗙 🚲 SP Ħ T

New Inn ⋀⋀
😊😊😊 COMMENDED

Cropton, Pickering YO18 8HH
☎ Lastingham (01751) 417330
Fax (01751) 417310
*Character inn in picturesque village
setting. Warm welcome, good food,
comfortable en-suite accommodation.
Award-winning ales from own brewery.
Rural location, convenient for moors
and coast.*
Bedrooms: 5 double, 2 twin, 1 triple;
suite available
Bathrooms: 8 private

Bed & breakfast

per night:	£min	£max
Single	25.00	35.00
Double	45.00	53.00

Half board

per person:	£min	£max
Daily	35.00	

Lunch available
Evening meal 1800 (last orders 2100)
Parking for 30
Cards accepted: Access, Visa

🥾🖭♿ S ⊁ Ħ TV 🛏 🅿 ∱40 ♦∪ ✿🗙🚲🅂 SP

EASINGWOLD

North Yorkshire
Map ref 5C3

Market town of charm and
character with a cobbled square
and many fine Georgian buildings.

The George ⋀⋀
😊😊😊

Market Place, Easingwold, York
YO6 3AD
☎ (01347) 821698
Fax (01347) 823448
*18th C coaching inn overlooking
cobbled square in delightful Georgian
market town. 15 minutes from York,
moors. Good food. Cask beers.*
Bedrooms: 1 single, 6 double, 5 twin,
2 triple
Bathrooms: 14 private

Bed & breakfast

per night:	£min	£max
Single	30.00	40.00
Double	45.00	60.00

Half board

per person:	£min	£max
Daily	37.50	37.50
Weekly	245.00	

Lunch available
Evening meal 1900 (last orders 2130)
Parking for 9
Cards accepted: Access, Visa, Diners,
Amex, Switch/Delta

🥾🖭♿📞🖭♿🐾🅂⊁Ħ🛏🅿∱50▶
🗙🚲 DAP 🅂 SP Ħ

The Old Vicarage ⋀⋀
😊😊 COMMENDED

Market Place, Easingwold, York
YO6 3AL
☎ (01347) 821015
*Delightful 18th C country house with
extensive lawned gardens and croquet
lawn. In centre of market town, 12
miles north of York, and ideal as a
touring centre for North Yorkshire.*
Bedrooms: 1 single, 2 double, 2 twin
Bathrooms: 5 private

Bed & breakfast

per night:	£min	£max
Single	21.00	24.00
Double	38.00	42.00

Parking for 5
Open February-November

🥾🖭♿🐾 UL ⊁ Ħ 🛏 🅿 ▶✿🗙🚲Ħ

EBBERSTON

North Yorkshire
Map ref 5D3

Picturesque village with a Norman
church and hall, overlooking the
Vale of Pickering.

Studley House ⋀⋀
Listed

67 Main Street, Ebberston,
Scarborough YO13 9NR
☎ Scarborough (01723) 859285
*43-acre beef farm. Very clean,
comfortable farmhouse in picturesque
village. Full breakfast, central heating,
tea makers. Own keys. Central for
moors, forests, sea and York.*
Bedrooms: 1 single, 1 double, 1 triple
Bathrooms: 1 private, 1 public

Bed & breakfast

per night:	£min	£max
Single	14.00	17.00
Double	28.00	35.00

Parking for 4

🥾5 ♿ UL 🅰 🅂 ⊁ Ħ TV 🛏 🍽 🅿∪▶✿
🗙🚲

National gradings and
classifications were correct
at the time of going to
press but are subject to
change. Please check at the
time of booking.

ELLERBY

North Yorkshire
Map ref 5C3

Hamlet 3 miles south of Staithes.

Ellerby Hotel ⋀⋀
😊😊😊 COMMENDED

Ellerby, Saltburn-by-the-Sea, Cleveland
TS13 5LP
☎ Whitby (01947) 840342
Fax (01947) 841221
*Residential country inn within the
North York Moors National Park, 9
miles north of Whitby, 1 mile inland
from Runswick Bay.*
Wheelchair access category 3 ♿
Bedrooms: 5 double, 4 triple
Bathrooms: 9 private

Bed & breakfast

per night:	£min	£max
Single	32.00	35.00
Double	46.00	54.00

Lunch available
Evening meal 1900 (last orders 2200)
Parking for 60
Cards accepted: Access, Visa, Switch/
Delta

🥾🖭♿📞🖭♿🐾🅰🅂Ħ🛏🅿∱40▶
✿🚲 SP Ħ

FLAXTON

North Yorkshire
Map ref 5C3

Attractive village with broad
greens, just west of the A64 York
to Malton highway.

Grange Farm ⋀⋀
😊😊

Oak Busk Lane, Flaxton, York
YO6 7RL
☎ York (01904) 468219
*130-acre arable & livestock farm. South-
facing, modernised farmhouse in its
own gardens. 8 miles from York, off the
A64 York to Scarborough road, through
Flaxton village and right down Oak
Busk Lane.*
Bedrooms: 2 double, 1 twin
Bathrooms: 1 private, 1 public

Bed & breakfast

per night:	£min	£max
Double	28.00	32.00

Parking for 10

🥾♿ UL 🅂 Ħ TV 🛏 🅿 ∕✿🗙🚲

The symbols ♿ ♿ ♿
indicate categories of
accessibility for wheelchair
users. They are explained in
full in the information pages
at the back of this guide.

GARFORTH

West Yorkshire
Map ref 4B1

Town 7 miles east of Leeds, between Temple Newsam Estate and Lotherton Hall.

Myrtle House ⋔
Listed
31 Wakefield Road, Garforth, Leeds LS25 1AN
☎ Leeds (0113) 286 6445
Spacious Victorian terraced house between M62 and A1. All rooms have tea and coffee making facilities, TV and vanity basins.
Bedrooms: 1 single, 1 double, 3 twin, 1 triple
Bathrooms: 3 public
Bed & breakfast

per night:	£min	£max
Single	15.00	
Double	30.00	

🛇🖵♿ⅧⅢ▦🚗✿🚐

GILLAMOOR

North Yorkshire
Map ref 5C3

Village much admired by photographers for its views of Farndale, including "Surprise View" from the churchyard.

Royal Oak Inn ⋔
COMMENDED
Gillamoor, York YO6 6HX
☎ Kirkbymoorside (01751) 431414
Old country inn on the edge of the North York Moors. Tastefully renovated, with plenty of character and charm. Open log fires.
Bedrooms: 5 double, 1 twin
Bathrooms: 6 private
Bed & breakfast

per night:	£min	£max
Single	25.00	34.00
Double	40.00	50.00

Lunch available
Evening meal 1900 (last orders 2100)
Parking for 9
🛇10🔌🖵♿🏴🖇️🔒Ⓢ✁Ⅲ✈🚐
🅂🅿🎣

GOLCAR

West Yorkshire
Map ref 4B1

Pennine hillside village. Colne Valley Museum - restored weavers' cottages of the 1840s.

14 Grandstand ⋔
Listed
Scapegoat Hill, Golcar, Huddersfield HD7 4NQ
☎ Huddersfield (01484) 658342
Yorkshire stone-built cottage in quiet Pennine village. Panoramic views.

Spacious, comfortable rooms with double glazing, central heating and colour TV. Excellent pub nearby.
Bedrooms: 1 double, 1 twin
Bathrooms: 2 public
Bed & breakfast

per night:	£min	£max
Single	16.00	18.00
Double	32.00	36.00

Evening meal from 1800
Parking for 2
🛇🖾🖇️🖵♿🏴🖇️🔒Ⓢ📺Ⅲ🚗🚐

GRASSINGTON

North Yorkshire
Map ref 5B3

Tourists visit this former lead-mining village to see its "smiddy", antique and craft shops and Upper Wharfedale Museum of country trades. Popular with fishermen and walkers. Numerous prehistoric sites. Grassington Feast in October. National Park Centre.

Clarendon Hotel ⋔
COMMENDED
Hebden, Grassington, Skipton BD23 5DE
☎ Skipton (01756) 752446
Yorkshire Dales village inn serving good food and ales. Personal supervision at all times. Steaks and fish dishes are specialities.
Bedrooms: 2 double, 1 twin
Bathrooms: 3 private
Bed & breakfast

per night:	£min	£max
Double	40.00	50.00

Lunch available
Evening meal 1900 (last orders 2100)
Parking for 30
🛇12🖵♿🔒ⓈⅢ✈🚐

Foresters Arms Hotel ⋔
Listed
20 Main Street, Grassington, Skipton BD23 5AA
☎ (01756) 752349
Formerly an old coaching inn, situated in picturesque village, serving lunch and evening meals and hand-pulled ales.
Bedrooms: 1 single, 4 double, 2 triple
Bathrooms: 1 private, 2 public
Bed & breakfast

per night:	£min	£max
Single	16.00	20.00
Double	32.00	50.00

Lunch available
Evening meal 1800 (last orders 2030)
Parking for 2
🛇🖵♿🔒📺🚗🔍🚐

Franor House
☺☺
3 Wharfeside Avenue, Threshfield, Skipton BD23 5BS
☎ (01756) 752115
Large semi-detached house in quiet surroundings. Take B6265 from

---

Skipton, turning right for Grassington. Wharfeside Avenue is half a mile - first turning on left.
Bedrooms: 1 single, 1 twin, 1 triple
Bathrooms: 3 private
Bed & breakfast

per night:	£min	£max
Single	17.00	18.00
Double	32.00	36.00

Parking for 4
🛇🖵♿Ⅷ🔒Ⅲ🚗🖑🎣🏹✿✕🚐

Grange Cottage ⋔
HIGHLY COMMENDED
Linton, Skipton BD23 5HH
☎ (01756) 752527
Stone-built cottage with open fires and warm hospitality. In a quiet backwater of a picture postcard village, perfect for hiking and car touring in the dales.
Bedrooms: 1 double, 1 twin
Bathrooms: 1 public, 1 private shower
Bed & breakfast

per night:	£min	£max
Single	20.00	25.00
Double	35.00	37.50

Parking for 4
Open March-October
🛇🖾♿🏴Ⅷ🔒Ⓢ✁🏴Ⅲ🚗✿🚐

New Laithe House ⋔
☺☺
Wood Lane, Grassington, Skipton BD23 5LU
☎ (01756) 752764
Situated in a quiet location. An ideal base for walking or fishing and for visiting the many historic towns in North and West Yorkshire.
Bedrooms: 3 double, 2 twin, 1 triple
Bathrooms: 5 private, 1 private shower
Bed & breakfast

per night:	£min	£max
Double	38.00	42.00

Parking for 8
🛇🖾🖵♿Ⅷ🔒ⓈⅢ🚗✿✕🚐🅂🅿

HALIFAX

West Yorkshire
Map ref 4B1

Founded on the cloth trade, and famous for its building society, textiles, carpets and toffee. Most notable landmark is Piece Hall where wool merchants traded, now restored to house shops, museums and art gallery. Home also to Eureka! The Museum for Children.
Tourist Information Centre
☎ *(01422) 368725*

Beech Court
Listed
40 Prescott Street, Halifax HX1 2QW
☎ (01422) 366004
Late Victorian residence, just off the town centre. Well furnished and decorated, with emphasis on high standards and good service.
Bedrooms: 1 single, 1 twin, 1 triple

Bathrooms: 2 public

Bed & breakfast

per night:	£min	£max
Single	18.00	18.00
Double	34.00	34.00

Parking for 3

⛺🚪♨♿🛈🍴�(?) 🚗🚲 SP

The Elms

♨♨

Keighley Road, Illingworth, Halifax HX2 8HT

☎ (01422) 244430

Victorian residence with gardens and original ornate ceilings, within 3 miles of Halifax.

Bedrooms: 2 single, 1 double, 1 triple

Bathrooms: 2 private, 1 public

Bed & breakfast

per night:	£min	£max
Single	18.00	18.50
Double	36.00	37.00

Half board

per person:	£min	£max
Daily	26.00	27.00

Evening meal 1800 (last orders 2000)

Parking for 14

⛺🍴🚪♨♿🛈🅂🅿📺🍴🚗🍽✿ 🚲 SP

HARPHAM

Humberside
Map ref 5D3

St Quintin Arms Inn ♨

Listed COMMENDED

Main Street, Harpham, Driffield, North Humberside YO25 0QY

☎ Burton Agnes (01262) 490329

Comfortable, spaciously furnished, family-run country inn, providing home-cooked food, three quarters of a mile off the A166. Between Driffield and Bridlington.

Bedrooms: 2 double, 1 twin

Bathrooms: 3 private, 1 public

Bed & breakfast

per night:	£min	£max
Single	22.50	22.50
Double	37.00	40.00

Half board

per person:	£min	£max
Daily	30.00	40.00
Weekly	161.00	230.00

Lunch available

Evening meal 1900 (last orders 2130)

Parking for 32

Cards accepted: Access, Visa

⛺🏤🚪♨🛈🅂🍴🚗🍽30🍷✿🚲

> The National Grading and Classification Scheme is explained in full at the back of this guide.

HARROGATE

North Yorkshire
Map ref 4B1

A major conference, exhibition and shopping centre, renowned for its spa heritage and award winning floral displays, spacious parks and gardens. Famous for antiques, toffee, fine shopping and excellent tea shops, also its Royal Pump Rooms and Baths.

Tourist Information Centre
☎ *(01423) 525666*

Alamah ♨

♨♨ COMMENDED

88 Kings Road, Harrogate HG1 5JX

☎ (01423) 502187

Fax (01423) 566175

Comfortable rooms, personal attention, friendly atmosphere and full English breakfast. 300 metres from town centre. Garages/parking.

Bedrooms: 2 single, 2 double, 2 twin, 1 family room

Bathrooms: 5 private, 2 private showers

Bed & breakfast

per night:	£min	£max
Single	22.00	24.00
Double	42.00	46.00

Half board

per person:	£min	£max
Daily	36.00	

Evening meal 1830 (last orders 1400)

Parking for 8

⛺⛺3🚪♨♿🛈🅂🅿🍴🚗🚲 SP T

Anro ♨

♨♨ COMMENDED

90 Kings Road, Harrogate HG1 5JX

☎ (01423) 503087

In a central position, 2 minutes from the conference centre and near Valley Gardens, town, bus and rail stations. Ideal for touring the dales. Home cooking.

Bedrooms: 3 single, 1 double, 2 twin, 1 family room

Bathrooms: 4 private, 1 public

Bed & breakfast

per night:	£min	£max
Single	19.50	
Double	39.00	

Half board

per person:	£min	£max
Daily	30.00	

Evening meal 1815 (last orders 1630)

⛺7🚪♨♿🅂🅿📺🍴🚗🍽🚲 SP

The Belfry

Listed

27 Belmont Road, Harrogate HG2 0LR

☎ (01423) 522783

Friendly, family guesthouse within easy walking distance of the town centre and all tourist amenities. A wide choice of cooked breakfast is offered.

Bedrooms: 2 single, 1 double, 1 twin

Bathrooms: 1 public

Bed & breakfast

per night:	£min	£max
Single	15.50	16.00
Double	30.00	30.00

⛺🏤🚪♨♿🛈🅂🍴🚗🍽🚲

Crescent Lodge ♨

♨♨ COMMENDED

20 Swan Road, Harrogate HG1 2SA

☎ (01423) 503688

Elegant and well-appointed town house, welcoming a maximum of 6 guests. Quiet, yet close to all amenities. Grade II listed.

Bedrooms: 2 single, 2 twin

Bathrooms: 2 private, 1 public

Bed & breakfast

per night:	£min	£max
Single	21.00	31.00
Double	46.00	46.00

Parking for 2

♨♿🅂🅿📺🍴🚗✿🍽🚲🎏

Knabbs Ash ♨

♨♨ HIGHLY COMMENDED

Skipton Road, Felliscliffe, Harrogate HG3 2LT

☎ (01423) 771040

Fax (01423) 771515

Set back off the A59 Harrogate to Skipton road, 6 miles west of Harrogate, in its own grounds. In a panoramic, tranquil setting. Ideal area for walking and exploring the Yorkshire Dales. Winner of White Rose Award for Tourism, 1995.

Bedrooms: 2 double, 1 twin

Bathrooms: 3 private

Bed & breakfast

per night:	£min	£max
Single	25.00	25.00
Double	40.00	40.00

Parking for 6

⛺10🚪♨♿🅂🅿📺🍴U✿🍽🚲 DAP

17 Peckfield Close ♨

🏠 APPROVED

Hampsthwaite, Harrogate HG3 2ES

☎ (01423) 770765

In picturesque village 4 miles from Harrogate off A59. Large, attractive garden. At start of Nidderdale Walk.

Bedrooms: 1 single, 2 twin

Bathrooms: 1 public

Bed & breakfast

per night:	£min	£max
Single	14.00	16.00
Double	28.00	32.00

Continued ▶

HARROGATE

Continued

Half board

per person:	£min	£max
Daily	19.00	21.00
Weekly	133.00	147.00

Parking for 2

HAWES

North Yorkshire
Map ref 5B3

The capital of Upper Wensleydale on the famous Pennine Way, renowned for great cheeses. Popular with walkers. Dales National Park Information Centre and Folk Museum. Nearby is spectacular Hardraw Force waterfall.

East House ▲
Gayle, Hawes DL8 3RZ
☎ Wensleydale (01969) 667405
Detached house in a quiet position, overlooking the fells. Ideal centre for touring or walking the dales.
Bedrooms: 1 single, 1 twin, 2 triple
Bathrooms: 2 private, 1 public

Bed & breakfast

per night:	£min	£max
Single	15.50	15.50
Double	31.00	35.00

Parking for 3
Open March-October

Ebor Guest House ▲
Burtersett Road, Hawes DL8 3NT
☎ Wensleydale (01969) 667337
Small, family-run guesthouse, double-glazed and centrally-heated throughout. Walkers are particularly welcome. Centrally located for touring the dales.
Bedrooms: 1 single, 2 double, 1 twin
Bathrooms: 2 private, 1 public

Bed & breakfast

per night:	£min	£max
Single	15.00	17.00
Double	34.00	36.00

Parking for 5

Springbank House ▲
COMMENDED
Springbank, Townfoot, Hawes
DL8 3NW
☎ Wensleydale (01969) 667376
Delightful Victorian house near the centre of Hawes with superb views over the surrounding fells.
Bedrooms: 2 triple
Bathrooms: 2 private

Bed & breakfast

per night:	£min	£max
Double	32.00	34.00

Parking for 3
Open February-October

Tarney Fors Farmhouse ▲
COMMENDED
Tarney Fors, Hawes DL8 3LY
☎ Wensleydale (01969) 667475

Grade II listed building. Former dales farmhouse situated in open countryside, yet with easy access. In heart of Dales National Park. Lunches and cream teas available. Parking.
Bedrooms: 2 double, 1 twin
Bathrooms: 3 private, 1 public

Bed & breakfast

per night:	£min	£max
Single	27.00	35.00
Double	44.00	50.00

Half board

per person:	£min	£max
Daily	35.50	45.00
Weekly	200.00	260.00

Lunch available
Evening meal from 1900
Parking for 9
Open March-October
Cards accepted: Access, Visa

White Hart Inn ▲
Main Street, Hawes DL8 3QL
☎ Wensleydale (01969) 667259
17th C coaching inn with a friendly welcome, offering traditional fare. Open fires, Yorkshire ales. Central for exploring the dales.
Bedrooms: 1 single, 4 double, 2 twin
Bathrooms: 2 public

Bed & breakfast

per night:	£min	£max
Single	17.50	
Double	35.00	

Lunch available
Evening meal 1900 (last orders 2100)
Parking for 7
Cards accepted: Access, Visa, Amex

All accommodation in this guide has been graded, or is awaiting a grading, by a trained Tourist Board inspector.

HAWORTH

West Yorkshire
Map ref 4B1

This Pennine town is famous as home of the Bronte family. The parsonage is now a Bronte Museum where furniture and possessions of the family are displayed. Moors and Bronte waterfalls nearby and steam trains on the Keighley and Worth Valley Railway pass through.
Tourist Information Centre
☎ *(01535) 642329*

Ashmount ▲
Mytholmes Lane, Haworth, Keighley
BD22 8EZ
☎ Keighley (01535) 645726
Victorian Gothic villa with half acre of garden. Outstanding views across Haworth and the moors. Three hundred yards from the village centre.
Bedrooms: 3 double, 3 twin; suite available
Bathrooms: 6 private

Bed & breakfast

per night:	£min	£max
Single	25.00	25.00
Double	35.00	35.00

Half board

per person:	£min	£max
Daily	27.50	39.00
Weekly	154.00	218.00

Evening meal 1800 (last orders 2000)
Parking for 6
Cards accepted: Access, Visa, Amex

Ebor House
APPROVED
Lees Lane, Haworth, Keighley
BD22 8RA
☎ Keighley (01535) 645869
Yorkshire stone-built house of character, conveniently placed for the main tourist attractions of Haworth, including the Worth Valley Railway and Bronte Parsonage and Museum.
Bedrooms: 3 twin
Bathrooms: 1 public

Bed & breakfast

per night:	£min	£max
Single		15.00
Double		28.00

Parking for 2

Hole Farm
COMMENDED
Dimples Lane, Haworth, Keighley
BD22 8QS
☎ Keighley (01535) 644755
8-acre smallholding. 17th C farmhouse, five minutes' walk from Bronte Parsonage and two minutes' walk from the moors. Panoramic views of Haworth. Farm has pigs, peacocks, geese, cattle and horses.
Bedrooms: 2 double
Bathrooms: 2 private

Bed & breakfast

per night:	£min	£max
Single		25.00
Double		36.00

Parking for 4

📼🖳⌨🖩ⓊⓁⓢ✠🛏️🎱Ｕ❄✕🍴

The Lee

Listed | **COMMENDED**

Lee Lane, Oxenhope, Keighley
BD22 9RB
☎ (01535) 646311
*Detached 17th C house with 6 acres of
land, 1.5 miles from the centre of
Haworth. Close to moors and waterfalls.*
Bedrooms: 1 double, 1 triple
Bathrooms: 2 private

Bed & breakfast

per night:	£min	£max
Single	16.00	20.00
Double	32.00	32.00

Parking for 4

🛏️4📼🖳🖩ⓊⓁ🎱 TV🎱❄🍴 DAP🏠

Old White Lion Hotel ⚑

😀😀😀😀 | **COMMENDED**

Haworth, Keighley BD22 8DU
☎ Keighley (01535) 642313
Fax (01535) 646222
*Family-run, centuries old coaching inn.
Candlelit restaurant using local fresh
produce, cooked to order and featured
in good food guides. Old world bars,
popular with locals, serving home-made
bar meals and traditional ales.*
Bedrooms: 3 single, 8 double, 1 twin,
2 triple
Bathrooms: 14 private

Bed & breakfast

per night:	£min	£max
Single	38.00	43.00
Double	50.00	60.00

Half board

per person:	£min	£max
Daily	37.50	55.50

Lunch available
Evening meal 1900 (last orders 2200)
Parking for 8
Cards accepted: Access, Visa, Diners,
Amex

🛏️📞📼🖳🖩🏠🎱 TV🖩🖩🎱🕯60✕
SP🏠

The symbol 🎯 within an
entry indicates participation
in the Welcome Host
programme – a nationally
recognised customer care
initiative which aims to
promote the highest
standards of service and a
warm welcome for all visitors.

HEBDEN BRIDGE

West Yorkshire
Map ref 4B1

Originally a small town on
packhorse route, Hebden Bridge
grew into a booming mill town in
18th C with rows of "up-and-down"
houses of several storeys built
against hillsides. Ancient "pace-
egg play" custom held on Good
Friday.
Tourist Information Centre
☎ *(01422) 843831*

Robin Hood Inn ⚑

Listed | **APPROVED**

Pecket Well, Hebden Bridge HX7 8QR
☎ (01422) 842593
*Traditional inn on the edge of
Calderdale and Pennine Way, Bronte
country, Hardcastle Crags. Near Hebden
Bridge. Real ale and home-made food.*
Bedrooms: 1 single, 1 double, 1 twin,
1 triple, 1 family room
Bathrooms: 1 private, 2 public

Bed & breakfast

per night:	£min	£max
Single	16.50	22.50
Double	33.00	39.50

Half board

per person:	£min	£max
Daily	21.00	27.50
Weekly	95.00	140.00

Lunch available
Evening meal 1700 (last orders 2130)
Parking for 28
Cards accepted: Visa, Switch/Delta

🛏️📼🖳🖩🏠ⓢ✠🖩🏠🎱▶❄🎱
DAP🎱SP🏠

HELLIFIELD

North Yorkshire
Map ref 4B1

Dales village on the edge of the
Yorkshire Dales National Park, 5
miles south-east of Settle.

Wenningber Farm ⚑

😀 | **HIGHLY COMMENDED**

Airton Road, Hellifield, Skipton
BD23 4JR
☎ (01729) 850856
*80-acre mixed farm. Charming
farmhouse, with log fire and oak beams,
just 5 miles from Malham in the heart
of the Yorkshire Dales.*
Bedrooms: 1 double, 1 twin
Bathrooms: 1 public

Bed & breakfast

per night:	£min	£max
Single	18.00	24.00
Double	34.00	36.00

Parking for 10

🛏️📼🖳🖩ⓊⓁⓢ✠🖩🖩🖩Ｕ▶❄
🎱🏠

HELMSLEY

North Yorkshire
Map ref 5C3

Pretty town on the River Rye at
the entrance to Ryedale and the
North York Moors, with large
square and remains of 12th C
castle, several inns and All Saints'
Church.

Mount Grace Farm ⚑

😀😀 | **COMMENDED**

Cold Kirby, Thirsk YO7 2HL
☎ Thirsk (01845) 597389

*120-acre mixed farm. Traditional stone
farmhouse in North York Moors
National Park. Peaceful location west of
Helmsley. Ideal touring/walking. Easy
access A1.*
Bedrooms: 1 double, 2 twin
Bathrooms: 3 private

Bed & breakfast

per night:	£min	£max
Single	18.00	25.00
Double	40.00	50.00

Half board

per person:	£min	£max
Daily	30.00	35.00
Weekly	186.00	200.00

Evening meal from 1800
Parking for 6

🛏️📼🖳🖩ⓊⓁ🏠ⓢ✠🖩 TV🖩🖩🎱Ｔ Ｕ▶
✓❄✕🎱SP

Stilworth House

😀😀 | **COMMENDED**

1 Church Street, Helmsley, York
YO6 5AD
☎ (01439) 771072 & 770507
*Comfortable relaxed atmosphere in
elegant Georgian town house off the
market square of Helmsley. Pretty en-
suite rooms, colour TV, tea/coffee
facilities. Private car park.*
Bedrooms: 3 double, 1 triple
Bathrooms: 4 private

Bed & breakfast

per night:	£min	£max
Double	35.00	45.00

Evening meal from 1830
Parking for 4

🛏️🖳📼🖳🖩ⓊⓁⓢ🖩 TV🖩🎱❄✕
🎱SP

Valley View Farm ⚑

😀😀 | **HIGHLY COMMENDED**

Old Byland, York YO6 5LG
☎ (01439) 798221
*230-acre mixed farm. Friendly, family-
run, relaxed and peaceful. 5 miles from*

Continued ▶

HELMSLEY

Continued

Helmsley. Beautiful views, home cooking, new en-suite accommodation. Brochure available.
Bedrooms: 1 double, 2 twin, 1 family room
Bathrooms: 4 private

Bed & breakfast

per night:	£min	£max
Double	44.00	54.00

Half board

per person:	£min	£max
Daily	34.00	39.00

Evening meal from 1900
Parking for 4
Cards accepted: Access, Visa
🏠🛍️💻📞🥂🍴§📺📺🖩 🛏️∪✓❀
🚲🐾SP

HOLMFIRTH

West Yorkshire
Map ref 4B1

This village has become famous as the location for the filming of the TV series "Last of the Summer Wine". It has a postcard museum and is on the edge of the Peak District National Park.
Tourist Information Centre
☎ *(01484) 687603*

Spring Head House ⋀
Listed

15 Holmfirth Road, Shepley, Huddersfield HD8 8BB
☎ Huddersfield (01484) 606300
Fax (01484) 608030
Large Georgian house with a garden, close to Holmfirth and "Summer Wine" country and with easy access to the M1 and M62.
Bedrooms: 1 single, 1 twin
Bathrooms: 1 private, 1 public

Bed & breakfast

per night:	£min	£max
Single	17.00	22.00
Double	33.00	33.00

Parking for 3
Cards accepted: Access, Visa
🏠🛍️💻📺🖩🛏️❀✕🚲

29 Woodhead Road
COMMENDED

Holmfirth, Huddersfield HD7 1JU
☎ (01484) 683962
200-year-old family home, 5 minutes' walk from Holmfirth. Tea and coffee available at any time. Good walking area and pleasant countryside.
Bedrooms: 1 twin
Bathrooms: 1 private

Bed & breakfast

per night:	£min	£max
Single	13.50	14.00
Double	27.00	28.00

Parking for 2
📞📠💻🐾🖩🛏️✕🚲

HOOTON PAGNELL

South Yorkshire
Map ref 4C1

Rock Farm
🏠

Hooton Pagnell, Doncaster DN5 7BT
☎ Pontefract (01977) 642200
200-acre mixed farm. Traditional farmhouse in an unspoilt, picturesque stone village on the B6422, 6 miles north-west of Doncaster and 1.5 miles west of the A1.
Bedrooms: 1 single, 1 family room
Bathrooms: 1 private, 1 public

Bed & breakfast

per night:	£min	£max
Single	16.00	20.00
Double	30.00	40.00

Parking for 20
🏠💻🐾🖩📞🍴📺🖩🛏️❀✕🚲🏰

HUDDERSFIELD

West Yorkshire
Map ref 4B1

Founded on wool and cloth, has a famous choral society. Town centre redeveloped, but several good Victorian buildings remain, including railway station, St Peter's Church, Tolson Memorial Museum, art gallery and nearby Colne Valley Museum.
Tourist Information Centre
☎ *(01484) 430808*

White House ⋀
🏠

Holthead, Slaithwaite, Huddersfield HD7 5TY
☎ (01484) 842245
Fax (01484) 842245
Lovely 18th C inn with traditional ale and comfortable en-suite accommodation. Notable cuisine in warm and friendly surroundings. In the country, only 4 miles from Huddersfield on the B6107 Meltham to Marsden road.
Bedrooms: 1 single, 6 double, 1 twin
Bathrooms: 6 private, 1 public

Bed & breakfast

per night:	£min	£max
Single	17.50	20.00
Double	38.00	40.00

Half board

per person:	£min	£max
Daily	26.50	60.00

Lunch available
Evening meal 1800 (last orders 2130)
Parking for 100
Cards accepted: Access, Visa, Diners, Amex
🏠📪💻🐾🍴§🖩📞🛎️▶🚲🚲SP🏰

HUNTON

North Yorkshire
Map ref 5C3

Typical dales village 5 miles east of Leyburn.

The Countryman's Inn
🏠🏠🏠 COMMENDED

Hunton, Bedale DL8 1PY
☎ Bedale (01677) 450554 & Mobile 0850 863153
Modernised village inn and restaurant, retaining its old world charm, with log fires and beamed ceilings. Four-poster room. Just off A684 between Bedale and Leyburn, convenient for Yorkshire Dales.
Bedrooms: 6 double, 1 twin
Bathrooms: 7 private

Bed & breakfast

per night:	£min	£max
Single	30.00	35.00
Double	45.00	60.00

Evening meal 1900 (last orders 2130)
Parking for 20
Cards accepted: Access, Visa, Amex
🖾💻🐾§🖩✕🖩📞🍴∪▶❀✕🚲SP

HUSTHWAITE

North Yorkshire
Map ref 5C3

Attractive village beneath Hambleton Hills, of weathered brickwork houses and a green dominated by medieval church of St Nicholas with some Norman features.

Flower of May
Listed

Husthwaite, York YO6 3SG
☎ Coxwold (01347) 868317
153-acre mixed farm. Family-run farm with beautiful views of the Vale of York. Convenient for North York Moors, York and coast.
Bedrooms: 1 single, 1 double, 1 twin
Bathrooms: 1 public

Bed & breakfast

per night:	£min	£max
Single	12.00	12.00
Double	24.00	24.00

Parking for 5
Open February-November
🏠🖾🐾🖩§🖩📺🖩🛏️❀✕🚲

Individual proprietors have supplied all details of accommodation. As changes can occur, we advise you to confirm the information at the time of booking.

ILKLEY

West Yorkshire
Map ref 4B1

This moorland town is famous for its ballad. The 16th C manor house, now a museum, displays local prehistoric and Roman relics. Popular walk leads up Heber's Ghyll to Ilkley Moor, with the mysterious Swastika Stone and White Wells, 18th C plunge baths.
Tourist Information Centre
☎ (01943) 602319

Briarwood

👑 COMMENDED

Queens Drive, Ilkley LS29 9QW
☎ (01943) 600870
Victorian ladies' residence with spacious rooms and excellent views. Visitors are entertained as house guests. 5 minutes' walk from Ilkley Moor and Ilkley College.
Bedrooms: 2 twin
Bathrooms: 2 private, 1 public

Bed & breakfast per night:	£min	£max
Single	15.00	17.00
Double	30.00	30.00

Parking for 5
🐴 [UL] 🔒 [S] 🛋 [TV] 🌡 👕 ✿ 🐕 🚌

INGLEBY GREENHOW

North Yorkshire
Map ref 5C3

Perched on the edge of Cleveland Hills, the village boasts the Norman church of St Andrew's with well-preserved carving and effigies of a priest and a knight. Ingleby Moor rises 1300 ft above village.

Manor House Farm ⛰

👑👑 HIGHLY COMMENDED

Ingleby Greenhow, Great Ayton TS9 6RB
☎ Great Ayton (01642) 722384

168-acre mixed farm. In a picture book setting surrounded by hills and forests, in North York Moors National Park. Ideal for nature lovers, walking, touring, riding and relaxing. Fine food and wines.
Bedrooms: 1 double, 2 twin
Bathrooms: 3 private

Half board per person:	£min	£max
Daily	37.50	42.50
Weekly	248.50	248.50

Evening meal 1900 (last orders 1600)
Parking for 66
🐴 12 🍴 ☕ 🔒 [S] 🚭 🛋 [TV] 🌡 👕 🐎 🐟 ⛳ 🔫 ✿ 🚌 🎄 🏛

INGLETON

North Yorkshire
Map ref 5B3

Thriving tourist centre for fell-walkers, climbers and pot-holers. Popular walks up beautiful Twiss Valley to Ingleborough Summit, Whernside, White Scar Caves and waterfalls.

Gatehouse Farm ⛰

👑👑 COMMENDED

Far Westhouse, Ingleton, Carnforth, Lancashire LA6 3NR
☎ (015242) 41458 & 41307
250-acre dairy & livestock farm. 1740 farmhouse with old oak beams and panoramic views over open countryside.
Bedrooms: 2 double, 1 twin
Bathrooms: 3 private

Bed & breakfast per night:	£min	£max
Single	16.00	18.00
Double	32.00	36.00

Half board per person:	£min	£max
Daily	25.00	27.00
Weekly	170.00	180.00

Evening meal 1900 (last orders 1200)
Parking for 5
🐴 🍴 ☕ [UL] 🔒 [S] 🛋 [TV] 🌡 👕 🚌

Langber Country Guest House ⛰

👑👑

Tatterthorne Road, Ingleton, Carnforth, Lancashire LA6 3DT
☎ (015242) 41587
Detached country house in hilltop position with panoramic views. Good touring centre for dales, lakes and coast. Comfortable accommodation. Friendly service - everyone welcome.
Bedrooms: 1 single, 2 double, 1 twin, 3 triple, 1 family room
Bathrooms: 4 private, 1 public

Bed & breakfast per night:	£min	£max
Single	15.50	21.00
Double	30.00	38.00

Half board per person:	£min	£max
Daily	21.50	28.00
Weekly	136.00	162.00

Evening meal 1830 (last orders 1700)
Parking for 6
🐴 ☕ [UL] 🔒 [S] 🚭 🛋 [TV] 🌡 👕 ✿ [OAP] [SP]

New Butts Farm ⛰

Listed APPROVED

High Bentham, Lancaster LA2 7AN
☎ (015242) 41238
16-acre mixed farm. Attractive stone-built farmhouse in an area of outstanding beauty. Good home cooking, open fires and a warm welcome.
Bedrooms: 2 double, 1 twin, 2 triple
Bathrooms: 2 private, 1 public

Bed & breakfast per night:	£min	£max
Single	14.50	15.50
Double	29.00	31.00

Half board per person:	£min	£max
Daily	24.00	25.00

Evening meal from 1900
Parking for 6
🐴 ☕ [UL] 🔒 [S] 🚭 🛋 [TV] 🌡 👕 ✿ 🚌 [OAP]

KIRKBYMOORSIDE

North Yorkshire
Map ref 5C3

Attractive market town with remains of Norman castle. Good centre for exploring moors. Nearby are wild daffodils of Farndale.

Low Northolme Farm ⛰

👑👑 HIGHLY COMMENDED

Salton, York YO6 6RP
☎ (01751) 432321
220-acre mixed farm. 18th C farmhouse set in peaceful area of Ryedale, 6 miles from Helmsley, just two miles south of A170.
Bedrooms: 1 twin, 1 triple
Bathrooms: 2 private

Bed & breakfast per night:	£min	£max
Single	18.00	
Double	36.00	

Half board per person:	£min	£max
Daily	28.00	

Evening meal 1830 (last orders 1930)
Parking for 6
Open March-October
🐴 5 🍴 ☕ 💨 [UL] 🚭 🛋 [TV] 🌡 👕 🐎 🐟 ✿ 🐕 🚌

LEEDS

West Yorkshire
Map ref 4B1

Large city with excellent modern shopping centre and splendid Victorian architecture. Museums and galleries including Temple Newsam House (the Hampton Court of the North) and Tetley's Brewery Wharf; also home of Opera North. The Royal Armouries opening in spring 1996.
Tourist Information Centre
☎ (0113) 242 5242

Eagle Tavern ⛰

Listed

North Street, Leeds LS7 1AF
☎ (0113) 245 7146

Continued ►

LEEDS

Continued

Traditional pub in a commercial district of Leeds, offering friendly service at reasonable rates. Close to the city centre. Colour TV in all rooms. Voted CAMRA pub of the year 1989, 1990 and 1992. Yorkshire pub of the year 1993.
Bedrooms: 1 single, 6 twin, 2 triple
Bathrooms: 2 public

Bed & breakfast

per night:	£min	£max
Single	20.00	25.00
Double	40.00	

Evening meal 1730 (last orders 1900)
Parking for 12

Moorlea Hotel ⋀
☵☵ APPROVED
146 Woodsley Road, Leeds LS2 9LZ
☎ (0113) 243 2653
Five minutes from the University and fifteen minutes from the city centre.
Bedrooms: 5 single, 2 double, 2 twin, 1 triple, 1 family room
Bathrooms: 6 private, 2 public

Bed & breakfast

per night:	£min	£max
Single	22.00	28.00
Double	30.00	40.00

Evening meal 1800 (last orders 1830)
Parking for 20

The White House ⋀
Listed APPROVED
157 Middleton Park Road, Leeds
LS10 4LZ
☎ (0113) 271 1231
Spacious, detached house. Excellent local transport from near the door. Convenient for M1, M62 and West Riding towns and ideal stopover for North/South travel. Non-smokers only, please.
Bedrooms: 3 twin
Bathrooms: 1 public

Bed & breakfast

per night:	£min	£max
Single	16.00	16.00
Double	32.00	32.00

Parking for 3

LEEDS/BRADFORD AIRPORT

See under Bingley, Bradford, Leeds, Otley

Half board prices shown are per person but in some cases may be based on double/twin occupancy.

LEYBURN

North Yorkshire
Map ref 5B3

Attractive dales market town where Mary Queen of Scots was reputedly captured after her escape from Bolton Castle. Fine views over Wensleydale from nearby.
Tourist Information Centre
☎ *(01969) 623069 or 622773*

Eastfield Lodge Private Hotel ⋀
☵☵ COMMENDED
St Matthews Terrace, Leyburn
DL8 5EL
☎ Wensleydale (01969) 623196
Family-run, private hotel, central for touring the dales. En-suite facilities, good car parking, garden, residential licence.
Bedrooms: 1 single, 4 double, 1 twin, 1 triple, 1 family room
Bathrooms: 7 private, 1 public, 1 private shower

Bed & breakfast

per night:	£min	£max
Single	16.00	19.00
Double	32.00	38.00

Parking for 11

LONG MARSTON

North Yorkshire
Map ref 4C1

Close to the site of the Battle of Marston Moor, a decisive Civil War battle of 1644. A monument commemorates the event.

Gill House Farm ⋀
☵☵☵ HIGHLY COMMENDED
Tockwith Road, Long Marston, York
YO5 8PJ
☎ Rufforth (01904) 738379 & Mobile 0850 511140
600-acre mixed farm. Peaceful period farmhouse set in glorious countryside overlooking the Vale of York. Warm welcome. Good bus route and lots of local eating places.
Bedrooms: 2 double, 1 triple, 1 family room
Bathrooms: 4 private

Bed & breakfast

per night:	£min	£max
Single	30.00	
Double	40.00	42.00

Parking for 5

Please mention this guide when making a booking.

LUND

Humberside
Map ref 4C1

Village near Beverley close to the route of "The Minster Way".

Clematis House, Farmhouse Bed & Breakfast ⋀
☵☵
1 Eastgate, Lund, Driffield, North Humberside YO25 9TQ
☎ Driffield (01377) 217204
Fax (01377) 217204
389-acre arable & livestock farm. Family-run working farm in pretty, rural village. Farmhouse with character, spacious yet cosy, with en-suite rooms and tea/coffee making facilities. Secluded walled garden, TV lounge.
Bedrooms: 1 double, 1 twin
Bathrooms: 2 private

Bed & breakfast

per night:	£min	£max
Single	18.50	18.50
Double	35.00	35.00

Evening meal 1800 (last orders 2000)
Parking for 4

MALHAM

North Yorkshire
Map ref 5B3

Hamlet of stone cottages amid magnificent rugged limestone scenery in the Yorkshire Dales National Park. Malham Cove is a curving, sheer white cliff 240 ft high. Malham Tarn, one of Yorkshire's few natural lakes, belongs to the National Trust. National Park Centre.

Beck Hall Guest House ⋀
☵
Malham, Skipton BD23 4DJ
☎ Settle (01729) 830332
Family-run guesthouse set in a spacious riverside garden. Homely atmosphere, four-poster beds, log fires and home cooking.
Bedrooms: 11 double, 3 twin
Bathrooms: 11 private, 1 public

Bed & breakfast

per night:	£min	£max
Single	15.00	25.00
Double	30.00	38.00

Half board

per person:	£min	£max
Daily	21.95	25.95

Lunch available
Evening meal 1900 (last orders 2000)
Parking for 30

Miresfield Farm ⚘
🏆🏆🏆

Malham, Skipton BD23 4DA
☎ Airton (01729) 830414
In national park. En-suite rooms, tea-making facilities, ground floor bedrooms, central heating. Two lounges. Home cooking. Private parking.
Bedrooms: 1 single, 5 double, 4 twin, 4 triple
Bathrooms: 14 private, 1 public

Bed & breakfast

per night:	£min	£max
Single	22.00	30.00
Double	40.00	44.00

Half board

per person:	£min	£max
Daily	30.00	34.00
Weekly	210.00	224.00

Evening meal 1830 (last orders 1200)
Parking for 16

🖤🖤🖤🖤🖤🖤🖤🖤🖤🖤🖤🖤🖤🖤🖤

MARKET WEIGHTON

Humberside
Map ref 4C1

Small town on the western side of the Yorkshire Wolds. A tablet in the parish church records the death of William Bradley in 1820 at which time he was 7 ft 9 in tall and weighed 27 stone!

Arras Farmhouse ⚘
Listed

Arras Farm, Market Weighton, York YO4 3RN
☎ (01430) 872404
Fax (01430) 871500

460-acre arable farm. Large farmhouse and grounds, peaceful and comfortable, on A1079 between Market Weighton and Beverley. 3 miles from Market Weighton at crossroads.
Bedrooms: 2 double, 1 twin
Bathrooms: 2 private, 1 public

Bed & breakfast

per night:	£min	£max
Single	18.00	20.00
Double	30.00	34.00

Parking for 5

🖤🖤🖤🖤🖤🖤🖤

> Map references apply to the colour maps at the back of this guide.

MASHAM

North Yorkshire
Map ref 5C3

Famous market town on the River Ure, with a large market square. St Mary's Church has Norman tower and 13th C spire. Theakston's "Old Peculier" ale is brewed here.

Pasture House ⚘
🏆 COMMENDED

Healey, Ripon HG4 4LJ
☎ Ripon (01765) 689149
Fax (01765) 689990
100-year-old detached house in 3.5 acres at the foot of Colsterdale, a beautiful, small and quiet dale leading to grouse moors. Fishing and golf available by arrangement.
Bedrooms: 2 double, 1 twin, 1 triple
Bathrooms: 2 public

Bed & breakfast

per night:	£min	£max
Single	14.00	
Double	28.00	

Half board

per person:	£min	£max
Daily	24.00	
Weekly	160.00	

Lunch available
Evening meal from 1900
Parking for 6

🖤🖤🖤🖤🖤🖤🖤🖤🖤🖤🖤🖤

MIDDLEHAM

North Yorkshire
Map ref 5C3

Town famous for racehorse training, with cobbled squares and houses of local stone. Norman castle, once principal residence of Warwick the Kingmaker and later Richard III. Ruins of Jervaulx Abbey nearby.

Black Swan Hotel ⚘
🏆🏆 COMMENDED

Market Place, Middleham DL8 4NP
☎ Wensleydale (01969) 622221
Unspoilt 17th C inn, with open fires and beamed ceilings, allied to 20th C comforts. Emphasis on food.
Bedrooms: 1 single, 4 double, 1 twin, 1 triple
Bathrooms: 7 private

Bed & breakfast

per night:	£min	£max
Single	26.00	29.00
Double	44.00	59.00

Half board

per person:	£min	£max
Daily	31.00	39.00

Lunch available
Evening meal 1830 (last orders 2100)
Parking for 3
Cards accepted: Access, Visa

🖤🖤🖤🖤🖤🖤🖤🖤🖤🖤🖤🖤🖤🖤

MYTHOLMROYD

West Yorkshire
Map ref 4B1

Situated in the Calder Valley, the meaning of the name originates from "a clearance of woodland where streams join".

Riga Rose ⚘
🏆🏆 COMMENDED

Scout Close, Mytholmroyd, Hebden Bridge HX7 5JU
☎ Halifax (01422) 885415
Homely bed and breakfast accommodation designed with the visitor in mind.
Bedrooms: 1 double
Bathrooms: 1 private

Bed & breakfast

per night:	£min	£max
Single	17.50	17.50
Double	35.00	35.00

Parking for 2
Open March-December

🖤🖤🖤🖤🖤🖤🖤🖤🖤🖤🖤🖤

MYTON-ON-SWALE

North Yorkshire
Map ref 5C3

Small village on the mighty River Swale.

Plump House Farm ⚘
🏆🏆

Myton-on-Swale, York YO6 2RA
☎ Boroughbridge (01423) 360650
160-acre mixed farm. A warm welcome with comfortable en-suite accommodation on a working family farm. Easy access to York and Harrogate and an ideal centre for the coast, dales and moors. Reductions for children.
Bedrooms: 1 double, 1 family room
Bathrooms: 2 private

Bed & breakfast

per night:	£min	£max
Single	14.00	
Double	28.00	

Half board

per person:	£min	£max
Daily	20.00	

Evening meal 1800 (last orders 2000)
Parking for 4

🖤🖤🖤🖤🖤🖤🖤🖤🖤🖤

> The symbols 🦽 🦽 🦽 indicate categories of accessibility for wheelchair users. They are explained in full in the information pages at the back of this guide.

NORTHALLERTON

North Yorkshire
Map ref 5C3

Formerly a staging post on coaching route to the North and later a railway town. Today a lively market town and administrative capital of North Yorkshire. Parish church of All Saints dates from 1200.
Tourist Information Centre
☎ (01609) 776864

Lovesome Hill Farm

COMMENDED

Lovesome Hill, Northallerton DL6 2PB
☎ (01609) 772311
165-acre mixed farm. 19th C farmhouse. Tastefully converted granary adjoins with spacious, quality en-suite rooms. North of Northallerton, twixt dales and moors. "You'll love it".
Bedrooms: 1 single, 1 double, 1 twin, 1 family room
Bathrooms: 4 private

Bed & breakfast per night:	£min	£max
Single	17.00	20.00
Double	34.00	40.00

Half board per person:	£min	£max
Daily	29.95	29.95
Weekly	188.65	188.65

Evening meal from 1900
Parking for 10
Open February-November
[UL] [S] [TV]

Porch House

HIGHLY COMMENDED

68 High Street, Northallerton DL7 8EG
☎ (01609) 779831 & Mobile 0589 776014

16th/17th C Grade II listed family house, with original beams, fireplaces and walled garden. Guests have included Charles I. Centrally positioned, ideal for discovering the Yorkshire dales, moors and coast.
Bedrooms: 4 double
Bathrooms: 4 private

Bed & breakfast per night:	£min	£max
Single	25.00	30.00
Double	38.00	42.00

Half board per person:	£min	£max
Daily	25.00	40.00
Weekly	160.00	255.00

Evening meal 1800 (last orders 1930)
Parking for 5
[S] 8 [OAP] [SP] [T]

NUNNINGTON

North Yorkshire
Map ref 5C3

On the River Rye, this picturesque village has a splendid Hall which houses some magnificent 17th C tapestries.

Sunley Court

COMMENDED

Nunnington, York YO6 5XQ
☎ (01439) 748233
200-acre arable and mixed farm. Modern farmhouse in open countryside. Home cooking, log fires and emphasis on comfort. Central to York, North York Moors and coast.
Bedrooms: 2 single, 1 double, 1 twin
Bathrooms: 2 private, 1 public

Bed & breakfast per night:	£min	£max
Single	15.00	
Double	30.00	

Half board per person:	£min	£max
Daily	25.00	
Weekly	175.00	

Lunch available
Evening meal 1800 (last orders 2100)
Parking for 9
Open March-October
[UL] [S] [TV]

OSMOTHERLEY

North Yorkshire
Map ref 5C3

The famous "Lyke Wake Walk", across the Cleveland Hills to Ravenscar 40 miles away, starts here in this ancient village. Attached to the village cross is a large stone table used as a "pulpit" by John Wesley.

Quintana House

Listed COMMENDED

Back Lane, Osmotherley, Northallerton DL6 3BJ
☎ (01609) 883258
Detached, stone cottage near national park village centre, within 90 metres of the Cleveland Way, affording panoramic views of Black Hambleton. Non-smokers only, please.
Bedrooms: 1 double, 1 twin
Bathrooms: 1 public

Bed & breakfast per night:	£min	£max
Double	30.00	31.00

Half board per person:	£min	£max
Daily	22.00	35.00
Weekly	154.00	245.00

Evening meal 1830 (last orders 2000)
Parking for 5
[UL] [S] [TV]

OTLEY

West Yorkshire
Map ref 4B1

Charming market and small manufacturing town in Lower Wharfedale, the birthplace of Thomas Chippendale, painted by Turner. Old inns, medieval 5-arched bridge, local history museum, maypole, historic All Saints' Church. Beautiful countryside. Location for "Emmerdale Farm" and "Heartbeat".
Tourist Information Centre
☎ (0113) 247 7707

Paddock Hill

APPROVED

Norwood, Otley LS21 2QU
☎ (01943) 465977
Converted farmhouse on the B6451 with open fires and lovely views. Within easy reach of Herriot, Bronte and Emmerdale country, the dales, Skipton, Harrogate and Leeds. Reservoir fishing nearby.
Bedrooms: 1 double, 2 twin
Bathrooms: 1 public, 1 private shower

Bed & breakfast per night:	£min	£max
Single	13.00	15.00
Double	26.00	32.00

Parking for 3
[UL] [S] [TV]

Wood Top Farm

COMMENDED

Off Norwood Edge, Lindley, Otley LS21 2QS
☎ (01943) 464010
Fax (01943) 464010
7-acre mixed farm. Quiet 18th C farmhouse in an Area of Outstanding Natural Beauty, half a mile off B6451. Ideal for country lovers and central for Leeds, Bradford, Harrogate, Skipton, York, Haworth and the dales. Cosy bedrooms with adjoining private bathroom/dressing room. Room service for tea and coffee, varied breakfast menu. Non-smoking. Stabling available.
Bedrooms: 1 single, 1 twin
Bathrooms: 2 private

Bed & breakfast per night:	£min	£max
Single	18.00	20.00
Double	36.00	40.00

Parking for 6
Open February-December
10 [UL] [S] [TV]

PATELEY BRIDGE

North Yorkshire
Map ref 5C3

Small market town at centre of Upper Nidderdale. Flax and linen industries once flourished in this remote and beautiful setting.

The Watermill Inn ♔

Foster Beck, Pateley Bridge,
Harrogate HG3 5AX
☎ Harrogate (01423) 711484
Fax (01423) 711484

18th C flax mill with giant working water wheel, converted into residential public house with function, games and family rooms.
Bedrooms: 5 double, 1 twin, 2 family rooms
Bathrooms: 8 private, 2 public

Bed & breakfast per night:	£min	£max
Single	25.00	30.00
Double	30.00	45.00

Half board per person:	£min	£max
Daily	32.00	40.00
Weekly	160.00	200.00

Lunch available
Evening meal 1830 (last orders 2000)
Parking for 120
Cards accepted: Access, Visa, Amex
🐴 🍴 ☐ ☕ 💨 🍷 [S] ◐ ▥ 🚗 ⊤150 ♠ U 🎣 ⛳ 🎾 ✿ [OAP] ✕ [SP] 🏠 [T]

PICKERING

North Yorkshire
Map ref 5D3

Market town and tourist centre on edge of North York Moors. Parish church has complete set of 15th C wall paintings depicting lives of saints. Part of 12th C castle still stands. Beck Isle Museum. The North York Moors Railway begins here.
Tourist Information Centre
☎ (01751) 473791

Eden House ♔

♛♛ COMMENDED
120 Eastgate, Pickering YO18 7DW
☎ (01751) 472289 & 477297
Fax (01751) 477297
Delightful listed cottage situated on the A170 road to the East Coast. On the outskirts of a small market town.
Bedrooms: 2 double, 1 twin
Bathrooms: 1 private, 1 public

Bed & breakfast per night:	£min	£max
Single	20.00	25.00
Double	32.00	35.00

Half board per person:	£min	£max
Daily	30.00	35.00

Evening meal 1830 (last orders 2000)
Parking for 3
🐴 🍴 ☐ ☕ 💨 [UL] 🍷 [S] 🚭 🛋 ▥ 🚗 ✿ 🚚 [SP] [T]

Grindale House ♔

♛♛ COMMENDED
123 Eastgate, Pickering YO18 7DW
☎ (01751) 476636
Beautiful 18th C stone/pantile townhouse. Lovely rooms with antique furniture, private facilities, TV. Car park. Friendly informal atmosphere. Non-smoking.
Bedrooms: 2 double, 1 twin
Bathrooms: 3 private

Bed & breakfast per night:	£min	£max
Single	20.00	25.00
Double	34.00	42.00

Parking for 8
🐴 ♿ ☐ ☕ [UL] 🚭 🛋 [TV] ▥ 🚗 U ✿ 🚚 [SP] [T]

Heathcote Guest House ♔

♛♛ COMMENDED
100 Eastgate, Pickering YO18 7DW
☎ (01751) 476991
Early Victorian house 5 minutes from town centre. Ideal for walking and touring. All bedrooms have private facilities. Optional dinners. Relaxed, friendly atmosphere. Secluded parking. Non-smoking throughout.
Bedrooms: 4 double, 1 twin
Bathrooms: 5 private

Bed & breakfast per night:	£min	£max
Single	20.00	22.00
Double	40.00	44.00

Half board per person:	£min	£max
Daily	30.00	32.00
Weekly	196.00	202.00

Evening meal 1900 (last orders 1100)
Parking for 7
Cards accepted: Access, Visa, Switch/Delta
🍴 ☐ ☕ 💨 🍷 [S] 🚭 🛋 [TV] ▥ 🚗 ✿ 🐕 🚚 [SP]

Marton Hill ♔

Listed
Marton, Sinnington, York YO6 6RG
☎ Kirkbymoorside (01751) 431418
55-acre livestock farm. 300-year-old country house with spectacular views. 3 miles from Kirkbymoorside on the Malton road, with good easy access.
Bedrooms: 1 double, 1 twin
Bathrooms: 1 public

Bed & breakfast per night:	£min	£max
Double	22.00	26.00

Parking for 2
Open April-October
🐴 ✗ ☕ [UL] [S] [TV] ▥ 🚗 ✿ 🐕 🚚

The Old Vicarage ♔

♛♛ COMMENDED
Yedingham, Malton YO17 8SL
☎ West Heslerton (01944) 728426
Delightful, Georgian former vicarage set in large gardens with panoramic views of moors and wolds. Pretty village, with local inn, approximately 7 miles from Pickering, on River Derwent in the heart of Ryedale. Dinner by arrangement.
Bedrooms: 2 double, 1 twin
Bathrooms: 1 private, 1 public

Bed & breakfast per night:	£min	£max
Single	14.00	18.00

Half board per person:	£min	£max
Daily	22.50	27.00

Parking for 4
🐴 5 ☕ [UL] 🍷 [S] 🚭 🛋 [TV] ▥ 🚗 U ⛳ ✿ [OAP] [SP] 🏠

Sunnyside ♔

♛♛ HIGHLY COMMENDED
Carr Lane, Middleton, Pickering YO18 8PD
☎ (01751) 476104
Fax (01751) 476104
Large, south-facing chalet bungalow with private parking and a garden, in an open country aspect. Some ground floor rooms.
Bedrooms: 1 double, 1 twin, 1 triple
Bathrooms: 3 private

Bed & breakfast per night:	£min	£max
Single	24.00	26.00
Double	36.00	38.00

Half board per person:	£min	£max
Daily	30.00	31.00
Weekly	190.00	210.00

Evening meal from 1930
Parking for 4
Open April-October
Cards accepted: Access, Visa
🐴 ♿ ☐ ☕ [UL] [S] 🚭 🛋 ▥ 🚗 ✿ 🚚

The symbol ❁ within an entry indicates participation in the Welcome Host programme – a nationally recognised customer care initiative which aims to promote the highest standards of service and a warm welcome for all visitors.

RAVENSCAR

North Yorkshire
Map ref 5D3

Splendidly-positioned small coastal resort with magnificent views over Robin Hood's Bay. Its Old Peak is the end of the famous Lyke Wake Walk or "corpse way".

Smugglers Rock Country Guest House ⋔

Ravenscar, Scarborough YO13 0ER
☎ Scarborough (01723) 870044
Georgian country house, reputedly a former smugglers' haunt, with panoramic views over the surrounding national park and sea. Half a mile from the village. Ideal centre for touring, walking and pony trekking.
Bedrooms: 2 single, 2 double, 2 twin, 1 triple, 1 family room
Bathrooms: 8 private

Bed & breakfast

per night:	£min	£max
Single	19.00	20.00
Double	38.00	40.00

Half board

per person:	£min	£max
Daily	27.50	28.50
Weekly	175.00	179.00

Evening meal 1830 (last orders 1630)
Parking for 12
Open March-November

RICHMOND

North Yorkshire
Map ref 5C3

Market town on edge of Swaledale with 11th C castle, Georgian and Victorian buildings surrounding cobbled market-place. Green Howards' Museum is in the former Holy Trinity Church. Attractions include the Georgian Theatre, Richmondshire Museum and Easby Abbey.
Tourist Information Centre
☎ *(01748) 850252 or 825994*

Browson Bank ⋔

Dalton, Richmond DL11 7HE
☎ Darlington (01325) 718504 & 718246

16th C converted barn, full of character, in beautiful farmland near Richmond and 6 miles west of Scotch Corner.
Bedrooms: 1 double, 2 twin
Bathrooms: 3 private, 1 public

Bed & breakfast

per night:	£min	£max
Single	15.00	18.00
Double	30.00	30.00

Parking for 4

Carlin House

COMMENDED

6 Frenchgate, Richmond DL10 4JG
☎ (01748) 826771
Grade II listed 18th C town house located at lower entrance to Richmond's market square. Geologists especially welcome.
Bedrooms: 1 single, 1 double
Bathrooms: 2 private

Bed & breakfast

per night:	£min	£max
Single	16.00	20.00
Double	32.00	36.00

Open January-November

Holmedale

COMMENDED

Dalton, Richmond DL11 7HX
☎ Teesdale (01833) 621236
Georgian house in a quiet village, midway between Richmond and Barnard Castle. Ideal for the Yorkshire and Durham dales.
Bedrooms: 1 double, 1 triple
Bathrooms: 1 public

Bed & breakfast

per night:	£min	£max
Single	15.00	
Double	26.00	

Half board

per person:	£min	£max
Daily	20.00	
Weekly	140.00	

Evening meal 1800 (last orders 1200)
Parking for 2

Mount Pleasant Farm ⋔

COMMENDED

Whashton, Richmond DL11 7JP
☎ (01748) 822784

280-acre mixed farm. Just the place for that special holiday or short break. En-suite rooms in a renovated stable. Well known for our farmer's breakfast and delicious dinners, warm welcome and personal service. Real peace and quiet in lovely countryside.
Wheelchair access category 3 ⋓
Bedrooms: 2 double, 1 twin, 2 triple, 1 family room
Bathrooms: 6 private

Bed & breakfast

per night:	£min	£max
Single	20.00	21.00
Double	34.00	36.00

Half board

per person:	£min	£max
Daily	27.50	28.50
Weekly	185.00	

Evening meal 1830 (last orders 1200)
Parking for 6

RIPON

North Yorkshire
Map ref 5C3

Small, ancient city with impressive cathedral containing Saxon crypt which houses church treasures from all over Yorkshire. "Setting the Watch" tradition kept nightly by horn-blower in Market Square. Fountains Abbey nearby.

The Coopers ⋔

36 College Road, Ripon HG4 2HA
☎ (01765) 603708
Spacious, comfortable Victorian house in quiet area. En-suite facilities available. Special rates for children. Cyclists welcome (storage for bicycles). Take-away meals acceptable in rooms.
Bedrooms: 1 single, 1 twin, 1 triple
Bathrooms: 1 private, 1 public

Bed & breakfast

per night:	£min	£max
Single	16.00	17.00
Double	28.00	34.00

Parking for 3

Lowgate Cottage ⋔

Listed COMMENDED

Lowgate Lane, Sawley, Ripon HG4 3EL
☎ Sawley (01765) 620302
Restored dwelling, peacefully located in one-third of an acre of beautiful gardens. 10 minutes' walking distance from Fountains Abbey and Studley Park.
Bedrooms: 1 double, 1 twin
Bathrooms: 1 public

Bed & breakfast

per night:	£min	£max
Double	30.00	

Parking for 4

Mallard Grange ⋔

Listed COMMENDED

Aldfield, Ripon HG4 3BE
☎ Sawley (01765) 620242

460-acre mixed farm. Set in the Yorkshire Dales, this peaceful 16th C farmhouse offers high quality traditionally furnished rooms. Historically linked to Fountains Abbey, just a few fields away.
Bedrooms: 1 double, 1 twin
Bathrooms: 1 public
Bed & breakfast

per night:	£min	£max
Single	23.00	
Double	36.00	

Parking for 4
Open April-October

Moor End Farm ⋀

Knaresborough Road, Littlethorpe, Ripon HG4 3LU
☎ (01765) 677419
41-acre livestock farm. Comfortable rooms, TV lounge with log fire. Home cooking and a warm Yorkshire welcome. Non-smokers only, please. Ideal centre for Yorkshire Dales, York and Harrogate.
Bedrooms: 2 double, 1 twin
Bathrooms: 1 private, 1 public
Bed & breakfast

per night:	£min	£max
Double	30.00	38.00

Half board

per person:	£min	£max
Daily	24.00	28.00
Weekly	161.00	189.00

Evening meal 1830 (last orders 1600)
Parking for 7
Open January-November

ROBIN HOOD'S BAY

North Yorkshire
Map ref 5D3

Picturesque village of red-roofed cottages with main street running from clifftop down ravine to seashore. Scene of much smuggling and shipwrecks in 18th C. Robin Hood reputed to have escaped to continent by boat from here.

The Flask Inn

Fylingdales, Whitby YO22 4QH
☎ Whitby (01947) 880305
Originally a 16th C monks' hostel, situated on the Whitby to Scarborough road (A171) in the glorious North York Moors National Park.

Bedrooms: 3 double, 1 twin, 1 triple, 1 family room
Bathrooms: 6 private
Bed & breakfast

per night:	£min	£max
Single	25.00	30.00
Double	40.00	50.00

Lunch available
Evening meal 1900 (last orders 2100)
Parking for 25

RUFFORTH

North Yorkshire
Map ref 4C1

Village west of York. There is a small airfield, and it is also the home of the York Gliding Centre.

Rosedale Guest House ⋀

COMMENDED
Wetherby Road, Rufforth, York YO2 3QB
☎ York (01904) 738297
Small, family-run guesthouse with a homely atmosphere and all facilities, in a delightful, unspoilt village 4 miles west of York on the B1224. Private parking available.
Bedrooms: 1 single, 3 double, 1 twin
Bathrooms: 1 private, 2 public, 2 private showers
Bed & breakfast

per night:	£min	£max
Single	16.00	18.00
Double	32.00	35.00

Parking for 5

SCARBOROUGH

North Yorkshire
Map ref 5D3

Large, popular East Coast seaside resort, formerly a spa town. Beautiful gardens and two splendid sandy beaches. Castle ruins date from 1100; fine Georgian and Victorian houses. Scarborough Millennium depicts 1,000 years of town's history. Sea Life Centre.
Tourist Information Centre
☎ *(01723) 373333*

Ambassador Hotel ⋀

COMMENDED
Esplanade, Scarborough YO11 2AY
☎ (01723) 362841
Fax (01723) 362841

Victorian hotel with en-suite bedrooms, offering unrivalled sea views, excellent cuisine, dinner/dances, leisure, entertainment, satellite, direct-dial telephone, lift, ample free parking and more!
Bedrooms: 12 single, 15 double, 12 twin, 7 triple, 3 family rooms
Bathrooms: 49 private
Bed & breakfast

per night:	£min	£max
Single	25.00	42.00
Double	50.00	84.00

Half board

per person:	£min	£max
Daily	30.00	52.00
Weekly	175.00	319.00

Evening meal 1800 (last orders 1930)
Cards accepted: Access, Visa, Amex, Switch/Delta

SELBY

North Yorkshire
Map ref 4C1

Small market town on the River Ouse, believed to have been birthplace of Henry I, with a magnificent abbey containing much fine Norman and Early English architecture.
Tourist Information Centre
☎ *(01757) 703263*

Hazeldene Guest House ⋀

Listed APPROVED
34 Brook Street, Doncaster Road, Selby YO8 0AR
☎ (01757) 704809
Fax (01757) 709300
Situated by the A19 in pleasant market town, only 12 miles from York. M62 and A1 are both 7 miles distant.
Bedrooms: 2 single, 1 double, 2 twin, 2 triple, 1 family room
Bathrooms: 1 private, 2 public
Bed & breakfast

per night:	£min	£max
Single	16.00	18.00
Double	28.00	36.00

Parking for 6

Judith Parish ⋀

Listed APPROVED
Villa Nuseries, 33 York Road, Riccall, York YO4 6QG
☎ (01757) 248257
Family-run house in a quiet village 9 miles south of York, offering comfortable, friendly accommodation. Kitchen and laundry facilities. Children and pets welcome.
Bedrooms: 1 single, 4 twin, 1 triple, 1 family room
Bathrooms: 3 private, 1 public

Continued ▶

SELBY

Continued

Bed & breakfast

per night:	£min	£max
Single	14.00	19.00
Double	26.00	36.00

Parking for 8

⚒ ♿ 🏠 Ⓤ ⓘ Ⓢ ⋈ 📺 ▥ ◨ ✿ ➤ ⛽ DAP SP 🔔

SETTLE

North Yorkshire
Map ref 5B3

Town of narrow streets and
Georgian houses in an area of
great limestone hills and crags.
Panoramic view from Castleberg
Crag which stands 300 ft above
town.
Tourist Information Centre
☎ *(01729) 825192*

Maypole Inn ♈

😀😀😀 COMMENDED

Maypole Green, Main Street, Long
Preston, Skipton BD23 4PH
☎ Long Preston (01729) 840219
*17th C inn, with open fires, on the
village green. Easy access to many
attractive walks in the surrounding
dales. 4 miles from Settle.*
Bedrooms: 1 single, 2 double, 1 twin,
1 triple, 1 family room
Bathrooms: 6 private

Bed & breakfast

per night:	£min	£max
Single	26.00	26.00
Double	39.00	39.00

Lunch available
Evening meal 1830 (last orders 2100)
Parking for 25
Cards accepted: Access, Visa, Diners,
Amex

⚒ ☎ 📞 ❑ ♿ ⓘ Ⓢ ⋈ 🗝 📺 ▥ ◨ 🎱60
● ✕ ⛽ SP 🔔 Ⓣ

Whitefriars Country Guest
House ♈

😀😀 APPROVED

Church Street, Settle BD24 9JD
☎ (01729) 823753
*Historic family-run guesthouse, set in
spacious gardens, in heart of Settle.
Ideal for exploring the Dales,
Settle/Carlisle Railway. Non-smokers
only, please.*
Bedrooms: 1 single, 3 double, 3 twin,
1 triple, 1 family room
Bathrooms: 3 private, 2 public

Bed & breakfast

per night:	£min	£max
Single	17.00	17.50
Double	34.00	42.00

We advise you to confirm
your booking in writing.

Half board

per person:	£min	£max
Daily	27.00	31.50
Weekly	167.10	195.30

Evening meal 1900 (last orders 2000)
Parking for 9

⚒ ♿ ⓘ Ⓢ ⋈ 🗝 📺 ▥ ◨ ✿ ✕ ⛽ SP 🔔

STARBOTTON

North Yorkshire
Map ref 5B3

Quiet, picturesque village midway
between Kettlewell and Buckden in
Wharfedale. Many buildings belong
to the 17th C and several have
dated lintels.

Bushey Lodge Farm

😀😀😀 HIGHLY COMMENDED

Starbotton, Skipton BD23 5HY
☎ Kettlewell (01756) 760424
*2000-acre mixed farm. Traditional dales
farmhouse in quiet position in Upper
Wharfedale village. Extensive views
along the valley. Both rooms are en-
suite with TV, tea/coffee facilities.*
Bedrooms: 1 double, 1 twin
Bathrooms: 2 private

Bed & breakfast

per night:	£min	£max
Double	36.00	40.00

Parking for 6

⚒ ☎ 📞 ❑ ♿ Ⓤ ⓘ Ⓢ ⋈ 📺 ▥ ◨ ✿ ✕
⛽ DAP

SUTTON BANK

North Yorkshire
Map ref 5C3

Escarpment of the Hambleton
Hills, 5 miles east of Thirsk.
Spectacular views. Gliding from
summit.

High House Farm ♈

😀

Sutton Bank, Thirsk YO7 2HA
☎ Thirsk (01845) 597557
*113-acre mixed farm. Family-run, set in
open countryside and offering
magnificent views. Splendid walking
country, ideal for quiet relaxing holiday.
Good food and hospitality. East Coast 1
hour, York and North York Moors half
an hour.*
Bedrooms: 2 triple
Bathrooms: 1 public

Bed & breakfast

per night:	£min	£max
Double	30.00	

Half board

per person:	£min	£max
Daily	38.00	39.00

Parking for 2
Open April-October

⚒ ✕ ❑ Ⓤ ⓘ 📺 ▥ ◨ ✿ U ✿ ✕ ⛽ DAP

TERRINGTON

North Yorkshire
Map ref 5C3

In the Howardian Hills, the name
of this picturesque village is said
to refer in Old English to the
practice of sorcery. There is a
church and an old rectory now
known as Terrington Hall.

Gate Farm ♈

😀😀

Ganthorpe, Terrington, York YO6 4QD
☎ Coneysthorpe (01653) 648269
*150-acre dairy farm. Stone-built
farmhouse offering traditional Yorkshire
hospitality in a quiet village near Castle
Howard. Convenient for the moors,
wolds, the East Coast and York.*
Bedrooms: 2 double, 1 twin, 1 family
room
Bathrooms: 2 private, 1 public,
2 private showers

Bed & breakfast

per night:	£min	£max
Single	15.00	
Double	30.00	

Half board

per person:	£min	£max
Daily	22.50	
Weekly	157.50	

Evening meal 1830 (last orders 1600)
Parking for 3
Open March-October

⚒ 📞 ❑ ♿ 🏠 ⓘ Ⓢ 🗝 📺 ▥ ◨ U 🎱
✿ ⛽

THIRSK

North Yorkshire
Map ref 5C3

Thriving market town with cobbled
square surrounded by old shops
and inns and also with a local
museum. St Mary's Church is
probably the best example of
Perpendicular work in Yorkshire.

Angel Inn ♈

😀😀😀

Long Street, Topcliffe, Thirsk
YO7 3RW
☎ (01845) 577237
Fax (01845) 578000
*Attractive village inn with a warm,
traditional atmosphere, renowned for
good food and traditional ales. Ideal
centre for touring York and Herriot
country.*
Bedrooms: 2 single, 8 double, 4 twin,
1 family room
Bathrooms: 15 private

Bed & breakfast

per night:	£min	£max
Single	35.00	39.50
Double	50.00	55.00

Lunch available
Evening meal 1830 (last orders 2130)
Parking for 150

Cards accepted: Access, Visa, Switch/
Delta

☎ 2 ୯ ⌨ 🖳 🖐 🐾 🛇 🅿 TV 🛏 🖨 ⌂
🍴150 ● ♪ ✿ ✕ ⛳ SP

Ashton House

☷☷ HIGHLY COMMENDED

166 Front Street, Sowerby, Thirsk
YO7 1JN
☎ (01845) 526803
*Late Georgian/early Victorian house,
bordering the village green, offering a
warm welcome and traditional
Yorkshire hospitality and comfort.*
Bedrooms: 2 double
Bathrooms: 2 private
Bed & breakfast

per night:	£min	£max
Single	18.15	18.50
Double	37.00	

Parking for 4

☷ 5 🐾 🖳 🖐 🛇 🅿 🐾 TV 🛏 ⌂ ∪ ▶ ✿ ✕
⛳ SP 🏠

Doxford House ⚠

☷☷ APPROVED

Front Street, Sowerby, Thirsk YO7 1JP
☎ (01845) 523238
*Handsome, Georgian house with
attractive garden, overlooking greens of
Sowerby. Comfortable rooms, all en-
suite. Ideal centre for touring moors
and dales.*
Wheelchair access category 3 ♿
Bedrooms: 1 double, 1 twin, 2 triple
Bathrooms: 4 private
Bed & breakfast

per night:	£min	£max
Single	21.00	22.00
Double	32.00	33.00

Half board

per person:	£min	£max
Daily	24.00	
Weekly	161.00	

Evening meal from 1830
Parking for 4

☷ 🐾 ⌨ 🖐 🐾 🖳 🖐 🛇 🅿 TV 🛏 ⌂ ✿ ⛳ 🏠

Garth House Farm ⚠

Listed

Dalton, Thirsk YO7 3HY
☎ (01845) 577310
Fax (01845) 577310
*50-acre livestock farm. Farmhouse set in
a country village. Central for York,
Harrogate and many historic,
interesting places. Friendly welcome
awaiting guests.*
Bedrooms: 1 twin, 1 family room
Bathrooms: 2 public
Bed & breakfast

per night:	£min	£max
Single	12.00	14.00
Double	24.00	28.00

Parking for 6
Open March-November

☷ ⌨ 🖐 🐾 🖳 TV 🛏 ⌂ ∪ ✿ ⛳

Low Paradise ⚠

Listed COMMENDED

Boltby, Thirsk YO7 2HS
☎ (01845) 537253
*17th C farmhouse offering warm
hospitality. A quiet haven with super
views towards the Vale of York, close to
moors and dales.*
Bedrooms: 1 double, 2 twin
Bathrooms: 1 public
Bed & breakfast

per night:	£min	£max
Single	18.00	18.00
Double	32.00	32.00

Half board

per person:	£min	£max
Daily	25.00	28.00
Weekly	160.00	180.00

Lunch available
Evening meal 1800 (last orders 2000)
Parking for 4
Open April-October
Cards accepted: Access, Visa

☷ 3 🖳 🖐 🛇 ✕ 🅿 TV 🛏 ⌂ ∪ ▶ ✿ ⛳ SP 🏠

Old Post Office House

Listed COMMENDED

Baldersby, Thirsk YO7 4PE
☎ Ripon (01765) 640215
*Former village post office, Grade II
listed, with pretty cottage garden. Ideal
centre for Yorkshire Dales and good
stopover point between London and
Scotland.*
Bedrooms: 1 double, 1 twin
Bathrooms: 2 private
Bed & breakfast

per night:	£min	£max
Single	18.00	18.00
Double	30.00	40.00

Parking for 2
Open February-November

☷ 12 ⌨ 🖐 🐾 🖳 ✕ TV 🛏 ⌂ ✿ ✕ ⛳ 🏠

Plump Bank ⚠

☷ COMMENDED

Felixkirk Road, Thirsk YO7 2EW
☎ (01845) 522406
*From Thirsk take the A170 Scarborough
road. After 1 mile turn left for Felixkirk
and Boltby and house is on the left
after 100 yards.*
Bedrooms: 2 double, 1 twin
Bathrooms: 3 private
Bed & breakfast

per night:	£min	£max
Double	32.00	36.00

Parking for 9
Open March-October

⌨ 🖐 🐾 🖐 🛏 ⌂ ∪ ✕ ⛳

Station House

☷☷

Station Road, Thirsk YO7 4LS
☎ (01845) 522063
*Old station-master's house with en-suite
rooms and orchard. Ideal base for
touring dales, moors and York. Private
car park.*
Bedrooms: 1 double, 1 triple
Bathrooms: 2 private

per night:	£min	£max
Single	16.00	16.00
Double	32.00	32.00

Parking for 3
Open April-October

☷ 🖐 🖳 🛇 🅿 TV 🛏 ⌂ ✿ ⛳ 🏠

Thornborough House Farm

☷☷ COMMENDED

South Kilvington, Thirsk YO7 2NP
☎ (01845) 522103
Fax (01845) 522103
*206-acre mixed farm. 200-year-old
farmhouse in an ideal position for
walking and touring in the North York
Moors and Yorkshire Dales.*
Bedrooms: 1 double, 1 twin, 1 family
room
Bathrooms: 3 private
Bed & breakfast

per night:	£min	£max
Single	15.00	17.00
Double	30.00	34.00

Half board

per person:	£min	£max
Daily	24.00	26.00
Weekly	135.00	155.00

Evening meal from 1830
Parking for 6
Cards accepted: Access, Visa

☷ ⌨ 🖐 🐾 🖳 🛇 ✕ 🅿 TV 🛏 ⌂ ✿
⛳ OAP ⌂ SP

Town Pasture Farm ⚠

Listed

Boltby, Thirsk YO7 2DY
☎ (01845) 537298
*180-acre mixed farm. Farmhouse with
views of the Hambleton Hills, in
picturesque Boltby village within the
boundary of the North Yorkshire Moors
National Park.*
Bedrooms: 1 twin, 1 triple
Bathrooms: 1 public
Bed & breakfast

per night:	£min	£max
Single	14.50	16.00

Half board

per person:	£min	£max
Daily	22.00	25.50
Weekly	154.00	178.00

Parking for 4

☷ 🖳 🛇 🅿 TV 🛏 ⌂ ∪ ✿ ⛳ OAP

THORNTON WATLASS

North Yorkshire
Map ref 5C3

Picturesque village in Lower
Wensleydale.

The Buck Inn ⚠

☷☷☷ COMMENDED

Thornton Watlass, Ripon HG4 4AH
☎ Bedale (01677) 422461
*Friendly village inn overlooking the
delightful cricket green in a small
village, 3 miles from Bedale on the*

Continued ▶

THORNTON WATLASS

Continued

Masham road, and close to the A1. In James Herriot country. Walking holidays with experienced leader.
Bedrooms: 1 single, 2 double, 1 twin, 1 triple
Bathrooms: 5 private
Bed & breakfast

per night:	£min	£max
Single	30.00	
Double	50.00	

Lunch available
Evening meal 1830 (last orders 2130)
Parking for 40
Cards accepted: Access, Visa, Diners, Amex

THURLSTONE

South Yorkshire
Map ref 4B1

On the River Don and close to the Peak District National Park. Has some 19th C weavers' cottages with long upper windows.

Weavers Cottages

3-5 Tenter Hill, Thurlstone, Sheffield S30 6RG
☎ Barnsley (01226) 763350
18th C weavers' cottages in conservation area and listed Grade II. Original workrooms converted into private suites with authentic furnishings.
Bedrooms: 1 single, 1 double, 1 twin
Bathrooms: 2 private, 1 public
Bed & breakfast

per night:	£min	£max
Single	19.00	23.00
Double	38.00	46.00

Parking for 2

WARTER

Humberside
Map ref 4C1

Picturesque Wolds village adjacent to the Wolds Way on the B1246 east coast road. Famous for its thatched cottages on the green and the priory, one of the "Lost great houses of East Yorkshire", destroyed in 1970.

Rickman House Bed & Breakfast

Listed COMMENDED
Huggate Road, Warter, York YO4 2SY
☎ Pocklington (01759) 304303
Secluded 17th C wolds farmhouse in large garden, surrounded by parkland overlooking Warter village. Period

furniture, log fires. Convenient for York, Beverley, Hull and East Coast.
Bedrooms: 3 double
Bathrooms: 3 private, 1 public
Bed & breakfast

per night:	£min	£max
Single	18.00	19.00
Double	32.00	34.00

Half board

per person:	£min	£max
Daily	28.50	39.50

Evening meal 1800 (last orders 1900)
Parking for 4
Cards accepted: Access, Visa

WETHERBY

West Yorkshire
Map ref 4B1

Prosperous market town on the River Wharfe, noted for horse-racing.
Tourist Information Centre
☎ *(01937) 582706*

Number Fifty

Listed HIGHLY COMMENDED
50 Westgate, Wetherby LS22 6NJ
☎ (01937) 583106
Elegant early Victorian town house with a large garden and within easy walking distance of market square, restaurants and pleasant riverside.
Bedrooms: 1 double, 2 twin
Bathrooms: 1 public
Bed & breakfast

per night:	£min	£max
Single	22.00	24.00
Double	34.00	36.00

Parking for 4

14 Woodhill View

Listed COMMENDED
Wetherby LS22 6PP
☎ (01937) 581200
Semi-detached house in a quiet residential area near the town centre.
Bedrooms: 1 double, 1 twin
Bathrooms: 1 public
Bed & breakfast

per night:	£min	£max
Single	18.50	20.00
Double	29.00	31.00

Parking for 2
Cards accepted: Access, Visa

National gradings and classifications were correct at the time of going to press but are subject to change. Please check at the time of booking.

YORK

North Yorkshire
Map ref 4C1

Ancient walled city nearly 2000 years old containing many well-preserved medieval buildings. Its Minster has over 100 stained glass windows. Attractions include Castle Museum, National Railway Museum, Jorvik Viking Centre and York Dungeon.
Tourist Information Centre
☎ *(01904) 621756 or 620557*

Arndale Hotel

HIGHLY COMMENDED
290 Tadcaster Road, York YO2 2ET
☎ (01904) 702424

Delightful Victorian house, directly overlooking racecourse. Beautiful enclosed walled gardens giving a country atmosphere within the city. Antiques, fresh flowers, four-poster beds, whirlpool baths. Enclosed gated car park.
Bedrooms: 7 double, 2 twin, 1 triple
Bathrooms: 10 private
Bed & breakfast

per night:	£min	£max
Single	29.00	39.00
Double	39.00	57.00

Parking for 20

Ashwood Place

19 Nunthorpe Avenue, Off Scarcroft Road, York YO2 1PF
☎ (01904) 623412
Fax (01904) 623412
Comfortable guesthouse, close to the city, racecourse and station. Families welcome. Low season breaks. Non-smokers. No parking restrictions.
Bedrooms: 2 double, 1 twin, 1 family room
Bathrooms: 4 private, 1 public
Bed & breakfast

per night:	£min	£max
Double	30.00	45.00

Half board

per person:	£min	£max
Daily	25.00	30.00
Weekly	157.50	196.00

Open February-November

Avimore House Hotel ⚊

 COMMENDED
78 Stockton Lane, York YO3 0BS
☎ (01904) 425556
Edwardian house, now a family-run hotel with quiet rooms, in a pleasant residential area on the east side of the city. Car park.
Bedrooms: 2 single, 1 double, 2 twin, 1 triple
Bathrooms: 6 private
Bed & breakfast

per night:	£min	£max
Single	20.00	26.00
Double	34.00	46.00

Evening meal 1800 (last orders 1200)
Parking for 6

Beech House ⚊

6-7 Longfield Terrace, Bootham, York YO3 7DJ
☎ (01904) 634581
Small, family-run guesthouse with a warm welcome and a relaxing atmosphere, only 5 minutes' walk from York Minster.
Bedrooms: 1 single, 5 double, 2 twin
Bathrooms: 8 private
Bed & breakfast

per night:	£min	£max
Single	20.00	25.00
Double	36.00	46.00

Evening meal from 1800
Parking for 5

Black Bull Inn ⚊

COMMENDED
Main Street, Escrick, York YO4 6JP
☎ (01904) 728245

Appealing cottage-style village inn close to York offers comfortable en-suite accommodation and fine food in its notable restaurant.
Bedrooms: 5 double, 2 twin, 1 family room
Bathrooms: 8 private
Bed & breakfast

per night:	£min	£max
Single	35.00	35.00
Double	48.00	58.00

Lunch available
Evening meal 1830 (last orders 2200)
Parking for 20
Cards accepted: Access, Visa

Bloomsbury Hotel ⚊

127 Clifton, York YO3 6BL
☎ (01904) 634031
Splendid large Victorian Bed and Breakfast with car park and cosy, well-appointed en-suite rooms. 12 minutes' walk from York Minster and city centre.
Bedrooms: 2 single, 3 double, 3 twin, 3 triple, 1 family room
Bathrooms: 12 private
Bed & breakfast

per night:	£min	£max
Single	20.00	36.00
Double	32.00	48.00

Parking for 14

Bowen House ⚊

4 Gladstone Street, Huntington Road, York YO3 7RF
☎ (01904) 636881

Close to York Minster, this late Victorian town house combines high quality facilities with old-style charm. Private car park. Traditional/vegetarian breakfasts. Non-smoking throughout.
Bedrooms: 1 single, 2 double, 1 twin, 1 family room
Bathrooms: 2 private, 1 public, 1 private shower
Bed & breakfast

per night:	£min	£max
Single	20.00	25.00
Double	31.00	45.00

Parking for 4
Cards accepted: Access, Visa

Burton Villa ⚊

Listed COMMENDED
22 Haxby Road, York YO3 7JX
☎ (01904) 626364

Noted for friendly atmosphere, good breakfasts and high standards. 7 minutes' walk from York Minster. Private parking.
Bedrooms: 1 single, 6 double, 2 twin, 1 triple, 2 family rooms
Bathrooms: 8 private, 1 public

Bed & breakfast

per night:	£min	£max
Single	16.00	22.50
Double	30.00	48.00

Parking for 7

City Centre Guest House ⚊

Listed
54 Walmgate, York YO1 2TJ
☎ (01904) 624048 & 652383
Fax (01904) 612494
Quiet, city centre guesthouse offering a warm welcome. Lunches available on request.
Bedrooms: 3 single, 3 double, 2 twin, 5 triple, 2 family rooms
Bathrooms: 5 private, 4 public
Bed & breakfast

per night:	£min	£max
Single	14.50	18.00
Double	25.00	29.00

Half board		
per person:	£min	£max
Daily	19.50	25.00
Weekly	125.00	150.00

Lunch available
Evening meal 1800 (last orders 2200)
Parking for 15
Cards accepted: Access, Visa, Switch/Delta

City Guest House ⚊

68 Monkgate, York YO3 7PF
☎ (01904) 622483
Small, friendly guesthouse, 5 minutes' walk from York Minster. Private parking. Most rooms en-suite, all with shower. Non-smoking.
Bedrooms: 1 single, 4 double, 2 twin, 2 triple, 1 family room
Bathrooms: 8 private, 2 private showers
Bed & breakfast

per night:	£min	£max
Single	12.00	22.00
Double	28.00	44.00

Parking for 5
Cards accepted: Access, Visa

Craig-Y-Don ⚊

Listed
3 Grosvenor Terrace, Bootham, York YO3 7AG
☎ (01904) 637186 & Mobile 0850 202795
Under the Oliver ownership since 1979, where guests have become friends. Early booking is advisable to prevent disappointment.
Bedrooms: 3 single, 3 double, 2 twin
Bathrooms: 1 private, 3 public

Continued ▶

YORK

Continued

Bed & breakfast

per night:	£min	£max
Single	15.00	19.00
Double	30.00	38.00

Parking for 5
Open January-October, December
Cards accepted: Access, Visa

🛏 10 💪 🖥 👜 ⓤⓛ ⓢ ▥ 🎁 🅂🄿

Cumbria House ⋀

Listed | COMMENDED

2 Vyner Street, Haxby Road, York
YO3 7HS
☎ (01904) 636817
*Family-run guesthouse, 12 minutes'
walk from York Minster. En-suites
available. Easily located from ring road.
Private car park. Brochure.*
Bedrooms: 1 single, 2 double, 1 twin,
1 triple, 1 family room
Bathrooms: 2 private, 2 public

Bed & breakfast

per night:	£min	£max
Single	15.00	20.00
Double	30.00	40.00

Parking for 5

🛏 🖥 ☍ ⓢ ⅄ ▥ 🚗 ✕ ▤ 🅳🅰🅿

Curzon Lodge and Stable Cottages ⋀

👑 👑 COMMENDED

23 Tadcaster Road, Dringhouses, York
YO2 2QG
☎ (01904) 703157

*Delightful 17th C listed house and
former stables in pretty conservation
area overlooking York racecourse, once
a home of the Terry "chocolate" family.
All en-suite, some four-posters. Many
antiques. Large enclosed car park.*
Bedrooms: 1 single, 4 double, 3 twin,
1 triple, 1 family room
Bathrooms: 10 private

Bed & breakfast

per night:	£min	£max
Single	30.00	39.00
Double	45.00	58.00

Parking for 16
Cards accepted: Access, Visa

🛏 8 💪 🖥 ☍ 🖥 ♦ ⅄ ⓤⓛ ⓢ ▥ 🚗 ✕ 🎁 🅂🄿

Hotel Fairmount ⋀

👑 👑 👑

230 Tadcaster Road, Mount Vale, York
YO2 2ES
☎ (01904) 638298
Fax (01904) 639724

---

*Large, tastefully furnished, Victorian
villa with open views over racecourse,
10 minutes from city centre. Ground
floor rooms available for people with
special needs.*
Bedrooms: 2 single, 6 double, 2 twin,
2 triple
Bathrooms: 12 private

Bed & breakfast

per night:	£min	£max
Single	20.00	30.00
Double	35.00	62.00

Half board

per person:	£min	£max
Daily	35.00	45.00

Lunch available
Evening meal 1900 (last orders 2100)
Parking for 12
Cards accepted: Access, Visa, Switch/
Delta

🛏 💪 🖥 ☍ 🖥 ♦ ⓢ 🖥 ⅄ ▥ ▥ 🚗
🎁 35 🅿 🎁 🅂🄿 🏮 🎫

Foss Bank Guest House

👑👑

16 Huntington Road, York YO3 7RB
☎ (01904) 635548
*Small Victorian family-run guesthouse,
comfortable and friendly, on the north-
east side of the city. 5 minutes' walk
from the city wall.*
Bedrooms: 2 single, 3 double, 1 twin
Bathrooms: 2 private, 4 private
showers

Bed & breakfast

per night:	£min	£max
Single	15.00	18.00
Double	30.00	38.00

Parking for 5
Open February-December

🛏 ♦ ⓤⓛ ⓢ ⅄ ▥ ⓉⓋ ▥ 🚗 🎁 🅂🄿 🎫

Four Seasons Hotel ⋀

👑 👑 COMMENDED

7 St Peter's Grove, Bootham, York
YO3 6AQ
☎ (01904) 622621
Fax (01904) 430565
*Beautiful, high-quality Victorian hotel,
in a quiet location 5 minutes' walk from
city centre. All rooms en-suite. Private
car park.*
Bedrooms: 2 double, 1 twin, 1 triple,
1 family room
Bathrooms: 5 private

Bed & breakfast

per night:	£min	£max
Double	44.00	56.00

Parking for 8
Cards accepted: Access, Visa

🛏 💪 🖥 ♦ 🖥 ⓢ 🖥 ⅄ ▥ ⓉⓋ ▥ 🚗 🏮
🅳🅰🅿 🅂🄿

Hillcrest Guest House ⋀

👑 👑 COMMENDED

110 Bishopthorpe Road, York
YO2 1JX
☎ (01904) 653160
*Two elegantly converted Victorian town
houses, close to city centre, race-course
and station. It is our pleasure to offer*

---

*individual attention, home cooking,
comfort and excellent value.*
Bedrooms: 3 single, 4 double, 2 twin,
2 triple, 2 family rooms
Bathrooms: 7 private, 3 public

Bed & breakfast

per night:	£min	£max
Single	15.00	19.00
Double	26.00	40.00

Evening meal 1800 (last orders 1500)
Parking for 8
Cards accepted: Access, Visa

🛏 💪 🖥 ♦ ⓤⓛ 🖥 ⓢ ⅄ 🖥 ⓉⓋ ▥ 🚗 🏮 🅳🅰🅿
🕯 🅂🄿

Holgate Hill Hotel ⋀

👑 👑 👑 👑 APPROVED

124 Holgate Road, York YO2 4BB
☎ (01904) 653786
Fax (01904) 643223
*Family hotel where home cooking is a
speciality. Close to the city centre,
points of historic interest and the
racecourse.*
Bedrooms: 6 single, 15 double, 7 twin,
4 triple, 1 family room
Bathrooms: 33 private, 2 public

Bed & breakfast

per night:	£min	£max
Single	34.00	
Double	54.00	

Half board

per person:	£min	£max
Daily	37.75	

Lunch available
Evening meal 1900 (last orders 2030)
Parking for 18
Cards accepted: Access, Visa, Diners,
Amex, Switch/Delta

🛏 💪 🖥 🖥 ☍ 🖥 ♦ 🖥 ⓢ 🖥 ⓉⓋ ▥ 🚗
🎁 40 ✕ 🅳🅰🅿 🕯 🏮

Holly Lodge ⋀

👑 👑 APPROVED

206 Fulford Road, York YO1 4DD
☎ (01904) 646005
*Listed Georgian building on the A19,
convenient for both the north and south
and within walking distance of the city
centre. Close to university, golf course
and Barbican centre. Quiet rooms and
private car park.*
Bedrooms: 3 double, 1 twin, 1 family
room
Bathrooms: 5 private

Bed & breakfast

per night:	£min	£max
Single	25.00	30.00
Double	30.00	50.00

Parking for 5
Open February-November
Cards accepted: Access, Visa

🛏 💪 🖥 ♦ ⓤⓛ 🖥 ⓢ 🖥 ▥ 🚗 🕯 ✕ 🏮
🅂🄿 🏮

Jacobean Lodge Hotel ⋀

👑 👑 👑 COMMENDED

Plainville Lane, Wigginton, York
YO3 8RG
☎ (01904) 762749
Fax (01904) 762749

Converted 17th C farmhouse, 4 miles north of York. Set in picturesque gardens with ample parking. Open log fire, warm, friendly atmosphere and traditional cuisine.
Bedrooms: 2 single, 8 double, 2 twin, 2 triple
Bathrooms: 14 private
Bed & breakfast

per night:	£min	£max
Single	25.00	33.00
Double	40.00	54.00

Lunch available
Evening meal 1900 (last orders 2200)
Parking for 70
Cards accepted: Access, Visa

The Lodge ᴀ
COMMENDED
Earswick Grange, Old Earswick, York YO3 9SW
☎ (01904) 761387
Modern family house in its own grounds. Large comfortable rooms ideal for families. No smoking establishment. Easy access to York.
Bedrooms: 1 double, 1 triple
Bathrooms: 2 private, 1 public
Bed & breakfast

per night:	£min	£max
Single	16.00	18.00
Double	32.00	32.00

Parking for 3

Midway House Hotel ᴀ
COMMENDED
145 Fulford Road, York YO1 4HG
☎ (01904) 659272
Fax (01904) 621799
Family-run Victorian hotel with spacious en-suite bedrooms, near city centre, university and Fulford golf-course. Private parking. Non-smokers only, please.
Bedrooms: 7 double, 3 twin, 2 triple
Bathrooms: 12 private, 1 public
Bed & breakfast

per night:	£min	£max
Single	20.00	37.00
Double	33.00	45.00

Half board

per person:	£min	£max
Daily	35.00	52.00

Evening meal 1730 (last orders 1900)
Parking for 14
Cards accepted: Access, Visa, Diners, Amex

Newton Guest House ᴀ
Neville Street, Haxby Road, York YO3 7NP
☎ (01904) 635627
Family-run, friendly guesthouse, a few minutes' walk from city centre. Private car park. Non-smoking. Breakfast menu. Your comfort is first priority.

Bedrooms: 1 single, 2 double, 1 twin, 1 triple
Bathrooms: 5 private
Bed & breakfast

per night:	£min	£max
Single	18.00	20.00
Double	32.00	36.00

Parking for 5

Oaklands Guest House
COMMENDED
351 Strensall Road, Old Earswick, York YO3 9SW
☎ (01904) 768443
Friendly, well-furnished house, 3 miles from the city and within easy reach of the A64 and A1237.
Bedrooms: 1 double, 1 twin, 1 triple
Bathrooms: 1 private, 1 public
Bed & breakfast

per night:	£min	£max
Single	18.00	21.00
Double	30.00	36.00

Parking for 7

Orillia House ᴀ
89 The Village, Stockton-on-the-Forest, York YO3 9UP
☎ (01904) 400600 & Mobile 0850 108181
A warm welcome awaits you in this 300-year-old house of charm and character, opposite church. Three miles north east of York.
Bedrooms: 2 double, 1 twin, 2 triple
Bathrooms: 5 private
Bed & breakfast

per night:	£min	£max
Single	22.50	
Double	34.00	

Parking for 10
Cards accepted: Access, Visa

Papillon Hotel ᴀ
Listed
43 Gillygate, York YO3 7EA
☎ (01904) 636505
Small, friendly guesthouse with personal attention at all times. 300 yards from York Minster. En-suite available. No smoking, please.
Bedrooms: 2 single, 1 double, 2 twin, 3 triple
Bathrooms: 3 private, 2 public
Bed & breakfast

per night:	£min	£max
Single	20.00	25.00
Double	35.00	50.00

Parking for 7

Stanley Guest House ᴀ
COMMENDED
Stanley Street, Haxby Road, York YO3 7NW
☎ (01904) 637111

Friendly, comfortable guesthouse, 10 minutes' walk to York Minster and city and close to many attractions. All rooms en-suite. Non-smokers only, please.
Bedrooms: 2 single, 2 double, 1 twin, 1 triple
Bathrooms: 6 private
Bed & breakfast

per night:	£min	£max
Single	17.50	20.00
Double	32.00	40.00

Parking for 5
Cards accepted: Access, Visa

Tower Guest House ᴀ
COMMENDED
2 Feversham Crescent, Wigginton Road, York YO3 7HQ
☎ (01904) 655571 & 635924
Comfortable and spacious 19th C guesthouse with friendly, friendly hosts. Strolling distance from York Minster and city centre attractions.
Bedrooms: 2 double, 1 twin, 2 triple
Bathrooms: 5 private
Bed & breakfast

per night:	£min	£max
Single	18.00	25.00
Double	35.00	40.00

Parking for 5
Cards accepted: Access, Visa

Vegetarian Guest House
COMMENDED
21 Park Grove, York, Norh Yorkshire YO3 7LG
☎ (01904) 644790
Exclusively vegetarian/vegan wholefood accommodation in Victorian town house, 10 minutes' walk from centre. Charming en-suite rooms.
Bedrooms: 1 double, 1 triple
Bathrooms: 2 private, 1 public
Bed & breakfast

per night:	£min	£max
Single	18.00	18.00
Double	36.00	36.00

Parking for 1

Victoria Villa
Listed
72 Heslington Road, York YO1 5AU
☎ (01904) 631647
Victorian town house, close to city centre. Offering clean and friendly accommodation and a full English breakfast.
Bedrooms: 1 single, 2 double, 1 twin, 2 triple
Bathrooms: 2 public
Bed & breakfast

per night:	£min	£max
Single	17.00	20.00
Double	28.00	34.00

Parking for 4

YORK

Continued

Wellgarth House 🅰

👑👑

Wetherby Road, Rufforth, York
YO2 3QB
☎ Rufforth (01904) 738592 & 738595
Fax (01904) 738595

Individual and attractive country guesthouse in the delightful village of Rufforth. Ideal touring base for York and the Yorkshire Dales.

Bedrooms: 1 single, 3 double, 2 twin, 1 triple
Bathrooms: 6 private, 1 public

Bed & breakfast per night:	£min	£max
Single	17.00	
Double	30.00	40.00

Parking for 10
Cards accepted: Access, Visa
🐴 2 🛏 📺 ☕ [UL] 🔒 [S] 🚭 [R] [TV] ▥ 🧺 🛎 20
∪ ✿ 🐕 [OAP] [SP] [T]

USE YOUR *i*'S

There are more than 550 Tourist Information Centres throughout England offering friendly help with accommodation and holiday ideas as well as suggestions of places to visit and things to do. There may well be a centre in your home town which can help you before you set out. You'll find the address of your nearest Tourist Information Centre in your local Phone Book.

Heart of England

From the cheery pubs and busy streets of Birmingham to the remote and beautiful hills of the western Marches, this is a region of sharp and splendid contrasts.

Here you can tour the Cotswolds with its exquisite villages, medieval wool churches and handsome market towns; visit Shakespeare's country, and treat yourself to a theatre ticket in Stratford; or discover the industrial heritage of the famous Potteries and Black Country regions with their factory visits, museums and canals.

But if you simply want to get away from it all for a while, then drive out and explore the wild spaces of the Staffordshire Peaks, walk the rolling slopes of the Malvern Hills or discover the quiet byways of the Welsh border country.

The Counties of Gloucestershire, Hereford & Worcester, Shropshire, Staffordshire, Warwickshire and West Midlands

For more information on the Heart of England, contact:

Heart of England Tourist Board
Lark Hill Road, Worcester WR5 2EF
Tel: (01905) 763436 or 763439
Fax: (01905) 763450
Where to Go in the Heart of England –
see pages 120–123
Where to Stay in the Heart of England –
see pages 124–176

Heart of England

Where to go and what to see

You will find hundreds of interesting places to visit during your stay in the Heart of England, just some of which are listed in these pages. The number against each name will help you locate it on the map (page 123). Contact any Tourist Information Centre in the region for more ideas on days out in the Heart of England.

1 Wedgwood Visitor Centre
Barlaston, Stoke-on-Trent, Staffordshire ST12 9ES
Tel: (01782) 204141
Located in the Wedgwood factory which lies within a 500-acre country estate. Potters and decorators can be seen at work. Museum and shop.

2 Alton Towers Theme Park
Alton, Staffordshire ST10 4DB
Tel: (01538) 702200
Over 125 rides and attractions including Haunted House, Runaway Mine Train, Congo River Rapids, Log Flume, The Beast, Corkscrew and Thunderlooper.

3 Bass Museum, Visitor Centre and Shire Horse Stables
Horninglow Street, Burton upon Trent, Staffordshire DE14 1JZ
Tel: (01283) 42031
First major museum of brewing industry. Exhibition and story of different methods of transporting beer since the early 1800s. Shire horse stables.

4 Shugborough Estate (National Trust)
Shugborough, Milford, Stafford, Staffordshire ST17 0XB
Tel: (01889) 881388
18th C mansion house with fine collection of furniture. Gardens and park contain beautiful neo-classical monuments. Also houses Staffordshire Country Museum.

5 Ironbridge Gorge Museum
Ironbridge, Shropshire TF8 7AW
Tel: (01952) 433522
World's first cast iron bridge, Museum of the River visitor centre, tar tunnel, Jackfield Tile Museum, Coalport China Museum, Rosehill House, Blists Hill Museum, Museum of Iron.

6 Black Country Museum
Tipton Road, Dudley, West Midlands DY1 4SQ
Tel: (0121) 557 9643
Open-air museum bringing Britain's industrial past to life. Shops, chapel, canal trip into limestone cavern houses, underground mining display and electric tramway.

7 Sandwell Park Farm Visitors Centre
Salters Lane, West Bromwich, West Midlands B71 4BG
Tel: (0121) 553 0220
Restored 19th C working farm with livestock breeds of the period, traditional farming methods, displays and exhibitions. Tearooms and Victorian kitchen garden.

8 Birmingham Museum of Science and Industry
146 Newhall Street, Birmingham B3 1RZ
Tel: (0121) 235 1661

Steam engines and locomotives, aircraft, veteran cars, motorcycles and other items of industrial or scientific interest. Interactive areas.

⑨ Cadbury World
Linden Road, Bournville, Birmingham, West Midlands B30 2LD
Tel: (0121) 451 4180
Story of chocolate from Aztec times to present day includes chocolate-making demonstration and children's fantasy factory.

⑩ National Motorcycle Museum
Coventry Road, Bickenhill, West Midlands B92 OEJ
Tel: (01675) 443311
Museum with a collection of 650 British machines from 1898–1993.

⑪ Museum of British Road Transport
St Agnes Lane, Hales Street, Coventry, West Midlands CV1 1NN
Tel: (01203) 832425
160 cars and commercial vehicles from 1896, 200 cycles from 1818 and 50 motorcycles from 1920. Also Thrust 2, holder of land speed record.

⑫ Midland Air Museum
Coventry Airport, Baginton, West Midlands CV8 3AZ
Tel: (01203) 301033
Collection of over 28 historic aeroplanes. Sir Frank Whittle Jet Heritage Centre includes early jet aircraft and aero engines.

⑬ Severn Valley Railway
The Railway Station, Bewdley, Worcestershire DY12 1BG
Tel: (01299) 403816
Preserved standard gauge steam railway running 16 miles between Kidderminster, Bewdley and Bridgnorth. Collection of locomotives and passenger coaches.

⑭ Warwick Castle
Warwick, Warwickshire CV34 4QU
Tel: (01926) 408000
Set in 60 acres of grounds. State rooms, armoury, dungeon, torture chamber, clock tower. Exhibits include "A Royal Weekend Party 1898", a preparation for battle scene and "Kingmaker Feasts".

⑮ Ashorne Hall Nickelodeon
Ashorne Hill, Nr Warwick, Warwickshire CV33 9QN
Tel: (01926) 651444
Britain's only "nickelodeon" with unique presentation of automatic musical instruments. Vintage cinema showing silent films with Compton organ accompaniment.

⑯ Heritage Motor Centre
Banbury Road, Gaydon, Warwickshire CV35 0BJ
Tel: (01926) 641188
Purpose-built transport museum on 63-acre site. Collection of historic British cars, 4-wheel drive circuit, playground, picnic area, nature reserve.

⑰ Shakespeare's Birthplace
Henley Street, Stratford-upon-Avon, Warwickshire CV37 6QW
Tel: (01789) 204016
Half-timbered building furnished in period style, containing many fascinating books, manuscripts and objects. BBC TV Shakespeare costume exhibition.

⑱ Elgar's Birthplace Museum
Crown East Lane, Lower Broadheath, Worcestershire WR2 6RH
Tel: (01905) 333224
Cottage in which Edward Elgar was born, now housing a museum of photographs, musical scores, letters and records associated with the composer.

⑲ The Commandery
Sidbury, Worcester, Worcestershire WR1 2HU
Tel: (01905) 355071
16th C timber-framed building with great hall and panelled rooms. Civil War audio-visual show and exhibition.

⑳ Worcester Cathedral
10A College Green, Worcester
WR1 2LH
Tel: (01905) 28854
Norman crypt and Chapter House, King John's tomb, Prince Arthur's chantry, medieval cloisters and buildings. Facilities available for visually impaired.

㉑ Three Choirs Vineyards Ltd
Baldwins Farm, Newent,
Gloucestershire GL18 1LS
Tel: (01531) 890555
Home of internationally-awarded Three Choirs wine. Visitors are welcome to look round the vineyards and taste the wines at no charge.

㉒ The Lost Street Museum
Palma Court, 27 Brookend Street,
Ross-on-Wye, Herefordshire
HR9 7EE
Tel: (01989) 62752
Complete Edwardian street of shops including tobacconist, glassware,
grocer, chemist, clothes store, pub and many others.

㉓ Jubilee Maze and Museum of Mazes
Jubilee Park, Symonds Yat,
Herefordshire HR9 6DA
Tel: (01600) 890360
Traditional hedge maze with carved stone temple centrepiece, created to celebrate Queen Elizabeth's Jubilee in 1977. World's only "hands-on interactive" Museum of Mazes.

㉔ National Waterways Museum
Llanthony Warehouse, Gloucester
Docks, Gloucester GL1 2EH
Tel: (01452) 318054
Three floors of dockside warehouse with lively displays telling the story of Britain's canals. Outside craft area with demonstrations, café and shop.

㉕ Robert Opie Collection – Museum of Advertising and Packaging
Albert Warehouse, Gloucester
Docks, Gloucester GL1 2EH
Tel: (01452) 302309
Steeped in nostalgia, the Robert Opie Collection of packaging and advertising brings over 100 years of shopping basket history vividly to life.

㉖ Slimbridge Wildfowl and Wetlands Centre
Slimbridge, Gloucester,
Gloucestershire GL2 7BT
Tel: (01453) 890065
Tropical house, hides, heated observatory, exhibits, shop and restaurant.

Find out more

Further information about holidays and attractions in the Heart of England is available from:
Heart of England Tourist Board, Lark Hill Road, Worcester WR5 2EF
Tel: (01905) 763436 (24 hours)

These publications are available free from the Heart of England Tourist Board:
- **Bed & Breakfast Touring Map**
- **Great Escapes** – short breaks and leisure holidays for all seasons
- **Events list**

Also available are:
- **Places to Visit in the Heart of England** – a comprehensive guide to over 750 varied attractions & things to see, also great ideas for where to go in winter, (over £40 in discount vouchers included). £3.50
- **Cotswolds map** £2.95
- **Cotswold/Wyedean map** £3.25
- **Shropshire/Staffordshire map** £3.25
Please add 60p postage for up to 3 items, plus 25p for each additional 3 items

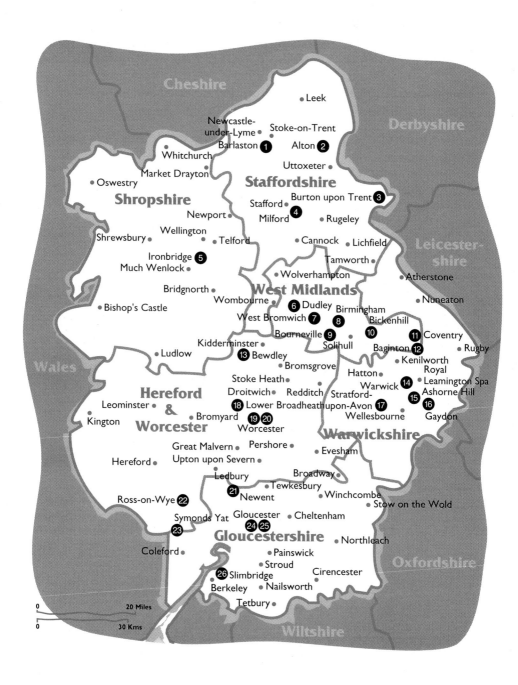

Cheshire

Leek

Newcastle-
under-Lyme
Stoke-on-Trent
Barlaston **1**   Alton **2**

Derbyshire

Whitchurch
Market Drayton
Oswestry

Uttoxeter

Staffordshire

Shrewsbury

Shropshire

Newport
Wellington
Telford

Stafford   Burton upon Trent **3**
Milford **4**
Rugeley

Ironbridge **5**
Much Wenlock

Cannock   Lichfield
Tamworth

Bridgnorth

Wolverhampton

West Midlands

Atherstone

**Leicester-
shire**

Bishop's Castle

Wombourne   Dudley **6**   Birmingham
West Bromwich **7**   Bickenhill **8**
Bourneville **9**   **10**   **11** Coventry
Solihull   Baginton **12**
Kidderminster
Bewdley **13**
Bromsgrove
Hatton
Kenilworth
Royal
Warwick **14**   Leamington Spa
Stratford-   Ashorne Hill
upon-Avon **17**   **15**   **16**
Wellesbourne   Gaydon

Nuneaton

Rugby

Ludlow

**Hereford
&
Worcester**

Leominster
Kington
Bromyard   **18** Lower Broadheath
19 20
Worcester

Stoke Heath
Droitwich
Redditch

Hereford

Great Malvern   Pershore
Upton upon Severn
Ledbury

Warwickshire

Evesham

Broadway
Tewkesbury
Winchcombe
Stow on the Wold
Cheltenham
Northleach

Ross-on-Wye **22**
Symonds Yat
23

Newent **21**

Gloucester
24 25

Coleford

Gloucestershire

Painswick
Stroud
Cirencester

Oxfordshire

Slimbridge **26**
Berkeley   Nailsworth
Tetbury

Wales

0 ——— 20 Miles
0 ——— 30 Kms

Wiltshire

123

WHERE TO STAY

Accommodation entries in this regional section are listed in alphabetical order of place name, and then in alphabetical order of establishment.

Map references refer to the colour location maps at the back of this guide. The first figure is the map number; the letter and figure which follow indicate the grid reference on the map.

At-a-glance symbols at the end of each accommodation entry give information about services and facilities. A handy guide to these symbols can be found inside the back cover flap, which can be kept open for easy reference.

ABBOTS BROMLEY

Staffordshire
Map ref 4B3

Attractive conservation village with a green, a Butter Cross and 18th C almshouses. Well-known for the ancient Horn Dance which takes place each year in September when dancers in Tudor dress bear reindeer antlers. Nearby are Shugborough Hall (National Trust) and Alton Towers.

Crown Inn ⋀
APPROVED

Market Place, Abbots Bromley, Rugeley WS15 3BS
☎ Burton upon Trent (01283) 840227
Fax (01283) 840227
Comfortable and friendly English country inn in centre of attractive village. Home-cooked food using local fresh produce, fully licensed.
Bedrooms: 1 single, 2 double, 2 twin, 1 triple
Bathrooms: 2 public

Bed & breakfast

per night:	£min	£max
Single	20.00	25.00
Double	40.00	40.00

Half board

per person:	£min	£max
Daily	27.50	40.00
Weekly	170.00	200.00

Lunch available
Evening meal 1800 (last orders 2100)
Parking for 30
Cards accepted: Access, Visa
⛷ 🖵 🕯 🦮 🛏 S 🎿 🖥 ▦ 🖳 ♿ ⌇40 ✿ �'' ◨ 🏛

ALCESTER

Warwickshire
Map ref 2B1

Town has Roman origins and many old buildings around the High Street. It is close to Ragley Hall, the 18th C Palladian mansion with its magnificent baroque Great Hall.

Hillcrest
Evesham Road, Arrow, Alcester
B49 5PH
☎ (01789) 762447
Spacious, detached family home, near attractive market town of Alcester, Ragley Hall and Stratford-upon-Avon. Pretty en-suite bedrooms with splendid views.
Bedrooms: 2 double
Bathrooms: 2 private

Bed & breakfast

per night:	£min	£max
Single	18.00	20.00
Double	36.00	40.00

Parking for 7
⛷ 🕯 ⅏ 🎿 🖥 ▦ 🖳 ✿ 🚶 🚵

Orchard Lawns ⋀
HIGHLY COMMENDED

Wixford, Alcester B49 6DA
☎ Stratford-on-Avon (01789) 772668
Charming house with character, set in delightful gardens, in small village on B4085, 7 miles from Stratford-upon-Avon. Ideal touring centre.
Bedrooms: 1 single, 1 double, 1 twin
Bathrooms: 1 private, 1 public

Please mention this guide when making a booking.

Bed & breakfast

per night:	£min	£max
Single	16.00	18.00
Double	32.00	36.00

Parking for 6
Cards accepted: Access, Visa
⛷ 5 🖵 S 🎿 🐾 🖥 ▦ 🖳 ♿ ✿ 🚶 ◨ 🏛

Sambourne Hall Farm ⋀
HIGHLY COMMENDED

Wike Lane, Sambourne, Redditch, Worcestershire B96 6NZ
☎ Studley (01527) 852151
315-acre arable & livestock farm. Mid-17th C farmhouse in a peaceful village, close to local pub. Just off the A435 between Alcester and Studley and 9 miles from Stratford-upon-Avon.
Bedrooms: 2 double, 1 twin
Bathrooms: 3 private

Bed & breakfast

per night:	£min	£max
Single	20.00	25.00
Double	35.00	35.00

Parking for 6
⛷ 🖵 🕯 🖵 S 🎿 🐾 🖥 ▦ 🖳 ♿ ✿ 🚵 🏛

ALDERTON

Gloucestershire
Map ref 2B1

Hillside village with wide views of Evesham Vale. The restored church has a 15th C tower, a broken Saxon font and some medieval glass. Some stone from the previous Norman church has been incorporated into its structure.

Corner Cottage ⋀
Listed

Stow Road, Alderton, Tewkesbury GL20 8NH
☎ Cheltenham (01242) 620630

Originally two farm cottages, now a family home. In large garden with views to surrounding Cotswold Hills and countryside.
Bedrooms: 1 single, 1 double, 1 twin
Bathrooms: 1 public
Bed & breakfast

per night:	£min	£max
Single	15.00	17.00
Double	30.00	34.00

Parking for 5
⌂⬚⌷♦Ⓤⓘ⬚Ⓢ✂️ℳⒸⓋ⬛.🛋☀✈
🚲 ⓈⓅ

ALTON

Staffordshire
Map ref 4B2

Alton Castle, an impressive 19th C building, dominates the village which is set in spectacular scenery. Nearby is Alton Towers, a romantic 19th C ruin with innumerable tourist attractions within one of England's largest theme parks in its 800 acres of magnificent gardens.

Bank House
👑👑 APPROVED
Smithy Bank, Alton, Stoke-on-Trent
ST10 4AA
☎ Oakamoor (01538) 702524
Central in Alton village, 1 mile from Alton Towers and close to Dovedale and Manifold Valley. 3 good inns serving meals within 200 metres. Family-run.
Bedrooms: 2 double, 1 twin, 3 family rooms
Bathrooms: 4 private, 1 public
Bed & breakfast

per night:	£min	£max
Double	38.00	38.00

Parking for 6
⌂⬚♦Ⓤⓘⓜ Ⓒⓥ⬛⬛.🛋🚲 ⓈⓅ

Bee Cottage ⋀⋀
Listed COMMENDED
Saltersford Lane, Alton, Stoke-on-Trent ST10 4AU
☎ Oakamoor (01538) 702802
Traditional stone-built cottage, extended over a period of 200 years. In countryside, 1 mile from Alton Towers. Adjoining paddock and orchard extending to 2 acres.
Bedrooms: 2 double, 1 twin
Bathrooms: 1 private, 2 public
Bed & breakfast

per night:	£min	£max
Single	15.00	20.00
Double	30.00	35.00

Parking for 5
Open March-November
⌂🍴♦Ⓤⓘ✂️ℳ⬛.🚲

Bradley Elms Farm ⋀⋀
👑👑👑 COMMENDED
Threapwood, Cheadle, Stoke-on-Trent
ST10 4RA
☎ Cheadle (01538) 753135

Well-appointed farm accommodation providing a comfortable and relaxing atmosphere for that well-earned break. On the edge of the Staffordshire Moorlands. 3 miles from Alton Towers, close to the Potteries and the Peak District National Park.
Bedrooms: 4 double, 3 twin, 1 triple, 1 family room
Bathrooms: 9 private, 1 public
Bed & breakfast

per night:	£min	£max
Double	35.00	40.00

Half board

per person:	£min	£max
Daily	37.00	39.00

Lunch available
Evening meal 1830 (last orders 2000)
Parking for 10
⌂🍴⬚⌷♦ⓘℳ☀⬛.🛋🍷10 🍽️🌟
☀✈Ⓣ

Bulls Head Inn ⋀⋀
👑👑👑 APPROVED
High Street, Alton ST10 4AQ
☎ Oakamoor (01538) 702307
Fax (01538) 702065
In the village of Alton close to Alton Towers, an 18th C inn with real ale and home cooking.
Bedrooms: 3 double, 1 twin, 2 family rooms
Bathrooms: 6 private, 1 public
Bed & breakfast

per night:	£min	£max
Single	30.00	35.00
Double	45.00	50.00

Lunch available
Evening meal 1900 (last orders 2200)
Parking for 10
Cards accepted: Access, Visa, Switch/ Delta
⌂⬚⌷♦ⓘⓜℳ⬛.🛋✈🚲 ⓈⓅ🎏

Cotton Lane Farm
👑👑 COMMENDED
Cotton, Oakamoor, Stoke-on-Trent
ST10 3DS
☎ Oakamoor (01538) 702033
10-acre horse farm. Character farmhouse with log fires, oak beams, patchwork quilts, home-made bread. Ideal for walking, cycling and riding. Alton Towers 2 miles.
Bedrooms: 1 double, 1 twin, 1 family room
Bathrooms: 1 private, 1 public
Bed & breakfast

per night:	£min	£max
Single	16.00	18.00
Double	32.00	34.00

Parking for 10
Open March-November
⌂⬚♦Ⓤⓘ Ⓢ Ⓒⓥ⬛.🛋∪↺✓☀
🚲 ⓈⓅ

Hillside Farm
Denstone, Uttoxeter ST14 5HG
☎ Rocester (01889) 590760
Victorian farmhouse with extensive views to the Weaver Hills and Churnet Valley. Situated 2 miles south of Alton Towers on B5032.

Bedrooms: 1 double, 2 family rooms
Bathrooms: 2 public
Bed & breakfast

per night:	£min	£max
Single	15.00	18.00
Double	30.00	35.00

Parking for 7
Open March-November
⌂⬚♦Ⓤⓘ Ⓢ Ⓒⓥ⬛.🛋☀✈🚲

Talbot Inn ⋀⋀
Listed
Red Road, Alton, Stoke-on-Trent
ST10 4BX
☎ Oakamoor (01538) 702767
Charming country inn, delightful setting within view of Alton Towers, offering varied, interesting home-cooked food, real ale and comfortable accommodation.
Bedrooms: 1 twin, 1 family room
Bathrooms: 1 public
Bed & breakfast

per night:	£min	£max
Double		40.00

Lunch available
Evening meal 1830 (last orders 2100)
Parking for 20
⌂⬚♦ⓘ Ⓢ✂️⬛.☀✈🚲 ⓈⓅ

ARLINGHAM

Gloucestershire
Map ref 2B1

Small, quiet village in a horseshoe bend of the River Severn. The parish church contains medieval glass and interesting sculptures. Berkeley Castle and the Wildfowl Trust at Slimbridge are nearby and there is easy access from the M5 and A38.

Horseshoe View ⋀⋀
Listed
Overton Lane, Arlingham, Gloucester
GL2 7JJ
☎ Gloucester (01452) 740293
Ideally situated for touring. Close to the Forest of Dean, Wildfowl Trust and the M5, with many other places of interest nearby.
Bedrooms: 1 single, 2 double, 1 twin
Bathrooms: 1 private, 2 public
Bed & breakfast

per night:	£min	£max
Single	12.50	12.50
Double	30.00	30.00

Parking for 5
⌂5🍴ⓊⓘℳⒸⓥ✈🚲 ⓄⒶⓅ ⓈⓅ

Individual proprietors have supplied all details of accommodation. As changes can occur, we advise you to confirm the information at the time of booking.

AVON DASSETT

Warwickshire
Map ref 2C1

Village on the slopes of the Dasset Hills, with good views. The church, with its impressive tower and spire, dates from 1868 but incorporates a 14th C window with 15th C glass.

Crandon House ⋀

⚜ ⚜ HIGHLY COMMENDED

Avon Dassett, Leamington Spa CV33 0AA
☎ Fenny Compton (01295) 770652
Fax (01295) 770652

20-acre mixed farm. Farmhouse offering a high standard of accommodation with superb views over unspoilt countryside. Quiet and peaceful. Easy access to Warwick, Stratford and Cotswolds. 4 miles from junctions 11 and 12 of M40.
Bedrooms: 1 double, 2 twin
Bathrooms: 3 private

Bed & breakfast per night:	£min	£max
Single	22.00	28.00
Double	36.00	42.00

Half board per person:	£min	£max
Daily	29.00	34.00
Weekly	206.00	234.00

Evening meal from 1900
Parking for 22
Cards accepted: Access, Visa
⛁ 8 ⬜ ♿ ⚲ ⓾ 🛁 ⓢ 🍴 ⏰ 📺 Ⓜ ▱ ✓ ✿ 🐎 SP

BALSALL COMMON

West Midlands
Map ref 4B3

Close to Kenilworth and within easy reach of Coventry.

Avonlea ⋀

Listed

135 Kenilworth Road, Balsall Common, Coventry CV7 7EU
☎ Berkswell (01676) 533003 & Mobile 0850 915611
Fax (01676) 533003
19th C cottage extended to provide spacious and comfortable accommodation, a walk back from main A425 road. Ample off-road parking.
Bedrooms: 1 double, 2 twin
Bathrooms: 1 public

Bed & breakfast per night:	£min	£max
Single	20.00	20.00
Double	40.00	40.00

Parking for 5
⛁ ⬜ ♿ 🛁 ⓾ ♿ ⓢ 🍴 📺 Ⓜ ✿ 🐎 🐎

Blythe Paddocks ⋀

⚜

Barston Lane, Balsall Common, Coventry CV7 7BT
☎ Berkswell (01676) 533050
Family home standing in 5 acres. Ten minutes from Birmingham Airport and the National Exhibition Centre. NAC Stoneleigh 8 miles. Countryside location.
Bedrooms: 2 single, 1 double, 1 twin
Bathrooms: 1 public

Bed & breakfast per night:	£min	£max
Single	16.00	20.00
Double	32.00	40.00

Parking for 10
⛁ ⚲ 🍴 ⬜ ♿ 🛁 ⓾ 📺 Ⓜ ▱ ✿ 🐎 Ⓣ

BARLASTON

Staffordshire
Map ref 4B2

Wedgwood Memorial College ⋀

⚜

Station Road, Barlaston, Stoke-on-Trent ST12 9DG
☎ Stoke-on-Trent (01782) 372105 & 373743
Fax (01782) 372393
Pleasant, well-appointed adult residential college with relaxed, homely ambience. In a quiet village, yet close to National Trust downs and Potteries. Convenient for Peak District, Alton Towers. Good quality, home-cooked food with an imaginative repertoire of vegetarian dishes. Limited facilities for the disabled.
Bedrooms: 9 single, 7 twin, 3 triple, 2 family rooms
Bathrooms: 3 private, 7 public

Bed & breakfast per night:	£min	£max
Single	12.50	
Double	25.00	

Half board per person:	£min	£max
Daily	18.50	
Weekly	129.50	

Lunch available
Evening meal 1830 (last orders 1830)
Parking for 40
Cards accepted: Access, Visa
⛁ ⚤ ♿ 🛁 ⓢ 🍴 📺 Ⓜ ▱ ⍌50 ♦ ♿ ✿ 🐎

We advise you to confirm your booking in writing.

BAYTON

Hereford and Worcester
Map ref 4A3

A north-west Worcestershire village on a hill, with some pretty cottages of half-timber and with fine distant views into Shropshire from the sloping field in which the church is set.

The Old Vicarage

⚜

Bayton, Kidderminster, Worcestershire DY14 9LP
☎ Clows Top (01299) 832257
Attractive, modern property with superb views over the Teme Valley. Take B4202 off A456 to Bayton.
Bedrooms: 1 double, 1 twin
Bathrooms: 1 private, 1 public

Bed & breakfast per night:	£min	£max
Single	13.00	16.00
Double	26.00	32.00

Half board per person:	£min	£max
Daily	22.00	25.00
Weekly	140.00	150.00

Evening meal 1800 (last orders 2030)
Parking for 6
⛁ 🍴 ⬜ 🛁 ⓾ ♿ ⓢ 📺 Ⓜ ▱ ✿ 🐎 OAP

BERKELEY

Gloucestershire
Map ref 2B1

Town dominated by the castle where Edward II was murdered. Dating from Norman times, it is still the home of the Berkeley family and is open to the public April to September and October Sundays. Slimbridge Wildfowl Trust is nearby.

Pickwick Farm

Listed COMMENDED

Berkeley GL13 9EU
☎ Dursley (01453) 810241
120-acre dairy farm. A warm welcome at this easily located family farm, formerly a coaching inn used by Charles Dickens. Close to Berkeley Castle, Slimbridge Wildfowl Trust and 3 golf courses. Non-smoking establishment.
Bedrooms: 1 double, 2 twin
Bathrooms: 1 public

Bed & breakfast per night:	£min	£max
Single	16.00	17.00
Double	32.00	34.00

Parking for 3
⛁ ♿ 🛁 ⓢ 🍴 ⏰ 📺 Ⓜ ▱ ✦ ✿ 🐎

BERKSWELL

West Midlands
Map ref 4B3

Pretty village with an unusual set of 5-holed stocks on the green. It has some fine houses, cottages, a 16th C inn and a windmill open to the public Sunday afternoons, May to end September. The Norman church is one of the finest in the area, with many interesting features.

Elmcroft Country Guesthouse ⋔

Listed HIGHLY COMMENDED

Elmcroft, Hodgetts Lane, Berkswell, Coventry CV7 7HO
☎ (01676) 535204
Country guesthouse in close proximity to the National Exhibition Centre and ideal base for all of Warwickshire's tourist attractions.
Bedrooms: 1 single, 2 double, 2 twin
Bathrooms: 5 private
Bed & breakfast

per night:	£min	£max
Single	25.00	
Double	40.00	

Evening meal 1800 (last orders 2000)
Parking for 8

BEWDLEY

Hereford and Worcester
Map ref 4A3

Attractive hillside town on the River Severn, approached by a bridge designed by Telford. The town has many elegant buildings and an interesting museum. It is the southern terminus of the Severn Valley Steam Railway.
Tourist Information Centre
☎ *(01299) 404740*

Clay Farm ⋔

HIGHLY COMMENDED

Clows Top, Kidderminster, Worcestershire DY14 9NN
☎ Clows Top (01299) 832421
98-acre mixed farm. Modern farmhouse with outstanding views. Bedrooms en-suite with tea-making facilities. TV lounge, central heating. Fly and coarse fishing pools. Brochures on request. On B4202 Clows Top to Cleobury Mortimer road.
Bedrooms: 2 double, 1 twin
Bathrooms: 3 private, 1 public
Bed & breakfast

per night:	£min	£max
Single	18.00	20.00
Double	34.00	

Parking for 10

BIBURY

Gloucestershire
Map ref 2B1

Village on the River Coln with stone houses and the famous 17th C Arlington Row, former weavers' cottages. Arlington Mill is now a folk museum. Trout farm and Bansley House Gardens nearby are open to the public.

Cotteswold House

HIGHLY COMMENDED

Arlington, Bibury, Cirencester GL7 5ND
☎ Cirencester (01285) 740609
Enjoy a relaxed friendly atmosphere in this family home. Ideally situated for touring the Cotswolds. All bedrooms en-suite with TV. Guest lounge/dining room. No smoking, please. Parking.
Bedrooms: 2 double, 1 twin
Bathrooms: 3 private
Bed & breakfast

per night:	£min	£max
Single		25.00
Double		38.00

Parking for 4

BIRDLIP

Gloucestershire
Map ref 2B1

Hamlet at the top of a very steep descent down to the Gloucester Vale with excellent viewpoint over Crickley Hill Country Park.

Beechmount ⋔

COMMENDED

Birdlip, Cirencester GL4 8JH
☎ Gloucester (01452) 862262
Family-run guesthouse with personal attention. Ideal centre for the Cotswolds. Choice of menu for breakfast, unrestricted access.
Bedrooms: 1 single, 2 double, 2 twin, 2 triple
Bathrooms: 2 private, 1 public
Bed & breakfast

per night:	£min	£max
Single	14.50	30.00
Double	28.00	42.00

Evening meal (last orders 1900)
Parking for 7

National gradings and classifications were correct at the time of going to press but are subject to change. Please check at the time of booking.

BIRMINGHAM

West Midlands
Map ref 4B3

Britain's second city, whose attractions include Centenary Square and the ICC with Symphony Hall, the NEC, the City Art Gallery, Barber Institute of Fine Arts, 17th C Aston Hall, science and railway museums, Jewellery Quarter, Cadbury World, 2 cathedrals and Botanical Gardens.
Tourist Information Centre
☎ *(0121) 643 2514 or 780 4321 or 693 6300*

Heath Lodge Hotel ⋔

Coleshill Road, Marston Green, Birmingham B37 7HT
☎ (0121) 779 2218
Fax (0121) 779 2218

Licensed family-run hotel, quietly situated less than 2 miles from the National Exhibition Centre and Birmingham Airport. Courtesy car to airport.
Bedrooms: 9 single, 3 double, 5 twin, 1 family room
Bathrooms: 13 private, 1 public, 1 private shower
Bed & breakfast

per night:	£min	£max
Single	25.00	39.50
Double	32.00	50.00

Evening meal 1830 (last orders 2030)
Parking for 24
Cards accepted: Access, Visa, Diners, Amex

Lyndhurst Hotel ⋔

135 Kingsbury Road, Erdington, Birmingham B24 8QT
☎ (0121) 373 5695
Fax (0121) 373 5695
Within half a mile of M6 (junction 6) and within easy reach of the city and National Exhibition Centre. Comfortable bedrooms, spacious restaurant. Personal service in a quiet friendly atmosphere.
Bedrooms: 10 single, 2 double, 2 twin
Bathrooms: 13 private, 1 public
Bed & breakfast

per night:	£min	£max
Single	25.00	39.00
Double	37.50	49.50

Continued ▶

BIRMINGHAM

Continued

Half board per person:	£min	£max
Daily	38.00	49.50
Weekly	250.00	295.00

Evening meal 1800 (last orders 2000)
Parking for 12
Cards accepted: Access, Visa, Diners, Amex

🛏️�️📞⌨️👜🐾🛎️📱 ⓣ30 ✿ 🐎 SP Ⓣ

BIRMINGHAM AIRPORT

West Midlands

See under Balsall Common, Berkswell, Coleshill, Coventry, Hampton in Arden, Solihull

BISHOP'S CASTLE

Shropshire
Map ref 4A3

A 12th C Planned Town with a castle site at the top of the hill and a church at the bottom of the main street. Many interesting buildings with original timber frames hidden behind present day houses. On the Welsh border close to the Clun Forest in quiet, unspoilt countryside.

Castle Hotel
👑👑 COMMENDED

The Square, Bishop's Castle SY9 5DG
☎ (01588) 638403
300-year-old unspoilt coaching inn. Large, well-kept garden with views over the town and valley.
Bedrooms: 1 single, 4 double, 2 twin
Bathrooms: 2 private, 2 public

Bed & breakfast per night:	£min	£max
Single	28.00	
Double	40.00	45.00

Lunch available
Evening meal 1830 (last orders 2100)
Parking for 40
Cards accepted: Access, Visa

🛏️📺👜📶👜🛎️📱ⓣ40 ✿🐎🐚Ⓣ

BISHOP'S CLEEVE

Gloucestershire
Map ref 2B1

Village close to Sudeley Castle, Cheltenham Spa and the Cotswolds.

Barn End
Listed

23 Cheltenham Road, Bishop's Cleeve, Cheltenham GL52 4LU
☎ Cheltenham (01242) 672404
Large, spacious, comfortable detached house. Convenient for Cheltenham and

its racecourse, Tewkesbury, Stratford-upon-Avon and the Cotswolds.
Bedrooms: 1 double, 2 twin
Bathrooms: 1 private, 1 public

Bed & breakfast per night:	£min	£max
Double	34.00	34.00

Parking for 7

🛏️3🏕️👜👜🛎️🐾🛎️📺👜📱🐾🛎️

BLEDINGTON

Gloucestershire
Map ref 2B1

Village close to the Oxfordshire border, with a pleasant green and a beautiful church.

Kings Head Inn & Restaurant 🅰
👑👑👑 COMMENDED

The Green, Bledington, Oxford OX7 6HD
☎ Kingham (01608) 658365
Fax (01608) 658902

15th C inn located in the heart of the Cotswolds, facing the village green. Authentic lounge bars, notable restaurant. Delightful en-suite rooms.
Bedrooms: 10 double, 2 twin
Bathrooms: 12 private

Bed & breakfast per night:	£min	£max
Single	40.00	42.00
Double	60.00	75.00

Lunch available
Evening meal 1900 (last orders 2200)
Parking for 60
Cards accepted: Access, Visa, Switch/Delta

🛏️🚾📞📺👜📶👜🛎️🐾🛎️📺📱
🍷🛎️✿🐎🐚 OAP SP 🐚Ⓣ

BLOCKLEY

Gloucestershire
Map ref 2B1

This village's prosperity was founded in silk mills and other factories but now it is a quiet, unspoilt place. An excellent centre for exploring pretty Cotswold villages, especially Chipping Campden and Broadway.

21 Station Road 🅰
👑👑 COMMENDED

Blockley, Moreton-in-Marsh GL56 9ED
☎ (01386) 700402
Beautifully presented Cotswold-stone house on edge of delightful village. Ideal base for touring Cotswolds and Shakespeare country. Tastefully

decorated, comfortable, non-smoking accommodation with full en-suite facilities. A warm welcome awaits you.
Bedrooms: 1 double, 2 twin
Bathrooms: 3 private

Bed & breakfast per night:	£min	£max
Single	20.00	20.00
Double	36.00	36.00

Parking for 9

🛏️📬📞👜👜S🐾🛎️📺📱🐾✿🗡️🐎

BODENHAM

Hereford and Worcester
Map ref 2A1

Attractive village with old timbered cottages and stone houses and an interesting church. Here the River Lugg makes a loop and flows under an ancient bridge at the end of the village.

Maund Court
👑👑👑 HIGHLY COMMENDED

Bodenham, Hereford HR1 3JA
☎ (01568) 797282
150-acre mixed farm. Attractive 15th C farmhouse with a large garden, swimming pool and croquet. Riding, golf and pleasant walks nearby. Ideal centre for touring.
Bedrooms: 1 single, 2 double, 1 twin
Bathrooms: 4 private

Bed & breakfast per night:	£min	£max
Single	18.00	20.00
Double	36.00	40.00

Evening meal from 1900
Parking for 8
Open March-October

🛏️🚾📞📬📞👜👜S🐾🛎️📺📱🐾🛝
🛎️🐾✿🐎🐚

BOURTON-ON-THE-WATER

Gloucestershire
Map ref 2B1

The River Windrush flows through this famous Cotswold village which has a green, and cottages and houses of Cotswold stone. Its many attractions include a model village, Birdland, a Motor Museum and the Cotswold Perfumery.

Berkeley Guesthouse 🅰
👑👑 COMMENDED

Moore Road, Bourton-on-the-Water, Cheltenham GL54 2AZ
☎ Cotswold (01451) 810388
Fax (01451) 810388
Detached house with a homely, relaxed atmosphere, furnished to a high standard. Personal attention. Attractive gardens, sun lounge, car park. No smoking.
Bedrooms: 2 double, 1 twin
Bathrooms: 3 private

Bed & breakfast

per night:	£min	£max
Single	17.50	20.00
Double	35.00	40.00

Parking for 4

🛇 4 🕭 🖭 🖵 ♨ UL S ⅙ ⅍ TV ● ▦. ▦ ▭ ♪ ⚘ ✕ 🛲 OAP ⚲ SP

Coombe House ⋀

🛏🛏 HIGHLY COMMENDED

Rissington Road, Bourton-on-the-Water, Cheltenham GL54 2DT
☎ Cotswold (01451) 821966
Fax (01451) 810477
Gentle elegance in quiet Cotswold home. Pretty, thoughtfully equipped en-suite bedrooms. Gardeners' garden. Ample parking. Non-smoking haven. Restaurants riverside walk away.
Bedrooms: 3 double, 2 twin, 2 triple
Bathrooms: 7 private

Bed & breakfast

per night:	£min	£max
Single	38.00	45.00
Double	52.00	64.00

Parking for 10
Cards accepted: Access, Visa, Amex

🛇 🕭 🖭 🖵 ♨ S ⅙ ▦. ▭ ⚘ ✕ 🛲 SP

Farncombe ⋀

🛏🛏

Clapton, Bourton-on-the-Water, Cheltenham GL54 2LG
☎ Cotswold (01451) 820120 & Mobile (01378) 843123
Fax (01451) 820120
Quiet comfortable accommodation with superb views of the Windrush Valley. In the hamlet of Clapton, 2.5 miles from Bourton-on-the-Water. No-smoking house.
Bedrooms: 2 double, 1 twin
Bathrooms: 1 private, 1 public, 2 private showers

Bed & breakfast

per night:	£min	£max
Single	17.50	30.00
Double	35.00	42.00

Parking for 3

🖭 ⚘ UL S ⅙ ⅍ TV ▦. ▭ ∪ ⚘ ✕ 🛲

Lamb Inn ⋀

🛏🛏🛏 COMMENDED

Great Rissington, Bourton-on-the-Water, Cheltenham GL54 2LP
☎ Cotswold (01451) 820388
Fax (01451) 820724
Country inn in rural setting, with home-cooked food, including steaks and local trout, served in attractive restaurant. Beer garden and real ale. Honeymoon suite also available.
Bedrooms: 11 double, 1 twin
Bathrooms: 12 private, 1 public

Bed & breakfast

per night:	£min	£max
Single	35.00	50.00
Double	44.00	75.00

Half board

per person:	£min	£max
Daily	45.00	65.00

Lunch available
Evening meal 1900 (last orders 2130)
Parking for 10
Cards accepted: Access, Visa, Amex

🛇 🕭 🕭 ♨ S ⅙ ⅍ TV ▦. ▭ ⚘ ✕ 🛲 SP 🏠

Lansdowne House ⋀

🛏 COMMENDED

Lansdowne, Bourton-on-the-Water, Cheltenham GL54 2AT
☎ Cotswold (01451) 820812

Large period stone family house. Tastefully furnished en-suite accommodation with a combination of old and antique furniture. Tea/coffee trays, colour TVs, parking, garden.
Bedrooms: 2 double, 1 triple
Bathrooms: 3 private

Bed & breakfast

per night:	£min	£max
Single	23.00	29.00
Double	30.00	35.00

Parking for 4

🛇 🕭 🖭 🖵 ⚘ UL ♨ S ⅙ ⅍ TV ▦. ▭ ⚘ ✕ 🛲 SP

Mousetrap Inn ⋀

🛏 APPROVED

Lansdowne, Bourton-on-the-Water, Cheltenham GL54 2AR
☎ Cotswold (01451) 820579
Small homely inn with beer garden. TV and tea/coffee makers in all rooms. Bar meals, and open fires in winter.
Bedrooms: 7 double, 2 twin
Bathrooms: 9 private

Bed & breakfast

per night:	£min	£max
Single	25.00	30.00
Double	40.00	45.00

Lunch available
Evening meal 1830 (last orders 2100)
Parking for 12

🛇 🕭 🖵 ⚘ S ⅙ ▦. ▭ ♦ ⚘

The Ridge ⋀

🛏🛏

Whiteshoots Hill, Bourton-on-the-Water, Cheltenham GL54 2LE
☎ Cotswold (01451) 820660
Large country house surrounded by beautiful grounds. Central for visiting many places of interest and close to all amenities. Ground floor en-suite bedrooms available.
Bedrooms: 3 double, 1 twin, 1 triple
Bathrooms: 4 private, 1 public

Please mention this guide when making a booking.

Bed & breakfast

per night:	£min	£max
Single	25.00	32.00
Double	32.00	38.00

Parking for 12

🛇 6 🕭 🖵 ⚘ UL ⅙ TV ▦. ▭ ⚘ ✕ 🛲 SP

Rooftrees Guesthouse ⋀

🛏🛏

Rissington Road, Bourton-on-the-Water, Cheltenham GL54 2DX
☎ Cotswold (01451) 821943
Detached Cotswold-stone family house, all rooms individually decorated, 8 minutes' level walk from village centre. Home cooking with fresh local produce. 3 en-suite bedrooms: 2 rooms are on ground floor, 2 rooms have four-posters. No smoking.
Bedrooms: 3 double
Bathrooms: 3 private

Bed & breakfast

per night:	£min	£max
Single	28.00	
Double	38.00	40.00

Half board

per person:	£min	£max
Daily	30.00	31.00
Weekly	200.00	205.00

Evening meal 1830 (last orders 1200)
Parking for 8
Cards accepted: Access, Visa, Switch/Delta

🛇 6 🕭 🕭 ⚲ 🖭 🖵 ⚘ UL ♨ S ⅙ TV ▦. ▭ ✕ 🛲

Strathspey ⋀

🛏 APPROVED

Lansdown, Bourton-on-the-Water, Cheltenham GL54 2AR
☎ Cotswold (01451) 820694
Character, Cotswold-stone house 400 yards' walk from village centre. Quiet location with pretty riverside walk.
Bedrooms: 3 double
Bathrooms: 3 private

Bed & breakfast

per night:	£min	£max
Double	32.00	36.00

Parking for 4
Open April-October

🛇 🕭 🖭 🖵 ⚘ UL ♨ S ⅙ ⅍ ▦. ▭ ✕ 🛲 OAP

Upper Farm

🛏🛏 COMMENDED

Clapton on the Hill, Bourton-on-the-Water, Cheltenham GL54 2LG
☎ Cotswold (01451) 820453
130-acre mixed farm. 17th C Cotswold farmhouse in a quiet, unspoilt village 2.5 miles from Bourton-on-the-Water. Magnificent views. Fresh farm produce.
Bedrooms: 3 double, 2 twin
Bathrooms: 3 private, 1 public

Continued ▶

BOURTON-ON-THE-WATER

Continued

Bed & breakfast

per night:	£min	£max
Single	20.00	
Double	32.00	40.00

Parking for 6
Open March-November

🛇5👤💷🖵♨🕭🛡⚡🐾📺🖼.🛈✓ ❋✖🛏🏮

Willow Crest

🏵🏵 COMMENDED

Rissington Road, Bourton-on-the-Water, Cheltenham GL54 2DZ
☎ Cotswold (01451) 822073
Chalet bungalow in a quiet position on the edge of the village.
Bedrooms: 2 double, 1 twin
Bathrooms: 3 private

Bed & breakfast

per night:	£min	£max
Double	33.00	35.00

Parking for 6

👤💷🖵♨🕭📶Ⓢ🐾📺🖼.🛒❋✖ 🛏SP

BRAILES

Warwickshire
Map ref 2C1

Agdon Farm

Listed

Brailes, Banbury, Oxfordshire
OX15 5JJ
☎ (01608) 685226 & Mobile 0850 847786
520-acre mixed farm. Old Cotswold-stone farmhouse in an Area of Outstanding Natural Beauty. We keep sheep, horses, cats and dogs. Well situated for touring the Cotswolds, Oxford, Warwick and Stratford-upon-Avon.
Bedrooms: 1 double, 1 twin, 1 triple
Bathrooms: 1 public

Bed & breakfast

per night:	£min	£max
Double	35.00	

Evening meal 1800 (last orders 2100)
Parking for 8

🛇🌂🖵♨🕭🛡⚡📺🖼.🛒🛈✓ ❋🛏

New House Farm 🅰

🏵🏵

Brailes, Banbury, Oxfordshire
OX15 5BD
☎ Little Cherington (01608) 686239
420-acre mixed farm. Quietly situated, comfortable Georgian farmhouse in an Area of Outstanding Natural Beauty. Within easy reach of the Cotswolds, 15 miles from Stratford-upon-Avon, 10 miles Banbury Cross, off B4035 and 4 miles from Shipston-on-Stour. 18-hole golf-course nearby.
Bedrooms: 2 double, 1 twin
Bathrooms: 2 private, 1 public

Bed & breakfast

per night:	£min	£max
Single	15.00	18.00
Double	30.00	36.00

Parking for 10

🛇2💷🖵♨🕭📶Ⓢ🐾📺🖼.🛈🛒❋ 🛏DAP🏮

BRIDGNORTH

Shropshire
Map ref 4A3

Red sandstone riverside town in 2 parts - High and Low - linked by a cliff railway. Much of interest including a ruined Norman keep, half-timbered 16th C houses, Midland Motor Museum and Severn Valley Railway.
Tourist Information Centre
☎ *(01746) 763358*

The Albynes

🏵🏵

Nordley, Bridgnorth WV16 4SX
☎ (01746) 762261

263-acre arable and mixed farm. Large country house, peacefully set in parkland with spectacular views of Shropshire countryside. On B4373 - Bridgnorth 3 miles, Ironbridge 4 miles.
Bedrooms: 1 double, 2 twin
Bathrooms: 3 private

Bed & breakfast

per night:	£min	£max
Single	20.00	22.00
Double	36.00	40.00

Parking for 8

🛇💷🖵♨🕭🛡Ⓢ🐾📺🖼.🛒❋✖ 🛏🏮

Aldenham Weir 🅰

🏵🏵 COMMENDED

Muckley Cross, Bridgnorth WV16 4RR
☎ Morville (01746) 714352
Superb country house, set in 11.5 acres, with working mill race, weir and trout stream for fishing. All rooms en-suite. Close to Ironbridge Gorge Museum. Quietly located off the A458, central between Much Wenlock and Bridgnorth.
Bedrooms: 3 double, 2 twin, 1 triple
Bathrooms: 6 private

Bed & breakfast

per night:	£min	£max
Single	25.00	25.00
Double	38.00	38.00

Parking for 7

🛇👤💷🖵♨🕭🛡Ⓢ🐾🕭📺🖼.🛒🛈 ✓❋🛏SP

Haven Pasture 🅰

🏵🏵 COMMENDED

Underton, Bridgnorth WV16 6TY
☎ Middleton Scriven (01746) 789632
Fax (01746) 789632
Large country bungalow, set in 1 acre of gardens, with panoramic views. Outdoor heated swimming pool. Trout pools 400 yards.
Wheelchair access category 3 ♿
Bedrooms: 1 triple
Bathrooms: 1 private, 1 public

Bed & breakfast

per night:	£min	£max
Single	28.00	28.00
Double	36.00	36.00

Parking for 8

🛇👤🌂☎💷🖵♨🕭📶Ⓢ🐾📺🖼.🛒⤵ ❋🛏

Middleton Lodge 🅰

🏵🏵 HIGHLY COMMENDED

Middleton Priors, Bridgnorth WV16 6UR
☎ Ditton Priors (01746) 712228
Imposing stone building in its own grounds, in a quiet hamlet in the Shropshire hills, 6 miles from Bridgnorth. Non-smokers only, please.
Bedrooms: 2 double, 1 twin
Bathrooms: 3 private

Bed & breakfast

per night:	£min	£max
Single	25.00	30.00
Double	45.00	50.00

Parking for 4

🛇12🖵🖵♨🕭🛡⚡📺🖼.🛒❋ ✖🛏

Park Grange Holidays 🅰

🏵🏵

Morville, Bridgnorth WV16 4RN
☎ Morville (01746) 714285
12-acre livestock farm. Splendid beamed family house, with goats, poultry, pony, wildlife and fishing pools. Children's play area. Glorious views. Quiet location midway between Bridgnorth and Much Wenlock just off A458. Look for holiday caravans sign.
Bedrooms: 1 family room
Bathrooms: 1 private

Bed & breakfast

per night:	£min	£max
Double	36.00	36.00

Parking for 10
Open March-October

🛇☎💷🖵♨🕭🛡Ⓢ✂📺🖼.🛒🛈🍴 ▸✓❋✖🛏

BROAD CAMPDEN

Gloucestershire
Map ref 2B1

Vine Cottage

Listed

Broad Campden, Chipping Campden GL55 6US
☎ Evesham (01386) 840282
Idyllic Cotswold cottage in quiet no-through lane in conservation village

one mile from Chipping Campden.
Pretty garden and beautiful countryside.
Bedrooms: 1 single, 1 twin
Bathrooms: 1 public
Bed & breakfast

per night:	£min	£max
Single		19.00
Double		38.00

Parking for 1

🛇🖭☐🖐🔌Ⓤ⼁🔲Ⓣ🖩⣿. 🚗✿🗡🐾📞

BROADWAY

Hereford and Worcester
Map ref 2B1

Beautiful Cotswold village called the "Show village of England", with 16th C stone houses and cottages. Near the village is Broadway Tower with magnificent views over 12 counties and a country park with nature trails and adventure playground.

Cinnibar Cottage 👭
`Listed` `HIGHLY COMMENDED`
45 Bury End, (Snowshill Rd.,),
Broadway, Worcestershire WR12 7AF
☎ (01386) 858 623
150-year-old Cotswold-stone cottage.
Quiet situation with open country views,
half a mile from Broadway village
green, along Snowshill road. Non-
smoking establishment.
Bedrooms: 1 double, 1 twin
Bathrooms: 1 public
Bed & breakfast

per night:	£min	£max
Double	32.00	36.00

Parking for 2

🛇6🏵🖐Ⓤ🔲Ⓢ⼁🔲Ⓣ🖩. 🚗🗡🐾

Crown and Trumpet Inn 👭
`APPROVED`
Church Street, Broadway,
Worcestershire WR12 7AE
☎ (01386) 853202
Fax (01386) 853874
Traditional English inn with log fires
and oak beams, quietly located just off
the village green. Home-cooked local
and seasonal English food.
Bedrooms: 3 double, 1 twin
Bathrooms: 4 private
Bed & breakfast

per night:	£min	£max
Double		39.00

Lunch available
Evening meal 1830 (last orders 2130)
Parking for 6

🛇☐🖐Ⓘ🔲Ⓢ🖩. 🚗📞Ս✿🐾🔲📞

Eastbank 👭
👑👑👑
Station Drive, Broadway,
Worcestershire WR12 7DF
☎ (01386) 852659
Quiet location, half a mile from village.
All rooms fully en-suite (bath/shower),
with colour TV and beverage facilities.
Homely atmosphere. Free brochure.
Bedrooms: 2 double, 2 twin, 2 triple

Bathrooms: 6 private
Bed & breakfast

per night:	£min	£max
Single	15.00	
Double	30.00	50.00

Evening meal 1900 (last orders 1000)
Parking for 6

🛇⼁2🖭🖭☐🖐Ⓤ🔲Ⓘ🔲Ⓢ⼁🔲🖩. 🚗✿
🐾 `OAP` `SP` `T`

Leasow House 👭
👑👑👑 `HIGHLY COMMENDED`
Laverton Meadow, Broadway,
Worcestershire WR12 7NA
☎ Stanton (01386) 584526
Fax (01386) 584596

17th C Cotswold-stone farmhouse
tranquilly set in open countryside close
to Broadway village.
Bedrooms: 3 double, 2 twin, 2 triple
Bathrooms: 7 private
Bed & breakfast

per night:	£min	£max
Single	30.00	48.00
Double	48.00	60.00

Parking for 14
Cards accepted: Access, Visa, Amex

🛇🏵📞🖭☐🖐🔌Ⓘ🔲Ⓢ🔲🖩. 🚗✿
🐾📞

Millhay Cottage
`Listed` `COMMENDED`
Bury End, Broadway, Worcestershire
WR12 7JS
☎ (01386) 858241
House set in a superb garden off the
Snowshill road and adjacent to
Cotswold Way. The suite of two
bedrooms, bathroom and WC is let as a
family unit (1-4 persons).
Bedrooms: 1 family room
Bathrooms: 1 private
Bed & breakfast

per night:	£min	£max
Single	18.00	22.00
Double	36.00	40.00

Parking for 12
Open January-February, April-
December

🛇☐🔲Ⓤ🔲Ⓘ🔲Ⓢ🖩. 🚗🔾🔾✿🐾

Mount Pleasant Farm 👭
👑👑👑 `HIGHLY COMMENDED`
Childswickham, Broadway,
Worcestershire WR12 7HZ
☎ (01386) 853424
250-acre mixed farm. Large Victorian
farmhouse with excellent views. Very
quiet accommodation with all modern
amenities. Approximately 3 miles from
Broadway.
Bedrooms: 2 double, 1 twin
Bathrooms: 3 private

Bed & breakfast

per night:	£min	£max
Single		25.00
Double	36.00	42.00

Parking for 8

🛇⼁3☐🖐🔌Ⓤ🔲🔲Ⓣ🖩. 🚗Ս✿🗡🐾

Olive Branch Guest House 👭
👑👑👑
78 High Street, Broadway,
Worcestershire WR12 7AJ
☎ (01386) 853440
Fax (01386) 853440

16th C house with modern amenities
close to centre of village. Traditional
English breakfast served. Reduced rates
for 3 nights or more.
Bedrooms: 1 single, 3 double, 2 twin,
1 triple
Bathrooms: 7 private, 1 public
Bed & breakfast

per night:	£min	£max
Single	16.00	19.50
Double	40.00	48.00

Half board

per person:	£min	£max
Daily	32.00	38.00

Evening meal 1900 (last orders 2000)
Parking for 8
Cards accepted: Amex

🛇🏵🖐Ⓤ🔲Ⓘ🔲Ⓢ🔲🔲Ⓣ🖩. 🚗Ս✿🐾
`SP` `T`

Orchard Grove 👭
👑👑👑 `HIGHLY COMMENDED`
Station Road, Broadway,
Worcestershire WR12 7DE
☎ Evesham (01386) 853834
Attractive detached Cotswold house, just
minutes from village centre, tastefully
appointed for guests' every comfort.
Warm welcome assured. Non-smokers
only, please.
Bedrooms: 1 double, 1 twin, 1 triple
Bathrooms: 3 private
Bed & breakfast

per night:	£min	£max
Double	40.00	45.00

Parking for 3

🛇10🖭☐🖐🔌Ⓤ🔲Ⓢ⼁🔲Ⓣ🖩. 🚗
🗡🐾

Pine Tree Cottage 👭
`Listed` `COMMENDED`
Laverton, Broadway, Worcestershire
WR12 7NA
☎ Stanton (01386) 584280
Fax (01386) 584280
Small family bed and breakfast, 2 miles
from Broadway in peaceful village.
Bedrooms: 1 double, 1 twin
Bathrooms: 2 private

Continued ▶

BROADWAY

Continued

Bed & breakfast

per night:	£min	£max
Single	21.00	21.00
Double	32.00	36.00

Parking for 3

❄🏠⊡📶🅿🔄🆄🅂🏧💷,🚗🛥🚶✖🚲

Shenberrow Hill

Listed

Stanton, Broadway, Worcestershire
WR12 7NE
☎ (01386) 584468
*9-acre horse farm. Attractive country
house, quietly situated in beautiful
unspoilt Cotswold village. Heated
swimming pool. Friendly, helpful
service. Inn nearby.*
Bedrooms: 2 twin, 2 family rooms
Bathrooms: 2 private, 2 public

Bed & breakfast

per night:	£min	£max
Single	25.00	25.00
Double	38.00	40.00

Half board

per person:	£min	£max
Daily	29.00	30.00

Evening meal 1800 (last orders 2000)
Parking for 6

❄3🌀🏠⊡📶🅿🔄🆄🛏🅂🏧,🚗🔌🛥❄✖🚲

Southwold House ⋀

COMMENDED

Station Road, Broadway,
Worcestershire WR12 7DE
☎ (01386) 853681
*Warm welcome, friendly service, good
cooking at this large Edwardian house,
only 4 minutes' walk from village
centre. Reductions for 2 or more nights;
bargain winter breaks.*
Bedrooms: 1 single, 5 double, 2 twin
Bathrooms: 5 private, 2 public

Bed & breakfast

per night:	£min	£max
Single	17.00	
Double	34.00	42.00

Parking for 8
Cards accepted: Access, Visa, Amex

❄🏠⊡📶🆄🅂🏧📺🏧,🚗❄🚲🚶🆂🅃

White Acres Guesthouse ⋀

COMMENDED

Station Road, Broadway,
Worcestershire WR12 7DE
☎ (01386) 852320
*Spacious Victorian house with en-suite
bedrooms, 3 with four-poster beds. Off-
road parking. 4 minutes' walk from
village centre. Reductions for 2 or more
nights. Bargain winter breaks.*
Bedrooms: 5 double, 1 twin
Bathrooms: 6 private

Bed & breakfast

per night:	£min	£max
Double	38.00	42.00

Parking for 8
Open March-November

🏠🏠⊡📶🅿🔄🆄🛏🏧,🚗❄✖🚲
🆂🅃

Windrush House ⋀

COMMENDED

Station Road, Broadway,
Worcestershire WR12 7DE
☎ (01386) 853577
*Edwardian guesthouse on the A44, 300
yards from the village centre, offering
personal service. Evening meals by
arrangement. 10 per cent reduction in
tariff after 2 nights. A no-smoking
establishment.*
Bedrooms: 4 double, 1 twin
Bathrooms: 5 private

Bed & breakfast

per night:	£min	£max
Single	18.00	25.00
Double	36.00	44.00

Half board

per person:	£min	£max
Daily	30.00	34.00
Weekly	200.00	220.00

Parking for 5

⊡📶🅿🔄🆂🅂🏧,🚗🚲🆂🅿

BROMSGROVE

Hereford and Worcester
Map ref 4B3

This market town near the Lickey
Hills has an interesting museum
and craft centre and 14th C
church with fine tombs and a
Carillon tower. The Avoncroft
Museum of Buildings is nearby
where many old buildings have
been re-assembled, having been
saved from destruction.
Tourist Information Centre
☎ *(01527) 831809*

The Barn ⋀

COMMENDED

Woodman Lane, Clent, Stourbridge,
Worcestershire DY9 9PX
☎ Hagley (01562) 885879 &
Kingswinford (01384) 401977
*Converted Georgian barn on
smallholding. At foot of Clent Hills with
access to the hills from property. Easy
access to Birmingham and National
Exhibition Centre.*
Bedrooms: 1 triple
Bathrooms: 1 private

Bed & breakfast

per night:	£min	£max
Single	20.00	20.00
Double	40.00	40.00

Evening meal 1900 (last orders 2100)
Parking for 11

❄🏠🏠⊡📶🆄🅂🔄🏧,🚗🛥❄
🚲🆎

The Grahams

Listed COMMENDED

95 Old Station Road, Bromsgrove,
Worcestershire B60 2AF
☎ (01527) 874463
*Modern house in quiet pleasant location
close to the A38, 3 miles from the M5
and 1.5 miles from the M42. Within
easy reach of National Exhibition
Centre, Worcester and Stratford. Car
parking, TV lounge, tea/coffee facilities.*
Bedrooms: 2 single, 1 twin
Bathrooms: 1 public

Bed & breakfast

per night:	£min	£max
Single	15.00	15.00
Double	30.00	30.00

Half board

per person:	£min	£max
Daily	20.00	20.00
Weekly	120.00	120.00

Evening meal 1800 (last orders 0900)
Parking for 2

❄2🌀🛥🅿🛏📺🏧,🚗✖🚲

Hill Farm ⋀

COMMENDED

Rocky Lane, Bournheath, Bromsgrove,
Worcestershire B61 9HU
☎ (01527) 872403
*50-acre market garden. Georgian listed
farmhouse, tastefully maintained
throughout. Traditional farmhouse fare.
Families welcome.*
Bedrooms: 2 single, 1 double, 2 twin
Bathrooms: 5 private

Bed & breakfast

per night:	£min	£max
Single	20.00	25.00
Double	40.00	50.00

Half board

per person:	£min	£max
Daily	31.50	35.00
Weekly	203.00	220.50

Evening meal 1800 (last orders 2000)
Parking for 6

❄3🌀🛥🔄🆄🛏🅂🔄🏧📺🏧,🚗❄
✖🚲🆎

BROMYARD

Hereford and Worcester
Map ref 2B1

Market town on the River Frome
surrounded by orchards, with black
and white houses and a Norman
church. Nearby at Lower
Brockhampton is a 14th C half-
timbered moated manor house
owned by the National Trust.
Heritage Centre.
Tourist Information Centre
☎ *(01885) 482038*

Park House ⋀

⛲⛲

28 Sherford Street, Bromyard,
Herefordshire HR7 4DL
☎ (01885) 482294

Close to town centre, restaurant and shops, and a desirable location for touring. Ample parking.
Bedrooms: 1 single, 1 double, 1 twin, 2 triple
Bathrooms: 3 private, 1 public
Bed & breakfast

per night:	£min	£max
Single	15.00	20.00
Double	28.00	30.00

Parking for 6

BROSELEY

Shropshire
Map ref 4A3

Lord Hill Guest House
Listed

Duke Street, Broseley TF12 5LU
☎ Telford (01952) 884270
Former public house renovated to a high standard. Easy access to Ironbridge, Bridgnorth, Shrewsbury and Telford town centre.
Bedrooms: 1 single, 1 double, 5 twin
Bathrooms: 3 private, 2 public, 1 private shower
Bed & breakfast

per night:	£min	£max
Single	16.00	19.00
Double	32.00	36.00

Parking for 9

BURTON UPON TRENT

Staffordshire
Map ref 4B3

An important brewing town with the Bass Museum of Brewing, where the Bass shire horses are stabled. There are 3 bridges with views over the river and some interesting public buildings including the 18th C St Modwen's Church.
Tourist Information Centre
☎ *(01283) 516609*

Hayfield House
Listed

13 Ashby Road, Woodville, Swadlincote, Derbyshire DE11 7BZ
☎ (01283) 225620
Victorian villa on the A50 in South Derbyshire, close to the Leicestershire/Staffordshire/Derbyshire border.
Bedrooms: 1 triple, 1 family room
Bathrooms: 1 private, 1 public
Bed & breakfast

per night:	£min	£max
Single	14.00	15.00
Double	28.00	30.00

Half board

per person:	£min	£max
Daily	20.00	21.00
Weekly	126.00	133.00

Evening meal 1800 (last orders 1900)
Parking for 3

CARDINGTON

Shropshire
Map ref 4A3

Grove Farm
Listed

Cardington, Church Stretton SY6 7JZ
☎ Longville (01694) 771451
7-acre mixed farm. Oak-beamed farmhouse built in 1667, in delightful village 5 miles from Church Stretton. Excellent walking country. Homely atmosphere.
Bedrooms: 1 twin, 1 triple
Bathrooms: 1 public
Bed & breakfast

per night:	£min	£max
Single	15.00	16.00
Double	26.00	30.00

Parking for 10

CHALFORD

Gloucestershire
Map ref 2B1

In the Stroud valley, with very steep little side streets, handsome Georgian cloth mills and their former owners' houses.

Millswood ⋀

Old Neighbouring, Chalford, Stroud GL6 8AA
☎ Stroud (01453) 883787
Fax (01453) 883787
Medieval long house, circa 1480, in wooded situation.
Bedrooms: 2 double
Bathrooms: 2 private
Bed & breakfast

per night:	£min	£max
Single	20.00	20.00
Double	38.00	38.00

Parking for 4

CHEDDLETON

Staffordshire
Map ref 4B2

Brook House Farm ⋀
COMMENDED

Cheddleton, Leek ST13 7DF
☎ Churnetside (01538) 360296
200-acre dairy farm. In a picturesque valley. Family rooms in a tastefully converted cowshed, other rooms in the farmhouse; all with private facilities.

Bedrooms: 2 double, 1 triple, 2 family rooms
Bathrooms: 5 private
Bed & breakfast

per night:	£min	£max
Single	16.00	18.00
Double	32.00	36.00

Half board

per person:	£min	£max
Daily	25.00	27.00
Weekly	175.00	185.00

Evening meal 1800 (last orders 1400)
Parking for 6

CHELMARSH

Shropshire
Map ref 4A3

An unspoilt village near the River Severn, with old timbered cottages and an imposing 14th C church.

Bulls Head Inn ⋀
COMMENDED

Chelmarsh, Bridgnorth WV16 6BA
☎ Highley (01746) 861469

17th C village inn with warm friendly atmosphere. All rooms en-suite. TV lounge, jacuzzi, solarium. Magnificent views.
Bedrooms: 1 single, 3 double, 1 twin, 1 triple
Bathrooms: 6 private
Bed & breakfast

per night:	£min	£max
Single	19.50	27.00
Double	29.50	41.00

Half board

per person:	£min	£max
Daily	27.50	35.00
Weekly	165.00	210.00

Lunch available
Evening meal 1900 (last orders 2130)
Parking for 50
Cards accepted: Access, Visa, Switch/Delta

Individual proprietors have supplied all details of accommodation. As changes can occur, we advise you to confirm the information at the time of booking.

CHELTENHAM

Gloucestershire
Map ref 2B1

Cheltenham was developed as a spa town in the 18th C and has some beautiful Regency architecture, in particular the Pittville Pump Room. It holds international music and literature festivals and is also famous for its race meetings and cricket.
Tourist Information Centre
☎ *(01242) 522878*

Beaumont House Hotel ♠
⚜⚜ COMMENDED

Shurdington Road, Cheltenham
GL53 0JE
☎ (01242) 245986
Fax (01242) 520044

Elegant Victorian hotel set in own picturesque gardens; comfortably relaxing, conveniently placed for town centre and Cotswolds; large private car park.
Bedrooms: 4 single, 5 double, 5 twin, 2 triple, 1 family room
Bathrooms: 14 private, 1 public, 2 private showers

Bed & breakfast

per night:	£min	£max
Single	25.00	38.00
Double	38.00	58.00

Half board

per person:	£min	£max
Daily	34.00	44.00

Evening meal 1900 (last orders 2000)
Parking for 20
Cards accepted: Access, Visa
🛇 ⚏ 🖭 ℄ 🖷 📵 ♨ ⓢ ⅂ ⁑ 📺 ⅲ. 🖧 ✿ ✕ ⤨ SP ㎡ T

Ham Hill Farm ♠
⚜⚜ COMMENDED

Whittington, Cheltenham GL54 4EZ
☎ (01242) 584415
160-acre mixed farm. Farmhouse, built in 1983 to a high standard, with good views of the Cotswolds. 2 miles from Cheltenham, on the Cotswold Way.
Bedrooms: 4 double, 2 twin, 1 family room
Bathrooms: 6 private, 1 public

Bed & breakfast

per night:	£min	£max
Single	20.00	20.00
Double	33.00	36.00

Parking for 7
🛇 7 ⚏ 🖷 📵 ♨ ⓤ ⅰ ⓢ ⅂ ⁑ 📺 ⅲ. 🖧 ∪ ✿ ⤨

Hamilton
⚜

46 All Saints Road, Cheltenham
GL52 2HA
☎ (01242) 582845
Fax (01242) 582845
Early Victorian town house, with spacious accommodation, near town centre. Ideal for visitors to Stratford-upon-Avon, the Cotswolds and Forest of Dean.
Bedrooms: 1 double, 1 twin
Bathrooms: 1 public

Bed & breakfast

per night:	£min	£max
Single	18.00	20.00
Double	34.00	50.00

Open January-November
🖷 📵 ♨ ⓤ ⅂ ⁑ 📺 ⅲ. 🖧 ✕ ⤨

Lonsdale House ♠
⚜⚜ COMMENDED

Montpellier Drive, Cheltenham
GL50 1TX
☎ (01242) 232379
Fax (01242) 232379
Regency house situated 5 minutes' walk from the town hall, promenade, shopping centre, parks and theatre. Easy access to all main routes.
Bedrooms: 5 single, 2 double, 1 twin, 2 triple, 1 family room
Bathrooms: 3 private, 4 public

Bed & breakfast

per night:	£min	£max
Single	18.00	28.00
Double	36.00	44.00

Parking for 6
Cards accepted: Access, Visa
🛇 3 🖭 🖷 📵 ♨ ⓤ ⅰ ⅰ 📺 ⅲ. 🖧 ✿ ✕ ⤨ SP ㎡ T

Old Rectory ♠
⚜⚜ COMMENDED

Woolstone, Cheltenham GL52 4RG
☎ Bishops Cleeve (0124267) 3766
Beautiful Victorian rectory in peaceful hamlet, 4 miles north of the Regency town of Cheltenham. Tranquil spot with lovely views.
Bedrooms: 2 double, 1 twin
Bathrooms: 3 private

Bed & breakfast

per night:	£min	£max
Single		27.00
Double		40.00

Parking for 6
🛇 ⚏ 🖭 🖷 📵 ♨ ⓤ ⅂ ⁑ 📺 🖧 ⅰ ∪ ✕ ⤨ ㎡

St. Michaels ♠
⚜⚜ COMMENDED

4 Montpellier Drive, Cheltenham
GL50 1TX
☎ (01242) 513587
Elegant Edwardian guesthouse 5 minutes' stroll from town centre. Delightful rooms with central heating, refreshment tray, colour TV, clock/radio, hairdryer. Quiet location.
Bedrooms: 2 double, 1 twin, 2 triple
Bathrooms: 2 private, 1 public

Bed & breakfast

per night:	£min	£max
Single	22.00	30.00
Double	36.00	42.00

Parking for 3
Cards accepted: Access, Visa
🛇 ⚏ 🖭 🖷 📵 ♨ ⓤ ⓢ ⅂ ⁑ ⅲ. 🖧 ⤨ OAP SP

Upper Farm
Listed

Brockhampton, Swindon Village,
Cheltenham GL51 9RS
☎ (01242) 525923
150-acre mixed farm. Historic farmhouse built in the 17th C, with inglenook fireplace and open fires, decorated throughout, with a warm family atmosphere.
Bedrooms: 1 single, 1 double, 1 twin
Bathrooms: 2 public

Bed & breakfast

per night:	£min	£max
Single	16.00	
Double	32.00	

Parking for 10
Open January-November
🛇 ⚒ 🗶 🖷 ⓤ 📺 ⅲ. 🖧 ✕ ⤨ ㎡

Willoughby House Hotel ♠
⚜⚜ COMMENDED

1 Suffolk Square, Cheltenham
GL50 2DR
☎ (01242) 522798
Fax (01242) 256369
Beautiful, listed Regency house, ideally situated within walking distance of town centre. Comfortable accommodation and full facilities.
Bedrooms: 1 single, 3 double, 3 twin, 2 family rooms; suite available
Bathrooms: 9 private, 1 public

Bed & breakfast

per night:	£min	£max
Single	39.00	50.00
Double	50.00	80.00

Half board

per person:	£min	£max
Daily	37.00	45.00
Weekly	345.00	380.00

Evening meal 1830 (last orders 2100)
Parking for 16
Cards accepted: Access, Visa, Amex
🛇 ⚏ ⚒ 🖭 🖷 📵 ♨ ⓤ ⓢ ⅂ ⁑ 📺 ⅲ. 🖧 ℡20 ▸ ⤨ OAP ⚏ SP ㎡ T

The Wynyards ♠
⚜⚜ COMMENDED

Butts Lane, Woodmancote,
Cheltenham GL52 4QH
☎ (01242) 673876
Secluded old Cotswold-stone house in elevated position with panoramic views. Set in open countryside on outskirts of small village, 4 miles from Cheltenham.
Bedrooms: 1 double, 2 twin
Bathrooms: 2 private, 2 public

Bed & breakfast

per night:	£min	£max
Single	16.00	18.00
Double	27.00	32.00

Parking for 6

🐕📞♿🅿️🖳Ⓢ✕🎃📺◐🕮⌂🔌↺∪▶ ✿✕🐾🅢🅟

CHIPPING CAMPDEN

Gloucestershire
Map ref 2B1

Outstanding Cotswold wool town with many old stone gabled houses, a splendid church, 17th C almshouses and Woolstaplers Hall Museum. Nearby are Kiftsgate Court Gardens and Hidcote Manor Gardens (National Trust).

Haydon House

⚜⚜ COMMENDED

Church Street, Chipping Campden
GL55 6JG
☎ Evesham (01386) 840275

Comfortable historic house, converted from a dairy and bakehouse, surrounding a secluded vine-hung courtyard. Centrally heated. No smoking.
Bedrooms: 1 single, 1 double, 1 twin
Bathrooms: 3 private

Bed & breakfast

per night:	£min	£max
Single	22.00	25.00
Double	42.00	44.00

Open March-December

🐕10🖳♿🅿️🖳🅢✕📺🕮🔌🎃✕ 🐾🕮

Holly House

Listed COMMENDED

Ebrington, Chipping Campden
GL55 6NL
☎ Broadway (01386) 593213
Set in centre of picturesque Cotswold village. Guest accommodation is on ground floor with private entrances. Car park. Short walk from pub.
Bedrooms: 1 double, 1 triple
Bathrooms: 2 private

Bed & breakfast

per night:	£min	£max
Single		25.00
Double	34.00	34.00

Parking for 4

🐕🖳⌂♿🖳✕🕮🔌🎃✕🐾

Manor Farm ⋔

⚜⚜ COMMENDED

Weston Subedge, Chipping Campden
GL55 6QH
☎ Evesham (01386) 840390 &
(mobile) (0589) 108812
600-acre mixed farm. Traditional 17th C farmhouse, an excellent base for touring the Cotswolds, Shakespeare country and Hidcote Gardens. Warm, friendly atmosphere. Walled garden. All rooms en-suite with tea/coffee making facilities, TV/radio. 1.5 miles from Chipping Campden.
Bedrooms: 2 double, 1 twin
Bathrooms: 3 private

Bed & breakfast

per night:	£min	£max
Single	25.00	25.00
Double	40.00	40.00

Parking for 8

🐕🖳⌂♿🖳🅿️📺🕮🔌⌂∪🎃🐾🕮

Orchard Hill House ⋔

Listed HIGHLY COMMENDED

Broad Campden, Chipping Campden
GL55 6UU
☎ Evesham (01386) 841473

17th C Cotswold-stone restored farmhouse. Breakfast in our flagstoned dining room with inglenook fireplace around our 10 ft elm farmhouse table.
Bedrooms: 1 double, 1 twin, 1 triple
Bathrooms: 3 private

Bed & breakfast

per night:	£min	£max
Single	35.00	45.00
Double	42.00	55.00

Parking for 6

🐕8🖳⌂♿🖳✕🕮🔌⌂✕🐾

Sparlings

⚜⚜ COMMENDED

Leysbourne, High Street, Chipping Campden GL55 6HL
☎ Evesham (01386) 840505

Fully centrally heated, comfortable, attractive 18th C Cotswold house in Chipping Campden High Street. Walled garden. Easy parking. Children over 6 welcome.
Bedrooms: 1 double, 1 twin
Bathrooms: 2 private

Bed & breakfast

per night:	£min	£max
Single	26.50	26.50
Double	43.50	45.50

🐕6🖳♿🅿️🖳🅢✕📺🕮🔌🎃✕ 🐾🕮Ⓣ

Weston Park Farm ⋔

⚜⚜

Dovers Hill, Chipping Campden
GL55 6UW
☎ Evesham (01386) 840835
20-acre mixed farm. Self-contained wing of secluded, magnificently situated farmhouse, 1 mile from Chipping Campden, adjacent to National Trust land.
Bedrooms: 1 triple
Bathrooms: 1 private

Bed & breakfast

per night:	£min	£max
Double	38.00	40.00

Parking for 10

🐕⌂♿🖳📺🕮🔌🚲⌂▶🎃✕ 🐾🕮

Wyldlands

Listed COMMENDED

Broad Campden, Chipping Campden
GL55 6UR
☎ Evesham (01386) 840478
Welcoming, comfortable house in picturesque village. Peaceful setting with lovely views. Ideal for walking and touring. Traditional inn nearby. Reduced rates for 3 nights or more.
Bedrooms: 2 double, 1 twin
Bathrooms: 1 private, 2 public

Bed & breakfast

per night:	£min	£max
Single	20.00	25.00
Double	34.00	40.00

Parking for 4

🐕🖳⌂♿🖳🅢✕📺🕮🔌🎃✕ 🐾🅾🅟

CHURCH STRETTON

Shropshire
Map ref 4A3

Church Stretton lies under the eastern slope of the Longmynd surrounded by hills. It is ideal for walkers, with marvellous views, golf and gliding. Wenlock Edge is not far away.

Acton Scott Farm ⋔

⚜⚜ COMMENDED

Acton Scott, Church Stretton SY6 6QN
☎ Marshbrook (01694) 781260
320-acre mixed farm. Conveniently situated 17th C farmhouse of character with comfortable, spacious rooms and log fires. Beautiful countryside.
Bedrooms: 1 double, 1 twin, 1 family room
Bathrooms: 1 private, 1 public

Continued ▶

CHURCH STRETTON

Continued

Bed & breakfast

per night:	£min	£max
Double	30.00	44.00

Parking for 6
Open March-October

Batchcott Hall

Listed HIGHLY COMMENDED

Picklescott, Church Stretton SY6 6NP
☎ Leebotwood (01694) 751234

350-acre mixed farm. Friendly atmosphere in a 16th C farmhouse. Well-appointed, comfortable rooms, colour TV. An idyllic spot on the edge of the Longmynd with excellent views.
Bedrooms: 1 double, 1 twin
Bathrooms: 2 private

Bed & breakfast

per night:	£min	£max
Single	15.00	25.00
Double	30.00	40.00

Parking for 6

The Elms ♠

Listed

Little Stretton, Church Stretton SY6 6RD
☎ (01694) 723084
Victorian country house in spacious grounds, decorated and furnished in Victorian style.
Bedrooms: 2 double, 1 twin
Bathrooms: 2 public

Bed & breakfast

per night:	£min	£max
Single	19.00	
Double	31.00	

Parking for 3

Gilberries Cottage ♠

COMMENDED

Wall-under-Heywood, Church Stretton SY6 7HZ
☎ Longville (01694) 771400
Country cottage adjoining family farm, in peaceful and beautiful countryside. Ideal for walking. Numerous places of interest nearby.
Bedrooms: 1 twin, 1 triple
Bathrooms: 1 public

Bed & breakfast

per night:	£min	£max
Single	20.00	20.00
Double	32.00	34.00

Parking for 8
Open February-November

Juniper Cottage

All Stretton, Church Stretton SY6 6HG
☎ (01694) 723427
Quality cottage-style house in lovely secluded grounds with outstanding views of Caer Caradoc. Attractive village adjacent Long Mynd. Church Stretton 1 mile.
Bedrooms: 1 double
Bathrooms: 1 private

Bed & breakfast

per night:	£min	£max
Double	30.00	32.00

Parking for 5

Sayang House

HIGHLY COMMENDED

Hope Bowdler, Church Stretton SY6 7DD
☎ (01694) 723981
Beautiful house in tranquil village in the Stretton Hills. 1.75 miles from town of Church Stretton. Residents' lounge with oak beams and inglenook fireplace. All accommodation en-suite and furnished to highest possible standard. Good local pub.
Bedrooms: 1 double, 2 twin
Bathrooms: 3 private

Bed & breakfast

per night:	£min	£max
Single	21.00	23.00
Double	41.00	46.00

Parking for 10
Open January-November

Wayside Inn

Listed

Marshbrook, Church Stretton SY6 6QE
☎ (01694) 781208
16th C inn, fully beamed and with log fires. Excellent walking area. Meals available 7 days a week.
Bedrooms: 1 single, 1 double, 1 triple
Bathrooms: 1 public

Bed & breakfast

per night:	£min	£max
Single	16.00	18.00
Double	32.00	36.00

Lunch available
Evening meal 1830 (last orders 2100)
Parking for 20

Willowfield Country Guest House

Lower Wood, All Stretton, Church Stretton SY6 6LF
☎ Leebotwood (01694) 751471

Quiet and idyllic, set in its own grounds, with beautiful rural views of surrounding hills. Traditional cooking, Elizabethan dining room, candlelit dinners. Warm and friendly atmosphere. Colour brochure.
Bedrooms: 3 double, 2 twin
Bathrooms: 5 private

Bed & breakfast

per night:	£min	£max
Double	44.00	52.00

Half board

per person:	£min	£max
Daily	41.00	
Weekly	254.00	

Evening meal 1830 (last orders 2030)
Parking for 5
Open March-November

Woolston Farm ♠

Church Stretton SY6 6QD
☎ Marshbrook (01694) 781201
350-acre mixed farm. Victorian farmhouse in the small hamlet of Woolston, off A49. Ideal position for touring Shropshire. Outstanding views and good farmhouse fare.
Bedrooms: 2 double, 1 twin
Bathrooms: 1 private, 1 public

Bed & breakfast

per night:	£min	£max
Single	14.50	
Double	29.00	

Half board

per person:	£min	£max
Daily	23.00	
Weekly	147.00	

Evening meal 1850 (last orders 2000)
Parking for 2
Open January-November

National gradings and classifications were correct at the time of going to press but are subject to change. Please check at the time of booking.

CHURCHAM

Gloucestershire
Map ref 2B1

Village a few miles west of Gloucester off the A40, making a delightful picture of church, court and willow-fringed pond.

Edgewood House ♠

Churcham, Gloucester GL2 8AA
☎ Gloucester (01452) 750232
Lovely country house in 2 acres of picturesque gardens opposite RSPB reserve. Spacious rooms furnished to a high standard. Special children's rates.
Bedrooms: 1 single, 1 double, 1 family room
Bathrooms: 3 private
Bed & breakfast

per night:	£min	£max
Single	17.50	18.50
Double	37.00	39.00

Parking for 6

CIRENCESTER

Gloucestershire
Map ref 2B1

"Capital of the Cotswolds", Cirencester was Britain's second most important Roman town with many finds housed in the Corinium Museum. It has a very fine Perpendicular church and old houses around the market place.
Tourist Information Centre
☎ *(01285) 654180*

Chesil Rocks

Listed COMMENDED
Baunton Lane, Stratton, Cirencester GL7 2LL
☎ (01285) 655031
Pleasant and friendly home in a quiet lane, with easy access to town and country walks. Cheltenham, Gloucester and Swindon within easy reach.
Bedrooms: 2 single, 1 twin
Bathrooms: 1 public
Bed & breakfast

per night:	£min	£max
Single	15.00	15.00
Double	30.00	30.00

Parking for 3

Eliot Arms Hotel Free House ♠

COMMENDED
Clarks Hay, South Cerney, Cirencester GL7 5UA
☎ (01285) 860215
Fax (01285) 860215
Dating from the 16th C, a comfortable Cotswold freehouse hotel, 2.5 miles from Cirencester, just off the A419.

Reputation for fine food and hospitality. Riverside gardens.
Bedrooms: 1 single, 5 double, 4 twin, 2 triple; suites available
Bathrooms: 12 private
Bed & breakfast

per night:	£min	£max
Single	35.00	
Double	49.50	

Lunch available
Evening meal 1830 (last orders 2200)
Parking for 30
Cards accepted: Access, Visa, Amex, Switch/Delta

The Masons Arms ♠

COMMENDED
High Street, Meysey Hampton, Cirencester GL7 5JT
☎ (01285) 850164
Fax (01285) 850164

Seeking peace and tranquillity? Treat yourself to a break in this 17th C inn set beside the village green. Oak beams and log fire. A warm welcome awaits you.
Bedrooms: 6 double, 1 twin, 1 triple
Bathrooms: 8 private
Bed & breakfast

per night:	£min	£max
Single	28.00	32.00
Double	44.00	54.00

Lunch available
Evening meal 1900 (last orders 2130)
Parking for 8
Cards accepted: Access, Visa

The Old Rectory ♠

COMMENDED
Rodmarton, Cirencester GL7 6PE
☎ (01285) 841246
Fax (01285) 841246
17th C rectory set in three-quarters of an acre of gardens. Cirencester 6 miles, Tetbury 5 miles. Equidistant Swindon, Cheltenham and Gloucester.
Bedrooms: 1 double, 1 twin
Bathrooms: 2 private
Bed & breakfast

per night:	£min	£max
Single	17.50	20.00
Double	35.00	40.00

Half board

per person:	£min	£max
Daily	32.50	
Weekly	204.75	

Evening meal 1900 (last orders 2100)
Parking for 6

Smerrill Barns ♠

COMMENDED
Kemble, Cirencester GL7 6BW
☎ (01285) 770907
Fax (01285) 770907
Accommodation in a listed barn, providing all modern facilities. Situated 3 miles from Cirencester on the A429.
Bedrooms: 1 single, 4 double, 1 twin, 1 family room
Bathrooms: 7 private, 1 public
Bed & breakfast

per night:	£min	£max
Single	25.00	35.00
Double	40.00	55.00

Parking for 7
Cards accepted: Access, Visa, Switch/Delta

Tally Cottage ♠

Listed
Woodmancote, Cirencester GL7 7EF
☎ North Cerney (01285) 831563
A typical 16th C Cotswold stone village cottage with mullioned windows, beams and inglenook. Centrally heated. Pretty, private small garden.
Bedrooms: 1 twin
Bathrooms: 1 public
Bed & breakfast

per night:	£min	£max
Single	17.50	17.50
Double	35.00	35.00

Parking for 1

The Village Pub

Listed APPROVED
Barnsley, Cirencester GL7 5EF
☎ (01285) 740421
The Village Pub has 5 rooms, all with private facilities, and is situated in a pretty Cotswold village.
Bedrooms: 4 double, 1 twin
Bathrooms: 5 private
Bed & breakfast

per night:	£min	£max
Single	30.00	35.00
Double	45.00	50.00

Lunch available
Evening meal 1900 (last orders 2130)
Parking for 40
Cards accepted: Access, Visa, Amex

Wimborne House ♠

COMMENDED
91 Victoria Road, Cirencester GL7 1ES
☎ (01285) 653890

Continued ►

CIRENCESTER

Continued

Cotswold-stone house, built in 1886, with a warm and friendly atmosphere and spacious rooms. Four-poster room. Non-smokers only, please.
Bedrooms: 4 double, 1 twin
Bathrooms: 5 private

Bed & breakfast per night:	£min	£max
Single	20.00	28.00
Double	28.00	35.00

Half board per person:	£min	£max
Daily	20.00	23.00
Weekly	140.00	156.00

Evening meal 1830 (last orders 1730)
Parking for 6

CLAINES

Hereford and Worcester
Map ref 2B1

Rose Place

Hindlip Lane, Claines, Worcester
WR3 8SA
☎ Worcester (01905) 451526
Grade II Georgian country house, close to Worcester. Set in 3 acres of walled gardens and grounds.
Bedrooms: 2 double, 1 twin
Bathrooms: 3 private

Bed & breakfast per night:	£min	£max
Single	30.00	35.00
Double	45.00	50.00

Parking for 20

CLAVERDON

Warwickshire
Map ref 2B1

Village with an old forge and some timbered cottages approached by winding, leafy Warwickshire lanes.

The Grange ⋀

APPROVED

Henley Road, Claverdon, Warwick
CV35 8PS
☎ (01926) 842313

Spacious country house in Shakespeare's Warwickshire, with delightful gardens and furnished with English antiques.
Bedrooms: 2 double
Bathrooms: 2 private

Bed & breakfast per night:	£min	£max
Double	47.50	49.50

Parking for 6

CLEEVE HILL

Gloucestershire
Map ref 2B1

Settlement with wonderful all-round views, above Cheltenham on the road to Winchcombe and Broadway.

Cleyne Hage ⋀

APPROVED

Southam Lane, Southam, Cheltenham
GL52 3NY
☎ Cheltenham (01242) 518569 &
Mobile 0850 285338
Fax (01242) 518569
Cotswold-stone house in secluded setting between B4632 and A435, on the Cotswold Way, 3 miles north of Cheltenham. Open view of hills and racecourse. Off-road parking. Non-smokers only, please.
Bedrooms: 1 single, 1 double, 1 twin
Bathrooms: 2 private, 2 public

Bed & breakfast per night:	£min	£max
Single	18.00	25.00
Double	30.00	45.00

Parking for 8
Cards accepted: Access, Visa

CLEOBURY MORTIMER

Shropshire
Map ref 4A3

Village with attractive timbered and Georgian houses and a church with a wooden spire. It is close to the Clee Hills with marvellous views.

Cox's Barn

Listed

Bagginswood, Cleobury Mortimer, Kidderminster, Worcestershire
DY14 8LS
☎ Stottesden (01746) 718415 &
Mobile Phone 0860 135011
*124-acre mixed farm. Converted barn on working farm with spacious gardens overlooking beautiful countryside. Good home cooking, centrally heated.
Evening meal optional.*
Bedrooms: 2 double, 1 twin
Bathrooms: 2 private, 1 public

Bed & breakfast per night:	£min	£max
Single	14.00	16.00
Double	28.00	32.00

Half board per person:	£min	£max
Daily	21.00	28.00

Lunch available
Evening meal 1800 (last orders 2000)
Parking for 6

The Old Bake House

♔♔

46/47 High Street, Cleobury
Mortimer, Kidderminster,
Worcestershire DY14 8DQ
☎ (01299) 270193
Grade II listed townhouse, formerly both a public house and bakery, with 18th C frontage. Home cooking. Vegetarians welcome, special diets by arrangement.
Bedrooms: 1 double, 2 twin
Bathrooms: 3 private

Bed & breakfast per night:	£min	£max
Single	15.00	18.00
Double	30.00	36.00

Half board per person:	£min	£max
Daily	25.00	28.00
Weekly	155.00	170.00

Evening meal 1900 (last orders 2000)
Parking for 2

CLUN

Shropshire
Map ref 4A3

Small, ancient town on the Welsh border with flint and stone tools in its museum and Iron Age forts nearby. The impressive ruins of a Norman castle lie beside the River Clun and there are some interesting 17th C houses.

Clun Farm

Listed

High Street, Clun, Craven Arms
SY7 8JB
☎ (01588) 640432
200-acre mixed farm. 16th C double cruck farmhouse situated in Clun High Street, within 200 metres of 3 public houses and restaurants.
Bedrooms: 2 single, 1 double, 1 twin
Bathrooms: 1 private, 1 public

Bed & breakfast per night:	£min	£max
Single	14.00	16.00
Double	30.00	34.00

Parking for 6

Hurst Mill Farm ⋀

♔

Clun, Craven Arms SY7 0JA
☎ (01588) 640224
100-acre mixed farm. Attractive farmhouse and old mill in the lovely

Clun Valley. River and woodland trails, 2 riding ponies, pets welcome. Previous winner of "Great Shropshire Breakfast" challenge.
Bedrooms: 1 double, 2 twin
Bathrooms: 1 private, 2 public

Bed & breakfast

per night:	£min	£max
Single	15.00	17.00
Double	30.00	34.00

Half board

per person:	£min	£max
Daily	24.00	25.00
Weekly	160.00	170.00

Evening meal 1800 (last orders 2000)
Parking for 8
⏣🖵♦🖵🛈S⊁🅿📺🛏🔌🛢⛵🚴🚲
✿🐾🛡

CLUNGUNFORD

Shropshire
Map ref 4A3

Village near the River Clun and Stokesay Castle, a 13th C fortified manor house with an Elizabethan gatehouse.

Broadward Hall **⋀**
Listed

Clungunford, Craven Arms SY7 0QA
☎ Bucknell (01547) 530357
176-acre mixed farm. Grade II listed, castellated building, 9 miles west of Ludlow in rural Clun Valley surroundings.
Bedrooms: 2 twin, 1 triple
Bathrooms: 2 public

Bed & breakfast

per night:	£min	£max
Single	14.00	
Double	28.00	

Half board

per person:	£min	£max
Daily	24.00	
Weekly	154.00	

Evening meal 1900 (last orders 0900)
Parking for 15
Open March-November
⏣🗐🖵⊁🅿📺🛢🚴✿🚲🛡

CODSALL

Staffordshire
Map ref 4B3

Expanding residential village a few miles from Wolverhampton.

Moors Farm and Country Restaurant
🗐🗐🗐

Chillington Lane, Codsall,
Wolverhampton WV8 1QF
☎ (01902) 847878
100-acre mixed farm. 200-year-old farmhouse, 1 mile from pretty village. All home produce used. Many local walks and places of interest.
Bedrooms: 3 double, 1 twin, 1 family room

Bathrooms: 3 private, 2 public

Bed & breakfast

per night:	£min	£max
Single	25.00	30.00
Double	42.00	50.00

Half board

per person:	£min	£max
Daily	35.00	40.00

Evening meal 1830 (last orders 1900)
Parking for 20
⏣🖵♦🖵🛈S🅿📺🛢⛵🚴🚲
🐾🛡🅣

COLEFORD

Gloucestershire
Map ref 2A1

Small town in the Forest of Dean with the ancient iron mines at Clearwell Caves nearby, where mining equipment and geological samples are displayed. There are several forest trails in the area.
Tourist Information Centre
☎ *(01594) 836307*

Millend House and Garden
🗐🗐 HIGHLY COMMENDED

Newland, Coleford GL16 8NF
☎ Dean (01594) 832128
250-year-old traditional stone-built house, in 2 acres of lovely hillside gardens and woodlands. Situated at the end of a valley looking down towards Newland and the "Cathedral of the Forest".
Bedrooms: 1 double, 2 twin
Bathrooms: 1 private, 1 public

Bed & breakfast

per night:	£min	£max
Single	23.00	27.00
Double	36.00	44.00

Parking for 4
🖵♦🖵⊁🛢🚴✿🚲🚴

COLESHILL

Warwickshire
Map ref 4B3

Close to Birmingham's many attractions including the 17th C Aston Hall with its plasterwork and furnishings, the Railway Museum and Sarehole Mill, an 18th C water-powered mill restored to working order.

Maxstoke Hall Farm
🗐🗐 COMMENDED

Maxstoke, Coleshill, Birmingham B46 2QT
☎ (01675) 463237
Fax (01675) 463237

> Check the introduction to this region for ideas on **Where to Go.**

230-acre arable farm. Elegant farmhouse, 1634, with en-suite rooms. 10 minutes from M42 and M6, 15 minutes from National Exhibition Centre and Birmingham Airport.
Bedrooms: 2 single, 1 twin
Bathrooms: 3 private, 1 public

Bed & breakfast

per night:	£min	£max
Single	25.00	25.00
Double	44.00	44.00

Half board

per person:	£min	£max
Daily	37.00	37.00

Evening meal 1830 (last orders 2000)
Parking for 30
⏣🖵♦🖵🛈⊁🅿📺🛢🚴🚲✿
🐾🅣

The Old Rectory **⋀**
🗐🗐 HIGHLY COMMENDED

Church Lane, Maxstoke, Coleshill,
Birmingham B46 2QW
☎ (01675) 462248
Fax (01675) 481615

Elegant Victorian rectory built from local sandstone, set in 5 acres of walled garden, originally the gardens of Maxstoke Priory.
Bedrooms: 1 double, 1 twin, 1 triple
Bathrooms: 3 private

Bed & breakfast

per night:	£min	£max
Single	28.00	30.00
Double	44.00	46.00

Parking for 10
⏣🖵♦🖵S📺🛢✿🐾🛡

Packington Lane Farm **⋀**
🗐 COMMENDED

Packington Lane, Coleshill,
Birmingham B46 3JJ
☎ (01675) 462228
Fax (01675) 462228
250-acre mixed farm. Traditional 17th C farmhouse where comfort, cleanliness and a friendly welcome are assured. 3 miles from National Exhibition Centre, airport and railway, half-a-mile from Coleshill. Secure car parking.
Bedrooms: 1 single, 2 twin
Bathrooms: 1 private, 1 public

Continued ▶

COLESHILL

Continued

Bed & breakfast

per night:	£min	£max
Single	18.00	
Double	36.00	

Parking for 8

🏡🖵☼🍴🔳☕📺🛋🚗✿🎣🐾

COLWALL

Hereford and Worcester
Map ref 2B1

Village on the slopes of the Malvern Hills close to the famous Herefordshire Beacon, site of a large Iron Age camp. The area offers excellent walks with the Worcestershire Beacon to the north.

Hacketts ♠

`Listed` `COMMENDED`

Mathon Road, Colwall, Malvern, Worcestershire WR13 6EW
☎ (01684) 540261
3-acre arable farm. Well-built black and white house, completely remodernised and tastefully decorated. Situated on the roadside, with pleasant garden.
Bedrooms: 1 single, 1 double, 1 twin
Bathrooms: 2 public

Bed & breakfast

per night:	£min	£max
Single	16.00	16.00
Double	32.00	32.00

Half board

per person:	£min	£max
Daily	24.00	24.00
Weekly	168.00	168.00

Parking for 6
Open April-October

🛏🖵☼🔳🛈📺🛋✿🎣

CORSE

Gloucestershire
Map ref 2B1

Kilmorie Guest House

☕☕

Gloucester Road, Corse, Snigs End, Staunton, Gloucester GL19 3RQ
☎ Gloucester (01452) 840224

7-acre livestock & fruit farm. Built by Chartists in 1847, Grade II listed smallholding in conservation area. Modernised, comfortable and friendly. TV all rooms. Ideally situated for touring Cotswolds, Forest of Dean and Malvern Hills.

Bedrooms: 1 single, 3 double, 1 twin, 1 family room
Bathrooms: 2 private, 1 public

Bed & breakfast

per night:	£min	£max
Single	13.50	
Double	27.00	

Half board

per person:	£min	£max
Daily	20.00	
Weekly	136.50	

Lunch available
Evening meal from 1800
Parking for 8

🛏5🛢🏡☼🔳🛈🅂🛌📺🛋🚗U✿🆂🏮

COTSWOLDS

See under Berkeley, Bibury, Birdlip, Bledington, Blockley, Bourton-on-the-Water, Broad Campden, Broadway, Cheltenham, Chipping Campden, Cirencester, Cleeve Hill, Didmarton, Donnington, Fairford, Gloucester, Great Rissington, Guiting Power, Lechlade, Long Compton, Minchinhampton, Moreton-in-Marsh, Nailsworth, Naunton, Northleach, Nympsfield, Painswick, Rendcomb, Slimbridge, Stonehouse, Stow-on-the-Wold, Stretton on Fosse, Stroud, Tetbury, Tewkesbury, Winchcombe, Wotton-under-Edge
See also Cotswolds in South of England region

COVENTRY

West Midlands
Map ref 4B3

Modern city with a long history. It has many places of interest including the post-war and ruined medieval cathedrals, art gallery and museums, some 16th C almshouses, St Mary's Guildhall, Lunt Roman fort and the Belgrade Theatre.
Tourist Information Centre
☎ (01203) 832303

Abigail Guesthouse

`Listed`

39 St. Patrick's Road, Coventry CV1 2LP
☎ (01203) 221378
Family-run establishment in centre of city, very clean and friendly. Convenient for station, cathedral and city centre shopping, also NEC and NAC.
Bedrooms: 2 single, 1 double, 1 twin, 1 triple
Bathrooms: 2 public

Bed & breakfast

per night:	£min	£max
Single	15.00	17.00
Double	30.00	34.00

🛏🖵☼🔳🛈🅂🛋🚗🐾

Mount Guest House ♠

`Listed`

9 Coundon Road, Coventry CV1 4AR
☎ (01203) 225998
Fax (01203) 225998
Family guesthouse within walking distance of city and cathedral. Easy reach of the National Exhibition Centre and the Royal Showground. Snacks available.
Bedrooms: 2 single, 5 twin, 2 triple
Bathrooms: 2 public

Bed & breakfast

per night:	£min	£max
Single	13.50	20.00
Double	27.00	27.00

🛏🖾🛢🖵☼🔳🛈🅂✂🛌📺🛋🚗🆂

Westwood Cottage

☕☕

79 Westwood Heath Road, Westwood Heath, Coventry CV4 8GN
☎ (01203) 471084
One of 4 sandstone farm cottages, circa 1834, in rural surroundings. Recently converted but with character maintained and offering comfortable accommodation for a small number of guests.
Bedrooms: 2 single, 1 double, 1 twin
Bathrooms: 4 private

Bed & breakfast

per night:	£min	£max
Single	18.00	18.00
Double	33.00	35.00

Parking for 5

🛏🛢🔳🛈🅂✂📺🛋🚗✿🎣🏮

Woodlands ♠

☕

Oak Lane, Allesley, Coventry CV5 9BX
☎ Meriden (01676) 522688 & Mobile (01585) 520147
Comfortable, detached and privately situated in a beautiful country lane only 150 yards from the A45. Ten minutes from NEC and Birmingham Airport, ideal for Coventry, Stratford-upon-Avon and Warwick.
Bedrooms: 3 twin
Bathrooms: 1 private, 1 public

Bed & breakfast

per night:	£min	£max
Single	19.00	19.00
Double	38.00	38.00

Parking for 6

🛏7🖵☼🔳🛈🅂✂🛌📺🛋🚗U♪▶🎣🐾

Individual proprietors have supplied all details of accommodation. As changes can occur, we advise you to confirm the information at the time of booking.

CRAVEN ARMS

Shropshire
Map ref 4A3

Busy village on A49 renowned for its sheep markets. Close to Wenlock Edge and the Longmynd and an ideal centre for walking with many fine views. Nearby Stokesay Castle, a 13th C fortified manor house, the ruins of Hopton Castle and Ludlow.

Castle View

Listed HIGHLY COMMENDED

148 Stokesay, Craven Arms SY7 9AL
☎ (01588) 673712
Large, comfortable stone-built Victorian house. Within easy walking distance of Stokesay Castle and on route of the Shropshire Way.
Bedrooms: 1 double, 1 twin
Bathrooms: 2 private
Bed & breakfast

per night:	£min	£max
Single	15.00	16.00
Double	32.00	34.00

Parking for 3

Strefford Hall ♠♠

♨♨ COMMENDED

Strefford, Craven Arms SY7 8DE
☎ (01588) 672383
350-acre mixed farm. Victorian farmhouse nestling at the foot of Wenlock Edge, 2 miles north of the market town of Craven Arms. Non-smokers only, please.
Bedrooms: 2 double, 1 twin
Bathrooms: 3 private
Bed & breakfast

per night:	£min	£max
Single	20.00	
Double	35.00	38.00

Parking for 6

DEERHURST

Gloucestershire
Map ref 2B1

Deerhurst House ♠♠

♨♨ HIGHLY COMMENDED

Deerhurst, Gloucester GL19 4BX
☎ Tewkesbury (01684) 292135 & Mobile 0850 520051
Classical Georgian country house set in 3 acres on edge of ancient riverside village of Deerhurst, midway between Cheltenham, Tewkesbury and Gloucester.
Bedrooms: 1 double, 1 twin
Bathrooms: 2 private
Bed & breakfast

per night:	£min	£max
Single	20.00	30.00
Double	40.00	50.00

Parking for 10

DIDMARTON

Gloucestershire
Map ref 2B2

Attractive village with stone houses and interesting architectural features. It has 2 churches, one of which has Georgian furnishings. Didmarton is close to Badminton House.

The Old Rectory ♠♠

♨♨

Didmarton GL9 1DS
☎ Chipping Sodbury (01454) 238233
Small former rectory in centre of village close to Westonbirt and Tetbury. Easy reach of Bath, M4 and Cirencester.
Bedrooms: 2 double
Bathrooms: 1 private, 1 public
Bed & breakfast

per night:	£min	£max
Single	17.00	19.00
Double	32.00	35.00

Parking for 4
Open January-October, December

DONNINGTON

Gloucestershire
Map ref 2B1

Holmleigh

Listed

Donnington, Moreton-in-Marsh GL56 0XX
☎ Cotswold (01451) 830792
15-acre dairy farm. Farmhouse accommodation with friendly welcome. In a peaceful setting with own private lane from the village of Donnington, 1 mile from Stow-on-the-Wold.
Bedrooms: 2 twin
Bathrooms: 1 private, 1 public
Bed & breakfast

per night:	£min	£max
Single	12.50	12.50
Double	25.00	25.00

Parking for 3
Open April-October

The symbol ⊛ within an entry indicates participation in the Welcome Host programme – a nationally recognised customer care initiative which aims to promote the highest standards of service and a warm welcome for all visitors.

DROITWICH

Hereford and Worcester
Map ref 2B1

Old town with natural brine springs, now incorporated into the Brine Baths Health Centre, developed as a spa at the beginning of the 19th C. Of particular interest is the Church of the Sacred Heart with splendid mosaics. Fine parks and a Heritage Centre.
Tourist Information Centre
☎ *(01905) 774312*

Church Farm

Elmbridge, Droitwich, Worcestershire WR9 0DA
☎ Cutnall Green (01299) 851627
Beautiful listed Georgian farmhouse with panoramic views of Malvern Hills. Situated in peaceful village of Elmbridge yet only 2 miles from M5.
Bedrooms: 2 twin
Bathrooms: 2 private
Bed & breakfast

per night:	£min	£max
Single	25.00	25.00
Double	40.00	40.00

Parking for 7

Foxbrook ♠♠

♨♨ COMMENDED

238A Worcester Road, Droitwich, Worcestershire WR9 8AY
☎ Worcester (01905) 772414
Detached residence, standing in an elevated position in its own delightful gardens. Ample car parking and 5 minutes from motorway network. Walking distance of station and town centre and on main bus route.
Bedrooms: 1 single, 1 double, 1 twin
Bathrooms: 1 private, 1 public, 1 private shower
Bed & breakfast

per night:	£min	£max
Single	17.00	30.00
Double	32.00	38.00

Parking for 8

Richmond Guest House ♠♠

Listed

3 Ombersley St. West, Droitwich, Worcestershire WR9 8HZ
☎ Worcester (01905) 775722
Fax (01905) 794500
Victorian-built guesthouse in the town centre, 5 minutes from railway station and bus route. English breakfast. 30 minutes from National Exhibition Centre via M5/M42.
Bedrooms: 6 single, 1 double, 2 twin, 5 triple
Bathrooms: 3 public

Continued ▶

DROITWICH

Continued

Bed & breakfast

per night:	£min	£max
Single	16.00	18.00
Double	28.00	30.00

Parking for 12

🛇🕭⌷🐾ｗ Ⓢ 뱀 📺 ▥, ◪

DUNCHURCH

Warwickshire
Map ref 4C3

The 14th C church has a sandstone tower, Norman doorway and Norman font. The northern chapel arcade is Victorian. Nearby is a statue of Lord John Scott, the seafaring sportsman, dating from 1867.

Toft Hill

| Listed | COMMENDED |

Dunchurch, Rugby CV22 6NR
☎ Rugby (01788) 810342
Large country house set in mature gardens, half a mile from the centre of Dunchurch on Southam road.
Bedrooms: 1 single, 1 double, 1 twin
Bathrooms: 1 private, 1 public

Bed & breakfast

per night:	£min	£max
Single	18.50	18.50
Double	37.00	37.00

Parking for 5

🛇8🐾ｗ📺▥, ◪ ⸜ ✿ 🚐

EASTCOMBE

Gloucestershire
2B1

Pretoria Villa

| Listed |

Wells Road, Eastcombe, Stroud
GL6 7EE
☎ Gloucester (01452) 770435
Cotswold-stone double-fronted detached house, built c1900, with private gardens. In quiet village lane with beautiful views.
Bedrooms: 1 single, 1 double, 1 twin
Bathrooms: 1 private, 1 public

Bed & breakfast

per night:	£min	£max
Single	20.00	20.00
Double	40.00	40.00

Half board

per person:	£min	£max
Daily	32.00	32.00
Weekly	210.00	210.00

Evening meal 1830 (last orders 2030)
Parking for 3

🛇5🖾🐾🐾🎇 Ⓢ ✂ 뱀 📺 ▥, ✿ ✗ 🚐

ECCLESHALL

Staffordshire
Map ref 4B3

Small market town has long associations with the Bishops of Lichfield, 6 of whom are buried in the large 12th C parish church. The ruined castle was formerly the residence of these bishops.

Cobblers Cottage

Kerry Lane, Eccleshall, Stafford
ST21 6EJ
☎ Stafford (01785) 850116
Country cottage with en-suite bedrooms, in a quiet lane on the edge of village, with several pubs and restaurants within walking distance.
Bedrooms: 1 double, 1 twin
Bathrooms: 2 private

Bed & breakfast

per night:	£min	£max
Single	18.00	23.00
Double	32.00	36.00

Parking for 3

🛇2⌷🐾ｗ Ⓢ ✂ ▥, 🔾 🚐 SP

Glenwood ⚠

| COMMENDED |

Croxton, Eccleshall, Stafford ST21 6PF
☎ Wetwood (01630) 620238

16th C timber-framed cottage in an ideal position for visiting the many attractions of Staffordshire and Shropshire.
Bedrooms: 1 double, 2 twin, 1 triple
Bathrooms: 1 private, 1 public

Bed & breakfast

per night:	£min	£max
Single	16.00	18.00
Double	28.00	36.00

Parking for 6

🛇🕭🖾🐾ｗ 🎇 Ⓢ ✂ 뱀 📺 ▥, ◪ 🔾 ✿ 🚐 OAP SP 🏮 🅣

The symbol 🌐 within an entry indicates participation in the Welcome Host programme – a nationally recognised customer care initiative which aims to promote the highest standards of service and a warm welcome for all visitors.

ECKINGTON

Hereford and Worcester
Map ref 2B1

Large and expanding village in a fruit growing and market gardening area beside the Avon, which is crossed here by a 15th C bridge. Half-timbered houses are much in evidence.

Sandrene ⚠

| Listed | COMMENDED |

Tewkesbury Road, Eckington, Pershore, Worcestershire WR10 3AW
☎ Evesham (01386) 750756
Relax in our small friendly country home, overlooking Bredon Hill. Good hospitality, accommodation and food. Within walking distance of two pubs.
Bedrooms: 1 double, 1 twin
Bathrooms: 2 private

Bed & breakfast

per night:	£min	£max
Single	25.00	30.00
Double	40.00	45.00

Half board

per person:	£min	£max
Daily	32.50	37.50
Weekly	162.50	187.50

Evening meal 1800 (last orders 2000)
Parking for 2

🛇🕭🖾⌷🐾ｗ 🛈 📺 ▥, ◪ ✿ 🚐 🐾

ELMLEY CASTLE

Hereford and Worcester
Map ref 2B1

Attractive black and white village at the foot of Bredon Hill. No castle exists but this is a popular place to start a walk over Bredon.

The Cloisters

| ⚠⚠ | HIGHLY COMMENDED |

Main Street, Elmley Castle, Pershore, Worcestershire WR10 3HS
☎ Pershore (01386) 710241
A stone and half-timbered Tudor house, part of which dates back to the 14th C. Located towards the end of the main street, on the left-hand corner of Ashton-under-Hill Lane. Elmley Castle, at the foot of Bredon Hill, is one of the most attractive villages in the Vale of Evesham.
Bedrooms: 1 double, 1 family room
Bathrooms: 2 private

Bed & breakfast

per night:	£min	£max
Single	22.00	22.00
Double	40.00	40.00

Parking for 3

🛇⌷🐾ｗ Ⓢ 뱀 ▥, ◪ ✿ ✗ 🚐 🐾 🏮

We advise you to confirm your booking in writing.

EVESHAM

Hereford and Worcester
Map ref 2B1

Market town in the centre of a fruit-growing area. There are pleasant walks along the River Avon and many old houses and inns. A fine 16th C bell tower stands between 2 churches near the medieval Almonry Museum.
Tourist Information Centre
☎ *(01386) 446944*

Chequers Inn ⋀

😊😊😊 COMMENDED

Fladbury, Pershore, Worcestershire
WR10 2PZ
☎ (01386) 860276 & 860527
Fax (01386) 861286
14th C inn between Evesham and Pershore, on the edge of the Cotswolds. Off B4084 and A44, in a quiet village location, 17 miles from Stratford-upon-Avon.
Bedrooms: 4 double, 4 twin
Bathrooms: 8 private
Bed & breakfast

per night:	£min	£max
Single	42.50	
Double	55.00	65.00

Lunch available
Evening meal 1830 (last orders 2130)
Parking for 30
Cards accepted: Access, Visa, Amex
🛏🦮📞🖭◻🚼♨📶🖩🛏♨🕯25🎵🏱❄✕
🐾🕭🆂🏮

The Croft ⋀

😊😊 HIGHLY COMMENDED

54 Greenhill, Evesham, Worcestershire
WR11 4NF
☎ (01386) 446035

Splendid Georgian home offering comfortable overnight and holiday accommodation. Large private garden and ample parking.
Bedrooms: 1 twin, 2 triple
Bathrooms: 3 private
Bed & breakfast

per night:	£min	£max
Single	26.00	35.00
Double	38.00	46.00

Parking for 6
🛏🦮🖭◻♨🗝🆂🏮📺🖩♨❄🐾

Far Horizon ⋀

😊😊 COMMENDED

Long Hyde Road, South Littleton,
Evesham, Worcestershire WR11 5TH
☎ (01386) 831691
Elegant family home of character, with fine views over surrounding Cotswolds

and Malvern Hills. Rural location 3 miles from Evesham.
Bedrooms: 1 single, 1 double, 1 twin
Bathrooms: 3 private
Bed & breakfast

per night:	£min	£max
Single	17.00	18.50
Double	34.00	37.00

Parking for 3
🛏10🖭◻♨🖭✕♨🖩🛏♨✕🐾

Fircroft ⋀

😊😊 COMMENDED

84 Greenhill, Evesham, Worcestershire
WR11 4NH
☎ (01386) 45828
Comfortable B & B offering a relaxed and unobtrusive environment. Elegant house in attractive gardens, situated three quarters of a mile north of town centre. No smoking.
Bedrooms: 1 double, 1 twin, 1 triple
Bathrooms: 1 private, 2 public
Bed & breakfast

per night:	£min	£max
Single	20.00	25.00
Double	35.00	42.00

Parking for 6
Open March-October
🛏◻♨🖭◻🆂♨✕♨❄✕🐾🆃

Glencoyne

Listed

Lenchwick, Evesham, Worcestershire
WR11 4TG
☎ (01386) 870901
Ground floor accommodation in large chalet bungalow. Beautiful gardens overlooking a lake, available to guests. Two miles from Evesham centre.
Bedrooms: 1 twin
Bathrooms: 1 public
Bed & breakfast

per night:	£min	£max
Single	15.00	15.00
Double	30.00	30.00

Parking for 5
🛏5🦮♨🆂♨📺🖩♨❄🐾

Park View Hotel ⋀

📶

Waterside, Evesham, Worcestershire
WR11 6BS
☎ (01386) 442639
Family-run hotel offering comfortable accommodation in a friendly atmosphere. Riverside situation, close to town centre. Ideal base for touring the Cotswolds and Shakespeare country.
Bedrooms: 10 single, 4 double, 10 twin, 1 triple, 1 family room
Bathrooms: 7 public
Bed & breakfast

per night:	£min	£max
Single	19.50	24.00
Double	34.00	41.00

Evening meal 1800 (last orders 1900)
Parking for 50
Cards accepted: Access, Visa, Diners, Amex
🛏🆂♨📺♨🕯30🆂🅿🆃

EWEN

Gloucestershire
Map ref 2B1

Village in the South Cotswolds of attractive stone cottages and houses.

Wild Duck Inn ⋀

😊😊😊 COMMENDED

Drakes Island, Ewen, Cirencester
GL7 6BY
☎ Cirencester (01285) 770310 & 770364
Fax (01285) 770310
15th C Cotswold-stone inn, set in a rural position in the village. Two four-poster rooms in the oldest part of the building. All rooms with private facilities. Delightful garden.
Bedrooms: 6 double, 3 twin
Bathrooms: 9 private
Bed & breakfast

per night:	£min	£max
Single	40.00	48.00
Double	55.00	75.00

Lunch available
Evening meal 1900 (last orders 2145)
Parking for 50
Cards accepted: Access, Visa, Amex, Switch/Delta
🛏🦮🕭📞🖭◻♨🖀🆂🛏📺🖩♨
🕯🖐❄🆂🏮🆃

FAIRFORD

Gloucestershire
Map ref 2B1

Small town with a 15th C wool church famous for its complete 15th C stained glass windows, interesting carvings and original wall paintings. It is an excellent touring centre and the Cotswolds Wildlife Park is nearby.

East End House

😊😊 COMMENDED

Fairford GL7 4AP
☎ Cirencester (01285) 713715

Spacious accommodation in large Georgian family home in peaceful conservation area. Private parking, gardens, tennis court. Listed building. Family run.
Bedrooms: 1 twin, 1 family room
Bathrooms: 2 private
Bed & breakfast

per night:	£min	£max
Single	20.00	25.00
Double	40.00	50.00

Continued ▶

FAIRFORD
Continued

Half board

per person:	£min	£max
Daily	35.00	40.00
Weekly	260.00	260.00

Parking for 8

🛏🍽📺🖥♿🕯📶⓾🅢✕🔖🛍🚗🔍✿✕🐾🎠🏠

Milton Farm
Listed **COMMENDED**
Fairford GL7 4HZ
☎ Cirencester (01285) 712205
Fax (01285) 712205
*840-acre arable farm. Large Georgian
farmhouse with ample sized rooms. Run
by farming family of Scottish ancestry.*
Bedrooms: 1 double, 2 twin
Bathrooms: 3 private, 1 public

Bed & breakfast

per night:	£min	£max
Single	20.00	22.00
Double	32.00	36.00

🛏♿🖥🅢🛍📺🛍🚗🎠

Waiten Hill Farm ⚘
👑👑
Fairford GL7 4JG
☎ Cirencester (01285) 712652
Fax (01285) 712652
*350-acre mixed farm. Imposing 19th C
farmhouse, overlooking River Coln, old
mill and famous church. Short walk to
shops and restaurants. Ideal for touring
the Cotswolds and water parks.*
Bedrooms: 2 double, 1 twin
Bathrooms: 1 private, 1 public

Bed & breakfast

per night:	£min	£max
Single	20.00	25.00
Double	30.00	35.00

Parking for 8

🛏📺♿🖥📺🛍✿🎠🔖🅣

FOREST OF DEAN
*See under Coleford, Corse,
Lydney, Newent, Newland,
Parkend*

FOWNHOPE
Hereford and Worcester
Map ref 2A1

Attractive village close to the River
Wye with black and white cottages
and other interesting houses. It
has a large church with a Norman
tower and a 14th C spire.

Green Man Inn ⚘
👑👑 **COMMENDED**
Fownhope, Hereford HR1 4PE
☎ Hereford (01432) 860243
Fax (01432) 860207

*15th C black and white coaching inn,
midway between Ross-on-Wye and
Hereford, in the picturesque village of
Fownhope. On B4224, close to the
River Wye and set in the beautiful Wye
Valley.*
Bedrooms: 1 single, 13 double, 1 twin,
4 triple
Bathrooms: 19 private

Bed & breakfast

per night:	£min	£max
Single	31.00	32.00
Double	50.00	51.50

Half board

per person:	£min	£max
Daily	36.50	37.75
Weekly	239.50	245.00

Lunch available
Evening meal 1900 (last orders 2100)
Parking for 80
Cards accepted: Access, Visa, Switch/
Delta

🛏🍽📺🕯🍽🖥♿🕯📶🅢✕🛍📺🛍
🚗🍴🔖✿🔍🔖🏠

GLOUCESTER
Gloucestershire
Map ref 2B1

A Roman city and inland port, its
cathedral is one of the most
beautiful in Britain. Gloucester's
many attractions include museums
and the restored warehouses in
the Victorian docks containing the
National Waterways Museum,
Robert Opie Collection and other
attractions.
*Tourist Information Centre
☎ (01452) 421188*

Gilbert's ⚘
👑👑 **HIGHLY COMMENDED**
Brookthorpe, Gloucester GL4 0UH
☎ Painswick (01452) 812364
Fax (01452) 812364

*4-acre organic farm. Grade II listed
Jacobean house near the Cotswolds,
Bath, Oxford and Stratford. A family
home, combining antiques with modern
amenities.*
Bedrooms: 1 single, 2 double, 1 twin
Bathrooms: 4 private

Bed & breakfast

per night:	£min	£max
Single	23.00	30.00
Double	46.00	55.00

Parking for 6

🛏🍴🍽📺♿🖥🕯🅢✕🛍⓾📺🚗
🍴⓾🔍✕🛍🏠

Merrivale ⚘
📺 **COMMENDED**
Tewkesbury Road, Norton, Gloucester
GL2 9LQ
☎ (01452) 730412
*Large private house with a pleasant
garden, 3 miles north of Gloucester. TV
and tea/coffee-making facilities in all
bedrooms.*
Bedrooms: 2 double, 3 twin, 1 triple
Bathrooms: 1 public, 2 private
showers

Bed & breakfast

per night:	£min	£max
Single	15.50	17.00
Double	31.00	34.00

Parking for 8

🛏🍴📺♿🖥🕯🛍📺📺🛍🚗✿🎠

Notley House and Coach House ⚘
👑👑👑 **COMMENDED**
93 Hucclecote Road, Hucclecote,
Gloucester GL3 3TR
☎ (01452) 611584
*Affordable quality accommodation. Ideal
for historic Gloucester and the
Cotswolds. Tastefully furnished en-suite
rooms, suites with four-poster bed.*
Bedrooms: 1 single, 2 double, 2 twin,
1 triple, 1 family room
Bathrooms: 4 private, 3 private
showers

Bed & breakfast

per night:	£min	£max
Single	23.50	41.12
Double	37.60	58.75

Half board

per person:	£min	£max
Daily	28.79	51.11
Weekly	181.38	321.99

Evening meal 1900 (last orders 2000)
Parking for 8
Cards accepted: Access, Visa

🛏🍽📺🕯🍽♿🖥📶🅢✕🛍📺🛍🚗
✿✕🏠

Severn Bank ⚘
👑👑 **COMMENDED**
Minsterworth, Gloucester GL2 8JH
☎ (01452) 750357
Fax (01452) 750357
*Fine riverside country house in 6 acres
of grounds, 4 miles west of Gloucester.
Viewpoint for Severn Bore Tidal Wave.
Ideal for touring Forest of Dean and
the Cotswolds.*
Bedrooms: 1 single, 2 double, 3 triple
Bathrooms: 4 private, 1 public

Bed & breakfast

per night:	£min	£max
Single	17.50	19.50
Double	35.00	39.00

Parking for 6

🌲🖵💧ⓤⓈ✗🅿🎢 ▄❄️✗🚲🏛

GREAT RISSINGTON

Gloucestershire
Map ref 2B1

One of two villages overlooking the River Windrush near Bourton-on-the-Water.

The Malthouse
♛♛

Great Rissington, Cheltenham
GL54 2LH
☎ Cotswolds (01451) 820582
Cotswold-stone malthouse built in 1648, in sought after, quiet Cotswold village. Accommodation is a private suite with gallery bedroom. Non-smokers only, please.
Bedrooms: 1 double
Bathrooms: 1 private

Bed & breakfast

per night:	£min	£max
Double	40.00	45.00

Parking for 2

🖵💧🍳ⓤⓈ✗🅿🎢▄ U❄️✗ 🚲🏛

GUITING POWER

Gloucestershire
Map ref 2B1

Unspoilt village with stone cottages and a green. The Cotswold Farm Park, with a collection of rare breeds, an adventure playground and farm trail, is nearby.

Farmers Arms
♛♛♛ APPROVED

Guiting Power, Cheltenham GL54 5TZ
☎ Cotswold (01451) 850358

Country pub in lovely unspoilt Cotswold village, 13 miles from Cheltenham. Good access to local places of interest.
Bedrooms: 1 double, 1 twin
Bathrooms: 1 private, 1 public

Bed & breakfast

per night:	£min	£max
Single	20.00	22.00
Double	35.00	40.00

Half board

per person:	£min	£max
Daily	30.00	42.00
Weekly	180.00	250.00

Lunch available
Evening meal 1900 (last orders 2115)
Parking for 24

🌲🖵💧🍳ⒶⓈ▥▄🍴60❄️✗🚲🖂 🏛Ⓣ

Halfway House
♛

Kineton, Guiting Power, Cheltenham
GL54 5UG
☎ Cotswold (01451) 850344
Fax (01451) 850344
17th C inn serving good food and offering a warm welcome.
Bedrooms: 1 single, 1 double, 1 twin
Bathrooms: 2 public

Bed & breakfast

per night:	£min	£max
Single	20.00	24.00
Double	36.00	40.00

Lunch available
Evening meal 1830 (last orders 2130)
Parking for 10
Cards accepted: Access, Visa, Switch/Delta

🌲💧✗▥▄❄️U P❄️🚲🐾 SP

HAMPTON IN ARDEN

West Midlands
Map ref 4B3

Midway between Birmingham and Coventry and with the National Exhibition Centre on the doorstep.

The Hollies 🅰
Listed COMMENDED

Kenilworth Road, Hampton in Arden, Solihull B92 0LW
☎ (01675) 442941 & 442681
Fax (01675) 442941
Home from home comfort, 2.5 miles from NEC and Birmingham International Airport. Sky TV, ample parking.
Bedrooms: 1 single, 3 double, 4 twin
Bathrooms: 8 private, 1 public

Bed & breakfast

per night:	£min	£max
Single	20.00	25.00
Double	36.00	40.00

Parking for 10

🌲🖴🖵💧🍳ⒶⓈ✗🅿📺▥▄ 🍴25❄️Ⓣ

Pear Tree House 🅰
♛♛♛

10 Station Road, Hampton in Arden, Solihull B92 0BJ
☎ (01675) 443993
Fax (01675) 443991
Comfortable Victorian house close to National Exhibition Centre and Birmingham Airport. All rooms en-suite and individually furnished. Near local railway station.
Bedrooms: 1 single, 2 twin

Bathrooms: 3 private

Bed & breakfast

per night:	£min	£max
Single	25.00	35.00
Double	40.00	45.00

Parking for 6
Cards accepted: Access, Visa

🌲5✆🖵🖵💧🍳ⓤ▥🛆▄❄️🚲

HARBURY

Warwickshire
Map ref 2C1

The Dog Inn
Listed

The Bull Ring, Harbury, Leamington Spa CV33 9EZ
☎ Leamington Spa (01926) 612599
100-year-old inn set in beautiful rural village, 3 miles from junction 12 of M40 and near Warwick, Stratford, Leamington and Coventry.
Bedrooms: 2 double
Bathrooms: 1 public

Bed & breakfast

per night:	£min	£max
Single	21.00	
Double	37.00	

Half board

per person:	£min	£max
Daily	25.50	28.00

Lunch available
Evening meal 1800 (last orders 2200)
Parking for 31
Cards accepted: Access, Visa

🌲🖵💧▥📺▥🍴30❄️🚲🐾

HENLEY-IN-ARDEN

Warwickshire
Map ref 2B1

Old market town which in Tudor times stood in the Forest of Arden. It has many ancient inns, a 15th C Guildhall and parish church. Coughton Court with its Gunpowder Plot connections is nearby.

Irelands Farm 🅰
♛♛ HIGHLY COMMENDED

Irelands Lane, Henley-in-Arden, Solihull, West Midlands B95 5SA
☎ (01564) 792476
220-acre arable & livestock farm. Secluded farmhouse in peaceful countryside. Close to Stratford, Warwick, National Exhibition Centre and the Cotswolds. 1 mile off A3400 between Henley and M42.
Bedrooms: 2 double, 1 twin
Bathrooms: 3 private

Bed & breakfast

per night:	£min	£max
Single	17.00	20.00
Double	30.00	35.00

Parking for 6

🖵🖵💧🍳ⓤⓈ✗🅿📺▥▄🖊❄️ 🚲🏛

HEREFORD

Hereford and Worcester
Map ref 2A1

Agricultural county town, its cathedral containing much Norman work and a large chained library. Among the city's varied attractions are several museums including the Cider Museum and the Old House.
Tourist Information Centre
☎ (01432) 268430

The Ancient Camp Inn ⋀

⛫⛫⛫ COMMENDED

Ruckhall, Eaton Bishop, Hereford HR2 9QX
☎ Golden Valley (01981) 250449
Fax (01981) 251581
This inn is on the site of an Iron Age fort dating from the 4th-5th C BC. Spectacular views of the River Wye. Restaurant and bar food a speciality.
Bedrooms: 4 double, 1 twin; suite available
Bathrooms: 5 private

Bed & breakfast

per night:	£min	£max
Single	35.00	45.00
Double	48.00	58.00

Lunch available
Evening meal 1900 (last orders 2130)
Parking for 45
Cards accepted: Access, Visa

Collins House ⋀

⛫⛫ COMMENDED

19 St Owen Street, Hereford HR1 2JB
☎ (01432) 272416
Fax (01432) 357717
Fully restored early Georgian town house, c1722, combining comfort, character and convenience in historic town centre. Private parking.
Bedrooms: 1 double, 2 twin
Bathrooms: 3 private

Bed & breakfast

per night:	£min	£max
Single	27.50	30.00
Double	35.00	39.00

Parking for 3
Cards accepted: Access, Visa

Cwm Craig Farm

⛫⛫ COMMENDED

Little Dewchurch, Hereford HR2 6PS
☎ Carey (01432) 840250
190-acre arable & livestock farm. Spacious Georgian farmhouse on edge of Wye Valley, surrounded by superb, unspoilt countryside. 5 miles south of Hereford. Easy access from M50.
Bedrooms: 1 double, 1 twin, 1 family room
Bathrooms: 1 private, 2 public

Bed & breakfast

per night:	£min	£max
Single	16.00	16.00
Double	30.00	34.00

Parking for 6

Felton House ⋀

⛫⛫ HIGHLY COMMENDED

Felton, Hereford HR1 3PH
☎ (01432) 820366
The tranquil charm of a Victorian/Edwardian stone rectory. Four-poster and brass beds. Wide breakfast choice. Modern comforts and warm welcome. Tiny hamlet 8 miles Hereford, Leominster, Bromyard off A417.
Bedrooms: 1 single, 2 double, 1 twin
Bathrooms: 3 private, 1 public

Bed & breakfast

per night:	£min	£max
Single	17.50	20.00
Double	35.00	40.00

Parking for 6
Open January-November

Grafton Villa Farm House

⛫⛫ HIGHLY COMMENDED

Grafton, Hereford HR2 8ED
☎ (01432) 268689
180-acre mixed farm. Character farmhouse beautifully furnished with antiques and lovely fabrics, surrounded by peaceful countryside. Ideal for touring Wye Valley. Set back off A49 Hereford/Ross-on-Wye road.
Bedrooms: 1 double, 1 twin, 1 triple
Bathrooms: 3 private

Bed & breakfast

per night:	£min	£max
Single	18.00	20.00
Double	32.00	36.00

Parking for 10
Open February-November

Lower Bartestree Farm

⛫

Bartestree, Hereford HR1 4DT
☎ (01432) 851005
Comfortable accommodation in a peaceful setting with splendid views. Home-made bread, preserves and crafts available. Off A438, 4 miles from city centre.
Bedrooms: 1 twin, 1 triple
Bathrooms: 1 public

Bed & breakfast

per night:	£min	£max
Single		16.00
Double		30.00

Parking for 5

Sink Green Farm

⛫⛫ COMMENDED

Rotherwas, Hereford HR2 6LE
☎ Holme Lacy (01432) 870223
170-acre livestock farm. 16th C farmhouse on family-run farm. Overlooking River Wye and 3 miles from Hereford city centre. Establishment is non-smoking.
Bedrooms: 2 double, 1 twin
Bathrooms: 3 private

Bed & breakfast

per night:	£min	£max
Single	20.00	25.00
Double	36.00	44.00

Parking for 10

IRONBRIDGE

Shropshire
Map ref 4A3

Small town on the Severn where the Industrial Revolution began. It has the world's first iron bridge built in 1779. The Ironbridge Gorge Museum, of exceptional interest, comprises a rebuilt turn-of-the-century town and sites spread over 6 square miles.
Tourist Information Centre
☎ (01952) 432166

The Golden Ball Inn

⛫⛫⛫ COMMENDED

1 Newbridge Road, Ironbridge, Telford TF8 7BA
☎ Telford (01952) 432179
Traditional character inn, full of beams and fireplaces. Ironbridge's oldest pub, serving good food and traditional ales 7 days a week.
Bedrooms: 1 single, 1 double, 1 twin
Bathrooms: 3 private

Bed & breakfast

per night:	£min	£max
Single	35.00	35.00
Double	45.00	45.00

Lunch available
Evening meal 1800 (last orders 2130)
Parking for 35
Cards accepted: Access, Visa

Hundred House Hotel ⋀

⛫⛫⛫ HIGHLY COMMENDED

Bridgnorth Rd., A442, Norton, Shifnal, Telford TF11 9EE
☎ Telford (01952) 730353
Fax (01952) 730355
Homely, family-run hotel, with atmospheric historic bars, interesting bar food and intimate restaurant. Antique patchwork themed bedrooms with all facilities. Beautiful, relaxing cottage gardens.
Bedrooms: 1 single, 2 double, 1 twin, 5 triple
Bathrooms: 9 private

Bed & breakfast

per night:	£min	£max
Single	59.00	69.00
Double	69.00	88.00

Half board

per person:	£min	£max
Daily	48.00	55.00
Weekly	302.00	346.00

Lunch available
Evening meal 1800 (last orders 2200)
Parking for 30
Cards accepted: Access, Visa, Amex,
Switch/Delta

🏠♿📠🖵♨🖊📺💻 ⚓🍴20🕭❀
🚳🐾 SP 🅿️ T

Orchard House

⚜️ ⚜️

40 King Street, Broseley TF12 5NA
☎ Telford (01952) 882684
*Three-storey Georgian family house with
large garden, in small historic town, 1
mile from Ironbridge Gorge and River
Severn.*
Bedrooms: 1 twin, 1 triple
Bathrooms: 1 private, 2 public

Bed & breakfast

per night:	£min	£max
Single	15.00	18.00
Double	30.00	35.00

Parking for 3

🏠🖵♨ UL 🖊 S 🖊 📺 💻 ⚓❀🚳🐾

46 Wigmore

Listed APPROVED

Woodside, Telford TF7 5NB
☎ Telford (01952) 583748
*Privately-owned house with garden and
garage at rear. TV in all rooms and hot
and cold water at all times.*
Bedrooms: 1 single, 1 twin
Bathrooms: 1 public

Bed & breakfast

per night:	£min	£max
Single	10.00	12.00
Double	20.00	24.00

Evening meal from 1700
Parking for 2

🖵🖵 UL 🖊 🖊 📺 💻 ⚓🚳

KENILWORTH

Warwickshire
Map ref 4B3

The main feature of the town is
the ruined 12th C castle. It has
many royal associations but was
damaged by Cromwell. A good
base for visiting Coventry,
Leamington Spa and Warwick.
Tourist Information Centre
☎ *(01926) 52595 or 50708*

Banner Hill Farmhouse

⚜️

Rouncil Lane, Kenilworth CV8 1NN
☎ (01926) 52850 changing to 852850
*250-acre mixed farm. Listed farmhouse
in Warwickshire countryside, also
mobile home. In middle of nowhere and
no distance from anywhere. NAC 10*

minutes, NEC and Stratford-upon-Avon
20 minutes.
Bedrooms: 3 twin
Bathrooms: 1 private, 1 public

Bed & breakfast

per night:	£min	£max
Single	15.00	22.50
Double	34.00	37.50

Half board

per person:	£min	£max
Daily	20.00	27.50
Weekly	87.50	140.00

Lunch available
Parking for 8

🏠🖵🖵♨ UL 🖊 S 🖊 📺 💻 ⚓🚲
❀🚳

Ravensbridge

⚜️ ⚜️ HIGHLY COMMENDED

Fernhill Lane, Fen End, Kenilworth
CV8 1NU
☎ Berkswell (01676) 533361
*15-acre horse farm. Farmhouse and
working stables in rural setting, yet
minutes from the National Exhibition
Centre, National Agricultural Centre
and motorway links.*
Bedrooms: 1 double
Bathrooms: 1 private

Bed & breakfast

per night:	£min	£max
Single	30.00	30.00
Double	39.99	39.99

Evening meal 1900 (last orders 2030)
Parking for 5

🏠🖵♨♨ UL 🖊 📺 💻 ⚓☄❀🦋🚳

KIDDERMINSTER

Hereford and Worcester
Map ref 4B3

The town is the centre for carpet
manufacturing. It has a medieval
church with good monuments and
a statue of Sir Rowland Hill, a
native of the town and founder of
the penny post. West Midlands
Safari Park is nearby. Severn
Valley railway station.

Cedars Hotel

⚜️ ⚜️ COMMENDED

Mason Road, Kidderminster,
Worcestershire DY11 6AG
☎ (01562) 515595
Fax (01562) 751103
*Charming conversion of a Georgian
building close to the River Severn,
Severn Valley Railway and
Worcestershire countryside. 15 minutes
from M5.*
Bedrooms: 2 single, 7 double, 7 twin,
4 triple, 2 family rooms
Bathrooms: 22 private

Bed & breakfast

per night:	£min	£max
Single	29.90	51.00
Double	42.00	62.00

Evening meal 1900 (last orders 2030)
Parking for 23

Cards accepted: Access, Visa, Diners,
Amex

🏠♿☎📠🖵♨♨🖊 S 🖊 💻 ⚓
🍴35❀ SP T

KINETON

Warwickshire
Map ref 2C1

Attractive old village in rolling
countryside. 1 mile from site of
famous battle of Edgehill. Medieval
church of St Peter.

Willowbrook Farmhouse ⋀

⚜️ ⚜️

Lighthorne Road, Kineton, Warwick
CV35 0JL
☎ (01926) 640475
Fax (01926) 641747
*4-acre smallholding. Very comfortable
house surrounded by lovely countryside,
3 miles to M40 (junction 12), half a
mile from Kineton village. Handy for
Stratford-upon-Avon, Warwick and
Cotswolds. Tea trays, antiques and
friendly service.*
Bedrooms: 2 double, 1 twin
Bathrooms: 1 private, 2 public

Bed & breakfast

per night:	£min	£max
Double	31.00	37.00

Parking for 6

🏠🖵♨ UL S 🖊 📺 💻 ⚓🖐❀🚳 SP

KINGS CAPLE

Hereford and Worcester
Map ref 2A1

Quiet village set in a loop of the
River Wye, one of the 3
Herefordshire parishes where pax
cakes are given out after the
service on Palm Sunday, together
with the greeting "Peace and Good
Neighbourhood".

Ruxton Farm

⚜️ ⚜️ COMMENDED

Kings Caple, Hereford HR1 4TX
☎ Carey (01432) 840493
Fax (01432) 840592
*18-acre horse farm. 17th C farmhouse
with original staircase and hound gate.
Quiet, tranquil location off the main
road in beautiful Wye Valley. Ample
parking. A non-smoking establishment.*
Bedrooms: 2 double, 1 twin
Bathrooms: 3 private

Bed & breakfast

per night:	£min	£max
Single	17.50	17.50
Double	35.00	35.00

Parking for 6

🏠🍴10🖵♨ UL S 🖊 📺 💻 ⚓🖐❀
🦋🚳🅿️

KNOCKDOWN

Gloucestershire
Map ref 2B2

Avenue Farm
Knockdown, Tetbury GL8 8QY
☎ Chipping Sodbury (01454) 238207
300-acre mixed farm. 300-year-old farmhouse, just off the A433, adjacent to Westonbirt Arboretum and 30 minutes' drive from Bath.
Bedrooms: 3 twin
Bathrooms: 1 public, 1 private shower

Bed & breakfast

per night:	£min	£max
Single	15.00	20.00
Double	30.00	35.00

Parking for 3

LEAMINGTON SPA

Warwickshire
Map ref 4B3

18th C spa town with many fine Georgian and Regency houses. Tea can be taken in the 19th C Pump Room. The attractive Jephson Gardens are laid out alongside the river and there is a museum and art gallery.
Tourist Information Centre
☎ *(01926) 311470*

8 Clarendon Crescent
Listed
Leamington Spa CV32 5NR
☎ (01926) 429840
Fax (01926) 451660

Elegant Regency house situated in a quiet backwater of Leamington Spa, 5 minutes' walk from town centre, overlooking private dell.
Bedrooms: 2 single, 1 double, 1 twin
Bathrooms: 4 private

Bed & breakfast

per night:	£min	£max
Single	25.00	30.00
Double	50.00	50.00

Parking for 1

Glendower Guesthouse ⋀
COMMENDED
8 Warwick Place, Leamington Spa
CV32 5BJ
☎ (01926) 422784
Charming Victorian building with many original features in a central but quiet location, offering comfortable accommodation. Ideal for National

Agricultural Centre, M40, NEC, Warwick Castle and for touring the Cotswolds.
Bedrooms: 3 single, 1 double, 2 twin, 2 triple, 1 family room
Bathrooms: 2 private, 2 public

Bed & breakfast

per night:	£min	£max
Single	16.00	20.00
Double	32.00	40.00

Parking for 4

Hill Farm ⋀
COMMENDED
Lewis Road, Radford Semele,
Leamington Spa CV31 1UX
☎ (01926) 337571
350-acre mixed farm. Farmhouse set in large attractive garden, 2 miles from Leamington town centre and close to Warwick Castle and Stratford-upon-Avon.
Bedrooms: 3 double, 2 twin
Bathrooms: 3 private, 1 public

Bed & breakfast

per night:	£min	£max
Single	18.00	20.00
Double	32.00	38.00

Parking for 10

Northton ⋀
COMMENDED
77 Telford Avenue, Lillington,
Leamington Spa CV32 7HQ
☎ (01926) 425609
Detached family home with large garden in quiet residential area off A445, 2.5 miles from National Agricultural Centre. No smoking and no pets, please.
Bedrooms: 1 single, 1 twin
Bathrooms: 2 private

Bed & breakfast

per night:	£min	£max
Single	17.50	
Double	35.00	

Parking for 4
Open February-October

The Orchard ⋀
Listed APPROVED
3 Sherbourne Terrace, Clarendon Street, Leamington Spa CV32 5SP
☎ (01926) 428198
Victorian double-fronted terrace with walled garden. 5 minutes' walk to town centre. Overseas visitors and children welcome.
Bedrooms: 1 single, 1 twin, 1 triple
Bathrooms: 2 public

Bed & breakfast

per night:	£min	£max
Single	15.00	18.00
Double	28.00	30.00

Half board

per person:	£min	£max
Daily	19.00	22.00
Weekly	110.00	120.00

Lunch available
Evening meal from 1800

Snowford Hall ⋀
COMMENDED
Snowford Hall Farm, Hunningham,
Leamington Spa CV33 9ES
☎ Marton (01926) 632297
200-acre arable and mixed farm. 18th C farmhouse off the Fosse Way, on the edge of Hunningham village. On elevated ground overlooking quiet surrounding countryside. Self-catering also available.
Bedrooms: 1 double, 1 twin, 1 triple
Bathrooms: 1 private, 1 public, 1 private shower

Bed & breakfast

per night:	£min	£max
Double	34.00	40.00

Parking for 4

Stonehouse Farm ⋀
Listed COMMENDED
Leicester Lane, Cubbington Heath,
Leamington Spa CV32 6QZ
☎ (01926) 336370
Friendly, Grade II listed Queen Anne farmhouse, with extensive views over Warwickshire's beautiful countryside. A mile from the Royal Showground and close to Leamington Spa, Warwick and Stratford.
Bedrooms: 3 twin
Bathrooms: 1 private, 1 public

Bed & breakfast

per night:	£min	£max
Single	21.00	26.50
Double	42.00	36.50

Half board

per person:	£min	£max
Daily	33.00	38.50

Evening meal from 1930
Parking for 6

LECHLADE

Gloucestershire
Map ref 2B1

Attractive village on the River Thames and a popular spot for boating. It has a number of fine Georgian houses and a 15th C church. Nearby is Kelmscott Manor, with its William Morris furnishings, and 18th C Buscot House (National Trust).

Apple Tree House
Buscot, Faringdon, Oxfordshire
SN7 8DA
☎ Faringdon (01367) 252592
Listed property offering comfortable B & B in National Trust village near Lechlade. River Thames 5 minutes' walk through village. Large garden.

Bedrooms: 2 double, 1 twin
Bathrooms: 1 private, 1 public

Bed & breakfast per night:	£min	£max
Double	33.00	38.00

Parking for 8

⛄🚗♿🅿️🔠🖊️🚭🌙📺🛏️🍴🍺❄️✕🐕🐎🏠

Cambrai Lodge 🏨

Listed

Oak Street, Lechlade GL7 3AY
☎ (01367) 253173 & Mobile 0860 150467
Family-run guesthouse, recently modernised, close to River Thames. Ideal base for touring the Cotswolds. Garden and ample parking.
Bedrooms: 1 double, 1 twin, 1 triple
Bathrooms: 3 private, 1 public

Bed & breakfast per night:	£min	£max
Single	20.00	25.00
Double	30.00	38.00

Parking for 13

⛄🚗♿🅿️🖊️🌙🔠🅿️📺🛏️🍴☀️🐎
🐕 SP

Hereford and Worcester
Map ref 2B1

Town with cobbled streets and many black and white timbered houses, including the 17th C market house and old inns. Nearby is Eastnor Castle with an interesting collection of tapestries and armour.
Tourist Information Centre
☎ *(01531) 636147*

Mainstone House

Listed

Trumpet, Ledbury, Herefordshire HR8 2RA
☎ Trumpet (01531) 670230
Large 17th C black and white timbered property, once the farmhouse to the adjacent court estate. Wealth of exposed beams.
Bedrooms: 1 double, 1 family room
Bathrooms: 2 private

Bed & breakfast per night:	£min	£max
Single	20.00	22.00
Double	30.00	33.00

Parking for 8

⛄🚗🌙🔠🅿️🍴🚭🛏️🍴🐎♦️☀️🐕 SP
🏠🅃

Priors Court

♿♿

Aylton, Ledbury, Herefordshire HR8 2QE
☎ Trumpet (01531) 670748
Fax (01531) 670860

11-acre mixed farm. Early 17th C half-timbered farmhouse, set in peaceful grounds with lake.
Bedrooms: 1 double, 1 triple
Bathrooms: 2 private

Bed & breakfast per night:	£min	£max
Single	20.00	25.00
Double	35.00	40.00

Half board per person:	£min	£max
Daily	27.00	35.00
Weekly		205.00

Evening meal 1800 (last orders 2100)
Parking for 10

⛄🚗🍴🌙🖊️🔠🚭✕🐎 SP 🏠

Staffordshire
Map ref 4B2

Old silk and textile town, with some interesting buildings and a number of inns dating from the 17th C. Its art gallery has displays of embroidery. Brindley Mill, designed by James Brindley, has been restored as a museum.
Tourist Information Centre
☎ *(01538) 381000*

Abbey Inn

♿♿ **COMMENDED**

Abbey Green Road, Leek ST13 8SA
☎ (01538) 382865
17th C inn with accommodation in a separate annexe, set in beautiful countryside, 1 mile from the town and just off the main A523.
Bedrooms: 2 single, 4 double, 1 twin
Bathrooms: 7 private

Bed & breakfast per night:	£min	£max
Single	27.00	30.00
Double	42.00	46.00

Lunch available
Evening meal 1830 (last orders 2100)
Parking for 60
Cards accepted: Access, Visa, Diners, Amex, Switch/Delta

⛄🚗♿🍴🌙🖊️🅿️🛏️☀️✕ SP 🏠

Bank End Farm Motel 🏨

♿♿♿ **COMMENDED**

Leek Old Road, Longsdon, Stoke-on-Trent ST9 9QJ
☎ (01538) 383638
62-acre mixed farm. Pleasant motel in converted dairy and old stone barn, in a quiet lane close to Leek, Peak District National Park and Alton Towers.
Bedrooms: 1 single, 3 double, 3 twin, 2 family rooms

Bathrooms: 7 private, 1 public

Bed & breakfast per night:	£min	£max
Single	28.00	31.00
Double	46.00	50.00

Half board per night:	£min	£max
Daily	39.00	43.00

Evening meal 1900 (last orders 2000)
Parking for 10
Cards accepted: Access, Visa

⛄🚗♿🍴🌙♦️🔠🅿️🛏️📺🛏️🅿️♦️
🍃🎣▶️✕☀️🐎🏠

Beechfields

♿♿

Park Road, Leek ST13 8JS
☎ (01538) 372825
Secluded Victorian house with large gardens, 50 yards Brough Park leisure facilities, close to town. Convenient for Alton Towers, Peak District, Potteries.
Bedrooms: 1 double, 2 triple
Bathrooms: 1 private, 2 public

Bed & breakfast per night:	£min	£max
Single	16.50	16.50
Double	33.00	33.00

Parking for 7

⛄6🅿️♦️🔠🚭✕🛏️📺🛏️🅿️☀️✕🐎

Three Horseshoes Inn & Restaurant 🏨

♿♿♿ **COMMENDED**

Buxton Road, Blackshaw Moor, Leek ST13 8TW
☎ (01538) 300296
Fax (01538) 300320

Log fire, slate floor, oak and pine beams, good food and wines. Cottage-style rooms. Convenient for Peak District National Park and Alton Towers.
Bedrooms: 4 double, 2 twin
Bathrooms: 6 private

Bed & breakfast per night:	£min	£max
Single	40.00	46.00
Double	46.00	54.00

Half board per person:	£min	£max
Daily	38.00	46.00

Lunch available
Evening meal 1900 (last orders 2100)
Parking for 100
Cards accepted: Access, Visa, Switch/Delta

⛄🚗🍴🌙♦️🔠🅿️🚭✕🛏️📺🛏️🅿️🔆♦️
SP 🅃

LEINTWARDINE

Hereford and Worcester
Map ref 4A3

Attractive border village where the Rivers Teme and Clun meet. It has some black and white cottages, old inns and an impressive church. It is near Hopton Castle and the beautiful scenery around Clun.

Lower House ⋀⋀
HIGHLY COMMENDED

Adforton, Leintwardine, Craven Arms, Shropshire SY7 0NF
☎ Wigmore (01568) 770223
House dates from early 17th C. Set in peaceful, unspoilt countryside. Excellent walking in surrounding hills. Home cooking using local produce. A no-smoking establishment.
Bedrooms: 2 double, 2 twin
Bathrooms: 4 private

Bed & breakfast

per night:	£min	£max
Single	22.00	24.00
Double	44.00	48.00

Half board

per person:	£min	£max
Daily	38.00	40.00
Weekly	255.00	255.00

Evening meal 1900 (last orders 1930)
Parking for 10

LEOMINSTER

Hereford and Worcester
Map ref 2A1

The town owed its prosperity to wool and has many interesting buildings, notably the timber-framed Grange Court, a former town hall. The impressive Norman priory church has 3 naves and a ducking stool. Berrington Hall (National Trust) is nearby.
Tourist Information Centre
☎ *(01568) 616460*

Bedford House

Dilwyn, Hereford HR4 8JJ
☎ Pembridge (01544) 388260
20-acre mixed farm. Small, friendly farm offering peace and quiet, excellent accommodation, and good home cooking. In village south-west of Leominster, central for exploring Herefordshire, Worcestershire, Gloucestershire and Radnorshire. Welcome cup of tea.
Bedrooms: 1 double, 1 twin, 1 triple
Bathrooms: 1 private, 1 public

Bed & breakfast

per night:	£min	£max
Single	18.00	
Double	32.00	

Half board

per person:	£min	£max
Daily		24.00

Evening meal from 1830
Parking for 3
Open March-November

Copper Hall ⋀⋀
COMMENDED

South Street, Leominster, Herefordshire HR6 8JN
☎ (01568) 611622
Comfortable 17th C house with spacious garden. Good English cooking and homely atmosphere. Convenient touring centre for Wales, Wye Valley and the Malverns.
Bedrooms: 1 double, 2 twin, 1 triple
Bathrooms: 1 public

Bed & breakfast

per night:	£min	£max
Single	20.00	20.00
Double	35.00	35.00

Half board

per person:	£min	£max
Daily	27.50	30.00
Weekly	165.00	180.00

Evening meal 1800 (last orders 1500)
Parking for 6

Heath House ⋀⋀
HIGHLY COMMENDED

Humber, Stoke Prior, Leominster, Herefordshire HR6 0NF
☎ Steens Bridge (01568) 760385
Attractive stone farmhouse full of beams and history, set in peaceful countryside. Room to move and relax in comfort.
Bedrooms: 1 double, 1 twin, 1 triple
Bathrooms: 3 private

Bed & breakfast

per night:	£min	£max
Single	17.00	23.50
Double	40.00	44.00

Half board

per person:	£min	£max
Daily	29.00	40.50
Weekly	182.00	252.00

Evening meal 1900 (last orders 2000)
Parking for 6
Open March-November

Lower Bache ⋀⋀
HIGHLY COMMENDED

Kimbolton, Leominster, Herefordshire HR6 0ER
☎ Leysters (01568) 750304

17th C farmhouse in tranquil valley, with annexe comprising 3 suites, each with bedroom, bath/shower and sitting room. Period country furniture, renowned food. Wildlife, walking, ideal as touring base. Please ring for brochure.
Bedrooms: 2 double, 1 twin
Bathrooms: 3 private

Bed & breakfast

per night:	£min	£max
Single	29.50	29.50
Double	49.00	49.00

Half board

per person:	£min	£max
Daily	36.00	47.00
Weekly	252.00	273.00

Lunch available
Evening meal 1950 (last orders 1230)
Parking for 5

Royal Oak Hotel ⋀⋀
APPROVED

South Street, Leominster, Herefordshire HR6 8JA
☎ (01568) 612610
Fax (01568) 612710
Grade II listed Georgian coaching house dating from 1723, with log fires in winter, real ales and an emphasis on good food and wines at reasonable prices.
Bedrooms: 2 single, 9 double, 5 twin, 2 triple
Bathrooms: 18 private

Bed & breakfast

per night:	£min	£max
Single	31.50	35.00
Double	45.00	45.00

Half board

per person:	£min	£max
Daily	32.50	41.50
Weekly	204.75	261.45

Lunch available
Evening meal 1830 (last orders 2130)
Parking for 25
Cards accepted: Access, Visa, Diners, Amex

LONG COMPTON

Warwickshire
Map ref 2B1

Village with a restored church displaying Norman doorways and a thatched room above the lych gate. Several interesting old houses exist in the area.

Ascott House Farm ⋀⋀

Whichford, Long Compton, Shipston-on-Stour CV36 5PP
☎ (01608) 684655

500-acre arable & livestock farm. Old stone farmhouse in beautiful countryside on edge of Cotswolds. 3 miles off A3400 between Stratford-upon-Avon and Oxford. 10 miles from M40 at Banbury. Swimming pool, games room and walks. Riding and golf within 3 miles.
Bedrooms: 2 double, 1 twin
Bathrooms: 2 private, 1 public

Bed & breakfast

per night:	£min	£max
Single	16.00	20.00
Double	30.00	36.00

Parking for 12

LONGDON

Staffordshire
Map ref 4B3

Longdon Old Hall

Listed

Thorleys Hill, Longdon, Rugeley
WS15 4NW
☎ Burntwood (01543) 682267
100-acre mixed farm. 300-year-old Grade II listed farm with panoramic views, set back along a quarter-mile drive in unspoilt countryside.
Bedrooms: 1 double, 2 twin, 2 family rooms
Bathrooms: 2 private, 2 public

Bed & breakfast

per night:	£min	£max
Single	20.00	25.00
Double	30.00	40.00

Parking for 24

LONGNOR

Staffordshire
Map ref 4B2

Remote village in farming country between Buxton and Hartington and close to the River Dove.

Mount Pleasant Farm

COMMENDED

Elkstone, Longnor, Buxton, Derbyshire
SK17 0LU
☎ Blackshaw (01538) 300380
Truly peaceful and very comfortable farmhouse with wonderful views. Delicious breakfast with local produce, free range eggs and home made preserves.
Bedrooms: 1 double, 1 twin
Bathrooms: 2 private

Bed & breakfast

per night:	£min	£max
Single	20.00	24.00
Double	40.00	48.00

Parking for 5
Open March-November

LOXLEY

Warwickshire
Map ref 2B1

There is an attractive black and white farmhouse and some cottages in this pleasant village overlooking a wooded valley, only a few miles from Stratford-upon-Avon and close to Warwick and Leamington Spa.

Loxley Farm

COMMENDED

Loxley, Warwick CV35 9JN
☎ Stratford-upon-Avon (01789) 840265

6-acre horse farm. Picturesque, half-timbered thatched farmhouse dating from the late 13th C, set in 2 acres of garden. Accommodation in converted 17th C thatched half-timbered barn next to house.
Bedrooms: 2 double
Bathrooms: 2 private

Bed & breakfast

per night:	£min	£max
Single	30.00	33.00
Double	42.00	45.00

Parking for 10

LUDLOW

Shropshire
Map ref 4A3

Outstandingly interesting border town with a magnificent castle high above the River Teme, 2 half-timbered old inns and an impressive 15th C church. The Reader's House, with its 3-storey Jacobean porch, should also be seen.
Tourist Information Centre
☎ (01584) 875053

Bull Hotel

14 The Bull Ring, Ludlow SY8 1AD
☎ (01584) 873611
Fax (01584) 873611

Oldest pub in Ludlow, earliest mention c1343. Was known as Peter of Proctors House and probably dates back to c1199.
Bedrooms: 2 double, 2 twin
Bathrooms: 4 private

Bed & breakfast

per night:	£min	£max
Single	30.00	30.00
Double	45.00	45.00

Lunch available
Parking for 8
Cards accepted: Access, Visa, Amex

The Church Inn

Butter Cross, Ludlow SY8 1AW
☎ (01584) 872174
Fax (01584) 877146
Georgian inn, centrally located on one of the most ancient sites in Ludlow. Good food and CAMRA listed for ales.
Bedrooms: 5 double, 2 twin, 1 triple
Bathrooms: 8 private

Bed & breakfast

per night:	£min	£max
Single	28.00	28.00
Double	40.00	40.00

Lunch available
Evening meal 1800 (last orders 2100)
Cards accepted: Access, Visa

Corndene

Coreley, Ludlow SY8 3AW
☎ (01584) 890324
Country house of character in the heart of rural Shropshire. Beautiful and secluded situation only 5 minutes off A4117 (Ludlow 7 miles). Spacious en-suite rooms, tasty home cooking and relaxing atmosphere. No smoking indoors please.
Bedrooms: 3 twin
Bathrooms: 3 private

Bed & breakfast

per night:	£min	£max
Single	21.00	23.00
Double	37.00	41.00

Half board

per person:	£min	£max
Daily	27.00	30.00
Weekly	166.00	185.00

Evening meal 1830 (last orders 2000)
Parking for 5

LUDLOW

Continued

Fairview ⋀

⛉⛉ HIGHLY COMMENDED

Green Lane, Onibury, Craven Arms
SY7 9BL
☎ Bromfield (01584) 856505
*5-acre smallholding. 300-year-old cottage
6 miles north of Ludlow. Panoramic
views of Wenlock Edge, Long Mynd and
Clee Hills.*
Bedrooms: 2 double, 1 twin
Bathrooms: 1 private, 1 public

Bed & breakfast

per night:	£min	£max
Single	16.50	18.00
Double	31.00	36.00

Half board

per person:	£min	£max
Daily	28.00	29.50
Weekly	190.25	200.25

Evening meal 1930 (last orders 1930)
Parking for 8
Open April-October
⛱ 12 ♣ ⌾ ▥ ⧠ ⑤ ⅄ ⋈ 📺 ▥ 🖃 ✤
✕ 🐾

Longlands

⛉⛉

Woodhouse Lane, Richards Castle,
Ludlow SY8 4EU
☎ Richards Castle (01584) 831636
*35-acre livestock farm. Farmhouse set in
lovely rural landscape. Home-grown
produce. Convenient for Ludlow,
Mortimer Forest and Croft Castle.
Interesting 14th C church and remains
of 11th C castle in village.*
Bedrooms: 1 double, 1 twin; suite
available
Bathrooms: 2 private

Bed & breakfast

per night:	£min	£max
Single	18.00	
Double	35.00	

Half board

per person:	£min	£max
Daily	26.00	

Evening meal 1830 (last orders 1930)
Parking for 2
⛱ ⛌ ⬚ ♣ ▥ ⧠ ⑤ ⅄ ⋈ 📺 ▥ 🖃 ∪
✤ 🐾

The Moor Hall

⛉⛉ HIGHLY COMMENDED

Cleedownton, Ludlow SY8 3EG
☎ Stoke St Millborough (01584)
823209 & 823333
Fax (01584) 823387

*Built in c1789, the Moor Hall is set in 5
acres of mature grounds with pools,
amid unspoilt countryside, yet close to
historic Ludlow. Relaxed, informal
atmosphere. Fishing.*
Bedrooms: 2 double, 1 twin
Bathrooms: 3 private

Bed & breakfast

per night:	£min	£max
Single	15.00	19.50
Double	18.50	22.00

Half board

per person:	£min	£max
Daily	27.00	30.50
Weekly	170.00	192.00

Evening meal 1900 (last orders 2000)
Parking for 12
⛱ ⛌ ⬚ ♣ ⌾ ⧠ ⑤ ⅄ ⋈ 📺 ▥ 🖃 ⚡25
♣ ∪ ✈ ✤ 🐾 ✎ SP

Number Twenty Eight ⋀

⛉⛉⛉ COMMENDED

28 Lower Broad Street, Ludlow
SY8 1PQ
☎ (01584) 876996
Fax (01584) 876996

*Listed town house of charm and
character. Secluded walled garden.
Emphasis on good food and wines,
warm hospitality and quiet relaxed
atmosphere.*
Bedrooms: 2 double, 1 twin, 1 triple
Bathrooms: 4 private, 1 public

Bed & breakfast

per night:	£min	£max
Single	30.00	55.00
Double	45.00	60.00

Half board

per person:	£min	£max
Daily	37.00	45.00
Weekly	250.00	300.00

Evening meal 1930 (last orders 2030)
Cards accepted: Access, Visa, Amex
⛱ ⛌ ⬚ ♣ ⌾ ⧠ ⑤ ⋈ ▥ 🖃 ✤ 🐾 SP
🏚 ⛾

Seifton Court ⋀

⛉⛉ COMMENDED

Culmington, Ludlow SY8 2DG
☎ Seifton (01584) 861214
*Period farmhouse, 5 miles from Ludlow
on the B4365 road. Set in the beautiful
Corve Dale valley. Near Longmynd,
Ironbridge. Ideal for walking and
visiting National Trust properties.
Farmhouse fare using home-grown
produce.*
Bedrooms: 1 single, 1 double, 1 twin
Bathrooms: 3 private, 1 public

Bed & breakfast

per night:	£min	£max
Single	18.50	25.00
Double	36.00	40.00

Half board

per person:	£min	£max
Daily	29.00	35.00
Weekly	185.00	196.00

Lunch available
Evening meal 1800 (last orders 1900)
Parking for 7
⛱ ⛌ ⬚ ♣ ⌾ ⧠ ⑤ ⅄ ⋈ 📺 ▥ 🖃 ✈ ✤
✕ 🐾 ✎ SP

The Wheatsheaf Inn ⋀

⛉⛉⛉

Lower Broad Street, Ludlow SY8 1PH
☎ (01584) 872980

*Family-run mid-17th C beamed inn, 100
yards from the town centre, nestling
under Ludlow's historic 13th C Broad
Gate, the last remaining of 7 town
gates.*
Bedrooms: 4 double, 1 twin
Bathrooms: 5 private, 1 public

Bed & breakfast

per night:	£min	£max
Single	25.00	30.00
Double	40.00	40.00

Lunch available
Evening meal 1830 (last orders 2100)
Cards accepted: Access, Visa, Switch/
Delta
⛱ ⛌ ⬚ ♣ ⧠ ⑤ ▥ 🐾 ✎ SP 🏚

LYDNEY

Gloucestershire
Map ref 2B1

Small town in the Forest of Dean
close to the River Severn, where
Roman remains have been found.
It has a steam centre with
engines, coaches and wagons.

Deanfield

Listed

Folly Road, Lydney GL15 4JF
☎ (01594) 562256
*Historic 1840 quarry master's village
residence. Set in heart of the Forest of
Dean, backing on to RSPB nature
reserve and cycle track. Special all-year
offer - 4 nights for the price of 3.*
Bedrooms: 1 single, 1 twin, 1 triple
Bathrooms: 1 private, 1 public

> Please mention this guide
> when making a booking.

Bed & breakfast

per night:	£min	£max
Single	15.00	20.00
Double	30.00	35.00

Parking for 8

🐕♿🖵♨🍳♨ⓌⅢ🛈Ⓢ⌫Ⅲ🚗✲🎿
🐾 ⓈⲢ 🏠

Treetops

Viney Hill, Lydney GL15 4LZ
☎ Dean (01594) 516149
Modern house with private facilities and own lounge. Lovely garden with ponds. Unspoilt and beautiful area, warm welcome.
Bedrooms: 1 single, 1 double, 1 twin
Bathrooms: 3 private
Bed & breakfast

per night:	£min	£max
Single	18.00	18.00
Double	36.00	36.00

Parking for 3

🐕5♨♨ⓌⓈ⌫Ⅲ☂Ⅲ🚗✲🎿
🐾 Ⓢ

MALVERN

Hereford and Worcester
Map ref 2B1

Spa town in Victorian times, its water is today bottled and sold worldwide. 6 resorts, set on the slopes of the Hills, form part of Malvern. Great Malvern Priory has splendid 15th C windows. It is an excellent walking centre.
Tourist Information Centre
☎ *(01684) 892289*

Chestnut Hill 🅰

🖥

Green Lane, Malvern Wells, Malvern, Worcestershire WR14 4HU
☎ (01684) 564648
House, garden and grounds just a mile from the Three Counties Showground, situated well away from the main road in a quiet but accessible position. Outdoor manege and stabling available for horse owners.
Bedrooms: 2 double, 1 twin
Bathrooms: 1 private, 2 public
Bed & breakfast

per night:	£min	£max
Single		18.00
Double	32.00	36.00

Parking for 4
Open March-November

♨♨ⓌⅢ🛈Ⓢ⌫Ⅲ☂Ⅲ🚗∪↑✲🎿🐾

Grove House Farm 🅰

😊😊 COMMENDED
Guarlford, Malvern, Worcestershire WR14 3QZ
☎ (01684) 574256
Fax (01684) 574256
370-acre mixed farm. Beautifully furnished large farmhouse in peaceful surroundings with glorious views of the Malvern Hills. Close to Three Counties Showground.

Bedrooms: 1 double, 1 twin, 1 family room
Bathrooms: 3 private, 1 public
Bed & breakfast

per night:	£min	£max
Double	38.00	42.00

Parking for 8
Open January-November

🐕🖵♨♨ⓌⅢ🛈Ⓢ⌫Ⅲ☂Ⅲ🚗✲
🎿🐾

Nags Head

😊😊
19-21 Bank Street, Malvern, Worcestershire WR14 2JG
☎ (01684) 574373
Self-contained bedroom with sofa bed in lounge, sleeping capacity for four people, private kitchen, bathroom and lounge.
Bedrooms: 1 double
Bathrooms: 1 private
Bed & breakfast

per night:	£min	£max
Single	20.00	25.00
Double	40.00	45.00

Half board

per person:	£min	£max
Daily	27.00	33.00
Weekly	135.00	165.00

Lunch available
Parking for 2

🐕🖵♨♨🛈Ⓢ⌫Ⅲ🛈Ⅲ🔦✲🐾

Rock House 🅰

😊 COMMENDED
144 West Malvern Road, Malvern, Worcestershire WR14 4NJ
☎ (01684) 574536
Early Victorian house on Malvern Hills with large garden and wonderful views. Ideal for rambling and touring. Comfortable bedrooms, excellent cuisine, licensed. Special midweek prices available.
Bedrooms: 5 double, 3 twin, 2 triple
Bathrooms: 1 private, 2 public, 2 private showers
Bed & breakfast

per night:	£min	£max
Single	22.00	26.00
Double	36.00	40.00

Half board

per person:	£min	£max
Daily	29.00	36.00
Weekly	195.00	240.00

Evening meal 1830 (last orders 1700)
Parking for 10

🐕3♨♨Ⓢ⌫Ⅲ🛈Ⅲ✲🐾 ⓄⲀⲢ Ⓢ

The Wyche Inn 🅰

😊😊😊 APPROVED
74 Wyche Road, Malvern, Worcestershire WR14 4EQ
☎ (01684) 575396 & Mobile (01831) 704124
The highest inn in Worcestershire, nestling on top of the Malvern Hills and with spectacular views across the Severn Valley.
Bedrooms: 2 twin, 3 triple

Bathrooms: 5 private
Bed & breakfast

per night:	£min	£max
Single	25.00	30.00
Double	40.00	45.00

Lunch available
Evening meal 1900 (last orders 2130)
Parking for 12
Cards accepted: Access, Visa

🐕🖵♨♨ⓌⅢ🛈Ⓢ⌫Ⅲ🛈Ⅲ🚗🔦
🐾 Ⓣ

MARKET DRAYTON

Shropshire
Map ref 4A2

Old market town with black and white buildings and 17th C houses, also acclaimed for its gingerbread. Hodnet Hall is in the vicinity with its beautiful landscaped gardens covering 60 acres.
Tourist Information Centre
☎ *(01630) 652139*

Heath Farm Bed and Breakfast

Listed
Heath Farm, Hodnet, Market Drayton TF9 3JJ
☎ Hodnet (01630) 685570
Fax (01743) 249970
60-acre mixed farm. Traditional farmhouse welcome. Situated 1.5 miles south of Hodnet off the A442, approached by private drive.
Bedrooms: 1 double, 2 twin
Bathrooms: 1 public
Bed & breakfast

per night:	£min	£max
Single	14.00	15.00
Double	28.00	30.00

Parking for 5

🐕5🐎♨ⓌⅢ🛈Ⅲ✲🐾

MINCHINHAMPTON

Gloucestershire
Map ref 2B1

Stone-built town, with many 17th/18th C buildings, owing its existence to the wool and cloth trades. A 17th C pillared market house may be found in the town square, near which is the Norman and 14th C church.

Hunters Lodge

😊😊 HIGHLY COMMENDED
Dr Brown's Road, Minchinhampton, Stroud GL6 9BT
☎ Brimscombe (01453) 883588
Fax (01453) 731449
Cotswold stone house adjoining Minchinhampton common and golf-course. Ideal centre for Bath, Gloucester, Cheltenham and Cotswolds. Located 2 miles from A419 Stroud-Cirencester road 1.5 miles from A46

Continued ▶

MINCHINHAMPTON

Continued

(first house on right going into Minchinhampton from common.)
Bedrooms: 2 twin, 1 triple
Bathrooms: 3 private
Bed & breakfast

per night:	£min	£max
Single	25.00	
Double	38.00	48.00

Parking for 8

MINSTERLEY

Shropshire
Map ref 4A3

Village with a curious little church of 1692 and a fine old black and white hall. The lofty ridge known as the Stiperstones is 4 miles to the south.

Cricklewood Cottage
HIGHLY COMMENDED

Plox Green, Minsterley, Shrewsbury
SY5 0HT
☎ Shrewsbury (01743) 791229
Delightful 18th C cottage with countryside views, at foot of Stiperstones Hills. Exposed beams, inglenook fireplace, traditional furnishings. Lovely cottage garden. Excellent restaurants and inns nearby.
Bedrooms: 2 double, 1 twin
Bathrooms: 3 private
Bed & breakfast

per night:	£min	£max
Single	18.00	30.00
Double	36.00	40.00

Half board

per person:	£min	£max
Daily	29.00	31.00
Weekly	203.00	217.00

Evening meal 1900 (last orders 1000)
Parking for 4

MORETON-IN-MARSH

Gloucestershire
Map ref 2B1

Attractive town of Cotswold stone with 17th C houses, an ideal base for touring the Cotswolds. Some of the local attractions include Batsford Park Arboretum, the Jacobean Chastleton House and Sezincote Garden.

Blue Cedar House ⚌

Stow Road, Moreton-in-Marsh
GL56 0DW
☎ (01608) 650299
Attractive detached residence set in half-acre garden in the Cotswolds, with pleasantly decorated, well-equipped

accommodation and garden room. Close to village centre.
Bedrooms: 1 single, 2 double, 1 family room
Bathrooms: 2 private, 2 public
Bed & breakfast

per night:	£min	£max
Single	18.00	28.00
Double	33.00	42.00

Evening meal 1800 (last orders 1800)
Parking for 7
Open February–November

Lower Farm Barn ⚌
⚌

Great Wolford, Shipston-on-Stour,
Warwickshire CV36 5NQ
☎ Barton on the Heath (01608) 674435
900-acre arable farm. 18th C converted barn combines modern comforts with exposed beams and ancient stonework. Use of attractive drawing room. Quiet village between A3400, A44 and A429.
Bedrooms: 1 single, 2 double
Bathrooms: 1 private, 1 public
Bed & breakfast

per night:	£min	£max
Single	18.00	20.00
Double	28.00	34.00

Parking for 10

Manor Farm ⚌
Listed

Great Wolford, Shipston-on-Stour,
Warwickshire CV36 5NQ
☎ Barton-on-the-Heath (01608) 674247
Fax (01608) 674247

270-acre mixed farm. Comfortable listed farmhouse in a small village with traditional pub, close to Moreton-in-Marsh. Open fire, TV lounge, lovely views. Ideal for Cotswolds and Stratford-upon-Avon.
Bedrooms: 1 double, 1 twin
Bathrooms: 1 public
Bed & breakfast

per night:	£min	£max
Single	16.00	18.00
Double	30.00	35.00

Parking for 12
Open March–November

New Farm ⚌
⚌ **COMMENDED**

Dorn, Moreton-in-Marsh GL56 9NS
☎ (01608) 650782

250-acre dairy farm. Old Cotswold farmhouse. All rooms spacious, en-suite and furnished with antiques and with colour TV, coffee and tea facilities. Dining room with large impressive fireplace. Full English breakfast served with hot crispy bread.
Bedrooms: 2 double, 1 twin
Bathrooms: 3 private
Bed & breakfast

per night:	£min	£max
Single	16.00	18.00
Double	32.00	34.00

Parking for 10

Old Farm ⚌
⚌ **COMMENDED**

Dorn, Moreton-in-Marsh GL56 9NS
☎ (01608) 650394
250-acre mixed farm. Enjoy the delights of a 15th C farmhouse - a comfortable family home. Spacious bedrooms. Tennis and croquet. Children welcome. Surrounded by beautiful Cotswolds scenery.
Bedrooms: 1 double, 1 twin, 1 triple
Bathrooms: 1 private, 1 public
Bed & breakfast

per night:	£min	£max
Single	20.00	
Double	32.00	34.00

Parking for 8
Open March–October

Red Lion Inn ⚌
⚌

Little Compton, Moreton-in-Marsh
GL56 0RT
☎ Barton-on-the-Heath (01608) 674397
Fax (01608) 674521
16th C village inn with large garden, offering comfortable accommodation, bar meals, home-made dishes and quality rump steaks. 4 miles from Moreton-in-Marsh off A44.
Bedrooms: 1 twin, 2 triple
Bathrooms: 1 public
Bed & breakfast

per night:	£min	£max
Single		24.00
Double		36.00

Lunch available
Evening meal 1900 (last orders 2045)
Parking for 20
Cards accepted: Access, Visa, Switch/Delta

Rest Harrow

📖 COMMENDED

Evenlode Road, Moreton-in-Marsh
GL56 0NJ
☎ (01608) 650653
*Large four-bedroomed house in rural
location. Take Evenlode turning by
Wellington public house on main A44
Oxford-London road, then half a mile
on left.*
Bedrooms: 1 double, 1 triple
Bathrooms: 1 public
Bed & breakfast

per night:	£min	£max
Single	14.00	16.00
Double	26.00	28.00

Parking for 3

Shropshire
Map ref 4A3

Small town close to Wenlock Edge
in beautiful scenery and full of
interest. In particular there are the
remains of an 11th C priory with
fine carving and the black and
white 16th C Guildhall.

The Old Barn

📖 📖 COMMENDED

45 Sheinton Street, Much Wenlock
TF13 6HR
☎ Telford (01952) 728191
*18th C barn, converted to cottage-style
accommodation, in the beautiful town of
Much Wenlock.*
Bedrooms: 2 double, 2 twin
Bathrooms: 4 private
Bed & breakfast

per night:	£min	£max
Single	25.00	28.00
Double	35.00	38.00

Parking for 4
Open January-November

Walton House

Listed COMMENDED

35 Barrow Street, Much Wenlock
TF13 6EP
☎ (01952) 727139
*Two minutes' walk from town centre. 5
miles from Ironbridge Gorge, 13 miles
from Shrewsbury, 8 miles from
Bridgnorth and 10 miles from Telford
town centre. Lawns and patio.*
Bedrooms: 1 single, 2 twin
Bathrooms: 1 public
Bed & breakfast

per night:	£min	£max
Single	15.00	15.00
Double	28.00	28.00

Parking for 2
Open April-October

Gloucestershire
Map ref 2B1

Ancient wool town with several
elegant Jacobean and Georgian
houses, surrounded by wooded
hillsides with fine views.

Aaron Farm (formerly North Farm)

📖 COMMENDED

Nympsfield Road, Nailsworth, Stroud
GL6 0ET
☎ Stroud (01453) 833598
Fax (01453) 836737
*Former farmhouse, with large en-suite
bedrooms and panoramic views of the
Cotswolds. Ideal touring centre. Many
walks and attractions. Home cooking.
Brochure on request.*
Bedrooms: 1 double, 2 twin
Bathrooms: 3 private
Bed & breakfast

per night:	£min	£max
Single	22.00	26.00
Double	32.00	36.00

Half board

per person:	£min	£max
Daily	32.00	36.00
Weekly	200.00	240.00

Evening meal 1800 (last orders 2000)
Parking for 4

Apple Orchard House

📖 📖 COMMENDED

Orchard Close, Springhill, Nailsworth,
Stroud GL6 0LX
☎ (01453) 832503
Fax (01453) 836213

*Elegant and spacious house in pretty 1
acre garden. Panoramic views from
bedrooms and sitting room of
picturesque Cotswold hills. Excellent
touring centre. In small, historic town,
close to restaurants. Easy access M5
and M4 (20 minutes).*
Wheelchair access category 3 ♿
Bedrooms: 1 single, 2 twin
Bathrooms: 3 private
Bed & breakfast

per night:	£min	£max
Single	18.00	28.00
Double	34.00	40.00

Half board

per person:	£min	£max
Daily	29.00	32.00
Weekly	182.70	201.60

Evening meal 1800 (last orders 1700)

Parking for 3
Cards accepted: Access, Visa, Amex

Gloucestershire
Map ref 2B1

A high place on the Windrush,
renowned for its wild flowers and
with an attractive dovecote.

Eastern Hill Farm

Listed

Naunton, Cheltenham GL54 3AF
☎ Guiting Power (01451) 850716
*77-acre arable and mixed farm. Recently
constructed traditional style Cotswolds
farmhouse. Within walking distance of
Bourton-on-the-Water and the
Slaughters.*
Bedrooms: 2 double, 1 triple
Bathrooms: 3 public
Bed & breakfast

per night:	£min	£max
Single	17.00	18.00
Double	34.00	36.00

Evening meal from 1900
Parking for 6

Gloucestershire
Map ref 2B1

Small town with the largest
collection of birds of prey in
Europe at the Falconry Centre.
Flying demonstrations daily. Glass
workshop where visitors can watch
glass being blown. There is a
"seconds" shop. North of the
village is the Three Choirs
Vineyards.
*Tourist Information Centre
☎ (01531) 822145*

Merton House

📖

7 Birches Lane, Newent GL18 1DN
☎ (01531) 820608
*Detached house in attractive gardens,
quiet rural setting, good view to the
Malverns and Cotswolds. 1.75 miles
from the market town of Newent.*
Bedrooms: 2 double
Bathrooms: 1 public
Bed & breakfast

per night:	£min	£max
Single	19.00	21.00
Double	30.00	32.00

Parking for 4

Old Court Hotel

📖 📖 📖 APPROVED

Church Street, Newent GL18 1AB
☎ (01531) 820522

Continued ▶

NEWENT

Continued

Magnificent manor house in 1 acre of walled gardens. Friendly, relaxed atmosphere in elegant surroundings. Good cuisine. Four poster available.
Bedrooms: 3 double, 1 twin, 1 triple
Bathrooms: 5 private

Bed & breakfast per night:	£min	£max
Single	29.00	37.50
Double	45.00	65.00

Half board per person:	£min	£max
Daily	36.25	46.25
Weekly	225.25	293.50

Evening meal 1930 (last orders 2030)
Parking for 21
Cards accepted: Access, Visa, Amex
🐴 🛏 🛌 🖥 ☕ [S] 🚭 🛏 [IIII] 🚗 ⊤40 ✽ 🚚 [SP] 🏛

5 Onslow Road

Listed

Newent GL18 1TL
☎ (01531) 821677
Modern 4-bedroomed house, on south side of Newent. Last right turn out of town off old Gloucester Road, third house on left.
Bedrooms: 1 single, 1 double, 1 twin
Bathrooms: 1 private, 1 public

Bed & breakfast per night:	£min	£max
Single	14.00	17.00
Double	28.00	34.00

Parking for 2
🐴 10 ☕ [UL] [TV] [IIII] 🚗 ✈ 🚚 [OAP] [SP]

NEWLAND

Gloucestershire
Map ref 2A1

Probably the most attractive of the villages of the Forest of Dean. The church is often referred to as "the Cathedral of the Forest"; it contains a number of interesting monuments and the Forest Miner's Brass. Almshouses nearby were endowed by William Jones, founder of Monmouth School.

Scatterford Farm

👑👑 COMMENDED

Newland, Coleford GL16 8NG
☎ Dean (01594) 836562
Fax (01594) 836323
Beautiful 15th C farmhouse with spacious rooms set in the midst of glorious walking country. Half-a-mile from Newland village.
Bedrooms: 2 double, 1 twin
Bathrooms: 3 private

Bed & breakfast per night:	£min	£max
Single	19.50	19.50
Double	39.00	39.00

Parking for 8
🐴 🖥 ☕ [UL] [S] 🚭 🛏 [TV] [IIII] 🚗 U ✽ ✈ 🚚 🏛

NEWPORT

Shropshire
Map ref 4A3

Small market town on the Shropshire Union Canal has a wide High Street and a church with some interesting monuments. Newport is close to Aqualate Mere which is the largest lake in Staffordshire.

Bridge Inn

Chetwynd End, Newport TF10 7JB
☎ (01952) 811785
Small, 17th C inn, friendly and comfortable, in good location. Home-cooked food using fresh local produce. Ample parking.
Bedrooms: 2 single, 1 double, 2 twin
Bathrooms: 2 private, 1 public

Bed & breakfast per night:	£min	£max
Single	16.00	19.00
Double	32.00	38.00

Evening meal 1900 (last orders 2130)
Parking for 30
Cards accepted: Access, Visa, Amex
🐴 🖥 ☕ [S] [IIII] 🚗 🚚 [T]

Lane End Farm

👑👑 COMMENDED

Chetwynd, Newport TF10 8BN
☎ Sambrook (01952) 550337
Delightful period farmhouse set in lovely countryside. Located on A41 near Newport. Ideal touring base and beautiful local walks.
Bedrooms: 2 double
Bathrooms: 2 private

Bed & breakfast per night:	£min	£max
Single	18.00	20.00
Double	35.00	40.00

Evening meal 1800 (last orders 2100)
Parking for 5
🐴 ☕ [UL] 🔒 [S] 🛏 [TV] [IIII] 🚗 ✽ 🚚 ↯ [SP] 🏛 [T]

Sambrook Manor

Listed

Sambrook, Newport TF10 8AL
☎ Sambrook (01952) 550256
260-acre mixed farm. Old manor farmhouse built in 1702. Close to Stoke Potteries, Shrewsbury, Ironbridge, Wolverhampton and many places of historic interest.
Bedrooms: 1 single, 1 double, 1 triple
Bathrooms: 2 public

Bed & breakfast per night:	£min	£max
Single	15.00	16.00
Double	30.00	32.00

Parking for 10
🐴 ☕ [UL] 🔒 🚭 🛏 [TV] [IIII] 🚗 U ⛳ ✽ ✈ 🚚 🏛

NORTHLEACH

Gloucestershire
Map ref 2B1

Village famous for its beautiful 15th C wool church with its lovely porch and interesting interior. There are also some fine houses including a 17th C wool merchant's house containing Keith Harding's World of Mechanical Music, and the Cotswold Countryside Collection is in the former prison.

Northfield Bed & Breakfast ♿

👑👑👑 COMMENDED

Cirencester Road (A429), Northleach, Cheltenham GL54 3JL
☎ Cotswold (01451) 860427
Detached family house in the country with large gardens and home-grown produce. Excellent centre for visiting the Cotswolds and close to local services.
Bedrooms: 1 double, 2 family rooms
Bathrooms: 3 private

Bed & breakfast per night:	£min	£max
Single	20.00	
Double	34.00	40.00

Half board per person:	£min	£max
Daily	30.00	32.00

Evening meal 1800 (last orders 1900)
Parking for 10
🐴 🛁 🛌 🖥 ☕ ⚲ 🔒 [S] 🚭 🛏 [TV] [IIII] 🚗 U ✽ ✈ 🚚 [SP]

NYMPSFIELD

Gloucestershire
Map ref 2B1

Pretty village high up in the Cotswolds, with a simple mid-Victorian church and a prehistoric long barrow nearby.

Rose and Crown Inn ♿

👑👑👑 COMMENDED

Nympsfield, Stonehouse GL10 3TU
☎ Dursley (01453) 860240
Fax (01453) 860240
300-year-old inn, in quiet Cotswold village, close to Cotswold Way. Easy access to M4/M5.
Bedrooms: 1 double, 3 triple
Bathrooms: 4 private

Bed & breakfast per night:	£min	£max
Single	24.00	28.00
Double	39.00	48.00

Lunch available
Evening meal 1830 (last orders 2130)
Parking for 30
Cards accepted: Access, Visa, Amex, Switch/Delta

OAKAMOOR

Staffordshire
Map ref 4B2

Small village below a steep hill amid the glorious scenery of the Churnet Valley. Its industrial links have now gone, as the site of the factory which made 20,000 miles of copper wire for the first Atlantic cable has been transformed into an attractive picnic site on the riverside.

Ribden Farm ⚠

HIGHLY COMMENDED

Oakamoor, Stoke-on-Trent ST10 3BW
☎ (01538) 702830

98-acre livestock farm. Grade II listed 18th C farmhouse in open countryside, one and a half miles from Alton Towers. TV and tea/coffee in all rooms.
Bedrooms: 1 double, 2 family rooms
Bathrooms: 3 private

Bed & breakfast

per night:	£min	£max
Single	25.00	25.00
Double	36.00	40.00

Parking for 3

OMBERSLEY

Hereford and Worcester
Map ref 2B1

A particularly fine village full of black and white houses including the 17th C Dower House and some old inns. The church contains the original box pews.

The Crown and Sandys Arms ⚠

Ombersley, Droitwich, Worcestershire WR9 0EW
☎ Worcester (01905) 620252
Fax (01905) 620769
Freehouse with comfortable bedrooms, draught beers and open fires. Home-cooked meals available lunchtime and evenings, 7 days a week.
Bedrooms: 1 single, 5 double, 1 twin
Bathrooms: 6 private, 1 public

Bed & breakfast

per night:	£min	£max
Single	25.00	30.00
Double	40.00	40.00

Lunch available
Evening meal 1800 (last orders 2145)
Parking for 100
Cards accepted: Access, Visa, Amex, Switch/Delta

ONNELEY

Staffordshire
Map ref 4A2

Village on the line between Shropshire and Staffordshire counties, within easy reach of Bridgemere Garden World.

The Wheatsheaf Inn at Onneley ⚠

COMMENDED

Bar Hill Road, Onneley, Madeley CW3 9QF
☎ Stoke-on-Trent (01782) 751581
Fax (01782) 751499
18th C country inn with bars, Spanish restaurant, conference and function facilities. On A525, 3 miles from Bridgemere and Keele University, 7 miles from Newcastle-under-Lyme. Prices are per room.
Bedrooms: 4 double, 1 twin
Bathrooms: 5 private

Bed & breakfast

per night:	£min	£max
Single	45.00	45.00
Double	45.00	55.00

Half board

per person:	£min	£max
Daily	45.00	57.00

Lunch available
Evening meal 1800 (last orders 2130)
Parking for 150
Cards accepted: Access, Visa, Diners, Amex

OSWESTRY

Shropshire
Map ref 4A3

Town close to the Welsh border, the scene of many battles. To the north are the remains of a large Iron Age hill fort. An excellent centre for exploring Shropshire and Offa's Dyke.
Tourist Information Centre
☎ *(01691) 662488 or 662753*

Frankton House

Welsh Frankton, Oswestry SY11 4PA
☎ (01691) 623422

Large old farmhouse, completely refurbished as a guesthouse. In rural Shropshire, close to A5. Canal and hire boats nearby, also riding stables and golf-course.
Bedrooms: 1 double, 2 twin
Bathrooms: 2 private, 1 public

Bed & breakfast

per night:	£min	£max
Single	16.00	17.50
Double	32.00	35.00

Parking for 14

Pant-Hir

Croesaubach, Oswestry SY10 9BH
☎ Llansilin (01691) 791457
25-acre horse farm. Just outside Oswestry in beautiful rural surroundings lies this attractive smallholding. The bedrooms are en-suite with TV. Added attraction is the miniature horse stud.
Bedrooms: 1 double, 1 twin
Bathrooms: 2 private

Bed & breakfast

per night:	£min	£max
Double		32.00

Half board

per person:	£min	£max
Daily		25.00
Weekly		165.00

Evening meal 1900 (last orders 2000)
Parking for 10
Open January-November

Rhoswiel Lodge ⚠

Weston Rhyn, Oswestry SY10 7TG
☎ Chirk (01691) 777609
Victorian country house in pleasant surroundings beside Llangollen Canal, 4 miles north of Oswestry. 300 yards from A5.
Bedrooms: 1 double, 1 twin
Bathrooms: 2 private

Bed & breakfast

per night:	£min	£max
Single	18.00	20.00
Double	32.00	36.00

Parking for 6

Please check prices and other details at the time of booking.

OXHILL

Warwickshire
Map ref 2C1

Village in the Vale of Red Horse not far from the battlefield of Edgehill. Its church retains much that is Norman.

Nolands Farm and Country Restaurant ⚔
👑👑

Oxhill, Warwick CV35 0RJ
☎ Kineton (01926) 640309
Fax (01926) 641662

300-acre arable farm. Situated in tranquil valley surrounded by fields. Most rooms in converted barn annexe. Peaceful and quiet, overlooking old stable yard. Stocked lake, woods, walks and wildlife. Elegant four-poster bedrooms. Cycles for hire, fishing, clay pigeon shooting, riding nearby.
Bedrooms: 5 double, 1 twin, 2 triple, 1 family room
Bathrooms: 9 private
Bed & breakfast

per night:	£min	£max
Single	20.00	
Double	30.00	44.00

Evening meal from 1900
Parking for 11
Open January-November
Cards accepted: Access, Visa, Switch/Delta
🕭🕗🗺🖾🎜📺🖵♿🛆📶🛏🗓📺🖩🛆🎕🎣♿✕ SP T

PAINSWICK

Gloucestershire
Map ref 2B1

Picturesque wool town with inns and houses dating from the 14th C. Painswick House is a Palladian mansion with Chinese wallpaper. The churchyard is famous for its yew trees.

The Dream Factory
👑👑 APPROVED

Friday Street, Painswick, Stroud GL6 6QJ
☎ (01452) 812379
Grade II listed building, in the centre of the village known as the "Queen of the Cotswolds".
Bedrooms: 1 double
Bathrooms: 1 private

Bed & breakfast per night:	£min	£max
Single	20.00	20.00
Double	30.00	40.00

🕭🖾♿🛆🛏🗓📺🖩🛆✳🐎

Hambutts Mynd
👑👑

Edge Road, Painswick, Stroud GL6 6UP
☎ (01452) 812352
Old corn windmill, c1700-50, with original beams. Panoramic views from all bedrooms. 200 yards from main road. Dogs accepted. Weekly rates available.
Bedrooms: 1 single, 1 double, 1 twin
Bathrooms: 1 private, 1 public

Bed & breakfast per night:	£min	£max
Single	19.00	22.00
Double	37.00	39.00

Parking for 3
Open February-December
🕭🕗🖵🗺🖾🛆🗓⊬🛏📺🖩🛆✳🐎🐾

Upper Doreys Mill ⚔
👑👑

Edge, Painswick, Stroud GL6 6NF
☎ (01452) 812459
18th C cloth mill with log fires and old beams. By a stream and in a rural setting. Half a mile from Painswick, down Edge Lane.
Bedrooms: 2 double, 1 twin
Bathrooms: 3 private

Bed & breakfast per night:	£min	£max
Single	25.00	
Double	38.00	

Parking for 6
🕭♿🗺🖾🛆⊬🛏📺🛆∪🎣✳✕🐎🎣

PARKEND

Gloucestershire
Map ref 2A1

Village in the Forest of Dean, once an important industrial and railway centre, but now quiet and peaceful and a good base for exploring the forest.

The Fountain Inn ⚔
👑👑

Fountain Way, Parkend, Lydney GL15 4JD
☎ Dean (01594) 562189
Fax (01594) 564438
Beautifully renovated village pub at Parkend, 3.5 miles from Lydney on the A48 Chepstow to Gloucester road. Ideal for walking and cycling.
Wheelchair access category 3 ♿
Bedrooms: 2 single, 4 double, 2 twin
Bathrooms: 8 private

Bed & breakfast per night:	£min	£max
Single	27.00	
Double	46.00	

Half board per person:	£min	£max
Daily	27.00	29.00
Weekly	170.10	182.70

Lunch available
Evening meal 1800 (last orders 2130)
Parking for 30
Cards accepted: Access, Visa, Diners, Amex
🕭🖾🖵🛆♿🛆🗓🛏📺🖩🛆🎕20✳🎣 SP 🐎 T

PONTESBURY

Shropshire
Map ref 4A3

With views of the Rea Valley from nearby Pontesford Hill, this village is the site of a 7th C battle between a King of Mercia and a King of the West Saxons. Most of the village church was rebuilt in the last century, except for the 13th C chancel which retains its original roof.

Marehay Farm
👑👑 HIGHLY COMMENDED

Ratlinghope, Pontesbury, Shrewsbury SY5 0SJ
☎ Linley (01588) 650289
5-acre livestock farm. Splendid isolation at 1,100ft in the Long Mynd and Stiperstones environmentally sensitive area. Peace and quiet. Good walking and bird-watching.
Bedrooms: 2 twin
Bathrooms: 2 private

Bed & breakfast per night:	£min	£max
Single	15.00	20.00
Double	30.00	40.00

Parking for 4
🕭🖾♿🗺🖾🛆⊬🛏📺🖩🛆∪✳🐎 SP 🐎

RENDCOMB

Gloucestershire
Map ref 2B1

On the river Churn north of Cirencester. Nearby are Chedworth Roman Villa and Fosse Way.

Shawswell Country House ⚔
👑👑 DE LUXE

Rendcomb, Cirencester GL7 7HD
☎ Cirencester (01285) 831779
17th C country house with quality accommodation. Idyllic setting in 25 acres offering peace and tranquillity and wonderful views. From A435 take turning to Rendcomb and follow "no through road" to the end.
Bedrooms: 1 single, 3 double, 1 twin
Bathrooms: 5 private

Bed & breakfast

per night:	£min	£max
Single	30.00	35.00
Double	45.00	55.00

Parking for 8
Open February-November

🏃 10 🏠🎕📞 ♨✕🏫⛿. ➡ ♨ ✿ 🚲
📠 🅿 🏢

ROCK

Hereford and Worcester
Map ref 4A3

The Old Forge

Listed

Gorst Hill, Rock, Kidderminster,
Worcestershire DY14 9YG
☎ (01299) 266745
*Recently renovated country cottage,
near the Wyre Forest. Ideal for country
walks and visiting local places of
interest. Short and midweek breaks.*
Bedrooms: 1 twin, 1 triple
Bathrooms: 1 public

Bed & breakfast

per night:	£min	£max
Single	15.00	
Double	28.00	

Parking for 5
Open January-November

🏃✕🎕📞 ♨⛿ 📞🏫 📺⛿. ➡ ✿✕🚲

ROSS-ON-WYE

Hereford and Worcester
Map ref 2A1

Attractive market town with a 17th
C market hall, set above the River
Wye. There are lovely views over
the surrounding countryside from
the Prospect and the town is close
to Goodrich Castle and the Welsh
border.
Tourist Information Centre
☎ *(01989) 562768*

The Arches Country House

👑👑

Walford Road, Ross-on-Wye,
Herefordshire HR9 5PT
☎ (01989) 563348
*Small family-run hotel set in half an
acre of lawned gardens, half a mile
from town centre. Warm, friendly
atmosphere. All rooms furnished to a
high standard and with views of the
garden. Victorian-style conservatory in
which to relax.*
Bedrooms: 1 single, 4 double, 2 twin,
1 triple
Bathrooms: 6 private, 2 public

Bed & breakfast

per night:	£min	£max
Single	16.00	21.00
Double	32.00	42.00

Half board

per person:	£min	£max
Daily	26.00	31.00
Weekly	109.50	143.00

Evening meal from 1900

Parking for 10
Cards accepted: Access, Visa

🏃🎕📞♨🛄🖍🅂🖍🏫⛿. ➡✿✕🚲
📠 🅿

Lavender Cottage

Listed

Bridstow, Ross-on-Wye, Herefordshire
HR9 6QB
☎ (01989) 562836
*Part 17th C character property, 1 mile
from Ross-on-Wye. Take Hereford road,
turn right to Foy and then first turning
on left.*
Bedrooms: 1 double, 2 twin
Bathrooms: 1 public

Bed & breakfast

per night:	£min	£max
Single	18.00	20.00
Double	30.00	34.00

Half board

per person:	£min	£max
Daily	26.00	28.00
Weekly	160.00	170.00

Evening meal from 1830
Parking for 3

🏃5📞♨🛄🛆♨📺⛿. ➡✿✕🚲🏢

Merrivale Place ⋀

👑 COMMENDED

The Avenue, Ross-on-Wye,
Herefordshire HR9 5AW
☎ (01989) 564929
*Fine Victorian house in quiet tree-lined
avenue. Large comfortable rooms and
lovely views. Home cooking. Near town
and river.*
Bedrooms: 1 double, 1 twin, 1 triple
Bathrooms: 2 public

Bed & breakfast

per night:	£min	£max
Single	18.00	18.00
Double	32.00	32.00

Evening meal 1830 (last orders 1600)
Parking for 6
Open March-October

🏃♨🛄🅂🖍🏫📺⛿. ➡✿✕🚲🏢

The Old Rectory

👑👑

Hope Mansell, Ross-on-Wye,
Herefordshire HR9 5TL
☎ (01989) 750382
Fax (01989) 750382
*Georgian house in beautiful rural
surroundings near Ross-on-Wye.
Friendly atmosphere, comfortable rooms
with period furniture. Lovely mature
gardens and all-weather tennis court.*
Bedrooms: 2 double, 1 twin
Bathrooms: 1 private, 2 public

Bed & breakfast

per night:	£min	£max
Single	18.50	20.00
Double	37.00	40.00

Parking for 4

🏃📞♨🛄📞🅂⛿. ⚲✿🚲🏢

Rudhall Farm

👑👑 HIGHLY COMMENDED

Ross-on-Wye, Herefordshire HR9 7TL
☎ Upton Bishop (01989) 780240 &
Mobile (0585) 871379

*Savour the tranquillity of our elegant
early-Georgian farmhouse, offering well-
appointed accommodation, country
house hospitality and comfort with style
- "somewhere special". In picturesque
valley with lake and millstream. Perfect
for exploring beautiful Wye Valley. Aga
cooked breakfasts.*
Bedrooms: 1 single, 2 double
Bathrooms: 1 private, 1 public

Bed & breakfast

per night:	£min	£max
Single	18.50	22.00
Double	37.00	40.00

Parking for 10
Open January-November

🎕📞♨🛄🅂🖍🏫📺⛿. ➡✿✕🚲🏢

The Skakes

👑👑

Glewstone, Ross-on-Wye, Herefordshire
HR9 6AZ
☎ (01989) 770456

*Country guesthouse combining 18th C
character with 20th C comforts. Perfect
for Symonds Yat, Wye Valley, Forest of
Dean. Home cooking.*
Bedrooms: 1 single, 5 double, 1 twin
Bathrooms: 4 private, 3 public

Bed & breakfast

per night:	£min	£max
Single	20.00	
Double	30.00	

Half board

per person:	£min	£max
Daily	30.00	

Evening meal 1900 (last orders 1000)
Parking for 8
Cards accepted: Access, Visa

🏃10🎕🎕📞♨🅂🏫⛿. ➡✿🚲
🖐️🅃

Thatch Close

👑👑 COMMENDED

Llangrove, Ross-on-Wye, Herefordshire
HR9 6EL
☎ Llangarron (01989) 770300
Continued ▶

ROSS-ON-WYE

Continued

13-acre mixed farm. Secluded Georgian country farmhouse midway between Ross-on-Wye and Monmouth. Home-produced vegetables and meat. Ideal for country lovers of any age. Guests welcome to help with animals. Map sent on request. Ordnance Survey: 51535196.
Bedrooms: 2 double, 1 twin
Bathrooms: 3 private

Bed & breakfast
per night:	£min	£max
Double	30.00	38.00

Half board
per person:	£min	£max
Daily	25.00	29.00
Weekly	170.00	190.00

Lunch available
Evening meal 1830 (last orders 1800)
Parking for 7

RUGBY

Warwickshire
Map ref 4C3

Town famous for its public school which gave its name to Rugby Union football and which featured in "Tom Brown's Schooldays".
Tourist Information Centre
☎ *(01788) 535348*

Avondale Guest House

16 Elsee Road, Rugby CV21 3BA
☎ (01788) 578639
Victorian town residence close to Rugby School, convenient for Warwick Castle, Coventry Cathedral, Leamington Spa, National Exhibition Centre and Birmingham.
Bedrooms: 3 twin, 1 triple
Bathrooms: 1 private, 2 public

Bed & breakfast
per night:	£min	£max
Single	20.00	
Double	35.00	

Parking for 8

Lawford Hill Farm ⋀

Lawford Heath Lane, Rugby CV23 9HG
☎ (01788) 542001
100-acre mixed farm. Bed and breakfast all the year round in this spacious Georgian farmhouse. Close to National Agricultural Centre, Stratford-upon-Avon and the Cotswolds.
Bedrooms: 2 double, 1 twin
Bathrooms: 1 public

Bed & breakfast
per night:	£min	£max
Single	16.00	20.00
Double	30.00	35.00

Parking for 6

White Lion Inn ⋀

Listed   APPROVED

Coventry Road, Pailton, Rugby CV23 0QD
☎ (01788) 832359
17th C coaching inn, recently refurbished but maintaining all old world features. Close to Rugby, Coventry and Stratford. Within 2 miles of motorways.
Bedrooms: 6 twin
Bathrooms: 2 public

Bed & breakfast
per night:	£min	£max
Single	17.50	18.50
Double	35.00	35.00

Half board
per person:	£min	£max
Daily	22.50	29.00
Weekly	157.50	203.00

Lunch available
Evening meal 1830 (last orders 2200)
Parking for 60
Cards accepted: Access, Visa

RUSHTON SPENCER

Staffordshire
Map ref 4B2

Village with an interesting church built in the 14th C of wood, some of which still remains. It is close to the pleasant Rudyard Reservoir.

Barnswood Farm

Listed

Rushton Spencer, Macclesfield, Cheshire SK11 0RA
☎ (01260) 226261
100-acre dairy farm. In a lovely setting overlooking Rudyard Lake 400 yards down the field. Alton Towers, Peak District and the Potteries all within a 15-mile radius. Homely welcome, English breakfast.
Bedrooms: 1 double, 1 triple, 1 family room
Bathrooms: 2 public

Bed & breakfast
per night:	£min	£max
Single	15.00	
Double	28.00	

Parking for 5

SEVERN STOKE

Hereford and Worcester
Map ref 2B1

Village to the south of Worcester with a picturesque group of houses surrounding the church and magnificent views across the Severn to the Malvern Hills.

Madge Hill House

Severn Stoke, Worcester WR8 9JN
☎ (01905) 371362
Georgian house in peaceful country setting, between Tewkesbury and Worcester on A38. En-suite bedrooms with TV.
Bedrooms: 1 double, 1 twin
Bathrooms: 2 private

Bed & breakfast
per night:	£min	£max
Single	17.00	
Double	34.00	

Parking for 2

SHIFNAL

Shropshire
Map ref 4A3

Small market town, once an important staging centre for coaches on the Holyhead road. Where industrialism has not prevailed, the predominating architectural impression is Georgian, though some timber-framed houses survived the Great Fire of 1591.

Village Farm Lodge ⋀

Sheriffhales, Shifnal TF11 8RD
☎ Telford (01952) 462763 & Mobile 0585 254528
Fax (01952) 677912
Tastefully converted farm buildings in Sheriffhales village, situated on the B4379 off the A5. Minutes from Telford and Ironbridge Gorge.
Bedrooms: 1 single, 2 double, 3 twin, 1 triple, 1 family room
Bathrooms: 8 private

Bed & breakfast
per night:	£min	£max
Single	25.00	28.50
Double	35.00	39.50

Parking for 8
Cards accepted: Access, Visa, Amex

At-a-glance symbols are explained on the flap inside the back cover.

The accommodation coupons at the back will help you when contacting proprietors.

SHREWSBURY

Shropshire
Map ref 4A3

Beautiful historic town on the River Severn retaining many fine old timber-framed houses. Its attractions include Rowley's Museum with Roman finds, remains of a castle, Clive House Museum, St Chad's 18th C round church and rowing on the river.
Tourist Information Centre
☎ *(01743) 350761*

Acton Burnell Farm

Listed

Acton Burnell, Shrewsbury SY5 7PQ
☎ Acton Burnell (01694) 731207
300-acre arable farm. Comfortable farmhouse in village. Residents' lounge with TV. 8 miles from Shrewsbury and 6 miles from Church Stretton. Ideal base for sightseeing and walking.
Bedrooms: 1 twin
Bathrooms: 1 private

Bed & breakfast per night:	£min	£max
Single	15.00	
Double	30.00	

Parking for 4
Open April-October

➤ 5 ♦ ⓤ ⅟ Ⓜ ⓉⓋ Ⅲ. ⌐ ✿ 🐾

Ashton Lees

Ⓒ COMMENDED

Dorrington, Shrewsbury SY5 7JW
☎ Dorrington (01743) 718378
Comfortable family home set in large secluded garden, 6 miles south of Shrewsbury on A49. Convenient for exploring the town and surrounding countryside.
Bedrooms: 2 double, 1 twin
Bathrooms: 1 private, 1 public

Bed & breakfast per night:	£min	£max
Single	17.00	20.00
Double	34.00	40.00

Half board per person:	£min	£max
Daily	24.50	27.50
Weekly	150.00	170.00

Evening meal 1830 (last orders 2030)
Parking for 6

➤ ⊑ Ⓔ ⌐ ♦ ⓠ ⅟ Ⓢ Ⅿ ⓉⓋ ⌐ ✿ 🐾 OAP SP

Chatford House ⋀

Ⓒ

Bayston Hill, Shrewsbury SY3 0AY
☎ (01743) 718301
5-acre mixed farm. Comfortable farmhouse built in 1776, 5.5 miles south of Shrewsbury off A49. Through Bayston Hill, take third right (Stapleton) then right to Chatford.
Bedrooms: 3 twin
Bathrooms: 1 public

Bed & breakfast per night:	£min	£max
Single	14.00	15.00
Double	28.00	30.00

Parking for 4
Open April-October

➤ ⊑ Ⓔ ♦ ⓤ Ⓢ ⓉⓋ Ⅲ. ⌐ Ս ⏐ ✿ 🐾 ⋒

166 Copthorne Rd

Listed

Shrewsbury SY3 8LP
☎ (01743) 353602
Situated in a quiet area of the town, within walking distance of the shops.
Bedrooms: 1 single, 1 twin
Bathrooms: 1 public

Bed & breakfast per night:	£min	£max
Single	15.50	16.00
Double	30.00	32.00

Parking for 2

❑ ⓤ ⅟ Ⅲ. ✕ 🐾

Glynndene

Listed

Abbey Foregate, Shrewsbury SY2 6BL
☎ (01743) 352488
Pleasant and friendly bed and breakfast, overlooking the Abbey church grounds. Ideal for touring "Brother Cadfael" country.
Bedrooms: 2 double, 1 twin
Bathrooms: 1 public

Bed & breakfast per night:	£min	£max
Single	14.00	16.00
Double	28.00	32.00

Parking for 3

➤ 3 ❑ ♦ ⓤ ⓠ Ⓢ Ⅲ. ⌐ 🐾

Hillsboro

Listed

1 Port Hill Gardens, Shrewsbury SY3 8SH
☎ (01743) 231033
Charming Edwardian private house in quiet residential area, near park, river and Shrewsbury School. 5 minutes from town centre. Traditional breakfast a speciality. Parking.
Bedrooms: 1 double, 1 twin
Bathrooms: 1 public

Bed & breakfast per night:	£min	£max
Single	15.00	15.00
Double	30.00	30.00

Parking for 2

➤ 8 ❑ ♦ ⓠ ⓤ Ⓢ ⅟ Ⅲ. ⌐ ✿ ✕ 🐾 T

Merevale House

Listed COMMENDED

66 Ellesmere Road, Shrewsbury SY1 2QP
☎ (01743) 243677
Lovely Victorian house. Attractive bedrooms with washbasins, TV, drinks and biscuits, hairdryer and many extra home comforts. Vegetarians catered for. 10 minutes from town. Private parking. Brochure.
Bedrooms: 3 double

Bathrooms: 1 public

Bed & breakfast per night:	£min	£max
Single	15.00	15.00
Double	30.00	30.00

Parking for 8

➤ ⊑ ❑ ♦ ⓠ ⓤ Ⓢ Ⅲ. ⌐ ✿ ✕ 🐾 SP

Shorthill Lodge ⋀

Ⓒ Ⓒ HIGHLY COMMENDED

Shorthill, Lea Cross, Shrewsbury SY5 8JE
☎ (01743) 860864
Attractive, comfortable house in open country setting, inglenook log fire and centrally heated in winter. Five miles south of Shrewsbury, off A488. Nearby pub, restaurant and golf course. Brochure available.
Bedrooms: 1 double, 1 twin
Bathrooms: 2 private, 1 public

Bed & breakfast per night:	£min	£max
Single	18.00	20.00
Double	32.00	36.00

Parking for 3

➤ ⊑ ❑ ♦ ⓤ Ⓢ ⅟ Ⓜ ⓉⓋ Ⅲ. ⊚ ⌐ ⏐ ✿ 🐾

The Stiperstones Guest House ⋀

Ⓒ COMMENDED

18 Coton Crescent, Coton Hill, Shrewsbury SY1 2NZ
☎ (01743) 246720 & 350303
Fax (01743) 350303

Always a warm welcome. Tastefully furnished, quality accommodation. Very comfortable and clean. Extensive facilities, off-road parking. Close to town centre and river. Special rates.
Bedrooms: 1 single, 3 double, 1 twin, 1 triple
Bathrooms: 3 public

Bed & breakfast per night:	£min	£max
Single	17.00	17.00
Double	32.00	32.00

Half board per person:	£min	£max
Daily	24.50	25.50
Weekly	160.00	166.00

Evening meal 1930 (last orders 1200)
Parking for 8

➤ ⚒ ❑ ♦ ⓤ Ⓢ ⅟ Ⓜ ⓉⓋ Ⅲ. ⌐ ✿ ✕
🐾 OAP ⚑ SP T

Bathrooms: 1 public

Bed & breakfast per night:	£min	£max
Single	15.00	15.00
Double	30.00	30.00

Parking for 8

➤ ⊑ ❑ ♦ ⓠ ⓤ Ⓢ Ⅲ. ⌐ ✿ ✕ 🐾 SP

We advise you to confirm your booking in writing.

SHREWSBURY

Continued

Upper Brompton Farm

COMMENDED

Brompton, Cross Houses, Shrewsbury
SY5 6LE
☎ Cross Houses (01743) 761629

*316-acre arable & livestock farm.
Elegant Georgian farmhouse with
relaxed friendly atmosphere and
delightful accommodation amid peace
and tranquillity. Home-cooked
farmhouse fare available by
arrangement.*
Bedrooms: 2 double, 1 twin
Bathrooms: 3 private
Bed & breakfast

per night:	£min	£max
Double	44.00	50.00

Evening meal from 1830
Parking for 10
🛇🏛️🖵♿🥤♨️🖵🔒📵⚡🖾✗🏥🔾⌀❈ 🐾 SP

SLIMBRIDGE

Gloucestershire
Map ref 2B1

The Wildfowl and Wetlands Trust
Centre was founded by Sir Peter
Scott and has the world's largest
collection of wildfowl. Of special
interest are the wild swans and the
geese which wander around the
grounds.

Tudor Arms Lodge

COMMENDED

Shepherds Patch, Slimbridge,
Gloucester GL2 7BP
☎ Dursley (01453) 890306
*Newly-built lodge adjoining an 18th C
freehouse, alongside Gloucester and
Sharpness Canal. Renowned Slimbridge
Wildfowl and Wetlands Trust centre
only 800 yards away.*
Bedrooms: 4 double, 5 twin, 2 triple,
1 family room
Bathrooms: 12 private
Bed & breakfast

per night:	£min	£max
Single	29.50	32.50
Double	39.50	42.50

Half board

per person:	£min	£max
Daily	28.50	38.00
Weekly	178.50	230.00

Lunch available
Evening meal 1900 (last orders 2200)

Parking for 70
Cards accepted: Access, Visa, Amex
🛇🏛️♿🖵🖵♿🥤🔒📵🖾✗🖵🖵♨️🐾▶️
✗🔾 SP

SOLIHULL

West Midlands
Map ref 4B3

On the outskirts of Birmingham.
Some Tudor houses and a 13th C
church remain amongst the new
public buildings and shopping
centre. The 16th C Malvern Hall is
now a school and the 15th C
Chester House at Knowle is now a
library.
Tourist Information Centre
☎ (0121) 704 6130

The Gate House

Listed

Barston Lane, Barston, Solihull
B92 0JN
☎ Barston (01675) 443274
*Early Victorian mansion house set in
beautiful countryside. Close to the
National Exhibition Centre,
International Convention Centre,
airport and motorway.*
Bedrooms: 1 single, 1 double, 2 twin
Bathrooms: 4 private, 1 public
Bed & breakfast

per night:	£min	£max
Single	20.00	25.00
Double	38.00	44.00

Parking for 20
🛇🖵🖵♿🥤🔒📵✗🏥📺🖾🖵❈✗🐾

STAFFORD

Staffordshire
Map ref 4B3

The town has a long history and
some half-timbered buildings still
remain, notably the 16th C High
House. There are several
museums in the town and
Shugborough Hall and the famous
angler Izaak Walton's cottage, now
a museum, are nearby.
Tourist Information Centre
☎ (01785) 40204

Littywood Farm M

COMMENDED

Bradley, Stafford ST18 9DW
☎ (01785) 780234
Fax (01785) 780770
*400-acre mixed farm. Beautiful 14th C
manor offering country house
accommodation, secluded yet easily
accessible from the M6.*
Bedrooms: 1 double, 1 twin
Bathrooms: 1 private, 1 public
Bed & breakfast

per night:	£min	£max
Single	15.00	18.00
Double	30.00	35.00

Parking for 6
🛇1🖵🖵♿🖾📺🖾🖵♨️✗🔾❈🖾🏮

Oakleigh

COMMENDED

Salters Lane, Enson, Stafford
ST18 9TA
☎ Sandon (01889) 508432
*A converted barn offering privacy and
quietness in the countryside. Fresh food
served in a large conservatory. 4 miles
north of Stafford off A34.*
Bedrooms: 1 double, 1 twin
Bathrooms: 2 private
Bed & breakfast

per night:	£min	£max
Single	22.00	25.00
Double	35.00	35.00

Parking for 4
🛇🖵🖵♿🥤🖾✗🖾🖵❈✗🐾

STIPERSTONES

Shropshire
Map ref 4A3

Below the spectacular ridge of the
same name, from which superb
views over moorland, forest and
hills may be enjoyed.

Tankerville Lodge M

COMMENDED

Stiperstones, Minsterley, Shrewsbury
SY5 0NB
☎ Shrewsbury (01743) 791401
*Country house noted for warm
hospitality, set in superb landscape
which offers breathtaking views. Ideal
touring base for Shropshire and Welsh
borderland. Adjacent to Stiperstones
Nature Reserve.*
Bedrooms: 1 double, 3 twin
Bathrooms: 2 public
Bed & breakfast

per night:	£min	£max
Single	15.75	18.25
Double	31.50	31.50

Half board

per person:	£min	£max
Daily	24.50	27.00
Weekly	160.51	178.01

Evening meal 1900 (last orders 0900)
Parking for 5
🛇5♿🖾🔒📺🖾🖵♨️🔾❈🐾 SP

STOKE LACY

Hereford and Worcester
Map ref 2A1

Small village by the River Leadon,
on the cider trail, a few miles from
Bromyard. The 14th C half-
timbered manor house of Lower
Brockhampton (National Trust) is
nearby.

Nether Court M

HIGHLY COMMENDED

Stoke Lacy, Bromyard, Herefordshire
HR7 4HJ
☎ Hereford (01432) 820247
*300-acre mixed farm. Victorian
farmhouse in peaceful village*

surroundings. Small lake for wildlife.
Good restaurant within walking
distance. Near Hereford, Ludlow,
Malvern, Leominster and Worcester.
Bedrooms: 3 double
Bathrooms: 3 private

Bed & breakfast

per night:	£min	£max
Single	22.00	
Double	35.00	35.00

Half board

per person:	£min	£max
Daily	34.00	

Evening meal from 1800

STOKE-ON-TRENT

Staffordshire
Map ref 4B2

Famous for its pottery. Factories of
several famous makers, including
Josiah Wedgwood, can be visited.
The City Museum has one of the
finest pottery and porcelain
collections in the world.
Tourist Information Centre
☎ *(01782) 284600*

The Hollies

Clay Lake, Endon, Stoke-on-Trent
ST9 9DD
☎ (01782) 503252
Delightful Victorian house in a quiet
country setting off B5051. Convenient
for M6, the Potteries and Alton Towers.
Non-smokers only, please.
Bedrooms: 2 double, 1 twin, 2 triple
Bathrooms: 5 private, 1 public

Bed & breakfast

per night:	£min	£max
Single	20.00	30.00
Double	32.00	40.00

Parking for 5

The Limes

Cheadle Road, Blythe Bridge, Stoke-
on-Trent ST11 9PW
☎ Blythe Bridge (01782) 393278
Victorian residence of quality and
character in large, landscaped gardens,
near Alton Towers, Wedgwood, the
Potteries and Staffordshire moorlands.
Bedrooms: 1 single, 1 double, 1 triple
Bathrooms: 1 public, 2 private
showers

Bed & breakfast

per night:	£min	£max
Single	20.00	22.00
Double	35.00	38.00

Parking for 8

STONE

Staffordshire
Map ref 4B2

Town on the River Trent with the
remains of a 12th C Augustinian
priory. It is surrounded by pleasant
countryside. Trentham Gardens
with 500 acres of parklands and
recreational facilities is within easy
reach.

Couldreys ♠♠

COMMENDED

8 Airdale Road, Stone ST15 8DW
☎ (01785) 812500
Fax (01785) 811761
Edwardian house quietly situated on
town outskirts, providing every comfort
plus home-made bread! Excellent
restaurants within walking distance.
Convenient for M6, Wedgwood and
Potteries. Non-smokers only, please.
Bedrooms: 1 twin
Bathrooms: 1 private

Bed & breakfast

per night:	£min	£max
Single	20.00	
Double	32.00	

Parking for 2

STONEHOUSE

Gloucestershire
Map ref 2B1

Village in the Stroud Valley with an
Elizabethan Court, later restored
and altered by Lutyens.

The Grey Cottage

HIGHLY COMMENDED

Bath Road, Leonard Stanley,
Stonehouse GL10 3LU
☎ Stroud (01453) 822515
1807 Cotswold cottage featuring
tessellated tiling, stonework and open
log fires. Charming garden with
distinctive Wellingtonia. Imaginative
cooking and presentation.
Bedrooms: 1 single, 1 double, 1 twin
Bathrooms: 3 private, 1 public

Bed & breakfast

per night:	£min	£max
Single	22.00	28.00
Double	45.00	48.00

Half board

per person:	£min	£max
Daily	36.00	44.00

Parking for 7

Merton Lodge

8 Ebley Road, Stonehouse GL10 2LQ
☎ (01453) 822018
Former gentleman's residence offering a
warm welcome. No smoking in the
house. Three miles from junction 13 of

M5. Take A419 to Stroud over 3
roundabouts, under footbridge - located
opposite garden centre. Short walk to
carvery/pub.
Bedrooms: 3 double
Bathrooms: 1 private, 2 public

Bed & breakfast

per night:	£min	£max
Single	14.00	16.00
Double	28.00	32.00

Parking for 6

STOULTON

Hereford and Worcester
Map ref 2B1

Caldewell

Pershore Road, Stoulton, Worcester
WR7 4RL
☎ Worcester (01905) 840894
Country house set in woodland
conservation area with lake. Farm
animals kept. Miniature steam railway
and excellent facilities for children.
Bedrooms: 3 double, 1 twin
Bathrooms: 3 private, 2 public

Bed & breakfast

per night:	£min	£max
Single	20.00	24.00
Double	35.00	40.00

Half board

per person:	£min	£max
Daily	24.50	31.00

Evening meal from 1830
Parking for 6
Open March-December

STOURBRIDGE

West Midlands
Map ref 4B3

Town on the River Stour, famous
for its glassworks. Several of the
factories can be visited and
glassware purchased at the factory
shops.

St. Elizabeth's Cottage

COMMENDED

Woodman Lane, Clent, Stourbridge
DY9 9PX
☎ Hagley (01562) 883883
Beautiful country cottage with lovely
gardens and interior professionally
decorated throughout. 20 minutes from
Birmingham and close to motorway
links.
Bedrooms: 1 double, 1 twin
Bathrooms: 2 private, 1 public

Bed & breakfast

per night:	£min	£max
Single	22.00	25.00
Double	44.00	50.00

Parking for 2

STOW-ON-THE-WOLD

Gloucestershire
Map ref 2B1

Attractive Cotswold wool town with a large market-place and some fine houses, especially the old grammar school. There is an interesting church dating from Norman times. Stow-on-the-Wold is surrounded by lovely countryside and Cotswold villages.
Tourist Information Centre
☎ *(01451) 831082*

Aston House

Broadwell, Moreton-in-Marsh
GL56 0TJ
☎ Cotswold (01451) 830475
Cotswold-stone chalet-bungalow in quiet village, 1.5 miles from Stow-on-the-Wold. Central for touring Cotswolds. Pub and good food within walking distance. Reduced rates for weekly B&B.
Bedrooms: 1 twin, 1 triple
Bathrooms: 2 private

Bed & breakfast

per night:	£min	£max
Double	17.50	20.00

Parking for 3
Open March-November

Corsham Field Farmhouse ⚌

Bledington Road, Stow-on-the-Wold,
Cheltenham GL54 1JH
☎ Cotswold (01451) 831750
100-acre mixed farm. Homely farmhouse with breathtaking views. Ideally situated for exploring the Cotswolds. En-suite and standard rooms. TVs, guest lounge, tea/coffee facilities. Good pub food 5 minutes' walk away.
Bedrooms: 1 double, 1 twin, 1 family room
Bathrooms: 1 private, 1 public

Bed & breakfast

per night:	£min	£max
Single	15.00	25.00
Double	27.00	37.00

Parking for 10

Crestow House ⚌ COMMENDED

Stow-on-the-Wold, Cheltenham
GL54 1JX
☎ (01451) 830969
Fax (01451) 832129

Large stone-built Victorian Cotswold country house. Large comfortable en-suite rooms. Conservatory and swimming pool.

Bedrooms: 4 double
Bathrooms: 4 private, 1 public

Bed & breakfast

per night:	£min	£max
Single	34.00	40.00
Double	50.00	68.00

Half board

per person:	£min	£max
Daily	50.00	55.00
Weekly	249.00	290.00

Lunch available
Evening meal 2000 (last orders 2000)
Parking for 4
Open February-December
Cards accepted: Access, Visa

Cross Keys Cottage ⚌ COMMENDED

Park Street, Stow-on-the-Wold,
Cheltenham GL54 1AQ
☎ Cotswold (01451) 831128
A warm welcome awaits you at our 17th C Cotswold cottage, close to the square in Stow-on-the-Wold.
Bedrooms: 2 double, 1 twin
Bathrooms: 1 private, 2 public

Bed & breakfast

per night:	£min	£max
Double	38.00	48.00

Journeys End ⚌ COMMENDED

Evenlode, Moreton-in-Marsh
GL56 0NN
☎ Moreton-in-Marsh (01608) 650786
20-acre mixed farm. Peaceful, gabled, Cotswold-stone farmhouse in quiet village. Approximately 3 miles from Moreton-in-Marsh and Stow-on-the-Wold. One bedroom is on ground floor.
Bedrooms: 3 double, 1 twin, 1 family room
Bathrooms: 5 private

Bed & breakfast

per night:	£min	£max
Single	17.00	25.00
Double	34.00	40.00

Parking for 5

Old Farmhouse Hotel ⚌⚌ COMMENDED

Lower Swell, Stow-on-the-Wold,
Cheltenham GL54 1LF
☎ Cotswold (01451) 830232
Fax (01451) 870962

Sympathetically converted 16th C Cotswold-stone farmhouse in a quiet hamlet, 1 mile west of Stow-on-the-Wold. Offers warm and unpretentious hospitality.

Bedrooms: 9 double, 4 twin, 1 family room; suite available
Bathrooms: 14 private, 1 public

Bed & breakfast

per night:	£min	£max
Single	20.00	60.00
Double	40.00	90.00

Half board

per person:	£min	£max
Daily	35.95	75.95
Weekly	240.00	500.00

Lunch available
Evening meal 1900 (last orders 2100)
Parking for 25
Cards accepted: Access, Visa, Switch/Delta

Pear Tree Cottage ⚌ APPROVED

High Street, Stow-on-the-Wold,
Cheltenham GL54 1DL
☎ Cotswold (01451) 831210
Period cottage with two nicely decorated bedrooms, both en-suite with TV and tea/coffee making facilities. Less than a minute's walk to market square. Off-street car parking.
Bedrooms: 2 double
Bathrooms: 2 private

Bed & breakfast

per night:	£min	£max
Single		30.00
Double		40.00

Parking for 1

Royalist Hotel ⚌

Digbeth Street, Stow-on-the-Wold,
Cheltenham GL54 1BN
☎ Cotswold (01451) 830670
Fax (01451) 970048
The oldest inn in England (947 AD) with all the inherent charm and character of the past, yet every modern-day facility as well.
Bedrooms: 1 single, 9 double, 2 twin
Bathrooms: 12 private

Bed & breakfast

per night:	£min	£max
Single	35.00	50.00
Double	50.00	75.00

Lunch available
Parking for 10
Cards accepted: Access, Visa

South Hill Farmhouse ⚌

Fosseway, Stow-on-the-Wold,
Cheltenham GL54 1JU
☎ Cotswold (01451) 831219
Fax (01451) 831554

Base your touring holiday in this Victorian farmhouse. Individually furnished and spacious rooms, a hearty breakfast, lounge with open fires.
Bedrooms: 3 double, 1 twin, 1 triple
Bathrooms: 5 private, 1 public
Bed & breakfast

per night:	£min	£max
Double	30.00	36.00

Parking for 6

There are separate sections in this guide listing groups specialising in farm holidays and accommodation which is especially suitable for young people and organised groups.

STRATFORD-UPON-AVON

Warwickshire
Map ref 2B1

Famous as Shakespeare's home town, Stratford's many attractions include his birthplace, New Place where he died, the Royal Shakespeare Theatre and Gallery, "The World of Shakespeare" 30 minute theatre and Hall's Croft (his daughter's house).
Tourist Information Centre
☎ *(01789) 293127*

Abberley

COMMENDED
12 Albany Road, Stratford-upon-Avon
CV37 6PG
☎ (01789) 295934
Comfortable home set in a quiet residential area yet within easy walking distance of theatres and town centre. Non-smokers only, please.
Bedrooms: 1 twin
Bathrooms: 1 private
Bed & breakfast

per night:	£min	£max
Double	42.00	44.00

Parking for 2

Allors

Listed
62 Evesham Road, Stratford-upon-Avon CV37 9BA
☎ (01789) 269982
Detached house, comfortable rooms with en-suite or private facilities. Dining room overlooking secluded garden. TV, parking, non-smoking. Special rates for 3-night breaks.
Bedrooms: 2 double
Bathrooms: 2 private
Bed & breakfast

per night:	£min	£max
Double	32.00	40.00

Parking for 3
Open February–November

Braeside Guest House

129 Shipston Road, Stratford-upon-Avon CV37 7LW
☎ (01789) 261648
Attractive detached family-run guesthouse, 10 minutes' walk from Royal Shakespeare Theatre and town centre along old tramway footpath. Double/family room and twin room are en-suite, single has private bathroom. Ample parking.
Bedrooms: 1 single, 1 double, 1 twin
Bathrooms: 3 private, 1 public

Continued ▶

STRATFORD-UPON-AVON

Continued

Bed & breakfast

per night:	£min	£max
Single	16.00	17.00
Double	30.00	34.00

Parking for 4

Bronhill House ⋀

Listed

260 Alcester Road, Stratford-upon-Avon CV37 9JQ
☎ (01789) 299169
Detached family house in elevated position, 1 mile from Stratford-upon-Avon. Family-run with relaxed friendly atmosphere. A non-smoking establishment.
Bedrooms: 1 single, 2 double
Bathrooms: 3 private, 2 public

Bed & breakfast

per night:	£min	£max
Single	15.00	20.00
Double	24.00	30.00

Parking for 5

Burton Farm

Bishopton, Stratford-upon-Avon CV37 0RW
☎ (01789) 293338

150-acre mixed farm. Elizabethan farmhouse with large gardens, in rural surroundings 1.5 miles from Stratford-upon-Avon.
Bedrooms: 2 double, 1 twin, 1 triple
Bathrooms: 4 private

Bed & breakfast

per night:	£min	£max
Single	25.00	30.00
Double	40.00	50.00

Parking for 22

Carlton Guest House ⋀

22 Evesham Place, Stratford-upon-Avon CV37 6HT
☎ (01789) 293548
Tasteful decor, elegantly furnished, combining Victorian origins with modern facilities. A peaceful home, happily shared with guests.
Bedrooms: 1 single, 3 double, 1 family room
Bathrooms: 3 private, 1 public

Bed & breakfast

per night:	£min	£max
Single	22.00	23.00
Double	38.00	48.00

Parking for 3

Chadwyns Guest House ⋀

Listed

6 Broad Walk, Stratford-upon-Avon CV37 6HS
☎ (01789) 269077

Traditionally furnished Victorian house, family-run, in old town near theatre. Colour TV and tea/coffee making facilities in all rooms. Vegetarian alternative breakfast.
Bedrooms: 1 single, 1 double, 2 twin, 2 family rooms
Bathrooms: 2 private, 2 public

Bed & breakfast

per night:	£min	£max
Single	16.00	16.00
Double	30.00	38.00

Parking for 2

Cherangani ⋀

COMMENDED

61 Maidenhead Road, Stratford-upon-Avon CV37 6XU
☎ (01789) 292655
Pleasant detached house in a quiet, residential area, offering warm, attractive accommodation. Within walking distance of the town and theatre.
Bedrooms: 1 twin
Bathrooms: 1 public

Bed & breakfast

per night:	£min	£max
Single	16.00	18.00
Double	32.00	36.00

Parking for 3

Church Farm ⋀

COMMENDED

Dorsington, Stratford-upon-Avon CV37 8AX
☎ (01789) 720471 & Mobile 0831 504194
Fax (01789) 720830
127-acre mixed farm. Situated in beautiful countryside, some rooms en-suite, TV, tea and coffee facilities. Close to Stratford-upon-Avon, Warwick, the Cotswolds and Evesham.
Wheelchair access category 3 ♿
Bedrooms: 3 double, 2 twin, 2 family rooms
Bathrooms: 4 private, 2 public

Bed & breakfast

per night:	£min	£max
Single	18.00	23.50
Double	24.00	36.00

Parking for 12

Church Farm ⋀

COMMENDED

Long Marston, Stratford-upon-Avon CV37 8RH
☎ (01789) 720275
A very friendly welcome at this old family farmhouse in quiet village. Close to Stratford-upon-Avon, Warwick Castle and the Cotswolds.
Bedrooms: 1 twin, 1 triple
Bathrooms: 2 private

Bed & breakfast

per night:	£min	£max
Single	26.00	
Double	35.00	

Parking for 4

Clomendy Guest House ⋀

157 Evesham Road, Stratford-upon-Avon CV37 9BP
☎ (01789) 266957

Small, detached, mock-Tudor family-run guesthouse, convenient for town centre, Anne Hathaway's cottage and theatres. Stratford-in-Bloom commendation winner. Rail/coach guests met and returned. No smoking, please.
Bedrooms: 1 single, 1 double, 1 twin
Bathrooms: 1 public, 1 private shower

Bed & breakfast

per night:	£min	£max
Single	14.00	17.00
Double	26.00	34.00

Parking for 5

Field View ⋀

APPROVED

35 Banbury Road, Stratford-upon-Avon CV37 7HW
☎ (01789) 292694
10 minutes' walk from Stratford town centre, offering comfortable, family-type accommodation.
Bedrooms: 1 double
Bathrooms: 1 public

Bed & breakfast

per night:	£min	£max
Single	14.00	16.00
Double	28.00	30.00

Parking for 3

Green Gables

 COMMENDED

47 Banbury Road, Stratford-upon-Avon CV37 7HW
☎ (01789) 205557
Edwardian house in a residential area, within 10 minutes' walk of the town centre and theatre.
Bedrooms: 3 double
Bathrooms: 1 private, 1 public

Bed & breakfast

per night:	£min	£max
Double	32.00	38.00

Parking for 3

Highcroft

COMMENDED

Banbury Road, Stratford-upon-Avon CV37 7NF
☎ (01789) 296293

Lovely country house in 2-acre garden, only 2 miles from Stratford-upon-Avon, on A422. Families welcome. Friendly, relaxed atmosphere.
Bedrooms: 1 double, 1 family room
Bathrooms: 2 private

Bed & breakfast

per night:	£min	£max
Single	20.00	25.00
Double	33.00	36.00

Parking for 3

Houndshill House

Banbury Road, Ettington, Stratford-upon-Avon CV37 7NS
☎ (01789) 740267
Family-run pub with restaurant. 4 miles from Stratford-upon-Avon. Informal and friendly atmosphere.
Bedrooms: 2 single, 3 double, 2 twin, 1 triple
Bathrooms: 8 private

Bed & breakfast

per night:	£min	£max
Single	30.00	
Double	48.00	

Lunch available
Evening meal 1900 (last orders 2200)
Parking for 50
Cards accepted: Access, Visa, Switch/Delta

Ingon Grange

Listed COMMENDED

Ingon Lane, Snitterfield, Stratford-upon-Avon CV37 0QF
☎ (01789) 731122

Spacious, traditional family home in quiet countryside. 3 miles from Stratford-upon-Avon, 6 miles from Warwick. Ample parking, large garden, tennis court.
Bedrooms: 1 single, 1 double, 1 twin
Bathrooms: 1 private, 1 public

Bed & breakfast

per night:	£min	£max
Single	20.00	28.00
Double	40.00	44.00

Parking for 21

Moonraker House

COMMENDED

40 Alcester Road, Stratford-upon-Avon CV37 9DB
☎ (01789) 299346 & 267115
Fax (01789) 295504
Family-run, near town centre. Beautifully co-ordinated decor throughout. Some rooms with four-poster beds and garden terrace available for non-smokers.
Bedrooms: 16 double, 2 twin, 4 triple
Bathrooms: 22 private

Bed & breakfast

per night:	£min	£max
Single	28.00	34.00
Double	39.00	60.00

Parking for 24
Cards accepted: Access, Visa

Moss Cottage

COMMENDED

61 Evesham Road, Stratford-upon-Avon CV37 9BA
☎ (01789) 294770
Pauline and Jim Rush welcome you to their charming detached cottage. Walking distance theatre/town. Spacious en-suite accommodation. Hospitality tray, TV. Parking.
Bedrooms: 2 double
Bathrooms: 2 private

Bed & breakfast

per night:	£min	£max
Single	25.00	30.00
Double	34.00	40.00

Parking for 3
Open March-December

The Myrtles Bed and Breakfast

Listed COMMENDED

6 Rother Street, Stratford-upon-Avon CV37 6LU
☎ (01789) 295511

Detached Victorian three storey building in town centre. Newly converted, three en-suite bedrooms, breakfast room and patio garden.
Bedrooms: 2 double, 1 twin
Bathrooms: 3 private

Bed & breakfast

per night:	£min	£max
Single	25.00	35.00
Double	40.00	50.00

Cards accepted: Access, Visa

Newlands

COMMENDED

7 Broad Walk, Stratford-upon-Avon CV37 6HS
☎ (01789) 298449
Park your car at Sue Boston's home and take a short walk to the Royal Shakespeare Theatre, town centre and Shakespeare properties.
Bedrooms: 1 single, 1 double, 2 triple
Bathrooms: 3 private, 1 public

Bed & breakfast

per night:	£min	£max
Single	18.00	20.00
Double	40.00	44.00

Parking for 2

The Poplars

Listed

Mansell Farm, Newbold-on-Stour, Stratford-upon-Avon CV37 8BZ
☎ (01789) 450540
172-acre dairy farm. Modern farmhouse in picturesque surroundings offers friendly welcome. Two hostelries within walking distance serve good food. Six miles south of Stratford-upon-Avon on A3400.
Bedrooms: 1 single, 1 twin, 1 triple
Bathrooms: 2 private, 1 public

Bed & breakfast

per night:	£min	£max
Single	14.00	15.00
Double	30.00	33.00

Half board

per person:	£min	£max
Daily	23.00	25.00
Weekly	147.00	170.00

Evening meal 1830 (last orders 2000)
Parking for 3
Open March-October

Ravenhurst

2 Broad Walk, Stratford-upon-Avon CV37 6HS
☎ (01789) 292515

Continued ►

Please mention this guide when making a booking.

STRATFORD-UPON-AVON

Continued

Quietly situated, a few minutes' walk from the town centre and places of historic interest. Comfortable home, with substantial breakfast provided. Four-poster en-suite available.
Bedrooms: 3 double, 2 twin
Bathrooms: 5 private

Bed & breakfast

per night:	£min	£max
Double	38.00	44.00

Parking for 4
Cards accepted: Access, Visa, Diners, Amex

Sequoia House ⋒
🏵🏵 COMMENDED

51-53 Shipston Road, Stratford-upon-Avon CV37 7LN
☎ (01789) 268852 & 294940
Fax (01789) 414559
Beautifully-appointed private hotel with large car park and delightful garden walk to the theatre, riverside gardens and Shakespeare properties. Fully air-conditioned dining room.
Bedrooms: 2 single, 10 double, 12 twin
Bathrooms: 20 private, 3 public

Bed & breakfast

per night:	£min	£max
Single	29.00	49.00
Double	39.00	72.00

Lunch available
Parking for 33
Cards accepted: Access, Visa, Diners, Amex, Switch/Delta

Whitchurch Farm ⋒
🏵🏵 APPROVED

Wimpstone, Stratford-upon-Avon CV37 8NS
☎ Alderminster (01789) 450275
260-acre mixed farm. Listed Georgian farmhouse set in park-like surroundings on the edge of the Cotswolds. Ideal for a touring holiday. Small village 4 miles south of Stratford-upon-Avon.
Bedrooms: 2 double, 1 triple
Bathrooms: 3 private, 1 public

Bed & breakfast

per night:	£min	£max
Single	17.00	18.00
Double	34.00	36.00

Half board

per person:	£min	£max
Daily	26.50	28.00

Evening meal from 1830
Parking for 3

Wood View ⋒
🏵🏵 HIGHLY COMMENDED

Pathlow, Stratford-upon-Avon CV37 0RQ
☎ (01789) 295778
Fax (01789) 295778
Beautifully situated comfortable home, with fine views over fields and woods. Ideal for touring Stratford-upon-Avon and the Cotswolds.
Bedrooms: 2 twin
Bathrooms: 2 private

Bed & breakfast

per night:	£min	£max
Single	25.00	30.00
Double	40.00	50.00

Parking for 6

STRETTON ON FOSSE

Warwickshire
Map ref 2B1

Village on the Warwickshire/Gloucestershire border, through which the Roman Fosse Way passes, and with a mixture of stone and brick houses.

Ditchford Farmhouse ⋒
🏵🏵 COMMENDED

Stretton on Fosse, Moreton-in-Marsh, Gloucestershire GL56 9RD
☎ Shipston-on-Stour (01608) 663307
Secluded Georgian farmhouse in lovely north Cotswold countryside. Large garden with children's corner. Home-grown produce and country cooking. Winter breaks with log fires. Private facilities available.
Bedrooms: 1 single, 3 double, 2 family rooms
Bathrooms: 6 private

Bed & breakfast

per night:	£min	£max
Single	17.95	19.45
Double	35.90	40.00

Half board

per person:	£min	£max
Daily	26.90	28.90
Weekly	181.65	202.65

Evening meal from 1900
Parking for 8

The town index at the back of this guide gives page numbers of all places with accommodation.

STROUD

Gloucestershire
Map ref 2B1

This old town has been producing broadcloth for centuries and the local museum has an interesting display on the subject. It is surrounded by attractive hilly country.
Tourist Information Centre
☎ *(01453) 765768*

Beechcroft
🏵 COMMENDED

Brownshill, Stroud GL6 8AG
☎ (01453) 883422
Edwardian house in quiet rural position, with open views. Evening meal by arrangement. Home-made bread and preserves. No smoking.
Bedrooms: 1 double, 1 twin
Bathrooms: 1 public

Bed & breakfast

per night:	£min	£max
Single		17.00
Double		30.00

Half board

per person:	£min	£max
Daily	25.00	27.00

Evening meal from 1900
Parking for 4

Cairngall Guest House
🏵 APPROVED

65 Bisley Old Road, Stroud GL5 1NF
☎ (01453) 764595
Listed house with panoramic views over Severn Vale. Spacious, warm rooms, comfortably furnished. Pleasant garden.
Bedrooms: 1 twin, 1 triple
Bathrooms: 1 public

Bed & breakfast

per night:	£min	£max
Single	14.00	15.00
Double	28.00	32.00

Parking for 3

Downfield Hotel ⋒
🏵🏵🏵

134 Cainscross Road, Stroud GL5 4HN
☎ (01453) 764496
Fax (01453) 753150

Imposing hotel in quiet location. Home cooking. 1 mile from town centre, 5 miles from M5 motorway, junction 13, on main A419 road.
Bedrooms: 4 single, 9 double, 7 twin, 1 triple
Bathrooms: 11 private, 3 public

Bed & breakfast per night:	£min	£max
Single	20.00	29.00
Double	29.00	35.00

Half board per person:	£min	£max
Daily	25.00	50.00
Weekly	175.00	273.00

Evening meal 1830 (last orders 2000)
Parking for 23
Cards accepted: Access, Visa, Switch/Delta
🐴 ♿ ☕ 🔒 [S] 🛏 [TV] ▥ 🚗 🚐

Hawthorns

👑👑

Lower Littleworth, Amberley, Stroud GL5 5AW
☎ (01453) 873535
Grade II listed Queen Anne house in National Trust setting. Glorious 20-mile views. Wild badgers (floodlit) feed at nightfall within touching distance. Exceptional walking country, riding, hot-air ballooning. Warm welcome.
Bedrooms: 2 double, 1 twin
Bathrooms: 3 private

Bed & breakfast per night:	£min	£max
Single	25.00	30.00
Double	28.00	38.00

Parking for 3
Open March-October
☕ [UL] 🔒 [S] 🛏 [TV] ▥ 🚗 U ⛳ ✿ 🚐 🏛

Whitegates Farm

👑👑 COMMENDED

Cowcombe Hill, Chalford, Stroud GL6 8HP
☎ Cirencester (01285) 760758
Peaceful hillside farmhouse with lovely views, gardens, orchards and 16 rambling acres. Good walking, central for touring. Non-smokers only, please. Spanish spoken.
Bedrooms: 2 double
Bathrooms: 2 private

Bed & breakfast per night:	£min	£max
Single	25.00	30.00
Double	38.00	43.00

Parking for 6
🐴 ▭ ☕ [UL] 🔒 [S] 🚭 ▥ 🚗 ✿ ✈ 🚐 [SP] 🏛

The symbol ⚙ within an entry indicates participation in the Welcome Host programme – a nationally recognised customer care initiative which aims to promote the highest standards of service and a warm welcome for all visitors.

TELFORD

Shropshire
Map ref 4A3

New Town named after Thomas Telford, the famous engineer who designed many of the country's canals, bridges and viaducts. It is close to Ironbridge with its monuments and museums to the Industrial Revolution, including restored 18th C buildings.
Tourist Information Centre
☎ (01952) 291370

Albion Inn

👑👑👑

West Street, St Georges, Telford TF2 9AD
☎ (01952) 614193
Friendly village pub offering accommodation and home-cooked food. Ten minute drive to Ironbridge, five minutes to town centre.
Bedrooms: 2 twin
Bathrooms: 2 private

Bed & breakfast per night:	£min	£max
Single	25.00	25.00
Double	40.00	40.00

Lunch available
Evening meal 1900 (last orders 2200)
Parking for 10
🐴 ▭ ☕ 🔒 [TV] ▥ 🚗 🔍 ✿ ✈ 🚐 [SP]

Allscott Inn

👑👑👑 APPROVED

Walcot, Wellington, Telford TF6 5EQ
☎ (01952) 248484
Homely country inn offering delicious food and comfortable accommodation. Beer garden. Easy access Shrewsbury, Ironbridge and Telford.
Bedrooms: 2 double, 2 twin
Bathrooms: 2 private, 1 public

Bed & breakfast per night:	£min	£max
Single	20.00	25.00
Double	35.00	40.00

Lunch available
Evening meal 1900 (last orders 2200)
Parking for 50
Cards accepted: Amex
🐴 ♿ ▭ ☕ [S] 🚭 🛏 [TV] ▥ 🚗 🔍 ✿ 🚐

There are separate sections in this guide listing groups specialising in farm holidays and accommodation which is especially suitable for young people and organised groups.

TENBURY WELLS

Hereford and Worcester
Map ref 4A3

Small market town on the Teme possessing many fine black and white buildings. In 1839 mineral springs were found here and there were hopes of a spa centre developing. The waters never became fashionable and today only the old Pump Room remains.

The White House

👑👑

White House Lane, Kyrewood, Tenbury Wells, Worcestershire WR15 8SQ
☎ (01584) 810694
Georgian country property, surrounded by orchards, situated on the completely unspoilt Shropshire/Worcestershire border. Golf-courses nearby.
Bedrooms: 1 single, 2 double, 1 twin
Bathrooms: 4 private

Bed & breakfast per night:	£min	£max
Single	20.00	20.00
Double	40.00	50.00

Parking for 6
🐴5 ▤ ▥ ▭ ☕ [UL] 🔒 🚭 🛏 ▥ 🚗 ⛳ ✿ ✈ 🚐 ⚲

TETBURY

Gloucestershire
Map ref 2B2

Small market town with 18th C houses and an attractive 17th C Town Hall. It is a good touring centre with many places of interest nearby including Badminton House and Westonbirt Arboretum.

Tavern House

👑👑 DE LUXE

Willesley, Tetbury GL8 8QU
☎ (01666) 880444
Fax (01666) 880254

A Grade II listed Cotswold stone house (formerly a staging post) on the A433 Bath road, 1 mile from Westonbirt Arboretum and 4 miles from Tetbury.
Bedrooms: 3 double, 1 twin
Bathrooms: 4 private

Continued ►

We advise you to confirm your booking in writing.

TETBURY

Continued

Bed & breakfast

per night:	£min	£max
Single	37.50	47.50
Double	55.00	69.00

Parking for 4
Cards accepted: Access, Visa

☜ 10 ☎ 🖭 ☐ ♦ 🖂 ⓊⓁ 🛉 ✗ 🐾 ⅲ, 🔌 🅿 ⋃
🏋 ☼ 🎿 🐎 🐕 🏢 🔲

TEWKESBURY

Gloucestershire
Map ref 2B1

Tewkesbury's outstanding possession is its magnificent church, built as an abbey, with a great Norman tower and beautiful 14th C interior. The town stands at the confluence of the Severn and Avon and has many medieval houses, inns and several museums.
Tourist Information Centre
☎ *(01684) 295027*

Abbots Court Farm ⋀

⬡⬡ COMMENDED

Church End, Twyning, Tewkesbury GL20 6DA
☎ (01684) 292515
Fax (01684) 292515

450-acre arable & dairy farm. Large, comfortable farmhouse in excellent touring area. Most rooms en-suite. 3 games rooms, grass tennis court, fishing available.
Bedrooms: 1 single, 1 double, 2 twin, 2 triple, 2 family rooms
Bathrooms: 6 private, 1 public
Bed & breakfast

per night:	£min	£max
Single	17.50	19.50
Double	29.00	33.00

Parking for 20
Cards accepted: Visa

☜ 🐾 ☐ ♦ 🖂 ⓘ 🅂 🛉 ⓉⓋ ⅲ, 🔌 🔦 ⋃
🎵 ☼ 🐎 ⒪Ⓐ⒫ 🔲 🏢

Lampitt House ⋀

⬡⬡ COMMENDED

Lampitt Lane, Bredon's Norton, Tewkesbury GL20 7HB
☎ Bredon (01684) 772295

Please mention this guide when making a booking.

Large house set in 1.5 acre garden in picturesque Cotswold village at the foot of Bredon Hill. Extensive views. Tewkesbury 4 miles. Beautiful hill and riverside walks.
Bedrooms: 2 double, 1 twin
Bathrooms: 3 private
Bed & breakfast

per night:	£min	£max
Single	24.00	26.00
Double	35.00	36.00

Half board

per person:	£min	£max
Daily	35.00	37.00
Weekly	245.00	259.00

Evening meal 1800 (last orders 2000)
Parking for 6

☜ 🐾 🖭 ☐ ♦ 🖂 ⓊⓁ ⓘ 🅂 ✗ 🛉 ⅲ, 🔌 ⋃
☼ 🐎

Personal Touch ⋀

Listed

37 Tirle Bank Way, Tewkesbury GL20 8ES
☎ (01684) 297692
Semi-detached overlooking farmland. Leave M5 at junction 9, Tewkesbury. Second left past traffic lights, then left and immediately right, follow road round to right.
Bedrooms: 2 twin
Bathrooms: 1 public
Bed & breakfast

per night:	£min	£max
Single	15.00	18.00
Double	30.00	30.00

Half board

per person:	£min	£max
Daily	23.00	25.00
Weekly	160.00	160.00

Lunch available
Evening meal from 1830
Parking for 2

☜ 3 ☐ ♦ 🖂 ⓘ 🅂 🛉 ⓉⓋ ⅲ, 🔌 🔦 🐎 ⒪Ⓐ⒫

Town Street Farm ⋀

⬡⬡ COMMENDED

Tirley, Gloucester GL19 4HG
☎ Gloucester (01452) 780442
Fax (01452) 780890

500-acre mixed farm. 18th C farmhouse set in beautiful surroundings and within half a mile of the River Severn.
Bedrooms: 1 double, 1 triple

Bathrooms: 2 private, 1 public
Bed & breakfast

per night:	£min	£max
Single	20.00	
Double	30.00	32.00

Parking for 4

☜ ☐ ♦ ⓊⓁ 🛉 🅂 🛉 ⓉⓋ ⅲ, 🔌 🔦 ⋃ ☼ 🐎

UPTON-UPON-SEVERN

Hereford and Worcester
Map ref 2B1

Attractive country town on the banks of the Severn and a good river cruising centre. It has many pleasant old houses and inns, and the pepperpot landmark is now the Heritage Centre.

Tiltridge Farm and Vineyard ⋀

⬡⬡ HIGHLY COMMENDED

Upper Hook Road, Upton-upon-Severn, Worcester WR8 0SA
☎ (01684) 592906
Fax (01684) 594142

9-acre vineyard & grazing farm. Fully renovated period farmhouse close to Upton and Malvern showground. Good food, warm welcome and wine from our own vineyard!
Bedrooms: 2 double, 1 triple
Bathrooms: 3 private
Bed & breakfast

per night:	£min	£max
Single	20.00	22.00
Double	36.00	36.00

Half board

per person:	£min	£max
Daily	30.50	32.50
Weekly	185.50	213.50

Lunch available
Evening meal 1800 (last orders 2000)
Parking for 12

☜ 🖭 ☐ ♦ 🐾 ⓘ 🅂 ✗ 🛉 ⓉⓋ ⅲ, 🔌 ☼ 🐎 🏢

Welland Court ⋀

⬡⬡ HIGHLY COMMENDED

Upton-upon-Severn, Worcester WR8 0ST
☎ (01684) 594426 & 594413
Fax (01684) 594426
Built c.1450 and enlarged in the 18th C. Rescued from a dilapidated state and modernised to a high standard. It lies at the foot of the Malvern Hills and is an ideal base for touring the Wye and Teme valleys.
Bedrooms: 2 double, 1 twin
Bathrooms: 3 private

Bed & breakfast

per night:	£min	£max
Single	40.00	40.00
Double	60.00	60.00

Half board

per person:	£min	£max
Daily	65.00	65.00
Weekly	390.00	390.00

Parking for 13

🐕🕭📬🖰🛏🗉Ⓢ🖳📺🎞🖀♟🍴❄✠🛒🏠🅣

UTTOXETER

Staffordshire
Map ref 4B2

Small market town, famous for its racecourse. There are half-timbered buildings around the Market Square.

West Lodge ⋀

Listed HIGHLY COMMENDED

Bramshall, Uttoxeter ST14 5BG
☎ (01889) 566000
Detached residence in 1 acre of attractive garden, on the B5027, 2 miles from Uttoxeter. Easy access to the Derbyshire Dales and Alton Towers.
Bedrooms: 1 double, 2 twin
Bathrooms: 2 public

Bed & breakfast

per night:	£min	£max
Single	20.00	20.00
Double	30.00	32.00

Parking for 8

🐕📬🖰🛏Ⓤ🖳Ⓢ✁🎞🖀❄✠🛒

VOWCHURCH

Hereford and Worcester
Map ref 2A1

Village in the Golden Valley by the River Dore and set in beautiful countryside. It has an interesting 14th C church and is close to Abbey Dore with its famous Cistercian church.

Sefton Cottage

Vowchurch Common, Vowchurch,
Hereford HR2 0RL
☎ Peterchurch (01981) 550319
Superb views in peaceful countryside. Many places of interest in the area. Good food.
Bedrooms: 1 double, 1 twin
Bathrooms: 1 public

Bed & breakfast

per night:	£min	£max
Single	15.00	15.00
Double	30.00	30.00

Half board

per person:	£min	£max
Daily	30.00	30.00
Weekly	210.00	210.00

Lunch available
Evening meal 1900 (last orders 2000)
Parking for 4

🛠📬⛛🖰🛏Ⓤ🖰✁🎞🖀♟❄🛒❄

Upper Gilvach Farm ⋀

👑 COMMENDED

St. Margarets, Vowchurch, Hereford
HR2 0QY
☎ Michaelchurch (0198123) 618
90-acre dairy farm. Between Golden Valley and Black Mountains. Very quiet with much historic interest. Family-run.
Bedrooms: 2 double, 1 triple
Bathrooms: 3 private

Bed & breakfast

per night:	£min	£max
Single	18.00	25.00
Double	36.00	50.00

Half board

per person:	£min	£max
Daily	25.00	35.00

Parking for 20

🐕📬🖰Ⓤ🛏🗉📺🎞❄✠🛒

WARWICK

Warwickshire
Map ref 2B1

Castle rising above the River Avon and 15th C Beauchamp Chapel attached to St Mary's Church, medieval Lord Leycester's Hospital almshouses and several museums. Nearby is Ashorne Hall Nickelodeon and the new National Heritage museum at Gaydon.
Tourist Information Centre
☎ (01926) 492212

The Croft ⋀

👑 COMMENDED

Haseley Knob, Warwick CV35 7NL
☎ Haseley Knob (01926) 484447
Fax (01926) 484447
Friendly family atmosphere in picturesque rural setting. In Haseley Knob village off the A4177 between Balsall Common and Warwick, convenient for NEC, National Agricultural Centre, Stratford and Coventry. 15 minutes from Birmingham Airport.
Bedrooms: 1 single, 2 double, 1 twin, 1 triple
Bathrooms: 5 private, 2 public

Bed & breakfast

per night:	£min	£max
Single	19.50	30.00
Double	40.00	44.00

Parking for 10

🐕📬⛛📬🖰🛏Ⓤ🖰✁📺🎞🖀❄🛒Ⓢ🅣

30 Eastley Crescent ⋀

👑 HIGHLY COMMENDED

Warwick CV34 5RX
☎ (01926) 496480
Next to A46 and 5 minutes from the M40. A comfortable, non-smoking establishment.
Bedrooms: 1 single, 1 double

Bathrooms: 1 private, 1 public

Bed & breakfast

per night:	£min	£max
Single	16.00	18.00
Double	32.00	34.00

Parking for 2

🐕8📬🖰🛏Ⓤ🖳Ⓢ✁📺🎞🖀❄✠🛒🆔

Forth House ⋀

👑👑 HIGHLY COMMENDED

44 High Street, Warwick CV34 4AX
☎ (01926) 401512
Ground floor and first floor guest suites with private sitting rooms and bathrooms at the back of the house. Overlooking peaceful garden, in town centre.
Bedrooms: 1 double, 1 twin
Bathrooms: 2 private

Bed & breakfast

per night:	£min	£max
Single	30.00	40.00
Double	40.00	50.00

Parking for 2

🐕📬❄📬🖰🛏Ⓤ🖰🗉✁📺🎞🖀Ⓤ🖊❄🛒Ⓢ🏠

Fulbrook Edge ⋀

👑 COMMENDED

Sherbourne Hill, Warwick CV35 8AG
☎ Barford (01926) 624242
Old-fashioned hospitality in spectacular panoramic surroundings. All rooms at ground level. Privately situated, midway Stratford/Warwick on A46, a few minutes from the M40, junction 15.
Wheelchair access category 3 ♿
Bedrooms: 1 double, 2 twin
Bathrooms: 1 public

Bed & breakfast

per night:	£min	£max
Single	25.00	31.00
Double	38.00	42.00

Parking for 6

❄📬🖰🛏Ⓤ✁📺🎞🖀Ⓤ🖊❄✠🛒🆔Ⓢ🏠

The Gate House ⋀

Listed HIGHLY COMMENDED

75 West Street, Warwick CV34 6AH
☎ (01926) 496965
Fax (01926) 411910

"Dangerfield" country. Centre of Warwick (A429) 15th C timbered property, 100 yards from Warwick Castle. One and a quarter miles from M40 motorway. Non-smoking. "Heartbeat" award 94/95.
Bedrooms: 1 double, 1 twin
Bathrooms: 2 private

Continued ▶

WARWICK
Continued

Bed & breakfast

per night:	£min	£max
Single	30.00	30.00
Double	45.00	50.00

Evening meal 1900 (last orders 2015)
Parking for 4

🛏🕻📠⌂♦🍴📶🛗🛆Ⓢ⊁🅿📺🗔,🛆
✿✕🚲🏧

Longbridge Farm
Listed

Stratford Road, Warwick CV34 6RB
☎ (01926) 401857
*Charming and comfortable 16th C
farmhouse set in 20 acres of meadows,
1.5 miles from Warwick town centre on
A429 and convenient for the M40.*
Bedrooms: 2 double, 1 twin; suite
available
Bathrooms: 1 private, 1 public

Bed & breakfast

per night:	£min	£max
Single	25.00	25.00
Double	36.00	40.00

Parking for 4

🛏🚲♦🅿📶Ⓢ⊁🅿📺🗔.🛆✕☍🔍♆🍴
✿🚲🏧

Lower Watchbury Farm ♈
☟☟ COMMENDED

Wasperton Lane, Barford, Warwick
CV35 1DH
☎ (01926) 624772
*50-acre mixed farm. Well-appointed
accommodation on working farm, in
rural surroundings outside Barford.
M40 2 miles, Stratford-upon-Avon 7
miles, Warwick 3 miles. All rooms en-
suite, large garden. Good pubs nearby.*
Bedrooms: 1 single, 1 double, 1 triple
Bathrooms: 3 private

Bed & breakfast

per night:	£min	£max
Single	19.50	21.50
Double	39.00	43.00

Parking for 3

🛏🚲🖳♦🅿📶Ⓢ⊁🅿📺🗔.🛆
🕯6✿🏧SP

Merrywood
Listed HIGHLY COMMENDED

Hampton on the Hill, Warwick
CV35 8QR
☎ (01926) 492766
*Family house in small village 2 miles
from Warwick, with open views from
both of the rooms.*
Bedrooms: 1 single, 1 twin
Bathrooms: 2 public

Bed & breakfast

per night:	£min	£max
Single	17.50	18.50
Double	27.50	30.00

Parking for 3

🛏1🗡🖳♦🅿📶Ⓢ🗔.🛆✿✕🏧

Northleigh House ♈
☟☟ HIGHLY COMMENDED

Five Ways Road, Hatton, Warwick
CV35 7HZ
☎ (01926) 484203 & Mobile 0374
101894
Fax (01926) 484006

*Comfortable, peaceful country house
where the elegant rooms are
individually designed and have en-suite
bathroom, fridge, kettle and remote-
control TV.*
Bedrooms: 1 single, 5 double, 1 twin
Bathrooms: 7 private

Bed & breakfast

per night:	£min	£max
Single	28.00	38.00
Double	38.00	55.00

Parking for 8
Open February-November
Cards accepted: Access, Visa

🛏🚲📠🖳♦🅿📶Ⓢ⊁🅿📺🗔.🛆✿🏧

Old Rectory ♈

Vicarage Lane, Sherbourne, Warwick
CV35 8AB
☎ Barford (01926) 624562
Fax (01926) 624562

*Georgian country house with beams and
inglenook fireplaces, furnished with
antiques. Well-appointed bedrooms,
many with brass beds, some with direct-
dial telephones, all with en-suite
facilities and colour TV. Hearty
breakfast, tray supper. Situated half a
mile from M40 junction 15.*
Bedrooms: 4 single, 6 double, 2 twin,
1 triple, 1 family room
Bathrooms: 14 private

Bed & breakfast

per night:	£min	£max
Single	32.50	39.00
Double	39.50	53.00

Evening meal 1800 (last orders 2200)
Parking for 14
Cards accepted: Access, Visa, Switch/
Delta

🛏🚲🖳♦Ⓢ🅿🗔.🛆🕯10✿SP🏧

The Seven Stars Public House
Listed

Friars Street, Warwick CV34 6HD
☎ (01926) 492658
*Black and white inn, built in 1610.
Near town centre and racecourse and*

*just a few minutes' walk from Warwick
Castle. Five minutes from M40.*
Bedrooms: 2 twin
Bathrooms: 1 public

Bed & breakfast

per night:	£min	£max
Single	16.00	20.00
Double	28.00	33.00

Half board

per person:	£min	£max
Daily	19.00	23.00
Weekly	133.00	161.00

Lunch available
Evening meal from 1900
Parking for 8
Cards accepted: Visa

🛏🗡🚲♦Ⓢ🗔.🛆✿🏧🏧

Shrewley House ♈
☟☟ HIGHLY COMMENDED

Hockley Road, Shrewley, Warwick
CV35 7AT
☎ Claverdon (0192684) 2549
Fax (0192684) 2216
*Listed 17th C farmhouse and home set
amidst beautiful 1.5 acre gardens. King-
sized four-poster bedrooms, all en-suite,
with many thoughtful extras. Four miles
from Warwick.*
Bedrooms: 3 double
Bathrooms: 3 private

Bed & breakfast

per night:	£min	£max
Single	42.00	
Double	62.00	

Evening meal from 1930
Parking for 17
Cards accepted: Access, Visa

🛏🚲🕻📠🖳♦🅿📶🛗Ⓢ⊁🅿📺🗔.
🛆☍✕🏧🏧

Shrewley Pools Farm ♈
Listed COMMENDED

Haseley, Warwick CV35 7HB
☎ (01926) 484315
*260-acre mixed farm. Traditional mid-
17th C beamed farmhouse set in 1 acre
of gardens. 5 miles north of Warwick
on the A4177.*
Bedrooms: 1 twin, 1 triple
Bathrooms: 1 private, 1 public

Bed & breakfast

per night:	£min	£max
Single	19.00	25.00
Double	36.00	45.00

Half board

per person:	£min	£max
Daily	25.00	33.00
Weekly	175.00	220.00

Lunch available
Evening meal 1800 (last orders 2100)
Parking for 10

🛏🚲♦📶🛗Ⓢ🅿⊁🅿📺🛆☍🏴✿DAP
SP🏧

Tudor House Inn ♈
☟☟

90-92 West Street, Warwick
CV34 6AW
☎ (01926) 495447
Fax (01926) 492948

Inn of character dating from 1472, with a wealth of beams. One of the few buildings to survive the great fire of Warwick in 1694. Opposite Warwick Castle and close to Warwick racecourse.
Bedrooms: 3 single, 5 double, 2 twin, 1 family room
Bathrooms: 6 private, 1 public, 2 private showers

Bed & breakfast

per night:	£min	£max
Single	24.00	
Double		54.00

Lunch available
Evening meal 1800 (last orders 2300)
Parking for 6
Cards accepted: Access, Visa, Diners, Amex, Switch/Delta

Woodside

Langley Road, Claverdon, Warwick CV35 8PJ
☎ Claverdon (0192684) 2446
Charming country house with acres of garden and woodland nature reserve. Full central heating, open fires, good home cooking. Very central for Stratford-upon-Avon and Warwick.
Wheelchair access category 3
Bedrooms: 1 single, 1 double, 2 twin, 1 triple
Bathrooms: 2 public

Bed & breakfast

per night:	£min	£max
Single	18.00	23.00
Double	36.00	40.00

Half board

per person:	£min	£max
Daily	26.00	35.00
Weekly	175.00	217.00

Lunch available
Evening meal 1930 (last orders 1400)
Parking for 13

WATERHOUSES

Staffordshire
Map ref 4B2

Village in the valley of the River Hamps, once the terminus of the Leek and Manifold Light Railway, 8 miles of which is now a macadamised walkers' path.

Ye Olde Crown

APPROVED

Leek Road, Waterhouses, Stoke-on-Trent ST10 3HL
☎ (01538) 308204
17th C coaching inn, on the edge of the Peak District National Park and at the start of the beautiful Manifold Valley. It is built of natural stone and has a wealth of original oak beams.
Bedrooms: 2 single, 3 double, 1 twin, 1 family room
Bathrooms: 5 private, 1 public

Bed & breakfast

per night:	£min	£max
Single	15.00	22.50
Double	30.00	35.00

Half board

per person:	£min	£max
Daily	21.00	35.00
Weekly	145.00	245.00

Lunch available
Evening meal 1900 (last orders 2200)
Parking for 50

WEM

Shropshire
Map ref 4A3

Small town connected with Judge Jeffreys who lived in Lowe Hall. Well known for its ales.

Chez Michael

Listed

23 Roden Grove, Wem, Shrewsbury SY4 5HJ
☎ (01939) 232947
Family-run, large bungalow and conservatory, suitable for the elderly - children welcome. Garden. Hawkstone Follies a short car ride away. Also convenient for medieval Shrewsbury. Local produce and meat used.
Bedrooms: 1 single, 2 double
Bathrooms: 1 private, 1 public

Bed & breakfast

per night:	£min	£max
Single	14.00	16.00
Double	28.00	34.00

Half board

per person:	£min	£max
Daily	20.00	22.00
Weekly	130.00	150.00

Evening meal 1700 (last orders 1830)
Parking for 2

Forncet

Listed COMMENDED

Soulton Road, Wem, Shrewsbury SY4 5HR
☎ (01939) 232996
Spacious, centrally heated Victorian house on the edge of this small market town, 200 yards from British Rail station.
Bedrooms: 1 single, 1 twin, 1 triple
Bathrooms: 2 public

Bed & breakfast

per night:	£min	£max
Single	12.00	15.00
Double	24.00	30.00

Half board

per person:	£min	£max
Daily		23.00
Weekly	140.00	

Evening meal 1830 (last orders 1930)
Parking for 6

Lowe Hall Farm

Wem, Shrewsbury SY4 5UE
☎ (01939) 232236
150-acre dairy farm. Historically famous Grade II listed farmhouse, once the country residence of Judge Jeffreys, 1648-1689. High standard of food, decor and accommodation guaranteed.
Bedrooms: 1 double, 1 twin, 1 triple
Bathrooms: 1 private, 1 public

Bed & breakfast

per night:	£min	£max
Single	17.50	17.50
Double	32.00	32.00

Half board

per person:	£min	£max
Daily	23.00	23.00
Weekly	147.00	147.00

Evening meal 1830 (last orders 1930)
Parking for 8

Soulton Hall

COMMENDED

Wem, Shrewsbury SY4 5RS
☎ (01939) 232786
Fax (01939) 234097
Super home cooking and en-suite rooms at this Tudor manor house ensure a relaxing holiday. Moated Domesday site in grounds, private riverside and woodland walks.
Bedrooms: 1 single, 3 double, 1 twin, 1 triple
Bathrooms: 6 private

Bed & breakfast

per night:	£min	£max
Single	23.50	35.00
Double	44.00	58.00

Half board

per person:	£min	£max
Daily	39.25	50.75
Weekly	247.00	319.72

Evening meal 1900 (last orders 2030)
Parking for 23
Cards accepted: Access, Visa, Diners

WEOBLEY

Hereford and Worcester
Map ref 2A1

One of the most beautiful Herefordshire villages, full of framed houses, at the heart of the Black and White Trail. It is dominated by the church which has a fine spire.

Hill Top Farm

COMMENDED

Wormsley, Hereford HR4 8LZ
☎ Bridge Sollars (01981) 590246
200-acre arable & livestock farm. Comfortable stone-built farmhouse under brow of hill, deep in the

Continued ►

WEOBLEY

Continued

*Herefordshire countryside. Magnificent
views over fields and woods to Black
Mountains. On Black and White Trail.*
Bedrooms: 1 twin, 1 triple
Bathrooms: 2 private

Bed & breakfast

per night:	£min	£max
Single		15.00
Double	30.00	35.00

Parking for 6
Open February-November
🐾 ♨ 🆄🅻 Ⓢ ⌨ 📺 🏧 ❀ 🚐

WHITNEY-ON-WYE

Hereford and Worcester
Map ref 2A1

Here the main Hereford to Brecon
road crosses into Wales and
nearby the Wye is spanned by its
only surviving toll bridge,
unfortunately damaged by floods,
the owners of which are exempt,
by the terms of an Act of George
III, from payment of taxes.

The Rhydspence Inn 𝔐
☗☗☗ HIGHLY COMMENDED

Whitney-on-Wye, Hereford HR3 6EU
☎ Clifford (01497) 831262
*14th C black and white country inn
offering food and hospitality, in superb
Wye Valley and Black Mountains
countryside.*
Bedrooms: 1 single, 4 double, 2 twin
Bathrooms: 7 private

Bed & breakfast

per night:	£min	£max
Single	27.50	32.50
Double	55.00	75.00

Lunch available
Evening meal 1900 (last orders 2130)
Parking for 60
Cards accepted: Access, Visa, Amex
🐾 🏠 🖵 ♨ Ⓢ 🏧 🏧 🚪 ♨ ❀ ✗ 🚐 🆂🅿 🏬

WHITTINGTON

Staffordshire
Map ref 4B3

The Dog Inn & Restaurant
☗ COMMENDED

Main Street, Whittington, Lichfield
WS14 9JU
☎ Lichfield (01543) 432252
*17th C inn with bar and restaurant.
Open seven days a week. Bar meals,
real ales. Off the A51 Lichfield to
Tamworth road.*
Bedrooms: 3 single, 1 double, 2 twin
Bathrooms: 6 private showers

Bed & breakfast

per night:	£min	£max
Single		28.20
Double		39.90

Lunch available
Evening meal 1800 (last orders 2130)

Parking for 40
Cards accepted: Access, Visa, Diners,
Amex, Switch/Delta
🐾 🖵 ♨ 🛈 Ⓢ ⌨ 📺 🏧 🚪 🍴 ✝ ❀ 🚐 ✗ 🏬

WIGMORE

Hereford and Worcester
Map ref 4A3

Village with a Norman church and
some attractive half-timbered
houses. There are the remains of
Wigmore Castle and Wigmore
Abbey. Croft Castle (National
Trust) is nearby.

Compasses Hotel 𝔐
Listed APPROVED

Ford Street, Wigmore, Leominster,
Herefordshire HR6 9UN
☎ (0156886) 203
*Hotel, country pub and restaurant, set
in rural surroundings. Ideal for touring
the Marches. Walkers and cyclists
welcome.*
Bedrooms: 1 double, 2 twin
Bathrooms: 1 public

Bed & breakfast

per night:	£min	£max
Single	18.00	18.00
Double	36.00	36.00

Half board

per person:	£min	£max
Daily	25.00	25.00
Weekly	157.50	157.50

Lunch available
Evening meal 1830 (last orders 2130)
Parking for 70
Cards accepted: Access, Visa, Diners,
Amex
🐾 🖵 ♨ 🍺 🛈 Ⓢ ⌨ 📺 🏧 🚪 🍴50 ♨ ♨ ❀ 🚐 🅾🅰🅿 🆂🅿 🏬

WILMCOTE

Warwickshire
Map ref 2B1

Village where Shakespeare's
mother, Mary Arden, lived. Her
home has an attractive cottage
garden and now houses a
museum of rural life.

Dosthill Cottage
☗☗

The Green, Wilmcote, Stratford-upon-
Avon CV37 9XJ
☎ Stratford-upon-Avon (01789)
266480
Fax (01789) 266480
*Old cottage on the village green,
overlooking Mary Arden's house, with
pleasant garden available to guests.*
Bedrooms: 2 double, 1 twin
Bathrooms: 3 private

Bed & breakfast

per night:	£min	£max
Double	38.00	42.00

Parking for 6
🐾 🚲 🖵 🖵 ♨ 🆄🅻 📺 🏧 🚪 ❀ 🚐 🏬

WINCHCOMBE

Gloucestershire
Map ref 2B1

Ancient town with a folk museum
and railway museum. To the south
lies Sudeley Castle with its fine
collection of paintings and toys
and an Elizabethan garden.

Isbourne Manor House
☗☗ DE LUXE

Castle Street, Winchcombe,
Cheltenham GL54 5JA
☎ Cheltenham (01242) 602281

*Listed part-Georgian, part-Elizabethan
house overlooking grounds of Sudeley
Castle and situated within attractive
gardens bordered by the River Isbourne.
2 minutes from both open countryside
and town centre. Spacious rooms with
en-suite facilities.*
Bedrooms: 2 double, 1 twin
Bathrooms: 3 private

Bed & breakfast

per night:	£min	£max
Single	30.00	45.00
Double	40.00	50.00

Parking for 5
🐾 10 🎛 🖵 ♨ 🍺 🆄🅻 🗡 📺 🏧 🚪 ♨ ❀ ✗ 🚐 🆂🅿 🏬

Manor Farm
☗☗

Greet, Winchcombe, Cheltenham
GL54 5BJ
☎ Cheltenham (01242) 602423
*400-acre mixed farm. Cotswolds manor
in quiet hamlet. Good views of Cotswold
Escarpment and steam railway. Near
racecourse. Picturesque, well-equipped
holiday cottages also available.*
Bedrooms: 2 double, 1 twin
Bathrooms: 3 private

Bed & breakfast

per night:	£min	£max
Single	20.00	
Double	40.00	

Parking for 10
Open January-November
🐾 🖵 ♨ 🆄🅻 🗡 📺 🏧 🚪 🍴10 ♨ 🔺 ❀ ✗ 🚐 🏬

Mercia
☗☗ COMMENDED

Hailes Street, Winchcombe,
Cheltenham GL54 5HU
☎ Cheltenham (01242) 602251
*Black and white Cotswold-stone Tudor
cottage with beamed walls and ceilings.
Private parking at rear. Pleasant garden
and views. 15 minutes from M5.*
Bedrooms: 2 double, 1 twin

Bathrooms: 3 private
Bed & breakfast

per night:	£min	£max
Single	18.00	20.00
Double	34.00	36.00

Parking for 3

☎ ♨ ⬚ 🛅 🅂 ⚡ 🅟 📺 🛏 ⬚ ⏰ ✿ 🐎 ⬚ 🅞🅐🅟 🏠

Old White Lion Inn ⋀

⬚ ⬚ ⬚ **COMMENDED**

37 North Street, Winchcombe,
Cheltenham GL54 5PS
☎ Cheltenham (01242) 603300
Fax (01242) 251694
Of 15th C origins and a coaching inn since 1700s. Recently refurbished and now operating as a small hotel and restaurant with public bar. In centre of town.
Bedrooms: 1 single, 4 double, 1 twin
Bathrooms: 6 private
Bed & breakfast

per night:	£min	£max
Single	32.50	38.50
Double	52.50	67.50

Lunch available
Evening meal 1900 (last orders 2230)
Cards accepted: Access, Visa, Amex, Switch/Delta

☎ 🛋 ⬚ ⬚ ♨ 🅂 🅟 🛏 ⬚ ⬚ ✿ 🐎 ⬚ 🆂🅿 🏠 🆃

The Plaisterers Arms ⋀

⬚ ⬚ **APPROVED**

Abbey Terrace, Winchcombe,
Cheltenham GL54 5LL
☎ Cheltenham (01242) 602358
Fax (01242) 602358

Old Cotswold stone inn with en-suite bed and breakfast accommodation, close to Sudeley Castle and town centre. Extensive menu, pub lunches, bar snacks and evening meals available every day. Large garden, patio and children's area.
Bedrooms: 2 double, 1 twin
Bathrooms: 3 private, 1 public
Bed & breakfast

per night:	£min	£max
Single	20.00	25.00
Double	30.00	40.00

Lunch available
Evening meal 1830 (last orders 2130)
Cards accepted: Access, Visa, Amex, Switch/Delta

☎ 🛋 ⬚ ♨ 🅂 🅟 ⬚ ⚡ ✿ 🐎 🅞🅐🅟 🆂🅿 🏠

Postlip Hall Farm ⋀

⬚ ⬚ **HIGHLY COMMENDED**

Winchcombe, Cheltenham GL54 5AQ
☎ Cheltenham (01242) 603351

300-acre mixed farm. Family farm in superb scenic location 1 mile from Winchcombe, on side of Cleeve Hill. Perfect centre for touring the Cotswolds, Bath, Warwick. Beautiful surroundings, wonderful atmosphere.
Bedrooms: 1 double, 1 twin, 1 triple
Bathrooms: 3 private
Bed & breakfast

per night:	£min	£max
Single	20.00	25.00
Double	36.00	40.00

Parking for 6

☎ ⬚ ⬚ ♨ ⚡ 🅟 🅂 ⚡ 📺 ⬚ ⬚ ⬚ 🅟 ✿ ✿ 🐎 🏠

WOOTTON WAWEN

Warwickshire
Map ref 2B1

Attractive village which has an unspoilt church with an Anglo-Saxon tower, the only chained library in Warwickshire and some good brasses and monuments.

Wootton Park Farm

⬚ ⬚

Alcester Road, Wootton Wawen,
Solihull, West Midlands B95 6HJ
☎ Henley-in-Arden (01564) 792673

340-acre arable & dairy farm. Delightful 16th C half-timbered farmhouse with a wealth of oak beams. 5 miles north of Stratford-upon-Avon in quiet countryside. Conveniently situated for National Agricultural Centre and National Exhibition Centre.
Bedrooms: 1 double, 1 triple, 1 family room
Bathrooms: 1 private, 1 public
Bed & breakfast

per night:	£min	£max
Single	22.00	25.00
Double	38.00	42.00

Parking for 6

☎ ⬚ ♨ 🅄🅻 🅂 🅟 📺 ⬚ ⬚ 🅣10 ⚡ ✿ ✿ 🐎 🏠

Yew Tree Farm ⋀

⬚ ⬚ **COMMENDED**

Wootton Wawen, Solihull, West Midlands B95 6BY
☎ Henley-in-Arden (01564) 792701
800-acre arable & dairy farm. Fine Georgian farmhouse conveniently situated in village on the A3400, 5 miles from Stratford-upon-Avon. Large en-suite bedrooms, with tea/coffee facilities. Hearty English breakfast. Farm walks.
Bedrooms: 1 double, 1 twin
Bathrooms: 2 private

Bed & breakfast

per night:	£min	£max
Single		22.50
Double		36.00

Parking for 12

☎ 5 ⬚ ⬚ ♨ ⚡ 🅄🅻 ⬚ 🅟 📺 ⬚ ⬚ ⬚ ✿ ✿ 🐎 🏠

WORCESTER

Hereford and Worcester
Map ref 2B1

Lovely riverside city dominated by its Norman and Early English cathedral, King John's burial place. Many old buildings including the 15th C Commandery and the 18th C Guildhall. There are several museums and the Royal Worcester porcelain factory.
Tourist Information Centre
☎ *(01905) 726311*

40 Britannia Square ⋀

⬚ ⬚ **HIGHLY COMMENDED**

Worcester WR1 3DN
☎ (01905) 611920
Fax (01905) 27152
Beautiful listed Georgian house in quiet conservation square, close to city centre and M5. Featured by interior design magazines and BBC. Lovely garden and courtyard.
Bedrooms: 1 double, 2 twin
Bathrooms: 3 private
Bed & breakfast

per night:	£min	£max
Single	30.00	40.00
Double	40.00	50.00

Half board

per person:	£min	£max
Daily	40.00	50.00

Parking for 2

☎ 5 ⬚ ⬚ ⬚ ♨ ⚡ 🅄🅻 ⚡ 🅟 📺 ⬚ ⬚ ✿ ✿ 🐎 🏠

Burgage House ⋀

Listed

4 College Precincts, Worcester
WR1 2LG
☎ (01905) 25396
Comfortable accommodation in elegant Georgian mews house in quiet cobbled street next to cathedral. Close to River Severn and cricket ground.
Bedrooms: 1 single, 1 double, 1 twin, 1 family room
Bathrooms: 1 private, 2 public
Bed & breakfast

per night:	£min	£max
Single	24.00	26.00
Double	36.00	44.00

☎ 🛋 ⬚ ♨ 🅄🅻 🅂 ⚡ 🅟 ⬚ ⬚ ✿ 🐎 🅞🅐🅟 🆂🅿 🏠 🆃

Ivy Cottage ⋀

⬚ ⬚ **COMMENDED**

Sinton Green, Hallow, Worcester
WR2 6NP
☎ (01905) 641123

Continued ▶

WORCESTER

Continued

Charming cottage in quiet village, 4 miles north of Worcester, off A443 Worcester to Tenbury road. Good local restaurants.
Bedrooms: 1 single, 1 double, 1 twin
Bathrooms: 3 private

Bed & breakfast

per night:	£min	£max
Single		20.00
Double		35.00

Parking for 4

Little Lightwood Farm

⚬⚬ COMMENDED

Lightwood Lane, Cotheridge,
Worcester WR6 5LT
☎ Cotheridge (01905) 333236
56-acre dairy farm. Farmhouse accommodation with en-suite rooms, tea-making facilities and heating in all bedrooms. Delightful views of the Malvern Hills. Just off the A44 from Worcester to Leominster, 3.5 miles from Worcester.
Bedrooms: 2 double, 1 twin
Bathrooms: 3 private

Bed & breakfast

per night:	£min	£max
Single	20.00	22.00
Double	34.00	36.00

Half board

per person:	£min	£max
Daily	49.00	51.00
Weekly	218.50	225.50

Evening meal from 1800
Parking for 6
Open February-November

Loch Ryan Hotel ⋀

⚬⚬⚬

119 Sidbury, Worcester WR5 2DH
☎ (01905) 351143
Fax (01905) 764407
Historic hotel, once home of Bishop Gore, close to cathedral, Royal Worcester Porcelain factory and Commandery. Attractive terraced garden. Imaginative food. Holders of Heartbeat and Worcester City clean food awards.
Bedrooms: 1 single, 3 double, 5 twin, 1 family room
Bathrooms: 10 private

Bed & breakfast

per night:	£min	£max
Single	30.00	40.00
Double	45.00	50.00

Evening meal 1800 (last orders 1900)
Parking for 10
Cards accepted: Access, Visa, Diners, Amex

Park House Hotel ⋀

⚬⚬ APPROVED

12 Droitwich Road, Worcester
WR3 7LJ
☎ (01905) 21816 & 612029
Fax (01905) 612178
Family-run Victorian guesthouse, near city centre, racecourse and cricket. Close junction 6 of M5. Friendly, informal atmosphere.
Bedrooms: 1 single, 3 double, 2 twin, 1 family room
Bathrooms: 4 private, 1 public

Bed & breakfast

per night:	£min	£max
Single	24.00	
Double	34.00	

Lunch available
Evening meal 1830 (last orders 1930)
Parking for 10
Cards accepted: Access, Visa

Retreat Farm ⋀

Listed HIGHLY COMMENDED

Camp Lane, Grimley, Worcester
WR2 6LU
☎ (01905) 640266
60-acre arable farm. 17th C farmhouse, overlooking River Severn and Bevere Lock. Within walking distance of the Camp House Inn and Wagon Wheel Restaurant.
Bedrooms: 2 double
Bathrooms: 2 private

Bed & breakfast

per night:	£min	£max
Single		20.00
Double		38.00

Parking for 14
Open April-October

WOTTON-UNDER-EDGE

Gloucestershire
Map ref 2B2

Small Cotswold town with a replica of the Orpheus Pavement, a Roman mosaic, in the Tabernacle Church. Berkeley Castle is within easy reach.

Hillesley Mill

⚬⚬

Alderley, Wotton-under-Edge
GL12 7QT
☎ Dursley (01453) 843258
Easily accessible converted cotton/woollen mill, nestling in undulating fields and prolific woodland, overlooking a mill lake and stream.
Bedrooms: 1 double, 1 twin
Bathrooms: 2 private

> We advise you to confirm your booking in writing.

Bed & breakfast

per night:	£min	£max
Single	20.00	23.00
Double	36.00	40.00

Parking for 8

WYE VALLEY

See under Fownhope, Hereford, Ross-on-Wye

YARKHILL

Hereford and Worcester
Map ref 2B1

Thatched cottages, oasthouses and a medieval church among the old hopfields and orchards.

Garford Farm ⋀

Listed

Yarkhill, Hereford HR1 3ST
☎ Tarrington (01432) 890226
Fax (01432) 890707
190-acre mixed farm. Picturesque black and white farmhouse on working farm. Very quiet but with easy access to the A4103 Hereford to Worcester road.
Bedrooms: 1 double, 1 family room
Bathrooms: 2 private, 1 public

Bed & breakfast

per night:	£min	£max
Double	32.00	40.00

Parking for 6

YOXALL

Staffordshire
Map ref 4B3

Small village near the Needwood Forest north of Lichfield. Once the home of Thomas Gisborne, booklover and campaigner against slavery.

The Moat ⋀

⚬⚬ HIGHLY COMMENDED

Town Hill, Yoxall, Burton upon Trent
DE13 8NN
☎ Burton upon Trent (01543) 472210
Country house sited in 2.5 acres of garden, dry moated, of historic interest. Grounds listed Grade II.
Wheelchair access category 3 ♿
Bedrooms: 3 twin
Bathrooms: 3 private, 1 public

Bed & breakfast

per night:	£min	£max
Single	25.00	30.00
Double	45.00	55.00

Half board

per person:	£min	£max
Daily	40.00	45.00

Parking for 6

Middle England

From the craggy heights of the High Peaks to the rich dark fenlands which run to the sea –
there are many landscapes to be discovered in Middle England.

Drive through gentle shire countryside and you'll find ancient forests and quiet waterways to explore. Here too are some of England's loveliest stately homes: treasure-filled Belvoir Castle; breathtaking Chatsworth; romantic Newstead Abbey.

Make sure you visit some of the region's fascinating towns – Lincoln for its vast cathedral, Buxton for its spa-town elegance, Skegness for a breezy, bracing day by the sea. Finally, of course, no visit to Middle England is complete without a merrie sortie to Robin Hood's Sherwood, or one of the region's many other family attractions.

The Counties of Derbyshire, Leicestershire, Lincolnshire, Northamptonshire and Nottinghamshire
For more information on Middle England, contact:
East Midlands Tourist Board
Exchequergate, Lincoln LN2 1PZ
Tel: (01522) 531521
Fax: (01522) 532501
Where to Go in Middle England –
see pages 178–181
Where to Stay in Middle England –
see pages 182–200

Middle England

Where to go and what to see

You will find hundreds of interesting places to visit during your stay in Middle England, just some of which are listed in these pages. The number against each name will help you locate it on the map (page 181). Contact any Tourist Information Centre in the region for more ideas on days out in Middle England.

1 Gainsborough Old Hall
Parnell Street, Gainsborough,
Lincolnshire DN21 2NB
Tel: (01427) 612669
Late medieval timber-framed manor house built c1460, with fine medieval kitchen. Displays on the building and its restoration.

2 Buxton Micrarium
The Crescent, Buxton,
Derbyshire SK17 6BQ
Tel: (01298) 78662
Unique exhibition of the natural world under the microscope, using special push-button projection microscopes operated by visitors.

3 Lincoln Cathedral
Lincoln LN2 1PZ
Tel: (01522) 544544
Medieval Gothic cathedral of outstanding historical and architectural merit.

4 Museum of Lincolnshire Life
Burton Road, Lincoln LN1 3LY
Tel: (01522) 528448
Agricultural, industrial and social history of Lincolnshire from 1800. Edwardian room setting. Display of craftwork in progress. World War I tank on display.

5 Chatsworth House and Garden, Farmyard and Adventure Playground
Chatsworth, Bakewell,
Derbyshire DE45 1PP
Tel: (01246) 582204
Built 1687–1707. Collection of fine pictures, books, drawings, furniture. Garden laid out by Capability Brown with fountains, cascade. Farmyard with livestock, adventure playground.

6 The Heights of Abraham
Matlock Bath, Matlock,
Derbyshire DE4 3PD
Tel: (01629) 582365
Cable car ride across Derwent Valley gives access to Alpine Centre with refreshments, superb views, woodland, prospect tower and two show caves.

7 The National Tramway Museum
Crich, Derbyshire DE4 5DP
Tel: (01773) 852565
Collection of 50 trams from Britain and overseas built 1873–1953. Tram rides on one-mile route, period street scene, depots, power station, workshops.

8 Midland Railway Centre
Butterley Station, Ripley,
Derbyshire DE5 3TL
Tel: (01773) 747674
Over 25 locomotives and over 80 items of historic rolling stock of Midland and LMS origin. Steam-hauled passenger service, museum site, country park.

⑨ White Post Modern Farm Centre
Farnsfield, Nr Newark,
Nottinghamshire
NG22 8HL
Tel: (01623) 882977
Working farm with over 2,000 animals, including llama. 8,000-egg incubator, free-range hens, lakes, picnic areas, tea gardens, indoor countryside night walk.

⑩ Southwell Minster
Bishop's Drive, Southwell,
Nottinghamshire NG25 0JP
Tel: (01636) 812649
Saxon tympanum, Norman nave and crossing, Early English choir, outstanding foliage carving in Chapter House. Ruins of archbishop's palace.

⑪ American Adventure
Pit Lane, Ilkeston, Derbyshire
DE7 5SX
Tel: (01773) 531521
American theme park with more than 100 rides including Nightmare Niagara, Log Flume, Rocky Mountain, Rapids Ride, The Missile. Motion Master Simulator Cinema and many other attractions.

⑫ Nottingham Industrial Museum
Courtyard Buildings, Wollaton Park, Nottingham NG8 2AE
Tel: (0115) 928 4602

18th C stables presenting history of Nottingham's industries: printing, pharmacy, hosiery and lace. Victorian beam engine, horse gin, transport.

⑬ The Tales of Robin Hood
30–38 Maid Marian Way,
Nottingham NG1 6GF
Tel: (0115) 941 4414
Join the world's greatest medieval adventure and hide out in the Sheriff's eerie cave. Ride through the magical Greenwood and play the Silver Arrow game.

⑭ Belvoir Castle
Belvoir, Lincolnshire NG32 1PD
Tel: (01476) 870262
Present castle is fourth to be built on the site, dating from 1816. Museum of Queen's Royal Lancers. Art treasures include works by Poussin, Rubens, Holbein, Reynolds.

⑮ Belton House, Park and Gardens
Belton, Lincolnshire NG32 2LS
Tel: (01476) 66116
The crowning achievement of Restoration country house architecture, built in 1685–88 for Sir John Brownlow. Alterations by James Wyatt in 1777.

⑯ Sudbury Hall
Sudbury, Derbyshire DE6 5HT
Tel: (01283) 585305
Grand 17th C house. Plasterwork

ceilings, ceiling paintings, carved staircase and overmantel. Museum of Childhood in former servants' wing.

⑰ Great Central Railway
Great Central Station, Great Central Road, Loughborough, Leicestershire LE11 1RW
Tel: (01509) 230726
Preserved mainline steam railway operating over 8.5 miles between Loughborough and Leicester North.

⑱ Ye Olde Pork Pie Shoppe
10 Nottingham Street, Melton Mowbray, Leicestershire
LE13 1NW
Tel: (01664) 62341
Pork pie shop and bakery in 17th C building. History of the town's pork pie industry, demonstrations of traditional craft of hand raising pork pies.

⑲ Spalding Tropical Forest
Glenside North, Pinchbeck,
Spalding, Lincolnshire PE11 3SD
Tel: (01775) 710882
One half acre glass house enclosing a tropical environment. Four zones including Tasmanian Rain Forest, Japanese and Australian Tropical plants and Mediterranean Temperate Zone.

⑳ Springfields
Camelgate, Spalding, Lincolnshire
PE12 6ET
Tel: (01775) 724843

25 acres of landscaped gardens with lake, woodland walk and palm house. New exhibition centre houses various events throughout the year.

21 Oakham Castle

Oakham, Leicestershire
Tel: (01572) 723654
Splendid 12th C great hall of fortified manor house. Unique horseshoe forfeits left by peers of the realm.

22 Newarke Houses Museum

The Newarke, Leicester LE2 7BY
Tel: (0116) 247 3222
Local history and crafts from 1485. Toys and games, clocks, mechanical instruments. 19th C street scene, early 20th C shop. Feature on Daniel Lambert, the 19th C giant.

23 Twycross Zoo

Twycross, Leicestershire
CV9 3PX
Tel: (01827) 880250
Gorillas, orang-utans, chimpanzees, modern gibbon complex, elephants, lions, cheetahs, giraffes, reptile house, pets' corner, rides.

24 Rockingham Castle

Rockingham, Leicestershire
LE16 8TH
Tel: (01536) 770240
Elizabethan house within walls of Norman castle. Fine pictures. Extensive views and gardens with roses and ancient yew hedge.

25 Stanford Hall and Motorcycle Museum

Lutterworth, Leicestershire
LE17 6DH
Tel: (01788) 860250
William and Mary house on River Avon. Family costumes, furniture and pictures. Replica 1898 flying machine, motorcycle museum, rose garden, nature trail. Craft centre most Sundays.

26 Holdenby House Gardens

Holdenby, Northampton
NN6 8DJ
Tel: (01604) 770074
Remains of Elizabethan gardens with original entrance arches and terraces. King Charles Walk. Museum, craft shop, rare breeds of farm animals, falconry centre.

27 Sulgrave Manor

Sulgrave, Northampton OX17 2SD
Tel: (01295) 760205
Small manor house of Shakespeare's time with furniture of period and fine kitchen. Early English home of ancestors of George Washington.

Find Out More

Further information about holidays and attractions in Middle England is available from:
East Midlands Tourist Board,
Exchequergate, Lincoln
LN2 1PZ
Tel: (01522) 531521

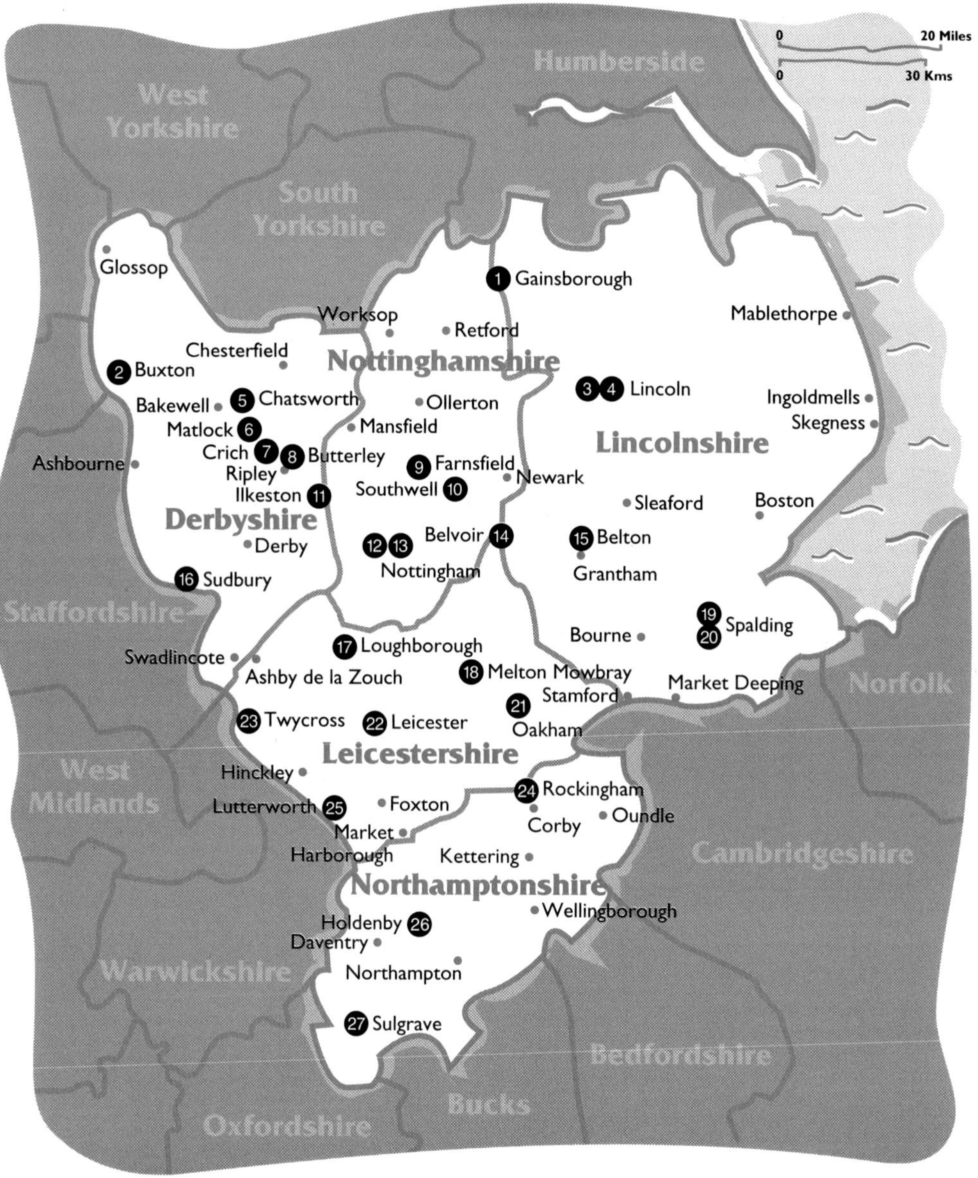

0
20 Miles
0
30 Kms
Humberside
West Yorkshire
South Yorkshire
Glossop
1 Gainsborough
Worksop
Retford
Mablethorpe
Chesterfield
2 Buxton
Nottinghamshire
3 4 Lincoln
Bakewell
5 Chatsworth
Ollerton
Ingoldmells
Matlock 6
Mansfield
Skegness
Lincolnshire
Crich 7
8 Butterley
9 Farnsfield
Ashbourne
Ripley
Newark
Ilkeston 11
Southwell 10
Sleaford
Boston
Derbyshire
Belvoir 14
15 Belton
Derby
12 13
Nottingham
Grantham
16 Sudbury
Staffordshire
19 Spalding 20
Bourne
17 Loughborough
Swadlincote
18 Melton Mowbray
Ashby de la Zouch
Market Deeping
Norfolk
Stamford
21
23 Twycross
22 Leicester
Oakham
Leicestershire
West Midlands
Hinckley
24 Rockingham
Lutterworth 25
Foxton
Corby
Oundle
Market Harborough
Kettering
Cambridgeshire
Northamptonshire
Wellingborough
Holdenby 26
Daventry
Warwickshire
Northampton
27 Sulgrave
Bedfordshire
Bucks
Oxfordshire

These publications are available free from the East Midlands Tourist Board:

- **Short Breaks and Holidays**
- **The Peak District 1996**
- **Bed and Breakfast Touring Map**
- **Camping and Caravaning Touring Map**
- **Events list**

Also available is (price includes postage and packing):

- **Places to Visit** £1.50

WHERE TO STAY

Accommodation entries in this regional section are listed in alphabetical order of place name, and then in alphabetical order of establishment.

Map references refer to the colour location maps at the back of this guide. The first figure is the map number; the letter and figure which follow indicate the grid reference on the map.

At-a-glance symbols at the end of each accommodation entry give information about services and facilities. A handy guide to these symbols can be found inside the back cover flap, which can be kept open for easy reference.

ABTHORPE

Northamptonshire
Map ref 2C1

Three miles south-west of Towcester, formerly owned by the Duke of Grafton.

Stone Cottage
Main Street, Abthorpe, Towcester
NN12 8QN
☎ Silverstone (01327) 857544
Fax (01327) 857544
Grade II listed cottage in delightful secluded position in conservation village. Convenient for Silverstone, Cotswolds, Oxford, M1 and M40 motorways.
Bedrooms: 1 single, 2 twin
Bathrooms: 2 public

Bed & breakfast

per night:	£min	£max
Single		20.00
Double		36.00

Parking for 8
🐎 🖵 💺 🏧 Ⓢ 🛂 ⅲ 🖾 🗖 ✿ 📮 🏦

ALDWARK

Derbyshire
Map ref 4B2

Tithe Farm ⋒
😊😊😊 COMMENDED
Aldwark, Grange Mill, Matlock
DE4 4HX
☎ Carsington (01629) 540263
Peacefully situated, within 10 miles of Matlock, Bakewell, Ashbourne, the dales and historic houses. Extensive breakfast menu with home-made bread and preserves.
Bedrooms: 1 twin, 1 triple
Bathrooms: 2 private

Bed & breakfast

per night:	£min	£max
Single	23.00	24.00
Double	36.00	38.00

Parking for 6
Open April-October
🐎 🖵 💺 🏧 Ⓢ 🛂 ⅲ 🖾 🗖 ✿ 📮 🏦 🏦 Ⓣ

ALKMONTON

Derbyshire
Map ref 4B2

At the end of a 5-mile stretch of straight Roman road, Alkmonton has fantastic views of the surrounding countryside as far as Staffordshire.

Dairy House Farm ⋒
😊😊😊 COMMENDED
Alkmonton, Longford, Ashbourne
DE6 3DG
☎ Ashbourne (01335) 330359
Fax (01335) 330359
82-acre livestock farm. Old red brick farmhouse with oak beams, inglenook fireplace and a comfortable atmosphere. Guests have their own lounge and dining room. Non-smokers only and no pets please. Children over 12 only.
Bedrooms: 3 single, 2 double, 1 twin
Bathrooms: 4 private, 1 public

Bed & breakfast

per night:	£min	£max
Single	16.00	23.00
Double	32.00	38.00

Half board

per person:	£min	£max
Daily	28.00	31.00
Weekly	189.00	210.00

Lunch available
Evening meal 1830 (last orders 1930)
Parking for 8
💺 ？ 🏧 Ⓢ 🛂 🏵 🖾 🖾 🗖 🖎 ✿ 🍴 🏦

ANCASTER

Lincolnshire
Map ref 3A1

Large village on the Roman Ermine Street, within easy drive of Belton House, Grantham and the cathedral city of Lincoln.

Woodlands ⋒
Listed
West Willoughby, Ancaster, Grantham
NG32 3SH
☎ Loveden (01400) 230340

12-acre mixed farm. Victorian stone farmhouse, in peaceful rural surroundings. A warm welcome, comfortable accommodation and traditional farmhouse breakfast. Within easy reach of A1, Grantham, Lincoln and many places of historic interest.
Bedrooms: 1 twin, 1 family room
Bathrooms: 1 public

Bed & breakfast

per night:	£min	£max
Single	16.00	18.00
Double	30.00	32.00

Evening meal 1700 (last orders 2000)
Parking for 6
Open March-November
🐎 🖵 💺 🏧 ⅲ 🏵 🖾 🗖 ✿ 📮

ASHBOURNE

Derbyshire
Map ref 4B2

Market town on the edge of the Peak District National Park and an excellent centre for walking. Its impressive church with 212-ft spire stands in an unspoilt old street. Ashbourne is well-known for gingerbread and its Shrovetide football match.
Tourist Information Centre
☎ *(01335) 343666*

Bentley Brook Inn ⚊

⚊⚊⚊ COMMENDED

Fenny Bentley, Ashbourne DE6 1LF
☎ (01335) 350278
Fax (01335) 350422

Traditional family-run country inn with large garden in Peak District National Park. Close to Dovedale, Alton Towers and Chatsworth.
Bedrooms: 1 single, 5 double, 3 twin; suites available
Bathrooms: 7 private, 2 public

Bed & breakfast

per night:	£min	£max
Single	25.00	37.00
Double	45.00	57.50

Half board

per person:	£min	£max
Daily	36.00	50.00
Weekly	175.00	199.00

Lunch available
Evening meal 1900 (last orders 2130)
Parking for 60
Cards accepted: Access, Visa, Diners, Amex, Switch/Delta

Collycroft Farm

Listed

Clifton, Ashbourne DE6 2GN
☎ (01335) 342187
260-acre mixed farm. A warm welcome is assured in this pleasant farmhouse. Lovely garden and excellent views across the surrounding countryside. South of Ashbourne on the A515 Lichfield road.
Bedrooms: 1 double, 1 twin, 1 triple
Bathrooms: 1 private, 1 public

Bed & breakfast

per night:	£min	£max
Single	15.00	17.00
Double	34.00	36.00

Parking for 8

Little Park Farm

⚊ COMMENDED

Mappleton, Ashbourne DE6 2BR
☎ Thorpe Cloud (01335) 350341
123-acre mixed farm. 300-year-old listed oak-beamed farmhouse, tastefully furnished. In the peaceful Dove Valley, 3 miles from Ashbourne. Superb views.
Bedrooms: 2 double, 1 twin
Bathrooms: 1 public

Bed & breakfast

per night:	£min	£max
Double	29.00	30.00

Evening meal from 1830
Parking for 3
Open March-October

Mercaston Hall ⚊

⚊⚊

Mercaston, Brailsford, Ashbourne DE6 3BL
☎ (01335) 360263 & Mobile 0836 648102
55-acre mixed farm. Listed buildings in attractive, quiet countryside. Hard tennis court. Kedleston Hall (National Trust) 1 mile, Carsington Reservoir 5 minutes away.
Bedrooms: 1 double, 1 twin
Bathrooms: 2 private, 1 public

Bed & breakfast

per night:	£min	£max
Single	20.00	22.50
Double	30.00	36.00

Parking for 16

Shirley Hall Farm

⚊⚊ HIGHLY COMMENDED

Shirley, Ashbourne DE6 3AS
☎ (01335) 360346
200-acre mixed farm. This peaceful timbered manor house, complete with part of its moat, is adjacent to superb woodland walks and makes an excellent centre for Sudbury and Kedleston Hall, Chatsworth and Alton Towers. Good pub food in Shirley village within walking distance.
Bedrooms: 2 double, 1 twin
Bathrooms: 2 private, 1 public

Bed & breakfast

per night:	£min	£max
Single	18.00	24.00
Double	30.00	36.00

Parking for 5

Stanshope Hall ⚊

⚊⚊ COMMENDED

Stanshope, Ashbourne DE6 2AD
☎ (01335) 310278
Fax (01335) 310470

18th C listed hall providing comfortable and imaginatively decorated bed and breakfast accommodation, with home cooking using garden and local produce.
Bedrooms: 2 double, 1 twin
Bathrooms: 3 private

Bed & breakfast

per night:	£min	£max
Single	20.00	30.00
Double	40.00	65.00

Half board

per person:	£min	£max
Daily	37.50	47.50

Evening meal 1900 (last orders 2000)
Parking for 3

ASHBY-DE-LA-ZOUCH

Leicestershire
Map ref 4B3

Lovely market town with late 15th C church, impressive ruined 15th C castle, an interesting small museum and a wide, sloping main street with Georgian buildings. Twycross Zoo is nearby.
Tourist Information Centre
☎ *(01530) 411767*

The Laurels Guesthouse

⚊⚊ APPROVED

17 Ashby Road, Measham, Swadlincote, Derbyshire DE12 7JR
☎ Measham (01530) 272567
A warm welcome awaits you at this modern guesthouse on the B5006, convenient for the M42/M1. Rural location.
Bedrooms: 1 double, 1 twin
Bathrooms: 2 private, 1 public

Bed & breakfast

per night:	£min	£max
Single	18.00	20.00
Double	36.00	40.00

Parking for 7

There are separate sections in this guide listing groups specialising in farm holidays and accommodation which is especially suitable for young people and organised groups.

ASHFORD IN THE WATER

Derbyshire
Map ref 4B2

Limestone village in attractive surroundings of the Peak District approached by 3 bridges over the River Wye. There is an annual well-dressing ceremony and the village was well-known in the 18th C for its black marble quarries.

Gritstone House

HIGHLY COMMENDED

Greaves Lane, Ashford in the Water, Bakewell DE45 1QH
☎ Bakewell (01629) 813563
Charming 18th C Georgian house offering friendly service and accommodation designed with comfort and style in mind. Ideal centre for exploring the Peak District's scenery and country houses, and close to an extensive range of dining-out facilities.
Bedrooms: 2 double, 1 twin
Bathrooms: 1 private, 1 public

Bed & breakfast per night:	£min	£max
Double	34.00	42.00

ASHOVER

Derbyshire
Map ref 4B2

Unspoilt village with a 13th C church.

Old School Farm

Uppertown, Ashover, Chesterfield S45 0JF
☎ Chesterfield (01246) 590813
25-acre mixed farm. A working farm welcoming children but not pets, suitable for visitors with their own transport. In a small hamlet bordering the Peak District, ideal for Chatsworth House, Chesterfield and Matlock Bath.
Bedrooms: 1 single, 1 double, 2 family rooms
Bathrooms: 2 private, 1 public

Bed & breakfast per night:	£min	£max
Single	16.00	18.00
Double	32.00	36.00

Half board per person:	£min	£max
Daily	22.00	24.00
Weekly	154.00	168.00

Evening meal 1900 (last orders 0930)
Parking for 10
Open March-November

Please mention this guide when making a booking.

BAKEWELL

Derbyshire
Map ref 4B2

Pleasant market town, famous for its pudding. It is set in beautiful countryside on the River Wye and is an excellent centre for exploring the Derbyshire Dales, the Peak District National Park, Chatsworth and Haddon Hall.
Tourist Information Centre
☎ (01629) 813227

The Ashford Hotel and Restaurant

COMMENDED

Church Street, Ashford in the Water, Bakewell DE4 1QB
☎ (01629) 812725

Traditional, friendly country hotel where you will receive personal attention throughout your stay. There are open fires and a wealth of oak beams. An ideal location to relax.
Bedrooms: 1 single, 5 double, 1 twin
Bathrooms: 7 private

Bed & breakfast per night:	£min	£max
Single	45.00	50.00
Double	70.00	80.00

Lunch available
Evening meal 1900 (last orders 2130)
Parking for 45
Cards accepted: Access, Visa, Diners, Amex

Castle Cliffe Private Hotel

COMMENDED

Monsal Head, Bakewell DE45 1NL
☎ Great Longstone (01629) 640258
A Victorian stone house overlooking beautiful Monsal Dale. Noted for its friendly atmosphere, good food and exceptional views.
Bedrooms: 3 double, 4 twin, 2 family rooms
Bathrooms: 4 private, 2 public, 4 private showers

Bed & breakfast per night:	£min	£max
Single	27.00	37.00
Double	44.00	50.00

Half board per person:	£min	£max
Daily	39.00	49.00
Weekly	220.00	260.00

Evening meal 1900 (last orders 1700)
Parking for 15
Cards accepted: Access, Visa
15

Croft Cottages

1 Croft Cottages, Coombs Road, Bakewell DE45 1AQ
☎ (01629) 814101
Fax (01629) 815001
17th C cottage beside River Wye. Charming rooms overlooking walled cottage garden or delightful suite in small converted barn. 100 yards Bakewell Bridge and town centre. Friendly welcome, excellent breakfasts.
Bedrooms: 1 double, 1 twin, 1 family room; suite available
Bathrooms: 3 private

Bed & breakfast per night:	£min	£max
Double	35.00	40.00

Melbourne House

Buxton Road, Bakewell DE45 1DA
☎ (01629) 815357
Listed Georgian house with character and history, spacious en-suite bedrooms, helpful tourist information, tasty breakfast menu and warm Derbyshire welcome.
Bedrooms: 2 double, 1 twin
Bathrooms: 3 private

Bed & breakfast per night:	£min	£max
Single	25.00	35.00
Double	36.00	44.00

5

Riversdale Farm

Coombs Road, Bakewell DE45 1AR
☎ (01629) 813586
Victorian farmhouse in a quiet area, surrounded by flat pastureland and wooded hills, close to Bakewell. Non-smokers only, please.
Bedrooms: 1 single, 1 double, 1 twin
Bathrooms: 2 public

Bed & breakfast per night:	£min	£max
Single	17.00	
Double	34.00	

Half board per person:	£min	£max
Daily	25.00	
Weekly	157.50	

Evening meal from 1830
Parking for 5
Open February-November

Rowland Cottage

Listed

Rowland, Bakewell DE45 1NR
☎ Great Longstone (01629) 640365

Nestling peacefully below Longstone Edge since 1667. A warm welcome, comfortable beds, delicious food and relaxation await you. Come and share our lovely home!
Bedrooms: 1 double, 1 triple
Bathrooms: 1 private, 1 public
Bed & breakfast

per night:	£min	£max
Double	30.00	35.00

Half board per person:	£min	£max
Daily	22.50	25.00
Weekly	157.50	175.00

Evening meal 1800 (last orders 2000)
Parking for 3

☎☺🖵🔌♨🔍Ⓤ🅐Ⓢ✠🅟Ⓣ🖿💷,🛏 ❄🚲🔌 🆂🅿🏠Ⓣ

Sheldon House
👑👑 HIGHLY COMMENDED
Chapel Street, Monyash, Bakewell DE45 1JJ
☎ (01629) 813067
Warm welcome in comfortable family home, 5 miles from Bakewell. Ideal for walking, good pub food locally, overseas visitors welcome.
Bedrooms: 3 double
Bathrooms: 3 private, 1 public
Bed & breakfast

per night:	£min	£max
Single	22.00	25.00
Double	35.00	38.00

Parking for 4

☎7🖵🖵🔌♨🔍Ⓤ🅐Ⓢ✠🅟🖿💷,🛏 Ⓤ🅿❄✠🏠

BAMFORD
Derbyshire
Map ref 4B2

Village in the Peak District near the Upper Derwent Reservoirs of Ladybower, Derwent and Howden. An excellent centre for walking.

Pioneer House ♨
👑👑 COMMENDED
Station Road, Bamford, Sheffield S30 2BN
☎ Hope Valley (01433) 650638
Comfortable, spacious rooms, all with private facilities, in Edwardian family home. Friendly atmosphere, hearty breakfasts. Central location in Peak District.
Bedrooms: 2 double, 1 twin
Bathrooms: 3 private
Bed & breakfast

per night:	£min	£max
Double	30.00	40.00

Evening meal 1800 (last orders 1930)
Parking for 8

☎🖵🖵🔌♨🔍Ⓤ🅐Ⓢ✠💷,🛏❄🚲🆂🅿

We advise you to confirm your booking in writing.

BARNBY MOOR
Nottinghamshire
Map ref 4C2

Village on the former Great North Road, within easy reach of Clumber Park, Sherwood Forest and Pilgrim Father country.

White Horse Inn and Restaurant ♨
👑👑
Great North Road, Barnby Moor, Retford DN22 8QS
☎ Retford (01777) 707721
An old converted farmhouse on the old Great North Road, 2 miles from the A1.
Bedrooms: 1 double, 1 twin, 1 triple
Bathrooms: 1 private, 1 public
Bed & breakfast

per night:	£min	£max
Single	20.00	23.00
Double	32.00	38.00

Half board per person:	£min	£max
Daily	22.50	36.95
Weekly	141.75	232.79

Lunch available
Evening meal 1700 (last orders 2200)
Parking for 30
Cards accepted: Access, Visa, Amex

☎🖵♨🅐Ⓢ✠💷,🍴❄🚲🏠

BELPER
Derbyshire
Map ref 4B2

Pleasant old market town in the valley of the River Derwent. Attractive scenery and a wealth of industrial history.

Chevin Green Farm ♨
👑👑 COMMENDED
Chevin Road, Belper, Derby DE56 2UN
☎ (01773) 822328
38-acre mixed farm. Extended and improved 300-year-old beamed farmhouse accommodation with all bedrooms en-suite, an ideal base for exploring Derbyshire.
Bedrooms: 2 single, 2 double, 1 twin, 1 family room
Bathrooms: 6 private
Bed & breakfast

per night:	£min	£max
Single	18.00	20.00
Double	32.00	36.00

Parking for 6

☎🖵🔌♨✠🅟Ⓣ💷,🛏Ⓤ🗡❄

Establishments should be open throughout the year unless otherwise stated in the entry.

BELTON
Lincolnshire
Map ref 3A1

Attractive village including 17th C Belton House and Park, owned by the National Trust.

Coach House ♨
👑👑
Belton, Grantham NG32 2LS
☎ Grantham (01476) 73636

Idyllically situated, surrounded by National Trust land and golf-courses. Guest lounge overlooks extensive gardens. Antique furnishings complement the rooms. Access at all times.
Bedrooms: 2 double, 2 twin
Bathrooms: 4 private
Bed & breakfast

per night:	£min	£max
Single	18.50	20.00
Double	34.00	37.00

Half board per person:	£min	£max
Daily	29.00	32.00

Parking for 6

☎🛁🖵🖵♨🅐Ⓢ✠🅟Ⓣ💷,🛏Ⓤ🅿 ❄🚲🆂🅿

BRACKLEY
Northamptonshire
Map ref 2C1

Historic market town of mellow stone, with many fine buildings lining the wide High Street and Market Place. Sulgrave Manor (George Washington's ancestral home) and Silverstone Circuit are nearby.
Tourist Information Centre
☎ *(01280) 700111*

Walltree House Farm ♨
👑👑👑
Steane, Brackley NN13 5NS
☎ Banbury (01295) 811235 & 0860 913399
Fax (01295) 811147
200-acre arable farm. Individual ground floor rooms in the courtyard adjacent to Victorian farmhouse, all en-suite. Gardens and woods to relax in. Near historic sites, shopping and sports. M40 junctions 10/11. County winners of Booker Silver Lapwing award for conservation.
Bedrooms: 2 double, 3 twin, 1 triple, 2 family rooms
Bathrooms: 8 private, 1 public

Continued ▶

BRACKLEY

Continued

Bed & breakfast per night:	£min	£max
Single	30.00	40.00
Double	40.00	60.00

Half board per person:	£min	£max
Daily	30.00	35.00

Evening meal 1900 (last orders 1900)
Parking for 10
Cards accepted: Access, Visa
🐎 🍴 📺 ☕ 🔒 [S] 🛏 [TV] ♨ 🚗 🏊 16 🐴 🎣
✿ 🐕 🚜 [OAP] [T]

BRADWELL

Derbyshire
Map ref 4B2

Small village in the beautiful Hope Valley. There is a well-dressing ceremony in August.

Stoney Ridge ♿

👑👑 HIGHLY COMMENDED

Granby Road, Bradwell, Sheffield
S30 2HU
☎ Hope Valley (01433) 620538
Split-level bungalow, with good views, established gardens and an indoor heated pool, close to Castleton.
Bedrooms: 2 double, 1 twin
Bathrooms: 3 private, 1 public

Bed & breakfast per night:	£min	£max
Single	23.00	23.00
Double	40.00	48.00

Parking for 8
Cards accepted: Access, Visa, Switch/Delta
🐎 10 📖 📺 ☕ 📞 [UL] 🔒 [S] 🛏 [TV] ♨ 🚗 🏊
🐴 ✿ 🚜 🚭 [SP]

BROUGHTON ASTLEY

Leicestershire
Map ref 4C3

First mentioned in the Domesday Book when it was three separate villages, Broctone, Sutone and Torp.

The Old Farm House

Listed

Old Mill Road, Broughton Astley, Leicester LE9 6PQ
☎ Sutton in the Elms (01455) 282254
Recently converted Georgian farmhouse overlooking fields. Quietly situated behind the church, near village centre. Near junctions 20/21 of M1, junction 1 of M69. Well-behaved pets welcome. French spoken.
Bedrooms: 3 twin
Bathrooms: 2 public

Bed & breakfast per night:	£min	£max
Single	17.00	20.00
Double	34.00	40.00

Half board per person:	£min	£max
Daily	25.00	28.00

Parking for 4
🐎 ☕ [UL] 🔒 [S] 🚭 [TV] ♨ 🚗 ✂ 🐴 🐕 🚜 🏠

BRUNTINGTHORPE

Leicestershire
Map ref 4C3

Knaptoft House Farm

👑👑 HIGHLY COMMENDED

Bruntingthorpe Road, Shearsby, Lutterworth LE17 6PR
☎ (0116) 247 8388
Fax (0116) 247 8388
145-acre mixed farm. Very quiet, warm, comfortable, beautifully appointed family home surrounded by farmland. Family historians welcome - many records on premises and only 4 miles from County Records Office. A14 junction 1, M1 junction 20, M6 junction 1, A50 Shearsby 1 mile. Ample parking.
Bedrooms: 2 double, 1 twin
Bathrooms: 1 private, 1 public, 2 private showers

Bed & breakfast per night:	£min	£max
Single	18.00	
Double	35.00	42.00

Parking for 5
🐎 5 ☕ [UL] [S] 🚭 🛏 [TV] ♨ 🚗 🎣 ✿ 🐕 🚜

BUXTON

Derbyshire
Map ref 4B2

The highest market town in England and one of the oldest spas, with an elegant Crescent, Poole's Cavern, Opera House and attractive Pavilion Gardens. An excellent centre for exploring the Peak District.
Tourist Information Centre
☎ (01298) 25106

Coningsby ♿

👑👑👑 HIGHLY COMMENDED

6 Macclesfield Road, Buxton
SK17 9AH
☎ (01298) 26735
Impressive Victorian detached house set in a pretty garden in a pleasant area. A friendly welcome, superior accommodation, good food and wine are assured but non-smoking guests only, please.
Bedrooms: 3 double
Bathrooms: 3 private

Bed & breakfast per night:	£min	£max
Double	36.00	45.00

Evening meal 1900 (last orders 1600)
Parking for 6
Open January-November
📖 📺 ☕ 📞 🔒 [S] 🚭 🛏 ♨ 🚗 ✿ 🐕 🚜

Cotesfield Farm ♿

Listed

Parsley Hay, Buxton SK17 0BD
☎ Longnor (01298) 83256 & Mobile 0850 051148
Fax (01298) 83256
300-acre mixed farm. In the Peak District National Park on the Tissington Trail, this farmhouse offers peace and quiet. Access from the A515 Buxton to Ashbourne road.
Bedrooms: 2 double, 1 twin
Bathrooms: 1 public

Bed & breakfast per night:	£min	£max
Single	13.00	17.00
Double	26.00	34.00

Parking for 6
🐎 ☕ [UL] 🔒 [S] 🛏 [TV] ♨ 🚗 ✿ 🚜 🚭 [SP] 🏠

Devonshire Arms ♿

👑👑👑

Peak Forest, Buxton SK17 8EJ
☎ (01298) 23875
17th C former coaching inn located in the heart of the Peak District, north-east of Buxton and close to all attractions. All rooms refurbished to a high standard offering en-suite facilities.
Bedrooms: 2 double, 1 twin
Bathrooms: 3 private

Bed & breakfast per night:	£min	£max
Single	25.00	25.00
Double	35.00	35.00

Half board per person:	£min	£max
Daily	22.50	

Lunch available
Evening meal 1830 (last orders 2145)
Parking for 40
🐎 📺 ☕ 📞 🔒 [S] ♨ 🚗 🐴 ✿ 🚜

Fairhaven ♿

Listed APPROVED

1 Dale Terrace, Buxton SK17 6LU
☎ (01298) 24481
Centrally placed with ample roadside parking, offering English home cooking in a warm and friendly atmosphere.
Bedrooms: 1 single, 1 double, 1 twin, 2 triple, 1 family room
Bathrooms: 1 public

Bed & breakfast per night:	£min	£max
Single	17.00	18.00
Double	30.00	32.00

Half board per person:	£min	£max
Daily	22.00	25.00
Weekly	147.00	168.00

Evening meal 1800 (last orders 1600)
Cards accepted: Access, Visa, Amex
🐎 📖 📺 ☕ [UL] 🔒 ♨ 🚗 🚜

Grendon

Bishops Lane, Buxton SK17 6UN
☎ (01298) 78831

Family-run, Edwardian, detached house set in lovely gardens with outstanding views to National Park. High standard of comfort and service. Easy walk to town and countryside.
Bedrooms: 1 double, 1 twin
Bathrooms: 2 private

Bed & breakfast

per night:	£min	£max
Single	20.00	30.00
Double	32.00	38.00

Parking for 8

Hawthorn Farm Guesthouse
COMMENDED

Fairfield Road, Buxton SK17 7ED
☎ (01298) 23230
A 400-year-old former farmhouse which has been in the family for 10 generations. Full English breakfast.
Bedrooms: 4 single, 2 double, 2 twin, 4 triple
Bathrooms: 5 private, 2 public

Bed & breakfast

per night:	£min	£max
Single	20.00	21.00
Double	40.00	46.00

Parking for 15
Open April-October

Lynstone Guesthouse

3 Grange Road, Buxton SK17 6NH
☎ (01298) 77043
A spacious homely house. Home cooking, traditional and vegetarian. Ideal base for touring and walking. Children welcome, cleanliness assured. Off-street parking. No smoking and no pets please.
Bedrooms: 1 double, 1 family room
Bathrooms: 1 private, 2 public

Bed & breakfast

per night:	£min	£max
Single	20.00	
Double	30.00	32.00

Evening meal 1800 (last orders 1800)
Parking for 3
Open March-December

Oldfield House
COMMENDED

8 Macclesfield Road, Buxton
SK17 9AH
☎ (01298) 24371

Attractive detached Victorian guesthouse with gardens, close to the town centre and Pavilion Gardens. Spacious en-suite bedrooms. Non-smoking.
Bedrooms: 3 double
Bathrooms: 3 private, 1 public

Bed & breakfast

per night:	£min	£max
Single	20.00	24.00
Double	34.00	37.00

Half board

per person:	£min	£max
Daily	28.00	30.00
Weekly	190.00	196.00

Parking for 8

Pedlicote Farm
Listed

Peak Forest, Buxton SK17 8EG
☎ (01298) 22241
1681 oak-beamed farmhouse conversion in the Peak Park, full of character, with a charming atmosphere and magnificent views.
Bedrooms: 1 double, 2 twin
Bathrooms: 2 public

Bed & breakfast

per night:	£min	£max
Single	18.00	20.00
Double	28.00	30.00

Half board

per person:	£min	£max
Daily	25.00	27.00
Weekly	175.00	175.00

Lunch available
Evening meal 1830 (last orders 2030)
Parking for 9

Stoneridge
COMMENDED

9 Park Road, Buxton SK17 6SG
☎ (01298) 26120

Edwardian stone-built house in quiet but central location. Opera House, station and all amenities within easy walking distance, yet ideally situated for walking the beautiful Peak District.
Bedrooms: 2 double, 1 twin, 1 triple
Bathrooms: 4 private

Bed & breakfast

per night:	£min	£max
Single	25.00	25.00
Double	35.00	40.00

Parking for 5
Open March-October

The Victorian Guesthouse
COMMENDED

5 Wye Grove, Off Macclesfield Road, Buxton SK17 9AJ
☎ (01298) 78759
Attractive and comfortable surroundings, furnished in a tasteful Victorian manner, with a beautiful conservatory to relax in. En-suite rooms. Diets catered for. In a quiet cul-de-sac near town centre. Telephone for brochure.
Bedrooms: 2 double, 1 twin, 1 triple
Bathrooms: 4 private, 1 public

Bed & breakfast

per night:	£min	£max
Double	34.00	39.00

Half board

per person:	£min	£max
Daily	29.00	31.50
Weekly	196.00	213.50

Evening meal 1800 (last orders 1600)
Parking for 4

Westlands
Listed

Bishops Lane, St. Johns Road, Buxton SK17 6UN
☎ (01298) 23242
Beautifully appointed small guesthouse on country lane 1 mile from town centre. Magnificent views overlooking golf-course. Non-smoking.
Bedrooms: 2 double, 1 twin
Bathrooms: 1 public

Bed & breakfast

per night:	£min	£max
Single	18.00	26.00
Double	28.00	32.00

Parking for 5

CASTLETON

Derbyshire
Map ref 4B2

Large village in a spectacular Peak District setting with ruined Peveril Castle and 4 great show caverns, where the Blue John stone and lead mines were mined. One cavern offers a mile-long underground boat journey.

Bargate Cottage
COMMENDED

Bargate, Pindale Road, Castleton, Sheffield S30 2WG
☎ Hope Valley (01433) 620201
Fax (01433) 621739
Unspoilt, renovated 17th C cottage adjacent to Peveril Castle in the centre of the village. An ideal base for relaxing, walking or touring. Many recreational facilities available locally. Non-smokers only, please, and sorry, no pets.
Bedrooms: 1 double, 2 triple
Bathrooms: 3 private

Continued ▶

CASTLETON

Continued

Bed & breakfast

per night:	£min	£max
Double	41.00	45.00

Half board

per person:	£min	£max
Daily	31.00	33.00

Evening meal from 1830
Parking for 6

🛥 3 🐴🖃 ✦♨♿🅸 Ⓢ ⊁ 🐾 🎢 ⚓ ∪
♪🏵 ✾ ✕ 🐎 🏮

CHAPEL-EN-LE-FRITH

Derbyshire
Map ref 4B2

Small market town and a good base for climbing and walking. Close to the show caverns at Castleton.

Slack Hall Farm

Listed

Castleton Road, Chapel-en-le-Frith, Stockport, Cheshire SK12 6QS
☎ (01298) 812845
550-acre mixed & dairy farm. Farmhouse built in 1727. 1 mile from Chapel-en-le-Frith and an ideal base for touring the Peak National Park.
Bedrooms: 1 double, 1 triple
Bathrooms: 1 public

Bed & breakfast

per night:	£min	£max
Double	30.00	32.00

Parking for 2

🛥 ♨♿ 📺 🖃 ✓ ✕ 🐎

CHESTERFIELD

Derbyshire
Map ref 4B2

Famous for the twisted spire of its parish church, Chesterfield has some fine modern buildings and excellent shopping facilities, including a large, traditional open-air market. Hardwick Hall and Bolsover Castle are nearby.
Tourist Information Centre
☎ *(01246) 207777 or 207778*

Eastview

Listed APPROVED

35 Holymoor Road, Holymoorside, Chesterfield S42 7EB
☎ (01246) 566925
Welcoming family home in quiet village on edge of Peak District. Ideal walking, touring, cycling. Special diets catered for especially vegetarian. Non-smoking. Dogs welcome.
Bedrooms: 1 single, 1 double, 1 twin
Bathrooms: 1 public

Bed & breakfast

per night:	£min	£max
Single	14.50	14.50
Double	28.00	28.00

Half board

per person:	£min	£max
Daily	19.50	19.50

Lunch available
Evening meal 1700 (last orders 1900)
Parking for 1

🛥 ✗♨♿📞 🖃 ∪ ✦♿ Ⓤ🅸 Ⓢ ⊁ 🐾 📺
◑ 🖃 ⚓ ✾ 🎈 ᴏᴀᴘ ꜱᴘ

CONINGSBY

Lincolnshire
Map ref 4D2

Large thriving village on the edge of the Lincolnshire Fens. It is within easy reach of main towns and has a pleasing church with an unusual one-handed clock.

White Bull Inn

⚑⚑ APPROVED

55 High Street, Coningsby, Lincoln LN4 4RB
☎ (01526) 342439
A warm welcome awaits at this friendly pub with real ale, riverside beer garden and large children's playground. Children's Certificate. Traditional home-made meals are available every day, lunch time and evening. Half a mile from RAF Coningsby. Family Pub of the Year finalist, 1995.
Bedrooms: 2 single, 1 double, 1 twin
Bathrooms: 2 private, 4 public

Bed & breakfast

per night:	£min	£max
Single	15.00	20.00
Double	28.00	36.00

Half board

per person:	£min	£max
Daily	19.00	24.00
Weekly	95.00	175.00

Lunch available
Evening meal 1900 (last orders 2200)
Parking for 60

🛥 ♨ 🐴 🖃 ✦🅸 ⊁ 🐾 📺 🖃 ⚓ ✦ ♪ ✾
✕ ꜱᴘ Ⓣ

COTGRAVE

Nottinghamshire
Map ref 4C2

In 1934 an Anglo-Saxon burial ground was discovered on Mill Hill, in this interesting, historic village.

Jerico Farm

⚑⚑ COMMENDED

Fosse Way, Cotgrave, Nottingham NG12 3HG
☎ Kinoulton (01949) 81733
Fax (01949) 81733
120-acre mixed farm. With lovely views over the Nottinghamshire Wolds, an excellent rural location for the business or holiday visitor yet only 8 miles from Nottingham with its universities, sports venues and tourist sites. Brochure available.
Bedrooms: 2 double, 1 twin
Bathrooms: 1 private, 1 public

Bed & breakfast

per night:	£min	£max
Single	18.00	
Double	32.00	36.00

Parking for 4

🛥 5 ✦♨🖃 Ⓢ ⊁ 🐾 📺 🖃 ⚓ ♪ ✾
✕ 🐎

DERBY

Derbyshire
Map ref 4B2

Modern industrial city but with ancient origins. There is a wide range of attractions including several museums (notably Royal Crown Derby), a theatre, a concert hall, and the cathedral with fine ironwork and Bess of Hardwick's tomb.
Tourist Information Centre
☎ *(01332) 255802*

Alambie ♈

⚑

189 Main Road, Morley, Derby DE7 6DG
☎ (01332) 780349
Friendly family bungalow in the country, facing the Rose & Crown public house on the Smalley crossroads, 6 miles from Derby. Non-smoking establishment.
Bedrooms: 1 double, 1 twin, 1 family room
Bathrooms: 3 private

Bed & breakfast

per night:	£min	£max
Single	20.00	
Double	32.00	

Parking for 4

🛥 ♨ 🖃 ✦♨ Ⓤ ⊁ 🐾 📺 🖃 ⚓ ✾ 🐎

Bonehill Farm

Listed

Etwall Road, Mickleover, Derby DE3 5DN
☎ (01332) 513553
120-acre mixed farm. A traditional farmhouse in a rural setting, 3 miles from Derby. Alton Towers, the Peak District, historic houses and the Potteries are all within easy reach.
Bedrooms: 1 double, 1 twin, 1 triple
Bathrooms: 1 private, 1 public

Bed & breakfast

per night:	£min	£max
Single	15.00	20.00
Double	30.00	36.00

Parking for 6

🛥 🐴 ♨ Ⓤ 🅸 Ⓢ 🐾 📺 🖃 ⚓ ♪ ✾ 🐎 🏮

Colour maps at the back of this guide pinpoint all places which have accommodation listings in the guide.

ELMESTHORPE

Leicestershire
Map ref 4C3

Silhouetted against the horizon, the picturesque church of St Mary has a 17th C tower and 12th or 13th C font and is set in a beautiful churchyard with lovely views.

Water Meadows Farm

Listed **COMMENDED**

22 Billington Road East, Elmesthorpe, Leicester LE9 7SB
☎ Earl Shilton (01455) 843417
15-acre smallholding. Tudor-style, oak-beamed farmhouse with extensive gardens, including private conservation area, woodland and stream. Own produce, home cooking. On a private road. Central for visiting many places of scenic and historic interest.
Bedrooms: 1 double, 1 family room
Bathrooms: 1 public
Bed & breakfast

per night:	£min	£max
Single	17.50	17.50
Double	29.00	29.00

Half board per person:	£min	£max
Daily	22.00	25.00
Weekly	140.00	160.00

Evening meal from 1900
Parking for 10
🛏 2 🖵 ♦ 🔟 🖀 🕭 🖣 🗠 📺 🖳, 🖴 ✿ 🚗 SP

EYAM

Derbyshire
Map ref 4B2

Attractive village famous for the courage it showed during the plague of 1665. The church has several memorials to this time and there is a well-dressing ceremony in August. The fine 17th C manor house of Eyam Hall is open in summer, and Chatsworth is nearby.

Royal Oak 🕭

≌≌ **APPROVED**

Town Head, Eyam, Sheffield S30 1RE
☎ Hope Valley (01433) 631390
A quaint pub in the historic and picturesque "plague village" of Eyam in the Peak Park, close to Bakewell and Buxton.
Bedrooms: 1 double, 1 twin, 1 triple
Bathrooms: 3 private
Bed & breakfast

per night:	£min	£max
Single	25.00	35.00
Double	35.00	45.00

Half board per person:	£min	£max
Daily	30.00	45.00
Weekly	190.00	280.00

Lunch available
Evening meal 1900 (last orders 2100)
Parking for 3
🛏 🖵 ♦ 🖀 🕭 🖣 🗠 📺 🖳, 🖴 ⋃ 🚗 DAP 🗠 SP T

FILLINGHAM

Lincolnshire
Map ref 4C2

Church Farm 🕭

Listed **HIGHLY COMMENDED**

Fillingham, Gainsborough DN21 5BS
☎ Hemswell (01427) 668279
Fax (01427) 668025
Large, comfortable stone farmhouse, set in peaceful gardens with lovely views. 5 minutes from Hemswell Antique Centre.
Bedrooms: 1 single, 1 double, 1 twin; suite available
Bathrooms: 1 private, 2 public
Bed & breakfast

per night:	£min	£max
Single	16.00	25.00
Double	30.00	35.00

Half board per person:	£min	£max
Daily	27.00	27.00
Weekly	182.00	189.00

Parking for 3
🛏 🖾 🖵 ♦ 🔟 🖀 🕭 📺 🖳, 🖴 ✿ 🗙 🚗 SP 🕭

FOXTON

Leicestershire
Map ref 4C3

Attractive village established in the 8th C. The 13th C church contains part of a Saxon Cross and a "lepers window". The Grand Union Canal passes through the village. Within walking distance is historic Foxton Locks with its unique staircase flight of 10 locks, and Inclined Plane Museum.

The Old Manse

≌≌

Swingbridge Street, Foxton, Market Harborough LE16 7RH
☎ Market Harborough (01858) 545456
Period house in large gardens with warm and friendly atmosphere, on edge of conservation village, 3 miles north of Market Harborough. Good food at both local inns.
Bedrooms: 1 double, 2 twin
Bathrooms: 1 private, 1 public
Bed & breakfast

per night:	£min	£max
Single	20.00	23.00
Double	35.00	39.00

Parking for 6
🛏 🖵 ♦ 🔟 🗠 🖣 📺 🖳, 🖴 ✿ 🗙 🚗

GOADBY

Leicestershire
Map ref 4C3

The Hollies

Listed

Goadby, Leicester LE7 9EE
☎ (0116) 259 8301 & Mobile 0374 871169
Comfortable, Grade II listed house, tastefully restored. In a quiet village in the heart of the Leicestershire countryside. Ideal base for walking and touring.
Bedrooms: 1 single, 1 double, 1 triple
Bathrooms: 3 private, 1 public
Bed & breakfast

per night:	£min	£max
Single	15.00	16.00
Double	30.00	32.00

Parking for 4
🛏 5 🖾 🖅 🖵 ♦ 🔟 🖣 📺 🖳, 🖴 ✿ 🚗 🕭

GUILSBOROUGH

Northamptonshire
Map ref 4C3

Lively village, situated 500 ft above sea level and close to two large reservoirs that have plenty of water activities. A very old village with much evidence of its history to be seen.

Seven Piers 🕭

Listed

Coton, Northampton NN6 8RF
☎ Northampton (01604) 740322
Detached, brick house with private garden, close to Ravensthorpe Reservoir and Althorpe House.
Bedrooms: 2 single, 1 twin, 1 triple
Bathrooms: 2 private, 1 public
Bed & breakfast

per night:	£min	£max
Single	15.00	18.00
Double	30.00	36.00

Parking for 3
🛏 🖅 🖵 ♦ 🖣 🔟 🖀 🗠 🖣 📺 🖳, 🖴 ✿ 🚗

HATHERSAGE

Derbyshire
Map ref 4B2

Hillside village in the Peak District, dominated by the church with many good brasses and monuments to the Eyre family which provide a link with Charlotte Bronte. Little John, friend of Robin Hood, is said to be buried here.

Hillfoot Farm 🕭

Listed **COMMENDED**

Castleton Road, Hathersage, Sheffield S30 1AH
☎ Hope Valley (01433) 651673
Recently built accommodation on the existing farmhouse. All rooms are en-
Continued ►

HATHERSAGE

Continued

suite with colour TV, tea/coffee facilities. 2 rooms on ground floor, 2 on first floor. Large car park.
Bedrooms: 2 double, 1 twin, 1 triple
Bathrooms: 4 private

Bed & breakfast

per night:	£min	£max
Single	20.00	37.00
Double	34.00	37.00

Lunch available
Evening meal 1800 (last orders 1900)
Parking for 13

Millstone Inn ⋀

COMMENDED

Sheffield Road, Hathersage, Sheffield
S30 1DA
☎ Hope Valley (01433) 650258
Fax (01433) 651664

Country inn with interesting food, traditional ales, function room and en-suite rooms with views of Hope Valley. All rooms have telephones and Sky TV.
Bedrooms: 3 double, 2 twin, 2 family rooms
Bathrooms: 7 private

Bed & breakfast

per night:	£min	£max
Single	30.00	
Double	49.50	

Half board

per person:	£min	£max
Daily	35.00	45.00

Lunch available
Evening meal 1800 (last orders 2100)
Parking for 75
Cards accepted: Access, Visa, Switch/Delta

The Old Vicarage ⋀

Church Bank, Hathersage, Sheffield
S30 1AB
☎ Hope Valley (01433) 651099
In 1845 Charlotte Bronte stayed in this listed building which is beside Little John's grave overlooking the Hope Valley. Central for Chatsworth House, the caves, fishing and walking.
Bedrooms: 2 double, 1 twin
Bathrooms: 1 private, 2 public, 1 private shower

Bed & breakfast

per night:	£min	£max
Single	20.00	21.00
Double	34.00	43.00

Parking for 3

The Scotsmans Pack ⋀

COMMENDED

School Lane, Hathersage, Sheffield
S30 1BZ
☎ Hope Valley (01433) 650253

Traditional country inn in the heart of the Peak District National Park, combining the unique blend of old world charm with modern fittings.
Bedrooms: 3 double, 1 twin
Bathrooms: 4 private

Bed & breakfast

per night:	£min	£max
Single	28.50	35.50
Double	52.00	57.00

Lunch available
Evening meal 1800 (last orders 2030)
Parking for 13

HAYFIELD

Derbyshire
Map ref 4B2

Village set in spectacular scenery at the highest point of the Peak District with the best approach to the Kinder Scout plateau via the Kinder Downfall. An excellent centre for walking. Three reservoirs close by.

The Royal Hotel ⋀

COMMENDED

Market Street, Hayfield, Stockport, Cheshire SK12 5EP
☎ Whaley Bridge (01663) 742721
Fax (01663) 742721
Centrally located in Hayfield at the foot of Kinder Scout in the High Peak district. Built in 1755, comprises oak panelled pub and restaurant with log fires, function room and accommodation.
Bedrooms: 2 double, 1 twin
Bathrooms: 3 private, 1 public

Bed & breakfast

per night:	£min	£max
Single	25.00	30.00
Double	40.00	45.00

Half board

per person:	£min	£max
Daily	34.00	37.00
Weekly	238.00	260.00

Lunch available
Evening meal 1900 (last orders 2145)
Parking for 100
Cards accepted: Access, Visa

HOLBECK

Nottinghamshire
Map ref 4C2

Browns ⋀

Listed HIGHLY COMMENDED

The Old Orchard Cottage, Holbeck, Worksop S80 3NF
☎ Worksop (01909) 720659
Fax (01909) 720659
1730 country cottage in delightful 1-acre garden. Previous winner of East Midlands B&B of the Year. Separate lodge accommodation. Cross through the ford in the driveway and stay "somewhere special".
Bedrooms: 1 family room
Bathrooms: 1 private

Bed & breakfast

per night:	£min	£max
Single	16.00	30.00
Double	38.00	40.00

Parking for 6

HOLMESFIELD

Derbyshire
Map ref 4B2

Halfway between Sheffield and Bakewell with easy access to Chesterfield. Consists of 14 hamlets, each with its place within the story of the village.

Springwood House ⋀

HIGHLY COMMENDED

Cowley Lane, Holmesfield, Sheffield
S18 5SD
☎ (0114) 289 0253 & Mobile 0831 398373
Fax (0114) 891365

Comfortable bungalow in 1.5 acres of garden with glorious views from all windows, in a quiet rural position.
Bedrooms: 1 double, 1 twin
Bathrooms: 2 private

Bed & breakfast

per night:	£min	£max
Single	17.50	20.00
Double	35.00	37.00

Parking for 12

HOPE

Derbyshire
Map ref 4B2

Village in the Hope Valley which is an excellent base for walking in the Peak District and for fishing and shooting. There is a well-dressing ceremony each June and its August sheep dog trials are well-known. Castleton Caves are nearby.

Mill Farm ⚠

Listed

Edale Road, Hope, Sheffield S30 2RF
☎ (01433) 621181
Stone-built, traditional farmhouse. Character property with oak beams and open log fire. Sunken garden overlooks herbaceous garden, shrubbery and lawn.
Bedrooms: 1 double, 2 twin
Bathrooms: 2 public

Bed & breakfast

per night:	£min	£max
Double	35.00	37.00

Parking for 4

Underleigh House ⚠

HIGHLY COMMENDED

Off Edale Road, Hope, Sheffield S30 2RF
☎ (01433) 621372

Secluded farmhouse-style home 1.5 miles from village. Magnificent countryside views from all rooms. En-suite facilities, colour TV and resident teddy bear. Gourmet houseparty dinners by owner-chef.
Bedrooms: 3 double, 2 twin
Bathrooms: 5 private

Bed & breakfast

per night:	£min	£max
Single	30.00	35.00
Double	50.00	56.00

Half board

per person:	£min	£max
Daily	40.00	43.00

Evening meal from 1930
Parking for 5
Cards accepted: Access, Visa

Woodroffe Arms ⚠

COMMENDED

1 Castleton Road, Hope, Sheffield S30 2RD
☎ (01433) 620351
A village pub which has been completely refurbished. Ideally located for visiting the caverns and Chatsworth

and for climbing and walking. Open all day.
Bedrooms: 2 double, 1 twin
Bathrooms: 3 private

Bed & breakfast

per night:	£min	£max
Double	45.00	52.00

Half board

per person:	£min	£max
Daily	28.00	31.50
Weekly	190.00	220.00

Lunch available
Evening meal 1900 (last orders 2100)
Parking for 25
Cards accepted: Access, Visa

HUSBANDS BOSWORTH

Leicestershire
Map ref 4C3

Mrs Armitage's

☎
31-33 High Street, Husbands Bosworth, Lutterworth LE17 6LJ
☎ Market Harborough (01858) 880066
Village centre home of character on A427, with wholesome cooking and warm welcome. Good choice of reasonably-priced evening meals at nearby inn.
Bedrooms: 3 twin
Bathrooms: 1 public

Bed & breakfast

per night:	£min	£max
Single	14.00	16.00
Double	28.00	32.00

Parking for 6

KETTERING

Northamptonshire
Map ref 3A2

Ancient industrial town based on shoe-making. Wicksteed Park to the south has many children's amusements. The splendid 17th C ducal mansion of Boughton House is to the north.
Tourist Information Centre
☎ *(01536) 410266 or 410333 ext 212*

Dairy Farm

COMMENDED

Cranford St Andrew, Kettering NN14 4AQ
☎ Cranford (01536) 330273
350-acre mixed farm. 17th C thatched house with inglenook fireplaces and a garden with an ancient circular dovecote and mature trees. Good food.
Bedrooms: 2 double, 1 twin
Bathrooms: 2 private, 1 public

Bed & breakfast

per night:	£min	£max
Single	18.00	30.00
Double	36.00	50.00

Half board

per person:	£min	£max
Daily	28.00	40.00

Evening meal 1900 (last orders 1200)
Parking for 5

The Wold

COMMENDED

34 Church Street, Burton Latimer, Kettering NN15 5LU
☎ Burton Latimer (01536) 722685
A detached house of generous proportions, in a semi-rural area in the old part of Burton Latimer. Non-smokers preferred. One mile from A14 junction 10.
Bedrooms: 1 single, 1 double, 1 twin
Bathrooms: 1 private, 2 public, 1 private shower

Bed & breakfast

per night:	£min	£max
Single	17.00	18.50
Double	30.00	33.00

Half board

per person:	£min	£max
Daily	24.50	26.00

Evening meal from 1900
Parking for 3

KEXBY

Lincolnshire
Map ref 4C2

Kexby Grange

Listed

Kexby, Gainsborough DN21 5PJ
☎ Gainsborough (01427) 788265
300-acre mixed farm. Pleasant, Victorian farmhouse offering a warm welcome. In rural surroundings, 4 miles from Gainsborough. Convenient for Lincoln and Hemswell Antique Centre.
Bedrooms: 1 single, 1 double
Bathrooms: 1 public

Bed & breakfast

per night:	£min	£max
Single	13.00	15.00
Double	26.00	30.00

Lunch available
Evening meal 1700 (last orders 2100)
Parking for 4

KIRKLINGTON

Nottinghamshire
Map ref 4C2

Archway House ⚠

Kirklington, Newark NG22 8NX
☎ Newark (01636) 812070 & 812280
Fax (01636) 812200
Edwardian house, characterful and atmospheric, with outstanding parkland views and large gardens. Close to Sherwood Forest and Southwell Minster.
Bedrooms: 2 double, 1 twin

Continued ▶

KIRKLINGTON

Continued

Bathrooms: 2 private, 1 private shower

Bed & breakfast

per night:	£min	£max
Single	18.00	18.00
Double	33.00	35.00

Half board

per person:	£min	£max
Daily	28.00	35.00
Weekly	150.00	175.00

Evening meal 1930 (last orders 2100)
Parking for 7

📺♨️🖨♿️♨️⬜️S✂️⛄️📺🕮 ⬛️🍴♟️❋🐎🐟T

LAXTON

Nottinghamshire
Map ref 4C2

The only village in England where medieval open-field strip farming is still practised, preserved as an official ancient monument. 3 large fields survive and there are remains of a splendid motte and bailey castle.

Manor Farm

Listed COMMENDED

Laxton, Newark NG22 0NU
☎ Tuxford (01777) 870417
137-acre mixed & dairy farm. In the historic, medieval village of Laxton, 10 miles north of Newark on the edge of Sherwood Forest.
Bedrooms: 1 double, 1 family room
Bathrooms: 1 public

Bed & breakfast

per night:	£min	£max
Single	15.00	
Double	30.00	

Half board

per person:	£min	£max
Daily	22.00	
Weekly	140.00	145.00

Evening meal 1800 (last orders 1900)
Parking for 6

📺🎿♟️⬜️♨️🕮📺⬛️🐎

The symbol 🌐 within an entry indicates participation in the Welcome Host programme – a nationally recognised customer care initiative which aims to promote the highest standards of service and a warm welcome for all visitors.

LINCOLN

Lincolnshire
Map ref 4C2

Ancient city dominated by the magnificent 11th C cathedral with its triple towers. A Roman gateway is still used and there are medieval houses lining narrow, cobbled streets. Other attractions include the Norman castle, several museums and the Usher Gallery.
Tourist Information Centre
☎ *(01522) 529828*

Garden House ⚑

👑👑 COMMENDED

Burton, Lincoln LN1 2RD
☎ (01522) 526120
Fax (01522) 523787
Fully restored 300-year-old house with oak beams. A stairlift and wheelchair ramp are available. 1 mile north of Lincoln off B1398.
Wheelchair access category 3 ♿️
Bedrooms: 1 double, 2 twin
Bathrooms: 2 private, 1 public

Bed & breakfast

per night:	£min	£max
Single	19.00	21.00
Double	38.00	42.00

Parking for 3

📺♨️🖨♿️♨️⬜️✂️🕮📺⧉🕮⬛️❋🐟 🐎SP🐎T

New Farm ⚑

📺

Burton, Lincoln LN1 2RD
☎ (01522) 527326
360-acre arable & dairy farm. Twin-bedded room with private bathroom. Use of lounge with colour TV. 2 miles north of Lincoln. Evening meal by prior arrangement. Coarse fishing in private lakes. Nature reserve close by.
Bedrooms: 1 twin
Bathrooms: 1 private

Bed & breakfast

per night:	£min	£max
Single	21.00	21.00
Double	34.00	34.00

Half board

per person:	£min	£max
Daily	26.00	30.00
Weekly	177.00	205.00

Parking for 3
Open March-November

📺🎿5♨️♿️♨️⬜️♨️S✂️📺🕮⬛️❋🐟 🐎

Newport Guesthouse ⚑

📮

26-28 Newport, Lincoln LN1 3DF
☎ (01522) 528590 & 0831 773622
Fax (01522) 542868
Part of a Victorian terrace, only 4 minutes' walk from cathedral and castle.
Bedrooms: 1 single, 1 double, 4 twin, 1 family room
Bathrooms: 2 public

Bed & breakfast

per night:	£min	£max
Single		18.00
Double		36.00

Parking for 6

📺♨️🖨♿️♨️⬜️S✂️📺🕮⬛️🍴

LONG BUCKBY

Northamptonshire
Map ref 4C3

Stretching for one and a half miles, this is a village with individuality and character.

Murcott Mill

👑👑 COMMENDED

Murcott, Long Buckby, Northampton NN6 7QR
☎ (01327) 842236
100-acre livestock farm. Imposing Georgian mill house overlooking open countryside. Recently renovated to a high standard, with open fires and en-suite bedrooms. Ideal stopover for M1 travellers.
Bedrooms: 1 double, 2 twin
Bathrooms: 3 private, 1 public

Bed & breakfast

per night:	£min	£max
Single	18.00	20.00
Double	35.00	35.00

Half board

per person:	£min	£max
Daily	21.50	21.50

Evening meal 1900 (last orders 2030)
Parking for 12

📺♨️♿️♨️⬜️♨️S♨️📺🕮⬛️❋🐎

LOUGHBOROUGH

Leicestershire
Map ref 4C3

Industrial town famous for its bell foundry and 47-bell Carillon Tower. The Great Central Railway operates steam railway rides of over 8 miles through the attractive scenery of Charnwood Forest.
Tourist Information Centre
☎ *(01509) 218113*

De Montfort Hotel ⚑

👑👑👑 COMMENDED

88 Leicester Road, Loughborough LE11 2AQ
☎ (01509) 216061
Fax (01509) 233667
Recently refurbished, friendly family-run hotel under new ownership. Close to town centre, Main Line Steam Trust, university and beautiful Leicestershire countryside.
Bedrooms: 2 single, 1 double, 5 twin, 1 triple
Bathrooms: 9 private, 1 public

Bed & breakfast

per night:	£min	£max
Single	20.00	28.00
Double	30.00	40.00

Half board

per person:	£min	£max
Daily	25.50	40.00

Evening meal 1830 (last orders 2030)
Cards accepted: Access, Visa, Amex
⛄ 🖪 🖵 ⚓ ♿ 🛈 Ⓢ 🅿 TV 🏛 🚗 ✿ SP

Peachnook 🏔

Listed

154 Ashby Road, Loughborough
LE11 3AG
☎ (01509) 264390
*Small, friendly guesthouse built around
1890. Near all amenities. TV and tea-
making facilities in all rooms. Ironing
facilities.*
Bedrooms: 1 single, 2 twin, 1 triple
Bathrooms: 2 private, 1 public,
1 private room
Bed & breakfast

per night:	£min	£max
Single	12.00	25.00
Double	28.00	35.00

⛄ 5 🏌 🖵 ⚓ 🔟 🛈 Ⓢ 🚗 ✿ ✕ 🐾 Ⓣ

LOUTH

Lincolnshire
Map ref 4D2

Attractive old market town set on
the eastern edge of the
Lincolnshire Wolds. St James's
Church has an impressive tower
and spire and there are the
remains of a Cistercian abbey. The
museum contains an interesting
collection of local material.
Tourist Information Centre
☎ *(01507) 609289*

Wickham House

Listed HIGHLY COMMENDED

Church Lane, Conisholme, Louth
LN11 7LX
☎ North Somercotes (01507) 358465
*Attractive 18th C cottage in country
lane. En-suite bedrooms. Beamed sitting
and dining room, separate tables,
library. No smoking please.*
Bedrooms: 1 single, 1 double, 1 twin
Bathrooms: 3 private
Bed & breakfast

per night:	£min	£max
Double	37.00	

Parking for 4
⛄ 8 🏌 🖪 🖵 ⚓ 🛈 ✕ 🔟 🏛 🚗 ✿ ✕
🐾 SP 🏮

LUDFORD

Lincolnshire
Map ref 4D2

The hamlets of Ludford Magna
and Ludford Parva combine to
form Ludford, situated on the busy
road from Market Rasen to Louth.

Hainton Walk Farm

Listed COMMENDED

Ludford, Lincoln LN3 6AP
☎ Burgh on Bain (01507) 313242

*4-acre smallholding. Very peaceful and
beautiful area on Lincolnshire Wolds.
Outstanding views. Good food and
homely atmosphere. Small pets
welcome.*
Bedrooms: 1 single, 1 double, 1 triple
Bathrooms: 1 public
Bed & breakfast

per night:	£min	£max
Single	15.00	15.00
Double	28.00	30.00

Half board

per person:	£min	£max
Daily	21.50	22.50
Weekly	125.00	131.00

Evening meal 1900 (last orders 2130)
Parking for 7
⛄ ⚡ 🖪 ⚓ ♿ 🏛 🛈 Ⓢ ✕ 🔟 TV 🏛 🚗 ✿
🐾 OAP SP

LUTTERWORTH

Leicestershire
Map ref 4C3

The Greyhound Coaching Inn 🏔

🏮🏮🏮🏮

9 Market Street, Lutterworth
LE17 4EJ
☎ (01455) 553307
Fax (01455) 554558
*Intimate restaurant which serves local
food and special conference facilities.
Adjacent to junction 20 of M1 and
junction 1 of M6 motorways.*
Bedrooms: 4 single, 22 double, 3 twin,
1 triple
Bathrooms: 30 private
Bed & breakfast

per night:	£min	£max
Single	25.00	39.00
Double	35.00	49.00

Half board

per person:	£min	£max
Daily	45.00	55.00

Lunch available
Evening meal 1900 (last orders 2200)
Cards accepted: Access, Visa, Diners,
Amex, Switch/Delta
⛄ 🏌 🖪 ⛽ 🖪 🖵 ⚓ ♿ 🛈 Ⓢ ✕ 🔟 TV ●
🏛 🚗 🏌 80 ✕ OAP 🐾 SP 🏮

There are separate
sections in this guide
listing groups specialising
in farm holidays and
accommodation which
is especially suitable
for young people and
organised groups.

MANSFIELD

Nottinghamshire
Map ref 4C2

Ancient town, now an industrial
and shopping centre, with a
popular market, in the heart of
Robin Hood country. There is an
impressive 19th C railway viaduct,
2 interesting churches, an 18th C
Moot Hall and a museum and art
gallery.

Dalestorth Guesthouse 🏔

Listed

Skegby Lane, Skegby, Sutton in
Ashfield NG17 3DH
☎ (01623) 551110
Fax (01623) 442241
*18th C ancestral house, modernised to a
high standard. Clean, comfortable and
friendly. 5 miles junction 28 of M1 and
central for Nottinghamshire and
Derbyshire.*
Bedrooms: 8 single, 2 double, 2 twin,
1 family room
Bathrooms: 7 public
Bed & breakfast

per night:	£min	£max
Single		16.00
Double		30.00

Half board

per person:	£min	£max
Daily	21.00	22.00

Evening meal 1900 (last orders 1730)
Parking for 100
⛄ 🏌 🖵 ⚓ 🔟 🛈 🏛 🚗 ✿ ✕ 🐾 🏮

MARKET HARBOROUGH

Leicestershire
Map ref 4C3

There have been markets here
since the early 13th C, and the
town was also an important
coaching centre, with several
ancient hostelries. The early 17th
C grammar school was once the
butter market.
Tourist Information Centre
☎ *(01858) 468106*

The Fox Inn 🏔

🏮🏮 COMMENDED

Church Street, Wilbarston, Market
Harborough LE16 8QG
☎ Rockingham (01536) 771270
*Old ironstone village inn offering home-
cooked food, real ales and traditional
pub games. Near Rockingham Forest
and Castle.*
Bedrooms: 2 double, 1 twin, 1 family
room
Bathrooms: 4 private
Bed & breakfast

per night:	£min	£max
Single	20.00	30.00
Double	30.00	40.00

Continued ▶

MARKET HARBOROUGH

Continued

Lunch available
Evening meal 1830 (last orders 2145)
Parking for 10
Cards accepted: Access, Visa

MARKET RASEN

Lincolnshire
Map ref 4D2

Market town on the edge of the Lincolnshire Wolds. The racecourse and the picnic site and forest walks at Willingham Woods are to the east of the town.

East Farm House **M**

HIGHLY COMMENDED

Middle Rasen Road, Buslingthorpe,
Market Rasen LN3 5AQ
☎ (01673) 842283
410-acre arable farm. In a pretty, rural location, 4 miles south-west of Market Rasen on the Middle Rasen to Lissington road. Guests' sitting room, colour TV, tea/coffee facilities. En-suite available.
Bedrooms: 1 double, 1 twin
Bathrooms: 2 private, 1 public

Bed & breakfast
per night:	£min	£max
Single	18.00	20.00
Double	36.00	37.00

Evening meal from 1800
Parking for 6

MARSTON

Lincolnshire
Map ref 3A1

Thorold Arms

Listed COMMENDED

Main Street, Marston, Grantham
NG32 2HH
☎ Honington (01400) 250899 & 0831 340018
Fax (01400) 251030
Typical inn, circa 1830, in middle of village on the Viking Way. Traditional cask ales plus guest ales. Home-cooked food.
Bedrooms: 1 double, 1 family room
Bathrooms: 2 private

Bed & breakfast
per night:	£min	£max
Single	25.00	30.00
Double	45.00	50.00

Half board
per person:	£min	£max
Daily	30.00	35.00
Weekly	150.00	175.00

Lunch available
Evening meal 1900 (last orders 2200)

Parking for 14
Cards accepted: Visa, Amex

MARTIN

Lincolnshire
Map ref 4D2

Beechwood Barn **M**

Listed COMMENDED

North Moor Farm, Linwood Road,
Martin, Lincoln LN4 3RA
☎ (01526) 378339
20-acre arable farm. An 1853 converted barn at the edge of a mixed wood. Cosy bedrooms. Delightful walks and central for touring.
Bedrooms: 1 double, 1 twin
Bathrooms: 2 private, 1 public

Bed & breakfast
per night:	£min	£max
Single	17.00	20.00
Double	32.00	38.00

Half board
per person:	£min	£max
Daily	25.00	27.00
Weekly	157.00	170.00

Evening meal 1700 (last orders 2000)
Parking for 4
Cards accepted: Access

MATLOCK

Derbyshire
Map ref 4B2

The town lies beside the narrow valley of the River Derwent surrounded by steep wooded hills. Good centre for exploring Derbyshire's best scenery.

Farley Farm

Farley, Matlock DE4 5LR
☎ (01629) 582533
250-acre mixed farm. Built in 1610 of natural stone, set in open countryside close to Peak District and many places of interest.
Bedrooms: 1 double, 1 twin, 1 family room
Bathrooms: 1 private, 2 public

Bed & breakfast
per night:	£min	£max
Single	17.00	17.00
Double	32.00	32.00

Half board
per person:	£min	£max
Daily	22.00	23.00
Weekly	154.00	161.00

Evening meal 1700 (last orders 1900)
Parking for 10

MELTON MOWBRAY

Leicestershire
Map ref 4C3

Close to the attractive Vale of Belvoir and famous for its pork pies and Stilton cheese which are the subjects of special displays in the museum. It has a beautiful church with a tower 100 ft high.
Tourist Information Centre
☎ *(01664) 480992*

Manor House **M**

HIGHLY COMMENDED

Church Lane, Saxelby, Melton
Mowbray LE14 3PA
☎ (01664) 812269
125-acre livestock farm. Home cooking and a warm welcome in this oak-beamed farmhouse. Parts date back several hundred years including a unique 400-year-old staircase.
Bedrooms: 2 double, 1 twin, 1 family room
Bathrooms: 1 private, 1 public

Bed & breakfast
per night:	£min	£max
Single	25.00	
Double	35.00	

Half board
per person:	£min	£max
Daily	27.50	
Weekly	175.00	

Evening meal 1900 (last orders 1200)
Parking for 6
Open April-October

MIDDLETON

Northamptonshire
Map ref 4C3

Valley View

COMMENDED

3 Camsdale Walk, Middleton, Market
Harborough, Leicestershire LE16 8YR
☎ Rockingham (01536) 770874
Elevated, stone-built house with panoramic views of the Welland Valley. Within easy distance of Market Harborough and Corby.
Bedrooms: 1 double, 1 twin
Bathrooms: 1 public

Bed & breakfast
per night:	£min	£max
Single	15.00	16.00
Double	30.00	32.00

Parking for 2

The symbol **M** after an establishment name indicates membership of a Regional Tourist Board.

MORETON PINKNEY

Northamptonshire
Map ref 2C1

Thriving village in the south west of the county. The annual summer fete is a major attraction.

Barewell Fields

Listed HIGHLY COMMENDED

Moreton Pinkney, Daventry NN11 3NJ
☎ Sulgrave (01295) 760754
200-acre mixed farm. In a peaceful corner of the conservation village of Moreton Pinkney, convenient for many National Trust properties, Stratford and Silverstone, M1 and M40.
Bedrooms: 1 single, 1 double, 1 twin
Bathrooms: 1 public
Bed & breakfast

per night:	£min	£max
Single	16.00	18.00
Double	32.00	36.00

Parking for 4
Open January-November

➤ 10 ⚒ ☕ ♿ 🅿 🛎 📺 🛏 🍴 ✕ 🐾

NEWARK

Nottinghamshire
Map ref 4C2

The town has many fine old houses and ancient inns near the large, cobbled market-place. Substantial ruins of the 12th C castle, where King John died, dominate the riverside walk and there are several interesting museums. Sherwood Forest is nearby.
Tourist Information Centre
☎ *(01636) 78962*

Willow Tree Inn ⚑

Listed

Front Street, Barnby-in-the-Willows, Newark NG24 2SA
☎ Fenton Claypole (01636) 626613
Fax (01636) 626613
17th C village inn, conveniently placed for historic Lincoln, Grantham, Newark and Sherwood. Known locally for good food and ales. Off the A17 and A1.
Bedrooms: 1 single, 2 double, 2 triple
Bathrooms: 2 private, 1 public
Bed & breakfast

per night:	£min	£max
Single	15.00	17.50
Double	30.00	35.00

Half board

per person:	£min	£max
Daily	20.00	32.50
Weekly	140.00	227.50

Lunch available
Evening meal 1900 (last orders 2230)
Parking for 50
Cards accepted: Access, Visa, Amex

➤ ⚒ ☕ 📺 🍴 🛎 💷 🛏 📺 🍴 ⚓ 🍴 🔔 ○ ✳ ✕
🐾 DAP ☟ SP 🏠 Ⓣ

NORTH WINGFIELD

Derbyshire
Map ref 4B2

South View ⚑

Listed COMMENDED

95 Church Lane, North Wingfield, Chesterfield S42 5HR
☎ Chesterfield (01246) 850091
Bed and breakfast in spacious late Victorian farmhouse. Peaceful position with off-road parking. Ideal for Peak District and Amber Valley.
Bedrooms: 1 single, 2 double
Bathrooms: 1 public
Bed & breakfast

per night:	£min	£max
Single	14.00	14.00
Double	28.00	28.00

Parking for 3
Open January-November

➤ 8 🍴 ☕ 📺 ♿ 🅿 ⚒ 💷 📺 ⊛ ⚓ ✕ 🐾 SP
🏠 Ⓣ

NORTHAMPTON

Northamptonshire
Map ref 2C1

A bustling town and a shoe manufacturing centre, with excellent shopping facilities, several museums and parks, a theatre and a concert hall. Several old churches include 1 of only 4 round churches in Britain.
Tourist Information Centre
☎ *(01604) 22677*

Quinton Green Farm ⚑

Quinton, Northampton NN7 2EG
☎ (01604) 863685
Fax (01604) 862230
1200-acre arable & dairy farm. Rambling 17th C farmhouse with lovely views over own farmland. Convenient for Northampton, M1 (junction 15) and Milton Keynes.
Bedrooms: 1 single, 1 double, 1 twin
Bathrooms: 2 private, 1 public
Bed & breakfast

per night:	£min	£max
Single	18.00	20.00
Double	36.00	40.00

Parking for 6

➤ 🍴 ☕ ♿ 💷 S 🛏 📺 🍴 ⚓ ○ ✳ 🐾

> There are separate sections in this guide listing groups specialising in farm holidays and accommodation which is especially suitable for young people and organised groups.

NOTTINGHAM

Nottinghamshire
Map ref 4C2

Attractive modern city with a rich history. Outside its castle, now a museum, is Robin Hood's statue. Attractions include "The Tales of Robin Hood"; the Lace Hall; Wollaton Hall; museums and excellent facilities for shopping, sports and entertainment.
Tourist Information Centre
☎ *(0115) 947 0661 or 977 3558 (West Bridgford)*

Adams Castle View Guesthouse

Listed

85 Castle Boulevard, Nottingham NG7 1FE
☎ (0115) 950 0022
Late-Victorian private dwelling, completely refurbished to accommodate guests. Close to city centre and railway station.
Bedrooms: 3 single, 1 twin
Bathrooms: 1 public
Bed & breakfast

per night:	£min	£max
Single	16.00	
Double	30.00	

⚒ ⚓ ♿ 💷 S 🍴 🛏 📺 🍴 ✕ 🐾 SP

Grantham Hotel ⚑

COMMENDED

24-26 Radcliffe Road, West Bridgford, Nottingham NG2 5FW
☎ (0115) 981 1373
Fax (0115) 981 8567
Family-run licensed hotel offering modern accommodation in a comfortable atmosphere. Convenient for the centre of Nottingham, Trent Bridge and the National Water Sports Centre.
Bedrooms: 13 single, 2 double, 4 twin, 2 triple, 1 family room
Bathrooms: 13 private, 3 public
Bed & breakfast

per night:	£min	£max
Single	18.50	26.00
Double	38.00	38.00

Half board

per person:	£min	£max
Daily	24.00	32.00
Weekly	120.00	142.00

Evening meal 1800 (last orders 1930)
Parking for 20
Cards accepted: Access, Visa, Amex, Switch/Delta

➤ 3 🍴 ☕ ♿ 🐟 💷 S 🍴 🛏 📺 🍴 ⚓ Ⓣ

Nelson & Railway Inn

Listed APPROVED

Station Road, Kimberley, Nottingham NG16 2NR
☎ (0115) 938 2177
A family-run village inn, 1 mile north of junction 26 of the M1. Listed in "Good Beer Guide" and "Good Pub Guide".

Continued ▶

NOTTINGHAM

Continued

Bedrooms: 2 twin, 1 triple
Bathrooms: 3 private, 1 public
Bed & breakfast

per night:	£min	£max
Single	18.00	18.00
Double	31.00	31.00

Lunch available
Evening meal 1700 (last orders 2200)
Parking for 50
Cards accepted: Access, Visa

OUNDLE

Northamptonshire
Map ref 3A1

Historic town situated on the River
Nene with narrow alleys and
courtyards and many stone
buildings, including a fine church
and historic inns.
Tourist Information Centre
☎ (01832) 274333

Lilford Lodge Farm

🏠🏠 COMMENDED

Barnwell, Peterborough PE8 5SA
☎ (01832) 272230

*305-acre mixed farm. 19th C farmhouse,
recently converted, in the Nene Valley.
On the A605, 3 miles south of Oundle,
5 miles north of A14.*
Bedrooms: 1 single, 1 double, 1 twin
Bathrooms: 3 private
Bed & breakfast

per night:	£min	£max
Single	16.00	18.00
Double	32.00	36.00

Parking for 13

PEAK DISTRICT

*See under Aldwark, Ashbourne,
Ashford in the Water, Bakewell,
Bamford, Buxton, Castleton,
Chapel-en-le-Frith, Eyam,
Hathersage, Hayfield, Hope,
Tideswell, Winster*

The National Grading and
Classification Scheme is
explained in full at the back
of this guide.

RAGNALL

Nottinghamshire
Map ref 4C2

Lying 4 miles north-east of
Tuxford, close to the Trent. Pretty
and interesting church.

Ragnall House 🏠

🏠🏠 COMMENDED

Ragnall, Newark NG22 0UR
☎ Dunham-on-Trent (01777) 228575
& Mobile 0374 455792
*Large listed Georgian family house in
over an acre of grounds in a small
village close to the River Trent. Good
local inns and restaurants nearby.*
Bedrooms: 1 single, 2 twin, 1 triple
Bathrooms: 1 private, 1 public,
1 private shower
Bed & breakfast

per night:	£min	£max
Single	14.00	16.00
Double	28.00	32.00

Parking for 8

RAITHBY

Lincolnshire
Map ref 4D2

Red Lion Inn/Le Baron Restaurant

Main Road, Raithby, Spilsby
PE23 4DS
☎ Spilsby (01790) 753727

*16th C listed country inn providing
comfortable accommodation. Restaurant
with traditional and continental cuisine.*
Bedrooms: 2 double, 1 twin
Bathrooms: 3 private
Bed & breakfast

per night:	£min	£max
Single	19.00	26.00
Double	30.00	37.00

Evening meal 1900 (last orders 2130)
Parking for 20
Cards accepted: Access, Visa, Amex,
Switch/Delta

SHERWOOD FOREST

*See under Barnby Moor, Laxton,
Mansfield, Newark, Ragnall,
Southwell*

Please mention this guide
when making a booking.

SKEGNESS

Lincolnshire
Map ref 4D2

Famous seaside resort with 6
miles of sandy beaches and
bracing air. Attractions include
swimming pools, bowling greens,
gardens, Natureland Marine Zoo,
golf-courses and a wide range of
entertainment at the Embassy
Centre. Nearby is Gibraltar Point
Nature Reserve.
Tourist Information Centre
☎ (01754) 764821

Top Yard Farm 🏠

🏠

Croft Bank, Croft, Skegness PE24 4RL
☎ (01754) 880189
*A farmhouse dated 1844 in a quiet
location, 2 miles from Skegness on the
A52 Boston to Skegness road.*
Bedrooms: 2 double, 1 twin
Bathrooms: 1 private, 1 public
Bed & breakfast

per night:	£min	£max
Single	15.00	24.00
Double	24.00	32.00

Half board		
per person:	£min	£max
Daily	16.00	20.00
Weekly	100.00	128.00

Lunch available
Evening meal 1200 (last orders 2000)
Parking for 10
Open March–November
Cards accepted: Access, Visa

Victoria Inn 🏠

Wainfleet Road, Skegness PE25 3RG
☎ (01754) 767333
*Friendly, traditional inn with hotel
annexe, providing home-cooked food.
Central for town and beach facilities.*
Bedrooms: 1 single, 3 double, 1 twin,
2 family rooms
Bathrooms: 4 private, 1 public
Bed & breakfast

per night:	£min	£max
Single	13.00	15.00
Double	25.00	28.00

Half board		
per person:	£min	£max
Daily	18.00	27.00
Weekly	108.00	135.00

Lunch available
Evening meal 1800 (last orders 2200)
Parking for 20
Cards accepted: Access, Visa

We advise you to confirm
your booking in writing.

SLEAFORD

Lincolnshire
Map ref 3A1

Market town whose parish church has one of the oldest stone spires in England and particularly fine tracery round the windows.
Tourist Information Centre
☎ *(01529) 414294*

The Tally Ho Inn

⬛⬛ COMMENDED

Aswarby, Sleaford NG34 8SA
☎ Culverthorpe (01529) 455205
Traditional, friendly 17th C listed country inn. En-suite rooms in carefully converted stables, a la carte restaurant and bar meals. Plenty of welcoming atmosphere and character.
Bedrooms: 2 double, 4 twin
Bathrooms: 6 private

Bed & breakfast

per night:	£min	£max
Single	30.00	32.00
Double	45.00	47.00

Lunch available
Evening meal 1900 (last orders 2200)
Parking for 50
Cards accepted: Access, Visa, Switch/Delta

SOUTH WITHAM

Lincolnshire
Map ref 3A1

The Blue Cow Inn ⋀

Listed

29 High Street, South Witham, Grantham NG33 5QB
☎ Grantham (01572) 768432
Fax (01572) 768432
13th C beamed freehouse with log fires, real ales and home-cooked meals. Restaurant and bar meals 7 days a week. Convenient for A1, Grantham, Oakham, Stamford and Melton Mowbray.
Bedrooms: 1 single, 3 twin
Bathrooms: 2 public

Bed & breakfast

per night:	£min	£max
Single	17.50	17.50
Double	35.00	35.00

Half board

per person:	£min	£max
Daily	22.50	26.50
Weekly	150.00	175.00

Lunch available
Evening meal 1800 (last orders 2130)
Parking for 45

SOUTHWELL

Nottinghamshire
Map ref 4C2

Town dominated by the Norman minster which has some beautiful 13th C stone carvings in the Chapter House. Charles I spent his last night of freedom in one of the inns. The original Bramley apple tree can still be seen.

Barn Lodge

Listed COMMENDED

Duckers Cottage, Brinkley, Southwell NG25 0TP
☎ (01636) 813435
Smallholding with panoramic views, 1 mile from the centre of Southwell and close to the racecourse, railway station and River Trent.
Bedrooms: 1 double, 1 twin, 1 triple
Bathrooms: 3 private

Bed & breakfast

per night:	£min	£max
Single	18.00	22.00
Double	36.00	40.00

Parking for 3

Upton Fields House ⋀

⬛⬛

Upton Fields, Southwell NG25 0QA
☎ (01636) 812303
Large country house with spacious rooms, open country views, an inlaid galleried staircase and stained glass windows.
Bedrooms: 3 double, 2 twin
Bathrooms: 5 private

Bed & breakfast

per night:	£min	£max
Single	28.00	30.00
Double	45.00	48.00

Parking for 7

SPALDING

Lincolnshire
Map ref 3A1

Fenland town famous for its bulbfields. A spectacular Flower Parade takes place at the beginning of May each year and the tulips at Springfields show gardens are followed by displays of roses and bedding plants in summer. Interesting local museum.
Tourist Information Centre
☎ *(01775) 725468 or 761161 ext 4297*

Travel Stop ⋀

②② APPROVED

Locks Mill Farm, 50 Cowbit Road, Spalding PE11 2RJ
☎ (01775) 767290 & 767716
Fax (01775) 767716

Converted from farm buildings, the motel complements 17th C farmhouse. Three-quarters of a mile from centre of Spalding on A1073 Peterborough road. Most units are on ground floor with own porches and all are equipped with refrigerator and colour TV.
Bedrooms: 3 single, 5 double, 2 twin
Bathrooms: 10 private, 2 public

Bed & breakfast

per night:	£min	£max
Single	20.00	42.00
Double	35.00	55.00

Parking for 25
Cards accepted: Access, Visa, Amex

STAMFORD

Lincolnshire
Map ref 3A1

Exceptionally beautiful and historic town with many houses of architectural interest, several notable churches and other public buildings all in the local stone. Burghley House, built by William Cecil, is a magnificent Tudor mansion on the edge of the town.
Tourist Information Centre
☎ *(01780) 55611*

Birch House ⋀

Listed COMMENDED

4 Lonsdale Road, Stamford PE9 2RW
☎ (01780) 54876 & 0850 185759
Comfortable, family-run detached house on the outskirts of Stamford. All rooms have TV and tea/coffee-making facilities. Non-smokers only, please.
Bedrooms: 2 single, 1 double, 1 twin
Bathrooms: 1 public

Bed & breakfast

per night:	£min	£max
Single	15.00	
Double	30.00	

Parking for 3

176 Casterton Road ⋀

Listed COMMENDED

Stamford PE9 2XX
☎ (01780) 63368
Homely, modern detached house, a mile from the A1 on the B1081 and 1 mile from town centre.
Bedrooms: 2 single, 1 double
Bathrooms: 1 public

Bed & breakfast

per night:	£min	£max
Single	16.00	16.00
Double	30.00	30.00

Parking for 3

STAMFORD

Continued

The Manor Cottage
Listed HIGHLY COMMENDED
Stamford Road, Collyweston, Stamford
PE9 3PN
☎ (01780) 444209
Large stone-built Georgian house, set in 2 acres of grounds, with panoramic views, in the picturesque village of Collyweston, just 3 miles from historic Stamford.
Bedrooms: 2 single, 1 double, 1 twin
Bathrooms: 1 private, 2 public

Bed & breakfast

per night:	£min	£max
Single	15.00	35.00
Double	30.00	60.00

Parking for 10

Martins
Listed
20 High Street, Saint Martin's,
Stamford PE9 2LF
☎ (01780) 52106
Elegant, 17th C house near the town centre. Large rooms furnished with antiques. Walled garden and croquet. Street parking.
Bedrooms: 3 twin
Bathrooms: 2 public

Bed & breakfast

per night:	£min	£max
Single	22.50	28.50
Double	45.00	50.00

Half board

per person:	£min	£max
Daily	37.50	43.50
Weekly	250.00	292.00

Evening meal 1930 (last orders 2030)
Parking for 3

Midstone Farm House
Listed COMMENDED
Southorpe, Stamford PE9 3BX
☎ (01780) 740136
Fax (01780) 740136
20-acre mixed farm. Grade II listed farmhouse in beautiful countryside with lovely walks. Adults and children will enjoy meeting George, the pot bellied pig.
Bedrooms: 2 double, 1 twin
Bathrooms: 1 private, 2 public

Bed & breakfast

per night:	£min	£max
Single	18.00	24.00
Double	35.00	40.00

Parking for 5

The Priory ⋀
HIGHLY COMMENDED
Church Road, Ketton, Stamford
PE9 3RD
☎ (01780) 720215
Fax (01780) 721881

Grade II listed 16th C licensed country house near Stamford. En-suite rooms overlooking splendid gardens. Colour brochure available.
Bedrooms: 2 double, 1 twin
Bathrooms: 3 private, 1 public

Bed & breakfast

per night:	£min	£max
Single	29.50	37.50
Double	38.00	55.00

Half board

per person:	£min	£max
Daily	31.50	40.00
Weekly	198.00	252.00

Lunch available
Evening meal 1900 (last orders 2000)
Parking for 10
Cards accepted: Access, Visa

Rock Lodge ⋀
1 Empingham Road, Stamford
PE9 2RH
☎ (01780) 64211
Fax (01780) 482442
Victorian former hunting lodge c1900, set within stone-walled gardens. En-suite rooms. Close to heart of Stamford.
Bedrooms: 2 double, 1 twin
Bathrooms: 3 private

Bed & breakfast

per night:	£min	£max
Single	25.00	35.00
Double	40.00	50.00

Parking for 3

STRETTON

Derbyshire
Map ref 4B2

Ivy Beech
Listed COMMENDED
Highstairs Lane, Stretton, Derby
DE55 6FD
☎ Chesterfield (01246) 863397
Private house in its own grounds, down a country lane but close to the main trunk road. An ideal centre for touring.
Bedrooms: 1 single, 2 twin
Bathrooms: 1 private, 2 public

Bed & breakfast

per night:	£min	£max
Single	15.50	15.50
Double	31.00	31.00

Evening meal 1900 (last orders 2000)
Parking for 5

SWAYFIELD

Lincolnshire
Map ref 3A1

The Royal Oak Inn ⋀
Listed COMMENDED
High Street, Swayfield, Grantham
NG33 4LL
☎ Corby Glen (01476) 550247
Fax (01476) 550996
Old world inn in country setting, 3.5 miles from A1. Well-appointed 1650 property with chalet accommodation. Separate restaurant.
Bedrooms: 2 double, 2 twin, 1 family room
Bathrooms: 5 private

Bed & breakfast

per night:	£min	£max
Single	29.75	29.75
Double	34.75	34.75

Lunch available
Evening meal 1830 (last orders 2230)
Parking for 40
Cards accepted: Access, Visa, Amex

TIDESWELL

Derbyshire
Map ref 4B2

Small town with a large 14th C church known as the "Cathedral of the Peak". There is a well-dressing ceremony each June with Morris dancing, and many choral events throughout the year.

Poppies
Listed APPROVED
Bank Square, Tideswell, Buxton
SK17 8LA
☎ (01298) 871083
Poppies offers a warm welcome, comfortable accommodation and good vegetarian and traditional home cooking in a small restaurant, at the centre of this picturesque mid Peak District village.
Bedrooms: 1 double, 1 twin, 1 triple
Bathrooms: 1 private, 1 public

Bed & breakfast

per night:	£min	£max
Single	14.00	18.50
Double	28.00	37.00

Half board

per person:	£min	£max
Daily	24.00	36.00
Weekly	154.00	220.00

Lunch available
Evening meal 1900 (last orders 2130)

Open February-December
Cards accepted: Access, Visa, Diners, Amex

TWO DALES

Derbyshire
Map ref 4B2

Village set in beautiful Derbyshire scenery and with easy access to the country houses of Haddon and Chatsworth.

Top 'O The Hill

Listed COMMENDED

Sydnope Hill, Two Dales, Matlock
DE4 2FN
☎ Matlock (01629) 734548

A modern, country residence overlooking the Peak Park border with superb views. On the B5057, Darley Dale to Chesterfield road.

Bedrooms: 2 double, 1 twin
Bathrooms: 1 public

Bed & breakfast per night:	£min	£max
Single	15.00	16.50
Double	30.00	33.00

Half board per person:	£min	£max
Daily	24.00	25.50
Weekly	161.00	171.50

Evening meal 1800 (last orders 2000)
Parking for 4

UPPINGHAM

Leicestershire
Map ref 4C3

Quiet market town dominated by its famous public school which was founded in 1584. It has many stone houses and is surrounded by attractive countryside.

Old Rectory

New Road, Belton in Rutland, Oakham
LE15 9LE
☎ Belton (01572) 717279
Fax (01572) 717343

14-acre smallholding. Large Victorian country house and annexe overlooking Eye Brook valley and rolling Rutland countryside. Cottage-style en-suite rooms, quiet friendly atmosphere and good food. Small farm environment. Families welcome.

Bedrooms: 1 single, 2 double, 2 twin, 1 triple, 1 family room
Bathrooms: 7 private

Bed & breakfast per night:	£min	£max
Single	25.00	
Double	36.00	44.00

Half board per person:	£min	£max
Daily	32.00	

Evening meal 1800 (last orders 1900)
Parking for 10
Cards accepted: Access, Visa

Rutland House

61 High Street East, Uppingham
LE15 9PY
☎ (01572) 822497
Fax (01572) 822497

Family-run B&B with all rooms en-suite. Close to Rutland Water. Full English or continental breakfast. Well-placed for exploring Rutland's villages and countryside.

Bedrooms: 2 single, 1 double, 1 twin
Bathrooms: 4 private

Bed & breakfast per night:	£min	£max
Single	29.00	29.00
Double	39.00	39.00

Parking for 3
Cards accepted: Access, Visa

WEEDON

Northamptonshire
Map ref 2C1

Old village steeped in history, with thatched cottages and several antique shops.

Globe Hotel

COMMENDED

High Street, Weedon, Northampton
NN7 4QD
☎ (01327) 340336
Fax (01327) 349058

19th C countryside inn. Old world atmosphere and freehouse hospitality with good English cooking, available all day. Meeting rooms. Close to M1, Stratford and many tourist spots. Send for information pack.

Bedrooms: 4 single, 6 double, 5 twin, 3 triple
Bathrooms: 18 private

Bed & breakfast per night:	£min	£max
Single	29.50	42.00
Double	39.50	49.50

Half board per person:	£min	£max
Daily	35.00	54.95
Weekly	245.00	384.65

Lunch available
Evening meal (last orders 2200)
Parking for 40
Cards accepted: Access, Visa, Diners, Amex

30

WESSINGTON

Derbyshire
Map ref 4B2

Small village between Alfreton and Matlock on the A615.

Crich Lane Farm

Listed

Moorwood Moor Lane, Wessington, Derby DE55 6DU
☎ Alfreton (01773) 835186

44-acre dairy farm. Large garden in peaceful surroundings, easy walking distance of village and pubs. Pet attractions and a warm and friendly welcome to all. Easy access to M1 and A38.

Bedrooms: 1 single, 1 double, 1 twin, 1 family room
Bathrooms: 2 public

Bed & breakfast per night:	£min	£max
Single	15.00	17.00
Double	30.00	34.00

Parking for 10

WEST HADDON

Northamptonshire
Map ref 4C3

A once rural community with the historic and attractive All Saints Church.

Pear Trees

APPROVED

31 Station Road, West Haddon, Northampton NN6 7AU
☎ (01788) 510389

Attractive 18th C Northamptonshire-stone detached house in village, with good pubs/restaurants within walking distance. Four miles junction 18 M1/M6. Rugby 10 miles, Daventry 7 miles, Northampton 13 miles, nearest main line station 2 miles.

Bedrooms: 1 double, 1 twin, 1 triple
Bathrooms: 3 private, 1 public

Bed & breakfast per night:	£min	£max
Single	18.00	20.00
Double	36.00	38.00

Half board per person:	£min	£max
Daily	25.00	27.00
Weekly	165.00	180.00

Evening meal 1900 (last orders 2030)

WESTON UNDERWOOD

Derbyshire
Map ref 4B2

Parkview Farm ⋏⋏

HIGHLY COMMENDED

Weston Underwood, Ashbourne
DE6 4PA
☎ Ashbourne (01335) 360352
*370-acre arable & dairy farm. Period
farmhouse with country house
atmosphere. Elegant four-poster
bedrooms overlooking the gardens and
the National Trust's Kedleston Hall and
Park.*
Bedrooms: 2 double, 1 twin
Bathrooms: 1 private, 2 public
Bed & breakfast

per night:	£min	£max
Single	22.00	25.00
Double	38.00	40.00

Parking for 10

WILLOUGHBY WATERLEYS

Leicestershire
Map ref 4C3

Mentioned in the Domesday Book,
village 8 miles due south of
Leicester. Its name comes from
the many springs that lie near the
surface and the two rivulets that
run through the parish.

The Old Rectory

Listed

Willoughby Waterleys, Leicester
LE8 6UF
☎ (0116) 247 8474
*A listed Georgian rectory with many
original features, in a conservation
village 7 miles south of Leicester.*
Bedrooms: 1 double, 1 twin
Bathrooms: 1 private, 1 public
Bed & breakfast

per night:	£min	£max
Single	20.00	20.00
Double	40.00	40.00

Parking for 4

> Please mention this guide
> when making a booking.

WINSTER

Derbyshire
Map ref 4B2

Village with some interesting old
gritstone houses and cottages,
including the 17th C stone market
hall now owned by the National
Trust. It is a former lead mining
centre.

Brae Cottage ⋏⋏

East Bank, Winster, Matlock DE4 2DT
☎ (01629) 650375
*Spacious, self contained cottage annexe,
ground level, with en-suite bathroom.
Garage, patio and picturesque garden.
Suitable for couple or small
family/group.*
Bedrooms: 1 family room
Bathrooms: 1 private
Bed & breakfast

per night:	£min	£max
Single	14.00	14.00
Double	28.00	28.00

Parking for 2

The Dower House

HIGHLY COMMENDED

Main Street, Winster, Matlock
DE4 2DH
☎ Matlock (01629) 650213
Fax (01629) 650894
*Elizabethan country house offering
peace and relaxation in a homely
atmosphere. Home-made jams and
marmalade. Close to Chatsworth and
Haddon Hall. Resident Blue Badge
Derbyshire tourist guide.*
Bedrooms: 1 double, 2 twin
Bathrooms: 3 private
Bed & breakfast

per night:	£min	£max
Double	36.00	55.00

Parking for 6
Open March-October

> All accommodation in this
> guide has been graded, or is
> awaiting a grading, by a trained
> Tourist Board inspector.

WINWICK

Northamptonshire
Map ref 4C3

Pleasant village, one of the most
rural in the county. Has a pretty,
medieval church at which much
restoration has been completed.

Winwick Mill ⋏⋏

Winwick, West Haddon NN6 7PD
☎ West Haddon (01788) 510613
Fax (01788) 510613
*Converted watermill in quiet, secluded
location. Ideal for rambling and touring.
All bedrooms en-suite. Good access to
M1, M6, A5 and A14.*
Bedrooms: 1 single, 1 double, 1 twin
Bathrooms: 3 private
Bed & breakfast

per night:	£min	£max
Double	36.00	

Evening meal 1800 (last orders 2000)
Parking for 10

YARDLEY GOBION

Northamptonshire
Map ref 2C1

Lying in the southern tip of the
county near the Grand Union
Canal, a relatively modern village
with much expansion since the
1950s.

Old Wharf Farm

Listed

Bridge 60, Grand Union Canal, Yardley
Gobion NN12 7UE
☎ Milton Keynes (01908) 542454 &
Mobile 0860 924782
*8-acre smallholding. This unique
complex of old farm buildings, with its
own working wharf and dry dock on to
the Grand Union Canal, is now a family
home, smallholding and canal boat
maintenance base.*
Bedrooms: 1 single, 1 double, 1 triple
Bathrooms: 2 public
Bed & breakfast

per night:	£min	£max
Single	18.00	20.00
Double	34.00	42.00

Parking for 5

East Anglia

This is a region of wide skies and broad-brush landscapes, a land with a character all of its own. Sandy heaths, wide fenlands and lush valleys are all waiting to be explored. To the southwest lies pretty Hertfordshire; to the east, the reed-murmuring watery Broads, England's newest National Park.

Along the coast discover sandy beaches and bird-haunted marshlands, havens for ornithologists. Head for the bright-light fun of Great Yarmouth, Clacton and Southend-on-Sea; genteel, pretty Southwold; Aldeburgh with its famous music festival.

Don't miss picturesque Constable country, where the painter lived and worked, and don't leave the region without first tasting succulent Cromer crab, Suffolk ham, and Colchester oysters.

The Counties of Bedfordshire, Cambridgeshire, Essex, Hertfordshire, Norfolk and Suffolk

For more information on East Anglia, contact:

East Anglia Tourist Board
Toppesfield Hall, Hadleigh,
Suffolk IP7 5DN
Tel: (01473) 822922
Fax: (01473) 823063

Where to Go in East Anglia – see pages 202–205
Where to Stay in East Anglia – see pages 206–236

East Anglia

Where to go and what to see

You will find hundreds of interesting places to visit during your stay in East Anglia, just some of which are listed in these pages. The number against each name will help you locate it on the map (page 205). Contact any Tourist Information Centre in the region for more ideas on days out in East Anglia.

1 Holkham Hall
Wells-next-the-Sea, Norfolk
NR23 1AB
Tel: (01328) 710733
Classic 18th C Palladian-style mansion, part of a great agricultural estate, and a living treasure house of artistic and architectural history.

2 Sea Life Centre
Southern Promenade, Hunstanton, Norfolk PE36 5BH
Tel: (01485) 533576
See a world only divers see, from the ocean tunnel. View and touch a variety of rock pool creatures. Also a seal rehabilitation centre.

3 Thursford Collection
Thursford, Norfolk NR21 0AS
Tel: (01328) 878477
Live musical shows, mechanical organs and Wurlitzer show.

4 Blickling Hall
Blickling, Norfolk NR11 6NF
Tel: (01263) 733084
Jacobean red brick mansion. Garden, orangery, parkland and lake. Fine tapestries and furniture.

5 Pensthorpe Waterfowl Park
Pensthorpe, Fakenham, Norfolk
NR21 0LN
Tel: (01328) 851465
Large waterfowl and wildfowl collection. Information centre, conservation shop, adventure play area, walks and nature trails. Licensed restaurant.

6 Sainsbury Centre for Visual Arts
University of East Anglia, Norwich, Norfolk NR4 7TJ
Tel: (01603) 56060
Robert and Lisa Sainsbury Collection is wide ranging and of international importance, housed in a remarkable building designed by N. Foster.

7 Sacrewell Farm and Country Centre
Sacrewell, Thornhaugh, Peterborough, Cambridgeshire
PE8 6HJ
Tel: (01780) 782222
500-acre farm, with working watermill, gardens, shrubberies, nature and general interest trails. 18th C buildings, displays of farm, rural and domestic bygones.

8 Oxburgh Hall
Oxborough, King's Lynn, Norfolk
PE33 9PS
Tel: (01366) 328258
15th C moated red brick fortified manor house. Magnificent 80ft gatehouse, Mary Queen of Scots needlework, priest's hole, garden.

9 Pleasure Beach
South Beach Parade, Great Yarmouth, Norfolk NR30 3EH
Tel: (01493) 844585
Roller coaster, terminator, log flume,

flipper, monorail, breakdance, galloping horses, caterpillar, ghost train and fun house.

⑩ Somerleyton Hall and Gardens
Somerleyton, Suffolk NR32 5QQ
Tel: (01502) 730224
Anglo-Italian style building with state rooms, maze, garden. Miniature railway, shop and refreshment room.

⑪ Pleasurewood Hills American Theme Park
Lowestoft, Suffolk NR32 5DZ
Tel: (01502)508200
Tempest, chair lift, cine 180, railway, pirate ship, fort, Aladdin's cave, parrot shows, rollercoaster, waveswinger, Eye in the Sky, star ride Enterprise.

⑫ Otter Trust
Earsham, Suffolk NR35 2AF
Tel: (01986) 893470
A breeding and conservation headquarters with the largest collection of otters in the world. Also lakes with collection of waterfowl, deer, etc.

⑬ Bressingham Steam Museum and Gardens
Bressingham, Norfolk IP22 2AB
Tel: (0137988) 386
Steam rides through 5 miles of woodland, garden and nursery. Mainline locomotive and over 50

steam engines. Alan Bloom's "Dell" garden.

⑭ Ancient House Museum
White Hart Street, Thetford, Norfolk IP24 1AA
Tel: (01842) 752599
Museum of Thetford and Breckland life in a remarkable early Tudor house. Displays on local history, flint, archaeology and natural history.

⑮ Ely Cathedral
Chapter House, The College, Ely, Cambridgeshire CB7 4DN
Tel: (01353) 667735
One of England's finest cathedrals. Octagon is the crowning glory. Fine outbuildings. Guided tours and tower tours available. Brass rubbing and stained glass museum.

⑯ Minsmere Nature Reserve (RSPB)
Westleton, Suffolk IP17 3BY
Tel: (0178873) 281
Two 2-mile walks, 6 hides on coastal lagoon walk, 2 hides on reed bed. Birds include avocet, marsh harrier, bittern. Shop and reception area.

⑰ Framlingham Castle
Framlingham, Suffolk IP8 9BT
Tel: (01728) 724189
12th C curtain walls with 13 towers and Tudor brick chimneys. Built by Bigod family, Earls of Norfolk, home of Mary Tudor in 1553.

⑱ Pakenham Watermill
Grimstone End, Pakenham, Bury St. Edmunds, Suffolk
Tel: (01787) 247179
Fine 18th C working watermill on Domesday site complete with oil engine and other subsidiary machinery. Restored by Suffolk Preservation Society.

⑲ Ickworth House, Park and Gardens
Ickworth, Bury St Edmunds, Suffolk IP29 5QE
Tel: (01284) 735270
Extraordinary oval house with flanking wings. Fine paintings and Georgian silver, Italian garden and park designed by Capability Brown.

⑳ The National Horseracing Museum
99 High Street, Newmarket, Suffolk CB8 8JL
Tel: (01638) 667333
5 permanent galleries telling the great story of the development of horseracing. British sporting art.

㉑ Helmingham Hall Gardens
Helmingham, Suffolk IP14 6EF
Tel: (01473) 890363
Moated and walled garden with many rare roses and possibly the best kitchen garden in Britain. Highland cattle, safari rides in park to view red and fallow deer.

a collection of manuscripts, portraits, Jacobean banqueting hall, adventure playground and gift shop.

27 Whipsnade Wild Animal Park
Zoological Society of London, Dunstable, Bedfordshire LU6 2LF
Tel: (01582) 872171
Over 2,000 animals of 200 species in 600 acres of parkland. Children's playground, railway, Tiger Falls, sea-lions and birds of prey.

28 The Gardens of the Rose
The Royal National Rose Society, Chiswell Green, St Albans, Hertfordshire AL2 3NR
Tel: (01727) 850461
The Royal National Rose Society's garden, 20 acres of showground and trial ground for new varieties of rose. 30,000 roses of all types with 1,700 different varieties.

29 Hatfield House
Hatfield Park, Hatfield, Hertfordshire AL9 5NQ
Tel: (01707) 262823
Jacobean house built in 1611 and Old Palace built in 1497. Contains famous paintings, fine furniture and possessions of Queen Elizabeth I. Park and gardens.

30 Aldenham Country Park
Dagger Lane, Elstree, Hertfordshire WD6 3AT
Tel: (0181) 953 9602
65-acre reservoir, circular footpath and 175 acres of woods. Adventure playground, rare breed cattle, sheep, pigs and chickens. Angling, nature trail, horse-riding.

22 Imperial War Museum
Duxford, Cambridgeshire CB2 4QR
Tel: (01223) 835000
Over 120 aircraft plus tanks, vehicles and guns on display. Adventure playground, shops, restaurant.

23 Woburn Abbey
Woburn, Bedfordshire MK43 0TP
Tel: (01525) 290666
18th C Palladian mansion altered by Henry Holland, the Prince Regent's architect. Contains a collection of English silver, French and English furniture and an important art collection.

24 Mountfitchet Castle
Stansted Mountfitchet, Essex CM24 8SP

Tel: (01279) 813237
Reconstructed Norman motte and bailey castle and village of Domesday period. Grand hall, church, prison, siege tower and weapons.

25 Colchester Castle
Colchester, Essex CO1 1TJ
Tel: (01206) 282931
Norman keep on foundations of Roman temple. Archaeological material includes much on Roman Colchester.

26 Knebworth House, Gardens and Park
Knebworth, Hertfordshire SG3 6PY
Tel: (01438) 812661
Tudor mansion house refashioned in the 19th C by Bulwer-Lytton. Houses

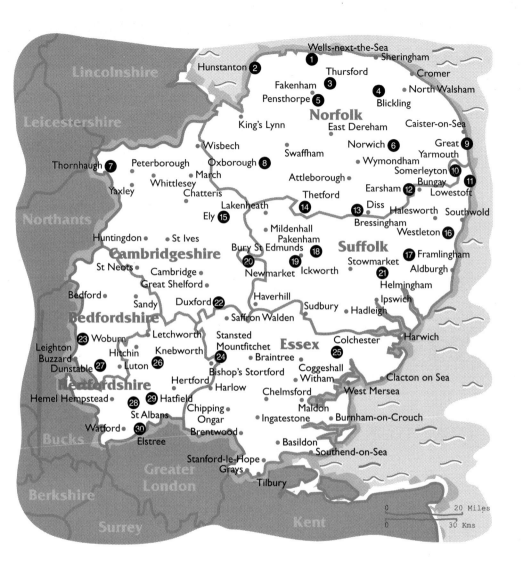

Find Out More

Further information about holidays and attractions in East Anglia is available from:

East Anglia Tourist Board, Toppesfield Hall, Hadleigh, Suffolk IP7 5DN
Tel: (01473) 822922

These publications are available from the East Anglia Tourist Board (post free):

- **Bed & Breakfast Touring Map**
- **Great Escapes** – short breaks
- **Places to Stay: Hotels, Guesthouses and Inns and Self-Catering**
- **Camping and Caravaning Touring Map**
- **Freedom Holiday Parks in Eastern England**

Also available are (prices include postage and packaging):

- **East Anglia Guide** £4.50
- **East Anglia Leisure Map** £4.50
- **A Day out of London Map** £4.00
- **Gardens to Visit in East Anglia** £1.50

WHERE TO STAY

Accommodation entries in this regional section are listed in alphabetical order of place name, and then in alphabetical order of establishment.

Map references refer to the colour location maps at the back of this guide. The first figure is the map number; the letter and figure which follow indicate the grid reference on the map.

At-a-glance symbols at the end of each accommodation entry give information about services and facilities. A handy guide to these symbols can be found inside the back cover flap, which can be kept open for easy reference.

ALDEBURGH

Suffolk
Map ref 3C2

A prosperous port in the 16th C, now famous for the Aldeburgh Music Festival held annually in June. The 16th C Moot Hall, now a museum, is a timber-framed building once used as an open market.

Faraway
Listed
28 Linden Close, Aldeburgh IP15 5JL
☎ (01728) 452571
Bungalow with garden and car parking. Very quiet, being off the main road. TV in all rooms.
Bedrooms: 1 single, 1 twin, 1 triple
Bathrooms: 2 public
Bed & breakfast

per night:	£min	£max
Single	14.00	15.00
Double	28.00	30.00

Parking for 4
⌂ ⛱ ♨ ❑ ⓤ Ⓢ ⅋ ⏢ ⅏ 🖳 ✿ 🐾

ALDHAM

Essex
Map ref 3B2

Old House ♠
😃 COMMENDED
Ford Street, Aldham, Colchester CO6 3PH
☎ Colchester (01206) 240456
Bed and breakfast in 14th C family home, listed as historic building, with friendly atmosphere, oak beams, log fires, large garden and ample parking. Between Harwich and Cambridge, Felixstowe and London. On A604, 5 miles west of Colchester.
Bedrooms: 1 single, 1 double, 1 twin
Bathrooms: 3 private, 1 public
Bed & breakfast

per night:	£min	£max
Single	25.00	30.00
Double	35.00	45.00

Parking for 8
⌂ ⅌ ❑ ♨ ⓤ ⅋ ✄ ⏢ 🖳 ⅏ ✿ ✕ 🐾 🏠

AMPTHILL

Bedfordshire
Map ref 2D1

Busy market town with houses of distinctive Georgian character. Market established in 13th C, where traders sell their wares around the town pump, a Portland-stone obelisk presented to the town in 1785 by Lord Ossory.

Pond Farm
Listed
7 High Street, Pulloxhill, Bedford MK45 5HA
☎ Flitwick (01525) 712316
70-acre arable & horse farm. Listed building, an ideal base for touring. Close to Woburn Abbey, Whipsnade Zoo, the Shuttleworth Collection of old aircraft and Luton Airport. Resident Great Dane. Tea/coffee and colour TV all rooms.
Bedrooms: 1 double, 1 twin, 1 triple
Bathrooms: 1 public
Bed & breakfast

per night:	£min	£max
Single	16.00	20.00
Double	30.00	

Parking for 6
⌂ ❑ ♨ ⓤ ⓘ Ⓢ ⏢ 🖳 ⅏ ✿ ✕ 🐾 🏠 Ⓣ

ARDLEIGH

Essex
Map ref 3B2

2.5 miles north-east of Colchester on the A137. Ardleigh Reservoir has a large bird-watching area.

Dundas Place ♠
😃 😃 COMMENDED
Colchester Road, Ardleigh, Colchester CO7 7NP
☎ Colchester (01206) 230625
300-year-old cottage with exposed oak beams throughout, a large open fireplace and a picturesque old world garden. Located in the centre of the village. Four night bed and breakfast package - £128 for 2 people, including use of Ordnance Survey maps and local information.
Bedrooms: 1 double, 2 twin
Bathrooms: 1 private, 1 public
Bed & breakfast

per night:	£min	£max
Single	20.00	23.00
Double	34.00	38.00

Parking for 2
⌂ 12 ❑ ♨ ⓤ Ⓢ ⅋ ⅋ 🖳 ⅏ ✿ 🐾 🏠

The symbol ⚙ within an entry indicates participation in the Welcome Host programme – a nationally recognised customer care initiative which aims to promote the highest standards of service and a warm welcome for all visitors.

AYLSHAM

Norfolk
Map ref 3B1

Small town on the River Bure with an attractive market place and interesting church. Nearby is Blickling Hall (National Trust). Also the terminal of the Bure Valley narrow gauge steam railway which runs on 9 miles of the old Great Eastern trackbed, between Wroxham and Aylsham.

The Old Bank House

3 Norwich Road, Aylsham, Norwich
NR11 6BN
☎ (01263) 733843

Relax in the comfort and traditional Victorian atmosphere of Aylsham's former private bank. We offer guests a friendly break, spacious welcoming bedrooms with TV and home-cooked meals. Lovely countryside nearby.
Bedrooms: 1 double, 1 twin, 1 triple
Bathrooms: 2 private, 2 public

Bed & breakfast

per night:	£min	£max
Single	17.00	20.00
Double	34.00	36.00

Half board

per person:	£min	£max
Daily	26.50	29.50
Weekly	156.00	174.00

Evening meal 1800 (last orders 2000)
Parking for 3

The Old Pump House ⋀

HIGHLY COMMENDED

Holman Road, Aylsham, Norwich
NR11 6BY
☎ (01263) 733789
Comfortable, rambling 1750s family home, opposite thatched pump and 1 minute from church and historic marketplace. Pine-shuttered breakfast room overlooks peaceful garden. Non-smoking.
Bedrooms: 3 double, 2 twin
Bathrooms: 3 private, 2 public

Bed & breakfast

per night:	£min	£max
Single	17.00	25.00
Double	34.00	42.00

Half board

per person:	£min	£max
Daily	27.00	35.00
Weekly	138.00	186.00

Evening meal from 1900
Parking for 7

BACTON

Suffolk
Map ref 3B2

Brickwall Farm

HIGHLY COMMENDED

Broad Road, Bacton, Stowmarket
IP14 4HP
☎ (01449) 780197
17th C listed farmhouse which has been sympathetically restored. Centrally situated for exploring Mid-Suffolk and the Heritage Coast.
Bedrooms: 3 double
Bathrooms: 3 private

Bed & breakfast

per night:	£min	£max
Double	35.00	

Half board

per person:	£min	£max
Weekly	150.00	

Evening meal 1900 (last orders 2100)
Parking for 5

BARNHAM

Suffolk
Map ref 3B2

Rymer Farm

COMMENDED

Barnham, Thetford, Norfolk IP24 2PP
☎ Elveden (01842) 890233
Fax (01842) 890653

550-acre arable farm. 17th C farmhouse welcomes guests with tea and log fire or summer garden room. Enjoy real "farmer's breakfast". Farm walks with wildlife, carp lake and gardens.
Bedrooms: 1 single, 1 double, 1 twin
Bathrooms: 3 private, 1 public

Bed & breakfast

per night:	£min	£max
Single	19.00	21.00
Double	36.00	40.00

Parking for 10

> Half board prices shown are per person but in some cases may be based on double/twin occupancy.

BECCLES

Suffolk
Map ref 3C1

Fire destroyed the town in the 16th C and it was rebuilt in Georgian red brick. The River Waveney, on which the town stands, is popular with boating enthusiasts and has an annual regatta. Home of Beccles and District Museum and the William Clowes Printing Museum.

Rose Cottage

Listed COMMENDED

21 Kells Way, Geldeston, Beccles
NR34 0LU
☎ Kirby Cane (01508) 518451
Parts of the cottage date back to 1600, with inglenook fireplaces, beams and studwork. Quiet Waveney Valley position in south Norfolk.
Bedrooms: 2 single, 2 double
Bathrooms: 1 public

Bed & breakfast

per night:	£min	£max
Single	15.00	15.00
Double	27.00	27.00

Parking for 3

BEDFORD

Bedfordshire
Map ref 2D1

Busy county town with interesting buildings and churches near the River Ouse which has pleasant riverside walks. Many associations with John Bunyan, including Bunyan Meeting House, museum and statue. The Bedford Museum and Cecil Higgins Art Gallery are of interest.
Tourist Information Centre
☎ (01234) 215226

Firs Farm

COMMENDED

Stagsden, Bedford MK43 8TB
☎ (01234) 822344
504-acre arable farm. Family-run, set in quiet surroundings quarter-of-a-mile south of A422, midway between Bedford and Milton Keynes (M1 junction 14).
Bedrooms: 2 double, 1 twin
Bathrooms: 1 private, 1 public

Bed & breakfast

per night:	£min	£max
Single	15.00	20.00
Double	30.00	40.00

Parking for 4

Jays End Guest House

Listed

13 Putnoe Heights, Bedford
MK41 8EB
☎ (01234) 359537

Continued ►

BEDFORD

Continued

Semi-detached house, within walking distance of the town centre. Both rooms en-suite. Small and friendly. Ample parking.
Bedrooms: 1 double, 1 twin
Bathrooms: 2 private

Bed & breakfast

per night:	£min	£max
Single	12.50	15.00
Double	25.00	30.00

Parking for 2

BEETLEY

Norfolk
Map ref 3B1

Peacock House ⋀

Listed | HIGHLY COMMENDED

Peacock Lane, Old Beetley, Dereham NR20 4DG
☎ Dereham (01362) 860371
Beautiful period farmhouse in rural setting, 3.5 miles from Dereham. Ideal for Norwich, Sandringham and coast. Full English breakfast and a warm welcome.
Bedrooms: 2 double, 1 twin
Bathrooms: 3 private

Bed & breakfast

per night:	£min	£max
Single	17.00	18.00
Double	34.00	36.00

Parking for 4

BELCHAMP ST PAUL

Essex
Map ref 3B2

Cherry Tree Inn ⋀

Listed

Knowl Green, Belchamp St Paul, Sudbury, Suffolk CO10 7BY
☎ Great Yeldham (01787) 237263
Friendly thatched freehouse in beautiful countryside. Delightful self-contained accommodation. Lovely views. Ideal for touring East Anglia. Good, inexpensive home-made food. 60 miles London, close Harwich and Felixstowe.
Bedrooms: 1 double, 1 twin
Bathrooms: 2 private

Bed & breakfast

per night:	£min	£max
Double	35.00	

Lunch available
Evening meal 1900 (last orders 2030)
Parking for 40

We advise you to confirm your booking in writing.

BIGGLESWADE

Bedfordshire
Map ref 2D1

Busy centre for market gardening set on the River Ivel spanned by a 14th C bridge. Some interesting old buildings in the market-place. Nearby are the Shuttleworth collection of historic aeroplanes and Jordan's Mill.

Old Warden Guest House

Listed

Shop and Post Office, Old Warden, Biggleswade SG18 9HQ
☎ Northill (01767) 627201
Listed, 19th C building, adjacent to shop and post office. Between Biggleswade and Bedford.
Bedrooms: 1 double, 2 twin
Bathrooms: 1 public

Bed & breakfast

per night:	£min	£max
Single	15.00	20.00
Double	34.00	34.00

Parking for 5

BISHOP'S STORTFORD

Hertfordshire
Map ref 2D1

Fine old town on the River Stort with many interesting buildings, particularly Victorian, and an imposing parish church. The vicarage where Cecil Rhodes was born is now a museum.
Tourist Information Centre
☎ *(01279) 652274*

The Thatch

Listed | HIGHLY COMMENDED

Cambridge Road, Ugley, Bishop's Stortford CM22 6HZ
☎ Rickling (01799) 543440
Situated in hamlet just north of Bishop's Stortford. Set in lovely countryside, with warm and friendly atmosphere. Convenient for Stansted airport and M11. Airport parking available.
Bedrooms: 2 double, 1 twin
Bathrooms: 2 private, 1 public

Bed & breakfast

per night:	£min	£max
Single	18.00	25.00
Double	36.00	40.00

Parking for 7

The accommodation coupons at the back will help you when contacting proprietors.

BLAKENEY

Norfolk
Map ref 3B1

Picturesque village on the north coast of Norfolk and a former port and fishing village. 15th C Guildhall. Marshy creeks extend towards Blakeney Point (National Trust) and are a paradise for naturalists, with trips to the reserve and to see the seals from Blakeney Quay.

Flintstones Guest House ⋀

Listed | COMMENDED

Wiveton, Holt NR25 7TL
☎ Cley (01263) 740337
Attractive licensed guesthouse in picturesque rural surroundings near village green. 1 mile from Cley and Blakeney with good sailing and bird-watching. All rooms with private facilities. Non-smokers only, please.
Bedrooms: 1 single, 1 double, 3 triple
Bathrooms: 5 private

Bed & breakfast

per night:	£min	£max
Single	21.00	23.00
Double	33.00	38.00

Half board

per person:	£min	£max
Daily	29.50	29.50
Weekly	189.00	189.00

Evening meal 1900 (last orders 1700)
Parking for 5

BLYTHBURGH

Suffolk
Map ref 3C2

Little Thorbyns

COMMENDED

The Street, Blythburgh, Halesworth IP19 9LS
☎ (01502) 478664
Good, comfortable accommodation and a warm welcome. Close to Minsmere RSPB sanctuary and Southwold, Walberswick and Dunwich beaches. Three-day mini-break £70 per person.
Bedrooms: 1 single, 1 double, 1 twin
Bathrooms: 2 private, 2 public

Bed & breakfast

per night:	£min	£max
Single	17.00	17.00
Double	33.00	36.00

Half board

per person:	£min	£max
Daily	25.00	25.00
Weekly	140.00	175.00

Parking for 4

BOURN

Cambridgeshire
Map ref 2D1

The Bungalow
5 Gills Hill, Bourn, Cambridge
CB3 7TS
☎ Elsworth (01954) 719463
Spacious modern bungalow overlooking golf-course at rear. Facilities suitable for disabled. Pleasant rural setting.
Bedrooms: 1 double, 1 triple
Bathrooms: 2 private, 1 public

Bed & breakfast

per night:	£min	£max
Single	16.00	18.00
Double	28.00	32.00

Parking for 2

BRACON ASH

Norfolk
Map ref 3B1

The Old Bakery
The Street, Bracon Ash, Norwich
NR14 8EL
☎ Mulbarton (01508) 570360
Fax (01508) 570360
Former village bakery dating from 1725 set in centre of pretty village, 5 miles from Norwich. All rooms en-suite. Hearty farmhouse-style breakfasts.
Bedrooms: 1 double, 1 twin, 1 triple
Bathrooms: 3 private

Bed & breakfast

per night:	£min	£max
Single	18.00	20.00
Double	33.00	35.00

Parking for 8

BRADFIELD

Essex
Map ref 3B2

Emsworth House
Listed
Bradfield, Manningtree CO11 2UP
☎ Clacton (01255) 870860
Formerly a vicarage, the spacious rooms look out over stunning countryside and the River Stour. 2 minutes' walk to shore. Near Colchester, Ipswich and Harwich. On business, holiday or en-route to the continent, it's perfect. Art tuition available.
Bedrooms: 3 double, 1 twin
Bathrooms: 1 private, 3 public

Bed & breakfast

per night:	£min	£max
Single	18.00	22.00
Double	38.00	42.00

Lunch available
Evening meal 1930 (last orders 2200)
Parking for 11

BRAINTREE

Essex
Map ref 3B2

The Heritage Centre in the Town Hall describes Braintree's former international importance in wool, silk and engineering. St Michael's parish church includes some Roman bricks and Braintree market was first chartered in 1199.
Tourist Information Centre
☎ *(01376) 550066*

Spicers Farm
HIGHLY COMMENDED
Rotten End, Wethersfield, Braintree
CM7 4AL
☎ Great Dunmow (01371) 851021
70-acre arable farm. Attractive farmhouse with large garden in area designated of special landscape value. Lovely views over quiet rural countryside, convenient for Harwich, Stansted, Cambridge. All rooms en-suite. 6 miles north-west of Braintree.
Bedrooms: 1 double, 2 twin
Bathrooms: 3 private

Bed & breakfast

per night:	£min	£max
Single	18.00	20.00
Double	30.00	34.00

Parking for 10

BROMESWELL

Suffolk
Map ref 3C2

Meadow View
Listed
School Lane, Bromeswell, Woodbridge
IP12 2PY
☎ Eyke (01394) 460635
400-year-old beamed cottage with heated swimming pool in a lovely village, 2 miles from Woodbridge, off the A1152.
Bedrooms: 1 single, 2 double, 1 twin
Bathrooms: 1 private, 2 public

Bed & breakfast

per night:	£min	£max
Single	16.00	18.00
Double	32.00	36.00

Parking for 6

The town index at the back of this guide gives page numbers of all places with accommodation.

BULPHAN

Essex
Map ref 3B3

Bonny Downs Farm
Listed APPROVED
Doesgate Lane, Bulphan, Upminster
RM14 3TB
☎ Basildon (01268) 542129
60-acre mixed farm. Large comfortable farmhouse offering home-cooked food. Conveniently placed for road links: M25, A13 and A127 to London and south-east England.
Bedrooms: 2 twin, 1 triple
Bathrooms: 1 private, 2 public

Bed & breakfast

per night:	£min	£max
Single	20.00	20.00
Double	30.00	30.00

Half board

per person:	£min	£max
Daily	28.00	30.00
Weekly	196.00	196.00

Evening meal 1800 (last orders 2000)
Parking for 4

BUNGAY

Suffolk
Map ref 3C1

Market town and yachting centre on the River Waveney with the remains of a great 12th C castle. In the market-place stands the Butter Cross, rebuilt in 1689 after being largely destroyed by fire. Nearby at Earsham is the Otter Trust.

Shoo-Devil Farmhouse
Ilketshall Saint Margaret, Bungay
NR35 1QU
☎ Ilketshall (01986) 781303
16th C thatched farmhouse with attractive gardens, set in peaceful surroundings. Ideal for touring East Anglia. Comfortable, spacious bedrooms with en-suite facilities.
Bedrooms: 1 double, 1 twin
Bathrooms: 2 private

Bed & breakfast

per night:	£min	£max
Single	16.50	16.50
Double	33.00	33.00

Parking for 6
Open March-October

Establishments should be open throughout the year unless otherwise stated in the entry.

BUNTINGFORD

Hertfordshire
Map ref 2D1

Buckland Bury Farm

Listed

Buckland Bury, Buntingford SG9 0PY
☎ Royston (01763) 272958 & 0850
638625
*5-acre arable farm. Farmhouse within
easy reach of Cambridge, Audley End,
Wimpole Hall, Duxford and plenty of
country walks.*
Bedrooms: 1 double, 1 twin
Bathrooms: 1 private, 1 public

Bed & breakfast

per night:	£min	£max
Single	15.00	20.00
Double	40.00	50.00

Half board

per person:	£min	£max
Daily	28.00	33.00
Weekly	176.40	207.90

Parking for 8

🛇 🕱 📷 ➡ 👌 🔌 ⌧ ⓘ 📺 ⬆ 🛢 ➡ ✳ ✕ 🛶

Southfields Farm

Listed

Throcking, Buntingford SG9 9RD
☎ Royston (01763) 281224 & (01589)
646759
*Warm, comfortable farmhouse 1.5 miles
off A10 midway between London and
Cambridge. TV, tea and coffee facilities.
Closed at Christmas. No smoking in
bedrooms.*
Bedrooms: 1 single, 1 twin
Bathrooms: 1 public

Bed & breakfast

per night:	£min	£max
Single	18.00	20.00
Double	36.00	40.00

Parking for 5

➡ 👌 🔌 ✕ 🖾 🛢 ✳ ✕ 🛶

BURNHAM OVERY STAITHE

Norfolk
Map ref 3B1

Unspoilt scenic village, steeped in
naval history, Lord Nelson's
playground as a boy. Captain
Woodgett of the Cutty Sark once
lived here and cargo ships visited
the harbour. Wonderful tidal inlet
with great variety of natural history.
Close to Roman fort at Brancaster
and famous Peddars Way.

Domville Guest House ⋔

COMMENDED

Glebe Lane, Burnham Overy Staithe,
King's Lynn PE31 8JQ
☎ Fakenham (01328) 738298
*Standing in own grounds in a quiet
lane, close to the sea. Closed for
Christmas.*
Bedrooms: 3 single, 2 double, 2 twin

Bathrooms: 2 private, 2 public

Bed & breakfast

per night:	£min	£max
Single	17.00	
Double	34.00	44.00

Half board

per person:	£min	£max
Daily	24.00	29.00
Weekly	171.50	203.00

Lunch available
Evening meal 1900 (last orders 1200)
Parking for 10

➡ 6 ➡ 👌 🔌 ⓘ 🔌 ✕ 🛢 📺 ✳ ✕ 🛶

BURY ST EDMUNDS

Suffolk
Map ref 3B2

Ancient market and cathedral town
which takes its name from the
martyred Saxon King, St Edmund.
Bury St Edmunds has many fine
buildings including the Athenaeum
and Moyses Hall, reputed to be
the oldest Norman house in the
county.
*Tourist Information Centre
☎ (01284) 764667*

Haygreen Farm

Whepstead, Bury St Edmunds
IP29 4UD
☎ (01284) 850567

*Typical, listed Suffolk farmhouse,
quietly situated off A143, 5 miles south
of Bury St Edmunds. Close to Ickworth
Park and an ideal base for exploring
East Anglia. Good evening meals in
local pubs.*
Bedrooms: 1 single, 1 double, 1 twin,
1 family room; suites available
Bathrooms: 1 public

Bed & breakfast

per night:	£min	£max
Single	20.00	20.00
Double	40.00	40.00

➡ 🕱 ➡ 👌 🔌 ⓢ ✕ 📺 🖾 U ✳ 🛶 SP 🏠

The Leys

COMMENDED

113 Fornham Road, Bury St Edmunds
IP32 6AT
☎ (01284) 760225
*Lovely, spacious Victorian house in own
grounds, close to the A45 and railway
station. Pay-phone, home-made bread
and preserves.*
Bedrooms: 1 double, 1 twin, 1 triple
Bathrooms: 1 private, 1 public

Bed & breakfast

per night:	£min	£max
Single	20.00	30.00
Double	34.00	40.00

Parking for 6

➡ ➡ 👌 🔌 ✕ 📺 🖾 🛶 🏠

Maundrell House

COMMENDED

109 Fornham Road, Bury St Edmunds
IP32 6AS
☎ (01284) 705884
*Large Edwardian semi-detached town
house. Twin rooms overlook garden.
Close to town centre, station and A45.
Guests are assured of a warm welcome
and good food. Meeting from coach or
train by arrangement.*
Bedrooms: 1 single, 2 twin
Bathrooms: 1 private, 1 public

Bed & breakfast

per night:	£min	£max
Single	15.00	25.00
Double	30.00	35.00

Parking for 2

➡ ➡ 👌 🔌 ⓘ ⓢ ✕ 🖾 🛢 ✳ ✕ 🛶

South Hill House

Listed **COMMENDED**

43 Southgate Street, Bury St
Edmunds IP33 2AZ
☎ (01284) 755650
Fax (01284) 755650
Grade II listed townhouse, reputed to
be the school mentioned in Charles
Dickens' Pickwick Papers. 10 minutes'
walk from town centre, 2 minutes' drive
from A14.*
Bedrooms: 1 twin, 1 family room
Bathrooms: 2 private

Bed & breakfast

per night:	£min	£max
Single	20.00	25.00
Double	35.00	40.00

Parking for 4

➡ ➡ 👌 🔌 ✕ 🖾 ✳ ✕ 🛶 SP 🏠

39 Well Street

Listed

Bury St Edmunds IP33 1EQ
☎ (01284) 768986
*Elegant 19th C town house within 100
yards of all amenities. Friendly
atmosphere, comfortable and well-
furnished rooms.*
Bedrooms: 1 single, 2 double
Bathrooms: 2 private, 1 public

Bed & breakfast

per night:	£min	£max
Single	18.00	18.50
Double	34.00	36.00

Parking for 2

➡ ➡ ➡ ➡ 👌 🔌 ⓘ ⓢ 🖾 🛢 ✳ ✕ 🛶 🏠

Please mention this guide
when making a booking.

BUXTON

Norfolk
Map ref 3C1

Belair

Listed

Crown Road, Buxton, Norwich
NR10 5EN
☎ Norwich (01603) 279637
*Central for Broads and Norfolk coast,
close to Buxton Mill/Restaurant. Steam
railway runs from Buxton to Aylsham,
where Blickling Hall can be visited, and
on to Wroxham where one can have a
trip on a cruiser or shop at the store.*
Bedrooms: 1 single, 2 double
Bathrooms: 2 private, 2 public

Bed & breakfast

per night:	£min	£max
Single	14.00	14.00
Double	28.00	32.00

Parking for 3

Kenwin

COMMENDED

Lamas, Buxton, Norwich NR10 5AF
☎ Norwich (01603) 279355

*Three-bedroomed en-suite bungalow
with colour TV, tea/coffee. In pleasant
rural area, Wroxham 10 minutes' drive.
Use of lounge and evening meal if pre-
booked.*
Bedrooms: 1 double, 1 twin
Bathrooms: 2 private, 1 public

Bed & breakfast

per night:	£min	£max
Single	14.00	17.00
Double	28.00	34.00

Half board

per person:	£min	£max
Daily	20.00	23.00
Weekly	120.00	139.00

Evening meal 1800 (last orders 2000)
Parking for 5

The symbols ☺ ☺ ☺
indicate categories of
accessibility for wheelchair
users. They are explained in
full in the information pages
at the back of this guide.

CAMBRIDGE

Cambridgeshire
Map ref 2D1

A most important and beautiful city
on the River Cam with 31 colleges
forming one of the oldest
universities in the world. Numerous
museums, good shopping centre,
restaurants, theatres, cinema and
fine bookshops.
Tourist Information Centre
☎ *(01223) 322640*

Antwerp Guest House ⋀

36 Brookfields, Mill Road, Cambridge
CB1 3NW
☎ (01223) 247690
*On A1134 ring road between
Addenbrookes Hospital and Cambridge
Airport. Near the city's amenities, and
bus and railway stations. Pleasant
gardens.*
Bedrooms: 4 double, 4 twin
Bathrooms: 2 private, 2 public

Bed & breakfast

per night:	£min	£max
Single	20.00	25.00
Double	30.00	35.00

Evening meal 1830 (last orders 1600)
Parking for 8
Open February-November

Carlton Lodge

Listed

245 Chesterton Road, Cambridge
CB4 1AS
☎ (01223) 367792 & 566877
*Small family-run business within 1 mile
of the city centre and with easy access
from M11 and A14.*
Bedrooms: 1 double, 1 twin, 1 triple
Bathrooms: 3 private, 1 public

Bed & breakfast

per night:	£min	£max
Double	38.00	42.00

Parking for 6

Cristinas

47 St. Andrews Road, Cambridge
CB4 1DL
☎ (01223) 365855 & 327700
*Small family-run business in quiet
location, a short walk from city centre
and colleges.*
Bedrooms: 2 double, 2 twin, 2 triple;
suites available
Bathrooms: 6 private, 1 public

Bed & breakfast

per night:	£min	£max
Single	25.00	26.00
Double	37.00	45.00

Parking for 8

Dykelands Guest House ⋀

157 Mowbray Road, Cambridge
CB1 4SP
☎ (01223) 244300
*Detached guesthouse offering modern
accommodation. On south side of city.
Ideally located for city centre and for
touring the secrets of the
Cambridgeshire countryside. Children
welcome.*
Bedrooms: 1 single, 2 double, 2 twin,
2 triple, 1 family room
Bathrooms: 4 private, 1 public,
2 private showers

Bed & breakfast

per night:	£min	£max
Single	19.75	25.00
Double	33.00	39.00

Parking for 7
Cards accepted: Access, Visa, Diners,
Amex, Switch/Delta

Foxhounds

Listed

71 Cambridge Road, New Wimpole/
Orwell, Royston, Hertfordshire
SG8 5QD
☎ (01223) 207344
*Former pub, part 17th C, now a family
home. On A603, 9 miles from
Cambridge and within easy reach of
Wimpole Hall (National Trust). Sitting
room for guests, large garden.*
Bedrooms: 1 single, 2 twin
Bathrooms: 2 public

Bed & breakfast

per night:	£min	£max
Single	17.00	17.00
Double	34.00	34.00

Evening meal 1930 (last orders 1930)
Parking for 3

Hamden Guest House

Listed

89 High Street, Cherry Hinton,
Cambridge CB1 4LU
☎ (01223) 413263
*High standard bed & breakfast
accommodation. Comfortable rooms
with private facilities, most with garden
view. Full English and continental
breakfast. Private car park. Frequent
bus service to city centre; close to
Addenbrookes Hospital, local shops,
pubs and restaurants. Easy access for
M11, A14 and A1303 junction.*
Bedrooms: 1 single, 1 double, 1 twin,
1 triple, 1 family room
Bathrooms: 5 private

Bed & breakfast

per night:	£min	£max
Single	20.00	25.00
Double	30.00	35.00

Parking for 7

CAMBRIDGE

Continued

Home From Home
39 Milton Road, Cambridge CB4 1XA
☎ (01223) 323555 & Mobile 0850
538712
Small, friendly B & B with 3 spacious rooms, located 10 minutes' walk from bus station and city centre.
Bedrooms: 2 double, 1 twin
Bathrooms: 1 private, 2 private showers
Bed & breakfast

per night:	£min	£max
Single	22.00	30.00
Double	35.00	40.00

Parking for 3

King's Tithe
⊟ HIGHLY COMMENDED
13a Comberton Road, Barton,
Cambridge CB3 7BA
☎ (01223) 263610
Up-market, very quiet, private homely house. Two twin bedrooms with adjacent bathroom and separate toilet. Good bar food available at local village pub. On B1046 off A603 (exit junction 12 of M11).
Bedrooms: 2 twin
Bathrooms: 1 public
Bed & breakfast

per night:	£min	£max
Single	25.00	28.00
Double	37.00	42.00

Parking for 3
Open February-December

Leys Cottage ⋀
Listed   APPROVED
56 Wimpole Road, Barton, Cambridge
CB3 7AB
☎ (01223) 262482
Fax (01223) 264166
Part 17th C house with modern extension in a quiet and secluded spot but within easy reach of Cambridge, M11 and A14. On A603 Cambridge-Sandy road.
Bedrooms: 1 single, 1 double, 1 twin
Bathrooms: 2 private, 1 public
Bed & breakfast

per night:	£min	£max
Single	20.00	25.00
Double	30.00	40.00

Half board

per person:	£min	£max
Daily	30.00	37.50

Evening meal 1900 (last orders 2030)
Parking for 4

Manor Farm
⊟⊟
Landbeach, Cambridge CB4 4ED
☎ (01223) 860165

620-acre mixed farm. Grade II listed, double-fronted, Georgian farmhouse, surrounded by enclosed garden, in centre of village next to church.
Bedrooms: 1 double, 1 triple
Bathrooms: 2 private
Bed & breakfast

per night:	£min	£max
Single	20.00	25.00
Double	34.00	40.00

Parking for 4
Open January-November

The Old Rectory
Listed
Green End, Landbeach, Cambridge
CB4 4ED
☎ (01223) 861507
Fax (01223) 441276
Only 10 minutes from Cambridge centre, historic spacious former rectory in secluded grounds. Donkeys and rare breed sheep. Antique furniture throughout. All rooms en-suite. Aga home cooking. Families welcome.
Bedrooms: 1 triple, 1 family room
Bathrooms: 2 private, 1 public
Bed & breakfast

per night:	£min	£max
Single	22.00	25.00
Double	37.50	37.50

Parking for 11

The Old Rectory
Listed   COMMENDED
High Street, Swaffham Bulbeck,
Cambridge CB5 0LX
☎ (01223) 811986 & 812009
Georgian former vicarage set in own grounds. Located 6 miles from Cambridge and 4 miles from Newmarket.
Bedrooms: 1 double, 1 twin, 1 triple
Bathrooms: 1 private, 1 public
Bed & breakfast

per night:	£min	£max
Single	20.00	25.00
Double	35.00	45.00

Parking for 10

Segovia Lodge
⊟⊟
2 Barton Road, Newnham, Cambridge
CB3 9JZ
☎ (01223) 354105 & 323011
Within walking distance of the city centre and colleges. Next to cricket and tennis fields. Warm welcome, personal service and both rooms with private facilities. Non-smokers only, please.
Bedrooms: 1 double, 1 twin
Bathrooms: 2 private, 1 public
Bed & breakfast

per night:	£min	£max
Double	40.00	45.00

Parking for 4

Woodfield House
⊟⊟
Madingley Hill, Coton, Cambridge
CB3 7PH
☎ Madingley (01954) 210265
Farmhouse set on a hill with beautiful views. 1.5 miles from Cambridge, half a mile from M11. Sorry, no smoking.
Bedrooms: 1 twin, 1 triple
Bathrooms: 1 private, 1 public
Bed & breakfast

per night:	£min	£max
Single	18.00	20.00
Double	32.00	36.00

Parking for 4

Worsted Barrows
⊟⊟
Babraham, Cambridge CB2 4AX
☎ (01223) 833298
Country house offering comfortable accommodation, 4 miles from Cambridge, Newmarket and for touring the pretty villages of Essex and Suffolk.
Bedrooms: 3 double, 3 twin, 1 triple
Bathrooms: 6 private, 1 public
Bed & breakfast

per night:	£min	£max
Single	17.00	20.00
Double	32.00	34.00

Evening meal 1700 (last orders 1930)
Parking for 9

CASTLE ACRE

Norfolk
Map ref 3B1

Remains of castle and priory. Possibly the grandest castle earthworks in England.

Lodge Farm
Listed
Castle Acre, King's Lynn PE32 2BS
☎ Swaffham (01760) 755506
Fax (01760) 755103
Farmhouse with large gardens, 1 mile north of Castle Acre on Rougham road.
Bedrooms: 3 twin
Bathrooms: 1 private, 1 public
Bed & breakfast

per night:	£min	£max
Double	36.00	40.00

Parking for 7

CASTLE HEDINGHAM

Essex
Map ref 3B2

Fishers
⊟⊟
St James Street, Castle Hedingham,
Halstead CO9 3EW
☎ Halstead (01787) 460382
Fax (01787) 460382

Attractive Georgian Grade II listed property located in the main street. Guest accommodation overlooks the garden and so offers a peaceful stay - suit garden enthusiasts.
Bedrooms: 1 twin
Bathrooms: 1 private
Bed & breakfast

per night:	£min	£max
Single	23.50	25.00
Double	37.00	40.00

The Old School House
Listed

St James Street, Castle Hedingham, Halstead CO9 3EW
☎ Hedingham (01787) 461629
Very comfortable self-contained converted coachhouse, set in delightful walled garden, with en-suite facilities and private sitting room, offering a little extra peace and privacy.
Bedrooms: 2 twin
Bathrooms: 2 private
Bed & breakfast

per night:	£min	£max
Single	20.00	25.00
Double	37.00	40.00

Parking for 1

CHATTERIS

Cambridgeshire
Map ref 3A2

Cross Keys Inn Hotel ♨
COMMENDED

16 Market Hill, Chatteris PE16 6BA
☎ March (01354) 693036 & 692644
Fax (01354) 693036

Elizabethan coaching inn built around 1540, Grade II listed. A la carte menu and bar meals. Friendly atmosphere, oak-beamed lounge with log fires. Ideally placed in the heart of the Fens.
Bedrooms: 1 double, 5 twin, 1 triple
Bathrooms: 5 private, 1 public
Bed & breakfast

per night:	£min	£max
Single	21.00	32.50
Double	32.50	45.00

Lunch available
Evening meal 1900 (last orders 2200)
Parking for 10
Cards accepted: Access, Visa, Diners, Amex, Switch/Delta

CHELMSFORD

Essex
Map ref 3B3

The county town of Essex, originally a Roman settlement, Caesaromagus, thought to have been destroyed by Boudicca. Growth of the town's industry can be traced in the excellent museum in Oaklands Park. 15th C parish church has been Chelmsford Cathedral since 1914.
Tourist Information Centre
☎ *(01245) 283400*

Neptune Cafe Motel
Listed

Burnham Road, Latchingdon, Chelmsford CM3 6EX
☎ Maldon (01621) 740770
Cafe with adjoining chalet block, which includes 2 units suitable for physically disabled. Village location between Maldon and Burnham-on-Crouch.
Bedrooms: 4 double, 2 twin, 4 triple
Bathrooms: 10 private
Bed & breakfast

per night:	£min	£max
Single	20.00	
Double	30.00	

Half board		
per person:	£min	£max
Daily	26.00	

Lunch available
Parking for 40

Springford ♨
Listed **APPROVED**

8 Well Lane, Galleywood, Chelmsford CM2 8QY
☎ (01245) 257821
Family home at Galleywood, south of Chelmsford. Take B1007 out of the town or Galleywood turn-off from A12. Well Lane is near White Bear pub.
Bedrooms: 1 single, 2 twin
Bathrooms: 1 public
Bed & breakfast

per night:	£min	£max
Single	14.00	15.00
Double	28.00	30.00

Half board		
per person:	£min	£max
Daily	22.00	23.00

Evening meal 1700 (last orders 2030)
Parking for 3

25 West Avenue
Listed

Maylandsea, Chelmsford CM3 6AE
☎ Maldon (01621) 740972
Fax (01621) 740945
Detached four-bedroomed private residence. From Maldon on B1018 or from South Woodham Ferrers on B1012 to Latchingdon, then on to Steeple Road to Maylandsea (about 2 miles).
Bedrooms: 1 double, 1 twin

Bathrooms: 1 public
Bed & breakfast

per night:	£min	£max
Single	15.00	17.00
Double	30.00	34.00

Parking for 5

CHOSELEY

Norfolk
Map ref 3B1

Choseley Farmhouse
Listed

Choseley, Docking, King's Lynn PE31 8PQ
☎ Thornham (01485) 512331
17th C Norfolk farmhouse with Tudor chimneys. Foundations are thought to date back to original abbey of 1250.
Bedrooms: 1 double, 2 twin
Bathrooms: 1 public
Bed & breakfast

per night:	£min	£max
Single	15.00	
Double	30.00	

Parking for 10
Open July-September

CLARE

Suffolk
Map ref 3B2

Attractive village with many of the houses displaying pargetting work and the site of a castle first mentioned in 1090. Clare Country Park occupies the site of the castle bailey and old railway station. Ancient House Museum in the 15th C priest's house contains local bygones.

Cobwebs
Listed

26 Nethergate Street, Clare, Sudbury CO10 8NP
☎ Sudbury (01787) 277539
Beamed Grade II listed family house near town centre on A1092. Excellent base for touring. Set in delightful walled garden.
Bedrooms: 1 single, 2 twin
Bathrooms: 1 private, 1 public
Bed & breakfast

per night:	£min	£max
Single	18.00	20.00
Double	36.00	40.00

Colour maps at the back of this guide pinpoint all places which have accommodation listings in the guide.

COLCHESTER

Essex
Map ref 3B2

Britain's oldest recorded town standing on the River Colne and famous for its oysters. Numerous historic buildings, ancient remains and museums. Plenty of parks and gardens, extensive shopping centre, theatre and zoo.
Tourist Information Centre
☎ *(01206) 282920*

The Chase
Listed **HIGHLY COMMENDED**
2 The Chase, Straight Road, Lexden, Colchester CO3 5BU
☎ (01206) 540587
Fax (01206) 44471

60-year-old house of real character. Quiet yet convenient for town and other facilities. In large, beautiful secluded gardens.
Bedrooms: 3 twin
Bathrooms: 3 private, 1 public

Bed & breakfast

per night:	£min	£max
Single	25.00	25.00
Double	35.00	35.00

Parking for 6

Fletchers Farm
Listed
Bergholt Road, Fordham, Colchester CO6 3NT
☎ (01206) 240262
250-acre dairy farm. Listed farmhouse on a family farm with animals in a lovely area. Close to Colchester and Harwich.
Bedrooms: 2 double, 1 twin
Bathrooms: 2 public

Bed & breakfast

per night:	£min	£max
Single	15.00	17.00
Double	30.00	34.00

Parking for 6

11 Harvest End
Listed
Stanway, Colchester CO3 5YX
☎ (01206) 43202
Comfortable family home with friendly atmosphere. Colour TV and tea/coffee facilities in rooms. Many local restaurants and take-aways nearby. No smoking, please.
Bedrooms: 1 single, 1 double, 1 twin
Bathrooms: 1 public

Bed & breakfast

per night:	£min	£max
Single	17.00	18.00
Double	34.00	34.00

Parking for 2

The Maltings
Listed
Mersea Road, Abberton, Colchester CO5 7NR
☎ (01206) 735780
Attractive period house with a wealth of beams and an open log fire, in walled garden with swimming pool.
Bedrooms: 1 single, 1 twin, 1 triple
Bathrooms: 2 public

Bed & breakfast

per night:	£min	£max
Single	15.00	18.00
Double	30.00	36.00

Parking for 8

Rose & Crown ⋔
COMMENDED
East Street, Colchester CO1 2TZ
☎ (01206) 866677
Fax (01206) 866616

The oldest inn in the oldest recorded town in England. Early 15th C inn with charming en-suite bedrooms, log fire bar and noted restaurant. On Ipswich road 2 miles off A12 and half a mile from town centre.
Bedrooms: 1 single, 20 double, 7 twin, 2 triple
Bathrooms: 30 private

Bed & breakfast

per night:	£min	£max
Single	45.00	55.00
Double	50.00	60.00

Half board

per person:	£min	£max
Daily	39.50	60.00

Lunch available
Evening meal 1900 (last orders 2200)
Parking for 60
Cards accepted: Access, Visa, Diners, Amex, Switch/Delta

Silver Springs Motel ⋔
Tenpenny Hill, Thorrington, Colchester CO7 8JG
☎ (01206) 250366
Fax (01206) 250700
A unique motel consisting of chalets set in 6 acres of landscaped grounds with separate restaurant, bar and conference facilities. On B1027, between Colchester and Clacton-on-sea.
Bedrooms: 11 double, 4 twin, 2 triple, 3 family rooms
Bathrooms: 20 private

Bed & breakfast

per night:	£min	£max
Single	24.95	34.95
Double	34.95	44.95

Evening meal 1830 (last orders 2100)
Parking for 50
Cards accepted: Access, Visa, Switch/ Delta

COLTISHALL

Norfolk
Map ref 3C1

On the River Bure, with an RAF station nearby. The village is attractive with many pleasant 18th C brick houses and a thatched church.

Broadgates
Listed
1 Wroxham Road, Coltishall, Norwich NR12 7DU
☎ Norwich (01603) 737598
Close to river. 3 miles from Wroxham and the Broads, 6 miles from Norwich.
Bedrooms: 1 single, 2 twin
Bathrooms: 1 public

Bed & breakfast

per night:	£min	£max
Single	18.50	18.50
Double	37.00	37.00

Half board

per person:	£min	£max
Daily	25.50	25.50
Weekly	170.00	170.00

Evening meal 1800 (last orders 1900)
Parking for 8

CROMER

Norfolk
Map ref 3C1

Once a small fishing village and now famous for its fishing boats that still work off the beach and offer freshly caught crabs. Excellent bathing on sandy beaches fringed by cliffs. The town boasts a fine pier, theatre, museum and a lifeboat station.
Tourist Information Centre
☎ *(01263) 512497*

The Crowmere
Listed
4 Vicarage Road, Cromer NR27 9DQ
☎ (01263) 513056
Charming Victorian residence in quiet road close to beach/town centre and all amenities. Tea/coffee making facilities and TV in all rooms. Most rooms are en-suite. Family suites available.

Bedrooms: 4 double, 2 twin, 3 family rooms
Bathrooms: 7 private, 1 public
Bed & breakfast

per night:	£min	£max
Single	16.00	19.00
Double	32.00	38.00

Parking for 6

🐾🐕🛏👶🖵🛎Ⓢ⅍🛏✕🐾

Shrublands Farm

🏆🏆 HIGHLY COMMENDED

Northrepps, Cromer NR27 0AA
☎ Overstrand (01263) 579297
Fax (01263) 579297
300-acre arable farm. Traditional Norfolk farmhouse in centre of Northrepps village, 1 mile off A149 and 2 miles from Cromer.
Bedrooms: 1 double, 2 twin
Bathrooms: 3 private
Bed & breakfast

per night:	£min	£max
Single	22.00	24.00
Double	36.00	40.00

Half board

per person:	£min	£max
Daily	31.00	35.00
Weekly	217.00	245.00

Evening meal 1900 (last orders 2000)
Parking for 4
Cards accepted: Diners

🐾 13 🖵👶🖵⅍🛏📺▥ 🍴❋✕🐾

DANBURY

Essex
Map ref 3B3

Southways

Listed

Copt Hill, Danbury, Chelmsford CM3 4NN
☎ Chelmsford (01245) 223428
Pleasant country house with large garden adjoining an area of National Trust common land.
Bedrooms: 2 twin
Bathrooms: 1 public
Bed & breakfast

per night:	£min	£max
Single	16.00	16.00
Double	30.00	30.00

Parking for 2

🐾🖵👶🖵▥❋🐾

DARSHAM

Suffolk
Map ref 3C2

Priory Farm 🏍

Listed COMMENDED

Darsham, Saxmundham IP17 3QD
☎ Yoxford (01728) 668459
40-acre mixed farm. Comfortable 17th C farmhouse, ideally situated for exploring Suffolk and heritage coast. Cycle hire available from own hire fleet.
Bedrooms: 1 single, 1 double, 1 twin
Bathrooms: 1 public

Bed & breakfast

per night:	£min	£max
Single	18.00	25.00
Double	36.00	40.00

Parking for 10
Open March-October

🐾👶🖵⅍📺▥ 🍴❋✕🐾◉

DEBDEN GREEN

Essex
Map ref 2D1

Wigmores Farm

Listed COMMENDED

Debden Green, Saffron Walden CB11 3LX
☎ Thaxted (01371) 830050
1000-acre farm. 16th C thatched farmhouse in open countryside, 1.5 miles from Thaxted, just off the Thaxted to Debden road.
Bedrooms: 2 double, 1 twin
Bathrooms: 2 public
Bed & breakfast

per night:	£min	£max
Single	19.00	19.00
Double	34.00	34.00

Half board

per person:	£min	£max
Daily	29.00	31.00
Weekly	200.00	220.00

Lunch available
Evening meal 1900 (last orders 2100)
Parking for 12

🐾🐕🖵👶🛎Ⓢ⅍🛏📺▥ 🍴❋🐾
🐟🏠

DEBENHAM

Suffolk
Map ref 3B2

The first trickles of the River Deben run beside the gently sloping tree-lined street of Debenham and it then weaves in and out of the town, among the colour-washed and timbered houses. Rush weaving is carried on in a building beside the bridge.

Kenton Hall

🏆🏆 COMMENDED

Debenham, Stowmarket IP14 6JU
☎ (01728) 860279
Fax (01728) 861246
460-acre arable farm. Beautiful moated Tudor hall set in peaceful surroundings. All rooms furnished to a high standard with en-suite facilities. Open log fire in panelled sitting room and separate dining room.
Bedrooms: 1 double, 1 family room
Bathrooms: 2 private, 4 public
Bed & breakfast

per night:	£min	£max
Single	17.50	22.50
Double	37.00	42.00

Parking for 7

🐾👶🖵👶🛎⅍🛏📺▥ 🍴❋✕🐾 SP🏠

DEDHAM

Essex
Map ref 3B2

A former wool town. Dedham Vale is an Area of Outstanding Natural Beauty and there is a countryside centre in the village. This is John Constable country and Sir Alfred Munnings lived at Castle House which is open to the public.

May's Barn Farm

🏆🏆 HIGHLY COMMENDED

May's Lane, Off Long Road West, Dedham, Colchester CO7 6EW
☎ Colchester (01206) 323191
300-acre arable farm. Tranquil old farmhouse with outstanding views over Dedham Vale in Constable country. Quarter mile down private lane. Comfortable, spacious rooms, with private facilities.
Bedrooms: 1 double, 1 twin
Bathrooms: 2 private
Bed & breakfast

per night:	£min	£max
Single	20.00	25.00
Double	36.00	40.00

Parking for 7

🐾 10 🖵👶🐕🖵Ⓢ⅍🛏📺▥ 🍴❋
✕🐾

DEREHAM

Norfolk
Map ref 3B1

East Dereham is famous for its associations with the poet William Cowper and also Bishop Bonner, chaplain to Cardinal Wolsey. His home is now a museum. Around the charming market-place are many notable buildings.

Chapel Farm

🏆🏆

Dereham Road, Whinburgh, Dereham NR19 1AA
☎ (01362) 698433
Farmhouse B & B with full facilities, including CH, outdoor heated swimming pool, international standard snooker table. En-suite rooms. Pub close by.
Bedrooms: 3 double
Bathrooms: 2 private, 1 public
Bed & breakfast

per night:	£min	£max
Single	17.00	17.00
Double	34.00	34.00

Parking for 10

🐾🐕🖵👶🖵Ⓢ🛏📺▥ 🍴⚓🚲∪↑
❋🐾

Clinton House

Listed HIGHLY COMMENDED

Well Hill, Clint Green, Yaxham, Dereham NR19 1RX
☎ (01362) 692079

Continued ▶

DEREHAM
Continued

Charming 18th C country house, full of character, in peaceful location. Tennis/croquet. Good touring centre. Breakfast served in beautiful conservatory.
Bedrooms: 1 single, 2 double, 1 twin
Bathrooms: 1 private, 2 public

Bed & breakfast

per night:	£min	£max
Single	20.00	22.00
Double	32.00	35.00

Parking for 10

Lynn Hill Guest House

Lynn Hill, Yaxham Road, Dereham NR19 1HA
☎ (01362) 696142
Modern establishment on approach road to East Dereham, 400 yards from the town centre, 300 yards from the by-pass exit.
Bedrooms: 2 single, 2 double, 4 twin, 1 triple
Bathrooms: 3 private, 2 public

Bed & breakfast

per night:	£min	£max
Single	15.00	20.00
Double	30.00	35.00

Half board

per person:	£min	£max
Daily	20.00	25.00
Weekly	120.00	140.00

Evening meal 1800 (last orders 2000)
Parking for 8

Park Farm
Listed

Bylaugh, East Dereham NR20 4QE
☎ Bawdeswell (01362) 688584
500-acre arable farm. Charming old family farmhouse, in country setting in the picturesque Wensum Valley. Located just off B1147 between Swanton Morley and Bawdeswell. Full English breakfast.
Bedrooms: 1 single, 1 double, 1 twin
Bathrooms: 1 private, 1 public

Bed & breakfast

per night:	£min	£max
Single	20.00	26.00
Double	29.00	36.00

Half board

per person:	£min	£max
Daily	24.50	30.00
Weekly	150.00	200.00

Evening meal 1930 (last orders 2130)
Parking for 6

Shillingstone ⋀

Church Road, Old Beetley, Dereham NR20 4AB
☎ (01362) 861099 & Mobile 0421 306190
Country house 3 miles from Dereham. Rural outlook, convenient for Norfolk Broads, coast, Sandringham. Large, sunny rooms, home cooking, warm welcome. Children welcome.
Bedrooms: 1 single, 1 double, 1 twin
Bathrooms: 1 public

Bed & breakfast

per night:	£min	£max
Single	15.00	16.00
Double	28.00	30.00

Half board

per person:	£min	£max
Daily	22.00	25.00
Weekly	140.00	150.00

Evening meal from 1830
Parking for 8
Cards accepted: Access, Visa, Amex

DISS
Norfolk
Map ref 3B2

Old market town built around 3 sides of the Mere, a placid water of 6 acres. Although modernised, some interesting Tudor, Georgian and Victorian buildings around the market-place remain. St Mary's church has a fine knapped flint chancel.
Tourist Information Centre
☎ *(01379) 650523*

Malt House ⋀
HIGHLY COMMENDED

Denmark Hill, Palgrave, Diss IP22 1AE
☎ (01379) 642107
Fax (01379) 640315
17th C malt house, beautifully renovated and with all modern amenities. Candlelit dinners in elegant dining room, after-dinner coffee in beamed lounge. 1 acre of landscaped garden with walled kitchen garden. 10 minutes' walk Diss, 2 miles Bressingham Gardens.
Bedrooms: 2 double, 1 twin
Bathrooms: 3 private

Bed & breakfast

per night:	£min	£max
Single	30.00	
Double	60.00	68.00

Half board

per person:	£min	£max
Daily	48.00	
Weekly	300.00	

Evening meal 1900 (last orders 2000)
Parking for 6
Cards accepted: Access, Visa, Diners

Rose Cottage
Diss Road, Burston, Diss IP22 3TP
☎ (01379) 740602
Fax (01379) 740602

Modernised timber-framed 18th C house, situated on Church Green, opposite famous Burston Strike School. Parking and garden.
Bedrooms: 1 single, 1 double
Bathrooms: 2 private, 1 public

Bed & breakfast

per night:	£min	£max
Single	19.00	21.00
Double	36.00	40.00

Parking for 3
Open April-September

DRINKSTONE
Suffolk
Map ref 3B2

Silver Trees
Listed

5 The Meadows, Drinkstone, Bury St Edmunds IP30 9TS
☎ Rattlesden (01449) 737994
Fax (01449) 737994
Quality bed & breakfast in large, modern, detached house in quiet village location, just off A14. Ideal for touring the area. Good local hostelries.
Bedrooms: 1 double, 1 twin
Bathrooms: 1 public

Bed & breakfast

per night:	£min	£max
Single		15.00
Double		30.00

Parking for 2

EARLS COLNE
Essex
Map ref 3B2

Drum Inn
COMMENDED

21 High Street, Earls Colne, Colchester CO6 2PA
☎ Bures (01787) 222368 & 222213
Traditional family-owned inn, on the A604 between Colchester and Halstead.
Bedrooms: 1 single, 2 double, 3 twin
Bathrooms: 6 private

Bed & breakfast

per night:	£min	£max
Single	19.00	22.00
Double	38.00	44.00

Lunch available
Evening meal 1900 (last orders 2200)
Parking for 6

Cards accepted: Access, Visa, Diners, Switch/Delta

EAST BERGHOLT

Suffolk
Map ref 3B2

John Constable, the famous East Anglian artist, was born here in 1776 and at the church of St Mary are reminders of his family's associations with the area. 1 mile south of the village are Flatford Mill and Willy Lott's cottage, both made famous by Constable in his paintings.

Rosemary
Listed

Rectory Hill, East Bergholt, Colchester CO7 6TH
☎ Colchester (01206) 298241
Pleasant family house in lovely 1-acre garden in the National Garden Scheme. Wide variety of plants and old-fashioned roses. In centre of Constable country. A non-smoking establishment.
Bedrooms: 1 single, 2 twin
Bathrooms: 1 public

Bed & breakfast

per night:	£min	£max
Single	17.00	17.00
Double	34.00	34.00

Parking for 2

ELY

Cambridgeshire
Map ref 3A2

Until the 17th C, when the Fens were drained, Ely was an island. The cathedral, completed in 1189, dominates the surrounding area. One particular feature is the central octagonal tower with a fan-vaulted timber roof and wooden lantern.
Tourist Information Centre
☎ (01353) 662062

The Black Hostelry
Listed **COMMENDED**

The Cathedral Close, The College, Firmary Lane, Ely CB7 4DL
☎ (01353) 662612
Fax (01353) 665658
One of the finest collections of medieval domestic buildings still in use in England. Situated on the south side of Ely Cathedral.
Bedrooms: 2 triple; suite available
Bathrooms: 2 private

Bed & breakfast

per night:	£min	£max
Single	49.00	49.00
Double	49.00	49.00

Parking for 6

Hill House Farm
HIGHLY COMMENDED

9 Main Street, Coveney, Ely CB6 2DJ
☎ (01353) 778369
240-acre arable farm. High quality en-suite accommodation and food, in fine Victorian farmhouse. Situated in unspoilt Fenland village 3 miles west of Ely, with open views of the surrounding countryside, and easy access to Cambridge. No smoking and no pets, please.
Bedrooms: 2 double, 1 twin
Bathrooms: 3 private

Bed & breakfast

per night:	£min	£max
Single	25.00	
Double	36.00	

Parking for 4

Spinney Abbey

Stretham Road, Wicken, Ely CB7 5XQ
☎ (01353) 720971

150-acre dairy farm. Spacious Georgian farmhouse set in 1 acre of garden. All rooms with private facilities. Farm borders Wicken Fen Nature Reserve.
Bedrooms: 1 double, 1 twin, 1 triple
Bathrooms: 3 private

Bed & breakfast

per night:	£min	£max
Double	36.00	40.00

Parking for 4

EPPING

Essex
Map ref 2D1

Epping retains its identity as a small market town despite its nearness to London. Epping Forest covers 2000 acres and at Chingford Queen Elizabeth I's Hunting Lodge houses a display on the forest's history and wildlife.

Uplands
Listed **APPROVED**

181a Lindsey Street, Epping CM16 6RF
☎ Waltham Cross (01992) 573733
Private house with rural views. Close to M25, M11 for Stansted Airport and Central Line underground for London. Pay phone available.
Bedrooms: 2 single, 2 triple
Bathrooms: 2 public

Bed & breakfast

per night:	£min	£max
Single	16.00	
Double	32.00	

Parking for 6

EYKE

Suffolk
Map ref 3C2

The Old House
COMMENDED

Eyke, Woodbridge IP12 2QW
☎ (01394) 460213
Lovely Grade II listed house, c1600. Comfortable and friendly, with beams, open fires, large, interesting garden and views over Deben Valley. Centre of village and edge of heritage coast. Good choice of food. All rooms also let as singles.
Bedrooms: 1 double, 2 triple
Bathrooms: 3 private

Bed & breakfast

per night:	£min	£max
Single	22.00	25.00
Double	37.00	40.00

Half board

per person:	£min	£max
Daily	29.00	35.00

Evening meal 1800 (last orders 1000)
Parking for 8

FAKENHAM

Norfolk
Map ref 3B1

Attractive, small market town dates from Saxon times and was a Royal Manor until the 17th C. Its market place has 2 old coaching inns, both showing traces of earlier work behind Georgian facades, and the parish church has a commanding 15th C tower.

Sculthorpe Mill ⚓

Lynn Road, Sculthorpe, Fakenham NR21 9QG
☎ (01328) 856161 & 862675
Fax (01328) 856651

Grade II listed watermill in 6 acres of watermeadows straddling the River Wensum. A la carte and set menus served in oak-beamed restaurant overlooking river. Extensive range of bar food. En-suite rooms, including four-poster. Open all day.

Continued ▶

FAKENHAM

Continued

Bedrooms: 2 single, 2 double, 1 twin,
1 triple; suite available
Bathrooms: 6 private

Bed & breakfast

per night:	£min	£max
Single	30.00	35.00
Double	50.00	65.00

Half board

per person:	£min	£max
Daily	37.50	55.00
Weekly	190.00	290.00

Lunch available
Evening meal 1830 (last orders 2130)
Parking for 50
Cards accepted: Access, Visa, Amex

FELIXSTOWE

Suffolk
Map ref 3C2

Seaside resort that developed at
the end of the 19th C. Lying in a
gently curving bay with a 2-mile-
long beach and backed by a wide
promenade of lawns and floral
gardens. Ferry links to the
continent.
Tourist Information Centre
☎ *(01394) 276770*

Fludyer Arms Hotel ♠

APPROVED

Undercliff Rd. East, Felixstowe
IP11 7LU
☎ (01394) 283279
Fax (01394) 670754
Closest hotel to the sea in Felixstowe.
Two fully licensed bars and family room
overlooking the sea. All rooms have
superb sea views. Colour TV. Specialises
in home-cooked food, with children's
and vegetarian menus available.
Bedrooms: 3 single, 5 double, 1 twin
Bathrooms: 9 private, 1 public

Bed & breakfast

per night:	£min	£max
Single	18.00	32.00
Double	38.00	46.00

Lunch available
Evening meal 1900 (last orders 2100)
Parking for 14
Cards accepted: Access, Visa, Amex

FELSTED

Essex
Map ref 3B2

Potash Farm

COMMENDED

Cobblers Green, Causeway End Road,
Felsted, Dunmow CM6 3LX
☎ Great Dunmow (01371) 820510
160-acre arable farm. Lovely old 15th C
listed farmhouse set in a large half

moated garden, within walking distance
of Felsted centre. Convenient for
Stansted and London.
Bedrooms: 1 double, 2 twin
Bathrooms: 1 public

Bed & breakfast

per night:	£min	£max
Single	15.00	17.00
Double	30.00	32.00

Parking for 6

FINCHINGFIELD

Essex
Map ref 3B2

Finchingfield House

Finchingfield, Braintree CM7 4JS
☎ Great Dunmow (01371) 810289
Fax (01371) 810289
Magnificent 400-year-old country house,
overlooking beautiful and famous village
green, set within 2 acres of mature,
landscaped gardens. Ideal centre for
numerous places of interest and leisure
activities.
Bedrooms: 2 double, 1 twin
Bathrooms: 1 private, 1 public

Bed & breakfast

per night:	£min	£max
Single	28.00	35.00
Double	38.00	45.00

Parking for 6

FRAMLINGHAM

Suffolk
Map ref 3C2

Pleasant old market town with an
interesting church, impressive
castle and some attractive houses
round Market Hill. The town's
history can be traced at the
Lanman Museum.

Boundary Farm

Listed COMMENDED

Saxmundham Road, Framlingham,
Woodbridge IP13 9NU
☎ (01728) 723401

17th C listed farmhouse in 1.5 acres of
garden amidst open countryside. Log
fires, warm, friendly atmosphere.
Pleasant stay is assured. 1.5 miles out
of Framlingham on B1119 road. Ideal
location for touring.
Bedrooms: 2 double, 1 twin
Bathrooms: 2 public

Bed & breakfast

per night:	£min	£max
Single	20.00	
Double	36.00	

Parking for 6

High House Farm ♠

COMMENDED

Cransford, Framlingham, Woodbridge
IP13 9PD
☎ Rendham (01728) 663461
240-acre arable farm. Beautifully
restored 15th C farmhouse featuring
exposed beams, inglenooks and
attractive gardens. Large family room.
Situated between Framlingham and
Saxmundham.
Bedrooms: 1 double, 1 family room
Bathrooms: 2 private

Bed & breakfast

per night:	£min	£max
Single	20.00	24.00
Double	32.00	36.00

Parking for 4

Shimmens Pightle ♠

Listed COMMENDED

Dennington Road, Framlingham,
Woodbridge IP13 9JT
☎ (01728) 724036
Brian and Phyllis Collett's home is set
in an acre of landscaped garden
overlooking fields, on outskirts of
Framlingham. Ground floor rooms with
washbasins. Locally-cured bacon and
home-made marmalade.
Bedrooms: 1 double, 2 twin
Bathrooms: 1 public

Bed & breakfast

per night:	£min	£max
Double	34.00	38.00

Parking for 4
Cards accepted: Diners

FRESSINGFIELD

Suffolk
Map ref 3C2

Chippenhall Hall ♠

HIGHLY COMMENDED

Fressingfield, Eye IP21 5TD
☎ Diss (01379) 586733 & 588180
Fax (01379) 586272
Listed Tudor manor, heavily beamed
and with inglenook fireplaces, in 7
secluded acres. Fine food and wines. 1
mile south of Fressingfield on B1116.
Bedrooms: 3 double
Bathrooms: 3 private

Bed & breakfast

per night:	£min	£max
Single	48.00	55.00
Double	55.00	62.00

Half board

per person:	£min	£max
Daily	50.00	54.00
Weekly	334.00	356.00

Lunch available
Evening meal 1930 (last orders 1600)
Parking for 12
Cards accepted: Access, Visa

⌨🖤🎣🅢💢🅜📺🛢🍳☀️🔥⛎▶️❄️
🔫🦽🐕🅗

FRINTON-ON-SEA

Essex
Map ref 3C2

Sedate town that developed as a resort at the end of the 19th C and still retains an air of Victorian gentility. Fine sandy beaches, good fishing and golf.

Hodgenolls Farmhouse

😺😺 COMMENDED

Pork Lane, Great Holland, Frinton-on-Sea CO13 0ES
☎ Clacton (01255) 672054
Early 17th C timber-framed farmhouse in rural setting close to sandy beaches, Constable country, historic Colchester and Harwich. Non-smoking establishment.
Bedrooms: 2 double, 1 twin
Bathrooms: 3 private, 1 public

Bed & breakfast

per night:	£min	£max
Single	20.00	
Double	36.00	38.00

Parking for 5
Open March-October

🛏️🖤🖵🅢🗝️🍳📺🛢🛢☀️🔫🦽

GARBOLDISHAM

Norfolk
Map ref 3B2

Ingleneuk Lodge 🕮

😺😺😺 COMMENDED

Hopton Road, Garboldisham, Diss IP22 2RQ
☎ (01953) 681541

Modern single-level home in 10 acres of wooded countryside. South-facing patio, riverside walk. Very friendly atmosphere. On B1111, 1 mile south of village.
Wheelchair access category 2 🐧
Bedrooms: 2 single, 3 double, 2 twin, 1 triple, 1 family room
Bathrooms: 9 private, 1 public

Bed & breakfast

per night:	£min	£max
Single	23.00	33.00
Double	37.50	51.00

Half board

per person:	£min	£max
Daily	33.25	47.50
Weekly	215.00	306.50

Evening meal 1830 (last orders 1300)
Parking for 20
Cards accepted: Access, Visa, Amex

🛏️🦽📞🖵🖤🅢🗝️🍳🛢🛢🛢12☀️🦽
🆂🅟🅗

GISSING

Norfolk
Map ref 3B2

Old Rectory 🕮

😺😺 HIGHLY COMMENDED

Gissing, Diss IP22 3XB
☎ Tivetshall (01379) 677575
Fax (01379) 674427
Elegant Victorian house in 3 acres. Peaceful, comfortable, exuberantly decorated and furnished, indoor pool. Four-course, candlelit dinner by arrangement. Tea/coffee-making facilities, colour TV. 3 nights for price of 2 December-March plus weekday breaks.
Bedrooms: 1 double, 2 twin
Bathrooms: 3 private, 1 public

Bed & breakfast

per night:	£min	£max
Single	36.00	42.00
Double	48.00	58.00

Half board

per person:	£min	£max
Daily	44.00	49.00
Weekly	268.00	303.00

Evening meal 1945 (last orders 1945)
Parking for 6
Cards accepted: Access, Visa

🛏️8🖵🖤🎣🅘🅢🗝️🍳🛢🛢☀️🔫
🦽🆂🅗

GREAT BIRCHAM

Norfolk
Map ref 3B1

King's Head Hotel 🕮

😺😺

Great Bircham, King's Lynn PE31 6RJ
☎ Syderstone (01485) 578265
Country inn with 3 bars, Italian restaurant and beer gardens, near Sandringham, King's Lynn and the coast. English and Italian cuisine, fresh Norfolk seafood and poultry, traditional Sunday lunch. Two-night breaks available.
Bedrooms: 2 double, 3 twin
Bathrooms: 5 private

Bed & breakfast

per night:	£min	£max
Single	30.00	33.00
Double	50.00	55.00

Half board

per person:	£min	£max
Daily	25.00	30.00
Weekly	175.00	210.00

Lunch available
Evening meal 1900 (last orders 2200)
Parking for 80
Cards accepted: Access, Visa

🛏️🖵🖤🎣🍳📺🛢🛢☀️🛢☀️🦽🆂🅟🆂🅟
🅗🅣

GREAT DUNMOW

Essex
Map ref 3B2

On the main Roman road from Bishop's Stortford to Braintree. Doctor's Pond near the square was where the first lifeboat was tested in 1785. Home of the Dunmow Flitch trials held every 4 years on Whit Monday.

Cowels Cottage

😺😺

Cowels Farm Lane, Lindsell, Dunmow CM6 3QG
☎ Gt Dunmow (01371) 870454
Pink cottage, overlooking farmland in tranquil, secluded garden. Centrally heated, private sitting room and bathrooms, TV. No traffic noise. 9 miles Stansted Airport but not on a flightpath.
Bedrooms: 2 single, 1 family room
Bathrooms: 3 private, 1 public

Bed & breakfast

per night:	£min	£max
Single	20.00	20.00
Double	36.00	40.00

Parking for 4

🛏️🦽⌨🖤🖵🍳📺🛢🛢☀️🔫🦽

Yarrow

😺😺 COMMENDED

27 Station Road, Felsted, Great Dunmow CM6 3HD
☎ (01371) 820878
Edwardian house. South-facing bedrooms with garden and countryside views. Ample parking. Quarter-of-a-mile to restaurants and pub in lovely village.
Bedrooms: 2 double, 1 twin
Bathrooms: 2 private, 2 public

Bed & breakfast

per night:	£min	£max
Single	16.00	18.00
Double	28.00	34.00

Parking for 6

🛏️⌨🖵🖤🖵🍳📺🛢🛢☀️🔫🦽

> National gradings and classifications were correct at the time of going to press but are subject to change. Please check at the time of booking.

GREAT YARMOUTH

Norfolk
Map ref 3C1

One of Britain's major seaside resorts with 5 miles of seafront and every possible amenity including an award winning leisure complex offering a huge variety of all-weather facilities. Busy harbour and fishing centre.

Spindrift Private Hotel M

≝≝ APPROVED

36 Wellesley Road, Great Yarmouth
NR30 1EU
☎ (01493) 858674
Attractively situated small private hotel, close to all amenities and with Beach Coach Station and car park at rear. Front bedrooms have sea views.
Bedrooms: 2 single, 2 double, 1 twin, 1 triple, 1 family room
Bathrooms: 5 private, 1 public

Bed & breakfast

per night:	£min	£max
Single	16.00	26.00
Double	28.00	40.00

Cards accepted: Access, Visa, Amex

HADLEIGH

Suffolk
Map ref 3B2

Former wool town, lying on a tributary of the River Stour. The church of St Mary stands among a remarkable cluster of medieval buildings.
Tourist Information Centre
☎ *(01473) 823824*

French's Farm

≝≝

Hadleigh, Ipswich IP7 5PQ
☎ Ipswich (01473) 824215
Large period country house set in magnificent grounds, offering well-appointed, peaceful accommodation and friendly service. Horse riding facilities available.
Bedrooms: 1 double, 2 triple
Bathrooms: 3 private

Bed & breakfast

per night:	£min	£max
Single	20.00	25.00
Double	38.00	48.00

Half board

per person:	£min	£max
Daily	25.00	30.00
Weekly	150.00	185.00

Evening meal 1800 (last orders 2000)
Parking for 15

The Marquis of Cornwallis M

≝≝ COMMENDED

Upper Layham, Hadleigh, Ipswich
IP7 5JZ
☎ (01473) 822051
Fax (01473) 822051
Large public house in 2 acres of grounds leading down to River Brett, between Constable country and Lavenham.
Bedrooms: 2 double, 1 twin
Bathrooms: 3 private, 1 public

Bed & breakfast

per night:	£min	£max
Single	27.00	27.00
Double	39.00	39.00

Lunch available
Evening meal 1900 (last orders 2130)
Parking for 22
Cards accepted: Access, Visa, Diners, Amex, Switch/Delta

Mount Pleasant Farm M

≝≝ COMMENDED

Offton, Ipswich IP8 4RP
☎ Ipswich (01473) 658896
Fax (01473) 658896

8-acre mixed farm. Genuinely secluded, typical Suffolk farmhouse. 30 minutes from the sea and 5 minutes from water park. Many local beauty spots. Evening meals a speciality.
Bedrooms: 2 double, 1 twin
Bathrooms: 3 private

Bed & breakfast

per night:	£min	£max
Single	18.00	20.00
Double	28.00	30.00

Half board

per person:	£min	£max
Daily	22.00	26.00
Weekly	154.00	182.00

Lunch available
Evening meal 1900 (last orders 1000)
Parking for 10

Town House Fruit Farm

Listed

Hook Lane, Hadleigh, Ipswich
IP7 5PH
☎ (01473) 823260
Fax (01473) 827161
85-acre fruit farm. Converted barn close to Constable country, Harwich and Felixstowe. Facilities for own horses. Studio tuition, painting, drawing.
Bedrooms: 2 double, 1 twin
Bathrooms: 2 public

Bed & breakfast

per night:	£min	£max
Single	15.00	18.00
Double	30.00	35.00

Parking for 6

HALSTEAD

Essex
Map ref 3B2

The Victory Inn & Gingerbreads Restaurant M

Listed COMMENDED

The Green, Wickham St. Paul's,
Halstead CO9 2PT
☎ Sudbury (01787) 269364
Original village ale house, now incorporating large lounge bar, restaurant and accommodation. In centre of triangle between Hedingham, Sudbury and Halstead.
Bedrooms: 2 double, 1 twin
Bathrooms: 1 private, 1 public

Bed & breakfast

per night:	£min	£max
Single	17.50	20.00
Double	28.00	30.00

Lunch available
Evening meal 1900 (last orders 2100)
Parking for 20
Cards accepted: Access, Visa

HARTEST

Suffolk
Map ref 3B2

Giffords Hall

≝≝ COMMENDED

Hartest, Bury St Edmunds IP29 4EX
☎ Bury St Edmunds (01284) 830464

Georgian farmhouse just outside Hartest village, operating a vineyard and small country living with flowers and animals on 33 acres.
Bedrooms: 1 double, 2 twin
Bathrooms: 3 private

Bed & breakfast

per night:	£min	£max
Single	20.00	22.00
Double	36.00	40.00

Parking for 20
Cards accepted: Access, Visa

HARWICH

Essex
Map ref 3C2

Port where the Rivers Orwell and Stour converge and enter the North Sea. The old town still has a medieval atmosphere with its narrow streets. To the south is the seaside resort of Dovercourt with long sandy beaches.
Tourist Information Centre
☎ *(01255) 506139*

Una House
Listed

1 Una Road, Parkeston, Harwich CO12 4PP
☎ (01255) 551390
Three storey end-of-terrace Victorian house within walking distance of ferries. Comfortable and friendly atmosphere. From A120 follow Parkeston Quay ferry terminal sign. First house on left from roundabout.
Bedrooms: 1 double, 2 twin
Bathrooms: 3 private
Bed & breakfast

per night:	£min	£max
Single	16.00	20.00
Double	30.00	45.00

Evening meal 1930 (last orders 2130)
Parking for 3
🛌 🕭 🖭 📺 🛒 🏧

HEMINGFORD GREY

Cambridgeshire
Map ref 3A2

38 High Street
COMMENDED

Hemingford Grey, Huntingdon PE18 9BJ
☎ St Ives (01480) 301203
Private detached house in centre of village, with large garden and quiet surroundings. All home cooking. 1 mile from the A14. Sorry, no smoking or pets.
Bedrooms: 2 single, 2 double
Bathrooms: 1 public
Bed & breakfast

per night:	£min	£max
Single	18.00	18.00
Double	36.00	36.00

Half board

per person:	£min	£max
Daily	28.00	28.00
Weekly	140.00	140.00

Evening meal 1930 (last orders 1600)
Parking for 4
Open January-November
🛌 10 🕭 🖭 🛡 🗟 🖍 📺 🛒 🏧

We advise you to confirm your booking in writing.

HETHERSETT

Norfolk
Map ref 3B1

Magnolia House
Listed

Cromwell Close, Hethersett NR9 3HD
☎ Norwich (01603) 810749
Fax (01603) 810749
Family-run B & B. All rooms centrally heated, colour TV, hot and cold water, tea/coffee making facilities, own key. Laundry available. Private car park.
Bedrooms: 2 single, 3 double, 1 twin
Bathrooms: 3 public
Bed & breakfast

per night:	£min	£max
Single	15.00	20.00
Double	28.00	32.00

Parking for 7
Cards accepted: Diners
🛌 6 🕭 🖭 🖍 📺 🛒 🏧
OAP SP

HEVINGHAM

Norfolk
Map ref 3B1

Marsham Arms Inn
COMMENDED

Holt Road, Hevingham, Norwich NR10 5NP
☎ (01603) 754268
Fax (01603) 754839
Set in peaceful Norfolk countryside within reach of Norwich, the Broads and the coast. Comfortable and spacious accommodation, good food and a fine selection of ales.
Bedrooms: 3 double, 5 twin; suites available
Bathrooms: 8 private
Bed & breakfast

per night:	£min	£max
Single	35.00	40.00
Double	45.00	52.00

Lunch available
Evening meal 1800 (last orders 2200)
Parking for 100
Cards accepted: Access, Visa, Amex, Switch/Delta
🛌 🕭 📞 🖭 🛡 🗟 🖍 📺 🛒 🏧
£50 🏧 SP 🏧

HIGHAM

Suffolk
Map ref 3B2

Bauble
HIGHLY COMMENDED

Higham, Colchester CO7 6LA
☎ (01206) 337254
Fax (01206) 337263
Modernised country house in mature gardens adjacent to the Rivers Brett and Stour. Ideal for touring Constable country and wool industry villages. Will accept children over 12 years old.
Bedrooms: 1 single, 2 twin
Bathrooms: 3 private

Bed & breakfast

per night:	£min	£max
Single	22.00	25.00
Double	40.00	45.00

Parking for 5
🛌 12 🖭 🕭 🖭 🛡 🖍 🛒 🏧 🏧

HINTLESHAM

Suffolk
Map ref 3B2

Birch Farm
🏠🏠

Silver Hill, Hintlesham, Ipswich IP8 3NJ
☎ (01473) 652249

80-acre mixed farm. Traditional farm cottage set in very picturesque, tranquil valley. Indoor heated swimming pool. En-suite bedrooms are in a beautifully converted annexe with own lounge, kitchen/dining room and courtyard. Excellent base for touring this beautiful part of Suffolk.
Bedrooms: 1 single, 1 double, 1 twin
Bathrooms: 3 private
Bed & breakfast

per night:	£min	£max
Single	20.00	25.00
Double	35.00	40.00

Parking for 6
🛌 🕭 🖭 🛡 🗟 🖍 📺 🛒 🏧 🏧

College Farm
🏠🏠 **HIGHLY COMMENDED**

Hintlesham, Ipswich IP8 3NT
☎ (01473) 652253
Fax (01473) 652253
600-acre arable & livestock farm. Beamed 15th C farmhouse in rural setting 6 miles west of Ipswich, offering a warm welcome and comfortable accommodation. Close to Constable country and Lavenham.
Bedrooms: 1 single, 1 double, 1 triple
Bathrooms: 1 private, 1 public
Bed & breakfast

per night:	£min	£max
Single	17.00	22.00
Double	34.00	39.00

Parking for 6
Cards accepted: Diners
🛌 8 🖭 🕭 🖭 🛡 🗟 🖍 📺 🛒 🏧 🏧
🏧 🏧

Please mention this guide when making a booking.

HITCHAM

Suffolk
Map ref 3B2

Pansy Cottage

Listed COMMENDED

The Causeway, Hitcham, Ipswich
IP7 7NE
☎ Bildeston (01449) 740858 & 0378 006195

Grade II listed timber-framed, thatched cottage.

Bedrooms: 1 single, 1 double, 1 twin
Bathrooms: 1 public

Bed & breakfast per night:	£min	£max
Single	14.00	20.00
Double	28.00	32.00

Parking for 1

Wetherden Hall

Listed APPROVED

Hitcham, Ipswich IP7 7PZ
☎ Bildeston (01449) 740412

270-acre arable and mixed farm. A warm welcome awaits you at this attractive farmhouse on the edge of a very pretty village. Private fishing. Good centre for visiting medieval Lavenham, Bury St Edmunds, Ipswich, Cambridge and Constable country.

Bedrooms: 1 double, 1 triple
Bathrooms: 1 public

Bed & breakfast per night:	£min	£max
Single	14.50	18.00
Double	27.00	32.00

Parking for 6
Open March-October

HITCHIN

Hertfordshire
Map ref 2D1

Once a flourishing wool town. Full of interest, with many fine old buildings around the market square. These include the 17th C almshouses, old inns and the Victorian Corn Exchange.

The Greyhound

London Road, St Ippolyts, Hitchin
SG4 7NL
☎ (01462) 440989

Lovely countryside views yet only 1.5 miles south of Hitchin. 15 minutes to Luton Airport, M1, 10 minutes to A1(M) or Stevenage. Personal service.

Bedrooms: 1 double, 1 twin
Bathrooms: 2 private

Bed & breakfast per night:	£min	£max
Single	20.00	35.00
Double	25.00	40.00

Lunch available
Evening meal 1800 (last orders 2230)
Parking for 25
Cards accepted: Access, Visa, Switch/Delta

HOLT

Norfolk
Map ref 3B1

Much of the town centre was destroyed by fire in 1708 but has since been restored. The famous Gresham's School founded by Sir Thomas Gresham is sited here.

Hempstead Hall

COMMENDED

Holt NR25 6TN
☎ (01263) 712224

300-acre arable farm. 1.5 miles off A148 near Holt. Elegant listed 19th C country house built from traditional Norfolk flint, conveniently situated near the north Norfolk coast and its many attractions.

Bedrooms: 1 double, 1 family room
Bathrooms: 2 private

Bed & breakfast per night:	£min	£max
Single	24.00	24.00
Double	32.00	40.00

Parking for 6

HORSEY

Norfolk
Map ref 3C1

Tranquil National Trust village in an Area of Outstanding Natural Beauty, half-a-mile from the sea and the Norfolk Broads (Horsey Mere).

The Old Chapel

Listed COMMENDED

Horsey Corner, Horsey NR29 4EH
☎ Winterton (01493) 393498 & Mobile 0589 404051

Converted Methodist chapel in quiet rural environment. Glorious sunsets, peaceful walks and abundant wildlife.

Bedrooms: 1 double, 1 twin, 1 family room
Bathrooms: 3 private, 1 public

Bed & breakfast per night:	£min	£max
Single	21.00	29.25
Double	28.00	39.00

Evening meal from 1900
Parking for 6

HUNTINGDON

Cambridgeshire
Map ref 3A2

Attractive, interesting town which abounds in associations with the Cromwell family. The town is connected to Godmanchester by a beautiful 14th C bridge over the River Great Ouse.
Tourist Information Centre
☎ *(01480) 388588*

Prince of Wales

COMMENDED

Potton Road, Hilton, Huntingdon
PE18 9NG
☎ (01480) 830257
Fax (01480) 830257

Village inn renowned for its traditional ales and good value food. Convenient for St Ives, Huntingdon, St Neots and Cambridge. On B1040, south-east of Huntingdon.

Bedrooms: 2 single, 1 double, 1 twin
Bathrooms: 4 private

Bed & breakfast per night:	£min	£max
Single	20.00	33.00
Double	40.00	48.00

Lunch available
Evening meal 1900 (last orders 2115)
Parking for 9
Cards accepted: Access, Visa, Amex, Switch/Delta

INGATESTONE

Essex
Map ref 3B3

Eibiswald

Listed HIGHLY COMMENDED

85 Mill Road, Stock, Ingatestone
CM4 9LR
☎ Stock (01277) 840631
Fax (01277) 840631

Anglo-Austrian hospitality. Comfortable, modern house in quiet, pleasant rural surroundings. Close to village centre. Railway 4 miles. Convenient for Chelmsford, Brentwood, Basildon. 5 minutes from A12 on B1007, signposted Billericay.

Bedrooms: 3 double
Bathrooms: 1 private, 1 public

Bed & breakfast per night:	£min	£max
Single	25.00	30.00
Double	35.00	40.00

Parking for 7

⛵ 12 🏧 ▢ 🖤 ⑱ 🛇 🍴 ✗ 📺 🛏 🚗 🕛 ✤ ✕ 🎠 ⓣ

IPSWICH

Suffolk
Map ref 3B2

Interesting county town and major port on the River Orwell. Birthplace of Cardinal Wolsey. Christchurch Mansion, set in a fine park, contains a good collection of furniture and pictures, with works by Gainsborough, Constable and Munnings.
Tourist Information Centre
☎ *(01473) 258070*

Redholme

😊😊 COMMENDED

52 Ivry Street, Ipswich IP1 3QP
☎ (01473) 250018 & 233174
Large Victorian house and garden in quiet residential area, near Christchurch Park and 10 minutes' walk from town centre.
Bedrooms: 3 twin, 1 triple
Bathrooms: 4 private

Bed & breakfast per night:	£min	£max
Single	22.00	27.00
Double	39.50	45.00

Half board per person:	£min	£max
Daily	27.00	37.00
Weekly	170.00	210.00

Evening meal 1830 (last orders 2100)
Parking for 4

⛵ 🏧 ▢ 🖤 ⑱ ⓢ 🛇 🍴 ✗ 📺 🛏 🚗 ✕ ✤ ✗ 🎠 ⓣ

KELVEDON

Essex
Map ref 3B3

Village on the old Roman road from Colchester to London. Many of the buildings are 18th C but there is much of earlier date. The famous preacher Charles Spurgeon was born here in 1834.

Highfields Farm

😊😊

Kelvedon, Colchester CO5 9BJ
☎ (01376) 570334
700-acre arable & horses farm. Farmhouse in quiet location in open countryside. Easy access to A12. Heating in all rooms.
Bedrooms: 2 twin, 1 triple
Bathrooms: 3 private, 1 public

Bed & breakfast per night:	£min	£max
Single	18.00	20.00
Double	32.00	34.00

Parking for 6

⛵ 🏧 ▢ 🖤 ⑱ ⑆ ✗ ✕ 📺 🚗 ✤ 🎠 🏘

KERSEY

Suffolk
Map ref 3B2

A most picturesque village, which was famous for cloth-making, set in a valley with a water-splash. The church of St Mary is an impressive building at the top of the hill.

Red House Farm

Listed COMMENDED

Kersey, Ipswich IP7 6EY
☎ Boxford (01787) 210245
Listed farmhouse between Kersey and Boxford, central for Constable country. Rooms with wash basins, TV and tea-making facilities. Twin bedroom and ground floor annexe single are en-suite. Swimming pool.
Bedrooms: 1 single, 1 double, 1 twin
Bathrooms: 3 private, 1 public

Bed & breakfast per night:	£min	£max
Single	18.00	20.00
Double	34.00	36.00

Half board per person:	£min	£max
Daily	26.00	28.00
Weekly	182.00	196.00

Evening meal 1900 (last orders 1000)
Parking for 5
Cards accepted: Diners

🏧 🏧 ▢ 🖤 ⑆ 🖤 ⑱ ⓢ 🛏 🚗 ✗ ∪ ➤ ✤ 🎠 🏘

KESSINGLAND

Suffolk
Map ref 3C1

Seaside village whose church tower has served as a landmark to sailors for generations. Nearby is the Suffolk Wildlife and Country Park.

The Old Rectory

😊😊 HIGHLY COMMENDED

157 Church Road, Kessingland, Lowestoft NR33 7SQ
☎ Lowestoft (01502) 740020
Beautiful late Georgian house in 2 acres of garden, well back from road ensuring peace and quiet. A warm welcome awaits. Spacious, comfortable, delightfully furnished rooms, most with antiques.
Bedrooms: 2 double, 1 twin
Bathrooms: 2 private, 2 public

Bed & breakfast per night:	£min	£max
Single	22.00	24.00
Double	40.00	44.00

Parking for 6
Open May-September

⛵ 6 🏧 ▢ ✆ ⑩ 🖤 ⑱ ⓢ 🛇 🍴 📺 🛏 🚗 ✤ ✕ 🎠 🏘

KING'S LYNN

Norfolk
Map ref 3B1

A busy town with many outstanding buildings. The Guildhall and Town Hall are both built of flint in a striking chequer design. Behind the Guildhall in the Old Gaol House the sounds and smells of prison life 2 centuries ago are recreated.
Tourist Information Centre
☎ *(01553) 763044*

Maranatha Guest House ⋀

😊 APPROVED

115 Gaywood Road, Gaywood, King's Lynn PE30 2PU
☎ (01553) 774596
Large carrstone and brick residence with gardens front and rear, 10 minutes' walk from town centre, Lynnsport and Queen Elizabeth Hospital. Direct road to Sandringham and the coast.
Bedrooms: 2 single, 2 double, 2 twin
Bathrooms: 2 private, 1 public

Bed & breakfast per night:	£min	£max
Single	17.00	
Double	28.00	

Half board per person:	£min	£max
Daily	22.00	

Lunch available
Evening meal 1800 (last orders 1800)
Parking for 9

⛵ ▢ ✆ ⑱ ⓢ ✕ 📺 🛏 🚗 🎠 ✎

The Tudor Rose Hotel ⋀

😊😊😊 COMMENDED

St. Nicholas Street, Off Tuesday Market Place, King's Lynn PE30 1LR
☎ (01553) 762824
Fax (01553) 764894
Built around 1500 by a local merchant and extended in 1640, the hotel offers comfortable accommodation, traditional British cooking and a choice of 4 real ale bars.
Bedrooms: 3 single, 6 double, 3 twin
Bathrooms: 12 private

Bed & breakfast per night:	£min	£max
Single	30.00	38.50
Double	50.00	50.00

Continued ▶

KING'S LYNN

Continued

Lunch available
Evening meal 1900 (last orders 2130)
Cards accepted: Access, Visa, Diners, Amex, Switch/Delta
🛏🍴🐾🍷📞🖵🔌♦🎣📶💷✕🎿📺🎲 🛍. 🌼 SP 🎏

KINGS LANGLEY

Hertfordshire
Map ref 2D1

Woodcote House

😄😄 COMMENDED

7 The Grove, Chipperfield Road, Kings
Langley WD4 9JF
☎ (01923) 262077
*Timber-framed house, sitting in 1 acre
of landscaped gardens with quiet rural
aspect. Convenient for M1 and M25 and
close to Watford and Hemel Hempstead.*
Bedrooms: 2 single, 1 double, 1 twin
Bathrooms: 4 private
Bed & breakfast

per night:	£min	£max
Single	20.00	24.00
Double	38.00	40.00

Evening meal 1800 (last orders 2100)
Parking for 8
🛏🍷📶💷✕🎿📺🛍. 🍴🎯🌼✈🎏

LAVENHAM

Suffolk
Map ref 3B2

A former prosperous wool town of
timber-framed buildings with the
cathedral-like church and its tall
tower. The market-place is 13th C
and the Guildhall now houses a
museum.

The Red House ⚑

😄😄 COMMENDED

29 Bolton Street, Lavenham, Sudbury
CO10 9RG
☎ (01787) 248074 & 0585 536148
*In the best of the medieval East Anglian
villages, a large Victorian house,
attractively redecorated. Full central
heating, large garden. Only a step from
pubs.*
Bedrooms: 2 double, 1 twin; suites
available
Bathrooms: 3 private
Bed & breakfast

per night:	£min	£max
Single	20.00	30.00
Double	40.00	

Half board

per person:	£min	£max
Daily	32.50	

Evening meal 1930 (last orders 2030)
Parking for 8
Open February-November and
Christmas
🛏♦📶💷✕🎿📺🛍. 🍴🌼🎏

LAWSHALL

Suffolk
Map ref 3B2

Brighthouse Farm

😄😄 COMMENDED

Melford Road, Lawshall, Bury St
Edmunds IP29 4PX
☎ Bury St Edmunds (01284) 830385
*300-acre arable & livestock farm. A
warm welcome awaits you at this 200-
year-old farmhouse set in 3 acres of
gardens. Close to many places of
historic interest. Good pubs and
restaurants nearby.*
Bedrooms: 2 double, 1 twin
Bathrooms: 1 private, 1 public
Bed & breakfast

per night:	£min	£max
Single	18.00	25.00
Double	36.00	40.00

Parking for 10
🛏🎣📶💷✕🎿📺🛍. 🍴🍷🌼✈🎏

LESSINGHAM

Norfolk
Map ref 3C1

The Seafarers

Listed

North Gap Eccles Beach, Lessingham,
Norwich NR12 0SW
☎ Hickling (01692) 598218
*18th C former farmhouse with sailing
ship mast beams in main rooms.
Furnished with antiques and shipping
memorabilia.*
Bedrooms: 1 single, 1 double, 1 twin
Bathrooms: 3 private, 1 public
Bed & breakfast

per night:	£min	£max
Single	18.00	22.00
Double	36.00	44.00

Parking for 5
🛏🍷📶♦📶✕🎿📺🛍. 🌼✈🎏🎏

LITTLE TEY

Essex
Map ref 3B2

Knaves Farm House

Listed

Great Tey Road, Little Tey, Colchester
CO6 1JA
☎ Colchester (01206) 211039
*Charming early Victorian farmhouse in
1 acre of well-kept garden with
traditional Essex barns. 400 yards from
A120 towards Great Tey.*
Bedrooms: 1 double, 1 twin
Bathrooms: 1 private, 1 public
Bed & breakfast

per night:	£min	£max
Single	20.00	25.00
Double	30.00	35.00

Parking for 1
🛏🍴🍷📞♦🎣📶💷🛍. 🍴🌼✈🎏🎏

LITTLE THETFORD

Cambridgeshire
Map ref 3A2

Quarterway House ⚑

😄😄

Ely Road, Little Thetford, Ely
CB6 3HP
☎ Ely (01353) 648964
*In 4 acres adjoining byway and open
countryside, 4 miles from Wicken Fen
nature reserve, 2 miles from Ely and
just off A10. Warm, comfortable rooms
with colour TV. Use of garden and
conservatory.*
Bedrooms: 1 double, 1 twin; suites
available
Bathrooms: 2 private, 1 public
Bed & breakfast

per night:	£min	£max
Single	19.00	19.00
Double	35.00	35.00

Half board

per person:	£min	£max
Daily	28.00	28.00

Parking for 7
🛏5🍷📞♦🎣📶♦💷✕🎿📺🛍. 🍴✕
🌙🎯🌼🎏

LITTLE WENHAM

Suffolk
Map ref 3B2

Grove Farm House

😄 COMMENDED

Little Wenham, Colchester CO7 6QB
☎ Great Wenham (01473) 310341

*190-acre arable farm. Comfortable listed
farmhouse in quiet rural setting, 15
minutes from Ipswich. Convenient for
Constable country and the coast.*
Bedrooms: 1 single, 1 double, 1 twin
Bathrooms: 1 public
Bed & breakfast

per night:	£min	£max
Single		16.00
Double		32.00

Half board

per person:	£min	£max
Daily		28.00
Weekly		175.00

Evening meal 1830 (last orders 2000)
Parking for 5
Open March-October
🍷♦📶♦💷✕🎿📺🛍. 🍴🌼✈🎏🎏

LONG MELFORD

Suffolk
Map ref 3B2

One of Suffolk's loveliest villages, remarkable for the length of its main street. Holy Trinity Church is considered to be the finest village church in England. The National Trust own the Elizabethan Melford Hall and nearby Kentwell Hall is also open to the public.

The George & Dragon

Long Melford, Sudbury CO10 9JB
☎ Sudbury (01787) 371285
Fax (01787) 312428
English country inn offering traditional service and hospitality. The best in both beer and beef.
Bedrooms: 2 double, 3 twin, 1 triple, 1 family room
Bathrooms: 6 private, 1 private shower

Bed & breakfast

per night:	£min	£max
Single	25.00	30.00
Double	45.00	50.00

Half board

per person:	£min	£max
Daily	35.00	45.00
Weekly	210.00	245.00

Lunch available
Evening meal 1800 (last orders 2200)
Parking for 20
Cards accepted: Access, Visa, Switch/Delta

LOWESTOFT

Suffolk
Map ref 3C1

Seaside town with wide sandy beaches. Important fishing port with picturesque fishing quarter. Home of the famous Lowestoft porcelain and birthplace of Benjamin Britten. East Point Pavilion's exhibition describes the Lowestoft story.
Tourist Information Centre
☎ *(01502) 523000*

Church Farm

Listed HIGHLY COMMENDED
Corton, Lowestoft NR32 5HX
☎ (01502) 730359
Fax (01502) 730359

220-acre arable farm. Victorian farmhouse with clean and comfortable

accommodation of high standard and a warm, welcoming atmosphere. Situated 3 miles north of Lowestoft near quiet, rural coastline and within easy reach of the beautiful Broadland and many local attractions. Traditional English breakfast. Non-smoking establishment.
Bedrooms: 3 double
Bathrooms: 3 private

Bed & breakfast

per night:	£min	£max
Single		25.00
Double		36.00

Parking for 4
Open March-October

Hall Farm

Listed COMMENDED
Jay Lane, Church Lane, Lound, Lowestoft NR32 5LJ
☎ (01502) 730415
101-acre arable farm. Traditional 16th C Suffolk farmhouse within 2 miles of the sea. Clean, comfortable accommodation with generous English breakfast. Farm down a quiet, private lane half-a-mile from A12.
Bedrooms: 2 single, 1 double, 1 triple
Bathrooms: 2 private, 1 public

Bed & breakfast

per night:	£min	£max
Single	16.00	18.00
Double	32.00	36.00

Parking for 6
Open March-October

Rockville House ⋒

COMMENDED
6 Pakefield Road, Lowestoft NR33 0HS
☎ (01502) 581011 & 0374 453687
Fax (01502) 581011
Victorian villa quietly situated in south Lowestoft near Suffolk Heritage Coast. Tastefully renovated throughout. Close to beach and gardens.
Bedrooms: 3 single, 2 double, 2 twin
Bathrooms: 3 private, 2 public

Bed & breakfast

per night:	£min	£max
Single	21.00	
Double	37.00	

Evening meal 1800 (last orders 1000)
Cards accepted: Access, Visa

MARGARET RODING

Essex
Map ref 2D1

Greys

Listed
Ongar Road, Margaret Roding, Dunmow CM6 1QR
☎ Good Easter (01245) 231509
340-acre arable and mixed farm. Formerly 2 cottages pleasantly situated

on family farm just off A1060 at telephone kiosk. Beamed throughout, large garden. Tea/coffee available. Singles by arrangement.
Bedrooms: 2 double, 1 twin
Bathrooms: 1 public

Bed & breakfast

per night:	£min	£max
Single	18.00	
Double	36.00	40.00

Parking for 6

MUNDESLEY

Norfolk
Map ref 3C1

Small seaside resort with a superb sandy beach and excellent bathing. Nearby is a smock-mill still with cap and sails.

The Grange

COMMENDED
High Street, Mundesley-on-Sea, Norwich NR11 8JL
☎ (01263) 721556
Beautiful, well-furnished house with friendly atmosphere, in attractive garden. Ideal for the Broads and Norwich, bird-watching, fishing and beach.
Bedrooms: 2 double, 1 twin, 1 triple
Bathrooms: 2 public

Bed & breakfast

per night:	£min	£max
Single	16.00	18.00
Double	32.00	36.00

Parking for 10

NAYLAND

Suffolk
Map ref 3B2

Charmingly located village on the River Stour owing its former prosperity to the cloth trade. The hub of the village is the 15th C Alston Court. The altar-piece of St James Church was painted by John Constable.

Gladwins Farm ⋒

COMMENDED
Harpers Hill, Nayland, Colchester CO6 4NU
☎ (01206) 262261
Fax (01206) 263001

22-acre smallholding. Timbered farmhouse in peaceful wooded surroundings in Constable country.

Continued ▶

NAYLAND

Continued

Entrance on A134. Trout fishing, tennis. Golf 2 miles. Home and local produce. Brochure.
Bedrooms: 1 single, 1 double, 1 twin, 1 family room
Bathrooms: 2 private, 1 public

Bed & breakfast

per night:	£min	£max
Single	18.00	20.00
Double	40.00	56.00

Half board

per person:	£min	£max
Daily	26.50	37.00
Weekly	175.00	210.00

Evening meal 1900 (last orders 2030)
Parking for 5
Cards accepted: Access, Visa, Switch/ Delta

Hill House

Listed COMMENDED

Gravel Hill, Nayland, Colchester CO6 4JB
☎ Colchester (01206) 262782
Comfortable 16th C home peacefully situated on edge of picturesque "Constable" village. Good local eating places. Ideal base for exploring.
Bedrooms: 1 single, 1 twin
Bathrooms: 2 private, 2 public

Bed & breakfast

per night:	£min	£max
Single	18.00	20.00
Double	36.00	38.00

Parking for 2

Leavenheath Farm

Listed HIGHLY COMMENDED

Locks Lane, Leavenheath, Colchester CO6 4PF
☎ Colchester (01206) 262322

30-acre mixed farm. Small fruit farm with pedigree sheep, free-range chickens, geese and ancient bluebell wood in Stour Valley. Lovely refurbished oak-beamed Suffolk farmhouse offering peace and tranquillity with home cooking. Winter log fires and a warm welcome.
Bedrooms: 2 double, 2 twin
Bathrooms: 3 private, 1 public

Bed & breakfast

per night:	£min	£max
Single	18.00	25.00
Double	36.00	40.00

Half board

per person:	£min	£max
Daily	30.00	32.00
Weekly	200.00	270.00

Lunch available
Evening meal 1900 (last orders 2100)
Parking for 26

NEWMARKET

Suffolk
Map ref 3B2

Centre of the English horse-racing world and the headquarters of the Jockey Club and National Stud. Racecourse and horse sales. The National Horse Racing Museum traces the history and development of the Sport of Kings.
Tourist Information Centre
☎ *(01638) 667200*

Westley House

Listed

Westley Waterless, Newmarket CB8 0RQ
☎ (01638) 508112
Fax (01638) 508113
Spacious Georgian-style former rectory in quiet rural area 5 miles south of Newmarket and convenient for Cambridge. Large comfortable bedrooms and drawing room opening on to 5 acres of garden, trees and paddocks. Visitors are our guests. Advance bookings only, please.
Bedrooms: 1 single, 2 twin
Bathrooms: 2 public

Bed & breakfast

per night:	£min	£max
Single	18.50	20.00
Double	37.00	40.00

Half board

per person:	£min	£max
Daily	32.00	32.00
Weekly	175.00	175.00

Evening meal 1930 (last orders 2100)
Parking for 6

NORFOLK BROADS

See under Aylsham, Beccles, Bungay, Coltishall, Great Yarmouth, Hevingham, Lowestoft, North Walsham, Norwich, Rackheath, Salhouse, South Walsham, Stalham, Wroxham

Individual proprietors have supplied all details of accommodation. As changes can occur, we advise you to confirm the information at the time of booking.

NORTH WALSHAM

Norfolk
Map ref 3C1

Weekly market has been held here for 700 years. 1 mile south of town is a cross commemorating the Peasants' Revolt of 1381. Nelson attended the local Paston Grammar School, founded in 1606 and still flourishing.

Geoffrey the Dyer House

Church Plain, Worstead, North Walsham NR28 9AL
☎ Smallburgh (01692) 536562
Carefully restored 17th C weaver's residence, full of character and comfort, close to beach, Broads and Norwich. In centre of conservation village.
Bedrooms: 2 double, 1 twin, 1 family room
Bathrooms: 4 private

Bed & breakfast

per night:	£min	£max
Single	17.50	23.00
Double	35.00	40.00

Half board

per person:	£min	£max
Daily	26.00	31.50

Lunch available
Evening meal 1830 (last orders 2200)
Parking for 4
Cards accepted: Diners

NORWICH

Norfolk
Map ref 3C1

Beautiful cathedral city and county town on the River Wensum with many fine museums and medieval churches. Norman castle, Guildhall and interesting medieval streets. Good shopping centre and market.
Tourist Information Centre
☎ *(01603) 666071*

Cavell House

Listed

Swardeston, Norwich NR14 8D2
☎ Mulbarton (01508) 578195
Birthplace of nurse Edith Cavell. Georgian farmhouse on edge of Swardeston village. Off B1113 south of Norwich, 5 miles from centre. Rural setting. Close to university.
Bedrooms: 1 single, 1 double, 1 twin
Bathrooms: 2 public

Bed & breakfast

per night:	£min	£max
Single	10.00	18.00
Double	30.00	35.00

Lunch available
Parking for 10

Cumberland Hotel and Restaurant ᴁ

ᵂᵂᵂ COMMENDED

212-216 Thorpe Road, Norwich
NR1 1TJ
☎ (01603) 434550 & 434560
Fax (01603) 433355
*Independently-run hotel offering
personal and friendly service, good
restaurant and full modern facilities.
Ample parking.*
Bedrooms: 9 single, 9 double, 3 twin,
3 triple, 1 family room
Bathrooms: 25 private, 3 public
Bed & breakfast

per night:	£min	£max
Single	34.90	
Double	44.00	

Half board

per person:	£min	£max
Daily	44.00	
Weekly	237.00	

Lunch available
Evening meal 1830 (last orders 2130)
Parking for 63
Cards accepted: Access, Visa, Diners,
Amex, Switch/Delta
ᴥᴥᴧ☐♨☎❡⑂S⌀㎧TV◑▥
🖪ⓣ30 ☀✕▥ ⒹⒶᴾ SP Ⓣ

Kingsley Lodge

ᵂᵂ COMMENDED

3 Kingsley Road, Norwich NR1 3RB
☎ (01603) 615819
*Quiet, friendly Edwardian house near
bus station, under 10 minutes' walk to
city centre. Spacious bedrooms with en-
suite bathrooms, TV, tea/coffee making
facilities. No smoking.*
Bedrooms: 1 single, 1 double, 1 twin
Bathrooms: 3 private
Bed & breakfast

per night:	£min	£max
Single	22.00	25.00
Double	36.00	38.00

Open February-December
🖳☐♨❡⑂S⌀㎧▥🖪✕�📦

Oakfield

ᵂᵂ HIGHLY COMMENDED

Yelverton Road, Framingham Earl,
Norwich NR14 7SD
☎ Framingham Earl (01508) 492605
*Superior accommodation in beautiful,
quiet setting on edge of village 4 miles
south-east of Norwich. Splendid
breakfasts. Local pubs serve good
evening meals.*
Bedrooms: 1 single, 1 double, 1 twin
Bathrooms: 1 private, 1 public
Bed & breakfast

per night:	£min	£max
Single	18.00	22.00
Double	35.00	40.00

Parking for 6
ᴥ12🖳🖳♨▥㎧⌀TV▥🖪☀
✕📦

Rosedale ᴁ

Listed

145 Earlham Road, Norwich NR2 3RG
☎ (01603) 453743
*Friendly, family-run Victorian
guesthouse and restaurant on main
B1108, 1 mile from city centre.
Shopping centre, restaurants and
university nearby.*
Bedrooms: 3 single, 2 double, 2 twin,
2 triple
Bathrooms: 2 public
Bed & breakfast

per night:	£min	£max
Single	14.00	18.00
Double	29.00	34.00

Parking for 2
ᴥ4☐♨▥S⌀▥🖪✕📦🏚

Witton Hall Farm

ᵂᵂ

Witton, Norwich NR13 5DN
☎ (01603) 714580
*500-acre dairy farm. Elegant Georgian
farmhouse in the heart of Norfolk.
Peaceful, mature grounds. Swimming
pool in walled garden.*
Bedrooms: 1 double, 1 twin, 1 family
room
Bathrooms: 3 private
Bed & breakfast

per night:	£min	£max
Single	20.00	22.00
Double	32.00	34.00

Parking for 4
Cards accepted: Diners
ᴥ☐♨▥🖪🖩TV▥🖪〰☀📦

OCCOLD

Suffolk
Map ref 3B2

The Cedars Guest House

ᵂᵂ COMMENDED

Church Street, Occold, Eye IP23 7PS
☎ (01379) 678439

*Georgian house dating from around
1730, set in pleasant wooded grounds
in quiet village close to the ancient
town of Eye. Ideally situated for
exploring the rural East Anglian
countryside.*
Bedrooms: 2 double, 1 twin
Bathrooms: 3 private
Bed & breakfast

per night:	£min	£max
Single	18.50	21.00
Double	37.00	42.00

Half board

per person:	£min	£max
Daily	31.00	33.50

Evening meal 1900 (last orders 2030)

Parking for 5
Open January-November
Cards accepted: Amex
ᴥ♨❡⑂S⌀㎧TV▥🖪🖪☀✕📦🏚

ONGAR

Essex
Map ref 3B3

Bumbles

Listed

Moreton Road, Ongar CM5 0EZ
☎ (01277) 362695
*2-acre smallholding. 200-year-old cottage
with beams and inglenook fireplace.
Easy access to London, M11, M25 and
main towns in area.*
Bedrooms: 3 twin
Bathrooms: 2 private, 2 public
Bed & breakfast

per night:	£min	£max
Single	20.00	20.00
Double	32.00	34.00

Parking for 6
ᴥ12🖳▥🖩S⌀TV▥∪☀📦🏚Ⓣ

POTTER HEIGHAM

Norfolk
Map ref 3C1

On the River Thurne, the village is
one of the most popular of the
Broadland centres and is well
known for its 13th C bridge and
boatyard. The thatched church has
a rare octagonal font made of
brick.

Falgate Inn

ᵂᵂ COMMENDED

Main Road, Potter Heigham, Great
Yarmouth NR29 5HZ
☎ (01692) 670003 & mobile 0585
735068
*Bed and breakfast, with restaurant, bar
snacks and beer garden. Open 7 days a
week, full on-licence.*
Bedrooms: 1 single, 1 double, 2 twin,
1 triple
Bathrooms: 2 private, 1 public
Bed & breakfast

per night:	£min	£max
Single	17.00	21.00
Double	34.00	42.00

Lunch available
Evening meal 1900 (last orders 2130)
Cards accepted: Access, Visa, Switch/
Delta
ᴥ☐♨S▥☀📦

National gradings and
classifications were correct
at the time of going to
press but are subject to
change. Please check at the
time of booking.

RACKHEATH

Norfolk
Map ref 3C1

Barn Court

Listed **APPROVED**

6 Back Lane, Rackheath, Norwich
NR13 6NN
☎ Norwich (01603) 782536
Fax (01603) 782536
*Spacious accommodation in a
traditional Norfolk barn conversion,
built around a courtyard. Ideal base for
exploring Norfolk - 3 miles Norwich.
Friendly atmosphere with good home
cooking.*
Bedrooms: 2 double, 1 twin
Bathrooms: 2 public

Bed & breakfast

per night:	£min	£max
Single	16.00	20.00
Double	32.00	40.00

Parking for 4

⏳♨♿👆📞♿ⓘ🅂⛱📺▥◻🚲❄
🚃🏵

RADWINTER

Essex
Map ref 3B2

The Plough Inn

Listed **APPROVED**

Sampford Road, Radwinter, Saffron
Walden CB10 2TL
☎ Saffron Walden (01799) 599222
*16th C inn with lovely garden views of
countryside. Self-contained
accommodation in garden. Lunch and
evening meal available in the pub. 5
miles from Saffron Walden and 6 miles
from Finchingfield.*
Bedrooms: 1 double, 1 twin
Bathrooms: 2 private

Bed & breakfast

per night:	£min	£max
Single	22.00	22.00
Double	40.00	40.00

Lunch available
Evening meal 1900 (last orders 2200)
Parking for 20

♿📞📞👆🅂▥❄🗡🚃🏵

RAMSEY

Cambridgeshire
Map ref 3A2

The Leys ♠♠

Listed

25 Bury Road, Ramsey, Huntingdon
PE17 1NE
☎ (01487) 813221 & 710053
*Large family house with a friendly
atmosphere. On B1040 on the southern
outskirts of Ramsey, between
Huntingdon and Peterborough.*
Bedrooms: 1 single, 1 twin, 2 triple
Bathrooms: 2 private, 1 public

Bed & breakfast

per night:	£min	£max
Single	13.00	25.00
Double	26.00	32.00

Half board

per person:	£min	£max
Daily	19.00	31.00
Weekly	126.00	

Evening meal from 1930
Parking for 10

⏳♨♿👆📞♨♿ⓘ🅂➰📺▥◻🚲♿❄
🚃ⓣ

REEDHAM

Norfolk
Map ref 3C1

A chain ferry crosses the River
Yare at this point.

Briars

♨♨♨

10 Riverside, Reedham, Norwich
NR13 3TF
☎ Great Yarmouth (01493) 700054
Fax (01493) 700054
*Accommodation over a "tea room" on
the riverside at Reedham between Great
Yarmouth and Norwich. Lounge and
sun balcony on upper floor with river
and open marshland views. Station
close by. Evening meals by
arrangement.*
Bedrooms: 3 double
Bathrooms: 3 private

Bed & breakfast

per night:	£min	£max
Single	30.00	30.00
Double	45.00	45.00

Lunch available
Evening meal 1800 (last orders 2100)
Parking for 6

⏳📞📞👆📞♿ⓘ🅂➰📺▥◻🚲🗡
❄🚃⏳

RICKMANSWORTH

Hertfordshire
Map ref 2D2

Old town, where 3 rivers meet,
now mainly residential. The High
Street is full of interesting
buildings, including the home of
William Penn. Moor Park Mansion,
a fine 18th C house, is now a golf
clubhouse.

6 Swallow Close

Listed

Nightingale Road, Rickmansworth
WD3 2DZ
☎ (01923) 720069
*In a quiet cul-de-sac, 5 minutes' walk
from underground station, 30 minutes
to London. Convenient for M25 and
Watford. All food home-made. Non-
smokers only, please.*
Bedrooms: 1 single, 1 double, 1 triple
Bathrooms: 1 private, 1 public

Bed & breakfast

per night:	£min	£max
Single	18.00	
Double	36.00	

Parking for 3

⏳5📞👆♨▥❄▥◻🚲❄🗡🚃

ROYSTON

Hertfordshire
Map ref 2D1

Old town lying at the crossing of
the Roman road Ermine Street and
the Icknield Way. It has many
interesting old houses and inns.

Hall Farm

Listed

Great Chishill, Royston SG8 8SH
☎ (01763) 838263
Fax (01763) 838263
*Homely accommodation on working
farm, in secluded gardens on the
highest point in Cambridgeshire.
Royston 5 miles, Duxford Museum 4
miles, Cambridge 11 miles.*
Bedrooms: 2 double, 1 twin
Bathrooms: 1 public

Bed & breakfast

per night:	£min	£max
Single	17.50	20.00
Double	30.00	35.00

Parking for 8

⏳📞📞👆▥ⓘ🅂➰▥◻🚲∪ℾ❄🗡
🚃🆂🅿🏵

SAFFRON WALDEN

Essex
Map ref 2D1

Takes its name from the saffron
crocus once grown around the
town. The church of St Mary has
superb carvings, magnificent roofs
and brasses. A town maze can be
seen on the common. Two miles
south-west is Audley End, a
magnificent Jacobean mansion
owned by English Heritage.
Tourist Information Centre
☎ *(01799) 510444*

Duddenhoe End Farm

♨♨ **COMMENDED**

Duddenhoe End, Saffron Walden
CB11 4UU
☎ Royston (01763) 838258
*230-acre mixed farm. 17th C farmhouse
with a wealth of beams and inglenook
fireplace, situated in a quiet rural area.*
Bedrooms: 2 double, 1 twin
Bathrooms: 3 private

Bed & breakfast

per night:	£min	£max
Single	25.00	
Double	36.00	

Parking for 3

⏳12📞👆▥❄▥📺▥◻🗡❄🗡🚃

Elmdon Bury

HIGHLY COMMENDED

Elmdon, Saffron Walden CB11 4NF
☎ Royston (01763) 838220
350-acre arable farm. Recently restored red brick Essex farmhouse with outstanding thatched barns. Set in beautiful grounds behind church, in centre of Elmdon village, to the West of Saffron Walden. Large spacious rooms.
Bedrooms: 2 double, 1 twin
Bathrooms: 3 private

Bed & breakfast per night:	£min	£max
Single	25.00	28.00
Double	40.00	44.00

Half board per person:	£min	£max
Daily	35.00	40.00

Evening meal 1930 (last orders 2030)
Parking for 10

Oak House

Listed

40 Audley Road, Saffron Walden CB11 3HD
☎ (01799) 523290
Modern conversion of stables adjacent to house. Centrally situated, with off-street parking and lock-up for bicycles.
Bedrooms: 1 double, 1 twin
Bathrooms: 1 public

Bed & breakfast per night:	£min	£max
Single	16.00	20.00
Double	32.00	40.00

Parking for 2

Pond Mead

Widdington, Saffron Walden CB11 3SB
☎ (01799) 540201
Comfortable old house on the edge of Widdington village, with its ancient tithe barn and wildlife park. Easy access to Stansted Airport, Cambridge and M11.
Bedrooms: 1 single, 1 double, 1 triple
Bathrooms: 3 private, 1 public

Bed & breakfast per night:	£min	£max
Single	14.00	19.00
Double		32.00

Parking for 5

Queens Head Inn

COMMENDED

Littlebury, Saffron Walden CB11 4TD
☎ (01799) 522251
Fax (01799) 513522
Family-run freehouse and hotel close to Audley End. All rooms en-suite. Good Pub Guide "Best Pub in Essex" 1995. Interesting and unusual menu.
Bedrooms: 2 single, 2 double, 1 twin, 1 triple
Bathrooms: 6 private

Bed & breakfast per night:	£min	£max
Single	29.95	36.50
Double	44.95	54.95

Lunch available
Evening meal 1900 (last orders 2100)
Parking for 30
Cards accepted: Access, Visa, Diners, Switch/Delta

Rowley Hill Lodge

COMMENDED

Little Walden, Saffron Walden CB10 1UZ
☎ (01799) 525975
Fax (01799) 516622
Quiet farm lodge with large garden, 1 mile from centre of Saffron Walden. Stansted Airport, Cambridge and Duxford 20 minutes.
Bedrooms: 1 double, 1 twin; suite available
Bathrooms: 2 private

Bed & breakfast per night:	£min	£max
Single	19.50	19.50
Double	35.00	35.00

Parking for 4

ST ALBANS

Hertfordshire
Map ref 2D1

As Verulamium this was one of the largest towns in Roman Britain and its remains can be seen in the museum. The Norman cathedral was built from Roman materials to commemorate Alban, the first British Christian martyr.
Tourist Information Centre
☎ *(01727) 864511*

Amaryllis

Listed

25 Ridgmont Road, St Albans AL1 3AG
☎ (01727) 862755 & Mobile 0850 662371
Friendly, informal family home close to city centre. Convenient for M1 and M25. Central London 20 minutes by train. Non-smokers only, please.
Bedrooms: 1 single, 1 twin, 1 triple
Bathrooms: 1 public

Bed & breakfast per night:	£min	£max
Single	16.00	25.00
Double	32.00	35.00

Parking for 1

Care Inns

29 Alma Road, St Albans AL1 3AT
☎ (01727) 867310
Comfortable family atmosphere. Ideally located close to station, city centre and cathedral. All rooms have en-suite bath/shower and toilet.
Bedrooms: 1 single, 1 double, 1 twin
Bathrooms: 3 private

Bed & breakfast per night:	£min	£max
Single		25.00
Double		39.00

Parking for 5

24 Kingshill Avenue

Listed

St Albans AL4 9QD
☎ (01727) 852647
A 3-bedroomed, semi-detached house.
Bedrooms: 2 single, 1 double
Bathrooms: 1 public

Bed & breakfast per night:	£min	£max
Single	14.00	14.00
Double	28.00	28.00

Parking for 1

2 The Limes

Listed

Spencer Gate, St Albans AL1 4AT
☎ (01727) 831080
Modern, detached house in a quiet cul-de-sac, within 10 minutes' walk of the city centre. Home-baked bread. Friendly atmosphere.
Bedrooms: 1 single, 1 twin
Bathrooms: 1 public

Bed & breakfast per night:	£min	£max
Single	15.00	17.00
Double	30.00	34.00

Parking for 2

The Squirrels

Listed APPROVED

74 Sandridge Road, St Albans AL1 4AR
☎ (01727) 840497
Edwardian terraced house, 10 minutes' walk from town centre.
Bedrooms: 1 twin
Bathrooms: 1 private

Bed & breakfast per night:	£min	£max
Single	17.50	20.00
Double	27.50	30.00

There are separate sections in this guide listing groups specialising in farm holidays and accommodation which is especially suitable for young people and organised groups.

SALHOUSE

Norfolk
Map ref 3C1

Village above the tree-fringed Salhouse Broad. The church of All Saints has a thatched roof and a 14th C arcade.

Brooks Bank

COMMENDED

Lower Street, Salhouse, Norwich NR13 6RW
☎ Norwich (01603) 720420
18th C house situated in the centre of Broadland. Guests' own private accommodation. Illustrated brochure. Our pleasure is your comfort.
Bedrooms: 1 single, 2 double, 1 twin
Bathrooms: 4 private

Bed & breakfast

per night:	£min	£max
Single	20.00	22.00
Double	32.00	36.00

Parking for 4

SANDRINGHAM

Norfolk
Map ref 3B1

Famous as the country retreat of Her Majesty the Queen. The house and grounds are open to the public at certain times.

Mill Cottage

Mill Cottage, Mill Road, Dersingham, King's Lynn PE31 6HY
☎ Dersingham (01485) 544411

"Seek peace and pursue it" Psalms 34: 14. By Sandringham, set amidst picturesque countryside with distant sea views, a Georgian cottage with lawned gardens, paddock and barn.
Bedrooms: 2 double
Bathrooms: 2 private

Bed & breakfast

per night:	£min	£max
Single	17.00	38.00
Double	30.00	58.00

Parking for 4

SANDY

Bedfordshire
Map ref 2D1

Small town on the River Ivel on the site of a Roman settlement. Sandy is mentioned in Domesday.
Tourist Information Centre
☎ (01767) 682728

Highfield Farm

HIGHLY COMMENDED

Great North Road, Sandy SG19 2AQ
☎ (01767) 682332

300-acre arable farm. Beautifully peaceful, comfortable farmhouse. Most rooms en-suite. Cambridge, the Shuttleworth Collection, RSPB and London all within easy reach. Most guests return.
Bedrooms: 2 double, 3 twin, 1 family room
Bathrooms: 4 private, 1 public

Bed & breakfast

per night:	£min	£max
Single	19.00	25.00
Double	32.00	38.00

Parking for 9

SAXMUNDHAM

Suffolk
Map ref 3C2

The church of St John the Baptist has a hammer-beam roof and contains a number of good monuments.

Little Orchard

Listed HIGHLY COMMENDED

Middleton, Saxmundham IP17 3NT
☎ Westleton (01728) 648385
Charming early 18th C house with open views all around. Ideally situated for sea and countryside, Snape Maltings and Concert Hall and Minsmere nature reserve. First house on left on B1125 coming from Theberton off the B1122.
Bedrooms: 2 double
Bathrooms: 2 private

Bed & breakfast

per night:	£min	£max
Single	17.00	17.00
Double	34.00	34.00

Half board

per person:	£min	£max
Daily	27.00	27.00

Evening meal 1900 (last orders 2000)
Parking for 3

SLOLEY

Norfolk
Map ref 3C1

Sloley Farm

COMMENDED

Sloley, Norwich NR12 8HJ
☎ Smallburgh (01692) 536281
Fax (01692) 535162
400-acre mixed farm. Comfortable farmhouse set in peaceful countryside, 4 miles from Norfolk Broads and within easy reach of the coast. Off B1150 Norwich to North Walsham road.
Bedrooms: 1 single, 2 double
Bathrooms: 3 private, 1 public

Bed &
breakfast

per night:	£min	£max
Single	17.50	
Double	30.00	32.00

Half board

per person:	£min	£max
Daily	26.00	27.50
Weekly	182.00	192.50

Evening meal from 1800
Parking for 5
Cards accepted: Diners

SOUTH LOPHAM

Norfolk
Map ref 3B2

Malting Farm

Blo Norton Road, South Lopham, Diss IP22 2HT
☎ Bressingham (01379) 687201
70-acre dairy farm. Recently renovated, timber-framed farmhouse with inglenook fireplaces and four-poster beds. Crafts, including embroidery, patchwork, spinning. See the cows being milked.
Bedrooms: 2 double, 1 twin
Bathrooms: 1 private, 1 public

Bed & breakfast

per night:	£min	£max
Single	20.00	25.00
Double	35.00	

Parking for 10
Cards accepted: Diners

SOUTH MIMMS

Hertfordshire
Map ref 2D1

Best known today for its location at the junction of the M25 and the A1M.
Tourist Information Centre
☎ (01707) 643233

The Black Swan

Listed

62-64 Blanche Lane, South Mimms, Potters Bar EN6 3PD
☎ Potters Bar (01707) 644180

Comfortable accommodation in oak-beamed bedrooms or self-contained flats in quietly located listed building. Breakfast provided.
Bedrooms: 2 double; suite available
Bathrooms: 2 private, 1 public
Bed & breakfast

per night:	£min	£max
Single	25.00	
Double	35.00	

Parking for 7
⛵🛁♿🖤📺🏧 🚗✿🍴🏤 T

SOUTH WALSHAM

Norfolk
Map ref 3C1

Village famous for having 2 churches in adjoining churchyards. South Walsham Broad consists of an inner and outer section, the former being private. Alongside, the Fairhaven Garden Trust has woodland and water-gardens open to the public.

Old Hall Farm ⋀
⛱⛱
South Walsham, Norwich NR13 6DT
☎ Norwich (01603) 270271
82-acre arable farm. Thatched farmhouse dating from 17th C on edge of Broadland village. Good centre for Norwich, Broads and coast.
Bedrooms: 1 single, 3 double, 1 twin
Bathrooms: 1 private, 1 public
Bed & breakfast

per night:	£min	£max
Single	13.50	20.00
Double	27.00	37.00

Parking for 5
Open April-October
⛵🛁📱⌨📺♿🖤ⓤⓈ✂🍴📺🏧 🚗✿🍴
🏤 T

STALHAM

Norfolk
Map ref 3C1

Lies on the edge of the Broads.

Bramble House
⛱⛱ COMMENDED
Cat's Common, Norwich Road, Smallburgh, Norwich NR12 9NS
☎ Smallburgh (01692) 535069
Friendliness and comfort guaranteed in this large country house. Set in 1.5 acres in the heart of Broadland but only 6 miles from sandy beaches.
Bedrooms: 1 single, 1 twin, 1 triple; suites available
Bathrooms: 3 private
Bed & breakfast

per night:	£min	£max
Single	17.00	25.00
Double	34.00	38.00

Parking for 8
Cards accepted: Diners
⛵⌨📱♿🖤ⓤ📱Ⓢ✂🍴📺🏧 🚗🚲
▶✿🚗

STEEPLE BUMPSTEAD

Essex
Map ref 3B2

An interesting building in the village is the Moot Hall, which in the 17th C served as a village school and was restored as part of the 1977 Jubilee celebrations.

Yew Tree House
⛱ COMMENDED
15 Chapel Street, Steeple Bumpstead, Haverhill, Suffolk CB9 7DQ
☎ (01440) 730364
Fax (01440) 730364
Charming Victorian house, with many period features, and comfortable accommodation, in the centre of Steeple Bumpstead.
Bedrooms: 1 double, 1 twin
Bathrooms: 1 private, 1 public
Bed & breakfast

per night:	£min	£max
Single	17.00	22.00
Double	29.00	36.00

Half board

per person:	£min	£max
Daily	23.00	26.50
Weekly	160.00	185.50

Evening meal 1800 (last orders 2000)
Parking for 3
⛵2♿🖤ⓤ📱Ⓢ✂🍴📺🏧 🚗🍴🚗🏤

STOKE HOLY CROSS

Norfolk
Map ref 3C1

Salamanca Farm ⋀
⛱⛱ COMMENDED
Stoke Holy Cross, Norwich NR14 8QJ
☎ Framingham Earl (01508) 492322
175-acre mixed farm. Picturesque village near Norwich. Comfortable Victorian farmhouse in a flower arranger's garden. Guests have been welcomed for 20 years.
Bedrooms: 3 double, 1 twin
Bathrooms: 4 private, 1 public
Bed & breakfast

per night:	£min	£max
Single	18.00	22.00
Double	36.00	42.00

Parking for 8
Cards accepted: Diners
⛵6♿ⓤⓈ✂🍴📺🏧 🚗🍴16✿🍴
🚗🍴

STOKE-BY-NAYLAND

Suffolk
Map ref 3B2

Picturesque village with a fine group of half-timbered cottages near the church of St Mary, the tower of which was one of Constable's favourite subjects. In School Street are the Guildhall and the Maltings, both 16th C timber-framed buildings.

Nether Hall
Listed
Thorington Street, Stoke-by-Nayland, Colchester, Essex CO6 4ST
☎ Higham (01206) 337373

Charming grade II listed 15th C country house with grounds adjoining the River Box and in the heart of Constable country. On B1068, 3 miles from A12. One double/twin room is on ground floor with private external access.
Bedrooms: 1 single, 2 double
Bathrooms: 3 private
Bed & breakfast

per night:	£min	£max
Single	21.00	21.00
Double	42.00	42.00

Parking for 6
⛵10🛁⌨🖤ⓤ⒮🍴🏧✿🚗 T

Ryegate House ⋀
⛱⛱ HIGHLY COMMENDED
Polstead Street, Stoke-by-Nayland, Colchester CO6 4RA
☎ Nayland (01206) 263679
Comfortable friendly house in Suffolk village within Dedham Vale. On the B1068, 5.5 miles from A12 and 2.5 miles from A134.
Bedrooms: 2 double, 1 twin
Bathrooms: 3 private
Bed & breakfast

per night:	£min	£max
Double	33.00	36.00

Parking for 4
⛵10⌨🖤ⓤ📺🏧✿🚗 SP

STRADBROKE

Suffolk
Map ref 3C2

Thought to be the birthplace of Robert Grosseteste, writer and once Bishop of Lincoln.

The Ivy House Public House
Listed

Wilby Road, Stradbroke, Eye IP21 5JN
☎ Diss (01379) 384634
Pretty, thatched public house in an award-winning Suffolk village. A la carte food and bar meals available during opening hours.
Bedrooms: 1 twin, 1 triple
Bathrooms: 1 public

Bed & breakfast

per night:	£min	£max
Single	18.00	
Double	35.00	

Lunch available
Evening meal 1830 (last orders 2200)
Parking for 20
Cards accepted: Access, Visa, Diners
🖵 ♿ ☆ Ⓢ 🏚 ✕ 🚜

STRATFORD ST MARY

Suffolk
Map ref 3B2

Set in countryside known as Constable country.

Teazles
Listed **APPROVED**

Stratford St Mary, Colchester CO7 6LU
☎ Colchester (01206) 323148
Attractive 16th C country house in heart of Constable country. Just off A12 on B1029 to Dedham, leaving church on right. Refurbished in 1971, now our family home to which we welcome guests.
Bedrooms: 1 single, 1 double, 1 twin
Bathrooms: 2 public

Bed & breakfast

per night:	£min	£max
Single	17.00	19.50
Double	32.00	37.00

Parking for 7
🖵 4 🖵 ♿ Ⓤ 🔓 Ⓢ ✂ 🖻 🏚 🖵 ✿ 🚜 ⊠ 🎣

The symbol ⊛ within an entry indicates participation in the Welcome Host programme – a nationally recognised customer care initiative which aims to promote the highest standards of service and a warm welcome for all visitors.

SWAFFHAM

Norfolk
Map ref 3B1

Busy market town with a triangular market-place, a domed rotunda built in 1783 and a number of Georgian houses. The 15th C church possesses a large library of ancient books.

Glebe Bungalow
COMMENDED

8a Princes Street, Swaffham PE37 7BP
☎ (01760) 722764

Quiet secluded town centre location on no-through road. Home-from-home accommodation with private parking. Ideal for discovering Norfolk.
Wheelchair access category 3 ♿
Bedrooms: 1 double, 1 twin, 1 triple
Bathrooms: 3 private

Bed & breakfast

per night:	£min	£max
Single	16.00	
Double	32.00	

Half board

per person:	£min	£max
Daily	22.00	24.00
Weekly	139.00	151.00

Evening meal 1700 (last orders 1900)
Parking for 6
🖵 ♿ 🖻 ♿ Ⓤ 🔓 Ⓢ ✂ 🖻 🆃🆅 🏚 🖵 ✿ ✕ 🚜

SWAFFHAM BULBECK

Cambridgeshire
Map ref 2D1

The Black Horse Village Pub and Restaurant
APPROVED

35 High Street, Swaffham Bulbeck, Cambridge CB5 0HP
☎ Cambridge (01223) 811366

Picturesque pub overlooking the village green offering accommodation in new stable block.
Bedrooms: 7 twin
Bathrooms: 7 private

Bed & breakfast

per night:	£min	£max
Single	35.00	
Double	45.00	

Lunch available
Evening meal 1900 (last orders 2100)
Parking for 16
Cards accepted: Access, Visa
🖵 🖻 🖵 ♿ 🏚 🖵 🖵 ♦ ✿

THAXTED

Essex
Map ref 3B2

Small town rich in outstanding buildings and dominated by its hilltop medieval church. The magnificent Guildhall was built by the Cutlers' Guild in the late 14th C. A windmill built in 1804 has been restored and houses a rural museum.

Piggots Mill
HIGHLY COMMENDED

Watling Lane, Thaxted, Dunmow CM6 2QY
☎ (01371) 830379
850-acre arable farm. Traditional Essex barn, now a secluded farmhouse offering excellent accommodation in the centre of Thaxted. Garden leads into meadow giving access to attractive walks.
Bedrooms: 1 double, 1 twin
Bathrooms: 2 private

Bed & breakfast

per night:	£min	£max
Single	30.00	32.00
Double	45.00	48.00

Parking for 10
🖵 12 🖻 🖻 🖵 ♿ Ⓤ Ⓢ ✂ 🏚 🖵 🖵 ♿ ✿ ✕ 🚜 🆂🅿 🏚 🆃

THETFORD

Norfolk
Map ref 3B2

Small, medieval market town with numerous reminders of its long history: the ruins of the 12th C priory, Iron Age earthworks at Castle Hill and a Norman castle mound. Timber-framed Ancient House is now a museum.

Church Cottage
COMMENDED

Breckles, Attleborough NR17 1EW
☎ Great Hockham (01953) 498286
Fax (01953) 498320
Charming 18th C home in beautiful Breckland. Ideal for touring East Anglia. Own coarse fishing. Heated outdoor swimming pool. Home-made bread. On B1111, 9 miles north-east of Thetford.
Bedrooms: 2 double, 1 twin
Bathrooms: 2 public

Bed & breakfast per night:	£min	£max
Single	17.00	17.00
Double	34.00	34.00

Parking for 10

🐕 10 ⛶ 🖥 🦻 Ⓢ 🏄 📺 ⅲ � ⟋ ✿ 🚲 ♨

THOMPSON

Norfolk
Map ref 3B1

College Farm ⋀

Listed

Thompson, Thetford IP24 1QG
☎ Caston (01953) 483318

14th C farmhouse, formerly a college of priests. In quiet village away from main road. Meals provided at nearby inns.
Bedrooms: 1 double, 2 twin
Bathrooms: 3 private, 1 public

Bed & breakfast per night:	£min	£max
Single	17.00	19.00
Double	34.00	38.00

Parking for 10

🐕 7 ☐ ⅲ Ⓢ ⅲ 🚲 ✿ 🏹 🚲 ♨

THORPE MORIEUX

Suffolk
Map ref 3B2

Mount Farm House
🍽️ 🍽️

Thorpe Morieux, Bury St Edmunds
IP30 0NQ
☎ Lavenham (01787) 248428
Fax (01787) 248428

19th C former farmhouse in quiet location, close to historic Lavenham. Full use of sauna, indoor swimming pool and tennis court. Non-smokers please.
Bedrooms: 3 double
Bathrooms: 3 private

Bed & breakfast per night:	£min	£max
Double	38.00	45.00

Evening meal 1930 (last orders 2130)
Parking for 12

☐ 🖐 🦻 ⅲ ⅙ 🏄 🌀 🏹 🔍 🏹 🚲

TIPTREE

Essex
Map ref 3B3

Linden
Listed   HIGHLY COMMENDED

8 Clarkesmead, Maldon Road, Tiptree,
Colchester CO5 OBX
☎ (01621) 819737 & 0585 243425
Fax (01621) 818033
Modern architect-designed house in quiet cul-de-sac, off Maldon Road on edge of Tiptree, near A12.
Bedrooms: 1 single, 1 double, 1 twin,
1 family room; suite available
Bathrooms: 1 private, 3 public,
1 private shower

Bed & breakfast per night:	£min	£max
Single	20.00	22.00
Double	38.00	44.00

Parking for 6
Cards accepted: Access, Visa

🐕 🎀 🦻 ⛶ ☐ 🖐 🦻 ⅲ 🛈 Ⓢ ⅙ ⅲ 🚲 ▶
✿ 🚲

TIVETSHALL ST MARY

Norfolk
Map ref 3B2

The Old Ram Coaching Inn
🍽️ 🍽️ 🍽️   HIGHLY COMMENDED

Ipswich Road, Tivetshall St Mary,
Norwich NR15 2DE
☎ Pulham Market (01379) 676794
Fax (01379) 608399
17th C coaching inn (15 miles south of Norwich) with oak beams and log fires. En-suite accommodation, extensive menu.
Bedrooms: 4 double, 1 triple
Bathrooms: 5 private

Bed & breakfast per night:	£min	£max
Single	43.00	48.00
Double	61.00	66.00

Lunch available
Evening meal 1800 (last orders 2200)
Parking for 150
Cards accepted: Access, Visa, Switch/
Delta

🐕 🎀 📞 ⛶ ☐ 🖐 🦻 🛈 Ⓢ ⅙ 🏄 ◑ ⅲ 🚲
🍴 ✿ 🏹 OAP 🔖 SP 🚲

TUDDENHAM

Suffolk
Map ref 3B2

Oakdene
Listed

Higham Road, Tuddenham, Bury St
Edmunds IP28 6SG
☎ Mildenhall (01638) 718822 &
Mobile 0860 732336
Fax (01638) 711784
Situated on the Icknield Way offering very comfortable accommodation. Friendly atmosphere, 400 yards from local pub and close to racing at Newmarket.

Bedrooms: 1 twin, 1 triple

Bathrooms: 2 private, 1 public

Bed & breakfast per night:	£min	£max
Single	16.50	18.50
Double	33.00	33.00

Half board per person:	£min	£max
Daily	24.00	26.00
Weekly	154.00	182.00

Evening meal 1830 (last orders 2000)
Parking for 2

🐕 ⛶ ☐ 🖐 ⅲ 🛈 ⅙ 📺 ⅲ 🚲 ✿ 🏹 🚲

WANSFORD

Cambridgeshire
Map ref 3A1

A terminus of the Nene Valley
Railway with British and
continental steam locomotives and
rolling-stock.

Stoneacre ⋀
🍽️ 🍽️

Elton Road, Wansford, Peterborough
PE8 6JT
☎ Stamford (01780) 783283
Modern country house in rural and secluded position with delightful views across the Nene Valley. Half a mile from A1, 10 minutes from Peterborough and Stamford. Large grounds with mini golf-course.
Bedrooms: 4 double, 1 twin
Bathrooms: 4 private, 2 public

Bed & breakfast per night:	£min	£max
Single	22.00	35.00
Double	28.00	42.00

Parking for 24

🐕 5 🦻 ⛶ ☐ 🖐 🦻 Ⓢ ⅙ 🏄 📺 ⅲ 🚲
🍴 20 🔍 🔔 🍴 ✿ 🚲 SP 🚲 🆃

WARE

Hertfordshire
Map ref 2D1

Interesting riverside town with
picturesque summer-houses lining
the tow-path of the River Lea. The
town has many timber-framed and
Georgian houses and the famous
Great Bed of Ware is now in the
Victoria and Albert Museum.

Ashridge
🍽️   COMMENDED

3 Belle Vue Road, Ware SG12 7BD
☎ (01920) 463895
Comfortable, Edwardian residence in quiet cul-de-sac. 10 minutes' walk from Ware and station. Non-smokers only, please.
Bedrooms: 2 single, 1 double, 1 twin
Bathrooms: 2 public

Continued ▶

WARE

Continued

Bed & breakfast

per night:	£min	£max
Single	16.50	20.00
Double	33.00	40.00

Half board

per person:	£min	£max
Daily	22.50	28.00

Evening meal 1830 (last orders 1200)
Parking for 4

🖙⛱️♨️♿🛈⑤✂️🎢⏛️🖨️✕🚗

WATFORD

Hertfordshire
Map ref 2D1

Large town with many industries but with some old buildings, particularly around St Mary's Church which contains some fine monuments. The grounds of Cassiobury Park, once the home of the Earls of Essex, form a public park and golf-course.

The Millwards

Listed

30 Hazelwood Road, Croxley Green, Rickmansworth WD3 3EB
☎ (01923) 226666 & 233751
*Quiet, homely canalside residence.
Pleasant location. Convenient London (Metropolitan line), Moor Park, Wembley, Heathrow, Rickmansworth, M1 and M25, Watford and Croxley Business Centre.*
Bedrooms: 1 single, 2 twin
Bathrooms: 2 public

Bed & breakfast

per night:	£min	£max
Single	17.00	17.00
Double	30.00	30.00

Parking for 2

🖙⛱️♨️♿🛈⑤✂️📺⏛️🖨️✕🚗

WELLS-NEXT-THE-SEA

Norfolk
Map ref 3B1

Seaside resort and small port on the north coast. The Buttlands is a large tree-lined green surrounded by Georgian houses and from here narrow streets lead to the quay.

Old Police House

COMMENDED

Polka Road, Wells-next-the-Sea
NR23 1ED
☎ Fakenham (01328) 710630
Purpose-built ground floor extension to former police house. Three en-suite double rooms, separate guest entrance.
Bedrooms: 3 twin
Bathrooms: 3 private

Bed & breakfast

per night:	£min	£max
Single	20.00	25.00
Double	36.00	36.00

Parking for 6

🖙10⛱️📧♨️♿🛈⑤SP

Scarborough House Hotel M

COMMENDED

Clubbs Lane, Wells-next-the-Sea
NR23 1DP
☎ Fakenham (01328) 710309 & 711661
*Licensed hotel with restaurant, log fires, four-poster beds, private parking.
Perfect for bird-watchers and ramblers.
Dogs welcome.*
Bedrooms: 9 double, 4 twin, 1 family room
Bathrooms: 14 private

Bed & breakfast

per night:	£min	£max
Single	29.00	34.00
Double	48.00	58.00

Half board

per person:	£min	£max
Daily	37.95	47.95
Weekly	235.00	305.00

Evening meal 1930 (last orders 2100)
Parking for 14
Cards accepted: Access, Visa, Diners, Amex, Switch/Delta

🖙⛱️🏇♨️♿🛈⑤🎢⏛️🖨️✕🍴SP

WESTLETON

Suffolk
Map ref 3C2

Has a number of fine buildings including the gabled Elizabethan Moot House and the Crown Inn. The unusual thatched church holds an annual wild flower festival. The large green is bordered by an avenue of limes and a large duckpond.

Pond House

COMMENDED

The Hill, Westleton, Saxmundham
IP17 3AN
☎ (01728) 73773
18th C beamed cottage by village green and duck pond. Just 2 miles from Minsmere and 3 miles from Dunwich.
Bedrooms: 3 twin
Bathrooms: 1 private, 1 public

Bed & breakfast

per night:	£min	£max
Single	24.00	28.00
Double	34.00	42.00

Parking for 5

🖙📧♨️♿⑤✂️📺⏛️🖨️✕🚗

We advise you to confirm your booking in writing.

WISBECH

Cambridgeshire
Map ref 3A1

The town is the centre of the agricultural and flower-growing industries of Fenland. Peckover House (National Trust) is an important example of domestic architecture.
Tourist Information Centre
☎ *(01945) 583263*

Crown Lodge Hotel M

COMMENDED

Downham Road, Outwell, Wisbech
PE14 8SE
☎ (01945) 773391
Fax (01945) 772668
*A warm welcome awaits you at this small hotel, which offers a relaxed, friendly atmosphere. Enjoy a meal in our bistro-style restaurant which uses only the best fresh local produce and prime select meats, poultry and fish.
Wheelchair access category 3* ♿
Bedrooms: 8 double, 2 twin
Bathrooms: 10 private

Bed & breakfast

per night:	£min	£max
Single	35.75	38.00
Double	48.00	54.00

Half board

per person:	£min	£max
Daily	46.70	48.95
Weekly	300.00	316.00

Lunch available
Evening meal 1830 (last orders 2230)
Parking for 100
Cards accepted: Access, Visa, Diners, Amex

🖙⛱️♨️♿🛈⑤✂️🎢⏛️🖨️🍴100🍷🎣❄️SP

Stratton Farm

HIGHLY COMMENDED

West Drove North, Walton Highway, Wisbech PE14 7DP
☎ (01945) 880162
*22-acre livestock farm. All ground floor en-suite accommodation in peaceful setting, with heated swimming pool and private fishing. Wheelchair facilities.
Non-smokers only, please. Home-produced sausages, bacon and eggs.
Wheelchair access category 3* ♿
Bedrooms: 2 double, 1 twin
Bathrooms: 3 private

Bed & breakfast

per night:	£min	£max
Single	20.70	23.00
Double	41.40	46.00

Parking for 6
Cards accepted: Diners

🖙6⛱️📧♨️♿🛈⑤✂️🎢⏛️🖨️🚗♨️🔧✕🚗SP

WIX

Essex
Map ref 3B2

New Farm House ⚑

😀😀😀

Spinnell's Lane, Wix, Manningtree
CO11 2UJ
☎ Clacton (01255) 870365
Fax (01255) 870837

*Modern comfortable farmhouse in large
garden, 10 minutes' drive to Harwich
and convenient for Constable country.
From Wix village crossroads, take
Bradfield Road, turn right at top of hill;
first house on left.*
Bedrooms: 3 single, 1 double, 3 twin,
5 family rooms
Bathrooms: 7 private, 2 public
Bed & breakfast

per night:	£min	£max
Single	20.00	24.00
Double	39.00	44.00

Half board

per person:	£min	£max
Daily	32.00	36.00
Weekly	321.30	352.80

Evening meal 1830 (last orders 1730)
Parking for 18
Cards accepted: Access, Visa, Amex
❆💁📧🖵🗢🏠🖪⌖📺🛏🍽💡❆🐾

WOODHAM FERRERS

Essex
Map ref 3B3

Woolfe's Cottage

Listed
The Street, Woodham Ferrers,
Chelmsford CM3 5RG
☎ Chelmsford (01245) 320037
*Large converted Victorian cottage in
historic village, 12 miles from
Chelmsford on the B1418. Many
excellent walking trails for ramblers.*
Bedrooms: 1 double, 2 twin
Bathrooms: 3 private, 1 public
Bed & breakfast

per night:	£min	£max
Single	16.00	17.00
Double	30.00	32.00

Parking for 2
❆📧🖵🗢⌖🖪📱🔒🍽📺🛏🖪🖵🗢🏠

Please mention this guide
when making a booking.

WOOLPIT

Suffolk
Map ref 3B2

Village with a number of attractive
timber-framed Tudor and Georgian
houses. St Mary's Church is one
of the most beautiful churches in
Suffolk and has a fine porch. The
brass eagle lectern is said to have
been donated by Elizabeth I.

Grange Farm

Listed
Woolpit, Bury St Edmunds IP30 9RG
☎ Elmswell (01359) 241143
*120-acre arable farm. Fine Victorian
farmhouse, three-quarters of a mile
from Woolpit village centre on the
Rattlesden road. Set in pleasant
grounds with surrounding ponds.*
Bedrooms: 1 double, 2 twin
Bathrooms: 2 public
Bed & breakfast

per night:	£min	£max
Single	17.50	
Double	30.00	

Parking for 10
❆🖾🖵🗢🖪⌖🍽📺🛏🖪📱❆🐾🏠

WRABNESS

Essex
Map ref 3B2

Glebe House

Listed
Rectory Road, Wrabness, Manningtree
CO11 2TX
☎ Ramsey (01255) 880354
*Country house in pleasant garden, close
to Stour Woods and Estuary (RSPB bird
reserve). Ideal for walking and
exploring unspoilt Essex. Dovercourt
Bay 5 miles. Convenient
Harwich/Dovercourt ferries.*
Bedrooms: 1 double, 1 triple
Bathrooms: 1 public
Bed & breakfast

per night:	£min	£max
Single	16.50	
Double	32.00	

Parking for 6
Open February-November
❆🖵🗢🖐🖪🖪❆🍽🐾

The symbol 🏵 within an
entry indicates participation
in the Welcome Host
programme – a nationally
recognised customer care
initiative which aims to
promote the highest
standards of service and a
warm welcome for all visitors.

WROXHAM

Norfolk
Map ref 3C1

Yachting centre on the River Bure
which houses the headquarters of
the Norfolk Broads Yacht Club.
The church of St Mary has a
famous doorway and the manor
house nearby dates back to 1623.

Holly Cottage

😀😀 COMMENDED
Church Lane, Wroxham, Norwich
NR12 8SH
☎ Norwich (01603) 783401
*Detached, modernised 200-year-old
riverside cottage with artist's studio,
near church in oldest part of Broadland
village of Wroxham. Ample parking and
beautiful gardens. Terraced down to
River Bure.*
Bedrooms: 1 double, 1 twin
Bathrooms: 2 private
Bed & breakfast

per night:	£min	£max
Single	22.00	24.00
Double	38.00	42.00

Parking for 5
❆10🖵🗢🖪⌖📺🛏💡❆🐾🏠🖪

Manor Barn House

😀😀 COMMENDED
Back Lane, Rackheath, Wroxham,
Norwich NR13 6NN
☎ Norwich (01603) 783543

*Traditional Norfolk barn conversion
with exposed beams, in quiet setting
with pleasant gardens. Just off the
A1151, 2 miles from Wroxham.*
Bedrooms: 3 double, 2 twin
Bathrooms: 5 private
Bed & breakfast

per night:	£min	£max
Single	18.00	25.00
Double	32.00	36.00

Parking for 8
❆3💁🖵🗢🖐🖪📱⌖🍽📺🛏🖪📱♡↻⌖
🐾❆🔒🏠

Wroxham Park Lodge ⚑

😀😀 COMMENDED
142 Norwich Road, Wroxham, Norwich
NR12 8SA
☎ (01603) 782991
*Comfortable Victorian house in lovely
gardens. All rooms en-suite. In Broads
capital of Wroxham, central for all
Broads amenities. Private parking.*
Bedrooms: 2 double, 1 twin
Bathrooms: 3 private

Continued ▶

WROXHAM

Continued

Bed & breakfast
per night:	£min	£max
Single	20.00	25.00
Double	38.00	38.00

Parking for 6

🛇 📠 ⛿ ♨ ⓤ 🛆 🗓 ❄ ⚲ 🆂🅿

WYMONDHAM

Norfolk
Map ref 3B1

Thriving historic market town of charm and architectural interest. The octagonal market cross, 12th C abbey and 15th C Green Dragon inn blend with streetscapes spanning three centuries. An excellent touring base.

Rose Farm

Listed

School Lane, Suton, Wymondham
NR18 9JN
☎ (01953) 603512
2-acre poultry farm. Homely farmhouse accommodation within easy reach of Norwich, Broads and Breckland. Bus

and train services close by. Ample parking.
Bedrooms: 2 single, 1 double, 1 triple
Bathrooms: 2 public
Bed & breakfast
per night:	£min	£max
Single	19.00	22.00
Double	38.00	44.00

Parking for 4
Cards accepted: Diners

🛇 🐾 ⛿ 🗖 ♨ ⓤ 🛆 🔋 ⑂ 🅜 📺 🖩 🚪 ∪ ♪ ❄ 🚜 🅃

Turret House

Listed

27 Middleton Street, Wymondham
NR18 0AB
☎ (01953) 603462
Fax (01953) 603462
Large Victorian house in centre of Wymondham within walking distance of shops, restaurants and historic abbey. Convenient for Norwich.
Bedrooms: 1 double, 1 twin
Bathrooms: 1 public
Bed & breakfast
per night:	£min	£max
Single	14.50	14.50
Double	29.00	29.00

Parking for 2

🛇 🐾 🖂 🗖 ♨ ⓤ ⑂ 🖩 ✕ 🚜

Willow Farm

Listed **COMMENDED**

Wattlefield, Wymondham NR18 9PA
☎ (01953) 604679

Comfortable farmhouse in 4 acres offering high standard of hospitality in relaxed atmosphere. Two miles south down B1135 from Wymondham, fork right. Willow Farm three quarters of a mile on the left.
Bedrooms: 1 single, 1 double, 1 twin
Bathrooms: 2 public
Bed & breakfast
per night:	£min	£max
Single	16.00	16.00
Double	32.00	32.00

Parking for 3

🛇 🐾 🗖 🔋 ⓤ 🅜 📺 🖩 🚪 ❄ 🚜

CHECK THE MAPS

The colour maps at the back of this guide show all the cities, towns and villages which have accommodation listings. They will enable you to check if there is suitable accommodation in the area that you plan to visit.

AT-A-GLANCE SYMBOLS

At-a-glance symbols at the end of each accommodation entry give information about services and facilities. A handy guide to these symbols can be found inside the back cover flap, which can be kept open for easy reference.

West Country

From high, raw-boned granite moorlands to rolling sheep-dotted chalk downs; from deep, lush Devon lanes to rocky, thunderous Cornish coves... the landscape of the West Country is a tapestry of character and variety.

Here the climate is softened by the warm Gulf Stream and the long coastline irresistibly lures holiday-makers with its busy resorts, pretty fishing villages, glinting sands and titanic cliffs.

Inland, there are the wild, wide landscapes of Dartmoor and Exmoor to explore; many prehistoric sites such as King Arthur's Tintagel and mysterious Stonehenge; historic towns such as maritime Plymouth, lovely old Salisbury, and perennially elegant Bath. With all this, and many family attractions too, no wonder the West Country is one of England's favourite holiday spots.

The Counties of Avon, Cornwall, Devon, Dorset (western), Somerset, Wiltshire and the Isles of Scilly

For more information on the West Country, contact:

West Country Tourist Board
60 St David's Hill, Exeter EX4 4SY
Tel: (01392) 76351
Fax: (01392) 420891

Where to Go in the West Country –
see pages 238–242

Where to Stay in the West Country –
see pages 243–294

West Country

Where to go and what to see

You will find hundreds of interesting places to visit during your stay in the West Country, just some of which are listed in these pages. The number against each name will help you locate it on the map (pages 240–241). Contact any Tourist Information Centre in the region for more ideas on days out in the West Country.

1 Lydiard Park
Lydiard Tregoze, Swindon, Wiltshire SN5 9PA
Tel: (01793) 770401
Fine 18thC house set in its own park, and originally the home of the St John family. Paintings and furniture on display in restored state rooms.

2 Clevedon Court
Tickenham Road, Clevedon, Avon BS21 6QU
Tel: (01275) 872257
Home of the Elton family. 14thC manor house, once partly fortified. Terraced garden and rare shrubs. Collection of Nailsea glass and Eltonware.

3 Bristol Zoo Gardens
Clifton, Bristol, Avon BS8 3HA
Tel: (0117) 973 8951
Set in beautiful gardens, the Zoo provides a haven for some of the world's most endangered wildlife. Plenty of activities and special events.

4 Avebury Stone Circles
Avebury, Marlborough, Wiltshire SN8 1RF
Tel: (016723) 250
One of the most important megalithic ceremonial monuments (in Europe) of the late Neolithic period. 28.5 acre site, stone circles enclosed by a bank and ditch with avenue of stones.

5 Corsham Court
Corsham, Wiltshire SN13 0BZ
Tel: (01249) 712214
Elizabethan house altered in 18thC, contains Methuen collection of Old Masters and 18thC furniture. Capability Brown gardens.

6 Museum of Costume
Assembly Rooms, Bennett Street, Bath, Avon BA1 2QH
Tel: (01225) 461111
Displays of fashionable dress for men, women and children from 16thC to present day.

7 Radford Children's Farm and Shire Horse Stables
Radford, Timsbury, Bath, Avon BA3 1QF
Tel: (01761) 470106
Hand-milked goats and other farm animals. Also home of Radford shire horse display team, vehicles, carts and blacksmith's shop.

8 The Woodland Park & Woodland Heritage Museum
Brokerswood, Westbury, Wiltshire BA13 4EH
Tel: (01373) 822238
80 acres of ancient woodland, lake, wildfowl, nature trails. Barbecue sites. 1.5 mile narrow gauge railway, adventure playground, coarse fishing, woodland museum.

9 Stourton House Flower Garden
Stourton, Warminster, Wiltshire BA12 6QF
Tel: (01747) 840417

4.5 acres of varied and colourful shrubs, borders, woodland glades, secret garden. Superb hydrangeas. Dried flowers and unusual plants a speciality. Colour and interest all year.

⑩ Watermouth Castle
Berrynarbor, Ilfracombe, Devon EX34 9SL
Tel: (01271) 863879
Mechanical music demonstrations, model railway, domestic dairy, cider-making exhibits, cycle museum, smugglers' dungeon and gardens. Children's animations. 'Merrygoland'.

⑪ West Somerset Railway
The Railway Station, Minehead, Somerset TA24 5BG
Tel: (01643) 704996
Preserved steam railway operating between Minehead and Bishops Lydeard, near Taunton. Longest independent railway in Britain – 20 miles.

⑫ Secret World
New Road Farm, East Huntspill, Highbridge, Somerset TA9 3PZ
Tel: (01278) 783250
300-year-old farm, many breeds of animals including rare breeds. Old and modern farm machinery on display. Play areas, gardens. Somerset Levels Visitor Centre.

⑬ Somerset Rural Life Museum
Abbey Farm, Chilkwell Street, Glastonbury, Somerset BA6 8DB
Tel: (01458) 831197
Magnificent 14thC abbey barn, also Victorian farmhouse and yard. Permanent exhibitions. Events programme throughout the summer.

⑭ Salisbury Cathedral
The Close, Salisbury, Wiltshire SP1 2EF
Tel: (01722) 328726
Gothic cathedral consecrated in 1258. Famous spire rising to record height of 404ft was added in 14thC. Ancient clock mechanism dates from 1386. One of 4 originals of Magna Carta.

⑮ Hestercombe Gardens
Cheddon Fitzpaine, Taunton, Somerset TA2 8LQ
Tel: (01823) 337222
Multi-terraced garden created by Sir Edwin Lutyens and Gertrude Jekyll at the turn of the century. Restored using the original plans and plants.

⑯ Clovelly Village
Clovelly, Bideford, Devon EX39 5SY
Tel: (01237) 431200
Unspoilt fishing village on North Devon coast with steep cobbled street and no vehicular access. Donkeys and sledges only means of transport. Visitor centre.

⑰ Montacute House
Montacute, Yeovil, Somerset TA15 6XP
Tel: (01935) 823289
Late 16thC house built of local golden Ham stone by Sir Edward Phelips. The Long Gallery houses a collection of Tudor and Jacobean portraits. Formal gardens. Park.

⑱ Sherborne Castle
Sherborne, Dorset
Tel: (01935) 813182
Built by Sir Walter Raleigh in 1594 to replace the old castle. The Elizabethan Hall and Jacobean Oak Room show two of the many styles of architecture.

⑲ Forde Abbey and Gardens
Chard, Somerset TA20 4LU
Tel: (01460) 220231
12thC Cistercian abbey converted during Commonwealth. Mortlake Tapestries, pictures. 30 acres of outstanding gardens. 14thC crucifixion painting in undercroft.

⑳ Coldharbour Mill Working Wool Museum
Coldharbour Mill, Uffculme, Cullompton, Devon EX15 3EE
Tel: (01884) 840960
Museum of the Devon wool textiles industry in an 18thC woollen mill. Working demonstrations of traditional textile machinery. Water-wheel and steam engines. Riverside walks.

㉑ Dorset County Museum
High West Street, Dorchester,
Dorset DT1 1XA
Tel: (01305) 262735
*Archaeology, natural history, and
geology of Dorset. Local and
agricultural history displays.
Exhibition gallery, Thomas Hardy
material and study reconstruction.*

㉒ Abbotsbury Swannery
New Barn Road, Abbotsbury,
Weymouth, Dorset DT3 4JG
Tel: (01305) 871684
*The only place in the world where
over 600 swans can be visited during
the nesting and hatching time (end
May-end June). Audio visual
presentation. Ugly duckling trail.*

**㉓ Brewers' Quay and
Timewalk**
Hope Square, Weymouth, Dorset
DT4 8TR
Tel: (01305) 777622
*Former brewery now housing The
Timewalk, depicting 600 years of
Weymouth's history, also The
Brewer's Tale exhibition and
shopping village with restaurants.*

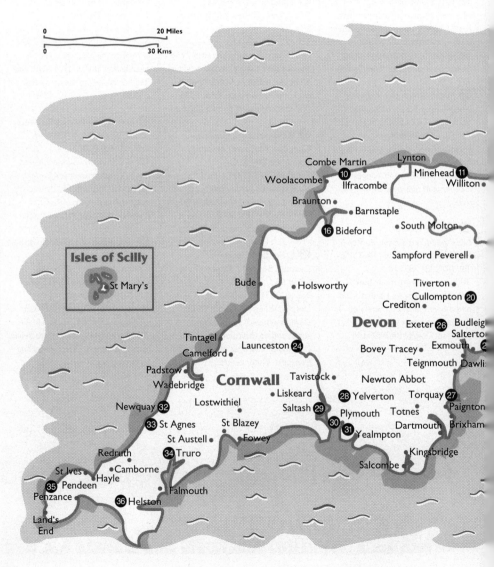

24 Launceston Castle
Castle Lodge, Launceston,
Cornwall PL15 7DR
Tel: (01566) 772365
*Castle overlooking Launceston, it was
the seat of Robert of Mortain,
brother of William I, but present
stone defences including keep on
summit are 12th/13thC.*

25 Bicton Park and Gardens
East Budleigh, Budleigh Salterton,
Devon EX9 7DP
Tel: (01395) 568465
*60 acres of garden includes Italian
garden laid out in 1735. James
Countryside collection, exhibition hall,
woodland railway and indoor and
outdoor children's play area. Maze.*

26 Royal Albert Memorial Museum
Queen Street, Exeter, Devon
EX4 3RX
Tel: (01392) 265858
*Largest museum in the south west.
Silver, natural history, ethnography,
local history, temporary exhibitions
and holiday activities.*

㉗ Torre Abbey Historic House and Gallery
The Kings Drive, Torquay, Devon TQ2 5JX
Tel: (01803) 293593
12thC monastery converted into a family home after the Dissolution in 1539. 19thC paintings and antiques, historic rooms, Agatha Christie room and colourful gardens.

㉘ Buckland Abbey
Yelverton, Devon PL20 6EY
Tel: (01822) 853607
Originally Cistercian monastery, then home of Sir Francis Drake. Craft workshops, exhibitions, herb garden and estate walks.

㉙ Cotehele
St Dominick, Saltash, Cornwall PL12 6TA
Tel: (01579) 50434
Medieval granite house. Watermill restored to working condition. Quay on River Tamar with small shipping museum. Sailing barge "Shamrock". Garden with pools and dovecote.

㉚ Crownhill Fort
Crownhill Fort Road, Plymouth, Devon PL6 5BX
Tel: (01752) 793754
Largest and least altered of Plymouth's great Victorian forts. Original features

include massive ditch and ramparts, gun towers, parade ground and barracks. 16-acre site, museum.

㉛ Kitley Caves and Country Park
Kitley Estate Office, Yealmpton, Plymouth, Devon PL8 2LT
Tel: (01752) 880885
Showcaves, museum, adventure play area, woodland and riverside walks.

㉜ Newquay Sea Life Centre
Towan Promenade, Newquay, Cornwall TR7 1DU
Tel: (01637) 872822
Journey beneath the ocean waves and encounter thousands of marine creatures; everything from shrimps to starfish and conger eels to octopus.

㉝ St Agnes Leisure Park
Penwinnick Road, St Agnes, Cornwall TR5 0PA
Tel: (01872) 552793
"Cornwall in Miniature", "Fairyland," "Lost World of the Dinosaurs," "Haunted House," grand animated circus. Beautiful land-scaped gardens. Super'X' simulator and much more.

㉞ Royal Cornwall Museum
River Street, Truro, Cornwall TR1 2SJ
Tel: (01872) 72205

World famous mineral collection, Old Master drawings, ceramics, oil paintings by the Newlyn School and others, including John Opie and Hogarth. Geneaology library.

㉟ Geevor Tin Mine Museum
Pendeen, Penzance, Cornwall TR19 7EW
Tel: (01736) 788662
Cornish mining museum, tours of surface plant and videofilm of surface. Underground operations by appointment.

㊱ Goonhilly Satellite Earth Station
Goonhilly Downs, Helston, Cornwall TR12 6LQ
Tel: (01326) 221333
The world's largest satellite earth station. Guided bus tour around the complex. Visitors' Centre with audio-visual show, inter-active displays and museum area. Children's play area.

Find Out More

Further information about holidays and attractions in West Country is available from:
West Country Tourist Board, 60 St David's Hill, Exeter EX4 4SY
Tel: (01392) 76351
Fax: (01392) 420891

These publications are available free from the West Country Tourist Board:
- **England's West Country – Holidays '96**
- **Bed & Breakfast Touring Map**
- **West Country Inspected Holiday Homes '96**
- **Activity and Leisure Holidays '96**
- **West Country Short Breaks '95/'96**
- **Commended Hotels and Guesthouses '95/'96**
- **West Country Gardens**

WHERE TO STAY

Accommodation entries in this regional section are listed in alphabetical order of place name, and then in alphabetical order of establishment.

Map references refer to the colour location maps at the back of this guide. The first figure is the map number; the letter and figure which follow indicate the grid reference on the map.

At-a-glance symbols at the end of each accommodation entry give information about services and facilities. A handy guide to these symbols can be found inside the back cover flap, which can be kept open for easy reference.

ABBOTSBURY

Dorset
Map ref 2A3

Beautiful village near Chesil Beach, with a long main street of mellow stone and thatched cottages and the ruins of a Benedictine monastery. High above the village on a hill is a prominent 15th C chapel. Abbotsbury's famous swannery and sub-tropical gardens lie just outside the village.

Linton Cottage

Listed COMMENDED

Abbotsbury, Weymouth DT3 4JL
☎ (01305) 871339
Victorian cottage in picturesque setting. Our own honey on the breakfast table, and dinners just that extra bit special.
Bedrooms: 2 double, 1 twin
Bathrooms: 1 private, 1 public

Bed & breakfast

per night:	£min	£max
Single	27.50	30.50
Double	35.00	38.00

Half board

per person:	£min	£max
Daily	30.00	31.50
Weekly	180.00	190.00

Evening meal from 1830
Parking for 4

🛇🛆♿🖃🖬§⊁🅟📺🛏. 🖫❅✕🏃

Swan Lodge 🅰

♔♔

Rodden Row, Abbotsbury, Weymouth DT3 4JL
☎ (01305) 871249
Fax (01305) 871249
Situated on the B3157 coastal road between Weymouth and Bridport. Swan Inn public house opposite, where food

is served all day, is under the same ownership.
Bedrooms: 2 double, 2 twin, 1 triple
Bathrooms: 2 private, 1 public

Bed & breakfast

per night:	£min	£max
Single	20.00	35.00
Double	40.00	50.00

Lunch available
Evening meal 1800 (last orders 2200)
Parking for 10
Cards accepted: Access, Visa

🛇🛆♿🖃§⊁🅟📺🛏.🖫🛋️🍴80♦🕻❅ 🖮 OAP 🛇 SP

ALLERFORD

Somerset
Map ref 1D1

Village with picturesque stone and thatch cottages and a packhorse bridge, set in the beautiful Vale of Porlock.

Fern Cottage 🅰

♔♔♔ COMMENDED

Allerford, Minehead TA24 8HN
☎ Porlock (01643) 862215

Large 16th C traditional Exmoor cottage in National Trust wooded vale. Dramatic scenery and wildlife. Fine classic cooking and comprehensive wine list.
Bedrooms: 2 double, 2 triple
Bathrooms: 4 private

Bed & breakfast

per night:	£min	£max
Single	28.50	28.50
Double	50.00	50.00

Half board

per person:	£min	£max
Daily	36.25	36.25
Weekly	228.40	228.40

Evening meal 1900 (last orders 1800)
Parking for 7
Cards accepted: Access, Visa, Switch/ Delta

🛇♿🖃§⊁🅟📺🛏.🖫🛋️🕻🍴 🖮 SP 🅣

AMESBURY

Wiltshire
Map ref 2B2

Standing on the banks of the River Avon, this is the nearest town to Stonehenge on Salisbury Plain. The area is rich in prehistoric sites.
Tourist Information Centre
☎ (01980) 622833

Church Cottage

♔ HIGHLY COMMENDED

Church Street, Amesbury, Salisbury SP4 7EY
☎ (01980) 624650
Period 18th C property with beams and antiques, only 2 miles from Stonehenge. Attractive patio and gardens, lovely bedrooms, delicious English breakfast. Superb service.
Bedrooms: 3 double; suite available
Bathrooms: 3 private

Continued ▶

We advise you to confirm your booking in writing.

AMESBURY

Continued

Bed & breakfast

per night:	£min	£max
Single	22.00	27.00
Double	30.00	38.00

Evening meal 1900 (last orders 2030)

🛇 10 📯 ❑ ♿ 🕯 ⑩ 🕯 ⓢ ⅟ ▥ ▦ 🗬 ✿ ✗ 🚿 SP 🐾 ⊤

Epworth House Bed and Breakfast ▲▲

👑👑 COMMENDED

21 Edwards Road, Amesbury,
Salisbury SP4 7LT
☎ (01980) 624242 & Mobile 0850 452829
Fax (01980) 624242
Restful house in quiet cul-de-sac, two minutes' level walk from Amesbury centre. Lovely enclosed garden, excellent breakfasts. Stonehenge nearby.
Bedrooms: 2 double, 1 twin
Bathrooms: 3 private

Bed & breakfast

per night:	£min	£max
Single	25.00	27.50
Double	35.00	40.00

Parking for 4

🛇 10 📯 ❑ ♿ 🕯 ⑩ ⅟ ▥ ▦ 🗬 ✿ ✗ 🚿

ASHBURTON

Devon
Map ref 1C2

Formerly a thriving wool centre and important as one of Dartmoor's four stannary towns. Today's busy market town has many period buildings. Ancient tradition is maintained in the annual ale-tasting and bread-weighing ceremony. Good centre for exploring Dartmoor or the south Devon coast.

New Cott Farm

👑👑 COMMENDED

Poundsgate, Newton Abbot TQ13 7PD
☎ Poundsgate (01364) 631421
Fax (01364) 631338
130-acre mixed farm. Enjoy the freedom, peace and tranquillity of moorland and valleys in the Dartmoor National Park. A warm welcome and lots of lovely home-made food to complete your stay.
Bedrooms: 2 double, 1 twin, 1 triple
Bathrooms: 4 private

Bed & breakfast

per night:	£min	£max
Double	33.00	34.00

Half board

per person:	£min	£max
Daily	26.00	27.00

Evening meal 1830 (last orders 1700)
Parking for 4

🛇 3 🖧 📯 ♿ 🕯 ⑩ 🕯 ⓢ ⅟ ▥ ▦ 🗬 🗬 U ♪ ✓ ✿ ✗ 🚿

Wellpritton Farm

👑👑 HIGHLY COMMENDED

Holne, Newton Abbot TQ13 7RX
☎ Poundsgate (01364) 631273
15-acre mixed farm. Plenty of mouthwatering farm-produced food in a tastefully modernised farmhouse on the edge of Dartmoor. Special diets catered for by arrangement. A warm welcome and caring personal attention.
Bedrooms: 2 double, 2 twin
Bathrooms: 3 private, 1 public

Bed & breakfast

per night:	£min	£max
Single	17.00	18.00
Double	34.00	36.00

Half board

per person:	£min	£max
Daily	25.00	26.00
Weekly	161.00	161.00

Evening meal from 1900
Parking for 4

🛇 🖧 📯 ♿ ⑩ ⓢ ▥ ⊤ ▦ 🗬 🗬 ✎ U ✿ ✗ 🚿

ASHTON KEYNES

Wiltshire
Map ref 2B2

Village beside the River Thames, with houses standing along the edge of the stream reached by bridges from the road on the opposite bank. Nearby stands the manor, Ashton House.

Corner Cottage

👑👑 APPROVED

Fore Street, Ashton Keynes, Swindon SN6 6NP
☎ Cirencester (01285) 861454
Homely 17th C Cotswold-stone cottage in centre of best kept village within the Cotswold Water Park. Ideal for water sports and touring the Cotswolds.
Bedrooms: 1 double, 1 family room; suite available
Bathrooms: 2 private

Bed & breakfast

per night:	£min	£max
Single	20.00	22.00
Double	35.00	38.00

Parking for 4

🛇 ♿ 🕯 ⑩ 🕯 ⓢ ▥ ⊤ ▦ 🗬 ✿ ✗ 🚿

> National gradings and classifications were correct at the time of going to press but are subject to change. Please check at the time of booking.

ASHWATER

Devon
Map ref 1C2

Village 6 miles south-east of Holsworthy, with a pleasant village green dominated by its church.

Renson Mill

👑👑 HIGHLY COMMENDED

Ashwater EX21 5ER
☎ Beaworthy (01409) 211665
Fax (01409) 211665
Fabulous view in the heart of West Devon countryside. Your welcome is second to none by your hosts, Sonia and Geoffrey Archer. Brochure available.
Bedrooms: 1 triple; suite available
Bathrooms: 1 private

Bed & breakfast

per night:	£min	£max
Single	20.00	25.00

Evening meal 1830 (last orders 2130)
Parking for 12

🛇 🖧 📯 ❑ ♿ 🕯 ⑩ 🕯 ⓢ ⅟ ▥ ▦ 🗬 U ⊦ ✿ ✗ 🚿 ⊤

AVEBURY

Wiltshire
Map ref 2B2

Set in a landscape of earthworks and megalithic standing stones, Avebury has a fine church and an Elizabethan manor. Remains from excavations may be seen in the museum. The area abounds in important prehistoric sites, among them Silbury Hill. Stonehenge stands about 20 miles due south.

New Inn

Listed APPROVED

Winterbourne Monkton, Swindon SN4 9NW
☎ (01672) 539240
Small and friendly country pub only 1 mile from Avebury. Good, central touring position.
Bedrooms: 2 double, 3 twin
Bathrooms: 5 private

Bed & breakfast

per night:	£min	£max
Double	33.00	38.00

Lunch available
Evening meal 1830 (last orders 2130)
Parking for 20
Cards accepted: Access, Visa, Switch/Delta

🛇 🖧 ❑ ♿ 🕯 ⓢ ▦ 🗬 ✎ ✿ ✗ 🚿

> The symbol ▲▲ after an establishment name indicates membership of a Regional Tourist Board.

BANWELL

Avon
Map ref 1D1

Banwell Castle

Listed

Banwell, Weston-super-Mare
BS24 6NX
☎ Weston-super-Mare (01934) 822263
Fax (01934) 823946

Romantic, tranquil castle furnished in Victorian style, set in 20 acres of grounds. Outstanding views to the Mendips and Welsh hills. Midway Cheddar Gorge and Weston-super-Mare
Bedrooms: 3 double
Bathrooms: 3 private

Bed & breakfast per night:	£min	£max
Single	20.00	25.00
Double	40.00	50.00

Half board per person:	£min	£max
Daily	30.00	35.00
Weekly	210.00	210.00

Lunch available
Evening meal (last orders 2100)
Parking for 3
Cards accepted: Access, Visa
ॐ🏠🍴📺📟↓🐾🖐ⓈⓊ📺▥🔲
📸50 ▶ ❄ 🚲 🔖 SP 🈺 Ⓣ

BARNSTAPLE

Devon
Map ref 1C1

At the head of the Taw Estuary, once a ship-building and textile town, now an agricultural centre with attractive period buildings, a modern civic centre and leisure centre. Attractions include Queen Anne's Walk, a charming colonnaded arcade and Pannier Market.
Tourist Information Centre
☎ *(01271) 388583 or 388584*

Cedars Lodge Inn

COMMENDED

Bickington Road, Barnstaple
EX31 2HP
☎ (01271) 71784
Fax (01271) 25733
Country house with lodges in 3 acres. All en-suite, satellite TV. Pub and restaurant. Just off North Devon link road.
Bedrooms: 9 double, 8 twin, 6 family rooms
Bathrooms: 23 private

Bed & breakfast per night:	£min	£max
Single	33.00	38.00
Double	45.00	55.00

Lunch available
Evening meal 1830 (last orders 2200)
Parking for 100
Cards accepted: Access, Visa, Amex, Switch/Delta
ॐ🏠&🍴📟↓🐾Ⓢ🖐▥◑▥.🔲
📸150 🎿❄🚲 SP Ⓣ

Home Park Farm Accommodation

COMMENDED

Lower Blakewell, Muddiford, Barnstaple EX31 4ET
☎ (01271) 42955
70-acre livestock farm. Paradise for the country and garden lover, with food and hospitality second to none. True tranquillity at the end of a no-through road. Take A39 Lynton road out of Barnstaple, left on to B3230, second left to Lower Blakewell.
Bedrooms: 1 double, 2 triple
Bathrooms: 3 private

Bed & breakfast per night:	£min	£max
Single	15.00	20.00
Double	30.00	35.00

Half board per person:	£min	£max
Daily	22.50	25.00
Weekly	150.00	160.00

Lunch available
Evening meal 1800 (last orders 1800)
Parking for 3
ॐ5🍴📟↓🐾▥🔲Ⓢ🖐▥▥.🔲
❄🚲 OAP SP Ⓣ

The Red House

HIGHLY COMMENDED

Brynsworthy, Roundswell, Barnstaple EX31 3NP
☎ (01271) 45966
Country house, panoramic views. Both rooms colour TV, shower, hairdryer, tea/coffee facilities, central heating. Good pub food nearby.
Bedrooms: 1 double, 1 twin
Bathrooms: 2 private showers

Bed & breakfast per night:	£min	£max
Single	15.00	18.00
Double	30.00	36.00

Parking for 7
ॐ12🍴📟↓🐾▥🖐▥▥.❄🎿🚲

The Spinney ▲

COMMENDED

Shirwell, Barnstaple EX31 4JR
☎ Shirwell (01271) 850282
Regency former rectory with spacious accommodation, set in over an acre of grounds with views of Exmoor. Meals made from local market-day produce.
Bedrooms: 1 single, 1 double, 1 twin, 2 triple
Bathrooms: 1 private, 2 public

Bed & breakfast per night:	£min	£max
Single	16.50	19.50
Double	33.00	39.00

Half board per person:	£min	£max
Daily	24.00	27.00
Weekly	144.00	162.00

Evening meal 1900 (last orders 1700)
Parking for 7
ॐ🍴↓🐾Ⓤ Ⓢ🖐📺▥.🔲❄🚲 SP 🈺

Waytown Farm

COMMENDED

Shirwell, Barnstaple EX31 4JN
☎ Shirwell (01271) 850396
240-acre mixed farm. Pleasantly situated 17th C farmhouse, 3 miles from Barnstaple. Exmoor and beaches within easy reach. Home cooking, comfortable accommodation. Access at all times.
Bedrooms: 1 single, 1 twin, 1 triple, 1 family room; suites available
Bathrooms: 2 private, 1 public

Bed & breakfast per night:	£min	£max
Single	18.00	20.00
Double	33.00	38.00

Half board per person:	£min	£max
Daily	24.00	27.00
Weekly	150.00	165.00

Evening meal 1830 (last orders 1600)
Parking for 6
Open January-November
ॐ🍴📟↓🐾Ⓤ🖐📺▥.🔲↺✓❄✖
🚲 🈺

BATH

Avon
Map ref 2B2

Georgian spa city beside the River Avon. Important Roman site with impressive reconstructed baths, uncovered in 19th C. Bath Abbey built on site of monastery where first king of England was crowned (AD 973). Fine architecture in mellow local stone. Pump Room and museums.
Tourist Information Centre
☎ *(01225) 462831*

Aaron House Number Ninety Three

COMMENDED

93 Wells Road, Bath BA2 3AN
☎ (01225) 317977
Pleasant Victorian house, all rooms en-suite. Within very easy walking distance of city centre, British Rail and national coach stations. Evening meals by arrangement. Special rates for 3 or more nights.
Bedrooms: 1 double, 1 twin, 1 triple
Bathrooms: 3 private

Continued ▶

BATH

Continued

Bed & breakfast per night:	£min	£max
Single	19.00	35.00
Double	38.00	47.00

Half board per person:	£min	£max
Daily	28.50	44.50
Weekly	199.50	311.50

Evening meal from 1830
Cards accepted: Access, Visa, Amex

Aimee's Guest House

6 Manvers Street, Bath BA1 1JQ
☎ (01225) 330133
Very central to all amenities and convenient for rail and bus stations.
Bedrooms: 5 double, 4 twin
Bathrooms: 4 private, 3 public

Bed & breakfast per night:	£min	£max
Single	16.00	24.00
Double	24.00	34.00

Cards accepted: Access, Visa, Diners

Astor House

COMMENDED
14 Oldfield Road, Bath BA2 3ND
☎ (01225) 429134
Fax (01225) 429134
Comfortable, spacious Victorian home with lovely views of the city and countryside yet only a short walk to the centre. Friendly welcome, varied delicious breakfasts.
Bedrooms: 4 double, 2 twin
Bathrooms: 4 private, 2 public

Bed & breakfast per night:	£min	£max
Single	18.00	26.00
Double	30.00	46.00

Parking for 4
Open February-December
Cards accepted: Access, Visa

Athelney Guest House

Listed
5 Marlborough Lane, Bath BA1 2NQ
☎ (01225) 312031
Comfortable Victorian home close to the Royal Crescent and just a short, pleasant walk from the city centre. Private car parking.
Bedrooms: 2 twin, 1 triple
Bathrooms: 2 public

Bed & breakfast per night:	£min	£max
Double	32.00	36.00

Parking for 3

Cedar Lodge

13 Lambridge, London Road, Bath BA1 6BJ
☎ (01225) 423468
Convenient for city centre, this beautiful detached Georgian house offers period elegance, combined with home comforts. Individually designed bedrooms, 1 with four-poster, 1 with half tester. No smoking or pets, please.
Bedrooms: 2 double, 1 twin
Bathrooms: 3 private, 1 public

Bed & breakfast per night:	£min	£max
Double	40.00	60.00

Evening meal 1930 (last orders 1100)
Parking for 8

Cherry Tree Villa

7 Newbridge Hill, Bath BA1 3PW
☎ (01225) 331671
Small, friendly, Victorian home, within easy walking distance of city centre through pleasant park.
Bedrooms: 1 single, 1 double, 1 triple
Bathrooms: 1 public

Bed & breakfast per night:	£min	£max
Single	15.00	18.00
Double	30.00	36.00

Parking for 4

Church Farm

Monkton Farleigh, Bradford-on-Avon, Wiltshire BA15 2QJ
☎ (01225) 858583 & Mobile (0589) 596929
52-acre mixed farm. Converted barn in Wiltshire countryside. Traditional facilities with guest lounge. Livery stables. 5 minutes to new 18-hole golf-course, 10 minutes to Bath.
Bedrooms: 3 double
Bathrooms: 3 private, 1 public

Bed & breakfast per night:	£min	£max
Single	22.50	22.50
Double	32.00	38.00

Parking for 5

Corston Fields Farm

Listed HIGHLY COMMENDED
Corston, Bath BA2 9EZ
☎ (01225) 873305 & Mobile (0421) 379294
Fax (01225) 873305

Map references apply to the colour maps at the back of this guide.

17 C farmhouse on working arable farm. Set in the countryside, 4 miles from Bath. Centrally heated with safe car parking.
Bedrooms: 2 double, 1 twin, 1 triple
Bathrooms: 1 private, 1 public

Bed & breakfast per night:	£min	£max
Double	36.00	48.00

Parking for 10

Dorset Villa

APPROVED
14 Newbridge Road, Bath BA1 3JX
☎ (01225) 425975
Victorian house half a mile from Royal Crescent. En-suite rooms available. TV and coffee/tea facilities in all rooms.
Bedrooms: 5 double, 1 twin, 1 family room
Bathrooms: 5 private, 1 public

Bed & breakfast per night:	£min	£max
Single	31.00	36.00
Double	38.00	46.00

Evening meal 1700 (last orders 2000)
Parking for 6
Cards accepted: Access, Visa

Edgar Hotel

64 Great Pulteney Street, Bath BA2 4DN
☎ (01225) 420619
Georgian town house hotel, close to city centre and Roman Baths. Privately run. All rooms with en-suite facilities.
Bedrooms: 2 single, 9 double, 4 twin, 1 triple
Bathrooms: 16 private

Bed & breakfast per night:	£min	£max
Single	25.00	35.00
Double	35.00	55.00

Cards accepted: Access, Visa

Fern Cottage

COMMENDED
74 Monkton Farleigh, Bradford-on-Avon, Wiltshire BA15 2QJ
☎ (01225) 859412
Fax (01225) 859018
Delightful stone-built 17th C cottage, set in fine gardens in peaceful conservation village between Bath and Bradford-on-Avon. Well-appointed rooms.
Bedrooms: 2 double, 1 twin
Bathrooms: 1 private, 1 public

Bed & breakfast per night:	£min	£max
Single	30.00	30.00
Double	45.00	50.00

Parking for 5

♿ ⌂ ♨ ☎ ⓊⓁ Ⓢ ✗ ♨ 🞑 ☎ ✿ ✈ ♠

Gainsborough Hotel ⋀
☸☸☸

Weston Lane, Bath BA1 4AB
☎ (01225) 311380
Fax (01225) 447411

Spacious and comfortable country house hotel in own lovely grounds near the botanical gardens, and within easy walking distance of the city. High ground, nice views, own large car park. 5-course breakfast, friendly staff, warm welcome.
Bedrooms: 2 single, 8 double, 4 twin, 1 triple, 1 family room
Bathrooms: 16 private

Bed & breakfast per night:	£min	£max
Single	25.00	40.00
Double	48.00	60.00

Evening meal 1900 (last orders 2000)
Parking for 18
Cards accepted: Access, Visa, Amex

♿ ♨ 🐾 ☎ ⌂ ♨ ☎ Ⓢ ♨ 🞑 ☎ ✿ ✗ ✈ ♠

Gardens Guest House
Listed

7 Pulteney Gardens, Bath BA2 4HG
☎ & (01225) 337642
5 minutes' walk to Roman Baths, Abbey, train/coach stations, city shops, tranquil canalside. Private parking and generous breakfasts.
Bedrooms: 2 single, 2 double, 1 twin, 1 family room
Bathrooms: 6 private showers

Bed & breakfast per night:	£min	£max
Double	30.00	38.00

Parking for 2

♿ ☐ ♨ ⓊⓁ ♨ Ⓜ ⓉⓋ 🞑 🞑 ✈ ⒹⒶⓅ Ⓢ Ⓣ

Haute Combe Hotel
☸☸☸

176 Newbridge Road, Bath BA1 3LE
☎ (01225) 420061 & Mobile 0831 379231
Fax (01225) 420061
Fully-equipped en-suite rooms in comfortable, period surroundings. Easy access to city attractions. Special off-season rates. Telephone for brochure.
Bedrooms: 2 single, 3 double, 2 twin, 2 triple, 2 family rooms
Bathrooms: 11 private

Bed & breakfast per night:	£min	£max
Single	32.00	39.00
Double	45.00	59.00

Evening meal 1900 (last orders 1800)
Parking for 11
Cards accepted: Access, Visa, Amex, Switch/Delta

♿ ♨ ☎ ⌂ ☐ ♨ ☎ ♨ Ⓢ ✗ ♨ Ⓜ 🞑 ☎ ♠ ✿ ✈ Ⓢ Ⓣ

Henrietta Hotel
☸☸

32 Henrietta Street, Bath BA2 6LR
☎ (01225) 447779
Privately-run Georgian town house hotel, close to city centre and Roman Baths. All rooms with en-suite facilities.
Bedrooms: 7 double, 3 twin
Bathrooms: 10 private

Bed & breakfast per night:	£min	£max
Single	25.00	35.00
Double	35.00	55.00

♿ ♨ ☐ ♨ ☎ ⓊⓁ Ⓜ ⓉⓋ 🞑 🞑 ✈ ✈ Ⓢ ♠

The Hollies
☸☸ COMMENDED

Hatfield Road, Wellsway, Bath BA2 2BD
☎ (01225) 313366

Grade II early Victorian family house, 15 minutes' walk to city centre, overlooking parish church and gardens. Pretty guest-rooms, comfortably furnished. Sunny secluded garden.
Bedrooms: 2 double, 1 twin
Bathrooms: 3 private

Bed & breakfast per night:	£min	£max
Single	20.00	25.00
Double	38.00	48.00

Parking for 6

♿ ☐ ♨ ☎ ⓊⓁ ♨ Ⓢ ✗ Ⓜ 🞑 🞑 ✿ ✗ ✈ Ⓢ ♠

Kennard Hotel ⋀
☸☸ COMMENDED

11 Henrietta Street, Bath BA2 6LL
☎ (01225) 310472
Fax (01225) 460054
Converted Georgian house in quiet street. A few minutes' level walk to city centre, abbey, Roman Baths, Pump Room and Henrietta Park.
Bedrooms: 2 single, 9 double, 1 twin, 1 family room
Bathrooms: 11 private, 1 public

Bed & breakfast per night:	£min	£max
Single	30.00	35.00
Double	52.00	62.00

Cards accepted: Access, Visa, Diners, Amex, Switch/Delta

♿ ☎ ⌂ ☐ ♨ ☎ ⓊⓁ ✗ Ⓜ 🞑 🞑 ✿ ✗ ✈ Ⓢ ♠ Ⓣ

Kinlet Villa Guest House
☸ COMMENDED

99 Wellsway, Bath BA2 4RX
☎ (01225) 420268
Edwardian villa retaining original features and antiques. Walking distance from city centre, good bus service, unrestricted parking. Non-smokers only, please.
Bedrooms: 1 double, 1 triple
Bathrooms: 2 public

Bed & breakfast per night:	£min	£max
Double	32.00	34.00

♿ ☐ ♨ ⓊⓁ Ⓢ ✗ Ⓜ 🞑 🞑 ✗ ✈ Ⓢ

Leighton House ⋀
☸☸ HIGHLY COMMENDED

139 Wells Road, Bath BA2 3AL
☎ (01225) 314769
Fax (01225) 443079

Enjoy a haven of friendliness in this elegant and spacious Victorian guesthouse with own car park, 10 minutes' walk from city centre.
Bedrooms: 3 double, 3 twin, 1 triple, 1 family room
Bathrooms: 8 private

Bed & breakfast per night:	£min	£max
Single	42.00	50.00
Double	60.00	65.00

Parking for 8
Cards accepted: Access, Visa

♿ ♨ ☎ ⌂ ☐ ♨ ☎ ⓊⓁ Ⓢ Ⓜ 🞑 🞑 ✿ ✗ ✈ Ⓢ Ⓣ

Lindisfarne
☸☸ COMMENDED

41a Warminster Road, Bathampton, Bath BA2 6XJ
☎ (01225) 466342
Modern property, all bedrooms en-suite with colour TV and tea/coffee facilities. Within walking distance of good eating places, about 1.5 miles from Bath city centre with a regular bus service. Large car park.
Bedrooms: 3 double, 1 twin
Bathrooms: 4 private

Bed & breakfast per night:	£min	£max
Single	25.00	35.00
Double	38.00	42.00

Parking for 6

♿ 3 ♨ ☐ ♨ ⓊⓁ Ⓢ 🞑 🞑 ✿ ✈ ♠ Ⓢ Ⓣ

BATH

Continued

The Manor House

👑👑 COMMENDED

Mill Lane, Monkton Combe, Bath
BA2 7HD
☎ (01225) 723128
Fax (01225) 723128

Restful, rambling 16th C manor beside mill stream in wooded valley designated as an Area of Outstanding Natural Beauty, just 2 miles south of city. Inglenook fires, Victorian conservatory, spacious bedrooms. Fine breakfasts served until noon.
Bedrooms: 2 double, 1 family room
Bathrooms: 3 private, 1 public

Bed & breakfast

per night:	£min	£max
Single	25.00	25.00
Double	45.00	45.00

Parking for 6

🛇♥️▨⊬⊬☺🇹🇻▥▦🝁🐾10 ⚲∪✿🐎
ⓄⒶⓅ SP 🏮

Marlborough House

👑👑 COMMENDED

1 Marlborough Lane, Bath BA1 2NQ
☎ (01225) 318175 & 466127
Recently renovated Victorian house 5 minutes' level walk from city centre and 2 minutes from Royal Crescent. Light and airy rooms, four-posters. Non-smoking, private parking. 10% discount for 3 nights or more.
Bedrooms: 2 single, 2 double, 1 twin
Bathrooms: 3 private, 1 public,
1 private shower

Bed & breakfast

per night:	£min	£max
Single	20.00	35.00
Double	40.00	55.00

Parking for 3
Cards accepted: Access, Visa, Amex

🛇🗗🎏🖃♥️🇹🇻▨Ⓢ⊬⊬☺▥▦🝁✕
🐾SP

Meadowland

👑👑 DE LUXE

36 Bloomfield Park, Bath BA2 2BX
☎ (01225) 311079
Set in quiet secluded grounds and offering the highest standard in de-luxe en-suite accommodation, Meadowland is elegantly furnished and decorated. Private parking, lovely gardens, non-smoking only. A peaceful retreat for discerning travellers.
Bedrooms: 2 double, 1 twin
Bathrooms: 3 private

Bed & breakfast

per night:	£min	£max
Single	35.00	40.00
Double	50.00	60.00

Parking for 6
Cards accepted: Access, Visa

🛇3🗗🖃♥️🇹🇻Ⓢ⊬☺🇹🇻▥▦◻∪
🏮✿✕🐎SP

Midway Cottage

👑👑 COMMENDED

10 Farleigh Wick, Bradford-on-Avon,
Wiltshire BA15 2PU
☎ Bradford-on-Avon (01225) 863932
Friendly, relaxed cottage with high standards of comfort and service. On A363 between Bath and Bradford-on-Avon, next door to a country inn serving excellent food.
Bedrooms: 2 double, 1 twin
Bathrooms: 3 private, 1 public

Bed & breakfast

per night:	£min	£max
Single	17.50	20.00
Double	35.00	35.00

Parking for 5

🛇🖃♥️🇹🇻🞐Ⓢ⊬⊬☺🇹🇻▥
🝁🐎SP

Oakleigh House ⚠

👑👑 COMMENDED

19 Upper Oldfield Park, Bath BA2 3JX
☎ (01225) 315698
Fax (01225) 448223
Quietly situated Victorian home only 10 minutes from city centre. All rooms en-suite with colour TV, tea/coffee making facilities, etc. Private car park.
Bedrooms: 3 double, 1 twin
Bathrooms: 4 private

Bed & breakfast

per night:	£min	£max
Single	35.00	45.00
Double	45.00	60.00

Parking for 4
Cards accepted: Access, Visa

🗗🖃♥️🇹🇻▨Ⓢ⊬☺▥▦🝁✕🐎ⒶⓅSP

The Old School House ⚠

👑👑👑 HIGHLY COMMENDED

Church Street, Bathford, Bath
BA1 7RR
☎ (01225) 859593
Fax (01225) 859590

Pretty Victorian schoolhouse of Bath stone in peaceful conservation area overlooking Avon Valley. 3 miles to Bath centre. Country house ambience with candlelit dinners and winter log fires. Ground floor en-suite rooms. Licensed, non-smoking.
Bedrooms: 3 double, 1 twin
Bathrooms: 4 private

Bed & breakfast

per night:	£min	£max
Single	45.00	50.00
Double	60.00	70.00

Evening meal 1900 (last orders 2000)
Parking for 6
Cards accepted: Access, Visa

🛇🝁🖃♥️🇹🇻Ⓢ⊬☺▥▦🝁✿✕🐎
🝁SP🏮

Paradise House Hotel

👑👑

86-88 Holloway, Bath BA2 4PX
☎ (01225) 317723
Fax (01225) 482005

Lovely Bath-stone house in very quiet cul-de-sac within 4 minutes' walk of city. Superb views from rear.
Bedrooms: 5 double, 4 twin
Bathrooms: 7 private, 1 public

Bed & breakfast

per night:	£min	£max
Single	30.00	45.00
Double	48.00	65.00

Parking for 6
Cards accepted: Access, Visa, Amex

🛇🝁🖃🗗♥️🇹🇻▨▥🝁✿✕
🐎🏮

Poplar Farm ⚠

Listed COMMENDED

Stanton Prior, Bath BA2 9HX
☎ Mendip (01761) 470382

350-acre mixed farm. 17th C farmhouse, 5 miles west of Bath and within easy reach of park-and-ride for Bristol and Bath. Idyllic village beneath Iron Age fort. Good walks, peace and quiet.
Bedrooms: 1 double, 1 twin, 1 family room
Bathrooms: 2 private, 1 public

Bed & breakfast

per night:	£min	£max
Single	18.00	22.00
Double	34.00	45.00

Parking for 10

🛇🇹⊬☺🇹🇻▥▦◻∪▶✿🐾🏮

The Priory Wing

👑👑 COMMENDED

54 Lyncombe Hill, Bath BA2 4PJ
☎ (01225) 336395
Peaceful Georgian listed building bordering meadowland yet only 10

minutes' walk from city centre and railway/bus stations. Original fireplaces. One bedroom adjoins flagstone, panelled, entrance hall. Non-smokers only, please.
Bedrooms: 1 double, 1 twin, 1 triple
Bathrooms: 3 private
Bed & breakfast

per night:	£min	£max
Single	20.00	25.00
Double	40.00	45.50

Parking for 3

⛶♿🖵📶📵📞🅂↗️📺▥🖨✳️🐾 🆂🅿️🛏️

Hotel Saint Clair

💀💀 COMMENDED

1 Crescent Gardens, Upper Bristol Road, Bath BA1 2NA
☎ (01225) 425543 & Mobile (01378) 834592
Fax (01225) 425543
Small family hotel 5 minutes' walk from city, 2 minutes from Royal Crescent. Large public car park 1 minute away. One-night stays welcome.
Bedrooms: 4 double, 2 twin, 2 triple, 1 family room
Bathrooms: 7 private, 1 public
Bed & breakfast

per night:	£min	£max
Single	22.00	38.00
Double	32.00	48.00

Cards accepted: Access, Visa, Amex

⛶3📞🖵📶📵▥🖨🅣

Sampford

💀

11 Oldfield Road, Bath BA2 3ND
☎ (01225) 310053
In a quiet residential area half a mile south of city centre off the A367 Exeter road.
Bedrooms: 1 double, 1 twin, 1 triple
Bathrooms: 1 public, 3 private showers
Bed & breakfast

per night:	£min	£max
Double	32.00	32.00

Parking for 2

⛶🖵📶📵▥🖨🚗

Sarnia

💀💀 HIGHLY COMMENDED

19 Combe Park, Weston, Bath BA1 3NR
☎ (01225) 424159
Large Victorian house, beautifully furnished. Spacious bedrooms with private facilities, TV, tea/coffee facilities. English, continental and vegetarian breakfasts. Off road parking. On bus route.
Bedrooms: 2 double, 1 twin
Bathrooms: 3 private
Bed & breakfast

per night:	£min	£max
Single	20.00	30.00
Double	40.00	50.00

Parking for 6

⛶🖵📶📵🅂↗️📵📺▥🖨✳️ 🆂🏮

Serendipity

Listed

19f Bradford Road, Winsley, Bradford-on-Avon, Wiltshire BA15 2HW
☎ (01225) 722380
Bungalow with beautiful secluded gardens 5 miles from Bath. 2 miles Bradford-on-Avon on B3108. Picturesque village location.
Bedrooms: 1 double, 1 twin
Bathrooms: 2 public
Bed & breakfast

per night:	£min	£max
Single	15.00	20.00
Double	30.00	32.00

Parking for 5

⛶🛁♿🖵📶🍴📵🅂↗️▥🖨✳️✠ 🐾 🆂🏮

Seven Springs

Listed APPROVED

4 High Street, Woolley, Bath BA1 8AR
☎ (01225) 858001

In small country hamlet of Woolley, 3 miles from Bath city centre and 4 miles from M4. Lovely walks on public footpaths. Ideal for touring West Country. Bedrooms can be let as twins, doubles or family rooms. Payphone available.
Bedrooms: 2 family rooms
Bathrooms: 2 private
Bed & breakfast

per night:	£min	£max
Double	35.00	40.00

Parking for 8

⛶♿🖵📶📶🅂↗️▥✳️✠🐾

Toghill House Farm

Listed COMMENDED

Doynton, Bristol BS15 5RT
☎ (01225) 891261
50-acre mixed farm. Warm and cosy 17th C farmhouse, formerly a resting home for monks travelling from Malmesbury to Glastonbury. Views over historic Bath, Bristol and Welsh hills.
Bedrooms: 1 double, 1 triple, 1 family room
Bathrooms: 3 private
Bed & breakfast

per night:	£min	£max
Single	25.00	25.00
Double	40.00	40.00

Parking for 50

⛶🖵📶📵🛏️🖨🚗✳️🐾🏮

Wansdyke Cottage

Listed COMMENDED

Marksbury Gate, Bath BA2 9HE
☎ Saltford (01225) 873674
Fax (01225) 873674

Grade II Georgian house in gardens with country views. 5 miles west of Bath on A39. Convenient for park and ride.
Bedrooms: 2 double, 1 twin
Bathrooms: 1 private, 2 public
Bed & breakfast

per night:	£min	£max
Single	15.00	18.00
Double	30.00	36.00

Half board

per person:	£min	£max
Daily	22.00	25.00

Evening meal 1900 (last orders 1700)
Parking for 4

⛶♿📶🅂📵📺▥🖨✳️🐾🏮

Wellsway Guest House

💀

51 Wellsway, Bath BA2 4RS
☎ (01225) 423434
Comfortable, clean, warm, small guesthouse on bus route. Colour TV in bedrooms. Close to local shops, only a few minutes' walk to city centre.
Bedrooms: 1 single, 1 double, 1 twin, 1 triple
Bathrooms: 1 public
Bed & breakfast

per night:	£min	£max
Single	16.00	18.00
Double	26.00	34.00

Parking for 3

⛶🖵📶🅂📵📺▥🖨🚗▸✳️🐾�🅣

Wheelwrights Arms 🏍

Listed

Monkton Combe, Bath BA2 7HD
☎ Limpley Stoke (01225) 722287
Ideal centre for sightseeing, a short distance from Bath. Guest rooms are in converted 17th C stables and barn.
Bedrooms: 6 double, 2 twin
Bathrooms: 8 private
Bed & breakfast

per night:	£min	£max
Single	35.00	35.00
Double	44.00	48.00

Lunch available
Evening meal 1930 (last orders 2100)
Parking for 30
Cards accepted: Access, Visa

⛶14♿📞🖵📶🍴🛏️▥🖨🚗✳️✠🐾🆂 🏮🅣

Whittington Farmhouse

Listed HIGHLY COMMENDED

Cold Ashton, Chippenham, Wiltshire SN14 8JS
☎ (01225) 891628
18th C farmhouse in a peaceful setting on the Cotswold Way, 5 miles north of
Continued ▶

BATH

Continued

Bath. Convenient also for Bristol and Chippenham.
Bedrooms: 2 double
Bathrooms: 2 private
Bed & breakfast

per night:	£min	£max
Single	25.00	30.00
Double	35.00	35.00

Parking for 6
Open February-November
☺ 10 ⌗ ▱ 🖵 ♨ 🕮 ⅍ 🅜 🕐 🎔 ✿ ✕ 🐾

BICKINGTON

Devon
Map ref 1D2

Gale Farm
🎓🎓 COMMENDED
Bickington, Newton Abbot TQ12 6PG
☎ (01626) 821273
Georgian farmhouse in sheltered valley just off A38. Comfortable sitting room and well-furnished rooms. Traditional cooking with home-grown produce.
Bedrooms: 2 double, 1 twin
Bathrooms: 3 private
Bed & breakfast

per night:	£min	£max
Single	18.00	
Double	30.00	

Half board

per person:	£min	£max
Daily	28.00	

Evening meal 1900 (last orders 1900)
Parking for 4
☺ ♨ 🖵 🅜 🅐 🅢 ⅍ 🅜 🎔 🎠 🐌 ♨ 🐾 🏠

BIDEFORD

Devon
Map ref 1C1

The home port of Sir Richard Grenville, the town with its 17th C merchants' houses flourished as a shipbuilding and cloth town. The bridge of 24 arches was built about 1460. Charles Kingsley stayed here while writing Westward Ho!
Tourist Information Centre
☎ *(01237) 477676 or 421853*

Sunset Hotel ⋔
🎓🎓🎓
Landcross, Bideford EX39 5JA
☎ (01237) 472962
Small, elegant country hotel in peaceful, picturesque location, specialising in home cooking. Delightful en-suite bedrooms with beverages and colour TV. Book with confidence. A non-smoking establishment.
Bedrooms: 1 double, 1 twin, 1 triple, 1 family room
Bathrooms: 4 private

Bed & breakfast

per night:	£min	£max
Single	25.00	28.00
Double	46.00	48.00

Half board

per person:	£min	£max
Daily	33.00	35.00
Weekly	217.50	222.50

Evening meal 1900 (last orders 1900)
Parking for 10
Open February-November
Cards accepted: Access, Visa
☺ 🖵 ♨ 🍴 🅢 ⅍ 🅜 📺 🕐 🎔, 🎠 🐾 ✿ 🐾 🅾🅐🅟 🆂🅿 🏠

BISHOP SUTTON

Avon
Map ref 2A2

Village at edge of Chew Valley Lake.

Centaur ⋔
🎓🎓 COMMENDED
Ham Lane, Bishop Sutton, Bristol BS18 4TZ
☎ Chew Magna (01275) 332321
Comfortable family house in the peaceful Chew Valley. Bishop Sutton is on the A368 between Bath and Weston-super-Mare.
Bedrooms: 1 twin, 1 triple
Bathrooms: 1 private, 1 public, 1 private shower
Bed & breakfast

per night:	£min	£max
Single	15.50	18.00
Double	30.00	35.00

Parking for 2
☺ 🖵 ♨ 🅜 🍴 📺 🎔 ✕ 🐾

BISHOP'S LYDEARD

Somerset
Map ref 1D1

Village 5 miles north-west of Taunton, the county town. Terminus for the West Somerset steam railway.

Slimbridge Station Farm
🎓 COMMENDED
Bishop's Lydeard, Taunton TA4 3BX
☎ Bishops Lydeard (01823) 432223
Fax (01823) 432223
120-acre mixed farm. Delightful Victorian house next to the privately-owned West Somerset Steam Railway, with a limited number of trains running in the summer.
Bedrooms: 1 single, 1 double, 1 twin
Bathrooms: 1 public
Bed & breakfast

per night:	£min	£max
Single	15.00	17.00
Double	30.00	34.00

Parking for 4
☺ 🖵 🖵 ♨ 🅜 🅢 ⅍ 🅜 📺 🎔 ✿ 🐾

BLAGDON

Avon
Map ref 2A2

Village beneath the north-facing slopes of the Mendips, in a countryside of woods and lanes. Just below the Yeo Valley is Blagdon Lake, a large reservoir.

Butcombe Farm
🎓🎓 COMMENDED
Aldwick Lane, Blagdon, Bristol BS18 6UW
☎ (01761) 462380
Fax (01761) 462300
Domesday Book manor house with 15th C Assize court and many historic features in an Area of Outstanding Natural Beauty in Mendip Hills.
Bedrooms: 4 double, 1 twin
Bathrooms: 5 private
Bed & breakfast

per night:	£min	£max
Single	39.00	39.00
Double	49.00	49.00

Evening meal 1800 (last orders 2130)
Parking for 28
Cards accepted: Access, Visa
☺ 🍴 ✆ 🖵 🖵 ♨ 🍴 🅢 📺 🎔, 🎠 🎯 ✕ ● 🐌 🕐 🎠 ✕ 🐾 🅢🅟 🏠

BODMIN

Cornwall
Map ref 1B2

County town south-west of Bodmin Moor with a ruined priory and church dedicated to St Petroc. Nearby are Lanhydrock House and Pencarrow House.
Tourist Information Centre
☎ *(01208) 76616*

Bokiddick Farm
🎓🎓 COMMENDED
Lanivet, Bodmin PL30 5HP
☎ (01208) 831481
185-acre dairy farm. The warmest of welcomes in central Cornwall awaits you. Two pretty en-suite bedrooms, colour TV, delicious farmhouse cooking.
Bedrooms: 1 double, 1 triple
Bathrooms: 2 private
Bed & breakfast

per night:	£min	£max
Double	38.00	42.00

Evening meal 1830 (last orders 1200)
Parking for 4
Open April-October
☺ 3 🖵 ♨ 🅜 🅜 📺 🎔, ✿ ✕ 🐾

Treffry Farm ⋔
🎓🎓🎓 HIGHLY COMMENDED
Lanhydrock, Bodmin PL30 5AF
☎ (01208) 74405
Fax (01208) 74405

200-acre dairy farm. Lovely Georgian farmhouse in beautiful countryside adjoining National Trust Lanhydrock. Central for coast, moors and walks.
Bedrooms: 1 double, 2 twin
Bathrooms: 2 private, 1 public, 1 private shower
Bed & breakfast

per night:	£min	£max
Single		25.00
Double		38.00

Parking for 3

⛺ 6 ♨ 📞 ☐ ♦ ♋ 🅿 ⓘ ✗ ⋈ 📺 🛏 🔌 ⋃ ✦ ♪ ☼ ✕ 🚲 ⛪

BOSCASTLE
Cornwall
Map ref 1B2

Small, unspoilt village in Valency Valley. Active as a port until onset of railway era, its natural harbour affords rare shelter on this wild coast. Attractions include spectacular blow-hole, Celtic field strips, part-Norman church. Nearby St Juliot Church was restored by Thomas Hardy.

The Old Coach House ⋀
⌂⌂
Tintagel Road, Boscastle PL35 0AS
☎ (01840) 250398
Fax (01840) 250346
Relax and enjoy this beautiful 300-year-old former coach house. All rooms en-suite with colour TV, teamaker, hairdryer, etc. Friendly and helpful owners.
Wheelchair access category 3 ♿
Bedrooms: 1 single, 3 double, 3 twin, 1 triple
Bathrooms: 8 private
Bed & breakfast

per night:	£min	£max
Double	34.00	50.00

Parking for 9
Open February-November
Cards accepted: Access, Visa, Amex

⛺ 6 ♨ 📞 ☐ ♦ ♋ 🅿 ⓘ 🆂 ✗ ⋈ 🛏 🔌 ⋃ ✦ ☼ ✕ 🚲 SP ⛪ Ⓣ

Tolcarne House Hotel and Restaurant ⋀
⌂⌂⌂ COMMENDED
Tintagel Road, Boscastle PL35 0AS
☎ (01840) 250654
Delightful late Victorian house in spacious grounds with lovely views to the dramatic Cornish coastline. All rooms en-suite. Restaurant and bar. Warm welcome.
Bedrooms: 1 single, 5 double, 2 twin
Bathrooms: 8 private

Bed & breakfast

per night:	£min	£max
Single	19.00	21.00
Double	38.00	52.00

Half board

per person:	£min	£max
Daily	30.00	37.00
Weekly	195.00	230.00

Evening meal 1900 (last orders 2130)
Parking for 15
Open January-October
Cards accepted: Access, Visa

⛺ ☐ ♦ ♋ ⓘ 🆂 ✗ ⋈ 📺 🛏 🔌 ⋃ 🅿 ✦ 🚲 SP

BOVEY TRACEY
Devon
Map ref 1D2

Standing by the river just east of Dartmoor National Park, this old town has good moorland views. Its church, with a 14th C tower, holds one of Devon's finest medieval rood screens.

Frost Farmhouse
⌂⌂ COMMENDED
Frost Farm, Hennock Road, Bovey Tracey, Newton Abbot TQ13 9PP
☎ (01626) 833266
220-acre mixed farm. Pretty pink-washed thatched farmhouse. Country furnishings, log fires, good country food. Quiet location, back to nature experience.
Bedrooms: 2 double, 1 twin
Bathrooms: 3 private
Bed & breakfast

per night:	£min	£max
Single	18.00	18.00
Double	36.00	36.00

Half board

per person:	£min	£max
Daily	27.50	27.50

Evening meal from 1900
Parking for 6

⛺ ♨ 📞 ☐ ♦ ♋ 🅿 🆂 ✗ 🛏 ☼ ✕ 🚲 ⛪

BRADFORD-ON-AVON
Wiltshire
Map ref 2B2

Huddled beside the river, the buildings of this former cloth-weaving town reflect continuing prosperity from the Middle Ages. There is a tiny Anglo-Saxon church, part of a monastery. The part-14th C bridge carries a medieval chapel, later used as a gaol.
Tourist Information Centre
☎ *(01225) 865797*

Brookfield House
⌂⌂ HIGHLY COMMENDED
Vaggs Hill, Southwick, Trowbridge BA14 9NA
☎ Frome (01373) 830615

150-acre dairy farm. Delightful converted country barn in quiet rural setting. Relaxed, warm and friendly atmosphere. Dairy farm 100 yards away.
Bedrooms: 2 double, 1 twin
Bathrooms: 1 private, 2 public
Bed & breakfast

per night:	£min	£max
Single	15.00	25.00
Double	34.00	40.00

Parking for 10

⛺ ☐ ♦ ♋ 🆄🅻 ⓘ 🆂 ✗ ⋈ 📺 🔌 ◉ 🛏 🔌 ⛵ ✦ 🚲 🅳🅰🅵 SP ⛪

BRANSCOMBE
Devon
Map ref 1D2

Scattered village of unusual character. Houses of cob and thatch are sited irregularly on the steep wooded slopes of a combe, which widens towards the sea. Much of Branscombe Estate is National Trust property.

Three Horseshoes ⋀
⌂⌂
Branscombe, Seaton EX12 3BR
☎ (01297) 680251

Family-run inn with beams, brasses, log fires. Short distance from several seaside resorts. Beautiful countryside with excellent walks. Close to 4 golf-courses.
Bedrooms: 5 single, 5 double, 1 twin, 1 triple, 1 family room
Bathrooms: 5 private, 2 public
Bed & breakfast

per night:	£min	£max
Single	16.50	20.50
Double	33.00	41.00

Half board

per person:	£min	£max
Daily	24.00	28.00
Weekly	140.00	160.00

Lunch available
Evening meal 1800 (last orders 2200)
Parking for 102
Cards accepted: Access, Visa, Diners, Amex

⛺ ♨ 📞 ☐ ♦ ♋ ✗ ⋈ 📺 🛏 🔌 🅿 ⏱75 ☎ ⋃ 🅿 ✗ ☼ ✦ 🅳🅰🅵 🚲 SP Ⓣ

> The National Grading and Classification Scheme is explained in full at the back of this guide.

BRIDESTOWE

Devon
Map ref 1C2

Small Dartmoor village with a much restored 15th C church, and Great Links Tor rising to the south-east.

White Hart Inn

⚜ ⚜

Fore Street, Bridestowe, Okehampton EX20 4EL
☎ (01837) 86318
17th C inn, family-run for 34 years, primarily noted for good food. En-suite accommodation. Close to Dartmoor National Park, Lydford Gorge and fishing at Roadford Lake.
Bedrooms: 2 double
Bathrooms: 2 private

Bed & breakfast

per night:	£min	£max
Single	26.00	
Double	42.50	

Lunch available
Evening meal 1900 (last orders 2130)
Parking for 20
Cards accepted: Access, Visa, Diners, Amex

📇⌨ ♦ Ⓢ 🅜 ⏰ 🖨 ❋ ✕ 🚜

BRIDGWATER

Somerset
Map ref 1D1

Former medieval port on the River Parrett, now small industrial town with mostly 19th C or modern architecture. Georgian Castle Street leads to West Quay and site of 13th C castle razed to the ground by Cromwell. Birthplace of Cromwellian Admiral Robert Blake is now museum. Arts centre.

Cokerhurst Farm

⚜ ⚜ COMMENDED

87 Wembdon Hill, Bridgwater TA6 7QA
☎ (01278) 422330 & Mobile 0850 692065

105-acre arable farm. West of Bridgwater, off A39. Old farmhouse set in quiet countryside with peaceful garden overlooking the lake and farm.
Bedrooms: 1 twin, 2 triple
Bathrooms: 1 private, 1 public

Bed & breakfast

per night:	£min	£max
Single	17.00	22.50
Double	34.00	45.00

Parking for 9

📇⌨ ♦ 🅦 ✕ 🅜 ⏰ 🖨 ⤳ ❋ ✕ 🚜

Wembdon Farm

⚜ ⚜ HIGHLY COMMENDED

Hollow Lane, Wembdon, Bridgwater TA5 2BD
☎ (01278) 453097

380-acre arable & dairy farm. Enjoy bed and breakfast at this homely farmhouse. En-suite rooms with tea/coffee making facilities, lounge, dining room and lovely gardens. Convenient for Quantock, Mendip and Polden Hills, Somerset Levels and coast. Golf and fishing nearby. Non-smokers only, please.
Bedrooms: 2 double; suites available
Bathrooms: 2 private

Bed & breakfast

per night:	£min	£max
Single	19.50	
Double		39.00

Parking for 4

📇⌨ ♦ 🅦 ✕ 🅜 ⏰ 🖨 ❋ ✕ 🚜

Woodlands

⚜ ⚜ HIGHLY COMMENDED

35 Durleigh Road, Bridgwater TA6 7HX
☎ (01278) 423442
Beautiful listed house in 2 acres of landscaped gardens, in convenient location for exploring Quantocks and north Somerset coastline. Tranquillity and seclusion yet close to town centre, only 3 miles from junction 24 of M5. Country house hotel quality at B & B prices.
Bedrooms: 1 single, 2 double, 1 twin
Bathrooms: 4 private, 1 public

Bed & breakfast

per night:	£min	£max
Single	18.00	25.00
Double	37.00	40.00

Half board

per person:	£min	£max
Daily	28.00	38.00
Weekly	170.00	225.00

Evening meal 1830 (last orders 2000)
Parking for 4
Cards accepted: Access, Visa

📇 10 📇⌨ ♦ 🐾 🅦 Ⓢ 🅜 ⏰ 🖨 ❋ ✕ 🚜 SP 🏛

BRIDPORT

Dorset
Map ref 2A3

Market town and chief producer of nets and ropes just inland of dramatic Dorset coast. Old, broad streets built for drying and twisting, long gardens for rope-walks. Grand arcaded Town Hall and Georgian buildings. Local history museum has Roman relics.
Tourist Information Centre
☎ (01308) 424901

Britmead House ⚔

⚜ ⚜ HIGHLY COMMENDED

West Bay Road, Bridport DT6 4EG
☎ (01308) 422941

Elegant, spacious, tastefully decorated house. Lounge and dining room overlooking garden. West Bay Harbour/Coastal Path, 10 minutes' walk away. Renowned for hospitality, delicious meals and comfort.
Bedrooms: 4 double, 3 twin
Bathrooms: 7 private

Bed & breakfast

per night:	£min	£max
Single	24.00	34.00
Double	38.00	54.00

Half board

per person:	£min	£max
Daily	31.00	39.00
Weekly	189.00	224.00

Evening meal 1900 (last orders 1700)
Parking for 8
Cards accepted: Access, Visa, Diners, Amex

📇 ♿ 📇⌨ ♦ 🐾 î Ⓢ ✕ 🅜 ⏰ 🖨 ▶ ❋ 🚜 SP T

New House Farm

⚜

Mangerton Lane, Bradpole, Bridport DT6 3SF
☎ (01308) 422884
Modern, comfortable farmhouse set in rural Dorset hills.
Bedrooms: 1 family room
Bathrooms: 1 private

Bed & breakfast

per night:	£min	£max
Single	16.00	19.00
Double	32.00	38.00

Half board

per person:	£min	£max
Daily	20.00	26.00

Lunch available
Evening meal 1800 (last orders 2000)

Parking for 10
Open March-November
🛏🛒📻🖥📶🔌🅢📺🖩🖨🚗∪♪▶
❄🎣

Rudge Farm 🏔

★★★ HIGHLY COMMENDED

Chilcombe, Bridport DT6 4NF
☎ Long Bredy (01308) 482630
Fax (01308) 482635

108-acre livestock farm. Large
comfortable farmhouse 2 miles from the
sea, enjoying spectacular views over the
Bride Valley. Good home cooking using
fresh local produce.
Bedrooms: 2 double, 1 twin
Bathrooms: 3 private
Bed & breakfast

per night:	£min	£max
Single	20.00	
Double	40.00	

Half board

per person:	£min	£max
Daily	32.50	

Evening meal from 1930
Parking for 12
Open March-October
🛒🌸🍴🅢🖊🍽🖩🚗🎣❄✕🖨🎣📶

BRISTOL

Avon
Map ref 2A2

Famous for maritime links, historic
harbour, Georgian terraces and
Brunel's Clifton suspension bridge.
Many attractions including SS
Great Britain, Bristol Zoo,
museums and art galleries and top
name entertainments. Events
include Balloon Fiesta and
Regatta.
Tourist Information Centre
☎ (0117) 926 0767

The Bowl Inn and Restaurant 🏔

★★★ COMMENDED

16 Church Road, Lower Almondsbury,
Bristol BS12 4DT
☎ Almondsbury (01454) 612757
Fax (01454) 619910
*12th C building, once a priory, nestling
on the edge of the Severn Vale. 3
minutes from M4/M5 interchange.*
Bedrooms: 3 double, 5 twin
Bathrooms: 8 private
Bed & breakfast

per night:	£min	£max
Single	20.00	48.50
Double	39.00	68.50

Half board

per person:	£min	£max
Daily	32.50	58.00
Weekly	355.00	355.00

Lunch available
Evening meal 1830 (last orders 2200)
Parking for 40
Cards accepted: Access, Visa, Diners,
Amex, Switch/Delta
🛏4🍴🖭🌸🍴🅢🖩🚗🍴30❄✕
🎣 SP 🐾 T

Crown and Anchor

6 Hotwell Road, Clifton Wood, Bristol
BS8 4UD
☎ (0117) 929 0304
*Family-run, welcoming public house in
150-year-old building. View of "SS
Great Britain" on River Avon in Bristol
Harbour.*
Bedrooms: 1 single, 6 twin, 1 triple
Bathrooms: 4 private, 4 private
showers
Bed & breakfast

per night:	£min	£max
Single	15.00	25.00
Double	25.00	35.00

Evening meal 1700 (last orders 2100)
🛏🛒🌸📺◐🖩🚗🍺🎣

Westbury Park Hotel

★★ HIGHLY COMMENDED

37 Westbury Road, Bristol BS9 3AU
☎ (0117) 9620465
Fax (0117) 9628607
*Friendly family-run hotel on Durdham
Downs, close to city centre and M5,
junction 17.*
Bedrooms: 1 single, 5 double, 2 twin
Bathrooms: 8 private
Bed & breakfast

per night:	£min	£max
Single	27.50	38.00
Double	43.00	48.00

Parking for 5
Cards accepted: Access, Visa, Diners,
Amex
🛏🍴🌸🍴🖩🅢🍴📺🖩🚗🍴20❄
🎣 T

BRIXHAM

Devon
Map ref 1D2

Famous for its trawling fleet in the
19th C, a steeply-built fishing port
overlooking the harbour and fish
market. A statue of William of
Orange recalls his landing here
before deposing James II. There is
an aquarium and museum. Good
cliff views and walks.
Tourist Information Centre
☎ (01803) 852861

Richmond House Private Hotel 🏔

★★ COMMENDED

Higher Manor Road, Brixham
TQ5 8HA
☎ (01803) 882391

*Detached Victorian house with well-
appointed accommodation, sun trap
garden and adjacent car park. En-suite
available. Convenient for shops and
harbour, yet quiet location. First left
after Golden Lion.*
Bedrooms: 1 single, 3 double, 1 twin,
1 triple, 1 family room
Bathrooms: 5 private, 1 public
Bed & breakfast

per night:	£min	£max
Single	16.00	18.00
Double	32.00	40.00

Parking for 5
Cards accepted: Access, Visa
🛏🍴🌸🖭🍴🅢🖊🍴📺🖩▶❄🎣🐾T

BROAD CHALKE

Wiltshire
Map ref 2B3

Delightful River Ebble Valley
village with a 13th C church
displaying a notable porch and
central tower.

The Queens Head Inn

★★★

Broad Chalke, Salisbury SP5 5EN
☎ Salisbury (01722) 780344

*15th C building with stone walls and
old beams. Set in the beautiful Chalke
Valley, 8 miles from Salisbury.*
Bedrooms: 3 double, 1 twin
Bathrooms: 4 private
Bed & breakfast

per night:	£min	£max
Single	22.50	22.50
Double	45.00	45.00

Lunch available
Evening meal 1900 (last orders 2115)
Parking for 40
Cards accepted: Access, Visa
🛏8🍴🖭🛒🌸🍴🖊🖩🚗🍴30
❄🎣

BROAD HINTON

Wiltshire
Map ref 2B2

Village 4 miles north of Avebury
with its stone circle, museum and
manor house. Good centre for
walking and cycling, with easy
access to the Ridgeway National
Trail 2 miles north west.

Weir Farm 🏔

Listed COMMENDED

Broad Hinton, Swindon SN4 9NE
☎ Swindon (01793) 731207
Fax (01793) 731207

Continued ▶

BROAD HINTON

Continued

800-acre mixed farm. Attractive, comfortable period farmhouse on working farm with lovely views. On A361, 6 miles from Swindon and near the Ridgeway, Avebury and Marlborough.
Bedrooms: 1 double, 2 twin
Bathrooms: 1 public
Bed & breakfast

per night:	£min	£max
Single	20.00	24.00
Double	32.00	38.00

Parking for 4
Open January, March-December

🛇 8 💶 🖐 ⛄ 📺 🖩 ⬛ ⊙ ► ✿ ✕ 🐾 🏠

BROUGHTON GIFFORD

Wiltshire
Map ref 2B2

Frying Pan Farm

😕😕

Broughton Gifford, Melksham
SN12 8LL
☎ Melksham (01225) 702343
70-acre livestock farm. House believed to be former coaching inn (1560s). Ideally situated for visiting Bath, Bradford-on-Avon and Lacock, also numerous National Trust properties.
Bedrooms: 1 single, 1 double, 1 twin
Bathrooms: 1 private, 1 public
Bed & breakfast

per night:	£min	£max
Single	19.00	22.00
Double	34.00	37.00

Parking for 4
Open February-December

🖵 🖐 ⛄ ⛄ 🖩 ✿ ✕ 🐾 🏠

BUCKFASTLEIGH

Devon
Map ref 1C2

Small manufacturing and market town just south of Buckfast Abbey on the fringe of Dartmoor. Return trips can be taken by steam train on a reopened line along the beautiful Dart Valley.

Wellpark Farm

Listed | HIGHLY COMMENDED

Dean Prior, Buckfastleigh TQ11 0LY
☎ (01364) 643775
500-acre arable & dairy farm. Set on the edge of Dartmoor. A warm and friendly welcome. Very comfortable rooms with colour TV and tea/coffee facilities. Log fires, farmhouse breakfast, large enclosed garden. Golf and horse riding nearby. Excellent local 11th C inn.
Bedrooms: 1 double, 1 family room
Bathrooms: 1 public

Bed & breakfast

per night:	£min	£max
Single	10.00	15.00
Double	20.00	30.00

Parking for 3
Open March-October

🛇 🖐 💶 🖐 🖩 ⛄ 📺 🖩 ⬛ ⊙ ✿ ✕ 🐾 [SP]

BUCKLAND MONACHORUM

Devon
Map ref 1C2

Village just north of Buckland Abbey, home of Sir Francis Drake. Founded by Cistercians, the building is of unique interest through its conversion into a country home by Sir Richard Grenville. Now a museum of Drake and Grenville mementoes, including Drake's drum. Beautiful gardens.

Store Cottage

😕😕

19 The Village, Buckland Monachorum, Yelverton PL20 7NA
☎ Yelverton (01822) 853117 & Mobile 0850 193495

South-facing listed stone house in centre of village. Excellent meals at village pub. Unspoilt countryside at western edge of Dartmoor National Park.
Bedrooms: 1 double, 1 twin
Bathrooms: 2 private
Bed & breakfast

per night:	£min	£max
Single	18.00	18.00
Double	36.00	36.00

Parking for 2
Open March-October

🛇 12 💶 🖵 🖐 ⛄ 🖩 📱 ⛄ ✕ ⛄ 🖩 ⬛ ⊙ ✿ 🐾 🏠

The symbol 🏵 within an entry indicates participation in the Welcome Host programme – a nationally recognised customer care initiative which aims to promote the highest standards of service and a warm welcome for all visitors.

BUDE

Cornwall
Map ref 1C2

Resort on dramatic Atlantic coast. High cliffs give spectacular sea and inland views. Golf-course, cricket pitch, folly, surfing, coarse-fishing and boating. Mother-town Stratton was base of Royalist Sir Bevil Grenville.
Tourist Information Centre
☎ *(01288) 354240*

Clovelly House

😕😕 | COMMENDED

4 Burn View, Bude EX23 8BY
☎ (01288) 352761
In a level location, opposite golf club and close to all amenities. All rooms with tea/coffee facilities, satellite TV, some en-suite.
Bedrooms: 2 single, 2 double, 1 twin, 1 triple
Bathrooms: 3 private, 1 public
Bed & breakfast

per night:	£min	£max
Single	13.50	19.00
Double	28.00	39.00

Parking for 2

🛇 3 🖵 🖐 ⛄ 🖐 📺 🖩 ► ✕ 🐾 [OAP]

Court Farm

😕😕

Marhamchurch, Bude EX23 0EN
☎ (01288) 361494
Fax (01288) 361494
18-acre beef farm. Lovely old farmhouse in the centre of a quiet village with pub and shop. Close to Bude and various beaches. Ideal for touring Cornwall and Devon.
Bedrooms: 2 double, 2 triple, 1 family room
Bathrooms: 5 private
Bed & breakfast

per night:	£min	£max
Single	15.00	17.00
Double	30.00	34.00

Half board per person:	£min	£max
Daily	22.50	23.50
Weekly	145.00	150.00

Evening meal from 1830
Parking for 6

🛇 1 🖵 🖐 ⛄ [S] 🖐 📺 ⬛ 🔍 🔆 🔍 ✿ 🐾 [SP]

Lower Northcott Farm

😕😕 | COMMENDED

Poughill, Bude EX23 9EL
☎ (01288) 352350
Fax (01288) 352350
400-acre mixed farm. Georgian farmhouse in secluded grounds with children's safe play area. Visitors welcome to wander around and meet the animals.
Bedrooms: 1 single, 1 twin, 3 family rooms
Bathrooms: 4 private, 1 public

Bed & breakfast per night:	£min	£max
Single	17.00	
Double	34.00	

Half board per person:	£min	£max
Daily	25.00	
Weekly	155.00	

Evening meal 1830 (last orders 1830)
Parking for 4

☎️🖥️♨️🎇🛉🆂💺🕊️📺🏧◻️🛋️●☕♨️🚲🅾️🅿️❄️🏮

BURBAGE

Wiltshire
Map ref 2B2

Village close to Savernake Forest, famous as a habitat for deer. Close by are the remains of Wolf Hall mansion, where a great banquet in honour of Jane Seymour took place in 1536.

The Old Vicarage ♈

🎖️🎖️🎖️ HIGHLY COMMENDED

Burbage, Marlborough SN8 3AG
☎ Marlborough (01672) 810495
Fax (01672) 810663
Victorian country house in 2-acre garden, offering peace, comfort and delicious food. Within easy reach of Avebury, Bath, Oxford and Salisbury.
Bedrooms: 1 single, 1 double, 1 twin
Bathrooms: 3 private

Bed & breakfast per night:	£min	£max
Single	30.00	40.00
Double	60.00	80.00

Parking for 10
Cards accepted: Access, Visa, Amex

📞🖥️♨️🎇🆂💺🕊️📺🏧◻️🛋️◗🕊️❄️🏮

BURNHAM-ON-SEA

Somerset
Map ref 1D1

Small Victorian resort famous for sunsets and sandy beaches, a few minutes from junction 22 of the M5. Ideal base for touring Somerset, Cheddar and Bath. Good sporting facilities, championship golf-course.
Tourist Information Centre
☎ *(01278) 787852*

Priors Mead

🎖️🎖️

23 Rectory Road, Burnham-on-Sea TA8 2BZ
☎ (01278) 782116 & Mobile 0860 573018
Fax (01934) 822392
Friendly, quiet quiet Edwardian house with beautiful grounds, croquet and swimming pool. Large rooms either en-suite or with private facilities. Near championship golf-course and sea. Ideal touring centre.

Bedrooms: 2 double, 1 twin
Bathrooms: 3 private

Bed & breakfast per night:	£min	£max
Single	17.00	20.00
Double	30.00	32.00

Parking for 3

🖥️10◻️♨️🎇💺🕊️📺🏧◻️🛋️◗🕊️❄️🏮🆂🏮

BURTON BRADSTOCK

Dorset
Map ref 2A3

Lying amid fields beside the River Bride, a village of old stone houses, a 14th C church and a village green. The beautiful coast road from Abbotsbury to Bridport passes by and Iron Age forts top the surrounding hills. The sheltered river valley makes a staging post for migrating birds.

Bridge Cottage Stores

Listed COMMENDED

87 High Street, Burton Bradstock, Bridport DT6 4RA
☎ Bridport (01308) 897222
Self-contained en-suite accommodation in rooms above village shop and tea room. Close to beach, on Bridport to Weymouth road.
Bedrooms: 2 double, 1 twin
Bathrooms: 3 private

Bed & breakfast per night:	£min	£max
Single	14.15	24.50
Double	28.30	39.00

Lunch available
Parking for 8

🖥️5🆂🖥️♨️🕊️🆂⊙🏧◻️🛋️❄️🏮🆂🆂

CALLINGTON

Cornwall
Map ref 1C2

A quiet market town standing on high ground above the River Lynher. The 15th C church of St Mary's has an alabaster monument to Lord Willoughby de Broke, Henry VII's marshal. A 15th C chapel, 1 mile east, houses Dupath Well, one of the Cornish Holy Wells.

Dozmary ♈

🎖️ COMMENDED

Tors View Close, Tavistock Road, Callington PL17 7DY
☎ Liskeard (01579) 383677
Deceptively spacious dormer bungalow providing comfortable accommodation with good facilities, just a few minutes from Callington town centre.
Bedrooms: 1 double, 1 twin, 1 family room; suites available
Bathrooms: 3 private

Bed & breakfast per night:	£min	£max
Single	17.00	17.00
Double	30.00	30.00

Parking for 4
Open January-November

🖥️🛎️🆂🖥️♨️🎇🆂💺🕊️🏧◻️🛋️❄️🕊️🆂

CASTLE CARY

Somerset
Map ref 2B2

One of south Somerset's most attractive market towns, with a picturesque winding high street of golden stone and thatch, markethouse and famous round 18th C lock-up.

George Hotel ♈

🎖️🎖️ COMMENDED

Market Place, Castle Cary BA7 7AH
☎ (01963) 350761

15th C thatched coaching inn with en-suite rooms, 2 bars and noted restaurant. Centrally located for many National Trust houses and gardens, Cheddar, Wells, Glastonbury and Bath.
Bedrooms: 4 single, 7 double, 3 twin, 1 family room
Bathrooms: 15 private

Bed & breakfast per night:	£min	£max
Single	37.00	45.00
Double	65.00	70.00

Half board per person:	£min	£max
Daily	48.50	53.50

Lunch available
Evening meal 1900 (last orders 2100)
Parking for 10
Cards accepted: Access, Visa, Amex, Switch/Delta

🖥️🛎️📞🖥️🖥️♨️🛎️🆂💺🕊️🏧◻️🛋️🎇20🕊️🕊️🏮🆂🏮🆃

There are separate sections in this guide listing groups specialising in farm holidays and accommodation which is especially suitable for young people and organised groups.

CASTLE COMBE

Wiltshire
Map ref 2B2

One of England's prettiest villages, in a steep woodland valley by a brook. The Perpendicular church recalls the village's prosperous times as a cloth-weaving centre. No trace remains of the castle, but the 13th C effigy of its founder Walter de Dunstanville lies in the church.

Goulters Mill Farm

[Listed]

Goulters Mill, Nettleton, Chippenham SN14 7LL
☎ (01249) 782555

Secluded 17th C mill cottage in garden and woodland open to public. On B4039 2 miles west of Castle Combe down track opposite turning to Littleton Drew.
Bedrooms: 1 single, 1 double, 1 triple
Bathrooms: 2 private, 1 public

Bed & breakfast per night:	£min	£max
Single	15.00	25.00
Double	30.00	50.00

Half board per person:	£min	£max
Daily	25.00	35.00
Weekly	95.00	165.00

Evening meal 1830 (last orders 2000)
Parking for 4
Open February-October
🐴 📻 ☕ [UL] 🔒 [S] 🪑 [TV] 🔥 🚗 ⛳ ✿ ✈ 🚌 [SP] 🏠

CHAGFORD

Devon
Map ref 1C2

Handsome stone houses, some from the Middle Ages, grace this former stannary town on northern Dartmoor. It is a popular centre for walking expeditions and for tours of the antiquities on the rugged moor. There is a splendid 15th C granite church, said to be haunted by the poet Godolphin.

St. Johns West

[👑👑]

Murchington, Chagford, Newton Abbot TQ13 8HJ
☎ (01647) 432468
Splendid country house within Dartmoor National Park, 1.5 miles north-west of Chagford. Walkers welcome. Sorry - non-smoking throughout. Brochure with pleasure.
Bedrooms: 1 double, 1 twin, 1 family room
Bathrooms: 3 private, 1 public

Bed & breakfast per night:	£min	£max
Single	16.00	
Double	40.00	44.00

Evening meal 1800 (last orders 2000)
Parking for 6
Open April-October
🐴 ☎ 📺 ☕ [UL] 🔒 [S] 🚭 🪑 [TV] 🔥 🚗 U ⛳ ✿ ✈ 🚌 🏠

Throwleigh Manor 🏔

[👑👑]

Throwleigh, Near Chagford, Okehampton EX20 2JF
☎ Whiddon (01647) 231630
Beautiful country house set in 12 acres in lovely countryside within Dartmoor National Park. Tasteful decor and excellent breakfasts. Swimming pool, games room, private lake.
Bedrooms: 1 single, 1 double, 1 triple; suite available
Bathrooms: 3 private, 3 public

Bed & breakfast per night:	£min	£max
Single	15.50	19.00
Double	31.00	38.00

Parking for 10
🐴 ☕ [UL] 🚭 🪑 [TV] 🔥 🚗 🎱 🎣 U ⛳ ✿ ✈ 🚌 [SP] 🏠

CHARD

Somerset
Map ref 1D2

Market town in hilly countryside. The wide main street has some handsome buildings, among them the Guildhall, court house and almshouses. Modern light industry and dairy produce have replaced 19th C lace making which came at decline of cloth trade.
Tourist Information Centre
☎ *(01460) 67463*

Wambrook Farm

[Listed]

Wambrook, Chard TA20 3DF
☎ (01460) 62371
300-acre mixed farm. Attractive listed farmhouse 2 miles from Chard in beautiful rural village. Children welcome. From Chard take A30 towards Honiton, follow signs.
Bedrooms: 1 double, 1 triple
Bathrooms: 1 private, 1 public

Bed & breakfast per night:	£min	£max
Single	18.00	22.00
Double	28.00	34.00

Parking for 8
Open April-November
Cards accepted: Visa
🐴 ☕ [UL] [S] 🪑 [TV] 🔥 🚗 ✿ ✈ 🚌 🏠

CHARMINSTER

Dorset
Map ref 2B3

Three Compasses Inn

Charminster, Dorchester DT2 9QT
☎ Dorchester (01305) 263618

Traditional village public house/inn with skittle alley, set in village square.
Bedrooms: 1 single, 1 double, 1 twin, 1 triple
Bathrooms: 2 private, 1 public

Bed & breakfast per night:	£min	£max
Single	15.00	17.50
Double	30.00	35.00

Lunch available
Evening meal 1900 (last orders 2200)
Parking for 50
🐴 📺 ☕ 🔒 🪑 [TV] 🔥 🚗 T15 🚌 🐕

CHEDDAR

Somerset
Map ref 1D1

Large village at foot of Mendips just south of the spectacular Cheddar Gorge. Close by are Roman and Saxon sites and famous show caves. Traditional Cheddar cheese is still made here.

Clementine

[👑👑]

Station Road, Cheddar BS27 3AH
☎ (01934) 743651
Very interesting home and garden. Easy walk to Gorge and pubs, satisfaction assured. So before you're lost and gone forever come and stay at Clementine.
Bedrooms: 1 double, 1 twin, 1 family room
Bathrooms: 3 private

Bed & breakfast per night:	£min	£max
Double	26.00	31.00

Parking for 5
Open April-September
🐴 ♿ ☎ 📺 ☕ [UL] 🚭 [TV] 🔥 ✿ 🚌

Constantine

[Listed] [COMMENDED]

Lower New Road, Cheddar BS27 3DY
☎ (01934) 742732
Very friendly family home, close to village and Gorge, with beautiful views. Large garden available to guests. Children welcome. Private sitting room.
Bedrooms: 1 single, 1 double, 1 triple
Bathrooms: 1 public, 1 private shower

Bed & breakfast per night:	£min	£max
Single	14.50	14.50
Double	29.00	29.00

Parking for 6

Tor Farm

HIGHLY COMMENDED

Nyland, Cheddar BS27 3UD
(01934) 743710

33-acre mixed farm. On A371 between Cheddar and Draycott (take the road signposted Nyland). Quiet and peaceful on Somerset Levels. Ideally situated for visiting Cheddar, Bath, Wookey Hole, Glastonbury, Wells and coast.

Bedrooms: 1 single, 5 double, 1 twin, 1 family room
Bathrooms: 5 private, 2 public

Bed & breakfast per night:	£min	£max
Single	19.00	27.00
Double	33.00	46.00

Evening meal 1900 (last orders 1800)
Parking for 10
Cards accepted: Access, Visa

CHEW MAGNA

Avon
Map ref 2A2

Prosperous redstone village in the Mendip Hills with fine houses, cottages and inns of varying periods. High Street rises between railed, raised pavements from a part-Norman church with lofty 15th C tower.

Valley Farm

HIGHLY COMMENDED

Sandy Lane, Stanton Drew, Bristol BS18 4EL
Pill (01275) 332723

64-acre beef farm. New farmhouse in old village with Druid stones. Quiet location, central for Bath, Wells, Cheddar. TV and tea/coffee facilities in bedrooms. TV lounge.

Bedrooms: 3 double
Bathrooms: 3 private, 1 public

Bed & breakfast per night:	£min	£max
Single	16.00	21.00
Double	32.00	36.00

Parking for 4

All accommodation in this guide has been graded, or is awaiting a grading, by a trained Tourist Board inspector.

CHICKERELL

Dorset
Map ref 2B3

8 miles south-west of Dorchester and close to the famous Chesil Beach, the popular resort of Weymouth and the Isle of Portland.

Stonebank

HIGHLY COMMENDED

14 West Street, Chickerell, Weymouth DT3 4DY
Weymouth (01305) 760120
Fax (01305) 760871

Charming 17th C former farmhouse, close to coastal path and Chesil Beach. Ideal for exploring the Dorset coast and countryside. Self-catering unit also available.

Bedrooms: 2 double
Bathrooms: 2 private

Bed & breakfast per night:	£min	£max
Double	35.00	40.00

Parking for 2
Open April-September

CHIDEOCK

Dorset
Map ref 1D2

Village of sandstone thatched cottages in a valley near the dramatic Dorset coast. The church holds an interesting processional cross in mother-of-pearl and the manor house close by is associated with the Victorian Roman Catholic church. Seatown has a pebble beach and limestone cliffs.

Park Farmhouse Bed and Breakfast

Park Farmhouse, Main Street, Chideock, Bridport DT6 6JD
Bridport (01297) 489157

Built around 1750, Grade II listed, partly thatched, former farmhouse and converted creamery in a conservation area. Resident Cordon Bleu cook!

Bedrooms: 1 single, 5 double, 1 twin, 1 triple
Bathrooms: 5 private, 1 public

Bed & breakfast per night:	£min	£max
Single	16.50	20.00
Double	33.00	45.00

Half board per person:	£min	£max
Daily	26.50	37.50
Weekly	171.50	248.50

Evening meal 1930 (last orders 2030)
Parking for 14
Cards accepted: Access, Visa, Switch/Delta

CHIPPENHAM

Wiltshire
Map ref 2B2

Ancient market town with modern industry. Notable early buildings include the medieval Town Hall and the gabled 15th C Yelde Hall, now a local history museum. On the outskirts Hardenhuish has a charming hilltop church by the Georgian architect John Wood of Bath.
Tourist Information Centre
(01249) 657733

Frogwell House

132 Hungerdown Lane, Chippenham SN14 0BD
(01249) 650328
Fax (01249) 650328

An imposing late 19th C house built of local stone, modernised to provide comfortable and appealing accommodation.

Bedrooms: 1 single, 1 double, 2 twin
Bathrooms: 4 private

Bed & breakfast per night:	£min	£max
Single	15.00	22.00
Double	30.00	40.00

Half board per person:	£min	£max
Daily	21.00	28.00

Evening meal from 1800
Parking for 6

75 Rowden Hill

Chippenham SN15 2AL
(01249) 652981

Near National Trust village of Lacock and attractive Castle Combe. Corsham Court also nearby. Friendly welcome assured.

Bedrooms: 2 double, 1 twin
Bathrooms: 1 public

Bed & breakfast per night:	£min	£max
Single	15.00	
Double	25.00	

Parking for 5
Open April-October

CHIPPENHAM

Continued

Stanton Court

Stanton St.Quintin, Chippenham
SN14 6DQ
☎ Malmesbury (01666) 837007 &
837210
Fax (01666) 837775

Set in delightful gardens and woodland, yet just off the M4 (junction 17) 4 miles north of Chippenham. A warm welcome awaits at this elegant country home.
Bedrooms: 2 double, 1 twin
Bathrooms: 3 private

Bed & breakfast

per night:	£min	£max
Single	18.00	22.00
Double	36.00	44.00

Half board

per person:	£min	£max
Daily	23.00	32.00

Evening meal 1800 (last orders 2000)
Parking for 6

🏠🛁📧☐♦♞🏧ⓢ🅿📺▥🛏⇦🗴U
❀✕🚗🏥

CHULMLEIGH

Devon
Map ref 1C2

Small, hilly town above the Little Dart River, long since by-passed by the main road. The large 15th C church is noted for its splendid rood screen and 38 carved wooden angels on the roof.

The Old Bakehouse 🔼

🏵🏵 HIGHLY COMMENDED

South Molton Street, Chulmleigh
EX18 7BW
☎ (01769) 580074

16th C merchant's house with licensed restaurant. En-suite bedrooms in converted bakehouse. Situated in beautiful Taw Valley between Dartmoor and Exmoor. Cosy wood burning stoves, unique atmosphere. Ideal centre for touring Devon.
Bedrooms: 1 double, 2 twin
Bathrooms: 3 private

Bed & breakfast

per night:	£min	£max
Single	17.00	22.00
Double	30.00	40.00

Half board

per person:	£min	£max
Daily	26.50	33.50
Weekly	185.50	234.50

Lunch available
Evening meal 1930 (last orders 2100)

🏠🛁5♨📧☐♦♞🏧ⓢ⤢🅿▥⇦U🗴
❀✕🚗🆂🅿🏥Ⓣ

CLEVEDON

Avon
Map ref 1D1

Handsome Victorian resort on shingly shores of Severn Estuary. Pier, golf links with ruined folly, part-Norman clifftop church. Tennyson and Thackeray stayed at nearby Clevedon Court just to the east. Medieval with later additions, the manor overlooks terraces with rare plants.

Apple Trees

Listed

161 Old Church Road, Clevedon
BS21 7UB
☎ (01275) 872919
Lovely Victorian house. Excellent beds, beautiful lounge, home-made bread and marmalade. Quiet location, warm welcome, backing on to headland, lovely walks.
Bedrooms: 1 double, 1 triple
Bathrooms: 1 public

Bed & breakfast

per night:	£min	£max
Single	12.00	20.00
Double	28.00	30.00

Parking for 3

🏠♦▥ⓢ⤢🅿📺▥⇦🚗

CLOVELLY

Devon
Map ref 1C1

Clinging to wooded cliffs, fishing village with steep cobbled street zigzagging, or cut in steps, to harbour. Carrying sledges stand beside whitewashed flower-decked cottages. Charles Kingsley's father was rector of the church set high up near the Hamlyn family's Clovelly Court.

Fuchsia Cottage

Listed COMMENDED

Burscott, Clovelly, Bideford EX39 5RR
☎ (01237) 431398
Private house with comfortable ground and first floor en-suite accommodation. Surrounded by beautiful views of sea and country. Evening meal by arrangement.
Bedrooms: 1 single, 1 double, 1 triple
Bathrooms: 2 private, 1 public

Bed & breakfast

per night:	£min	£max
Single		13.00
Double		30.00

Half board

per person:	£min	£max
Daily		21.00
Weekly		147.00

Evening meal from 1830
Parking for 3
Open April-October

🏠🛁☐♦▥ⓢ⤢📺▥⇦🚗

COLYTON

Devon
Map ref 1D2

Surrounded by fertile farmland, this small riverside town was an early Saxon settlement. Medieval prosperity from the wool trade built the grand church tower with its octagonal lantern and the church's fine west window.

Smallicombe Farm

🏵🏵 COMMENDED

Northleigh, Colyton EX13 6BU
☎ Wilmington (01404) 831310
17-acre mixed farm. Relax watching cows and sheep graze in glorious rural setting. Meet our prize-winning rare breed pigs. Convenient for coast from Lyme Regis to Sidmouth.
Bedrooms: 1 double, 1 family room; suite available
Bathrooms: 2 private

Bed & breakfast

per night:	£min	£max
Single	17.50	19.50
Double	35.00	39.00

Half board

per person:	£min	£max
Daily	26.50	28.50

Evening meal (last orders 1600)
Parking for 10

🏠🛁📧☐♦♞▥ⓢ🅿📺▥⇦🔍
U🗴❀✕🚫🆂🅿🏥

CORSHAM

Wiltshire
Map ref 2B2

Growing town with old centre showing Flemish influence, legacy of former prosperity from weaving. The church, restored last century, retains Norman features. The Elizabethan Corsham Court, with additions by Capability Brown, has fine furniture.

Halfway Firs

Listed

5 Halfway Firs, Corsham SN13 0PJ
☎ Bath (01225) 810552
Situated 7 miles from Bath on A4, 5 miles from Chippenham and 1 mile from Corsham, overlooking open farmland.

Bedrooms: 1 single, 1 double, 1 triple
Bathrooms: 1 public

Bed & breakfast

per night:	£min	£max
Single	15.00	16.00
Double	26.00	30.00

Parking for 4

⟲ 8 ♨ ⬆ ⬜ ⌁ 📺 ⊞ ✿ ✕ ⇄

CRACKINGTON HAVEN

Cornwall
Map ref 1C2

Tiny village on the North Cornwall coast, with a small sandy beach and surf bathing. The highest cliffs in Cornwall lie to the south.

Coombe Barton Inn

⚇⚇⚇

Crackington Haven, Bude EX23 0JG
☎ St. Gennys (01840) 230345
Fax (01840) 230788
Warm and friendly inn beside the beach, serving good food, local ales and fine wines and offering comfortable accommodation.
Bedrooms: 1 single, 2 double, 1 twin, 1 family room
Bathrooms: 3 private, 2 public

Bed & breakfast

per night:	£min	£max
Single	16.50	19.50
Double	38.00	55.00

Lunch available
Evening meal 1800 (last orders 2200)
Parking for 40
Open March-October
Cards accepted: Access, Visa, Diners, Amex, Switch/Delta

⟲ ⬇ ⓘ S 🏵 📺 ⊞ ⌁ ⛵ ♦ ⚘ ∪ ⟆ ⇄ ⊞

Tregather

Listed COMMENDED

Crackington Haven, Bude EX23 0LQ
☎ St Gennys (01840) 230667

500-acre dairy farm. Tastefully furnished home offering peace and comfort situated on north Cornish coastal farm. Dramatic cliffs and two sandy beaches within walking distance.
Bedrooms: 2 double, 1 twin
Bathrooms: 1 private, 1 public

Bed & breakfast

per night:	£min	£max
Single	15.00	20.00
Double	28.00	36.00

Parking for 3
Open March-November

⟲ ⚒ ♨ ⬜ ⓘ S 🏵 📺 ⊞ ✿ ✕ ⇄

CREDITON

Devon
Map ref 1D2

Ancient town in fertile valley, once prosperous from wool, now active in cider-making. Said to be the birthplace of St Boniface. The 13th C Chapter House, the church governors' meeting place, holds a collection of armour from the Civil War.

Birchmans Farm

⚇⚇ COMMENDED

Colebrooke, Crediton EX17 5AD
☎ Bow (01363) 82393
200-acre mixed farm. In the centre of Devon within easy reach of Exeter and Dartmoor. Home produce. All rooms en-suite with tea and coffee-making facilities.
Bedrooms: 2 double, 1 twin
Bathrooms: 3 private

Bed & breakfast

per night:	£min	£max
Single	14.00	15.00
Double	28.00	30.00

Half board

per person:	£min	£max
Daily	21.00	21.00

Evening meal (last orders 1830)
Parking for 6

⟲ ⛌ ◻ ♦ ⚘ ⬜ ⓘ ✕ 🏵 📺 ⊞ ⌁ ⛵ ✿ ✕ ⇄ SP

CREWKERNE

Somerset
Map ref 1D2

This charming little market town on the Dorset border nestles in undulating farmland and orchards in a conservation area. Built of local sandstone with Roman and Saxon origins. The magnificent St Bartholomew's Church dates from 15th C; St Bartholomew's Fair is held in September.

Broadview ⋀

⚇⚇⚇ DE LUXE

43 East Street, Crewkerne TA18 7AG
☎ (01460) 73424
Friendly, informal atmosphere. Extremely comfortable and relaxing in an unusual Colonial ambience. Set in an acre of secluded feature gardens. Quality traditional English home cooking. Truly perfect touring base.
Bedrooms: 1 double, 2 twin
Bathrooms: 3 private

Bed & breakfast

per night:	£min	£max
Single		35.00
Double	46.00	50.00

Half board

per person:	£min	£max
Daily	35.00	37.00
Weekly	245.00	259.00

Evening meal 1830 (last orders 1200)
Parking for 6

⟲ ♨ ◻ ⬜ ♦ ⚘ ⬜ ✕ 🏵 ⊞ ⌁ ⛵ ✿ ⇄
✕ ⊞

CROYDE

Devon
Map ref 1C1

Pretty village with thatched cottages near Croyde Bay. To the south stretch Saunton Sands and their dunelands Braunton Burrows with interesting flowers and plants, nature reserve and golf-course. Cliff walks and bird-watching at Baggy Point, west of the village.

Combas Farm

Listed COMMENDED

Putsborough, Croyde, Braunton EX33 1PH
☎ (01271) 890398
140-acre mixed farm. Old world 16th C farmhouse, in secluded situation only three-quarters of a mile from Woolacombe Bay "Blue Flag" beach. Home cooking using own produce.
Bedrooms: 1 single, 2 double, 1 twin, 1 triple, 1 family room
Bathrooms: 2 public

Bed & breakfast

per night:	£min	£max
Single	15.50	18.50
Double	31.00	37.00

Half board

per person:	£min	£max
Daily	23.50	26.50
Weekly	148.00	166.50

Evening meal 1830 (last orders 1630)
Parking for 10
Open March-November

⟲ ♨ ⚘ ⬜ S 🏵 📺 ⌁ ∪ ⟆ ⚘ ✕
⇄ OAP SP ⌂ ⊞

Denham Farm and Country House ⋀

⚇⚇ COMMENDED

North Buckland, Braunton EX33 1HY
☎ (01271) 890297
Fax (01271) 890297

160-acre mixed farm. Sample home cooking in this delightful country house, a "little gem" off the beaten track. Enjoy peace and tranquillity amid beautiful unspoilt countryside, near miles of golden sands.
Bedrooms: 6 double, 1 twin, 1 triple, 2 family rooms
Bathrooms: 10 private, 1 public
Continued ▶

CROYDE

Continued

Bed & breakfast

per night:	£min	£max
Double	46.00	50.00

Half board

per person:	£min	£max
Daily	35.00	37.00
Weekly	198.00	220.00

Evening meal 1900 (last orders 1900)
Parking for 8
Cards accepted: Access, Visa
☎🏠🖵🖤🖳ⓢ⅄🖳ⓣⓥ🖳▥,🛋🏮❀🗙
🐴 ⓄⒶⓅ ↘ ⒮Ⓟ

Fig Tree Farmhouse
Listed COMMENDED

St Mary's Road, Croyde, Braunton
EX33 1PJ
☎ (01271) 890204
Fax (01271) 890204
*400-year-old thatched Devon longhouse,
fully restored yet retaining charm and
character. On the edge of Croyde
village.*
Bedrooms: 2 double, 1 triple
Bathrooms: 1 private, 1 public

Bed & breakfast

per night:	£min	£max
Single	16.00	20.00

Parking for 6
Cards accepted: Access, Visa
☎ ▥ 🖤⅄🖳ⓣⓥ🛋🏮❀🐴 ⓄⒶⓅ 🎏

CULLOMPTON

Devon
Map ref 1D2

Market town on former coaching
routes, with pleasant tree-shaded
cobbled pavements and some
handsome 17th C houses. Earlier
prosperity from the wool industry is
reflected in the grandness of the
church with its fan-vaulted aisle
built by a wool-stapler in 1526.

Weir Mill Farm
HIGHLY COMMENDED

Jaycroft, Willand, Cullompton
EX15 2RE
☎ Tiverton (01884) 820803
Fax (01884) 820973

*105-acre livestock farm. Farmhouse
accommodation in the beautiful Culm
Valley. Only 3 miles from junction 27 of
M5, giving easy access to coast, moors
and National Trust properties.*
Bedrooms: 2 double, 1 family room
Bathrooms: 1 private, 1 public

Bed & breakfast

per night:	£min	£max
Single	18.00	20.00
Double	32.00	36.00

Half board

per person:	£min	£max
Daily	26.00	28.00
Weekly	167.00	180.00

Evening meal 1830 (last orders 0900)
Parking for 5
☎🖵🖤🖳🖳⅄🖳ⓣⓥ▥,❀🗙🐴

DARTMOOR

*See under Ashburton, Bickington,
Bovey Tracey, Bridestowe,
Buckfastleigh, Buckland
Monachorum, Chagford, Dousland,
Dunsford, Holne, Lustleigh,
Moretonhampstead, Okehampton,
Peter Tavy, Tavistock,
Widecombe-in-the-Moor, Yelverton*

DARTMOUTH

Devon
Map ref 1D3

Ancient port at mouth of Dart. Has
fine period buildings, notably town
houses near Quay and Butterwalk
of 1635. Harbour castle ruin. In
12th C Crusader fleets assembled
here. Royal Naval College
dominates from Hill. Carnival,
June; Regatta, August.
Tourist Information Centre
☎ *(01803) 834224*

Boringdon House
HIGHLY COMMENDED

1 Church Road, Dartmouth TQ6 9HQ
☎ (01803) 832235
*Welcoming Georgian house in large
secluded garden overlooking Dartmouth
town and harbour. Spacious attractive
rooms. Courtyard parking. Short walk
to town centre. No smoking please.*
Bedrooms: 1 double, 2 twin
Bathrooms: 3 private

Bed & breakfast

per night:	£min	£max
Single	39.00	45.00
Double	45.00	55.00

Parking for 3
Open March-December
🖵🖵🖤▥⅄▥,🛋🏮❀🗙🐴🎏ⓣ

Royal Castle Hotel Ⓜ
HIGHLY COMMENDED

11 The Quay, Dartmouth TQ6 9PS
☎ Torbay (01803) 833033
Fax (01803) 835445

Historic 17th C quayside coaching inn,
famous for traditional-style food and
service. Antiques, open fires, character
bars and restaurant, delightful
accommodation.
Bedrooms: 4 single, 10 double, 7 twin,
4 triple
Bathrooms: 25 private

Bed & breakfast

per night:	£min	£max
Single	45.00	59.00
Double	76.00	100.00

Half board

per person:	£min	£max
Daily	45.00	69.00
Weekly	270.00	370.00

Lunch available
Evening meal 1845 (last orders 2200)
Parking for 4
Cards accepted: Access, Visa, Switch/
Delta
☎🖅📞🖵🖤🖳ⓢ🖳Ⓞ▥,🛋
🍴70 Ⓤ🏮🐴↘ⓈⓅ🎏ⓣ◉

DEVIZES

Wiltshire
Map ref 2B2

Old market town standing on the
Kennet and Avon Canal. Rebuilt
Norman castle, good 18th C
buildings. St John's church has
12th C work and Norman tower.
Museum of Wiltshire's archaeology
and natural history reflects wealth
of prehistoric sites in the county.
Tourist Information Centre
☎ *(01380) 729408*

Pinecroft
♨♨

Potterne Road (A360), Devizes
SN10 5DA
☎ (01380) 721433
Fax (01380) 728368
*Comfortable Georgian family house with
spacious rooms, exquisite garden and
private parking. Only 3 minutes' walk
from town centre.*
Bedrooms: 2 double, 2 twin, 1 family
room; suite available
Bathrooms: 5 private

Bed & breakfast

per night:	£min	£max
Single	20.00	25.00
Double	32.00	40.00

Parking for 7
Cards accepted: Access, Visa, Amex
☎🏠🖵🖤▥🖳ⓢ⅄Ⓞ▥,🛋🍴8Ⓤ🏮
❀🗙ⓄⒶⓅ↘ⓈⓅ🎏ⓣ

Individual proprietors
have supplied all details of
accommodation. As changes
can occur, we advise you to
confirm the information at
the time of booking.

DODDISCOMBSLEIGH

Devon
Map ref 1D2

Riverside village amid hilly countryside just east of Dartmoor. Former manor house stands beside granite church. Spared from the Roundheads by its remoteness, the church's chief interest lies in glowing 15th C windows said to contain Devon's finest collection of medieval glass.

Great Leigh Farm & Guesthouse

Doddiscombsleigh, Exeter EX6 7RF
☎ Christow (01647) 252058 & 253008
Fax (01647) 252058

180-acre livestock farm. Secluded farmhouse and converted barns, traditionally furnished. Beams in bedrooms, inglenook fireplace and beams in dining room. Snooker room. Fishing on River Teign.
Bedrooms: 3 double, 1 twin
Bathrooms: 4 private
Bed & breakfast

per night:	£min	£max
Single	24.00	34.50
Double	45.00	60.00

Half board

per person:	£min	£max
Daily	42.50	54.50
Weekly	270.00	381.50

Lunch available
Evening meal 1930 (last orders 2100)
Parking for 10
Cards accepted: Access, Visa, Switch/Delta

Whitemoor Farm

APPROVED
Doddiscombsleigh, Exeter EX6 7PU
☎ Christow (01647) 252423

284-acre mixed farm. Homely 16th C thatched farmhouse, surrounded by garden and own farmland. Within easy reach of Dartmoor, the coast, Exeter, forest walks, birdwatching and Haldon Racecourse. Evening meal on request

with good local inn nearby. Swimming pool available.
Bedrooms: 2 single, 1 double, 1 twin
Bathrooms: 1 public
Bed & breakfast

per night:	£min	£max
Single	16.50	17.50
Double	33.00	35.00

Half board

per person:	£min	£max
Daily	41.00	43.00
Weekly	246.00	258.00

Evening meal 1900 (last orders 2000)
Parking for 5
Cards accepted: Visa

DORCHESTER

Dorset
Map ref 2B3

Busy medieval county town destroyed by fires in 17th and 18th C. Cromwellian stronghold and scene of Judge Jeffrey's Bloody Assize after Monmouth Rebellion of 1685. Tolpuddle Martyrs were tried in Shire Hall. Museum has Roman and earlier exhibits and Hardy relics.
Tourist Information Centre
☎ (01305) 267992

Castleview

APPROVED
8 Edward Road, Dorchester DT1 2HJ
☎ (01305) 263507
Excellent base for touring beautiful Dorset, offering TV, washbasin with softened water and tea/coffee-making facilities in all rooms.
Bedrooms: 2 single, 1 double, 1 twin
Bathrooms: 2 private, 1 public
Bed & breakfast

per night:	£min	£max
Single	15.00	16.00
Double	34.00	36.00

Parking for 4

The Dower House

COMMENDED
Bradford Peverell, Dorchester DT2 9SF
☎ (01305) 266125
Comfortable Grade II listed house. Pleasant village setting, 3 miles Dorchester. Warm welcome. Guest sitting room. Home baking. Cotton sheets.
Bedrooms: 1 single, 1 double, 1 twin
Bathrooms: 3 private
Bed & breakfast

per night:	£min	£max
Single	16.50	18.00
Double	33.00	36.00

Parking for 3
Open March-October

Maumbury Cottage

Listed COMMENDED
9 Maumbury Road, Dorchester DT1 1QW
☎ (01305) 266726
Homely town centre Victorian house, convenient for all public transport. Dorset owner has intimate local knowledge.
Bedrooms: 1 single, 1 double, 1 twin
Bathrooms: 1 public
Bed & breakfast

per night:	£min	£max
Single	14.00	16.00
Double	30.00	32.00

Parking for 2

Mountain Ash ▲

APPROVED
30 Mountain Ash Road, Dorchester DT1 2PB
☎ (01305) 264811
Comfortable accommodation close to transport, Records Office and museums. Washbasins, TV, beverage facilities in bedrooms. Owner knowledgeable about Dorset.
Bedrooms: 1 single, 1 double, 1 twin
Bathrooms: 1 public
Bed & breakfast

per night:	£min	£max
Single	15.00	18.00
Double	30.00	36.00

Parking for 5

The Old Rectory

HIGHLY COMMENDED
Winterbourne Steepleton, Dorchester DT2 9LG
☎ Martinstown (01305) 889468
Fax (01305) 889468

Built 1850 - 8 miles from beaches, 6 miles from historic Dorchester. Surrounded by spectacular walks. Excellent local pubs. French spoken.
Bedrooms: 3 double, 1 triple, 2 family rooms
Bathrooms: 6 private
Bed & breakfast

per night:	£min	£max
Single	25.00	35.00
Double	27.00	80.00

Evening meal 1930 (last orders 2100)
Parking for 14

DOUSLAND

Devon
Map ref 1C2

Peek Hill Farm
COMMENDED
Dousland, Yelverton PL20 6PD
☎ Yelverton (01822) 852908

*300-acre livestock farm. Working farm
abutting Dartmoor. From Yelverton,
take Princetown road for 2 miles, farm
is 2nd on left after Dousland Garage.
Cycle hire from farm.*
Bedrooms: 1 double, 1 twin
Bathrooms: 2 private, 1 public
Bed & breakfast

per night:	£min	£max
Single	18.00	
Double	30.00	

Parking for 4
Open February-November

DULVERTON

Somerset
Map ref 1D1

Set among woods and hills of
south-west Exmoor, a busy
riverside town with a 13th C
church. The Rivers Barle and Exe
are rich in salmon and trout. The
information centre at the Exmoor
National Park Headquarters at
Dulverton is open throughout the
year.

Town Mills
HIGHLY COMMENDED
High Street, Dulverton TA22 9HB
☎ (01398) 323124
*Secluded 18th C millhouse in centre of
town. Spacious bedrooms, some with
log fires, providing bedsitting facilities
with breakfast served in rooms.*
Bedrooms: 4 double, 1 twin; suite
available
Bathrooms: 2 private, 1 public
Bed & breakfast

per night:	£min	£max
Single	17.00	32.00
Double	32.00	41.00

Parking for 5

Check the introduction to
this region for ideas on
Where to Go.

DUNSFORD

Devon
Map ref 1D2

Picturesque village of thatched
white walled cottages 4 miles
north-east of Moretonhampstead
and on the edge of the Dartmoor
National Park.

Royal Oak Inn ⋀
Listed **APPROVED**
Dunsford, Exeter EX6 7DA
☎ Christow (01647) 252256
Fax (01647) 252256
*Beautiful en-suite rooms in Victorian
country inn, in the heart of a charming
thatched village in the Teign Valley.
Always 6 real ales and unusual home-
made meals served 7 days a week.*
Bedrooms: 4 double, 2 twin, 2 triple
Bathrooms: 5 private, 1 public
Bed & breakfast

per night:	£min	£max
Single	18.00	25.00
Double	31.50	40.00

Lunch available
Evening meal 1830 (last orders 2100)
Parking for 40
Cards accepted: Access, Visa

DUNSTER

Somerset
Map ref 1D1

Ancient town with views of
Exmoor. The hilltop castle has
been continuously occupied since
1070. Medieval prosperity from
cloth built 16th C octagonal Yarn
Market and the church. A riverside
mill, packhorse bridge and 18th C
hilltop folly occupy other
interesting corners in the town.

Woodville House
Listed **COMMENDED**
25 West Street, Dunster, Minehead
TA24 6SN
☎ (01643) 821228
*Georgian house in the residential end
of the village. Warm welcome,
comfortable accommodation, good
breakfast, homely relaxing atmosphere
assured. Parking available in courtyard.*
Bedrooms: 1 single, 1 double, 1 twin
Bathrooms: 1 public
Bed & breakfast

per night:	£min	£max
Single	15.00	16.00
Double	34.00	38.00

Parking for 4
Open March-November

Please mention this guide
when making a booking.

EAST ALLINGTON

Devon
Map ref 1C3

Village 3 miles north-east of
Kingsbridge and within easy reach
of the South Devon coast.

Cuttery House
Listed
East Allington, Totnes TQ9 7QN
☎ (01548) 521259
*200-year-old farmhouse refurbished to a
high standard. In a charming rural
setting, offering a quiet comfortable
base from which to explore the beautiful
South Hams.*
Bedrooms: 1 single, 1 double, 1 twin,
1 triple
Bathrooms: 4 private
Bed & breakfast

per night:	£min	£max
Single	15.00	20.00
Double	30.00	40.00

Evening meal 1800 (last orders 2000)
Parking for 10

EXETER

Devon
Map ref 1D2

University city rebuilt after the
1940s around its cathedral.
Attractions include 13th C
cathedral with fine west front;
notable waterfront buildings;
Maritime Museum; Guildhall; Royal
Albert Memorial Museum;
underground passages; Northcott
Theatre.
*Tourist Information Centre
☎ (01392) 265700 or 437581
(Exeter Services)*

Clock Tower Hotel ⋀
16 New North Road, Exeter EX4 4HF
☎ (01392) 424545
Fax (01392) 218445
*Homely accommodation in the city
centre. Coach and railway stations
within 10 minutes' walk. All modern
facilities. En-suite rooms.*
Bedrooms: 4 single, 8 double, 2 twin,
1 triple, 1 family room
Bathrooms: 11 private, 2 public
Bed & breakfast

per night:	£min	£max
Single	15.00	16.50
Double	25.00	45.00

Half board

per person:	£min	£max
Daily	17.50	27.50
Weekly	112.00	171.50

Evening meal 1800 (last orders 1600)
Cards accepted: Access, Visa, Diners,
Amex

Culm Vale Country House
😑 😑

Stoke Canon, Exeter EX5 4EG
☎ (01392) 841615
Comfortable accommodation in beautiful old country house 4 miles north east of Exeter. Friendly relaxed atmosphere, lovely gardens, ample free parking. Ideal touring centre.
Bedrooms: 2 double, 1 twin
Bathrooms: 1 private, 1 public
Bed & breakfast

per night:	£min	£max
Single	15.00	17.50
Double	30.00	35.00

Half board

per person:	£min	£max
Daily	22.00	24.00
Weekly	140.00	160.00

Evening meal from 1830
Parking for 6
🐕 ⓦ ⓤ ⓝ ⓣⓥ �🖩 🔌 ⚱ ∪ ✿ ✗ 🚗 🏠 Ⓣ

Danson House
😑 😑 COMMENDED

Marsh Green, Exeter EX5 2ES
☎ Whimple (01404) 823260

Country house in grounds of 1.5 acres. Excellent en-suite accommodation. Rural location, 2 miles from A30 and with easy access from M5.
Bedrooms: 1 single, 1 double, 1 triple
Bathrooms: 3 private
Bed & breakfast

per night:	£min	£max
Single	17.00	19.00
Double	32.00	34.00

Half board

per person:	£min	£max
Weekly	150.00	165.00

Evening meal 1900 (last orders 2000)
Parking for 4
🐕 ⓤ ▯ ✤ ⓦ ⓤ ⓘ ✗ ⓣⓥ �🖩 🔌 ✿ ✗
🚗 SP

The Grange
😑 😑 COMMENDED

Stoke Hill, Exeter EX4 7JH
☎ (01392) 59723
Country house set in 3 acres of woodlands, 1.5 miles from the city centre. Ideal for holidays and off-season breaks. En-suite rooms available.
Bedrooms: 2 double, 1 twin
Bathrooms: 3 private
Bed & breakfast

per night:	£min	£max
Single	20.00	22.00
Double	30.00	37.00

Parking for 11
🐕 ▯ ✤ ⓤ ✗ ⓝ ⓣⓥ �🖩 🔌 ∪ ✿ ✗ 🚗
DAP SP

Hayne Barton
😑 😑 😑 COMMENDED

Whitestone, Exeter EX4 2JN
☎ Longdown (01392) 811268
16-acre mixed farm. Listed farmhouse dating from 1086 (Domesday Book), set in gardens, woodland and fields overlooking Alphinbrook Valley. 4 miles from Exeter Cathedral and convenient for Dartmoor and Torquay.
Bedrooms: 2 double, 1 twin
Bathrooms: 3 private
Bed & breakfast

per night:	£min	£max
Single	24.00	26.00
Double	40.00	44.00

Half board

per person:	£min	£max
Daily	32.00	34.00
Weekly	175.00	189.00

Evening meal 1930 (last orders 2030)
Parking for 10
🐕 ⓪ ▯ ✤ ⓤ ▯ Ⓢ ✗ ⓝ ⓣⓥ �🖩 🔌 ∪ ▶
✏ ✿ 🚗 DAP 🖉 SP 🏠

Rydon Farm
😑 😑 COMMENDED

Woodbury, Exeter EX5 1LB
☎ Woodbury (01395) 232341

280-acre dairy farm. 16th C Devon longhouse with exposed beams and inglenook fireplace. Spacious individually furnished and decorated rooms, one with romantic four-poster. En-suite facilities.
Bedrooms: 1 double, 1 twin, 1 triple
Bathrooms: 3 private
Bed & breakfast

per night:	£min	£max
Single	17.00	23.00
Double	34.00	46.00

Parking for 5
🐕 ⓪ ✤ ⓠ ⓤ Ⓢ ⓝ ⓣⓥ �🖩 🔌 ✿ 🚗 DAP
SP 🏠 Ⓣ

EXMOOR

See under Allerford, Brayford, Dulverton, Dunster, Lynmouth, Lynton, Parracombe, West Anstey, Winsford

National gradings and classifications were correct at the time of going to press but are subject to change. Please check at the time of booking.

EXMOUTH

Devon
Map ref 1D2

Developed as a seaside resort in George III's reign, set against the woods of the Exe Estuary and red cliffs of Orcombe Point. Extensive sands, small harbour, chapel and almshouses, a model railway and A la Ronde, a 16-sided house.
Tourist Information Centre
☎ (01395) 263744

The Mews
😑

Knappe Cross, Brixington Lane, Exmouth EX8 5DL
☎ (01395) 272198
Large part of a delightfully secluded mews building in a country setting. Midway between Exmouth and Woodbury Common. We ask that guests refrain from smoking.
Bedrooms: 1 single, 1 double, 1 twin
Bathrooms: 1 public
Bed & breakfast

per night:	£min	£max
Single	14.00	15.50
Double	28.00	31.00

Parking for 10
🐕 4 ⓤ ▯ Ⓢ ✗ ⓝ ⓣⓥ �🖩 ✿ ✗ 🚗

The Swallows
😑 😑 COMMENDED

11 Carlton Hill, Exmouth EX8 2AJ
☎ (01395) 263937
Attractive Georgian house only 300 yards from seafront, pleasantly converted to modern standards and providing comfortable guest accommodation.
Bedrooms: 1 single, 2 double, 2 twin, 1 family room
Bathrooms: 6 private
Bed & breakfast

per night:	£min	£max
Single	18.00	25.00
Double	34.00	40.00

Parking for 3
🐕 ▯ ✤ ⓤ Ⓢ ⓝ �🖩 🔌 ✿ ✗ 🚗 SP

FALMOUTH

Cornwall
Map ref 1B3

Busy port and fishing harbour, popular resort on the balmy Cornish Riviera. Henry VIII's Pendennis Castle faces St Mawes Castle across the broad natural harbour and yacht basin Carrick Roads, which receives 7 rivers.
Tourist Information Centre
☎ (01326) 312300

Ivanhoe Guest House ⚑
😑 😑 COMMENDED

7 Melvill Road, Falmouth TR11 4AS
☎ (01326) 319083

Continued ▶

FALMOUTH

Continued

Charming Edwardian town house situated minutes from the beaches and town centre. Most rooms are en-suite with colour TV and all amenities.
Bedrooms: 2 single, 2 double, 2 twin, 1 family room
Bathrooms: 4 private, 2 public, 1 private shower

Bed & breakfast

per night:	£min	£max
Single	13.00	18.00
Double	26.00	38.00

Parking for 4
Cards accepted: Access, Visa, Diners, Amex, Switch/Delta

FENNY BRIDGES

Devon
Map ref 1D2

Village on the River Otter, 2 miles north-east of Ottery St Mary.

Skinners Ash Farm
Listed COMMENDED

Fenny Bridges, Honiton EX14 0BH
☎ Honiton (01404) 850231
127-acre mixed farm. Traditional farmhouse offering cream teas to order and with rare animals and birds. Situated on A30, 3 miles from Honiton and close to local beaches.
Bedrooms: 1 twin, 1 family room
Bathrooms: 2 public

Bed & breakfast

per night:	£min	£max
Single		15.50
Double		31.00

Half board

per person:	£min	£max
Daily		22.50
Weekly		154.00

Lunch available
Evening meal 1900 (last orders 2100)
Parking for 7

FIGHELDEAN

Wiltshire
Map ref 2B2

Village on the River Avon, 4 miles north of Amesbury. Stonehenge 6 miles south west.

Vale House
Listed

Figheldean, Salisbury SP4 8JJ
☎ Stonehenge (01980) 670713
Secluded house in centre of picturesque village, 4 miles north of Amesbury on A345. Pub food nearby. Stonehenge 2 miles.
Bedrooms: 1 single, 2 twin

Bathrooms: 2 private, 1 public

Bed & breakfast

per night:	£min	£max
Single	14.00	16.00
Double	28.00	32.00

Parking for 3

FROME

Somerset
Map ref 2B2

Old market town with modern light industry, its medieval centre watered by the River Frome. Above Cheap Street with its flagstones and watercourse is the church showing work of varying periods. Interesting buildings include 18th C wool merchants' houses.
Tourist Information Centre
☎ *(01373) 467271*

Fourwinds Guest House
😋😋😋 COMMENDED

19 Bath Road, Frome BA11 2HJ
☎ (01373) 462618
Fax (01373) 453029
Chalet bungalow with some bedrooms on ground floor. TV and tea-making facilities. Licensed, good food.
Bedrooms: 1 single, 2 double, 2 twin, 1 family room
Bathrooms: 4 private, 2 public

Bed & breakfast

per night:	£min	£max
Single	20.00	30.00
Double	40.00	45.00

Half board

per person:	£min	£max
Daily		40.00
Weekly		245.00

Lunch available
Evening meal 1800 (last orders 1900)
Parking for 12
Cards accepted: Access, Visa

GLASTONBURY

Somerset
Map ref 2A2

Market town associated with Joseph of Arimathea and the birth of English Christianity. Built around its 7th C abbey said to be the site of King Arthur's burial. Glastonbury Tor with its ancient tower gives panoramic views over flat country and the Mendip Hills.
Tourist Information Centre
☎ *(01458) 832954*

Meadow Barn
😋😋

Middlewick Farm, Wick Lane, Glastonbury BA6 8JW
☎ (01458) 832351

20-acre beef farm. Idyllically situated amidst apple orchards and gardens, Meadow Barn has country-style ground-floor accommodation with indoor heated swimming pool. From Glastonbury take A361 Shepton Mallet road for 1.5 miles, take left turn signposted Wick, continue for 1.5 miles.
Bedrooms: 2 double, 1 twin
Bathrooms: 3 private

Bed & breakfast

per night:	£min	£max
Single	19.00	24.00
Double	34.00	36.00

Half board

per person:	£min	£max
Daily	27.00	34.00
Weekly	189.00	238.00

Evening meal 1900 (last orders 2030)
Parking for 20

Pippin
Listed APPROVED

4 Ridgeway Gardens, Glastonbury BA6 8ER
☎ (01458) 834262
Peaceful location within a short walk of town centre and the Tor. Superb views over Chalice Hill. Every comfort.
Bedrooms: 1 single, 1 double, 1 twin; suite available
Bathrooms: 1 private, 1 public

Bed & breakfast

per night:	£min	£max
Single	12.50	14.00
Double	25.00	30.00

Parking for 2

Wick Hollow House
😋😋

8 Wick Hollow, Glastonbury BA6 8JJ
☎ (01458) 833595
Peaceful, self-contained accommodation with private sitting room, on ground floor of lovely house overlooking Chalice Hill and the Tor. Special rates for stays of more than 3 nights. Children half price.
Bedrooms: 1 family room; suite available
Bathrooms: 1 private

Bed & breakfast

per night:	£min	£max
Single	27.50	30.00
Double	35.00	40.00

Parking for 2

> Half board prices shown are per person but in some cases may be based on double/twin occupancy.

GRAMPOUND

Cornwall
Map ref 1B3

Village on the River Fal, 6 miles south-west of St Austell. Probus Gardens 3 miles south-west.

Perran House
👑 👑

Fore Street, Grampound, Truro TR2 4RS
☎ St. Austell (01726) 882066
Delightful listed cottage in the pretty village of Grampound, between St Austell and Truro. Central for touring.
Bedrooms: 1 single, 3 double, 1 twin
Bathrooms: 3 private, 1 public
Bed & breakfast

per night:	£min	£max
Single	14.00	16.00
Double	28.00	36.00

Parking for 6
Cards accepted: Access, Visa
🛇 📞 🖵 ♦ ⑪ 🅂 ⅄ 🅟 📺 ⅲ, 🚗 ✳ ✈ 🚲 🐾 🆃

GREINTON

Somerset
Map ref 1D1

Village on the southern slopes of the Polden Hills, within easy reach of Bridgwater and the historic town of Glastonbury.

West Town Farm
👑 👑 COMMENDED

Greinton, Bridgwater TA7 9BW
☎ Ashcott (01458) 210277

Original part of house is over 200 years old, with large inglenook fire and bread oven, flagstone floors and Georgian front. Listed building. Non-smoking establishment.
Bedrooms: 1 double, 1 twin
Bathrooms: 2 private
Bed & breakfast

per night:	£min	£max
Single	18.00	20.00
Double	36.00	40.00

Parking for 2
Open March-September
🛇 03 🖵 ♦ 🖥 ⑪ 🅂 ⅄ 🅟 🚗 ✳ ✈ 🚲

> Please check prices and other details at the time of booking.

HARTLAND

Devon
Map ref 1C1

Hamlet on high, wild country near Hartland Point. Just west, the parish church tower makes a magnificent landmark; the light, unrestored interior holds one of Devon's finest rood screens. There are spectacular cliffs around Hartland Point and the lighthouse.

Elmscott Farm
👑 👑

Hartland, Bideford EX39 6ES
☎ (01237) 441276
650-acre mixed farm. In a coastal setting, quietly situated near the Devon/Cornwall border. Signposted from the main A39, about 4 miles away.
Bedrooms: 2 double, 1 twin
Bathrooms: 1 private, 1 public
Bed & breakfast

per night:	£min	£max
Single	15.00	18.00
Double	30.00	36.00

Evening meal 1800 (last orders 2000)
Parking for 8
Open April-October
🛇 ♦ ⑪ 🅂 🅟 📺 🚗 ♦ ◖ ∪ ┃ ✳ ✈ 🚲

HELSTON

Cornwall
Map ref 1B3

Handsome town with steep, main street and narrow alleys. In medieval times it was a major port and stannary town. Most buildings date from Regency and Victorian periods. The famous May dance, the Furry, is thought to have pre-Christian origins. A museum occupies the old Butter Market.
Tourist Information Centre
☎ *(01326) 565431*

Longstone Farm
👑 👑 COMMENDED

Trenear, Helston TR13 0HG
☎ (01326) 572483
62-acre dairy farm. In peaceful countryside in west Cornwall. Ideal for touring and beaches. Flambards, horse riding and swimming pool nearby. B3297 to Redruth, left for Coverack Bridges. Right at bottom of hill, continue left for about 1.5 miles to Longstone Farm.
Bedrooms: 1 double, 1 twin, 2 triple, 1 family room
Bathrooms: 5 private
Bed & breakfast

per night:	£min	£max
Single	18.00	
Double	32.00	

Half board

per person:	£min	£max
Daily	24.00	
Weekly	145.00	

Evening meal 1800 (last orders 0900)
Parking for 6
Open March-October
🛇 ♦ ♦ ⑪ 🅂 🅟 📺 ⅲ, 🚗 ◖ ✳ 🚲 ᴼᴬᴾ

HENSTRIDGE

Somerset
Map ref 2B3

Village with a rebuilt church containing the Tudor Carent tomb.

Fountain Inn Motel
👑 👑

High Street, Henstridge, Templecombe BA8 0RA
☎ Stalbridge (01963) 362722
Just off the A30 on the A357 Henstridge to Stalbridge road. Country inn (1700) with modern en-suite motel-type accommodation.
Bedrooms: 6 double
Bathrooms: 6 private
Bed & breakfast

per night:	£min	£max
Single	14.00	22.00
Double	25.00	33.00

Lunch available
Evening meal 1800 (last orders 2230)
Parking for 28
Cards accepted: Access, Visa, Diners, Amex, Switch/Delta
🛇 📞 ◖ 📞 🖵 ♦ 🅂 ⅲ, 🚗 ◖ ✳ 🚲 🆂🅿

Quiet Corner Farm
👑 👑 COMMENDED

Henstridge BA8 0RA
☎ Stalbridge (01963) 363045
Fax (01963) 363400
5-acre livestock & fruit farm. Comfortable, welcoming 18th C farmhouse and lovely old barns, some converted to holiday cottages. In conservation village with excellent eating places and shops. Beautiful gardens and orchards. Miniature Shetland pony stud.
Bedrooms: 2 double, 1 triple
Bathrooms: 1 private, 1 public, 1 private shower
Bed & breakfast

per night:	£min	£max
Single	22.00	25.00
Double	36.00	40.00

Parking for 8
🛇 📞 ♦ 🖥 ⑪ 🅂 🅟 📺 ⅲ, 🚗 ∪ ┃ ✳ ✈ 🚲 🆂🅿 🐾 🆃

HIGHBRIDGE

Somerset
Map ref 1D1

Alstone Court Farm
Listed

Alstone Lane, Highbridge TA9 3DS
☎ Burnham-on-Sea (01278) 789417
250-acre mixed farm. 17th C farmhouse with a warm and friendly atmosphere. Horse riding on farm, qualified instructors available.

Continued ▶

HIGHBRIDGE

Continued

Bedrooms: 1 double, 2 triple
Bathrooms: 3 public

Bed & breakfast

per night:	£min	£max
Single	14.50	14.50
Double	28.00	28.00

Parking for 6
Open April-November

HIGHWORTH

Wiltshire
Map ref 2B2

Small town 6 miles north-east of Swindon with square of 17th C and 18th C buildings close to the church.

Roves Farm

COMMENDED

Sevenhampton, Highworth, Swindon SN6 7QG
☎ Swindon (01793) 763939
Fax (01793) 763939
450-acre arable & livestock farm. Spacious, comfortable, quiet accommodation surrounded by beautiful countryside. Panoramic views, farm trail to woods, ponds and river. Signposted in Sevenhampton village.
Bedrooms: 1 twin, 1 triple
Bathrooms: 2 private

Bed & breakfast

per night:	£min	£max
Single	20.00	21.00
Double	33.00	34.00

Parking for 5

HITTISLEIGH

Devon
Map ref 1C2

Hill Farm

Listed

Hittisleigh, Exeter EX6 6LQ
☎ Cheriton Bishop (01647) 24149
47-acre livestock & horse farm. 17th C farmhouse in peaceful country environment. Gardens, swimming pool, fields and woods to explore, home cooking. Central position.
Bedrooms: 1 double, 1 twin
Bathrooms: 1 public

Bed & breakfast

per night:	£min	£max
Single	15.00	15.00
Double	30.00	30.00

We advise you to confirm your booking in writing.

Half board

per person:	£min	£max
Daily	23.00	23.00
Weekly	150.00	150.00

Evening meal 1800 (last orders 2030)
Parking for 7

HOLFORD

Somerset
Map ref 1D1

Sheltered in a wooded combe on the edge of the Quantocks, small village near Alfoxden House where William Wordsworth and his sister Dorothy lived in the late 1790s. Samuel Coleridge occupied a cottage at Nether Stowey during the same period. Nearby Quantock Forest has nature trails.

Forge Cottage

Listed

Holford, Bridgwater TA5 1RY
☎ (01278) 741215
Comfortable family home in beautiful Quantock village. H & C, tea/coffee, facilities. Guests' lounge and dining room. Children and well behaved pets welcome. Ideal for walking and mountain biking.
Bedrooms: 2 double, 1 twin
Bathrooms: 1 public

Bed & breakfast

per night:	£min	£max
Single	13.00	15.00
Double	25.00	28.00

Half board

per person:	£min	£max
Daily	18.00	20.00
Weekly	130.00	140.00

Evening meal 1800 (last orders 1900)
Parking for 2

HOLNE

Devon
Map ref 1C2

Woodland village on south-east edge of Dartmoor. Its 15th C church has a painted medieval screen. Charles Kingsley was born at the vicarage. Holne Woods slope to the River Dart.

Dodbrooke Farm

Listed   APPROVED

Michelcombe, Holne, Newton Abbot TQ13 7SP
☎ Poundsgate (01364) 631461
23-acre livestock farm. Listed 17th C longhouse in idyllic setting at foot of Dartmoor, on farm with animals and large gardens. From Ashburton on A38 take road to Two Bridges, fork left for Holne then follow signs to Michelcombe.
Bedrooms: 2 single, 2 twin
Bathrooms: 1 public

Bed & breakfast

per night:	£min	£max
Single	14.50	15.50
Double	30.00	32.00

Half board

per person:	£min	£max
Daily	20.50	26.00
Weekly	143.50	182.00

Evening meal from 1930
Parking for 3
Open January-November

Hazelwood

Listed   APPROVED

Holne, Newton Abbot TQ13 7SJ
☎ Poundsgate (01364) 631235
Near Ashburton, family-run bed and breakfast in village with panoramic views. Village amenities include shop, post office and period pub.
Bedrooms: 1 single, 1 double
Bathrooms: 1 public

Bed & breakfast

per night:	£min	£max
Single	14.00	15.00
Double	28.00	30.00

Parking for 3

HOLNEST

Dorset
Map ref 2B3

Village 5 miles south-east of Sherborne.

Bookham Stud and Ryewater Farm

Listed   COMMENDED

Holnest, Sherborne DT9 5PL
☎ (01963) 210248
80-acre stud farm. Delightful period stone farmhouse in idyllic setting in the centre of a small thoroughbred stud. Easy access to historic town of Sherborne.
Bedrooms: 1 single, 2 twin; suite available
Bathrooms: 2 private, 1 public

Bed & breakfast

per night:	£min	£max
Single	12.00	16.00
Double	30.00	50.00

Parking for 6
Open March-October

The symbols ◐ ◖ ◗ indicate categories of accessibility for wheelchair users. They are explained in full in the information pages at the back of this guide.

HOLSWORTHY

Devon
Map ref 1C2

Busy rural town and centre of a large farming community. Market day attracts many visitors.

The Barton

👑👑

Pancrasweek, Holsworthy EX22 7JT
☎ Bridgerule (01288) 381315
200-acre dairy farm. At the Devon/Cornwall border on the A3072, 3.5 miles from Holsworthy and 6 miles from the Cornish coast. Friendly atmosphere and home cooking with home-produced vegetables.
Bedrooms: 2 double, 1 twin
Bathrooms: 3 private

Bed & breakfast per night:	£min	£max
Single	14.00	14.50
Double	28.00	29.00

Half board per person:	£min	£max
Daily	21.00	21.50
Weekly	147.00	150.00

Evening meal 1800 (last orders 1600)
Parking for 5
Open April-September
🐴 ☕ [UL] [S] 🚭 [TV] 🚗 🎣 U ✓ ✿ 🏛

Elm Park Farm

👑👑 APPROVED

Bridgerule, Holsworthy EX22 7EL
☎ Bridgerule (01288) 381231
208-acre mixed farm. Relax at this character farmhouse, near village and 6 miles from Bude and beaches. En-suite family rooms with colour TV, tea-making. Pony. Games room.
Bedrooms: 1 triple, 2 family rooms
Bathrooms: 2 private, 1 public

Bed & breakfast per night:	£min	£max
Single	14.00	16.00
Double	28.00	32.00

Half board per person:	£min	£max
Daily	20.00	22.00
Weekly	138.00	145.00

Evening meal 1830 (last orders 1830)
Parking for 4
Open March-November
🐴 ☐ ☕ [UL] [TV] 🚗 U ✓ ✿ [SP]

Individual proprietors have supplied all details of accommodation. As changes can occur, we advise you to confirm the information at the time of booking.

HONITON

Devon
Map ref 1D2

Old coaching town in undulating farmland. Formerly famous for lace-making, it is now an antiques trade centre and market town. Small museum.
Tourist Information Centre
☎ (01404) 43716

Lelamarie

👑👑 COMMENDED

Awliscombe, Honiton EX14 0PP
☎ (01404) 44646 & 42308
Fax (01404) 44646
Detached bungalow with conservatory, patio, garden and parking. Exit junction 28 M5, A373 to Honiton for 7 miles. From Honiton, A373 for 2.5 miles.
Bedrooms: 1 double, 1 twin
Bathrooms: 2 private

Bed & breakfast per night:	£min	£max
Double	28.00	30.00

Parking for 4
🐴 1 ☐ ☕ [UL] 🚭 [TV] 🚗 ✿ [SP]

IVYBRIDGE

Devon
Map ref 1C2

Town set in delightful woodlands on the River Erme. Brunel designed the local railway viaduct. South Dartmoor Leisure Centre.
Tourist Information Centre
☎ (01752) 897035

Hillhead Farm

👑 COMMENDED

Ugborough, Ivybridge PL21 0HQ
☎ Plymouth (01752) 892674
77-acre mixed farm. Spacious family farmhouse, surrounded by fields. All home-cooked and largely home-grown food. From A38 turn off at Wrangton Cross, turn left, take third right over crossroads, after half a mile go straight over next crossroads, after three-quarters of a mile turn left, farm is 75 yards on left.
Bedrooms: 2 double, 1 twin
Bathrooms: 1 public

Bed & breakfast per night:	£min	£max
Single	14.00	16.00
Double	28.00	32.00

Half board per person:	£min	£max
Daily	23.00	25.00
Weekly		161.00

Evening meal 1900 (last orders 2100)
Parking for 5
🐴 ☐ ☕ [UL] [S] [TV] 🚗 ✓ ✿

Strashleigh Farmhouse Bed & Breakfast

Listed COMMENDED

Strashleigh, Ivybridge PL21 9JP
☎ Plymouth (01752) 892226
420-acre dairy & livestock farm. 13th C house with high ceilings and well-appointed rooms. Strashleigh is a working farm, situated between Dartmoor and Bigbury Bay. Perfect base, near A38.
Bedrooms: 2 double, 1 twin
Bathrooms: 1 public

Bed & breakfast per night:	£min	£max
Single	17.00	17.00
Double	34.00	34.00

Parking for 5
Open April-September
🐴 ☕ [UL] 🚭 [TV] 🚗 ✿ 🏛

KENTISBEARE

Devon
Map ref 1D2

Pretty village at the foot of the Blackdown Hills. The church has a magnificent carved 15th C screen, and nearby is a medieval priest's house with a minstrels' gallery and oak screens.

Knowles House

Listed

Broad Road, Kentisbeare, Cullompton EX15 2EU
☎ (01884) 266209
Country house with beautiful gardens and woodland on edge of the Blackdown Hills. 5 minutes M5, junction 28, left on A373, left to Sheldon, 1.5 miles on left.
Bedrooms: 1 double, 1 twin
Bathrooms: 2 private

Bed & breakfast per night:	£min	£max
Single	16.00	16.00
Double	32.00	32.00

Parking for 4
🐴 ☐ ☕ [UL] ✿

KINGSBRIDGE

Devon
Map ref 1C3

Formerly important as a port, now a market town overlooking head of beautiful, wooded estuary winding deep into rural countryside. Summer art exhibitions; Cookworthy Museum.
Tourist Information Centre
☎ (01548) 853195

The Ashburton Arms

Listed COMMENDED

West Charleton, Kingsbridge TQ7 2AH
☎ (01548) 531242
Fax (01548) 531189

Continued ▶

KINGSBRIDGE

Continued

Friendly village freehouse serving real ale and home-cooked food. Comfortable accommodation. Sorry, no pets. No smoking on first floor.
Bedrooms: 2 single, 1 double, 1 twin
Bathrooms: 1 public

Bed & breakfast

per night:	£min	£max
Single	19.00	24.00
Double	35.00	45.00

Half board

per person:	£min	£max
Daily	24.00	40.00
Weekly	168.00	280.00

Lunch available
Evening meal 1900 (last orders 2100)
Parking for 15
Cards accepted: Access, Visa

Court Barton Farmhouse ⚑

COMMENDED

Aveton Gifford, Kingsbridge TQ7 4LE
☎ (01548) 550312

40-acre mixed farm. Beautiful 16th C manor farmhouse, below the church, 100 yards from A379. Splendid hospitality guaranteed.
Bedrooms: 1 single, 2 double, 2 twin, 2 family rooms
Bathrooms: 6 private, 1 public, 1 private shower

Bed & breakfast

per night:	£min	£max
Single	16.00	24.00
Double	32.00	48.00

Parking for 10

Sloop Inn ⚑

COMMENDED

Bantham, Kingsbridge TQ7 3AJ
☎ (01548) 560489 & 560215
Fax (01548) 561940
Part 16th C inn in old world fishing village west of Kingsbridge. Some rooms overlook sea and estuary. Menu majors on local seafood. Featured in pub guides.
Bedrooms: 3 double, 2 triple
Bathrooms: 5 private

Bed & breakfast

per night:	£min	£max
Single	27.00	54.00
Double	54.00	59.00

Half board

per person:	£min	£max
Daily	38.00	40.00

Lunch available
Evening meal 1900 (last orders 2200)
Parking for 35
Cards accepted: Access, Visa, Switch/Delta

Tor Cottage

COMMENDED

The Mounts, East Allington, Totnes TQ9 7QJ
☎ East Allington (01548) 521316 & Mobile 0836 359320
Fax (01548) 521316
Small, friendly guesthouse in rural setting. Guests' lounge and garden with pleasant, relaxing views. Close to Dartmouth and Salcombe. Ideal for touring and long stay.
Bedrooms: 2 double, 1 twin
Bathrooms: 3 private

Bed & breakfast

per night:	£min	£max
Single	24.00	30.00
Double	32.00	40.00

Half board

per person:	£min	£max
Daily	25.00	29.00
Weekly	178.00	199.00

Evening meal from 1800
Parking for 5
Open February-November

Tunley Farm

Loddiswell, Kingsbridge TQ7 4ED
☎ (01548) 550279
180-acre dairy farm. Enjoy comfortable, spacious accommodation in relaxed family atmosphere. Splendid breakfasts. Peaceful countryside near coast and Dartmoor.
Bedrooms: 1 double, 1 twin
Bathrooms: 2 private

Bed & breakfast

per night:	£min	£max
Double	33.00	34.00

Parking for 3
Open March-October

KINGSHEANTON

Devon
Map ref 1C1

Heaton House ⚑

Listed

Kingsheanton, Barnstaple EX31 4ED
☎ Barnstaple (01271) 46342
Fax (01271) 46342
Quiet, comfortable North Devon country family house. Spacious garden, guest lounge, TV, fine home cooking. Local walks near coast and Exmoor.
Bedrooms: 2 single, 2 double, 1 twin

Bathrooms: 3 public

Bed & breakfast

per night:	£min	£max
Single	16.00	19.00

Half board

per person:	£min	£max
Daily	21.00	27.00
Weekly	125.00	160.00

Lunch available
Evening meal 1900 (last orders 2000)
Parking for 7

LACOCK

Wiltshire
Map ref 2B2

Village of great charm. Medieval buildings of stone, brick or timber-frame have jutting storeys, gables, oriel windows. Magnificent church has perpendicular fan-vaulted chapel with grand tomb to benefactor who, after Dissolution, bought Augustinian nunnery, Lacock Abbey.

Old Rectory

COMMENDED

Cantax Hill, Lacock, Chippenham SN15 2JZ
☎ (01249) 730335

11-acre mixed farm. As the name implies, shares in the history of Lacock. Located at the approach to the village and set in grounds complete with tennis and croquet. Elegant accommodation with private facilities.
Bedrooms: 2 double, 1 twin
Bathrooms: 3 private

Bed & breakfast

per night:	£min	£max
Double	40.00	45.00

Parking for 10
Open February-December

There are separate sections in this guide listing groups specialising in farm holidays and accommodation which is especially suitable for young people and organised groups.

LAUNCESTON

Cornwall
Map ref 1C2

Medieval "Gateway to Cornwall", county town until 1838, founded by the Normans under their hilltop castle near the original monastic settlement. This market town, overlooked by its castle ruin, has a square with Georgian houses and an elaborately-carved granite church.
Tourist Information Centre
☎ (01566) 772321 or 772333

The Old Vicarage ⚤

HIGHLY COMMENDED

Treneglos, Launceston PL15 8UQ
☎ Canworthy Water (01566) 781351
Elegant Georgian vicarage set in peaceful seclusion near spectacular north Cornwall coast. Renowned for hospitality and good food. High standard of furnishings and personal attention. Non-smoking.
Bedrooms: 2 double
Bathrooms: 2 private
Bed & breakfast

per night:	£min	£max
Double	40.00	40.00

Half board

per person:	£min	£max
Daily	32.00	32.00
Weekly	213.50	213.50

Evening meal 1800 (last orders 2130)
Parking for 10
Open April-October

LEIGH

Wiltshire
Map ref 2B2

Village 3 miles west of Cricklade and close to the River Thames and the Cotswold Water Park.

Leighfield Lodge Farm

Listed

Leigh, Swindon SN6 6RH
☎ Malmesbury (01666) 860241 & (01378) 521154
Fax (01666) 860241
104-acre mixed farm. Relaxed, comfortable farmhouse accommodation, peacefully situated. Convenient for Cotswolds and Wiltshire Downs. Near junction 16 M4.
Bedrooms: 1 double, 1 twin
Bathrooms: 2 private, 1 public
Bed & breakfast

per night:	£min	£max
Single	17.50	20.00
Double	32.00	40.00

Evening meal 1800 (last orders 2000)
Parking for 12

LEWDOWN

Devon
Map ref 1C2

Small village on the very edge of Dartmoor. Lydford Castle is 4 miles to the east.

Stowford Grange Farm

Listed

Stowford, Lewdown, Okehampton EX20 4BZ
☎ (01566) 783298
240-acre mixed farm. Listed building, quiet village. Home-cooked food, fresh vegetables and poultry. 10 miles from Okehampton and 7 miles from Launceston. Half a mile from old A30, turn right at Royal Exchange.
Bedrooms: 3 double
Bathrooms: 2 public
Bed & breakfast

per night:	£min	£max
Single	16.00	18.00
Double	30.00	34.00

Half board

per person:	£min	£max
Daily	17.50	18.50
Weekly	110.00	112.00

Evening meal from 1900
Parking for 5
Open February-November

LISKEARD

Cornwall
Map ref 1C2

Former stannary town with a livestock market and light industry, at the head of a valley running to the coast. Handsome Georgian and Victorian residences and a Victorian Guildhall reflect the prosperity of the mining boom. The large church has an early 20th C tower and a Norman font.

Tregondale Farm

HIGHLY COMMENDED

Menheniot, Liskeard PL14 3RG
☎ (01579) 342407
180-acre mixed farm. Characteristic farmhouse in beautiful countryside. En-suite bedrooms with TV and tea/coffee. Home-produced food our speciality. Log fires, tennis court. North east of Menheniot, between A38 and A390.
Bedrooms: 1 double, 1 twin, 1 triple
Bathrooms: 3 private
Bed & breakfast

per night:	£min	£max
Single	18.00	20.00
Double	35.00	40.00

Half board

per person:	£min	£max
Daily	27.00	29.00
Weekly	178.00	182.00

Evening meal 1900 (last orders 1800)
Parking for 3

Tresulgan Farm

HIGHLY COMMENDED

Menheniot, Liskeard PL14 3PU
☎ Widegates (01503) 240268
Fax (01503) 240268

145-acre mixed farm. Picturesque views from modernised 17th C farmhouse which has retained its character. Lots to do in this beautiful area and a warm and friendly welcome awaits you.
Bedrooms: 1 double, 1 triple, 1 family room
Bathrooms: 3 private
Bed & breakfast

per night:	£min	£max
Single	19.00	20.00
Double	36.00	38.00

Half board

per person:	£min	£max
Daily	25.00	27.50
Weekly	175.00	192.50

Evening meal 1830 (last orders 1900)
Parking for 3

LITTLE BEDWYN

Wiltshire
Map ref 2C2

Village on the banks of the Kennet and Avon Canal, 4 miles south-west of Hungerford and close to the Wiltshire/Berkshire border.

Harrow Inn

COMMENDED

Little Bedwyn, Marlborough SN8 3JP
☎ Marlborough (01672) 870871
Fax (01672) 870401
Country inn on south-east side of quiet, unspoilt village close to Kennet and Avon Canal. Excellent restaurant, attractive garden.
Bedrooms: 1 single, 1 double, 1 twin
Bathrooms: 3 private
Bed & breakfast

per night:	£min	£max
Single	22.00	28.00
Double	37.00	45.00

Lunch available
Evening meal 1930 (last orders 2100)
Parking for 1
Cards accepted: Access, Visa

LONGDOWN

Devon
Map ref 1D2

Willhayes Farm

⛫⛫ COMMENDED

Longdown, Exeter EX6 7BN
☎ Exeter (01392) 832636
45-acre mixed farm. Mainly sheep grazing. Carp and trout ponds. Wild flowers and butterflies abound and birds of prey are often seen.
Bedrooms: 1 double, 2 twin
Bathrooms: 3 private
Bed & breakfast

per night:	£min	£max
Single	15.00	18.00
Double	30.00	36.00

Open February-November

LOOE

Cornwall
Map ref 1C2

Small resort developed around former fishing and smuggling ports occupying the deep estuary of the East and West Looe Rivers. Narrow winding streets, with old inns; museum and art gallery are housed in interesting old buildings. Shark fishing centre, boat trips; busy harbour.

Bucklawren Farm ⋒

⛫⛫⛫ HIGHLY COMMENDED

St. Martin-by-Looe, Looe PL13 1NZ
☎ Widegates (01503) 240738
Fax (01503) 240481

534-acre arable & dairy farm. Set in glorious countryside with beautiful sea views. Only 1.5 miles from beach. Family and en-suite accommodation with colour TV. Delicious farmhouse cooking.
Bedrooms: 2 double, 2 triple, 1 family room
Bathrooms: 5 private, 1 public
Bed & breakfast

per night:	£min	£max
Single	17.00	23.00
Double	34.00	38.00

Half board

per person:	£min	£max
Daily	26.50	28.50
Weekly	171.50	182.00

Evening meal 1800 (last orders 1800)
Parking for 10

Open March-October
Cards accepted: Access, Visa

Coombe Farm ⋒

⛫⛫⛫ HIGHLY COMMENDED

Widegates, Looe PL13 1QN
☎ Widegates (01503) 240223

Country house in lovely grounds with superb views to sea. All rooms en-suite. Candlelit dining. Home cooking. Glorious walks and beaches nearby. 3.5 miles east of Looe on the B3253.
Bedrooms: 1 single, 2 double, 2 twin, 2 triple, 3 family rooms
Bathrooms: 10 private
Bed & breakfast

per night:	£min	£max
Single	20.00	26.00
Double	40.00	52.00

Half board

per person:	£min	£max
Daily	32.00	38.00
Weekly	210.00	258.00

Evening meal 1900 (last orders 1900)
Parking for 12
Open March-October

Kantara Guest House ⋒

⛫ COMMENDED

7 Trelawney Terrace, Looe PL13 2AG
☎ (01503) 262093
Licensed guesthouse close to beach and shops. Informal, friendly atmosphere. Ideal family holiday setting and touring base. Satellite TV in all rooms.
Bedrooms: 1 single, 1 double, 1 twin, 1 triple, 2 family rooms
Bathrooms: 2 public
Bed & breakfast

per night:	£min	£max
Single	13.00	15.50
Double	26.00	31.00

Half board

per person:	£min	£max
Daily	22.00	24.50
Weekly	150.00	167.00

Evening meal 1800 (last orders 1900)
Parking for 1
Cards accepted: Access, Visa, Amex

Little Larnick Farm

⛫⛫

Pelynt, Looe PL13 2NB
☎ (01503) 262837
200-acre mixed & dairy farm. Spacious, character en-suite accommodation in the beautiful West Looe River Valley.

Peaceful and relaxing. Superb farmhouse breakfast.
Bedrooms: 1 double, 1 twin, 1 triple
Bathrooms: 3 private
Bed & breakfast

per night:	£min	£max
Single	16.00	18.00
Double	32.00	36.00

Parking for 3
Open February-November

Stonerock Cottage

⛫⛫ COMMENDED

Portuan Road, Hannafore, Looe PL13 2DN
☎ (01503) 263651
Modernised, old world cottage facing south to the Channel. Ample free parking. 2 minutes from the beach, shops, tennis and other amenities.
Bedrooms: 1 single, 2 double, 1 twin
Bathrooms: 1 private, 2 public
Bed & breakfast

per night:	£min	£max
Double	30.00	38.00

Parking for 4
Open February-October

LUSTLEIGH

Devon
Map ref 1D2

Riverside village of pretty thatched cottages gathered around its 15th C church. The traditional Mayday festival has dancing round the maypole. Just west is Lustleigh Cleave, where Dartmoor is breached by the River Bovey which flows through a deep valley of boulders and trees.

The Mill

Listed

Lustleigh, Newton Abbot TQ13 9SS
☎ (016477) 357
12-acre smallholding. Historic riverside millhouse on edge of beautiful Dartmoor village. Exposed beams, antique furniture, home-grown produce.
Bedrooms: 1 single, 2 double
Bathrooms: 2 public
Bed & breakfast

per night:	£min	£max
Single	17.50	
Double	33.00	

Half board

per person:	£min	£max
Daily	26.50	
Weekly	180.00	

Evening meal from 1830
Parking for 3

LYME REGIS

Dorset
Map ref 1D2

Pretty, historic fishing town and resort set against the fossil-rich cliffs of Lyme Bay. In medieval times it was an important port and cloth centre. The Cobb, a massive stone breakwater, shelters the ancient harbour which is still lively with boats.
Tourist Information Centre
☎ *(01297) 442138*

Coverdale Guest House

🏵🏵 COMMENDED

Woodmead Road, Lyme Regis
DT7 3AB   ·
☎ (01297) 442882
Bright, spacious, non-smoking 1920s house. Well furnished, comfortable bedrooms with sea or pretty garden/country views. Short walk to town and beach.
Bedrooms: 2 single, 2 double, 1 twin, 3 triple
Bathrooms: 6 private, 1 public
Bed & breakfast

per night:	£min	£max
Single	15.00	17.00
Double	26.00 ·	40.00

Evening meal 1830 (last orders 1630)
Parking for 12
Open March-October
🛇3🔌♿📺Ⓢ✑🅿📺📖🛏♿⛟ OAP SP

The Red House 🅰

🏵🏵 HIGHLY COMMENDED

Sidmouth Road, Lyme Regis DT7 3ES
☎ (01297) 442055
Superb coastal views, large garden, parking.
Bedrooms: 2 twin, 1 triple
Bathrooms: 3 private
Bed & breakfast

per night:	£min	£max
Single	24.00	35.00
Double	36.00	48.00

Parking for 4
Open March-November
🛇8💳🔌♿📺📖🛏🅿✿✗🛏

Southernhaye

🏵 COMMENDED

Pound Road, Lyme Regis DT7 3HX
☎ (01297) 443077
Fax (01297) 443077
Distinctive Edwardian house in quiet location with panoramic views over Lyme Bay, about 10 minutes' walk from town and beach.
Bedrooms: 1 double, 1 twin
Bathrooms: 1 public
Bed & breakfast

per night:	£min	£max
Single	18.00	18.00
Double	30.00	34.00

Parking for 2
♿📺Ⓢ📖📺📖🅿✿✗🛏🏠

Springfield

🏵🏵 COMMENDED

Woodmead Road, Lyme Regis DT7 3LJ
☎ (01297) 443409

Elegant Georgian house and conservatory in partly walled garden, with well-proportioned rooms, many enjoying views over the sea.
Bedrooms: 1 single, 2 double, 2 twin, 1 triple, 1 family room
Bathrooms: 3 private, 2 public
Bed & breakfast

per night:	£min	£max
Single	15.00	18.00
Double	26.00	40.00

Parking for 9
Open February-November
🛇🔌♿📺📖📺📖🅿✿🛏🏠

White House

🏵🏵 COMMENDED

47 Silver Street, Lyme Regis DT7 3HR
☎ (01297) 443420
Fine views of Dorset coastline from rear of this 18th C guesthouse. A short walk from beach, gardens and shops.
Bedrooms: 5 double, 2 twin
Bathrooms: 7 private
Bed & breakfast

per night:	£min	£max
Double	32.00	40.00

Parking for 6
Open April-October
💳♿🔌♿📖✑📺📖🅿🛏 SP 🏠

LYNMOUTH

Devon
Map ref 1C1

Resort set beneath bracken-covered cliffs and pinewood gorges where 2 rivers meet, and cascade between boulders to the town. Lynton, set on cliffs above, can be reached by water-operated cliff railway from the Victorian esplanade. Valley of the Rocks, to the west, gives dramatic walks.

The Village Inn

Listed COMMENDED

Lynmouth Street, Lynmouth EX35 6EH
☎ (01598) 752354
Refurbished without sacrificing the atmosphere of a traditional inn. Open stone fire, good home-cooked food, en-suite rooms with facilities. Centrally located.
Bedrooms: 6 double
Bathrooms: 6 private

Bed & breakfast

per night:	£min	£max
Double	40.00	70.00

Half board

per person:	£min	£max
Daily	27.50	45.00
Weekly	150.00	250.00

Lunch available
Evening meal 1830 (last orders 2130)
Cards accepted: Access, Visa, Switch/Delta
💳📺🔌♿📺📖✿✗🛏♿ SP

LYNTON

Devon
Map ref 1C1

Hilltop resort on Exmoor coast linked to its seaside twin, Lynmouth, by a water-operated cliff railway which descends from the town hall. Spectacular surroundings of moorland cliffs with steep chasms of conifer and rocks through which rivers cascade.
Tourist Information Centre
☎ *(01598) 752225*

Ingleside Hotel 🅰

🏵🏵🏵

Lynton EX35 6HW
☎ (01598) 752223
Family-run hotel with high standards in elevated position overlooking village. Ideal centre for exploring Exmoor.
Bedrooms: 4 double, 1 twin, 2 triple
Bathrooms: 7 private
Bed & breakfast

per night:	£min	£max
Single	22.00	27.00
Double	36.00	48.00

Half board

per person:	£min	£max
Daily	31.00	36.00
Weekly	203.00	238.00

Evening meal 1900 (last orders 1800)
Parking for 10
Open March-October
Cards accepted: Access, Visa
🛇12💳📺🔌♿📺Ⓢ✑📺📖✿✗🛏 OAP SP Ⓣ

Sandrock Hotel 🅰

🏵🏵🏵 COMMENDED

Longmead, Lynton EX35 6DH
☎ (01598) 753307
Fax (01598) 752665

Comfortable family-run hotel, quietly situated near local beauty spots, bowls green and tennis courts.

Continued ▶

LYNTON

Continued

Bedrooms: 2 single, 4 double, 3 twin
Bathrooms: 7 private, 1 public
Bed & breakfast

per night:	£min	£max
Single	20.00	22.00
Double	40.00	48.50

Half board

per person:	£min	£max
Daily	32.00	36.50
Weekly	205.00	230.00

Evening meal 1900 (last orders 2000)
Parking for 9
Open February-November
Cards accepted: Access, Visa, Amex
🛏🗝📞☎♨♿🅿🛎💺🅿🖼▥📠🔍🐕🐴 DAP SP T

MALMESBURY

Wiltshire
Map ref 2B2

Overlooking the River Avon, an old town dominated by its great church, once a Benedictine abbey. The surviving Norman nave and porch are noted for fine sculptures, 12th C arches and musicians' gallery.
Tourist Information Centre
☎ *(01666) 823748*

Flisteridge Cottage
Listed COMMENDED

Flisteridge Road, Upper Minety,
Malmesbury SN16 9PS
☎ (01666) 860343
Warm welcome at cottage overlooking lovely landscaped gardens and open countryside. Choice of breakfasts. Good food nearby. Ideal touring base for Cotswolds and surrounding area.
Bedrooms: 1 single, 1 double, 1 twin
Bathrooms: 1 private, 1 public
Bed & breakfast

per night:	£min	£max
Single	14.00	17.50
Double	28.00	35.00

Parking for 5
🛏11🏠📞🗝▥🔍📺▥💺🌸🐴 SP

Lovett Farm
Listed COMMENDED

Little Somerford, Malmesbury
SN15 5BP
☎ (01666) 823268
65-acre livestock farm. Delightful farmhouse with superb views and pretty en-suite accommodation. Ideally positioned for visiting Bath and Cotswolds. Local pubs serve excellent food.
Bedrooms: 1 double, 1 twin
Bathrooms: 1 private, 1 public

Bed & breakfast

per night:	£min	£max
Single	17.00	20.00
Double	30.00	34.00

Parking for 5
🛏🗝📞♨♿▥🅿📷🛎💺🔍💺📺▥💺🅿🌸 🐴🐴

Manor Farm
COMMENDED

Corston, Malmesbury SN16 0HF
☎ (01666) 822148 & Mobile 0374 675783

436-acre mixed farm. Relax and unwind in charming 17th C Cotswolds farmhouse. Excellent meals available in village pub. Ideally situated for visiting Cotswolds, Bath and Stonehenge.
Bedrooms: 1 single, 2 double, 1 triple, 2 family rooms
Bathrooms: 3 private, 1 public, 2 private showers
Bed & breakfast

per night:	£min	£max
Single	16.00	24.00
Double	32.00	40.00

Parking for 12
Cards accepted: Access, Visa
🛏🗝📞♨♿▥📠📺▥💺🅿🔍🐕🐴🏠

MARLBOROUGH

Wiltshire
Map ref 2B2

Important market town, in a river valley cutting through chalk downlands. The broad main street, with colonnaded shops on one side, shows a medley of building styles, mainly from the Georgian period. Lanes wind away on either side and a church stands at each end.
Tourist Information Centre
☎ *(01672) 513989*

Laurel Cottage Guest House
HIGHLY COMMENDED

Southend, Ogbourne St George,
Marlborough SN8 1SG
☎ Ogbourne St George (01672) 841288

16th C thatched cottage, in a delightful rural setting. Low beamed ceilings and

inglenook fireplace. Non-smokers only, please.
Bedrooms: 2 double, 2 twin
Bathrooms: 2 private, 1 public
Bed & breakfast

per night:	£min	£max
Single	26.00	34.00
Double	33.00	50.00

Parking for 5
Open April-October
Cards accepted: Access, Visa, Switch/ Delta
🛏🗝📞♨♿▥🅿💺🔍📺▥💺🅿🌸 🐴🐴🏠

MARTINSTOWN

Dorset
Map ref 2B3

Village 3 miles west of Dorchester. Maiden Castle Iron Age fort lies to the east of the village and the Hardy Monument stands on Black Down to the south west.

Old Post Office
Listed

Martinstown, Dorchester DT2 9LF
☎ (01305) 889254
Grade II listed Georgian cottage tastefully modernised throughout. Large garden with many small animals. Good rural base, children and pets welcome.
Bedrooms: 1 double, 2 twin
Bathrooms: 2 public
Bed & breakfast

per night:	£min	£max
Single	17.50	21.00
Double	30.00	35.00

Half board

per person:	£min	£max
Daily	25.00	27.50
Weekly	175.00	192.50

Evening meal 1900 (last orders 1630)
Parking for 3
🛏📞♨♿▥🅿💺📺▥💺🅿🌸🐴🏠

MARTOCK

Somerset
Map ref 2A3

Small town with many handsome buildings of Ham stone and a beautiful old church with tie-beam roof. Medieval treasurer's house, Georgian market house, 17th C manor.

Wychwood ♨
HIGHLY COMMENDED

7 Bearley Road, Martock TA12 6PG
☎ (01935) 825601
Small, quality B & B in quiet position just off A303 between Montacute and Tintinhull. Ideal for visiting the eight classic gardens of South Somerset. Near Glastonbury and Wells. Brochure.
Bedrooms: 2 double, 1 twin
Bathrooms: 3 private

Bed & breakfast

per night:	£min	£max
Double	34.00	37.00

Half board

per person:	£min	£max
Daily	30.00	31.50

Evening meal 1900 (last orders 2000)
Parking for 3
Cards accepted: Access, Visa, Switch/
Delta
🛇 8 💷 ⛶ 📺 ♨ 🅂 ✕ ⊨ 📺 🏛 🖆
🏃 ✿ ✕ 🛋

MERE

Wiltshire
Map ref 2B2

Small town with a grand
Perpendicular church surrounded
by Georgian houses, with old inns
and a 15th C chantry house. On
the chalk downs overlooking the
town is an Iron Age fort.
Tourist Information Centre
🕾 *(01747) 861211*

Talbot Hotel
👑 👑 👑 APPROVED

The Square, Mere BA12 6DR
🕾 (01747) 860427
Fax (01747) 861210
*16th C coaching inn with interesting
features. Ideal for visits to Stourhead,
Longleat, Stonehenge, Salisbury, Bath,
Sherborne and Cheddar areas. Two-
night breaks available.*
Bedrooms: 1 single, 2 double, 1 twin,
3 triple
Bathrooms: 7 private

Bed & breakfast

per night:	£min	£max
Single	25.00	32.50
Double	40.00	53.00

Half board

per person:	£min	£max
Weekly	157.50	210.00

Lunch available
Evening meal 1830 (last orders 2130)
Parking for 20
Cards accepted: Access, Visa, Amex
🛇 2 💷 ⛶ ♨ 🅂 ✕ ⊨ 🏛 🖆 🛋 ✿
🆂🅿 🏧

The symbol ⊛ within an
entry indicates participation
in the Welcome Host
programme – a nationally
recognised customer care
initiative which aims to
promote the highest
standards of service and a
warm welcome for all visitors.

MEVAGISSEY

Cornwall
Map ref 1B3

Small fishing town, a favourite with
holidaymakers. Earlier prosperity
came from pilchard fisheries, boat-
building and smuggling. By the
harbour are fish cellars, some
converted, and a local history
museum is housed in an old boat-
building shed. Handsome
Methodist chapel; shark fishing,
sailing.

Auraville
👑

The Drive, Trevarth, Mevagissey, St
Austell PL26 6RX
🕾 (01726) 843293
*Homely accommodation in quiet and
peaceful surroundings, a short walk
from quaint fishing village and harbour.
Central for touring Cornwall.*
Bedrooms: 1 single, 2 double, 1 twin
Bathrooms: 2 public

Bed & breakfast

per night:	£min	£max
Single	13.50	15.00
Double	27.00	30.00

Parking for 4
🛇 📤 💷 ⛶ ♨ 🅆 ♨ 🅂 ✕ ⊨ 📺 🏛 🛋 ✿ ✕
🛋 🆂🅿 🅃

Polrudden Farm ⋀
Listed

Pentewan, Near Mevagissey, St Austell
PL26 6BJ
🕾 St Austell (01726) 843213
*75-acre mixed farm. Modern farmhouse
with fantastic views and walks, 3 miles
from St Austell and 2 miles from
Mevagissey. Peace and tranquillity.*
Bedrooms: 1 double, 2 twin
Bathrooms: 1 private, 2 public

Bed & breakfast

per night:	£min	£max
Single	16.00	18.00
Double	32.00	35.00

Parking for 13
🛇 📤 💷 ⛶ ♨ 🅆 ♨ 🅂 ✕ 📺 🏛 🛋 🙂
✿ 🛋

Rising Sun Inn
👑

Portmellon Cove, Mevagissey, St
Austell PL26 6PL
🕾 (01726) 843235
*17th C inn right next to the beach at
Portmellon Cove, and overlooking
Chapel Point and surrounding
countryside.*
Bedrooms: 3 double, 1 twin, 1 triple
Bathrooms: 5 private

Bed & breakfast

per night:	£min	£max
Single	17.50	25.00
Double	33.00	44.00

Lunch available
Evening meal 1830 (last orders 2130)

Parking for 60
Open March-September
Cards accepted: Access, Visa
🛇 📤 ⛶ ♨ 🅂 ✕ 🏛 🛋 ✕ ♨ ✕ 🆂🅿 🏧

Steep House ⋀
👑 👑

Portmellon Cove, Mevagissey, St
Austell PL26 2PH
🕾 (01726) 843732

*Refreshingly clean and comfortable
house with large garden and covered
(summertime) pool. Superb seaside
views, licensed, free off-road parking.*
Bedrooms: 5 double, 1 twin, 1 triple
Bathrooms: 2 private, 2 public,
1 private shower

Bed & breakfast

per night:	£min	£max
Single	16.50	
Double	33.00	

Half board

per person:	£min	£max
Daily	27.50	

Parking for 12
Cards accepted: Access, Visa, Amex
🛇 10 ⛶ ♨ 🅂 ✕ ⊨ 📺 🏛 🔌 ✿ ✕ 🛋 🆂🅿

MINETY

Wiltshire
Map ref 2B2

Equidistant (7 miles) from
Malmesbury and Cricklade, the
village is spread over 1.5 miles.
The church contains a 17th C
canopied pulpit, Jacobean pews
and 15th C screen.

The White Horse
Listed

Minety, Malmesbury SN16 9QY
🕾 Malmesbury (01666) 860284
Fax (01666) 860468
*Recently refurbished country pub with
accommodation, restaurant and function
room. Two pleasant beamed bars with
open fires. Lakeside setting.*
Bedrooms: 2 double
Bathrooms: 2 private

Bed & breakfast

per night:	£min	£max
Single	28.00	
Double	38.00	

Lunch available
Evening meal 1900 (last orders 2200)
Parking for 50
Cards accepted: Access, Visa
🛇 ⛶ ♨ 🅂 ✕ ⊨ 🏛 🛋 🍴40 🔌 ✕ ∪
🎵 ✿ 🛋 🆂🅿 🏧 🅃

MISTERTON

Somerset
Map ref 2A3

Dryclose

Listed | **HIGHLY COMMENDED**

Newbery Lane, Misterton, Crewkerne
TA18 8NE
☎ Crewkerne (01460) 73161

Grade II 16th C farmhouse set in 2 acres of garden. A356 from Crewkerne to Misterton, turn left into Silver Street, then left into Newbery Lane.
Bedrooms: 1 single, 2 twin
Bathrooms: 1 private, 1 public

Bed & breakfast

per night:	£min	£max
Single	16.50	18.00
Double	32.00	40.00

Evening meal from 1900
Parking for 9

MORETONHAMPSTEAD

Devon
Map ref 1C2

Small market town with a row of 17th C almshouses standing on the Exeter road. Surrounding moorland is scattered with ancient farmhouses, prehistoric sites.

Great Doccombe Farm

Doccombe, Moretonhampstead,
Newton Abbot TQ13 8SS
☎ (01647) 40694
8-acre mixed farm. 300-year-old farmhouse in Dartmoor National Park. Comfortable rooms, farmhouse cooking. Ideal for walking the Teign Valley and Dartmoor.
Bedrooms: 1 double, 1 triple
Bathrooms: 2 private, 2 public

Bed & breakfast

per night:	£min	£max
Double	32.00	36.00

Parking for 6

Great Sloncombe Farm ⋀

HIGHLY COMMENDED

Moretonhampstead, Newton Abbot
TQ13 8QF
☎ (01647) 440595
170-acre dairy farm. 13th C Dartmoor farmhouse. Comfortable rooms, central heating, en-suite. Large wholesome

farmhouse breakfasts and delicious dinners. Friendly Devonshire welcome.
Bedrooms: 2 double, 1 twin
Bathrooms: 3 private

Bed & breakfast

per night:	£min	£max
Single	19.00	20.00
Double	38.00	40.00

Half board

per person:	£min	£max
Daily	29.00	31.00

Evening meal 1830 (last orders 1000)
Parking for 3

Wooston Farm

HIGHLY COMMENDED

Moretonhampstead, Newton Abbot
TQ13 8QA
☎ (01647) 440367
Fax (01647) 440367
280-acre mixed farm. Situated within Dartmoor National Park above the Teign Valley, with scenic views and walks. Two rooms are en-suite, one with four-poster bed.
Bedrooms: 2 double, 1 twin
Bathrooms: 3 private

Bed & breakfast

per night:	£min	£max
Single	18.00	20.00
Double	34.00	40.00

Half board

per person:	£min	£max
Daily	27.00	31.00

Evening meal 1800 (last orders 1830)
Parking for 3

MORWENSTOW

Cornwall
Map ref 1C2

Scattered parish on the wild north Cornish coast. The church, beautifully situated in a deep combe by the sea, has a fine Norman doorway and 15th C bench-ends. Its unique vicarage was built by the 19th C poet-priest Robert Hawker. Nearby are Cornwall's highest cliffs.

Cornakey Farm

Morwenstow, Bude EX23 9SS
☎ (01288) 331260
220-acre mixed farm. Convenient coastal walking area with extensive views of sea and cliffs from bedrooms. Home cooking, games room. Reduced rates for children. Good touring centre.
Bedrooms: 2 triple
Bathrooms: 2 private, 1 public

Bed & breakfast

per night:	£min	£max
Single	15.00	16.00
Double	30.00	32.00

Half board

per person:	£min	£max
Daily	21.00	
Weekly	140.00	

Evening meal 1830 (last orders 1730)
Parking for 2

MYLOR BRIDGE

Cornwall
Map ref 1B3

Penmere Guest House

COMMENDED

10 Rosehill, Mylor Bridge, Falmouth
TR11 5LZ
☎ Falmouth (01326) 374470
Beautifully restored Victorian property enjoying splendid creek views, close to yachting centres. Lovely garden, perfect for a relaxing stay.
Bedrooms: 3 double, 2 twin, 2 triple
Bathrooms: 5 private, 1 public

Bed & breakfast

per night:	£min	£max
Single	22.00	25.00
Double	40.00	47.00

Parking for 6

NETHER STOWEY

Somerset
Map ref 1D1

Winding village below east slopes of Quantocks with attractive old cottages of varying periods. A Victorian clock tower stands at its centre, where a village road climbs the hill beside a small stream.

Mount Cottage

HIGHLY COMMENDED

Castle Hill, Nether Stowey, Bridgwater
TA5 1ET
☎ Bridgwater (01278) 732477
Period cottage with beams and inglenook, situated in beautiful Quantock Hills, ideal for walking or touring Somerset and Exmoor.
Bedrooms: 1 double, 1 twin, 1 triple
Bathrooms: 3 private

Bed & breakfast

per night:	£min	£max
Single	17.00	20.00
Double	34.00	36.00

Parking for 5

NETTLECOMBE

Dorset
Map ref 2A3

The Marquis of Lorne

COMMENDED

Nettlecombe, Bridport DT6 3SY
☎ Powerstock (01308) 485236
Fax (01308) 485666

Idyllic country inn just 4 miles from coast and Bridport. Good food and a warm welcome. Large gardens and car park.
Bedrooms: 5 double, 1 twin
Bathrooms: 6 private
Bed & breakfast

per night:	£min	£max
Single	35.00	35.00
Double	55.00	55.00

Lunch available
Evening meal 1900 (last orders 2130)
Parking for 50
Cards accepted: Access, Visa
☎ 10 📞 ❌ 🅿 🛈 S ⊁ ♨ 🛏, ♨ ◐ U ❋ ✕ ⚑ SP ℍ T

NEWQUAY

Cornwall
Map ref 1B2

Popular resort spread over dramatic cliffs around its old fishing port. Many beaches with abundant sands, caves and rock pools; excellent surf. Pilots' gigs are still raced from the harbour and on the headland stands the stone Huer's House from the pilchard-fishing days.
Tourist Information Centre
☎ *(01637) 871345*

Degembris Farmhouse ⋀
🍳🍳 HIGHLY COMMENDED
St Newlyn East, Newquay TR8 5HY
☎ Mitchell (01872) 510555
Fax (01872) 510230
165-acre arable farm. Cosy south-facing farmhouse offering welcoming log fires in winter, comfortable en-suite bedrooms and delicious home cooking. "A wonderful oasis from 23 million cars".
Bedrooms: 1 single, 1 double, 1 twin, 1 triple, 1 family room
Bathrooms: 3 private, 1 public
Bed & breakfast

per night:	£min	£max
Single	18.00	20.00
Double	36.00	40.00

Half board

per person:	£min	£max
Daily	26.50	28.50
Weekly	185.50	199.50

Evening meal from 1830
Parking for 8
☎ 🖵 ❌ 🆙 🛈 ♨ 🆃🆅 🛏, ♨ ◐ ✓ ❋ ✕ ⚑ ℍ

Manuels Farm
🍳🍳 HIGHLY COMMENDED
Quintrell Downs, Newquay TR8 4NY
☎ (01637) 873577
44-acre mixed farm. In a sheltered valley 2 miles inland from Newquay, offering the peace of the countryside with the charm of a traditional 17th C farmhouse. Beautifully furnished, log fires and delicious country cooking.
Bedrooms: 1 double, 1 triple, 1 family room
Bathrooms: 1 private, 2 public
Bed & breakfast

per night:	£min	£max
Single		19.00
Double		38.00

Half board

per person:	£min	£max
Daily		31.00
Weekly	185.00	207.50

Evening meal 1830 (last orders 1630)
Parking for 6
☎ 📞 📭 ❌ 🅿 🛈 S ⊁ ♨ 🆃🆅 🛏, ♨ ✓ ❋ ⚑ SP ℍ

Rose Cottage
🍳🍳
Shepherds Farm, St Newlyn East, Newquay TR8 5NW
☎ Zelah (01872) 540502
600-acre mixed farm. Decorated and furnished to a high standard, all rooms en-suite with colour TV and tea-making facilities. Ideal for touring and beaches, 1 mile from A30 in little hamlet of Fiddlers Green. A warm welcome awaits.
Bedrooms: 2 double, 1 twin
Bathrooms: 3 private
Bed & breakfast

per night:	£min	£max
Single	15.00	17.00
Double	30.00	34.00

Half board

per person:	£min	£max
Daily	22.50	
Weekly	100.00	115.00

Evening meal 1800 (last orders 1000)
Parking for 3
☎ 🖵 ❌ 🆙 🛈 S ♨ 🆃🆅 🛏, ♨ ◐ U ❋ ⚑ OAP SP

NEWTON FERRERS

Devon
Map ref 1C3

Hillside village overlooking wooded estuary of the River Yealm, with attractive waterside cottages and yacht anchorage.

Maywood Cottage
🍳🍳 COMMENDED
Bridgend, Newton Ferrers, Plymouth PL8 1AW
☎ Plymouth (01752) 872372
Cottage on 3 levels, close to River Yealm estuary. Part old, all modernised. Take Bridgend - Noss Mayo road off

B3186 (leading to Newton Ferrers). Maywood is at bottom of hill on right just before estuary.
Bedrooms: 2 twin
Bathrooms: 2 private
Bed & breakfast

per night:	£min	£max
Single	20.00	25.00
Double	35.00	50.00

Half board

per person:	£min	£max
Daily	28.50	33.50
Weekly	170.00	200.00

Evening meal 1800 (last orders 2030)
Parking for 3
☎ ❌ �🦆 🆙 🛈 S 🅿 🆃🆅 🛏, ♨ ❋ ⚑ OAP ↘ SP ℍ

NORTH CADBURY

Somerset
Map ref 2B3

Hill Ash Farm
🍳 COMMENDED
Woolston, North Cadbury, Yeovil BA22 7BL
☎ (01963) 440332
30-acre hill farm. 1766 Grade II listed thatched farmhouse. Beautiful rural setting in peaceful hamlet.
Bedrooms: 2 single, 2 double
Bathrooms: 2 private, 1 public
Bed & breakfast

per night:	£min	£max
Single	16.00	18.00
Double	32.00	36.00

Parking for 4
Open March-October
☎ ❌ 🆙 ⊁ ♨ 🆃🆅 🛏, ♨ ❋ ✕ ⚑ ℍ

OKEHAMPTON

Devon
Map ref 1C2

Busy market town near the high tors of northern Dartmoor. The Victorian church, with William Morris windows and a 15th C tower, stands on the site of a Saxon church. A Norman castle ruin overlooks the river to the west of the town. Museum of Dartmoor Life in a restored mill.

Higher Cadham Farm
🍳🍳🍳 COMMENDED
Jacobstow, Okehampton EX20 3RB
☎ Exbourne (01837) 851647
Fax (01837) 851410

139-acre mixed farm. 16th C farmhouse on a traditional Devon farm, 5 miles
Continued ►

275

OKEHAMPTON

Continued

from Dartmoor and within easy reach of coast. On the Tarka trail.
Bedrooms: 1 single, 3 double, 2 twin, 3 family rooms
Bathrooms: 5 private, 1 public

Bed & breakfast

per night:	£min	£max
Single	16.50	22.50
Double	33.00	45.00

Half board

per person:	£min	£max
Daily	24.50	30.50
Weekly	155.00	195.00

Lunch available
Evening meal 1900 (last orders 2000)
Parking for 6
Cards accepted: Access, Visa, Amex, Switch/Delta

Oxenham Arms ⚑
👑👑 COMMENDED

South Zeal, Okehampton EX20 2JT
☎ (01837) 840244
Fax (01837) 840791
In the centre of Dartmoor village, originally built in the 12th C. Wealth of granite fireplaces, oak beams, mullion windows. Various diets available on request.
Bedrooms: 3 double, 3 twin, 2 triple
Bathrooms: 8 private

Bed & breakfast

per night:	£min	£max
Single	40.00	45.00
Double	50.00	60.00

Half board

per person:	£min	£max
Daily	40.00	45.00
Weekly	210.00	227.50

Lunch available
Evening meal 1930 (last orders 2100)
Parking for 8
Cards accepted: Access, Visa, Diners, Amex

Week Farm
👑👑 COMMENDED

Bridestowe, Okehampton EX20 4HZ
☎ 01837 (01837) 861221

180-acre dairy & livestock farm. A warm welcome awaits you at this homely 17th C farmhouse three-quarters of a mile from the old A30 and 6 miles from Okehampton. Home cooking and

every comfort. Come and spoil yourselves.
Bedrooms: 3 double, 1 triple, 1 family room
Bathrooms: 5 private

Bed & breakfast

per night:	£min	£max
Single	20.00	22.00

Half board

per person:	£min	£max
Daily	30.00	34.00

Evening meal 1900 (last orders 1700)
Parking for 10

OTTERY ST MARY

Devon
Map ref 1D2

Former wool town with modern light industry set in countryside on the River Otter. The Cromwellian commander, Fairfax, made his headquarters here briefly during the Civil War. The interesting church, dating from the 14th C, is built to cathedral plan.

Fluxton Farm Hotel ⚑
👑👑

Ottery St Mary EX11 1RJ
☎ (01404) 812818
Former farmhouse in beautiful country setting. Comfortable en-suite bedrooms, 2 sitting rooms, large gardens. Home-cooked food served in candlelit dining room. Log fires in season. Cat lovers' paradise.
Bedrooms: 3 single, 3 double, 4 twin, 2 triple
Bathrooms: 10 private, 1 public

Bed & breakfast

per night:	£min	£max
Single	23.00	25.00
Double	46.00	50.00

Half board

per person:	£min	£max
Daily	29.50	33.00
Weekly	195.00	220.00

Evening meal 1850 (last orders 1800)
Parking for 20

Pitt Farm ⚑
👑👑 COMMENDED

Ottery St Mary EX11 1NL
☎ (01404) 812439
190-acre mixed farm. 16th C thatched farmhouse. En-suite rooms available, log fires in season. Half-a-mile off A30 on B3176.
Bedrooms: 1 single, 1 double, 2 twin, 2 family rooms
Bathrooms: 2 private, 3 public

Bed & breakfast

per night:	£min	£max
Single	16.00	20.00
Double	32.00	40.00

Half board

per person:	£min	£max
Daily	23.00	28.00

Evening meal 1900 (last orders 1700)
Parking for 6
Cards accepted: Amex

PADSTOW

Cornwall
Map ref 1B2

Old town encircling its harbour on the Camel Estuary. The 15th C church has notable bench-ends. There are fine houses on North Quay and Raleigh's Court House on South Quay. Tall cliffs and golden sands along the coast and ferry to Rock. Famous 'Obby 'Oss Festival on 1 May.

Old Mill Country House ⚑
👑👑👑 COMMENDED

Little Petherick, Padstow PL27 7QT
☎ Rumford (01841) 540388
16th C listed corn mill with waterwheel. Set in own gardens by stream in country village. Retains original character, period furnishings.
Bedrooms: 4 double, 2 twin
Bathrooms: 5 private, 1 public

Bed & breakfast

per night:	£min	£max
Double	47.00	55.00

Evening meal 1900 (last orders 1800)
Parking for 15
Open March-October
Cards accepted: Access, Visa, Amex

Trevorrick Farm ⚑
👑👑 COMMENDED

St Issey, Wadebridge PL27 7QH
☎ Rumford (01841) 540574
11-acre mixed farm. Delightful, comfortable farmhouse where quality and service come first. Located 1 mile from Padstow, overlooking Little Petherick Creek and the Camel Estuary.
Bedrooms: 1 double, 1 twin, 1 family room
Bathrooms: 3 private

Bed & breakfast

per night:	£min	£max
Single	17.50	19.00
Double	35.00	38.00

Half board

per person:	£min	£max
Daily	24.50	27.00

Evening meal 1800 (last orders 2030)
Parking for 20

Please mention this guide when making a booking.

PARRACOMBE

Devon
Map ref 1C1

Pretty village spreading over the slopes of a river valley on the western edge of Exmoor.

Fox and Goose Inn

👑

Parracombe, Barnstaple EX31 4PE
☎ (01598) 763239
19th C country coaching inn next to Heddon River, set in Exmoor National Park in the quiet village of Parracombe. Good home-cooked food.
Bedrooms: 3 double, 1 twin
Bathrooms: 1 public, 4 private showers

Bed & breakfast per night:	£min	£max
Single	17.00	18.00
Double	32.00	33.00

Lunch available
Evening meal 1900 (last orders 2100)
Parking for 20
Cards accepted: Access, Visa
2 [S] [TV]

PELYNT

Cornwall
Map ref 1C2

Trenake Farm

👑 COMMENDED

Pelynt, Looe PL13 2LT
☎ Lanreath (01503) 220216
Fax (01503) 220216
286-acre mixed farm. 14th C farmhouse, 5 miles from Looe and 3 miles from Talland Bay beach.
Bedrooms: 1 single, 1 double, 1 triple
Bathrooms: 1 private, 1 public

Bed & breakfast per night:	£min	£max
Single	15.00	18.50
Double	30.00	37.00

Parking for 6
Open April-October
[UL] [TV]

PENSFORD

Avon
Map ref 2A2

Green Acres

Listed APPROVED

Stanton Wick, Pensford BS18 4BX
☎ Mendip (01761) 490397
A friendly welcome awaits you in peaceful setting, off A37/A368. Relax and enjoy panoramic views across Chew Valley to Dundry Hills.
Bedrooms: 2 single, 2 double, 1 twin
Bathrooms: 1 private, 4 public

Bed & breakfast per night:	£min	£max
Single	16.00	18.00
Double	32.00	34.00

Parking for 21
[UL] [S] [TV]

PENZANCE

Cornwall
Map ref 1A3

Resort and fishing port on Mount's Bay with mainly Victorian promenade and some fine Regency terraces. Former prosperity came from tin trade and pilchard fishing. Grand Georgian style church by harbour. Georgian Egyptian building at head of Chapel Street and Morrab Gardens.
Tourist Information Centre
☎ (01736) 62207

Halcyon Guest House

👑👑

6 Chyandour Square, Penzance TR18 3LW
☎ (01736) 66302
Granite Tudor-style house overlooking Mount's Bay and St Michael's Mount in a private road between town and beach. Private parking.
Bedrooms: 1 double, 1 twin, 1 triple, 1 family room
Bathrooms: 4 private

Bed & breakfast per night:	£min	£max
Single	20.00	23.00
Double	36.00	40.00

Half board per person:	£min	£max
Daily	25.00	27.00
Weekly	154.00	160.00

Evening meal 1830 (last orders 1830)
Parking for 4
Open March-October
[UL] [TV]

Menwidden Farm

Listed APPROVED

Ludgvan, Penzance TR20 8BN
☎ (01736) 740415
40-acre mixed farm. Centrally situated in west Cornwall. Warm family atmosphere and home cooking. Turn right at Crowlas crossroads on the A30 from Hayle, signpost Vellanoweth on right turn. Last farm on left.
Bedrooms: 1 single, 2 double, 1 twin, 1 family room
Bathrooms: 2 public

Bed & breakfast per night:	£min	£max
Single	14.00	
Double	28.00	

Half board per person:	£min	£max
Daily	21.00	
Weekly	126.00	

Evening meal 1800 (last orders 1800)
Parking for 8
Open February-November
[UL] [TV]

Penalva

👑👑👑 APPROVED

Alexandra Road, Penzance TR18 4LZ
☎ (01736) 69060
Well positioned imposing Victorian hotel, near all amenities, offering full central heating, good food and service. Non-smokers only, please.
Bedrooms: 1 single, 3 double, 1 twin
Bathrooms: 5 private

Bed & breakfast per night:	£min	£max
Single	11.00	16.00

Half board per person:	£min	£max
Daily	21.00	26.00

Evening meal 1830 (last orders 1900)
5 ☎ [UL] [S] [TV] [OAP] [SP]

Tregoddick House

Listed

Madron, Penzance TR20 8SS
☎ (01736) 62643
Detached period house with walled gardens. Interior has some original fittings, granite fireplaces, etc. Located in attractive village close to West Penwith moors.
Bedrooms: 2 twin
Bathrooms: 2 private

Bed & breakfast per night:	£min	£max
Single	16.00	17.50
Double	32.00	35.00

Parking for 2
Open January-November
[UL] [TV]

Woodstock Guest House

👑👑

29 Morrab Road, Penzance TR18 4AZ
☎ (01736) 69049
Fax (01736) 69049
Well-appointed, centrally situated guesthouse. Helpful, friendly service. Tea-making facilities, radio, TV and hairdryer all inclusive.
Bedrooms: 1 single, 1 double, 2 twin, 1 triple
Bathrooms: 2 private, 2 public

Bed & breakfast per night:	£min	£max
Single	11.00	18.00
Double	22.00	36.00

Cards accepted: Access, Visa, Diners, Amex
[UL] [S] [TV] [SP]

PERRANUTHNOE

Cornwall
Map ref 1B3

Small village on Mount's Bay, with lovely cliff walks.

Ednovean House

♛♛♛

Perranuthnoe, Penzance TR20 9LZ
☎ Penzance (01736) 711071

Stands in 1 acre of gardens, with superb views of St Michael's Mount and Mount's Bay. Ideal centre for touring and walking.
Bedrooms: 2 single, 4 double, 2 twin, 1 triple
Bathrooms: 6 private, 1 public

Bed & breakfast per night:	£min	£max
Single	21.00	23.00
Double	38.00	46.00

Half board per person:	£min	£max
Daily	33.00	37.00
Weekly	208.00	233.00

Lunch available
Evening meal 1900 (last orders 2000)
Parking for 12
Cards accepted: Access, Visa, Amex
[S] [TV] [SP]

PETER TAVY

Devon
Map ref 1C2

Churchtown

[Listed]

Peter Tavy, Tavistock PL19 9NN
☎ Mary Tavy (01822) 810477
Peaceful Victorian house in own grounds on edge of village. Beautiful moorland views. 5 minutes' walk to excellent pub food.
Bedrooms: 2 single, 2 double
Bathrooms: 2 public, 3 private showers

Bed & breakfast per night:	£min	£max
Single	12.00	14.00
Double	24.00	28.00

Parking for 6
10 [UL] [S]

At-a-glance symbols are explained on the flap inside the back cover.

PIDDLETRENTHIDE

Dorset
Map ref 2B3

The Poachers Inn

♛♛♛ [COMMENDED]

Piddletrenthide, Dorchester DT2 7QX
☎ (01300) 348358
Country inn with riverside garden, in beautiful Piddle Valley. Swimming pool. All rooms en-suite, colour TV, tea-making facilities, telephone. Residents' lounge. Brochure available.
Bedrooms: 8 double, 1 twin, 2 family rooms
Bathrooms: 11 private

Bed & breakfast per night:	£min	£max
Double	42.00	46.00

Half board per person:	£min	£max
Daily	31.00	33.00
Weekly	196.00	208.00

Lunch available
Evening meal 1700 (last orders 2130)
Parking for 30
Cards accepted: Access, Visa
[S] [TV] [SP]

PILLATON

Cornwall
Map ref 1C2

Peaceful village on the slopes of the River Lynher in steeply-wooded country near the Devon border. Within easy reach of the coast and rugged walking country on Bodmin Moor.

The Weary Friar Inn

♛♛♛ [COMMENDED]

Pillaton, Saltash PL12 6QS
☎ Liskeard (01579) 50238
Charming country inn noted for its quality food and interesting combination of modern comforts with 12th C character. Ideally placed for exploring inland and coastal areas.
Bedrooms: 2 single, 7 double, 2 twin, 1 triple
Bathrooms: 12 private

Bed & breakfast per night:	£min	£max
Single	30.00	35.00
Double	40.00	50.00

Lunch available
Evening meal 1900 (last orders 2130)
Parking for 30
Cards accepted: Access, Visa
[S] [TV] 20 [T]

We advise you to confirm your booking in writing.

PLYMOUTH

Devon
Map ref 1C2

Devon's largest city, major port and naval base. Old houses on the Barbican and ambitious architecture in modern centre, with aquarium, museum and art gallery, the Dome - a heritage centre on the Hoe. Superb coastal views over Plymouth Sound from the Hoe.
Tourist Information Centre
☎ (01752) 264849 or 266030

Bowling Green Hotel

♛♛ [HIGHLY COMMENDED]

9-10 Osborne Place, Lockyer Street, Plymouth PL1 2PU
☎ (01752) 667485
Fax (01752) 255150
Rebuilt Victorian property with views of Dartmoor. Overlooking Sir Francis Drake's bowling green on beautiful Plymouth Hoe. Centrally situated for the Barbican, Theatre Royal and leisure/conference centre.
Bedrooms: 1 single, 6 double, 2 twin, 3 triple
Bathrooms: 8 private, 4 private showers

Bed & breakfast per night:	£min	£max
Single	28.00	34.00
Double	36.00	46.00

Parking for 4
Cards accepted: Access, Visa, Diners, Amex, Switch/Delta
[UL] [S] [TV] [OAP] [SP] [T]

Gabber Farm

♛♛ [COMMENDED]

Down Thomas, Plymouth PL9 0AW
☎ (01752) 862269
120-acre mixed & dairy farm. On the south Devon coast, near Bovisand and Wembury. Lovely walks in the area. Near diving centre. Directions are provided. Friendly welcome assured. Special weekly rates, especially for OAPs and children.
Bedrooms: 1 double, 2 twin, 1 triple, 1 family room
Bathrooms: 2 private, 1 public

Bed & breakfast per night:	£min	£max
Single	15.50	17.50
Double	30.00	34.00

Half board per person:	£min	£max
Daily	23.50	25.50
Weekly	145.00	155.00

Evening meal 1900 (last orders 1800)
Parking for 4
[UL] [S] [TV] [OAP] [T]

Lamplighter Hotel

103 Citadel Road, The Hoe, Plymouth PL1 2RN
☎ (01752) 663855
Small friendly hotel on Plymouth Hoe, 5 minutes' walk from the city centre and seafront.
Bedrooms: 5 double, 2 twin, 1 triple, 1 family room
Bathrooms: 9 private, 1 public

Bed & breakfast per night:	£min	£max
Single	20.00	25.00
Double	30.00	35.00

Parking for 4
Cards accepted: Access, Visa

Phantele Guest House

COMMENDED
176 Devonport Road, Stoke, Plymouth PL1 5RD
☎ (01752) 561506
Small family-run guesthouse about 2 miles from city centre. Convenient base for touring. Close to continental and Torpoint ferries.
Bedrooms: 2 single, 1 double, 1 twin, 2 triple
Bathrooms: 2 private, 2 public

Bed & breakfast per night:	£min	£max
Single	15.00	23.00
Double	28.00	37.00

Half board per person:	£min	£max
Daily	21.00	30.00
Weekly	126.00	180.00

Evening meal 1830 (last orders 1700)

PORTREATH

Cornwall
Map ref 1B3

Formerly developed as a mining port, small resort with some handsome 19th C buildings. Cliffs, sands and good surf.

Bensons

Listed COMMENDED
1 The Hillside, Portreath, Redruth TR16 4LL
☎ Redruth (01209) 842534
Situated in a valley overlooking the sea. Close to beach and harbour. Ideally suited for touring Cornwall. Lovely clifftop walks in surrounding National Trust land.
Bedrooms: 2 double, 2 twin
Bathrooms: 4 private

Bed & breakfast per night:	£min	£max
Single		25.00
Double		35.00

Parking for 5
12

PRIDDY

Somerset
Map ref 2A2

Village in the Mendips, formerly a lead-mining centre, with old inns dating from the mining era. The area is rich in Bronze Age remains, among them the Priddy nine barrows. There is a sheep fair in the village every August.

Highcroft

COMMENDED
Wells Road, Priddy, Wells BA5 3AU
☎ Wells (01749) 673446
A natural stone country house with large lawns. From Wells take A39 to Bristol for 3 miles, turn left to Priddy and Highcroft is on right after about 2 miles.
Bedrooms: 1 single, 1 double, 1 twin, 1 triple
Bathrooms: 2 private, 1 public

Bed & breakfast per night:	£min	£max
Single	18.00	18.00
Double	34.00	36.00

Parking for 5

ST AGNES

Cornwall
Map ref 1B3

Small town in a once-rich mining area on the north coast. Terraced cottages and granite houses slope to the church. Some old mine workings remain, but the attraction must be the magnificent coastal scenery and superb walks. St Agnes Beacon offers one of Cornwall's most extensive views.

Penkerris

Penwinnick Road, St Agnes TR5 0PA
☎ (01872) 552262

Enchanting Edwardian residence with own grounds in unspoilt Cornish village. Beautiful rooms, log fires in winter, good home cooking. Dramatic cliff walks and beaches nearby.
Bedrooms: 1 single, 3 double, 1 twin, 2 triple
Bathrooms: 2 private, 3 public

Bed & breakfast per night:	£min	£max
Single	15.00	20.00
Double	25.00	35.00

Half board per person:	£min	£max
Daily	20.00	25.00
Weekly	125.00	160.00

Lunch available
Evening meal from 1830
Parking for 8
Cards accepted: Access, Visa, Amex

ST AUSTELL

Cornwall
Map ref 1B3

Leading market town, the meeting point of old and new Cornwall. One mile from St Austell Bay with its sandy beaches, old fishing villages and attractive countryside. Ancient narrow streets, pedestrian shopping precincts. Fine church of Pentewan stone and Italianate Town Hall.

Poltarrow Farm

HIGHLY COMMENDED
St Mewan, St Austell PL26 7DR
☎ (01726) 67111
45-acre mixed farm. Delightful farmhouse on South Coast. Comfortable accommodation, charming bedrooms and traditional farmhouse cooking. Excellent central position for touring Cornwall.
Bedrooms: 3 double, 1 twin, 1 family room
Bathrooms: 5 private

Bed & breakfast per night:	£min	£max
Single	19.00	22.00
Double	36.00	40.00

Half board per person:	£min	£max
Daily	29.00	32.00
Weekly	195.00	210.00

Evening meal from 1830
Parking for 5
Cards accepted: Access, Visa

ST IVES

Cornwall
Map ref 1B3

Old fishing port, artists' colony and holiday town with good surfing beach. Fishermen's cottages, granite fish cellars, a sandy harbour and magnificent headlands typify a charm that has survived since the 19th C pilchard boom. Tate Gallery opened in 1993.
Tourist Information Centre
☎ (01736) 796297

The Anchorage Guest House

COMMENDED
5 Bunkers Hill, St Ives TR26 1LJ
☎ Penzance (01736) 797135

Continued ▶

ST IVES

Continued

*18th C fisherman's cottage guesthouse
with exceptional decor. Short walk to
beach. Full of old world charm,
centrally heated.*
Bedrooms: 1 single, 4 double, 1 twin
Bathrooms: 4 private, 1 public
Bed & breakfast

per night:	£min	£max
Single	15.00	19.00
Double	30.00	38.00

Cards accepted: Access, Visa, Amex

Seagulls Guest House

4 Godrevy Terrace, St Ives TR26 1JA
☎ Penzance (01736) 797273
*Panoramic sea views, 2 minutes to
beaches, town centre and Tate Gallery.
Superior rooms with private facilities.
Free parking.*
Bedrooms: 1 single, 4 double; suites
available
Bathrooms: 2 private, 1 public,
2 private showers
Bed & breakfast

per night:	£min	£max
Single	14.00	22.00
Double	28.00	44.00

Parking for 10

ST KEW

Cornwall
Map ref 1B2

Old village sheltered by trees
standing beside a stream. The
church is noted for its medieval
glass showing the Passion and the
remains of a scene of the Tree of
Jesse.

Tregellist Farm

COMMENDED

Tregellist, St Kew, Bodmin PL30 3HG
☎ Bodmin (01208) 880537
*125-acre mixed farm. Farmhouse, built
in 1989, offering old-fashioned
hospitality. Set in tiny hamlet with
lovely views and pleasant walks. Central
for coast and moors. Children welcome.
1.5 miles from A39.*
Bedrooms: 1 double, 1 twin, 1 family
room
Bathrooms: 3 private
Bed & breakfast

per night:	£min	£max
Single	18.00	18.00
Double	36.00	36.00

Half board

per person:	£min	£max
Daily	27.00	

Evening meal from 1800
Parking for 6
Open February-October

ST MAWGAN

Cornwall
Map ref 1B2

Pretty village on wooded slopes in
the Vale of Lanherne. At its
centre, an old stone bridge is
overlooked by the church with its
lofty buttressed tower. Among the
ancient stone crosses in the
churchyard is a 15th C lantern
cross with carved figures.

The Falcon Inn

St Mawgan, Newquay TR8 4EP
☎ Newquay (01637) 860225
*16th C wisteria-covered inn with
beautiful gardens in the vale of
Lanherne. Unspoilt peaceful situation.*
Bedrooms: 1 single, 2 double, 1 twin
Bathrooms: 2 private, 1 public
Bed & breakfast

per night:	£min	£max
Single	17.00	17.00
Double	42.00	48.00

Lunch available
Evening meal 1830 (last orders 2200)
Parking for 25
Cards accepted: Access, Visa

ST NEOT

Cornwall
Map ref 1C2

Colliford Tavern 🏔

COMMENDED

Colliford Lake, St Neot, Liskeard
PL14 6PZ
☎ Cardinham (01208) 821335
Fax (01208) 821335
*"An oasis on Bodmin Moor". Friendly
country pub, ideally situated for
exploring Cornwall. Immaculate
facilities. Good home-cooked meals and
fine traditional ales. Colour brochure
available.*
Bedrooms: 3 double, 2 twin
Bathrooms: 5 private
Bed & breakfast

per night:	£min	£max
Double	39.00	49.00

Lunch available
Evening meal 1900 (last orders 2130)
Parking for 50
Open April-December
Cards accepted: Access, Visa, Amex

> Map references apply to
> the colour maps at the
> back of this guide.

SALCOMBE

Devon
Map ref 1C3

Sheltered yachting resort of
whitewashed houses and narrow
streets in a balmy setting on the
Salcombe Estuary. Palm, myrtle
and other Mediterranean plants
flourish. There are sandy bays and
creeks for boating.

Torre View Hotel

COMMENDED

Devon Road, Salcombe TQ8 8HJ
☎ (01548) 842633
Fax (01548) 842633
*Detached Victorian residence with every
modern comfort, commanding extensive
views of the estuary and surrounding
countryside. Congenial atmosphere. No
smoking, please.*
Bedrooms: 6 double, 2 twin; suites
available
Bathrooms: 8 private
Bed & breakfast

per night:	£min	£max
Single	24.00	29.00
Double	45.00	52.00

Half board

per person:	£min	£max
Daily	32.50	36.50
Weekly	218.00	242.00

Evening meal 1900 (last orders 1800)
Parking for 5
Open February-October
Cards accepted: Access, Visa

SALISBURY

Wiltshire
Map ref 2B3

Beautiful city and ancient regional
capital set amid water meadows.
Buildings of all periods are
dominated by the cathedral whose
spire is the tallest in England. Built
between 1220 and 1258, it is one
of the purest examples of Early
English architecture.
Tourist Information Centre
☎ *(01722) 334956*

The Bell Inn

Warminster Road, South Newton,
Salisbury SP2 0QD
☎ (01722) 743336
*300-year-old roadside inn offering full
en-suite facilities. Extensive range of bar
meals. 6 miles north west of Salisbury.*
Bedrooms: 1 single, 1 double, 1 twin
Bathrooms: 3 private
Bed & breakfast

per night:	£min	£max
Single	20.00	20.00
Double	32.00	34.00

Lunch available
Evening meal 1900 (last orders 2100)
Parking for 60

🛇 5 ⛔ 👃 ⛱ ✑ ✂ Ⅲ. ◖ ∪ ♪ ✿ ✗ 🛒 Ⓣ

Beulah

Listed

144 Britford Lane, Salisbury SP2 8AL
☎ (01722) 333517
*Bungalow in quiet road 1.25 miles from
city centre, overlooking meadows. No-
smoking establishment.*
Bedrooms: 1 single, 1 family room
Bathrooms: 1 public

Bed & breakfast

per night:	£min	£max
Single	15.00	15.00
Double	30.00	30.00

Parking for 4

🛇 2 ⛺ ⅶ ✓ ✂ ☎ Ⅲ. ◻ ✿ ✗ 🛒

Brickworth Farmhouse

Listed COMMENDED

Brickworth Lane, Whiteparish,
Salisbury, Wilts SP5 2QE
☎ Whiteparish (01794) 884663
Fax (01794) 884581

*Charming 18th C listed farmhouse,
featured in "Ideal Home": perfect
location off A36 south-east of Salisbury.
Ideal for visiting Wiltshire, Hampshire
and Dorset.*
Bedrooms: 1 single, 1 double, 1 family
room
Bathrooms: 1 private, 1 public

Bed & breakfast

per night:	£min	£max
Single	18.00	22.00
Double	30.00	36.00

Parking for 20

🛇 ⛭ 👃 ⅶ ☎ Ⅲ. ◻ ✿ ✗ 🛒 🏛

Byways House

🏚🏚

31 Fowlers Road, City Centre,
Salisbury SP1 2QP
☎ (01722) 328364
Fax (01722) 322146
*Attractive family-run Victorian house
close to cathedral in quiet area of city
centre. Car park. Bedrooms en-suite
with colour TV. Traditional English and
vegetarian breakfasts.*
Bedrooms: 4 single, 8 double, 8 twin,
2 triple, 1 family room
Bathrooms: 20 private, 1 public

Bed & breakfast

per night:	£min	£max
Single	22.00	
Double	39.00	

Parking for 15
Cards accepted: Access, Visa

🛇 ⛺ ⛘ ⛔ 👃 ✑ 🛎 Ⓢ ✓ ⅶ Ⅲ. ◻ 🍴43 ∪
▸ ✿ ᴼᴬᴾ ꜱᴘ 🏛 Ⓣ

Castlewood

🏚🏚

45 Castle Road, Salisbury SP1 3RH
☎ (01722) 421494 & 324809
*Large Edwardian house, tastefully
restored throughout. Pleasant 10
minutes' riverside walk to city centre
and cathedral.*
Bedrooms: 1 single, 1 double, 1 twin,
1 triple, 1 family room
Bathrooms: 4 private, 1 public

Bed & breakfast

per night:	£min	£max
Single	18.00	25.00
Double	30.00	35.00

Parking for 4

🛇 ⛔ 👃 ⅶ ✓ ⅶ ☎ Ⅲ. ◻ ✗ 🛒

Cranston Guest House

🏚🏚 APPROVED

5 Wain-a-Long Road, Salisbury
SP1 1LJ
☎ (01722) 336776
*Large detached town house covered in
Virginia creeper. 10 minutes' walk from
town centre and cathedral.*
Bedrooms: 2 single, 1 double, 2 twin,
2 family rooms
Bathrooms: 5 private, 1 public

Bed & breakfast

per night:	£min	£max
Single	16.00	18.00
Double	32.00	36.00

Half board

per person:	£min	£max
Daily	22.00	24.00

Evening meal 1800 (last orders 1900)
Parking for 4

🛇 ⛺ ⛔ 👃 ⅶ Ⓢ ✓ ✂ ☎ ◻ ✿ 🛒 ꜱᴘ

The Gallery

Listed COMMENDED

36 Wyndham Road, Salisbury
SP1 3AB
☎ (01722) 324586
Fax (01722) 324586
*Experience our warm hospitality and
delicious breakfasts in a non-smoking
environment. Well situated for exploring
Salisbury and the many attractions in
the area.*
Bedrooms: 1 double, 2 twin
Bathrooms: 3 private

Bed & breakfast

per night:	£min	£max
Double	28.00	34.00

🛇 12 ⛭ ⛔ 👃 ⅶ 🛎 Ⓢ ✓ Ⅲ. ◻ ✿ 🛒
ᴼᴬᴾ ꜱᴘ

Hayburn Wyke Guest House

🏚

72 Castle Road, Salisbury SP1 3RL
☎ (01722) 412627
*Family-run spacious guesthouse
adjacent to Victoria Park. Short walk
from the cathedral and city centre and
Old Sarum. Stonehenge 9 miles.*

Bedrooms: 2 double, 2 twin, 2 triple
Bathrooms: 2 private, 1 public

Bed & breakfast

per night:	£min	£max
Single	21.00	30.00
Double	31.00	40.00

Parking for 6

🛇 ⛔ 👃 ⅶ 🛎 Ⓢ ✓ ✂ ☎ ◖ Ⅲ. ◻ ✿ ꜱᴘ 🏛

Kelebrae

🏚🏚

101 Castle Road, Salisbury SP1 3RP
☎ (01722) 333628
*Family home, opposite Victoria Park
and within walking distance of city
centre. Convenient for Stonehenge.
Parking.*
Bedrooms: 2 double, 1 twin
Bathrooms: 2 private, 1 public

Bed & breakfast

per night:	£min	£max
Double	34.00	36.00

Parking for 4

🛇 10 ⛔ 👃 ⅶ ✑ ✂ ☎ Ⅲ. ◻ ✿ ✗
🛒 ᴼᴬᴾ Ⓣ

Leena's Guest House

🏚🏚

50 Castle Road, Salisbury SP1 3RL
☎ (01722) 335419
*Attractive Edwardian house with
friendly atmosphere, close to riverside
walks and park. Modern facilities
include en-suite and ground-floor
rooms.*
Bedrooms: 1 single, 2 double, 2 twin,
1 family room
Bathrooms: 4 private, 1 public,
1 private shower

Bed & breakfast

per night:	£min	£max
Single	18.00	
Double	29.00	

Parking for 7

🛇 ⛺ ⛔ 👃 ⅶ Ⓢ ✓ ✂ ☎ ◖ Ⅲ. ◻ ✿ ✗
🛒 ꜱᴘ

Old Mill Hotel ⋒

🏚🏚🏚 COMMENDED

Town Path, Harnham, Salisbury
SP2 8EU
☎ (01722) 327517
Fax (01722) 333367
*Former mill, peacefully located on River
Nadder, surrounded by water meadows
and with views of Salisbury Cathedral.
Restaurant, dating from 1135,
specialises in traditional English fare.
Freehouse offers local real ale.*
Bedrooms: 2 single, 6 double, 2 twin
Bathrooms: 10 private

Bed & breakfast

per night:	£min	£max
Single	40.00	40.00
Double	50.00	65.00

Half board

per person:	£min	£max
Daily	50.00	55.00

Continued ▶

SALISBURY

Continued

Lunch available
Evening meal 1830 (last orders 2145)
Parking for 16
Cards accepted: Access, Visa, Amex

Richburn Guest House

APPROVED

23 & 25 Estcourt Road, Salisbury
SP1 3AP
☎ (01722) 325189
*Large, tastefully renovated Victorian
house with homely family atmosphere.
All modern amenities and large car
park. Close to city centre and parks.*
Bedrooms: 2 single, 4 double, 2 twin,
1 triple, 1 family room
Bathrooms: 2 private, 2 public

Bed & breakfast

per night:	£min	£max
Single	16.50	17.00
Double	29.00	39.00

Parking for 10

Swaynes Firs Farm

APPROVED

Grimsdyke, Coombe Bissett, Salisbury
SP5 5RF
☎ Martin Cross (01725) 519240

*15-acre mixed farm. Country farmhouse
in pleasant position with good views.
Ancient Roman ditch on farm.
Peacocks, ducks, chickens and horses
are reared on the farm.*
Bedrooms: 2 twin, 1 family room
Bathrooms: 3 private

Bed & breakfast

per night:	£min	£max
Single	18.00	20.00
Double	36.00	40.00

Parking for 9

SALISBURY PLAIN

*See under Amesbury, Figheldean,
Salisbury, Shrewton, Warminster,
Winterbourne Stoke*

The accommodation
coupons at the back will
help you when contacting
proprietors.

SENNEN COVE

Cornwall
Map ref 1A3

The Old Success Inn ⚠

COMMENDED

Sennen Cove, Lands End TR19 7DG
☎ (01736) 871232
Fax (01736) 871457
*Attractively modernised old fisherman's
inn nestles in one of Cornwall's most
beautiful bays. Restaurant, Cornish fish
specialities, locals' bar.*
Bedrooms: 2 single, 8 double, 2 twin
Bathrooms: 10 private, 1 public

Bed & breakfast

per night:	£min	£max
Single	26.00	34.00
Double	52.00	80.00

Half board

per person:	£min	£max
Daily	38.00	46.00
Weekly	213.00	279.00

Lunch available
Evening meal 1900 (last orders 2130)
Parking for 14
Cards accepted: Access, Visa

SHALDON

Devon
Map ref 1D2

Pretty resort facing Teignmouth
from the south bank of the Teign
Estuary. Regency houses
harmonise with others of later
periods; there are old cottages and
narrow lanes. On the Ness, a
sandstone promontory nearby, a
tunnel built in the 19th C leads to
a beach revealed at low tide.

Fonthill

HIGHLY COMMENDED

Torquay Road, Shaldon, Teignmouth
TQ14 0AX
☎ (01626) 872344
Fax (01626) 872344
*Lovely Georgian family home in superb
grounds overlooking River Teign. Very
comfortable rooms in a peaceful setting.
Restaurants nearby.*
Bedrooms: 3 twin
Bathrooms: 3 private

Bed & breakfast

per night:	£min	£max
Single	28.00	32.00
Double	46.00	52.00

Parking for 5

Please mention this guide
when making a booking.

SHEPTON MALLET

Somerset
Map ref 2A2

Important, stone-built market town
beneath the south-west slopes of
the Mendips. Thriving rural
industries include glove and shoe
making, dairying and cider making;
the remains of a medieval
"shambles" in the square date
from the town's prosperity as a
wool centre.

Hurlingpot Farm

COMMENDED

Chelynch, Doulting, Shepton Mallet
BA4 4PY
☎ (01749) 880256
Fax (01749) 880256
*Lovely 300-year-old farmhouse in a
peaceful country setting, 2 miles east of
Shepton Mallet. A361 to Doulting, then
take Chelynch road. Turn left past
Poachers Pocket pub and left again into
farm entrance.*
Bedrooms: 1 double, 1 twin, 1 triple;
suites available
Bathrooms: 3 private

Bed & breakfast

per night:	£min	£max
Single	20.00	25.00
Double	30.00	35.00

Parking for 6

Northover

COMMENDED

Charlton Road, Shepton Mallet
BA4 4PR
☎ (01749) 346856
*Lovely 17th C country house on the
outskirts of Shepton Mallet. Very
comfortable, very relaxing. Good centre
for interesting countryside.*
Bedrooms: 1 single, 2 double; suites
available
Bathrooms: 3 private

Bed & breakfast

per night:	£min	£max
Single	16.00	20.00
Double	38.00	45.00

Parking for 5

Temple House Farm ⚠

COMMENDED

Doulting, Shepton Mallet BA4 4RQ
☎ (01749) 880294
Fax (01749) 880688
*200-acre dairy farm. 400-year-old listed
farmhouse with all facilities. In rural
area within easy reach of Wells, Bath,
Shepton Mallet, the walking delights of
the Mendips and plenty of tourist
attractions.*
Bedrooms: 2 triple
Bathrooms: 2 private

Bed & breakfast per night:	£min	£max
Single		20.00
Double		32.00

Half board per person:	£min	£max
Daily		24.00
Weekly		160.00

⌂ 🕮 ⌷ ♦ ♛ Ⓤⓛ ⓐ Ⓢ ⓉⓋ ▥ 🖥 🎠 ✿ ✕ 🐾 🎏

SHERBORNE

Dorset
Map ref 2B3

Dorset's "Cathedral City" of medieval streets, golden Hamstone buildings and great abbey church, resting place of Saxon kings. Formidable 12th C castle ruins and Sir Walter Raleigh's splendid Tudor mansion and deer park. Street markets, leisure centre, many cultural activities.
Tourist Information Centre
☎ *(01935) 815341*

The Alders

😊😊 COMMENDED

Sandford Orcas, Sherborne DT9 4SB
☎ (01963) 220666
Secluded stone house set in old walled garden, in picturesque conservation village near Sherborne. Excellent food available in friendly village pub.
Bedrooms: 1 double, 1 twin
Bathrooms: 2 private

Bed & breakfast per night:	£min	£max
Single	18.50	25.00
Double	37.00	42.00

Parking for 6

⌂ 🕮 ⌷ ♦ Ⓤⓛ ✕ ⓉⓋ ▥ 🖥 ⌖ ✿ ✕ 🐾

The Queens Head

😊

High Street, Milborne Port, Sherborne DT9 5DQ
☎ Milborne Port (01963) 250314
Grade 11 listed village inn with 2 bars, separate restaurant and comfortable accommodation. 7 real ales and log fires.
Bedrooms: 1 single, 2 double
Bathrooms: 1 public, 1 private shower

Bed & breakfast per night:	£min	£max
Single		21.00
Double		35.00

Lunch available
Evening meal 1900 (last orders 2130)
Parking for 10
Cards accepted: Access, Visa, Diners, Amex

⌂ ⌷ ♦ ⓐ Ⓢ ▥ 🖥 ⌗40 🍷 🐾 🎏

Quinns

😊😊😊 HIGHLY COMMENDED

Marston Road, Sherborne DT9 4BL
☎ (01935) 815008

Delightful accommodation in modern house. All rooms en-suite, TV, tea/coffee making facilities. Spacious lounge. Dinners by arrangement. Car park.
Bedrooms: 1 single, 1 double, 1 twin
Bathrooms: 3 private

Bed & breakfast per night:	£min	£max
Single	21.00	25.00
Double	42.00	50.00

Half board per person:	£min	£max
Daily	35.00	39.00

Evening meal from 1900
Parking for 4

⌂ 8 ⌷ ♦ Ⓤⓛ ⓐ Ⓢ ⓅⓂ ▥ 🖥 🐾 SP

Wheatsheaf House

😊 COMMENDED

Corton Denham, Sherborne DT9 4LQ
☎ Corton Denham (0196322) 0207
Large country house in attractive grounds, 3 miles north of Sherborne. Spacious accommodation with use of kitchen, lounges and gardens.
Bedrooms: 1 double, 1 twin, 1 triple
Bathrooms: 2 public

Bed & breakfast per night:	£min	£max
Single	16.00	20.00
Double	32.00	40.00

Parking for 10
Open March-November

⌂ 🖑 Ⓤⓛ Ⓢ ⓅⓂ ⓉⓋ ▥ 🖥 ✿ 🐾

SHREWTON

Wiltshire
Map ref 2B2

Ashwick House

😊😊 COMMENDED

Upper Backway, Shrewton, Salisbury SP3 4DE
☎ (01980) 621138
Fax (01980) 620152
Large village house in quiet position. Ideal touring centre for Salisbury, Bath, New Forest, Stonehenge (2 miles). Walking distance of 2 pubs. Parking in driveway.
Bedrooms: 2 twin
Bathrooms: 1 private, 1 public

Bed & breakfast per night:	£min	£max
Single	14.00	16.00
Double	28.00	32.00

Half board per person:	£min	£max
Daily	22.00	30.00
Weekly	135.00	160.00

Evening meal 1900 (last orders 2030)
Parking for 5

⌂ 🕮 ♦ ♛ Ⓤⓛ ⓐ Ⓢ ✕ ⓅⓂ ▥ 🖥 ✿ ✕ 🐾 ⟨ SP Ⓣ

Maddington House

Listed APPROVED

Shrewton, Salisbury SP3 4JD
☎ (01980) 620406
Fax (01980) 620406

Beautiful listed 17th C family home, with attractive period hall and dining room. Stonehenge 2 miles, Salisbury 9 miles.
Bedrooms: 1 double, 1 twin, 1 family room
Bathrooms: 1 private, 1 public, 2 private showers

Bed & breakfast per night:	£min	£max
Single	20.00	
Double	32.00	35.00

Parking for 7

⌂ ⌷ ♦ Ⓤⓛ Ⓢ ✕ ▥ 🖥 ✿ ✕ 🐾 🎏 Ⓣ

SIDMOUTH

Devon
Map ref 1D2

Charming resort set amid lofty red cliffs where the River Sid meets the sea. The wealth of ornate Regency and Victorian villas recalls the time when this was one of the south coast's most exclusive resorts. Museum; August International Festival of Folk Arts.
Tourist Information Centre
☎ *(01395) 516441*

Broad Oak

😊😊 HIGHLY COMMENDED

Sid Road, Sidmouth EX10 8QP
☎ (01395) 513713

Listed Victorian villa in delightful gardens overlooking "The Byes". A peaceful location, only a short stroll from the town centre and Esplanade.
Bedrooms: 1 single, 1 double, 1 twin
Bathrooms: 2 private, 1 public

Bed & breakfast per night:	£min	£max
Single	20.00	20.00
Double	46.00	50.00

Parking for 4
Open February-November

🕮 ⌷ ♦ ♛ Ⓢ ✕ ⓅⓂ ▥ ✿ ✕ 🐾 🎏

Lower Pinn Farm

😊😊 COMMENDED

Pinn, Sidmouth EX10 0NN
☎ (01395) 513733
220-acre mixed farm. Situated 2 miles west of Sidmouth, comfortable accommodation with substantial breakfast. Bedrooms have TV, tea/coffee facilities, central heating. Access at all times.
Bedrooms: 2 double, 1 twin
Bathrooms: 2 private, 1 public

Continued ▶

SIDMOUTH

Continued

Bed & breakfast

per night:	£min	£max
Double	34.00	38.00

Parking for 3

🚫♿📧☐♨⚲ ⓤⓁ Ⓢ 🅿 ▥ ⚓ ◡ ⚓ SP

SOUTH MOLTON

Devon
Map ref 1C1

Busy market town at the mouth of the Yeo Valley near southern Exmoor. Wool, mining and coaching brought prosperity between the Middle Ages and the 19th C and the fine square with Georgian buildings, a Guildhall and Assembly Rooms reflect this former affluence.

Kerscott Farm ⚠

👑👑 HIGHLY COMMENDED

Ash Mill, South Molton EX36 4QG
☎ Bishops Nympton (01769) 550262
70-acre livestock farm. Peaceful, welcoming working farm mentioned in Domesday Book, overlooking Exmoor. Superb views. Beautiful old world antique interior. Home farm cooking. Non-smokers only.
Bedrooms: 2 double, 1 twin
Bathrooms: 3 private

Bed & breakfast

per night:	£min	£max
Double		34.00

Half board

per person:	£min	£max
Daily	23.00	26.00

Evening meal 1830 (last orders 1400)
Parking for 8

🚫 8 🏠 ♨ ⓤⓁ Ⓢ 🅿 ▥ 📺 ▥ ⚓ ※ ✕ ⚓ 🏠

SOUTH PETHERTON

Somerset
Map ref 1D2

Small town with a restored 15th C house, King Ina's Palace. The Roman Fosse Way crosses the River Parrett to the east by way of an old bridge on which there are 2 curious carved figures.

Kings Pleasure

👑👑 COMMENDED

24 Silver Street, South Petherton
TA13 5BZ
☎ (01460) 241747

> Check the introduction to this region for ideas on Where to Go.

Listed hamstone house in conservation area within 1 minute of village centre. Four-poster bed, garden chess and use of bicycles.
Bedrooms: 1 double, 1 twin
Bathrooms: 2 private

Bed & breakfast

per night:	£min	£max
Single	25.00	25.00
Double	35.00	38.00

Parking for 2

🚫🏠📧☐♨⚲ ⓤⓁ Ⓢ ✕ 🅿 ▥ ⚓ ※ ⚓ 🏠

STARCROSS

Devon
Map ref 1D2

Small village on the western shore of the Exe Estuary, with a harbour and 19th C seaside villas. Powderham Castle and Park, just north, make a pleasant excursion and a pedestrian ferry crosses the water to Exmouth.

The Old Vicarage ⚠

👑👑 COMMENDED

Starcross, Exeter EX6 8PX
☎ (01626) 890206

Enjoy the relaxed, friendly atmosphere of this interesting old house set in 3 acres on Exe Estuary village edge. River views from some bedrooms. Easy access to Exeter, beaches and Dartmoor. Good local inns nearby.
Bedrooms: 2 double, 2 twin, 1 family room
Bathrooms: 3 private, 1 public

Bed & breakfast

per night:	£min	£max
Single	15.00	22.00
Double	30.00	40.00

Parking for 6

🚫📧♨⚲ ⓤⓁ 🅿 📺 ▥ ⚓ ※ ✕ ⚓

> The town index at the back of this guide gives page numbers of all places with accommodation.

STOKE-IN-TEIGNHEAD

Devon
Map ref 1D2

Deane Thatch Accommodation ⚠

👑👑 COMMENDED

Deane Road, Stoke-in-Teignhead,
Newton Abbot TQ12 4QU
☎ Shaldon (01626) 873724
Fax (01626) 873724

Picturesque, period cob thatched cottage and linhay in secluded rural position. King size bed, own spring water, barbecue, large gardens. Sea 2 miles.
Bedrooms: 1 double, 1 family room
Bathrooms: 2 private

Bed & breakfast

per night:	£min	£max
Single	20.00	25.00
Double	30.00	36.00

Parking for 3

🚫♿📧☐♨⚲ ⓤⓁ Ⓢ ✕ 🅿 📺 ▥ ⚓ ◡ ▷ ※ ⚓ ◊ SP 🏠

SWINDON

Wiltshire
Map ref 2B2

Wiltshire's industrial and commercial centre, an important railway town in the 19th C, situated just north of the Marlborough Downs. The railway village created in the mid-19th C has been preserved. Railway museum, art gallery, theatre and leisure centre.
Tourist Information Centre
☎ *(01793) 530328 or 493007*

Internos

📺

3 Turnpike Road, Blunsdon, Swindon, Wilshire SN2 4EA
☎ (01793) 721496
Detached red brick house off A419, 4 miles north of Swindon and 6 miles from M4 junction 15.
Bedrooms: 1 single, 1 twin, 1 triple
Bathrooms: 2 public

Bed & breakfast

per night:	£min	£max
Single	19.00	22.00
Double	32.00	32.00

Parking for 6

🚫📧☐♨⚲ ⓤⓁ 🅰 Ⓢ 🅿 📺 ▥ ⚓ ※ ✕ ⚓

Relian Guest House
☺☺

151-153 County Road, Swindon
SN1 2EB
☎ (01793) 521416
Quiet house adjacent to Swindon Town Football Club and short distance from town centre. Close to bus and rail stations, and A345. Free car park at rear.
Bedrooms: 4 single, 2 double, 2 twin; suites available
Bathrooms: 3 private, 2 public, 3 private showers
Bed & breakfast

per night:	£min	£max
Single	17.00	
Double	32.00	

🐾 2 ⛭ 🖵 ♨ ⑪ ♿ ⚡ 🅿 📺 🏛 ✕ 🚗

The School House Hotel & Restaurant ⋀
☺☺☺ COMMENDED

Hook Street, Hook, Swindon SN4 8EF
☎ (01793) 851198
Fax (01793) 851025
Charming country house hotel in a converted 1860 school house. Combining modern facilities and Victorian decor. In rural hamlet but close to M4, Swindon and Cotswolds.
Bedrooms: 1 single, 8 double, 1 twin
Bathrooms: 10 private
Bed & breakfast

per night:	£min	£max
Single	59.50	72.50
Double	70.00	81.00

Half board

per person:	£min	£max
Daily	78.50	99.50
Weekly	392.50	497.50

Lunch available
Evening meal 1800 (last orders 2200)
Parking for 40
Cards accepted: Access, Visa, Diners, Amex, Switch/Delta

🐾 ⛭ ⍾ 📞 🖵 ♨ ⚱ ♿ 🅰 🔒 ✕ 📺 ◑ 🖶, 🚗 🍴 60 ∪ ✿ ✕ 🚗 [DAP] ⅍ [SP] 🏛 [T]

SYDLING ST NICHOLAS
Dorset
Map ref 2B3

Magiston Farm
Listed

Sydling St Nicholas DT2 9NR
☎ Maiden Newton (01300) 320295
400-acre arable farm. 350-year-old farmhouse set beside the Sydling River, in the heart of Dorset 5 miles north of Dorchester.
Bedrooms: 2 single, 1 double, 2 twin
Bathrooms: 1 private, 1 public
Bed & breakfast

per night:	£min	£max
Single	16.50	
Double	33.00	

Half board

per person:	£min	£max
Daily		27.00

Evening meal from 1900
Parking for 10

🐾 10 ♨ ⑪ 🔒 [S] 🖵, 🚗 ⍾ ✎ ∪ 🅿 ✿ 🚗 🏛

TAUNTON
Somerset
Map ref 1D1

County town, well-known for its public schools, sheltered by gentle hill-ranges on the River Tone. Medieval prosperity from wool has continued in marketing and manufacturing and the town retains many fine period buildings.
Tourist Information Centre
☎ *(01823) 274785*

Higher Dipford Farm
☺☺☺ COMMENDED

Dipford, Trull, Taunton TA3 7NU
☎ (01823) 275770 & 257916
120-acre dairy farm. 14th C listed Somerset longhouse with magnificent walks and views. Antique furniture, log fires and spacious en-suite rooms. Renowned for high class cuisine using fresh dairy produce.
Bedrooms: 1 double, 1 triple, 1 family room
Bathrooms: 3 private
Bed & breakfast

per night:	£min	£max
Single	28.00	32.00
Double	46.00	54.00

Half board

per person:	£min	£max
Daily	39.00	43.00
Weekly	266.00	294.00

Lunch available
Evening meal 1900 (last orders 2130)
Parking for 6
Open January, March-December
Cards accepted: Amex

🐾 🖵 ♨ ⍾ 🇼 ⑪ 🔒 ✕ 📺 🖵, 🚗 ⍾ ∪ 🅿 ✎ ✓ ✿ 🚗 [DAP] ⅍ 🏛 [T]

Prockters Farm
☺☺

West Monkton, Taunton TA2 8QN
☎ West Monkton (01823) 412269
300-acre mixed farm. 300-year-old farmhouse, 3 miles from M5. Inglenook fireplaces, brass beds, collection of farm antiques. Large garden. Ground floor en-suite bedrooms. Tea and cake on arrival.
Bedrooms: 2 double, 2 twin, 1 triple
Bathrooms: 2 private, 2 public
Bed & breakfast

per night:	£min	£max
Single	18.00	25.00
Double	34.00	42.00

Parking for 6
Cards accepted: Amex

🐾 ⛭ 🖵 ♨ ⍾ 🇼 ⑪ 🔒 [S] ♿ 📺 🚗 🍴 15 ∪ 🅿 ✿ 🚗 [SP] 🏛

Town End Farm
☺☺

Crowcombe, Taunton TA4 4AA
☎ Crowcombe (01984) 618655
17th C thatched farmhouse set in Quantock Hills and on edge of village. Outdoor heated pool and games room. Ideal walking country, 5 miles coast.
Bedrooms: 1 double, 1 triple
Bathrooms: 2 private, 2 public
Bed & breakfast

per night:	£min	£max
Single	15.00	17.50
Double	30.00	35.00

Half board

per person:	£min	£max
Daily	21.00	23.50

Parking for 4
Open March-October

🐾 Ⓜ ♨ ⍾ 🇼 ⑪ 🖵, 🚗 ⚱ ⍾ ∪ ✿ 🚗 🏛

TAVISTOCK
Devon
Map ref 1C2

Old market town beside the River Tavy on the western edge of Dartmoor. Developed around its 10th C abbey, of which some fragments remain, it became a stannary town in 1305 when tin-streaming thrived on the moors. Tavistock Goose Fair, October.

April Cottage
☺☺ HIGHLY COMMENDED

Mount Tavy Road, Tavistock PL19 9JB
☎ (01822) 613280
Restored Victorian riverside character cottage in pretty garden setting. Dining-room overlooks river. 5 minutes' level walk from town centre and excellent pub food. Modern comforts include en-suite. Homely and welcoming.
Bedrooms: 2 double, 1 twin
Bathrooms: 1 private, 1 public
Bed & breakfast

per night:	£min	£max
Single	16.00	18.00
Double	26.00	32.00

Parking for 4

🐾 🖵 ♨ ⍾ 🇼 ⑪ 🔒 ✕ 📺 🖵, 🚗 ✿ 🚗 [DAP] [SP]

Langstone House
☺

Moortown, Whitchurch, Tavistock
PL19 9JZ
☎ (01822) 615100
Wing of house built for Duke of Bedford in 1871. Just below Pew Tor, south of Tavistock-Princetown road.
Bedrooms: 1 single, 2 double
Bathrooms: 1 public

Continued ▶

We advise you to confirm your booking in writing.

TAVISTOCK

Continued

Bed & breakfast

per night:	£min	£max
Single	16.50	
Double	30.00	33.00

Evening meal 1830 (last orders 2000)
Parking for 6
Open April-October

🛥️4♿♨️🅿️🔌📶🍴🚭📺🛏️❄️✂️🐴🐎

TINTAGEL

Cornwall
Map ref 1B2

Coastal village near the legendary home of King Arthur. There is a lofty headland with the ruin of a Norman castle and traces of a Celtic monastery are still visible in the turf.

Castle Villa

COMMENDED

Molesworth Street, Tintagel PL34 0BZ
☎ Camelford (01840) 770373 & 770203

Over 160 years old, Castle Villa is within easy walking distance of the 11th C church, post office and King Arthur's castle.
Bedrooms: 1 single, 3 double, 1 twin
Bathrooms: 1 private, 2 public

Bed & breakfast

per night:	£min	£max
Single	14.50	16.50
Double	29.00	38.00

Evening meal 1900 (last orders 2100)
Parking for 6
Cards accepted: Access, Visa, Switch/Delta

🛥️📻🖥️♿♨️🅿️🔌🍴🚭📺🛏️🚿🐎📇 🔧🆑

TIVERTON

Devon
Map ref 1D2

Busy market and textile town, settled since the 9th C, at the meeting of 2 rivers. Town houses, Tudor almshouses and parts of the fine church were built by wealthy cloth merchants; a medieval castle is incorporated into a private house; Blundells School.
Tourist Information Centre
☎ *(01884) 255827*

Great Bradley Farm

HIGHLY COMMENDED

Withleigh, Tiverton EX16 8JL
☎ (01884) 256946

Please mention this guide when making a booking.

155-acre dairy farm. Enjoy peaceful, beautiful countryside, 20 minutes from M5. Lovely, historic farmhouse offering comfortable, attractive bedrooms and delicious food. Non-smokers only, please.
Bedrooms: 1 double, 1 twin
Bathrooms: 2 private

Bed & breakfast

per night:	£min	£max
Single	17.50	19.50
Double	35.00	39.00

Half board

per person:	£min	£max
Daily	27.50	29.50
Weekly	182.00	185.00

Parking for 2
Open March-November

🛥️10📞♿♨️🅿️🍴🚭🛏️📺🛏️❄️✂️🐴🐎🆑

Hornhill

HIGHLY COMMENDED

Exeter Hill, Tiverton EX16 4PL
☎ (01884) 253352

75-acre mixed farm. Country house with superb views. Home cooking using local produce. Comfortable bedrooms, one with Victorian four-poster. Peaceful relaxed atmosphere. Ten minutes from M5.
Bedrooms: 2 double, 1 twin
Bathrooms: 3 private

Bed & breakfast

per night:	£min	£max
Single	17.50	19.00
Double	34.00	38.00

Half board

per person:	£min	£max
Daily	27.50	29.00
Weekly	180.00	185.00

Evening meal 1830 (last orders 1930)
Parking for 4

🛥️12📻🐴📻🖥️♿♨️🔌🍴🛏️🅿️🍴12❄️🐎

Lower Collipriest Farm

HIGHLY COMMENDED

Tiverton EX16 4PT
☎ (01884) 252321
221-acre dairy & livestock farm. Thatched farmhouse built around courtyard garden. All rooms en-suite. Super fresh home cooking using local

---

produce. Walks on farm by pond and river. Brochure.
Bedrooms: 2 single, 2 twin
Bathrooms: 4 private

Bed & breakfast

per night:	£min	£max
Single	20.00	22.50
Double	40.00	45.00

Half board

per person:	£min	£max
Daily	28.00	30.00
Weekly		196.00

Evening meal 1900 (last orders 1200)
Parking for 4
Open February-November

🖥️♿🐿️🔌♨️🅿️🍴🚭📺🛏️🍴🎣🚶‍♂️ ❄️✂️🐎🅿️

TORQUAY

Devon
Map ref 1D2

Devon's grandest resort, developed from a fishing village. Smart apartments and terraces rise from the seafront and Marine Drive along the headland gives views of beaches and colourful cliffs.
Tourist Information Centre
☎ *(01803) 297428*

Barn Hayes Country Hotel ⚑

HIGHLY COMMENDED

Brim Hill, Maidencombe, Torquay TQ1 4TR
☎ (01803) 327980

Warm, friendly and comfortable country house hotel in an Area of Outstanding Natural Beauty overlooking countryside and sea. Relaxation is guaranteed in these lovely surroundings by personal service, good food and fine wines.
Bedrooms: 2 single, 4 double, 2 twin, 2 triple, 2 family rooms
Bathrooms: 11 private, 1 public

Bed & breakfast

per night:	£min	£max
Single	25.00	28.00
Double	50.00	56.00

Half board

per person:	£min	£max
Daily	38.00	41.00
Weekly	238.00	266.00

Lunch available
Evening meal 1830 (last orders 1900)
Parking for 16
Open February-December
Cards accepted: Access, Visa

🛥️📻♿🐿️♨️🅿️🍴🚭📺🛏️🍴🚶‍♀️▶ ❄️🐎🅿️🆑📵

Chelston Manor Hotel

😋😋😋

Old Mill Road, Torquay TQ2 6HW
☎ (01803) 605142
*Old world bed and breakfast inn.
Reputation for good pub food and
hospitality. Sun-trap gardens with
heated swimming pool.*
Bedrooms: 1 single, 9 double, 3 twin,
1 triple
Bathrooms: 11 private, 1 public
Bed & breakfast

per night:	£min	£max
Single	20.00	28.00
Double	40.00	56.00

Lunch available
Evening meal 1800 (last orders 2130)
Parking for 40
Open April-October

🏃 12 🖳 🖵 ♨ Ⓢ 🅜 📺 🛒 📠 ❊ ❦ 🔑
♌ ✿ 🗡 📧 SP 🛏

Claver Guest House 🏍

Listed

119 Abbey Road, Torquay TQ2 5NP
☎ (01803) 297118
*A warm welcome awaits you. Close to
beach, harbour and all entertainments.
Home-cooked food, you'll never leave
the table hungry!*
Bedrooms: 1 single, 2 double, 1 twin,
2 triple, 2 family rooms
Bathrooms: 2 private, 2 public
Bed & breakfast

per night:	£min	£max
Single	12.00	
Double	24.00	

Half board

per person:	£min	£max
Daily	18.50	
Weekly	110.00	

Evening meal 1800 (last orders 1800)
Parking for 4
Open February-October

🏃 🕯 🖵 ♨ 🖳 Ⓢ 🅜 📺 🛒 📠 🗡 OAP SP

Gainsboro Hotel

😋😋 COMMENDED

22 Rathmore Road, Torquay TQ2 6NY
☎ (01803) 292032
*Family-run hotel providing friendly
atmosphere. Close to station, seafront
and amenities.*
Bedrooms: 1 single, 5 double, 1 twin
Bathrooms: 3 private, 1 public
Bed & breakfast

per night:	£min	£max
Single	11.00	14.00
Double	22.00	32.00

Parking for 5
Open March-September
Cards accepted: Access, Visa

🏃 6 🕯 🖵 ♨ 🖳 🅜 📺 🛒 📠 ❊ 🗡 📧 OAP

Kingston House 🏍

😋😋

75 Avenue Road, Torquay TQ2 5LL
☎ (01803) 212760

*Elegant Victorian building, tastefully
modernised. Conveniently situated for
the town and seafront. Family-run,
offering traditional home cooking, with
a choice of daily menu.*
Bedrooms: 1 single, 2 double, 1 twin,
1 triple, 1 family room
Bathrooms: 6 private
Bed & breakfast

per night:	£min	£max
Single	15.50	22.50
Double	28.00	35.00

Half board

per person:	£min	£max
Daily	21.50	25.00
Weekly	135.00	165.00

Evening meal 1800 (last orders 1630)
Parking for 6
Open April-October
Cards accepted: Access, Visa

🏃 8 🕯 🖵 ♨ 🖳 🔒 Ⓢ 🅜 🛒 📠 🗡 📧
OAP SP

Maple Lodge

😋😋 COMMENDED

36 Ash Hill Road, Torquay TQ1 3JD
☎ (01803) 297391
*Detached guesthouse with beautiful
views. Relaxed atmosphere, home
cooking, en-suite rooms. Centrally
situated for town and beaches.*
Bedrooms: 1 single, 2 double, 1 twin,
2 triple, 1 family room
Bathrooms: 7 private, 1 public
Bed & breakfast

per night:	£min	£max
Single	12.50	16.00
Double	25.00	32.00

Half board

per person:	£min	£max
Daily	18.00	21.50
Weekly	120.00	149.00

Evening meal from 1800
Parking for 5
Open March-October

🏃 🕯 🖵 ♨ 🖳 Ⓢ 🅜 📺 🛒 📠 🗡 📧 OAP SP

The symbol 🌐 within an
entry indicates participation
in the Welcome Host
programme – a nationally
recognised customer care
initiative which aims to
promote the highest
standards of service and a
warm welcome for all visitors.

Perched high above the River
Torridge, with a charming market
square, Georgian Town Hall and a
museum. The famous Dartington
Crystal Factory, Rosemoor
Gardens and Plough Arts Centre
are all located in the town.

Flavills Farm

Listed

Kingscott, St Giles in the Wood,
Torrington EX38 7JW
☎ (018056) 23530 & 23250
*125-acre mixed farm. 15th C farmhouse
in conservation area of picturesque
hamlet. Peaceful atmosphere.*
Bedrooms: 1 single, 1 double, 1 triple
Bathrooms: 1 public
Bed & breakfast

per night:	£min	£max
Single	14.00	14.00
Double	28.00	28.00

Parking for 6
Open April-October

🏃 🐾 🖳 🅜 📺 🛒 📠 ▶ ❊ 📧 🛏

Old market town steeply built near
the head of the Dart Estuary.
Remains of medieval gateways, a
noble church, 16th C Guildhall and
medley of period houses recall
former wealth from cloth and
shipping, continued in rural and
water industries.
*Tourist Information Centre
☎ (01803) 863168*

Buckyette Farm

😋😋

Buckyette, Totnes TQ9 6ND
☎ Staverton (01803) 762638
*51-acre arable farm. Victorian
farmhouse in large garden in Devon
valley. Children welcome. Central
heating.*
Bedrooms: 1 double, 1 twin, 4 triple
Bathrooms: 6 private
Bed & breakfast

per night:	£min	£max
Single	21.50	21.50
Double	35.00	36.00

Evening meal 1830 (last orders 1830)
Parking for 8
Open March-October

🏃 ♨ Ⓢ 🅜 📺 🛒 ✿ 📧 🆃

Old Church House Inn 🏍

😋😋😋 COMMENDED

Torbryan, Newton Abbot TQ12 5UR
☎ Ipplepen (01803) 812372
*13th C coaching house of immense
character and old world charm with*

Continued ▶

TOTNES

Continued

inglenook fireplaces, stone walls and oak beamed ceilings. Situated in a beautiful valley between Dartmoor and Torquay.
Bedrooms: 1 single, 5 double, 2 twin, 2 triple
Bathrooms: 10 private

Bed & breakfast

per night:	£min	£max
Single	30.00	40.00
Double	45.00	55.00

Half board

per person:	£min	£max
Daily	32.50	40.00
Weekly	195.00	240.00

Lunch available
Evening meal 1800 (last orders 2130)
Parking for 30
Cards accepted: Access, Visa

The Old Forge at Totnes ⋏

👑👑 HIGHLY COMMENDED

Seymour Place, Totnes TQ9 5AY
☎ (01803) 862174
Delightful 600-year-old stone building, with walled garden, cobbled driveway and working smithy. Cottage suite suitable for family or disabled guests. No smoking indoors. Extensive breakfast menu including traditional, vegetarian, fish, continental and special diet.
Bedrooms: 1 single, 5 double, 2 twin, 2 family rooms; suites available
Bathrooms: 8 private, 1 public

Bed & breakfast

per night:	£min	£max
Single	30.00	45.00
Double	42.00	62.00

Parking for 10
Cards accepted: Access, Visa, Switch/Delta

Sea Trout Inn ⋏

👑👑👑 COMMENDED

Staverton, Totnes TQ9 6PA
☎ (01803) 762274
Fax (01803) 762506
Delightful beamed country inn, in attractive village by the River Dart, offering good food and friendly atmosphere. Good base for walking and touring Dartmoor and South Devon.
Bedrooms: 6 double, 3 twin, 1 triple
Bathrooms: 10 private

Bed & breakfast

per night:	£min	£max
Single	39.50	42.50
Double	44.00	60.00

Half board

per person:	£min	£max
Daily	37.50	42.50
Weekly	240.00	275.00

Lunch available
Evening meal 1900 (last orders 2145)
Parking for 50
Cards accepted: Access, Visa, Amex

The Watermans Arms ⋏

👑👑👑 HIGHLY COMMENDED

Bow Bridge, Ashprington, Totnes TQ9 7EG
☎ Harbertonford (01803) 732214
Fax (01803) 732214

Ancient inn nestling by the river, with picturesque gardens, comfortable beamed bar with log fires and award winning accommodation.
Bedrooms: 10 double, 3 twin, 2 triple
Bathrooms: 15 private

Bed & breakfast

per night:	£min	£max
Single	32.00	38.00
Double	54.00	66.00

Half board

per person:	£min	£max
Daily	42.00	50.00
Weekly	260.00	290.00

Lunch available
Evening meal 1830 (last orders 2130)
Parking for 60
Cards accepted: Access, Visa, Switch/Delta

TROWBRIDGE

Wiltshire
Map ref 2B2

Wiltshire's administrative centre, a handsome market and manufacturing town with a wealth of merchants' houses and other Georgian buildings.
Tourist Information Centre
☎ (01225) 777054

Welam House

👑👑 COMMENDED

Bratton Road, West Ashton, Trowbridge BA14 6AZ
☎ (01225) 755908
Located in quiet village, garden with trees and lawn with a view of Westbury White Horse. Ideally situated for touring. Bowls and mini-golf for guests.
Bedrooms: 1 double, 1 twin, 1 triple
Bathrooms: 3 private, 1 public

Bed & breakfast

per night:	£min	£max
Single	16.00	20.00
Double	32.00	32.00

Parking for 6
Open March-November and Christmas

TRURO

Cornwall
Map ref 1B3

Cornwall's administrative centre and cathedral city, set at the head of Truro River on the Fal Estuary. A medieval stannary town, it handled mineral ore from west Cornwall; fine Georgian buildings recall its heyday as a society haunt in the second mining boom.
Tourist Information Centre
☎ (01872) 74555

Arrallas ⋏

👑👑 HIGHLY COMMENDED

Ladock, Truro TR2 4NP
☎ Mitchell (01872) 510379
Fax (01872) 510200
320-acre arable farm. Signed from opposite the Clock Garage, Summercourt. Farmhouse accommodation set in truly rural situation. Good food, warm welcome, attention to detail. Listed building.
Bedrooms: 2 double, 1 twin
Bathrooms: 3 private

Bed & breakfast

per night:	£min	£max
Double	36.00	40.00

Half board

per person:	£min	£max
Daily	27.50	32.50
Weekly	185.50	216.50

Evening meal from 1900
Parking for 8
Open February-November

Marcorrie Hotel ⋏

👑👑👑

20 Falmouth Road, Truro TR1 2HX
☎ (01872) 77374
Fax (01872) 41666
Family-run hotel 5 minutes' walk from city centre and cathedral. Ideal for business or holiday, central for visiting the country houses and gardens of Cornwall.
Bedrooms: 3 single, 3 double, 2 twin, 1 triple, 3 family rooms
Bathrooms: 9 private, 1 public, 1 private shower

Bed & breakfast

per night:	£min	£max
Single	19.75	35.00
Double	39.50	45.00

Half board

per person:	£min	£max
Daily	28.50	44.00

Evening meal 1900 (last orders 1600)

Parking for 16
Cards accepted: Access, Visa, Amex
🛌🚪📞🖥📶🔣✂🎗📺🛏 🚗🅿20 ⛾❄♿ SP 🏠 T

Rock Cottage ⚠

HIGHLY COMMENDED

Blackwater, Truro TR4 8EU
☎ (01872) 560252
Fax (01872) 560252

18th C beamed cottage, old world charm. Formerly village schoolmaster's home. Haven for non-smokers. Comfort, hospitality, friendly service, a la carte menu.
Bedrooms: 2 double, 1 twin
Bathrooms: 3 private

Bed & breakfast

per night:	£min	£max
Single	23.50	
Double	39.00	

Evening meal 1900 (last orders 1500)
Parking for 4

♿📧🚪♿🎗✂🎗📺🛏🚗❄🗡♿

Trevispian-Vean Farm Guest House ⚠

COMMENDED

St. Erme, Truro TR4 9BL
☎ (01872) 79514
300-acre mixed farm. Beautifully situated 7 miles from the coast in the heart of the countryside, the farmhouse combines modern comforts with all the charm of a 300-year-old farm. Ideal for touring Cornwall.
Bedrooms: 4 double, 2 twin, 4 triple, 2 family rooms
Bathrooms: 12 private, 2 public

Bed & breakfast

per night:	£min	£max
Single	18.00	21.00
Double	34.00	38.00

Half board

per person:	£min	£max
Daily	24.00	26.00
Weekly	138.00	152.00

Evening meal 1830 (last orders 1600)
Parking for 15
Open March–October

🛌🚪♿🔣✂🎗📺🛏🚗🅿50♦🗡❄ 🗡♿

UPWEY

Dorset
Map ref 2B3

Friars Way

Listed

190 Church Street, Upwey, Weymouth
DT3 5QE
☎ (01305) 813243

17th C thatched cottage in idyllic, peaceful surroundings. Ideal for garden lovers, walking or exploring Dorset's fascinating villages. Fine hospitality and cuisine. Log fires in winter. Half board available October–April only.
Bedrooms: 3 double
Bathrooms: 1 private, 1 public

Bed & breakfast

per night:	£min	£max
Double	33.00	40.00

Half board

per person:	£min	£max
Daily	29.00	32.50

Evening meal 1945 (last orders 1945)
Parking for 4

♿📧🚪♿🔣🅰🔣✂🛏🚗❄🗡❄ SP 🏠

WARMINSTER

Wiltshire
Map ref 2B2

Attractive stone-built town high up to the west of Salisbury Plain. A market town, it originally thrived on cloth and wheat. Many prehistoric camps and barrows nearby, along with Longleat House and Safari Park.
Tourist Information Centre
☎ (01985) 218548

Belmont Bed & Breakfast

🛏

9 Boreham Road, Warminster
BA12 9JP
☎ (01985) 212799 & Mobile (0378) 391188
Enjoy a friendly welcome in comfortable, spacious and well-appointed accommodation. Ideal for Stonehenge, Longleat and Stourhead. Centrally placed for the historic towns of Bath and Salisbury. Non-smoking.
Bedrooms: 2 double, 1 twin
Bathrooms: 1 public

Bed & breakfast

per night:	£min	£max
Single	20.00	30.00
Double	30.00	36.00

Parking for 4

🛌🚪♿🅰🔣✂📺🛏🚗❄🗡❄ OAP ♿ SP

Establishments should be open throughout the year unless otherwise stated in the entry.

WATCHET

Somerset
Map ref 1D1

Small port on Bridgwater Bay, sheltered by the Quantocks and the Brendon Hills. A thriving paper industry keeps the harbour busy; in the 19th C it handled iron from the Brendon Hills. Cleeve Abbey, a ruined Cistercian monastery, is 3 miles to the south-west.

Wood Advent Farm

COMMENDED

Roadwater, Watchet TA23 0RR
☎ Washford (01984) 640920
Fax (01984) 640920
350-acre mixed farm. Situated in Exmoor National Park and ideal for touring the many beauty spots. Country cooking, using mostly home-produced food.
Bedrooms: 3 double, 2 twin
Bathrooms: 5 private

Bed & breakfast

per night:	£min	£max
Single	18.50	19.50
Double	38.00	44.00

Half board

per person:	£min	£max
Daily	30.50	34.00
Weekly	175.00	220.00

Lunch available
Evening meal 1900 (last orders 2100)
Parking for 13

🛌♿🔣🅰🔣✂🛏📺🛏🚗♦🗡♿U 🗡🎗✂❄🏠T

WELLINGTON

Somerset
Map ref 1D1

Pinksmoor Millhouse

COMMENDED

Pinksmoor Farm, Wellington
TA21 0HD
☎ Greenham (01823) 672361
Fax (01823) 672361
98-acre dairy & livestock farm. Personal service and home cooking. House adjoins old mill and stream with abundant wildlife and scenic walks. Conservation awards 1991 and 1992. En-suite bedrooms with beverage-making facilities and TV.
Bedrooms: 1 double, 1 twin, 1 triple
Bathrooms: 3 private

Bed & breakfast

per night:	£min	£max
Single	21.00	
Double	37.00	

Continued ▶

We advise you to confirm your booking in writing.

WELLINGTON

Continued

Half board

per person:	£min	£max
Daily	30.00	32.50
Weekly	206.50	220.50

Evening meal 1900 (last orders 1600)
Parking for 5

🛏🚳🖵♨♿ⓊⓁⓈ½⚑📺🅸🖩🔌∪🏃❄ 🚜🅿

WELLS

Somerset
Map ref 2A2

Small city set beneath the southern slopes of the Mendips. Built between 1180 and 1424, the magnificent cathedral is preserved in much of its original glory and with its ancient precincts forms one of our loveliest and most unified groups of medieval buildings.
Tourist Information Centre
☎ *(01749) 672552*

Beaconsfield Farm ⋀
♨♨ HIGHLY COMMENDED
Easton, Wells BA5 1DU
☎ (01749) 870308
Period character farmhouse in 4 acres of gardens and grounds with magnificent views. Beautifully decorated rooms, en-suite bathrooms. Village pub/restaurant 100 yards.
Bedrooms: 3 double
Bathrooms: 3 private

Bed & breakfast

per night:	£min	£max
Double	34.00	36.00

Parking for 10
Open April-October

🛏5🕭🖵♨♿ⓊⓁⓈ🅸📺🖩🔌●❄ ✗🚜

Bekynton House
♨♨ COMMENDED
7 St Thomas Street, Wells BA5 2UU
☎ (01749) 672222 & 672061
Comfortable well-appointed house with cathedral views makes this an ideal place to park your car and walk to the cathedral, Bishop's Palace and market place in a couple of minutes.
Bedrooms: 1 single, 3 double, 2 twin, 2 triple
Bathrooms: 6 private, 2 public

Bed & breakfast

per night:	£min	£max
Single	22.00	30.00
Double	38.00	46.00

Parking for 6
Cards accepted: Access, Visa

🛏5🖵♨ⓊⓁ🅸Ⓢ½⚑📺🖩🔌❄✗ 🚜🅾🆂🅿🆃

Burcott Mill
♨♨ COMMENDED
Burcott, Wells BA5 1NJ
☎ (01749) 673118
Restored working watermill with attached house and craft workshops. Friendly country atmosphere. Birds and animals. Home cooking. Opposite good country pub.
Bedrooms: 1 single, 1 double, 2 triple, 1 family room; suite available
Bathrooms: 5 private, 1 public

Bed & breakfast

per night:	£min	£max
Single	19.00	30.00
Double	32.00	50.00

Half board

per person:	£min	£max
Daily	26.00	40.00
Weekly		160.50

Evening meal 1800 (last orders 2000)
Parking for 10
Cards accepted: Access, Visa, Diners, Amex

🛏🕭🖵♨ⓊⓁ🅸Ⓢ½⚑📺🖩🔌∪🏃❄ 🚜🆂🅿🆁

Fenny Castle House ⋀
♨♨ COMMENDED
Fenny Castle, Wookey, Wells BA5 1NN
☎ (01749) 672265 & Mobile (0585) 616140
Fax (01749) 676799
Riverside setting overlooking motte and bailey castle. Country house in 60 acres on boundary of Levels. Restaurant, lounge bar, delightful accommodation.
Bedrooms: 1 single, 3 double, 2 twin; suites available
Bathrooms: 6 private

Bed & breakfast

per night:	£min	£max
Single	25.00	
Double	50.00	

Half board

per person:	£min	£max
Daily	38.00	
Weekly	245.00	

Lunch available
Evening meal 1800 (last orders 2130)
Parking for 60
Cards accepted: Access, Visa, Amex

📞🖵♨🅸Ⓢ½⚑🖩🔌●🍴100∪🏃 ❄✗🚜🆂🅿🆁🆃

Franklyns Farm
♨♨ HIGHLY COMMENDED
Chewton Mendip, Bath BA3 4NB
☎ Chewton Mendip (01761) 241372
350-acre arable & dairy farm. Comfortable and cosy modern farmhouse in heart of Mendips, in a peaceful setting with superb views. Situated on Emborough B3114 road. Ideal for touring Wells, Cheddar and Bath. Delicious breakfast.
Bedrooms: 1 double, 2 twin
Bathrooms: 3 private, 1 public

Bed & breakfast

per night:	£min	£max
Single	20.00	
Double		34.00

Parking for 5

🛏5🖵♨♿ⓊⓁⓈ📺🖩🔌●🍴♨ ❄🚜

Home Farm
♨♨
Stoppers Lane, Coxley, Wells BA5 1QS
☎ (01749) 672434
15-acre pig farm. 1.5 miles from Wells, in a quiet spot just off A39. Extensive views of Mendip Hills. Pleasant rooms.
Bedrooms: 1 single, 3 double, 2 twin, 2 triple
Bathrooms: 3 private, 2 public

Bed & breakfast

per night:	£min	£max
Single	16.50	17.50
Double	33.00	38.00

Parking for 12

🛏🕭Ⓢ⚑📺🖩🔌●∪❄🚜🆁

Littlewell Farm Guest House
♨♨ HIGHLY COMMENDED
Coxley, Wells BA5 1QP
☎ (01749) 677914
Converted 200-year-old farmhouse enjoying extensive rural views of beautiful countryside. All bedrooms have shower or bathroom en-suite. Located 1 mile south-west of Wells.
Bedrooms: 1 single, 2 double, 2 twin
Bathrooms: 5 private

Bed & breakfast

per night:	£min	£max
Single	21.00	24.00
Double	37.00	42.00

Half board

per person:	£min	£max
Daily	34.00	36.00

Evening meal 1900 (last orders 2000)
Parking for 11

🛏10🕭🖵♨🅸½⚑🖩🔌●∪🏃❄✗ 🚜🆂🆂

Manor Farm
♨
Old Bristol Road, Upper Milton, Wells BA5 3AH
☎ (01749) 673394
130-acre beef farm. Elizabethan manor house, Grade II listed, on the southern slopes of the Mendips, 1 mile north of Wells. Superb view.*
Bedrooms: 1 double, 1 twin, 1 triple
Bathrooms: 1 public

Bed & breakfast

per night:	£min	£max
Single	16.50	17.00
Double	29.00	30.00

Parking for 6

🛏♨ⓊⓁ½⚑📺🖩🔌●∪🏃❄✗🚜 🆂🆁

Tor House

HIGHLY COMMENDED

20 Tor Street, Wells BA5 2US
☎ (01749) 672322 & 672084
Fax (01749) 672322
*Historic, sympathetically restored 17th
C building in delightful grounds
overlooking the cathedral and Bishop's
Palace. Attractive, comfortable and
tastefully furnished throughout. 3
minutes' walk to town centre. Ample
parking.*
Bedrooms: 1 single, 3 double, 1 twin,
3 family rooms
Bathrooms: 5 private, 2 public
Bed & breakfast

per night:	£min	£max
Single	22.00	38.00
Double	35.00	50.00

Evening meal 1830 (last orders 1000)
Parking for 12
Cards accepted: Access, Visa
⌂ 3 🖥 ☐ ♥ 🗲 UL 🅐 S ⅙ ♙ TV Ⅲ. ◳
📶 8 ▸ ✤ ✕ 🛒 DAP SP 📠

WEST ANSTEY

Devon
Map ref 1D1

Partridge Arms Farm ⋀

COMMENDED

Yeo Mill, West Anstey, South Molton
EX36 3NU
☎ Anstey Mills (01398) 341217
Fax (01398) 341217
*200-acre mixed farm. Old established
family farm. Well placed for touring,
walking, riding, fishing, Exmoor
National Park, north Devon, west
Somerset and coastal resorts.*
Bedrooms: 3 double, 2 twin, 2 family
rooms
Bathrooms: 4 private, 1 public
Bed & breakfast

per night:	£min	£max
Single	18.50	23.00
Double	37.00	46.00

Half board

per person:	£min	£max
Daily	27.50	32.00
Weekly	192.50	217.00

Evening meal 1930 (last orders 1600)
Parking for 10
⌂ 🖥 ☐ ♥ 🅐 S ♙ TV Ⅲ. ◳ ∪ ♫ ✿
🛒 📠

The symbol 🔘 within an
entry indicates participation
in the Welcome Host
programme – a nationally
recognised customer care
initiative which aims to
promote the highest
standards of service and a
warm welcome for all visitors.

WESTON-SUPER-MARE

Avon
Map ref 1D1

Large, friendly resort developed in
the 19th C. Traditional seaside
attractions include theatres and a
dance hall. The museum shows a
Victorian seaside gallery and has
Iron Age finds from a hill fort on
Worlebury Hill in Weston Woods.
Tourist Information Centre
☎ *(01934) 626838*

Braeside Hotel ⋀

COMMENDED

2 Victoria Park, Weston-super-Mare
BS23 2HZ
☎ (01934) 626642
Fax (01934) 626642
*Delightful, family-run hotel, ideally
situated near seafront. All rooms en-
suite. Single rooms always available.*
Bedrooms: 2 single, 4 double, 1 twin,
1 triple, 1 family room
Bathrooms: 9 private
Bed & breakfast

per night:	£min	£max
Single	22.50	22.50
Double	45.00	45.00

Half board

per person:	£min	£max
Daily	31.00	31.00
Weekly	186.00	186.00

Lunch available
Evening meal 1830 (last orders 1800)
⌂ ☐ ♥ 🅐 S ⅙ ♙ Ⅲ. ◳ 🛒 ◈ SP T

Conifers

63 Milton Road, Weston-super-Mare
BS23 2SP
☎ (01934) 624404
*Semi-detached corner guesthouse
standing back in a large garden.
Completely refurbished for bed and
breakfast use. 24 years' experience.*
Bedrooms: 2 double, 1 twin
Bathrooms: 1 private, 1 public
Bed & breakfast

per night:	£min	£max
Single	15.00	20.00
Double	30.00	36.00

Parking for 4
Open January-November
☐ ♥ UL Ⅲ. ◳ ✕ 🛒 SP

Purn House Farm

COMMENDED

Bleadon, Weston-super-Mare
BS24 0QE
☎ (01934) 812324
*700-acre mixed farm. Comfortable 17th
C farmhouse only 3 miles from Weston-
super-Mare. En-suite available with TV.
1 ground floor room. Peaceful yet not
isolated, on bus route to town centre
and station.*
Bedrooms: 1 twin, 2 triple, 3 family
rooms
Bathrooms: 4 private, 1 public

Bed & breakfast

per night:	£min	£max
Single	16.00	24.00
Double	32.00	40.00

Half board

per person:	£min	£max
Daily	23.00	27.00
Weekly	135.00	155.00

Evening meal 1830 (last orders 1000)
Parking for 10
Open February-November
⌂ 🖥 ♥ UL S ⅙ ♙ TV Ⅲ. ◳ ◀ ∪ ♫ ✿
✕ 🛒 SP 📠

WEYMOUTH

Dorset
Map ref 2B3

Ancient port and one of the
south's earliest resorts. Curving
beside a long, sandy beach, the
elegant Georgian esplanade is
graced with a statue of George III
and a cheerful Victorian Jubilee
clock tower.
Tourist Information Centre
☎ *(01305) 765221*

Fairlight

Listed

50 Littlemoor Road, Preston,
Weymouth DT3 6AA
☎ (01305) 832293
*Homely atmosphere in family bungalow.
Children and one-nighters welcome.
Freshly cooked food. Half a mile
Boleaze Cove, 3 miles Weymouth.*
Bedrooms: 1 double, 1 family room
Bathrooms: 1 public
Bed & breakfast

per night:	£min	£max
Single	14.50	17.00
Double	29.00	34.00

Half board

per person:	£min	£max
Daily	21.50	24.50
Weekly	129.00	147.00

Evening meal from 1900
Parking for 2
Open March-October
⌂ 4 🖥 ☐ ♥ UL 🅐 S ⅙ Ⅲ. ✿ ✕ 🛒 DAP

WHIMPLE

Devon
Map ref 1D2

Down House

COMMENDED

Whimple, Exeter EX5 2QR
☎ (01404) 822860
*Elegant and comfortable Edwardian
country house in the style of Charles
Rennie Mackintosh. Five acres of
gardens and orchard. Splendid views.
Exeter, Honiton and Sidmouth 7 miles.*
Bedrooms: 3 double, 2 twin
Bathrooms: 5 private, 3 public

Continued ▶

WHIMPLE

Continued

Bed & breakfast

per night:	£min	£max
Single	18.00	22.00
Double	36.00	44.00

Parking for 8

☎ 4 ♨ ⬟ ⬚ ♦ ⬚ UL ⚡ ⬚ TV ⬚ , ⬛ ❋ 🚐 SP

WIDECOMBE-IN-THE-MOOR

Devon
Map ref 1C2

Old village in pastoral country under the high tors of East Dartmoor. The "Cathedral of the Moor" stands near a tiny square, once used for archery practice, which has a 16th C Church House among other old buildings.

Buzzards Reach 🅼

Listed COMMENDED

Widecombe Hill, Widecombe-in-the-Moor, Newton Abbot TQ13 7TE
☎ (01364) 621205
Extensive views from comfortable en-suite accommodation with own access, adjoining moorland house overlooking the Widecombe Valley. Private parking and access to open moorland. Ideal for touring Dartmoor, Devon and Cornwall.
Bedrooms: 3 double
Bathrooms: 3 private

Bed & breakfast

per night:	£min	£max
Double	32.00	

Parking for 20

⬚ ♦ ⬚ UL S ⬚ ✂ ⬚ , ⬛ ❋ ✗ 🚐 ⬚

Higher Venton Farm

Listed APPROVED

Widecombe-in-the-Moor, Newton Abbot
TQ13 7TF
☎ (01364) 631235
40-acre beef farm. 17th C thatched farmhouse with a homely atmosphere and farmhouse cooking. Ideal for touring Dartmoor. 16 miles from the coast.
Bedrooms: 2 double, 1 twin
Bathrooms: 1 private, 1 public

Bed & breakfast

per night:	£min	£max
Single	18.00	20.00
Double	30.00	38.00

Parking for 5

⬚ 5 ♦ ⬚ UL ⬚ 🛏 ⬚ TV ⬚ , ⬚ ▶ 🚐 ⬚

Sheena Tower 🅼

☺☺

Widecombe-in-the-Moor, Newton Abbot
TQ13 7TE
☎ (01364) 621308
Comfortable moorland guesthouse overlooking Widecombe village, offering a relaxed holiday in picturesque

---

surroundings. Well placed for discovering Dartmoor.
Bedrooms: 1 single, 2 double, 1 twin, 1 triple, 1 family room
Bathrooms: 2 private, 2 public

Bed & breakfast

per night:	£min	£max
Single	15.00	17.00
Double	30.00	34.00

Half board

per person:	£min	£max
Daily	23.50	25.50
Weekly	161.50	175.50

Evening meal 1900 (last orders 1200)
Parking for 6
Open February-October

⬚ ♨ ♦ ⬚ S 🅟 ⬚ TV ⬚ , ⬛ ❋ 🚐

WINCANTON

Somerset
Map ref 2B3

Thriving market town, rising from the rich pastures of Blackmoor Vale near the Dorset border, with many attractive 18th C stone buildings. Steeplechase racecourse.

Lower Church Farm

☺☺

Rectory Lane, Charlton Musgrove, Wincanton BA9 8ES
☎ (01963) 32307
60-acre livestock farm. 18th C brick farmhouse with beams and inglenooks, in a quiet area surrounded by lovely countryside. Ideal for touring.
Bedrooms: 2 double, 1 twin
Bathrooms: 3 private

Bed & breakfast

per night:	£min	£max
Double		30.00

Parking for 4

⬚ 6 ♦ ⬚ 🛏 S ✂ ⬚ TV ⬚ , ⬛ ❋ 🚐 🏠

WINSFORD

Somerset
Map ref 1D1

Small village on the River Exe in splendid walking country under Winsford Hill. On the other side of the hill is a Celtic standing stone, the Caratacus Stone, and nearby across the River Barle stretches an ancient packhorse bridge, Tarr Steps, built of great stone slabs.

Larcombe Foot

☺☺ **HIGHLY COMMENDED**

Winsford, Minehead TA24 7HS
☎ (01643) 851306
Comfortable country house in tranquil, beautiful setting, overlooking River Exe. Lovely walks on doorstep. Ideal for touring Exmoor and north Devon coast.
Bedrooms: 1 single, 1 double, 1 twin
Bathrooms: 3 private

Bed & breakfast

per night:	£min	£max
Single		18.00
Double		36.00

Evening meal (last orders 1930)
Parking for 3
Open April-October

☎ 6 ♦ ⬚ UL ⬚ TV ⬚ , ⬛ ⚲ ▶ 🚐

WINTERBOURNE ABBAS

Dorset
Map ref 2A3

Main road village with numerous prehistoric remains nearby. Maiden Castle 3 miles south-east.

Valley House

☺

Higher Kingston Russell, Winterbourne Abbas, Dorchester DT2 9EE
☎ Long Bredy (01308) 482646
Fax (01308) 482647
Listed stone farmhouse in peaceful West Dorset countryside, halfway between Dorchester and Bridport.
Bedrooms: 1 family room
Bathrooms: 1 private

Bed & breakfast

per night:	£min	£max
Single	20.00	22.00
Double	36.00	44.00

Parking for 8
Open April-October

⬚ 6 ⬟ ⬚ ♦ ⚡ 🛏 S ✂ ⬚ , ⬛ ❋ ✗ 🚐 OAP SP 🏠

WINTERBOURNE STOKE

Wiltshire
Map ref 2B2

Scotland Lodge 🅼

☺☺ **COMMENDED**

Winterbourne Stoke, Salisbury SP3 4TF
☎ Shrewton (01980) 620943 & Mobile 0860 272599
Fax (01980) 620943
Historic, comfortable country house with private bathrooms. Helpful service, delicious breakfasts. Ideal touring base. French and some German spoken. Self-contained unit also available for self-catering.
Bedrooms: 1 double, 2 twin
Bathrooms: 3 private

Bed & breakfast

per night:	£min	£max
Single	24.99	30.00
Double	35.00	45.00

Parking for 5

⬚ ⬟ ⬚ ♦ ⚡ ⬚ UL S ✂ ⬚ , ⬛ 🏇12 ❋ ✗ 🚐 SP 🏠

Please mention this guide when making a booking.

WOODBURY

Devon
Map ref 1D2

Attractive village, with Woodbury Common to the east, affording a panoramic coastal view from Berry Head to Portland Bill. Woodbury Castle Iron Age fort lies at a height of some 600 ft.

Lochinvar ⋀

[COMMENDED]

Shepherds Park Farm, Woodbury, Exeter EX5 1LA
☎ (01395) 232185
250-acre dairy farm. Rural setting near Woodbury Village. Three miles from M5 junction 30. Take A376 towards Exmouth then B3179 towards Woodbury, take second turning right then first right.
Bedrooms: 1 double, 1 twin, 1 triple
Bathrooms: 3 private
Bed & breakfast

per night:	£min	£max
Single	17.00	20.00
Double	34.00	38.00

Parking for 4

WOOTTON BASSETT

Wiltshire
Map ref 2B2

Small hillside town with attractive old buildings and a 13th C church. The church and the half-timbered town hall were both restored in the 19th C and the stocks and ducking pool are preserved.

Tockenham Court Farm

[Listed] [HIGHLY COMMENDED]

Tockenham, Wootton Bassett, Swindon SN4 7PH
☎ Swindon (01793) 852315 & Mobile 0836 241686
Fax (01793) 852315

250-acre dairy farm. 16th C listed building. Visitors are welcome to walk the fields.
Bedrooms: 2 double, 1 twin
Bathrooms: 2 public
Bed & breakfast

per night:	£min	£max
Single	18.00	
Double	36.00	

Parking for 4

YARCOMBE

Devon
Map ref 1D2

Tiny village between Honiton and Chard.

Crawley Farm ⋀

[APPROVED]

Yarcombe, Honiton EX14 9AX
☎ Chard (01460) 64760
Fax (01460) 64760

200-acre mixed farm. 17th C thatched farmhouse with old world charm in the Yarty Valley. Working, family-run farm, farmhouse breakfast, en-suite available. Excellent pub food available locally.
Bedrooms: 1 double, 1 twin, 1 triple
Bathrooms: 1 private, 2 public
Bed & breakfast

per night:	£min	£max
Single	14.00	16.00
Double	28.00	32.00

Parking for 6
Open March-November

YELVERTON

Devon
Map ref 1C2

Village on the edge of Dartmoor, where ponies wander over the flat common. Buckland Abbey is 2 miles south-west, while Burrator Reservoir is 2 miles to the east.

Greenwell Farm

[COMMENDED]

Meavy, Yelverton PL20 6PY
☎ (01822) 853563
Fax (01822) 853563
220-acre livestock farm. Fresh country air, breathtaking views and scrumptious farmhouse cuisine. This busy family farm welcomes you to share our countryside and wildlife.
Bedrooms: 2 double, 1 twin
Bathrooms: 3 private
Bed & breakfast

per night:	£min	£max
Double	38.00	44.00

Half board

per person:	£min	£max
Daily	30.50	33.50
Weekly	199.00	210.00

Evening meal 1900 (last orders 1200)
Parking for 8

YEOVIL

Somerset
Map ref 2A3

Lively market town, famous for glove making, set in dairying country beside the River Yeo. Interesting parish church. Museum of South Somerset at Hendford Manor.
Tourist Information Centre
☎ (01935) 71279

Holywell House

[HIGHLY COMMENDED]

Holywell, East Coker, Yeovil BA22 9NQ
☎ West Coker (01935) 862612
Fax (01935) 863035

Beautifully renovated country home with fine amenities. Three acres of lovely grounds, tennis court, idyllic rural setting. Quiet location off A30, 2 miles west of Yeovil.
Bedrooms: 2 double, 1 twin; suite available
Bathrooms: 3 private
Bed & breakfast

per night:	£min	£max
Single	35.00	40.00
Double	60.00	70.00

Half board

per person:	£min	£max
Daily	52.50	57.50
Weekly	330.00	360.00

Evening meal 1900 (last orders 2030)
Parking for 15

YEOVILTON

Somerset
Map ref 2A3

Cary Fitzpaine

Yeovilton, Yeovil BA22 8JB
☎ Charlton Mackerell (0145822) 3250
Fax (0145822) 3250
600-acre mixed farm. Elegant Georgian manor farmhouse in idyllic setting. 2 acres of gardens. High standard of accommodation, all bedrooms with en-suite bath.
Bedrooms: 1 single, 1 double, 1 twin, 1 triple
Bathrooms: 4 private

Continued ▶

YEOVILTON

Continued

Bed & breakfast per night:

	£min	£max
Single	17.50	20.00
Double	35.00	35.00

Parking for 14

🐾🖥👶🧺🆔Ⓢ🅟📺▦🖨➡♈✿ 🚐 SP

Courtry Farm
Listed

Bridgehampton, Yeovil BA22 8HF
☎ Ilchester (01935) 840327
590-acre mixed farm. Farmhouse with ground floor rooms, en-suite, TV, tea-making facilities. Tennis court. Fleet Air Arm Museum half a mile.
Bedrooms: 1 twin, 1 triple
Bathrooms: 2 private

Bed & breakfast per night:

	£min	£max
Single	20.00	
Double	32.00	

Parking for 20

🐾🛁🖥👶Ⓤ📺✂▦ ➡♈✿🚐🏠

ZEALS

Wiltshire
Map ref 2B2

Pretty village of thatched cottages set high over the Dorset border. Zeals House dates from the medieval period and has some 19th C work. The Palladian Stourhead House (National Trust), in its magnificent gardens, lies further north.

Cornerways Cottage ⚠
🛏🛏

Longcross, Zeals, Warminster BA12 6LL
☎ Bourton (01747) 840477
Fax (01747) 840477

18th C cottage with original beams. Ideal position for touring Stourhead, Stonehenge, Shaftesbury and other local attractions. Riding, fishing, golf and walking locally. Close to A303, midway for London or Devon and Cornwall. Two miles from Stourhead House and Gardens, 4 miles from Longleat.
Bedrooms: 3 double
Bathrooms: 2 private, 3 public

Bed & breakfast per night:

	£min	£max
Single	17.00	18.00
Double	32.00	34.00

Half board per person:

	£min	£max
Daily	24.00	25.00
Weekly	140.00	145.00

Evening meal 1830 (last orders 1930)
Parking for 6

🐾🚗👶🧺Ⓤ🆔Ⓢ✂🅟📺▦🖨➡♈♪🕨 ✿🎿🚐 OAP

AT-A-GLANCE SYMBOLS

At-a-glance symbols at the end of each accommodation entry give information about services and facilities. A handy guide to these symbols can be found inside the back cover flap, which can be kept open for easy reference.

COUNTRY CODE

🍃 Enjoy the countryside and respect its life and work 🍃 Guard against all risk of fire 🍃 Fasten all gates 🍃 Keep your dogs under close control 🍃 Keep to public paths across farmland 🍃 Use gates and stiles to cross fences, hedges and walls 🍃 Leave livestock, crops and machinery alone 🍃 Take your litter home 🍃 Help to keep all water clean 🍃 Protect wildlife, plants and trees 🍃 Take special care on country roads 🍃 Make no unnecessary noise

South of England

There is exquisitely pretty countryside to be explored here – from the autumn-liveried beechwoods of the Chilterns, to the thatch-topped cottages of Dorset; from the pony-cropped New Forest to the vales and hills of Thomas Hardy country. Tour the historic cities and towns – Oxford, Winchester, Windsor, and stop for cream teas at village tea shops.

The coastline of the region has character all of its own – with high cliffs, dramatic stacks, long beaches and deep rounded bays. Stop to watch the bobbing yachts of Poole Harbour; visit Weymouth and Bournemouth with its bustling seafront. Or pop across to the Isle of Wight, one of England's pleasantest seaside spots with its creeks and woods, flower-scattered clifftops and attractive resorts.

The Counties of Berkshire, Buckinghamshire, Dorset (eastern), Hampshire, Isle of Wight and Oxfordshire

For more information on the South of England, contact:

Southern Tourist Board
40 Chamberlayne Road, Eastleigh,
Hampshire SO50 5JH
Tel: (01703) 620555
Fax: (01703) 620010

Where to Go in the South of England – see pages 296–299
Where to Stay in the South of England – see pages 300–329

South of England

Where to go and what to see

You will find hundreds of interesting places to visit during your stay in the South of England, just some of which are listed in these pages. The number against each name will help you locate it on the map (page 299). Contact any Tourist Information Centre in the region for more ideas on days out in the South of England.

❶ Broughton Castle
Banbury, Oxfordshire OX15 5EB
Tel: (01295) 262624
Medieval moated house built in 1300 and enlarged between 1550 and 1600. The home of Lord and Lady Saye and Sele. Civil War connections.

❷ Blenheim Palace
Woodstock, Oxfordshire OX20 1PX
Tel: (01993) 811091
Birthplace of Sir Winston Churchill, designed by Vanbrugh with park designed by Capability Brown. Adventure play area, maze, butterfly house and Churchill exhibition.

❸ Cotswold Wildlife Park
Bradwell Grove, Burford, Oxfordshire OX18 4JW
Tel: (01993) 823006
Wildlife park in 200 acres of gardens and woodland, with a variety of animals from all over the world.

❹ Waterperry Gardens
Waterperry, Oxfordshire OX33 1JZ
Tel: (01844) 339254
Ornamental gardens covering 6 acres of 83-acre 18th C Waterperry House estate. Saxon village church, garden shop, tea shop.

❺ The Oxford Story
6 Broad Street, Oxford, Oxfordshire OX1 3AJ
Tel: (01865) 728822
Heritage centre depicting 800 years of university history in sights, sounds, personalities and smells. Visitors are transported in moving desks with commentary of their choice.

❻ Didcot Railway Centre
Great Western Railway, Didcot, Oxfordshire OX11 7NJ
Tel: (01235) 817200
Living museum recreating the golden age of the Great Western Railway. Steam locomotives and trains, engine shed and small relics museum. Steam days and gala events.

❼ Bekonscot Model Village
Warwick Road, Beaconsfield, Buckinghamshire HP9 2PL
Tel: (01494) 672919
A complete model village of the 1930s, with zoo, cinema, minster, cricket match and 1,400 inhabitants.

❽ Beale Park
The Child-Beale Wildlife Trust, Church Farm, Lower Basildon, Berkshire RG8 9NH
Tel: (01734) 845172
Established 36 years ago, the park features wildfowl, pheasants,

Highland cattle, rare sheep, llamas. Narrow gauge railway and pets' corner.

⑨ The Vyne
Sherborne St John, Hampshire RG26 5DX
Tel: (01256) 881337
Original house dating back to Henry VII's time, extensively altered in mid 17th C. Tudor chapel, beautiful gardens and lake.

⑩ Andover Museum
6 Church Close, Andover, Hampshire SP10 1DP
Tel: (01264) 366283
The "Story of Andover" galleries. The Museum of the Iron Age – life as revealed by excavations at Iron Age hill fort, Danebury Ring.

⑪ Museum of Army Flying
Middle Wallop, Hampshire SO20 8DY
Tel: (01264) 384421
Award-winning and unique collection of flying machines and displays depicting the role of army flying since the late 19th C.

⑫ Jane Austen's House
Chawton, Hampshire GU34 1SD
Tel: (01420) 83262
17th C house where Jane Austen lived from 1809–1817, and wrote or revised her 6 great novels. Letters, pictures, memorabilia, garden.

⑬ Romany Folklore Museum and Workshop
Limesend Yard, High Street, Selborne, Hampshire GU34 3JW
Tel: (01420) 511486
Museum depicting all aspects of gypsy life in Great Britain. Van builder's workshops.

⑭ Gilbert White's House and Garden and the Oates Museum
The Wakes, Selborne, Hampshire GU34 3JH
Tel: (01420) 511275
Historic house and garden, home of Gilbert White, author of "The Natural History of Selborne". Exhibition on Frank Oates, explorer, and Captain Oates of Antarctic fame.

⑮ Marwell Zoological Park
Colden Common, Winchester, Hampshire SO21 1JH
Tel: (01962) 777407
Large zoo breeding endangered species. Over 800 animals including big cats, giraffes, deer, zebras, monkeys, hippos and birds.

⑯ The Sir Harold Hillier Gardens and Arboretum
Jermyns Lane, Ampfield, Hampshire SO51 0QA
Tel: (01794) 368787
The largest collection of trees and shrubs of its kind in the British Isles.

⑰ Broadlands
Romsey, Hampshire SO51 9ZD
Tel: (01794) 516878
Home of the late Lord Mountbatten. Magnificent 18th C house and contents. Superb views across River Test. Mountbatten exhibition and audio-visual presentation.

⑱ Tudor House Museum
St Michael's Square, Bugle Street, Southampton SO1 0AD
Tel: (01703) 332513
Large half-timbered Tudor house with exhibitions on Tudor, Georgian and Victorian domestic and local history. Unique Tudor garden.

⑲ Staunton Country Park
Middle Park Way, Havant, Hampshire PO9 5HB
Tel: (01705) 453405
Reconstructed Victorian glasshouses with displays of exotic plants in the charming setting of the historic walled gardens. Ornamental farm with wide range of farm animals.

⑳ Royal Signals Museum
Blandford Camp, Blandford Forum, Dorset DT11 8RH
Tel: (01258) 482248
History of Army communication from Crimea to the Gulf. Vehicles, uniforms, medals and badges on display.

㉑ The New Forest Owl Sanctuary
Crow Lane, Crow, Ringwood,
Hampshire BH24 3EA
Tel: (01425) 476487
Sanctuary for barn owls destined to be released into the wild. Incubation room, hospital unit and 100 aviaries.

㉒ Kingston Lacy
Wimborne Minster, Dorset
BH21 4EA
Tel: (01202) 883402
17th C house designed for Sir Ralph Bankes by Sir Roger Pratt, altered by Sir Charles Barry in the 19th C. Collection of paintings, 250 acres of wooded park and herd of Devon cattle.

㉓ Beaulieu Palace House
Beaulieu, Hampshire SO42 7ZN
Tel: (01590) 612345
Home of Lord and Lady Montagu. National Motor Museum, monastic life exhibition.

㉔ The D Day Museum and Overlord Embroidery
Clarence Esplanade, Portsmouth,
Hampshire PO5 3PA
Tel: (01705) 827261
Incorporates Overlord embroidery depicting Allied invasion of Normandy.

㉕ Compton Acres
Canford Cliffs, Poole, Dorset
BH13 7ES
Tel: (01202) 700778
Gardens include Italian, Japanese, sub-tropical glen, rock, water and heather. Collection of statues.

㉖ The Tank Museum
Bovington Camp, Wareham,
Dorset BH20 6JG
Tel: (01929) 463953
Largest and most comprehensive museum collection of armoured fighting vehicles in the world.

㉗ Butterfly World and Fountain World
Staplers Road, Wootton,
Ryde, Isle of Wight
PO33 4RW
Tel: (01983) 883430
Tropical indoor garden with butterflies from around the world. Fountain World has water features and huge fish. Italian and Japanese garden.

Find out more
Further information about holidays and attractions in Central Southern England is available from:
Southern Tourist Board, 40 Chamberlayne Road, Eastleigh, Hampshire SO50 5JH
Tel: (01703) 620555

Hereford & Worcester

Warwickshire

Northants

• Cropredy
Newport Pagnell

• Wolverton
• Milton Keynes

Banbury ❶

Buckingham •
Bletchley •

Beds

Chipping Norton •

Bucks

Bicester •

Aylesbury •

Gloucestershire

❷ Woodstock •
Waterperry

Wendover •

❸ Burford •
Witney •
❹
Thame •

Chesham •
Princes Risborough

Oxford ❺

Oxfordshire

Faringdon •

Abingdon •

High Wycombe •
Beaconsfield ❼

Avon

Wantage •

Didcot ❻
Wallingford •

Marlow •

Maidenhead •
Slough •

Hungerford •

Henley-on-Thames •
Lower Basildon ❽
Twyford •
Windsor •

Berkshire

Reading •

Newbury •
Wokingham •
Bracknell •

Wiltshire

Stratfield Saye •

Farnborough •
Fleet •
Aldershot •

Sherborne St John ❾

Basingstoke •

Surrey

❿ Andover •

Hampshire

Alton •

⓫
Middle Wallop

Chawton ⓬

⓭ ⓮ Selborne

Winchester •

Liss •

Gillingham •

Ampfield •
Colden Common •

Shaftesbury •

Romsey ⓱ ⓰
⓯

Petersfield •

West Sussex

Dorset (eastern)

Fordingbridge •
Totton •
Lyndhurst •

Eastleigh
⓲ Southampton

Blandford Forum ⓴

Ringwood ㉑

Fawley •
Waterlooville •
Locks Heath
Lee-on-the-Solent
Havant ⓳

Wimborne Minster ㉒
West Moors •
Brockenhurst •
Beaulieu •
Gosport •
㉓
Portsmouth ㉔

Poole ㉕
Lymington •
Christchurch •
Cowes •
Newport •

Ryde •
㉗ Wootton

Wareham ㉖
Bournemouth •
Yarmouth •
Freshwater •

Isle of Wight

Sandown
Shanklin
Ventnor •

Swanage •

| 0 | 20 Miles |
| 0 | 30 Kms |

WHERE TO STAY

Accommodation entries in this regional section are listed in alphabetical order of place name, and then in alphabetical order of establishment.

Map references refer to the colour location maps at the back of this guide. The first figure is the map number; the letter and figure which follow indicate the grid reference on the map.

At-a-glance symbols at the end of each accommodation entry give information about services and facilities. A handy guide to these symbols can be found inside the back cover flap, which can be kept open for easy reference.

ABBOTTS ANN

Hampshire
Map ref 2C2

Virginia Lodge 🏧
COMMENDED

Salisbury Road, Abbotts Ann, Andover
SP11 7NX
☎ Andover (01264) 710713
Genuine welcome at comfortable bungalow (non-smoking), with large gardens, on edge of picturesque Abbotts Ann. On A343, 1 mile from A303 and convenient stop-over east/west. Central for Salisbury, Winchester, Stonehenge.
Bedrooms: 1 double, 2 twin
Bathrooms: 1 private, 1 public

Bed & breakfast

per night:	£min	£max
Single	19.00	25.00
Double	32.00	36.00

Parking for 6

ABINGDON

Oxfordshire
Map ref 2C1

Attractive former county town on River Thames with many interesting buildings, including 17th C County Hall, now a museum, in the market-place and the remains of an abbey.
Tourist Information Centre
☎ *(01235) 522711*

1 Long Barn
Listed

Sutton Courtenay, Abingdon
OX14 4BQ
☎ (01235) 848251
17th C village house 8 miles from Oxford, 2 miles from Abingdon. Easy access to Henley and the Cotswolds.

Bedrooms: 1 twin
Bathrooms: 1 private

Bed & breakfast

per night:	£min	£max
Single	15.00	15.00
Double	30.00	30.00

Parking for 3

ADSTOCK

Buckinghamshire
Map ref 2C1

The Folly Inn
APPROVED

Buckingham Road, Adstock,
Buckingham MK18 2HS
☎ Winslow (01296) 712671
Family-run roadside inn serving quality bar and restaurant food, with motel-type accommodation.
Bedrooms: 5 double
Bathrooms: 5 private

Bed & breakfast

per night:	£min	£max
Single		24.95
Double		39.80

Lunch available
Evening meal 1830 (last orders 2200)
Parking for 30
Cards accepted: Access, Visa, Amex,
Switch/Delta

National gradings and classifications were correct at the time of going to press but are subject to change. Please check at the time of booking.

ALTON

Hampshire
Map ref 2C2

Pleasant old market town standing on the Pilgrim's Way, with some attractive Georgian buildings. The parish church still bears the scars of bullet marks, evidence of a bitter struggle between the Roundheads and the Royalists.
Tourist Information Centre
☎ *(01420) 88448*

Glen Derry
Listed COMMENDED

52 Wellhouse Road, Beech, Alton
GU34 4AG
☎ (01420) 83235
Peaceful, secluded family home set in 3.5 acres of garden. Warm welcome assured. Ideal base for Watercress Steam Railway, Winchester and Portsmouth.
Bedrooms: 1 twin, 1 family room
Bathrooms: 1 private, 1 public

Bed & breakfast

per night:	£min	£max
Single	20.00	26.00
Double	30.00	36.00

Parking for 13

The symbols 🦽 🦽 🦽 indicate categories of accessibility for wheelchair users. They are explained in full in the information pages at the back of this guide.

AMERSHAM

Buckinghamshire
Map ref 2D1

Old town with many fine buildings, particularly in the High Street. There are several interesting old inns.

The Barn

`Listed` `HIGHLY COMMENDED`

Rectory Hill, Old Amersham, Amersham HP7 0BT
☎ (01494) 722701
Fax (01494) 728826
Restored 17th C heavily beamed tithe barns with warm and friendly atmosphere. Short walk from Amersham Station, excellent pubs and restaurants. Easy access to M25 and M40.
Bedrooms: 1 double, 2 twin
Bathrooms: 1 public
Bed & breakfast

per night:	£min	£max
Single	30.00	32.00
Double	48.00	50.00

Parking for 7

♿ 8 ⌨ ⏹ ♨ ⚑ ⓤⓛ ⅄ Ⓜ ⦿ ▥ ☎ ❀ ✕ ⚕ ♠

AMPORT

Hampshire
Map ref 2C2

Broadwater ₳

`COMMENDED`

Amport, Andover SP11 8AY
☎ Andover (01264) 772240
Fax (01264) 772240

Grade II listed thatched cottage. From A303 (from Andover) take turn off to Hawk Conservancy/Amport. At T-junction, turn right, take first road right (East Cholderton). Broadwater is first cottage on the right.
Bedrooms: 2 twin
Bathrooms: 2 private, 1 public
Bed & breakfast

per night:	£min	£max
Single	20.00	25.00
Double	40.00	

Half board

per person:	£min	£max
Daily	30.00	35.00
Weekly	210.00	240.00

Evening meal 1830 (last orders 2030)
Parking for 3

♿ ⚑ ♨ ⓤⓛ ⓘ Ⓢ Ⓜ ⦿ ▥ ☎ ❀ ✕ ⚕ ♠

ANDOVER

Hampshire
Map ref 2C2

Town that achieved importance from the wool trade and now has much modern development. A good centre for visiting places of interest.
Tourist Information Centre
☎ *(01264) 324320*

Malt Cottage ₳

`HIGHLY COMMENDED`

Upper Clatford, Andover SP11 7QL
☎ (01264) 323469
Fax (01264) 334100
Country house with idyllic 6-acre garden, lake and stream. Set in charming Hampshire village within easy reach of Salisbury, Romsey, Stonehenge and London/Exeter road.
Bedrooms: 1 single, 1 double, 1 twin
Bathrooms: 3 private
Bed & breakfast

per night:	£min	£max
Single	26.00	35.00
Double	37.00	44.00

Evening meal from 1800
Parking for 5

♿ ⚴ ⌨ ♨ ⓤⓛ Ⓜ ⦿ ▥ ☎ ❀ ✕ ⚕ ♠

The Old Barn ₳

`Listed` `HIGHLY COMMENDED`

Amport, Andover SP11 8AE
☎ (01264) 710410 & Mobile 0860 844772
Fax (01264) 710410
Converted old barn, in small village approximately 3 miles south west of Andover. Secluded, but only three-quarters of a mile from A303.
Bedrooms: 1 double, 1 triple
Bathrooms: 2 private
Bed & breakfast

per night:	£min	£max
Single	20.00	23.00
Double	30.00	34.00

Parking for 4

♿ 8 ⌨ ⏹ ♨ ⚑ ⓤⓛ Ⓢ ⅄ ▥ ☎ ❀ ✕ ⚕ SP ♠

ASCOT

Berkshire
Map ref 2C2

Small country town famous for its racecourse which was founded by Queen Anne. The race meeting each June is attended by the Royal Family.

Birchcroft House ₳

`HIGHLY COMMENDED`

Birchcroft, Brockenhurst Road, South Ascot, Ascot SL5 9HA
☎ (01344) 20574
Charming Edwardian country house in beautiful, peaceful wooded gardens. Ample parking. Warm welcome. Superb quality en-suite bedrooms. Ideal base for

London, (30 minutes by train), Windsor (6 miles), Heathrow (25 minutes).
Bedrooms: 1 double, 2 twin
Bathrooms: 3 private
Bed & breakfast

per night:	£min	£max
Single	28.00	35.00
Double	38.00	46.00

Parking for 6

♿ 7 ⌨ ⏹ ♨ ⚑ ⓤⓛ Ⓢ ⅄ Ⓜ ⦿ ▥ ☎ ❀ ✕ ⚕

Tanglewood ₳

♙♙

Birch Lane, off Longhill Road, Chavey Down, Ascot SL5 8RF
☎ Bracknell (01344) 882528
En-suite bedrooms in spacious, modern bungalow. Quiet secluded location, large wooded garden. Four miles from Windsor and 15 miles from Heathrow (pick up possible). Convenient for Wentworth, Sunningdale, Ascot, Bracknell, Thames Valley and London. Telephone for directions/map as hidden away.
Bedrooms: 1 single, 2 twin
Bathrooms: 3 private, 1 public
Bed & breakfast

per night:	£min	£max
Single	17.50	25.00
Double	35.00	50.00

Evening meal 1900 (last orders 2000)
Parking for 6

⚴ ⌨ ♨ ⓤⓛ Ⓢ ⅄ Ⓜ ⦿ ▥ ☎ ❀ ● ► ❀ ✕ ⚕ SP

ASHURST

Hampshire
Map ref 2C3

Small village on the A35, on the edge of the New Forest and three miles north-east of Lyndhurst. Easy access to beautiful forest lawns.

Forest Gate Lodge ₳

`Listed`

161 Lyndhurst Road, Ashurst, Lyndhurst SO4 2AA
☎ Southampton (01703) 293026
Large, comfortable house, with direct access to New Forest. Restaurants and public houses nearby. Central to all New Forest attractions.
Bedrooms: 2 double
Bathrooms: 2 private, 1 public
Bed & breakfast

per night:	£min	£max
Single	15.00	
Double	34.00	

Parking for 8

♿ ⏹ ♨ ⓤⓛ ⓘ ⅄ Ⓜ ⦿ ▥ ✕ ⚕ DAP ✎

We advise you to confirm your booking in writing.

AYLESBURY

Buckinghamshire
Map ref 2C1

Historic county town in the Vale of
Aylesbury. The cobbled market
square has a Victorian clock tower
and the 15th C King's Head Inn
(National Trust). Interesting county
museum and 13th C parish church.
Twice-weekly livestock market.
Tourist Information Centre
☎ *(01296) 330559*

Longmoor Farm

HIGHLY COMMENDED

Cublington Road, Aston Abbotts,
Aylesbury HP22 4ND
☎ (01296) 681010
Fax (01296) 688594
*Spacious, Victorian country house,
completely refurbished, built around
handsome enclosed courtyard. Four
acres of lovely gardens including 2
giant cedar trees.*
Bedrooms: 2 double, 1 twin
Bathrooms: 1 public
Bed & breakfast

per night:	£min	£max
Single	20.00	25.00
Double	35.00	40.00

Evening meal 1800 (last orders 2000)
Parking for 10

The Old Wheatsheaf Inn

Listed COMMENDED

Weedon, Aylesbury HP22 4NS
☎ (01296) 641581

*Old Elizabethan coaching inn, furnished
with antiques. Courtyard surrounded by
self-catering cottage and stable-cots.
Home-from-home treatment and
atmosphere. Garden with National
Gardens Scheme and featured by
Which? magazine.*
Bedrooms: 1 single, 1 double, 2 twin,
1 triple
Bathrooms: 3 private, 3 public
Bed & breakfast

per night:	£min	£max
Single	35.00	35.00
Double	60.00	60.00

Lunch available
Evening meal 1830 (last orders 2200)
Parking for 14

Wallace Farm

Dinton, Aylesbury HP17 8UF
☎ (01296) 748660
Fax (01296) 748851
*34-acre mixed farm. 16th C farmhouse
offers comfortable en-suite
accommodation in a quiet rural setting.
Self-catering cottages also available for
weekly rental.*
Bedrooms: 1 double, 2 twin
Bathrooms: 3 private
Bed & breakfast

per night:	£min	£max
Single	28.00	28.00
Double	40.00	42.00

Parking for 6
Cards accepted: Access, Visa

BANBURY

Oxfordshire
Map ref 2C1

Famous for its cattle market,
cakes and nursery rhyme Cross.
Founded in Saxon times, it has
some fine houses and interesting
old inns. A good centre for touring
Warwickshire and the Cotswolds.
Tourist Information Centre
☎ *(01295) 259855*

The Lodge

HIGHLY COMMENDED

Main Road, Middleton Cheney,
Banbury OX17 2PP
☎ (01295) 710355
*200-year-old lodge in lovely countryside,
on outskirts of historic village, 3 miles
east of Banbury on A422 and 1 mile
from M40.*
Bedrooms: 1 double, 1 twin
Bathrooms: 2 private
Bed & breakfast

per night:	£min	£max
Double	46.00	48.00

Parking for 5

The Old Manor

Listed HIGHLY COMMENDED

Cropredy, Banbury OX17 1PS
☎ (01295) 750235
Fax (01295) 758479
*Partially moated manor house alongside
Oxford Canal and in centre of village.
Rare breed farm animals and private
motor museum.*
Bedrooms: 1 double, 1 twin
Bathrooms: 2 private
Bed & breakfast

per night:	£min	£max
Single	22.00	28.00
Double	44.00	48.00

Parking for 20
Cards accepted: Access, Visa, Amex

Roxtones

Listed

Malthouse Lane, Shutford, Banbury
OX15 6PB
☎ (01295) 788240
*Stone-fronted semi-bungalow with
garden surrounds, orchard and lawns. 6
miles from Banbury, 16 miles from
Stratford-upon-Avon and 2 miles from
Broughton Castle.*
Bedrooms: 2 single, 1 double
Bathrooms: 1 public
Bed & breakfast

per night:	£min	£max
Single		15.00
Double		25.00

Half board

per person:	£min	£max
Daily		22.50
Weekly		140.00

Evening meal 1900 (last orders 2100)
Parking for 3
Open April-September

Studleigh Farm

Listed

Wales Street, King's Sutton, Banbury
OX17 3RR
☎ (01295) 811979
*Renovated and modernised farmhouse,
built circa 1700, on 8 acres of
pastureland in a picturesque village. On
direct Oxford-London rail line. Non-
smokers only, please.*
Bedrooms: 1 double, 1 twin
Bathrooms: 2 private
Bed & breakfast

per night:	£min	£max
Single	27.00	30.00
Double	40.00	44.00

Parking for 3

Treetops Guest House

28 Dashwood Road, Banbury
OX16 8HD
☎ (01295) 254444
*Comfortable accommodation. En-suite
facilities available. Pets welcome. In an
elegant Victorian town house on the
A361, 5 minutes' walk from town
centre.*
Bedrooms: 1 single, 1 double, 2 triple,
1 family room
Bathrooms: 4 private, 2 public
Bed & breakfast

per night:	£min	£max
Single	18.00	25.00
Double	36.00	40.00

Half board

per person:	£min	£max
Daily	24.00	31.00

Lunch available
Parking for 2

BARTON ON SEA

Hampshire
Map ref 2B3

Seaside village with views of the Isle of Wight. Within easy driving distance of the New Forest.

Bank Cottage ⛰

♔♔♔ COMMENDED

Grove Road, Barton on Sea, New Milton BH25 7DN
☎ New Milton (01425) 613677

Spacious en-suite rooms with every comfort and facility. Very warm welcome. Secure parking. Delicious home-made food. Close to pub and beach.
Bedrooms: 2 double, 1 twin
Bathrooms: 3 private, 1 public

Bed & breakfast per night:	£min	£max
Single	17.00	23.00
Double	35.00	39.00

Half board per person:	£min	£max
Daily	22.00	30.00
Weekly	154.00	210.00

Evening meal from 1900
Parking for 6
[UL] [S] [SP]

BEAULIEU

Hampshire
Map ref 2C3

Beautifully situated among woods and hills on the Beaulieu river, the village is both charming and unspoilt. The 13th C ruined Cistercian abbey and 14th C Palace House stand close to the National Motor Museum. There is a maritime museum at Bucklers Hard.

Leygreen Farm House ⛰

♔♔

Lyndhurst Road, Beaulieu, Brockenhurst SO42 7YP
☎ Lymington (01590) 612355
Comfortable Victorian farmhouse with large garden. Convenient for Beaulieu, Bucklers Hard museums and Exbury Gardens. Reductions for 3 days or more.
Bedrooms: 2 double, 1 twin
Bathrooms: 3 private, 1 public

Bed & breakfast per night:	£min	£max
Single	15.00	25.00
Double	28.00	38.00

Parking for 6
[UL] [S] [TV] [OAP] [SP]

BLANDFORD FORUM

Dorset
Map ref 2B3

Almost completely destroyed by fire in 1731, the town was rebuilt in a handsome Georgian style. The church is large and grand and the town is the hub of a rich farming area.
Tourist Information Centre
☎ *(01258) 454770*

Church House

♔♔ COMMENDED

Church Road, Shillingstone, Blandford Forum DT11 0SL
☎ Child Okeford (01258) 860646
Fax (01258) 860646

Charming, 18th C thatched farmhouse, near Blandford. Pretty gardens, en-suite bathrooms, four-poster, log fires, home cooking. Ideal for touring, walking, exploring.
Bedrooms: 1 double, 1 twin, 1 triple
Bathrooms: 3 private, 2 public

Bed & breakfast per night:	£min	£max
Single	22.00	25.00
Double	33.00	44.00

Half board per person:	£min	£max
Daily	27.00	38.00
Weekly	189.00	266.00

Lunch available
Evening meal 1800 (last orders 1930)
Parking for 3
10 [UL] [S] [TV] [SP] [T]

Farnham Farm House

Listed APPROVED

Farnham, Blandford Forum DT11 8DG
☎ Tollard Royal (01725) 516254
Fax (01725) 516254
350-acre arable farm. 19th C farmhouse in the Cranborne Chase with extensive views to the south. Within easy reach of the coast.
Bedrooms: 2 double, 1 twin
Bathrooms: 1 private, 1 public

Bed & breakfast per night:	£min	£max
Single	17.50	20.00
Double	35.00	40.00

Parking for 7
[UL] [S] [TV]

Home Farm

♔♔ HIGHLY COMMENDED

Bryanston, Blandford Forum DT11 0PR
☎ (01258) 452919
800-acre arable & dairy farm. Attractive Georgian farmhouse with walled garden in quiet hamlet. Area of Outstanding Natural Beauty. Half a mile from Blandford.
Bedrooms: 1 double, 2 twin
Bathrooms: 3 private

Bed & breakfast per night:	£min	£max
Single	17.50	
Double	35.00	

Parking for 10
[UL] [S] [TV]

Meadow House

♔

Tarrant Hinton, Blandford Forum DT11 8JG
☎ Tarrant Hinton (01258) 830498
17th-18th C brick and flint farmhouse set in 4.5 acres. Warm welcome in peaceful, comfortable family home. Noted for delicious home-produced English breakfast. Excellent base for touring.
Bedrooms: 1 single, 1 double, 1 triple
Bathrooms: 3 public

Bed & breakfast per night:	£min	£max
Single	16.50	22.00
Double	33.00	44.00

Parking for 6
[UL] [S] [TV]

BOURNEMOUTH

Dorset
Map ref 2B3

Seaside town set among the pines with a mild climate, sandy beaches and fine coastal views. The town has wide streets with excellent shops, a pier, a pavilion, museums and conference centre.
Tourist Information Centre
☎ *(01202) 789789*

Bay View Hotel ⛰

♔♔♔ COMMENDED

Southbourne Overcliff Drive, Bournemouth BH6 3QB
☎ (01202) 429315 & Mobile (01585) 488150
Fax (01202) 424385
Clifftop location on more relaxing side of Bournemouth. Scrumptious home-cooked food. Panoramic sea views from

Continued ►

BOURNEMOUTH

Continued

most rooms. Special Christmas programme.
Bedrooms: 2 single, 9 double, 3 twin
Bathrooms: 12 private, 1 public
Bed & breakfast

per night:	£min	£max
Single	19.00	24.00
Double	30.00	50.00

Half board

per person:	£min	£max
Daily	22.50	32.50
Weekly	142.50	166.50

Evening meal 1830 (last orders 1930)
Parking for 12
Cards accepted: Access, Visa, Switch/Delta

The Cottage ⚞
COMMENDED
12 Southern Road, Southbourne, Bournemouth BH6 3SR
☎ (01202) 422764

Charming character family-run hotel. Restful location. Noted for home-prepared fresh cooking, cleanliness and tastefully furnished accommodation. Ample parking. Non-smoking.
Bedrooms: 1 single, 1 double, 2 twin, 1 triple, 2 family rooms
Bathrooms: 4 private, 2 public, 1 private shower
Bed & breakfast

per night:	£min	£max
Single	17.00	21.00
Double	34.00	46.00

Half board

per person:	£min	£max
Daily	25.00	29.00
Weekly	162.00	184.00

Evening meal 1800 (last orders 1800)
Open February-November

Downside Private Hotel
52 Westbourne Park Road, Bournemouth BH4 8HQ
☎ (01202) 763109
Small, friendly, licensed hotel in quiet position near chines, close to sea. Special 5-day breaks out of season. Ideal for Poole and local beauty spots.
Bedrooms: 2 single, 2 double, 1 twin, 3 family rooms
Bathrooms: 5 private, 2 public

Bed & breakfast

per night;	£min	£max
Single	12.50	17.50
Double	25.00	35.00

Half board

per person:	£min	£max
Daily	18.50	23.50
Weekly	120.50	155.00

Evening meal from 1800
Parking for 5
Cards accepted: Amex

The Garthlyn Hotel ⚞
COMMENDED
6 Sandbourne Road, Alum Chine, Westbourne, Bournemouth BH4 8JH
☎ (01202) 761016
Hotel of character with award-winning gardens. Good quality beds. 4 minutes' walk to beaches (hut available). Car park in grounds.
Bedrooms: 1 single, 5 double, 1 twin, 1 triple, 2 family rooms
Bathrooms: 9 private, 1 public

Bed & breakfast

per night:	£min	£max
Single	21.00	34.00
Double	40.00	66.00

Half board

per person:	£min	£max
Daily	27.50	41.50
Weekly	171.50	230.00

Evening meal 1800 (last orders 1900)
Parking for 9
Cards accepted: Access, Visa, Switch/Delta

The Golden Sovereigns Hotel ⚞
97 Alumhurst Road, Alum Chine, Bournemouth BH4 8HR
☎ (01202) 762088
Attractively decorated Victorian hotel of character, in a quiet yet convenient location 4 minutes' walk from beach. Comfortable rooms, traditional and Old English home-cooked food.
Bedrooms: 1 single, 2 double, 1 twin, 2 triple, 2 family rooms
Bathrooms: 6 private, 2 public

Bed & breakfast

per night:	£min	£max
Single	15.00	28.00
Double	28.00	46.00

Half board

per person:	£min	£max
Daily	20.00	29.50
Weekly	125.00	185.00

Lunch available
Evening meal 1800 (last orders 1600)
Parking for 9
Cards accepted: Access, Visa

Mayfield Private Hotel ⚞
46 Frances Road, Bournemouth BH1 3SA
☎ (01202) 551839
Overlooking public gardens with tennis, bowling greens, crazy-golf. Central for sea, shops and main rail/coach stations. Some rooms have shower or toilet/shower. Licensed.
Bedrooms: 1 single, 4 double, 2 twin, 1 family room
Bathrooms: 4 private, 2 public, 3 private showers

Bed & breakfast

per night:	£min	£max
Single	13.00	16.00
Double	26.00	32.00

Half board

per person:	£min	£max
Daily	19.00	22.00
Weekly	110.00	128.00

Evening meal from 1800
Parking for 5
Open January-November

Pinewood ⚞
Listed COMMENDED
197 Holdenhurst Road, Bournemouth BH8 8DG
☎ (01202) 292684
Friendly guesthouse, close to rail, coach stations and all amenities. Tea, coffee and satellite TV in all rooms.
Bedrooms: 1 single, 3 double, 1 twin, 3 triple
Bathrooms: 2 public

Bed & breakfast

per night:	£min	£max
Single	15.00	16.00
Double	30.00	32.00

Parking for 8

Rosedene Cottage Hotel
Listed
St Peter's Road, Bournemouth BH1 2LA
☎ (01202) 554102
Old world cottage hotel, quiet, yet in the heart of Bournemouth. A short stroll to pier, shops, gardens, Bournemouth International Centre, theatres and beaches. 20 minutes from Bournemouth International Airport.
Bedrooms: 2 single, 5 double, 1 triple, 1 family room
Bathrooms: 6 private, 1 public

Bed & breakfast

per night:	£min	£max
Single	15.00	23.00
Double	30.00	46.00

Evening meal 1700 (last orders 1700)
Parking for 8
Cards accepted: Access, Visa, Diners, Amex

Willowdene Hotel

⌷⌷ HIGHLY COMMENDED

43 Grand Avenue, Southbourne,
Bournemouth BH6 3SY
☎ (01202) 425370
*Detached Edwardian house, for those
who require quality accommodation
with a happy relaxed atmosphere. 200
yards from sandy beach, with views
over Poole Bay, Isle of Wight Needles
and Purbeck Hills. 5 miles from New
Forest. Non smoking.*
Bedrooms: 3 double, 1 twin, 1 triple
Bathrooms: 5 private, 1 public
Bed & breakfast

per night:	£min	£max
Single	16.00	18.00
Double	32.00	36.00

Parking for 7
Open March-October
🏃♻⌨🖫🅂✂🎔📺 🛏 🚗✿✈🐾
🅿 SP

Woodside Hotel ⋀

⌷⌷ COMMENDED

29 Southern Road, Southbourne,
Bournemouth BH6 3SR
☎ (01202) 427213
*Between Bournemouth and
Christchurch. Family-run hotel.
Licensed bar. Good home cooking and
friendly atmosphere. Bargain breaks
October-May inclusive.*
Bedrooms: 2 single, 3 double, 2 twin,
1 triple, 2 family rooms
Bathrooms: 2 private, 1 public,
3 private showers
Bed & breakfast

per night:	£min	£max
Single	14.00	20.00
Double	28.00	40.00

Half board

per person:	£min	£max
Daily	21.00	27.00
Weekly	120.00	162.00

Evening meal from 1800
Parking for 5
Cards accepted: Access, Visa
🏃♻🅂🎔📺🛏🅿↘SP

BRAMDEAN

Hampshire
Map ref 2C3

Village astride the A272, 1 mile
west of the site of a Roman villa.

Dean Farm

Listed

Kilmeston, Alresford SO24 0NL
☎ (01962) 771286
*200-acre mixed farm. Comfortable, 18th
C farmhouse in Kilmeston, a small and
peaceful village 1.5 miles off the A272
between Petersfield and Winchester.*
Bedrooms: 3 double
Bathrooms: 1 public

Bed & breakfast

per night:	£min	£max
Single	18.00	22.00
Double	36.00	36.00

Parking for 3
🏃10♻⌨🖫🅸🅂✂📺🛏🚗✿✈🐾

BRANSGORE

Hampshire
Map ref 2B3

Situated in extensive woodlands.
In the church of St Mary is a
lovely Perpendicular font which is
said to have come from
Christchurch.

Wiltshire House ⋀

⌷⌷ HIGHLY COMMENDED

West Road, Bransgore, Christchurch,
Dorset BH23 8BD
☎ (01425) 672450
*Friendly, informal accommodation in
an early Victorian gentleman's
residence, set in a large secluded
garden.*
Bedrooms: 2 double, 1 family room
Bathrooms: 3 private
Bed & breakfast

per night:	£min	£max
Single	16.00	20.00
Double	29.00	32.00

Parking for 4
🏃🖩🖫⌨♻🅂✂🎔📺🛏🚗∪✿
✈🐾🅿SP🅃

BROCKENHURST

Hampshire
Map ref 2C3

Attractive village with thatched
cottages and a ford in its main
street. Well placed for visiting the
New Forest.

Evergreen ⋀

⌷⌷ COMMENDED

Sway Road, Brockenhurst SO42 7RX
☎ (01590) 623411
Fax (01590) 623411
*Lovely house, 10 minutes' walk from
village centre/station. Two friendly
ponies and donkey. Beautiful rooms, all
en-suite. Safe, off-road parking.*
Bedrooms: 3 double
Bathrooms: 3 private
Bed & breakfast

per night:	£min	£max
Double	34.00	34.00

Parking for 3
🏃🖩🛏♻⌨🖫🅸✂🛏🚗✿✈🐾

Garlands Cottage ⋀

Listed COMMENDED

2 Garlands Cottage, Lyndhurst Road,
Brockenhurst SO42 7RH
☎ Lymington (01590) 623250
*200-year-old cottage in the heart of the
New Forest, close to all forest facilities
and centre of Brockenhurst. Non-
smokers only, please and no pets.*

Bedrooms: 2 double, 1 twin, 1 triple
Bathrooms: 4 private
Bed & breakfast

per night:	£min	£max
Double	38.00	38.00

Parking for 6
Open January-November
🏃5🖩⌨🖫♻⌨🖫🛏🚗✈🐾

Little Prescotes

Listed

Tile Barn Lane, Brockenhurst
SO42 7UE
☎ Lymington (01590) 623352

*Beautiful country house set in 8 acres
of grounds and stabling. Direct access
to forest, walking, cycling and riding. 4
miles from Lymington.*
Bedrooms: 1 double, 1 triple
Bathrooms: 2 private
Bed & breakfast

per night:	£min	£max
Single	20.00	22.00
Double	36.00	40.00

Parking for 3
🏃🖫♻⌨✂✿✈🐾🖩🏰

BUCKINGHAM

Buckinghamshire
Map ref 2C1

Interesting old market town
surrounded by rich farmland. It has
many Georgian buildings, including
the Town Hall and Old Jail and
many old almshouses and inns.
Stowe School nearby has
magnificent 18th C landscaped
gardens.

Folly Farm ⋀

⌷⌷ COMMENDED

Padbury, Buckingham MK18 2HS
☎ Winslow (01296) 712413
*500-acre arable farm. On A413 between
Winslow and Padbury, 2 miles south of
Buckingham. Substantial farmhouse
opposite Folly Inn. Convenient for
Stowe Landscape Gardens, Silverstone
circuit and Addington Equestrian
Centre. Evening meals by arrangement.*
Bedrooms: 3 double
Bathrooms: 3 private
Bed & breakfast

per night:	£min	£max
Single	18.00	20.00
Double	32.00	34.00

Continued ▶

BUCKINGHAM

Continued

Half board per person:	£min	£max
Daily	26.00	28.00

Evening meal 1830 (last orders 1200)
Parking for 10
[UL] [S] [TV]

BURFORD

Oxfordshire
Map ref 2B1

One of the most beautiful Cotswold wool towns with Georgian and Tudor houses, many antique shops and a picturesque High Street sloping to the River Windrush.
Tourist Information Centre
☎ (01993) 823558 or 823590

The Dower House

Westhall Hill, Fulbrook, Oxford OX18 4BJ
☎ (01993) 822596
Elegant, restored period accommodation in an imposing Cotswold dower house. Superb and tranquil setting, with commanding views over Burford and beautiful surrounding countryside. South-facing bedrooms and picturesque gardens.
Bedrooms: 2 double
Bathrooms: 1 private, 1 public

Bed & breakfast per night:	£min	£max
Single	18.00	30.00
Double	34.00	36.00

Parking for 3
[UL] [S] [TV]

Romany Inn

[Listed]
Bridge Street, Bampton, Oxford OX18 2HA
☎ Bampton Castle (01993) 850237
17th C listed Georgian building, just refurbished, at nearby Bampton. Lounge bar, separate restaurant, chef/proprietor. Noted in pub and beer guides. Brochure available.
Bedrooms: 3 double, 2 twin, 3 triple
Bathrooms: 8 private

Bed & breakfast per night:	£min	£max
Single	21.00	21.00
Double	30.00	30.00

Half board per person:	£min	£max
Daily	26.00	30.00
Weekly	160.00	

Lunch available
Evening meal 1830 (last orders 2200)
Parking for 6
Cards accepted: Access, Visa
[TV]

St Winnow

[Listed] [COMMENDED]
160 The Hill, Burford OX18 4QY
☎ (01993) 823843

Listed Cotswold property in conservation area, on the hill above the High Street. Terraced house with garden and garage, plus limited parking, at rear.
Bedrooms: 1 single, 1 double, 1 twin
Bathrooms: 1 public

Bed & breakfast per night:	£min	£max
Single	20.00	25.00
Double	35.00	40.00

Parking for 2
[UL] [S] [TV]

BURLEY

Hampshire
Map ref 2B3

Attractive centre from which to explore the south-west part of the New Forest. There is an ancient earthwork on Castle Hill nearby, which also offers good views.

Brandon Thatch

[HIGHLY COMMENDED]
Charles' Lane, Bagnum, Ringwood BH24 3DA
☎ Ringwood (01425) 474256
Fax (01425) 478452

A warm, friendly welcome awaits you at this delightful 17th C thatched country house set in 3.5 acres of garden and woodlands. Guest sitting room with TV, video and sky TV. Horses and dogs by arrangement. A non-smoking house.
Bedrooms: 2 double, 1 twin
Bathrooms: 3 private, 1 public

Bed & breakfast per night:	£min	£max
Single	40.00	
Double	48.00	60.00

Parking for 13
Open April-October
[UL] [S] [TV] [SP]

CHANDLERS FORD

Hampshire
Map ref 2C3

Landfall

[Listed]
133 Bournemouth Road, Chandlers Ford, Eastleigh SO53 3HA
☎ Southampton (01703) 254801
Three bedroom, detached, family home. Situated in service road, with easy access to all routes. Pleasant garden with solar heated swimming pool.
Bedrooms: 1 single, 1 triple
Bathrooms: 1 public

Bed & breakfast per night:	£min	£max
Single	15.00	16.00
Double	28.00	30.00

Parking for 2
[UL] [S] [TV]

St Lucia

[Listed]
68 Shaftesbury Avenue, Chandlers Ford, Eastleigh SO53 3BP
☎ (01703) 262995 & Mobile (01589) 392765
Fax (01703) 262995

Homely accommodation well placed for touring, near Winchester, South Coast and New Forest. Evening meals, home-grown produce in season. Non-smokers only, please.
Bedrooms: 2 single, 1 double, 1 twin
Bathrooms: 1 public

Bed & breakfast per night:	£min	£max
Single	13.00	16.50
Double	28.00	30.00

Half board per person:	£min	£max
Daily	16.50	20.00
Weekly	105.00	125.00

Evening meal 1830 (last orders 1830)
Parking for 5
10 [UL] [S] [OAP] [SP]

The symbols ♿ ♿ ♿ indicate categories of accessibility for wheelchair users. They are explained in full in the information pages at the back of this guide.

CHARLBURY

Oxfordshire
Map ref 2C1

Large Cotswold village with beautiful views of the Evenlode Valley just outside the village and close to the ancient Forest of Wychwood.

Banbury Hill Farm 🏵

👑👑 COMMENDED

Enstone Road, Charlbury, Oxford OX7 3JH
☎ (01608) 810314
54-acre mixed farm. Cotswold-stone farmhouse with extensive views across Evenlode Valley. Ideal touring centre for Blenheim Palace, Oxford and the Cotswolds.
Bedrooms: 1 single, 2 double, 1 twin, 1 triple
Bathrooms: 3 private, 1 public

Bed & breakfast per night:	£min	£max
Single	16.00	20.00
Double	32.00	40.00

Evening meal 1830 (last orders 2100)
Parking for 6
🛏 ☐ ☕ 🔒 [S] ⚡ 🥐 [TV] ▥ 🚗 ✂ ❀ ✈ 🚜

CHOLDERTON

Hampshire
Map ref 2B2

Parkhouse Motel

👑👑👑

Cholderton, Salisbury, Wiltshire SP4 0EG
☎ (01980) 629256
Fax (01980) 629256
17th C former coaching inn built of brick and flint with slate roof. 5 miles east of Stonehenge, 10 miles north of Salisbury and 9 miles west of Andover.
Bedrooms: 6 single, 18 double, 6 twin, 3 triple; suites available
Bathrooms: 33 private, 3 public

Bed & breakfast per night:	£min	£max
Single	21.00	33.00
Double	40.00	44.00

Half board per person:	£min	£max
Daily	27.00	39.00
Weekly	189.00	273.00

Evening meal 1900 (last orders 2030)
Parking for 30
Cards accepted: Access, Visa
🛏 ♿ ☐ ☕ 🔒 🥐 [TV] ▥ 🚗 🍸 ❀ [OAP] ✂ [SP] 🏛

CHURCH HANBOROUGH

Oxfordshire
Map ref 2C1

1 Mansell Close

Listed HIGHLY COMMENDED

Church Hanborough, Witney OX8 8AU
☎ Freeland (01993) 881914
Detached house in a pretty village near Woodstock (Blenheim Palace) and only 7 miles west of Oxford. Easily accessible from A40 and A44.
Bedrooms: 2 double
Bathrooms: 2 private

Bed & breakfast per night:	£min	£max
Single	22.50	25.00
Double	36.00	40.00

Parking for 2
☐ ☕ [UL] ⚡ ▥ 🚗 ✈ 🚜 [T]

CHURCH KNOWLE

Dorset
Map ref 2B3

Cartshed Cottage

Listed

Whiteway Farm, Church Knowle, Wareham BH20 5NX
☎ Corfe Castle (01929) 480801
Beamed Tudor cottage with panoramic views of Purbeck Hills.
Bedrooms: 1 double, 2 twin
Bathrooms: 2 private, 1 private shower

Bed & breakfast per night:	£min	£max
Single	18.00	21.00
Double	36.00	42.00

Parking for 4
🛏 ☕ 🔨 [UL] ⚡ [TV] ▥ 🚗 ❀ 🚜 🏛

COMPTON

Berkshire
Map ref 2C2

Village lies above a hollow on the eastern slope of the Berkshire Downs, a little south of the Ridgeway and the ancient British stronghold of Perborough Castle.

The Compton Swan Hotel 🏵

High Street, Compton, Newbury RG16 0NH
☎ Newbury (01635) 578269
Fax (01635) 578269
Recently refurbished country hotel with games room, lounge, restaurant, extensive a la carte menu, large garden and a bar with a range of real ales. Close to the Ridgeway.
Bedrooms: 1 double, 3 twin, 1 family room
Bathrooms: 3 private, 1 public, 2 private showers

Bed & breakfast per night:	£min	£max
Single	30.00	33.00
Double	40.00	44.00

Half board per person:	£min	£max
Daily	35.00	50.00
Weekly	175.00	195.00

Lunch available
Evening meal 1800 (last orders 2200)
Parking for 30
Cards accepted: Access, Visa
🛏 ☎ ☐ ☕ 🔒 [S] ⚡ ▥ 🚗 🍸30 🎱 ♠ U ⛳ ❀ 🚜 [OAP] ✂ [SP]

COMPTON

Hampshire
Map ref 2C3

Manor House

Listed

Place Lane, Compton, Winchester SO21 2BA
☎ Twyford (01962) 712162
Comfortable country house, 8 minutes from Shawford railway station and 2 miles from city of Winchester. Non-smokers preferred.
Bedrooms: 1 double
Bathrooms: 1 public

Bed & breakfast per night:	£min	£max
Single	12.00	12.00
Double	24.00	24.00

Parking for 1
☐ ☕ [UL] ⚡ ▥ 🚗 ❀ ✈ 🚜 🏛

COOKHAM DEAN

Berkshire
Map ref 2C2

Primrose Hill

Listed

Bradcutts Lane, Cookham Dean, Cookham, Maidenhead SL6 9TL
☎ Bourne End (01628) 528179
Large country house, surrounded by beautiful countryside, adjacent to the historic village of Cookham and convenient for Windsor, London, Bath and Oxford. Good train service to Paddington.
Bedrooms: 1 single, 1 triple
Bathrooms: 1 public

Bed & breakfast per night:	£min	£max
Single	17.50	20.00
Double	35.00	40.00

Parking for 3
🛏 ☐ [UL] [S] ⚡ 🥐 [TV] ▥ 🚗 ❀ 🚜

The symbol 🏵 within an entry indicates participation in the Welcome Host programme – a nationally recognised customer care initiative which aims to promote the highest standards of service and a warm welcome for all visitors.

CORFE CASTLE

Dorset
Map ref 2B3

One of the most spectacular ruined castles in Britain. Norman in origin, the castle was a Royalist stronghold during the Civil War and held out until 1645. The village had a considerable marble-carving industry in the Middle Ages.

Bradle Farmhouse
COMMENDED

Bradle Farm, Church Knowle,
Wareham BH20 5NU
☎ (01929) 480712
Fax (01929) 480712

550-acre mixed farm. Picturesque farmhouse in the heart of Purbeck. Superb views of castle and surrounding countryside, beach 2 miles. Warm family atmosphere with evening meals arranged at local inn.
Bedrooms: 2 double, 1 twin
Bathrooms: 2 private, 1 public

Bed & breakfast

per night:	£min	£max
Single	18.00	25.00
Double	34.00	38.00

Half board

per person:	£min	£max
Weekly	180.00	200.00

Parking for 3

COTSWOLDS

*See under Burford, Charlbury, Church Hanborough, Deddington, Leafield, Middle Barton, Minster Lovell, Witney, Woodstock
See also Cotswolds in Heart of England region*

CRANBORNE

Dorset
Map ref 2B3

Village with an interesting Jacobean manor house. Lies south-east of Cranborne Chase, formerly a forest and hunting preserve.

Sheaf of Arrows ⚔

4 The Square, Cranborne, Wimborne
Minster BH21 5PR
☎ (01725) 517456
Fax (01725) 517456

Old village coaching inn with Victorian frontage. In country setting, with easy access to Poole, Bournemouth, Salisbury and Cranborne Chase.
Bedrooms: 1 double, 1 twin, 1 triple
Bathrooms: 3 private

Bed & breakfast

per night:	£min	£max
Single	25.00	35.00
Double	35.00	45.00

Half board

per person:	£min	£max
Daily	22.50	30.00
Weekly	150.00	200.00

Lunch available
Evening meal 1900 (last orders 2130)
Parking for 6

DEDDINGTON

Oxfordshire
Map ref 2C1

Attractive former market town with a large market square and many fine old buildings.

Hill Barn
Listed

Milton Gated Road, Deddington,
Banbury OX15 0TS
☎ (01869) 338631
Converted barn set in open countryside with views overlooking valley and hills. Banbury-Oxford road, half a mile before Deddington, turn right to Milton Gated Road. Hill Barn is 100 yards on the right.
Bedrooms: 1 double, 2 twin
Bathrooms: 1 public

Bed & breakfast

per night:	£min	£max
Single	15.00	20.00
Double	30.00	36.00

Parking for 6

Stonecrop Guest House

Hempton Road, Deddington, Banbury
OX15 0QH
☎ (01869) 338335 & 338496
Fax (01869) 338335
Modern, detached accommodation, close to major roads, shops and places of interest.
Bedrooms: 1 single, 1 double, 1 twin, 1 triple
Bathrooms: 1 public

Bed & breakfast

per night:	£min	£max
Single	15.00	17.00
Double	30.00	34.00

Parking for 6

DENMEAD

Hampshire
Map ref 2C3

Comparatively modern town, south-west of the original settlement.

Forest Gate
Listed

Hambledon Road, Denmead,
Waterlooville PO7 6EX
☎ Waterlooville (01705) 255901
Listed Georgian house in large garden, on outskirts of village. Within easy reach of maritime Portsmouth and continental ferries. Dinner by arrangement.
Bedrooms: 2 twin
Bathrooms: 2 private

Bed & breakfast

per night:	£min	£max
Single	22.00	24.00
Double	36.00	40.00

Half board

per person:	£min	£max
Daily	32.00	35.50
Weekly	202.00	224.00

Evening meal from 1930
Parking for 4

DIBDEN

Hampshire
Map ref 2C3

Small village on the edge of the New Forest with a full recreation centre. Picturesque 13th C church overlooks Southampton Water.

Dale Farm Guest House ⚔

Manor Road, Applemore Hill, Dibden,
Southampton SO45 5TJ
☎ Southampton (01703) 849632
Friendly, family-run 18th C converted farmhouse in wooded setting. Large garden with play area. 250 yards from A326, adjacent to riding stables and 15 minutes from beach. Children welcome.
Bedrooms: 1 single, 2 double, 2 twin, 1 triple
Bathrooms: 1 public, 1 private shower

Bed & breakfast

per night:	£min	£max
Single	16.00	19.00
Double	32.00	34.00

Half board

per person:	£min	£max
Daily	26.50	
Weekly	160.00	

Evening meal 1800 (last orders 1100)
Parking for 20

EAST MEON

Hampshire
Map ref 2C3

Set in one of the prettiest river valleys in Hampshire, with quiet lanes leading over the downs. The village is unspoilt and has some delightful cottages. The church has a magnificent black marble font with scenes from the life of Adam and Eve.

Drayton Cottage ⚊

Listed

East Meon, Petersfield GU32 1PW
☎ (01730) 823472
Flint period cottage overlooking river. Victorian-type conservatory and beautiful garden. Situated on road joining East Meon and West Meon. Brochure available.
Bedrooms: 1 double, 1 twin
Bathrooms: 1 private, 1 public

Bed & breakfast per night:	£min	£max
Single	22.00	22.00
Double	36.00	44.00

Half board per person:	£min	£max
Daily	30.00	34.00

Parking for 3

FLEET

Hampshire
Map ref 2C2

Tourist Information Centre
☎ *(01252) 811151*

The Webbs ⚊

Listed **COMMENDED**

12 Warren Close, Fleet, Aldershot GU13 9LT
☎ Aldershot (01252) 615063
Fax (01252) 629873
Homely, friendly atmosphere. Families welcome (no age limit). Close to Fleet station, A30 and M3, exit 4A.
Bedrooms: 2 single, 1 twin
Bathrooms: 2 public

Bed & breakfast per night:	£min	£max
Single	17.50	
Double	35.00	

Half board per person:	£min	£max
Daily	26.50	
Weekly	180.00	

Evening meal 1830 (last orders 1700)
Parking for 2

Please mention this guide when making a booking.

FORDINGBRIDGE

Hampshire
Map ref 2B3

On the north-west edge of the New Forest. A medieval bridge crosses the Avon at this point and gave the town its name. A good centre for walking, exploring and fishing.

Hillbury

Listed

2 Fir Tree Hill, Camel Green Road, Alderholt, Fordingbridge SP6 3AY
☎ (01425) 652582
Fax (01425) 652582
Bungalow in quiet situation with easy access to M27. Ideal touring base for New Forest and South Coast. Riding, swimming, golf and fishing nearby. Sorry, no pets or smokers.
Bedrooms: 1 single, 1 twin, 1 triple
Bathrooms: 1 private, 2 public

Bed & breakfast per night:	£min	£max
Single	15.00	18.00
Double	32.00	36.00

Parking for 5

GERRARDS CROSS

Buckinghamshire
Map ref 2D2

On the London Road, Gerrards Cross is distinguished by its wide gorse and beech tree common.

Dovetails

Listed

Upway, Chalfont Heights, Chalfont St Peter, Gerrards Cross SL9 0AS
☎ (01753) 882639
60-year-old detached house in large garden, on a quiet, private estate.
Bedrooms: 2 twin
Bathrooms: 2 private

Bed & breakfast per night:	£min	£max
Single	20.00	25.00
Double	35.00	40.00

Half board per person:	£min	£max
Daily	28.50	33.50
Weekly	195.00	210.00

Evening meal 1800 (last orders 2000)
Parking for 2

Colour maps at the back of this guide pinpoint all places which have accommodation listings in the guide.

GORING

Oxfordshire
Map ref 2C2

Riverside town on the Oxfordshire/ Berkshire border, linked by an attractive bridge to Streatley with views to the Goring Gap.

The John Barleycorn

Manor Road, Goring, Reading, Berkshire RG8 9DP
☎ (01491) 872509
16th C inn with exposed beams. Real ale, home-cooked food. Close to the river, lovely walks.
Bedrooms: 1 single, 2 double, 1 triple
Bathrooms: 2 public

Bed & breakfast per night	£min	£max
Single	23.00	
Double	39.00	

Lunch available
Evening meal 1900 (last orders 2200)
Parking for 2
Cards accepted: Access, Visa, Switch/ Delta

HAMBLE

Hampshire
Map ref 2C3

Set almost at the mouth of the River Hamble, this quiet fishing village has become a major yachting centre.

Braymar

Listed

35 Westfield Close, Hamble, Southampton SO30 5LG
☎ Southampton (01703) 453831
Private house, in peaceful position, 5 minutes from quiet beach and pretty, sailing village of Hamble, where "Howards Way" was filmed. 15 minutes' drive from Southampton and Portsmouth. Near M27.
Bedrooms: 1 single, 1 double, 2 twin
Bathrooms: 1 public

Bed & breakfast per night:	£min	£max
Single	14.00	15.00
Double	28.00	28.00

Parking for 3

Individual proprietors have supplied all details of accommodation. As changes can occur, we advise you to confirm the information at the time of booking.

HAMBLEDON

Hampshire
Map ref 2C3

In a valley, surrounded by wooded downland and marked by an air of Georgian prosperity. It was here that cricket was given its first proper rules. The Bat and Ball Inn at Broadhalfpenny Down is the cradle of cricket.

Cams
Hambledon, Waterlooville PO7 4SP
☎ Portsmouth (01705) 632865
Fax (01705) 632691
Comfortable, listed family house in beautiful setting with large garden on the edge of Hambledon village. Two pubs within walking distance. Evening meal by arrangement.
Bedrooms: 1 double, 2 twin
Bathrooms: 1 private, 1 public, 1 private shower

Bed & breakfast

per night:	£min	£max
Single	16.00	18.00
Double	32.00	36.00

Evening meal from 1900
Parking for 6

Mornington House
Listed
Speltham Hill, Hambledon, Waterlooville PO7 4RU
☎ Portsmouth (01705) 632704
18th C private house with 2 acres of garden and paddock, in the centre of Hambledon behind the George Inn, 2 miles from famous Bat and Ball Inn.
Bedrooms: 2 twin
Bathrooms: 1 public

Bed & breakfast

per night:	£min	£max
Single	16.00	20.00
Double	30.00	30.00

Parking for 6

Nightingale Cottage ⋀
HIGHLY COMMENDED
Hoegate, Hambledon, Waterlooville PO7 4RD
☎ Portsmouth (01705) 632447
Fax (01705) 632027
Country house with picturesque garden on outskirts of Hambledon, adjacent to Hoegate Common but only half a mile from B2150. In an Area of Outstanding Natural Beauty.
Bedrooms: 2 double, 1 twin
Bathrooms: 3 private, 1 public

Bed & breakfast

per night:	£min	£max
Single	20.00	25.00
Double	38.00	50.00

Parking for 8
Cards accepted: Access, Visa

HAVANT

Hampshire
Map ref 2C3

Once a market town famous for making parchment. Nearby at Leigh Park extensive early 19th C landscape gardens and parklands are open to the public. Right in the centre of the town stands the interesting 13th C church of St Faith.
Tourist Information Centre
☎ *(01705) 480024*

High Towers ⋀
14 Portsdown Hill Road, Bedhampton, Havant PO9 3JY
☎ Portsmouth (01705) 471748
Large, detached residence, located on Portsdown Hill, with magnificent views overlooking Portsmouth, the sea and surrounding countryside. Near ferries. Non-smokers only, please.
Bedrooms: 2 single, 2 double
Bathrooms: 4 private, 1 public

Bed & breakfast

per night:	£min	£max
Single	20.00	26.00
Double	36.00	40.00

Parking for 6

The Old Mill Guest House ⋀
Mill Lane, Bedhampton, Havant PO9 3JH
☎ Portsmouth (01705) 454948
Fax (01705) 499677
Georgian house in large grounds by a lake abundant in wildlife. Modernised, comfortable retreat. John Keats rested here.
Bedrooms: 1 double, 4 triple
Bathrooms: 5 private

Bed & breakfast

per night:	£min	£max
Single	23.00	25.00
Double	36.00	39.00

Parking for 10

The symbol 🌐 within an entry indicates participation in the Welcome Host programme – a nationally recognised customer care initiative which aims to promote the highest standards of service and a warm welcome for all visitors.

HAYLING ISLAND

Hampshire
Map ref 2C3

Small, flat island of historic interest, surrounded by natural harbours and with fine sandy beaches, linked to the mainland by a road.

Cockle Warren Cottage Hotel ⋀
HIGHLY COMMENDED
36 Seafront, Hayling Island PO11 9HL
☎ (01705) 464961
Fax (01705) 464838

Lovely seaside farmhouse-style hotel with large garden and heated swimming pool. French and English country cooking, home-made bread, four-poster and Victorian beds, log fires in winter.
Bedrooms: 5 double
Bathrooms: 5 private

Bed & breakfast

per night:	£min	£max
Single	45.00	65.00
Double	64.00	84.00

Half board

per person:	£min	£max
Daily	56.50	66.50

Evening meal 2000 (last orders 1600)
Parking for 11
Cards accepted: Access, Visa, Amex

Newtown House Hotel ⋀
Manor Road, Hayling Island PO11 0QR
☎ Portsmouth (01705) 466131
Fax (01705) 461366
18th C converted farmhouse, set in own grounds a quarter of a mile from seafront. Indoor leisure complex with heated pool, gym, steamroom, jacuzzi and sauna. Tennis.
Bedrooms: 9 single, 9 double, 4 twin, 3 triple
Bathrooms: 25 private, 2 public

Bed & breakfast

per night:	£min	£max
Single	35.00	
Double	55.00	

Half board

per person:	£min	£max
Daily	48.00	
Weekly	290.00	

Lunch available
Evening meal 1900 (last orders 2130)
Parking for 45

Cards accepted: Access, Visa, Diners, Amex

ᏉᏆᏉᏓᏉᏫ▢▧ᏛᏛᏉᏆᏉᏉᏉᏉᏉᏉᏉᏉᏉ
▥ᏝᏆᏉᏉᏉᏉᏉᏉᏉᏉᏉᏉᏉᏉᏉᏉ

HENLEY-ON-THAMES

Oxfordshire
Map ref 2C2

The famous Thames Regatta is held in this prosperous and attractive town at the beginning of July each year. The town has many Georgian buildings and old coaching inns and the parish church has some fine monuments.
Tourist Information Centre
☎ *(01491) 578034*

Alftrudis

☖ HIGHLY COMMENDED

8 Norman Avenue, Henley-on-Thames RG9 1SG
☎ (01491) 573099
Friendly detached Victorian house in quiet, private road, centrally situated two minutes' walk from the station, town centre and the river. Easy parking.
Bedrooms: 2 double, 1 triple
Bathrooms: 2 private, 1 public

Bed & breakfast

per night:	£min	£max
Single	22.00	30.00
Double	32.00	45.00

Parking for 2

Holmwood ⋀

☖☖ HIGHLY COMMENDED

Shiplake Row, Binfield Heath, Henley-on-Thames RG9 4DP
☎ Reading (01734) 478747
Fax (01734) 478637
Large Georgian country house in beautiful surroundings, equidistant from Henley and Reading, off A4155. Binfield Heath is signposted.
Wheelchair access category 3 ♿
Bedrooms: 1 single, 2 double, 2 twin
Bathrooms: 5 private

Bed & breakfast

per night:	£min	£max
Single	27.50	27.50
Double	45.00	45.00

Parking for 8

Lenwade ⋀

☖ HIGHLY COMMENDED

3 Western Road, Henley-on-Thames RG9 1JL
☎ (01491) 573468 & Mobile 0374 941629
Victorian house in quiet surroundings, within walking distance of the River Thames and town centre. Children welcome. Parking available.
Bedrooms: 2 double, 1 twin
Bathrooms: 1 private, 2 public

Bed & breakfast

per night:	£min	£max
Single	25.00	30.00
Double	35.00	45.00

Parking for 2

Mervyn House ⋀

☖ COMMENDED

4 St Marks Road, Henley-on-Thames RG9 1LJ
☎ (01491) 575331 & Mobile 0374 771513
Fax (01491) 411747
Victorian house, situated in a residential road, very close to Henley town centre, station, restaurants, pubs and river. Convenient for Windsor, Oxford and London, M4 and M40.
Bedrooms: 2 double, 1 twin; suite available
Bathrooms: 3 private, 1 public

Bed & breakfast

per night:	£min	£max
Single	22.00	27.00
Double	32.00	43.00

New Lodge ⋀

☖ COMMENDED

Henley Park, Henley-on-Thames RG9 6HU
☎ (01491) 576340
Victorian lodge in parkland in Area of Outstanding Natural Beauty. Lovely walks and views. Only 1 mile from Henley, 45 miles from Heathrow.
Bedrooms: 2 double
Bathrooms: 2 private

Bed & breakfast

per night:	£min	£max
Single	22.00	26.00
Double	29.00	39.00

Parking for 7

HOOK NORTON

Oxfordshire
Map ref 2C1

Quiet town with a history dating back 1000 years when the Normans built and buttressed its chancel walls against attack from the invading Danes.

Pear Tree Inn

☖☖ COMMENDED

Scotland End, Hook Norton, Banbury OX15 5NU
☎ (01608) 737482
Old beamed pub, near famous Hook Norton brewery. 5 miles from Chipping Norton, close to Banbury and the Cotswolds.
Bedrooms: 1 double
Bathrooms: 1 private

Bed & breakfast

per night:	£min	£max
Single	20.00	20.00
Double	35.00	35.00

Lunch available
Evening meal 1900 (last orders 2100)
Parking for 11
Cards accepted: Amex

HUNGERFORD

Berkshire
Map ref 2C2

Attractive town on the Avon Canal and the River Kennet, famous for its fishing. It has a wide High Street and many antique shops. Nearby is the Tudor manor of Littlecote with its large Roman mosaic.

Marshgate Cottage Hotel ⋀

☖☖ COMMENDED

Marsh Lane, Hungerford RG17 0QX
☎ (01488) 682307
Fax (01488) 685475
Family-run canalside hotel ranged around south-facing courtyard, linked to 350-year-old thatched cottage. Overlooks marshland and trout streams. Lovely walks, bike hire, bird watching. Important antiques centre. 1 hour from Heathrow. French, German and Scandinavian languages spoken.
Bedrooms: 1 single, 4 double, 2 twin, 1 triple, 1 family room
Bathrooms: 7 private, 2 public

Bed & breakfast

per night:	£min	£max
Single	25.50	35.50
Double	39.50	48.50

Half board

per person:	£min	£max
Daily	36.00	46.00

Evening meal 1900 (last orders 2100)
Parking for 9
Cards accepted: Access, Visa, Amex

HYTHE

Hampshire
Map ref 2C3

Changri-La

☖ HIGHLY COMMENDED

12 Ashleigh Close, Hythe, Southampton SO45 3QP
☎ Southampton (01703) 846664
Spacious comfortable home, in unique position on edge of New Forest, a few minutes' drive from Beaulieu and other places of interest. Golf-course, pony trekking and sports complex nearby.
Bedrooms: 1 double, 1 twin
Bathrooms: 2 public

Continued ▶

HYTHE

Continued

Bed & breakfast

per night:	£min	£max
Single	14.50	15.00
Double	28.00	30.00

Parking for 3

🅰♿🛏♿ⓊⓁ Ⓢ Ⓜ ⓉⓋ ⅢⅢ, 🚗✕ 🚲

IDBURY

Oxfordshire
Map ref 2B1

Bould Farmhouse ⋀

Listed · COMMENDED

Bould, Nr Idbury, Chipping Norton
OX7 6RT
☎ Chipping Norton (01608) 658850
*300-acre mixed farm. Listed Cotswold
farmhouse, 10 minutes' drive to Stow-
on-the-Wold, Bourton-on-the-Water and
Burford. Nature trails adjoining wood.*
Bedrooms: 1 double, 1 family room
Bathrooms: 2 private, 2 public

Bed & breakfast

per night:	£min	£max
Single	20.00	25.00
Double	36.00	40.00

Parking for 6
Open February-November

🛏🖙♿ⓊⓁ🔒Ⓢ✕ ⅢⅢ, 🚗⋃✿✕ 🚲🏠

ISLE OF WIGHT

*See under Ryde, Shalfleet,
Shanklin*

KIMMERIDGE

Dorset
Map ref 2B3

Kimmeridge Farmhouse

Listed

Kimmeridge, Wareham BH20 5PE
☎ Corfe Castle (01929) 480990

*750-acre mixed farm. Farmhouse built
in the 16th C, with lovely views of
surrounding countryside and the sea
within short walking distance. Warm
family atmosphere and spacious
facilities. Evening meals by
arrangement with local inn.*
Bedrooms: 2 double, 1 twin
Bathrooms: 1 private, 1 public

Bed & breakfast

per night:	£min	£max
Single	20.00	25.00
Double	34.00	37.00

Parking for 3

🛏♿Ⓤ🖙♿ⓊⓁⓈⅢⅢ, 🚗✿✕ 🚲🏠

KINGSCLERE

Hampshire
Map ref 2C2

Cleremede ⋀

⌘⌘ COMMENDED

Fox's Lane, Kingsclere, Newbury,
Berkshire RG20 5SL
☎ (01635) 297298 & Mobile 0374
280716
*Near Watership Down and Wayfarers
Walk. Breakfast in conservatory in
summer overlooking large garden.*
Bedrooms: 1 single, 2 twin
Bathrooms: 1 private, 1 public

Bed & breakfast

per night:	£min	£max
Single	19.00	20.00
Double	36.00	38.00

Parking for 6

🛏10🖙♿ⓊⓁ✕ Ⓜ ⅢⅢ, 🚗Ⓠ✿ 🚲

11 Hook Road

Listed

Kingsclere, Newbury, Berkshire
RG20 5PD
☎ (01635) 298861
Fax (01635) 298861
*Comfortable, modern house in historic
Kingsclere at the foot of the beautiful
Hampshire Downs. Convenient for M3,
M4 and A34 and all local amenities.
Hook Road is off Basingstoke Road, half
a mile east of Kingsclere village square.*
Bedrooms: 1 single, 1 double, 1 twin
Bathrooms: 1 private, 1 public

Bed & breakfast

per night:	£min	£max
Single	18.00	18.00
Double	30.00	30.00

Half board

per person:	£min	£max
Daily	28.00	28.00
Weekly	196.00	196.00

Lunch available
Evening meal 1900 (last orders 2100)
Parking for 2

🛏🖾♿ⓊⓁⓈ✕ ⓉⓋ ⅢⅢ, 🚗▶✿ 🚲Ⓣ

LAMBOURN

Berkshire
Map ref 2C2

Attractive village among the
Downs on the River Lambourn.
Famous for its racing stables.

Lodge Down ⋀

⌘⌘ COMMENDED

Lambourn, Newbury RG16 7BJ
☎ Marlborough (01672) 40304
Fax (01672) 40304

---

*70-acre arable farm. Country house with
quality accommodation and en-suite
bathrooms, set in lovely grounds. Exit
junction 14 of M4, take B4000 and
follow signs to Baydon. Lodge Down is
1 mile before Baydon (300 metres down
drive).*
Bedrooms: 1 double, 2 twin
Bathrooms: 3 private, 1 public

Bed & breakfast

per night:	£min	£max
Single	20.00	25.00
Double	40.00	50.00

Parking for 11

🛏🖙♿ⓆⓊⓁ✕ Ⓜ ⓉⓋ ⅢⅢ, 🚗⌇Ⓠ⌘⋃
▶✿ 🚲⌇ ⓈⓅ

LEAFIELD

Oxfordshire
Map ref 2C1

The Farm

Lower Farm, Witney Lane, Leafield,
Witney OX8 5PG
☎ Astall Leigh (01993) 878287
Fax (01993) 878042
*17th C farmhouse and outbuildings
nestled on the edge of the Cotswolds
and surrounded by 24 acres of pastures
and woodland. Only 10 minutes from
A40.*
Bedrooms: 9 single, 1 double, 2 twin
Bathrooms: 12 private

Bed & breakfast

per night:	£min	£max
Single	40.00	
Double	55.00	

Half board

per person:	£min	£max
Daily	55.00	

Evening meal 1900 (last orders 2200)
Parking for 50

🛏10🖾♿Ⓛ🖙♿Ⓢ ⅢⅢ, 🍴60✿✕
🚲 ⓈⓅ

LITTLE LONDON

Hampshire
Map ref 2C2

Bangla ⋀

Listed

Silchester Road, Little London, Tadley
RG26 5EP
☎ Basingstoke (01256) 850735
*Modern, chalet bungalow in village of
Little London, 6 miles from
Basingstoke. Adjacent to Pamber Forest
Nature Reserve.*
Bedrooms: 1 single, 1 double, 1 twin
Bathrooms: 2 public

Bed & breakfast

per night:	£min	£max
Single	13.50	17.50
Double		30.00

Parking for 4

🛏🖾🅰♿🖙♿ⓆⓊⓁ🔒Ⓢ✕ ⓉⓋ ⅢⅢ, 🚗
✿ 🚲

LITTLE WITTENHAM

Oxfordshire
Map ref 2C2

Rooks Orchard

HIGHLY COMMENDED

Little Wittenham, Abingdon OX14 4QY
☎ Clifton Hampden (01865) 407765
*Attractive, peaceful and welcoming
listed 17th C family house and garden,
in pretty Thameside village next to
nature reserve and Wiltenham Clumps.
"Splendid breakfasts". Abingdon, Didcot
and Wallingford approximately 4 miles,
Oxford 9 miles.*
Bedrooms: 1 single, 1 double
Bathrooms: 1 private, 1 public
Bed & breakfast

per night:	£min	£max
Single	20.00	24.00
Double	38.00	44.00

Evening meal from 1900
Parking for 6

LYMINGTON

Hampshire
Map ref 2C3

Small, pleasant town with bright
cottages and attractive Georgian
houses, lying on the edge of the
New Forest with a ferry service to
the Isle of Wight. A sheltered
harbour makes it a busy yachting
centre.

Admiral House

Listed

5 Stanley Road, Lymington SO41 3SJ
☎ (01590) 674339
*House exclusively for guests, with the
owner next door. 200 yards from
countryside conservation area and
marinas. Many pubs and restaurants
nearby.*
Bedrooms: 1 single, 1 twin, 1 triple
Bathrooms: 1 public
Bed & breakfast

per night:	£min	£max
Single	11.00	12.50
Double	22.00	25.00

Altworth

Listed **APPROVED**

12 North Close, Lymington SO41 9BT
☎ (01590) 674082
*Near centre of town in quiet residential
street, 5 minutes from bus/railway
stations and Isle of Wight ferry. Within
30 minutes of Southampton and
Bournemouth, with Brockenhurst and
New Forest area only 10 minutes away.*
Bedrooms: 1 single, 1 double, 1 triple
Bathrooms: 1 public

Bed & breakfast

per night:	£min	£max
Single	14.00	14.50
Double	25.00	26.00

Open April-October

Efford Cottage

COMMENDED

Everton, Lymington SO41 0JD
☎ (01590) 642315 & Mobile 0374
703075
Fax (01590) 642315

*Friendly, spacious, part Georgian family
home. Four course (five choice)
breakfast, home-made bread and
preserves. Traditional country cooking
by qualified chef using home-grown
produce when available. Parking.*
Bedrooms: 3 double, 1 twin, 1 triple
Bathrooms: 5 private
Bed & breakfast

per night:	£min	£max
Single	18.00	23.00
Double	34.00	42.00

Half board

per person:	£min	£max
Daily	28.00	33.50
Weekly	164.00	245.00

Lunch available
Evening meal 1800 (last orders 1900)
Parking for 4

Our Bench

COMMENDED

9 Lodge Road, Pennington, Lymington
SO41 8HH
☎ (01590) 673141
Fax (01590) 673141

*All en-suite bedrooms, separate TV
lounge, indoor heated pool, jacuzzi and
sauna. Non-smokers only, please. Sorry,
no children. Large quiet garden.*
Bedrooms: 1 single, 1 double, 1 twin
Bathrooms: 3 private
Bed & breakfast

per night:	£min	£max
Single	18.00	25.00
Double	38.00	42.00

Half board

per person:	£min	£max
Daily	25.00	32.00
Weekly	175.00	224.00

Evening meal 1800 (last orders 2000)
Parking for 5

LYNDHURST

Hampshire
Map ref 2C3

The "capital" of the New Forest,
surrounded by attractive woodland
scenery and delightful villages. The
town is dominated by the Victorian
Gothic-style church where the
original Alice in Wonderland is
buried.
*Tourist Information Centre
☎ (01703) 282269*

Burton House

Romsey Road, Lyndhurst SO43 7AA
☎ Southampton (01703) 282445
*Lovely house in half-acre garden, near
the village centre. All rooms with en-
suite shower, WC and washbasin.
Parking in grounds.*
Bedrooms: 1 single, 3 double, 1 triple,
1 family room
Bathrooms: 6 private
Bed & breakfast

per night:	£min	£max
Single	21.00	
Double	32.00	42.00

Parking for 8

Forest Cottage

Listed

High Street, Lyndhurst SO43 7BH
☎ Southampton (01703) 283461
*Charming 300-year-old cottage with
welcoming atmosphere, in the village,
yet open forest only yards away. Guest
lounge with open fire and TV.*
Bedrooms: 1 single, 1 double, 1 twin
Bathrooms: 2 public
Bed & breakfast

per night:	£min	£max
Single	17.00	18.00
Double	32.00	34.00

Parking for 3

Little Hayes

HIGHLY COMMENDED

43 Romsey Road, Lyndhurst
SO43 7AR
☎ Southampton (01703) 283000
Continued ▶

Continued ▶

> We advise you to confirm
> your booking in writing.

LYNDHURST

Continued

Lovely Victorian home, beautifully restored and furnished. Spacious rooms, friendly atmosphere and wonderful breakfast. Close to village centre and forest walks.
Bedrooms: 2 double, 1 twin
Bathrooms: 1 private, 1 public

Bed & breakfast

per night:	£min	£max
Single	20.00	
Double	34.00	

Parking for 4
Open March-October
Cards accepted: Access, Visa, Switch/ Delta

The Penny Farthing Hotel ⋀

⚜⚜ COMMENDED
Romsey Road, Lyndhurst SO43 7AA
☎ Southampton (01703) 284422
Fax (01703) 284488

Perfectly situated small hotel, 1 minute's walk from village centre, shops, restaurants, 2 minutes from open forest. Tastefully furnished rooms ensure a comfortable stay.
Bedrooms: 3 single, 5 double, 1 twin, 1 triple, 1 family room
Bathrooms: 11 private

Bed & breakfast

per night:	£min	£max
Single	25.00	35.00
Double	45.00	70.00

Parking for 15
Cards accepted: Access, Visa
Ad Display advertisement appears on this page

Reepham House

Listed HIGHLY COMMENDED
12 Romsey Road, Lyndhurst SO43 7AA
☎ (01703) 283091
Fax (01703) 283091

An attractive, refurbished Victorian house. Spacious bedrooms with colour TV. Private car park. Village shops and open forest are nearby.
Bedrooms: 2 double, 1 twin
Bathrooms: 1 public

Bed & breakfast

per night:	£min	£max
Double	32.00	35.00

Parking for 6
Open January-November

The symbol ⊛ within an entry indicates participation in the Welcome Host programme – a nationally recognised customer care initiative which aims to promote the highest standards of service and a warm welcome for all visitors.

MAIDENHEAD

Berkshire
Map ref 2C2

Attractive town on the River Thames which is crossed by an elegant 18th C bridge and by Brunel's well-known railway bridge. It is a popular place for boating with delightful riverside walks. The Courage Shire Horse Centre is nearby.
Tourist Information Centre
☎ *(01628) 781110*

Cartlands Cottage

⚜ APPROVED
Kings Lane, Cookham Dean, Cookham, Maidenhead SL6 9AY
☎ Marlow (01628) 482196
Family room in self-contained garden studio. Meals in delightful timbered character cottage with exposed beams. Traditional cottage garden. National Trust common land. Very quiet.
Bedrooms: 1 triple
Bathrooms: 1 private, 1 public

Bed & breakfast

per night:	£min	£max
Single	16.00	20.00
Double	30.00	40.00

Parking for 4

Moor Farm ⋀

⚜⚜ HIGHLY COMMENDED
Ascot Road, Holyport, Maidenhead SL6 2HY
☎ (01628) 33761
Fax (01628) 33761
100-acre mixed farm. 700-year-old medieval manor in picturesque Holyport village. 4 miles from Windsor, 12 miles from Heathrow.
Bedrooms: 1 double, 2 twin
Bathrooms: 3 private

Bed & breakfast

per night:	£min	£max
Double	39.00	46.00

Parking for 4

Sheephouse Manor ⋀⋀

Listed: ⚜⚜ COMMENDED

Sheephouse Road, Maidenhead
SL6 8HJ
☎ (01628) 776902
Fax (01628) 25138
Charming 16th C farmhouse in tranquil setting, close to River Thames. All rooms en-suite. Sauna, jacuzzi and gym available. Easy access to M4/M40.
Bedrooms: 2 single, 2 double, 1 twin
Bathrooms: 5 private
Bed & breakfast

per night:	£min	£max
Single	28.00	32.00
Double	40.00	45.00

Parking for 12
Cards accepted: Access, Visa, Switch/Delta

MARLOW

Buckinghamshire
Map ref 2C2

Attractive Georgian town on the River Thames, famous for its 19th C suspension bridge. The High Street contains many old houses and there are connections with writers including Shelley and the poet T S Eliot.

Acha Pani ⋀⋀

Listed COMMENDED

Bovingdon Green, Marlow SL7 2JL
☎ (01628) 483435
Modern house with large garden, in quiet location 1 mile north of Marlow. No children or dogs please.
Bedrooms: 1 single, 1 double, 1 twin
Bathrooms: 1 private, 1 public
Bed & breakfast

per night:	£min	£max
Single	15.00	
Double	30.00	32.00

Half board

per person:	£min	£max
Daily	20.00	

Parking for 3

2 Hyde Green

Listed

Marlow SL7 1QL
☎ (01628) 483526 & Mobile (01378) 178802
Comfortable family home. Quietly situated yet only a few minutes' level walk from town centre, River Thames and station (Paddington 1 hour).
Bedrooms: 1 double, 2 twin
Bathrooms: 2 private, 1 public
Bed & breakfast

per night:	£min	£max
Single	22.00	25.00
Double	32.00	36.00

Parking for 2

Monkton Farmhouse

Listed COMMENDED

Monkton Farm, Little Marlow, Marlow
SL7 3RF
☎ High Wycombe (01494) 521082
Fax (01494) 443905
150-acre dairy farm. 14th C cruckhouse set in beautiful countryside. Easily reached by motorway and close to shopping and sporting facilities.
Bedrooms: 1 single, 1 twin, 1 triple
Bathrooms: 1 public
Bed & breakfast

per night:	£min	£max
Single	20.00	22.00
Double	38.00	40.00

Parking for 6

5 Pound Lane

Listed

Marlow SL7 2AE
☎ (01628) 482649
Older style house, just off town centre, 2 minutes from River Thames and leisure complex. Double room has own balcony with delightful view.
Bedrooms: 1 double, 1 twin
Bathrooms: 1 public
Bed & breakfast

per night:	£min	£max
Single	22.00	25.00
Double	35.00	38.00

Parking for 2

MIDDLE BARTON

Oxfordshire
Map ref 2C1

Cottage-by-the-Ford

⚜

Mill Lane, Middle Barton, Chipping Norton OX7 7BT
☎ Steeple Aston (01869) 347150
Fax (01869) 347150
Cotswold-stone house with separate guest cottage in gardens with stream. Quiet village location. Convenient for Oxford, Stratford and Cotswolds.
Bedrooms: 1 twin
Bathrooms: 1 private
Bed & breakfast

per night:	£min	£max
Single	18.00	20.00
Double	30.00	34.00

Parking for 1

National gradings and classifications were correct at the time of going to press but are subject to change. Please check at the time of booking.

MILTON ABBAS

Dorset
Map ref 2B3

Sloping village street of thatched houses. A boys' school lies in Capability Brown's landscaped gardens amid hills and woods where the town once stood. The school chapel, former abbey church, can be visited.

Dunbury Heights

⚜⚜ HIGHLY COMMENDED

Winterborne Stickland, Blandford Forum DT11 0DH
☎ (01258) 880445
Always a friendly welcome at this brick and flint cottage. Outstanding views to Poole and Isle of Wight. 6 miles from Blandford Forum and 1 mile from the picturesque village of Milton Abbas.
Bedrooms: 1 double, 1 twin
Bathrooms: 1 private, 1 public
Bed & breakfast

per night:	£min	£max
Single	20.00	20.00
Double	35.00	35.00

Parking for 10

MILTON KEYNES

Buckinghamshire
Map ref 2C1

Designated a New Town in 1967, Milton Keynes offers a wide range of housing and is abundantly planted with trees. It has excellent shopping facilities and 3 centres for leisure and sporting activities. The Open University is based here.
Tourist Information Centre
☎ *(01908) 232525 or 231742*

Chantry Farm

⚜⚜ COMMENDED

Pindon End, Hanslope, Milton Keynes
MK19 7HL
☎ (01908) 510269 & Mobile 0850 166122
600-acre mixed farm. Stone farmhouse, built in 1650, with inglenook fireplaces. Surrounded by open countryside yet only 15 minutes to city centre. Swimming pool, trout lake, table tennis, clay pigeon shooting.
Bedrooms: 1 double, 2 twin
Bathrooms: 1 private, 1 public
Bed & breakfast

per night:	£min	£max
Single	20.00	22.00
Double	35.00	40.00

Parking for 7

MILTON KEYNES

Continued

Haversham Grange

Haversham, Milton Keynes MK19 7DX
☎ (01908) 312389
Fax (01908) 221554
Large 14th C stone house with many interesting features. Set in own gardens backing on to lakes.
Bedrooms: 3 twin
Bathrooms: 3 private, 1 public

Bed & breakfast

per night:	£min	£max
Single	20.00	25.00
Double	40.00	45.00

Parking for 4

Manor Farm House ⋀

South Street, Castlethorpe, Milton Keynes MK19 7EL
☎ (01908) 510216
Three-storey Grade II listed stone building, about 350 years old. In a small village approximately 5 miles north of central Milton Keynes.
Bedrooms: 1 double, 1 twin, 1 family room
Bathrooms: 1 private, 1 public, 1 private shower

Bed & breakfast

per night:	£min	£max
Single	17.50	27.50
Double	35.00	47.50

Parking for 3

Michelville House

Newton Road, Bletchley, Milton Keynes MK3 5BN
☎ (01908) 371578
Clean, compact establishment within easy reach of railway station, M1, shopping and sporting facilities. 10 minutes from Milton Keynes shopping centre.
Bedrooms: 10 single, 6 twin
Bathrooms: 4 public

Bed & breakfast

per night:	£min	£max
Single	15.00	22.00
Double	30.00	40.00

Parking for 16

Mill Farm

COMMENDED

Gayhurst, Newport Pagnell MK16 8LT
☎ Newport Pagnell (01908) 611489
Fax (01908) 611489
505-acre mixed farm. 17th C farmhouse. Tennis, riding and fishing available. Good touring centre for Oxford, Cambridge, Woburn, Whipsnade. City centre 7 minutes.
Bedrooms: 1 single, 1 twin, 1 family room

Bathrooms: 3 private, 2 public

Bed & breakfast

per night:	£min	£max
Single	15.00	20.00
Double	30.00	40.00

Half board

per person:	£min	£max
Daily	25.00	30.00

Parking for 12

The Old Rectory

Drayton Road, Newton Longville, Milton Keynes MK17 0BH
☎ (01908) 375794

Brick-built, listed Georgian house (1769), in village setting to the south of Milton Keynes.
Bedrooms: 2 single, 1 double, 1 twin
Bathrooms: 1 private, 2 public, 3 private showers

Bed & breakfast

per night:	£min	£max
Single	17.00	18.00
Double	36.00	44.00

Half board

per person:	£min	£max
Daily	22.00	23.00
Weekly	140.00	154.00

Evening meal 1800 (last orders 2000)
Parking for 6

Swan Revived Hotel ⋀

HIGHLY COMMENDED

High Street, Newport Pagnell, Milton Keynes MK16 8AR
☎ (01908) 610565
Fax (01908) 210995
Independently owned and family-run, town house hotel, renowned former coaching inn, where guests can enjoy every modern comfort. Convenient for thriving new city of Milton Keynes.
Bedrooms: 17 single, 19 double, 4 twin, 2 triple; suites available
Bathrooms: 42 private

Bed & breakfast

per night:	£min	£max
Single	39.50	58.00
Double	60.00	65.00

Half board

per person:	£min	£max
Daily	45.00	70.00

Lunch available
Evening meal 1915 (last orders 2200)
Parking for 18

Cards accepted: Access, Visa, Diners, Amex, Switch/Delta

MINSTEAD

Hampshire
Map ref 2C3

Cluster of thatched cottages and detached period houses. The church, listed in the Domesday Book, has private boxes - one with its own fireplace.

Acres Down Farm ⋀

Listed

Minstead, Lyndhurst SO43 7GE
☎ Southampton (01703) 813693
50-acre mixed farm. Homely New Forest working commoners' farm, in quiet surroundings opening directly on to open forest. Also self-catering cottage.
Bedrooms: 2 double, 1 twin
Bathrooms: 2 public

Bed & breakfast

per night:	£min	£max
Single	16.00	
Double	32.00	

Parking for 6

Grove House

Listed

Newtown, Minstead, Lyndhurst SO43 7GG
☎ Southampton (01703) 813211
9-acre smallholding. Attractive family home, in quiet, rural position 3 miles from Lyndhurst, with superb walking, birdwatching and riding (stabling available).
Bedrooms: 1 triple
Bathrooms: 1 private

Bed & breakfast

per night:	£min	£max
Double	32.00	35.00

Parking for 1

MINSTER LOVELL

Oxfordshire
Map ref 2C1

Picturesque village on the River Windrush with thatched cottages and 19th C houses. Minster Lovell Hall, built in the 15th C by the Lovell family, is the subject of several legends and now stands in ruins in a beautiful riverside setting.

Hill Grove Farm ⋀

HIGHLY COMMENDED

Crawley Road, Minster Lovell, Oxford OX8 5NA
☎ Witney (01993) 703120
Fax (01993) 700528

300-acre mixed farm. Cotswold farmhouse run on a family basis, in an attractive rural setting overlooking the Windrush Valley. Pleasant country walks.
Bedrooms: 1 double, 1 twin
Bathrooms: 2 private
Bed & breakfast

per night:	£min	£max
Single	18.00	26.00
Double	38.00	44.00

Parking for 4

NETHER WALLOP

Hampshire
Map ref 2C2

Winding lane leads to thatched cottages, cob walls of clay and straw and colourful gardens with the Wallop Brook running by St Andrew's Church. This has 11th C origins and a fine mural urging Sunday observance.

The Great Barn

Five Bells Lane, Nether Wallop, Stockbridge SO20 8EN
☎ Andover (01264) 782142
16th C barn, self-contained unit with private bathrooms. In picturesque village of Nether Wallop, setting for Agatha Christie's "Miss Marple" stories.
Bedrooms: 1 double, 1 twin
Bathrooms: 2 private
Bed & breakfast

per night:	£min	£max
Single	23.00	25.00
Double	34.00	35.00

Parking for 2

NEW FOREST

See under Ashurst, Barton on Sea, Beaulieu, Bransgore, Brockenhurst, Burley, Dibden, Fordingbridge, Hythe, Lymington, Lyndhurst, Minstead, Ringwood, Sway, Totton

NEWBURY

Berkshire
Map ref 2C2

Ancient town surrounded by the Downs and on the Kennet and Avon Canal. It has many buildings of interest, including the 17th C Cloth Hall, which is now a museum. The famous racecourse is nearby.
Tourist Information Centre
☎ *(01635) 30267*

The Old Farmhouse

Downend Lane, Chieveley, Newbury RG20 8TN
☎ Chieveley (01635) 248361

Small country farmhouse on edge of village. Within 1 mile of M4/A34 (junction 13) and close to Newbury. Accommodation in self-contained annexe.
Bedrooms: 1 family room; suite available
Bathrooms: 1 private
Bed & breakfast

per night:	£min	£max
Single	18.00	20.00
Double	36.00	40.00

Parking for 5

Thurston House ⋀

9 Stanley Road, Newbury RG14 7PB
☎ (01635) 38271 & Mobile (01370) 268574
Small, family-run B&B near the town centre. 5 minutes' walk to Newbury racecourse.
Bedrooms: 2 single, 1 twin
Bathrooms: 1 public, 2 private showers
Bed & breakfast

per night:	£min	£max
Single	17.00	18.00
Double	34.00	35.00

Parking for 4

White Cottage ⋀

Listed APPROVED
Newtown, Newbury RG20 9AP
☎ (01635) 43097
Delightful cottage in semi-rural position, just 2 miles south of Newbury. Comfortable, quiet accommodation. Children and dogs welcome.
Bedrooms: 1 double, 1 twin
Bathrooms: 2 private, 1 public
Bed & breakfast

per night:	£min	£max
Single	18.50	
Double	36.00	

Parking for 2

NORTH NEWINGTON

Oxfordshire
Map ref 2C1

Watered by a confluent of the Sor Brook. The ancient track known as the Salt Way passes through the village. Close by is Broughton Castle, a moated 14th C manor house with fine Elizabethan additions, including ceilings, panelling and fireplaces.

Mole End Cottage

Listed
Mole End, North Newington, Banbury OX15 6AA
☎ Banbury (01295) 258565

Fully modernised and extended Horton stone cottage, 2.5 miles from Banbury Cross, just off B4035.
Bedrooms: 2 double
Bathrooms: 2 private
Bed & breakfast

per night:	£min	£max
Single	15.00	18.00
Double	30.00	35.00

Parking for 3

OLNEY

Buckinghamshire
Map ref 2C1

Clifton Pastures ⋀

Clifton Reynes, Olney MK46 5DW
☎ Bedford (01234) 711287
Fax (01234) 711233
900-acre mixed farm. Large farmhouse set in own grounds with superb views. Delicious meals using home produce. Log fires burn and a warm welcome awaits. Only 6 miles from M1, junction 14.
Bedrooms: 1 twin
Bathrooms: 1 private, 1 public
Bed & breakfast

per night:	£min	£max
Single	30.00	35.00
Double	50.00	55.00

Half board

per person:	£min	£max
Daily	40.00	50.00

Evening meal 1900 (last orders 2000)
Parking for 6

OXFORD

Oxfordshire
Map ref 2C1

Beautiful university town with many ancient colleges, some dating from the 13th C, and numerous buildings of historic and architectural interest. The Ashmolean Museum has outstanding collections. Lovely gardens and meadows with punting on the Cherwell.
Tourist Information Centre
☎ *(01865) 726871*

Acorn Guest House

Listed
260 Iffley Road, Oxford OX4 1SE
☎ (01865) 247998
Situated midway between the centre of town and the ring-road and therefore convenient for local amenities and more distant attractions.
Bedrooms: 2 single, 1 twin, 3 triple
Bathrooms: 2 public

Continued ▶

OXFORD

Continued

Bed & breakfast

per night:	£min	£max
Single	20.00	25.00
Double	34.00	40.00

Parking for 5
Cards accepted: Access, Visa, Diners

Becket House
Listed

5 Becket Street, Oxford OX1 7PP
☎ (01865) 724675
Friendly guesthouse convenient for rail and bus station, within walking distance of city centre and colleges. Good, clean accommodation, en-suite rooms.
Bedrooms: 4 single, 1 double, 3 twin, 1 triple
Bathrooms: 6 private, 3 public

Bed & breakfast

per night:	£min	£max
Single	20.00	35.00
Double	36.00	50.00

Cards accepted: Access, Visa, Switch/Delta

Beinn Bheag ♠
Listed

96 Oxford Road, Cumnor, Oxford OX2 9PQ
☎ (01865) 864020 & 241381
Detached bungalow with large garden in quiet village just outside the city. Comfortable accommodation, warm welcome. Wide choice of breakfasts. Non smoking.
Bedrooms: 1 single, 1 double, 1 family room
Bathrooms: 2 private, 1 public

Bed & breakfast

per night:	£min	£max
Single	19.00	25.00
Double	35.00	45.00

Parking for 4
Open January-November

The Bungalow ♠
Listed

Cherwell Farm, Mill Lane, Old Marston, Oxford OX3 0QF
☎ (01865) 57171
Modern bungalow set in 5 acres, in quiet location with views over open countryside, but within 3 miles of city centre. No smoking.
Bedrooms: 2 double, 1 twin
Bathrooms: 3 private, 1 public

Bed & breakfast

per night:	£min	£max
Single	20.00	20.00
Double	35.00	45.00

Parking for 4
Open April-October

High Hedges
COMMENDED

8 Cumnor Hill, Oxford OX2 9HA
☎ (01865) 863395
Close to city centre, offering a high standard of accommodation for a comfortable and happy stay in Oxford.
Bedrooms: 2 double, 1 twin
Bathrooms: 1 private, 1 public

Bed & breakfast

per night:	£min	£max
Double	38.00	42.00

Parking for 3

Isis Guest House ♠
Listed APPROVED

45-53 Iffley Road, Oxford OX4 1ED
☎ (01865) 248894 & 242466
Fax (01865) 243492
Modernised, Victorian, city centre guesthouse within walking distance of colleges and shops. Easy access to ring road.
Bedrooms: 12 single, 6 double, 17 twin, 2 triple
Bathrooms: 14 private, 10 public

Bed & breakfast

per night:	£min	£max
Single	19.00	25.00
Double	38.00	42.00

Parking for 18
Open June-September
Cards accepted: Access, Visa

Mount Pleasant ♠
APPROVED

76 London Road, Headington, Oxford OX3 9AJ
☎ (01865) 62749
Fax (01865) 62749
Small, family-run hotel offering full facilities. On the A40 and convenient for Oxford shopping, hospitals, colleges, visiting the Chilterns and the Cotswolds.
Bedrooms: 2 double, 5 twin, 1 triple
Bathrooms: 8 private

Bed & breakfast

per night:	£min	£max
Single	37.50	55.00
Double	45.00	75.00

Half board

per person:	£min	£max
Daily	37.50	52.50
Weekly	262.50	367.50

Lunch available
Evening meal 1800 (last orders 2130)
Parking for 6
Cards accepted: Access, Visa, Diners, Amex

Newton House ♠
⌂⌂

82-84 Abingdon Road, Oxford OX1 4PL
☎ (01865) 240561

Centrally located, Victorian townhouse with comfortable homely accommodation, warm welcome and friendly atmosphere. Special diets catered for on request.
Bedrooms: 7 double, 4 twin, 2 family rooms
Bathrooms: 5 private, 3 public

Bed & breakfast

per night:	£min	£max
Single	21.00	47.00
Double	32.00	47.00

Parking for 8
Cards accepted: Access, Visa, Amex, Switch/Delta

7 Princes Street
Listed

Oxford OX4 1DD
☎ (01865) 726755
Restored Victorian artisan's cottage, furnished with many antiques. Short walk from Magdalen Bridge and central Oxford.
Bedrooms: 1 single, 1 double
Bathrooms: 1 public

Bed & breakfast

per night:	£min	£max
Single	16.00	20.00
Double	28.00	34.00

Parking for 2

PANGBOURNE

Berkshire
Map ref 2C2

A pretty stretch of river where the Pang joins the Thames with views of the lock, weir and toll bridge. Once the home of Kenneth Grahame, author of "Wind in the Willows".

Weir View Guest House
⌂⌂

9 Shooters Hill, Pangbourne, Reading RG8 7DZ
☎ (01734) 842120
House with superb views overlooking falling waters of weir and river. Adjacent to excellent village shops, restaurants and rail-link.
Bedrooms: 1 double, 2 twin
Bathrooms: 1 private, 1 public

Bed & breakfast

per night:	£min	£max
Single	25.00	40.00
Double	40.00	50.00

Parking for 4
Cards accepted: Access, Visa

Please mention this guide when making a booking.

PETERSFIELD

Hampshire
Map ref 2C3

Grew prosperous from the wool trade and was famous as a coaching centre. Its attractive market square is dominated by a statue of William III. Close by are Petersfield Heath with numerous ancient barrows and Butser Hill with magnificent views.
Tourist Information Centre
☎ *(01730) 268829*

Westmark House

Listed | **HIGHLY COMMENDED**

Sheet, Petersfield GU31 5AT
☎ (01730) 263863
Pleasant Georgian country house, with hard tennis court and heated pool. Take the A3 north from Petersfield. Turn right on to A272 towards Rogate and Midhurst. Westmark House is first house on the left.
Bedrooms: 1 single, 1 double, 1 twin
Bathrooms: 1 public
Bed & breakfast

per night:	£min	£max
Single	22.00	24.00
Double	44.00	48.00

Half board

per person:	£min	£max
Daily	34.50	39.00
Weekly	241.50	273.00

Evening meal 1900 (last orders 2030)
Parking for 3
ੲ 8 ⫐⊡ ♦ ⊡ ⛤ ▥ ▦. ☎ ⚒ ⚹ ⵗ ⚘ ⵝ
⛆ ⋒

POOLE

Dorset
Map ref 2B3

Tremendous natural harbour makes Poole a superb boating centre. The harbour area is crowded with historic buildings including the 15th C Town Cellars housing a maritime museum.
Tourist Information Centre
☎ *(01202) 673322*

Cramond

HIGHLY COMMENDED

9 Whitecliff Road, Poole BH14 8DU
☎ (01202) 730465
Fax (01202) 730465
A pleasant detached house, with beautiful uninterrupted views of the bay, Brownsea Island and Poole Harbour. Sandbanks' beaches are nearby.
Bedrooms: 1 double, 1 family room
Bathrooms: 1 private, 2 public

We advise you to confirm your booking in writing.

Bed & breakfast

per night:	£min	£max
Single	19.00	21.00
Double	36.00	48.00

Parking for 4
Open March–November
ੲ ♦ ▥ Ⓢ ⛤ ⵝ ⊡ ▦. ☎ ⚹ ⵗ ⛆

Homeleigh

Listed

105 Wimborne Road, Poole BH15 2BP
☎ (01202) 673697
Small, friendly, non-smoking establishment, near town centre, harbour, beaches and bus/rail stations. Within easy reach of coast and New Forest.
Bedrooms: 2 twin
Bathrooms: 1 public
Bed & breakfast

per night:	£min	£max
Single	14.00	15.00
Double	28.00	30.00

Parking for 2
ੲ ⛴ ♦ ▥ Ⓢ ⛤ ⵝ ▥ ▦. ☎ ⵗ ⛆

The Inn in the Park

⛉⛉

26 Pinewood Road, Branksome Park, Poole BH13 6JS
☎ Bournemouth (01202) 761318
Small, friendly, family-owned pub with sun terrace, log fire and easy access to the beach. Recommended in all leading pub guides.
Bedrooms: 3 double, 1 twin, 1 triple
Bathrooms: 5 private
Bed & breakfast

per night:	£min	£max
Single	27.50	35.00
Double	35.00	50.00

Lunch available
Evening meal 1900 (last orders 2130)
Parking for 15
Cards accepted: Access, Visa
ੲ ⊡ ♦ ▦. ☎ ⛆

The Rosemount Hotel

Listed

167 Bournemouth Road, Lower Parkstone, Poole BH14 9HT
☎ Bournemouth (01202) 732138
Small, family-run hotel on main road between Poole and Bournemouth, offering varied food, cleanliness and friendly service. Colour TV in all rooms, some en-suite.
Bedrooms: 1 single, 4 double, 2 twin, 1 triple
Bathrooms: 1 private, 2 public, 1 private shower
Bed & breakfast

per night:	£min	£max
Single	15.00	17.00
Double	30.00	35.00

Half board

per person:	£min	£max
Daily	21.00	23.00

Parking for 6
Cards accepted: Access, Visa
ੲ ⛴ ⊡ ♦ ▥ Ⓢ ▥ ⊡ ▦. ☎ ⛆ ⏾

Vernon

Listed

96 Blandford Road North, Beacon Hill, Poole BH16 6AD
☎ Lytchett Minster (01202) 625185
Comfortable bed and breakfast with relaxed atmosphere, in rural setting. Own key. Ideal base for touring Dorset. 10 minutes from Poole on A350 to Blandford.
Bedrooms: 2 double, 1 twin
Bathrooms: 1 private, 2 public
Bed & breakfast

per night:	£min	£max
Single	13.00	17.00
Double	20.00	28.00

Parking for 5
ੲ ⛴ ⊡ ♦ ▥ ▦. ☎ ⚹ ⛆ ⏾

PORTSMOUTH & SOUTHSEA

Hampshire
Map ref 2C3

The first dock was built in 1194. HMS Victory, Nelson's flagship, is here and Charles Dickens' former home is open to the public. Neighbouring Southsea has a promenade with magnificent views of Spithead.
Tourist Information Centre
☎ *(01705) 826722*

Hamilton House ⋀

⛉⛉ | **COMMENDED**

95 Victoria Road North, Southsea, Portsmouth, Hampshire PO5 1PS
☎ (01705) 823502
Fax (01705) 823502
Delightful family-run guesthouse, 5 minutes by car to ferry terminals and tourist attractions. Some en-suite rooms available. Breakfast served from 6am.
Bedrooms: 1 single, 2 double, 2 twin, 1 triple, 2 family rooms
Bathrooms: 3 private, 2 public
Bed & breakfast

per night:	£min	£max
Single	16.00	18.00
Double	32.00	36.00

Half board

per person:	£min	£max
Daily	21.00	23.00
Weekly	144.00	158.00

Evening meal from 1800
ੲ ⫐⊡ ♦ ⵡ ▥ Ⓢ ⛤ ▥ ⊡ ▦. ☎ ⚹ ⵗ
⏾ ⏼

Individual proprietors have supplied all details of accommodation. As changes can occur, we advise you to confirm the information at the time of booking.

319

READING

Berkshire
Map ref 2C2

Busy, modern county town with large shopping centre and many leisure and recreation facilities. There are several interesting museums and the Duke of Wellington's Stratfield Saye is nearby.
Tourist Information Centre
☎ *(01734) 566226*

Belstone ♠
Listed HIGHLY COMMENDED

36 Upper Warren Avenue, Caversham, Reading RG4 7EB
☎ (01734) 477435
Friendly welcome in elegant Victorian family house. Quiet tree-lined avenue near river and farmland. Convenient for town centre by car. Non-smokers only, please.
Bedrooms: 1 double, 1 twin
Bathrooms: 1 public

Bed & breakfast

per night:	£min	£max
Single	26.00	28.00
Double	37.00	42.00

Parking for 2

Dittisham Guest House
Listed COMMENDED

63 Tilehurst Road, Reading RG3 2JL
☎ (01734) 569483 & Mobile 0850 767029
Renovated Edwardian property with garden, in a quiet but central location. Good value, excellent quality.
Bedrooms: 4 single, 1 twin
Bathrooms: 3 private, 1 public

Bed & breakfast

per night:	£min	£max
Single	20.00	27.50
Double	32.50	45.00

Parking for 7
Cards accepted: Access, Visa

The Elms ♠
COMMENDED

Gallowstree Road, Rotherfield Peppard, Henley-on-Thames, Oxfordshire RG9 5HT
☎ (01734) 723164
Bed and breakfast near Reading. Heated swimming pool. All normal services, large garden, good parking. Excellent pub close by.
Bedrooms: 1 single, 1 double, 1 twin
Bathrooms: 2 private, 1 public

Bed & breakfast

per night:	£min	£max
Single	15.00	25.00
Double	30.00	40.00

Half board

per person:	£min	£max
Daily	24.50	34.50
Weekly	147.00	207.00

Evening meal 1930 (last orders 2000)
Parking for 13

10 Greystoke Road
Listed COMMENDED

Caversham, Reading RG4 0EL
☎ (01734) 475784
Private home in quiet, residential area. TV lounge, tea and coffee-making facilities. Non-smokers only, please.
Bedrooms: 1 single, 1 double
Bathrooms: 2 public

Bed & breakfast

per night:	£min	£max
Single	16.00	19.00
Double	27.00	30.00

Parking for 2

Warren Dene Hotel ♠
COMMENDED

1017 Oxford Road, Tilehurst, Reading RG3 6TL
☎ (01734) 422556
Fax (01734) 422556
Small, elegant Victorian hotel on the outskirts of Reading. Period bar lounge and decor throughout. Most rooms en-suite, family rooms available. Conveniently situated for Heathrow Airport and motorway access to Gatwick.
Bedrooms: 1 single, 2 double, 2 twin, 1 triple, 1 family room
Bathrooms: 3 private, 2 public

Bed & breakfast

per night:	£min	£max
Single	24.00	35.00
Double	35.00	42.00

Half board

per person:	£min	£max
Daily	30.00	45.00
Weekly	200.00	300.00

Lunch available
Evening meal 1800 (last orders 2100)
Parking for 9

RINGWOOD

Hampshire
Map ref 2B3

Market town by the River Avon comprising old cottages, many of them thatched. Although just outside the New Forest, there is heath and woodland nearby and it is a good centre for horse-riding and walking.

Picket Hill House ♠
COMMENDED

Picket Hill, Ringwood BH24 3HH
☎ (01425) 476173

Large country house, with direct access to New Forest, offering comfortable accommodation and good breakfast. Ideal for walkers/riders. Overseas guests particularly welcome. Accommodation for 2 horses by prior arrangement.
Bedrooms: 2 double, 1 twin
Bathrooms: 3 private

Bed & breakfast

per night:	£min	£max
Double	34.00	40.00

Parking for 6

ROMSEY

Hampshire
Map ref 2C3

Town grew up around the important abbey and lies on the banks of the River Test, famous for trout and salmon. Broadlands House, home of the late Lord Mountbatten, is open to the public.
Tourist Information Centre
☎ *(01794) 512987*

Country Accommodation ♠
COMMENDED

The Old Post Office, New Road, Michelmersh, Romsey SO51 0NL
☎ (01794) 368739

Converted 19th C post office, bakery and forge in pretty village location. All ground-floor rooms, some beamed. On-site parking. Excellent local pubs and restaurants.
Bedrooms: 2 double, 1 twin, 1 triple
Bathrooms: 4 private

Bed & breakfast

per night:	£min	£max
Single	25.00	25.00
Double	40.00	40.00

Parking for 10
Cards accepted: Access, Visa

Pyesmead Farm
Listed

Plaitford, Romsey SO51 6EE
☎ West Wellow (01794) 323386
70-acre livestock farm. Small, family-run stock farm, situated on edge of the New Forest, west of Romsey. Easy access from A36, Southampton to Salisbury road.
Bedrooms: 2 double, 1 twin
Bathrooms: 1 private, 1 public

Bed & breakfast

per night:	£min	£max
Single	17.00	
Double	27.00	32.00

Half board per person:	£min	£max
Daily	21.00	24.50

Evening meal from 1900
Parking for 10
🛇♿⬛✕📺▦₳🗲✿✖🚐

RYDE

Isle of Wight
Map ref 2C3

The island's chief entry port, connected to Portsmouth by ferries and hovercraft. 7 miles of sandy beaches with a half-mile pier, esplanade and gardens.
Tourist Information Centre
☎ *(01983) 562905*

Sillwood Acre ⋀

 HIGHLY COMMENDED
Church Road, Binstead, Ryde
PO33 3TB
☎ Isle of Wight (01983) 563553
Large Victorian house near Ryde, convenient for the ferry and hovercraft terminals. Two spacious en-suite rooms. Non-smoking.
Bedrooms: 1 double, 1 triple
Bathrooms: 2 private
Bed & breakfast

per night:	£min	£max
Single	16.00	18.00
Double	32.00	36.00

Parking for 3
🛇📬🖵♿▦🅰ⓈⒾ✕▦.₳✖🚐

SAUNDERTON

Buckinghamshire
Map ref 2C1

Small village close to the Ridgeway long distance footpath. The site of a Roman villa is near the church.

Hunter's Gate

 Listed
Deanfield, Saunderton, High Wycombe
HP14 4JR
☎ High Wycombe (01494) 481446
6-acre smallholding. 4-bedroomed house with a 1 bedroom flat above garage, in a valley overlooked by Bledlow Ridge, half-a-mile from Wycombe/Princes Risborough road. Set in 5 acres in a quiet area but only half-a-mile to BR station for London.
Bedrooms: 1 double, 1 twin
Bathrooms: 2 private, 1 public
Bed & breakfast

per night:	£min	£max
Single	15.00	17.50
Double	30.00	35.00

Parking for 4
🛇🖵♿ⒾⓈ📺▦.₳✕✿🚐

SELBORNE

Hampshire
Map ref 2C2

Village made famous by Gilbert White, who was a curate here and is remembered for his classic book "The Natural History of Selborne", published in 1788. His house is now a museum.

8 Goslings Croft

 Listed HIGHLY COMMENDED
Selborne, Alton GU34 3HZ
☎ (01420) 511285
Fax (01420) 577451
Family home, set on edge of historic village, adjacent to National Trust land. Ideal base for walking and touring. Non-smokers only, please.
Bedrooms: 1 twin
Bathrooms: 1 private
Bed & breakfast

per night:	£min	£max
Single	19.50	19.50
Double	29.50	29.50

Parking for 1
🛇📬🖵♿ⒾⓈ✕▦.₳✖🚐

SHALFLEET

Isle of Wight
Map ref 2C3

The Old Malthouse ⋀

 COMMENDED
1 Mill Road, Shalfleet, Newport
PO30 4NE
☎ Isle of Wight (01983) 531329
Family-run B & B in 250-year-old character house, in conservation village, opposite the New Inn. Cyclists and walkers welcome.
Bedrooms: 1 double, 1 triple
Bathrooms: 2 private
Bed & breakfast

per night:	£min	£max
Single	17.00	21.00
Double	30.00	34.00

Parking for 2
🛇📬♿ⒾⓈ✕📺◑▦.₳✖🚐🏢

Orchard Cottage

 COMMENDED
2 Mill Road, Shalfleet, Newport
PO30 4NE
☎ Isle of Wight (01983) 531589
Enjoy a warm welcome and pretty, comfortable rooms. Breakfast a speciality. Lovely surroundings and garden. By village pub, parking. Estuary, coastal trail. Touring, sailing, walking.
Bedrooms: 1 double, 1 twin, 1 triple
Bathrooms: 1 private, 1 public

Bed & breakfast per night:	£min	£max
Single	18.00	25.00
Double	32.00	40.00

Parking for 4
🛇🖵♿▦ⒾⓈ✕🏵◑▦.₳ᴗ✿✖🚐🏢

SHANKLIN

Isle of Wight
Map ref 2C3

Set on a cliff with gentle slopes leading down to the beach, esplanade and marine gardens. The picturesque, old thatched village nestles at the end of the wooded chine.
Tourist Information Centre
☎ *(01983) 862942*

Culham Lodge Hotel ⋀

 COMMENDED
31 Landguard Manor Road, Shanklin
PO37 7HZ
☎ Isle of Wight (01983) 862880
Fax (01983) 865858
Charming hotel in beautiful tree-lined road. Heated swimming pool, solarium, conservatory, home cooking and personal service. TV in all rooms with Sky movies and sport.
Bedrooms: 1 single, 6 double, 3 twin
Bathrooms: 10 private, 2 public

Bed & breakfast per night:	£min	£max
Single	17.00	21.00
Double	34.00	42.00

Half board per person:	£min	£max
Daily	22.00	26.00
Weekly	144.00	180.00

Evening meal 1800 (last orders 1600)
Parking for 8
Cards accepted: Access, Visa
🛇12🏵🖵♿🏵▦ⒾⓈ✕🏵📺▦.₳
ᴗ🏵✖🚐 ᴅᴀᴘ ꜱᴘ Ⓣ

Hazelwood Hotel ⋀

14 Clarence Road, Shanklin
PO37 7BH
☎ Isle of Wight (01983) 862824
Fax (01983) 862824
Detached, friendly, comfortable hotel in a quiet tree-lined road, close to all amenities. Daily bookings taken. Parking available.
Bedrooms: 1 single, 5 double, 3 triple, 1 family room
Bathrooms: 8 private, 1 public

Bed & breakfast per night:	£min	£max
Single	16.00	19.50
Double	32.00	39.00

Half board per person:	£min	£max
Daily	23.00	26.50
Weekly	146.00	173.50

Continued ▶

SHANKLIN

Continued

Evening meal 1800 (last orders 1600)
Parking for 5
Open February-October
Cards accepted: Access, Visa, Diners,
Amex

SHIPTON BELLINGER

Hampshire
Map ref 2B2

Parsonage Farm
COMMENDED

Shipton Bellinger, Tidworth SP9 7UF
☎ Stonehenge (01980) 842404
Former farmhouse of 16th/17th C
origins in quiet village. Walled garden,
stables, paddocks. Situated off A338
opposite parish church and Boot Inn.
Bedrooms: 1 single, 1 twin, 1 triple
Bathrooms: 1 private, 2 public

Bed & breakfast
per night:	£min	£max
Single	15.00	18.00
Double	30.00	35.00

Parking for 6

SIXPENNY HANDLEY

Dorset
Map ref 2B3

The Barleycorn House

Deanland, Sixpenny Handley,
Salisbury, Wiltshire SP5 5PD
☎ Handley (01725) 552583
Fax (01725) 552090
Converted 17th C inn retaining original
period features, in peaceful
surroundings with many nearby walks.
Relaxed atmosphere and home cooking.
Bedrooms: 1 single, 1 double, 1 twin
Bathrooms: 2 private, 1 public

Bed & breakfast
per night:	£min	£max
Single	18.00	18.00
Double	36.00	36.00

Half board
per person:	£min	£max
Daily	26.50	26.50
Weekly	172.90	172.90

Evening meal from 1830
Parking for 5

The symbol after an
establishment name
indicates membership of a
Regional Tourist Board.

SOULDERN

Oxfordshire
Map ref 2C1

Tower Fields

Tusmore Road, Souldern, Bicester
OX6 9HY
☎ Bicester (01869) 346554
Fax (01869) 345157
Converted 18th C cottages on 14-acre
smallholding with rare breeds of
poultry, sheep and cattle. Small
collection of vintage cars.
Bedrooms: 1 double, 1 twin
Bathrooms: 2 private

Bed & breakfast
per night:	£min	£max
Single	22.00	22.00
Double	40.00	44.00

Parking for 4

SOUTHAMPTON

Hampshire
Map ref 2C3

One of Britain's leading seaports
with a long history, now a major
container port. In the 18th C it
became a fashionable resort with
the assembly rooms and theatre.
The old Guildhall and the Wool
House are now museums.
Sections of the medieval wall can
still be seen.
Tourist Information Centre
☎ *(01703) 221106*

Ashelee Lodge ⚘
Listed COMMENDED

36 Atherley Road, Shirley,
Southampton SO15 5DQ
☎ (01703) 222095
Homely guesthouse, garden with pool.
Half a mile from city centre, near
station, M27 and Sealink ferryport.
Good touring base for New Forest,
Salisbury and Winchester.
Bedrooms: 1 single, 1 double, 1 twin,
1 triple
Bathrooms: 1 public

Bed & breakfast
per night:	£min	£max
Single	14.00	15.00
Double	28.00	30.00

Evening meal from 1800
Parking for 2
Cards accepted: Access, Visa

Madison House ⚘

137 Hill Lane, Southampton
SO15 5AF
☎ (01703) 333374
Fax (01703) 322264
Elegant Victorian house in tree
conservation area three-quarters of a

---

mile from centre. Ideal for touring the
south or relishing Southampton's
medieval history. Friendly family
atmosphere.
Bedrooms: 2 single, 3 double, 3 twin,
1 triple
Bathrooms: 3 private, 2 public

Bed & breakfast
per night:	£min	£max
Single	15.00	22.00
Double	30.00	40.00

Parking for 6
Cards accepted: Access, Visa

Mayview Guest House
Listed

30 The Polygon, Southampton
SO15 2BN
☎ (01703) 220907 & Mobile (0589)
680868
Small, family-run guesthouse in the city
centre, providing a comfortable stay in
clean and friendly surroundings.
Bedrooms: 1 single, 1 double, 2 twin,
1 triple
Bathrooms: 2 public

Bed & breakfast
per night:	£min	£max
Single	16.00	17.50
Double	30.00	32.00

SOUTHSEA

Hampshire

See under Portsmouth & Southsea

STOCKBRIDGE

Hampshire
Map ref 2C2

Set in the Test Valley which has
some of the best fishing in
England. The wide main street has
houses of all styles, mainly Tudor
and Georgian.

Carbery Guest House ⚘
COMMENDED

Salisbury Hill, Stockbridge SO20 6EZ
☎ Andover (01264) 810771
Fax (01264) 811022
Fine old Georgian house in an acre of
landscaped gardens and lawns,
overlooking the River Test. Games and
swimming facilities, riding and fishing
can be arranged. Ideal for touring the
south coast and the New Forest.
Bedrooms: 4 single, 3 double, 2 twin,
1 triple, 1 family room
Bathrooms: 8 private, 1 public

Bed & breakfast
per night:	£min	£max
Single	23.00	30.00
Double	46.00	49.00

Half board per person:	£min	£max
Daily	34.50	41.50
Weekly	239.50	288.50

Evening meal 1900 (last orders 1800)
Parking for 12

🔣🚪🔲👟🐾🛆🔲🔲🔲🍴🛏🔲✕🌼✕🏚

STONY STRATFORD

Buckinghamshire
Map ref 2C1

Saracen House
Listed

21 London Road, Old Stratford, Stony Stratford, Milton Keynes MK19 6AE
☎ Milton Keynes (01908) 562343
300-year-old former inn, with genuine stone walls, oak beams etc. All modern facilities. Easy to find on main road.
Bedrooms: 1 single, 1 twin
Bathrooms: 2 private, 1 public

Bed & breakfast

per night:	£min	£max
Single	16.00	20.00
Double	36.00	40.00

Parking for 4

🔣5👟🔲🍴🔲🔲🛆✕🏚

STUDLAND

Dorset
Map ref 2B3

On a beautiful stretch of coast and good for walking, with a National Nature Reserve to the north. The Norman church is the finest in the country, with superb rounded arches and vaulting. Brownsea Island, where the first scout camp was held, lies in Poole Harbour.

Bankes Arms Hotel ⋀
🏆🏆

Manor Road, Studland, Swanage BH19 3AU
☎ (01929) 450225

Lovely old inn with large gardens, overlooking the sea. En-suite rooms with colour TV and tea-making. Real ales, log fires, home-cooked lunches, evening bar meals (food all day during season). Sandy beaches, water sports, golf, riding, coastal walks.
Bedrooms: 1 single, 3 double, 2 twin, 3 triple
Bathrooms: 5 private, 1 public

Bed & breakfast

per night:	£min	£max
Single	15.00	25.00
Double	35.00	54.00

Lunch available
Evening meal 1900 (last orders 2130)
Parking for 12
Cards accepted: Access, Visa

🔣4🔲👟🔲🛡✕🍴🔲🛆🔲🛏🌼✕🏚
🆂🅿🏚

STURMINSTER NEWTON

Dorset
Map ref 2B3

Every Monday this small town holds a livestock market. One of the bridges over the River Stour is a fine medieval example and bears a plaque declaring that anyone "injuring" it will be deported.

Swan Inn
🏆🏆🏆 **COMMENDED**

Market Place, Sturminster Newton DT10 1AR
☎ Blandford (01258) 472208
Old coaching inn, located in the heart of Thomas Hardy's Blackmore Vale. All rooms en-suite with remote-control TV. Extensive a la carte menu plus bar meals.
Bedrooms: 1 single, 3 double, 1 twin
Bathrooms: 5 private

Bed & breakfast

per night:	£min	£max
Single	39.00	42.00
Double	52.50	55.00

Half board

per person:	£min	£max
Daily	35.00	38.00

Lunch available
Evening meal 1830 (last orders 2100)
Parking for 20
Cards accepted: Access, Visa, Diners, Amex

🔣🛆📞🚪👟🛡🔲🛆🍴🔲🔲🛆🍴
🛏🌼🏚🔲🆂🏚

SUTTON SCOTNEY

Hampshire
Map ref 2C2

Knoll House
🏆🏆 **COMMENDED**

Wonston, Sutton Scotney, Winchester SO21 3LR
☎ Winchester (01962) 760273 & 883550
Take Andover road from Winchester to Sutton Scotney. Turn right at village hall to Wonston. Situated on right hand side almost opposite Wonston Arms.
Bedrooms: 1 double, 1 twin
Bathrooms: 2 private

Bed & breakfast

per night:	£min	£max
Single	17.00	17.00
Double	34.00	34.00

Half board per person:	£min	£max
Daily	25.00	25.00
Weekly	169.00	169.00

Evening meal 1830 (last orders 2030)
Parking for 2

🔣🛆🚪👟🔲🆂🍴🔲🔲🛆🏚

SWANAGE

Dorset
Map ref 2B3

Began life as an Anglo-Saxon port, then a quarrying centre of Purbeck marble. Now the safe, sandy beach set in a sweeping bay and flanked by downs is good walking country, making it an ideal resort.
Tourist Information Centre
☎ *(01929) 422885*

Maycroft
🛆

Old Malthouse Lane, Langton Matravers, Swanage BH19 3HH
☎ (01929) 424305
Comfortable Victorian home in quiet village position, with magnificent views of sea and countryside. Close to coastal path and the amenities of the Isle of Purbeck, 2 miles from Swanage.
Bedrooms: 1 double, 1 twin
Bathrooms: 1 public

Bed & breakfast

per night:	£min	£max
Single	20.00	
Double	30.00	34.00

Parking for 4
Open February-November

🔣🔲👟🔲🔲🛆🛆🖰✕🏚🏚

SWAY

Hampshire
Map ref 2C3

Small village on the south-western edge of the New Forest. It is noted for its 220-ft tower, Peterson's Folly, built in the 1870s by a retired Indian judge to demonstrate the value of concrete as a building material.

The Forest Heath Hotel ⋀
Station Road, Sway, Lymington SO41 6BA
☎ Lymington (01590) 682287 & Mobile 0860 732469
Fax (01590) 682287
Victorian village inn with good food and lively bars. Lots to do, close to coast and scenic areas. Large garden. Families welcome.
Bedrooms: 2 double, 1 twin, 2 family rooms
Bathrooms: 2 public

Bed & breakfast

per night:	£min	£max
Single	25.00	30.00
Double	40.00	47.50

Continued ▶

SWAY

Continued

Half board

per person:	£min	£max
Daily	32.50	35.50
Weekly	200.00	220.00

Lunch available
Evening meal 1900 (last orders 2130)
Parking for 30
Cards accepted: Access, Visa, Amex
⌂⑄☐♦♨⒮⌨✂⑁⑃◐▥.🎔
☏25 ☎☺♪✝❀🖾♿⑄⒮⒫

Manor Farm ⋀
Listed

Coombe Lane, Sway, Lymington
SO41 6BP
☏ Lymington (01590) 683542
*30-acre beef farm. 18th C, Grade II
listed farmhouse, surrounded by open
fields and forest. Off B3055 Sway-
Brockenhurst road.*
Bedrooms: 1 double, 1 twin, 1 family
room
Bathrooms: 2 private, 1 public
Bed & breakfast

per night:	£min	£max
Single	18.00	22.00
Double	34.00	40.00

Parking for 15
⌂☐♦⑁🅸✂▥.🎔☺❀✝🖾🅿

TOTTON

Hampshire
Map ref 2C3

Jubilee Cottage
⚜⚜

303 Salisbury Road, Totton,
Southampton SO40 3LZ
☏ Southampton (01703) 862397
*Victorian house convenient for Romsey,
M27, New Forest, continental and Isle
of Wight ferries. Bed and breakfast
accommodation with private facilities.
French spoken.*
Bedrooms: 1 twin, 1 triple
Bathrooms: 2 private
Bed & breakfast

per night:	£min	£max
Single	15.00	18.00
Double	30.00	36.00

Parking for 2
⌂☐♦⑁✂▥.🎔❀✝🖾

WARBOROUGH

Oxfordshire
Map ref 2C2

Blenheim House ⋀
⚜⚜ HIGHLY COMMENDED

11-13 The Green North, Warborough,
Wallingford OX10 7DW
☏ (01865) 858445
Fax (01865) 858445
*Old village house set in 2.5 acres of
garden. Swimming pool.*
Bedrooms: 1 double, 1 twin

Bathrooms: 2 private
Bed & breakfast

per night:	£min	£max
Single	22.50	30.00
Double	45.00	50.00

Parking for 4
⌂⑄☐♦⑁▥.🎔☺☋❀✝🖾🅿

WARNFORD

Hampshire
Map ref 2C3

Paper Mill
Listed COMMENDED

Peake Lane, Warnford, Southampton
SO32 3LA
☏ West Meon (01730) 829387

*Self-contained mill house in unique
setting on River Meon. Take A272 from
Petersfield or Winchester to West Meon
Hut traffic lights, turn south on A32,
follow road to Warnford, past George
and Falcon and turn left into Peake
Lane.*
Bedrooms: 1 double
Bathrooms: 1 private
Bed & breakfast

per night:	£min	£max
Single	25.00	
Double	45.00	

Parking for 1
Open April-September
⌂⑄☐♦⑁🅸⒮🎔🖾🅿

WARSASH

Hampshire
Map ref 2C3

On the edge of Southampton
Water. Warships were built here in
Napoleonic times.

Jolly Farmer Country Inn ⋀
⚜⚜

Fleet End Road, Warsash,
Southampton SO31 6JH
☏ Locks Heath (01489) 572500
Fax (01489) 885847
*Country inn close to the banks of the
River Hamble and Warsash Pier. Ample
car parking, large garden and patio.*
Bedrooms: 2 single, 1 double, 1 twin
Bathrooms: 1 private, 3 private
showers
Bed & breakfast

per night:	£min	£max
Single	30.00	35.00
Double	40.00	45.00

Lunch available
Evening meal 1800 (last orders 2215)
Parking for 60

Cards accepted: Access, Visa, Diners,
Amex
⌂⑄☐♦⑁⒮◐▥.🎔☏35❀🖾
🅿⑁

WENDOVER

Buckinghamshire
Map ref 2C1

Historic town on the Icknield Way
set amid beautiful scenery and
spectacular views of the Chilterns.
There are many old timbered
cottages and inns, one visited by
Oliver Cromwell. The church has
some interesting carving.
Tourist Information Centre
☏ *(01296) 696759*

The Red Lion Hotel
⚜⚜⚜ COMMENDED

9 High Street, Wendover, Aylesbury
HP22 6DU
☏ (01296) 622266
Fax (01296) 625077

*17th C coaching inn. Great location for
walking in Chilterns. Excellent
reputation for food and drink. Popular
with locals.*
Bedrooms: 3 single, 12 double, 4 twin,
4 triple
Bathrooms: 23 private
Bed & breakfast

per night:	£min	£max
Single	40.00	45.00
Double	50.00	55.00

Lunch available
Evening meal 1800 (last orders 2200)
Parking for 60
Cards accepted: Access, Visa, Diners,
Amex, Switch/Delta
⌂⚒⑄☋♦⑁⒮▥.🎔☏35🖾
⑄⒮🅿

WEST LULWORTH

Dorset
Map ref 2B3

Well-known for Lulworth Cove, the
almost landlocked circular bay of
chalk and limestone cliffs.

Graybank Guest House
Listed

Main Road, West Lulworth, Wareham
BH20 5RL
☏ (01929) 400256
*Victorian guesthouse in beautiful
countryside, 5 minutes' walk from
Lulworth Cove. TV in most bedrooms.
Ideal walking and touring base.*
Bedrooms: 1 single, 2 double, 1 twin,
1 triple, 2 family rooms

Bathrooms: 3 public
Bed & breakfast

per night:	£min	£max
Single	17.00	18.00
Double	34.00	36.00

Parking for 7
Open February-November

Newlands Farm

Listed	COMMENDED

West Lulworth, Wareham BH20 5PU
☎ (01929) 400376
Fax (01929) 400536
750-acre arable & livestock farm. 19th C farmhouse, with outstanding views to sea and distant Purbeck Hills. At Durdle Door, 1 mile west of Lulworth Cove.
Bedrooms: 1 double, 1 triple
Bathrooms: 1 public, 2 private showers
Bed & breakfast

per night:	£min	£max
Double	36.00	40.00

Parking for 10
Open January-November

The Old Barn ♠

Listed

Lulworth Cove, West Lulworth,
Wareham BH20 5RL
☎ (01929) 400305

Converted old barn in peaceful, picturesque coastal village. Choice of rooms with continental breakfast or please-yourself-rooms with light self-catering facilities. Large gardens. Ideal base for touring Dorset. Restaurants nearby.
Bedrooms: 2 single, 2 double, 1 twin, 1 triple, 1 family room
Bathrooms: 3 public
Bed & breakfast

per night:	£min	£max
Single	16.00	20.00
Double	32.00	40.00

Parking for 9
Cards accepted: Access, Visa

WEST STOUR

Dorset
Map ref 2B3

The Ship Inn

☺☺☺	COMMENDED

West Stour, Gillingham SP8 5RP
☎ East Stour (01747) 838640
18th C mail coach inn with fine views over the Dorset countryside. Log fires during winter and traditional hand-pumped ales throughout the year.

Central for touring the West Country. Good home-cooked food served 7 days a week.
Bedrooms: 1 single, 3 double, 1 twin, 1 triple, 1 family room
Bathrooms: 7 private, 1 public
Bed & breakfast

per night:	£min	£max
Single	28.00	30.00
Double	38.00	45.00

Lunch available
Evening meal 1900 (last orders 2130)
Parking for 50
Cards accepted: Access, Visa

WESTBURY

Buckinghamshire
Map ref 2C1

Mill Farm House

☺☺

Westbury, Brackley, Northamptonshire
NN13 5JS
☎ Brackley (01280) 704843
1000-acre mixed farm. Grade II listed farmhouse, overlooking a colourful garden including a covered heated swimming pool. Situated in the centre of Westbury village.
Bedrooms: 1 single, 1 double, 1 triple
Bathrooms: 3 private, 1 public
Bed & breakfast

per night:	£min	£max
Single	18.00	20.00
Double	34.00	45.00

Half board

per person:	£min	£max
Daily	30.00	40.00

Evening meal 1930 (last orders 2130)
Parking for 6

WICKHAM

Hampshire
Map ref 2C3

Lying in the Meon Valley, this market town is built around the Square and in Bridge Street can be seen some timber-framed cottages. Still the site of an annual horse fair.

Montrose ♠

☺☺	HIGHLY COMMENDED

Solomons Lane, Shirrell Heath,
Southampton SO32 2HU
☎ (01329) 833345
Attractive, comfortable accommodation in lovely Meon Valley, offering comfort and personal attention. Equidistant from main towns and convenient for continental ferries and motorway links.
Bedrooms: 2 double, 1 twin
Bathrooms: 1 private, 1 public

Bed & breakfast

per night:	£min	£max
Single	22.00	27.00
Double	40.00	45.00

Parking for 6

WIMBORNE MINSTER

Dorset
Map ref 2B3

Market town centred on the twin-towered Minster Church of St Cuthberga which gave the town the second part of its name. Good touring base for the surrounding countryside, depicted in the writings of Thomas Hardy.
Tourist Information Centre
☎ *(01202) 886116*

Acacia House

☺☺	HIGHLY COMMENDED

2 Oakley Road, Wimborne Minster
BH21 1QJ
☎ Bournemouth (01202) 883958
Fax (01202) 881943

Beautifully decorated rooms are what the discerning traveller expects. What comes as a surprise is Eveline Stimpson's tea and cake welcome.
Bedrooms: 1 single, 1 double, 1 twin, 1 triple
Bathrooms: 3 private, 1 public
Bed & breakfast

per night:	£min	£max
Single	16.00	24.00
Double	34.00	40.00

Parking for 3

Ashton Lodge ♠

☺☺	COMMENDED

10 Oakley Hill, Wimborne Minster
BH21 1QH
☎ Bournemouth (01202) 883423
Fax (01202) 886180
Large, detached, family house, with attractive gardens and relaxed, friendly atmosphere. Off-street parking available. Pay phone. Children welcome.
Bedrooms: 1 single, 1 twin, 2 triple
Bathrooms: 3 private, 2 public
Bed & breakfast

per night:	£min	£max
Single	17.50	17.50
Double	18.50	20.00

Parking for 4

WIMBORNE MINSTER
Continued

Northill House ⋔
COMMENDED

Horton, Wimborne Minster BH21 7HL
☎ Witchampton (01258) 840407

*Mid-Victorian former farmhouse,
modernised to provide comfortable
bedrooms, all en-suite. Log fires and
cooking using fresh produce. Ideal
touring centre.*
Wheelchair access category 1 ♿
Bedrooms: 5 double, 3 twin, 1 triple
Bathrooms: 9 private

Bed & breakfast

per night:	£min	£max
Single	38.00	38.00
Double	67.00	67.00

Half board

per person:	£min	£max
Daily	47.50	52.00
Weekly	299.25	327.60

Evening meal 1930 (last orders 1830)
Parking for 12
Open February-December
Cards accepted: Access, Visa, Amex

Twynham
Listed

67 Poole Road, Wimborne Minster
BH21 1QB
☎ (01202) 887310
*Friendly, family home, recently
refurbished. Vanity unit, TV and
beverages in rooms. Within walking
distance of town centre.*
Bedrooms: 2 double
Bathrooms: 2 public

Bed & breakfast

per night:	£min	£max
Single	15.00	18.00
Double	28.00	32.00

Parking for 2

> There are separate
> sections in this guide
> listing groups specialising
> in farm holidays and
> accommodation which
> is especially suitable
> for young people and
> organised groups.

WINCHESTER

Hampshire
Map ref 2C3

King Alfred the Great made
Winchester the capital of Saxon
England. A magnificent Norman
cathedral, with one of the longest
naves in Europe, dominates the
city. Home of Winchester College
founded in 1382.
*Tourist Information Centre
☎ (01962) 840500 or 848180*

Cathedral View ⋔
COMMENDED

9A Magdalen Hill, Winchester
SO23 0HJ
☎ (01962) 863802
*Guesthouse with views across historic
city and cathedral. 5 minutes' walk from
city centre. En-suite facilities, TV,
parking.*
Bedrooms: 3 double, 1 twin, 1 family
room
Bathrooms: 5 private

Bed & breakfast

per night:	£min	£max
Single	30.00	35.00
Double	40.00	45.00

Parking for 4

85 Christchurch Road ⋔
COMMENDED

Winchester SO23 9QY
☎ (01962) 868661
Fax (01962) 868661
*Comfortable, friendly Victorian family
house in St Cross, Winchester. Ideal for
exploring city and Hampshire. Off-street
parking. Non-smokers only, please.*
Bedrooms: 1 single, 1 double, 1 twin
Bathrooms: 1 private, 2 public

Bed & breakfast

per night:	£min	£max
Single	17.00	20.00
Double	34.00	40.00

Parking for 3

Dellbrook ⋔
COMMENDED

Hubert Road, St Cross, Winchester
SO23 9RG
☎ (01962) 865093 & 841472
Fax (01962) 865093
*Comfortable, spacious, welcoming
Edwardian house in quiet area of
Winchester close to water meadows and
12th C St Cross Hospital.*
Bedrooms: 1 twin, 2 triple
Bathrooms: 2 private, 1 public

Bed & breakfast

per night:	£min	£max
Single	23.00	28.00
Double	38.00	42.00

Half board

per person:	£min	£max
Daily		31.00
Weekly	196.00	224.00

Evening meal 1800 (last orders 1400)
Parking for 4
Cards accepted: Access, Visa

The Farrells ⋔
COMMENDED

5 Ranelagh Road, St Cross,
Winchester SO23 9TA
☎ (01962) 869555
*A warm welcome awaits you at this
comfortable Victorian house close to
city centre, St Cross Hospital and water
meadows.*
Bedrooms: 2 double, 1 twin; suite
available
Bathrooms: 2 private, 2 public

Bed & breakfast

per night:	£min	£max
Single	17.00	19.00
Double	34.00	40.00

Parking for 2

32 Hyde Street
Winchester SO23 7DX
☎ (01962) 851621
*Attractive 18th C town house close to
city centre and recreational amenities.*
Bedrooms: 1 double, 1 triple
Bathrooms: 1 public

Bed & breakfast

per night:	£min	£max
Single	17.00	18.00
Double	28.00	30.00

Ivy House
Listed **HIGHLY COMMENDED**

45 Vernham Road, Greenacres,
Winchester SO22 6BS
☎ (01962) 855512
*Situated in quiet residential road, 5
minutes' drive from city centre. Family-
run house, decorated and furnished to a
high standard.*
Bedrooms: 1 single, 1 double, 1 twin
Bathrooms: 1 public

Bed & breakfast

per night:	£min	£max
Single	17.50	
Double		35.00

Half board

per person:	£min	£max
Daily	27.50	

Evening meal from 1930
Parking for 3

Markland House
44 St Cross Road, Winchester
SO23 9PS
☎ (01962) 854901

Delightful Victorian house, close to cathedral, college, St Cross Hospital, water meadows and town centre. A warm welcome awaits you.
Bedrooms: 2 double, 2 twin
Bathrooms: 4 private

Bed & breakfast

per night:	£min	£max
Single		35.00
Double		45.00

Parking for 3
Cards accepted: Access, Visa

Orchard House

Sleepers Hill, Winchester SO22 4NA
☎ (01962) 860176
Individual, modern, large detached family residence enjoying a secluded position within a mile of the city centre. Ample parking.
Bedrooms: 1 single, 1 double
Bathrooms: 1 public

Bed & breakfast

per night:	£min	£max
Single	18.00	
Double	30.00	36.00

67 St Cross Road

Winchester SO23 9RE
☎ (01962) 863002
Fax (01962) 863002
Large, terraced town house, with comfortable rooms, good food and a friendly atmosphere.
Bedrooms: 1 double, 1 family room
Bathrooms: 2 private, 1 public

Bed & breakfast

per night:	£min	£max
Double		30.00

Shawlands ⚠

COMMENDED

46 Kilham Lane, Winchester
SO22 5QD
☎ (01962) 861166
Fax (01962) 861166
Attractive, modern house, situated in a quiet, elevated position overlooking open countryside. Delightful garden. 1.5 miles from city centre.
Wheelchair access category 3 ♿
Bedrooms: 2 double, 2 twin, 1 triple
Bathrooms: 1 private, 3 public

Bed & breakfast

per night:	£min	£max
Single	20.00	23.00
Double	36.00	38.00

Parking for 4

Please mention this guide
when making a booking.

Stratton House ⚠

Stratton Road, St Giles Hill,
Winchester SO23 0JQ
☎ (01962) 863919 & 864529
Fax (01962) 842095
Lovely old Victorian house with an acre of grounds, in an elevated position on St Giles Hill.
Bedrooms: 1 single, 2 double, 2 twin, 1 triple, 1 family room
Bathrooms: 7 private

Bed & breakfast

per night:	£min	£max
Single	22.00	30.00
Double	44.00	50.00

Half board

per person:	£min	£max
Daily	29.00	37.00
Weekly	199.00	249.00

Evening meal 1800 (last orders 1600)
Parking for 8
Cards accepted: Access, Visa

WINDSOR

Berkshire
Map ref 2D2

Town dominated by the spectacular castle and home of the Royal Family for over 900 years. Parts are open to the public. There are many attractions including the Great Park, Eton and trips on the river.
Tourist Information Centre
☎ *(01753) 852010*

Barbara Clemens

49 Longmead, Windsor SL4 5PZ
☎ (01753) 866019
Fax (01753) 830964
A home-from-home with private facilities in quiet residential area. 1.25 miles from town centre and Windsor Castle.
Bedrooms: 1 double, 1 triple
Bathrooms: 2 private

Bed & breakfast

per night:	£min	£max
Single	22.00	22.00
Double	38.00	38.00

Parking for 2

Chasela

Listed

30 Convent Road, Windsor SL4 3RB
☎ (01753) 860410
Warm, modern house a mile from the castle. Easy access M4, M40, M25, M3, Heathrow. TV, tea/coffee facilities in rooms. Breakfast room overlooks lovely garden. Payphone.
Bedrooms: 1 single, 1 twin
Bathrooms: 1 public

Bed & breakfast

per night:	£min	£max
Single	16.00	20.00
Double	32.00	40.00

Parking for 5

Halcyon House

COMMENDED

131 Clarence Road, Windsor SL4 5AR
☎ (01753) 863262
A warm welcome at a family-run guesthouse, 10 minutes' walk from the town centre and river. Ideal base for London. Off-street parking.
Bedrooms: 2 double, 2 twin
Bathrooms: 3 private, 1 public

Bed & breakfast

per night:	£min	£max
Single	28.00	38.00
Double	36.00	44.00

Parking for 6

1 Stovell Road

Listed

Windsor SL4 5JB
☎ (01753) 852055
A separate, self-contained garden flat with its own lounge. Only 100 yards to the river and the leisure centre and 7 minutes' walk to the town centre.
Bedrooms: 1 double, 1 twin
Bathrooms: 2 private

Bed & breakfast

per night:	£min	£max
Single	20.00	30.00
Double	40.00	40.00

Parking for 2

Tanglewood

Listed **HIGHLY COMMENDED**

Oakley Green, Windsor SL4 4PZ
☎ (01753) 860034
Picturesque chalet-style guesthouse in beautiful garden. Rural area overlooking open fields on B3024. Windsor 10 minutes' drive, Heathrow 15 miles. Excellent meals at nearby pub.
Bedrooms: 2 twin
Bathrooms: 1 public

Bed & breakfast

per night:	£min	£max
Double	36.00	36.00

Parking for 2
Open May-September

Trinity Guest House ⚠

18 Trinity Place, Windsor SL4 3AT
☎ (01753) 831283
Fax (01753) 862640
Comfortable guesthouse in the heart of Windsor, close to castle, river and stations, run by traditional English family and with a worldwide reputation.

Continued ▶

WINDSOR

Continued

Bedrooms: 1 single, 3 double, 2 twin, 2 family rooms
Bathrooms: 4 private, 2 public
Bed & breakfast

per night:	£min	£max
Single	25.00	40.00
Double	40.00	48.00

Parking for 4
Cards accepted: Access, Visa

WINFRITH NEWBURGH

Dorset
Map ref 2B3

Village 4 miles south-west of Wool, and within easy reach of Lulworth Cove by car.

Fossil Farmhouse

Winfrith Newburgh, Dorchester DT2 8DB
☎ Dorchester (01305) 853355 & Mobile 0378 940924
Fax (01305) 854524
880-acre arable & dairy farm. Enjoy the views in this tranquil setting on family farm 4 miles from coast. Relaxed, friendly atmosphere and hearty breakfasts.
Bedrooms: 1 double
Bathrooms: 1 private, 1 public
Bed & breakfast

per night:	£min	£max
Double	36.00	40.00

Parking for 4
Open March-October

WINSLOW

Buckinghamshire
Map ref 2C1

Small town with Georgian houses, a little market square and a fine church with 15th C wall-paintings. Winslow Hall, built to the design of Sir Christopher Wren in 1700, is open to the public.

Manor Farm Stables
Listed

High Street, North Marston, Buckingham MK18 3PS
☎ North Marston (01296) 670252 & 670708
Comfortable converted stables within easy reach of National Trust properties, Milton Keynes and Aylesbury. Breakfast served in farmhouse.
Bedrooms: 1 single, 2 double, 2 twin, 1 triple
Bathrooms: 6 private

Bed & breakfast

per night:	£min	£max
Single	20.00	25.00
Double	39.00	45.00

Parking for 8

WINTERBORNE STICKLAND

Dorset
Map ref 2B3

Restharrow
HIGHLY COMMENDED

North Street, Winterborne Stickland, Blandford Forum DT11 0NH
☎ Milton Abbas (01258) 880936 & Mobile 0850 285645
Comfortable accommodation in pretty village at head of Winterborne Valley, in the "Heart of Dorset". Friendly base for exploring the county.
Bedrooms: 2 double
Bathrooms: 2 private
Bed & breakfast

per night:	£min	£max
Single	22.00	28.00
Double	32.00	38.00

Parking for 3

WITNEY

Oxfordshire
Map ref 2C1

Town famous for its blanket-making and mentioned in the Domesday Book. The market-place contains the Butter Cross, a medieval meeting place, and there is a green with merchants' houses.
Tourist Information Centre
☎ *(01993) 775802*

Ducklington Farm
COMMENDED

Coursehill Lane, Ducklington, Witney OX8 7YG
☎ (01993) 772175
1000-acre mixed farm. A modern farmhouse in open countryside, surrounded by mature trees and woodland. 1.5 miles from the town of Witney.
Bedrooms: 1 single, 1 twin, 1 triple
Bathrooms: 3 private
Bed & breakfast

per night:	£min	£max
Single	18.00	20.00
Double	36.00	40.00

Parking for 6

Field View
HIGHLY COMMENDED

Wood Green, Witney OX8 6DE
☎ (01993) 705485

Situated in 2 acres on edge of the bustling market town of Witney. Ideal for Oxford University and the Cotswolds.
Bedrooms: 1 double, 2 twin
Bathrooms: 3 private
Bed & breakfast

per night:	£min	£max
Single	25.00	25.00
Double	40.00	44.00

Parking for 10

Hawthorn House
COMMENDED

79 Burford Road, Witney OX8 5DR
☎ (01993) 772768
Modernised Victorian house.
Bedrooms: 2 double, 2 twin
Bathrooms: 4 private, 1 public
Bed & breakfast

per night:	£min	£max
Single	25.00	35.00
Double	45.00	50.00

Parking for 4
Cards accepted: Access, Visa, Amex

North Leigh Guest House
HIGHLY COMMENDED

28 Common Road, North Leigh, Witney OX8 6RA
☎ Freeland (01993) 881622
Near centre of friendly village. A warm and welcoming family home. Bedrooms are cosy and cheerful. Looks out over country views. Uncommonly good food is a speciality.
Bedrooms: 1 double, 1 triple
Bathrooms: 2 private
Bed & breakfast

per night:	£min	£max
Single	25.00	28.00
Double		38.00

Half board

per person:	£min	£max
Daily		29.50

Lunch available
Evening meal 1900 (last orders 1900)
Parking for 5

WOODCOTE

Oxfordshire
Map ref 2C2

Hedges ⋀

South Stoke Road, Woodcote, Reading, Berkshire RG8 0PL
☎ Checkendon (01491) 680461
Comfortable family house in rural situation on edge of village. Area of Outstanding Natural Beauty. Reading 10 miles, Oxford 18 miles. Easy access to London and M4.
Bedrooms: 1 single, 2 twin
Bathrooms: 1 private, 2 public

Bed & breakfast per night:	£min	£max
Single	15.00	15.00
Double	30.00	30.00

Parking for 3

ॸ ⭒ ⬓ 🛁 ♿ 🅿️ 📺 ⅲ. ➡️ ✿ 🐾

WOODSTOCK

Oxfordshire
Map ref 2C1

Small country town clustered around the park gates of Blenheim Palace, the superb 18th C home of the Duke of Marlborough. The town has well-known inns and an interesting museum. Sir Winston Churchill was born and buried nearby.
Tourist Information Centre
☎ *(01993) 811038*

Gorselands Farmhouse Auberge ᴍ

♛♛

Boddington Lane, Long Hanborough, Witney OX8 6PU
☎ Freeland (01993) 881895
Fax (01993) 882799
Stone country farmhouse with exposed beams, snooker room, conservatory. Convenient for Blenheim Palace, Oxford and Cotswold villages. Evening meals available. Licensed for wine and beer. Grass tennis court.
Bedrooms: 2 double, 1 twin, 1 family room; suite available
Bathrooms: 4 private

Bed & breakfast per night:	£min	£max
Single	20.00	25.00
Double	34.00	40.00

Half board per person:	£min	£max
Daily	28.95	33.95
Weekly	175.00	200.00

Evening meal 1900 (last orders 2100)
Parking for 7
Cards accepted: Access, Visa, Amex

ॸ ⬓ ♿ 🛁 🅂 ⅄ 🍴 📺 ◑ ⅲ. ➡️ ● ☍ ✿ 🐾 [SP] 🀫 [T]

The Laurels

♛♛ HIGHLY COMMENDED

Hensington Road, Woodstock
OX20 1JL
☎ (01993) 812583
Fax (01993) 812583
Fine Victorian house, charmingly furnished with an emphasis on comfort and quality. Just off town centre and a short walk from Blenheim Palace.
Bedrooms: 2 double, 1 twin
Bathrooms: 3 private

Bed & breakfast per night:	£min	£max
Single	30.00	40.00
Double	36.00	46.00

Parking for 3
Cards accepted: Access, Visa

ॸ 7 ⬓ ⭒ 🆄 🆂 ⅄ 🍴 ⅲ. 🍴 🐾 [OAP] [T]

Punch Bowl Inn ᴍ

Listed APPROVED

12 Oxford Street, Woodstock, Oxford
OX20 1TR
☎ (01993) 811218
Fax (01993) 811393
Family-run pub in the centre of Woodstock, close to Blenheim Palace. A good touring centre for Oxford and the Cotswolds.
Bedrooms: 2 single, 4 double, 2 twin, 1 triple, 1 family room
Bathrooms: 3 private, 3 public

Bed & breakfast per night:	£min	£max
Single	28.00	32.00
Double	38.00	42.00

Lunch available
Evening meal 1800 (last orders 2130)

Parking for 20
Cards accepted: Access, Visa, Amex, Switch/Delta

ॸ ⬓ ⬓ ⭒ 🛁 🅂 ⅲ. ➡️ ☍ 🀫 [T]

The Ridings

♛♛

32 Banbury Road, Woodstock
OX20 1LQ
☎ (01993) 811269
Detached house in a quiet, rural setting. 10 minutes' walk to town centre and Blenheim Palace. Go past the Tourist Information Centre for 300 yards then take left fork along Banbury Road.
Bedrooms: 1 double, 2 twin, 1 triple
Bathrooms: 2 private, 1 public

Bed & breakfast per night:	£min	£max
Single	25.00	42.00
Double	36.00	38.00

Parking for 4
Open March–November

ॸ ⬓ ⬓ ⭒ 🆄 ⅄ 🍴 📺 ⅲ. ✿ ✕ 🐾

Shepherds Hall Inn

♛♛

Witney Road, Freeland, Witney
OX8 8HQ
☎ Freeland (01993) 881256
Well-appointed inn offering good accommodation. All rooms en-suite. Ideally situated for Oxford, Woodstock and the Cotswolds, on the A4095 Woodstock to Witney road.
Bedrooms: 1 single, 1 double, 2 twin, 1 triple
Bathrooms: 5 private

Bed & breakfast per night:	£min	£max
Single	20.00	30.00
Double	38.50	40.00

Lunch available
Evening meal 1900 (last orders 2200)
Parking for 50
Cards accepted: Access, Visa

ॸ ✆ ⬓ ⬓ ⭒ ☍ 🛁 ⅲ. ● ✿ 🐾

AT-A-GLANCE SYMBOLS

At-a-glance symbols at the end of each accommodation entry give information about services and facilities. A handy guide to these symbols can be found inside the back cover flap, which can be kept open for easy reference.

USE YOUR *i*'S

There are more than 550 Tourist Information Centres throughout England offering friendly help with accommodation and holiday ideas as well as suggestions of places to visit and things to do. There may well be a centre in your home town which can help you before you set out. You'll find the address of your nearest Tourist Information Centre in your local Phone Book.

COUNTRY CODE

♣ Enjoy the countryside and respect its life and work ♣ Guard against all risk of fire ♣ Fasten all gates ♣ Keep your dogs under close control ♣ Keep to public paths across farmland ♣ Use gates and stiles to cross fences, hedges and walls ♣ Leave livestock, crops and machinery alone ♣ Take your litter home ♣ Help to keep all water clean ♣ Protect wildlife, plants and trees ♣ Take special care on country roads ♣ Make no unnecessary noise

South East England

What could be more delightfully English
than the gentle countryside of the Southeast?
This is the garden of England, a land of
oasthouses, vineyards and orchards; tile-hung
Sussex farmhouses, Kentish weatherboard cottages,
unspoilt villages with duckponds and greens. Come in
spring for the glorious, drenching blossom; in summer for the fruit harvests.

Make sure you visit the region's many sturdy old manor houses and
gardens open to the public, and the magnificent castles and cathedrals.

Ramble over Surrey heathland or the sheep-cropped Sussex Downs, then
head for the coast – Dover's white cliffs and busy harbour; Margate's
nine-mile long sands; the quaint prettiness of the medieval Cinque ports;
Brighton for its regency charm.

**The Counties of East Sussex, Kent,
Surrey and West Sussex**
For more information on South East
England, contact:
South East England Tourist Board
The Old Brewhouse, Warwick Road
Tunbridge Wells, Kent TN2 5TU
Tel: (01892) 540766
Fax: (01892) 511008
Where to Go and What to See in South
East England – see pages 332–335
Where to Stay in South East England –
see pages 336–360

South East England

Where to go and what to see

You will find hundreds of interesting places to visit during your stay in South East England, just some of which are listed here. The number against each name will help you locate it on the map (page 335). Any Tourist Information Centre in the region will be happy to help with more ideas on days out.

❶ Powell Cotton Museum, Quex House and Gardens
Quex Park, Birchington, Kent
CT7 0BH
Tel: (01843) 842168
Regency house with period furniture. Museum with ethnograhic collections, diorama of African and Asian animals, weapons, archaeology, Chinese porcelain.

❷ Royal Engineers Museum
Prince Arthur Road, Gillingham, Kent
Tel: (01634) 406397
The characters, lives and work of Britain's soldier-engineers, 1066–1945. Medals, uniforms, scientific and technical equipment. Collection of ethnography and decorative arts.

❸ The Historic Dockyard
Chatham, Kent ME4 4TE
Tel: (01634) 812551
Historic 18th C 80-acre dockyard, now a museum. Eight galleries including the award-winning "Wooden Walls". Sail and colour loft, ordnance mews, ropery, wagon rides.

❹ Brogdale Horticultural Trust
Brogdale Farm, Brogdale Road, Faversham, Kent ME13 8XZ
Tel: (01795) 535286
National Fruit Collection with 4,000 varieties of fruit in 30 acres of orchard: apples, pears, cherries, plums, currants, quinces, medlars, etc.

❺ The Royal Horticultural Society's Garden
Wisley, Surrey GU23 6QB
Tel: (01483) 224234
RHS establishment with 250 acres of vegetable, fruit and ornamental gardens. Trial grounds, glasshouses, rock garden, ponds, rose gardens, model and specialist gardens.

❻ Belmont
Belmont Park, Throwley, Kent
ME13 0HH
Tel: (01795) 890202
Late 18th C country mansion designed by Samuel Wyatt, seat of the Harris family since 1801. Harris clock collection, mementoes of connections with India. Gardens and pinetum.

❼ Guildford Cathedral
Stag Hill, Guildford, Surrey
GU2 5UP
Tel: (01483) 65287
Anglican cathedral, foundation stone laid in 1936 and consecrated in 1961. Notable glass engravings, embroidered kneelers, modern furnishings. Brass rubbing centre.

❽ Birdworld and Underwaterworld
Holt Pound, Farnham, Surrey
GU10 4LD

Tel: (01420) 22140
20 acres of garden and parkland with ostriches, flamingoes, hornbills, parrots, emus, pelicans, etc. Penguin island, tropical and marine fish, plant area, seashore walk.

9 Headcorn Flower Centre & Vineyard
Grigg Lane, Headcorn, Ashford, Kent TN27 9LX
Tel: (01622) 890250
Walk around 6 acres of vines, pausing at reservoir to watch wildlife. Weekend and group tours visit flower houses with chrysanthemums and orchid lilies flowering all year. Wine tasting.

10 Iden Croft Herbs
Frittenden Road, Staplehurst, Kent TN12 0DH
Tel: (01580) 891432
Large fresh herb farm with walled garden and variety of aromatic gardens, demonstrating the beauty and use of herbs. Thyme rockery of special interest.

11 Dover Castle and Hellfire Corner
Dover, Kent CT16 1HU
Tel: (01304) 201628
One of most powerful medieval fortresses in Western Europe. St Mary in Castro Saxon church, Roman lighthouse, Hellfire Corner. All the Queen's Men exhibition and Battle of Waterloo model.

12 Bedgebury National Pinetum
Goudhurst, Kent TN17 2SL
Tel: (01580) 211044
Forestry Commission's superb collection of specimen conifers in 150 acres, with lake and stream. Also many rhododendrons and azaleas. Visitor centre.

13 Leonardslee Gardens
Lower Beeding, West Sussex RH13 6PP
Tel: (01403) 891212
Renowned spring-flowering shrub garden in a valley: rhododendrons, camellias, azaleas, lakes, paths. Good views, autumn tints, rock garden, bonsai exhibition, alpine house.

14 The Bluebell Railway – Living Museum
Sheffield Park Station, Sheffield Park, East Sussex TN22 3QL
Tel: (01825) 722370
7.5-mile standard gauge track from Sheffield Park to Horsted Keynes with extension to New Coombe Bridge. Largest collection of engines in the south. Victorian stations and museum.

15 Brickwall House and Gardens
Northiam, East Sussex TN31 6NL
Tel: (01797) 223329
Formal garden with terracotta entrance gates. 18th C bowling alley, sunken topiary garden, yew hedges, chess garden, arboretum. Jacobean house with 17th C plaster ceilings.

16 Great Dixter House and Gardens
Northiam, East Sussex TN31 6PH
Tel: (01797) 252878
Fine example of 15th C manor house with antique furniture and needlework. Unique great hall restored by Lutyens, who also designed the garden – topiary, meadow garden, flower beds.

17 Rye Town Model Sound and Light Show
The Heritage Centre, Strand Quay, Rye, East Sussex TN31 7AY
Tel: (01797) 226696
Fascinating combination of detailed model of the ancient town with dramatic sound and light effects, telling the story of Rye through the ages.

18 Buckleys Yesterday's World
89–90 High Street, Battle, East Sussex TN33 0AQ
Tel: (01424) 775378
Over 50,000 exhibits in a Wealden hall house recall shopping and domestic life from 1850 to 1950 with smells and commentaries. Railway station, play village, garden.

⑲ Bignor Roman Villa
Bignor, West Sussex RH20 1PH
Tel: (017987) 259
Remains of large villa containing probably the finest mosaic pavements outside Italy. Hypocaust under-floor heating system, Roman artefacts.

⑳ Weald and Downland Open Air Museum
Singleton, West Sussex PO18 0EU
Tel: (01243) 811348
Open-air museum of over 35 rescued historic buildings from South East England reconstructed on downland country park site, including medieval farmstead and watermill.

㉑ A Smuggler's Adventure at St Clement's Caves
West Hill, Hastings, East Sussex TN34 3HY
Tel: (01424) 422964
One acre of caves, housing the largest smuggling exhibition in the country. Museum, audio-visual show and 50 life-size figures with dramatic sound and lighting effects.

㉒ The Wildfowl and Wetlands Centre
Mill Road, Arundel, West Sussex BN18 9PB
Tel: (01903) 883355
Reserve in 60 acres of watermeadows. Tame swans, ducks, geese and many wild birds. Film theatre and visitor centre with gallery.

㉓ Denmans Garden
Denmans, Fontwell, West Sussex BN18 0SU
Tel: (01243) 542808
Walled, gravel and water gardens, natural layout of trees, climbers and wall shrubs for all-year interest. Glass areas. School of Garden Design.

㉔ Pallant House
9 North Pallant, Chichester, West Sussex PO19 1TJ
Tel: (01243) 774557
Queen Anne residence containing Bow Porcelain collection, Hussey and Kearley painting collections, Rembrandt to Picasso, sculptures by Moore. Temporary exhibitions. Old kitchen.

㉕ Charleston Farmhouse
Firle, Lewes, East Sussex BN8 6LL
Tel: (01323) 811265
17th–18th C farmhouse, home of Vanessa and Clive Bell and Duncan Grant. House and contents decorated by the artists. Newly restored garden room. Traditional flint-walled garden.

㉖ Brighton Sea Life Centre
Marine Parade, Brighton BN2 1TB
Tel: (01273) 604234
Ocean life on a grand scale featuring over 35 displays of fascinating marine creatures with underwater tunnel.

㉗ Foredown Tower Countryside Centre
Foredown Road, Portslade, East Sussex BN41 2EW
Tel: (01273) 422540
Converted water tower 1909, housing exhibitions on the Downs and water. Camera obscura gives views of South Downs and coast. Touch-screen computer, weather station with satellite, slide shows.

㉘ Smarts Amusement Park
Seafront, Littlehampton, West Sussex BN17 5LL
Tel: (01903) 721200
Large indoor and outdoor amusement park for all ages. Many rides including dodgems, Waltzer, Cyclone Roller Coaster, waterslides.

㉙ Eastbourne Pier
Grand Parade, Eastbourne, East Sussex BN21 3EL
Tel: (01323) 410466
Well-preserved Victorian seaside pier with coastal views, family amusement arcade, disco, family entertainment room, shops, fishing and boats.

㉚ Earnley Butterflies and Gardens
133 Almodington Lane, Earnley, West Sussex PO20 7JR
Tel: (01243) 512637
Ornamental butterfly house, covered theme gardens, exotic bird garden, children's play area, small animal farm, pottery.

Find out more

Further information about holidays and attractions in South East England is available from:
South East England Tourist Board, The Old Brew House, Warwick Park, Tunbridge Wells, Kent TN2 5TU
Tel: (01892) 540766

These publications are available free from the South East England Tourist Board:
- **Holiday Selector**
- **Accommodation Guide**
- **Short Breaks South East**
- **Diary of Events**
- **Favourite Gardens and Garden Hotels**
- **Bed and Breakfast Touring Map**
- **Holidays for Walkers**
- **Holidays for Cyclists**

Also available is (price includes postage and packing):
- **South East England Leisure Map £4**

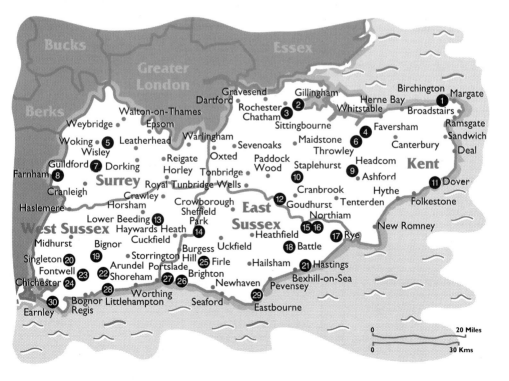

WHERE TO STAY

Accommodation entries in this regional section are listed in alphabetical order of place name, and then in alphabetical order of establishment.

Map references refer to the colour location maps at the back of this guide. The first figure is the map number; the letter and figure which follow indicate the grid reference on the map.

At-a-glance symbols at the end of each accommodation entry give information about services and facilities. A handy guide to these symbols can be found inside the back cover flap, which can be kept open for easy reference.

ALDINGTON

Kent
Map ref 3B4

Once the home of Elizabeth Barton, the "Holy Maid" or "Nun of Kent".

Hogben Farm

Listed **COMMENDED**

Church Lane, Aldington, Ashford TN25 7EH
☎ (01233) 720219
Small 16th C country house, surrounded by pretty garden and 17 acres of farmland. Convenient for Channel ports, Channel Tunnel, Canterbury, Rye, Tenterden and Romney Marsh. Evening meals by prior arrangement.
Bedrooms: 1 double, 2 twin
Bathrooms: 2 public

Bed & breakfast

per night:	£min	£max
Single	17.00	20.00
Double	34.00	40.00

Half board

per person:	£min	£max
Daily	25.00	27.50
Weekly	150.00	165.00

Evening meal 1800 (last orders 2000)
Parking for 6

National gradings and classifications were correct at the time of going to press but are subject to change. Please check at the time of booking.

ARDINGLY

West Sussex
Map ref 2D3

Famous for the South of England Agricultural Showground and public school. Nearby is Wakehurst Place (National Trust), the gardens of which are administered by the Royal Botanic Gardens, Kew.

Jordans

Church Lane, Ardingly, Haywards Heath RH17 6UP
☎ (01444) 892681
Fax (01444) 414269
Victorian country house set in beautiful gardens opposite medieval village church. Behind South of England Showground, close to many facilities and 20 minutes from Gatwick.
Bedrooms: 1 single, 1 twin
Bathrooms: 2 private, 1 public

Bed & breakfast

per night:	£min	£max
Single	21.00	23.00
Double	36.00	38.00

Parking for 5

There are separate sections in this guide listing groups specialising in farm holidays and accommodation which is especially suitable for young people and organised groups.

ARUNDEL

West Sussex
Map ref 2D3

Picturesque, historic town on the River Arun, dominated by Arundel Castle, home of the Dukes of Norfolk. There are many 18th C houses, the Toy and Military Museum, Wildfowl and Wetlands Centre and Museum and Heritage Centre.
Tourist Information Centre
☎ (01903) 882268

Arundel Park Inn & Travel Lodge

Station Approach, Arundel BN18 9JL
☎ (01903) 882588
Fax (01903) 883808
Refurbished to a high standard. 3 bedrooms on ground floor. Pleasant lounge bar, informal restaurant serving high quality food. Central to many places of interest. Two minutes from station, 5 minutes from centre of Arundel.
Bedrooms: 1 single, 8 double, 2 twin, 1 family room
Bathrooms: 12 private

Bed & breakfast

per night:	£min	£max
Single	34.00	38.00
Double	44.00	48.00

Lunch available
Evening meal 1830 (last orders 2100)
Parking for 60
Cards accepted: Access, Visa, Amex, Switch/Delta

Arundel Vineyards ⚑

📛 COMMENDED

The Vineyard, Church Lane,
Lyminster, Arundel BN17 7QF
☎ (01903) 883393
*3-acre fruit farm. Modern farmhouse in
English vineyard in beautiful
countryside. From Arundel, turn south
on to A284 Littlehampton/Lyminster
road (new split junction). Signposted 1
mile on right.*
Bedrooms: 1 double, 1 twin
Bathrooms: 2 private

Bed & breakfast

per night:	£min	£max
Single	24.00	
Double	36.00	

Parking for 15

🛏 10 ♨ ⊑ ☐ ➤ ♍ ⓘ ⓢ ⅍ ⅀ ◐ ▥
🖴 ❀ ✕ 🖙 ♿

Mill Lane House ⚑

📛📛

Slindon, Arundel BN18 0RP
☎ Slindon (01243) 814440
*18th C house in beautiful National Trust
village. Magnificent views to coast. Pubs
within easy walking distance. One mile
from A29/A27 junction.*
Wheelchair access category 3 ♿
Bedrooms: 1 single, 3 double, 2 twin,
1 triple; suite available
Bathrooms: 7 private, 1 public

Bed & breakfast

per night:	£min	£max
Single	24.25	24.25
Double	37.00	37.00

Half board

per person:	£min	£max
Daily	28.00	33.75
Weekly	182.50	220.50

Evening meal 1900 (last orders 1000)
Parking for 7

🛏 ♨ ⊑ ☐ ⅏ ⓘ ⓢ ⅍ ⅀ ▥ 🖴 ❀ 🖙 ⒹⒶⓅ
⒮Ⓟ ♿

Pindars ⚑

📛 HIGHLY COMMENDED

Lyminster, Arundel BN17 7QF
☎ (01903) 882628
*Charming country house in small
village offers comfortable bedrooms,
good food and warm hospitality.
Beautiful garden. Non-smoking. On
A284 off A27.*
Bedrooms: 2 double, 1 twin
Bathrooms: 3 private, 1 public

Bed & breakfast

per night:	£min	£max
Double	30.00	40.00

Half board

per person:	£min	£max
Daily	25.00	30.00

Evening meal from 1900
Parking for 7
Cards accepted: Access, Visa

🛏 10 ⊑ ☐ ➤ ♍ ⓤⓛ ⓢ ⅍ ▥ 🖴 ⟲
✕ 🖙

ASHFORD

Kent
Map ref 3B4

Once a market centre for the
farmers of the Weald of Kent and
Romney Marsh. The town centre
has a number of Tudor and
Georgian houses.
Tourist Information Centre
☎ *(01233) 629165*

Fishponds Farm

📛📛

Pilgrims Way, Brook, Ashford
TN25 5PP
☎ (01233) 812398
*Rural farmhouse with lake in Wye
Downs Nature Reserve, 3 miles south-
east of Wye on lane to Brabourne.*
Bedrooms: 1 double, 1 twin
Bathrooms: 2 private

Bed & breakfast

per night:	£min	£max
Single		20.00
Double		32.00

Parking for 10

🛏 ☐ ➤ ⓤⓛ ▥ ❀ ✕ 🖙

61 Magazine Road ⚑

Listed

Ashford TN24 8NR
☎ (01233) 621959
*Family-run establishment, all rooms
with colour TV and tea/coffee making
facilities. Friendly atmosphere.*
Bedrooms: 2 single, 1 double
Bathrooms: 1 public

Bed & breakfast

per night:	£min	£max
Single	14.00	15.00
Double	27.00	29.00

Half board

per person:	£min	£max
Daily	21.00	22.00
Weekly	147.00	154.00

Evening meal 1830 (last orders 2000)

🛏 ⌘ ⊑ ☐ ➤ ♍ ⓘ ⓢ ⓣⓥ ▥ ❀ ✕ 🖙

Meadowside ⚑

📛 HIGHLY COMMENDED

Church Road, Mersham, Ashford
TN25 6NT
☎ (01233) 502458
Fax (01233) 502458
*Two miles from junction 10 M20,
convenient for Channel Tunnel and
ports, Leeds and Sissinghurst Castles,
Canterbury and Tenterden. Large
comfortable rooms with en-suite shower,
tea-making, colour TV. Non-smokers
only, please.*
Bedrooms: 1 double, 1 twin
Bathrooms: 2 private

Bed & breakfast

per night:	£min	£max
Single	21.00	21.00
Double	38.00	38.00

Parking for 2

🛏 12 ⊑ ☐ ➤ ♍ ⓤⓛ ▥ ⅍ ▥ 🖴 ❀ ✕ 🖙

Warren Cottage ⚑

📛📛📛 APPROVED

136 The Street, Willesborough,
Ashford TN24 0NB
☎ (01233) 621905 & 632929
Fax (01233) 623400

*300-year-old guesthouse with oak beams,
open fireplaces and a cosy atmosphere.
On old coaching route with easy access
to M20 and a short drive from many
places of interest.*
Bedrooms: 2 single, 2 double
Bathrooms: 4 private, 1 public

Bed & breakfast

per night:	£min	£max
Single	25.00	29.90
Double	50.00	60.00

Half board

per person:	£min	£max
Daily	34.00	38.90
Weekly	238.00	272.30

Lunch available
Evening meal 1830 (last orders 2130)
Parking for 8
Cards accepted: Access, Visa, Switch/
Delta

🛏 ⌘ ≋ ⊑ ☐ ➤ ♍ ⓘ ⓢ ⅍ ⅀ ⓣⓥ ▥ 🖴 ∪
❀ ⚲ ♿

BATTLE

East Sussex
Map ref 3B4

The Abbey at Battle was built on
the site of the Battle of Hastings,
when William defeated Harold II
and so became the Conqueror in
1066. The museum has a fine
collection relating to the Sussex
iron industry.
Tourist Information Centre
☎ *(01424) 773721*

Kitchenham Farm

Listed

Ashburnham, Battle TN33 9NP
☎ Ninfield (01424) 892221
Fax (01424) 892221
*800-acre arable and mixed farm.
Friendly family atmosphere in beautiful
18th C farmhouse on working farm.
Traditional buildings offer perfect
backdrop for stunning views. Large
comfortable rooms.*
Bedrooms: 1 double, 2 twin
Bathrooms: 1 public

Bed & breakfast

per night:	£min	£max
Single	20.00	25.00
Double	34.00	35.00

Continued ▶

BATTLE

Continued

Half board

per person:	£min	£max
Daily	27.00	27.00
Weekly	170.00	170.00

Evening meal 1900 (last orders 2000)
Parking for 7

🛏🍴♿🔌♨📶✖🎱, ♨Ụ♪✻🚗 📠🏮

Moons Hill Farm ⚫

⚜⚜

The Green, Ninfield, Battle TN33 9LH
☎ Ninfield (01424) 892645
*10-acre mixed farm. Modernised
farmhouse in Ninfield village centre, in
the heart of "1066" country. A warm
welcome and Sussex home cooking. Pub
opposite.*
Bedrooms: 1 double, 2 twin
Bathrooms: 3 private, 1 public

Bed & breakfast

per night:	£min	£max
Single	15.00	17.50
Double	30.00	35.00

Parking for 12
Open January–November

🛏🔥🍴🖥♿🔅♨🔌🛁📺🏠, ♨Ụ♪✻
🚗Ⓣ

BEACHY HEAD

East Sussex
Map ref 3B4

Black Robin Farm

Listed COMMENDED

Beachy Head, Eastbourne BN20 7XX
☎ Eastbourne (01323) 643357 &
Mobile 0973 418654
*1000-acre livestock farm. Farmhouse B
& B. Peaceful location with excellent
views. Full English or vegetarian
breakfast. Close to town, beach and
South Downs Way.*
Bedrooms: 1 double, 2 twin
Bathrooms: 1 public

Bed & breakfast

per night:	£min	£max
Double	34.00	36.00

Parking for 4

🛏🖥♿🔌♨🔅♨, ♨✻🚗 SP

The symbol 🏵 within an
entry indicates participation
in the Welcome Host
programme – a nationally
recognised customer care
initiative which aims to
promote the highest
standards of service and a
warm welcome for all visitors.

BIDDENDEN

Kent
Map ref 3B4

Perfect village with black and
white houses, a tithe barn and a
pond. Part of the village is grouped
around a green with a village sign
depicting the famous Biddenden
Maids. It was an important centre
of the Flemish weaving industry,
hence the beautiful Old Cloth Hall.

Bettmans Oast ⚫

⚜⚜ HIGHLY COMMENDED

Hareplain Road, Biddenden, Ashford
TN27 8LJ
☎ (01580) 291463
*Grade II listed oast house and
converted barn set in 10 acres near
Sissinghurst Castle, a quarter of a mile
from Three Chimneys pub. Lovely
gardens and log fires in winter.*
Bedrooms: 1 single, 1 twin, 1 family
room
Bathrooms: 1 private, 1 public

Bed & breakfast

per night:	£min	£max
Single	20.00	20.00
Double	35.00	40.00

Half board

per person:	£min	£max
Daily	27.50	30.00
Weekly	192.50	210.00

Evening meal 1900 (last orders 2100)
Parking for 4

🛏🔥🍴🖥♿🔅♨🔌🍴✖🛁📺🏠, ♨
✻✖🚗🏮Ⓣ

BIRCHINGTON

Kent
Map ref 3C3

Town on the north coast of Kent
with sandy beaches and rock
pools. Powell Cotton Museum is in
nearby Quex Park.

Woodchurch Farmhouse

Listed

Woodchurch, Birchington CT7 0HE
☎ Thanet (01843) 832468
*6-acre arable farm. This Elizabethan
farmhouse provides a warm welcome
and ensures a comfortable stay. An
excellent base for exploring south-east
Kent.*
Bedrooms: 1 double, 2 twin
Bathrooms: 1 public

Bed & breakfast

per night:	£min	£max
Single		15.00
Double		30.00

Parking for 6

🛏🗾🔥♿🔌🛁📺🖥♨, ♨Ụ✻✖
🚗🏮

BRIGHTON & HOVE

East Sussex
Map ref 2D3

Brighton's attractions include the
Royal Pavilion, Volks Electric
Railway, Sea Life Centre and
Marina Village, Conference Centre
and "The Lanes" and several
theatres. Neighbouring Hove is a
resort in its own right.
Tourist Information Centre
☎ *(01273) 323755; for Hove
(01273) 746100 or 778087*

'Brighton' Marina House Hotel ⚫

⚜⚜⚜

8 Charlotte Street, Marine Parade,
Brighton BN2 1AG
☎ (01273) 605349 & Freephone 0500
099989
Fax (01273) 605349

*Cosy, elegantly furnished, well-equipped,
clean, comfortable, caring, family-run.
Near sea, central for Palace Pier, Royal
Pavilion, conference and exhibition
halls, the famous Lanes, tourist
attractions. Flexible breakfast, check-
in/out times. Offering all facilities. Free
street parking. Best in price range.*
Bedrooms: 3 single, 4 double, 3 triple
Bathrooms: 7 private, 1 public

Bed & breakfast

per night:	£min	£max
Single	13.50	27.00
Double	33.00	48.00

Half board

per person:	£min	£max
Daily	25.00	38.00
Weekly	160.00	240.00

Lunch available
Evening meal 1830 (last orders 1700)
Cards accepted: Access, Visa, Diners,
Amex

🛏🗾🔥🍴♿🔌♨🔅🛁🏠, ♨✖
✖ 📶 SP Ⓣ

Cavalaire House ⚫

⚜⚜ COMMENDED

34 Upper Rock Gardens, Brighton
BN2 1QF
☎ (01273) 696899
Fax (01273) 600504
*Victorian townhouse, close to sea and
town centre. Resident proprietors offer
comfortably furnished rooms with or
without private facilities. Book 7 nights
and get 1 night free.*
Bedrooms: 1 single, 3 double, 3 twin,
2 triple
Bathrooms: 3 private, 1 public,
3 private showers

Bed & breakfast

per night:	£min	£max
Single	18.00	25.00
Double	34.00	44.00

Cards accepted: Access, Visa, Amex

⌐ 5 🍴☐📞🐕🖤 UL S 🅿 IIII. 🚗 ✕ 🚲 🅃

Diana House ᐰ

Listed

25 St. Georges Terrace, Brighton
BN2 1JJ
☎ (01273) 605797
*Large, friendly guesthouse close to sea,
town and conference centre. All rooms
have TV, hospitality tray, clock/radio,
shaver point. Some rooms en-suite. 24-
hour access.*
Bedrooms: 4 double, 2 twin, 2 triple,
1 family room
Bathrooms: 3 private, 1 public,
5 private showers

Bed & breakfast

per night:	£min	£max
Single	15.00	19.00
Double	30.00	38.00

Half board

per person:	£min	£max
Daily	21.50	25.50
Weekly	135.00	160.00

Evening meal 1800 (last orders 2000)
Cards accepted: Access, Visa

⌐ 🍴☐🐕🖤 UL 🔒 S ⏰ 🌙 IIII. 🚗 🚲 DAP
SP 🅃

Melford Hall Hotel ᐰ

☺☺

41 Marine Parade, Brighton BN2 1PE
☎ (01273) 681435
Fax (01273) 624186
*Listed building, well positioned on
seafront and within easy walking
distance of all the entertainment that
Brighton has to offer. Many rooms with
sea views.*
Bedrooms: 4 single, 16 double, 4 twin,
1 triple
Bathrooms: 23 private, 1 public,
2 private showers

Bed & breakfast

per night:	£min	£max
Single	28.00	32.00
Double	46.00	54.00

Parking for 12
Cards accepted: Access, Visa, Diners,
Amex

⌐ 2 🎿🍴🚗🍴☐🐕🖤 UL 🅿 IIII. 🚗
✕ 🚲 DAP SP 🐟 🅃

There are separate
sections in this guide
listing groups specialising
in farm holidays and
accommodation which
is especially suitable
for young people and
organised groups.

Village of old houses, many from
the Tudor and Stuart periods. One
of the old ironmasters' houses is
Bateman's (National Trust) which
was the home of Rudyard Kipling.

Woodlands Farm

Listed

Heathfield Road, Burwash,
Etchingham TN19 7LA
☎ (01435) 882794

*55-acre mixed farm. Modernised 16th C
farmhouse set away from road, amidst
fields and woods. Friendly welcome and
fresh food. Near Bateman's.*
Bedrooms: 2 double, 1 twin
Bathrooms: 1 private, 2 public

Bed & breakfast

per night:	£min	£max
Single	16.00	20.00
Double	33.00	37.00

Parking for 4
Open April-December

⌐ 🎿🚗🍴 UL 🔒 🅿 ⏰ IIII. 🌸 🚲 🐟

Place of pilgrimage since the
martyrdom of Becket in 1170 and
the site of Canterbury Cathedral.
Visit St Augustine's Abbey, St
Martin's (the oldest church in
England), Royal Museum and Art
Gallery and the Canterbury Tales.
Nearby is Howletts Wild Animal
Park.
Tourist Information Centre
☎ *(01227) 766567*

Abberley House ᐰ

Listed

115 Whitstable Road, Canterbury
CT2 8EF
☎ (01227) 450265

*Family-run guesthouse within easy
walking distance of the city and
university. Tea/coffee-making facilities,
wash-basins. Non-smokers only, please.*

Bedrooms: 2 double, 1 twin
Bathrooms: 1 public, 1 private shower

Bed & breakfast

per night:	£min	£max
Single	18.00	20.00
Double	32.00	37.00

Parking for 3

🖤 UL ✂ IIII. 🚗 ✕ 🚲 🅃

Bower Farm House

☺☺ HIGHLY COMMENDED

Stelling Minnis, Canterbury CT4 6BB
☎ Stelling Minnis (01227) 709430
*Delightful heavily beamed 17th C
farmhouse between the villages of
Stelling Minnis and Bossingham.
Canterbury and Hythe are
approximately 7 miles away.*
Bedrooms: 1 double, 1 twin
Bathrooms: 2 private

Bed & breakfast

per night:	£min	£max
Single	18.00	18.00
Double	36.00	36.00

Parking for 8

⌐ 🍴🖤 UL S 🅿 📺 IIII. 🚗 🐈 🌸 🚲 🐟

Bridge House

Listed

The Green, Chartham, Canterbury
CT4 7JW
☎ (01227) 738354
*Well-equipped house on banks of River
Stour, next to village green. Tea/coffee
upon request. Colour TV. Canterbury 3
miles on A28.*
Bedrooms: 2 twin
Bathrooms: 2 public

Bed & breakfast

per night:	£min	£max
Single	20.00	22.00
Double	30.00	32.00

Parking for 5

⌐ 🎿🍴☐ UL 🔒 IIII. 🚗 🚕 🚲

Castle Court Guest House ᐰ

Listed

8 Castle Street, Canterbury CT1 2QF
☎ (01227) 463441
*Friendly family-run guesthouse in listed
Georgian building, close to cathedral,
parks, restaurants and bus/railway
station. Full English breakfast.*
Bedrooms: 3 single, 4 double, 3 twin,
1 triple
Bathrooms: 2 public

Bed & breakfast

per night:	£min	£max
Single	18.00	22.00
Double	28.00	34.00

Parking for 4
Cards accepted: Access, Visa

⌐ 2 ☐🖤 UL 🅿 📺 IIII. 🚗 DAP SP 🐟 🅃

Cathedral Gate Hotel ᐰ

☺☺☺

36 Burgate, Canterbury CT1 2HA
☎ (01227) 464381
Fax (01227) 462800

Continued ▶

CANTERBURY

Continued

Central position at main entrance to the cathedral. Car parking nearby. Baby listening service. Old world charm at reasonable prices. English breakfast extra.
Bedrooms: 5 single, 7 double, 8 twin, 2 triple, 2 family rooms
Bathrooms: 12 private, 3 public, 2 private showers

Bed & breakfast

per night:	£min	£max
Single	21.00	46.00
Double	40.00	70.00

Evening meal 1900 (last orders 2100)
Parking for 12
Cards accepted: Access, Visa, Diners, Amex, Switch/Delta

Clare-Ellen Guest House ⋔

HIGHLY COMMENDED

9 Victoria Road, Wincheap, Canterbury
CT1 3SG
☎ (01227) 760205
Fax (01227) 784482

Victorian house with large, elegant en-suite rooms, 6 minutes' walk to town centre. 5 minutes to BR Canterbury East station. Car park and garage available.
Bedrooms: 1 single, 2 double, 1 twin, 1 family room
Bathrooms: 4 private, 2 public

Bed & breakfast

per night:	£min	£max
Single	20.00	24.00
Double	40.00	46.00

Parking for 9
Cards accepted: Access, Visa, Switch/Delta

The Corner House ⋔

Listed

113 Whitstable Road, Canterbury
CT2 8EF
☎ (01227) 761352
Just a few minutes' walking distance from city, university, shops and restaurants. Spacious family house and friendly hospitality.
Bedrooms: 1 double, 2 twin
Bathrooms: 2 public

Bed & breakfast

per night:	£min	£max
Double	30.00	36.00

Parking for 4

Crossways

Field Way, Sturry, Canterbury
CT2 0BH
☎ (01227) 711059
Small, family-run early Victorian home, 3 miles from Canterbury on A28 Margate road. On main bus and rail routes.
Bedrooms: 1 single, 1 double, 1 twin
Bathrooms: 1 public, 1 private shower

Bed & breakfast

per night:	£min	£max
Single	15.00	18.00
Double	30.00	36.00

Parking for 6

The Farmhouse

HIGHLY COMMENDED

Upper Mystole Park Farm, Pennypot Lane, Mystole, Canterbury CT4 7BT
☎ (01227) 730589
90-acre fruit farm. Modern farmhouse in the heart of Kent and with magnificent views. Set between historic Canterbury and beautiful Chilham (A28). Dover 25 minutes. Good home cooking.
Bedrooms: 2 double, 1 twin
Bathrooms: 3 private

Bed & breakfast

per night:	£min	£max
Single	18.00	20.00
Double	34.00	38.00

Half board

per person:	£min	£max
Daily	26.00	46.00
Weekly	175.00	315.00

Evening meal 1830 (last orders 2000)
Parking for 6

Lindens Guest House

Listed COMMENDED

38b St. Dunstans Street, Canterbury
CT2 8BY
☎ (01227) 462339
Victorian house offering high standard of service and cleanliness, 5 minutes' walk from city centre. Full English breakfast. Private car park at rear.
Bedrooms: 2 double, 1 twin
Bathrooms: 1 private, 2 private showers

Bed & breakfast

per night:	£min	£max
Single	18.00	23.00
Double	32.00	38.00

Parking for 4

Magnolia House ⋔

HIGHLY COMMENDED

36 St Dunstans Terrace, Canterbury
CT2 8AX
☎ (01227) 765121 & Mobile 0585 595970
Fax (01227) 765121

Georgian house in attractive city street. Close to university, gardens, river and city centre. Very quiet house within a walled garden, ideal for guests to relax in. Four-poster suite available.
Bedrooms: 1 single, 4 double, 2 twin
Bathrooms: 7 private

Bed & breakfast

per night:	£min	£max
Single	36.00	45.00
Double	50.00	80.00

Half board

per person:	£min	£max
Daily	40.00	55.00

Evening meal 1800 (last orders 1900)
Parking for 4
Cards accepted: Access, Visa, Amex, Switch/Delta

Old House ⋔

Listed

Garlinge Green, Canterbury CT4 5RT
☎ (01227) 700284

Charming Grade II listed 16th C cottage in tranquil 1.5 acre garden, on the downs in Area of Outstanding Natural Beauty. Antiques, log fire, beams, croquet. Convenient for Canterbury and Channel ports.
Bedrooms: 2 double
Bathrooms: 1 private, 1 public

Bed & breakfast

per night:	£min	£max
Single	20.00	30.00
Double	35.00	45.00

Parking for 2

Old Stone House ⋔

Listed COMMENDED

The Green, Wickhambreaux, Canterbury CT3 1RQ
☎ (01227) 728591

One of the oldest houses in Kent, parts dating from 12th C. Once the home of Joan Plantagenet, wife of the Black Prince. Ten minutes east of Canterbury, 30 minutes from Folkestone and Dover.
Bedrooms: 1 single, 2 double, 1 twin
Bathrooms: 2 private, 1 public
Bed & breakfast

per night:	£min	£max
Single	18.00	25.00
Double	36.00	40.00

Parking for 4

Oriel Lodge ᴹ
HIGHLY COMMENDED
3 Queens Avenue, Canterbury
CT2 8AY
☎ (01227) 462845
Edwardian house in residential area near city centre. Clean, well-furnished rooms, lounge area with log fire. Private parking. Smoking in lounge area only.
Bedrooms: 1 single, 3 double, 1 twin, 1 triple
Bathrooms: 2 private, 2 public
Bed & breakfast

per night:	£min	£max
Single	20.00	26.00
Double	35.00	55.00

Parking for 6
Cards accepted: Visa

Pointers Hotel ᴹ
COMMENDED
1 London Road, Canterbury CT2 8LR
☎ (01227) 456846
Fax (01227) 831131

Family-run Georgian hotel close to city centre, cathedral and university.
Bedrooms: 1 single, 6 double, 2 twin, 2 triple, 1 family room
Bathrooms: 12 private
Bed & breakfast

per night:	£min	£max
Single	35.00	40.00
Double	45.00	58.00

Half board

per person:	£min	£max
Daily	38.00	48.00
Weekly	266.00	280.00

Evening meal 1930 (last orders 2030)
Parking for 10
Cards accepted: Access, Visa, Diners, Amex

St Stephens Guest House ᴹ
Listed   COMMENDED
100 St Stephens Road, Canterbury
CT2 7JL
☎ (01227) 767644
Mock-Tudor house set in attractive garden within easy walking distance of city centre and cathedral. Colour TV in rooms. Car park.
Bedrooms: 3 single, 8 double, 1 twin
Bathrooms: 4 private, 3 public
Bed & breakfast

per night:	£min	£max
Single	20.00	27.00
Double	35.00	44.00

Parking for 10
Cards accepted: Access, Visa

Thanington Hotel ᴹ
HIGHLY COMMENDED
140 Wincheap, Canterbury CT1 3RY
☎ (01227) 453227
Fax (01227) 453225

Lovely bed and breakfast hotel close to city centre. Indoor pool, snooker room, bar. 30 minutes' drive Dover and Channel Tunnel.
Bedrooms: 5 double, 3 twin, 2 family rooms
Bathrooms: 10 private
Bed & breakfast

per night:	£min	£max
Single	40.00	48.00
Double	58.00	64.00

Parking for 12
Cards accepted: Access, Visa, Diners, Amex

Well House
The Green, Chartham, Canterbury
CT4 7JW
☎ (01227) 738762
In a very quiet position, on village green next to 15th C church. Just off A28, 2 miles from Canterbury.
Bedrooms: 1 double, 1 twin
Bathrooms: 2 private
Bed & breakfast

per night:	£min	£max
Single	20.00	20.00
Double	30.00	30.00

Parking for 2

Wingham Well Farmhouse ᴹ
Listed   COMMENDED
Wingham, Canterbury CT3 1NW
☎ (01227) 720253
15th C half-timbered farmhouse, listed Grade II, on 160-acre arable farm. Off

A257 between Canterbury and Sandwich. Channel ports and tunnel 30 minutes' drive.
Bedrooms: 1 double, 1 twin
Bathrooms: 2 private
Bed & breakfast

per night:	£min	£max
Single	18.50	22.50
Double	40.00	44.00

Parking for 4

Yorke Lodge ᴹ
COMMENDED
50 London Road, Canterbury CT2 8LF
☎ (01227) 451243
Fax (01227) 462006
Spacious, elegant Victorian town house close to city centre. Relax and enjoy a special bed and breakfast.
Bedrooms: 1 single, 4 double
Bathrooms: 5 private
Bed & breakfast

per night:	£min	£max
Single	24.00	30.00
Double	40.00	45.00

Parking for 4
Cards accepted: Access, Visa, Amex

CHICHESTER

West Sussex
Map ref 2C3

The county town of West Sussex with a beautiful Norman cathedral. Noted for its Georgian architecture but also has modern buildings like the Festival Theatre. Surrounded by places of interest, including Fishbourne Roman Palace and Weald and Downland Open-Air Museum.
Tourist Information Centre
☎ *(01243) 775888*

Hedgehogs
Listed
45 Whyke Lane, Chichester PO19 2JT
☎ (01243) 780022
About half-a-mile from city centre, bus/railway stations and theatre. Secluded garden, TV lounge. Parking. Weekly terms available. Cyclists and hikers welcome. No smoking.
Bedrooms: 2 double, 1 twin
Bathrooms: 2 public
Bed & breakfast

per night:	£min	£max
Single	21.00	23.00
Double	32.00	36.00

Parking for 4

Meadow Corner ᴹ
Listed
The Street, Boxgrove, Chichester
PO18 0DY
☎ (01243) 774134

Continued ▶

CHICHESTER

Continued

Comfortable accommodation and excellent breakfast in family home, in attractive village 3 miles east of Chichester. Well placed for all local amenities and countryside.
Bedrooms: 1 single, 1 twin; suite available
Bathrooms: 2 private, 2 public

Bed & breakfast

per night:	£min	£max
Single	16.00	18.00
Double	36.00	40.00

Parking for 3

Stanes Farm

Hares Lane, Funtington, Chichester PO18 9DW
☎ Bosham (01243) 575558
Fax (01243) 575701
Comfortable accommodation in peaceful secluded family home with large garden, situated at foot of the South Downs, three quarters of a mile north of Funtington.
Bedrooms: 1 double, 1 twin
Bathrooms: 1 public

Bed & breakfast

per night:	£min	£max
Double	36.00	36.00

Parking for 6

CHIDDINGSTONE

Kent
Map ref 2D2

Pleasant village of 16th and 17th C, preserved by the National Trust, with an 18th C "castle" and attractive Tudor inn.

Hoath Holidays

Listed **APPROVED**

Hoath House, Chiddingstone Hoath, Edenbridge TN8 7DB
☎ Cowden (01342) 850362
Tudor family house with beamed and panelled rooms and extensive gardens. Convenient for Chartwell, Hever, Penshurst, Gatwick and London.
Bedrooms: 2 twin
Bathrooms: 2 private, 1 public

Bed & breakfast

per night:	£min	£max
Single	19.50	23.00
Double	39.00	46.00

Parking for 8

We advise you to confirm your booking in writing.

CHILHAM

Kent
Map ref 3B3

Extremely pretty village of mostly Tudor and Jacobean houses. The village rises to the spacious square with the castle and the 15th C church.

The Woolpack Inn

COMMENDED

High Street, Chilham, Canterbury CT4 8DL
☎ Canterbury (01227) 730208 & 730351
Fax (01227) 731053
Ancient inn, c 1422, with inglenook fireplaces and oak-beamed restaurant, in picturesque Chilham. Regional specialities, locally brewed ales. Halfboard daily prices are for a minimum 2-night stay.
Bedrooms: 7 double, 3 twin, 3 family rooms; suites available
Bathrooms: 13 private

Bed & breakfast

per night:	£min	£max
Single	37.50	39.50
Double	47.50	49.50

Half board

per person:	£min	£max
Daily	37.50	39.50
Weekly	262.50	276.50

Lunch available
Evening meal 1900 (last orders 2130)
Parking for 30
Cards accepted: Access, Visa, Amex, Switch/Delta

CLIFTONVILLE

Kent

See under Margate

CRANBROOK

Kent
Map ref 3B4

Old town, a centre for the weaving industry in the 15th C. The 72-ft high Union Mill is a 3-storey windmill, still in working order.

Tolehurst Barn

COMMENDED

Cranbrook Road, Frittenden, Cranbrook TN17 2BP
☎ (01580) 714385

Converted 17th C beamed barn in farmland - quiet and rural, all modern conveniences. On A229, convenient for the heart of Kent and places of historic interest. Only 5 minutes from Sissinghurst. Languages spoken.
Bedrooms: 2 double, 1 twin
Bathrooms: 3 private

Bed & breakfast

per night:	£min	£max
Single	15.00	17.50
Double	30.00	35.00

Half board

per person:	£min	£max
Daily	23.00	25.50
Weekly	150.00	170.00

Evening meal 1900 (last orders 2100)
Parking for 6

The White Horse Inn

High Street, Cranbrook TN17 3EX
☎ (01580) 712615
Victorian public house and restaurant in the centre of the smallest town in Kent, once the "capital" of the Weald.
Bedrooms: 1 single, 1 twin, 1 triple
Bathrooms: 1 public

Bed & breakfast

per night:	£min	£max
Single	24.00	
Double	34.00	

Half board

per person:	£min	£max
Daily	23.00	36.00
Weekly	138.00	216.00

Lunch available
Evening meal 1830 (last orders 2130)
Parking for 12
Cards accepted: Access, Visa

CRANLEIGH

Surrey
Map ref 2D2

White Hart Hotel

Listed **APPROVED**

Ewhurst Road, Cranleigh GU6 7AE
☎ (01483) 268647
Bed and breakfast in country village pub. En-suite facilities, satellite TV, lunch/evening meals available. 10 miles south of Guildford, off A281. Brochure available.
Bedrooms: 1 single, 5 double, 4 twin, 1 triple
Bathrooms: 11 private, 3 public

Bed & breakfast

per night:	£min	£max
Single	25.54	25.54
Double	39.86	39.86

Lunch available
Evening meal 1800 (last orders 2300)
Parking for 20

Cards accepted: Access, Visa, Switch/ Delta
🐴 ☐ ☕ ☏ 🔒 [S] 🚿 [TV] ◐ ▥ ⊜ 🚗 ⊤20 ● ⚑ ⁄ ✿ 🏛

CRAWLEY

West Sussex
Map ref 2D2

One of the first New Towns built after World War II, but it also has some old buildings. Set in magnificent wooded countryside.

Caprice Guest House 𝐀

Listed COMMENDED

Bonnetts Lane, Ifield, Crawley RH11 0NY
☎ (01293) 528620
Small, friendly, family-run guesthouse surrounded by farmland and close to all amenities. 10 minutes south of Gatwick Airport.
Bedrooms: 1 double, 2 twin
Bathrooms: 1 private, 1 public

Bed & breakfast per night:	£min	£max
Single	25.00	35.00
Double	35.00	45.00

Parking for 6
Cards accepted: Access, Visa, Amex
🐴 ♿ ⛽ ☐ ☕ [UL] [S] 🚭 🚿 [TV] ▥ 🚗 ✿ ✈ 🐕 [T]

The Manor House 𝐀

👑👑 COMMENDED

Bonnetts Lane, Ifield, Crawley RH11 0NY
☎ (01293) 510000 & 512298
100-year-old manor house in pleasant rural surroundings on Gatwick's doorstep. Family-run establishment offering comfortable and spacious accommodation.
Bedrooms: 1 single, 1 double, 2 twin, 1 family room
Bathrooms: 5 private, 1 public

Bed & breakfast per night:	£min	£max
Single	17.50	35.00
Double	35.00	40.00

Parking for 25
Cards accepted: Access, Visa
🐴 ☰ ☐ ☕ [UL] 🚭 ▥ 🚗 ✿ ✈ 🐕 [SP] [T]

The symbol ⊛ within an entry indicates participation in the Welcome Host programme – a nationally recognised customer care initiative which aims to promote the highest standards of service and a warm welcome for all visitors.

DEAL

Kent
Map ref 3C4

Coastal town and popular holiday resort. Deal Castle was built by Henry VIII as a fort and the museum is devoted to finds excavated in the area. Also the Time-Ball Tower museum. Angling available from both beach and pier.
Tourist Information Centre
☎ (01304) 369576

Hardicot Guest House

👑👑 COMMENDED

Kingsdown Road, Walmer, Deal CT14 8AW
☎ (01304) 373867

Large, quiet, detached Victorian house with Channel views and secluded garden. Ideal for sea fishing, cliff walks and golfing.
Bedrooms: 1 double, 2 twin
Bathrooms: 3 private

Bed & breakfast per night:	£min	£max
Single	17.00	20.00
Double	34.00	40.00

Parking for 4
🐴 5 ☕ [UL] 🔒 [S] 🚭 🚿 [TV] ▥ 🚗 ✿ ✈ 🐕 [OAP] [SP] [T]

DORKING

Surrey
Map ref 2D2

Ancient market town and a good centre for walking, delightfully set between Box Hill and the Downs.

Bulmer Farm

👑👑

Holmbury St Mary, Dorking RH5 6LG
☎ (01306) 730210
30-acre beef farm. 17th C character farmhouse with beams and inglenook fireplace, in the Surrey hills. Choice of twin rooms in the house or double/twin en-suite rooms in tastefully converted barn adjoining the house. Village is 5 miles from Dorking.
Bedrooms: 3 double, 5 twin
Bathrooms: 5 private, 2 public

Bed & breakfast per night:	£min	£max
Single	18.00	30.00
Double	36.00	40.00

Parking for 12
🐴 12 ⛽ ☕ [UL] [S] 🚭 [TV] ▥ 🚗 ⊤12 ✿ ✈ 🐕 🏛

Crossways Farm

👑👑

Raikes Lane, Abinger Hammer, Dorking RH5 6PZ
☎ (01306) 730173
200-acre arable & livestock farm. 17th C listed farmhouse in a small village south-west of Dorking. Good centre for London, the South East and airports. Large, comfortable rooms.
Bedrooms: 1 double, 1 family room
Bathrooms: 1 private, 1 public

Bed & breakfast per night:	£min	£max
Single	21.00	25.00
Double	34.00	38.00

Parking for 3
🐴 ☕ [UL] 🔒 🚭 [TV] ▥ 🚗 ∪ ✿ ✈ 🐕 🏛

Mark Ash

Listed

Abinger Common, Dorking RH5 6JA
☎ (01306) 731326
Victorian house in lovely garden opposite village green. Area of Outstanding Natural Beauty. One mile off A25. Dorking 4 miles, Guildford 8 miles. Convenient for Gatwick Airport.
Bedrooms: 1 single, 1 double, 1 twin
Bathrooms: 2 public

Bed & breakfast per night:	£min	£max
Single	20.00	25.00
Double	40.00	40.00

Parking for 4
Open March-November
🐴 ☰ ☐ ☕ ☏ [UL] 🚭 🚿 [TV] ▥ 🚗 ● ⁄ ⚲ ✿ ✈ 🐕

Steyning Cottage

Listed

Horsham Road, South Holmwood, Dorking RH5 4NE
☎ (01306) 888481
Detached tile-hung house adjacent to A24 and within walking distance of Leith Hill. Gatwick Airport approximately 20 minutes away, Heathrow 45 minutes. French spoken.
Bedrooms: 1 single, 2 twin
Bathrooms: 1 public

Bed & breakfast per night:	£min	£max
Single	15.00	20.00
Double	28.00	34.00
Half board per person:	**£min**	**£max**
Daily	23.00	28.00
Weekly	105.00	206.00

Evening meal 1900 (last orders 2000)
Parking for 4
🐴 ♿ [UL] 🔒 [TV] ▥ 🚗 🐕

The Volunteer 𝐀

Listed

Water Lane, Sutton Abinger, Dorking RH4 6PR
☎ (01306) 730798
17th C picturesque building set in rural hamlet.

Continued ▶

DORKING

Continued

Bedrooms: 1 double, 2 twin
Bathrooms: 1 public

Bed & breakfast

per night:	£min	£max
Single	20.00	25.00
Double	35.00	40.00

Half board

per person:	£min	£max
Daily	30.00	35.00
Weekly	150.00	200.00

Lunch available
Evening meal 1830 (last orders 2130)
Parking for 30
Cards accepted: Access, Visa

🛏 12 🕯 ♿ 🅿 Ⓢ ⚡ 🍴 Ⓤ ▸ ❀ ✕ 🐾 🎣

The Waltons

Listed

5 Rose Hill, Dorking RH4 2EG
☎ (01306) 883127
*House retains all its period features.
Central location with beautiful views.
Surrounded by National Trust land.
Friendly atmosphere.*
Bedrooms: 1 double, 1 twin
Bathrooms: 2 public

Bed & breakfast

per night:	£min	£max
Single	17.50	20.00
Double	30.00	35.00

Half board

per person:	£min	£max
Daily	25.50	28.00
Weekly	178.50	196.00

Evening meal 1800 (last orders 2100)
Parking for 3

🛏 ♨ 📺 🖥 🔌 📵 ♿ Ⓢ ⚡ 🍴 📺 �Ⅲ 🅿 ♦ ❀ 🐾 🎣

DOVER

Kent
Map ref 3C4

A Cinque Port and busiest
passenger port in the world. Still a
historic town and seaside resort
beside the famous White Cliffs.
The White Cliffs Experience
attraction traces the town's history
through the Roman, Saxon,
Norman and Victorian periods.
Tourist Information Centre
☎ *(01304) 205108*

Cliffe Tavern Hotel

♛♛♛

High Street, St-Margarets-at-Cliffe,
Dover CT15 6AT
☎ (01304) 852749 & 852400
Fax (01304) 852400
*Ancient, privately-run village inn
serving the best of English/French
dishes, fine wines and traditional ales,
with en-suite accommodation.*
Bedrooms: 3 single, 5 double, 1 twin,
1 triple, 2 family rooms
Bathrooms: 12 private

Bed & breakfast

per night:	£min	£max
Single	31.90	41.90
Double	44.80	54.80

Lunch available
Evening meal 1900 (last orders 2130)
Parking for 40
Cards accepted: Access, Visa, Switch/
Delta

🛏 ♨ 📵 ♿ ♦ Ⓢ ⚡ Ⅲ 🅿 🍴 Ⓤ ❀ 🎣 ⋈
Ⓢ🅿 🎣

Coldred Court Farm ⚑

♛♛♛ **HIGHLY COMMENDED**

Church Road, Coldred, Dover
CT15 5AQ
☎ (01304) 830816
Fax (01304) 830816
*7-acre mixed farm. 1620 farmhouse full
of old world charm, with modern
facilities. Situated 1 mile from the A2,
10 minutes from Dover.*
Bedrooms: 2 double, 1 twin
Bathrooms: 3 private

Bed & breakfast

per night:	£min	£max
Single	30.00	45.00
Double	40.00	50.00

Half board

per person:	£min	£max
Daily	42.50	57.50
Weekly	270.00	370.00

Evening meal 1800 (last orders 2030)
Parking for 13

🛏 ♨ 📵 ♿ ♦ 🖥 Ⓤ ♦ ♿ Ⓢ ⚡ 📺 📺 Ⅲ 🅿 🍴
♦ ❀ ✕ 🐾 Ⓢ🅿 🎣 Ⓣ

Elmo Guest House ⚑

♛

120 Folkestone Road, Dover
CT17 9SP
☎ (01304) 206236
*Conveniently situated for ferries and
Hoverport terminals and 10 minutes'
drive to Channel Tunnel. Within easy
reach of town centre and railway
station. Overnight stops our speciality.*
Bedrooms: 1 single, 2 double, 1 triple,
1 family room
Bathrooms: 2 public

Bed & breakfast

per night:	£min	£max
Single	12.00	16.00
Double	24.00	30.00

Parking for 7

🛏 📵 ♦ Ⅲ 📺 Ⅲ 🅿 ✕ 🐾 🅿 Ⓢ🅿 Ⓣ

Esther House

Listed **COMMENDED**

55 Barton Road, Dover CT16 2NF
☎ (01304) 241332
Fax (01304) 241332
*Non-smoking B and B with warm
Christian atmosphere. Close to ferries
and town centre. Ideal base for touring
and 15 minutes from Channel Tunnel.
Early breakfasts. Evening meals by
arrangement. Special and weekend
breaks from £11 per person per night.*
Bedrooms: 1 single, 1 twin, 1 triple
Bathrooms: 1 public

Bed & breakfast

per night:	£min	£max
Single	13.00	18.00
Double	26.00	34.00

Evening meal 1830 (last orders 1930)

🛏 📵 ♦ ♿ Ⓢ 🅿 ⚡ ✕ Ⅲ 🅿 ✕ 🐾 📺 Ⓢ🅿

The Norman Guest House

Listed

75 Folkestone Road, Dover CT17 9RZ
☎ (01304) 207803
*Opposite Dover Priory railway station
and close to shops, ferries, hovercraft
ports and all amenities. Only 15
minutes' drive to Eurotunnel.*
Bedrooms: 2 double, 2 twin, 1 triple,
2 family rooms
Bathrooms: 2 public

Bed & breakfast

per night:	£min	£max
Single	12.00	16.00
Double	24.00	32.00

Parking for 6

🛏 📵 ♦ ♿ Ⅲ Ⅲ 🅿 ✕ 🐾

Owler Lodge ⚑

♛♛♛ **HIGHLY COMMENDED**

Alkham Valley Road, Alkham, Dover
CT15 7BX
☎ (01304) 826375
*Small family run guesthouse with
inglenook and beams. In the middle of
the village of Alkham on B2060 between
Dover and Folkestone. 3 miles from
Channel Tunnel, 4 miles from Dover
Docks.*
Bedrooms: 2 double, 1 twin
Bathrooms: 3 private

Bed & breakfast

per night:	£min	£max
Single	25.00	30.00
Double	38.00	42.00

Half board

per person:	£min	£max
Daily	28.00	30.00
Weekly	186.00	200.00

Evening meal 1800 (last orders 2100)
Parking for 6

🛏 📵 ♦ ♿ 🖥 ⚡ ♿ ✕ 📺 📺 Ⅲ 🅿 ❀ ✕ 🐾 Ⓢ🅿

Tower Guest House

♛♛

98 Priory Hill, Dover CT17 0AD
☎ (01304) 208212
*Charmingly converted water tower in
quiet surroundings. Non-smoking
establishment. 6 minutes' drive to docks,
12 minutes to Channel Tunnel. Lock-up
garages available.*
Bedrooms: 1 double, 2 twin, 1 triple,
1 family room
Bathrooms: 3 private, 1 public

Bed & breakfast

per night:	£min	£max
Double	30.00	40.00

Parking for 2

🛏 📵 ♦ ♿ 🖥 Ⅲ 🅿 ❀ ✕ 🐾 Ⓢ🅿 🎣 Ⓣ

Woodpeckers

Chapel Lane, St-Margarets-at-Cliffe,
Dover CT15 6BQ
☎ (01304) 852761

*10 minutes from Dover docks, in the
quiet village of St Margarets, behind the
village pond. En-suite facilities.*
Bedrooms: 1 twin, 1 triple
Bathrooms: 2 private
Bed & breakfast

per night:	£min	£max
Single	20.00	20.00
Double	34.00	34.00

Parking for 4

EAST DEAN

East Sussex
Map ref 2D3

Pretty village on a green near
Friston Forest and Birling Gap.

Birling Gap Hotel

APPROVED

East Dean, Eastbourne BN20 0AB
☎ Eastbourne (01323) 423197
Fax (01323) 423030

*Magnificent Seven Sisters clifftop
position, with views of country, sea,
beach. Superb downland walks. Old
world "Thatched Bar" and "Oak Room
Restaurant". Coffee shop and games
room, function and conference suite.*
Bedrooms: 1 single, 5 double, 2 twin,
2 triple
Bathrooms: 10 private, 1 public
Half board

per person:	£min	£max
Weekly	365.00	460.00

Lunch available
Parking for 100
Cards accepted: Access, Visa, Diners,
Amex, Switch/Delta

Please mention this guide
when making a booking.

EAST GRINSTEAD

West Sussex
Map ref 2D2

A number of fine old houses stand
in the High Street, one of which is
Sackville College, founded in 1609.

Hammerwood Park

COMMENDED

East Grinstead RH19 3QE
☎ (01342) 850594
Fax (01342) 850864

*Built in 1792 by Latrobe who was
responsible for the White House,
Washington DC. Originally a hunting
lodge, now a hotel in magnificent
parkland.*
Bedrooms: 2 double
Bathrooms: 2 private
Bed & breakfast

per night:	£min	£max
Single	25.00	27.00
Double	54.00	54.00

Parking for 60
Open April-October

Middle House Cookhams

COMMENDED

Sharpthorne, East Grinstead
RH19 4HU
☎ (01342) 810566
*Central portion of large 100-year-old
country house, with open southerly
aspect. In village south of East
Grinstead.*
Bedrooms: 1 single, 1 double, 1 twin
Bathrooms: 2 private, 1 public
Bed & breakfast

per night:	£min	£max
Single	20.00	25.00
Double	40.00	50.00

Parking for 4

White Horse Inn

APPROVED

Holtye, Cowden, Edenbridge, Kent
TN8 7ED
☎ Cowden (01342) 850640
Fax (01342) 850032

---

*Built in the 13th C. Refurbished with
every modern facility yet retaining its
old world charm. New restaurant,
beamed and with oak furniture. Bar has
underwater fish tank with koi carp.
Every assistance for the disabled.*
Bedrooms: 7 double, 1 twin
Bathrooms: 8 private
Bed & breakfast

per night:	£min	£max
Single	35.00	40.00
Double	45.00	50.00

Lunch available
Evening meal 1800 (last orders 2200)
Parking for 40
Cards accepted: Access, Visa, Amex,
Switch/Delta

EASTBOURNE

East Sussex
Map ref 3B4

One of the finest, most elegant
resorts on the south-east coast
situated beside Beachy Head.
Long promenade, plenty of
gardens, theatres, Towner Art
Gallery, "How We Lived Then"
museum of shops and social
history.
Tourist Information Centre
☎ *(01323) 411400*

Bay Lodge Hotel

COMMENDED

61-62 Royal Parade, Eastbourne
BN22 7AQ
☎ (01323) 732515
Fax (01323) 735009
*Small seafront hotel opposite Redoubt
Gardens, close to bowling greens and
entertainments. Large sun-lounge. All
double/twin bedrooms are en-suite.
Non-smokers' lounge.*
Bedrooms: 3 single, 5 double, 4 twin
Bathrooms: 9 private, 2 public
Bed & breakfast

per night:	£min	£max
Single	20.00	25.00
Double	39.00	46.00

Half board

per person:	£min	£max
Daily	28.00	35.00
Weekly	169.00	209.00

Evening meal 1800 (last orders 1800)
Open March-October and Christmas
Cards accepted: Access, Visa

Chalk Farm Hotel

COMMENDED

Coopers Hill, Willingdon, Eastbourne
BN20 9JD
☎ (01323) 503800
Fax (01323) 520331
*A converted 17th C farmhouse set in 2
acres, on the edge of the Sussex Downs,
only a few miles from Eastbourne.*

Continued ▶

EASTBOURNE

Continued

Bedrooms: 1 single, 5 double, 1 twin,
2 triple
Bathrooms: 6 private, 1 public

Bed & breakfast

per night:	£min	£max
Single	30.00	37.00
Double	43.00	49.50

Lunch available
Evening meal 1830 (last orders 2100)
Parking for 20
Cards accepted: Access, Visa, Diners,
Amex

🛏 📞 ☐ ♨ 🛎 🗲 🎱 📺 Ⅲ 🚗 ♈70 ✿ 🐾
⊙ₐₚ 🏳 SP ⌂ T

ELHAM

Kent
Map ref 3B4

In the Nailbourne Valley on the
chalk downlands, this large village
has an outstanding collection of
old houses. Abbot's Fireside, built
in 1614, has a timbered upper
storey resting on brackets carved
into figures.

Tye
Listed

Collards Lane, Elham, Canterbury
CT4 6UF
☎ (01303) 840271
Fax (01303) 840271
*Country house, less than a mile from
the village, beautifully situated on top of
a hill with lovely views and walks. Very
quiet.*
Bedrooms: 1 single, 2 twin
Bathrooms: 1 public

Bed & breakfast

per night:	£min	£max
Single	17.00	17.00
Double	34.00	34.00

Parking for 6

🛏 10 🎱 🛎 ⓘ 🗲 🎱 📺 Ⅲ ✿ ✕ 🐾

ENGLEFIELD GREEN

Surrey
Map ref 2D2

Suburban village 3 miles west of
Staines.

4 Fircroft ⚠
Listed

Bagshot Road, Englefield Green,
Egham TW20 0RS
☎ Egham (01784) 432893
*Detached house, 10 minutes from
Windsor, 15 minutes from M25, near
Wentworth Golf Club. Convenient for
trains to Waterloo. Also near Ascot and
Saville Gardens.*
Bedrooms: 1 single, 1 twin
Bathrooms: 1 public

Bed & breakfast

per night:	£min	£max
Single	17.00	17.00
Double	32.00	32.00

Parking for 3

🛏 📭 ☐ ♨ 🛎 📺 Ⅲ ✕ 🐾

ETCHINGHAM

East Sussex
Map ref 3B4

Pleasant village at the confluence
of the Rivers Rother and Dudwell,
with a fine old church, once
surrounded by a moat, considered
the best 14th C church in the
county.

King Johns Lodge ⚠
Listed

Sheepstreet Lane, Etchingham
TN19 7AZ
☎ (01580) 819232
Fax (01580) 819127
*Listed Jacobean house with National
Garden Scheme garden. Take Church
lane off A265 by Etchingham church.
Continue into Sheepstreet Lane, King
Johns is 1 mile on the left.*
Bedrooms: 1 single, 2 double, 1 twin
Bathrooms: 4 private

Bed & breakfast

per night:	£min	£max
Single	25.00	30.00
Double	45.00	50.00

Half board

per person:	£min	£max
Daily	40.00	45.00
Weekly	240.00	260.00

Evening meal 1930 (last orders 2030)
Parking for 12

🛏 ♨ Ⅶ 🛏 📺 Ⅲ 🚗 ❧ ✿ ✕ 🐾 ⌂

FARNHAM

Surrey
Map ref 2C2

Town noted for its Georgian
houses. Willmer House (now a
museum) has a facade of cut and
moulded brick with fine carving
and panelling in the interior. The
12th C castle has been occupied
by Bishops of both Winchester and
Guildford.
Tourist Information Centre
☎ *(01252) 715109*

High Wray ⚠
Listed COMMENDED

73 Lodge Hill Road, Farnham
GU10 3RB
☎ (01252) 715589 & 724386
*Visitors welcome as family guests.
Gracious house with interesting garden.
Wing purpose built for disabled guests.
Home-grown vegetables and eggs.*
Bedrooms: 1 single, 2 twin
Bathrooms: 3 private, 1 public

Bed & breakfast

per night:	£min	£max
Single	16.00	16.00
Double	40.00	40.00

Half board

per person:	£min	£max
Daily	22.00	26.00
Weekly	142.80	168.00

Evening meal 1830 (last orders 2000)
Parking for 7

🛏 ♨ Ⅶ Ⅲ ⓘ S 🗲 📺 🚗 ♈ ✿ 🐾

FAVERSHAM

Kent
Map ref 3B3

Historic town, once a port, dating
back to prehistoric times. Abbey
Street has more than 50 listed
buildings. Roman and Anglo-Saxon
finds and other exhibits can be
seen in a museum in the Maison
Dieu at Ospringe. Fleur de Lis
Heritage Centre.
Tourist Information Centre
☎ *(01795) 534542*

Barnsfield ⚠
Listed

Hernhill, Faversham ME13 9JH
☎ Canterbury (01227) 750973 & Deal
(01304) 368550
*Listed Grade II country cottages, just off
A299, set in 3 acres of orchards, 6
miles from Canterbury.*
Bedrooms: 1 single, 2 double, 1 twin
Bathrooms: 1 private, 1 public

Bed & breakfast

per night:	£min	£max
Single	16.00	20.00
Double	28.00	40.00

Parking for 10
Cards accepted: Access, Visa

🛏 ⌘ ☐ ♨ Ⅶ ⓘ 🛏 📺 Ⅲ ✿ 🐾 ⌂

The Granary ⚠
🏆🏆 HIGHLY COMMENDED

Plumford Lane, Ospringe, Faversham
ME13 0DS
☎ (01795) 538416 & Mobile 0860
817713
Fax (01795) 538416
*Delightfully converted granary in
peaceful setting with large garden. Own
lounge with colour TV. Close to M2 and
Canterbury. Friendly welcome.*
Bedrooms: 1 double, 1 twin, 1 triple
Bathrooms: 3 private

Bed & breakfast

per night:	£min	£max
Single	25.00	30.00
Double	39.00	39.00

Parking for 8
Cards accepted: Access, Visa, Switch/
Delta

🛏 📭 ☐ ♨ Ⅶ S 🗲 🛏 📺 Ⅲ ✿ ✕ 🐾

Leaveland Court ⚠
🏆 HIGHLY COMMENDED

Leaveland, Faversham ME13 0NP
☎ Challock (01233) 740596

300-acre arable farm. Enchanting Grade II* listed 15th C timbered farmhouse in quiet rural setting adjacent to Leaveland church. 5 minutes from M2 Faversham, 20 minutes from Canterbury.
Bedrooms: 1 double, 2 twin
Bathrooms: 3 private, 1 public
Bed & breakfast

per night:	£min	£max
Single	20.00	25.00
Double	38.00	44.00

Evening meal 1830 (last orders 1800)
Parking for 6
Open February-November
Cards accepted: Access, Visa

Owens Court Farm
COMMENDED

Selling, Faversham ME13 9QN
☎ Canterbury (01227) 752247
Fax (01227) 752247
265-acre fruit farm. Comfortable Georgian farmhouse in quiet lane, 1 mile off A2. 3 miles from Faversham, 9 miles from Canterbury.
Bedrooms: 1 single, 1 twin, 1 triple
Bathrooms: 1 public
Bed & breakfast

per night:	£min	£max
Single	17.00	17.00
Double	34.00	34.00

Parking for 4
Open January-August, October-December

Preston Lea
HIGHLY COMMENDED

Canterbury Road, Faversham ME13 8XA
☎ (01795) 535266
Fax (01795) 533388

Beautiful, imposing Victorian house with turrets and other interesting features, set in large secluded grounds. Only 15 minutes from Canterbury and 30 minutes from Channel ports and Eurotunnel.
Bedrooms: 2 double, 1 twin
Bathrooms: 3 private
Bed & breakfast

per night:	£min	£max
Single	25.00	35.00
Double	40.00	60.00

Parking for 11
Cards accepted: Access, Visa

White Horse Inn
COMMENDED

Boughton, Faversham ME13 9AX
☎ Canterbury (01227) 751700 & 751343
Fax (01227) 751090
15th C coaching inn with oak beams and inglenook fireplaces. Freshly prepared regional specialities, locally brewed award-winning ales. Halfboard daily prices are for a minimum 2-night stay.
Bedrooms: 7 double, 4 twin, 2 triple; suites available
Bathrooms: 13 private
Bed & breakfast

per night:	£min	£max
Single	37.50	39.50
Double	47.50	49.50

Half board

per person:	£min	£max
Daily	37.50	39.50
Weekly	262.50	276.50

Lunch available
Evening meal 1900 (last orders 2130)
Parking for 50
Cards accepted: Access, Visa, Amex, Switch/Delta

FINDON
West Sussex
Map ref 2D3

Downland village well-known for its annual sheep fair and its racing stables. The ancient landmarks, Cissbury Ring and Chanctonbury Ring, and the South Downs Way are nearby.

Findon Tower
COMMENDED

Cross Lane, Findon, Worthing BN14 0UG
☎ (01903) 873870
Elegant Edwardian country house in large secluded garden. Spacious accommodation with en-suite facilities. Warm, friendly welcome, relaxed and peaceful atmosphere. Rural views, snooker room. Excellent selection of food in village restaurants and pubs.
Bedrooms: 2 double, 1 twin
Bathrooms: 3 private, 1 public
Bed & breakfast

per night:	£min	£max
Single	20.00	30.00
Double	35.00	45.00

Parking for 10

> The National Grading and Classification Scheme is explained in full at the back of this guide.

FOLKESTONE
Kent
Map ref 3C4

Popular resort and important cross-channel port. The town has a fine promenade, the Leas, from where orchestral concerts and other entertainments are presented. Horse-racing at Westenhanger.
Tourist Information Centre
☎ *(01303) 258594 or 270547 (Eurotunnel Exhibition Centre)*

Abbey House Hotel

5-6 Westbourne Gardens, off Sandgate Road, Folkestone CT20 2JA
☎ (01303) 255514
Fax (01303) 245098
Pleasant garden square location in residential West End, close to Leas Cliff Hall and bandstand. Easy access to ferry and Channel Tunnel. Unlimited street parking.
Bedrooms: 3 single, 2 double, 5 twin, 4 family rooms
Bathrooms: 3 private, 4 public
Bed & breakfast

per night:	£min	£max
Single	18.00	28.00
Double	35.00	45.00

Half board

per person:	£min	£max
Daily	28.00	38.00
Weekly	176.00	220.00

Evening meal 1830 (last orders 1930)
Cards accepted: Visa

FULKING
West Sussex
Map ref 2D3

Small, pretty village nestling on the north side of the South Downs near the route of the South Downs Way.

Downers Vineyard
Listed APPROVED

Clappers Lane, Fulking, Henfield BN5 9NH
☎ Brighton (01273) 857484 & Mobile 0850 122991
Fax (01273) 857068
18-acre vineyard & grazing farm. Quiet rural position, 1 mile north of the South Downs and Devil's Dyke, 8 miles from Brighton.
Bedrooms: 2 triple
Bathrooms: 2 public

Continued ▶

> We advise you to confirm your booking in writing.

FULKING

Continued

Bed & breakfast

per night:	£min	£max
Single	17.00	20.00
Double	30.00	35.00

Parking for 6

GATWICK AIRPORT

West Sussex

See under Crawley, East Grinstead, Horley, Horsham, Newdigate, Smallfield

GODALMING

Surrey
Map ref 2D2

Several old coaching inns are reminders that the town was once a staging point. The old Town Hall is now the local history museum. Charterhouse School moved here in 1872 and is dominated by the 150-ft Founder's Tower.

Fairfields

The Green, Elstead, Godalming
GU8 6DF
☎ Farnham (01252) 702345
High quality facilities in quiet modern detached house with 1 acre of grounds in centre of village. Excellent pub food nearby. Non-smokers only, please. Godalming 5 miles.
Bedrooms: 1 double, 2 twin
Bathrooms: 3 private
Bed & breakfast

per night:	£min	£max
Single	29.00	35.00
Double	32.00	39.50

Parking for 4

GOUDHURST

Kent
Map ref 3B4

Village on a hill surmounted by a square-towered church with fine views of orchards and hopfields. Achieved prosperity through weaving in the Middle Ages. Finchcocks houses a museum of historic keyboard instruments.

Mill House M

COMMENDED

Church Road, Goudhurst, Cranbrook
TN17 1BN
☎ (01580) 211703
16th C former mill with lots of history and a smugglers' tunnel. Beautiful grounds and views. Close to Sissinghurst, good base for exploring the Weald.

Bedrooms: 1 double, 1 family room
Bathrooms: 2 private
Bed & breakfast

per night:	£min	£max
Double	35.00	40.00

Parking for 6

GUILDFORD

Surrey
Map ref 2D2

Bustling town with many historic monuments, one of which is the Guildhall clock jutting out over the old High Street. The modern cathedral occupies a commanding position on Stag Hill.
Tourist Information Centre
☎ *(01483) 444333*

Beevers Farm

Listed

Chinthurst Lane, Bramley, Guildford
GU5 0DR
☎ (01483) 898764
In peaceful surroundings 2 miles from Guildford, near villages with pubs and restaurants. Convenient for Heathrow and Gatwick. Friendly atmosphere. Non-smokers only.
Bedrooms: 3 twin
Bathrooms: 1 public
Bed & breakfast

per night:	£min	£max
Single	20.00	20.00
Double	26.00	39.00

Parking for 10
Open February-November

HAILSHAM

East Sussex
Map ref 2D3

An important market town since Norman times and still one of the largest markets in Sussex. Two miles west, at Upper Dicker, is Michelham Priory, an Augustinian house founded in 1229.
Tourist Information Centre
☎ *(01323) 844426*

Sandy Bank M

COMMENDED

Old Road, Magham Down, Hailsham
BN27 1PW
☎ (01323) 842488
Fax (01323) 842488
Well-appointed en-suite rooms in recent development adjacent to cottage, plus one en-suite in cottage, in attractive Sussex countryside with easy access to Downs and sea. Ideal base for touring Sussex. Friendly atmosphere. Evening meals by prior arrangement.
Bedrooms: 3 twin
Bathrooms: 3 private

Bed & breakfast

per night:	£min	£max
Single	22.00	24.00
Double	40.00	45.00

Evening meal 1900 (last orders 2030)
Parking for 3

HARTFIELD

East Sussex
Map ref 2D2

Pleasant village in Ashdown Forest, the setting for A A Milne's "Winnie the Pooh" stories.

Stairs Farmhouse and Tea Room M

Listed COMMENDED

High Street, Hartfield TN7 4AB
☎ (01892) 770793
17th C modernised farmhouse with various period features, in picturesque village. Close to Pooh Bridge and Hever Castle. Views over open countryside. Home produced additive-free meals provided. Tea room and farm shop.
Bedrooms: 1 double, 1 twin
Bathrooms: 1 private, 2 public
Bed & breakfast

per night:	£min	£max
Single	25.00	35.00
Double	40.00	42.00

Half board

per person:	£min	£max
Daily	30.00	45.00

Lunch available
Evening meal 1800 (last orders 1930)
Parking for 16
Cards accepted: Access, Visa, Switch/Delta

HASLEMERE

Surrey
Map ref 2C2

Town set in hilly, wooded countryside, much of it in the keeping of the National Trust. Its attractions include the educational museum and the annual music festival.

Town House

Listed COMMENDED

High Street, Haslemere GU27 2JY
☎ (01428) 643310
Fax (01428) 641080
Period house in centre of quiet town. Panelled reception rooms, period furniture throughout. Easy walking to restaurants and pubs.
Bedrooms: 2 single, 1 double, 1 twin
Bathrooms: 2 private, 1 public

Bed & breakfast per night:	£min	£max
Single	20.00	22.00
Double	38.00	40.00

Parking for 3
Open February-December

⌂4 ♿♜ⓦ✂♨ⓉⓋ▥ ❦☼✗🚍⌂

HASTINGS

East Sussex
Map ref 3B4

Ancient town which became famous as the base from which William the Conqueror set out to fight the Battle of Hastings. Later became one of the Cinque Ports, now a leading resort. Castle, Hastings Embroidery inspired by the Bayeux Tapestry and Sea Life Centre.
Tourist Information Centre
☎ *(01424) 781111*

Eagle House Hotel ⋀
♛♛♛

12 Pevensey Road, St. Leonards-on-Sea, Hastings TN38 0JZ
☎ (01424) 430535 & 441273
Fax (01424) 437771

Large Victorian residence in its own grounds. Well placed for most local amenities and for visiting "1066" country.
Bedrooms: 14 double, 4 twin
Bathrooms: 18 private, 2 public

Bed & breakfast per night:	£min	£max
Single	31.60	31.60
Double	49.00	49.00

Half board per person:	£min	£max
Daily	50.55	50.55

Lunch available
Evening meal 1830 (last orders 2030)
Parking for 14
Cards accepted: Access, Visa, Diners, Amex

⌂5♿☎⌨⌂♜♨⌖♨▥ ⌂☰☼ ✗🚍

Tower House ⋀
♛♛♛ HIGHLY COMMENDED

28 Tower Road West, St Leonards-on-Sea, Hastings TN38 0RG
☎ (01424) 427217 & 423771
Elegant Victorian house situated half a mile from seafront. Pleasant gardens. Separate licensed bar leading to garden patio. Freshly-cooked meals. Ample parking.
Bedrooms: 1 single, 7 double, 2 twin
Bathrooms: 10 private

Bed & breakfast per night:	£min	£max
Single	25.00	35.00
Double	42.00	50.00

Half board per person:	£min	£max
Daily	36.50	46.50
Weekly	206.50	290.50

Evening meal 1800 (last orders 1900)
Cards accepted: Access, Visa, Diners, Amex

⌂⌨⌂♿♜⌖♨✂♨ⓉⓋ▥ ⌂☰14 ❦✗ ⌂▥ ⌂

HAYWARDS HEATH

West Sussex
Map ref 2D3

Busy market town and administrative centre of mid-Sussex, with interesting old buildings and a modern shopping centre.

The Anchorhold ⋀
Listed APPROVED

35 Paddock Hall Road, Haywards Heath RH16 1HN
☎ (01444) 452468
Fax (01444) 453350
Religious community providing bed and breakfast in a separate cottage within the grounds. Main line station is a quarter of a mile away.
Bedrooms: 2 single, 2 twin
Bathrooms: 1 public

Bed & breakfast per night:	£min	£max
Single	16.00	
Double	32.00	

Parking for 3

⌂♿⌨⌂♜ⓦ Ⓢ✂♨▥ ⌂☰✗🚍 SP ⌂

HENFIELD

West Sussex
Map ref 2D3

In flat or gently sloping countryside with views to the Downs. Early English church with a fine Perpendicular tower.

Lyndhurst
Listed

38 Broomfield Road, Henfield BN5 9UA
☎ (01273) 494054
Elegant Victorian house, decorated in traditional country style, offering family, double and single rooms. Convenient for coast and Gatwick Airport.
Bedrooms: 1 single, 1 double, 1 triple
Bathrooms: 3 public

Bed & breakfast per night:	£min	£max
Single	17.50	20.00
Double	35.00	40.00

Half board per person:	£min	£max
Daily	24.00	26.50
Weekly	160.00	175.00

Evening meal 1600 (last orders 2200)
Parking for 7

⌂⌨⌂♿ⓦ⌂Ⓢ✂ⓉⓋ▥ ⌂☰❦✗🚍⌂

HERSTMONCEUX

East Sussex
Map ref 3B4

Pleasant village noted for its woodcrafts and the beautiful 15th C moated Herstmonceux Castle (gardens only open to visitors).

The Stud Farm
♨♨ COMMENDED

Bodle Street Green, Herstmonceux, Hailsham BN27 4RJ
☎ (01323) 833201
Fax (01323) 833201
70-acre mixed farm. Upstairs, 2 bedrooms and bathroom let as one unit to party of 2, 3 or 4. Downstairs, twin-bedded en-suite room. Guests' sitting room and sunroom.
Bedrooms: 1 double, 2 twin
Bathrooms: 1 private, 1 public

Bed & breakfast per night:	£min	£max
Single	22.00	25.00
Double	34.00	38.00

Half board per person:	£min	£max
Daily	27.50	33.50
Weekly	178.50	213.50

Evening meal from 1830
Parking for 3

⌂♿⌨⌂♜⌂Ⓢ✂ⓉⓋ▥ ✗🚍

HOLLINGBOURNE

Kent
Map ref 3B3

Pleasant village near romantic Leeds Castle in the heart of orchard country at the foot of the North Downs. Some fine half-timbered houses and a flint and ragstone church.

Woodhouses ⋀
Listed

49 Eyhorne Street, Hollingbourne, Maidstone ME17 1TR
☎ Maidstone (01622) 880594
Interconnected listed cottages dating from 17th C, with inglenook fireplace and exposed wooden beams. Well-stocked cottage garden.
Bedrooms: 1 double, 2 twin
Bathrooms: 3 private

Continued ▶

HOLLINGBOURNE

Continued

Bed & breakfast

per night:	£min	£max
Single	17.50	18.50
Double	34.00	36.00

Evening meal 1800 (last orders 2000)
Parking for 4

🛇📭🔌🏠ℹ️🅂🏃‍♂️🛍️📺🛏️🚗🏃🦽🐾🏇

HORLEY

Surrey
Map ref 2D2

Town on the London to Brighton road, just north of Gatwick Airport, with an ancient parish church and 15th C inn.

Chalet Guest House ⋀

😁😁 COMMENDED

77 Massetts Road, Horley RH6 7EB
☎ (01293) 821666
Fax (01293) 821619
Comfortable modern guesthouse. Convenient for Gatwick Airport, motorways, railway station, local bus, shops, pubs and restaurants.
Bedrooms: 3 single, 1 double, 1 twin, 1 triple
Bathrooms: 5 private, 1 public

Bed & breakfast

per night:	£min	£max
Single	24.00	32.00
Double	42.00	42.00

Parking for 14
Cards accepted: Access, Visa

🛇🅂📭🗝️🔌🏠ℹ️🏃‍♂️🛍️📺🛏️🚗🏃🦽📞

The Lawn Guest House ⋀

😁😁 HIGHLY COMMENDED

30 Massetts Road, Horley RH6 7DE
☎ (01293) 775751
Fax (01293) 821803
Ideal for travellers using Gatwick. Pleasantly situated, few minutes' walk to town centre, pubs and restaurants. Good base for London and the south coast. Non-smokers only, please.
Bedrooms: 3 double, 4 twin, 1 family room
Bathrooms: 3 private, 2 public

Bed & breakfast

per night:	£min	£max
Double	35.00	42.00

Parking for 10
Cards accepted: Access, Visa, Diners, Amex

🛇📭🗝️🔌🏠ℹ️🏃‍♂️🛍️📺🛏️🚗🏃🦽📞

Prinsted Guest House

Listed

Oldfield Road, Horley RH6 7EP
☎ (01293) 785233
Detached Edwardian guesthouse in a quiet position, with spacious accommodation, including large family rooms. Close to Gatwick, London 30 minutes by train.

Bedrooms: 1 double, 2 twin, 1 triple, 2 family rooms
Bathrooms: 3 public, 1 private shower

Bed & breakfast

per night:	£min	£max
Single	27.00	37.00
Double	37.00	37.00

Parking for 10
Cards accepted: Amex

🛇🅂📭🗝️🔌🏠ℹ️🏃‍♂️🛍️📺🛏️🚗🏃🦽📞

Springwood Guest House ⋀

Listed APPROVED

58 Massetts Road, Horley RH6 7DS
☎ (01293) 775998
Elegant, detached Victorian house in pleasant residential road 1 mile from Gatwick Airport. Long-term car parking, courtesy transport. Five minutes from town centre, shops and pubs.
Bedrooms: 1 single, 1 double, 3 twin, 1 triple
Bathrooms: 1 private, 2 public

Bed & breakfast

per night:	£min	£max
Single	22.00	25.00
Double	34.00	42.00

Parking for 30

🛇📭🔌🗝️🔌🏠🛍️🚗🦽📞

HORSHAM

West Sussex
Map ref 2D2

Busy town with much modern development but still retaining its old character. The museum in Causeway House is devoted chiefly to local history and the agricultural life of the county.
Tourist Information Centre
☎ *(01403) 211661*

Brookfield Farm Hotel ⋀

Winterpit Lane, Plummers Plain, Horsham RH13 6LU
☎ Lower Beeding (01403) 891645 & 891568
Fax (01403) 891499
In beautiful countryside in central position, ideal for touring. Convenient for Gatwick Airport, lift service and long-term car parking available. Family-run and warm welcome assured. Golf-course, driving range and fishing.
Bedrooms: 6 single, 6 double, 5 twin, 2 triple
Bathrooms: 17 private, 1 public, 2 private showers

Bed & breakfast

per night:	£min	£max
Single	35.00	41.00
Double	47.00	70.00

Lunch available
Evening meal 1850 (last orders 2150)
Parking for 100
Cards accepted: Access, Visa, Diners, Amex, Switch/Delta

🛇🅂🐎📭📞🗝️🔌ℹ️🅂🏃‍♂️📺🛏️🚗📞90🏃🦽↻🏠♪🏇🦽🐾SP📞

HOVE

East Sussex

See under Brighton & Hove

LEATHERHEAD

Surrey
Map ref 2D2

Old county town in the Green Belt, with the modern Thorndike Theatre.

Bookham Grange Hotel ⋀

😁😁😁 APPROVED

Little Bookham Common, Bookham, Leatherhead KT23 3HS
☎ Bookham (01372) 452742
Fax (01372) 450080
Country house hotel in ideal location for M25, A3, Gatwick, Heathrow and central London. Good food and friendly service.
Bedrooms: 3 single, 10 double, 5 twin
Bathrooms: 18 private

Bed & breakfast

per night:	£min	£max
Single	55.00	
Double	65.00	

Half board

per person:	£min	£max
Daily	37.50	
Weekly	225.00	

Lunch available
Evening meal 1900 (last orders 2200)
Parking for 100
Cards accepted: Access, Visa, Diners, Amex

🛇🐎📭📞🗝️🔌🏠ℹ️🅂🛏️🚗🍽️100🏇🦽SP📞

Bronwen

Listed

Crabtree Drive, Givons Grove, Leatherhead KT22 8LJ
☎ (01372) 372515
Large family house in the Green Belt at Leatherhead. Adjoins open farmland and is close to National Trust areas of Headley Heath and Box Hill. 20 minutes from Gatwick, 30 minutes from Heathrow, 40 minutes from central London.
Bedrooms: 1 single, 1 double, 1 triple
Bathrooms: 1 private, 1 public

Bed & breakfast

per night:	£min	£max
Single	18.00	22.00
Double	36.00	44.00

Half board

per person:	£min	£max
Daily	26.00	28.00
Weekly	140.00	160.00

Lunch available
Evening meal 1900 (last orders 2100)
Parking for 4

🛇🅂📭📞🗝️🔌🏠ℹ️🅂🏃‍♂️🛏️📺🛏️🚗🍽️🦽🐾🏇SP

LENHAM

Kent
Map ref 3B4

Shops, inns and houses, many displaying timber-work of the late Middle Ages, surround a square which is the centre of the village. The 14th C parish church has one of the best examples of a Kentish tower.

Dog and Bear Hotel ⋒

😃😃😃 COMMENDED

The Square, Lenham, Maidstone ME17 2PG
☎ Maidstone (01622) 858219
Fax (01622) 859415
15th C coaching inn retaining its old world character and serving good Kent ale, lagers and fine wines with home cooking. En-suite rooms. 5 minutes' drive from Leeds Castle. Halfboard daily prices are for a minimum 2-night stay.
Wheelchair access category 3 ⓦ
Bedrooms: 3 single, 13 double, 5 twin, 2 triple, 1 family room; suites available
Bathrooms: 24 private

Bed & breakfast

per night:	£min	£max
Single	37.50	39.50
Double	47.50	49.50

Half board

per person:	£min	£max
Daily	37.50	39.50
Weekly	262.50	276.50

Lunch available
Evening meal 1900 (last orders 2130)
Parking for 26
Cards accepted: Access, Visa, Amex, Switch/Delta
🛏️🕭🛋️🕻⌂📠🖨️⌂💷📺🖥️💻📀 🕮50 SP 🏮 T

LEWES

East Sussex
Map ref 2D3

Historic county town with Norman castle. The steep High Street has mainly Georgian buildings. There is a folk museum at Anne of Cleves House and the archaeological museum is in Barbican House.
Tourist Information Centre
☎ *(01273) 483448*

Felix Gallery

Listed

2 Sun Street, (Corner Lancaster Street), Lewes BN7 2QB
☎ (01273) 472668
Fully-modernised period house in quiet location 3 minutes' walk from town centre, Records Office and castle. Full English breakfast.
Bedrooms: 1 single, 1 twin
Bathrooms: 1 public

Bed & breakfast

per night:	£min	£max
Single	23.00	25.00
Double	36.00	38.00

Cards accepted: Access, Visa
🛏️4⌂📠💷S💻📀🗙🐾

LIMPSFIELD

Surrey
Map ref 2D2

Arawa ⋒

Listed

58 Granville Road, Limpsfield, Oxted RH8 0BZ
☎ Oxted (01883) 714104
Family home near North Downs Way, Chartwell and Hever. Near rail service to London and 30 minutes to Gatwick by car. Friendly and comfortable.
Bedrooms: 2 twin
Bathrooms: 2 public

Bed & breakfast

per night:	£min	£max
Single	15.00	20.00
Double	30.00	40.00

Parking for 1
🛏️🕭🖃⌂📠💷📀🗙📺💻📀❋ 🐾T

LINGFIELD

Surrey
Map ref 2D2

Wealden village with many buildings dating back to the 15th C. Nearby there is horse racing at Lingfield Park.

The Old Cage ⋒

😃😃

Plaistow Street, Lingfield RH7 6AU
☎ (01342) 834271
Fax (01342) 832112

Restored timbered English pub, dating from 1592, with restaurant and en-suite accommodation. Ideal for M25, Gatwick and London connections.
Bedrooms: 3 twin
Bathrooms: 3 private

Bed & breakfast

per night:	£min	£max
Single	27.50	30.00
Double	37.50	40.00

Half board

per person:	£min	£max
Daily	25.00	40.00
Weekly	175.00	280.00

Lunch available
Evening meal (last orders 2100)
Parking for 30
Cards accepted: Access, Visa, Amex
🛏️🕭⌂💦🕻📠💷💻📀📀🐾 SP 🏮

LITTLEHAMPTON

West Sussex
Map ref 2D3

Ancient port at the mouth of the River Arun, now a popular holiday resort, offering flat, sandy beaches, sailing, fishing and boat trips. The Sussex Downs are a short walk inland.

Bracken Lodge Guest House ⋒

😃😃😃 HIGHLY COMMENDED

43 Church Street, Littlehampton BN17 5PU
☎ (01903) 723174
Warm welcome, first class service. Beach, town, swimming/sports facilities nearby. Comfortable rooms (1 suitable for disabled). Ideal touring base. Attractive house and gardens.
Wheelchair access category 2 ⓦ
Bedrooms: 2 double, 2 twin, 1 triple
Bathrooms: 5 private

Bed & breakfast

per night:	£min	£max
Single	29.00	30.00
Double	45.00	47.50

Evening meal 1815 (last orders 1600)
Parking for 6
Cards accepted: Access, Visa
🛏️2🕭🖃⌂💦🕻💷S🗙📺💻📀 ❋🗙🐾

LYMINSTER

West Sussex
Map ref 2D3

Links up with Littlehampton looking inland, and across the watermeadows to the churches and towers of Arundel.

Sandfield House ⋒

Listed COMMENDED

Lyminster, Littlehampton BN17 7PG
☎ Littlehampton (01903) 724129
Spacious country-style family house in 2 acres. Between Arundel and sea, in area of great natural beauty.
Bedrooms: 1 double
Bathrooms: 1 public

Bed & breakfast

per night:	£min	£max
Double	34.00	40.00

Parking for 4
🛏️🖃⌂💦📠💷📀💻📀❋🗙🐾

Please mention this guide when making a booking.

LYNSTED

Kent
Map ref 3B3

Village noted for its charming half-timbered houses and cottages, many of which date from the Tudor period.

Forge Cottage ♠

Listed

Lynsted, Sittingbourne ME9 0RH
☎ Teynham (01795) 521273
Historic half-timbered cottage with oak beams, in a picturesque village. Walled garden with terraced lawns. Good touring centre. Strictly non-smoking.
Bedrooms: 1 double, 1 twin, 1 triple
Bathrooms: 2 public

Bed & breakfast

per night:	£min	£max
Single	20.00	
Double	28.00	30.00

⌂ 10 ⚴ ⅏ 🛏 ⚒ ⅍ 🔌 📺 🛋 📞 ☼ 🐾 SP
🐟 T

MAIDSTONE

Kent
Map ref 3B3

Busy county town of Kent on the River Medway has many interesting features and is an excellent centre for excursions. Museum of Carriages, Museum and Art Gallery, Archbishop's Palace, Mote Park.
Tourist Information Centre
☎ *(01622) 673581*

Willington Court ♠

HIGHLY COMMENDED

Willington Street, Maidstone
ME15 8JW
☎ (01622) 738885

Charming Grade II listed building. Antiques, four-poster bed. Friendly and relaxed atmosphere. Adjacent to Mote Park and near Leeds Castle.
Bedrooms: 2 double, 1 twin
Bathrooms: 3 private

Bed & breakfast

per night:	£min	£max
Single	25.00	33.00
Double	38.00	46.00

Parking for 6
Cards accepted: Access, Visa, Diners, Amex

🏠 🍴 📺 🛋 ⅍ 🖥 S ⅏ 📺 🔌 📞 ☼ ✕
🐾 SP 🐟 T

MARDEN

Kent
Map ref 3B4

The village is believed to date back to Saxon times, though today more modern homes surround the 13th C church.

Great Cheveney Farm ♠

Listed **HIGHLY COMMENDED**

Goudhurst Road, Marden, Tonbridge TN12 9LX
☎ Maidstone (01622) 831207
Fax (01622) 831786

300-acre arable & fruit farm. 16th C farmhouse in Kent Weald, between Marden and Goudhurst villages on B2079. Comfortable, friendly accommodation in peaceful surroundings. Close to Sissinghurst, Scotney and Leeds Castle.
Bedrooms: 1 single, 1 double
Bathrooms: 1 public, 2 private showers

Bed & breakfast

per night:	£min	£max
Single	21.00	25.00
Double	36.00	40.00

Parking for 3
Open January-November

⌂ 10 🍴 ⅏ 🍵 🖥 ⅍ 📺 🛋 📞 ☼ ✕ 🐾 🐟

MARGATE

Kent
Map ref 3C3

Oldest and most famous resort in Kent. Many Regency and Victorian buildings survive from the town's early days. There are 9 miles of sandy beach. "Dreamland" is a 20-acre amusement park and the Winter Gardens offers concert hall entertainment.
Tourist Information Centre
☎ *(01843) 220241*

The Malvern Hotel ♠

COMMENDED

29 Eastern Esplanade, Cliftonville, Margate CT9 2HL
☎ Thanet (01843) 290192
Overlooking the sea, promenade and lawns. Close indoor/outdoor bowls complex, Margate Winter Gardens, amenities and Channel ports. Parking (unrestricted) outside and opposite hotel. TV and tea-making facilities - most rooms en-suite with shower and toilet (no baths).
Bedrooms: 1 single, 6 double, 2 twin, 1 family room

Bathrooms: 8 private, 1 public

Bed & breakfast

per night:	£min	£max
Double	35.00	45.00

Evening meal 1800 (last orders 1000)
Cards accepted: Access, Visa, Diners, Amex

⌂ ⅏ 🛏 ⅍ 🔌 📺 🛋 📞 ✕ 🐾 SP

MIDHURST

West Sussex
Map ref 2C3

Historic, picturesque town just north of the South Downs, with the ruins of Cowdray House, medieval castle and 15th C parish church. Polo at Cowdray Park. Excellent base for Chichester, Petworth, Glorious Goodwood and the South Downs Way.
Tourist Information Centre
☎ *(01730) 817322*

Crown Inn

Listed

Edinburgh Square, Midhurst GU29 9NL
☎ (01730) 813462
16th C freehouse behind and below the church. Large selection of real ales, good wine list, open fires. TV and central heating.
Bedrooms: 1 single, 1 double, 1 twin
Bathrooms: 1 public

Bed & breakfast

per night:	£min	£max
Single	15.00	17.50
Double	30.00	35.00

Lunch available
Evening meal 1900 (last orders 2000)

⚴ 📺 🛏 S ⅍ 🛋 ⚬ ✕ 🐾 🐟

NEWDIGATE

Surrey
Map ref 2D2

Village concerned with the old Wealden iron industry. The attractive 13th C church was once called "Hunter's Church" because of its connections with deer hunting.

Sturtwood Farm

COMMENDED

Partridge Lane, Newdigate, Dorking RH5 5EE
☎ Dorking (01306) 631308
140-acre mixed farm. Attractive 18th C farmhouse where you are assured of a warm welcome. 12 minutes from Gatwick. Many National Trust properties in the area.
Bedrooms: 2 single, 1 twin
Bathrooms: 3 private, 1 public

Bed & breakfast

per night:	£min	£max
Single	20.00	25.00
Double	35.00	40.00

Evening meal from 1900
Parking for 6

🛇🗁🖰🆄🅂✂️🏭▥🚗✿🚬🏠

OLD ROMNEY

Kent
Map ref 3B4

Village on the Romney Marsh with a 13th C church, 2 miles from the Cinque Port of New Romney.

Rose & Crown Inn ⋀
Listed

Old Romney, Romney Marsh
TN29 9SQ
☎ New Romney (01797) 367500
17th C traditional country inn with modern chalet accommodation, 100 yards south of A259 at Old Romney crossroad (2.25 miles west of New Romney).
Bedrooms: 5 twin
Bathrooms: 5 private
Bed & breakfast

per night:	£min	£max
Single	23.00	28.00
Double	35.00	40.00

Lunch available
Evening meal 1900 (last orders 2100)
Parking for 20

🛇1🖧🗁🖰🆂✂️▥🌡30🔔✿🚬

OXSHOTT

Surrey
Map ref 2D2

Suburban area 3 miles north-west of Leatherhead.

Apple Tree Cottage ⋀
Listed

3 Oakshade Road, Oxshott,
Leatherhead KT22 0LF
☎ (01372) 842087
Fax (01372) 842101

Attractive cottage accommodation in a quiet location, convenient for London (30 minutes), Wisley RHS Gardens and many National Trust properties. Non-smokers only, please.
Bedrooms: 1 single, 1 twin
Bathrooms: 1 public

Bed & breakfast

per night:	£min	£max
Single	29.50	41.50
Double	51.00	57.00

Parking for 2

🖂🗁🖰🆄🅹🍴🅿️📺▥🚗✿🚬🏠

OXTED

Surrey
Map ref 2D2

Pleasant town on the edge of National Trust woodland and at the foot of the North Downs. Chartwell (National Trust), the former home of Sir Winston Churchill, is close by.

The New Bungalow Old Hall Farm ⋀
Listed

Tandridge Lane, Oxted RH8 9NS
☎ South Godstone (01342) 892508
Fax (01342) 892508
40-acre livestock farm. Spacious, modern bungalow set in green fields and reached by a private drive. 5 minutes' drive from M25.
Bedrooms: 1 twin, 1 family room
Bathrooms: 1 public

Bed & breakfast

per night:	£min	£max
Single	22.00	25.00
Double	32.00	35.00

Parking for 5

🛇🖧🖰🆄🅰🅂✂️📺▥🚗✿🚬

PARTRIDGE GREEN

West Sussex
Map ref 2D3

Small village between Henfield and Billingshurst.

Pound Cottage Bed and Breakfast ⋀
COMMENDED

Mill lane, Littleworth, Partridge Green,
Horsham RH13 8JU
☎ (01403) 710218 & 711285
Pleasant country house in quiet surroundings. 8 miles from Horsham, 25 minutes from Gatwick. Just off the West Grinstead to Steyning road.
Bedrooms: 1 single, 1 double, 1 twin
Bathrooms: 1 public

Bed & breakfast

per night:	£min	£max
Single	16.00	16.00
Double	32.00	32.00

Half board

per person:	£min	£max
Daily	22.00	22.00
Weekly	154.00	154.00

Evening meal from 1830
Parking for 8

🛇🗁🖰🆄🅰🅂✂️📺▥✿🍴🚬

PETWORTH

West Sussex
Map ref 2D3

Town dominated by Petworth House (National Trust), the great 17th C mansion, set in 2000 acres of parkland laid out by Capability Brown. The house contains wood-carvings by Grinling Gibbons.
Tourist Information Centre
☎ *(01798) 343523*

White Horse Inn ⋀
👑👑👑 **HIGHLY COMMENDED**

The Street, Sutton, Pulborough
RH20 1PS
☎ Sutton (01798) 869221
Fax (01798) 869291

Pretty Georgian village inn close to South Downs Way. Roman villa 1 mile. Garden, log fires. 4 miles Petworth, 5 miles Pulborough.
Bedrooms: 3 double, 2 twin
Bathrooms: 5 private

Bed & breakfast

per night:	£min	£max
Single	48.00	48.00
Double	58.00	58.00

Half board

per person:	£min	£max
Daily	41.00	60.00
Weekly	206.00	290.00

Lunch available
Evening meal 1900 (last orders 2145)
Parking for 10
Cards accepted: Access, Visa, Diners, Amex

📞🗁🖰🅰🅂▥🚗✿🍴🚬📶🆂🏠🆃

POYNINGS

West Sussex
Map ref 2D3

Set in the South Downs behind Brighton, with Dyke Hill above, on which there was an Iron Age camp, and the Devil's Dyke along the southern side.

Poynings Manor Farm
👑

Poynings, Brighton BN45 7AG
☎ Brighton (01273) 857371
Fax (01273) 857371
260-acre mixed farm. Charming old farmhouse in quiet scenic surroundings. Ideal for walkers, riders and country lovers. Coast 15 minutes, Gatwick 30 minutes.
Bedrooms: 1 double, 2 twin

Continued ▶

POYNINGS

Continued

Bathrooms: 2 public

Bed & breakfast

per night:	£min	£max
Single		25.00
Double	38.00	

Half board

per person:	£min	£max
Daily	29.00	35.00

Evening meal from 1900
Parking for 6

🏃🍽️📺♿🧤♒UL📶S✂🖂📷,🚗U▶❄✖🚲

RAMSGATE

Kent
Map ref 3C3

Popular holiday resort with good sandy beaches. At Pegwell Bay is a replica of a Viking longship. Terminal for car-ferry service to Dunkirk and Ostend.
Tourist Information Centre
☎ *(01843) 583333*

Eastwood Guest House ⋀

`Listed` `COMMENDED`

28 Augusta Road, Ramsgate CT11 8JS
☎ Thanet (01843) 591505
Fax (01843) 591505

Pretty Victorian villa, close to ferry port and amenities. Comfortable rooms, mostly en-suite. Lock-up garages available. Breakfast served from 6.45 am, dinner available.
Bedrooms: 1 single, 4 double, 4 twin, 6 family rooms
Bathrooms: 10 private, 3 public

Bed & breakfast

per night:	£min	£max
Single	18.00	25.00
Double	30.00	40.00

Half board

per person:	£min	£max
Daily	23.00	30.00
Weekly	135.00	150.00

Evening meal 1830 (last orders 1930)
Parking for 20

🏃🍽️📺♿🧤♒UL🛈S✂♒📺🖂,🚗♟
♦❄🅾🌂SP🅣

> **Please check prices and other details at the time of booking.**

ROGATE

West Sussex
Map ref 2C3

On the main road between Midhurst and Petersfield, Rogate probably gets its name from its position as gateway to wooded hill slopes, the habitat of deer.

Trotton Farm

👑 `COMMENDED`

Trotton, Petersfield, Hampshire
GU31 5EN
☎ Midhurst (01730) 813618
Fax (01730) 816093
Farmhouse just off the A272, access through yard. Accommodation and lounge/games room in a converted cartshed adjoining farmhouse. All rooms with en-suite shower.
Bedrooms: 1 double, 2 twin
Bathrooms: 3 private

Bed & breakfast

per night:	£min	£max
Single	25.00	30.00
Double	35.00	40.00

🏃🍽️🍴📺♿🧤♒UL🛈S✂📺📷,🚗♦♟
✒❄🚲

ROTTINGDEAN

East Sussex
Map ref 2D3

The quiet High Street contains a number of fine old buildings and the village pond and green are close by.

Braemar Guest House

📺

Steyning Road, Rottingdean, Brighton
BN2 7GA
☎ Brighton (01273) 304263
Family-run guesthouse, proud of its cheerful atmosphere, in an old world village where Rudyard Kipling once lived.
Bedrooms: 5 single, 5 double, 2 twin, 2 triple
Bathrooms: 3 public, 2 private showers

Bed & breakfast

per night:	£min	£max
Single	15.00	16.00
Double	30.00	32.00

🏃🍴UL♒📺🖂,🅾🅿SP

> **The symbols ♿ ♿ ♿ indicate categories of accessibility for wheelchair users. They are explained in full in the information pages at the back of this guide.**

ROYAL TUNBRIDGE WELLS

Kent
Map ref 2D2

This "Royal" town became famous as a spa in the 17th C and much of its charm is retained, as in the Pantiles, a shaded walk lined with elegant shops. Heritage attraction "A Day at the Wells". Rich in parks and gardens and a good centre for walks.
Tourist Information Centre
☎ *(01892) 515675*

Chequers

👑👑 `HIGHLY COMMENDED`

Camden Park, Royal Tunbridge Wells
TN2 5AD
☎ (01892) 532299
Friendly family house, origins 1840. Part-walled garden. Unique private location, 10 minutes from Pantiles, high street, railway station. Peaceful, comfortable, central base. Non-smokers, only please.
Bedrooms: 1 single, 1 twin
Bathrooms: 2 private

Bed & breakfast

per night:	£min	£max
Single	18.00	20.00
Double	35.00	38.00

Parking for 5

🏃🍽️♿🧤S✂📺📷,🚗❄🚲

Jordan House ⋀

👑 `COMMENDED`

68 London Road, Royal Tunbridge Wells TN1 1DT
☎ (01892) 523983
17th C town house with old world ambience, overlooking Tunbridge Wells Common and near town centre and station. Non-smokers preferred.
Bedrooms: 1 double, 1 twin
Bathrooms: 2 private

Bed & breakfast

per night:	£min	£max
Single	20.00	25.00
Double	36.00	40.00

🏃10♿🧤🛈S♒📺📷,🚗🚲🌂SP🏠

Manor Court Farm ⋀

👑👑

Ashurst, Royal Tunbridge Wells
TN3 9TB
☎ Fordcombe (01892) 740279
350-acre mixed farm. Georgian farmhouse with friendly atmosphere. Spacious rooms and lovely views overlooking Medway Valley. Good base for walking and touring. Weekend cream teas. On A264, half a mile east of Ashurst village (Tunbridge Wells to East Grinstead road).
Bedrooms: 1 double, 2 twin
Bathrooms: 1 private, 2 public

Bed & breakfast

per night:	£min	£max
Single	18.00	25.00
Double	36.00	38.00

Parking for 19

☙ ♦ 🅆 🛆 🅂 ✂ 🅜 📺 ⊞ 🚭 ✖ ♨ ⏻ ♪ ✿ 🎮 🅞🅐🅟 🅢🅟 🏥

Nellington Mead

♨♨

Nellington Road, Royal Tunbridge Wells TN4 8SQ
☎ (01892) 545037
Comfortable modern house with extensive garden. Easy access to Kent/Sussex countryside, historic houses and gardens. London and coast easily accessible.
Bedrooms: 1 twin
Bathrooms: 1 private

Bed & breakfast

per night:	£min	£max
Single	18.50	20.00
Double	37.50	37.50

Half board

per person:	£min	£max
Daily	28.50	33.50

Evening meal from 1900
Parking for 5
Open January-November

☙ 🗆 ♦ 🅆 🛆 🅂 ✂ 📺 ⊞ 🚭 ✿ ✖ 🎮

The Old Parsonage ⋀

♨♨ DE LUXE

Church Lane, Frant, Royal Tunbridge Wells TN3 9DX
☎ Frant (01892) 750773
Fax (01892) 750773
Peacefully situated by the village church (2 pubs and restaurant nearby), this classic Georgian country house provides superior accommodation: en-suite bedrooms, antique-furnished reception rooms, spacious conservatory and ballustraded terrace overlooking the secluded walled garden. SEETB 1995 "Bed and Breakfast of the Year" Award winner.
Bedrooms: 2 double, 1 twin
Bathrooms: 3 private

Bed & breakfast

per night:	£min	£max
Single	32.00	39.00
Double	52.00	59.00

Parking for 12
Cards accepted: Access, Visa

☙ 🎩 🕮 🗆 ♦ 🅁 🅆 🅂 ✂ 🅜 📺 ⊞ 🚭 ✿ 🎮 🏥 🅣

> Individual proprietors have supplied all details of accommodation. As changes can occur, we advise you to confirm the information at the time of booking.

RYE

East Sussex
Map ref 3B4

Cobbled, hilly streets and fine old buildings make Rye, once a Cinque Port, a most picturesque town. Noted for its church with ancient clock, potteries and antique shops. Town Model Sound and Light Show gives a good introduction to the town.
Tourist Information Centre
☎ (01797) 226696

Aviemore Guest House ⋀

♨♨ APPROVED

28/30 Fishmarket Road, Rye TN31 7LP
☎ (01797) 223052

Owner-run, friendly guesthouse offering a warm welcome and hearty breakfast. Overlooking "Town Salts" and the River Rother. 2 minutes from town centre.
Bedrooms: 1 single, 4 double, 3 twin
Bathrooms: 4 private, 2 public

Bed & breakfast

per night:	£min	£max
Single	17.00	28.00
Double	30.00	42.00

Half board

per person:	£min	£max
Daily	26.00	37.00
Weekly	152.00	183.00

Evening meal 1800 (last orders 2200)
Cards accepted: Access, Visa, Amex

☙ ♦ 🛆 🅂 🅜 📺 ⊞ 🚭 ✖ 🅞🅐🅟 🅢🅟 🅣

Camber Sands Lodge ⋀

Camber Sands Leisure Park, 93 Lydd Road, Camber, Rye TN31 7RS
☎ (01797) 225555
Fax (01797) 225756
Modern, friendly hotel situated 100 yards from sandy beach. Ancient Rye a short ride away. Health club, swimming pools adjacent.
Bedrooms: 4 double, 4 twin, 1 triple
Bathrooms: 9 private

Bed & breakfast

per night:	£min	£max
Single	30.00	30.00
Double	40.00	40.00

Parking for 14
Open March-October
Cards accepted: Access, Visa

☙ 🍴 🗆 ♦ 🅜 📺 ⊞ 🎱 ✳ 🎿 ⤢ ♨ ✖ 🎮

Green Hedges ⋀

♨♨ HIGHLY COMMENDED

Hillyfields, Rye Hill, Rye TN31 7NH
☎ (01797) 222185

Country house in a private road. 1.5 acres of landscaped gardens with heated swimming pool. Short stroll to town centre. Ample parking. Home- grown organic produce.
Bedrooms: 2 double, 1 twin
Bathrooms: 3 private, 1 public

Bed & breakfast

per night:	£min	£max
Double	47.00	57.00

Parking for 7
Cards accepted: Access, Visa

☙ 🕛12 🕮 🗆 ♦ 🎱 🅆 🅂 ✂ 🅜 🚭 🚭 ✿ ✖ 🎮 🅢🅟

Jeake's House ⋀

♨♨ HIGHLY COMMENDED

Mermaid Street, Rye TN31 7ET
☎ (01797) 222828
Fax (01797) 222623

Recapture the past in this historic building, in a cobblestoned street at the heart of the old town. Honeymoon suite available.
Bedrooms: 1 single, 7 double, 1 twin, 2 triple, 1 family room
Bathrooms: 8 private, 2 public, 2 private showers

Bed & breakfast

per night:	£min	£max
Single	22.50	50.00
Double	41.00	59.00

Cards accepted: Access, Visa, Amex

☙ 🎩 🥂 🕮 🗆 ♦ 🎱 🅂 🅜 ⊞ 🚭 🎮 🅢🅟 🏥 🅣

Kimblee ⋀

♨♨ COMMENDED

Main Street, Peasmarsh, Rye TN31 6UL
☎ Peasmarsh (01797) 230514 & Mobile 0831 841004
Country house with views from all aspects, 250 metres from pub/restaurant and 5 minutes' drive on the A268 from Rye. Warm welcome.
Bedrooms: 3 double
Bathrooms: 3 private

Bed & breakfast

per night:	£min	£max
Single	17.50	25.00
Double	34.00	36.00

Parking for 4
Cards accepted: Access, Visa

☙ 🕮 🗆 ♦ 🎱 🅆 🅂 🅜 ⊞ 🚭 ✿ ✖ 🎮 🅞🅐🅟 🅢🅟 🅣

The Old Vicarage

Listed COMMENDED

Rye Harbour, Rye TN31 7TT
☎ (01797) 222088
Imposing Victorian former vicarage, quietly situated close to sea and nature

Continued ▶

RYE

Continued

reserve. Antique furniture and open
fires. Good English breakfast.
Bedrooms: 1 double, 1 twin
Bathrooms: 1 public

Bed & breakfast

per night:	£min	£max
Single	16.00	20.00
Double	32.00	36.00

Parking for 4
🛇🚭♿🛎ꔪ🅂🄰⚡✂🛏️🚗♿🆂🅿️

Saint Margarets ⋀

Listed

Dumbwomans Lane, Udimore, Rye
TN31 6AD
☎ (01797) 222586
*Comfortable, friendly chalet bungalow
with sea views. Car parking. En-suite
facilities. B2089, 2 miles west of Rye.*
Bedrooms: 2 double, 1 twin; suites
available
Bathrooms: 3 private

Bed & breakfast

per night:	£min	£max
Double	29.00	30.00

Parking for 3
Open February-November
🛇🚭♿⚡✂🛏️🚗

Strand House ⋀

😄😄😄 **COMMENDED**

Winchelsea TN36 4JT
☎ (01797) 226276
Fax (01797) 224806

*The old-world charm of one of
Winchelsea's oldest houses, dating from
the 15th C, with oak beams and
inglenooks. Overlooking National Trust
pastureland, four-poster bedroom.
Residents' licence.*
Bedrooms: 8 double, 1 twin, 1 triple
Bathrooms: 8 private, 1 public

Bed & breakfast

per night:	£min	£max
Single	28.00	32.00
Double	40.00	60.00

Evening meal 1800 (last orders 1900)
Parking for 12
Cards accepted: Access, Visa
🛇♿5🚭🛎⚡♿⚡🅂✂🛏️📺🛏️
🚗♿🚗🆂🅿️

Top o'The Hill at Rye ⋀

😄😄😄 **COMMENDED**

Rye Hill, Rye TN31 7NH
☎ (01797) 223284
Fax (01797) 227030
*Small friendly inn offering fine
traditional food and cottage-style
accommodation. Central for touring*

*Kent and Sussex, Channel ports nearby.
Large car park, garden.*
Bedrooms: 3 double, 2 twin, 1 triple
Bathrooms: 6 private

Bed & breakfast

per night:	£min	£max
Single	24.00	25.00
Double	40.00	44.00

Lunch available
Evening meal 1900 (last orders 2100)
Parking for 32
Cards accepted: Access, Visa
🛇♿⚡🛎♿⚡🛎️📺🛏️🚗♿12☺♿
♿🆂🅿️

ST NICHOLAS AT WADE

Kent
Map ref 3C3

Village in the Isle of Thanet with
ancient church built of knapped
flint.

Streete Farm House

Listed

Court Road, St Nicholas at Wade,
Birchington CT7 0NH
☎ Thanet (01843) 847245
*50-acre arable and mixed farm. 16th C
farmhouse on the outskirts of the
village, with original oak-panelled
dining room.*
Bedrooms: 1 single, 2 double
Bathrooms: 1 public

Bed & breakfast

per night:	£min	£max
Single	15.00	15.00
Double	30.00	30.00

Parking for 4
🛇3♿🛎📺🛏️♿✂🚗🆂

SARRE

Kent
Map ref 3C3

Attractive Dutch-gabled houses
can be seen in this Thanet village.
Names of many famous people
are inscribed on the walls of the
16th C Crown Inn, noted for the
manufacture of cherry brandy.

Crown Inn (The Famous
Cherry Brandy House) ⋀

😄😄😄 **COMMENDED**

Ramsgate Road, Sarre, Birchington
CT7 0LF
☎ Birchington (01843) 847808
Fax (01843) 847914
*An ancient traditional inn close to
Canterbury. Inglenook fireplaces,
gleaming brasses, freshly prepared
regional specialities. Excellent locally
brewed ales. Halfboard daily prices are
for a minimum 2-night stay.*
Wheelchair access category 3 ♿
Bedrooms: 9 double, 2 twin, 1 triple;
suites available
Bathrooms: 12 private

Bed & breakfast

per night:	£min	£max
Single		43.50
Double		56.50

Half board

per person:	£min	£max
Daily	37.50	39.50
Weekly	262.50	276.50

Lunch available
Evening meal 1900 (last orders 2200)
Parking for 40
Cards accepted: Access, Visa, Amex,
Switch/Delta
🛇♿🛎♿⚡🛎🅂✂🛏️🚗🍴10
♿🚗♿🆂🅿️🅃

SEAFORD

East Sussex
Map ref 2D3

The town was a bustling port until
1579 when the course of the River
Ouse was diverted. The downlands
around the town make good
walking country, with fine views of
the Seven Sisters cliffs.
*Tourist Information Centre
☎ (01323) 897426*

Rowans ⋀

Listed **HIGHLY COMMENDED**

5 Grove Road, Seaford BN25 1TP
☎ (01323) 896883

*Early 1930s character home. Many
original features, set in pleasant garden
of 0.75 acre. Peaceful, yet close to town
centre.*
Bedrooms: 1 single, 1 double, 1 twin
Bathrooms: 1 public

Bed & breakfast

per night:	£min	£max
Single	18.00	18.00
Double	36.00	36.00

Half board

per person:	£min	£max
Daily	32.00	32.00
Weekly	206.00	206.00

Evening meal 1800 (last orders 1900)
Parking for 2
🛇12🗝️♿🅂✂🛏️🛏️🚗♿✂🚗♿

> National gradings and
> classifications were correct
> at the time of going to
> press but are subject to
> change. Please check at the
> time of booking.

SEVENOAKS

Kent
Map ref 2D2

Set in pleasant wooded country, with a distinctive character and charm. Nearby is Knole (National Trust), home of the Sackville family and one of the largest houses in England, set in a vast deer park.
Tourist Information Centre
☎ *(01732) 450305*

The Bull Hotel ⋀

🏵🏵🏵 APPROVED

Wrotham, Sevenoaks TN15 7RF
☎ (01732) 885522 & 883092
Fax (01732) 886288

Privately-run 14th C coaching inn, in secluded historic village 15 minutes from Sevenoaks. Just off M20 and M25/26, 30 minutes from Gatwick and London. Oak beams and inglenook fireplaces. Ideal for local places of interest.
Bedrooms: 1 single, 3 double, 6 twin
Bathrooms: 10 private, 1 public
Bed & breakfast

per night:	£min	£max
Single	35.00	40.00
Double	45.00	50.00

Half board

per person:	£min	£max
Daily	30.00	42.00

Lunch available
Evening meal 1900 (last orders 2200)
Parking for 50
Cards accepted: Access, Visa, Diners, Amex

🛇🛋🏃🖳 ♦ 🛉 S 👑 Ⅲ, 🖧 ⚓ 🍴50 ✿ 🚲 🖎 SP 🏮 T

Mooring Hotel ⋀

🏵🏵🏵

97 Hitchen Hatch Lane, Sevenoaks TN13 3BE
☎ (01732) 452589 & 742323
Fax (01732) 456462
Friendly family hotel offering high standard accommodation for tourists and business travellers. 30 minutes from London. Close to BR station.
Bedrooms: 5 single, 4 double, 10 twin, 2 triple
Bathrooms: 21 private, 1 public
Bed & breakfast

per night:	£min	£max
Single	25.00	42.00
Double	35.00	59.00

Half board

per person:	£min	£max
Daily	35.00	52.00
Weekly	205.00	309.00

Evening meal 1900 (last orders 2100)
Parking for 22
Cards accepted: Access, Visa, Diners, Amex, Switch/Delta

🛇🛋🏃🖳 ♦ 🛉 S 👑 Ⅲ, ⓥ ♦ Ⅲ, 🖧
🍴45 ∪ 🏮 ✿ ⚓ SP T

SIDLESHAM

West Sussex
Map ref 2C3

Sidlesham has a nucleus of picture-postcard thatched houses and a harbour a mile south of the village on a creek of Pagham Harbour.

Muttons Farmhouse

Listed

Keynor Lane, Sidlesham, Chichester PO20 7NG
☎ (01243) 641703
18th C listed house off B2145, 4 miles south of Chichester. Rural surroundings near Pagham Harbour reserve. Ideal for Goodwood, beach and countryside.
Bedrooms: 1 single, 1 double, 2 twin
Bathrooms: 2 public
Bed & breakfast

per night:	£min	£max
Single	16.00	18.00
Double	32.00	36.00

Parking for 7

🛇🛋 ♦ 🖳 S Ⅳ Ⅲ, ✿ ⚓ 🏮

SITTINGBOURNE

Kent
Map ref 3B3

The town's position and its ample supply of water make it an ideal site for the paper-making industry. Delightful villages and orchards lie round about.

The Beaumont ⋀

🏵🏵🏵 COMMENDED

74 London Road, Sittingbourne ME10 1NS
☎ (01795) 472536
Fax (01795) 425921
Comfortable, friendly 17th C former farmhouse, conveniently located for historic Canterbury, Rochester and Leeds Castle. Superb prize-winning breakfast menu and private car park.
Bedrooms: 3 single, 3 double, 1 twin, 1 triple, 1 family room
Bathrooms: 6 private, 1 public, 2 private showers
Bed & breakfast

per night:	£min	£max
Single	23.00	42.00
Double	44.00	55.00

Parking for 9

Cards accepted: Access, Visa, Switch/Delta

🛇🛋🏃🖳 ♦ 🖳 🛉 S 👑 Ⅳ Ⅲ, 🖧 ⚓
🍴 ✿ ⚓ OAP SP 🏮 T

SMALLFIELD

Surrey
Map ref 2D2

Small village between Horley and Lingfield, named after local estate.

Chithurst Farm

Listed

Chithurst Lane, Horne, Smallfield, Horley RH6 9JU
☎ (01342) 842487
92-acre dairy farm. Recently renovated 16th C listed farmhouse, with genuine beamed rooms, inglenook fireplaces and attractive garden. Set in a quiet country lane, yet convenient for Gatwick and motorways.
Bedrooms: 1 single, 1 double, 1 triple
Bathrooms: 1 public
Bed & breakfast

per night:	£min	£max
Single	15.50	17.50
Double	30.00	34.00

Parking for 3
Open February-November

🛇🛋 ♦ 🖳 Ⅳ 🖧 ⚓ ✿ 🚲 ⚓ 🏮

SMARDEN

Kent
Map ref 3B4

Pretty village with a number of old, well-presented buildings. The 14th C St Michael's Church is sometimes known as the "Barn of Kent" because of its 36-ft roof span.

Chequers Inn ⋀

🏵🏵🏵 COMMENDED

Smarden, Ashford TN27 8QA
☎ Ashford (01233) 770217 & 770623
Fax (01233) 770623
Listed 14th C inn, wealth of oak beams, in heart of the Weald. Ideal for touring and visiting many places of historic interest. 5 golf-courses nearby. Good food always available - fresh fish a speciality.
Bedrooms: 1 single, 2 double, 2 twin
Bathrooms: 5 private, 1 public
Bed & breakfast

per night:	£min	£max
Single	22.00	35.00
Double	36.00	48.00

Lunch available
Evening meal 1800 (last orders 2200)
Parking for 18
Cards accepted: Access, Visa, Switch/Delta

🛇🛋 ♦ 🏃 🛉 S Ⅳ 🖧 🍴∪ 🏮 ✿ 🚲 SP 🏮

SOUTHBOROUGH

Kent
Map ref 2D2

Small town between Royal Tunbridge Wells and Tonbridge with an attractive common and cricket pitch where matches can be seen regularly.

Nightingales

Listed COMMENDED

London Road, Southborough, Royal Tunbridge Wells TN4 0UJ
☎ Tunbridge Wells (01892) 528443
Fax (01892) 511376
Georgian house situated on A26, convenient for A21, M25 and Tonbridge/Royal Tunbridge Wells. Attractive rooms, extensive breakfast menu. Parking.
Bedrooms: 1 single, 1 double, 1 triple
Bathrooms: 1 public

Bed & breakfast

per night:	£min	£max
Single	16.00	18.00
Double	30.00	34.00

Parking for 3

STELLING MINNIS

Kent
Map ref 3B4

Off the Roman Stone Street, this quiet, picturesque village lies deep in the Lyminge Forest, south of Canterbury.

Great Field Farm

Listed

Misling Lane, Stelling Minnis, Canterbury CT4 6DE
☎ (01227) 709223
42-acre mixed farm. Lovely spacious farmhouse with wealth of old pine, fine furnishings, pleasant gardens, paddocks with friendly ponies. Self-contained flat available for B&B or self catering. Quiet location midway Canterbury/Folkestone, adjacent B2068.
Bedrooms: 2 double, 1 twin
Bathrooms: 3 private

Bed & breakfast

per night:	£min	£max
Single	15.50	20.00
Double	36.00	40.00

Parking for 6

SWANLEY

Kent
Map ref 2D2

West of Farningham off the A20, Swanley village consists of a narrow street of old houses and an odd little Victorian church down a by-road.

The Dees

Listed COMMENDED

56 Old Chapel Road, Crockenhill, Swanley BR8 8LJ
☎ (01322) 667645
Crockenhill is 2 miles from M25 and M20. Easy access to Brands Hatch, London, Kent and Sussex coast and country. Nice double room with full private facilities plus single rooms.
Bedrooms: 2 single, 1 double
Bathrooms: 3 private, 1 public

Bed & breakfast

per night:	£min	£max
Single	12.50	17.50
Double	30.00	35.00

Parking for 2

TENTERDEN

Kent
Map ref 3B4

Most attractive market town with a broad main street full of 16th C houses and shops. The tower of the 15th C parish church is the finest in Kent.

Finchden Manor

HIGHLY COMMENDED

Appledore Road, Tenterden TN30 7DD
☎ (01580) 764719
Early 15th C manor house, Grade II listed, with inglenook fireplaces, panelled rooms and beams. Set in 4 acres of gardens and grounds.*
Bedrooms: 1 single, 2 double
Bathrooms: 2 private, 3 public

Bed & breakfast

per night:	£min	£max
Single	16.00	18.00
Double	32.00	36.00

Parking for 3

TUNBRIDGE WELLS

See under Royal Tunbridge Wells

UCKFIELD

East Sussex
Map ref 2D3

Once a medieval market town and centre of the iron industry, Uckfield is now a busy country town on the edge of the Ashdown Forest.

Dale Hamme

Listed APPROVED

Piltdown, Uckfield TN22 3XY
☎ Nutley (01825) 712422
15th C hall house with oak beams and inglenook fireplaces in idyllic rural location. On A272 going east, take second left after Piltdown Man pub into Down Street. After 1 mile turn left, house on left hand side.
Bedrooms: 2 single, 2 twin
Bathrooms: 2 private, 1 public

Bed & breakfast

per night:	£min	£max
Single	15.00	15.00
Double	34.00	34.00

Parking for 14

Old Mill Farm

High Hurstwood, Uckfield TN22 4AD
☎ Buxted (01825) 732279
Fax (01825) 732279
50-acre beef farm. Situated in picturesque valley, off A26. Gatwick, Crowborough, Uckfield and Ashdown Forest nearby. All rooms have private facilities.
Bedrooms: 1 single, 1 twin, 1 triple
Bathrooms: 3 private

Bed & breakfast

per night:	£min	£max
Single	18.00	20.00
Double	36.00	36.00

Half board

per person:	£min	£max
Daily	26.00	26.00
Weekly	182.00	182.00

Evening meal 1800 (last orders 2030)
Parking for 6

South Paddock

HIGHLY COMMENDED

Maresfield Park, Uckfield TN22 2HA
☎ (01825) 762335
Comfortable quiet country house accommodation set in 3.5 acres of landscaped gardens. Home-made preserves and log fires. Within easy reach of Gatwick, Brighton, Glyndebourne, Hever Castle.
Bedrooms: 1 double, 2 twin
Bathrooms: 1 private, 1 public

Individual proprietors have supplied all details of accommodation. As changes can occur, we advise you to confirm the information at the time of booking.

All accommodation in this guide has been graded, or is awaiting a grading, by a trained Tourist Board inspector.

We advise you to confirm your booking in writing.

Bed & breakfast per night:	£min	£max
Single	32.00	36.00
Double	50.00	54.00

Parking for 6

5 [UL] [TV] [OAP] [SP]

WADHURST

East Sussex
Map ref 3B4

Village in the Sussex Weald. The village sign depicts an anvil, recalling the iron industry, and also an oasthouse, showing that this is hop country.

Best Beech Inn

Best Beech, Wadhurst TN5 6JH
☎ (01892) 782046
Fax (01892) 785092
Quiet, rural public house set in pretty Sussex countryside and surrounded by beech trees.
Bedrooms: 1 single, 3 double, 2 twin, 1 family room
Bathrooms: 3 private, 1 public

Bed & breakfast per night:	£min	£max
Single	20.00	25.00
Double	32.50	40.00

Half board per person:	£min	£max
Daily	27.50	42.00
Weekly	175.00	266.00

Lunch available
Evening meal 1900 (last orders 2130)
Parking for 30
Cards accepted: Access, Visa

WALTON-ON-THAMES

Surrey
Map ref 2D2

Busy town beside the Thames, retaining a distinctive atmosphere despite being only 12 miles from central London. Close to Hampton Court Palace, Sandown Park racecourse and Claremont Landscape Garden (National Trust), Esher.

Beech Tree Lodge

Listed

7 Rydens Avenue, Walton-on-Thames KT12 3JB
☎ (01932) 242738
Edwardian house in tree-lined avenue near buses, trains, shops, pubs. Handy for London, Hampton Court, Kingston and country.
Bedrooms: 2 twin, 1 triple
Bathrooms: 2 public

Bed & breakfast per night:	£min	£max
Single	16.00	20.00
Double	32.00	34.00

Parking for 8

[UL] [S]

WARNINGLID

West Sussex
Map ref 2D3

Hamlet guarded by a village sign depicting a spear- brandishing Saxon.

Gillhurst

The Street, Warninglid, Haywards Heath RH17 5SZ
☎ Haywards Heath (01444) 461388
Quiet setting outside beautiful village. Extensive grounds, hard tennis court, lovely decor, large rooms. Walks and lovely gardens in vicinity.
Bedrooms: 1 double, 2 twin
Bathrooms: 3 private

Bed & breakfast per night:	£min	£max
Single	20.00	30.00
Double	40.00	50.00

Parking for 10

12 [UL] [S] [TV] [SP]

WEST CHILTINGTON

West Sussex
Map ref 2D3

Well-kept village caught in the maze of lanes leading to and from the South Downs.

New House Farm

COMMENDED

Broadford Bridge Road, West Chiltington, Pulborough RH20 2LA
☎ (01798) 812215
50-acre mixed farm. 15th C farmhouse with oak beams and inglenook for log fires. 40 minutes' drive from Gatwick. Within easy reach of local inns and golf-course.
Bedrooms: 1 double, 2 twin
Bathrooms: 3 private

Bed & breakfast per night:	£min	£max
Single	18.00	25.00
Double	36.00	50.00

Parking for 6

10 [UL] [TV] [SP]

Half board prices shown are per person but in some cases may be based on double/twin occupancy.

WEST CLANDON

Surrey
Map ref 2D2

Home of Clandon Park (National Trust), the Palladian mansion built in the early 1730s and home of the Queen's Royal Surrey Regiment Museum.

Ways Cottage

Listed COMMENDED

Lime Grove, West Clandon, Guildford GU4 7UT
☎ Guildford (01483) 222454
Rural detached house in quiet location, 5 miles from Guildford. Easy reach of A3 and M25. Close to station on Waterloo/Guildford line.
Bedrooms: 1 single, 2 twin
Bathrooms: 2 private, 1 public

Bed & breakfast per night:	£min	£max
Single	17.00	19.00
Double	30.00	33.00

Half board per person:	£min	£max
Daily	27.00	29.00
Weekly	189.00	203.00

Evening meal 1800 (last orders 2100)
Parking for 2

[UL]

WEST MALLING

Kent
Map ref 3B3

Became prominent in Norman times when an abbey was established here.

Westfields Farm

Listed

St. Vincents Lane, Addington, West Malling ME19 5BW
☎ (01732) 843209
Farmhouse of character, approximately 500 years old, in rural setting. Within easy reach of London, Canterbury, Tunbridge Wells and the coast. Reductions for children. Golf nearby.
Bedrooms: 1 single, 1 twin, 1 triple
Bathrooms: 2 public

Bed & breakfast per night:	£min	£max
Single	18.00	18.00
Double	36.00	36.00

[UL] [TV]

The accommodation coupons at the back will help you when contacting proprietors.

WHITSTABLE

Kent
Map ref 3B3

Seaside resort and yachting centre on Kent's north shore. The beach is shingle and there are the usual seaside amenities and entertainments and a museum.
Tourist Information Centre
☎ *(01227) 275482*

Copeland House

Listed COMMENDED

4 Island Wall, Whitstable CT15 1EP
☎ (01227) 266207
Fax (01227) 266207
Twenty yards from beach. Beautiful rooms, private facilities, central heating, tea/coffee facilities, fabulous breakfast. Close to town centre. Deck chairs for the beach.
Bedrooms: 1 double, 1 twin, 2 triple
Bathrooms: 4 private
Bed & breakfast

per night:	£min	£max
Single	20.00	30.00
Double	30.00	39.00

☎4🏠🍴📺♨♍🖥 ⓈⅢ 🛏❄🚐 ᴰᴬᴾ
♨ 🆂🅿

Marine ⋀

COMMENDED

Marine Parade, Tankerton, Whitstable CT5 2BE
☎ Canterbury (01227) 272672
Fax (01227) 264721
A hotel of original character recently refurbished with every modern facility. Good food, Kentish beers, comfortable en-suite accommodation, sea-facing bedrooms.
Bedrooms: 5 double, 6 twin
Bathrooms: 11 private
Bed & breakfast

per night:	£min	£max
Single	35.00	37.50
Double	49.50	51.50

Half board per person:	£min	£max
Daily	46.95	49.45
Weekly	245.00	262.50

Lunch available
Evening meal 1900 (last orders 2100)
Parking for 20
Cards accepted: Access, Visa, Switch/Delta
☎🛥📞🍴📺♨♍Ⓢ⅄♍ ⷮⅢ🚐
🍴200❄♨ 🆂🅿

The town index at the back of this guide gives page numbers of all places with accommodation.

WITTERSHAM

Kent
Map ref 3B4

Village in the Isle of Oxney with a well-preserved 18th C post mill, Stocks Mill, open to the public.

Isle of Oxney Shetland Centre ⋀

HIGHLY COMMENDED

Oxney Farm, Moons Green, Wittersham, Tenterden TN30 7PS
☎ (01797) 270558 & Mobile 0850 219830
11-acre livestock farm. Farmhouse in peaceful, rural setting. Warm welcome, high-class food. Convenient for Channel Tunnel, numerous historic and scenic places, variety of good golf-courses.
Bedrooms: 1 double, 1 twin
Bathrooms: 2 private
Bed & breakfast

per night:	£min	£max
Single	25.00	30.00
Double	50.00	60.00

Half board per person:	£min	£max
Daily	40.00	45.00
Weekly	255.00	290.00

Lunch available
Evening meal 1830 (last orders 2100)
Parking for 6
☎🛥10🍴♨♍ⷮ Ⓢ🅰⅄♍ⷮ Ⅲ🚐♨
❄🍴🐾

WOKING

Surrey
Map ref 2D2

One of the largest towns in Surrey, which developed with the coming of the railway in the 1830s. Old Woking was a market town in the 17th C and still retains several interesting buildings.

Elm Lodge ⋀

Listed

Elm Road, Horsell, Woking GU21 4DY
☎ (01483) 763323
Fax (01344) 845656
Comfortable Victorian home in a quiet location overlooking woodland, yet just a few minutes from town centre and British Rail main line station.
Bedrooms: 3 twin
Bathrooms: 2 public
Bed & breakfast

per night:	£min	£max
Single	28.00	28.00
Double	40.00	40.00

Parking for 6
Ⅲ Ⓢ⅄♍ⷮ Ⅲ🚐🐾

WORTHING

West Sussex
Map ref 2D3

Largest town in West Sussex, a popular seaside resort with extensive sand and shingle beaches. Seafishing is excellent here. The museum contains finds from Cissbury Ring.
Tourist Information Centre
☎ *(01903) 210022*

Tudor Guest House ⋀

👑

5 Windsor Road, Worthing BN11 2LU
☎ (01903) 210265
Ideally situated! 1 minute from seafront, restaurants, pubs, entertainment, etc. Very friendly atmosphere, top class service. Comfortable bedrooms with free trays tea/coffee/chocolate. 3 satellite channels in all rooms. Parking on premises. En-suite rooms available. English or continental breakfast.
Bedrooms: 5 single, 2 double, 1 twin
Bathrooms: 2 private, 1 public, 1 private shower
Bed & breakfast

per night:	£min	£max
Single	12.50	17.50
Double	24.00	36.00

Parking for 5
Cards accepted: Access, Visa
☎1🏠🍴📺♨🅰Ⓢ⅄♍ⷮ Ⅲ🚐❄
🐾 ᴰᴬᴾ 🆂🅿

WYE

Kent
Map ref 3B4

New Flying Horse Inn ⋀

COMMENDED

Upper Bridge Street, Wye, Ashford TN25 5AN
☎ (01233) 812297
Fax (01233) 813487
17th C former coaching inn with oak beams and gleaming brasses. Ideal for touring and walking the Kent countryside and coast. Halfboard daily prices are for a minimum 2-night stay.
Bedrooms: 1 single, 4 double, 4 twin, 1 triple; suites available
Bathrooms: 10 private
Bed & breakfast

per night:	£min	£max
Single	37.50	39.50
Double	47.50	49.50

Half board per person:	£min	£max
Daily	37.50	39.50
Weekly	262.50	276.50

Lunch available
Evening meal 1830 (last orders 2130)
Parking for 30
Cards accepted: Access, Visa, Amex, Switch/Delta
☎🏠🚗📞🍴📺♨🅰Ⓢ⅄Ⅲ🚐🛥U❄
🐾 🆂🅿♨ Ⓣ

Farm Holiday Groups

This section of the Guide lists groups specialising in farm and country-based holidays. Most offer bed and breakfast accommodation (some with evening meal) and self-catering accommodation.

To obtain further details of individual properties please contact the group(s) direct, indicating the time of year when the accommodation is required and the number of people to be accommodated. You may find the Accommodation Coupons towards the back of this Guide helpful when making contact.

The cost of sending out brochures is high, and the groups would appreciate written enquiries being accompanied by a stamped and addressed envelope (at least 9" x 5").

The 'b&b' prices shown are per person per night; the self-catering prices are weekly terms per unit.

The symbol 🐄 before the name of a group indicates that it is a member of the Farm Holiday Bureau, set up by the Royal Agricultural Society of England in conjunction with the English Tourist Board.

🐄 East Devon Farm Holidays Group

Mrs Brenda Northam,
Bodmiscombe Farm,
Blackborough, Cullompton,
Devon EX15 2HR
Tel: Kentisbeare (01884) 266315

A warm welcome and high standards assured in family-run farm and country homes. Explore East Devon's unspoilt rolling countryside with picturesque thatched villages and miles of sandy and pebble beaches. Caravan and tent pitches also available.

16 properties offering bed and breakfast: £15–£24 b&b.

13 self-catering units (sleeping 4–13): £100–£700 depending on size and season.

Short breaks also available.

🐄 Eden Valley & North Pennines

Mrs Ruth Tuer, Meaburn Hill,
Maulds Meaburn, Penrith,
Cumbria CA10 3HN
Tel: (01931) 715205
Fax: (01931) 715205

Whether you choose to stay in the caring family atmosphere of a farmhouse bed & breakfast, or a cosy sandstone self-catering cottage, the discerning visitor will appreciate the peace and tranquillity of 'England's last wilderness'. Members are renowned for their hospitality, fresh food and home cooking. Phone or write for brochure.

11 properties offering bed and breakfast: £13–£20 b&b.

27 self-catering units: low season £92–£150; high season £180–£480.

Short breaks also available.

🐄 Heart of Dorset

Clyffe Farm, Tincleton,
Dorchester, Dorset DT2 8QR
Tel: Puddletown (01305) 848252

We offer a wide choice of high quality accommodation, at very good value, in beautiful, peaceful countryside. Dorset is renowned for its traditional villages, excellent pubs and stunning coastline. Come and see for yourselves.

5 properties offering bed and breakfast: £15–£24 b&b.

25 self-catering units: low season (October–March) £100–£180; high season (July–September) £200–£425.

Short breaks also available.

Kent Farm Holidays

Mrs R. Bannock, Court Lodge Farm, Teston, Maidstone, Kent ME18 5AQ

Tel: (01622) 812570

Fax: (01622) 814200

Mrs S.A. Marsh, Newhouse Farm, Leysdown-on-Sea, Sheerness, Kent ME12 4BA

Tel: (01795) 510201

Fax: (01795) 880379

Wide selection, from traditional farm cottages to modern farm-building conversions. Many with interesting architectural features and leisure facilities, many welcome non-smokers. Peaceful touring caravan and camping park.

20 properties offering bed and breakfast: £18–£32 b&b.

21 self-catering units: low season (October–April) from £95; high season (May–September) £150–£600.

Discounted short breaks available in low season.

 Norfolk & Suffolk Farm Holiday Group

Mrs R Bryce, College Farm, Hintlesham, Ipswich, Suffolk IP8 3NT

Tel: Hintlesham (01473) 652253

Fax: (01473) 652253

Come to Norfolk & Suffolk and experience farmhouse hospitality on a working farm. We offer quality accommodation in a friendly atmosphere. Enjoy exploring picturesque market towns, heritage coastline and 'Constable country'. Caravan and tent pitches also available.

34 properties offering bed and breakfast: £14–£22 b&b.

18 self-catering units: low season (October–March) £90–£195; high season (April–September)

£160–£380.

Short breaks also available.

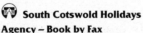 **North Pennines Area of Outstanding Natural Beauty**

Middle Bayles Farm, Alston, Cumbria CA9 3BS

Tel: Alston (01434) 381383

1st class farmhouse bed & breakfast (some en-suite) with optional dinners, or cater for yourselves in our luxury self-catering homes. Easily accessible yet far from the maddening crowds. Excellent area for touring the Lakes, Hadrian's Wall, Northumbria and Durham. Many footpaths criss-cross our beautiful homeland.

4 properties offering bed & breakfast (plus optional dinner): £12–£18 b&b.

2 self-catering units: low season (October–May) £160–£240; high season (June–September) £240–£350.

Short breaks also available.

South Cotswold Holidays Agency – Book by Fax

Mrs Victoria Jennings, Apple Orchard House, Springhill, Nailsworth, Stroud, Gloucestershire GL6 0LX

Tel: Stroud (01453) 832503 Fax: (01453) 836213

Variety of superior quality bed and breakfast establishments including inns and hotels, ranging from 17th C to modern, in the centre of an area with many visitor attractions, half an hour from Bath and Cirencester and convenient for Cheltenham, Gloucester, Stratford-upon-Avon, Oxford, Wells and Worcester. All have private bathrooms, tea/coffee facilities, friendly, helpful hosts. Half- or full-day driver and guided tours available. Colour brochure. Immediate bookings by fax at no

charge to you.

45 properties offering bed and breakfast: £15–£21 b&b. Some ground floor rooms for disabled guests. American Express/Visa/Mastercard accepted.

20 self-catering units: low season (November–April) £100–£200; high season (May–October) £200–£450 (sleeps 10).

Short breaks also available.

South Lakeland Farm & Country Holidays

Tranthwaite Hall, Underbarrow, nr Kendal, Cumbria LA8 8HG

Tel: Crossthwaite (015395) 68285

Treat yourself to a relaxing stay on one of South Lakeland's traditional working farms – full of character and tucked away in peaceful and picturesque valleys. Whatever the season there's always plenty to do and see. Ideal location for walking or touring the dramatic Lakeland scenery or, alternatively, exploring Windermere, Hill Top (Beatrix Potter's house) and many National Trust houses. Caravans available.

6 properties offering bed and breakfast: £14–£19 b&b.

4 self-catering units: £100–£300 depending on season.

Short breaks also available.

Vale of York and the Wolds

Church Farm, Scackleton, York, North Yorkshire YO6 4NB

Tel: (01653) 628403

Yorkshire farmhouse hospitality. Stay on a working farm amidst hills and dales, wolds and moors with historic York and heritage coast nearby. Caravan pitches also available.

9 properties offering bed and breakfast: £13–£22 b&b.

4 self-catering units: low season (October–March) £130–£240;

high season (April–September) £160–£340.
Short breaks also available.

 **Warwickshire Farm Holidays**
The Secretary, Crandon House, Avon Dassett, Leamington Spa, Warwickshire CV33 0AA
Tel: (01295) 770652

A warm welcome at farmhouses offering serviced and self-catering accommodation in comfortable and homely surroundings, situated in historic and picturesque 'Shakespeare country'. Caravan and tent pitches also available.
24 properties offering bed and breakfast: £12–£27 b&b.
25 self-catering units: low season (October–April) £70–£350; high season (May–September) £80–£450.

A D V E R T I S E R S

If you would like further information from any of the advertisers in this guide, you may find it helpful to use the advertisement coupons towards the end of the guide. These should be mailed direct to the companies in which you are interested. Do please remember to include your name and address.

B O O K I N G   E N Q U I R I E S

When enquiring about accommodation you may find it helpful to use the accommodation coupons towards the end of the guide. These should be mailed direct to the establishments in which you are interested. Do please remember to include your name and address.

C O U N T R Y   C O D E

🌳 Enjoy the countryside and respect its life and work 🌳 Guard against all risk of fire 🌳 Fasten all gates 🌳 Keep your dogs under close control 🌳 Keep to public paths across farmland 🌳 Use gates and stiles to cross fences, hedges and walls 🌳 Leave livestock, crops and machinery alone 🌳 Take your litter home 🌳 Help to keep all water clean 🌳 Protect wildlife, plants and trees 🌳 Take special care on country roads 🌳 Make no unnecessary noise

IS IT ACCESSIBLE?

If you are a wheelchair user or someone who has difficulty walking, look for the national 'Accessible' symbol when choosing where to stay.

All the places that display a symbol have been checked by a Tourist Board inspector against standard criteria that reflect the practical needs of wheelchair users.

There are three categories of accessibility:

 Accessible to all wheelchair users including those travelling independently

 Accessible to a wheelchair user with assistance

 Accessible to a wheelchair user able to walk short distances and up at least three steps

Establishments in this guide which have a wheelchair access category are listed on pages 10 and 11.

USE YOUR *i*'S

There are more than 550 Tourist Information Centres throughout England offering friendly help with accommodation and holiday ideas as well as suggestions of places to visit and things to do. You'll find the address of your nearest Tourist Information Centre in your local Phone Book.

CHECK THE MAPS

The colour maps at the back of this guide show all the cities, towns and villages which have accommodation listings. They will enable you to check if there is suitable accommodation in the area that you plan to visit.

Group and Youth Section

Most of the accommodation establishments listed in this Guide are particularly suitable for people looking for relatively low-cost places to stay in England. Some establishments make a special point of providing safe, budget-priced accommodation for young people, for families or for large groups. These places, ranging from Youth Hostels, YMCA and YWCA residences and budget and student hotels to the seasonally available campuses of universities and colleges, are listed individually in the pages which follow.

Information on organisations which specialise in accommodation for young people, families and groups is given below – please contact them direct for further details.

Youth Hostels

The Youth Hostels Association (England and Wales) provides basic accommodation, usually in single-sex bunk-bedded rooms or dormitories, with self-catering facilities. Most hostels also provide low-cost meals or snacks. At the time of going to press, a night's stay at a Youth Hostel will cost between £3.60 and £16.00 (under 18) and between £5.35 and £19.10 (over 18).

In spite of the word 'youth' in the name, there is in fact no upper age limit. Indeed, many Youth Hostels also offer family accommodation, either in self-contained annexes (with kitchen, living room and bathroom) or by letting the smaller, four-to-six bed dormitories as private units. Groups are very welcome at Youth Hostels, whether for educational or leisure pursuits: some hostels offer field study facilities and many more have classrooms. The YHA also offers a wide range of adventure holidays and special interest breaks.

Youth Hostels – from medieval castles to shepherds' huts – can be found all over the country, both in countryside and coastal locations and in towns and cities.

You need to be a member of the YHA in order to take advantage of the facilities. Membership entitles you to use not only the 240 hostels in England and Wales but also the thousands of Youth Hostels in other parts of the British Isles and around the world. Membership costs £3 (under 18) or £9 (over 18). Family membership is available at £9 (single-parent family) or £18 (two-parent family).

Further information from:
Youth Hostels Association
Trevelyan House, 8 St Stephen's Hill, St Albans, Hertfordshire AL1 2DY
Tel: (01727) 855215
Fax: (01727) 844126

YWCA and YMCA

The Young Women's Christian Association, founded in 1855, has grown into the world's largest women's organisation. Among its many activities is the running of over 60 houses in Britain which offer safe, reasonably priced self-catering accommodation, mostly in single rooms, either on a permanent or temporary basis.

Most houses take short-stay visitors only during the summer months. However, some of the houses do accept short-stay visitors all the year round. Although the word 'women' appears in the name of the organisation, many of the residences now take men and boys as well as women and girls.

365

The Young Men's Christian Association (YMCA), founded in 1844, operates on much the same basis as the YWCA, taking people of both sexes at its more than 70 residences around the country either on a permanent or short-stay basis.

Special budget accommodation is also available in July and August at some YMCAs as part of the Inter-Point Programme, set up to provide accommodation and advice for Inter-Railers.

Further information from:
YWCA HQ
Clarendon House, 52 Cornmarket Street, Oxford OX1 3EJ
Tel: (01865) 726110
YMCA
National Council,
640 Forest Road, Walthamstow, London E17 3DZ
Tel: (0181) 520 5599
For details of the Inter-Point Programme, please contact Brian Welters at YMCA on the above telephone number.

Universities and Colleges

Accommodation in universities and colleges offers excellent value for money at dozens of city centre, seaside and countryside campus locations around England. This type of accommodation is particularly suitable for groups, whether on a leisure trip or participating in a conference or seminar. Beds available on campus vary from 30 to 3,000. There is a wide selection of meeting room facilities to choose from, with a maximum capacity of 2,000 people, and banqueting facilities for up to 1,500.

Most accommodation is in single 'study bedrooms', with a limited number of twin and family rooms. Availability is mainly during the academic vacation periods (usually July to September and for four-week periods at Christmas and Easter), with some venues offering short-stay accommodation throughout the year.

For relaxation, there is a wide choice of recreational facilities, with most venues providing TV rooms, bars and restaurants and a variety of sporting activities, ranging from tennis, squash and swimming to team sports. Activity and special interest holidays are also on offer as are many self-catering flats and houses.

Further information from:
British Universities Accommodation Consortium (BUAC)
Box No 1150, University Park, Nottingham NG7 2RD
Tel: (0115) 950 4571
Fax: (0115) 942 2505
Connect Venues
36 Collegiate Crescent, Sheffield S10 2BP
Tel: (0114) 268 3759
Fax: (0114) 266 1203

Other Accommodation

In addition to the above main providers on a countrywide basis of budget accommodation for young people and groups, there are, of course, the many individual student and budget hotels around England and also such places as outdoor and field study centres. Some of these feature in the following pages but for more information on what is available in a particular area, please contact a local Tourist Information Centre.

WHERE TO STAY

Accommodation entries in this section are listed in alphabetical order of place name, and then in alphabetical order of establishment.

Map references refer to the colour location maps at the back of this guide. The first figure is the map number; the letter and figure which follow indicate the grid reference on the map.

At-a-glance symbols at the end of each accommodation entry give information about services and facilities. A handy guide to these symbols can be found inside the back cover flap, which can be kept open for easy reference.

ABINGDON

Oxfordshire
Map ref 2C1

Attractive former county town on River Thames with many interesting buildings, including 17th C County Hall, now a museum, in the market-place and the remains of an abbey.
Tourist Information Centre
☎ *(01235) 522711*

Kingfisher Barn
Rye Farm, Culham, Abingdon OX14 3NN
☎ (01235) 527567 & 527590
Contact: Ms Liz Beaumont or Dee O'Dell
Renovated barn and farm buildings with many activities, fully accessible to all. Accommodation for families, groups or individuals.
Bedrooms: 10 double/twin. Total number of beds: 20
Bathrooms: 10 private

Bed & breakfast

per person:	£min	£max
Daily	25.00	35.00

Full board

per person:	£min	£max
Weekly	250.00	400.00

Lunch available
Parking for 50
🛇 4 🛇 🛇 🖵 🖤 🛋 🛇 📶 🗕 🛇 🗢 ⋃ ↱ ✓ 📠 🛇 SP 🛇

Establishments should be open throughout the year unless otherwise stated in the entry.

AMBLESIDE

Cumbria
Map ref 5A3

Market town situated at the head of Lake Windermere and surrounded by fells. The historic town centre is now a conservation area and the country around Ambleside is rich in historic and literary associations. Good centre for touring, walking and climbing.

Ambleside Youth Hostel
Waterhead, Ambleside LA22 0EU
☎ (015394) 32304
Fax (015394) 34408
Situated on the shores of Windermere, with own waterfront and jetty. Panoramic views of Lakeland fells. Family rooms, friendly atmosphere, dining room overlooking lake.
Bedrooms: 18 double/twin, 9 triple, 14 quadruple, 22 dormitories. Total number of beds: 286
Bathrooms: 20 public

Bed only

per person:	£min	£max
Daily	6.15	9.10

Bed & breakfast

per person:	£min	£max
Daily	8.95	11.90

Full board

per person:	£min	£max
Weekly	108.00	129.00

Evening meal 1730 (last orders 1930)
Open March-December
Cards accepted: Access, Visa, Switch/Delta
🛇 5 📶 🛋 S ✂ 🛏 📶 🛇 🗢 🖢 ✗ 🛇 🛇 T

BASSENTHWAITE

Cumbria
Map ref 5A2

Standing in an idyllic setting, nestled at the foot of Skiddaw and Ullock Pike, this village is just a mile from Bassenthwaite Lake, the one true "lake" in the Lake District. The area is visited by many varieties of migrating birds.

Bassenthwaite Parish Rooms
Bassenthwaite, Keswick CA12
Contact: Miss Helen Reb, Bassenthwaite Parish Rooms, Management Committee, 1 The Avenue, Bassenthwaite, Keswick, Cumbria CA12 4QJ
☎ (017687) 76222
Village Hall. School Road off A591. Minimum booking is for 12 people, 3 nights.
Total number of beds: 50
Bathrooms: 1 public

Bed only

per person:	£min	£max
Daily	2.00	

Parking for 10
🛇 7 📶 📶 🛇

Kiln Hill Barn
Bassenthwaite, Keswick CA12 4RG
☎ (017687) 76454
Contact: Mr. J K Armstrong
Converted barn in the country. Owned and run by the Armstrongs. Ideal for leisure and activity holidays.
Bedrooms: 1 single, 2 double/twin, 2 dormitories. Total number of beds: 39
Bathrooms: 4 public

Bed & breakfast

per person:	£min	£max
Daily	11.00	11.00

Continued ▶

BASSENTHWAITE

Continued

Full board

per person:	£min	£max
Weekly	120.00	120.00

Evening meal 1830 (last orders 1830)
Parking for 15
Open February-November

🛏🖵📶🛈Ⓢ🅿📺🛆🔌♨☎Ⓣ

BATH

Avon
Map ref 2B2

Georgian spa city beside the River Avon. Important Roman site with impressive reconstructed baths, uncovered in 19th C. Bath Abbey built on site of monastery where first king of England was crowned (AD 973). Fine architecture in mellow local stone. Pump Room and museums.
Tourist Information Centre
☎ *(01225) 462831*

Bath Youth Hostel

Bathwick Hill, Bath BA2 6JZ
☎ (01225) 465674
Fax (01225) 482947
Contact: Mr Bob Newsom
Youth hostel occupying a handsome Italianate mansion set in large grounds overlooking the historic city of Bath.
Bedrooms: 2 double/twin, 10 quadruple, 6 dormitories. Total number of beds: 121
Bathrooms: 15 public

Bed only

per person:	£min	£max
Daily	5.50	8.30

Bed & breakfast

per person:	£min	£max
Daily	8.30	11.10

Full board

per person:	£min	£max
Weekly	103.60	123.20

Evening meal 1800 (last orders 1930)
Cards accepted: Access, Visa, Switch/Delta

🛏🖵📶🛈Ⓢ🅿📺🛆🔌☎♨Ⓢ⒫🏮

The City of Bath YMCA ⋔

International House, Broad Street Place, Bath BA1 5LN
☎ (01225) 460471
Fax (01225) 462065
Contact: Mr A Teasdale
Open to those of both sexes and all ages. Centrally located and only minutes away from Bath's major attractions. A convenient base for city and West Country tours.
Bedrooms: 38 single, 36 double/twin, 8 triple, 3 dormitories. Total number of beds: 190
Bathrooms: 30 public

Bed & breakfast

per person:	£min	£max
Daily	10.00	12.50

Full board

per person:	£min	£max
Weekly	126.00	143.50

Lunch available
Evening meal 1700 (last orders 1900)

🛏🖵📶🛈Ⓢ🅿📺🛆🔌☎♨✕🏮

BELFORD

Northumberland
Map ref 5B1

Small market town on the old coaching road, close to the coast, the Scottish border and the north-east flank of the Cheviots. Built mostly in stone and very peaceful now that the A1 has by-passed the town, Belford makes an ideal centre for excursions to the moors and coast.

Bearsports Outdoors

The Windy Gyle, Belford NE70 7QE
Contact: Mrs P M Clark, Bearsports Outdoors, Windy Gyle, Belford, Northumberland NE70 7QE
☎ (01668) 213289
Fax (01668) 213289
Outdoor activity courses for individuals, families and groups. Expert instruction, excellent equipment and locations. Quality accommodation and food. Approved by RYA, BCU and BAHA.
Bedrooms: 6 dormitories. Total number of beds: 42
Bathrooms: 8 public

Bed & breakfast

per person:	£min	£max
Daily	14.50	

Full board

per person:	£min	£max
Weekly	96.00	

Lunch available
Evening meal from 1830
Parking for 5

🛏⛄🛈Ⓢ🅿📺🛆🔌♨Ⓟ🔧Ⓢ⒫Ⓣ

BIRMINGHAM

West Midlands
Map ref 4B3

Britain's second city, whose attractions include Centenary Square and the ICC with Symphony Hall, the NEC, the City Art Gallery, Barber Institute of Fine Arts, 17th C Aston Hall, science and railway museums, Jewellery Quarter, Cadbury World, 2 cathedrals and Botanical Gardens.
Tourist Information Centre
☎ *(0121) 643 2514 or 780 4321 or 693 6300*

The University of Birmingham ⋔

Edgbaston, Birmingham B15 2TT

Contact: Mr E Farrar, Residences and Conferences, University of Birmingham, Edgbaston, Birmingham B15 2TT
☎ (0121) 454 6022
Fax (0121) 456 2415
Accommodation is provided in single and twin study bedrooms with washbasins, in parkland area in the attractive suburb of Edgbaston.
Bedrooms: 1050 single, 300 double/twin. Total number of beds: 1650
Bathrooms: 160 private, 100 public

Bed only

per person:	£min	£max
Daily	21.70	

Bed & breakfast

per person:	£min	£max
Daily	26.15	

Lunch available
Evening meal 1800 (last orders 2000)
Parking for 1000
Open January, March-April, July-September, December

🛏♦🛈Ⓢ🅿📺🛆🔌♨✕🔧♨♨🪑
♿✕Ⓢ⒫Ⓣ

BISHOP AUCKLAND

Durham
Map ref 5C2

Busy market town on the bank of the River Wear. The Palace, a castellated Norman manor house altered in the 18th C, stands in beautiful gardens. Entered from the market square by a handsome 18th C gatehouse, the park is a peaceful retreat of trees and streams.
Tourist Information Centre
☎ *(01388) 604922*

Weardale House ⋔

Ireshopeburn, Bishop Auckland, County Durham DL13 1HB
Contact: Mr C Jones, Y.M.C.A. Residential Office, Herrington Burn, Houghton-le-Spring, Tyne and Wear DH4 4JW
☎ (0191) 385 2822 & 385 3085
Fax (0191) 385 2267
Multi-activity outdoor centre. Prices quoted are for full board Monday-Friday and include all catering, accommodation and multi-activity course.
Bedrooms: 3 single, 8 dormitories. Total number of beds: 70
Bathrooms: 8 public

Full board

per person:	£min	£max
Weekly	128.00	141.00

Lunch available
Parking for 10

🛏7⛄🛈Ⓢ🅿📺🛆🔌🔌♨♨
✕🔧

BRADFORD

West Yorkshire
Map ref 4B1

City founded on wool, with fine Victorian and modern buildings. Attractions include the cathedral, city hall, Cartwright Hall, Lister Park, Moorside Mills Industrial Museum and National Museum of Photography, Film and Television.
Tourist Information Centre
☎ *(01274) 753678*

University of Bradford ⋀

Bradford BD7 1DP
Contact: Ms A Milton & Ms E Fazakerley, Conference Officer, University of Bradford, Bradford, West Yorkshire BD7 1DP
☎ (01274) 384889 & 733466
Fax (01274) 385505
Telex 51309
Attractive, compact campus in a convenient location for touring the peaks, dales and Bronte country. Sports facilities including swimming pool, sauna and solarium.
Bedrooms: 1300 single. Total number of beds: 1300
Bathrooms: 85 private, 200 public
Bed only

per person:	£min	£max
Daily	12.30	28.80

Bed & breakfast

per person:	£min	£max
Daily	15.90	33.00

Lunch available
Evening meal from 1800
Parking for 150
Open January, March-April, July-September, December
⚒ 10 ♨ 🛏 🖥 S 📺 💻 ▣ 🛍 ✕ ● 🔍 🎿 ☿ ✕

BRIGHTON & HOVE

East Sussex
Map ref 2D3

Brighton's attractions include the Royal Pavilion, Volks Electric Railway, Sea Life Centre and Marina Village, Conference Centre and "The Lanes" and several theatres. Neighbouring Hove is a resort in its own right.
Tourist Information Centre
☎ *(01273) 323755; for Hove (01273) 746100 or 778087*

University of Brighton ⋀

Circus Street, Brighton BN2 2QF
Contact: Mrs Evelyn Mohan, University of Brighton, Conference Office, Circus Street, Brighton, East Sussex BN2 2DF
☎ (01273) 643167 & 643168
Fax (01273) 643149
The university has a variety of residential accommodation in Brighton and Eastbourne available to groups and conference organisers in April, July, August and September.

Bedrooms: 416 single.
Bed only

per person:	£min	£max
Daily	10.00	16.00

Bed & breakfast

per person:	£min	£max
Daily	16.00	19.50

Lunch available
Evening meal 1800 (last orders 1900)
Parking for 230
Open April, July-September
Cards accepted: Access, Visa
⚒ 14 ♨ 🛏 🖥 S ✕ 📺 💻 ▣ 🛍 ☿ ✕ 🔍 ✕

BRISTOL

Avon
Map ref 2A2

Famous for maritime links, historic harbour, Georgian terraces and Brunel's Clifton suspension bridge. Many attractions including SS Great Britain, Bristol Zoo, museums and art galleries and top name entertainments. Events include Balloon Fiesta and Regatta.
Tourist Information Centre
☎ *(0117) 926 0767*

Youth Hostel - Bristol Centre

Hayman House, 14 Narrow Quay, Bristol BS1 4QA
☎ (0117) 922 1659
Fax (0117) 927 3789
Contact: Mr A Lamb
Impressive refurbished warehouse on the quayside in Bristol's historic harbour set in the heart of the city. Good value accommodation. Several rooms have en-suite facilities.
Bedrooms: 4 double/twin, 16 quadruple, 9 dormitories. Total number of beds: 120
Bathrooms: 12 private, 20 public
Bed only

per person:	£min	£max
Daily	7.50	11.00

Bed & breakfast

per person:	£min	£max
Daily	10.30	13.80

Full board

per person:	£min	£max
Weekly	117.60	142.10

Lunch available
Evening meal 1800 (last orders 1945)
Cards accepted: Access, Visa, Switch/Delta
⚒ 🛏 S ✕ 📺 💻 ▣ ● ✕ 🚲

Individual proprietors
have supplied all details of
accommodation. As changes
can occur, we advise you to
confirm the information at
the time of booking.

CAMBRIDGE

Cambridgeshire
Map ref 2D1

A most important and beautiful city on the River Cam with 31 colleges forming one of the oldest universities in the world. Numerous museums, good shopping centre, restaurants, theatres, cinema and fine bookshops.
Tourist Information Centre
☎ *(01223) 322640*

Cambridge Y.M.C.A.

Queen Anne House, Gonville Place, Cambridge CB1 1ND
☎ (01223) 356998
Fax (01223) 312749
Contact: Mrs P Bishop
Young people's residency, in the centre of Cambridge overlooking Parkers Piece. Near railway and bus stations. Very busy - not suitable for guests expecting peace and quiet.
Bedrooms: 95 single, 31 double/twin. Total number of beds: 157
Bathrooms: 24 public
Bed & breakfast

per person:	£min	£max
Daily	19.00	23.00

Lunch available
Evening meal 1715 (last orders 1845)
⚒ 🛏 ♨ S ✕ 📺 💻 ▣ ✕ ✕

Youth Hostel Cambridge ⋀

97 Tenison Road, Cambridge CB1 2DN
Contact: Miss Carol Hancock, Youth Hostel Association, 97 Tenison Road, Cambridge CB1 2DN
☎ (01223) 354601
Fax (01223) 312780
Youth hostel offering a high standard of comfort and facilities, including relaxing lounges, small rooms, an excellent cafeteria and courtyard garden.
Bedrooms: 23 dormitories. Total number of beds: 128
Bathrooms: 8 public
Bed only

per person:	£min	£max
Daily	6.80	10.05

Bed & breakfast

per person:	£min	£max
Daily	9.60	12.85

Full board

per person:	£min	£max
Weekly	112.70	135.45

Evening meal 1800 (last orders 2000)
Cards accepted: Access, Visa, Switch/Delta
⚒ ♨ 🛏 S ✕ 📺 💻 ▣ ✕ 🔍 SP

At-a-glance symbols are
explained on the flap inside
the back cover.

CANTERBURY

Kent
Map ref 3B3

Place of pilgrimage since the martyrdom of Becket in 1170 and the site of Canterbury Cathedral. Visit St Augustine's Abbey, St Martin's (the oldest church in England), Royal Museum and Art Gallery and the Canterbury Tales. Nearby is Howletts Wild Animal Park.
Tourist Information Centre
☎ *(01227) 766567*

Focus Canterbury
Tanglewood, The University, Canterbury CT2 7LX
Contact: Mr I M Sheridan, Focus Canterbury, The University, Canterbury, Kent CT2 7LX
☎ (01227) 769186
Fax (01227) 475432
During University vacations you can enjoy the flexible and comfortable accommodation facilities in one of our four colleges in the attractively situated parkland campus overlooking the Cathedral. Sports facilities also available.
Bedrooms: 1490 single, 31 double/twin. Total number of beds: 1552
Bathrooms: 268 private, 160 public
Bed & breakfast

per person:	£min	£max
Daily	15.00	17.00

Lunch available
Evening meal 1800 (last orders 1900)
Parking for 1200
Open January, March, July-September, December
Cards accepted: Access, Visa
♨ 10 ♿ ⓘ Ⓢ ⊬ ⓜ 🅣Ⅶ ⅢⅢ. ◨ ⅌ ✕ ◵ ⚓ ℺ Ü ⴼ ✕ 🅓🅐🅟 🆂🅿 🅣

Parkwood Village At The University of Kent, Canterbury ⋔
Focus Canterbury, Tanglewood, The University, Canterbury CT2 7LZ
Contact: Mr I M Sheridan, Focus Canterbury, Tanglewood, The University, Canterbury, Kent CT2 7LZ
☎ (01227) 769186
Fax (01227) 475432
The University, with its fine views of Canterbury, offers value-for-money self-catering accommodation in 5/6-bedded houses, ideal for families. Prices are based on a minimum 4-night stay for 4 people.
Minimum age 16
Bedrooms: 1400 single, 20 double/twin. Total number of beds: 1440
Bathrooms: 103 private, 160 public
Bed only

per person:	£min	£max
Daily	6.25	9.40

Lunch available
Evening meal 1800 (last orders 1900)

Parking for 1997
Open January, March-April, July-September, December
♨ ⓘ Ⓢ ⊬ 🅣Ⅶ ⅢⅢ. ◨ ⅌ ✕ ◵ ⚓ ⴼ ✕

CARNFORTH

Lancashire
Map ref 5B3

Permanent home of the "Flying Scotsman" in Steamtown Railway Museum. Nearby are Borwick Hall, an Elizabethan manor house, and Leighton Hall which has good paintings and early furniture and is open to the public.

Borwick Hall Residential Centre
Borwick, Carnforth LA6 1JU
☎ (01524) 732508
Fax (01524) 732590
Contact: Mrs Foster
Residential training centre for organised and accompanied groups with their own training programme. 2 separate buildings. M6 exit 35, A6 to Milnthorpe, first right, one mile.
For groups only
Bedrooms: 5 single, 24 double/twin, 5 triple, 2 quadruple, 4 dormitories. Total number of beds: 98
Bathrooms: 13 public
Bed only

per person:	£min	£max
Daily	9.10	20.20

Bed & breakfast

per person:	£min	£max
Daily	11.15	23.30

Full board

per person:	£min	£max
Weekly	147.70	314.30

Lunch available
Evening meal 1700 (last orders 1900)
Parking for 60
♨ ⏏ ⚲ ⅃ ⓘ Ⓢ ⊬ 🅣Ⅶ ⅢⅢ. ◨ ◵ ⴼ ✕ 🚲 🅕

CASTLETON

Derbyshire
Map ref 4B2

Large village in a spectacular Peak District setting with ruined Peveril Castle and 4 great show caverns, where the Blue John stone and lead were mined. One cavern offers a mile-long underground boat journey.

Castleton Youth Hostel
Castleton Hall, Castle Street, Castleton, Sheffield S30 2WG
Contact: The Warden, Castleton Youth Hostel, Castleton Hall, Castle Street, Castleton, Sheffield S30 2WG
☎ Hope Valley (01433) 620235
Fax (01433) 621767
Situated in the heart of village, offering low cost accommodation with family rooms and excellent meals.

Bedrooms: 4 double/twin, 7 quadruple, 9 dormitories. Total number of beds: 108
Bathrooms: 7 private, 7 public
Bed only

per person:	£min	£max
Daily	5.55	8.25

Bed & breakfast

per person:	£min	£max
Daily	8.35	11.05

Full board

per person:	£min	£max
Weekly	100.00	123.00

Lunch available
Evening meal 1800 (last orders 2000)
Open February-December
Cards accepted: Access, Visa, Switch/Delta
♨ 5 ⏏ ⚲ ⓘ Ⓢ ⊬ 🅣Ⅶ ⅢⅢ. ◵ Ü ✕ 🅓🅐🅟 ℺ 🆂🅿 🅕 🅣

CHALFONT ST GILES

Buckinghamshire
Map ref 2D2

Pretty, old village in wooded Chiltern Hills yet only 20 miles from London and a good base for visiting the city. Excellent base for Windsor, Henley, the Thames Valley, Oxford and the Cotswolds.

Buckinghamshire College
Newland Park, Gorlands Lane, Chalfont St Giles HP8 4AD
☎ (01494) 603064
Fax (01494) 603078
Contact: Facilities Office
15 minutes from M25, in 300 acres of parkland, at the centre of which is an 18th C manor house. 500 single bedrooms, especially suitable for groups. Extensive catering and conference facilities.
Bedrooms: 500 single. Total number of beds: 500
Bathrooms: 47 public
Bed only

per person:	£min	£max
Daily	12.00	16.00

Bed & breakfast

per person:	£min	£max
Daily	16.00	22.00

Full board

per person:	£min	£max
Weekly	120.00	200.00

Lunch available
Parking for 800
Open June-September
Cards accepted: Access, Visa
♨ ⏏ ⓘ Ⓢ ⊬ ⓜ ⅢⅢ. ◨ ✕ ◵ ⚓ ↺ ◵ Ü ✕ 🚲 ℺ 🆂🅿 🅕

Colour maps at the back of this guide pinpoint all places which have accommodation listings in the guide.

CHORLEY

Lancashire
Map ref 4A1

Set between the Pennine moors and the Lancashire Plain, Chorley has been an important town since medieval times, with its "Flat-Iron" and covered markets. The rich heritage includes Astley Hall and Park, Hoghton Tower, Rivington Country Park and the Leeds-Liverpool Canal.

Lancashire College
Southport Road, Chorley PR7 1NB
☎ (01257) 276719
Fax (01257) 241370
Contact: Mrs A Bithell
Purpose-built adult residential college. Lounge/bar, well designed and equipped teaching suite and conference accommmodation.
For groups only
Minimum age 18
Bedrooms: 46 single. Total number of beds: 53
Bathrooms: 6 private, 12 public
Bed & breakfast

per person:	£min	£max
Daily	13.00	15.00

Lunch available
Evening meal from 1830
Parking for 100

CIRENCESTER

Gloucestershire
Map ref 2B1

"Capital of the Cotswolds", Cirencester was Britain's second most important Roman town with many finds housed in the Corinium Museum. It has a very fine Perpendicular church and old houses around the market place.
Tourist Information Centre
☎ *(01285) 654180*

Royal Agricultural College Enterprises Limited ⋒
Cirencester GL7 6JS
☎ (01285) 652531
Fax (01285) 654214
Contact: Ms T North
Conference or touring centre in the heart of the Cotswolds offering a very personalised service to all guests.
Bedrooms: 50 single, 170 double/twin, 20 dormitories. Total number of beds: 430
Bathrooms: 44 private, 53 public
Bed & breakfast

per person:	£min	£max
Daily	20.00	30.00

Full board

per person:	£min	£max
Weekly	210.00	280.00

Lunch available
Evening meal 1800 (last orders 2000)
Parking for 700

Open January, March-April, July-September, December

CRANFIELD

Bedfordshire
Map ref 2D1

Apart from a very few small cottages and some Victorian almshouses, there is little evidence of Cranfield's past. This is now one of the most quickly growing and heavily populated towns in Bedfordshire.

Cranfield University
Cranfield, Bedford MK43 0AL
Contact: Miss Jane Horriben, Cranfield University, Mitchell Hall, Cranfield, Bedford MK43 0AL
☎ Bedford (01234) 750111 & 754300
Fax (01234) 752287
Cranfield, Europe's postgraduate university. Campus offers an excellent range of conference facilities, attractive comfortable accommodation and dining rooms.
Minimum age 16
Bedrooms: 80 single, 22 double/twin.
Bathrooms: 63 private
Bed & breakfast

per person:	£min	£max
Daily	21.00	50.55

Lunch available
Evening meal 1830 (last orders 1930)
Parking for 300
Cards accepted: Access, Visa

DONCASTER

South Yorkshire
Map ref 4C1

Ancient Roman town famous for its heavy industries, butterscotch and racecourse (St Leger), also centre of agricultural area. Attractions include 18th C Mansion House, Cusworth Hall Museum, Doncaster Museum, St George's Church, The Dome and Doncaster Leisure Park.
Tourist Information Centre
☎ *(01302) 734309*

Doncaster College Conference Centre
Doncaster College, High Melton, Doncaster DN5 7SZ
☎ (01302) 553715
Fax (01302) 553717
Contact: Mr David Mantell
Centre for residential short courses and conferences. In a central position and pleasant surroundings. Six miles west of Doncaster town centre.
Bedrooms: 28 single, 3 double/twin.
Total number of beds: 34
Bathrooms: 31 private

Bed only

per person:	£min	£max
Daily	30.00	

Bed & breakfast

per person:	£min	£max
Daily	35.00	

Full board

per person:	£min	£max
Weekly	330.00	

Lunch available
Evening meal 1800 (last orders 2030)
Parking for 450

DURHAM

Durham
Map ref 5C2

Ancient city with its Norman castle and cathedral set on a bluff high over the Wear. A market and university town and regional centre, spreading beyond the market-place on both banks of the river.
Tourist Information Centre
☎ *(0191) 384 3720*

College of St Hild and St Bede ⋒
University of Durham, Leazes Road, Durham, County Durham DH1 1SZ
☎ (0191) 374 3069
Contact: Mr P A Warburton
College set in spacious grounds in the medieval City of Durham, providing a splendid base for exploring Northumbria.
Bedrooms: 370 single, 45 double/twin, 1 triple. Total number of beds: 463
Bathrooms: 53 public
Bed & breakfast

per person:	£min	£max
Daily	13.50	16.50

Full board

per person:	£min	£max
Weekly	94.50	115.50

Lunch available
Evening meal 1800 (last orders 1900)
Parking for 200
Open March-April, July-September

Collingwood College ⋒
South Road, Durham, County Durham DH1 3LT
Contact: Mrs Sally Hewlett, Collingwood College, South Road, Durham, County Durham DH1 3LT
☎ (0191) 374 7397
Fax (0191) 374 4595
Durham's newest residential college, set in woodland 1 mile south of the city.
Bedrooms: 527 single, 16 double/twin, 1 triple. Total number of beds: 301
Bathrooms: 215 private, 56 public
Bed & breakfast

per person:	£min	£max
Daily	16.00	26.00

Continued ▶

DURHAM

Continued

Full board

per person:	£min	£max
Weekly	150.00	200.00

Lunch available
Evening meal 1800 (last orders 1900)
Parking for 120
Open January, March-April, July-
September, December

Grey College ⚲

University of Durham, South Road,
Durham, County Durham DH1 3LG
☎ (0191) 374 2900
Fax (0191) 374 2992
Contact: Miss S Wroe
*Attractive venue, just 15 minutes' walk
from the city centre. Reasonable single
and double room rates. Lounge, TV
room, bar and sports facilities.*
Bedrooms: 275 single, 12 double/twin,
1 dormitory. Total number of beds:
300
Bathrooms: 97 private, 28 public

Bed & breakfast

per person:	£min	£max
Daily	16.45	28.20

Full board

per person:	£min	£max
Weekly	246.75	329.00

Lunch available
Evening meal 1800 (last orders 2000)
Parking for 60
Open March-April, June-September,
December

St. Aidans College ⚲

University of Durham, Windmill Hill,
Durham, County Durham DH1 3LJ
☎ (0191) 374 3269
Contact: Lt. Cdr. J C Bull
*Modern college in beautiful landscaped
gardens overlooking the cathedral.
Comfortable standard and en-suite
single and twin-bedded rooms, bar, TV
lounge, free tennis. Adjacent golf-course.*
Bedrooms: 293 single, 66 double/twin.
Total number of beds: 425
Bathrooms: 94 private, 48 public

Bed & breakfast

per person:	£min	£max
Daily	15.00	25.00

Full board

per person:	£min	£max
Weekly	186.00	230.00

Lunch available
Evening meal 1830 (last orders 1900)
Parking for 80
Open March-April, July-September,
December
Cards accepted: Visa

St. Cuthberts Society

12 South Bailey, Durham, County
Durham DH1 3EE
☎ (0191) 374 3464
Contact: Mrs H Bowler

*Situated in the heart of the old town
and 5 minutes' walk from the cathedral
and city centre. Riverside gardens.*
Bedrooms: 50 single, 23 double/twin,
3 triple. Total number of beds: 114
Bathrooms: 21 public

Bed & breakfast

per person:	£min	£max
Daily	16.00	16.00

Full board

per person:	£min	£max
Weekly	182.00	182.00

Open July-September

St John's College ⚲

University of Durham, 3 South Bailey,
Durham, County Durham DH1 3RJ
☎ (0191) 374 3566
Fax (0191) 374 3573
Contact: Mr Martin Clemmett
*In the heart of the city, alongside
Durham Cathedral and Castle. Offering
good quality student accommodation to
individuals, families and groups.*
Bedrooms: 100 single, 13 double/twin,
1 triple. Total number of beds: 129
Bathrooms: 42 public

Bed only

per person:	£min	£max
Daily	14.00	14.00

Bed & breakfast

per person:	£min	£max
Daily	16.50	16.50

Full board

per person:	£min	£max
Weekly	217.00	217.00

Evening meal 1800 (last orders 1930)
Open March-April, July-September,
December

St Marys College ⚲

Elvet Hill Road, Durham, County
Durham DH1 3LR
☎ (0191) 374 2700
Fax (0191) 374 7473
Contact: Miss P Aynesworth
*Imposing, stone-built college in beautiful
grounds overlooking the cathedral. 7
minutes from the city centre and on a
bus route. En-suite rooms available.*
Bedrooms: 212 single, 29 double/twin.
Total number of beds: 270
Bathrooms: 48 private, 36 public

Bed & breakfast

per person:	£min	£max
Daily	17.90	28.00

Lunch available
Evening meal from 1900
Parking for 35
Open January, March-April, July-
September, December

Van Mildert College ⚲

University of Durham, Durham,
County Durham DH1 3LH
Contact: Mr J Hirst, Van Mildert
College, University of Durham,
Durham, County Durham DH1 3LH
☎ (0191) 374 3963
Fax (0191) 384 7764

*College and conference centre in
beautiful lakeside surroundings,
adjacent to golf course, opposite
Botanical Gardens. Half a mile from
Durham Cathedral and Castle World
Heritage Site. Families and small
groups welcome.*
Minimum age 17
Bedrooms: 390 single, 48 double/twin.
Total number of beds: 438
Bathrooms: 48 private, 68 public

Bed & breakfast

per person:	£min	£max
Daily	16.50	27.50

Full board

per person:	£min	£max
Weekly	99.00	165.00

Lunch available
Evening meal from 1800
Parking for 100

GIGGLESWICK

North Yorkshire
Map ref 5B3

Picturesque Pennine village of
period stone cottages with ancient
market cross, stocks and tithe
barn. Parish church is dedicated to
St Alkeda, an Anglo-Saxon saint.
During restoration work the tomb
of a 15th C knight with his horse
was discovered.

Yorkshire Dales Field Centre

Square House, 17 Church Street,
Giggleswick, Settle BD24 OBE
☎ Settle (01729) 822965 & (bookings)
824180
Fax (01729) 824180
Contact: Mr Peter Fish & Mrs A
Barbour

*Comfortable dales barn in quiet corner
of renowned village, Three Peaks area
of Yorkshire Dales. Any group of 10
people-plus. Good food provided or self-
catering basis.*
Bedrooms: 2 single, 2 quadruple,
4 dormitories. Total number of beds:
35
Bathrooms: 4 public

Bed only

per person:	£min	£max
Daily	8.00	10.00

Bed & breakfast

per person:	£min	£max
Daily	11.00	12.00

Full board

per person:	£min	£max
Weekly	102.00	114.00

Lunch available
Evening meal 1730 (last orders 1930)
Parking for 8

💶 ⚒ ♿ ⓤ🇮 🛈 Ⓢ ✂ ♨ ⓉⓋ �🖼 ⌷ ▤ 🞂 Ⓤ🇮 🛄
🆂🅿 🏮

GUILDFORD

Surrey
Map ref 2D2

Bustling town with many historic
monuments, one of which is the
Guildhall clock jutting out over the
old High Street. The modern
cathedral occupies a commanding
position on Stag Hill.
Tourist Information Centre
☎ *(01483) 444333*

University of Surrey ⋀⋀
Guildford GU2 5XH
☎ (01483) 259352
Fax (01483) 579266
Contact: Miss J Peberdy
The university and cathedral occupy
commanding positions on a hill
overlooking this historic town. London
30 miles, coast 40 miles. Self-catering
accommodation also available. Special
weekly rates.
Bedrooms: 6 double/twin. Total
number of beds: 2001
Bathrooms: 360 private, 491 public
Bed & breakfast

per person:	£min	£max
Daily	13.25	22.57

Lunch available
Evening meal 1800 (last orders 1930)
Parking for 1400
Open January, March-April, June-
September
Cards accepted: Access, Visa

💶 14 ⚒ ♿ 🛈 Ⓢ ♨ ⓉⓋ ⌷ ▤ ✕ 🞂 🎋 ♨
🏹 ✕ 🄳🄰🄿 🆂🅿 🏮

HARROGATE

North Yorkshire
Map ref 4B1

A major conference, exhibition and
shopping centre, renowned for its
spa heritage and award winning
floral displays, spacious parks and
gardens. Famous for antiques,
toffee, fine shopping and excellent
tea shops, also its Royal Pump
Rooms and Baths.
Tourist Information Centre
☎ *(01423) 525666*

West End Outdoor Centre ⋀⋀
West End, Summerbridge, Harrogate
HG3 4BA
Contact: Mrs M Verity, West End
Outdoor Centre, Whitmoor Farm, West
End, Summerbridge, Harrogate, North
Yorkshire HG3 4BA
☎ Blubberhouses (01943) 880207
Self-catering bunkhouse with panoramic
views over Thruscross reservoir. Well-
appointed facilities, 12 miles from
Harrogate and Skipton, 30 miles from
York.

Bedrooms: 4 double/twin,
4 quadruple, 1 dormitory. Total
number of beds: 30
Bathrooms: 1 private, 4 public
Bed only

per person:	£min	£max
Daily	5.00	7.00

Parking for 15

💶 ⚒ ♿ ⓤ🇮 ✂ ♨ ⌷ 🞂 🆂🅿

HEBDEN BRIDGE

West Yorkshire
Map ref 4B1

Originally a small town on
packhorse route, Hebden Bridge
grew into a booming mill town in
18th C with rows of "up-and-down"
houses of several storeys built
against hillsides. Ancient "pace-
egg play" custom held on Good
Friday.
Tourist Information Centre
☎ *(01422) 843831*

Hebden Hey Activity Centre
Hardcastle Crags, Hebden Bridge
HX7 7AW
Contact: Mr & Mrs A P Garside,
26 Carlton House Terrace, Haugh
Shaw Road, Halifax, West Yorkshire
HXL 3LD
☎ Halifax (01422) 347408
Two purpose-built hostels providing
accommodation for up to 28 and 46
persons, in bunk rooms. Price is per
person as part of group.
Bedrooms: 8 dormitories. Total
number of beds: 72
Bathrooms: 7 public
Bed only

per person:	£min	£max
Daily	1.57	2.16

Parking for 15

💶 ⚒ ⓤ🇮 ♨ 🖼

HECKFIELD

Hampshire
Map ref 2C2

Wellington Riding Ltd ⋀⋀
Basingstoke Road, Heckfield,
Basingstoke RG27 OLJ
☎ (01734) 326308
Fax (01734) 326661
Contact: Mr John Goodman & Miss
Linda Sawyer
Equestrian centre. Accommodation only
for unaccompanied juniors taking
riding holidays and for adults on
equestrian courses.
Minimum age 8
Bedrooms: 5 double/twin,
4 dormitories. Total number of beds:
49
Bathrooms: 4 public
Full board

per person:	£min	£max
Weekly	124.00	

Lunch available

Parking for 40
Cards accepted: Access, Visa, Switch/
Delta

💶 Ⓢ ✂ ♨ ⓉⓋ ⌷ ▤ Ⓤ ✕ 🖼 🄳🄰🄿 🆂🅿 Ⓣ

ILKLEY

West Yorkshire
Map ref 4B1

This moorland town is famous for
its ballad. The 16th C manor
house, now a museum, displays
local prehistoric and Roman relics.
Popular walk leads up Heber's
Ghyll to Ilkley Moor, with the
mysterious Swastika Stone and
White Wells, 18th C plunge baths.
Tourist Information Centre
☎ *(01943) 602319*

Glenmoor Centre/City of Bradford Metropolitan Council ⋀⋀
Wells Road, Ilkley LS29 9JF
☎ (01943) 816359
Fax (01943) 816359
Contact: Mrs M Cairns
Attractive accommodation for residential
and day conferences in a beautiful
setting, just on the edge of Ilkley Moor.
Special rates for voluntary
organisations and registered charities.
Tariffs shown based on minimum 10
delegates.
For groups only
Bedrooms: 8 single, 12 double/twin.
Total number of beds: 32
Bathrooms: 6 private, 7 public
Bed only

per person:	£min	£max
Daily	9.00	16.50

Bed & breakfast

per person:	£min	£max
Daily	12.50	20.00

Full board

per person:	£min	£max
Weekly	164.50	263.90

Lunch available
Evening meal 1700 (last orders 1900)
Parking for 14

⚒ ♿ 🛈 Ⓢ ✂ ♨ ⓉⓋ ⌷ ▤ 🆂🅿 🏮

INGLETON

North Yorkshire
Map ref 5B3

Thriving tourist centre for fell-
walkers, climbers and pot-holers.
Popular walks up beautiful Twiss
Valley to Ingleborough Summit,
Whernside, White Scar Caves and
waterfalls.

The Barnstead
Stackstead Farm, Ingleton, Carnforth,
Lancashire LA6 3HS
☎ (015242) 41386
Contact: Mr & Mrs J Charlton
Well-equipped, bunk-style, self-catering
accommodation for groups of 2-22 with
4 bedrooms, a communal kitchen and a
Continued ▶

373

INGLETON

Continued

lounge/dining area. Panoramic views of surrounding limestone countryside. Separate one-bedroomed fully equipped accommodation to sleep 6 also available.
Bedrooms: 5 dormitories. Total number of beds: 28
Bathrooms: 5 public

Bed only

per person:	£min	£max
Daily	7.00	

Parking for 10

♿🛆Ⅶ⅍🗲🅟Ⅲ,🖳Ʊ⸾🛩

KESWICK

Cumbria
Map ref 5A3

Beautifully positioned town beside Derwentwater and below the mountains of Skiddaw and Blencathra. Excellent base for walking, climbing, watersports and touring. Motor-launches operate on Derwentwater and motor boats, rowing boats and canoes can be hired.
Tourist Information Centre
☎ *(017687) 72645*

Castlerigg Manor Catholic Residential Youth Centre ⋀

Manor Brow, Keswick CA12 4AR
☎ (017687) 72711
Fax (017687) 75302
Contact: The Booking Secretary
Occupies a commanding position in Keswick with views of Derwentwater and the Borrowdale Valley.
Bedrooms: 8 single, 11 double/twin, 4 triple, 4 quadruple, 7 dormitories. Total number of beds: 75
Bathrooms: 12 private, 9 public

Bed only

per person:	£min	£max
Daily	12.00	18.00

Bed & breakfast

per person:	£min	£max
Daily	15.00	17.50

Full board

per person:	£min	£max
Weekly	189.00	189.00

Lunch available
Evening meal from 1830

♿🛆🛆🅸🅂⅍🗲Ⅳ Ⅲ,🗨⸾🛩

Individual proprietors have supplied all details of accommodation. As changes can occur, we advise you to confirm the information at the time of booking.

LEICESTER

Leicestershire
Map ref 4C3

Modern industrial city with a wide variety of attractions including Roman remains, ancient churches, Georgian houses and a Victorian clock tower. Excellent shopping precincts, arcades and market, museums, theatres, concert hall and sports and leisure centres.
Tourist Information Centre
☎ *(0116) 265 0555 or 251 1301*
(St Margaret's Bus Station)

Richards Backpackers Hostel

157 Wanlip Lane, Birstall, Leicester LE4 4GL
☎ (0116) 267 3107
Contact: Mr Richard Allen
Small, cosy, independent hostel catering for backpackers, cyclists and other young tourists. Tent space and camping chalet available. On a bus route. Home-made bread.
Bedrooms: 1 double/twin, 1 triple, 1 dormitory. Total number of beds: 10
Bathrooms: 1 public

Bed only

per person:	£min	£max
Daily	8.00	8.00

Bed & breakfast

per person:	£min	£max
Daily	9.00	10.50

Full board

per person:	£min	£max
Weekly	71.00	92.00

Evening meal 1800 (last orders 2000)

♿🛆6🛆🍳🍴🅰Ⅶ🅸🅂⅍🗲🅿Ⅲ,🗨⸾🛩

LIVERPOOL

Merseyside
Map ref 4A2

Exciting city, famous for the Beatles, football, the Grand National, theatres and nightlife. Liverpool has a magnificent waterfront, 2 cathedrals, 3 historic houses, museum, galleries and a host of attractions.
Tourist Information Centre
☎ *(0151) 709 3631 or 708 8854*

City of Liverpool Y.M.C.A.

56 Mount Pleasant, Liverpool L3 5SH
☎ (0151) 709 9516
City centre hostel catering for all ages. Basic accommodation and services at a reasonable cost. Climbing wall and 5-a-side. Restaurant open 5 - 6.30pm.
Bedrooms: 99 single, 6 double/twin, 3 triple. Total number of beds: 124
Bathrooms: 15 public

Bed & breakfast

per person:	£min	£max
Daily	10.00	12.50

Evening meal 1700 (last orders 1830)

♿🛆Ⅶ🅰🅸🅂🅿Ⅳ Ⅲ,🗨✻🔍⸾🛩🅰🛩

Embassie Youth Hostel ⋀

1 Faulkner Square, Toxteth, Liverpool L8 7NU
☎ (0151) 707 1089
Contact: Mr Kevin Murphy
Large Georgian hostel 10 minutes' walk from Liverpool's Anglican Cathedral. Cheap, clean and friendly.
Bedrooms: 1 double/twin, 3 dormitories. Total number of beds: 32
Bathrooms: 4 public

Bed & breakfast

per person:	£min	£max
Daily	9.50	9.50

Parking for 10

♿10🍳Ⅶ🅸⅍Ⅳ Ⅲ,🗨⸾⸾🅰🅃

Liverpool John Moores University JMU Services Limited

Egerton Court, 3rd Floor, 2 Rodney Street, Liverpool L3 5UX
Contact: Mr Jonathan Chinn, Liverpool John Moores University, 3rd Floor, 2 Rodney Street, Liverpool L3 5UX
☎ (0151) 231 3369 & 0860 924464
Accommodation available mid-June to mid-September.
Bedrooms: 1350 single. Total number of beds: 1350
Bathrooms: 800 public

Bed only

per person:	£min	£max
Daily	16.50	18.50

Bed & breakfast

per person:	£min	£max
Daily	18.00	22.50

Lunch available
Parking for 800
Open June-August

♿7⚓🅸🅂⅍Ⅲ,🗨⸾✻🔍🔍⸾Ʊ⸾🄳🄰🄿

LONDON

Brunel University Conference Centre ⋀

Conference Office, Brunel University, Uxbridge, Middlesex UB8 3PH
☎ Uxbridge (01895) 274 000
Fax (01895) 203 142
Telex 261173 G
Contact: Mr Carl Woodall
En-suite or standard bedrooms, cafeteria or silver service meals, purpose-built theatres and classrooms, audio and visual aids and sports facilities all available.
Bedrooms: 971 single. Total number of beds: 971
Bathrooms: 499 private, 85 public

Bed only

per person:	£min	£max
Daily	19.85	27.70

Bed & breakfast

per person:	£min	£max
Daily	24.55	32.40

Full board

per person:	£min	£max
Weekly	282.87	337.82

Lunch available
Evening meal 1800 (last orders 2000)

Parking for 2000
Open June-September
Cards accepted: Access, Visa

🛏 12 ♨ ♥ ⓘ Ⓢ ✂ 🅜 TV 🛗 🖳 📱 ☆ 🕯 ☔ 🎿 ∪ Ⓟ 🕂 OAP SP

Campbell House

Taviton Street, London WC1H 0BX
☎ (0171) 391 1479
Fax (0171) 388 0060
Contact: Mr. R L Sparvell
Specially reconstructed Georgian housing providing self-catering accommodation in a peaceful, central London location.
Bedrooms: 60 single, 40 double/twin.
Total number of beds: 140
Bathrooms: 25 public

Bed only

per person:	£min	£max
Daily	13.50	16.00

Open June-September

🛏 10 ♨ ♥ Ⓤ ✂ 🅜 TV 🛗 🖳 📱 🕯 🕂

Cartwright University Halls ⋀

36 Cartwright Gardens, London WC1H 9BZ
☎ (0171) 388 3757
Fax (0171) 388 2552
Contact: Mr Tom Kingsley
Centrally located accommodatiion at affordable prices, near mainline stations and tourist attractions. Reception, bar, restaurant, launderette, TV/games room and self-catering facilities.
Bedrooms: 140 single, 39 double/twin.
Total number of beds: 218
Bathrooms: 40 public

Bed & breakfast

per person:	£min	£max
Daily	15.00	25.00

Evening meal 1800 (last orders 2100)
Open March-April, July-September, December
Cards accepted: Access, Visa, Switch/Delta

🛏 8 ♨ Ⓢ 🅜 TV 🛗 🖳 📱 🕯 ☔ 🕂 Ⓣ

Central University of Iowa Hostel

7 Bedford Place, London WC1B 5JA
☎ (0171) 580 1121
Contact: Mr Roy Oliver
Old Georgian house near the British Museum. Closest underground stations are Russell Square and Holborn.

Bedrooms: 1 single, 6 double/twin, 2 triple, 3 quadruple, 5 dormitories.
Total number of beds: 30
Bathrooms: 7 public

Bed & breakfast

per person:	£min	£max
Daily	15.00	18.00

Open May-August
Cards accepted: Access, Visa, Switch/Delta

🛏 Ⓤ 🅜 TV 🛗 📱 🕯 🕂 ⚓ 🏮

City of London YHA ⋀

36 Carter Lane, London EC4V 5AD
☎ (0171) 236 4965
Fax (0171) 236 7681
Contact: Mr R E Stackhouse
In the centre of the City of London, in an area of winding narrow streets. Former school for choirboys of St Paul's Cathedral. Good central location for sightseeing.
Bedrooms: 4 single, 5 double/twin, 7 triple, 10 quadruple, 16 dormitories.
Total number of beds: 191
Bathrooms: 2 private, 10 public

Bed & breakfast

per person:	£min	£max
Daily	16.60	19.80

Full board

per person:	£min	£max
Weekly	161.70	184.10

Lunch available
Evening meal 1700 (last orders 2000)
Cards accepted: Access, Visa, Switch/Delta

🛏 ♨ ♥ ✂ 🅜 TV 🛗 🖳 📱 🕯 ☔ ✎ SP 🏮 Ⓣ

Driscoll House Hotel

172 New Kent Road, London SE1 4YT
☎ (0171) 703 4175
Fax (0171) 703 8013
Contact: Mr. T Driscoll
Long or short term accommodation offered to teachers, students and tourists. Weekly full-board price below excludes weekday lunch. During the past 80 years we have accommodated more than 50,000 people from 178 different countries.
Bedrooms: 200 single, 6 double/twin.
Total number of beds: 200
Bathrooms: 14 public

Bed & breakfast

per person:	£min	£max
Daily	27.00	27.00

Full board

per person:	£min	£max
Weekly	150.00	150.00

Lunch available
Evening meal 1730 (last orders 1900)
Parking for 10

🍷 Ⓤ ♥ Ⓢ ✂ 🅜 TV 🛗 📱 🕯 🕂 Ⓣ

Ealing YMCA

25 St Marys Road, Ealing, London W5 5RE
☎ (0181) 579 6946
Fax (0181) 579 1129
Contact: Judith Birch
A new residential centre, each room with colour TV. Le Jardin restaurant on premises. Weekly prices shown below are for half board only.
Bedrooms: 129 single, 13 double/twin, 13 triple. Total number of beds: 155
Bathrooms: 13 private, 28 public

Bed & breakfast

per person:	£min	£max
Daily	20.00	24.00

Full board

per person:	£min	£max
Weekly	95.00	115.00

Lunch available
Evening meal 1745 (last orders 1855)
Parking for 26
Cards accepted: Access, Visa

🛏 ♨ 🖥 ♥ ⓘ Ⓢ 🅜 🛗 📱 ☆ 🕯 🕂

Earls Court Youth Hostel ⋀

38 Bolton Gardens, London SW5 0AQ
☎ (0171) 373 7083
Fax (0171) 835 2034
Contact: Mr Nick Christian
Victorian town house in a residential area. Close to shops, restaurants, nightlife and all major tourist attractions. Comfortable dormitory accommodation.
Bedrooms: 1 triple, 4 quadruple, 15 dormitories. Total number of beds: 155
Bathrooms: 22 public

Bed & breakfast

per person:	£min	£max
Daily	15.55	17.70

Continued ▶

LONDON

Continued

Full board

per person:	£min	£max
Weekly	154.35	169.40

Lunch available
Evening meal 1700 (last orders 2000)
Cards accepted: Access, Visa, Switch/Delta

Elizabeth House Hostel ⋀
118 Warwick Way, London SW1V 1SD
☎ (0171) 630 0741
Contact: Ms. F McGinlay
Clean and secure basic bed and breakfast accommodation in central London for men, women and families. Garden available for guests. Recently refurbished with improved facilities.
Bedrooms: 10 single, 13 double/twin, 1 triple, 3 quadruple. Total number of beds: 51
Bathrooms: 9 private, 8 public

Bed & breakfast

per person:	£min	£max
Daily	10.00	23.00

Cards accepted: Access, Visa, Switch/Delta

Hampstead Heath Youth Hostel ⋀
4 Wellgarth Road, Golders Green, London NW11 7HR
☎ (0181) 458 7196 & 458 9054
Fax (0181) 209 0546
Contact: Ms Bev Robinson
Attractive building in well-kept gardens in an area of conserved architectural and natural beauty. Good value accommodation, just 20 minutes by tube from central London.
Bedrooms: 14 double/twin, 8 triple, 14 quadruple. Total number of beds: 198
Bathrooms: 2 private, 23 public

Bed only

per person:	£min	£max
Daily	12.30	14.50

Bed & breakfast

per person:	£min	£max
Daily	15.10	17.30

Full board

per person:	£min	£max
Weekly	151.20	166.60

Evening meal 1700 (last orders 2000)
Parking for 14
Cards accepted: Access, Visa, Switch/Delta

Highgate Village Youth Hostel ⋀
84 Highgate West Hill, London N6 6LU
☎ (0181) 340 1831
Fax (0181) 341 0376
Contact: Mrs Melanie Brigden

Offers traditional comfortable dormitory rooms to visitors of all ages. Just 20 minutes from central London by tube.
Bedrooms: 1 double/twin, 1 triple, 7 dormitories. Total number of beds: 72
Bathrooms: 6 public

Bed only

per person:	£min	£max
Daily	8.20	12.30

Bed & breakfast

per person:	£min	£max
Daily	11.00	15.10

Cards accepted: Access, Visa, Switch/Delta

Holland House Youth Hostel ⋀
Holland Walk, Kensington, London W8 7QN
☎ (0171) 937 0748
Fax (0171) 376 0667
Contact: Mr Steve Collier
Modern hostel incorporating part of Jacobean mansion, set in park with woodland, lawns and playing field. Within easy reach of all London's attractions - especially the museums!
Bedrooms: 1 single, 1 double/twin, 1 triple, 1 quadruple, 14 dormitories. Total number of beds: 23
Bathrooms: 36 public

Bed & breakfast

per person:	£min	£max
Daily	15.50	17.70

Full board

per person:	£min	£max
Weekly	154.00	169.40

Lunch available
Evening meal 1700 (last orders 2000)
Cards accepted: Access, Visa, Switch/Delta

International House Woolwich ⋀
109 Brookhill Road, London SE18 6RZ
☎ (0181) 854 1418
Fax (0181) 855 9257
Contact: Mr B Siderman
Purpose-built student hostel. Self-contained flats for married couples and children. Full en-suite facilities also available. Short-term visitor accommodation available July-September.
Bedrooms: 85 single, 21 double/twin. Total number of beds: 127
Bathrooms: 21 private, 18 public

Bed & breakfast

per person:	£min	£max
Daily	8.74	12.82

Parking for 21
Open April, July-September, December

International Students Hostel Frognal House
99 Frognal, Hampstead, London NW3 6XR
☎ (0171) 794 6893 & 794 8095
Contact: Sr. P S Taylor

Historic, listed building in attractive grounds. Family atmosphere. Five minutes Hampstead Heath and underground, 15 minutes central London. Budget rates for long-term students.
For females only
Minimum age 16
Bedrooms: 17 single, 2 double/twin, 4 dormitories. Total number of beds: 40
Bathrooms: 15 public

Bed only

per person:	£min	£max
Daily	9.50	15.00

Bed & breakfast

per person:	£min	£max
Daily	10.00	16.00

Full board

per person:	£min	£max
Weekly	65.00	90.00

Evening meal from 1845

International Students House ⋀
229 Great Portland Street, London W1N 5HD
☎ (0171) 631 8300
Fax (0171) 631 8315
Contact: Ms Martina Downes
Comfortable accommodation centrally located in West End. Allows easy access to all London's tourist attractions. Close to underground and other public transport. Restaurant and bar on premises.
Minimum age 17
Bedrooms: 159 single, 107 double/twin, 3 triple, 5 quadruple. Total number of beds: 421
Bathrooms: 4 private, 95 public

Bed & breakfast

per person:	£min	£max
Daily	10.00	25.00

Lunch available
Evening meal 1800 (last orders 1930)
Parking for 10
Cards accepted: Access, Visa, Switch/Delta

John Adams Hall (Institute of Education)

15-23 Endsleigh Street, London
WC1H ODH
☎ (0171) 387 4086
Fax (0171) 383 0164
Telex 94016519 DICE G
Contact: Mr M Lam-Hing
An assembly of Georgian houses, the hall retains its old glory. Close to Euston, King's Cross and St Pancras stations.
Bedrooms: 127 single, 22 double/twin.
Total number of beds: 171
Bathrooms: 1 private, 26 public

Bed & breakfast

per person:	£min	£max
Daily	19.00	21.40

Evening meal 1730 (last orders 1830)
Open January, March-April, July-September, December
Cards accepted: Access, Visa
[S] [TV] [T]

Kent House

325 Green Lanes, London N4 2ES
☎ (0181) 802 0800 & 802 5100
Fax (0181) 802 9070
Special off-season and weekly rates for young tourists. Facilities for self-catering. Adjacent to Manor House underground station and 10 minutes from central London.
Minimum age 16
Bedrooms: 3 single, 13 double/twin, 3 dormitories. Total number of beds: 34
Bathrooms: 6 public

Bed only

per person:	£min	£max
Daily	12.00	22.00

Bed & breakfast

per person:	£min	£max
Daily	14.00	25.00

Parking for 4
[UL] [TV] [SP] [T]

Lancaster Hall Hotel (Youth Annexe)

35 Craven Terrace, Lancaster Gate, London W2 3EL
☎ (0171) 723 9276
Fax (0171) 706 2870
Contact: Mr U Maynard
Within easy walking distance of Hyde Park, Kensington Gardens and Marble Arch. Close to public transport.
Bedrooms: 3 single, 7 double/twin, 4 triple, 3 quadruple. Total number of beds: 41
Bathrooms: 4 public

Bed & breakfast

per person:	£min	£max
Daily	18.00	20.00

Evening meal 1800 (last orders 2100)
Parking for 13
Cards accepted: Access, Visa, Switch/Delta
[S] [TV] [T]

Lee Abbey International Students Club

57-67 Lexham Gardens, Kensington, London W8 6JJ
☎ (0171) 373 7242
Fax (0171) 244 8702
Contact: Mr Colin Ross
Hostel, run by Christian Community, providing long-term accommodation for students of all nationalities and faiths and short-term accommodation for anyone. Standard accommodation is half-board weekdays and full-board weekends. Weekly full-board available by special arrangement, normally during vacations.
Minimum age 18
Bedrooms: 60 single, 28 double/twin, 10 triple. Total number of beds: 146
Bathrooms: 19 private, 28 public

Bed & breakfast

per person:	£min	£max
Daily	13.35	21.70

Lunch available
Evening meal 1800 (last orders 1900)
Parking for 1
[UL] [S] [TV] [SP]

Lightfoot Hall

King's College London, Manresa Road, London SW3 6LX
Contact: King's Campus Vacation Bureau, King's College London, Manresa Road, London SW3 6LX
☎ (0171) 351 6011
Fax (0171) 352 7376
Modern 10-storey building in the famous King's Road, Chelsea. Other Halls of Residence in Westminster, Wandsworth, Denmark Hill, Hampstead and Kensington.
Bedrooms: 174 single, 24 double/twin.
Total number of beds: 222
Bathrooms: 30 public

Bed only

per person:	£min	£max
Daily	12.50	14.50

Bed & breakfast

per person:	£min	£max
Daily	16.50	23.00

Lunch available
Evening meal 1800 (last orders 1900)
Open April, June-September, December
Cards accepted: Access, Visa, Switch/Delta
[S] [TV] [SP] [T]

London House Hotel

81 Kensington Gardens Square, London W2 4DJ
Contact: Miss Jackie Boughton, 16 Leinster Square, London W2 4DJ
☎ (0171) 221 1400
Fax (0171) 229 3917
Telex 24923 VIEHTL G
Friendly, comfortable budget hotel, convenient for shops, theatres and sightseeing.
Bedrooms: 4 single, 32 double/twin, 6 triple, 14 quadruple, 11 dormitories.
Total number of beds: 201
Bathrooms: 7 public

Bed & breakfast

per person:	£min	£max
Daily	24.25	36.00

Cards accepted: Access, Visa, Diners, Amex
[UL] [TV] [T]

Lords Hotel

20-22 Leinster Square, London
W2 4PR
☎ (0171) 229 8877
Fax (0171) 229 8377
Telex 298716 LORDS G
Contact: Mr. N G Ladas
Bed and breakfast accommodation in central London. Direct-dial telephone, radio. Most rooms with private facilities.
Bedrooms: 9 single, 29 double/twin, 12 triple, 17 quadruple. Total number of beds: 175
Bathrooms: 43 private, 7 public

Bed & breakfast

per person:	£min	£max
Daily	15.00	40.00

Cards accepted: Access, Visa, Diners, Amex, Switch/Delta
[UL] [TV] [SP] [T]

Oxford Street Youth Hostel

14-18 Noel Street, London W1V 3PD
☎ (0171) 734 1618
Fax (0171) 734 1657
Contact: Mr Peter Kane
In the heart of Soho and Oxford Street, this hostel is a perfect sightseeing base for individual travellers. Sleeping accommodation is in small bedrooms with individual security lockers.
For individuals only
Bedrooms: 13 double/twin, 16 triple, 4 quadruple. Total number of beds: 89
Bathrooms: 10 public

Bed only

per person:	£min	£max
Daily	14.10	17.30

Cards accepted: Access, Visa, Switch/Delta
5 [UL] [TV]

Passfield Hall

1 Endsleigh Place, London
WC1H 0PW
☎ (0171) 387 7743 & 387 3584
Fax (0171) 387 0419
University hall of residence with washbasin in all rooms, suitable for families. Central for Oxford Street and the West End.
Bedrooms: 100 single, 34 double/twin, 10 triple. Total number of beds: 198
Bathrooms: 36 public

Bed & breakfast

per person:	£min	£max
Daily	19.40	22.50

Open March-April, July-September
Cards accepted: Access, Visa, Switch/Delta
[UL] [S] [TV] [T]

LONDON

Continued

"Peace Haven"
London Friendship Centre, 3 Creswick Road, London W3 9HE
☎ (0181) 992 0221
Fax (0181) 992 0221
Contact: Mr. P O'Nath
Comfortable residence suitable for groups and school parties, open throughout the year. Individuals and families also welcome. Parking facilities now available.
Bedrooms: 2 single, 15 double/twin, 1 triple, 3 quadruple, 2 dormitories. Total number of beds: 53
Bathrooms: 6 private, 8 public
Bed & breakfast

per person:	£min	£max
Daily	10.50	19.00

Lunch available
Evening meal 1700 (last orders 1900)
Parking for 10
☐ 10 ☐ ☐ ☐ ☐ ☐ ☐ ☐ ☐ ☐ ☐ ☐ ☐
☐ ☐

Queen Alexandra's House ⋀
Bremner Road, Kensington Gore, London SW7 2QT
☎ (0171) 589 3635
Fax (0171) 589 3177
Contact: Mrs C J Raymond
Fine example of Victorian architecture and a long established hostel for women students of all ages in South Kensington.
For females only
Minimum age 17
Bedrooms: 75 single, 2 double/twin.
Total number of beds: 81
Bathrooms: 20 public
Bed & breakfast

per person:	£min	£max
Daily	23.00	25.00

Open May-August
☐ ☐ ☐ ☐ ☐ ☐ ☐ ☐ ☐ ☐

Ramsay Hall ⋀
20 Maple Street, London W1P 5GB
☎ (0171) 387 4537
Contact: Mr Hugh Ewing
Central London location, good value, comfortable accommodation in pleasant surroundings.
Bedrooms: 364 single, 20 double/twin, 2 triple. Total number of beds: 410
Bathrooms: 70 public
Bed & breakfast

per person:	£min	£max
Daily	18.50	20.00

Evening meal 1800 (last orders 1900)
Open January, March-April, June-September, December
☐ 11 ☐ ☐ ☐ ☐ ☐ ☐ ☐ ☐ ☐ ☐

Rotherhithe Youth Hostel and Conference Centre ⋀
Salter Road, London SE16 1PP
☎ (0171) 232 2114
Fax (0171) 237 2919
Contact: Mr Frank Velander

Ultra-modern building with every facility for families and individuals. All rooms have en-suite facilities, there is a restaurant and ample street parking. Special prices for family rooms. Within easy reach of central London.
Bedrooms: 22 double/twin, 16 quadruple, 32 dormitories. Total number of beds: 320
Bathrooms: 70 private
Bed & breakfast

per person:	£min	£max
Daily	16.60	19.80

Full board

per person:	£min	£max
Weekly	161.70	184.10

Lunch available
Evening meal 1730 (last orders 2030)
Cards accepted: Access, Visa, Switch/Delta
☐ 5 ☐ ☐ ☐ ☐ ☐ ☐ ☐ ☐ ☐ ☐

Rywin House
36 Christchurch Avenue, Brondesbury, London NW6 7BE
☎ (0181) 459 5434
Contact: Mr. P Horsley
In a quiet residential area with British Rail and London Transport stations nearby. Short walk to local tennis courts.
Bedrooms: 2 single, 1 double/twin, 6 dormitories. Total number of beds: 23
Bathrooms: 3 public
Bed only

per person:	£min	£max
Daily	13.50	13.50

Bed & breakfast

per person:	£min	£max
Daily	15.50	15.50

Cards accepted: Amex
☐ ☐ ☐ ☐ ☐ ☐ ☐

Hotel Saint Simeon ⋀
38 Harrington Gardens, London SW7 4LT
☎ (0171) 373 0505 & 370 4708
Fax (0171) 589 6412
Contact: Mr. J Gojkovic
Rooms for one, two or three people in central London. Nearest underground station is Gloucester Road.
Bedrooms: 6 single, 10 double/twin, 5 dormitories. Total number of beds: 41
Bathrooms: 4 private, 6 public
Bed & breakfast

per person:	£min	£max
Daily	9.00	14.00

Full board

per person:	£min	£max
Weekly	56.00	84.00

Cards accepted: Access, Visa, Amex
☐ ☐ ☐ ☐ ☐ ☐ ☐ ☐ ☐ ☐ ☐ ☐

Tent City ⋀
Old Oak Common Lane, East Acton, London W3 7DP
☎ (0181) 743 5708
Fax (0181) 749 9074
Contact: Ms Maxine Lambert

"Tented" hostel and campsite close to East Acton tube. On-site snackbar, free baggage and valuables store. Young and fun!
Bedrooms: 14 dormitories. Total number of beds: 448
Bathrooms: 24 public
Bed only

per person:	£min	£max
Daily	5.50	5.50

Lunch available
Parking for 30
Open June-September
☐ ☐ ☐ ☐ ☐ ☐ ☐ ☐ ☐ ☐ ☐

University of Westminster ⋀
International House, 1-5 Lambeth Road, London SE1 6HU
Contact: Ms Nicole Chanson, University of Westminster, Luxborough Suite, 35 Marylebone Road, London NW1 5LS
☎ (0171) 911 5000
Fax (0171) 911 5141
Telex 25964
Hall of Residence offering good quality accommodation in single and twin rooms on a self-catering or bed and breakfast basis. Four tube stops away from Piccadilly Circus and within a few minutes' walk of the River Thames, the Houses of Parliament and Westminster Abbey. Ideal for sightseeing and for London's theatreland.
Bedrooms: 63 single, 9 double/twin.
Total number of beds: 81
Bathrooms: 18 public
Bed only

per person:	£min	£max
Daily	13.25	19.50

Bed & breakfast

per person:	£min	£max
Daily	15.75	21.95

Lunch available
Evening meal 1730 (last orders 1930)
Parking for 2
Open April, July-September
Cards accepted: Access, Visa, Switch/Delta
☐ 7 ☐ ☐ ☐ ☐ ☐ ☐ ☐ ☐ ☐ ☐ ☐

University of Westminster ⋀
Furnival House, Cholmley Park, Highgate, London N6 5EU
Contact: Ms Nicole Chanson, University of Westminster, Luxborough Suite, 35 Marylebone Road, London NW1 5LS
☎ (0171) 911 5000
Fax (0171) 911 5141
Telex 25964
Refurbished Edwardian Hall of Residence in Highgate village, situated in its own grounds. Good quality accommodation on self-catering or meals basis. Within easy walking distance of Waterlow Park and Hampstead Heath and half-an-hour from the West End. Some rooms offer panoramic views of London.
Bedrooms: 85 single, 28 double/twin.
Total number of beds: 141
Bathrooms: 16 public

Bed only

per person:	£min	£max
Daily	13.25	19.50

Bed & breakfast

per person:	£min	£max
Daily	15.75	21.95

Lunch available
Evening meal 1730 (last orders 1930)
Parking for 6
Open April, July-September
Cards accepted: Access, Visa, Switch/
Delta

🛏7👤♿Ⓤ🛈Ⓢ✂️🅿️📺🏠🚗✈️⭐🏨Ⓣ

Urban Learning Foundation 🔺
56 East India Dock Road, London
E14 6JE
☎ (0171) 987 0033
Fax (0171) 538 2620
Contact: Ms Jacqui Duggan
*Purpose-built residential training centre,
close to central London. Single study
bedrooms arranged in 4-7 bedded
apartments.*
Bedrooms: 47 single. Total number of
beds: 47
Bathrooms: 1 private, 18 public

Bed only

per person:	£min	£max
Daily	10.00	20.00

Lunch available
Cards accepted: Access, Visa, Amex

🛏12🔌♿🛈Ⓢ✂️📺🏠✈️DAP🗄️SP🏨

Wimbledon YMCA
200 The Broadway, Wimbledon,
London SW19 1RY
☎ (0181) 542 9055
Fax (0181) 542 1086
Contact: Mr. A C Rothery
*Modern, purpose-built residence with
sports hall, fitness studio, saunas, dance
studio, coffee bar, restaurant and
laundry.*
Bedrooms: 106 single, 34 double/twin.
Total number of beds: 170
Bathrooms: 1 private, 20 public

Bed & breakfast

per person:	£min	£max
Daily	13.00	21.00

Lunch available
Evening meal 1700 (last orders 1850)
Parking for 30
Cards accepted: Access, Visa

🛏12🔌♿Ⓤ🛈Ⓢ✂️📺📺🏠🚗⭐
⭐✈️🚲🗄️SP

Y.M.C.A.
Rush Green Road, Romford RM7 0PH
☎ Romford (01708) 766211
Fax (01708) 754211
Contact: Mr Dave Ball
*8 minutes' walk from Romford British
Rail station, 25 minutes from Liverpool
Street station. Easy access to M25 and
south coast. Easy travel into London by
underground (Elm Park). International
hostel with many sports facilities.
Minimum age 18*
Bedrooms: 148 single, 2 double/twin.
Total number of beds: 150
Bathrooms: 4 private, 24 public

Bed & breakfast

per person:	£min	£max
Daily	16.50	19.50

Full board

per person:	£min	£max
Weekly	54.80	118.99

Lunch available
Evening meal 1730 (last orders 1845)
Parking for 120
Cards accepted: Access, Visa

🔌Ⓤ🛈Ⓢ✂️📺🏠🚗⭐🏨⭐🎣🔍✈️

MANCHESTER
Greater Manchester
Map ref 4B1

The Gateway to the North, offering
one of Britain's largest selections
of arts venues and theatre
productions, a wide range of chain
stores and specialist shops, a
legendary, lively nightlife,
spectacular architecture and a
plethora of eating and drinking
places.
Tourist Information Centre
☎ *(0161) 234 3157 or 234 3158 or
436 3344 (Manchester Airport
Terminal 1)*

The Manchester Conference Centre and Hotel 🔺
P.O. Box 88, Sackville Street,
Manchester M60 1QD
☎ (0161) 200 4065
Fax (0161) 200 4090
Contact: Mr A F Yates
*Modern year-round conference centre
and hotel, in Manchester city centre.
Standard and en-suite rooms.
Conferences and groups a speciality.
Restaurant and bar. Campus
accommodation during vacations.*
Bedrooms: 2226 single, 74 double/
twin. Total number of beds: 2374
Bathrooms: 700 private, 300 public

Bed only

per person:	£min	£max
Daily		60.00

Bed & breakfast

per person:	£min	£max
Daily	22.50	66.50

Full board

per person:	£min	£max
Weekly	150.00	752.58

Lunch available
Evening meal 1830 (last orders 2100)
Parking for 700
Cards accepted: Access, Visa, Diners,
Amex, Switch/Delta

🛏♿🛈Ⓢ✂️📺🏠🚗⭐🏨⭐🎣🔍✈️
🗄️SPⓉ

Manchester Youth Hostel 🔺
Potato Wharf, Castlefield, Manchester
M3 4NB
☎ (0161) 839 9960
Fax (0161) 835 2054
Contact: Mr I Hampson
*A brand new purpose built youth hostel
sleeping up to 150 people in four
bedded rooms all with en-suite facilities.*

*Centrally located to all the major
attractions in the city.*
Bedrooms: 3 double/twin,
28 quadruple, 6 dormitories. Total
number of beds: 150
Bathrooms: 37 private

Bed only

per person:	£min	£max
Daily	7.45	11.00

Bed & breakfast

per person:	£min	£max
Daily	10.25	13.80

Full board

per person:	£min	£max
Weekly	117.25	142.10

Lunch available
Evening meal 1900 (last orders 2100)
Parking for 25
Cards accepted: Access, Visa, Switch/
Delta

🛏5🛈Ⓢ✂️📺🏠🚗⭐✈️🗄️SPⓉ

MARKET HARBOROUGH
Leicestershire
Map ref 4C3

There have been markets here
since the early 13th C, and the
town was also an important
coaching centre, with several
ancient hostelries. The early 17th
C grammar school was once the
butter market.
Tourist Information Centre
☎ *(01858) 468106*

Hothorpe Hall 🔺
Theddingworth, Lutterworth
LE17 6QX
☎ (01858) 880257
Fax (01858) 880979
*Country house conference hotel, west of
Market Harborough, offering overnight
and full board accommodation for
individuals and groups. Delightful rural
setting with good road and rail access.*
Bedrooms: 2 single, 34 double/twin,
8 triple, 13 quadruple. Total number
of beds: 150
Bathrooms: 34 private, 7 public

Bed & breakfast

per person:	£min	£max
Daily	15.00	25.00

Lunch available
Evening meal 1800 (last orders 1800)
Parking for 60

🛏♿♿Ⓤ🛈Ⓢ✂️📺🏠🚗⭐✈️SP🏨

MATFIELD
Kent
Map ref 3B4

Village with Georgian houses,
green and pond.

Old Cryals
Cryals Road, Matfield, Tonbridge
TN12 7HN
☎ Brenchley (0189272) 2372
Fax (0189272) 3311
Contact: Mr C Charrington

Continued ▶

MATFIELD

Continued

Hostel-type accommodation for 12, in two rooms for 4 and 8. Comfortable sitting/dining room with microwave oven, TV, freezer, dishwasher. Self-catering only.
Bedrooms: 2 dormitories. Total number of beds: 12
Bathrooms: 2 public
Bed only

per person:	£min	£max
Daily	5.00	6.50

Parking for 12
Open March-November

MIDDLESBROUGH

Cleveland
Map ref 5C3

Boom-town of the mid 19th C, today's Teesside industrial and conference town has a modern shopping complex and predominantly modern buildings. An engineering miracle of the early 20th C is the Transporter Bridge which replaced an old ferry.
Tourist Information Centre
☎ *(01642) 243425 or 264330*

University of Teesside ⋒

Borough Road, Middlesbrough
TS1 3BA
☎ (01642) 218121
Fax (01642) 342067
Telex 587537 TP LB
Contact: Mrs J Murphy
The University of Teesside is located in Middlesbrough. All accommodation is within walking distance of the town centre.
Minimum age 16
Bedrooms: 473 single. Total number of beds: 473
Bathrooms: 252 private, 39 public
Bed only

per person:	£min	£max
Daily	10.23	19.63

Bed & breakfast

per person:	£min	£max
Daily	14.10	23.50

Lunch available
Evening meal 1800 (last orders 2030)
Parking for 855
Open March, July-September

Individual proprietors have supplied all details of accommodation. As changes can occur, we advise you to confirm the information at the time of booking.

NEWCASTLE UPON TYNE

Tyne and Wear
Map ref 5C2

Commercial and cultural centre of the North East, with a large indoor shopping centre, Quayside market, museums and theatres which offer an annual 6 week season by the Royal Shakespeare Company. Norman castle keep, medieval alleys, old Guildhall.
Tourist Information Centre
☎ *(0191) 261 0610 or 230 0030 or 214 4422 (Newcastle Airport)*

Newcastle Youth Hostel

107 Jesmond Road, Jesmond, Newcastle upon Tyne NE2 1NJ
☎ (0191) 281 2570
Fax (0191) 281 8779
Contact: Mr L Heslop
Large town house close to city centre. Families, individuals and groups welcome. Comfortable bunk-bedded accommodation.
Bedrooms: 11 dormitories. Total number of beds: 60
Bathrooms: 4 public
Bed only

per person:	£min	£max
Daily	5.00	7.45

Bed & breakfast

per person:	£min	£max
Daily	7.80	10.25

Full board

per person:	£min	£max
Weekly	100.00	117.00

Evening meal 1800 (last orders 1800)
Parking for 6
Open February-November
Cards accepted: Access, Visa

University of Northumbria Newcastle ⋒

Coach Lane Campus Halls of Residence, Coach Lane, Newcastle upon Tyne, Tyne & Wear NE7 7XA
Contact: Mrs S Cowell, University of Northumbria, Newcastle, Ellison Place, Newcastle upon Tyne, Tyne & Wear NE1 8ST
☎ (0191) 227 4024
Fax (0191) 227 3197
Accommodation in modern halls of residence, set in pleasant grounds, 3 miles from the city centre. Bed and breakfast with or without evening meal for groups or parties.
Minimum age 16
Bedrooms: 186 single, 50 double/twin. Total number of beds: 286
Bathrooms: 44 public
Bed & breakfast

per person:	£min	£max
Daily	13.50	14.50

Full board

per person:	£min	£max
Weekly	179.20	186.20

Lunch available
Evening meal 1730 (last orders 1930)
Parking for 100
Open April, July-September

NEWPORT

Shropshire
Map ref 4A3

Small market town on the Shropshire Union Canal has a wide High Street and a church with some interesting monuments. Newport is close to Aqualate Mere which is the largest lake in Staffordshire.

Harper Adams ⋒

Newport TF10 8NB
☎ (01952) 815201 & 815319
Fax (01952) 814783
Contact: Mr I & Ms C Barnard/ Skinner

A country estate of 600 acres. Renaissance architecture with 180 en-suite rooms (300 others). Conference, tutorial and all sports. Groups only.
Bedrooms: 443 single, 60 double/twin. Total number of beds: 503
Bathrooms: 180 private, 60 public
Bed only

per person:	£min	£max
Daily	18.80	

Bed & breakfast

per person:	£min	£max
Daily	21.15	

Lunch available
Evening meal 1700 (last orders 2200)
Parking for 4000
Open January, April, July-September, December

NORWICH

Norfolk
Map ref 3C1

Beautiful cathedral city and county town on the River Wensum with many fine museums and medieval churches. Norman castle, Guildhall and interesting medieval streets. Good shopping centre and market.
Tourist Information Centre
☎ *(01603) 666071*

City College Norwich

Southwell Lodge, Ipswich Road, Norwich NR2 2LL
☎ (01603) 618327 & 660011
Fax (01603) 760326
Contact: Mr John Wheeler

College halls of residence set in a rural tree-screened setting within 10 minutes' walk of Norwich city centre.
Bedrooms: 270 single, 8 double/twin.
Total number of beds: 286
Bathrooms: 13 private, 32 public
Bed only

per person:	£min	£max
Daily	12.00	18.00

Bed & breakfast

per person:	£min	£max
Daily	16.00	22.00

Lunch available
Evening meal 1730 (last orders 1900)
Parking for 500
Cards accepted: Access, Visa, Switch/Delta

≿┷🅸🅱🔆🅼📺▥◨♣◗◔

University of East Anglia
Norwich NR4 7TJ
☎ (01603) 593277
Fax (01603) 250585
Telex 14237
Contact: Ms J Court
A modern university in parkland 2 miles from the centre of Norwich. Comfortable, convenient and compact. En-suite and family accommodation available.
Bedrooms: 1300 single, 50 double/twin. Total number of beds: 1300
Bathrooms: 600 private, 70 public
Bed & breakfast

per person:	£min	£max
Daily	21.20	30.50

Lunch available
Evening meal 1700 (last orders 1915)
Parking for 700
Open March-April, July-August
Cards accepted: Visa

≿14┷♦🅸🆂🅼▥◨◨🗗🔆✳♣◔◑
◗✕🆂🅿🏠

YWCA
Marjorie Hinde House, 61 Bethel Street, Norwich NR2 1NR
☎ (01603) 625982
Contact: S. Williams
Comfortable hostel for long or short stays. Central position near shops, theatres, gardens, library and public transport.
For females only
Bedrooms: 20 single, 7 double/twin.
Total number of beds: 34
Bathrooms: 7 public
Bed only

per person:	£min	£max
Daily	10.71	10.71

▥🔆🅼📺▥◨◗✕🏠

The symbols 🅲 🅲 🅲 indicate categories of accessibility for wheelchair users. They are explained in full in the information pages at the back of this guide.

OTTERBURN
Northumberland
Map ref 5B1

Small village set at the meeting of the River Rede with Otter Burn, the site of the Battle of Otterburn in 1388. A peaceful tradition continues in the sale of Otterburn tweeds in this beautiful region, which is ideal for exploring the Border country and the Cheviots.

Otterburn Hall
Otterburn NE19 1HE
☎ Freephone 0800 591527
Fax (0191) 385 2267
Contact: Mrs K Hutchinson
Family holiday hotel, conference venue and training establishment in 100 acres. Offering special interest holidays. Prices quoted include dinner.
Bedrooms: 6 single, 53 double/twin, 7 triple. Total number of beds: 130
Bathrooms: 66 private, 8 public
Bed & breakfast

per person:	£min	£max
Daily	35.00	38.50

Lunch available
Evening meal 1900 (last orders 1900)
Parking for 100
Cards accepted: Access, Visa

≿8┷🗗♦🅸🆂🅼📺▥◨♣✲◔◔◔⛵
◗🅳🄰🄿◆🆂🅿🏠◨

OXFORD
Oxfordshire
Map ref 2C1

Beautiful university town with many ancient colleges, some dating from the 13th C, and numerous buildings of historic and architectural interest. The Ashmolean Museum has outstanding collections. Lovely gardens and meadows with punting on the Cherwell.
Tourist Information Centre
☎ (01865) 726871

Oxford Youth Hostel
32 Jack Straws Lane, Oxford OX3 0DW
☎ (01865) 62997
Fax (01865) 69402
Contact: Mr Mark Stanley
Victorian mansion converted into a lively hostel, ideal for groups and individuals.
Bedrooms: 3 double/twin, 4 quadruple, 11 dormitories. Total number of beds: 114
Bathrooms: 8 public
Bed only

per person:	£min	£max
Daily	6.20	9.15

Bed & breakfast

per person:	£min	£max
Daily	9.00	11.95

Full board

per person:	£min	£max
Weekly	108.50	129.15

Evening meal 1700 (last orders 1930)
Parking for 8
Cards accepted: Access, Visa, Switch/Delta

≿5┷🗗🅸🆂🔆🅼📺▥♣✕🆂🅿◨

POOLE
Dorset
Map ref 2B3

Tremendous natural harbour makes Poole a superb boating centre. The harbour area is crowded with historic buildings including the 15th C Town Cellars housing a maritime museum.
Tourist Information Centre
☎ *(01202) 673322*

Rockley Point Sailing School ⛵
Rockley Park, Hamworthy, Poole BH15 4LZ
☎ Bournemouth (01202) 677272
Fax (01202) 668268
Contact: Ms Barbara Gordon
RYA sailing school catering for all abilities and ages. Accommodation of various types available and residential children's courses. Also windsurfing and yacht courses. Adult all-in courses in bed and breakfast accommodation.
Minimum age 8
Bedrooms: 30 single, 16 dormitories.
Total number of beds: 80
Bathrooms: 5 public
Bed & breakfast

per person:	£min	£max
Daily	10.00	12.00

Full board

per person:	£min	£max
Weekly	110.00	125.00

Lunch available
Parking for 10
Open March-October
Cards accepted: Access, Visa

≿8┷🗗🅸🆂🔆📺♣✲✳◔◑✕🏠
🆂🅿◨

The symbol 🏵 within an entry indicates participation in the Welcome Host programme – a nationally recognised customer care initiative which aims to promote the highest standards of service and a warm welcome for all visitors.

PORTSMOUTH & SOUTHSEA

Hampshire
Map ref 2C3

The first dock was built in 1194. HMS Victory, Nelson's flagship, is here and Charles Dickens' former home is open to the public. Neighbouring Southsea has a promenade with magnificent views of Spithead.
Tourist Information Centre
☎ *(01705) 826722*

Southsea Lodge
4 Florence Road, Southsea, Hampshire PO5 2NE
☎ (01705) 832495
Contact: Mr & Mrs Peter Viner
Family-run, independent hostel for self-catering travellers, centrally situated for all attractions. Large social areas indoors/outdoors. Secure cycle storage.
Minimum age 16
Bedrooms: 8 double/twin, 4 triple, 2 quadruple, 1 dormitory. Total number of beds: 40
Bathrooms: 4 private, 4 public

Bed only

per person:	£min	£max
Daily	9.00	12.00

Parking for 5

University of Portsmouth ♠
Central Reservations, Nuffield Centre, St Michaels Road, Portsmouth, Hampshire PO1 2ED
☎ (01705) 843178
Fax (01705) 843182
Contact: Ms Elizabeth Jackson
Conference and holiday venue in self-catering flats or serviced accommodation, with sport and lecture facilities.
Bedrooms: 755 single, 30 double/twin. Total number of beds: 815
Bathrooms: 343 private, 82 public

Bed only

per person:	£min	£max
Daily	11.25	11.25

Bed & breakfast

per person:	£min	£max
Daily	14.25	14.25

Full board

per person:	£min	£max
Weekly	156.56	156.56

Lunch available
Evening meal 1700 (last orders 1830)
Open March-April, July-September
Cards accepted: Access, Visa

At-a-glance symbols are explained on the flap inside the back cover.

RINGWOULD

Kent
Map ref 3C4

Between Deal and Dover, a tight-knit cluster of houses off the main road. The church tower with its lead-capped corner turret is a great landmark.

Ripple Down House Environmental Education Centre ♠
Dover Road, Ringwould, Deal CT14 8HE
☎ Dover (01304) 364854
Fax (01304) 364820
Contact: Mr Chas Matthews
A residential/day centre for individuals and groups to study all aspects of the local environment at all levels. Six miles from Dover, 3 miles from Deal on A258.
Bedrooms: 1 single, 1 double/twin, 1 triple, 1 quadruple, 4 dormitories.
Total number of beds: 42
Bathrooms: 7 public

Bed only

per person:	£min	£max
Daily	10.00	20.00

Bed & breakfast

per person:	£min	£max
Daily	15.00	30.00

Lunch available
Evening meal 1730 (last orders 1830)
Parking for 15

ROBIN HOOD'S BAY

North Yorkshire
Map ref 5D3

Picturesque village of red-roofed cottages with main street running from clifftop down ravine to seashore. Scene of much smuggling and shipwrecks in 18th C. Robin Hood reputed to have escaped to continent by boat from here.

Old School House
Fisherhead, Robin Hood's Bay, Whitby YO22 4ST
Contact: Mrs. L Derry, The Old School House, PO Box 8, Willerby, Hull, North Humberside HU10 7DN
☎ Hull (01482) 650432
Former old school, expertly converted, offering accommodation specialising in educational and recreational groups. Prices include a packed lunch. Also offer B&B for walkers and casual stays.
Bedrooms: 1 double/twin, 2 triple, 4 quadruple, 3 dormitories. Total number of beds: 40
Bathrooms: 4 public

Bed & breakfast

per person:	£min	£max
Daily	11.75	18.80

Full board

per person:	£min	£max
Weekly	90.47	135.71

Parking for 12
Open February-November

SCARBOROUGH

North Yorkshire
Map ref 5D3

Large, popular East Coast seaside resort, formerly a spa town. Beautiful gardens and two splendid sandy beaches. Castle ruins date from 1100; fine Georgian and Victorian houses. Scarborough Millennium depicts 1,000 years of town's history. Sea Life Centre.
Tourist Information Centre
☎ *(01723) 373333*

University College Scarborough The North Riding College ♠
Filey Road, Scarborough YO11 3AZ
☎ (01723) 362392
Fax (01723) 370815
Contact: Miss E McAdam
Overlooking the cliffs of South Bay, the college is an ideal conference venue, with emphasis on the standard of catering.
Bedrooms: 292 single, 12 double/twin, 2 triple. Total number of beds: 322
Bathrooms: 214 private, 37 public

Bed only

per person:	£min	£max
Daily	10.00	15.00

Bed & breakfast

per person:	£min	£max
Daily	20.26	24.67

Full board

per person:	£min	£max
Weekly	273.49	291.99

Lunch available
Evening meal 1800 (last orders 2000)
Parking for 97
Open January, March-April, July-September, December

The symbol ⊛ within an entry indicates participation in the Welcome Host programme – a nationally recognised customer care initiative which aims to promote the highest standards of service and a warm welcome for all visitors.

SHEFFIELD

South Yorkshire
Map ref 4B2

Local iron ore and coal gave Sheffield its prosperous steel and cutlery industries. The modern city centre has many interesting buildings - cathedral, Cutlers' Hall, Crucible Theatre, Graves and Mappin Art Galleries - and Meadowhall shopping centre nearby.
Tourist Information Centre
☎ *(0114) 273 4671 or 273 4672 or 279 5901*

University of Sheffield ⋀⋀
Octagon Centre, Western Bank, Sheffield S10 2TQ
Contact: Ms C Davies, University of Sheffield, Conference Office, Octogan Centre, Western Bank, Sheffield, South Yorkshire S10 2TQ
☎ (0114) 282 4080 & 282 4949
Fax (0114) 272 9097
Telex 547216
Six halls of residence in a quiet suburb near the city centre and close to the Peak District National Park.
Wheelchair access category 3 💷
Bedrooms: 1886 single, 106 double/twin. Total number of beds: 1992
Bathrooms: 300 public
Bed & breakfast

per person:	£min	£max
Daily	19.50	

Lunch available
Evening meal 1730 (last orders 1830)
Parking for 600
Open January, March-April, June-August
⏃⛱⭍⊜️⌰✂⊬⋀⏺⎁⬛◻️⬛✖✦⛬✾⛇
✖ SP ⛩

SILSOE

Bedfordshire
Map ref 2D1

Silsoe College
Silsoe, Bedford MK45 3DT
☎ Leighton Buzzard (01525) 860428
Fax (01525) 861527
Contact: Mrs Sue Whittaker
We have an all-year-round residential facility with 38 bedrooms offering a high standard of accommodation. There is excellent on-site catering available and the college has a licensed bar.
Bedrooms: 38 single.
Bathrooms: 16 public
Bed only

per person:	£min	£max
Daily	19.39	25.26

Bed & breakfast

per person:	£min	£max
Daily	23.50	29.38

Lunch available
Evening meal 1700 (last orders 1830)
⏃8⛱⭍⊜️⌰⬛◻️⬛✦⚲

STOKE ROCHFORD

Lincolnshire
Map ref 3A1

Stoke Rochford Hall ⋀⋀
Stoke Rochford, Grantham NG33 5EJ
☎ Grantham (01476) 530337
Fax (01476) 530534
Contact: Peter Robinson
Elegant Victorian mansion house in 28 acres of beautiful parkland and formal gardens, an idyllic setting for that sought-after country holiday retreat. Creche and activity weeks for children in summer, extensive leisure club with indoor heated swimming pool, 18-hole golf-course adjacent.
Bedrooms: 86 single, 100 double/twin.
Total number of beds: 233
Bathrooms: 68 private, 27 public
Bed & breakfast

per person:	£min	£max
Daily	30.00	45.50

Lunch available
Evening meal 1830 (last orders 2030)
Parking for 500
Cards accepted: Access, Visa, Diners, Amex, Switch/Delta
⏃⛱⭍⊜️⌰✂⋀⬛◻️⬛⬛✂✖✦⚲
✖⚲⛫⊬✖ SP ⛩ ⛢

STRATFORD-UPON-AVON

Warwickshire
Map ref 2B1

Famous as Shakespeare's home town, Stratford's many attractions include his birthplace, New Place where he died, the Royal Shakespeare Theatre and Gallery, "The World of Shakespeare" 30 minute theatre and Hall's Croft (his daughter's house).
Tourist Information Centre
☎ *(01789) 293127*

Stratford-upon-Avon Youth Hostel
Hemmingford House, Alveston, Stratford-upon-Avon CV37 7RG
☎ (01789) 297093
Fax (01789) 205513
Contact: The Manager
Large house in attractive grounds, in village 2 miles from Stratford-upon-Avon. Convenient for visits to Shakespeare's birthplace and other famous properties including Royal Shakespeare Theatre and Warwick Castle.
Bedrooms: 5 double/twin, 8 quadruple, 15 dormitories. Total number of beds: 154
Bathrooms: 6 private, 9 public
Bed & breakfast

per person:	£min	£max
Daily	9.35	12.65

Full board

per person:	£min	£max
Weekly	109.90	133.00

Lunch available
Evening meal 1700 (last orders 2000)

Parking for 20
Cards accepted: Access, Visa, Switch/Delta
⏃5⛱⊎⎁⊜️⌰✂⋀⊬⬛◻️⬛✦✖ SP ⛩

STREET

Somerset
Map ref 2A2

Busy shoe-making town set beneath the Polden Hills. A museum at the factory, which was developed with the rest of the town in the 19th C, can be visited. Just south, the National Trust has care of woodland on Ivythorn Hill which gives wide views northward.

Millfield School Village of Education
Millfield School, Street BA16 0YD
☎ (01458) 45823
Fax (01458) 840584
Contact: Mrs C Steer
Famous independent school with a wealth of facilities and an international reputation as a centre of excellence. Accommodation in association with vast programme of holiday courses.
Bedrooms: 50 single, 150 double/twin, 150 dormitories. Total number of beds: 800
Bathrooms: 80 public
Full board

per person:	£min	£max
Weekly	146.00	166.00

Lunch available
Open January, April, July-September, December
Cards accepted: Access, Visa, Switch/Delta
⏃3⛱⊜️⋀⎁⬛◻️⬛✖✦⚲✾⛇⚲⊬✖⛲ DAP ⛩

TODMORDEN

West Yorkshire
Map ref 4B1

In beautiful scenery on the edge of the Pennines at junction of 3 sweeping valleys. Until 1888 the county boundary between Yorkshire and Lancashire cut this old cotton town in half, running through the middle of the Town Hall.
Tourist Information Centre
☎ *(01706) 818181*

Lumbutts Mill Activity Centre ⋀⋀
Lumbutts House, Lumbutts, Todmorden, Lancashire OL14 6JE
☎ (01706) 814536
Fax (01706) 819391
Contact: Mrs S Schofield
Purpose-built outdoor activity centre. Own lakes, beautiful countryside. Catered and self-catering programmes. Groups of 20-30, all ages, including disabled.
For groups only

Continued ▶

TODMORDEN

Continued

Minimum age 10
Bedrooms: 3 single, 2 double/twin, 4 dormitories. Total number of beds: 33
Bathrooms: 3 private, 11 public

Bed only per person:	£min	£max
Daily	11.00	14.00

Bed & breakfast per person:	£min	£max
Daily	14.00	17.00

Full board per person:	£min	£max
Weekly	157.50	192.50

Parking for 10
🐴 🔒 [S] 🚭 🛏 [TV] ▥ U ⛳ ✈ 🚐 🎣 🏛

WINDSOR

Berkshire
Map ref 2D2

Town dominated by the spectacular castle and home of the Royal Family for over 900 years. Parts are open to the public. There are many attractions including the Great Park, Eton and trips on the river.
Tourist Information Centre
☎ (01753) 852010

Youth Hostel Windsor

Edgeworth House, Mill Lane, Clewer, Windsor SL4 5JE
☎ (01753) 861710
Fax (01753) 832100
Contact: Mr Craig Thomas
A Queen Anne residence, near Windsor Castle, Legoland, Crown Jewels and Windsor leisure pool. We are only a 2 minute walk from River Thames.
Bedrooms: 10 dormitories. Total number of beds: 82
Bathrooms: 5 public

Bed only per person:	£min	£max
Daily	6.20	9.15

Bed & breakfast per person:	£min	£max
Daily	9.00	11.95

Full board per person:	£min	£max
Weekly	108.50	129.15

Evening meal 1900 (last orders 1800)
Parking for 8
Open February-December
Cards accepted: Access, Visa, Switch/Delta
🐴 5 [UL] 🔒 [S] 🚭 🛏 [TV] ▥ 🚘 🔍 ✈ [SP] 🏛

WYE

Kent
Map ref 3B4

Well known for its agricultural and horticultural college. The Olantigh Tower, with its imposing front portico, is used as a setting for part of the Stour Music Festival held annually in June.

Wye College (University of London) ⛰

Wye, Ashford TN25 5AH
☎ (01233) 812401
Fax (01233) 813320
Telex 96118
Contact: Mr David Traske
Close to the A28 between Ashford and Canterbury, Wye College offers excellent conference facilities with friendly service, in picturesque surroundings.
Minimum age 16
Bedrooms: 189 single, 11 double/twin. Total number of beds: 211
Bathrooms: 55 private, 24 public

Bed & breakfast per person:	£min	£max
Daily	19.95	23.00

Full board per person:	£min	£max
Weekly		308.00

Lunch available
Parking for 150
Cards accepted: Access, Visa, Switch/Delta
♿ 🔒 [S] 🛏 [TV] ▥ 🚘 🏋 🔍 🏊 🎾 🎣 ✈ 🏛

YORK

North Yorkshire
Map ref 4C1

Ancient walled city nearly 2000 years old containing many well-preserved medieval buildings. Its Minster has over 100 stained glass windows. Attractions include Castle Museum, National Railway Museum, Jorvik Viking Centre and York Dungeon.
Tourist Information Centre
☎ (01904) 621756 or 620557

Fairfax House ⛰

99 Heslington Road, York YO1 5BJ
☎ (01904) 432095
Contact: Mrs. A E Glover
Student residence in quiet spacious grounds, within walking distance of town centre. Reduced rates for children under 12 and senior citizens.
Bedrooms: 93 single. Total number of beds: 93
Bathrooms: 14 public

Bed & breakfast per person:	£min	£max
Daily	15.00	17.00

Open March-April, July-September
🐴 ♿ ☕ [UL] 🛏 [TV] ▥ 🚘 🚐 [OAP]

York International YHA

Haverford, Water End, Clifton, York YO3 6LT
☎ (01904) 653147
Fax (01904) 651230
Contact: Mr D Wood
Large house with a modern annexe in extensive grounds on the banks of the River Ouse; a gentle walk from the centre of historic York.
Bedrooms: 35 dormitories. Total number of beds: 156
Bathrooms: 1 private, 10 public

Bed & breakfast per person:	£min	£max
Daily	10.05	13.60

Full board per person:	£min	£max
Weekly	115.85	140.70

Lunch available
Evening meal 1730 (last orders 2200)
Parking for 30
Cards accepted: Access, Visa, Switch/Delta
🐴 3 ♿ 🔒 [S] 🚭 🛏 [TV] ▥ 🚘 🔍 ✈ [SP] 🏛

York Youth Hotel ⛰

11-13 Bishophill Senior, York YO1 1EF
☎ (01904) 625904 & 630613
Fax (01904) 612494
Contact: Ms Maureen Sellers
Dormitory-style accommodation in the city centre. Private rooms, TV lounge, snack shop, evening meals, packed lunches, games room, residential licence, disco and 24-hour service.
Bedrooms: 7 single, 14 double/twin, 1 triple, 4 quadruple, 5 dormitories. Total number of beds: 120
Bathrooms: 8 public

Bed only per person:	£min	£max
Daily	8.00	12.00

Bed & breakfast per person:	£min	£max
Daily	9.30	14.50

Full board per person:	£min	£max
Weekly	148.00	148.00

Lunch available
Evening meal 1700 (last orders 1900)
Cards accepted: Access, Visa, Switch/Delta
🐴 2 ♿ 🔒 [S] 🚭 🛏 [TV] ▥ 🚘 🔍 ✈ [SP] 🏛 [T]

Information Pages

National Grading and Classification Scheme

Sure Signs

The Tourist Boards in Britain operate a National Quality Grading and Classification Scheme for all types of accommodation. The purpose of the scheme is to identify and promote those establishments that the public can use with confidence. The system of facility classification and quality grading also acknowledges those that provide a wider range of facilities and services and higher quality standards.

Over 30,000 places to stay are inspected under the scheme and offer the reassurance of a national grading and classification.

For 'serviced' accommodation (which includes hotels, motels, guesthouses, inns, B&Bs and farmhouses) there are six classification bands, starting with LISTED and then from ONE to FIVE CROWN. For the new generation of 'lodges', offering budget accommodation along major roads and motorways, there are three classification bands, from ONE to THREE MOON.

Quite simply, the more Crowns or Moons, the wider the range of facilities and services offered.

Quality Grading

To help you find accommodation that offers even higher standards than those required for a Crown or Moon rating, there are four levels of quality grading, using the terms DE LUXE, HIGHLY COMMENDED, COMMENDED and APPROVED.

Wherever you see a national grading and classification sign, you can be sure that a Tourist Board inspector has been there before you, checking the place on your behalf – and will be there again, because every place with a national rating is inspected annually. Establishments that apply for quality grading – which until April 1996 was optional – are subject to a more detailed inspection that assesses the quality standard of the facilities and services provided. The initial inspection invariably involves the Tourist Board inspector staying overnight, as a normal guest, until the bill is paid the following morning. This quality assessment includes such aspects as warmth of welcome and efficiency of service, as well as the standard of the furnishings, fittings and decor. The standard of meals and their presentation is also taken into account. Everything that impinges on the experience of a guest is included in the assessment. Tourist Board inspectors receive careful training to enable them to apply the quality standards consistently and fairly. Only those facilities and services that are provided are assessed, and due consideration is given to the style and nature of the establishment. B&Bs, farmhouses and guesthouses are not expected to operate in the style of large city centre hotels, and vice versa. This means that all types of establishment, whatever their Crown or Moon classification, can achieve a high quality grade if the facilities and services they provide, however limited in range, are to a high quality standard.

The quality grade that is awarded to an establishment is a reflection of the overall standard, taking everything into account. It is a balanced view of what is provided and, as such, cannot acknowledge individual areas of excellence. Quality grades are not intended to indicate value for money. A high quality product can be over-priced; a product of modest quality, if offered at a low price, can represent good value. The information provided by the combination of the classification and quality grade will enable you to determine for yourself what represents good value for money.

All Inspected

All establishments listed in this guide have been inspected or are awaiting inspection under the National Grading and Classification Scheme. The ratings that appear in the accommodation entries were correct at the time of going to press but are subject to change. If no rating appears in an entry it means that the inspection had not been carried out by the time of going to press. An information leaflet giving full details of the National Grading and Classification Scheme – which also covers self-catering holiday homes and caravan, chalet and camping parks – is available from any Tourist Information Centre.

General Advice and Information

Making a booking

When enquiring about accommodation, make sure you check prices and other important details. You will also need to state your requirements, clearly and precisely – for example:

- **Arrival and departure dates**, with acceptable alternatives if appropriate.
- **The type of accommodation** you need; for example, room with twin beds, private bathroom.
- **The terms** you want; for example, room only, bed and breakfast, half board, full board.
- **If you have children** with you: their ages, whether you want them to share your room or be next door, any other special requirements, such as a cot.
- **Particular requirements** you may have, such as a special diet.

Booking by letter

Misunderstandings can easily happen over the telephone, so we strongly advise you to confirm your booking in writing if there is time.

If you decide to enquire in writing in the first place, you might find it helpful to use the Accommodation Coupons on pages 399–402, which can be cut out and posted to the places of your choice.

Remember to include your name and address, and a stamped self-addressed envelope, or an international reply coupon if you are writing from outside Britain.

Please note that the English Tourist Board does not make reservations – you should write direct to the accommodation.

Deposits

If you make your reservation weeks or months in advance, you will probably be asked for a deposit. The amount will vary according to the time of year, the number of people in your party and how long you plan to stay. The deposit will then be deducted from the final bill when you leave.

Payment on Arrival

Some establishments, especially large hotels in big towns ask you to pay for your room on arrival if you have not booked it in advance. This is especially likely to happen if you arrive late and with little or no luggage.

If you are asked to pay on arrival, it is a good idea to see your room first, to make sure it meets your requirements.

Cancellations

Legal contract

When you accept accommodation that is offered to you, by telephone or in writing, you enter a legally binding contract with the proprietor.

This means that if you cancel your booking, fail to take up the accommodation or leave early, the proprietor may be entitled to compensation if he cannot re-let for all or a good part of the booked period. You will probably forfeit any deposit you have paid, and may be asked for an additional payment.

The proprietor cannot make a claim until after the booked period, however, and during that time every effort should be made by the proprietor to re-let the accommodation.

The reasons for cancelling may also need to be taken into account in this kind of situation, so if there is a dispute it is sensible for both sides to seek legal advice on the matter.

If you do have to change your travel plans, it is in your own interests to let the proprietors know in writing as soon as possible, to give them a chance to re-let your accommodation.

And remember, if you book by telephone and are asked for your credit card number, you should check whether the proprietor intends charging your credit card account should you later cancel your reservation. A proprietor should not be able to charge your credit card account with a cancellation unless he or she has made this clear at the time of your booking and you have agreed. However, to avoid later disputes, we suggest you check with the proprietor whether he or she intends to charge your credit card account if you cancel, and if you do not agree to this then you should state so.

Insurance

A travel or holiday insurance policy will safeguard you if you have to cancel or change your holiday plans. You can arrange a policy quite cheaply through your insurance company or travel agent. Some hotels also offer their own insurance schemes.

Arriving Late

If you know you will be arriving late in the evening, it is a good idea to say so when you book. If you are delayed on your way, a telephone call to say that you will be late will help prevent any problems when you arrive.

Service Charges and Tipping

These days many places levy service charges automatically. If they do, they must clearly say so in their offer of accommodation, at the time of booking. Then the service charge becomes part of the legal contract when you accept the offer of accommodation.

If a service charge is levied automatically, there is no need to tip the staff, unless they provide some exceptional service. The usual tip for meals is ten per cent of the total bill.

Telephone Charges

Hotels can set their own charges for telephone calls made through their switchboard or from direct-dial telephones in bedrooms. These charges are often much higher than telephone companies' standard charges (to defray the cost of providing the service).

Comparing costs

It is a condition of the National Grading and Classification Scheme, that a hotel's unit charges are on display, by the telephones or with the room information. But in practice it is not always easy to compare these charges with standard telephone rates. Before using a hotel telephone for long-distance calls, you may decide to ask how the charges compare.

Security of Valuables

You can deposit your valuables with the proprietor or manager during your stay, and we recommend that you do this as a sensible precaution. Make sure you obtain a receipt for them.

Some places do not accept articles for safe custody, and in that case it is wisest to keep your valuables with you.

Disclaimer

Some proprietors put up a notice which disclaims liability for property brought on to their premises by a guest. In fact, they can only restrict their liability to a minimum laid down by law (The Hotel Proprietors Act, 1956).

Under that Act, a proprietor is liable for the value of the loss or damage to any property (except a motor car or its contents) of a guest who has engaged overnight accommodation, but if the proprietor has the prescribed notice on display as prescibed under that Act, liability is limited to £50 for one article and a total of £100 for any one guest. The notice must be prominently displayed in the reception area or main entrance. These limits do not apply to valuables you have deposited with the proprietor for safe-keeping, or to property lost through the default, neglect or wilful act of the proprietor or his staff.

Code of Conduct

All the places featured in this Guide have agreed to observe the following Code of Conduct:

1 To ensure high standards of courtesy and cleanliness, catering and service appropriate to the type of establishment.

2 To describe fairly to all visitors and prospective visitors the amenities, facilities and services provided by the establishment, whether by advertisement, brochure, word of mouth or any other means. To allow visitors to see accommodation, if requested, before booking.

3 To make clear to visitors exactly what is included in all prices quoted for accommodation, meals and refreshments, including service charges, taxes and other surcharges. Details of charges, if any, for heating or additional services or facilities should also be made clear.

4 To adhere to, and not to exceed, prices current at time of occupation for accommodation or other services.

5 To advise visitors at the time of booking, and subsequently of any change, if the accommodation offered is in an unconnected annexe, or similar, or by boarding out; and to indicate the location of such accommodation and any difference in comfort or amenities from accommodation in the main establishment.

6 To give each visitor, on request, details of payments due and a receipt if required.

7 To deal promptly and courteously with all enquiries, requests, reservations, correspondence and complaints from visitors.

8 To allow an English Tourist Board representative reasonable access to the establishment, on request, to confirm that the Code of Conduct is being observed.

Comments and Complaints

Hotels and the law

Places that offer accommodation have legal and statutory responsibilities to their customers, such as providing information about prices, providing adequate fire precautions and safeguarding valuables. Like other businesses, they must also abide by the Trades Description Acts 1968 and 1972 when they describe their accommodation and facilities.

All the places featured in this Guide have declared that they do fulfil all applicable statutory obligations.

Information

The proprietors themselves supply the descriptions of their establishments and other information for the listing, and they pay to have their entries included in the Guide. All the places featured in the Guide have been inspected or have applied for inspection under the National Grading and Classification Scheme.

The English Tourist Board cannot guarantee accuracy of information in this guide, and accepts no responsibility for any error or misrepresentation. All liability for loss, disappointment, negligence or other damage caused by reliance on the information contained in this Guide, or in the event of bankruptcy or liquidation or cessation of trade of any company, individual or firm mentioned, is hereby excluded.

We strongly recommend that you carefully check prices and other details when you book your accommodation.

Problems

Of course, we hope that you will not have cause for complaint, but problems do occur from time to time.

If you are dissatisfied with anything, make your complaint to the management immediately. Then the management can take action at once to investigate the matter and put things right. The longer you leave a complaint, the harder it is to deal with effectively.

In certain circumstances, the English Tourist Board may look into complaints. However, the Board has no statutory control over establishments or their methods of operating. The Board cannot become involved in legal or contractual matters.

Feedback Questionnaire

We find it very helpful to receive your comments about the places featured in *Where to Stay* and your suggestions on how to improve the Guide. Please send us your views using the Customer Feedback Questionnaire on pages 415–416 – we would like to hear from you.

Return it to: Department AS, English Tourist Board, Thames Tower, Black's Road, Hammersmith, London W6 9EL.

About the Guide Entries

Locations

Places to stay are listed under the town, city or village where they are located. If a place is out in the countryside, you will find it listed under its nearest village or town.

Town names are listed alphabetically within each regional section of the Guide, along with the name of the county they fall under, and their map reference.

Map references

These refer to the colour location maps at the back of the Guide. The first figure shown is the map number, the following letter and figure indicate the grid reference on the map.

Some entries were included just before the Guide went to press, so they do not appear on the maps.

Addresses

County names, which appear in the town headings, are not repeated in the entries. When you are writing, you should of course make sure you use the full address and postcode.

Telephone Numbers

Telephone numbers are listed below the accommodation address for each entry. Area codes are shown in brackets, and the exchange name is also included (before the code) if it differs from that of the town under which a place is listed.

Price

The prices shown in *Where to Stay 1996* are only a general guide; they were supplied to us by proprietors in summer of 1995. Remember, changes may occur after the Guide goes to press, so we strongly advise you to check prices when you book your accommodation.

Prices are shown in pounds sterling and include VAT where applicable. Some places also include a service charge in their standard tariff so check this when you book.

Standardised method

There are many different ways of quoting prices for accommodation. We use a standardised method in the Guide to allow you to compare prices. For example when we show: **Bed and breakfast**, the prices shown are for overnight accommodation with breakfast, for single and double rooms. **The double-room price** is for two people. If a double room is occupied by one person there is sometimes a reduction in price. **Half board**, the prices shown are for room, breakfast and evening meal, per person per day and per person per week.

Some places provide only a continental breakfast in the set price, and you may have to pay extra if you want a full English breakfast.

Checking prices

According to the law, hotels with at least four bedrooms or eight beds must display their overnight accommodation charges in the reception area or entrance. In your own interests, do make sure you check prices and what they include.

Children's rates

You will find that many places charge a reduced rate for children especially if they share a room with their parents. Some places charge the full rate, however, when a child occupies a room which might otherwise have been let to an adult.

The upper age limit for reductions for children varies from one hotel to another, so check this when you book.

Seasonal packages

Prices often vary through the year, and may be significantly lower outside peak holiday weeks. Many places offer special package rates – fully inclusive weekend breaks, for example – in the autumn, winter and spring.

You can get details of bargain packages from the the the establishment themselves, the Regional Tourist Boards or your local Tourist Information Centre (TIC). Your local travel agent may also have information, and can help you make bookings.

Bathrooms

Each accommodation entry shows you the number of private bathrooms available, the number of private showers, and the number of public bathrooms.

'Private bathroom' means a bath and/or shower with a WC en-suite with the bedroom, or a separate bathroom with a bath plus a WC solely for the occupants of that bedroom; 'private shower' means a shower en-suite but no WC.

Public bathrooms normally have a bath, sometimes with a shower attachment. If the availability of a bath is important to you, remember to check when you book.

Meals

If an establishment serves evening meals, you will find the starting time and last order times shown in the listing; some smaller places may ask you at breakfast or at midday whether you want an evening meal.

The prices shown in each entry are for bed and breakfast or half board, but many places also offer lunch, as you will see indicated in the listing.

Opening Period

All places are open all year, except where a specific opening period is indicated.

Symbols

The at-a-glance symbols included at the end of each entry show many of the services and facilities available at each place.

You will find the key to these symbols on the back cover flap.

Open out the flap and you can check the meanings of the symbols as you go.

Alcoholic Drinks

All the places listed in the Guide are licensed to serve alcohol, unless the symbol UL appears. The license may be restricted – to diners only, for example – so you may want to check this when you book.

Smoking

Many places provide no-smoking areas – from no-smoking bedrooms and lounges to no-smoking sections of the restaurant. Some places prefer not to accommodate smokers, and in such cases the listing information makes this clear.

Pets

Many places accept guests with pets, but we do advise you to check this when you book, and ask about any extra charges or any rules about exactly where your pet is allowed.

Some establishments do not accept dogs at all, and these places are marked with the symbol 🐕.

Visitors from overseas must not bring pets of any kind into Britain, unless they are prepared for the animals to go into lengthy quarantine. Because of the continuing threat of rabies, the penalties for ignoring these regulations are extremely severe.

Credit and Charge Cards

The credit and charge cards accepted by a place are listed immediately above the line of symbols at the end of each entry.

The abbreviations used are:
Access – Access/Eurocard/Mastercard
Visa – Visa/Barclaycard
Diners – Diners
Amex – American Express
Switch/Delta – Direct debit cards
If you do plan to pay by card, check that the establishment will take your card before you book.

Some proprietors will charge you a higher rate if you pay by credit card rather than cash or cheque. The difference is to cover the percentage paid by the proprietor to the credit card company.

If you are planning to pay by credit card, you may want to ask whether it would, in fact, be cheaper to pay by cheque or cash. When you book by telephone, you may be asked for your credit card number as 'confirmation'. *But remember, the proprietor may then charge your credit card account if you cancel your booking. See under Cancellations on page 387.*

Events for 1996

This is a selection of the many cultural, sporting and other events that will be taking place throughout England during 1996. Dates marked with an asterisk* were provisional at the time of going to press.

January 1996

1 January
London Parade
Starts from Westminster Abbey,
Parliament Square, London SW1
Contact: (0181) 566 8586

4–14 January
London International Boat Show
Earls Court Exhibition Centre,
Warwick Road, London SW5
Contact: (01784) 473377

4–29 January
Holiday on Ice 1996
Brighton Centre, Kings Road,
Brighton, East Sussex
Contact: (01273) 203131

6 January
Haxey Hood Game
Haxey, Humberside
Contact: (01427) 752845

February 1996

4–9 February
Wordsworth Winter School
Dove Cottage and Wordsworth
Museum, Town End, Grasmere,
Cumbria
Contact: (01539) 435544

10–17 February
Jorvik Festival
Various venues, York, North
Yorkshire
Contact: (01904) 643211

17–18 February
Primrose Festival
By Pass Nurseries, Dobbies Lane,
Marks Tey, Essex
Contact: (01206) 210400

24 February–2 March
Bedfordshire Music Festival
St Pauls Complex, St Pauls
Square, Bedford, Bedfordshire
Contact: (01234) 708566

25 February*
Chinese New Year – Year of the Rat
Leicester Square, London WC2
Contact: (0171) 734 5161

27 February–3 March
British Philatelic Exhibition, Spring Stampex
Royal Horticultural Halls,
Greycoat Street and Vincent
Square, London SW1
Contact: (0171) 490 1005

March 1996

4–9 March
A Celebration of Schools Music
Snape Maltings Concert Hall,
Snape Maltings, Suffolk
Contact: (01728) 452935

28–30 March
Horseracing: Martell Grand National Meeting
Aintree Racecourse, Liverpool,
Merseyside
Contact: (0151) 523 2600

29–31 March
Clacton Traditional Ale and Traditional Jazz Weekend
West Cliff Theatre, Tower Road,
Clacton-on-Sea, Essex
Contact: (01255) 474000

30–31 March
Thriplow Daffodil Weekend
Various venues, Thriplow,
Cambridgeshire
Contact: (01763) 208132

April 1996

1 April–31 May
Cornwall Gardens Festival
Various venues throughout
Cornwall
Contact: (01872) 74057

5–8 April
Lancaster Easter Maritime Festival
Various venues, Lancaster,
Lancashire
Contact: (01524) 32878

5–12 April
Harrogate International Youth Music Festival
Various venues, Harrogate, North
Yorkshire
Contact: (0171) 401 9941

6 April
Rowing: Oxford v Cambridge University Boat Race
Putney to Mortlake, River Thames, London
Contact: (0171) 379 3234

6–8 April
A Celebration of Easter
Leeds Castle, Leeds, Maidstone, Kent
Contact: (01622) 765400

25–28 April
Harrogate Spring Flower Festival
Valley Gardens, Harrogate, North Yorkshire
Contact: (01423) 561049

27–28 April
St George's Spring Festival
Various venues, Salisbury, Wiltshire
Contact: (01722) 434300

May 1996

3–6 May
Great Cornwall Balloon Festival
Varies venues, St Austell and Newquay, Cornwall
Contact: (01637) 872211

3–26 May
Brighton Festival
Various venues, Brighton, East Sussex
Contact: (01273) 676926

4–5 May
Nottingham County Show
Newark and Nottinghamshire Showground, Winthorpe, Newark, Nottinghamshire
Contact: (01636) 702627

4–6 May
Rochester Sweeps Festival
Various venues, Rochester, Kent
Contact: (01634) 843666

4–6 May
Spalding Flower Parade and Springfields Country Fair
Various venues, Spalding, Lincolnshire
Contact: (01775) 724843

5–6 May
Kids International
Telford Town Park, Telford, Shropshire
Contact: (01952) 203009

8–12 May
Showjumping: Royal Windsor Horse Show
Home Park, Windsor, Berkshire
Contact: (01753) 860633

17–19 May
Keswick Jazz Festival
Keswick, Cumbria
Contact: (01900) 602122

17 May–2 June
Bath International Music Festival
Various venues, Bath, Avon
Contact: (01225) 462231

21–24 May
Chelsea Flower Show (members only on 21–22 May)
Royal Hospital, Royal Hospital Road, Chelsea, London SW3
Contact: (0171) 834 4333

24–27 May
International Festival of the Sea – Bristol '96
Various venues, Bristol, Avon
Contact: (0117) 923 7996

24 May–2 June*
Coniston Water Festival
Coniston, Cumbria
Contact: (01539) 441707

25–27 May*
Liverpool Show
Wavertree Playground, Liverpool, Merseyside
Contact: (0151) 225 6354

26–27 May
North Shields Fishquay Festival
North Shields, Tyne and Wear
Contact: (0191) 257 5544

26–27 May
Wirral Countryside Fair
Wirral Country Park, Wallasey, Wirral, Merseyside
Contact: (0151) 648 4371

27 May
Northumberland County Show
Overdean Park, Ovington, Northumberland
Contact: (01434) 344443

29–30 May
Suffolk Show
Suffolk Showground, Bucklesham Road, Ipswich, Suffolk
Contact: (01473) 726847

29 May–1 June
Royal Bath and West of England Show
Royal Bath and West Showground, Shepton Mallet, Somerset
Contact: (01749) 822200

31 May–2 June
Great Garden and Countryside Festival
Holker Hall and Gardens, Cark in Cartmel, Cumbria
Contact: (01539) 558838

June 1996

1–2 June
Balloon and Vintage Car Fiesta
Leeds Castle, Leeds, Maidstone,
Kent
Contact: (01622) 765400

6–8 June
South of England Agricultural Show
Ardingly Showground, Haywards
Heath, West Sussex
Contact: (01444) 892700

6–12 June
Appleby Horse Fair
Appleby, Cumbria
Contact: (01325) 362933

7–9 June
Wimborne Folk Festival
Wimborne Minster, Dorset
Contact: (01202) 740792

7–23 June
Aldeburgh Festival of Music and the Arts
Various venues, Aldeburgh,
Suffolk
Contact: (01728) 452935

8–11, 13–16, 18, 19, 22.,23, 26, 30 June
Football: European Football Championship – EURO '96
Various venues
Contact: (01782) 741996

9 June
Bristol to Bournemouth Car Rally
Starts Bristol, Avon, and finishes
at Pier Approach, Bournemouth,
Dorset
Contact: (01935) 25597

14–16 June
Silloth Victorian Weekend
Silloth Green, Criffel Street,
Silloth, Cumbria
Contact: (016973) 32580

15–16 June
Durham Regatta
River Wear, Durham
Contact: (0191) 383 1594

15–16 June
Middle Wallop International Air Show 1996
Army Air Corps Centre, Middle
Wallop, Hampshire
Contact: (01264) 384461

16 June

Royal Air Force Cosford Open Day
Aerospace Museum, Cosford,
Shifnal, Shropshire
Contact: (01902) 374872

16 June
Sailing: Singlehanded Transatlantic Race
Starts Plymouth, Devon and
finishes Newport, Rhode Island,
USA
Contact: (01752) 660077

18–19 June
Cheshire County Show
Tabley House, Northwich Road,
Knutsford, Cheshire
Contact: (01829) 760020

18–21 June
Horseracing: Royal Ascot
Ascot Racecourse, Ascot,
Berkshire
Contact: (01344) 22211

19–20 June
Lincolnshire Show
Lincolnshire Showground,
Grange-de-Lings, Lincoln,
Lincolnshire
Contact: (01522) 524240

21 June–6 July
Bradford Festival
Various venues, Bradford, West
Yorkshire
Contact: (01274) 309199

22 June–7 July
Ludlow Festival
Ludlow Castle, Ludlow,
Shropshire
Contact: (01584) 872150

26–27 June
Royal Norfolk Show
The Showground, Dereham Road,
Norwich, Norfolk
Contact: (01603) 748931

29–30 June
Middlesex County Show
Middlesex Showground, Park
Road, Uxbridge, Greater London
Contact: (01895) 252131

29 June
Open Air Concert
Leeds Castle, Leeds, Maidstone,
Kent
Contact: (01622) 765400

30 June–7 July
Alnwick Medieval Fair
Various venues, Alnwick,
Northumberland
Contact: (01665) 605004

30 June–16 July
Chichester Festivities
Various venues, Chichester,
West Sussex
Contact: (01243) 785718

July 1996

1–4 July
The Royal Show
National Agricultural Centre,
Stoneleigh Park, Kenilworth,
Warwickshire
Contact: (01203) 696969

July*
Cumberland Agricultural Show
Rickerby Park, Carlisle, Cumbria
Contact: (01228) 560364

3–7 July
Henley Royal Regatta
Henley-on-Thames, Oxfordshire
Contact: (01491) 572153

4–21 July
Exeter Festival
Various venues, Exeter, Devon
Contact: (01392) 265613

5–7 July*
Ely Folk Weekend
Cresswells Lane Site, Ely,
Cambridgeshire
Contact: (01353) 698171

5–7 July
Grimsby International Jazz Festival
King George V Stadium, Weelsby
Road, Grimsby, Humberside
Contact: (01472) 242000

5–14 July
Hereford Summer Festival
Various venues, Hereford,
Hereford and Worcester
Contact: (01432) 268430

6 July
Open Air Concert
Leeds Castle, Leeds, Maidstone,
Kent
Contact: (01622) 765400

9–11 July
Great Yorkshire Show
Great Yorkshire Showground,
Wetherby Road, Harrogate,
North Yorkshire
Contact: (01423) 561536

10–13 July
Henley Festival of Music and the Arts
Various venues, Henley-on-
Thames, Oxfordshire
Contact: (01491) 411353

12–14 July
Motor Racing: British Grand Prix
Silverstone Circuit, Towcester,
Northamptonshire
Contact: (01327) 857271

13–14 July
Wirral Show
The Promenade, New Brighton,
Merseyside
Contact: (0151) 639 2718

14–15 July
Durham County Agricultural Show
Lambton Park, Chester-le-Street,
Durham
Contact: (0191) 388 5459

16–27 July
Royal Tournament
Earls Court Exhibition Centre,
Warwick Road, London SW5
Contact: (0171) 373 8141

20 July–3 August
King's Lynn Festival
Various venues, King's Lynn,
Norfolk
Contact: (01553) 773578

21 July
Tolpuddle Martyrs Rally
Tolpuddle, Dorset
Contact: (01202) 294333

26–28 July
Royal Lancashire Show
Astley Hall, Astley Park, Chorley,
Lancashire
Contact: (01254) 813769

29 July–4 August
Stockton Riverside International Festival
Dovecote Arts Centre, Dovecote
Street, Stockton-on-Tees,
Cleveland
Contact: (01642) 670067

30 July–1 August
New Forest and Hampshire County Show
New Park, Brockenhurst,
Hampshire
Contact: (01590) 622400

August 1996

August*
Robin Hood Festival
Sherwood Forest Visitor Centre
and Country Park, Edwinstowe,
Mansfield, Nottinghamshire
Contact: (0115) 977 4374

2–4 August
Portsmouth and Southsea Show
Southsea Common, Southsea,
Hampshire
Contact: (01705) 834146

2–9 August
Sidmouth International Festival of Folk Arts
Various venues, Sidmouth, Devon
Contact: (01296) 433669

3–4 August
Sunderland International Air Show
Seaburn and Roker, Coast Road, Sunderland, Tyne and Wear
Contact: (0191) 510 9317

3–10 August
Sailing: Cowes Week
Cowes, Isle of Wight
Contact: (01983) 295744

3–18 August
Women's World Bowls Championships
Victoria Park Bowling Greens, Victoria Park, Archery Road, Leamington Spa, Warwickshire
Contact: (01297) 21317

7–8 August
Bakewell Show
The Showground, Coombs Road, Bakewell, Derbyshire
Contact: (01629) 812736

9–11 August
Ambleside Great Summer Flower Show and Craft Fair
Ambleside Rugby Field, Borrans Road, Ambleside, Cumbria
Contact: (01539) 432904

9–18 August
Broadstairs Folk Week
Various venues, Broadstairs, Kent
Contact: (01843) 865650

10–17 August
Billingham International Folklore Festival
Various venues, Billingham, Cleveland
Contact: (01642) 558212

16–18 August
Northampton Hot Air Balloon Festival
Northampton Racecourse, St George's Avenue, Northampton, Northamptonshire
Contact: (01604) 233500

22 August
Grasmere Sports
Sports Field, Stock Lane, Grasmere, Cumbria
Contact: (01539) 432127

22–24 August
Southport Flower Show
Victoria Park, Rotten Row, Southport, Merseyside
Contact: (01704) 547147

23–26 August*
Clacton Jazz Festival
Various venues, Clacton-On-Sea, Essex
Contact: (01225) 253208

24–31 August
Bude Jazz Festival
Various venues, Bude, Cornwall
Contact: (01684) 566956

30 August–3 November
Blackpool Illuminations
The Promenade, Blackpool, Lancashire
Contact: (01253) 25212

September 1996

2–8 September*
Farnborough International – Aerospace Exhibition and Flying Display
Defence Research Agency, Farnborough, Hampshire
Contact: (0171) 839 3231

7–9 September
Wolsingham and Wear Valley Agricultural Show
Scotch Isle Farm, Wolsingham, Durham
Contact: (01388) 527862

8–9 September
Castlefield Carnival
Castlefield Urban Heritage Park, Castlefield Centre, 10 Liverpool Road, Castlefield, Manchester, Greater Manchester
Contact: (0161) 834 4026

13–15 September
Great Autumn Flower Show
Great Yorkshire Showground, Hookstone Oval, Harrogate, North Yorkshire
Contact: (01423) 561049

14–15 September
Royal Air Force Waddington Air Show
RAF Waddington, Waddington, Lincolnshire
Contact: (01522) 720271

14–16 September
Stanhope Agricultural Show
Unthank Park, Stanhope, Durham
Contact: (01388) 528347

15 September
Great North Run – Official World Half-Marathon
Various venues, Newcastle upon Tyne, Tyne and Wear
Contact: (0191) 261 2707

15–23 September
Southampton International Boat Show
Mayflower Park, Southampton, Hampshire
Contact: (01784) 473377

21–29 September
Scarborough Angling Festival
Scarborough, North Yorkshire
Contact: (01723) 859480

28 September
Eskdale Show
Brotherilkeld Farm, Boot, Holmrook, Cumbria
Contact: (01946) 723269

29 September
Urswick Rushbearing
Urswick Church, Church Road,
Urswick, Ulverston, Cumbria

4–6 October
**Concert: Music and
'A Shropshire Lad'**
Spadesbourne Hall, Burcot Lane,
Bromsgrove, Hereford and
Worcester
Contact: (01527) 874136

5–19 October
Writearound
Various venues throughout
Cleveland
Contact: (01642) 264341

10–20 October
Norfolk and Norwich Festival
Various venues, Norwich,
Norfolk
Contact: (01603) 614921

10–26 October
**Leeds International Film
Festival**
Various venues, Leeds, West
Yorkshire
Contact: (0113) 247 6962

12–26 October
Canterbury Festival
Various venues, Canterbury, Kent
Contact: (01227) 455600

13 October
World Conker Championship
Village Green, Ashton, Oundle,
Northamptonshire

Contact: (01832) 272735

20–25 October
Carnival Championships
Spa Royal Hall, South Marine
Drive, Bridlington, Humberside
Contact: (01262) 678255

22–27 October
**British Philatelic Exhibition,
Autumn Stampex**
Royal Horticultural Halls,
Greycoat Street and Vincent
Square, London SW1
Contact: (0171) 490 1005

2 November
**Leeds Castle Grand Firework
Spectacular**
Leeds Castle, Leeds, Maidstone,
Kent
Contact: (01622) 765400

7 November
**Bridgwater Guy Fawkes
Carnival**
Bridgwater, Somerset
Contact: (01278) 429288

10 November
**Lord Mayor's Procession and
Show**
The City, London

18 November
**Weston-super-Mare Guy
Fawkes Carnival**
Town centre, Weston-super-Mare,
Avon
Contact: (01278) 425344

24–27 November
**Royal Smithfield Show and
Agricultural Machinery
Exhibition**
Earls Court Exhibition Centre,
Warwick Road, London SW5
Contact: (0171) 370 8226

5–7 December
Worcester Christmas Fayre
City Centre, Cornmarket, New
Street and Friar Street,
Worcester, Hereford and
Worcester
Contact: (01905) 722320

6 December–5 January 97*
**Trafalgar Square Christmas
Tree**
Trafalgar Square, London WC2
Contact: (0171) 211 6393

7–8 December
Dickensian Christmas
Various venues, Rochester, Kent
Contact: (01634) 843666

7, 8, 14, 15, 21, 22 December*
Santa Specials
South Tynedale Railway, Alston,
Cumbria
Contact: (01434) 381696

31 December
Allendale Baal Festival
Market Square, Allendale,
Northumberland

IS IT ACCESSIBLE?

If you are a wheelchair user or someone who has difficulty walking, look for the national 'Accessible' symbol when choosing where to stay.

All the places that display a symbol have been checked by a Tourist Board inspector against standard criteria that reflect the practical needs of wheelchair users.

There are three categories of accessibility:

 Accessible to all wheelchair users including those travelling independently

 Accessible to a wheelchair user with assistance

 Accessible to a wheelchair user able to walk short distances and up at least three steps

Establishments in this guide which have a wheelchair access category are listed on pages 10 and 11.

ADVERTISERS

If you would like further information from any of the advertisers in this guide, you may find it helpful to use the advertisement coupons towards the end of the guide. These should be mailed direct to the companies in which you are interested. Do please remember to include your name and address.

BOOKING ENQUIRIES

When enquiring about accommodation you may find it helpful to use the accommodation coupons towards the end of the guide. These should be mailed direct to the establishments in which you are interested. Do please remember to include your name and address.

Accommodation Coupons

▶ *Complete this coupon and mail it direct to the establishment in which you are interested. Do not send it to the English Tourist Board. Remember to enclose a stamped addressed envelope (or international reply coupon).*

▶ *Tick as appropriate and complete the reverse side if you are interested in making a booking.*

❏ *Please send me a brochure or further information, and details of prices charged.*
❏ *Please advise me, as soon as possible, if accommodation is available as detailed overleaf.*

Name: *(BLOCK CAPITALS)*

Address:

                                                    Postcode:

Telephone number: Date:

Where to Stay 1996
Bed & Breakfast, Farmhouses, Inns & Hostels

English Tourist Board

▶ *Complete this coupon and mail it direct to the establishment in which you are interested. Do not send it to the English Tourist Board. Remember to enclose a stamped addressed envelope (or international reply coupon).*

▶ *Tick as appropriate and complete the reverse side if you are interested in making a booking.*

❏ *Please send me a brochure or further information, and details of prices charged.*
❏ *Please advise me, as soon as possible, if accommodation is available as detailed overleaf.*

Name: *(BLOCK CAPITALS)*

Address:

                                                    Postcode:

Telephone number: Date:

Where to Stay 1996
Bed & Breakfast, Farmhouses, Inns & Hostels

English Tourist Board

Accommodation Coupons

▶ **Complete this side if you are interested in making a booking.**

▶ **Please read the information on pages 387–391 before confirming any booking.**

Please advise me if accommodation is available as detailed below.

From (date of arrival): _____ To (date of departure): _____

or alternatively from: _____ To: _____

Adults _____ Children _____ (ages _____)

Please give the number of people and ages of children

Accommodation required: _____

_____

Meals required: _____

Other/special requirements: _____

▶ **Please enclose a stamped addressed envelope (or international reply coupon).**

▶ **Complete this side if you are interested in making a booking.**

▶ **Please read the information on pages 387–391 before confirming any booking.**

Please advise me if accommodation is available as detailed below.

From (date of arrival): _____ To (date of departure): _____

or alternatively from: _____ To: _____

Adults _____ Children _____ (ages _____)

Please give the number of people and ages of children

Accommodation required: _____

_____

Meals required: _____

Other/special requirements: _____

▶ **Please enclose a stamped addressed envelope (or international reply coupon).**

Accommodation Coupons

▶ Complete this coupon and mail it direct to the establishment in which you are interested. Do not send it to the English Tourist Board. Remember to enclose a stamped addressed envelope (or international reply coupon).

▶ Tick as appropriate and complete the reverse side if you are interested in making a booking.

❑ Please send me a brochure or further information, and details of prices charged.
❑ Please advise me, as soon as possible, if accommodation is available as detailed overleaf.

Name: _____ (BLOCK CAPITALS)

Address: _____

_____

_____ Postcode: _____

Telephone number: _____ Date: _____

Where to Stay 1996
Bed & Breakfast, Farmhouses, Inns & Hostels

English Tourist Board

▶ Complete this coupon and mail it direct to the establishment in which you are interested. Do not send it to the English Tourist Board. Remember to enclose a stamped addressed envelope (or international reply coupon).

▶ Tick as appropriate and complete the reverse side if you are interested in making a booking.

❑ Please send me a brochure or further information, and details of prices charged.
❑ Please advise me, as soon as possible, if accommodation is available as detailed overleaf.

Name: _____ (BLOCK CAPITALS)

Address: _____

_____

_____ Postcode: _____

Telephone number: _____ Date: _____

Where to Stay 1996
Bed & Breakfast, Farmhouses, Inns & Hostels

English Tourist Board

Accommodation Coupons

▶ **Complete this side if you are interested in making a booking.**

▶ **Please read the information on pages 387–391 before confirming any booking.**

Please advise me if accommodation is available as detailed below.

From (date of arrival): _____ To (date of departure): _____

or alternatively from: _____ To: _____

Adults _____ Children _____ (ages _____)
Please give the number of people and ages of children

Accommodation required: _____

_____

Meals required: _____

Other/special requirements: _____

▶ **Please enclose a stamped addressed envelope (or international reply coupon).**

▶ **Complete this side if you are interested in making a booking.**

▶ **Please read the information on pages 387–391 before confirming any booking.**

Please advise me if accommodation is available as detailed below.

From (date of arrival): _____ To (date of departure): _____

or alternatively from: _____ To: _____

Adults _____ Children _____ (ages _____)
Please give the number of people and ages of children

Accommodation required: _____

_____

Meals required: _____

Other/special requirements: _____

▶ **Please enclose a stamped addressed envelope (or international reply coupon).**

Advertisement Coupons

► **Complete this coupon and mail it direct to the advertiser from whom you would like to receive further information. Do not send it to the English Tourist Board.**

To (advertiser's name): _____

Please send me a brochure or further information on the following, as advertised by you in the English Tourist Board's **Where to Stay 1996** Guide:

_____

_____

My name and address are on the reverse.

► **Complete this coupon and mail it direct to the advertiser from whom you would like to receive further information. Do not send it to the English Tourist Board.**

To (advertiser's name): _____

Please send me a brochure or further information on the following, as advertised by you in the English Tourist Board's **Where to Stay 1996** Guide:

_____

_____

My name and address are on the reverse.

► **Complete this coupon and mail it direct to the advertiser from whom you would like to receive further information. Do not send it to the English Tourist Board.**

To (advertiser's name): _____

Please send me a brochure or further information on the following, as advertised by you in the English Tourist Board's **Where to Stay 1996** Guide:

_____

_____

My name and address are on the reverse.

Advertisement Coupons

Name: _____ (BLOCK CAPITALS)

Address: _____

_____

_____ Postcode: _____

Telephone number: _____ Date: _____

Where to Stay 1996
Bed & Breakfast, Farmhouses, Inns & Hostels

English Tourist Board

Name: _____ (BLOCK CAPITALS)

Address: _____

_____

_____ Postcode: _____

Telephone number: _____ Date: _____

Where to Stay 1996
Bed & Breakfast, Farmhouses, Inns & Hostels

English Tourist Board

Name: _____ (BLOCK CAPITALS)

Address: _____

_____

_____ Postcode: _____

Telephone number: _____ Date: _____

Where to Stay 1996
Bed & Breakfast, Farmhouses, Inns & Hostels

English Tourist Board

Advertisement Coupons

▶ **Complete this coupon and mail it direct to the advertiser from whom you would like to receive further information. Do not send it to the English Tourist Board.**

To (advertiser's name): _____

Please send me a brochure or further information on the following, as advertised by you in the English Tourist Board's **Where to Stay 1996** *Guide:*

_____

_____

My name and address are on the reverse.

▶ **Complete this coupon and mail it direct to the advertiser from whom you would like to receive further information. Do not send it to the English Tourist Board.**

To (advertiser's name): _____

Please send me a brochure or further information on the following, as advertised by you in the English Tourist Board's **Where to Stay 1996** *Guide:*

_____

_____

My name and address are on the reverse.

▶ **Complete this coupon and mail it direct to the advertiser from whom you would like to receive further information. Do not send it to the English Tourist Board.**

To (advertiser's name): _____

Please send me a brochure or further information on the following, as advertised by you in the English Tourist Board's **Where to Stay 1996** *Guide:*

_____

_____

My name and address are on the reverse.

Advertisement Coupons

Name: _____ (BLOCK CAPITALS)

Address: _____

_____

_____ Postcode: _____

Telephone number: _____ Date: _____

Where to Stay 1996
Bed & Breakfast, Farmhouses, Inns & Hostels

English Tourist Board

Name: _____ (BLOCK CAPITALS)

Address: _____

_____

_____ Postcode: _____

Telephone number: _____ Date: _____

Where to Stay 1996
Bed & Breakfast, Farmhouses, Inns & Hostels

English Tourist Board

Name: _____ (BLOCK CAPITALS)

Address: _____

_____

_____ Postcode: _____

Telephone number: _____ Date: _____

Where to Stay 1996
Bed & Breakfast, Farmhouses, Inns & Hostels

English Tourist Board

TOWN INDEX

The following cities, towns and villages all have accommodation listed in this guide. If the place where you wish to stay is not shown, the location maps (starting on page 417) will help you to find somewhere suitable in the same area.

CHECK THE MAPS

The colour maps at the back of this guide show all the cities, towns and villages which have accommodation listings. They will enable you to check if there is suitable accommodation in the area that you plan to visit.

AT-A-GLANCE SYMBOLS

At-a-glance symbols at the end of each
accommodation entry give information about
services and facilities. A handy guide to these
symbols can be found inside the back cover flap,
which can be kept open for easy reference.

COUNTRY CODE

🍀 Enjoy the countryside and respect its life and work
🍀 Guard against all risk of fire 🍀 Fasten all gates
🍀 Keep your dogs under close control 🍀 Keep to
public paths across farmland 🍀 Use gates and stiles
to cross fences, hedges and walls 🍀 Leave livestock,
crops and machinery alone 🍀 Take your litter home
🍀 Help to keep all water clean 🍀 Protect wildlife,
plants and trees 🍀 Take special care on country
roads 🍀 Make no unnecessary noise

INDEX TO ADVERTISERS

Mileage Chart

The distances between towns on the mileage chart are given to the nearest mile, and are measured along routes based on the quickest travelling time, making maximum use of motorways or dual-carriageway roads. The chart is based upon information supplied by the Automobile Association.

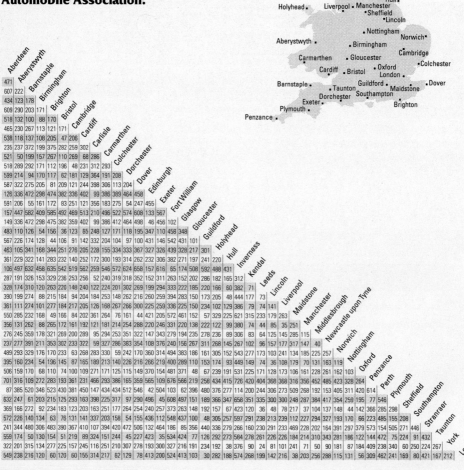

Aberystwyth — Aberdeen: 471
Barnstaple — 607 222
Birmingham — 434 123 178
Brighton — 609 290 203 171
Bristol — 518 132 100 88 170
Cambridge — 465 230 267 113 121 171
Cardiff — 538 118 137 108 205 47 206
Carlisle — 235 237 372 199 375 282 259 302
Carmarthen — 521 50 199 157 267 110 269 68 286
Colchester — 518 289 292 171 112 196 48 231 312 293
Dorchester — 599 214 94 170 117 62 181 129 364 191 208
Dover — 587 322 275 205 81 209 121 244 398 306 113 204
Edinburgh — 126 336 472 298 474 382 336 402 99 386 389 464 458
Exeter — 591 206 55 161 172 83 251 121 356 183 275 54 247 455
Fort William — 157 447 582 409 585 492 469 513 210 496 522 574 608 133 567
Glasgow — 149 336 472 298 475 382 359 402 99 386 412 464 498 46 456 102
Gloucester — 483 110 126 54 156 36 123 65 248 127 171 118 195 347 110 458 348
Guildford — 567 226 174 128 44 106 91 142 332 204 104 97 100 431 146 522 431 101
Holyhead — 463 105 341 168 344 251 276 205 228 155 334 333 367 327 326 439 328 217 301
Hull — 361 229 322 141 283 232 140 252 172 300 193 314 262 232 306 382 271 197 241 220
Inverness — 106 497 632 458 635 542 519 562 260 546 572 624 658 157 616 65 174 508 592 488 431
Kendal — 287 191 326 153 329 236 253 256 52 240 319 318 352 152 311 263 152 202 286 182 165 312
Leeds — 328 174 310 120 263 220 148 240 122 224 201 302 269 199 294 333 222 185 220 166 60 382 71
Lincoln — 390 199 274 88 215 184 94 204 184 253 148 262 216 260 259 394 283 150 173 205 48 444 177 73
Liverpool — 361 111 274 101 277 184 217 205 126 168 267 266 300 225 259 336 225 150 234 102 129 386 79 74 141
Maidstone — 550 285 232 168 49 166 84 202 361 264 76 161 44 421 205 572 461 152 57 329 225 621 315 233 179 263
Manchester — 356 131 262 88 265 172 161 192 121 181 214 254 288 220 246 331 220 138 222 122 99 380 74 44 85 35 251
Middlesbrough — 276 245 359 178 321 269 200 289 95 294 253 351 322 147 343 279 194 235 278 236 89 306 83 64 125 145 285 115
Newcastle upon Tyne — 237 277 391 211 353 302 233 322 59 327 286 383 354 108 376 240 156 267 311 268 121 267 102 96 157 177 317 147 40
Norwich — 489 293 319 172 130 63 268 283 330 59 242 170 360 314 494 383 186 161 305 152 543 277 173 103 241 134 185 225 257
Nottingham — 335 160 234 54 196 145 87 165 189 213 140 252 219 140 266 219 400 289 110 153 174 93 449 149 74 36 108 179 70 131 163 119
Oxford — 506 159 170 68 110 74 100 109 271 171 125 115 149 370 154 481 371 48 67 239 191 531 225 171 128 173 106 161 228 261 162 103
Penzance — 701 316 109 272 283 193 361 231 466 293 565 359 565 219 676 566 219 256 435 726 420 404 368 356 452 485 423 328 264
Perth — 87 385 520 346 523 430 381 450 147 434 434 512 546 42 504 103 62 396 480 376 277 114 200 244 306 273 509 268 192 153 405 311 420 614
Plymouth — 632 247 61 203 215 125 293 163 398 225 317 97 290 496 45 608 497 151 189 366 347 658 351 335 300 300 248 287 384 417 354 259 195 77 546
Sheffield — 369 166 272 92 234 183 123 203 163 251 177 264 240 257 373 263 148 192 157 67 423 120 36 48 78 217 37 104 137 148 44 142 366 285 259 205
Southampton — 572 226 140 134 63 76 131 141 337 203 158 54 155 436 112 548 437 100 48 305 278 213 239 213 230 172 227 294 327 193 170 66 223 485 155 208
Stranraer — 241 344 480 306 483 390 367 410 107 394 420 472 506 132 464 186 85 356 440 336 279 266 160 230 291 233 469 228 202 164 391 297 379 573 154 505 271 446
Taunton — 559 174 50 130 151 72 219 89 324 151 244 45 227 423 35 534 444 77 126 292 373 584 286 184 214 310 343 188 122 144 472 75 224 91 432
York — 322 201 315 134 277 225 157 245 116 251 210 307 278 193 300 327 216 191 234 192 38 376 90 24 81 101 241 71 50 90 181 87 184 409 238 340 60 250 224 267
London — 549 238 216 120 60 120 60 155 314 217 62 129 78 413 200 524 413 103 30 282 188 574 268 199 142 216 38 203 256 288 115 131 56 309 462 241 169 80 421 167 212

Customer Feedback Questionnaire

We hope you have found this guide useful in selecting accommodation in England which suits your needs.

It is very helpful to the English Tourist Board to receive comments about establishments in *Where to Stay* and suggestions on how to improve the guide, and also on the National Grading and Classification Schemes.

We would like to hear from you. It you wish to do so, you can send us your views using this questionnaire. You need not name the establishment concerned.

Q1 Did you use the *Where to Stay* guide to find:
Holiday accommodation .... ☐
Business accommodation .... ☐
Both... ☐

Q2 Did you use the establishment's Quality Grading / Crown or Key Classification to help you in making your choice?
Yes... ☐
No... ☐

Q3 If you did, was it the Quality Grading (Approved, Commended, Highly Commended or De Luxe) or the number of Crowns or Keys for facilities that influenced you most?
The Quality Grading .... ☐
The number of Crowns / Keys................. ☐
Both... ☐

Q4 What was the Quality Grading and Crown or Key Classification of the establishment you chose?

....

Q5 Do you find the National Grades and Classifications:
Very easy to understand .... ☐
Fairly easy to understand .... ☐

Difficult to understand .... ☐
If you find them difficult to understand, please specify why:

....

....

Q6 Was the accommodation you used:
Hotel .... ☐
Guesthouse .... ☐
Farmhouse .... ☐
Bed & Breakfast...................................... ☐
Self-Catering Holiday Home .... ☐

Q7 Did the establishment chosen:
Exceed your expectations........................ ☐
Meet your expectations .... ☐
Fail to meet your expectations .... ☐
If it failed to meet your expectations, please specify how:

....

....

Q8 Would you say the establishment offered good value for money?
Yes... ☐
No... ☐

PLEASE CUT ALONG DOTTED LINE

Q9 Was there any feature of your stay that you would particularly praise or criticise (please specify):

....

....

....

Q10 Have you bought a *Where to Stay* guide before?
Yes .... ☐
No .... ☐
If yes, how long ago:
Last Year.. ☐
2 Years ago .... ☐
More than 2 years ago .... ☐

Q11 Did you find the *Where to Stay* guide:
Very easy to use...................................... ☐
Fairly easy to use .... ☐
Difficult to use.. ☐

Q12 Are there any aspects of the *Where to Stay* guide that you would particularly praise or criticise (please specify):

....

....

....

Q13 Is there any additional information not already featured in this guide that you would find helpful (please specify):

....

....

....

**Thank you for giving us your views.
Please return this questionnaire to:
Department AS, English Tourist Board,
Thames Tower, Black's Road,
Hammersmith, London W6 9EL**

Please would you give us a few details about yourself:
Q14 Are you:
Married .... ☐
Single .... ☐

Q15 Do you have dependent children?
Yes.. ☐
No .... ☐
If yes, how many ....

Q16 Into which age group do you fall?
17-24 .... ☐
25–34.. ☐
35–44.. ☐
45-54 .... ☐
55 + ... ☐

Q17 Are you an overseas visitor (i.e. from outside the UK visiting this country)?
Yes.. ☐
No .... ☐

Q18 Did you travel alone or with a party?
Alone .... ☐
Party of people .... ☐
of which ....were adults
and ....were children

Q19 How long did you stay in the establishment?
....nights

Q20 Do you plan to use the guide to book any further stays this year?
Yes.. ☐
No .... ☐
If yes, how many .... ☐

Q21 What other sources of information did you use in selecting your accommodation (please specify):

....

....

Q22 Did you obtain your copy of *Where to Stay* from
Bookshop .... ☐
Tourist Information Centre...................... ☐
Other (please specify) .... ☐

PLEASE CUT ALONG DOTTED LINE

Location Maps

Every place name featured in the accommodation listings pages of this *Where to Stay* guide has a map reference to help you locate it on the maps which follow. For example, to find Colchester, Essex, which has 'Map ref 3B2', turn to Map 3 and refer to grid square B2.

All place names in the listings pages are shown in black type on the maps. This enables you to find other places in your chosen area which may have suitable accommodation – the Town Index (preceding pages) gives page numbers.

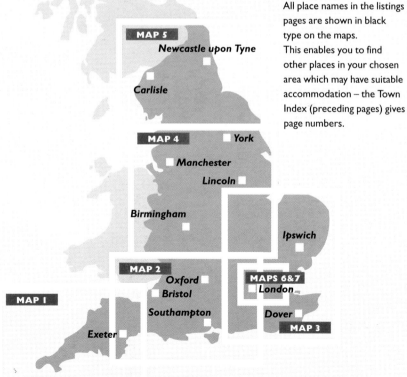

MAP 5

Newcastle upon Tyne

Carlisle

MAP 4 York

Manchester

Lincoln

Birmingham

Ipswich

MAP 2

Oxford

Bristol

MAPS 6&7

London

MAP 1

Southampton

Dover

MAP 3

Exeter

MAP 1

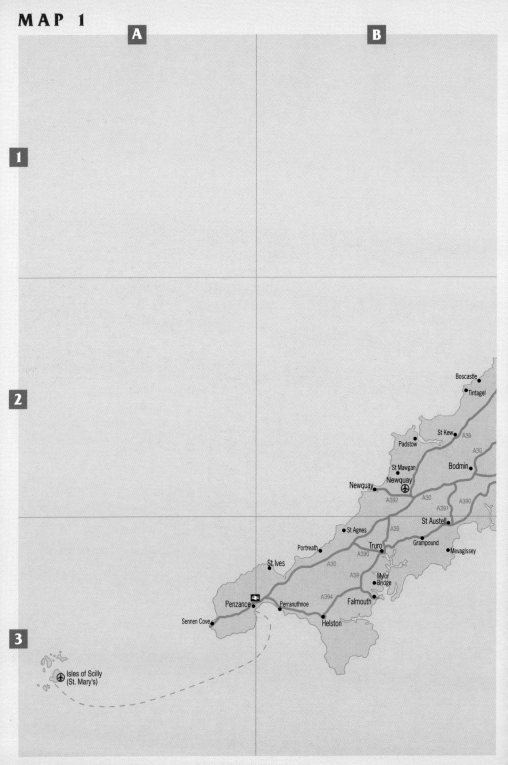

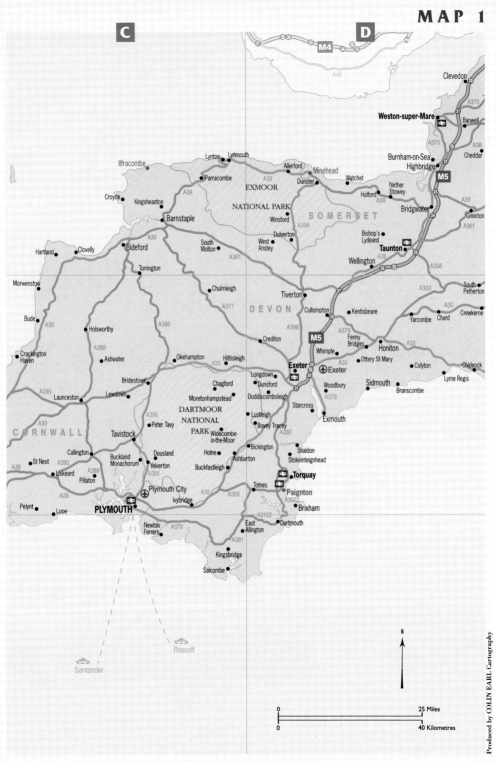

MAP 1

C   D

Clevedon

Weston-super-Mare   Banwell

Burnham-on-Sea   Cheddar
Highbridge   S
M5

Ilfracombe   Lynton   Lynmouth
Allerford   Minehead   Watchet
Parracombe   EXMOOR   Dunster   Nether
Croyde   Kingsheanton   NATIONAL PARK   Holford   Stowey   Bridgwater
Barnstaple   Winsford   S O M E R S E T   Greinton
West   Dulverton
Hartland   Clovelly   South   Anstey   Bishop's
Bideford   Molton   Lydeard   Taunton
Torrington   Wellington
Morwenstow   Chulmleigh   South
Petherton
Tiverton   D E V O N   Cullompton   Kentisbeare   Yarcombe   Chard   Crewkerne
Bude   Crediton   Whimple   Fenny   Honiton   Chideock
Holsworthy   Bridges   Ottery St Mary   Colyton   Lyme Regis
Crackington   Ashwater   Okehampton   Hittisleigh   Exeter   Woodbury   Sidmouth
Haven   Chagford   Longdown   Exeter   Branscombe
Bridestowe   Dunsford   Starcross
Launceston   Lewdown   Moretonhampstead   Doddiscombsleigh   Exmouth
DARTMOOR   Lustleigh
C O R N W A L L   NATIONAL   Bovey Tracey
Tavistock   PARK   Widecombe-   Shaldon
Peter Tavy   in-the-Moor   Bickington   Stokeinteignhead
Callington   Dousland   Holne   Ashburton   Torquay
St Neot   Buckland   Yelverton   Buckfastleigh   Paignton
Liskeard   Monachorum   Plymouth City   Totnes
Pillaton   Ivybridge   Brixham
Pelynt   Looe   PLYMOUTH   East   Dartmouth
Newton   Allington
Ferrers   Kingsbridge
Salcombe

N

Roscoff

Santander

0   25 Miles
0   40 Kilometres

Produced by COLIN EARL Cartography

419

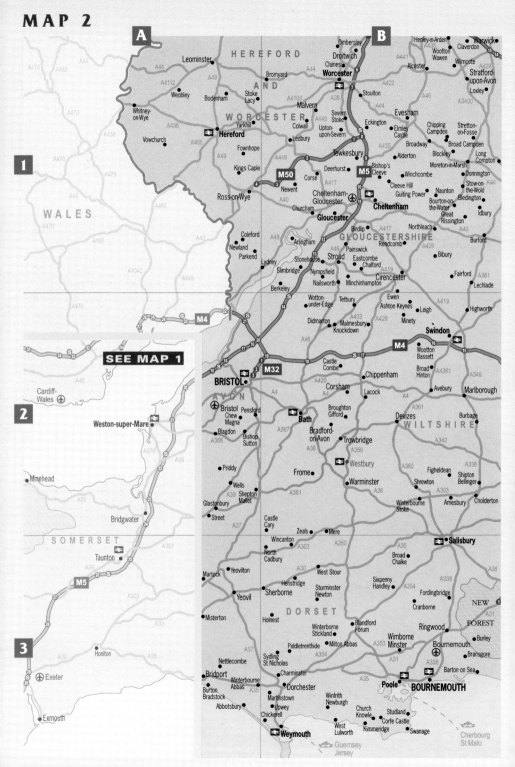

MAP 2

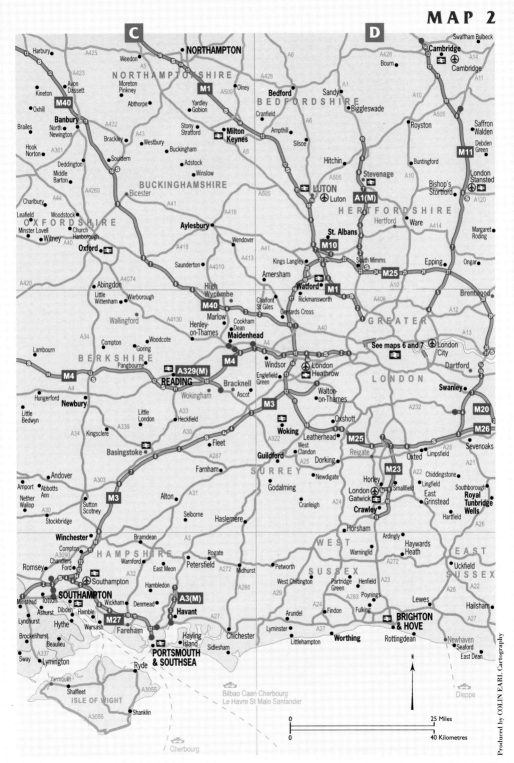

MAP 2

MAP 3

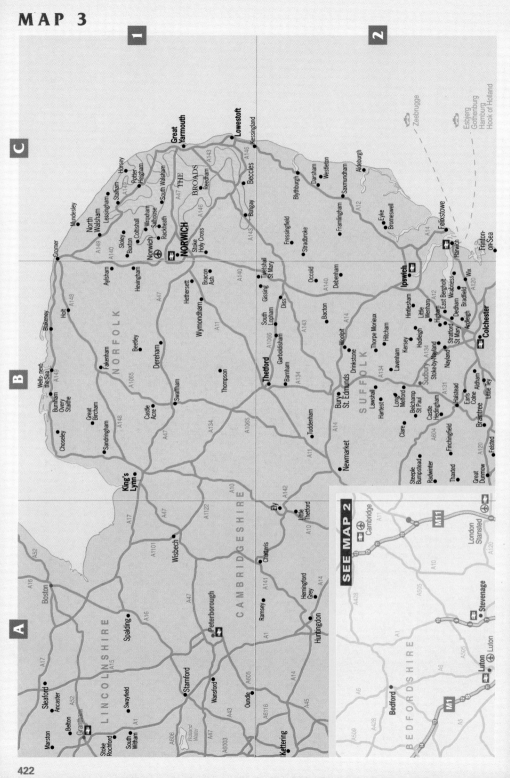

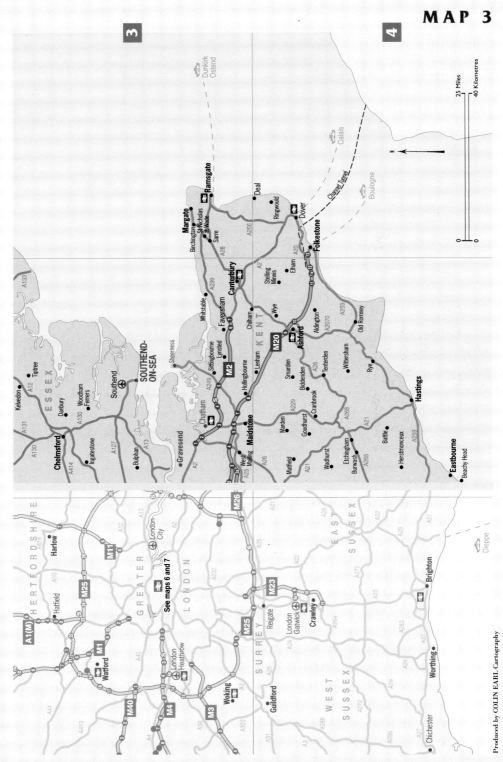

MAP 3

3

4

Dunkirk
Ostend

Calais

Boulogne

Channel Tunnel

25 Miles
40 Kilometres

Ramsgate

Margate
St Nicholas
at Wade
Birchington
Sarre

Deal

Ringwould

Dover

Folkestone

A256

A28

A2

Elham

Stelling
Minnis

A20

Canterbury

A299

Whitstable

Faversham

Wye

A259

Chilham

Aldington

A2070

Old Romney

Sheerness

KENT

Sittingbourne
Lynsted

Lenham

M2

M20
Ashford

A251

A28

Tenterden

Wittersham

Rye

Hollingbourne

Smarden

Biddenden

Cranbrook

A268

A21

Hastings

SOUTHEND-
ON-SEA

Southend

Chatham

Maidstone

Marden

Goudhurst

Battle

Herstmonceux

Eastbourne

Beachy Head

ESSEX

Kelvedon

A12

Tiptree

Danbury

Woodham
Ferrers

A130

A131

Chelmsford

A414

Ingatestone

A127

Bulphan

A13

Gravesend

West
Malling

A26

Matfield

A21

Wadhurst

Etchingham

Burwash

A265

A133

A131

A130

Steelmess

A249

A2

M26

A13

A12

A2

London
City

A10

HERTFORDSHIRE

Harlow

M11

M25

Hatfield

A1(M)

M1

Watford

M40

M4

M3

Woking

London
Heathrow

A40

A41

A413

A4

A30

See maps 6 and 7

GREATER
LONDON

A25

A232

A21

M26

A26

A22

EAST
SUSSEX

A26

A27

Dieppe

Brighton

Reigate

M23

London
Gatwick

Crawley

M25

SURREY

Guildford

A3

A31

A281

A272

WEST
SUSSEX

A286

A27

Chichester

A29

A24

A283

A264

A23

A22

A24

Worthing

Ramsgate

Produced by COLIN EARL Cartography

423

MAP 4

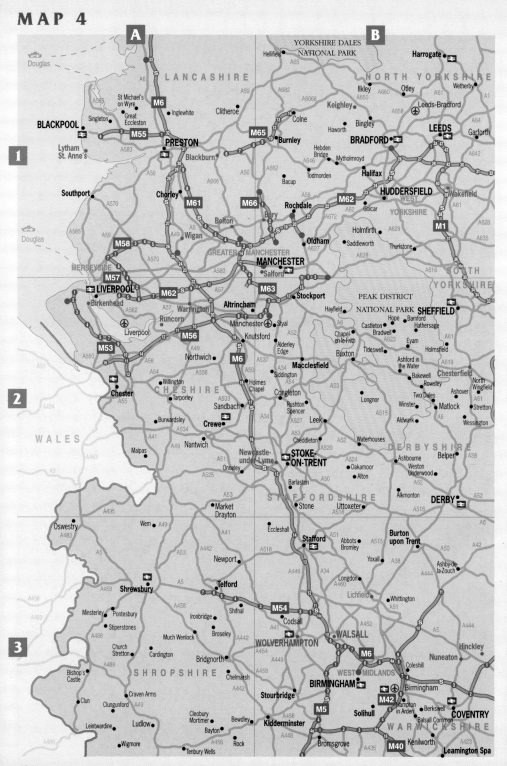

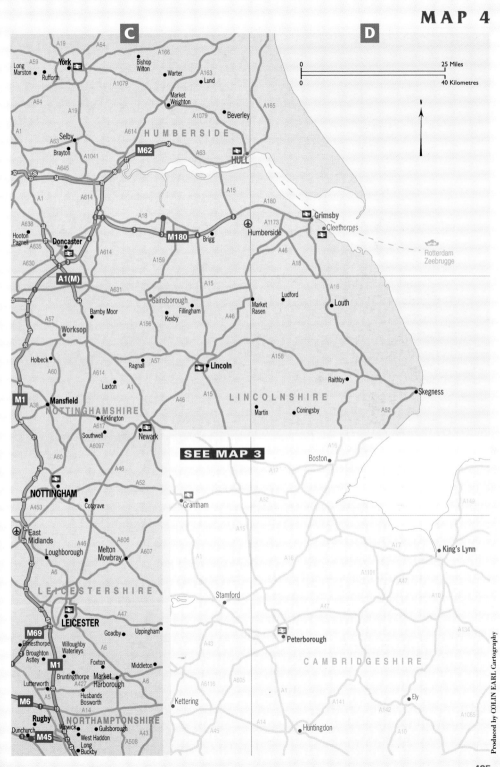

MAP 4

C

D

25 Miles
40 Kilometres

N

Long Marston
A59
York
A19
A64
Rufforth
Bishop Wilton
A166
Warter
A163
Lund
A64
A19
Market Weighton
A1079
Beverley
A1079
A165
A1
Selby
A63
HUMBERSIDE
A614
Brayton
A1041
M62
A63
Hull
A645
A15
S
A1
A614
A18
M180
A180
Grimsby
Cleethorpes
Hooton Pagnell
A635
Doncaster
A1173
Humberside
Rotterdam
Zeebrugge
A638
Brigg
A46
A630
A614
A158
A18
A1(M)
A631
A15
Gainsborough
A16
33
Barnby Moor
A57
Fillingham
Ludford
Louth
Worksop
A156
Kexby
A46
Market Rasen
Holbeck
A60
Ragnall
A57
Lincoln
A158
A614
Laxton
A1
Raithby
M1
A38
Mansfield
A15
A15
LINCOLNSHIRE
Skegness
NOTTINGHAMSHIRE
Kirklington
A617
Martin
Coningsby
A52
Southwell
A6097
Newark
A60
A46
Boston
A16
A453
A52
SEE MAP 3
NOTTINGHAM
Cotgrave
Grantham
A52
East Midlands
A46
A15
A17
King's Lynn
Loughborough
Melton Mowbray
A606
A607
A1
A16
A1101
A6
A47
A10
LEICESTERSHIRE
A47
Stamford
A47
Leicester
A47
M69
Goadby
Uppingham
A43
Peterborough
A134
Enderby
Willoughby Waterleys
Foxton
Middleton
CAMBRIDGESHIRE
Broughton Astley
M1
A6
Lutterworth
Bruntingthorpe
A427
Market Harborough
A6116
A605
M6
A5
Husbands Bosworth
A141
Ely
A1065
Rugby
NORTHAMPTONSHIRE
A14
Dunchurch
Warwick
Guilsborough
A43
Huntington
A10
M45
West Haddon
A14
Long Buckby
A508
A45

Produced by COLIN EARL Cartography

425

MAP 5

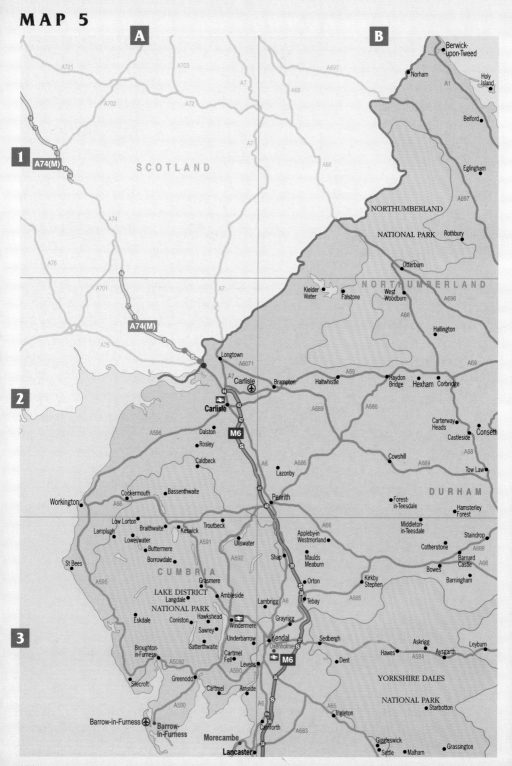

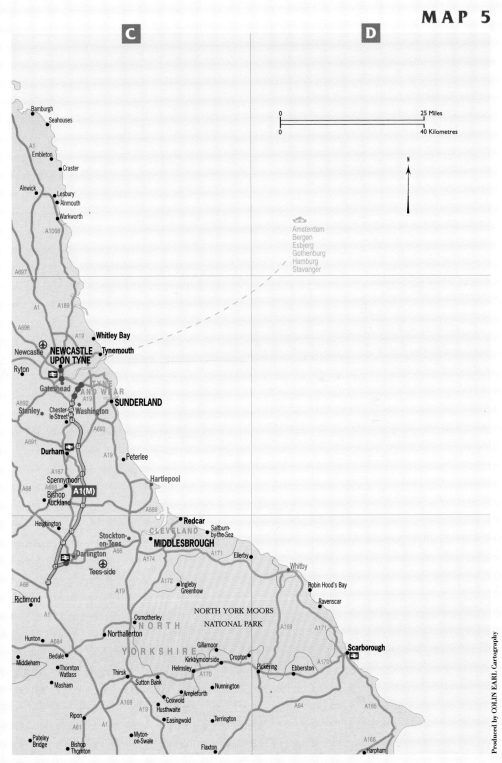

MAP 5

C

D

0   25 Miles

0   40 Kilometres

N

Amsterdam
Bergen
Esbjerg
Gothenburg
Hamburg
Stavanger

Bamburgh
Seahouses
A1
Embleton
Craster
Alnwick
Lesbury
Alnmouth
Warkworth
A1068
A697
A1   A189
A696
A19   Whitley Bay
Newcastle   NEWCASTLE   Tynemouth
UPON TYNE
Ryton
TYNE
Gateshead   AND WEAR
A692   A19   **SUNDERLAND**
Stanley   Chester-   Washington
le-Street
A691   A690
A68   A19   Peterlee
Durham
A167
Spennymoor   Hartlepool
A688
Bishop   **A1(M)**
Auckland
A689
Heighington   **Redcar**
Stockton-   Saltburn-
CLEVELAND   by-the-Sea
on-Tees
MIDDLESBROUGH
Darlington   A66   A174   A171   Ellerby
Tees-side   Whitby
A66   A172   Ingleby
Richmond   Greenhow   Robin Hood's Bay
A1   A19   Ravenscar
Hunton   A684   Gillamoor   NORTH YORK MOORS
Bedale   NATIONAL PARK   A169   A171
Middleham   Osmotherley
Thornton   NORTH   Kirkbymoorside   Cropton
Watlass   **Scarborough**
Masham   YORKSHIRE   A170
Thirsk   Helmsley   Pickering   Ebberston
Sutton Bank   A170
Coxwold   Ampleforth   Nunnington
Ripon   Husthwaite
A168   A19
Pateley   Easingwold   Terrington   A64   A165
Bridge   A61   A1   Myton-
Bishop   on-Swale   A166
Thornton   Flaxton   Harpham

Northallerton

Produced by COLIN EARL Cartography

MAP 6

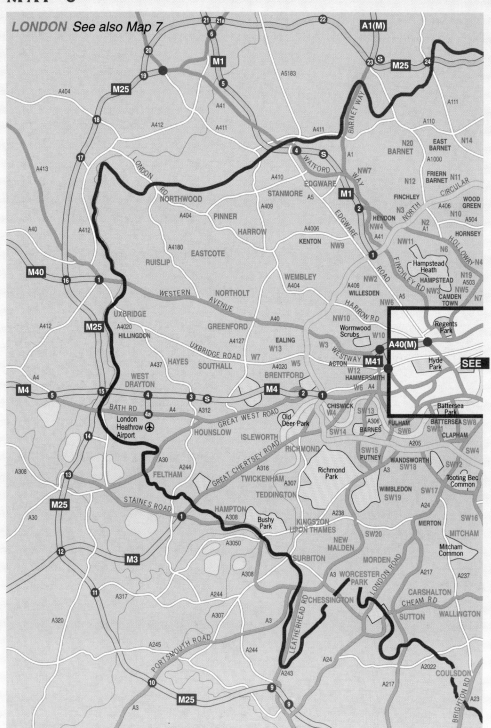

MAP 6

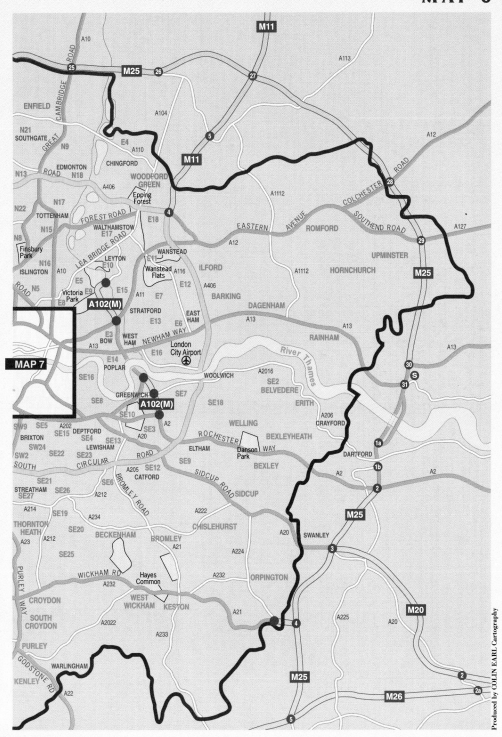

Produced by COLIN EARL Cartography

MAP 7

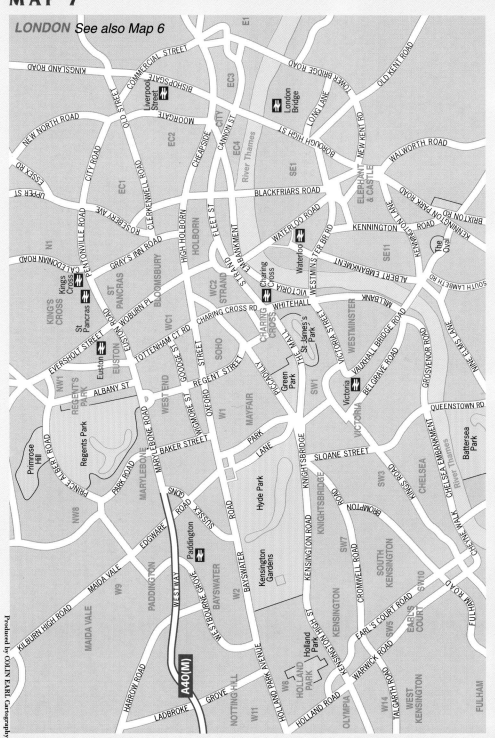

KINGSLAND ROAD

COMMERCIAL STREET

BISHOPSGATE

E1

OLD KENT ROAD

TOWER BRIDGE ROAD

EC3

London Bridge

LONG LANE

NEW NORTH ROAD

OLD STREET

MOORGATE

CITY

CANNON ST

WALWORTH ROAD

NEW KENT RD

Liverpool Street

CITY ROAD

CHEAPSIDE

EC4

BOROUGH HIGH ST

ELEPHANT & CASTLE

KENNINGTON PARK ROAD

BRIXTON RD

ESSEX RD

EC2

EC1

CLERKENWELL ROAD

SE1

River Thames

KENNINGTON LANE

UPPER ST

N1

CALEDONIAN ROAD

PENTONVILLE ROAD

ROSEBERY AVE

GRAY'S INN ROAD

HIGH HOLBORN

HOLBORN

BLACKFRIARS ROAD

WATERLOO ROAD

WESTMINSTER BR RD

KENNINGTON ROAD

SE11

The Oval

Kings Cross

ST PANCRAS

BLOOMSBURY

FLEET ST

STRAND EMBANKMENT

Waterloo

ALBERT EMBANKMENT

SOUTH LAMBETH RD

KING'S CROSS

St Pancras

EUSTON ROAD

WOBURN PL

WC1

STRAND WC2

Charing Cross

VICTORIA

MILLBANK

EVERSHOLT STREET

Euston

EUSTON ROAD

TOTTENHAM CT RD

CHARING CROSS RD

SOHO

WHITEHALL

CHARING CROSS

St James's Park

VICTORIA STREET

WESTMINSTER

NINE ELMS LANE

NW1

ALBANY ST

WEST END

GOODGE ST RD

STREET

REGENT STREET

PICCADILLY

THE MALL

Green Park

SW1

Victoria

VAUXHALL BRIDGE ROAD

GROSVENOR ROAD

REGENT'S PARK

WIGMORE ST

OXFORD

W1

MAYFAIR

St James's Park

VICTORIA

BELGRAVE ROAD

Primrose Hill

Regents Park

MARYLEBONE ROAD

BAKER STREET

PARK LANE

KNIGHTSBRIDGE

SLOANE STREET

SW3

QUEENSTOWN RD

Battersea Park

PRINCE ALBERT ROAD

PARK ROAD

MARYLEBONE

Hyde Park

KNIGHTSBRIDGE

KINGS ROAD

CHELSEA

CHELSEA EMBANKMENT

River Thames

NW8

EDGWARE ROAD

SUSSEX GDNS

KENSINGTON ROAD

SW7

BROMPTON ROAD

CHEYNE WALK

SW10

NW9

Paddington

WESTWAY

BAYSWATER ROAD

Kensington Gardens

KENSINGTON ROAD

CROMWELL ROAD

SOUTH KENSINGTON

FULHAM ROAD

MAIDA VALE

PADDINGTON

WESTBOURNE GROVE

W2

BAYSWATER

KENSINGTON HIGH ST

KENSINGTON

EARL'S COURT ROAD

SW5

EARL'S COURT

A40(M)

KILBURN HIGH ROAD

HARROW ROAD

LADBROKE GROVE

NOTTING HILL

W11

HOLLAND PARK AVENUE

W8

Holland Park

HOLLAND PARK

HOLLAND ROAD

OLYMPIA

W14

WARWICK ROAD

TALGARTH ROAD

WEST KENSINGTON

FULHAM

Produced by COLIN EARL Cartography

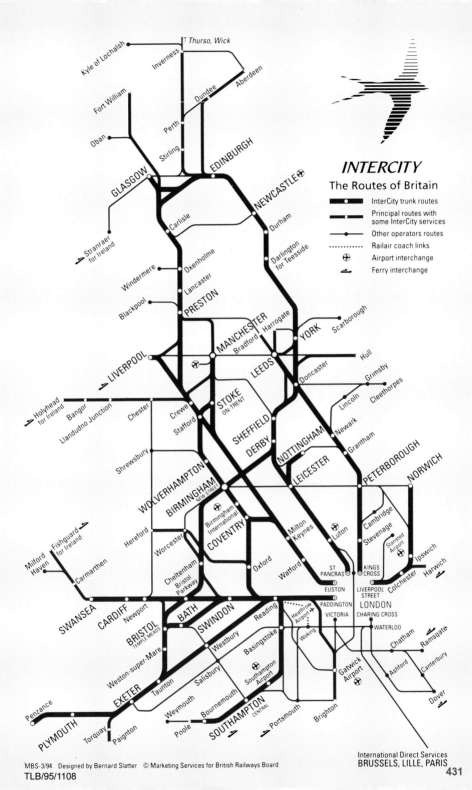

INTERCITY

The Routes of Britain

━━●━━	InterCity trunk routes
━━┿━━	Principal routes with some InterCity services
─●─	Other operators routes
··········	Railair coach links
✈	Airport interchange
⛴	Ferry interchange

International Direct Services
BRUSSELS, LILLE, PARIS

MBS-3/94   Designed by Bernard Slatter   © Marketing Services for British Railways Board
TLB/95/1108

Your Quick Guide...

Where to Stay makes it quick and easy to find a place to stay that offers the standard of quality and facilities you're looking for.

The TOWN INDEX (starting on page 407) and the LOCATION MAPS (starting on page 417) show all cities, towns and villages with accommodation listings in this guide.

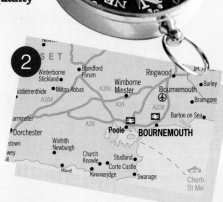

❶ Town Index

If the place you plan to visit is included in the town index, turn to the page number given to find accommodation available there. Also check that location on the colour maps to find other places nearby which also have accommodation listings in this guide.

❷ Location Maps

If the place you want is not in the town index – or you only have a general idea of the area in which you wish to stay – use the colour location maps to find places in the area which have accommodation listings in this guide.

When you have found suitable accommodation, check its availability with the establishment and also confirm any other information in the published entry which may be important to you (price, whether bath and/or shower available, children/dogs/credit cards welcome, months open, etc).

If you are happy with everything, make your booking and, if time permits, confirm it in writing.